Emerging Markets and the **Global Economy**

Emerging Markets and the
Global Economy

MOHAMED AROURI

SABRI BOUBAKER

DUC KHUONG NGUYEN

Amsterdam • Boston • Heidelberg • London • New York • Oxford
Paris • San Diego • San Francisco • Singapore • Sydney • Tokyo

Academic Press is an imprint of Elsevier

Academic Press is an imprint of Elsevier
The Boulevard, Langford Lane, Oxford, Kidlington, OX5 1GB, UK
225 Wyman Street, Waltham, MA 02451, USA
525 B Street, Suite 1800, San Diego, CA 92101-4495, USA

British Library Cataloguing-in-Publication Data
A catalogue record for this book is available from the British Library

Library of Congress Cataloging-in-Publication Data
A catalog record for this book is available from the Library of Congress

ISBN: 978-0-12-411549-1

For information on all Academic Press publications
visit our website at store.elsevier.com

Typeset by SPS
www.sps.co.in

Printed and bound by CPI Group (UK) Ltd, Croydon, CR0 4YY

14 15 16 17 10 9 8 7 6 5 4 3 2 1

CONTENTS

Foreword xv
Acknowledgments xvii
About the Editors xix
List of contributors xxi
Author Biographies xxix

PART I – COUNTRY-SPECIFIC EXPERIENCES

1 Robust Measures of Hybrid Emerging Market Mutual Funds Performance 3

Mohamed A. Ayadi

1 Introduction 3
2 Stochastic Discount Factors and Benchmark Models 5
3 Performance Evaluation of Managed Portfolios 7
4 Econometric Methodology and Tests 9
5 Conclusion 13

Acknowledgment 14
References 14

2 Emerging Countries Sovereign Rating Adjustment using Market Information: Impact on Financial Institutions' Investment Decisions 17

Dominique Guégan, Bertrand K. Hassani, Xin Zhao

1 Introduction 17
2 The δ-Rating Methodology 20
3 Rating Evaluation: Carrying Out the Methodology 24
4 Discussion and Conclusion 46

References 48

3 Emerging Markets Banks Performance Evidence from China's Banks in Hong Kong 51

Xiaoxi Zhang, Kevin Daly

1 Introduction 51
2 Foreign Banks in Hong Kong 52
3 Hypothesis Testing 53
4 Data and Methodology 55
5 Empirical Results 58
6 Conclusion 64

References 65

4 Determinants of the Real Rate of Return: Evidence from Cross-Country Panel Data **67**

Marcelo Sánchez

1 Introduction 67
2 The Data 69
3 The Methodology 71
4 Determinants of Asset Returns: Some Basic Results 76
5 Determinants of Asset Returns: Some Refinements 81
6 Conclusions 89

Appendix 92
References 97

5 Understanding the Relationship Between Liquidity and Inflation in the Post Crisis Period in India: from Bank Dealers' Perspectives **99**

Rituparna Das, Michael C.S. Wong

1 Introduction 99
2 The Scenario 100
3 The Existing Literature on Economic Games 101
4 Features of the Game in Decision Making of a Dealer in the Government Security Desk 101
5 Forecasting Liquidity 103
6 Decision Making of a Dealer in the Equity Desk 106
7 Conclusion 110

Appendix 111
References 111

6 Demographic Transition and Savings Behavior in Mauritius **115**

Rafael Munozmoreno, Verena Tandrayen-Ragoobur, Boopendra Seetanah, Raja Vinesh Sannassee

1 Introduction 115
2 Literature Survey 117
3 Savings Trends 121
4 Methodology 123
5 Findings—Macroeconomic Modeling 132
6 Findings—Microeconomic Modeling 135
7 Conclusion 136

References 139

7 An Investigation of the Deviation from the Market Efficiency and its Implications for Capital Market Development: The DSE Evidence **143**

A.S.M. Sohel Azad, Amirul Ahsan, Victor Fang

1 Introduction 143
2 Background of DSE 145

3 Testing Methodologies 148
4 Data, Econometric Packages, and Descriptive Statistics 150
5 Results and Analysis 152
6 Conclusion and Policy Implications 156

Acknowledgments 158
References 158

8 An Econometric Analysis of the Impact of Oil Prices on Stock Markets in Gulf Cooperation Countries 161

Mohamed El Hedi Arouri, Christophe Rault

1 Introduction 161
2 GCC Stock Markets and Oil 163
3 Transmission Channels 165
4 Empirical Investigation 166
5 Policy Discussion 173
6 Conclusion 175

Appendix 175
Acknowledgment 177
References 177

9 Trading Intensity and Informed Trading in the Tunis Stock Exchange 179

Rabaa Karaa, Skander Slim, Dorra Mezzez Hmaied

1 Introduction 179
2 Institutional Features of the Tunis Stock Exchange 182
3 Econometric Models 183
4 Empirical Analysis 187
5 Conclusion 196

Acknowledgments 198
References 198

10 Energy Sector Companies of the BRICS: Systematic and Specific Financial Risks and Value at Risk 201

Marcelo Bianconi, Joe A. Yoshino

1 Introduction 201
2 Literature Review 203
3 The Role of Gas and Oil in the BRICS 204
4 Data 207
5 Econometric Models 216
6 Empirical Results 220
7 Conclusions and Future Research 233

Appendix 238

Acknowledgment 239
References 239

11 Developed and Emerging Equity Market Tail Risk: Is it Constant? 241

Stefan Straetmans, Bertrand Candelon

1 Introduction 241
2 Testing Structural Change in Tail Behavior: Theory 243
3 Monte Carlo Experiments 247
4 Empirical Application 260
5 Conclusions 263

Appendix A. Calibration of GARCH(1,1) Parameters 265
Appendix B. Derivations of Second Order Expansion Parameters 266

Acknowledgment 268
References 268

12 Measuring Systemic Risk in Emerging Markets Using CoVaR 271

Anastassios A. Drakos, Georgios P. Kouretas

1 Introduction 271
2 Review of the Literature 274
3 Econometric Methodology 277
4 Data and Empirical Results 280
5 Summary and Concluding Remarks 304

Acknowledgments 305
References 306

13 An Empirical Study on Mutual Funds Performance Persistence in China 309

Dawei Chen, Christopher Gan, Baiding Hu

1 Introduction 309
2 Literature Review 310
3 Methodology 314
4 Research Findings 318
5 Conclusions 323

References 324

14 Cultural Behavioral Finance in Emerging Markets 327

Brian M. Lucey, Michael Dowling

1 Introduction 327
2 Culture and Financial Decision Making 328
3 Behavioral Finance in Emerging Markets: A Cultural Perspective 331

4 The Future of Cultural Behavioral Finance Research in Emerging Markets 341

References 342

15 Early Warning System for Financial Crisis: Statistical Classification Approach 347

Young Min Kim, Kyong Joo Oh, Tae Yoon Kim

1 Introduction 347
2 Procedure Description 348
3 Oracle Classifier 349
4 Lag-*l* Forecasting Classifier 353
5 Linking Various Classifiers 355
6 Empirical Example and Experiment 357
7 Conclusion 368

Acknowledgments 368
References 368

16 Comovements and Volatility Spillovers Between Oil Prices and Stock Markets: Further Evidence for Oil-Exporting and Oil-Importing Countries 371

Khaled Guesmi

1 Introduction 371
2 Data and Methodology 373
3 Empirical Results 378
4 Conclusion 381

References 381

17 Collateral in Emerging Economies 383

Elmas Yaldız Hanedar, Eleonora Broccardo, Flavio Bazzana

1 Introduction 383
2 Literature on Collateral 384
3 Empirical Analysis 391
4 Robustness Checks 400
5 Policy Implication 408
6 Conclusions 409

References 409

18 Tactical Risk Analysis in Emerging Markets in the Wake of the Credit Crunch and Ensuing Sub-prime Financial Crisis 413

Mazin A.M. Al Janabi

1 Introduction 413
2 Related Literature Review and Purpose of Present Study 416

3 Methodology and Research Design 420
4 Results and Discussion of Findings 426
5 Discussion and Conclusion 439
Appendix A. Derivation of Liquidity-Adjusted Value-at-Risk (LVaR) Mathematical Structure During the Close-Out (Unwinding) Period 442
Acknowledgment 445
References 445

PART II – DYNAMIC INTERACTIONS WITH THE GLOBAL ECONOMY

19 Volatility and Spillover Effects of Central and Eastern Europe: Impact of EU Enlargement 449

A. Golab, D.E. Allen, R. Powell, G. Yap

1 Introduction 449
2 Literature Review 450
3 Data and Summary Statistics 452
4 Multivariate GARCH Models 458
5 Empirical Results 460
6 Conclusion 479
References 480

20 Price Jump Behavior During Financial Distress: Intuition, Analysis, and a Regulatory Perspective 483

Jan Novotný, Jan Hanousek

1 Introduction 483
2 Price Jumps and Financial Crisis 485
3 Methodology 492
4 Data Description 494
5 Results 497
6 Regulatory Consequences 501
7 Conclusion 504
References 505

21 Are Emerging Markets Exposed to Contagion from the United States: Evidence from Stock and Sovereign Bond Markets 509

Hakimzadi Wagan, Zulfiqar Ali

1 Introduction 509
2 Some Theoretical Underpinnings 511
3 Some Amplifications on Recent Crisis 514
4 Methodology 515
5 Data and Descriptive Statistics 517

6 Empirical Results 521
7 Implications and Conclusion 533

References 535

22 Assessing the Effects of the Global Financial Crisis on the East Asian Equity Markets 537

Tran Phuong Thao, Kevin Daly, Craig Ellis

1 Introduction 537
2 Literature Review 538
3 Data and Methodology 540
4 Empirical Results 546
5 Conclusion 551

References 552

23 Contagion versus Interdependence: The Case of the BRIC Countries During the Subprime Crises 555

Mrabet Zouhair, Charfeddine Lanouar, Ahdi Noomen Ajmi

1 Introduction 555
2 BRIC Countries 557
3 A Brief Review of Literature 560
4 The Empirical Methodology 562
5 Empiricals Results 564
6 Interdependence versus Contagion 570
7 Summary and Implications 575

References 580

24 On the Importance of Trend Gaps in Assessing Equity Market Correlations 583

Jarkko Peltomäki, Michael Graham

1 Introduction 583
2 Measuring Market Correlation 585
3 Defining Stock Market Trends 588
4 Data and Descriptive Statistics 589
5 Results 590
6 Conclusion 598

References 599

25 Stock Market Co-movement in ASEAN and China 603

Hooi Hooi Lean, Russell Smyth

1 Introduction 603
2 Theoretical Underpinnings of Stock Market Linkages 605
3 Existing Literature on Stock Market Linkages 605

4 Overview of the Markets and Bilateral Trade and Investment 607
5 Data 609
6 Empirical Specification and Methodology 612
7 Results 614
8 Conclusion 617

References 620

26 Stock and Bond Markets Co-movements in Selected MENA Countries: A Dynamic Coherence Function Approach 623

Jamel Boukhatem, Zied Ftiti

1 Introduction 623
2 Related Literature 625
3 Empirical Analysis and Data 630
4 Results and Discussions 635
5 Conclusion 638

Appendix 639
References 639

27 Equity Market Comovements Among Selected Emerging Countries from Long- and Short-Run Perspectives 643

Jamel Jouini, Jihed Majdoub, Ines Ben Bouhouch

1 Introduction 643
2 Integration of Equity Markets 645
3 Empirical Methods 647
4 Data and Results 649
5 Conclusion 662

References 662

28 Stock Market Volatility and Contagion Effects in the Financial Crisis: The Case of South-Eastern Europe 665

Theodore Syriopoulos

1 Introduction 665
2 Recent Economic Developments in the SEE Countries 666
3 SEE Stock Market Growth and Prospects 679
4 An Empirical Analysis of the SEE Stock Markets 690
5 Conclusions 696

Acknowledgment 697
References 697

29 Emerging Market Stocks in Global Portfolios: A Hedging Approach **701**

Imad Moosa, Vikash Ramiah

1 Introduction 701
2 The Available Evidence 702
3 Methodology 704
4 An Informal Examination of the Data 707
5 Empirical Results 712
6 Robustness Test 1: The Conventional Mean-Variance Approach 717
7 Robustness Test 2: Alternative Estimates of the Hedge Ratio 718
8 Conclusion 721

References 722

30 The Behavior of International Stock Market Excess Returns in an Increasingly Integrated World **725**

Michael Donadelli

1 Introduction 725
2 Summary Statistics and Preliminary Analysis 727
3 A Time-Varying Analysis 737
4 Conclusion 746

References 747

31 Determinants of International Financial Integration of GCC Markets **749**

Abdullah R. Alotaibi, Anil V. Mishra

1 Introduction 749
2 Literature Review of Financial Integration 751
3 Measures of International Financial Integration 753
4 Analysis of Determinants of International Financial Integration in GCC 757
5 Conclusions and Policy Implications 768

References 770

32 Asset Return and Volatility Spillovers Between Big Commodity Producing Countries **773**

Perry Sadorsky

1 Introduction 773
2 Selected Literature Review 775
3 The Econometric Model 777
4 Data 778
5 Empirical Results for Returns Spillovers 781

6 Empirical Results for Volatility Spillovers 784
7 Conclusions 788

Acknowledgment 791
References 792

33 Correlation and Network Structure of International Financial Markets in Times of Crisis **795**

Leonidas Sandoval

1 Introduction 795
2 The Data 796
3 Random Matrix Theory 797
4 Correlation and Volatility of the Market 802
5 Network Structure 804
6 Conclusion 809

Acknowledgments 809
References 809

34 Financial Development and its Effects on Economic Growth: A Dynamic Analysis **811**

Christophe Rault, Anamaria Sova, Robert Sova, Guglielmo Maria Caporale

1 Introduction 811
2 Literature Review 812
3 Empirical Analysis of the Financial Development and Economic Growth Nexus 814
4 Conclusions 821

Appendix 822
Acknowledgment 823
References 823

35 Financial Market Integration of ASEAN-5 with China and India **825**

Kee Tuan Teng, Siew Hwa Yen, Soo Y. Chua, Hooi Hooi Lean

1 Introduction 825
2 Literature review 828
3 Data and Methodology 829
4 Findings 835
5 Conclusion 852

Appendix 857
References 858

Index **861**

FOREWORD

Emerging markets countries are expected to play a crucial role in international trade and finance as well as to contribute significantly to the global economic growth. Assets issued by emerging financial markets have, over the last three decades, been selected by both individual and professional investors to design dedicated investment portfolio strategies. While it is common that emerging markets can provide substantial diversification benefits at international level, their financial characteristics and links to the global economy tend to be country-specific, owing to an important degree of heterogeneity across these markets in terms of market size, financial depth, and international investment barriers, among others. The disparity between regional and global integration processes is also a source of differences in the functioning of emerging markets economies and the behavior of their financial markets. Looking ahead to the future of emerging markets, this handbook is thus a tasteful collection of 35 papers on emerging markets' specificities and their interactions with the global economy. The editors of the book are well-known experts in the field with significant contributions to emerging markets finance literature.

The volume contains empirical studies on macro- and microeconomic issues, covering many regions and individual countries. One of the uniquenesses of the studies is that each offers a well-thought testing of economics and finance theories and application of the most recent econometric methodologies. The papers in the volume are clearly written and nicely articulated. The volume can thus serve as a useful reference for both masters and PhD level students in terms of finding suitable research or thesis topics, as well as writing a review of literature chapter. It can be adopted by instructors to teach seminar courses as well. As the papers in the volume offer plenty of comparative studies, instructors may also find it useful in their comparative studies courses.

The regions studied in the volume are quite rich, including the Middle East and North Africa (MENA), Latin America, Gulf region, Asia, European Union, and Central, South, and Eastern Europe. There are many interesting cases on individual countries, including China, India, Hong Kong, Tunisia, Mauritius, and many others. In doing so, the volume allows for quite diverse empirical evidence on a variety of issues facing policymakers, investors, and other stakeholders.

The volume consists of two parts. The first part focuses on individual country experiences. The papers examine critical issues and/or offer useful case studies in different areas in economics and finance. For example, finance studies include mutual fund performance, bank performance, market efficiency, informed trading, systematic risk, and behavioral finance. Macro studies include the effect of inflation asset returns, sovereign rating methods, liquidity management, savings behavior, early warning systems for financial crises, and the link between oil prices and stock market returns. This part of the volume may be used in courses emphasizing case studies or individual country experiences.

The second part of the volume is a collection of papers examining dynamic interactions of emerging markets with the global economy. They are concerned with very timely issues including volatility and spillovers effects of the European Union enlargement and of financial crises, integration between emerging and advance markets, contagion effects, and stock and bond market co-movements. Many papers rely on a rich application of modern time series methodologies and this part of the volume would therefore be beneficial for applied econometrics and time series courses as very useful application cases.

Overall, the edited volume is an excellent handbook for graduate students and academicians doing research on emerging markets. It provides readers with a comprehensive understanding of emerging markets as well as their challenging problems in the years to come. Findings offer important implications for policymakers, investors, traders, financial analysts, regulators, and other key stakeholders. The handbook can thus be adopted in many courses including econometrics, time series, comparative studies, and research seminar courses. Useful case studies and individual country experiences also allow for a rich platform to test different theories in economics and finance and provide application of the most up-to-date econometrics techniques.

For all these reasons, this is a handbook that any scholar or professional focusing on emerging markets should have on his desk.

Ali M. Kutan
Professor of Economics and Finance at
Southern Illinois University at Edwardsville
Editor of *Emerging Markets Finance and Trade*
Editor of *Borsa Istanbul Review*
Co-editor of *Economic Systems*

ACKNOWLEDGMENTS

We would like to thank Dr. J. Scott Bentley, Melissa Murray, and Kathie Paoni at Elsevier Inc. (San Diego, United States) for their helpful comments and excellent editorial assistance. We are grateful to Professor Campbell R. Harvey who kindly agreed to write the foreword to this edited volume. Our sincere thanks also go to all the contributing authors for their intellectual contribution.

The contents of each chapter remain the sole responsibility of each contributor.

Mohamed Arouri, Sabri Boubaker, and Duc Khuong Nguyen

ABOUT THE EDITORS

Mohamed Arouri is a Professor of Finance at the University of Auvergne and a Researcher at EDHEC Business School, France. He holds a PhD in Economics from the University of Paris X Nanterre and a HDR degree (Habilitation for Supervising Doctoral Research) in management science from the University of Orléans. His research focuses on energy finance, the cost of capital, stock market integration, and international portfolio choice. He published articles in refereed journals such as *Journal of Banking and Finance*, *Journal of International Money and Finance*, *Journal of Macroeconomic Dynamics*, *Managerial Finance*, and *Macroeconomic Dynamics*.

Sabri Boubaker is an Associate Professor of Finance at Champagne School of Management (Groupe ESC Troyes en Champagne, France) and Research Fellow at the Institut de Recherche en Gestion (University of Paris Est). He holds a PhD in Finance from University of Paris Est (2006) and a HDR degree (Habilitation for Supervising Doctoral Research) in 2010 from the same university. He is a Visiting Professor at IESEG School of Management (France) and IAE Paris Gustave Eiffel (France). He has recently published several academic papers in international refereed journals including *Journal of Banking and Finance*, *Review of Accounting and Finance*, *Multinational Finance Journal*, *International Journal of Business*, and *Journal of International Financial Markets, Institutions and Money*. Dr. Boubaker has also edited several books on corporate governance and corporate social responsibility issues.

Duc Khuong Nguyen is a Professor of Finance and Deputy Director for Research at IPAG Business School (France). He holds a PhD in Finance from the University of Grenoble II (France) and a HDR degree (Habilitation for Supervising Scientific Research) from University of Cergy-Pontoise (France). His research articles are published in various refereed journals such as *Journal of Banking and Finance*, *Journal of International Money and Finance*, *Journal of International Financial Markets, Institutions and Money*, *Journal of Macroeconomics*, *Macroeconomic Dynamics*, *Quarterly Review of Economics and Finance*, and *Review of Accounting and Finance*. Dr. Nguyen has also edited several books on corporate governance and corporate social responsibility issues.

LIST OF CONTRIBUTORS

Amirul Ahsan
School of Accounting, Economics and Finance, Faculty of Business and Law, Deakin University, Melbourne, Australia.

Ahdi Noomen Ajmi
College of Science and Humanities in Slayel, Business Administration Department, Salman bin Abdulaziz University, Saudi Arabia.

Mazin A.M. Al Janabi
College of Business and Economics, Department of Economics and Finance, United Arab Emirates University, United Arab Emirates.

Zulfiqar Ali
University of Sindh Jamshoro, Department of Business Administration, Pakistan.

D.E. Allen
School of Accounting, Finance, & Economics, Edith Cowan University, Joondalup, Australia.

Abdullah R. Alotaibi
School of Business, University of Western Sydney, Sydney, Australia.

Mohamed El Hedi Arouri
CRCGM, University of Auvergne, Clermont-Ferrand, France

Mohamed A. Ayadi
Department of Finance, Operations, and Information Systems, Goodman School of Business, Brock University, St. Catharines, ON, Canada.

Flavio Bazzana
Department of Economics and Management, University of Trento, Via Inama, Trento, Italy.

Marcelo Bianconi
Associate Professor of Economics, Department of Economics, Tufts University, Medford, MA, USA.

Ines Ben Bouhouch
Faculty of Economics and Management of Nabeul, University of Carthage, Tunisia.

Jamel Boukhatem
Faculty of Islamic Economics and Finance, Umm Al-Qura University, Mecca, Saudi Arabia. URMOFIB, FSEG University of Tunis El Manar, Tunisia.

Eleonora Broccardo
Department of Economics and Management, University of Trento, Via Inama, Trento, Italy.
Cefin, Centro Studi Banca e Finanza, Modena, Italy.

Bertrand Candelon
Maastricht University, School of Business and Economics, Maastricht, The Netherlands.

Guglielmo Maria Caporale
Professor of Economics and Finance, Brunel University-London, Uxbridge, United Kingdom.

Dawei Chen
Department of Accounting, Economics and Finance, Lincoln University, Canterbury, New Zealand.

Soo Y. Chua
Economics Programme, School of Social Sciences, Universiti Sains Malaysia, Penang, Malaysia.

Kevin Daly
School of Economics and Finance, Campbelltown Campus, University of Western Sydney, Sydney, Australia.

Rituparna Das
Centre for Studies in Banking and Finance, National Law University, Jodhpur, Rajasthan, India.

Michael Donadelli
Department of Economics and Finance, LUISS Guido Carli, Rome, Italy.

Michael Dowling
DCU Business School, Dublin City University, Dublin, Ireland.

Anastassios A. Drakos
Department of Business Administration, Athens University of Economics and Business, Athens, Greece.

Craig Ellis
School of Business, University of Western Sydney, Sydney, Australia.

Victor Fang
School of Accounting, Economics and Finance, Faculty of Business and Law, Deakin University, Melbourne, Australia.

Zied Ftiti
IPAG Business School, IPAG lab, Paris, France.
High Institute of Management, University of Tunis, Tunis, Tunisia.

Christopher Gan
Department of Accounting, Economics and Finance, Lincoln University, Canterbury, New Zealand.

A. Golab
School of Accounting, Finance, & Economics, Edith Cowan University, Joondalup, Australia.

Michael Graham
School of Business, Stockholm University, Sweden.

Dominique Guégan
Université Paris, Panthéon-Sorbonne, France.

Khaled Guesmi
IPAG Business School, IPAG—Lab & EconomiX, University of Paris, France.

Elmas Yaldız Hanedar
Department of Economics and Management, University of Trento, Via Inama, Trento, Italy.

Jan Hanousek
CERGE-EI, Joint Workplace of the Charles University and Academy of Sciences of the Czech Republic, Prague, Czech Republic.

Bertrand K. Hassani
Santander UK, United Kingdom, and Université Paris, Panthéon-Sorbonne, France.

DorraMezzez Hmaied
Department of Finance, Institut des Hautes Etudes Commerciales de Carthage, Tunisia.

Baiding Hu
Department of Accounting, Economics and Finance, Lincoln University, Canterbury, New Zealand.

Jamel Jouini
Department of Economics, College of Business Administration, King Saud University, Riyadh, Saudi Arabia.

Rabaa Karaa
Department of Finance, Institut des Hautes Etudes Commerciales de Carthage, Tunisia.

Young Min Kim
Department of Information and Industrial Engineering, Yonsei University, Seoul, South Korea.

Tae Yoon Kim
Department of Statistics, Keimyung University, Daegu, South Korea.

Georgios P. Kouretas
Department of Business Administration, Athens University of Economics and Business, Athens, Greece.

Charfeddine Lanouar
College of Administrative Sciences, Najran University, Najran, Saudi Arabia.
Quantitatives Methods Department, Institut Supérieur de Gestion de Gabès, Université de Gabès, Gabès, Tunisia.

Hooi Hooi Lean
Economics Program, School of Social Sciences, Universiti Sains Malaysia, Malaysia.

Brian M. Lucey
School of Business Studies, Trinity College Dublin, Dublin, Ireland.

Jihed Majdoub
High School of Management of Tunis, University of Tunis, Tunisia.

Anil V. Mishra
School of Business, University of Western Sydney, Sydney, Australia.

Imad Moosa
School of Economics, Finance and Marketing, Royal Melbourne Institute of Technology (RMIT), Melbourne, Australia.

Rafael Munozmoreno
World Bank, Mauritius.

Jan Novotný
Centre for Econometric Analysis, Faculty of Finance, Cass Business School, City University London, London, UK.

CERGE-EI, Charles University and the Economics Institute of the Academy of Sciences of the Czech Republic, Prague, Czech Republic.

Kyong Joo Oh
Department of Information and Industrial Engineering, Yonsei University, Seoul, South Korea.

Jarkko Peltomäki
Stockholm University, School of Business, Sweden.

Tran Phuong Thao
School of Business, University of Western Sydney, Sydney, Australia.
Department of Banking, University of Economics, Ho Chi Minh City, Vietnam.

R. Powell
School of Accounting, Finance, & Economics, Edith Cowan University, Joondalup, Australia.

Vikash Ramiah
School of Economics, Finance and Marketing, Royal Melbourne Institute of Technology (RMIT), Melbourne, Australia.

Christophe Rault
Université d'Orléans, Orléans, France.
Toulouse Business School, France.

Perry Sadorsky
Schulich School of Business, York University, Toronto, Ontario, Canada.

Marcelo Sánchez
European Central Bank, Frankfurt, Germany.

Leonidas Sandoval
Insper Instituto de Ensino e Pesquisa, Brazil.

Raja Vinesh Sannassee
Department of Economics and Statistics, Faculty of Social Studies and Humanities, University of Mauritius, Reduit, Mauritius.

Boopendra Seetanah
Department of Economics and Statistics, Faculty of Social Studies and Humanities, University of Mauritius, Reduit, Mauritius.

Skander Slim
University of Sousse, Sousse, Tunisia.

Russell Smyth
Department of Economics, Clayton Campus, Monash University, Melbourne, Australia.

A.S.M. Sohel Azad
School of Accounting, Economics and Finance, Faculty of Business and Law, Deakin University, Melbourne, Australia.

Anamaria Sova
Economic Business Research Centre, Bucharest, Romania ASE, Bucharest University of Economics Studies, Romania Brunel University, London.
UK CESifo, Munich, Germany.
DIW, Berlin, Germany.

Robert Sova
The Bucharest University of Economic Studies, Bucharest, Romania, Sorbonne.
Economic Centre, University of Paris, Paris, France.

Stefan Straetmans
Maastricht University, School of Business and Economics, Maastricht, The Netherlands.

Theodore Syriopoulos
Department of Shipping, Trade and Transport, School of Business Studies, University of the Aegean, Chios, Greece.
Audencia School of Management, Department of Finance, Nantes, France.

Verena Tandrayen-Ragoobur
Department of Economics and Statistics, Faculty of Social Studies and Humanities, University of Mauritius, Reduit, Mauritius.

Kee Tuan Teng
Economics & Corporate Administration Department, Faculty of Accountancy, Finance & Business, Tunku Abdul Rahman University College, Penang, Malaysia.

Hakimzadi Wagan
University of Paris, France.

Michael C.S. Wong
Department of Economics and Finance, College of Business, City University of Hong Kong, Tat Chee Avenue, Hong Kong.

G. Yap
School of Accounting, Finance, & Economics, Edith Cowan University, Joondalup, Australia.

Siew Hwa Yen
Economic Section, School of Distance Education, Universiti Sains Malaysia, Penang, Malaysia.

Joe A. Yoshino
Associate Professor of Economics, Department of Economics, FEA, University of Sao Paulo, Sao Paulo, Brazil.

Xiaoxi Zhang
School of Economics and Finance, Campbelltown Campus, University of Western Sydney, Sydney, Australia.

Xin Zhao
Université Paris, Panthéon-Sorbonne, France.

Mrabet Zouhair
College of Business and Economics, Department of Finance and Economics, Qatar University, Qatar.

AUTHOR BIOGRAPHIES

Mohamed A. Ayadi

Dr. Mohamed A. Ayadi is an Associate Professor of Finance at the Goodman School of Business at Brock University (Ontario, Canada). He received his PhD in Finance from Concordia University and M.Sc. in Finance from HEC Montreal. Prior to joining Brock, he taught at Concordia University and University of Quebec. His research interests are in the area of investment management, mutual funds, corporate governance, financial markets regulation, and derivative securities. He has made numerous presentations at several domestic and international finance conferences. His papers have been published in journals/books such as the Journal of Banking and Finance, Computers and Operations Research, Quarterly Journal of Business and Economics, Numerical Methods in Finance, Journal of Financial Services Research, and Journal of Empirical Finance. He is an active reviewer for a number of finance and OR journals, books, conferences, FQRSC, Social Sciences and Humanities Research Council of Canada, and the Romanian National Council for Scientific Research.

Dominique Guégan

Dominique Guégan is currently a Professor of Mathematics at the University Paris 1 Panthéon-Sorbonne. She is the Director of the Doctorate school of Economics of University Paris 1, the head of the team of finance inside the research laboratory Centre d'Economie de la Sorbonne (CES), and the head of the master formation quantitative finance. Her domains of research are non-linear econometrics modeling, extreme value theory and risk measure in finance, pricing theory in incomplete markets, deterministic dynamical systems, non-parametric statistical tools, contagion, business cycle, and forecasting. She has already published eight books in statistics theory, time series, and finance, 100 academic papers and chapters of books. She also participates in several international projects supported by the French government, or European Commission, or International institutions.

Bertrand K. Hassani

Bertrand K. Hassani is a specialist of Basel II/III risk and capital modeling (Credit, Market, Operational, Liquidity, Counterparty, etc.) for SIFIs. He is also an active associate researcher at Paris 1 Pantheon-Sorbonne University in the LaBex ReFi. He has written several articles dealing with Risk Measures, Risk Modeling, and Risk Management. He spent two years working in the Bond/Structure notes market (Eurocorporate), four years in the banking industry in a Risk Management/Modelling department (BPCE), and one year as a Consultant (Aon-AGRC). Since 2012, he is the Head of Major Risk Management at Santander UK.

Xin Zhao

Xin Zhao is a PhD candidate from University Paris 1 Pantheon-Sorbonne, majored in applied mathematics. The topic of her thesis is "Long Term Risk Analysis and Modeling". The domains of her study cover long-memory modeling applied on risk measures, sovereign ratings, and corporate ratings. She has been actively participating in seminars and conferences worldwide. She also teaches for some master lectures in University Paris 1 Pantheon-Sorbonne.

Xiaoxi Zhang

Xiaoxi Zhang recently graduated with a PhD (Commerce) titled "China's outward FD1 and Bank Performance"' from the University of Western Sydney. She has published in professional journals on several aspects of China's Foreign Direct Investment including the Emerging Markets Review (2011), Journal of International Finance and Economics (2010), and forthcoming publications in the Chinese Economy (2013) and Journal of Modern Accounting and Auditing (2013). Currently she is researching on a global study that investigates successful case studies where the FDI Incentive has been applied.

Kevin Daly

Kevin Daly is Associate Professor and teaches International Finance and Investment in the School of Business University of Western Sydney (Macarthur), prior appointments included the University of Adelaide, University of Brighton (UK), and Sussex University. Before joining academia he worked at various positions in Merchant Banking in the City of London. He holds a BA (Hons in Political Economy), and MA (Economics Analysis and Policy) University of Sussex and a PhD (Commerce) University of Western Sydney (Macarthur). His research passion revolves around applied finance and open economy macroeconomics; researching the effects of financial volatility on real economic activity. Examples of his research are included in the following journals: Japan and the World Economy, Journal of Asia Pacific Economy, Asia Pacific Journal of Economics and Business, International Review of Financial Analysis, Emerging Markets Review, and the Australian Economic Review. His current research interests focus on banking in China and Vietnam, foreign direct investment in China and Vietnam, and financial volatility of stock markets in South East Asia.

Marcelo Sánchez

Marcelo Sánchez holds a PhD degree in Economics from the University of California at Berkeley. He currently works in the Euro Area Macroeconomic Developments Division, at the European Central Bank. His areas of expertise are monetary economics, international macroeconomics (with a focus on emerging market economies and currency unions), and the impact of oil shocks on advanced economies.

Rituparna Das

Dr. Rituparna Das is the Executive Director of the Centre of Risk Management and Derivatives and Associate Professor at the National Law University Jodhpur, India. His

PhD on Econometrics is preceded by dual Masters in Economics and Management. His prior academic associations include Centre for Studies in Banking and Finance (established by the Reserve Bank of India) at National Law University Jodhpur, National Institute of Bank Management (established by the Reserve Bank of India), National University of Juridical Sciences, and Indian Institute of Social Welfare and Business Management. His areas of preference and international publications include Strategies, Bank Risk Management, Financial Economics, and Policy Research. He is Life Member of the Indian Statistical Institute and the Indian Econometric Society. He received the Honors of being "Financial Economics and Risk Educator and Author" from Marquis Who's Who in 2012 and "One of the IBC's Leading Educators of the World" from International Biographical Centre in 2013.

Michael C.S. Wong

Dr. Michael C.S. Wong is the Founding Chairman of CTRISKS Rating, a licensed credit rating agency in Hong Kong. He graduated from the University of Cambridge, University of Essex, and Chinese University of Hong Kong and is an elected Fellow of Royal Statistical Society (UK). Prior to his academic and consulting career, he spent seven years on investment banking, specializing on currencies, precious metals, and derivatives trading. He was granted the "Teaching Excellence Award" by the City University of Hong Kong in 1999. In the same year, his PhD thesis won the "Young Scholar Dissertation Award" of the Chinese University of Hong Kong. He served as a founding member of GARP's FRM Committee, an examiner of Hong Kong Institute of Bankers' examinations, and a member of examination panel of Hong Kong Securities Institute and Stock Exchange of Hong Kong. He has published more than 60 academic papers in Finance and Risk Management and frequently serves as an invited speaker in professional risk conferences in the Asian region.

Rafael Munoz Moreno

Rafael Muñoz Moreno is Senior Country Economist at the World Bank. He holds a PhD in Economics from University of Louvain (Belgium), and a European Doctoral Program in Quantitative Economic after visiting the London School of Economics. He has published several research papers, mostly on labor economics and business cycles. Prior to joining the World Bank, he worked in the Spanish Embassy in Tokyo as Economist and the European Commission as Operation Officer in charge of development projects in Latin America. Since joining the World Bank in 2005, he has worked in the office of the Vice-President of the Economic Department and has served as country economist in the Africa Region. He is now based in Mauritius as Country Economist and Resident Representative.

Verena Tandrayen-Ragoobur

Verena Tandrayen-Ragoobur is Senior Lecturer in Economics in the Department of Economics and Statistics at the University of Mauritius. She has a Masters in

Economics and International Economics, from the University of Nottingham, UK and has completed a PhD in Economics from the University of Mauritius. She was a Commonwealth Scholar under the Split-Doctoral Scholarship tenable at the University of Nottingham. Her research areas are international trade, foreign direct investment, labor markets, public sector reforms, poverty, economic development, climate change, and gender issues. She has published in the Review of Development Economics, Research Journal of International Studies, Journal of Internet Banking and Commerce, International Research Journal of Finance and Economics, and Journal of Economic Research, among others. She has been involved in a number of research projects and consultancies funded by international and regional institutions like CEEPA, AERC, BIDPA, TIPS, among others. She has been involved in consultancies at the national level namely in the Maurice Ile Durable initiative, the Rio+20 report, and with the Truth and Justice Commission. She has also been the chair of the WTO Chairs Programme and has organized a number of workshops, lectures by eminent Professors, and International Conferences on International Trade and Investment.

Boopendra Seetanah

Boopen Seetanah is a Senior Lecturer in Economics and Finance and the Faculty Research Advisor at the Faculty of Law and Management of the University of Mauritius. His research interests are transport and tourism economics, development economics, and financial economics. He is a reviewer for a number of refereed journals including Annals of Tourism Research, Tourism Management, Tourism Economics, Journal of Transport, Economics, and Policy, and Empirical Economics, among others. He has been consulting with both the government of Mauritius and with international organization including UNCTAD, World Bank, UNDP, African Development Bank, and COMESA, among others.

Raja Vinesh Sannassee

Raja Vinesh Sannassee is an Associate Professor of the Department of Finance at the University of Mauritius. He holds a PhD in Economics from the University of Reading, UK and currently lectures International Business both at undergraduate and postgraduate levels. In addition, He has several publications in the areas of finance, economics, and trade. He is also presently the Director of Programme for the M.Sc. in Social Protection Financing, a joint initiative by the UoM and the ILO, funded by the IDRC. In addition, he is due to take over the Deanship of the Faculty of Law and Management in March of next year. Furthermore, he presently sits on various committees both at the University and at national level, and he is due to take up the Chair of the WTO Chairs Programme in July of this year. Finally, he has also acted as a consultant for various international organizations which include the World Bank, the UNDP, and the AfDB among others.

A.S.M. Sohel Azad

Dr. Sohel Azad joined Deakin University as Lecturer in Finance in 2011. Before joining Deakin, he held faculty and research positions at different universities in Bangladesh and Japan. His current research interests are in volatility and risk modeling, asset pricing, and financial integration. He has published his research works in International Review of Financial Analysis, International Review of Finance, Asian Economic Journal, Research in International Business and Finance, and other peer-reviewed finance and economics journals and books.

Amirul Ahsan

Dr. Amirual Ahsan joined Deakin University as Lecturer in Finance in 2009. Before joining Deakin, he held faculty and research positions at Dhaka University, Bangladesh. His research outputs have appeared in various peer-reviewed international journals including Journal of administration & governance and edited books.

Victor Fang

Victor Fang is an Associate Professor of Finance in the School of Accounting, Economics and Finance at Deakin University. He has spent more than 20 years teaching in various universities in Australia and abroad. In addition, he conducts professional training courses to professional bodies in China and Vietnam (such as CPA Beijing, Bank of Communication, Shanghai and China Civil Aviation Authority (CCAA, Beijing), and Ho Chi Minh Stock exchange and Security Research Training Centre (SRTC, Vietnam)). Prior to that, Victor has worked with various large international banks (HSBC, Chase Manhattan, and Deutsche Bank) for a period of 10 years. His prior appointments in the banking industry include the position of chief treasury officer, senior bank trader, and assistant bank manager. His research interests focus particularly on the valuation of interest rate swaps, the determinants of swap spreads, and modeling the term structure of interest rates. Victor has published his research works in International Review of Financial Analysis, International Review of Finance, Research in International Business and Finance, Pacific Basin Finance Journal, Journal of Fixed Income, Accounting and Finance, and other peer-reviewed finance and economics journals and books.

Mohamed El Hedi Arouri

Dr. Arouri is currently a Professor of Finance at the Université d'Auvergne, a Researcher at CRCGM, and an Associate Researcher at EDHEC Financial Analysis and Accounting Research Centre. He holds an M.Sc. in Economics and a PhD in Financial Economics from Université de Paris X (France) and obtained his HDR (Habilitation for Supervising Doctoral Research) in Management Sciences from the Université d'Orléans. Winner of the AFFI-Euronext 2006 Prize, his currently serves as member of editorial and scientific committee of various academic international journals and conferences. His research works' focus is on the cost of capital, risk management, energy Finance, and international portfolio choice. His most recent articles are published in refereed journals such as Journal of Macroeconomics, Journal of Banking & Finance, Ecological Economics, Journal of International Money & Finance, Energy Economics, Macroeconomic Dynamics, Revue Finance, and Annales d'Economie et de Statistiques.

Christophe Rault
Dr. Christophe Rault is Professor of Economics at the University of Orléans in France. He earned his PhD in economics from the University of Paris 1, Panthéon-Sorbonne in December 2000 and his HDR (Habilitation for Supervising Doctoral Research) in November 2003. His affiliated research group is LEO (Laboratoire d'Economie d'Orléans of the University of Orléans, CNRS UMR 7322). He is also a member of the Financial Economics research group at Toulouse Business School, France. He has been a Senior Expert for the European Central Bank (since 2007), for «l'Ecole Nationale d'Administration (ENA)» (since 2010), for «l'Institut Supérieur de Gestion et de Planification (ISGP) », of Alger (since 2010). His applied research interests include energy economics, labor economics, international macroeconomics, and transition economics. He has published articles in numerous international journals such as Economics Letters, Ecological Economics, Economic Modelling, Energy Policy, Oxford Bulletin of Economics and Statistics, Oxford Economic Papers, Journal of Comparative Economics, Journal of Economic Integration, Journal of Economic Surveys, the Journal of Economic History, and Review of World Economics among others.

Rabaa Karaa
Rabaa Karaa is a PhD researcher at the Institute of the Higher Commercial Studies of Carthage. She is also a teaching assistant at the Higher Institute of Transport and Logistics of Sousse. Her principal research areas concern financial crisis, market microstructure, and stock market volatility.

Skander Slim
Skander Slim is Assistant Professor of finance at the Institute of Higher Commercial Studies of Sousse and served as Head of department of economics and statistics. He holds a PhD in finance from the University of Paris X-Nanterre (France). His main research interests include risk evaluation, option pricing, and market microstructure. He has recently published academic papers in refereed journals including Quantitative Finance, International Journal of Theoretical and Applied Finance, and International Journal of Economics and Finance.

Dorra Mezzez Hmaied
Dorra Mezzez Hmaied is Associate Professor and Head of department of finance at the Institute of the Higher Commercial Studies of Carthage. She is also a Director of the training Institute of the Tunis Stock Exchange (IFBT). Her research interests

are mergers and acquisitions, market microstructure, and behavioral finance. She has published papers in Journal of Finance Regulation and Compliance, Banque et Marchés, Review of Middle East Economics and Finance, Quarterly Journal of Finance India, and Electronic Markets-the International Journal.

Marcelo Bianconi

Marcelo Bianconi is Associate Professor of Economics at Tufts University, in Medford, MA. He holds a PhD in Economics from University of Illinois at Urbana-Champaign. His fields of academic research are theoretical and applied economic models with particular attention to domestic and international aspects of financial economics, risk methods in economics and finance, applied econometrics and time series analysis, and monetary and fiscal policies. He has published books and academic papers in several professional journals. He also serves in the editorial council of the Review of International Economics since 1997 and is an associate editor of the International Review of Economics and Finance since 2002. In the years 2000–2003, he was elected and served as executive secretary of the International Economics and Finance Society (IEFS).

Joe Akira Yoshino

Joe Akira Yoshino is Associate Professor at FEA-Economics Department USP (Universidade de Sao Paulo) and researcher and project coordinator at FIPE-USP. He holds a PhD economics from University of Chicago (USA). He teaches undergraduate and graduate courses in capital markets, derivatives, money and banking, corporate finance, fixed-income analysis, and the economics of regulation. He is also Editor of Economic Studies (Estudos Economicos) for 2011 and has published in several academic journals.

Bertrand Candelon

Bertrand Candelon is a Professor, holding the chair in International Monetary Economics at the University Maastricht. Before, he received a PhD from Universite Catholique de Louvain, and was Pierre and Marie Curie post-doctoral fellowship at the Humboldt Universität zu Berlin. He has been Invited Professor in numerous universities as the University of Orleans, Macquarie University in Sydney, and City University of Hong-Kong. He has published and presented numerous works in the area of macroeconomics (Money demand, fiscal policy, raw commodities) and international finance (financial crisis early warning systems, the financial markets co-movements). He is also consultant at the European Commission, at the IMF, and one of the founders of the Methods in International Finance Network.

Stefan Straetmans

Stefan Straetmans is an Associate Professor of finance at the Maastricht University School of Business and Economics in the Netherlands. He received an MA in Economics from the University of Leuven in Belgium and a PhD in Economics from Erasmus University Rotterdam in the Netherlands. Before joining Maastricht University he was an Assistant Professor at the Free University Amsterdam. His research interests include, inter alia, exchange rate behavior, banking system stability and the modeling and measurement of systemic risk, financial risk and financial crisis management, financial market contagion, linkages, and integration. His work has resulted in numerous publications in international academic journals like the Review of Economics and Statistics, the Journal of Applied Econometrics, Oxford Bulletin of Economics and Statistics, the Journal of International Money and Finance, and the Journal of Banking and Finance.

Anastassios A. Drakos

Anastassios A. Drakos is Assistant Professor of Finance at the Department of Business Administration of the Athens University of Economics and Business. He holds a PhD in Finance from the Department of Business Administration, AUEB. He also holds an MA in International and European Economic Studies, AUEB and a B.Sc. in Regional Engineering, University of Thessaly. His main research interests are: Valuation of securities, money and capital markets, investments, corporate finance, and corporate governance. He has published in several refereed journals such as: Journal of Policy Modeling, International Journal of Finance and Economics, International Review of Financial Analysis, Research in International Business and Finance, Managerial and Decisions Economics.

Georgios P. Kouretas

Georgios P. Kouretas is currently Professor of International Finance at the Department of Business Administration at the Athens University of Economics and Business and holder of the Jean Monnet Chair on European Economic Policy. He obtained a BA in Economics from the University of Piraeus (1981), MA in Economics from the University of Notre Dame (1983), MA in Economics from Wayne State University (1985), and a PhD in Economics from the University of Birmingham (1988). His main research interests cover international finance, European financial markets and monetary issues, international money and capital markets, open economy macroeconomics, portfolio management, financial management, risk management, and applied econometrics. He has over 70 publications in refereed international journals and collective volumes. He is also co-organizer of the internationally recognized for their high-quality Annual Conference on Macroeconomic Analysis and International Finance and Advanced Summer School in Economics and Econometrics. He has acted as guest editor for high-quality international journals in economics and finance such as Macroeconomic Dynamics, Journal of Banking and Finance, North American Journal of Economics and Finance, Review of International Economics, Journal of International Money and Finance, International Journal of Finance and Economics, Open Economies Review, and Journal of Common Market Studies.

David Chen

David Chen received his Master of Commerce and Management in finance specializing in stock market and his Bachelor of Commerce in Finance from Lincoln University, Christchurch, New Zealand. His research interests are in the areas of emerging financial markets.

Christopher Gan

Christopher Gan is a Professor of accounting and finance in the Department of Accounting, Economics and Finance at Lincoln University, New Zealand. He is also the Director of Lincoln University Center for International Development. His research interests are in Asian economics, finance, and banking. He is the Chief Editor of the Review of Applied Economics.

Baiding Hu

Baiding Hu is a senior Lecturer in the Department of Accounting, Economics and Finance at Lincoln University, New Zealand. His research interests are in productivity and efficiency estimation, Chinese economy, and energy economics.

Brian M. Lucey

Brian M. Lucey is Professor of finance in Trinity College Dublin, Ireland. He obtained his PhD from the University of Stirling on the topic of behavioral asset pricing. His research output of more than 80 peer-reviewed publications covers behavioral finance, economic integration, and international finance, trade, and development. Brian is currently the editor of International Review of Financial Analysis and founder of the INFINITI Conference on International Finance.

Michael Dowling

Michael Dowling is Lecturer in finance in Dublin City University Business School, Ireland. He completed his PhD and post-doctoral studies on the influence of emotions in investor decision making in Trinity College Dublin, Ireland. His research covers emotion, heuristic, gender, and cultural influences on financial decision making, and has been published in journals including Journal of Economic Surveys, International Review of Financial Analysis, and Journal of Multinational Financial Management.

Kyong Joo OH

Kyong Joo OH is an Associate Professor in the Department of Information and Industrial Engineering at Yonsei University, South Korea. He received his BA (1991) and MA (1993) degrees in Applied Statistics at Yonsei University and PhD degree (2000) in Management Information Engineering at Korea Advanced Institute of Science and Technology (KAIST). He served as a researcher at Research Center of Hyundai Securities Co. (2001). He has published over 30 technical articles. His research fields are financial information systems, financial engineering, artificial intelligence in finance, and system trading.

Young Min Kim

Young Min Kim is a PhD degree student in the Department of Information and Industrial Engineering at Yonsei University, South Korea. He has submitted some technical articles to major journals and conferences. His research fields are financial information systems, financial engineering, and artificial intelligence applications.

Tae Yoon Kim

Tae Yoon Kim is a Professor in the Department of Statistics at Keimyung University, South Korea. He got his PhD in statistics at University of Illinois at Urbana-Champaign (1990). His research interest includes unit root test, nonparametric function estimation, bootstrap, neural network, and time series analysis of financial markets. He served as visiting research scholar at The Bank of Korea (2001) and Department of Statistics at Rice University (1998) and Seoul National University (2006).

Khaled Guesmi

Khaled Guesmi was an Associate Researcher at the University of Paris Ouest Naterre la Défense (France) where he obtained his PhD in Economics. His research interest covers the fields of international finance, market integration, and asset pricing. He has published articles in several peer-reviewed journals such as Economic Modelling, International Economics, Journal of Economic Integration, and Journal of International Financial Markets, Institutions and Money.

Flavio Bazzana

Flavio Bazzana is Associate Professor in Finance and Director of Studies of the Master in Finance at the University of Trento (Italy) where he teaches International Corporate Finance, Corporate Finance, and Investment and derivatives. He graduated in Economics at the University of Siena (Italy) with Prof. Frank H. Hahn and continued his academic training achieving the M.Phil. In Economic Theory and Econometrics at the University of Cambridge (UK), the M.Sc. in Banking and Finance, and the PhD in Finance, both at the University of Siena (Italy). His main interests are on corporate finance, contract theory, risk management, and microstructure of financial markets.

Eleonora Broccardo

Eleonora Broccardo is Assistant Professor in Finance at the University of Trento (Italy) where she teaches Advanced Corporate Finance. She graduated in Economics at the University of Trento (Italy) and achieved the PhD in Markets and Financial Intermediaries at the Catholic University of Milan (Italy). Her main interests are on small corporate finance, securitization, credit derivatives, and bank's risk management.

Elmas Yaldız

Elmas Yaldız received her first MA in Applied Economics from Dokuz Eylul University (Turkey), and her second MA in Financial Economics from Izmir University of

Economics (Turkey), where she was a research and teaching assistant, and her PhD in Economics and Management at the University of Trento (Italy). She taught econometrics, managerial economics, and finance for undergraduate and master students as teaching assistant both in Izmir and Trento. Her research interests include experimental economics, econometrics, and financial economics.

Mazin A. M. Al Janabi

Mazin A.M. Al Janabi has over 28 years of real-world experience in financial sectors and academic institutions and in many different roles in USA, Mexico, and UK. He has worked for top international financial groups and has held several senior finance and banking positions. He has served as consultant in finance/banking and as advisor for the creation of new financial markets within emerging economies. He has written on finance and banking and contemporary topics in trading, market, and credit risk management as well as on strategic assets allocation and modern portfolio management. His research interests, teaching and consulting activities address practitioners and regulatory issues in finance and banking, financial risk management, derivative securities, portfolio management, and financial engineering.

Anna Golab

Anna Golab has recently completed her PhD at Edith Cowan University. Her research field is of European emerging markets and economies. Her research adopted a time-series framework and extensive econometrics analysis.

David E. Allen

David E. Allen is Professor of Finance at Edith Cowan University, Perth, Western Australia. He is the author of three monographs and over 80 refereed publications on a diverse range of topics covering corporate financial policy decisions, asset pricing, business economics, funds management and performance bench marking, volatility modeling and hedging, and market microstructure and liquidity.

Robert Powell

Robert Powell has 20 years of banking experience in South Africa, New Zealand, and Australia. He has been involved in the development and implementation of several credit and financial analysis models in Banks. He has a PhD from Edith Cowan University, where he currently works as an Associate Professor, teaching and researching in banking and finance.

Ghialy Yap

Ghialy Yap is an Economics Lecturer at Edith Cowan University. Her main research interests are applied economics including economics of superannuation and tourism economics. Furthermore, she has extensive knowledge in applied time-series and panel data econometrics.

Jan Hanousek

Jan Hanousek is a Professor of Economics at Charles University, CERGE, and a Senior Researcher in the Economics Institute (EI) of the Czech Academy of Sciences. His research interests include applied econometrics and corporate finance, while his teaching includes various topics in statistics and econometrics. He has published in the Journal of Economic Literature, Journal of Corporate Finance, Journal of Economic Perspectives, Review of International Economics, European Economic Review, Economics of Transition, Journal of Comparative Economics, and other specialized journals. He has taught at the University of Pennsylvania and Anglo-American University. He has a PhD in statistics and an undergraduate degree in probability theory both from Charles University.

Jan Novotný

Jan Novotný is a Post-Doctoral Research Fellow at the Cass Business School, City University London funded from the European Community's Seventh Framework Program FP7-PEOPLE-2011-IEF under Grant Agreement Number PIEF-GA-2011-302098 (Price Jump Dynamics), and a Researcher at CERGE-EI, Charles University. His research interests include financial econometrics, financial engineering, risk, finance, and econophysics. He has published in Emerging Markets Review, Monte Carlo Methods and Applications, and Physica A. He has co-authored papers in physics journals. He has a M.Sc. in experimental nuclear physics from Czech Technical University and a MA from CERGE-EI and a PhD in economics from Charles University.

Hakimzadi Wagan

Hakimzadi Wagan is a postdoctoral fellow at HEC Montreal, Quebec, Canada. She received her Master's degree in Business Administration from the University of Sindh Jamshoro, Pakistan and the MPhil/MS degree in Money, Banking and Finance from the University of Paris 1, Panthéon-Sorbonne, Paris, France in 2009. She obtained her PhD degree from the University of Paris 1, Panthéon-Sorbonne, Paris, France in 2013. She worked on Monetary Policy Transmission in OECD and G-7 countries. She also worked on the contagion during recent global financial crisis in advanced and emerging countries. Her research interests include corporate finance, bank and money, exchange rates risk, portfolio diversification, stock markets integration versus segmentation, international multifactor asset pricing, and econometrics applied to finance.

Zulfiqar Ali

Zulfiqar Ali received his Master's degree in Business Administration from the University of Sindh Jamshoro, Pakistan. He is also visiting research fellow at University of Sindh Jamshoro, Pakistan. His research interests include monetary policy transmission, asset pricing, financial contagion, international finance, and econometrics of time series analysis applied to macroeconomics and finance.

Kevin Daly

Kevin Daly is Associate Professor and teaches International Finance and Investment in the School of Business University of Western Sydney (Macarthur), prior appointments included the University of Adelaide, University of Brighton (UK), and Sussex University. Before joining academia Kevin worked at various positions in Merchant Banking in the City of London. Kevin holds a BA (Hons in Political Economy), and MA (Economics Analysis and Policy) University of Sussex and a PhD (Commerce) University of Western Sydney (Macarthur). His research passion revolves around applied finance and open economy macroeconomics; researching the effects of financial volatility on real economic activity. Examples of his research are included in the following journals: Japan and the World Economy, Journal of Asia Pacific Economy, Asia Pacific Journal of Economics and Business, International Review of Financial Analysis, Emerging Markets Review, and the Australian Economic Review.

Tran Phuong Thao

Tran Phuong Thao recently graduated with a DBA (Commerce) titled "Impacts of the Global Financial Crisis on an Emerging Market: The Case of Vietnam" from the University of Western Sydney. She recently presented a paper titled "Post Global Financial Crisis and dynamic linkages among the East Asian equity markets" at the 3rd Annual International Conference on Qualitative and Quantitative Economic Research in Bangkok. Currently She is researching on dynamic linkages between Asian Equity Markets.

Craig Ellis

Craig Ellis graduated from the University of Western Sydney with PhD Commerce; his research field includes Corporate Governance and Firm Performance and Valuation of Companies in Emerging Markets.

Ahdi Noomen Ajmi

Ahdi Noomen Ajmi received the PhD degree in Economics from the University of the Mediterranean (France) and the University of Tunis (Tunisia). He also obtained this HDR (Habilitation for Supervising Doctoral Research) in Economics from University de la Manouba (Tunisia) in June 2013. He is an affiliated researcher with the Business and Economics Statistics Modeling Laboratory (University of Tunisia). He is currently an Assistant Professor at the College of Science and Humanities in Slayel, Salman bin Abdulaziz University (Kingdom of Saudi Arabia). His main research interests are: time-series models, causality analysis, long memory, and volatility analysis. The author's publications have appeared in Economic Modelling, Emerging Markets Review, Computational Economics, Mathematics and Social Sciences, Empirical Economics Letters, Applied Mathematical Sciences, and Economics Bulletin.

Charfeddine Lanouar

Charfeddine Lanouar is an Assistant Professor of Applied Econometrics in the College of Administrative Sciences, Department of Business Administration, Najran University, Saudi Arabia and Institut Supérieur de Gestion de Gabes, Tunisie. He has published several papers in international journals such as Physica A, Emerging Market Review, Journal of High Technology Management Research, and Région et Développement.

Zouhair Mrabet

Zouhair Mrabet is an Assistant Professor of Economics at the Department of Finance and Economics, College of Business and Economics, Qatar University. His research covers the fields of international trade and finance. He has published several papers in journals such as Région et Développement, African Journal of Economic and Management, and Journal of Economics and Behavioral Studies.

Jarkko Peltomäki

Jarkko Peltomäki is an Associate Professor at the Stockholm University, School of Business. His research interests focus on hedge funds, investment strategies, emerging markets, and performance measurement. His articles have appeared in the Journal of Behavioral Finance, Managerial Finance, Journal of Wealth Management, and Emerging Markets Review.

Michael Graham

Michael Graham is an Associate Professor at the School of Business, Stockholm University. His key research areas include financial market co-movement, corporate restructuring and governance, and working capital management corporate. He has published in several reputable journals including the European Finance Journal, Corporate Governance: An International Review, Quantitative Finance, Quarterly Review of Economics and Finance, Journal of Multinational Financial Management, Research in International Business and Finance, and Global Finance Journal. He has wide international experience and has taught in Australia, Finland, Hong Kong, Malaysia, and Singapore. He has also worked for several reputable institutions including the UN World Institute for Development Economics Research and the Australian Competition and Consumer Commission.

Hooi Hooi Lean

Hooi Hooi Lean is an Associate Professor at the School of Social Sciences (Economics Program), Universiti Sains Malaysia. She has published more than 60 book chapters and journal articles in many reputed international journals such as Applied Economics, Economics Letters, Energy Economics, Journal of Financial Markets, Journal of Economic Behavior & Organization, Pacific Basin Finance Journal, and Tourism Economics. She is listed in the Who'sWho in the World 2009 and Researcher of the Week in GDNet East Asia for her excellent contributions. She has been awarded the ASEAN-ROK

Academic Exchange Fellowship Program in 2007, the Democratic Pacific Union Visiting Fellowship in 2008, and the International HERMES Fellowship Program in 2009. She has also won the "Sanggar Sanjung" Excellent Award for Publication since 2009 and "Hadiah Sanjungan" Best Award for Publication since 2006 from Universiti Sains Malaysia. There are 730 citations to her research on Google Scholar.

Russell Smyth

Russell Smyth is Professor and Head of the Department of Economics Monash Univeristy, Australia. He has published approximately 300 book chapters and journal articles in the fields of economics, law, and political science. His research interests encompass Asian economies, Chinese economic reform, and financial economics, among others. From 1998 to 2008, he was Editor of Economic Papers, the policy journal of the Economic Society of Australia and was a member of the Central Council of the Economic Society of Australia. In 2008, he received the Honorary Fellow Award of the Economic Society of Australia. He is currently an Associate Editor of Energy Economics and a member of seven editorial boards. There are 3600 citations to his research on Google Scholar.

Zied Ftiti

Zied Ftiti is Associate Professor and teaches Econometrics, mathematics, statisticals, and monetary economic in High Institute of Management (Tunisia). Actually, he is an associate researcher at IPAG Business School in Paris (France). Before joining Higher Institute of Management, he has had various teaching experiences in many universities (such as Universities of Lyon 2 & Lyon 1, University of Poitiers…). He holds a Master degree on applied macroeconomics at the University of Lyon 2 and a PhD (Economics) at the University of Lyon 2 (France). His research passion revolves around applied economics and Finance and open economy macroeconomics; researching the robustness of monetary policy and the transmission channel. His research papers have appeared in journals such as Economic Modelling and Journal of Economic Integration.

Jamel Boukhatem

Jamel Boukhatem is Associate Professor and teaches Principles of Economics, International Economics, and Monetary and Financial Macroeconomics in the High School of Management (Tunisia). Prior appointments included the High Business School, the High School of Business and Economic Sciences. He holds a Master degree on Money Banking and Finance (University of Tunis El Manar) and a PhD on Economics (University of Paris West Nanterre la Defense and University of Tunis El Manar). His research passion revolves around applied economics and monetary and financial macroeconomics; researching the effects of bond market development on real economic activity. Examples of his research are included in the Journal of Development Economics, Panoeconomicus Review, Savings and Development, and

Finance Research Letters. Current research interests focus on bond markets integration and macroeconomic stability, financial accelerator and macroeconomic dynamics, and public debt and economic growth.

Ines Ben Bouhouch

Ines Ben Bouhouch is Research Assistant in Finance at the Faculty of Economics and Management of Nabeul (University of Carthage, Tunisia) since September 2008, and Research Fellow at Laboratory for Research on Quantitative Development Economics, Faculty of Economics and Management of Tunis.

Jamel Jouini

Jamel Jouini is Associate Professor of Economics at College of Business Administration (King Saud University, Saudi Arabia) since September 2011, and Research Fellow at Laboratory of Economics and Management (Polytechnic School of Tunisia) since September 2005. He holds a PhD in Economics from the University of Aix-Marseille II in France, and an Habilitation to Supervise Doctoral Researches in Economics from the University of Tunis El Manar (Tunisia). His research focuses on Time Series Econometrics, Macroeconometrics and Financial Econometrics. He has published several papers in international scientific reviews such as Journal of International Money and Finance, Energy Economics, Economic Modelling, Journal of Policy Modeling, Applied Economics, Journal of Applied Statistics, Statistical Papers, etc.

Jihed Majdoub

Jihed Majdoub is Assistant Professor of Finance at Higher Institute of Management (University of Tunis, Tunisia) since September 2011, and Research Fellow at Laboratory for Research on Quantitative Development Economics, Faculty of Economics and Management of Tunis. He holds a PhD in Economics from the University of Cergy-Pontoise, France. His research focuses on international diversification, financial econometrics, and behavioral finance. He has published several papers in international scientific reviews such as Journal of Computations & Modeling and Business Quarterly Studies.

Theodore Syriopoulos

Theodore Syriopoulos is Professor of Finance at the School of Business Studies, University of the Aegean, Greece. He also holds adjunct and visiting posts at Audencia Nantes School of Management, France, Newcastle University, UK, Shanghai Maritime University, China, Athens University of Economics and Business, Greece, International Hellenic University, Greece, and Hellenic Open University, Greece. Before joining the academia, he held top executive management posts in banking, investment, asset management, and consulting business. He publishes regularly in accredited international financial journals as well as in edited volumes and books in topics of applied finance.

Imad Moosa

Imad Moosa is a professor of finance at RMIT, Melbourne. He has held positions at Monash University (Melbourne), La Trobe University (Melbourne) and the University of Sheffield (UK). He holds a BA in Economics and Business Studies, MA in the Economics of Financial Intermediaries, and a PhD in Financial Economics from the University of Sheffield (UK). He has received formal training in model building, exchange rate forecasting, and risk management at the Claremont Economics Institute (United States), Wharton Econometrics (United States), and the Center for Monetary and Banking Studies (Switzerland). Before turning to academia in 1991, he worked as a financial analyst, a financial journalist, and an investment banker for over 10 years. He has also worked at the International Monetary Fund in Washington DC and acted as an advisor to the US Treasury. His work encompasses the areas of International Finance, Banking, Risk Management, Macroeconomics, and Applied Econometrics. His papers have appeared in the Journal of Applied Econometrics, Canadian Journal of Economics, IMF Staff Papers, Journal of Futures Markets, Quantitative Finance, Southern Economic Journal, American Journal of Agricultural Economics, Journal of Development Economics, Journal of Comparative Economics, Journal of Economic Organization and Behavior, and Journal of Banking and Finance. He has also written for the prestigious Euromoney Magazine. His recent books include Quantification of Operational Risk under Basel II: The Good, Bad and Ugly, The Myth of Too Big to Fail (both published by Palgrave in 2008 and 2009, respectively), and The US-China Trade Dispute: Facts, Figure and Myths, published by Edward Elgar in 2012. His forthcoming book, Quantitative Easing as a Highway to Hyperinflation will be published by World Scientific towards the end of 2012.

Vikash Ramiah

Vikash Ramiah is currently an Associate Professor of Finance at RMIT University. He has a Diploma of Management, B. Sc. (Hons) Economics, Master of Finance program, and Doctor of Philosophy from RMIT University. He has received numerous awards for outstanding performance in teaching and supervision. He taught economics and finance courses at RMIT, University of Melbourne, La Trobe University, and Australian Catholic University since 1999. He has published in academic journals (e.g. Journal of Banking and Finance, Journal of Behavioral Finance, Applied Economics, Pacific Basin Finance Journal, and Journal of International Financial Market, Institution and Money), industry reports, one book, book chapters, and over 35 conference papers. His supervises numerous PhD students and regularly attracts research funding. He is an expert reviewer for 13 finance journals and for the Mauritius Research Council. He serves on the editorial board of two finance journals. He was an elected board member of the RMIT University Business Board, program Director of Open Universities Australia, and acting Board member at the Australian Centre For Financial Studies. He was as a junior auditor at H&A Consultant, manager at Intergate PTY Limited, quantitative analyst at ANZ, Investment Banking Division, provided consultancy services to the Australian Stock Exchange and worked in collaboration with the Finance and Treasury Association of Australia and the Australian Centre for Financial Studies. His research areas are financial markets, behavioral finance, and environmental finance.

Michael Donadelli

Michael Donadelli is currently a PhD Candidate in Economics at LUISS Guido Carli in Rome (Italy) and Post-Doc research fellow at the Center of Excellence SAFE, Goethe University Frankfurt. His research interests are empirical asset pricing, international macro-finance and poor economics. He received a Master in Quantitative Finance from the University of Venice, Italy, in 2008; received a MSc in Economics in Finance from the University of Venice in 2007; and received a BSc in Economics from the University of Venice in 2005.

Anil Mishra

Anil Mishra is a financial economist at the School of Business, University of Western Sydney, specializing in cross border investment. His research interests include cross border investment, international financial integration, home bias, cross border taxation, and asset allocation. He has published in journals such as Journal of International Money and Finance, Research in International Business and Finance, Review of Quantitative Finance and Accounting, Review of Pacific Basin Financial Markets and Policies, Emerging Markets Review, Australian Economic Papers, Australian Economic Review, Journal of International Trade and Economic Development, Journal of Asia Pacific Economy, and others. He has served as referee for several journals including Economic Modelling, World Development, Journal of International Financial Markets Institutions & Money, Emerging Markets Review, Journal of Economic Structure & Change, Physica A, and others. He is examiner for PhD and honors thesis and is on the supervisory panel for several PhD students.

Abdullah Alotaibi

Abdullah Alotaibi is a PhD student at the School of Business, University of Western Sydney, Australia. His research work is related to financial integration in GCC markets.

Perry Sadorsky

Perry Sadorsky is an Associate Professor of Economics at the Schulich School of Business at York University, Toronto, Ontario, Canada. He teaches courses in Applied Macroeconomics, Economic Forecasting and Analysis and Sustainability and Carbon Finance at the undergraduate and graduate (MBA) level. His research focuses on business issues related to energy, the natural environment, and financial markets. He has published extensively in these areas. I also have an interest in technology and innovation management.

Leonidas Sandoval Junior

Leonidas Sandoval Junior holds a PhD in Mathematics from King's College London, a M.A.St. from the University of Cambridge, a M.Sc. and graduation in the University of São Paulo. He works on the interrelations between international financial markets in the field of Complex Systems.

Christophe Rault

Christophe Rault is Full Professor of Economics at the University of Orléans in France. He earned his PhD in economics from the University of Paris 1, Panthéon-Sorbonne in December 2000 and his Habilitation Thesis to supervise PhD students in November 2003. His affiliated research group is LEO (Laboratoire d'Economie d'Orléans of the University of Orléans, CNRS UMR 7322). He is also a member of the Financial Economics research group at Toulouse Business School, France. He has been a Senior Expert for the European Central Bank (since 2007), for «l'Ecole Nationale d'Administration (ENA)», (since 2010), for «l'Institut Supérieur de Gestion et de Planification (ISGP) », of Alger (since 2010). His applied research interests include energy economics, labour economics, international macroeconomics, and transition economics. He has published articles in numerous international journals such as Economics Letters, Ecological Economics, Economic Modelling, Energy Policy, Oxford Bulletin of Economics and Statistics, Oxford Economic Papers, Journal of Comparative Economics, Journal of Economic Integration, Journal of Economic Surveys, Journal of Economic History, and Review of World Economics.

Robert Sova

Robert Sova is Full Professor of Economics and Vice-rector of the Bucharest University of Economic Studies (ASE). His research interests include Macroeconomics, International Finance, Econometrics, and Environment Economics. He has published papers in academic journals such as Ecological Economics, Review of World Economics, Environmental and Resource Economics, Economic Modelling, International Journal of Finance and Economics Applied Economic Letters, Journal for Economic Forecasting, Review of International Comparative Management, and Journal of International Trade and Economic Development.

Anamaria Sova

Anamaria Sova is researcher at the Economic Business Research Centre in Bucharest, Romania. Her research interests include Macroeconomics, International Finance, and Environment Economics. Her articles are focalized generally on the studies concerning Central and Eastern European Countries, and specifically their financial and economic evolution in the context of the economic integration to EU-15. Her papers have been published in academic journals such as Review of World Economics, Ecological Economics, Environmental and Resource Economics, Economic Modelling,

International Journal of Finance and Economics Applied Economic Letters Journal International Trade and Economic Development, and Journal for Economic Forecasting.

Guglielmo Maria Caporale

Guglielmo Maria Caporale is Professor of Economics and Finance and Director of the Centre for Empirical Finance at Brunel University, London. He is also a Visiting Professor at London South Bank University and London Metropolitan University, a Research Professor at DIW Berlin, and a CESifo Research Network Fellow. His research interests include Econometrics, Macroeconomics, Monetary and Financial Economics, International Finance. He has published papers in numerous books and leading academic journals, such as Journal of International Money and Finance, Economics Letters, Canadian Journal of Economics, Journal of Macroeconomics, Econometric Reviews, Oxford Bulletin of Economics and Statistics, Journal of Forecasting, Computational Statistics and Data Analysis, Journal of Empirical Finance, Journal of Financial Econometrics, Southern Economic Journal, Eastern Economic Journal, Quarterly Review of Economics and Finance, Empirical Economics, Scottish Journal of Political Economy, Manchester School of Economic and Social Studies, and International Journal of Finance and Economics.

Kee Tuan Teng

Kee Tuan Teng is currently a Senior Lecturer in Economics at the School of Business Studies in Tunku Abdul Rahman University College, Malaysia. She obtained her PhD from Universiti Sains Malaysia. She teaches International Economics, Macroeconomics, Microeconomics, and Business Economics. Her research interest and areas of specialisation include international trade and finance and economic interdependence and integration. Her research articles have been published in international journals such as Economic Modelling, Prague Economic Papers, and Margin: the Journal of Applied Economic Research.

Siew Hwa Yen

Siew Hwa Yen is currently a Senior Lecturer in economics at the School of Distance Education in Universiti Sains Malaysia. She obtained her M.Sc. from Iowa State University, USA and PhD from Universiti Sains Malaysia. Her research interests focus on macroeconomics, international economics, and socio-economic studies. Her research articles have been published in some international and local journals such as Bulletin of the Malaysian Mathematical Sciences Society, Prague Economic Papers, Margin: The Journal of Applied Economic Research, The Indian Economic Journal, Singapore Economic Review, The Malaysian Journal of Economic Studies, Journal of Malaysian Studies, and Malaysian Economics Journal.

Soo Y. Chua

Soo Y. Chua is a Senior Lecturer in Economics at the School of Social Sciences, Universiti Sains Malaysia. He earned both M.Sc. and PhD in Economics from Southern Illinois University at Carbondale, USA. His areas of specialization are International Economics, Development Economics, and Applied Econometrics and Statistics. He teaches International Economics and Southeast Asian Economy at undergraduate and graduate levels. His research interests are economic interdependence, trade flows, economic shocks, and exchange rates in East Asia. He has published articles in journals such as Asian Economic Journal, Applied Economics, Applied Economics Letters, Margin: The Journal of Applied Economic Research, Asia-Pacific Journal of Accounting & Economics, and The Journal of International Trade & Economic Development.

Hooi Hooi Lean

Hooi Hooi Lean is an Associate Professor at the School of Social Sciences (Economics Program), Universiti Sains Malaysia. She has published more than 60 book chapters and journal articles in many reputed international journals such as Applied Economics, Economics Letters, Energy Economics, Journal of Financial Markets, Journal of Economic Behavior & Organization, Pacific Basin Finance Journal, and Tourism Economics. She is listed in the Who's Who in the World 2009 and Researcher of the Week in GDNet East Asia for her excellent contributions. She has been awarded the ASEAN-ROK Academic Exchange Fellowship Program in 2007, the Democratic Pacific Union Visiting Fellowship in 2008, and the International HERMES Fellowship Program in 2009. She has also won the "Sanggar Sanjung" Excellent Award for Publication since 2009 and "Hadiah Sanjungan" Best Award for Publication since 2006 from Universiti Sains Malaysia. There are 730 citations to her research on Google Scholar.

PART *One*

Country-Specific Experiences

CHAPTER 1

Robust Measures of Hybrid Emerging Market Mutual Funds Performance

Mohamed A. Ayadi

Department of Finance, Operations, and Information Systems, Goodman School of Business, Brock University, St. Catharines, ON, Canada

1. INTRODUCTION

Emerging market mutual funds are investment portfolios that offer foreign investors opportunities to invest in alternative markets in Asia, Latin America, and Eastern Europe. These funds are particularly attractive to both individual and institutional investors seeking to increase their returns and diversify risks. Such funds have experienced a rapid growth over the past 20 years following the liberalization of economic and financial policies in various countries in Asia, Latin American, and Eastern Europe.[1]

The growing literature on emerging market investments and mutual funds has addressed several issues, and the ultimate objective of such a literature was to assess the selectivity, timing, and persistence performance of these portfolios (van der Hart et al., 2003; Gottesman and Morey, 2007; Huij and Post, 2011; Banegas, 2011). Other studies in this research stream have also examined the determinants of stock returns, the potential role of risk factors in the underlying return generating process of these special investment funds, and the validity of the benchmark models (Harvey, 1995; Rouwenhorst, 1999; Abel and Fletcher, 2004; Phylaktis and Xia, 2006; Iqbal et al., 2007, 2010). However, most of the academic and practitioners' attention has focused on equity or bond (fixed-income) funds rather than balanced or hybrid funds. This class of emerging market funds is very popular with risk-averse investors because these funds offer lower volatility and moderate returns. In addition, such funds have experienced strong inflows ever since the last financial crisis.

The literature on US-based balanced mutual funds is very limited and consists of a few articles that rely on traditional multifactor asset pricing models adapted to equity and fixed-income pricing. These articles also extend the basic market-timing models used in the performance measurement of equity funds. For example, Aragon (2005) derives new performance measures from a theoretical model with multiple market exposures and finds balanced funds show a positive (negative) timing (selection) ability over the period 1976–2004. Using a multifactor benchmark specification, Comer (2006) reports significant timing performance over the period 1992–2000 for a large sample of US

[1] See Kaminsky et al. (2001) for an excellent review of the structure and working of emerging market mutual funds.

Emerging Markets and the Global Economy
http://dx.doi.org/10.1016/B978-0-12-411549-1.00001-6

hybrid and asset allocation mutual funds. More recently, Comer et al. (2009) recommend using bond indices and factors to evaluate the performance of managed portfolios with substantial holdings in fixed-income securities.

All of these papers derive performance metrics by comparing the portfolio's average excess return to that implied by a benchmark model that reflects the risks related to equity and fixed-income exposures. These benchmark models fail to deliver reliable measures of performance and sometimes generate misleading inferences where the rankings can change essentially due to the choice and efficiency of the chosen benchmarks. Other potential sources of false performance inferences include possible misspecifications of the proposed return dynamics. Finally, the proposed tests are based on unconditional performance metrics that fail to produce a robust measure of abnormal performance when the expected returns and/or risk are time-varying. It is because these metrics are not able to isolate the impact of the superior abilities of portfolio managers from inherent time variation in the underlying assets. All of these problems suggest the need to develop an asset pricing model-free measure, which can control for conditioning information to assess the performance of this hybrid type of emerging market funds.

This alternative methodology relies on the fundamental asset-pricing theorem known as the stochastic discount factor (SDF) representation of asset prices introduced by Harrison and Kreps (1979). The above-cited theorem states that any gross return discounted by a market-wide random variable has a constant conditional expectation. Furthermore, the proposed framework allows for an integration of the role of conditioning information with various structures (Hansen and Richard, 1987).

Thus, the objective of this chapter is to introduce a conditional SDF that is adapted to performance evaluation of emerging market hybrid funds. This SDF efficiently accounts for the time variation in expected returns and risk, and does not rely on the linear information scaling used in most SDF-based performance tests reported in the literature. This approach has the advantage of not being dependent on any asset pricing model or any distributional assumptions. The proposed SDF is further differentiated from most of the existing SDF models owing to its a unique structure that reflects the nonlinear interdependences between its conditional and unconditional versions caused essentially by the time variability in the optimal risky asset allocation. The framework is also suitable for performing unconditional evaluations of fixed-weight strategies and (un)conditional evaluations of dynamic strategies of hybrid emerging market mutual funds.[2] We also develop the appropriate empirical framework for estimating the performance measures. We advocate the use of a flexible estimation methodology using Hansen's (1982) (un)conditional Generalized Method of Moments (GMM). We estimate the empirical performance measures and perform their associated tests. The estimation of the GMM system is discussed and relies on a one-step method.

[2] See Ayadi and Kryzanowski (2005) for an application to Canadian equity mutual funds.

The remainder of the chapter is organized as follows: Section 2 presents the general asset-pricing framework and we derive the SDF in the presence of time-varying returns. An (un)conditional portfolio performance evaluation using the developed normalized pricing operator is carried out in Section 3. In Section 4, we develop and explain the econometric methodology and the performance tests. Finally, Section 5 concludes the chapter.

2. STOCHASTIC DISCOUNT FACTORS AND BENCHMARK MODELS

The fundamental theorem of asset pricing states that the price of a security is determined by the conditional expectations of its discounted future payoffs in frictionless markets. The stochastic discount factor (SDF) is a random variable that reflects the fundamental economy-wide sources of risk. The basic asset pricing equation is written using gross returns as:

$$E_t(Q_{t+1}R_{i,t+1}) = 1, \quad \text{all } i = 1, \ldots, N. \tag{1}$$

The conditional expectation is defined with respect to the sub-sigma field on the set of states of nature, I_t, which represents the information available to investors at time t. $P_{i,t}$ is the price of asset i at time t, $R_{i,t+1} = X_{i,t+1}/P_{i,t}$ represents a gross return at time $t+1$, defined as the ratio of a future payoff ($X_{i,t+1}$) on the price of asset i ($P_{i,t}$), and Q_{t+1} is the SDF or the pricing kernel.[3] The prices, returns, and discount factors can be real or nominal, and the general assumption is that the asset payoffs have finite second moments.[4]

2.1. The Model

When investment opportunities are time-varying, the SDFs or the period weights can be interpreted as the conditional marginal utilities of an investor with isoelastic preferences described by a power utility function that exhibits constant relative risk aversion (CRRA), given by[5]:

$$U(W_t) = \frac{1}{1-\gamma} W_t^{1-\gamma},$$

where W_t is the level of wealth at t, and γ is the relative risk aversion coefficient. In a single period model, the uninformed investor who holds the benchmark portfolio composed

[3] The SDF has various other names such as the intertemporal marginal rate of substitution in the consumption-based model, the equivalent martingale measure for allowing the change of measure from the actual or objective probabilities to the risk-neutral probabilities, or the state price density when the Arrow-Debreu or state-contingent price is scaled by the associated state probability. See Cochrane (1996) for more details.

[4] See Ayadi and Kryzanowski (2005) for a discussion of the advantages of the SDF representation.

[5] This is not a restrictive assumption on the investor preferences and the proposed setting can accommodate alternative specifications of utility functions such as the constant absolute risk aversion family (see Proposition A1 in Grinblatt and Titman (1989)). Moreover, Grinblatt and Titman (1994) construct their unconditional performance measures for an investor with power utility to study the performance of 270 US equity funds during the period 1975–1984.

of emerging markets securities (the risky asset) maximizes the conditional expectation of the utility of his or her terminal wealth:

$$E[U(W_{t+1})|I_t]. \tag{2}$$

The conditional expectation is based upon the information set I_t.

The investor with such preferences decides on the fraction δ_t of wealth to allocate to the risky asset (hybrid or balanced portfolio of emerging markets of equity and fixed-income securities) with gross return $R_{B,t+1}$, and any remaining wealth is invested in a risk-free security. The return on wealth is given by:

$$R_{w,t+1} = \kappa\delta_t(R^1_{B,t+1} - R^2_{B,t+1}) + \delta_t r^2_{B,t+1} + R_{f,t+1}, \tag{3}$$

where $R_{B,t+1} = \kappa(R^1_{B,t+1} - R^2_{B,t+1}) + R^2_{B,t+1}$ is the gross return on the benchmark portfolio of the balanced investment from t to $(t+1)$. $R^1_{B,t+1}$ and $R^2_{B,t+1}$ are the gross returns on the equity and fixed-income portfolios, respectively. κ is the proportion of investment in the equity portfolio. $R_{f,t+1}$ is the gross risk-free rate from t to $t+1$ that is known one period in advance at time t; and δ_t is the proportion of total wealth invested in the benchmark portfolio.

The optimal risky asset allocation or portfolio policy is no longer a constant parameter when emerging market asset returns are predictable. Harvey (1995) and Iqbal et al. (2010) document evidence of significant return predictability for long and short horizons where the means and variances of asset returns are time-varying and depend on some key variables such as lagged returns, dividend yield, term structure variables, and interest rate variables. Moreover, Brennan et al. (1997), Brandt (1999), and Aït-Sahalia and Brandt (2001) show that the optimal portfolio weight is a function of the state variable(s) that forecast the expected returns when stock returns are predictable. It follows that the optimal portfolio weight is a random variable measurable with respect to the set of state or conditioning variables and is consistent with a conditional Euler equation[6]:

$$\delta_t \equiv \delta(I_t). \tag{4}$$

Thus, considering a constant optimal portfolio weight when returns are predictable affects the construction of any measure based on this variable and distorts inferences related to the use of such a measure. In addition, the functional form and the parameterization of the optimal portfolio allocation depend on the relationship between asset returns and the predicting variables.[7]

[6] See Ayadi and Kryzanowski (2005) for a proof that the optimal risky asset allocation is a nonlinear function of the first and second conditional moments of asset returns.

[7] Brandt (1999) conducts a standard non-parametric estimation of the time-varying portfolio choice using four conditioning variables; namely, dividend yield, default premium, term premium, and lagged excess return.

2.2. Robust Performance Measures

Assuming initial wealth at time t equals one, the conditional optimization problem for the uninformed investor, as described in Brandt (1999), Aït-Sahalia and Brandt (2001), and Ayadi and Kryzanowski (2005), is:

$$\delta_t^* = \underset{\delta_t}{\arg\max}\, E[U(\kappa\delta_t(R_{B,t+1}^1 - R_{B,t+1}^2) + \delta_t r_{B,t+1}^2 + R_{f,t+1})|I_t]. \quad (5)$$

The first-order condition gives the conditional Euler equation:

$$E\{(\kappa\delta_t(R_{B,t+1}^1 - R_{B,t+1}^2) + \delta_t r_{B,t+1}^2 + R_{f,t+1})^{-\gamma}(\kappa(R_{B,t+1}^1 - R_{B,t+1}^2) + r_{B,t+1}^2)|I_t\} = 0. \quad (6)$$

Now define $Q_{t+1}^c \equiv [\kappa\delta_t(R_{B,t+1}^1 - R_{B,t+1}^2) + \delta_t r_{B,t+1}^2 + R_{f,t+1}]^{-\gamma}$, which is a strictly positive conditional SDF consistent with the no-arbitrage principle. This ensures that if a particular fund has a higher positive payoff than another fund, then it must have a higher positive performance. Grinblatt and Titman (1989) and Chen and Knez (1996) stress the importance of this positivity property in providing reliable performance measures. Q_{t+1}^c can be normalized such that:

$$q_{t+1}^c \equiv Q_{t+1}^c / E_t(Q_{t+1}^c) = Q_{t+1}^c R_{f,t+1}. \text{ Then } E_t(q_{t+1}^c) = 1. \quad (7)$$

The new conditional normalized SDF plays a central role in the construction of the portfolio performance measure. The unconditional normalized SDF is given by:

$$q_{t+1}^u \equiv Q_{t+1}^u / E(Q_{t+1}^u) = Q_{t+1}^u R_{f,t+1}. \text{ Then } E(q_{t+1}^u) = 1. \quad (8)$$

Let $\alpha_t^i,\ i = (u, c)$ be the (un)conditional portfolio performance measure, depending on the use of the appropriate SDF. It is an admissible positive performance measure with respect to Chen and Knez's (1996) definition. If $r_{x,t+1}$ is the excess return on any particular portfolio x, then:

$$\alpha_t^u = E(q_{t+1}^u r_{x,t+1}) = E(r_{x,t+1}) + \text{Cov}(q_{t+1}^u, r_{x,t+1}), \text{ and} \quad (9)$$

$$\alpha_t^c = E_t(q_{t+1}^c r_{x,t+1}) = E_t(r_{x,t+1}) + \text{Cov}_t(q_{t+1}^c, r_{x,t+1}). \quad (10)$$

It follows that the expected performance measure reflects an average value plus an adjustment for the riskiness of the portfolio measured by the covariance of its excess return with the appropriate normalized SDF.

3. PERFORMANCE EVALUATION OF MANAGED PORTFOLIOS

3.1. Unconditional Setting

When uninformed investors do not incorporate public information, the portfolio weights are fixed or constant. The gross return on such a portfolio is: $R_{p,t+1} = w' R_{1,t+1}$, with $w' 1_N = 1$, R_1 being an N-vector of gross security returns, and 1_N being an N-vector of ones. We define $r_{B,t+1} = R_{B,t+1} - R_{f,t+1} = \kappa(R^1_{B,t+1} - R^2_{B,t+1}) + r^2_{B,t+1}$. We assume that the portfolio weights w are chosen one period before. The corresponding unconditional performance measure is:

$$\alpha^u_t = E(q^u_{t+1} r_{B,t+1}) = E(q^u_{t+1} R_{B,t+1}) - R_{f,t+1} = 0,$$
$$q^u_{t+1} \equiv q(R^1_{B,t+1}, R^2_{B,t+1}, R_{f,t+1}, \kappa, \delta, \gamma). \tag{11}$$

This suggests that the risk-adjusted return on the passive portfolio held by the uninformed investor is equal to the risk-free rate.

The parameters of q^u_{t+1} are chosen such that $E(q^u_{t+1} r_{B,t+1}) = 0$. If $r_{B,t+1}$ is of dimension K, then $E(q^u_{t+1} r_{B,t+1}) = 0_K$ and $E(q^u_{t+1}) = 1$. Informed investors, such as possibly some mutual fund managers, trade based on private information or signals implying non-constant weights for their portfolios. The gross return on an actively managed portfolio is given by:

$$R_{a,t+1} = w(I^a_t)' R_{1,t+1}, \quad \text{with } w(I^a_t)' 1_N = 1,$$

where I^p and I^a represent public and private information sets, respectively.

The unconditional performance measure is given by:

$$\alpha^u_t = E(q^u_{t+1} r_{B,t+1}) = E(q^u_{t+1} R_{B,t+1}) - R_{f,t+1} = E(w(I^a_t)' q^u_{t+1} R_{1,t+1}) - R_{f,t+1}. \tag{12}$$

When informed investors optimally exploit their private information or signals, this measure is expected to be strictly positive.

3.2. Conditional Setting

When uninformed investors use publicly known information, I^p, in constructing their portfolios, the weights are a function of the information variables. The gross return is given by:

$$R_{p,t+1} = w(I^p_t)' R_{1,t+1}, \text{ with } w(I^p_t)' 1_N = 1, \quad \text{and} \quad I^p_t \subset I^a_t.$$

Consistent with the semi-strong form of the efficient market hypothesis, the conditional SDF prices the portfolio such that:

$$\alpha^c_t = E_t(q^c_{t+1} r_{p,t+1}) = E_t(q^c_{t+1} R_{p,t+1}) - R_{f,t+1} = 0,$$
$$q^c_{t+1} \equiv q(R^1_{B,t+1}, R^2_{B,t+1}, R_{f,t+1}, I^p_t, \kappa, \delta, \gamma). \tag{13}$$

To model conditioning information, we define $Z_t \in I^p_t$, where Z_t is a L-vector of the conditioning variables containing unity as its first element. The conditional expectations are analyzed by creating general managed portfolios with linear scaling and then examining the implications for the unconditional expectations as in Cochrane (1996). The new scaled returns can be interpreted as payoffs to managed portfolios or conditional assets. The payoff space is expanded to NL dimensions to represent the number of trading strategies available to uninformed investors.

The conditional performance measure can be written as:

$$\alpha_t^c = E_t(q_{t+1}^c R_{1,t+1}) \otimes Z_t - R_{f,t+1} 1_N \otimes Z_t = 0 \quad \text{and} \tag{14}$$

$$E_t(q_{t+1}^c) Z_t = Z_t. \tag{15}$$

Assuming stationarity and applying the law of iterated expectations yields:

$$E[q_{t+1}^c (R_{1,t+1} \otimes Z_t)] = E(R_{f,t+1} 1_N \otimes Z_t) \quad \text{and} \tag{16}$$

$$E(q_{t+1}^c Z_t) = E(Z_t), \tag{17}$$

where $\otimes$ is the Kronecker product obtained by multiplying every asset return by every instrument. These two conditions ensure that the conditional mean of the SDF is one, and that these managed portfolios are correctly priced. The conditional normalized SDF is only able to price any asset or portfolio whose returns are attainable from the dynamic trading strategies of the original N assets with respect to the defined conditioning information set.

The conditional performance for the actively managed portfolio is given by:

$$\alpha_t^c = E_t(q_{t+1}^c r_{a,t+1}) = E_t(q_{t+1}^c R_{a,t+1}) - R_{f,t+1}. \tag{18}$$

This conditional test determines whether the private information or signal contains useful information beyond that which is publicly available, and whether or not this information has been used profitably.

4. ECONOMETRIC METHODOLOGY AND TESTS

In this section, the empirical framework for the estimation of the performance measures and for the tests of the different hypotheses and specifications using Hansen's (1982) generalized method of moments (GMM) is detailed. Important issues associated with the estimation procedure and the optimal weighting or distance matrix are also dealt with.

4.1. The General Framework

The estimation of the performance of actively managed portfolios (such as mutual funds) is based on a one-step method using a GMM system approach. The one-step method jointly and simultaneously estimates the normalized SDF parameters and the performance measures by augmenting the number of moment conditions in the initial system with the actively managed fund(s) or portfolio(s) of funds.[8] This multivariate framework incorporates all of the cross-equation correlations. By construction, such estimations account

[8] Farnsworth et al. (2002) show that the performance estimates and associated standard errors are invariant to the number of actively managed individual funds or portfolios of funds in the GMM system.

for the restriction on the mean of the normalized (un)conditional SDF,[9] which Dahlquist and Soderlind (1999), Farnsworth et al. (2002), and Ayadi and Kryzanowski (2005) show is important in order to obtain reliable estimates.

We now present the general steps and expressions leading primarily to the general case of conditional GMM estimation relevant for the conditional evaluation of dynamic trading-based portfolios. The unconditional GMM estimation is obtained as a special case.

Let $\phi \equiv (\kappa\ \delta\ \gamma)'$ be the vector of unknown SDF parameters to be estimated. Our model implies the following conditional moment restriction:

$$E_t[q^c(R^1_{B,t+1}, R^2_{B,t+1}, R_{f,t+1}, Z_t, \phi_0)r_{p,t+1}] = 0_N \tag{19}$$

such that $E_t[q^c(R^1_{B,t+1}, R^2_{B,t+1}, R_{f,t+1}, Z_t, \phi_0)] = 1$.

Now define $u^c_{t+1} = q^c(R^1_{B,t+1}, R^2_{B,t+1}, R_{f,t+1}, Z_t, \phi)r_{p,t+1} \equiv u(R^1_{B,t+1}, R^2_{B,t+1}, R_{f,t+1}, r_{p,t+1}, Z_t, \phi)$ as an N-vector of residuals or pricing errors, which depends on the set of unknown parameters, the excess returns on the benchmark portfolio(s), the conditioning variables, and the excess returns on passive trading strategy-based portfolios.

Assume that the dimensions of the benchmark excess return and the conditioning variables are K and L, respectively. Then, the dimension of the vector of unknown parameters is $(KL + 1)$. We then have:

$$\begin{aligned} &E_t[u(R^1_{B,t+1}, R^2_{B,t+1}, R_{f,t+1}, r_{p,t+1}, Z_t, \phi_0)] \\ &\quad = E[u(R^1_{B,t+1}, R^2_{B,t+1}, R_{f,t+1}, r_{p,t+1}, Z_t, \phi_0)] = 0_N. \end{aligned} \tag{20}$$

Define $h(R^1_{B,t+1}, R^2_{B,t+1}, R_{f,t+1}, r_{p,t+1}, Z_t, \phi) = u^c_{t+1} \otimes Z_t = u(R^1_{B,t+1}, R^2_{B,t+1}, R_{f,t+1}, r_{p,t+1}, Z_t, \phi) \otimes Z_t$. Our conditional and unconditional moment restrictions can be written as:

$$\begin{aligned} &E_t[h(R^1_{B,t+1}, R^2_{B,t+1}, R_{f,t+1}, r_{p,t+1}, Z_t, \phi_0)] \\ &\quad = E[h(R^1_{B,t+1}, R^2_{B,t+1}, R_{f,t+1}, r_{p,t+1}, Z_t, \phi_0)] = 0_{NL} \quad \text{and} \end{aligned} \tag{21}$$

$$\begin{aligned} &E_t[q^c(R^1_{B,t+1}, R^2_{B,t+1}, R_{f,t+1}, Z_t, \phi_0)Z_t - Z_t] \\ &\quad = E[q^c(R^1_{B,t+1}, R^2_{B,t+1}, R_{f,t+1}, Z_t, \phi_0)Z_t - Z_t] = 0_L. \end{aligned} \tag{22}$$

Because the model is overidentified, the GMM system is estimated by setting the $(KL+1)$ linear combinations of the NL moment conditions equal to zero. When the system estimation of the performance measures is completed in one step, the number of moment conditions $L(N+1)$ and the number of unknown parameters $(KL+2)$ are augmented.

[9] The means of the normalized and non-normalized SDFs are equal to one and the inverse of the gross return on the risk-free asset, respectively.

Following Hansen (1982), the GMM estimator is obtained by selecting $\hat{\phi}_T$ that minimizes the sample quadratic form J_T given by[10]:

$$J_T(\phi) \equiv g_T(\phi)' \Lambda_T g_T(\phi), \tag{23}$$

where Λ_T is a symmetrical and non-singular positive semi-definite $NL \times NL$ weighting matrix and $g_T(\phi)$ is given by $\frac{1}{T}\sum_{t=1}^{T} h(R_{B,t+1}^1, R_{B,t+1}^2, R_{f,t+1}, r_{p,t+1}, Z_t, \phi)$.

Let $J_T(\hat{\phi}_T)$ be the minimized value of the sample quadratic form.[11] When the optimal weighting matrix or the inverse of the variance-covariance matrix of the orthogonality conditions is used, $TJ_T(\hat{\phi}_T)$ has an asymptotic standard central chi-square distribution with $((N-K)L-1)$ degrees of freedom. This is the well-known Hansen J_T-statistic. This estimation can handle the assumption that the vector of disturbances exhibits non-normality, conditional heteroskedasticity, and/or serial correlation even with an unknown form.

4.2. The Estimation Procedure and the Optimal Weighting Matrix

The estimates of the portfolio performance measure are obtained by minimizing the GMM criterion function constructed from a set of moment conditions in the system. This requires a consistent estimate of the weighting matrix that is a general function of the true parameters, at least in an efficient case. Hansen (1982) proves that the GMM estimator is asymptotically efficient when the weighting matrix is chosen to be the inverse of the variance-covariance matrix of the moment conditions.[12] This covariance matrix is defined as the zero-frequency spectral density of the pricing errors vector $h(R_{B,t+1}^1, R_{B,t+1}^2, R_{f,t+1}, r_{p,t+1}, Z_t, \phi_0)$. A consistent estimate of this spectral density is used herein to construct a heteroskedastic and autocorrelation consistent (HAC) or robust variance-covariance matrix in the presence of heteroskedasticity and autocorrelation of unknown forms. Chen and Knez (1996), Dahlquist and Soderlind (1999), Farnsworth et al. (2002), Ayadi and Kryzanowski (2005, 2008) construct robust t-statistics for their estimates of performance by using the modified Bartlett kernel proposed by Newey and West (1987) to construct a robust estimator for the variance-covariance matrix.[13]

The variance-covariance matrix of $g_T(\phi_0)$ can be written as:

$$S_0 \equiv \sum_{j=-\infty}^{+\infty} \Gamma_0(j), \tag{24}$$

[10] Under some regularity conditions, Hansen (1982) has shown that the GMM estimator is consistent and asymptotically normal for any fixed weighting matrix.

[11] Jagannathan and Wang (1996) show that T times the minimized GMM criterion function is asymptotically distributed as a weighted sum of central chi-squared random variables.

[12] The choice of the weighting matrix only affects the efficiency of the GMM estimator. Newey (1993) shows that the estimator's consistency only depends on the correct specification of the residuals and the information or conditioning variables.

[13] The higher-order sample autocovariances are downweighted using linear declining weights, and those with an order exceeding a certain parameter receive zero weight.

where $\Gamma_0(j) \equiv E[h(R^1_{B,t+1}, R^2_{B,t+1}, R_{f,t+1}, r_{p,t+1}, Z_t, \phi_0)h(R^1_{B,t-j+1}, R^2_{B,t-j+1}, R_{f,t-j+1}, r_{p,t-j+1}, Z_{t-j}, \phi_0)']$ is the jth autocovariance matrix of $h(R^1_{B,t+1}, R^2_{B,t+1}, R_{f,t+1}, r_{p,t+1}, Z_t, \phi_0)$.

This expression is difficult to estimate with an infinite number of terms. An estimate of S_0 is obtained by using a finite number of lags and by replacing the true autocovariances by their sample analogs, or:

$$\hat{S}_T \equiv \hat{\Gamma}_T(0) + \sum_{j=1}^{T-1} [\hat{\Gamma}_T(j) + \hat{\Gamma}_T(j)'], \tag{25}$$

where:
$\hat{\Gamma}_T(j) \equiv \frac{1}{T}\sum_{t=j+1}^{T} h(R^1_{B,t+1}, R^2_{B,t+1}, R_{f,t+1}, r_{p,t+1}, Z_t, \hat{\phi}_T)h(R^1_{B,t-j+1}, R^2_{B,t-j+1}, R_{f,t-j+1}, r_{p,t-j+1}, Z_{t-j}, \hat{\phi}_T)']$ for $j = 0, 1, \ldots, T-1$; and $\hat{\Gamma}_T(j) = \hat{\Gamma}_T(-j)'$ for $j = -1, -2, \ldots, -T+1$. A small sample correction $\frac{1}{T-NL+KL+1}$ may be used instead of $\frac{1}{T}$.

In the absence of serial correlation, a consistent estimate of S_0 is equal to the sample autocovariance of order zero. More formally:

$$\hat{S}_T \equiv \frac{1}{T}\sum_{t=1}^{T}[u(R^1_{B,t+1}, R^2_{B,t+1}, R_{f,t+1}, r_{p,t+1}, Z_t, \hat{\phi}_T)$$
$$u(R^1_{B,t+1}, R^2_{B,t+1}, R_{f,t+1}, r_{p,t+1}, Z_t, \hat{\phi}_T)' \otimes Z_t Z_t']. \tag{26}$$

However, two difficulties are associated with the estimation of the general expression. First, the sample autocovariance matrix $\hat{\Gamma}_T(j)$ is not a consistent estimator of the true autocovariance matrix $\Gamma_0(j)$ for some j with respect to the sample size T.[14] Second, the estimated variance-covariance matrix may not be positive definite, particularly for finite samples. We estimate the zero-frequency spectral density and overcome difficulties in the estimation by using a non-parametric or kernel-based approach.

A non-parametric or kernel-based robust estimator has the following general expression:

$$\hat{S}_T = \sum_{j=-T+1}^{T-1} w(j/\xi_T)\hat{\Gamma}_T(j), \tag{27}$$

where $w(.)$ is a real-valued kernel, weighting function, or lag window,[15] and ξ_T is a data-dependent bandwidth or lag truncation parameter. This particular structure imposes different weights on different sample autocovariances. Several estimators associated with different kernel functions are proposed in the spectral density function estimation literature. Only kernels that are relevant for portfolio performance measurement are presented next.

[14] A limited number of observations are available to complete the estimation, and the law of large numbers cannot be applied.

[15] Andrews (1991) and Newey and West (1994) derive conditions for admissible kernel functions.

Newey and West (1987) use the modified Bartlett or triangular kernel to construct a robust estimator of the variance-covariance matrix. They demonstrate that this estimator, unlike the truncated kernel-based one, is positive definite given the assigned weighting structure. This property (together with its simple tractability) results in the popular use of this estimator for the estimation of portfolio performance evaluation models. Examples include Chen and Knez (1996), Ferson and Schadt (1996), Farnsworth et al. (1999), Dahlquist and Soderlind (1999), Abel and Fletcher (2004), and Ayadi and Kryzanowski (2005, 2008, 2011).

4.3. Optimal Risky Asset Allocation Specifications

In a conditional setting, the optimal risky asset allocation of the uninformed investor is a function of the conditional moments of asset returns. We assume that these conditional moments are linear in the state variables:

$$\delta_t = Z_t'\delta, \tag{28}$$

where δ is a vector of unknown parameters, and Z_t is a vector of instruments (including a constant) with a dimension equal to that of the retained conditioning variables. When an unconditional evaluation is conducted, the uninformed investor's portfolio policy is a constant.

5. CONCLUSION

This paper uses the general asset-pricing or SDF framework to derive a conditional SDF that is suitable for measuring the performance of emerging market hybrid funds. Our approach reflects the predictability of this group of asset returns and accounts for conditioning information. Three robust performance measures are constructed and are related to the unconditional evaluation of fixed-weight strategies, and the unconditional and conditional evaluations of dynamic strategies. An appropriate empirical framework for estimating and implementing the proposed performance measures and their associated tests using the GMM method is developed.

Our approach may be extended in various directions. First, we can adopt a *continuous* SDF methodology adapted to the pricing of hybrid emerging market securities. Second, we can examine potential relationships between the performance measures and some business cycle indicators to determine more effectively if the performance of active portfolio management differs during periods of expansion and contraction in emerging markets. Third, we may assess the market-timing behavior of emerging market fund managers, and identify the determinants of fund flows based on several fund characteristics. These alternative directions are opportunities for future research.

ACKNOWLEDGMENT

Financial support from the Brock University SSHRC funds is gratefully acknowledged.

REFERENCES

Abel, E., Fletcher, J., 2004. An empirical examination of U.K. emerging market unit trust performance. Emerging Markets Review 5, 389–408

Aït-Sahalia, Y., Brandt, M.W., 2001. Variable selection and portfolio choice. Journal of Finance 56, 1297–1351

Andrews, D.W.K., 1991. Heteroskedasticity and autocorrelation consistent covariance matrix estimation. Econometrica 59, 817–858

Aragon, G., 2005. Timing multiple markets: theory and evidence from balanced mutual funds. Working Paper, Arizona State University.

Ayadi, M.A., Kryzanowski, L., 2005. Portfolio performance measurement using APM-free kernel models. Journal of Banking and Finance 29, 623–659

Ayadi, M.A., Kryzanowski, L., 2008. Portfolio performance sensitivity for various asset pricing kernels. Computers and Operations Research 35, 171–185

Ayadi, M.A., Kryzanowski, L., 2011. Fixed-income fund performance: role of luck and ability in tail membership. Journal of Empirical Finance 18, 379–392

Banegas, A., 2011. Emerging market mutual fund performance and the state of the economy. Working Paper, University of California, San Diego, CA, USA.

Brandt, M.W., 1999. Estimating portfolio and consumption choice: a conditional Euler equations approach. Journal of Finance 54, 1609–1645

Brennan, M.J., Schwartz, E.S., Lagnado, R., 1997. Strategic asset allocation. Journal of Economic Dynamics and Control 21, 1377–1403

Chen, Z., Knez, P.J., 1996. Portfolio performance measurement: theory and applications. Review of Financial Studies 9, 511–555

Cochrane, J.H., 1996. A cross-sectional test of an investment-based asset pricing model. Journal of Political Economy 104, 572–621

Comer, G., 2006. Hybrid mutual funds and market timing performance. Journal of Business 79, 771–797

Comer, G., Larrymore, N., Rodriguez, J., 2009. Controlling for fixed-income exposure in portfolio evaluation: evidence from hybrid mutual funds. Review of Financial Studies 22, 481–507

Dahlquist, M., Soderlind, P., 1999. Evaluating portfolio performance with stochastic discount factors. Journal of Business 72, 347–384

Farnsworth, H., Ferson, W.E., Jackson, D., Todd, S., 2002. Performance evaluation with stochastic discount factors. Journal of Business 75, 473–503

Ferson, W.E., Schadt, R., 1996. Measuring fund strategy and performance in changing economic conditions. Journal of Finance 51, 425–461

Gottesman, A., Morey, M.R., 2007. Predicting emerging market mutual fund performance. Journal of Investing 16, 111–122

Grinblatt, M., Titman, S., 1989. Portfolio performance evaluation: old issues and new insights. Review of Financial Studies 2, 393–422

Grinblatt, M., Titman, S., 1994. A study of monthly mutual fund returns and performance evaluation techniques. Journal of Financial and Quantitative Analysis 3, 419–444

Hansen, L.P., 1982. Large sample properties of generalized method of moments estimators. Econometrica 50, 1029–1054

Hansen, L.P., Richard, S.F., 1987. The role of conditioning information in deducing testable restrictions implied by dynamic asset pricing models. Econometrica 55, 587–613

Harrison, M., Kreps, D., 1979. Martingales and arbitrage in multiperiod security markets. Journal of Economic Theory 20, 381–408

Harvey, C., 1995. Predictable risk and returns in emerging markets. Review of Financial Studies 8, 773–816

Huij, J., Post, T., 2011. On the performance of emerging market equity mutual funds. Emerging Markets Review 12, 238–249

Iqbal, J., Brooks, R., Galagedera, D.U.A., 2007. Testing asset pricing models in emerging markets: an examination of higher order co-moments and alternative factor models. Working Paper, Monash University, Melbourne, Australia.

Iqbal, J., Brooks, R., Galagedera, D.U.A., 2010. Testing conditional asset pricing models: an emerging market perspective. Journal of International Money and Finance 29, 897–918

Jagannathan, R., Wang, Z., 1996. The conditional CAPM and the cross-section of expected returns. Journal of Finance 51, 3–35

Kaminsky, G.L., Lyons, R.K., Schmukler, S.L., 2001. Mutual fund investment in emerging markets: an overview. World Bank Economic Review 15, 315–340

Newey, W.K., 1993. Efficient estimation of models with conditional moment restriction. Handbook of Statistics 11, 419–445

Newey, W.K., West, K.D., 1987. A simple positive semi-definite heteroskedasticity and autocorrelation consistent covariance matrix. Econometrica 55, 703–708

Newey, W.K., West, K.D., 1994. Automatic lag selection in covariance matrix estimation. Review of Economic Studies 61, 631–653

Phylaktis, K., Xia, L., 2006. Sources of firms' industry and country effects in emerging markets. Journal of International Money and Finance 25, 459–475

Rouwenhorst, K.G., 1999. Local return factors and turnover in emerging stock markets. Journal of Finance 54, 1439–1464

van der Hart, J., Slagter, E., van Dijk, D., 2003. Stock selection strategies in emerging markets. Journal of Empirical Finance 10, 105–135

CHAPTER 2

Emerging Countries Sovereign Rating Adjustment using Market Information: Impact on Financial Institutions' Investment Decisions

Dominique Guégan[*], Bertrand K. Hassani[*,†], and Xin Zhao[*]
[*]Université Paris, Panthéon-Sorbonne, France
[†]Santander UK, United Kingdom

1. INTRODUCTION

Emerging markets are usually considered relatively riskier than developed markets as they carry additional political, economical, and currency risks. The term of emerging markets or emerging economies[1] refers to the nations with social or business activity in the process of rapid growth and industrialization. The seven largest emerging economies according to nominal gross domestic product (GDP) are Brazil, Russia, India, China (the BRICs), Mexico, Indonesia, and Turkey. Investing in emerging markets may lead to volatile returns, i.e., the probabilities of both large profits and large losses are high. The upside of investing in emerging markets is that their performance is considered usually less correlated with developed markets. As a result, these markets may be good investments for diversification purposes. Consequently, nowadays developing countries are major investment targets, and these fast-growing economies are usually a growth relay for major banks. The second criterion highlights the fact that these economies are growing so fast that the information characterizing them is rapidly outdated as their structure is quickly evolving. Therefore, relying on the traditional rating agencies (e.g., Fitch, Moody's and S&P's) to evaluate the risk of investing in these economies may be misleading, especially when the investment horizon is short or medium term. Indeed, by not integrating the latest information contained in the market, they may not provide the freshest points of view. It is important to recall that the rating is supposed to reflect the creditworthiness of a country, i.e., its probability of default. The consideration of fast-growing economies allows us to assume

[1] S&P/IFC index considers a market to be emerging if it satisfies at least one of the criteria: it is in a low- or middle-income country, as defined by the World Bank, and its investable market capitalization is low relative to its most recent GDP figures. In contrast, S&P/IFC defines a market as developed if it is in a country where gross national product (GNP) per capita exceeds the World Bank upper-income threshold for at least three consecutive years and the investable market capitalization-to-GDP ratio is in the top 25% of the emerging market universe for more than three consecutive years.

Emerging Markets and the Global Economy
http://dx.doi.org/10.1016/B978-0-12-411549-1.00002-8

that the related quickly growing cash flows generated decrease the probability of default of these countries on a constant basis.

Although there are papers doubting the quality of evaluations provided by rating agencies, investors keep relying on them. The problems of their evaluations have been largely unveiled during the East Asian Crisis and the recent European Sovereign Debt Crisis. Regulators and market practitioners have acknowledged the problems caused by external analysis, and as a consequence financial institutions developed internal rating methodologies.[2] External ratings, however, are still used as benchmark or important input of inside rating models. Possible explanations are that ratings provided by the major agencies are widely spread, easy to understand, and as a result contribute to limit information bias. Moreover, discussions concerning the problems of the rating system and propositions of new rating methods in recent literature have not reached any consensus. There are two schools of thought: the first states that the credit of a country is determined by its fundamental economic condition, therefore, ratings should rely on country-specific fundamentals; the second argues that economic fundamentals are insufficient to model sovereign credit risk and they propose to use market information.

In order to construct a rating methodology, the causal factors of sovereign default need to be analyzed, and these are different from the determinants of corporate defaults (Duffie et al., 2003). The risk of investing in a country is linked to its economic condition. Therefore, it is natural to start analyzing the credit quality of a country using its fundamental indicators. Literatures discussing the relationship between country fundamentals and ratings include Cantor and Packer (1996), Ferri et al. (1999), Mellios and Paget-Blanc (2006), and many others. Cantor and Packer (1996) have shown that Moody's and S&P's ratings can be explained by a number of well-defined economic criteria. Ferri et al. (1999) used these indicators to compare the ratings pre- and post-East Asian Crisis. They reached the conclusion that rating agencies failed to predict the emergence of the East Asian Crisis and attributed worse ratings than what the countries' fundamental economic condition deserved. They also argued that this undervaluation amplified the East Asian Crisis. To solve the problems engendered by the previous approach, Mellios and Paget-Blanc (2006) suggested to add other indicators, through which they emphasized the importance of political variables. However, the second school of thought claims that sovereign risk cannot be fully explained by country-specific fundamentals, especially for the risk in emerging market, as market opinions may influence the perception of a country credit quality up to a certain extent. This argument partially explains the inertia of agencies' rating. It is generally accepted that markets react faster than agencies to evaluate the creditworthiness of sovereigns. Hettenhouse and Sartoris (1976) and Weinstein (1977) have shown that bond prices are systematically reacting to the signals implying a credit-quality variation before agencies modify the ratings. Ederington et al. (1987) stated that market practitioners evaluate issuer's creditworthiness according to their expectations

[2] Basel II/III: banks meeting certain conditions are allowed to use internal risk parameters calculating regulatory capital.

and the market risk perception, and these are not considered by rating agencies. To capture market's attitude toward sovereign risk, Cunningham et al. (2001) discussed the relationship between government bonds yield spreads and the corresponding default risks on emerging market, where they claimed that information contained in yield spreads are multi-faceted. They mentioned the importance of investors' appetite for risk evaluation and the value of liquidity for specific instruments. Perraudin and Taylor (2004) have shown that sovereign bond valuations are inconsistent with their ratings. They claimed that the inconsistency can be eliminated by adjusting the prices for the effects of taxes, liquidity, and other risk premia. They also proved the inconsistencies between ratings and spreads are naturally eliminated over time. Mainstream discussions concerning market evaluated sovereign risk focus on detecting determinants of risk proxy from market, such as bond yields and credit default swaps. Baek et al. (2005) claimed that risk appetite can explain the movement of bond yields. They further proved that investors' risk attitude was not considered in public ratings. Longstaff et al. (2011) decomposed credit spreads into several risk premia. They found that sovereign credit risk was more driven by market factors, risk premia and investment flows than by country-specific fundamentals. Moreover, they found strong relationship between credit spreads and VIX index. In summary, movements of market indicators are closely related to agencies' ratings, but ratings issued by agencies are not consistent with investors' perceptions as fundamental indicators cannot fully explain the part of sovereign risk nested in market sentiments.

Therefore, this chapter presents a methodology to combine information obtained from macroeconomic indicators (fundamental rating) on the first hand and financial market (market implied rating) on the other hand in order to construct a rating reflecting both the targeted state's economic health and the global market evaluation of the sovereign's creditworthiness. This approach is referred to as the δ-Rating approach in the following. By means of this hybrid approach, it is possible to offer more timeless ratings compared to agencies' valuations and provide prompt signals for investment opportunities or necessity to sell. Therefore, this approach enables us to improve the investment strategy in emerging countries as being a more reality and reactive methodology compared to the traditional approaches.

To create the δ-Ratings, three steps are required. In the first step, country-specific fundamental information is modeled using a general panel model to obtain a basic long-term country-specific implied rating. In the second step, a multi-factor model is applied to decompose bond yields into different risk premia. Then, market implied ratings are computed from the stripped credit risk premium. In the final step, the δ-Rating is evaluated by applying a simplified version of the Bühlmann-Straub Credibility Theory (Bühlmann and Alois, 2005), which may be summarized by the following formula:

$$\delta\text{-Rating} = \omega \cdot \text{Fundamental Rating} + (1 - \omega) \cdot \text{Market Implied Rating},$$

where ω is the credibility weight calculated by the Bühlmann-Straub method.

This chapter proposes a method that systematically matches low-frequency macroeconomic data with high-frequency financial market data in the modeling of sovereign rating; it analyzes how market demands and risk appetite affect market implied rating, and their impact on financial institutions' investments in developing countries.[3] The novelty of our hybrid methodology stands in the combined information from data having different frequencies. Therefore, the Section 2 introduces the methodology, the Section 3 presents our results and the Section 4 concludes.

2. THE δ-RATING METHODOLOGY

This section details how a fundamental rating and a market implied rating are combined. In the first step, the next subsections present the methodologies carried out to evaluate each component. The third subsection outlines the Credibility Theory approach used to bring together the two elements.

2.1. Country-Specific Fundamental Rating

Sovereign credit risk can be captured by a relative by small number of economic variables. These do not dramatically differ among studies (Cantor and Packer, 1996; Ferri et al., 1999; Mellios and Paget-Blanc, 2006, etc.). Table 1 summarizes these macroeconomic variables. Nonetheless, the model used to analyze these variables varies among the studies. Cantor and Packer (1996)[4] tested the variables with cross-sectional data.[5] Ferri et al. (1999)[6] applied panel data[7] and performed regression analysis with random effect. Mellios and Paget-Blanc (2006) used a principal component analysis (PCA) method, a linear regression, and an ordered logistic modeling to analyze the indicators.

The relationship between explanatory variables and historical ratings on a special day is not the focal point of this paper, whereas we are interested in the explanatory power of fundamental economic indicators during a relatively long period, and panel analysis is more appropriate for this purpose. Therefore, a general panel model is applied to regress fundamental economic indicators on the numerical mappings of agencies' historical rating, which can be expressed by equation (1):

$$S_t = \alpha_0 + \beta_1' \cdot X_t + \epsilon_t', \tag{1}$$

where α_0 is an intercept vector, β_1 is a vector of the coefficients of the explanatory variables, ϵ_t is a white noise residual, and X_t is a matrix of economic indicators listed in Table 1. S_t represents the rating of each sovereign. Parameters and vectors are real

[3] Our empirical analysis covers an extent range of countries and time period which includes the peaks of recent crisis.

[4] Cantor and Packer (1996) use the notation external balance refer to the current account deficit.

[5] Data of 49 countries at September 29, 1995.

[6] Ferri et al. (1999) use the notation of GDP per capita instead of Per capital income; notation of budget deficit instead of fiscal balance; development indicator instead of economic development.

[7] 10 years time period (1989–1998) data of 17 countries.

Table 1 Fundamental explanatory variables introduced in literature.

Variable	Corr.*	Economic principle	Literature
Per capita income	+	The increase of the per capita income implies a larger tax base and stronger ability to honor the debt obligation.	Cantor and Packer (1996) Ferri et al. (1999) Mellios and Paget-Blanc (2006) Gärtner et al. (2011)
GDP growth rate	+	The higher growth rate of GDP indicates a better ability of the country to face their debt burden.	Cantor and Packer (1996) Ferri et al. (1999) Mellios and Paget-Blanc (2006) Gärtner et al. (2011)
Inflation	−	High inflation rate indicates government financial structure problem and low creditworthiness.	Cantor and Packer (1996) Ferri et al. (1999) Mellios and Paget-Blanc (2006) Gärtner et al. (2011)
Fiscal balance	+	Fiscal surplus indicates the government has the financial capacity to pay their debts. Fiscal deficit indicates less capital to pay the debts.	Cantor and Packer (1996) Ferri et al. (1999) Gärtner et al. (2011)
External debt	−	The higher external debt causes higher intensity to default and lower creditworthiness.	Cantor and Packer (1996) Ferri et al. (1999) Gärtner et al. (2011)
Economic development	+	Industrialized or developed countries have higher creditworthiness than the developing countries.	Cantor and Packer (1996) Ferri et al. (1999) Mellios and Paget-Blanc (2006)
Default History	−	Defaulting sovereigns suffer a severe decline in their reputation with creditors.	Ozler (1991) Cantor and Packer (1996)
Current Account Balances (CAB)	+	The larger current account indicates the more sufficient capital to pay the debt. A persistent deficit indicates the poor creditworthiness.	Cantor and Packer (1996) Ferri et al. (1999) Mellios and Paget-Blanc (2006)
Corruption Index	+	Higher index indicates less corruption and better policy operation.	Mellios and Paget-Blanc (2006) Michaelides et al. (2012)

Note: the literature is not the complete review, we only give relevant references.
*"Corr." refers to the correlation between the variable and the creditworthiness of the government. "+" means the bigger the variable the higher the credit. "−" means the lower the variable the higher the credit.

numbers. The techniques of analysis used in the empirical study include PCA and panel regression methods. To explore the fittest regression method of equation (1), the pooling regression has been tested against random and cross-sectional effects using Breusch-Pagan Lagrange Multiplier Test (Breusch and Pagan, 1980). Fixed effect against random effect of the selected data will be analyzed using the Hausman Test (Hausman, 1978). The time-fixed effect is tested using both the *F*-test and the serial correlation using Breusch-Godfrey/Wooldridge test (Godfrey, 1996).

2.2. Market Implied Rating

In this study, government bond yields are used as a representation of market perceptions of the risk. Government bonds are a publicly traded financial product. Their prices are related to a government's creditworthiness. Though many papers use credit default swap (CDS) as the proxy of credit risk, these are less resourceful data of CDS than bonds, especially for emerging countries. Secondly, sovereign bond spreads are less subject to liquidity frictions than CDS, therefore they provide a better representation of sovereign risk (Badaoui et al., 2012). Moreover as highlighted by Hull et al. (2004), bond yield and CDS contain almost the same information, government bond yield is a good proxy of sovereign risk.

Generally, the higher the rating of a sovereign, the lower the bond yields, and vice versa, therefore, bond yields' movements can reflect the shift of market attitude toward the credit quality of a sovereign. On the other hand, the movements are influenced by other factors than only government repayment capability. When an investor lends money to a government by buying bonds, he exposes himself to many risks, such as credit risk, market risk, and liquidity risk. Perraudin and Taylor (2004) have shown that the inconsistencies[8] between credit ratings and corporate bond yields come from non-credit-related factors of spreads such as tax, liquidity, and other risk premia. Ejsing et al. (2012) discussed liquidity and credit premia for the Euro Zone sovereign bonds. Bonds are traded in the secondary market, which simultaneously reflects the market risk perception and delivers timeless information to evaluate the credit risk. Agencies, however, evaluate countries' credit quality on a frequency from quarterly to annually. Hence, some discordances are observed between agencies' ratings and bond yields primarily. Rating agencies advocate that they provide less precise point-in-time measures of risk since the ratings reflect the credit quality in the long term. However, and despite the fact that the previous statement is questionable, market practitioners may be more interested in short- to medium-term investments. The inconsistence comes from non-credit reasons rather than only horizon difference.

To improve the analysis, a multi-factor approach is carried out. It is commonly accepted in the literature that credit spreads can be expressed as a linear combination of default-related components and other associated risk premia (Longstaff et al., 2011; Collin-Dufresne et al., 2001; Beber et al., 2009, etc.). Accordingly, the non-credit reasons

[8] The term "inconsistencies" refers to the disordered ordering classification of average price of bond according to ratings.

are considered as liquidity risk premium, market demands, and investors' risk appetite. Then, yield spreads are decomposed into credit, liquidity, market demand premia, and risk appetite using a multi-factor model:

$$y_{i,t} = a_{i,0} + a_{i,1}L_{i,t} + a_{i,2}MP_{i,t} + a_{i,3}RA_{i,t} + \varepsilon_t, \quad (2)$$

where $y_{i,t}$ refers to yield spreads of bond i at time t, $a_{i,0}$ represents the averaged credit risk premium, $L_{i,t}$ is the sign of liquidity risk and $MP_{i,t}$ represents the market demand of government bonds and denotes the market appetite, $RA_{i,t}$ measures investors' risk appetite, and ε_t is a standard white noise, which is independent from other explanatory variables. Proxies of each indicator in equation (2) are as follows:

1. Bid-ask spreads for liquidity risk.
2. FTSE-Index for the market demand of government bonds.
3. Implied volatility of S&P 500 index options (VIX) for the global risk aversion.

2.3. Credible Weights

The "δ-Rating" is obtained through the average of fundamental ratings and market implied ratings using the credibility weight ω. Bühlmann-Straub method,[9] the most extensively used and important model in Credibility Theory, is applied to compute the weight ω (Bühlmann and Alois, 2005).

Theorem 1 (Bühlmann-Straub). *The credibility estimator μ in the simple Bühlmann-Straub model:*

A.1 The random variables X_{kj} ($j = 1, \ldots, n$) are, conditional on $\Theta_k = \vartheta$, independent with the same distribution function F_ϑ and conditional moments:

$$\mu(\vartheta) = E[X_{kj}|\Theta_k = \vartheta],$$
$$\sigma^2(\vartheta) = Var[X_{kj}|\Theta_k = \vartheta].$$

A.2 The pairs $(\Theta_1, X_1), \ldots, (\Theta_K, X_K)$ are independent and identically distributed.

is given by the following formula:

$$\mu = \omega\overline{X_i} + (1 - \omega)\overline{X}, \quad (3)$$

where:

$$\omega = \frac{n}{n + \frac{\sigma^2}{\tau^2}}, \quad \sigma^2 = E[\sigma^2(\Theta)], \quad \tau^2 = Var(\mu(\Theta)).$$
$$\overline{X_i} = \frac{1}{n}\sum_{j=1}^{n} X_{i,j}, \quad \overline{X} = \frac{1}{Kn}\sum_{i=1}^{K}\sum_{j=1}^{n} X_{ij}. \quad (4)$$

[9] This approach is also called empirical Bayesian method.

Practically, in our case, $\overline{X_j}$ is the rating implied by the specific market information and $\overline{X}$ is the long-term fundamental rating estimated through country-specific economic data. Moreover, ω is the weight given to market implied rating and leads to the "δ-Rating", as it is the weighted average of the two previous components.

3. RATING EVALUATION: CARRYING OUT THE METHODOLOGY

3.1. Country-Specific Implied Rating

The data used to estimate country-specific rating have annual frequency and belong to the period between 2001 and 2012. Historical rating scores are derived from Fitch Sovereign Historical Ratings[10] using the mapping exhibited in Table 14. Economic indicators, except for the "corruption index," are collected from the International Money Fund (IMF) WEO Database. Corruption Perceptions Index (CPI) has been obtained from Transparency International.[11] The sample includes 20 advanced countries and 8 emerging countries, according to the IMF classification.[12]

Statistics of data are presented in Table 8. The rating of advanced economies is higher than emerging economies'. Advanced economies usually have smaller GPD growth rate, larger external debts, higher per capita income, lower inflation rates, greater fiscal balance, better current account balance, and higher corruption perceptions index than emerging economies.

In the first step, the multicollinearity and the correlation of the indicators with the ratings have been analyzed. There is no sufficient evidence supporting a linear relationship between indicators (Figure 1). Moreover, the value of correlations and variance inflation factors (VIF) presented in Table 6 shows that there is no significant multicollinearity. The cumulative explanatory proposition of indicators is given in Table 7 and computed implementing a principal component analysis. The results indicate that the first seven components can explain up to 99% of the information. The fittest regression method of equation (1) is obtained using the tests introduced in Section 2. The tests are implemented on both subgroups of countries and the whole data set. Results are presented in Table 9. The p-values of Breusch-Pagan and Breusch-Godfrey/Wooldridge tests indicate that there are cross-sectional dependencies and serial correlations in the advanced economies data set, emerging economies data sets and the whole sample, therefore an OLS regression is not reliable. This is confirmed by using an F-statistic to test fixed effects against the OLS, and Breusch-Pagan LM test of the random effects against the OLS. The p-values of

[10] http://www.fitchratings.com/web_content/ratings/sovereign_ratings_history.xls. The annual minimum ratings have been used when there were multiple rating assignments during 1 year.

[11] Transparency International (2010) Corruption Perceptions Index 2010. Retrieved 24 Aug 2011.

[12] Though there is plenty of macroeconomic data available for a larger number of countries, it is difficult to collect the market information for the same group of countries. The sample used in this part of analysis is in line with the sample used for the market implied rating. Thus, whether a country is selected in our sample depends on the limit of our access to its pertaining market indicators. Therefore, some interested candidates, such as Greece, China, and Argentina are missing.

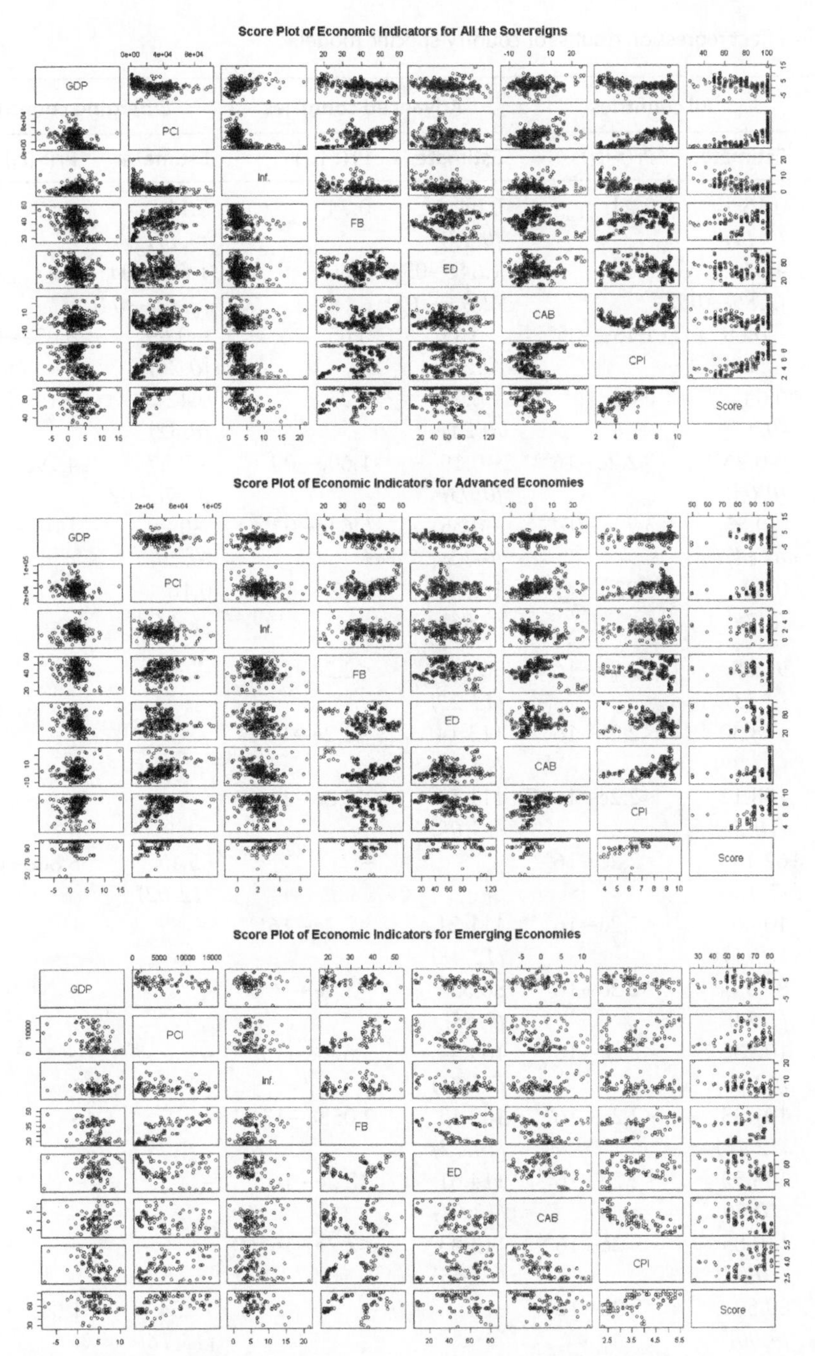

Figure 1 Score plot of economic indicators. This figure presents the economic indicators exhibited in Table 1 except for the two dummy variables (economic development and default history) and the rating scores. The upper, medium, and lower plots are, respectively, the score plots of the variables of all the sovereigns, the advanced economies, and the emerging economies.

Table 2 Fix-effect regression results for country-specific model.

	All countries		Advanced countries		Emerging countries	
	Estimate	**Pr(>|*t*|)**	**Estimate**	**Pr(>|*t*|)**	**Estimate**	**Pr(>|*t*|)**
GDP	0.13	0.24	0.04	0.74	0.11	0.52
	(0.11)		*(0.13)*		*(0.17)*	
PCI	4.84e−05	0.09	1.64e−05	0.56	1.68e−04	0.43
	(2.89e−05)		*(2.83e−05)*		*(2.12e−04)*	
Inf.	−0.68	1.15e−05***	−0.12	0.65	−0.69	8.02e−04***
	(0.15)		*(0.27)*		*(0.20)*	
FB	0.04	0.80	−0.25	0.23	0.42	0.19
	(0.17)		*(0.21)*		*(0.32)*	
ED	−0.26	<2.2e−16***	−0.19	1.60e−09***	−0.47	4.79e−12***
	(0.03)		*(0.03)*		*5.77e−02*	
CAB	−0.55	3.79e−07***	−0.35	6.64e−04**	−0.80	1.02e−04***
	(0.11)		*(0.13)*		*(0.20)*	
CPI	0.89	0.25	1.46	0.12	0.16	0.91
	(0.78)		*(0.93)*		*(1.44)*	
Australia	91.88	<2.2e−16***	96.85	<2.2e−16***	–	–
	(9.33)		*(11.29)*			
Austria	108.30	<2.2e−16***	113.14	<2.2e−16***	–	–
	(10.99)		*(13.28)*			
Belgium	108.12	<2.2e−16***	111.55	<2.2e−16***	–	–
	(10.85)		*(13.08)*			
Brazil	62.10	<2.2e−16***	–	–	65.17	5.86e−08***
	(7.18)				*(12.02)*	
Canada	109.67	<2.2e−16***	111.21	<2.2e−16***	–	–
	(10.33)		*(12.48)*			
Czech	81.59	<2.2e−16***	88.53	<2.2e−16***	–	–
	(7.94)		*(9.55)*			
Denmark	102.39	<2.2e−16***	109.44	3.670e−13***	–	–
	(12.45)		*(15.06)*			
Finland	101.38	<2.2e−16***	108.13	2.058e−13***	–	–
	(12.18)		*(14.72)*			
France	108.52	<2.2e−16***	114.61	<2.2e−16***	–	–
	(10.70)		*(12.91)*			
Germany	110.85	<2.2e−16***	113.83	<2.2e−16***	–	–
	(10.32)		*(12.46)*			
Hungary	80.50	<2.2e−16***	–	–	79.34	1.659e−07***
	(9.00)				*(15.16)*	
India	71.96	<2.2e−16***	–	–	83.10	<2.2e−16***
	(4.89)				*(8.09)*	

(*Continued*)

Table 2 (Continued)

	All countries		Advanced countries		Emerging countries	
	Estimate	**Pr(>|*t*|)**	**Estimate**	**Pr(>|*t*|)**	**Estimate**	**Pr(>|*t*|)**
Italy	108.50 *(9.52)*	<2.2e−16***	111.34 *(11.40)*	<2.2e−16***	–	–
Netherlands	107.02 *(10.91)*	<2.2e−16***	110.32 *(13.18)*	<2.2e−16***	–	–
New Zealand	101.96 *(17.96)*	<2.2e−16 ***	95.95 *(11.47)*	<2.2e−16***	–	–
Norway	93.2745 *(9.48)*	<2.2e−16***	114.43 *(15.21)*	<2.2e−16***	–	–
Philippines	65.57 *(4.18)*	<2.2e−16***	–	–	72.25 *(6.77)*	<2.2e−16***
Poland	81.70 *(7.82)*	<2.2e−16***	–	–	78.41 *(13.14)*	2.414e−09 ***
Portugal	89.25 *(9.15)*	<2.2e−16***	93.51 *(11.03)*	<2.2e−16***	–	–
Russia	67.29 *(7.05)*	<2.2e−16***	–	–	60.10 *(11.22)*	8.367e−08 ***
Singapore	125.25 *(9.19)*	<2.2e−16***	116.22 *(10.93)*	<2.2e−16***	–	–
South Africa	76.78 *(6.14)*	<2.2e−16***	–	–	77.42 *(10.10)*	2.953e−14***
Spain	96.94 *(8.75)*	<2.2e−16***	101.18 *(10.57)*	<2.2e−16***	–	–
Sweden	103.56 *(11.92)*	<2.2e−16***	109.52 *(14.40)*	2.864e−14***	–	–
Switzerland	109.64 *(9.94)*	<2.2e−16***	110.26 *(11.95)*	<2.2e−16***	–	–
Thailand	81.23 *(4.95)*	<2.2e−16***	–	–	85.87 *(8.09)*	<2.2e−16***
United Kingdom	103.30 *(9.51)*	<2.2e−16***	106.17 *(11.50)*	<2.2e−16***	–	–
United States	108.33 *(8.73)*	<2.2e−16***	109.34 *(10.54)*	<2.2e−16***	–	–
R-Square	0.37725		0.25517		0.68366	
Adj. R-Square	0.33795		0.22646		0.57684	

The regression is implemented with the data set of all countries, advanced countries, and emerging countries, respectively. In this table, the coefficient estimate of the corresponding variable is provided in the column labeled "Estimate" along with their standard errors in brackets. The *p*-values are given on the right of each estimate. The symbol "*" refers to significance level 0.05; **significance level 0.01; ***significance level 0.001.

Hausman tests reveal that a fixed effect model is more appropriate. The p-values of the F-tests reject time-fixed effect. Thus, the fixed-effect approach is the best regression method for fundamental rating model (equation (1)). The results are presented in Table 2. External debt (ED) and current account balance (CAB) are significant factors and exhibit negative effects considering advanced economies, emerging economies, and the whole data set. The negative effect of ED is consistent with the discussion mentioned in Section 2. Indeed, higher external debt causes higher debt burden and leads to lower creditworthiness. A possible explanation of negative CAB is that domestic investments are financed by foreigners' savings, and this implies a higher confidence in sovereigns' creditworthiness. Although the averaged CAB of advanced countries is higher than that of emerging economies, the regression results suggest that the CAB indicator alone is not sufficient to characterize a country credit quality.

Secondly, the inflation rate (denoted as Inf.) factor is significant for both the whole sample and the emerging economies subsample. It has a negative sign, as a high inflation rate is a negative indicator for the economic development of a country. Investing in countries where the inflation rate is uncontrolled is highly risky. Nevertheless, the causal factor of inflation is ambiguous, especially for the developed countries. It could be the result of a monetary policy aiming at improving the economic condition of a country rather than deteriorating it. However, GDP growth rate, fiscal balance (FB), and Corruption Perceptions Index (CPI) factors are not statistically significant. As a result, the GDP growth rate is not a suitable explanatory variable for rating scores, although it is an important index to characterize the development speed of a country. This result is not entirely counterintuitive as reviewing international GDP growth rate during 2012, we observed that most countries with high GDP growth rate, such as Qatar, Ghana, Turkmenistan, etc., are countries with poor credit quality. On the contrary, countries with good ratings, such as Germany, Finland, or Canada, have GDP growth rate under the world average. However, sovereigns with negative growth rate (recession), such as Sudan, Andorra, Syria, etc., are very risky investment choices, as these countries are not creating any value. Consequently, the influence of GDP growth rate on a country credit quality is not linearly related. Though these high scored countries generally have high and positive FB, the difference is not significant in our sample. Regarding the CPI, contrary to the results obtained by Mellios and Paget-Blanc (2006), this factor is positively significant for the whole sample at a 90% confidence level. Our results indicate that the PCI factor is appropriate to explain the rating scores if the countries are not split in different subsets. Finally, R^2 and Adjusted R^2 lie between 0.23 and 0.68 for the estimation of equation (1) on the three data sets. Moreover, R^2 and adjusted[13] R^2 cannot be improved by changing regression methods. It indicates that using these indicators cannot fully explain the ratings issued by agencies during the recent 10 years. These statistics suggest that during

[13] Here we assume the linear relation among the variables as model 1.

the selected time period some macroeconomic indicators, which were explanatory variables in previous analysis, cannot explain the rating in ours. This intermediate conclusion should be related to the fact that our analysis is performed during a global downturn and this affects the data. But this result supports the paper's objective of adjusting this fundamental rating using the market information.

3.2. Market Implied Rating

The data used in market implied rating analysis characterized by (2) include bond yields, bid-ask spreads of bond, FTSE-Global Index, and VIX index. These contain the market-related information of 20 advanced countries and 8 emerging countries and start from 01/01/2001 to 30/09/2012 on a daily basis. Concretely, the government benchmark bond index provided by Reuters *EcoWin* with a 10-years maturity, along with their local currencies is used to capture bond yields movements. The two main advantages of using this index than computing the term structure of a specific bond are the following. Firstly, it is much easier to match other market indicators with the selected bond yields. Secondly, this bond index is a reference to which investors benchmark the performance of individual market sectors as it is neither polluted by coupons nor taxes. Most bond yield indexes are provided by Reuters *EcoWin*, however, for some emerging economies, the data have been obtained from *Datastream*. The bid-ask spreads of bonds have been obtained from Bloomberg. The FTSE-Global Index for each sovereign provided by Reuters *EcoWin* is used as a proxy for the variation of market demands. VIX indexes obtained from *Datastream* are used as a measure of the market risk appetite.

Statistics of government benchmark bond index of the selected sovereigns with 10-years maturity are given in Table 10. To facilitate the comparison, a dichotomic approach has been undertaken, splitting advanced and emerging countries into two subgroups. Generally, higher rating leads to lower yields. Consequently, means of high rated sovereign bond yields are generally lower than means of those from low rated governments, however, the watershed is not clearly identified. There are intersections of the averaged yields between the high and low rated sovereign bond yields. For example, average yields of Thailand which has the highest rating of A/Stable are lower than the mean yields of Australia which is rated AAA/Stable in the period of analysis. Moreover, among the high rated bonds, the movements are not uniform. Figure 2 represents the time series of the government benchmark bond yields of 11 countries whose ratings remained AAA/Stable during the considered period. Although, they hold the same rating during the same period, the movements and ranges of their yields were varying. Switzerland bonds moved relatively smoothly during the observed period, however, on the same period Norway's government bonds fluctuations were significant. Moreover, all bond yields show clear upward movements from 2007 to 2009, except for Canada. Figure 3 exhibits the remaining nine advanced economies' government bond yields. These nine time series show more diverse features, since their ratings were varying during this period.

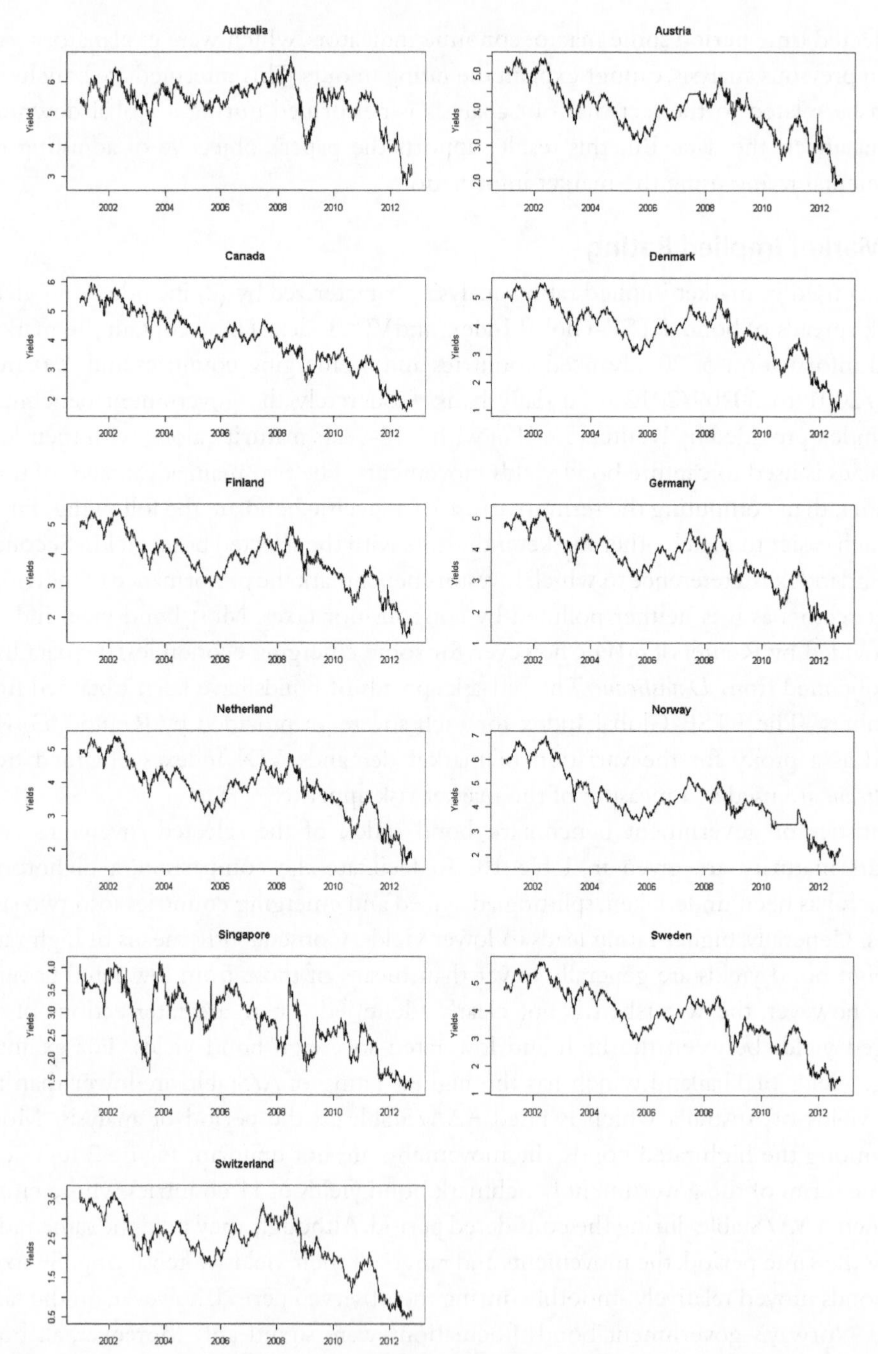

Figure 2 Government benchmark 10-year bond yields of the advanced AAA/Stable rated countries. These eleven countries: Australia, Austria, Canada, Denmark, Finland, Germany, Netherlands, Norway, Singapore, Sweden, and Switzerland are the countries which have had an AAA/Stable rating during the whole period from 2001 to 2012.

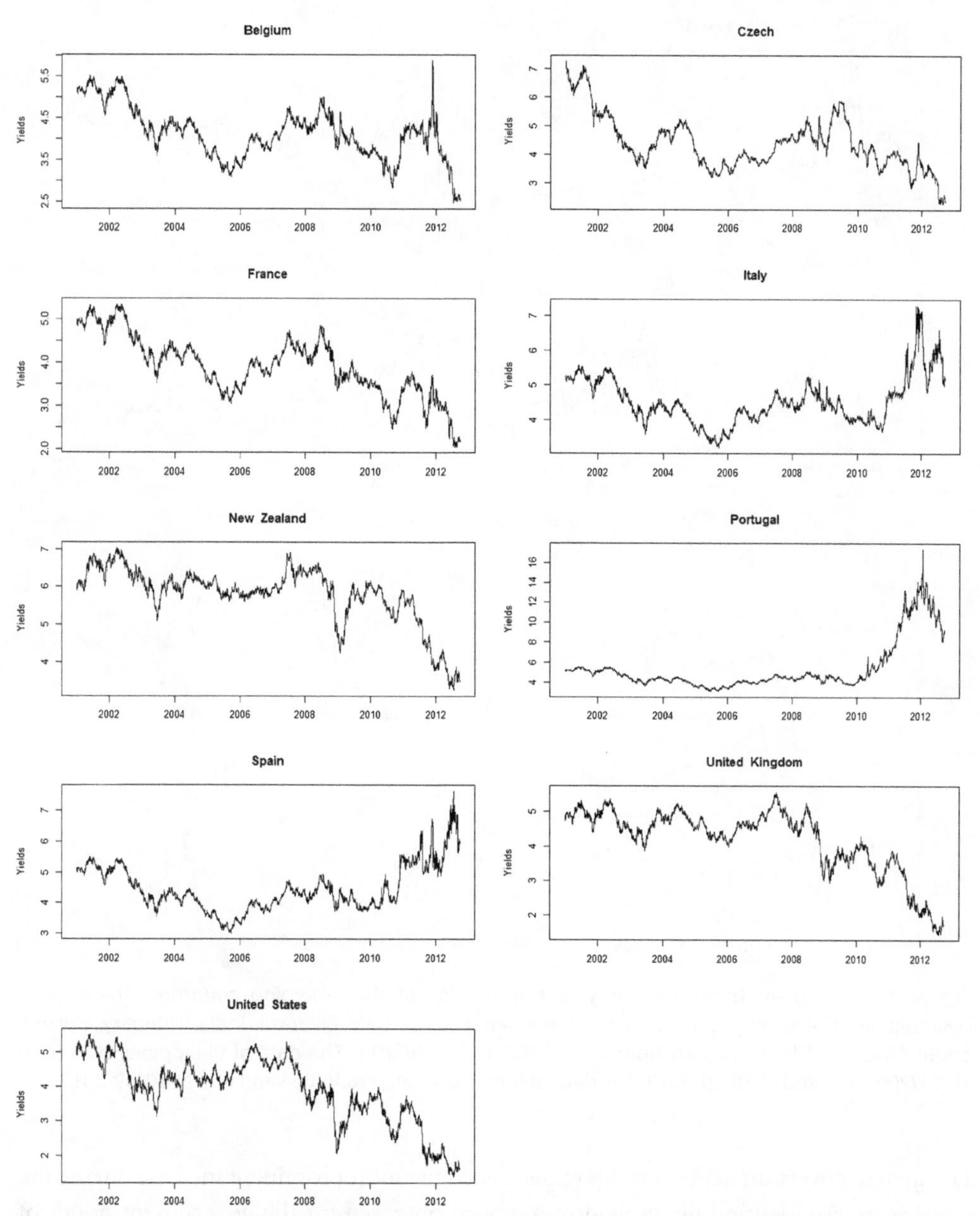

Figure 3 Government bond yields with 10 years maturity of the downgraded advanced countries. These nine countries: Belgium, Czech, France, Italy, New Zealand, Portugal, Spain, United Kingdom, and United States are the countries in the advanced economies group which have been downgraded during the sample period.

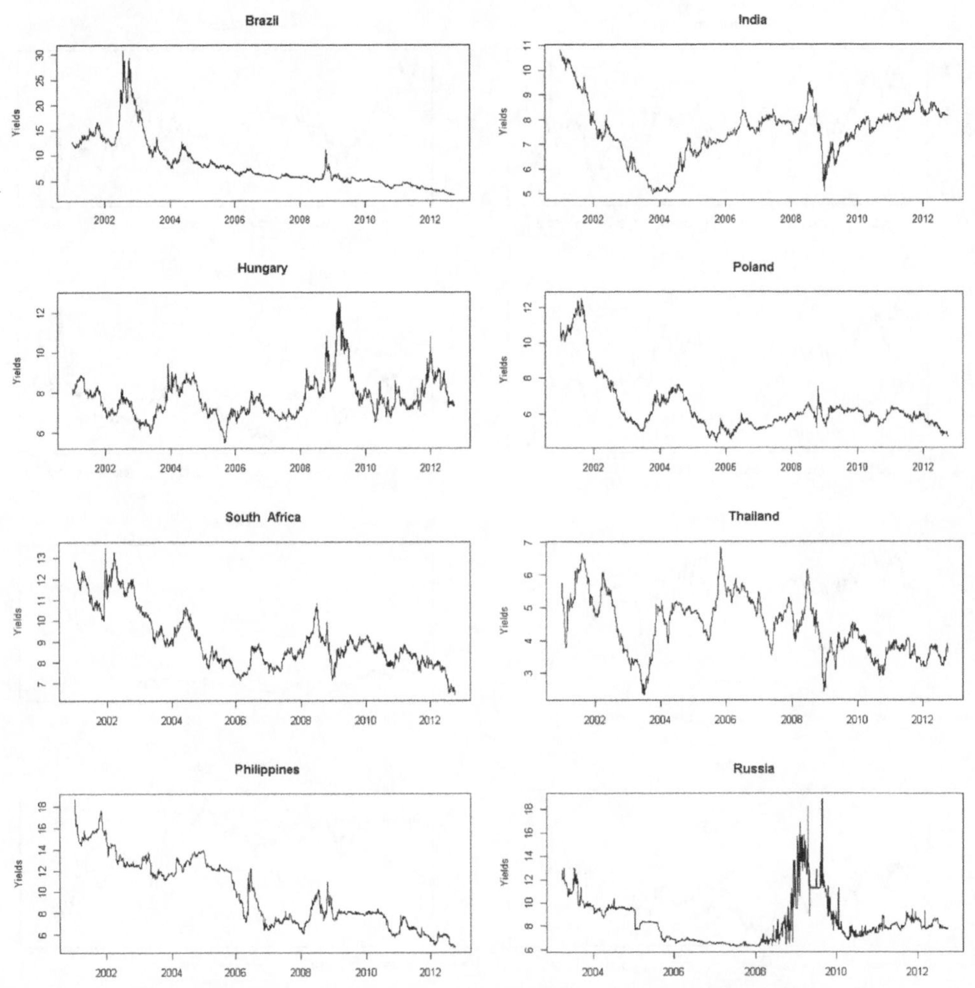

Figure 4 Government benchmark 10-year bond yields of the emerging countries. These eight countries are the emerging economies in the sample. The data of Brazil, India, Hungary, Poland, South Africa, and Thailand start from 01/01/2001 to 30/09/2012. The data of Philippines start from 16/01/2001 and end at 30/09/2012. The data of Russia start at 21/03/2003 and end at 30/09/2012.

Portuguese government bond yields experienced the most prominent increase during the last 2 years. An identical phenomenon has been observed for the government bonds of Belgium, Italy, and Spain. However, these countries have been dramatically impacted by the recent European Sovereign-Debt Crisis (Movements of emerging countries' bond yields are plotted in Figure 4). Though there is no tendency for these bond yields, behaviors, they are more volatile than those of advanced economies.

Chicago Board Options Exchange Volatility Index (VIX) of the same period is presented in Figure 5. Statistics of bid-ask spread of bonds and market capitalizations of

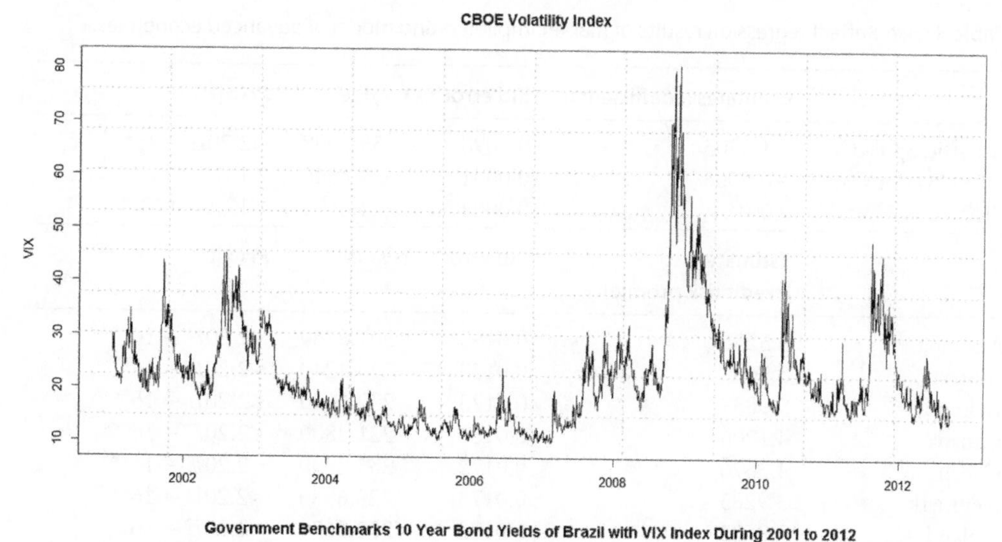

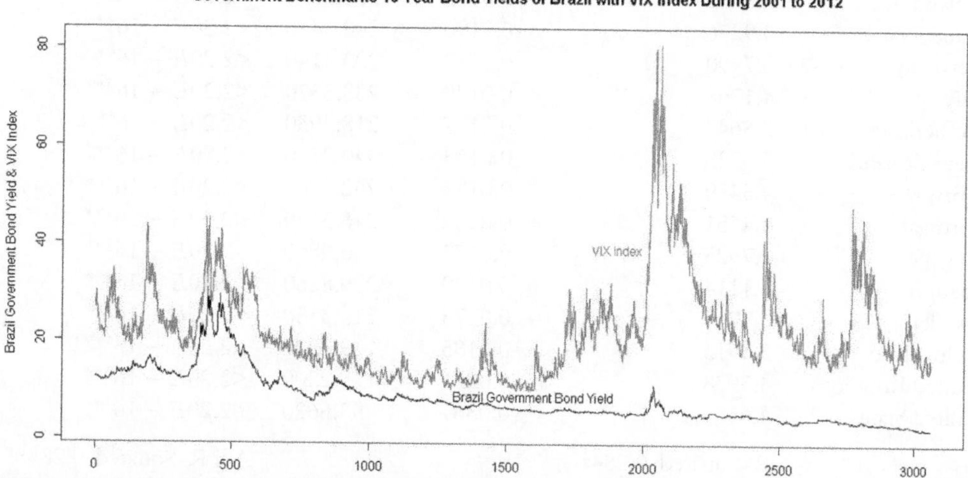

Figure 5 10-year government bond yields of Brazil with rating announcements and VIX Index. The upper graph illustrates the movement of the VIX index during the sample period. The lower graph plots the times series of Brazil bond yields and VIX.

FTSE-Global Equity Index are given in Table 11. Statistics of these two market indicators are presented in two groups following the country's economic development level. Italian, Portuguese, and Spanish bonds are relatively more liquid than others among the advanced economies. Meanwhile, the Hungarian, Philippians, and Polish bonds are more liquid compared to those of other emerging countries. The interesting observation in the results presented in Tables 3 and 4 is that the liquidity has different impact on the ratings depending on the group the country belongs to. The results show that liquid bonds issued by advanced economies, i.e., characterized by low bid-ask spreads, bear lower yields. This

Table 3 Fixed-effect regression results of market implied rating model of advanced economies.

	Estimates (coefficients)	**Std error**	***t*-value**	***Pr*(>|*t*|)**
Ask-Bid Spread	−1.5303	0.0098	−155.5998	$<2.20E-16^{***}$
FTSE Maket Cap.	−0.0006	0.0001	−7.9346	$2.15E-15^{***}$
VIX	0.0018	0.0004	4.8693	$1.12E-06^{***}$
	Estimates (credit risk premia)	**Std error**	***t*-value**	***Pr*(>|*t*|)**
Australia	5.5258	0.0183	301.8760	$<2.20E-16^{***}$
Austria	3.9067	0.0173	226.4240	$<2.20E-16^{***}$
Belgium	3.9839	0.0173	230.1640	$<2.20E-16^{***}$
Canada	4.1206	0.0186	221.4800	$<2.20E-16^{***}$
Czech	4.3676	0.0172	253.2900	$<2.20E-16^{***}$
Denmark	3.9283	0.0173	226.6980	$<2.20E-16^{***}$
Finland	3.8605	0.0173	222.5650	$<2.20E-16^{***}$
France	3.9276	0.0196	200.7410	$<2.20E-16^{***}$
Germany	3.7990	0.0187	203.4140	$<2.20E-16^{***}$
Italy	4.1761	0.0179	233.5370	$<2.20E-16^{***}$
Netherlands	3.8647	0.0177	218.3950	$<2.20E-16^{***}$
New Zealand	5.8735	0.0173	340.2560	$<2.20E-16^{***}$
Norway	4.5459	0.0173	262.0960	$<2.20E-16^{***}$
Portugal	4.4751	0.0182	246.5230	$<2.20E-16^{***}$
Singapore	2.7923	0.0173	160.9860	$<2.20E-16^{***}$
Spain	4.1114	0.0179	229.8260	$<2.20E-16^{***}$
Sweden	3.7717	0.0175	215.3550	$<2.20E-16^{***}$
Switzerland	2.5913	0.0185	139.7220	$<2.20E-16^{***}$
United Kingdom	4.3938	0.0251	175.2200	$<2.20E-16^{***}$
United States	4.6549	0.0867	53.6620	$<2.20E-16^{***}$
	R-Squared: 0.2849			Adj R-Squared: 0.2848

This table presents the result of the regression of the market implied rating model with the data of 20 advanced economies. Credit risk premia of each country are given in the second column.
***Significance level 0.001.

result is consistent with the fact that the more liquid the asset, the lower the transaction costs, the lower the risk, and consequently the lower the return. However, a negative bid-ask spread has been observed in the result of the regression regarding these emerging economies. A possible interpretation of this result is that the liquidity factor for emerging market[14] works in a different way than for the intuitive approach. When investing in emerging markets, which are relatively riskier than advanced markets, investors may hold more active and sensitive investment strategies than investing in advanced economies.

[14] Or the emerging markets in our sample.

Table 4 Fixed-effect regression results of market-implied rating model of emerging economies.

	Estimates (coefficients)	**Std error**	***t*-value**	***Pr*(>|*t*|)**
Ask-Bid Spread	2.8778	0.0686	41.9800	$<2.20E-16^{***}$
FTSE Maket Cap.	−0.1210	0.0011	−107.7100	$<2.20E-16^{***}$
VIX	0.0344	0.0013	27.1910	$<2.20E-16^{***}$
	Estimates (credit risk premia)	**Std error**	***t*-value**	***Pr*(>|*t*|)**
Brazil	9.7298	0.0628	154.8320	$<2.20E-16^{***}$
Hungary	6.7608	0.0692	97.6460	$<2.20E-16^{***}$
India	7.5942	0.0457	166.2740	$<2.20E-16^{***}$
Philippines	9.1144	0.0492	185.4130	$<2.20E-16^{***}$
Poland	6.0675	0.0428	141.8240	$<2.20E-16^{***}$
Russia	9.2199	0.0501	184.1090	$<2.20E-16^{***}$
South Africa	10.8099	0.0484	223.4070	$<2.20E-16^{***}$
Thailand	4.1275	0.0429	96.1070	$<2.20E-16^{***}$
	R-Squared: 0.3505			Adj. R-Squared: 0.3503

This table presents the results obtained from the regression of the market implied rating model with the data of eight emerging economies. Credit risk premia of each country are given in the second column.
***Significance level 0.001.

Therefore, even though investors prefer to choose more liquid bonds, they are more sensitive to losses than in advanced market such that they actively trade the bonds. Active trading contributes to a higher liquidity and the yields generated by these bonds are not necessarily very high. Secondly, the market requirement indicator (FTSE-Global Market Capitalization Index) is significant in both regressions with negative signs. This indicates that when investors are willing to invest but are "disappointed" by equity markets, they turn to other markets such as the bonds. Similarly, investors will leave the bond market if it becomes depressed. The p-values of the t-tests confirm that this indicator has a significant influence for the bond yields. While, comparing coefficients of the FTSE Market Capitalization in the two regressions, we observe that the influence of market requirements is more significant for the emerging economies than for advanced markets. Finally, the VIX index, which measures the risk appetite of market practitioners, has a significant positive coefficient in both regressions. This is consistent with the fact that investors tend to be more conservative when the markets are turbulent, i.e., they tend to demand higher returns for the same level of risk under a volatile market than under bullish market conditions. Moreover, the influence of this indicator is stronger for emerging markets than for advanced economies, as people usually have more confidence in advanced economies during crisis (e.g., "fly to quality" behaviors).

Table 5 Fundament implied rating, market implied rating, adjusted rating, and agency rating.

Country	Country-specific rating		Market implied rating		δ-rating		Fitch's rating	
Australia	AA−	Watch negative	A+	Watch positive	AA−	Watch negative	AAA	Stable
Austria	AA+	Watch positive	AA−	Watch positive	AA+	Watch positive	AAA	Stable
Belgium	AA+	Positive	AA−	Watch positive	AA+	Positive	AA	Negative
Canada	AA+	Positive	AA−	Positive	AA+	Stable	AAA	Stable
Czech	A	Positive	AA−	Negative	A	Positive	AA−	Stable
Denmark	AA+	Negative	AA−	Watch positive	AA+	Negative	AAA	Stable
Finland	AA+	Watch negative	AA−	Watch positive	AA+	Watch negative	AAA	Stable
France	AAA	Negative	AA−	Watch positive	AAA	Watch negative	AAA	Negative
Germany	AAA	Watch negative	AA	Negative	AAA	Watch negative	AAA	Stable
Italy	AA+	Positive	AA−	Stable	AA	Stable	A−	Negative
Netherlands	AA+	Stable	AA−	Watch positive	AA+	Stable	AAA	Stable
New Zealand	AA−	Watch negative	A+	Positive	A+	Watch positive	AA+	Stable
Norway	AAA	Watch negative	AA−	Watch negative	AA+	Watch positive	AAA	Stable
Portugal	A+	Stable	AA−	Negative	AA−	Watch negative	BB+	Negative
Singapore	AAA	Stable	AAA	Negative	AAA	Stable	AAA	Stable
Spain	AA−	Watch positive	AA−	Positive	AA−	Positive	BBB	Negative
Sweden	AA+	Negative	AA	Negative	AA+	Negative	AAA	Stable
Switzerland	AA+	Stable	AAA	Stable	AA+	Stable	AAA	Stable
UK	AA	Positive	AA−	Negative	AA	Positive	AAA	Negative
US	AA+	Negative	AA−	Watch negative	AA+	Watch negative	AAA	Negative
Brazil	BBB−	Positive	BBB	Watch positive	BBB−	Positive	BBB	Stable
Hungary	A−	Watch negative	A−	Stable	A−	Negative	BBB−	Negative
India	A−	Watch positive	BBB+	Watch positive	A−	Negative	BBB−	Negative
Philippines	BBB−	Watch positive	BBB+	Negative	BBB−	Watch positive	BBB−	Stable
Poland	BBB+	Watch positive	A	Watch negative	A−	Watch negative	A	Stable
Russia	BB+	Watch positive	BBB+	Watch negative	BB+	Watch positive	BBB	Stable
South Africa	BBB+	Positive	BBB	Positive	BBB+	Stable	A	Negative
Thailand	A	Negative	AA−	Positive	A	Positive	A−	Stable

This table compares the ratings obtained from the different sources. In the first two columns, the country-specific ratings and the market implied ratings of both the 20 advanced economies and the 8 emerging economies are provided using the regression results obtained in the previous section. The weighted averaged ratings obtained using the Credibility Theory are listed in the third column. The Fitch's history rating is given in the last column.

3.3. Implied Ratings and Credibility Weights

Here, we give the two implied ratings and the δ-Ratings in the standard alphabets fashion in order to compare the results with agency's ratings. Country-specific implied rating and market implied rating are derived from previous results listed in Tables 2, 3, and 4. The two

Table 6 Correlation among economic indicators and rating scores (2001–2012).

	GDP	PCI	Inf.	FB	ED	CAB	CPI	Score
			Advanced economies					
GDP	1.00	−0.09	0.11	−0.25	−0.15	0.23	0.18	0.13
PCI	−0.09	1.00	−0.14	0.29	−0.02	0.46	0.44	0.41
Inf.	0.11	−0.14	1.00	−0.09	−0.11	−0.29	−0.12	−0.13
FB	−0.25	0.29	−0.09	1.00	−0.05	0.08	0.01	0.02
ED	−0.15	−0.02	−0.11	−0.05	1.00	0.19	−0.30	−0.23
CAB	0.23	0.46	−0.29	0.08	0.19	1.00	0.48	0.33
CPI	0.18	0.44	−0.12	0.01	−0.30	0.48	1.00	0.69
Score	0.13	0.41	−0.13	0.02	−0.23	0.33	0.69	1.00
VIF	1.29	1.57	1.14	1.20	1.53	2.32	1.91	
			Emerging economies					
GDP	1.00	−0.36	0.08	−0.30	0.02	0.09	−0.32	−0.12
PCI	−0.36	1.00	−0.11	0.81	−0.15	−0.29	0.52	0.41
Inf.	0.08	−0.11	1.00	0.16	−0.20	0.30	−0.22	−0.45
FB	−0.30	0.81	0.16	1.00	−0.09	−0.21	0.50	0.23
ED	0.02	−0.15	−0.20	−0.09	1.00	−0.34	0.20	−0.37
CAB	0.09	−0.29	0.30	−0.21	−0.34	1.00	−0.73	−0.46
CPI	−0.32	0.52	−0.22	0.50	0.20	−0.73	1.00	0.54
Score	−0.12	0.41	−0.45	0.23	−0.37	−0.46	0.54	1.00
VIF	1.23	3.84	1.38	3.89	1.28	2.60	3.21	
			All sovereigns					
GDP	1.00	−0.35	0.30	−0.41	−0.16	0.12	−0.28	−0.32
PCI	−0.35	1.00	−0.50	0.56	0.11	0.37	0.77	0.75
Inf.	0.30	−0.50	1.00	−0.29	−0.20	−0.10	−0.56	−0.66
FB	−0.41	0.56	−0.29	1.00	0.04	0.08	0.48	0.50
ED	−0.16	0.11	−0.20	0.04	1.00	0.12	0.02	0.02
CAB	0.12	0.37	−0.10	0.08	0.12	1.00	0.29	0.16
CPI	−0.28	0.77	−0.56	0.48	0.02	0.29	1.00	0.88
Score	−0.32	0.75	−0.66	0.50	0.02	0.16	0.88	1.00
VIF	1.38	3.26	1.63	1.63	1.13	1.37	2.95	

PCI is per capita income; Inf. means inflation; FB refers to fiscal balance; ED indicates external debt; CAB is the abbreviation of current account balance; CPI is the Corruption Perceptions Index published by Transparency International; DH denotes default history; Score is the numerical value of the corresponding rating. The correlations are computed for all the sovereigns, advanced economies, and emerging economies, and listed in the three subtables.

Table 7 Principal component analysis of economic indicators (2001–2012).

Importance of components:

	PC1	PC2	PC3	PC4	PC5	PC6	PC7	PC8
				All economies				
Standard deviation	1.9281	1.0897	1.0377	0.8948	0.71550	0.62213	0.46419	0.3213
Proportion of variance	0.4647	0.1484	0.1346	0.1001	0.06399	0.04838	0.02693	0.0129
Cumulative proportion	0.4647	0.6131	0.7477	0.8478	0.91178	0.96017	0.98710	1.0000
				Advanced economies				
Standard deviation	1.5973	1.2271	1.1086	0.9247	0.86485	0.68678	0.63403	0.48714
Proportion of variance	0.3189	0.1882	0.1536	0.1069	0.09349	0.05896	0.05025	0.02966
Cumulative proportion	0.3189	0.5071	0.6607	0.7676	0.86113	0.92009	0.97034	1.00000
				Emerging economies				
Standard deviation	1.7672	1.2814	1.1289	0.9353	0.7818	0.46764	0.37059	0.34435
Proportion of variance	0.3904	0.2053	0.1593	0.1094	0.0764	0.02734	0.01717	0.01482
Cumulative proportion	0.3904	0.5956	0.7549	0.8643	0.9407	0.96801	0.98518	1.00000

This table gives the principal component analysis results of the economic indicators listed in Table 1 with the three sample sets. Here PC1 to PC8 refers to Rating Scores, GDP growth rate, Per capita income, inflation rate, fiscal balance, external debts, current balance accounts, and corruption perceptions index.

ratings are both calculated from an ordinal scale method[15] with the inputs of the previous by obtained implied credit premium. The outcomes are credit scores showed in the first two columns of Table 13. Credibility weights, i.e., ω in equation (4), are listed in the fifth column of Table 13.[16] Alphabets given in Table 5 are the scaled results according to the mapping given in Table 14.

Firstly, fundamental ratings listed in the second column of Table 5 are compared with Fitch's ratings, the last column. Rating agencies tend to rate the advanced countries higher than what is implied by the related economic data, except for the countries like Belgium, Italy, Portugal, and Spain affected by the crisis. However, this optimistic attitude is not observed while evaluating the ratings of emerging countries. Emerging countries with higher agency's ratings than fundamental ratings are usually believed to have good economic perspectives, while those with higher fundamental ratings than agency's ratings usually recently experienced an economic turmoil.

Secondly, we compared the market implied ratings and agency's ratings (third and last column in Table 5). Similarly, Fitch gave better ratings to advanced economies than the ratings implied by their market indicators, except for the countries believed to be in trouble, such as Italy, Spain, and Portugal. However, this tendency is not particularly clear in

[15] The scales are different since the difference of models of the two ratings. We separate the two economies groups to compute market implied ratings since the different sign of liquidity. Credit rankings are given in Table 12.

[16] The value of σ^2 is calculated by bootstrapping.

Table 8 Statistics of economic indicator data (2001–2012).

	GDP	PCI*	Inf.*	FB*	ED*	CAB*	CPI*	DH*	Score*	Rating
					Advanced economies					
Min	−8.3540	6270	−0.903	18.01	9.709	−12.638	3.700	0.0	49.00	AA−/stable
1st qu.	0.7505	27146	1.575	36.47	42.511	−3.201	7.100	0.0	99.00	–
Median	1.9195	37293	2.184	43.58	58.422	1.012	8.500	0.5	100.00	–
Mean	1.7465	38335	2.180	42.60	60.735	1.847	7.921	0.5	96.72	–
3rd qu.	3.0595	46329	2.784	49.59	77.138	5.788	9.000	1.0	100.00	–
Max.	14.7630	99665	6.612	58.53	123.357	25.813	9.900	1.0	100.00	AAA/stable
					Emerging economies					
Min.	−7.800	467.2	−0.846	17.00	7.876	−8.4270	2.300	1	26.0	BBB−/negative
1st qu.	2.851	2118.7	3.703	20.28	40.096	−3.3453	2.700	1	54.0	–
Median	4.325	5080.5	4.944	31.84	50.806	−0.2730	3.500	1	62.5	–
Mean	4.194	5861.7	5.871	30.27	51.529	−0.1983	3.652	1	61.8	–
3rd qu.	6.118	8768.7	7.099	38.58	66.929	2.8727	4.525	1	74.0	–
Max.	10.623	15354.3	21.461	52.40	84.300	11.0690	5.500	1	80.0	A/stable
					All countries					
Min.	−8.3540	467.2	−0.903	17.00	7.876	−12.638	2.300	0.0000	26.00	BBB−/negative
1st qu.	0.9423	11248.1	1.780	33.78	41.700	−3.248	4.600	0.0000	75.00	–
Median	2.5165	30152.8	2.479	39.34	55.836	0.285	7.300	1.0000	100.00	–
Mean	2.4459	29056.8	3.234	39.08	58.105	1.262	6.701	0.6429	86.75	–
3rd qu.	3.9000	43394.7	3.814	47.68	72.164	4.697	8.800	1.0000	100.00	–
Max.	14.7630	99664.5	21.461	58.53	123.357	25.813	9.900	1.0000	100.00	AAA/stable

*In this table, PCI is the per capita income; Inf. means inflation; FB refers to fiscal balance; ED indicates external debt; CAB is the abbreviation of current account balance; CPI is the Corruption Perceptions Index published by Transparency International; DH denotes default history; Score is the numerical value of the corresponding rating. It includes 20 advanced economies: Australia, Austria, Belgium, Canada, Czech, Denmark, Finland, France, Germany, Italy, Netherlands, New Zealand, Norway, Portugal, Singapore, Spain, Sweden, Switzerland, United Kingdom, United States; and 8 emerging economies: Brazil, Hungary, India, Philippines, Poland, Russia, South Africa, and Thailand. The data are from 2001 to 2012, annually.

Table 9 Tests for regression method of country-specific model.

	Fixed vs. OLS *F*-test	Fixed or random Hausman test	Time-fixed *F*-test	Random or OLS Breusch-Pagan LM test	Cross-sectional Breusch-Pagan LM test	Serial correlation Breusch-Godfrey/ Wooldridge test
Advanced economies	F = 9.61 df1 = 18 df2 = 213 *p*-value < 2.2e−16	chisq = 37.35 df = 7 *p*-value = 4.03e−06	F = 1.22 df1 = 11 df2 = 202 *p*-value = 0.28	chisq = 69.41 df = 1 *p*-value < 2.2e−16	chisq = 605.93 df = 190 *p*-value < 2.2e−16	chisq = 69.93 df = 12 *p*-value = 3.3e−10
Emerging economies	F = 20.81 df1 = 7 df2 = 81 *p*-value < 9.44e−16	chisq = 3.43 df = 6 *p*-value = 1.83e−11	F = 1.33 df1 = 11 df2 = 70 *p*-value = 0.23	chisq = 159.34 df = 1 *p*-value < 2.2e−16	chisq = 65.84 df = 28 *p*-value = 6.95e−05	chisq = 40.20 df = 12 *p*-value = 6.66e−05
All countries	F = 26.75 df1 = 26 df2 = 301 *p*-value < 2.2e−16	chisq = 97.18 df = 7 *p*-value < 2.2e−16	F = 1.64 df1 = 11 df2 = 290 *p*-value = 0.09	chisq = 468.72 df = 1 *p*-value < 2.2e−16	chisq = 1137.98 df = 378 *p*-value < 2.2e−16	chisq = 143.84 df = 12 *p*-value < 2.2e−16

*Breusch-Pagan Lagrange Multiplier method tests the pooling regression vs. random effect; The Hausman Test checks the fixed effect vs. the random effect. The Breusch-Pagan Lagrange Multiplier test checks the cross-sectional effect. The time-fixed effect is tested using an *F*-test and the serial correlation is tested using the Breusch-Godfrey/Wooldridge test. All the tests are implemented on the entire data set, the advanced economies, and the emerging countries.

Table 10 Statistics of government benchmarks 10-Year Bond Yields of 28 countries (2001–2012).

		Min	1st qu.	Median	Mean	3rd qu.	Max	Std	Highest rating	Lowest rating
1	Australia	2.73	5.21	5.51	5.39	5.81	6.79	0.70	AAA/stable	AAA/stable
2	Austria	1.87	3.50	4.02	3.96	4.42	5.47	0.74	AAA/stable	AAA/stable
3	Belgium	2.47	3.71	4.14	4.13	4.46	5.88	0.61	AA+/stable	AA−/stable
4	Canada	1.58	3.37	4.11	4.00	4.74	5.97	1.01	AAA/stable	AAA/stable
5	Czech	2.29	3.77	4.22	4.38	4.85	7.27	0.91	AA−/positive	A/stable
6	Denmark	0.97	3.35	3.97	3.83	4.48	5.51	0.98	AAA/stable	AAA/stable
7	Finland	1.34	3.36	3.95	3.85	4.39	5.48	0.85	AAA/stable	AAA/stable
8	France	2.06	3.46	3.94	3.91	4.36	5.35	0.69	AAA/stable	AAA/negative
9	Germany	1.16	3.19	3.85	3.67	4.28	5.28	0.90	AAA/stable	AAA/stable
10	Italy	3.21	4.08	4.43	4.55	4.92	7.30	0.68	AA/stable	A−/negative
11	Netherlands	1.54	3.39	3.93	3.84	4.36	5.40	0.82	AAA/stable	AAA/stable
12	New Zealand	3.24	5.66	5.94	5.79	6.24	7.03	0.76	AAA/stable	AA+/stable
13	Norway	1.61	3.69	4.24	4.37	4.96	6.97	1.17	AAA/stable	AAA/stable
14	Portugal	3.10	4.07	4.46	5.39	5.24	17.36	2.50	AA/stable	BB−/negative
15	Singapore	1.30	2.37	2.86	2.82	3.38	4.13	0.68	AAA/stable	AAA/stable
16	Spain	3.00	3.96	4.27	4.46	5.02	7.64	0.75	AAA/stable	BBB/negative
17	Sweden	1.13	3.20	3.87	3.80	4.59	5.77	1.05	AAA/stable	AAA/stable
18	Switzerland	0.45	1.97	2.44	2.36	2.86	3.73	0.74	AAA/stable	AAA/stable
19	United Kingdom	1.44	3.69	4.49	4.18	4.84	5.58	0.92	AAA/stable	AAA/negative
20	United States	1.39	3.40	4.07	3.90	4.60	5.51	0.95	AAA/stable	AAA/negative
1	Brazil	2.26	5.10	6.38	8.19	10.44	30.78	4.76	BBB/stable	B+/negative
2	India	4.96	6.92	7.62	7.50	8.15	10.82	1.15	A+/stable	BBB−/negative
3	Hungary	5.49	7.04	7.54	7.72	8.22	12.72	1.00	BBB−/stable	BB+/stable
4	Philippines	4.85	7.23	8.75	9.84	12.48	18.64	3.16	BBB/stable	BB+/negative
5	Poland	4.39	5.50	5.90	6.37	6.47	12.54	1.57	A+/stable	A/stable
6	Russia	6.26	6.84	7.91	8.36	9.43	18.90	1.90	BBB+/stable	B−
7	South Africa	6.44	8.06	8.67	9.07	9.80	13.50	1.39	A/positive	BBB+/stable
8	Thailand	2.35	3.73	4.42	4.42	5.07	6.84	0.88	A/stable	BBB+/stable

*There are statistics of 20 advanced economies and 8 emerging economies government benchmark bond yields with 10-years maturity. 1st Qu. and 3rd Qu. means the first quartile and third quartile; Std. refers to the standard error. The data set starts from Jan. 2001 to Sep. 2012. We give the highest rating and lowest rating from Fitch History Rating during this period in the last two columns. For the lack of data, the statistics of Philippine and Russia start from 16/01/2001 to 21/03/2003, respectively.

Table 11 Statistics of market indicators (2001–2012).

		Ask-bid spreads					FTSE-global market CAP				
		Min	Median	Mean	Max	Std	Min	Median	Mean	Max	Std
1	Australia	0.99	1.09	1.10	1.32	0.04	20.42	61.88	63.07	111.28	27.34
2	Austria	0.61	1.02	0.99	1.12	0.08	0.75	3.40	3.61	8.90	2.12
3	Belgium	0.31	1.01	0.94	1.08	0.15	3.59	7.83	8.04	12.11	1.86
4	Canada	0.87	1.07	1.08	1.24	0.05	26.92	78.68	74.44	134.39	28.98
5	Czech	0.78	1.00	1.02	1.42	0.13	0.17	1.41	1.24	3.24	0.77
6	Denmark	0.97	1.08	1.09	1.54	0.08	3.80	8.55	9.17	16.29	3.29
7	Finland	0.84	1.03	1.03	1.27	0.04	6.58	11.75	12.62	26.39	3.85
8	France	0.62	1.03	1.00	1.12	0.08	46.85	100.92	104.75	179.16	31.70
9	Germany	1.02	1.07	1.09	1.39	0.90	28.60	75.69	76.89	138.34	24.65
10	Italy	0.06	0.99	0.86	1.04	0.24	19.24	35.54	38.37	65.67	12.21
11	Netherlands	0.84	1.03	1.03	1.15	0.04	15.80	35.90	36.31	57.24	8.77
12	New Zealand	0.92	1.09	1.08	1.22	0.06	0.79	1.63	1.63	2.55	0.42
13	Norway	1.02	1.12	1.15	1.60	0.11	2.58	7.52	7.61	16.34	3.58
14	Portugal	0.00	1.01	0.82	1.06	0.35	1.88	3.52	3.76	6.87	1.10
15	Singapore	0.75	1.00	1.00	1.18	0.01	4.14	10.13	12.10	23.00	5.66
16	Spain	0.04	1.02	0.89	1.09	0.27	16.35	39.96	39.71	73.11	14.21
17	Sweden	0.75	1.01	1.00	1.24	0.03	9.39	25.73	25.44	43.04	8.43
18	Switzerland	1.00	1.14	1.17	1.69	0.10	34.96	72.44	70.89	101.92	17.67
19	United Kingdom	0.94	1.08	1.08	1.28	0.04	118.8	224.4	225.0	345.1	48.68
20	United States	0.95	1.10	1.10	1.22	0.04	642.3	1142.8	1131.3	1513.1	196.30
1	Brazil	1.16	1.72	1.74	2.13	0.16	3.12	27.15	32.04	75.75	23.44
2	India	2.72	2.72	2.72	2.72	5.70E−07	3.68	27.23	24.63	46.10	12.06
3	Hungary	0.69	0.96	0.95	1.16	0.08	0.36	1.65	1.65	3.60	0.82
4	Philippines	0.38	0.73	0.73	1.08	0.16	0.34	1.00	1.16	3.38	0.73
5	Poland	0.72	0.98	0.96	1.13	0.06	0.64	2.68	2.78	6.44	1.65
6	Russia	0.49	1.23	1.23	1.80	0.15	2.59	20.10	17.66	40.29	10.35
7	South Africa	0.91	1.00	1.01	1.15	0.04	4.41	22.34	20.89	38.52	10.21
8	Thailand	0.61	0.99	1.00	1.50	0.13	0.59	3.30	3.53	8.86	2.12

Market capitalizations of the country's equity market issued by FTSE-Global Equity Index for each sovereign are normalized into the common scale as bond yields and liquidity spreads. Statistics of two market indicators of the 28 economies. The ask-bid spread is calculated using the following formula: $\frac{\text{Ask}-\text{Bid}}{\text{Ask}} \times 100\%$ using data collected from Bloomberg. The equity market capitalizations of sovereign are measured by the FTSE-Global market cap index. Std means standard deviation. These data start from Jan. 2001 to Sep. 2012. The data of Philippines and Russia follow the same period as the data of their government benchmark bond yields. They are all daily data.

Table 12 Country-specific implied and market implied ranks.

	Country-specific rank	Market implied rank	Rank splits
Advanced economies			
Australia	17	19	2
Austria	5	7	2
Belgium	6	10	4
Canada	8	12	4
Czech Republic	20	14	−6
Denmark	12	9	−3
Finland	14	5	−9
France	2	8	6
Germany	4	4	0
Italy	7	13	6
Netherlands	9	6	−3
New Zealand	18	20	2
Norway	3	17	14
Portugal	19	16	−3
Singapore	1	2	1
Spain	16	11	−5
Sweden	11	3	−8
Switzerland	10	1	−9
United Kingdom	15	15	0
United States	13	18	5
Emerging economies			
Brazil	7	7	0
Hungary	3	3	0
India	4	2	−2
Philippines	5	6	1
Poland	2	4	2
Russia	6	8	2
South Africa	8	5	−3
Thailand	1	1	0

In this table, the implied credit ranks of the 20 advanced economies and the 8 selected emerging economies have been provided. The number in the first column is the country-specific ranks computed from the results of Table 2. The market implied ranks are listed in the second column calculated from the implied credit premia in Tables 3 and 4. In the last column, the differences between the two ranks have been provided.

the emerging group. Comparing fundamental and market implied ratings, we found that market implied ratings are lower than their fundamental ratings for advanced economies, except for Czech Republic, Portugal, and Switzerland. For emerging economies, however, market implied ratings are higher than country-specific implied ratings except for India and South Africa.

Table 13 Fundamental and market implied ratings scores.

Country	Fundamental score	Market score	Averaged scores	Fitch's score	δ-score	Weight
Australia	0.83	0.82	0.83	1.00	0.83	0.311901195
Austria	0.97	0.87	0.92	1.00	0.97	0.039688222
Belgium	0.96	0.87	0.91	0.89	0.96	0.003523232
Canada	0.96	0.86	0.91	1.00	0.95	0.056833804
Czech Republic	0.76	0.84	0.80	0.85	0.76	0.007325898
Denmark	0.94	0.87	0.91	1.00	0.94	0.050539811
Finland	0.93	0.87	0.90	1.00	0.93	0.057606644
France	0.99	0.87	0.93	0.99	0.98	0.023910266
Germany	0.98	0.89	0.93	1.00	0.98	0.019197356
Italy	0.96	0.85	0.90	0.69	0.90	0.529180125
Netherlands	0.95	0.87	0.91	1.00	0.95	0.044894827
New Zealand	0.83	0.81	0.82	0.95	0.82	0.122773553
Norway	0.98	0.83	0.91	1.00	0.97	0.104713107
Portugal	0.80	0.84	0.82	0.49	0.83	0.851728728
Singapore	1.00	0.99	1.00	1.00	1.00	1.23082E−06
Spain	0.87	0.86	0.87	0.59	0.86	0.736500433
Sweden	0.94	0.89	0.92	1.00	0.94	0.028099158
Switzerland	0.95	1.00	0.97	1.00	0.95	0.00088457
United Kingdom	0.91	0.84	0.88	0.99	0.91	0.091735941
United States	0.94	0.83	0.89	0.99	0.93	0.095308758
Brazil	0.56	0.62	0.59	0.60	0.56	0.002671929
Hungary	0.68	0.7	0.69	0.54	0.69	0.626134691
India	0.72	0.67	0.69	0.54	0.69	0.644876707
Philippines	0.62	0.64	0.63	0.55	0.62	0.113775216
Poland	0.67	0.73	0.70	0.75	0.68	0.027353724
Russia	0.52	0.63	0.57	0.60	0.52	0.051003205
South Africa	0.66	0.61	0.64	0.74	0.65	0.276121817
Thailand	0.74	0.86	0.80	0.70	0.76	0.159453856

*The advanced and emerging economies are listed in the first column separated by a horizontal line. The upper 20 countries are the advanced economies considered in our study and the lower 8 countries are the emerging countries. Fundamental credit scores and market credit scores are given in the second and the third column. The Fitch's scores are the score obtained from Fitch's rating using the mapping given in Table 14. Weights are the credibility weights (ω in Equation (4)) computed by $\frac{2}{2+\frac{\sigma^2}{\tau^2}}$. The δ-scores listed in the last column is the weighted averaged scores of fundamental and market credit scores using the credibility weights.

Credibility weights are given in Table 13, applying the algorithm expressed in equation (4) and the bootstrapping results of $E(\sigma^2)$. Market implied ratings bear lower weights for the states with stable ratings through years and higher weights for the countries with volatile ratings. The δ-Ratings provided in the fourth column are obtained using

Table 14 Ratings and corresponding scores.

1	AAA	Stable	0.67	BBB+	Watch positive	0.34	B+	Negative
0.99	AAA	Negative	0.66	BBB+	Positive	0.33	B+	Watch negative
0.98	AAA	Watch negative	0.65	BBB+	Stable	0.32	B	Watch positive
0.97	AA+	Watch positive	0.64	BBB+	Negative	0.31	B	Positive
0.96	AA+	Positive	0.63	BBB+	Watch negative	0.3	B	Stable
0.95	AA+	Stable	0.62	BBB	Watch positive	0.29	B	Negative
0.94	AA+	Negative	0.61	BBB	Positive	0.28	B	Watch negative
0.93	AA+	Watch negative	0.6	BBB	Stable	0.27	B−	Watch positive
0.92	AA	Watch positive	0.59	BBB	Negative	0.26	B−	Positive
0.91	AA	Positive	0.58	BBB	Watch negative	0.25	B−	Stable
0.9	AA	Stable	0.57	BBB−	Watch positive	0.24	B−	Negative
0.89	AA	Negative	0.56	BBB−	Positive	0.23	B−	Watch negative
0.88	AA	Watch negative	0.55	BBB−	Stable	0.22	CCC	Watch positive
0.87	AA−	Watch positive	0.54	BBB−	Negative	0.21	CCC	Positive
0.86	AA−	Positive	0.53	BBB−	Watch negative	0.2	CCC	Stable
0.85	AA−	Stable	0.52	BB+	Watch positive	0.19	CCC	Negative
0.84	AA−	Negative	0.51	BB+	Positive	0.18	CCC	Watch negative
0.83	AA−	Watch negative	0.5	BB+	Stable	0.17	CC	Watch positive
0.82	A+	Watch positive	0.49	BB+	Negative	0.16	CC	Positive
0.81	A+	Positive	0.48	BB+	Watch negative	0.15	CC	Stable
0.8	A+	Stable	0.47	BB	Watch positive	0.14	CC	Negative
0.79	A+	Negative	0.46	BB	Positive	0.13	CC	Watch negative
0.78	A+	Watch negative	0.45	BB	Stable	0.12	C	Watch positive
0.77	A	Watch positive	0.44	BB	Negative	0.11	C	Positive
0.76	A	Positive	0.43	BB	Watch negative	0.1	C	Stable
0.75	A	Stable	0.42	BB−	Watch positive	0.09	C	Negative
0.74	A	Negative	0.41	BB−	Positive	0.08	C	Watch negative
0.73	A	Watch negative	0.4	BB−	Stable	0.07	D	Watch positive
0.72	A−	Watch positive	0.39	BB−	Negative	0.06	D	Positive
0.71	A−	Positive	0.38	BB−	Watch negative	0.05	D	Stable
0.7	A−	Stable	0.37	B+	Watch positive	0.04	D	Negative
0.69	A−	Negative	0.36	B+	Positive	0.03	D	Watch negative
0.68	A−	Watch negative	0.35	B+	Stable			

*This table shows the mapping from numerical credit score between 0 and 1 to the standard alphabets ratings from D watch negative to AAA stable.

the credibility weights between the fundamental ratings and the market implied ratings. Comparing the δ-Ratings and Fitch's ratings, we observe that the adjusted ratings are usually lower than agency's ratings for advanced economies, but they exhibit different aspects whether the countries are facing financial or economic trouble. This phenomenon indicates that rating agencies may overreact to these countries' problems than what their economic and financial indicators imply. For emerging countries, rating agencies give higher ratings to the countries which are believed to have better economic perspectives than the averaged ratings we proposed and lower ratings to these countries facing or under economic or financial difficulties. Therefore, we believe rating agencies are driven by public belief or mass media and partially lose their objectivity. Combining the two implied ratings using credibility weights enables assessing the underlying credit risk of the sovereign.

4. DISCUSSION AND CONCLUSION

As investment opportunities become more global and diverse, it is important to decide which countries represent good investment opportunities. There are advantages to invest in foreign markets, but the risks associated may be considerably higher when investing in emerging economies. To secure the advantage of foreign investment, investors should ensure that the return generated is sufficient to offset the risk they are taking. Measuring the ability of a country to face its financial commitments, i.e., its debts, ratings are essential tools to support investment decisions. Traditional ratings are issued by credit rating agencies (CRAs), which are painfully recovering their credibility after the crisis. The recent remedial regulations such as the Sarbanes-Oxley Act or the Code of Conduct for CRAs[17] cannot solve the problems completely. Hence, it is necessary to challenge CRAs' fundamental methodologies. In this paper, we proposed an hybrid method using public information to evaluate sovereign's credit. We find several interesting results supporting the idea that investors should rethink the credibility or the objectivity of the ratings issued by CRAs.

Firstly, some macroeconomic indicators, which have proved to be useful (indeed used by CRAs in their quantitative models), do not really explain the ratings issued by them nowadays. As mentioned above, ratings are a combination of quantitative and qualitative evaluation approach, but the results of country-specific implied rating in Section 3.1 tend to show that agencies' models tend to improve the ratings of advanced economies and lower the ratings of emerging economies. While it is interesting to notice that there are three exceptions, Italy, Portugal, and Spain, who have the agencies' ratings lower than both their country-specific ratings and market implied ratings. This finding confirms the belief that CRAs tend to become more conservative during the crisis and by the way, may adopt a pro-cyclical attitude toward these economies. This attitude justifies the need of alternative approach. Indeed, they tend to give conservative ratings to the countries who are "believed" to be in trouble even though both economic indicators and market perceptions do not acknowledge them. On the other hand, fundamental rating obtained in our study offers investors an overview of sovereigns credit risk implied by their economic profile. Therefore, an investor holding a long-term investment project may rely more on the fundamental ratings in order to screen the subjective biases released in agencies' ratings.

[17] The code published by the International Organization of Securities Commissions.

Secondly, market implied ratings are generally lower than country-specific implied ratings for advanced economies, but higher than the corresponding fundamental ratings for emerging markets. This finding indicates that market has different opinion concerning the difference of credibility between developed and developing sovereigns. Besides, the influence of bond liquidity exhibits different roles in advanced and emerging economies. This outcome suggests that in practice, investors use different trading strategies for emerging markets than for developed economies, since these markets work in another way than the traditional ones. This finding shows that investors who are attracted by the advantages of investing in emerging countries should consider alternative trading strategies than traditional developed markets'. Therefore, investors having a more complex business model should pay more attention to the market implied ratings approach which allows quicker updates regarding the tendency of the uncertain markets. Moreover, the overvalued risk of investing in emerging countries according to CRAs' ratings may offer arbitrage opportunity to short-term oriented investors.

Additionally, the δ-Rating approach proposed in this paper gives a weighted average of the long-term fundamental ratings and the updated market implied ratings through credibility weight. We believe the δ-Rating can provide better information to investors to make investment decisions. The pure quantitative approach combines the information contained in the low-frequency macroeconomic data which provides a long-term through-the-cycle credit evaluation and the timeless market cognition of the risk of investing in the country. The credibility factor grants higher weight to market implied rating when the market is facing turmoil and less weight when the market is stable. We believe the quantitative adjustment from market implied rating is more objective than the qualitative adjustment implemented by rating agencies, and therefore provides better ratings to investors. Accordingly, the $\delta-$rating can correct the subjective biases of agencies' ratings and offer better information to investors to make their investment decision. This statement is even more important, as to optimize a portfolio allocation considering the financial assets issued by the fast-growing emerging countries, a more reactive analysis is required.

Furthermore, having used a data set from 2001 to 2012 which covers the turmoil period of the recent European Sovereign Debt Crisis, our results show that CRAs cannot justify themselves by claiming that they focus on a long-term horizon in using a through-the-cycle rating methodology. Their ratings seem distorted by certain subjective decisions which may be questionable. The statement that they aim to respond only to the perceived permanent component of credit-quality changes is suspect as well since they give the ratings to Italy, Portugal, and Spain lower than the ratings implied by their economic and market indicators. The debt problem experienced by the PIGS (Portugal, Italy, Greece, and Spain) justifies the concerns, but the pressures from public opinions seem aggravating their predicaments. It is interesting to notice that according to CRAs the PIGS are not investment grade while considering our analysis they are. Consequently, from a credit point of view, the PIGS are ranked among emerging economies. Relying on CRAs may lead to arbitrage opportunities as the yield of bonds issued by the new pool of emerging countries (i.e., PIGS and traditional emerging countries) is too high considering the inherent risk highlighted by our study; therefore, it could be very interesting to invest in these countries, as the bonds are underpriced according to our analysis. The crisis of these sovereigns, however, could be chances for investors, since hidden opportunities during crises discovered and highlighted by alternative risk evaluation may be the way to the success. Emerging Markets today will become tomorrows' developed countries. From a credit point of view, without considering any political aspects, these changes may come faster than expected. Besides, considering that some developed countries may do a backward journey toward uncertainty, the definition of emerging countries should be revised, and should be disconnected to the definition underlying investment/non-investment grade assets.

These results stimulate further interests in studies. Firstly, we have not discussed the problem of forward-looking ratings which could be achieved by a quantitative analysis. Since the macroeconomic forecasts for the coming 5 years from are available from worldwide banks and IMF, we are able to derive a forward-looking perspective of country-specific implied ratings. Difficulty may arise from forecasting the market information. Secondly, the correlations between the ratings and the loss given defaults have not been dealt with. We believe these ratings combined practitioners' expectations of the two important factors of counterpart risk. It could be interesting to study the implied default probability and loss given defaults using public available information which is more practicable for investors and risk managers.

Lastly, our studies are limited by the availability of market data for emerging markets. The study will be extended considering a larger group of emerging countries when there are more resourceful data for emerging markets. Furthermore, as some non-linearity exists in both the fundamental and the market implied models' factors, it will be interesting to extend the methodology to non-linear approaches.

REFERENCES

Badaoui, S., Cathcart, L., El-Jahel, L., 2012. Do sovereign credit default swaps represent a clean measure of sovereign default risk? A Factor Model Approach. SSRN Working Papers, UK.

Baek, I.M., Bandopadhyaya, A., Du, C., 2005. Determinants of market-assessed sovereign risk: economic fundamentals or market risk appetite? Journal of International Money and Finance 24, 533–548

Beber, A., Brandt, M.W., Kavajecz, K.A., 2009. Flight-to-quality or flight-to-liquidity? Evidence from the Euro-area bond market. Review of Financial Studies 22 (3), 925–957

Breusch, T.S., Pagan, A.R., 1980. The lagrange multiplier test and its applications to model specification in econometrics. Review of Economic Studies 47 (1), 239–253 Wiley Blackwell

Bühlmann, H., Alois, G., 2005. A Course in Credibility Theory. Springer-Verlag, New York

Cantor, R., Packer, F., 1996. Determinants and impact of sovereign credit ratings. Economic Policy Review 2 (2), 37–53

Collin-Dufresne, P., Goldstein, R.S., Martin, J.S., 2001. The determinants of credit spread changes. Journal of Finance 56 (6), 2177–2207

Cunningham, A., Dixon, L., Hayes, S., 2001. Analysing yield spreads on emerging market sovereign bonds. Financial Stability Review. Bank of England, London, UK, pp 175–186

Duffie, D., Pedersen, L.H., Singleton, K., 2003. Modeling sovereign spreads: a case study of Russian Debt. Journal of Finance 58, 119–159

Ederington, L.H., Yawitz, J.B., Roberts, B.E., 1987. The information content of bond ratings. Journal of Financial Research 10, 211–226

Ejsing, J, Grothe, M., Grothe, O., 2012. Liquidity and credit risk premia in government bond yields. European Central Bank Working Paper Series No. 1440, Frankfurt, Germany.

Ferri, G., Liu, L.-G., Stiglitz, J.E., 1999. The procyclical role of rating agencies: evidence from the East Asian Crisis. Economic Notes 3, 335–355

Gärtner, M., Griesbach, B., Jung, F., 2011. PIGS or lambs? The European Sovereign Debt Crisis and the role of rating agencies. International Advances in Economic Research 17 (3), 288–299

Hausman, J.A., 1978. Specification tests in econometrics. Econometrica 46 (6), 1251–1271

Hettenhouse, G., Sartoris, W., 1976. An analysis of the information value of bond rating changes. Quarterly Review of Economics and Business 16, 65–78

Godfrey, L.G., 1996. Misspecification tests and their uses in econometrics. Journal of Statistical Planning and Inference 49 (2), 241–260

Hull, J., Predescu, M., White, A., 2004. The relationship between credit default swap spreads, bond yields, and credit rating announcements. Journal of Banking and Finance 28 (11), 2789–2811

Longstaff, F.A., Pan, J., Pedersen, L.H., Singleton, K.J., 2011. How sovereign is sovereign credit risk? American Economic Journal 3, 75–103

Mellios, C., Paget-Blanc, E., 2006. Which factors determine sovereign credit ratings? European Journal of Finance 12 (4), 361–377

Michaelides, A., Milidonis, A., Nishiotis, G., Papakyriacou, P., 2012. Sovereign debt rating changes and the stock market. CEPR Discussion Papers with No. 8743, Cyprus.

Ozler, S., 1991. Evolution of credit terms: an empirical examination of commercial bank lending to developing countries. Journal of Development Economics 38, 79–97

Perraudin, W., Taylor, A.P., 2004. On the consistency of ratings and bond market yields. Journal of Banking & Finance 28 (11), 2769–2788

Weinstein, M., 1977. The effect of a rating change announcement on bond price. Journal of Financial Economics 5, 329–350

CHAPTER 3

Emerging Markets Banks Performance Evidence from China's Banks in Hong Kong

Xiaoxi Zhang[*] and Kevin Daly[†]

[*]School of Economics and Finance, Campbelltown Campus, University of Western Sydney, Penrith, NSW, Australia
[†]Institute of Economic Research, Chinese Academy of Social Sciences, Beijing, China

1. INTRODUCTION

Compared with other industries, China's outward investment across its financial sector represents a relatively small proportion of its total dollar investment abroad. However, China's outward financial investment has been increasing gradually, especially since 2006. Figure 1 indicates that China's total outward financial investment for the period over 2006–2009 experienced an almost threefold increase, with the vast majority of this outward financial investment represented by mainland China's banking business operations in Hong Kong.

The objective of this research is to analyze and compare the performance of China's banks operating in (HKSAR) relative local and foreign banks. The motivation for conducting this research relates to providing an analysis of how China's mainland banks perform in the highly competitive Hong Kong banking sector relative to foreign and Hong Kong banks. By using firm-level data across a range of performance indicators, this research enables researchers to discover the key performance indicators of China's outward investment in the banking sector.

Chinese owned banks comprise approximately 25% of all HKSAR banking assets. The presence of Chinese owned banks operating in HKSAR allows us to apply firm-specific data, in particular, parent-specific characteristics of Chinese banks performance. In order to investigate this issue fully, we compared Chinese owned banks with two other groups, namely local owned banks and foreign owned banks.

The rest of the paper is structured as follows: Section 2 provides an overview of foreign banks (including China's owned banks) operating in HKSAR; Section 3 reviews previous studies conducted into measuring banks performance in HK including hypotheses testing; Section 4 provides a description of the data sources and methodology; Section 5 discusses the empirical results; finally Section 6 offers some concluding comments and provides some suggestions for Chinese bank expansion overseas in the future.

Emerging Markets and the Global Economy
http://dx.doi.org/10.1016/B978-0-12-411549-1.00003-X

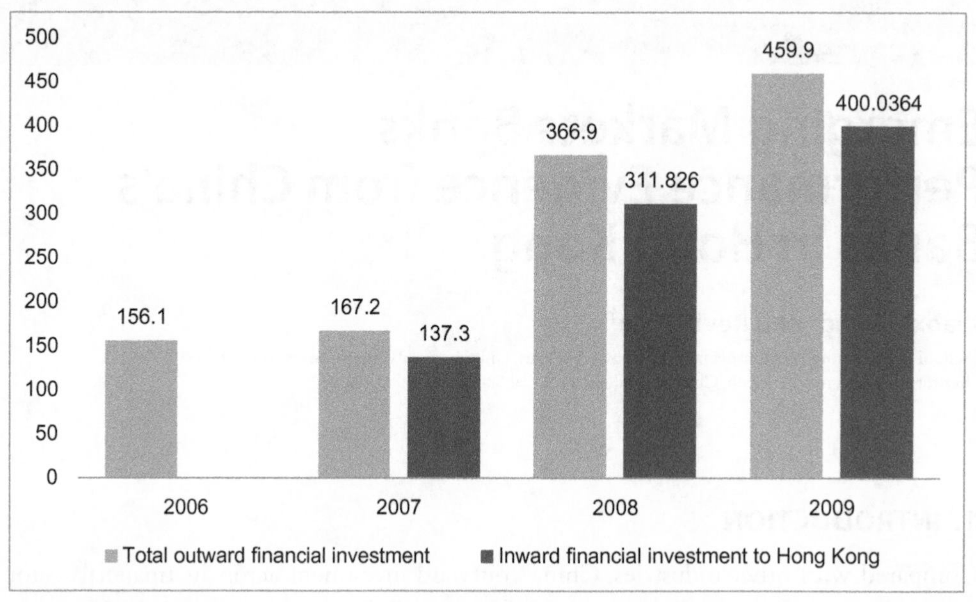

Figure 1 Chinese outward investment in financial industry stocks, total and in Hong Kong, 2006–2009, $100 million.
Source: Statistical Bulletin of China's outward Foreign Direct Investment, 2006, 2007, 2008, 2009.

2. FOREIGN BANKS IN HONG KONG

Hong Kong is one of the world's largest offshore banking centers with approximately 60 of the world's largest banks operating within the SAR of Hong Kong.

One reveals that in 2005 Hong Kong was host to 133 incorporated licensed banks, 39 restricted license banks, and 35 deposit-taking companies; in addition to the 207 authorized institutions, 182 were foreign owned.

Traditionally Hong Kong has been acknowledged globally as having a strong, independent, and stable banking system; in addition, the HK dollar has over time been recognized as a stable managed currency. The HK economic model is viewed by foreigners as somewhat more liberal than that of mainland China; in addition, HK administers a lower taxation regime relative to most developed economies. Taken together these characteristics make HK an attractive financial investment destination for multinational banks.

Hong Kong as an offshore banking center operates a three-tier banking system that includes licensed banks,[1] restricted license banks (RLBs),[2] and deposit-taking companies (DTCs).[3] This three-tier banking system allows Hong Kong authorities to keep domestic

[1] They can accept deposits of any size and maturity. They are also allowed to provide current and savings accounts to their clients.

[2] They are allowed to accept deposits of HK$500,000 and above.

[3] They are licensed to accept deposits of HK$100,000 and above with the minimum maturity of 3 months.

Table 1 Selected list of licensed banks incorporated in Hong Kong.

Name	Type	Country/region
Bank of China (Hong Kong)	Limited	China
Bank of East Asia	Limited	Hong Kong
China Construction Bank (Asia)	Corporation Limited	China
Chiyu Banking Corporation	Limited	China
Chong Hing Bank	Limited	Hong Kong
Citibank (Hong Kong)	Limited	United States
CITIC Ka Wah Bank	Limited	China
Dah Sing Bank	Limited	Hong Kong
DBS Bank (Hong Kong)	Limited	Singapore
Fubon Bank (Hong Kong)	Limited	Taiwan
Hang Seng Bank	Limited	Hong Kong
Hongkong and Shanghai Banking Corporation	Limited	United Kingdom
Industrial and Commercial Bank of China (Asia)	Limited	China
MEVAS Bank	Limited	Hong Kong
Nanyang Commercial Bank	Limited	China
Public Bank (Hong Kong)	Limited	Malaysia
Shanghai Commercial Bank	Limited	Hong Kong
Standard Chartered Bank (Hong Kong)	Limited	United Kingdom
Tai Sang Bank	Limited	Hong Kong
Tai Yau Bank	Limited	Hong Kong
Wing Hang Bank	Limited	Hong Kong
Wing Lung Bank	Limited	China

Source: The Financial Services Sector in Hong Kong, Hong Kong Monthly Digest of Statistics; http://www.censtatd.gov.hk/gb/?param=b5uniS&url=http://www.censtatd.gov.hk/hkstat/sub/sp110_tc.jsp?productCode=B1010002.

and offshore banking sectors separate from each other. Foreign banks, which do not qualify for a full bank license, usually get Restricted Licensed Banks (RLB) or Deposit-Taking Companies (DTC) license status, which allows them to conduct wholesale and investment banking business on the Asian Dollar Market.

Hong Kong emerged from the global financial crisis relatively unscathed due in part to both the strong local banking regulatory environment and enhanced management practices adopted by HK domiciled banks following the Asian financial crisis (see Table 1).

3. HYPOTHESIS TESTING

This research employs firm-level panel data to examine several performance specific hypotheses. Relatively few studies employ industry-level data to test other countries' financial institutions performance in a third country. The data employed in this study are sourced from Chinese, Foreign, and Hong Kong owned banks operating in Hong Kong from 2004 to 2010.

3.1. Profitability Measures

The profitability of banks operating across borders can be measured by several variables. This study considers the following dimensions: Return on Assets (ROA) and Return on Equities (ROE): the ROA is used to measure the earning ability, which is the net income after taxes for the year relative to total average assets. ROA is an internal performance measure of shareholder value, and it is by far the most popular measure of performance because ROA proposes a direct assessment of the financial return of a shareholder's investment, ROA is easily available for analysts, only relying upon public information; and ROA allows for comparison between different companies or different sectors of the economy. The Return on Equity (ROE) is used to measure bank's profitability, which is the net income after taxes divided by total equity. However, ROA is biased upwards for banks that earn significant profits from off-balance sheet operations such as derivative activities, as these activities generate revenue and expenses but are not recorded as assets (Rhoades, 1998). Therefore, we employ ROE as an alternative measure of profitability.

3.2. Hypotheses

In the context of factors within the control of management, the immediate factors that would have an impact on bank profitability would be those factors that affect a bank's net interest income (Guru et al., 2000). To this extent, the net interest margin could be expected to have a positive influence on the bank's profitability.

Hypothesis 1. Net interest margin has a positive impact on profitability in Hong Kong.

Generally, a bank's efficiency regarding cost control would be reflected in profit. A Federal Reserve Bank of New York study found that enhanced expenses, such as salaries and wages, pensions, and other (non-interest) expenses, resulted in a relatively slower growth in profitability (Federal Reserve Bank of New York 1973, pp. 70–71).

Hypothesis 2. Non-interest expense has a negative impact on profitability in Hong Kong.

Licensed banks are expected to have some positive value; otherwise, no institution would be willing to bear the regulatory costs associated with gaining a license. Previous research has indicated that foreign banks expressed a strong preference for the banking license status upon entering into a foreign market, Davis and Lewis (1982). Thus a bank license may be considered as a firm-specific advantage. In our model, a bank license is treated as an exogenous variable, as the Chinese banks applied for a bank license, but the decision as to their success or failure was outside their control.

Hypothesis 3. The possession of a bank license has a positive impact on profitability in Hong Kong.

The ratio of impaired loans to gross loans (NPL) is included to capture the effect of credit risk on bank profitability. Evidence suggests that impaired loans may increase after periods of increased lending often when senior bank managers under competitive pressure to satisfy short-term profit targets imposed by owners employ less rigorous lending standards (Salas and Saurina, 2002; Berger and Udell, 2006; Ruckes, 2004). Petersen and Rajan (1994) posited that banks in pursuit of short-run reputation will ease credit standards to boost assets growth and profitability in order to maintain comparability with peer banks. Furthermore, disaster myopia may occur when banks find it difficult to acknowledge and assess the possibility of a major shock to their loan books (Guttentag and Herring, 1986; Herring, 1999). Consequently, decisions are based on recent information, which is assumed to continue into the future. This myopia may be accompanied by overconfidence (where bank managers believe in their investing skills), which leads them to undertake excessive lending and risk leading to increases in impaired loans in the longer term. Overall, we expect a negative relationship between NPL and profitability.

Hypothesis 4. Impaired loans ratio has a negative impact on profitability in Hong Kong.

The equity multiplier (defined as assets divided by equity) is the reciprocal of the capital-to-asset ratio. It provides a gauge of bank's leverage (debt-to-asset ratio), or the dollar amount of assets pyramided on the bank's base of equity capital. A higher EM indicates that the bank has borrowed more funds to convert into asset with the share capital. The higher value of EM indicates greater risk for a bank. Samad and Hassan (2000) found that the higher returns might have been due to higher risky investments by the bank. This is supported by the increased debt equity and equity multiplier ratio.

Hypothesis 5. Equity multiplier has a positive impact on profitability in Hong Kong.

4. DATA AND METHODOLOGY

This research considers the period from 2004 to 2010; the data were provided by BankScope, the Hong Kong Monetary Authority, and the Chinese Financial Yearbooks.

The general consensus from the literature regarding modeling bank profitability favors a linear analysis approach. To this extent, Short (1978) and Bourke (1989) considered several functional forms and concluded that the linear model produced results as good as any other functional form. In support of this, Molyneux et al. (1994) and Guru et al. (2000) had also considered a linear model in their studies on bank profitability. This study considers a linear model to analyze pooled cross-section time series data.

Our modeling begins with running four regressions simultaneously. Using return on assets (ROA) and return on equity (ROE) as dependent variables, we itemized our independent variables as net interest margin (MARGIN), non-interest expense (NIE), and the ratio of impaired loans to gross loans (NPL). Net interest margin is a measure of the difference between the interest income generated by banks and the amount of

Table 2 Top 7 China's owned banks in Hong Kong.

Bank name	Licensed/ Unlicensed	Chinese shareholder name	Latest total assets (Mil HKD)
CITIC Bank International Limited	Licensed	CHINA CITIC BANK CORPORATION LIMITED	148,209
Wing Lung Bank Ltd	Licensed	CHINA MERCHANTS BANK CO LTD	137,075
China Construction Bank (Asia) Corporation Limited	Licensed	CHINA CONSTRUCTION BANK CORPORATION	102,728
Industrial and Commercial Bank of China (Asia) Limited - ICBC (Asia)	Licensed	INDUSTRIAL & COMMERCIAL BANK OF CHINA (THE) - ICBC	266,939
BOC Hong Kong (Holdings) Ltd	Unlicensed	BANK OF CHINA LIMITED	1,661,040
Bank of China (Hong Kong) Limited	Licensed		1,612,194
Nanyang Commercial Bank Ltd	Licensed		192,175

Source: Bankscope database, Financial Services Sector in Hong Kong, and Hong Kong Monthly Digest of Statistics.

interest paid out to their lenders (for example, deposits), relative to the amount of their (interest-earning) assets. Based on the definition, we expect there is a positive relationship between profitability and net interest margin if the ratio is bigger the ROA and ROE should be larger. Theoretically, higher non-interest expense (including employee salaries and benefits, equipment and property leases, taxes, loan loss provisions, and professional service fees) will reduce bank profitability, which is showed by ROA and ROE in our study. Impaired loans ratio represents banks' loan quality, which we expect has a negative effect on ROA and ROE.

Our initial empirical model considered seven of China's largest owned banks operating in Hong Kong (Table 2). Since licensed banks in Hong Kong can accept deposits of any size and maturity, we also separated our banks into licensed/non-licensed groups to find if having a license can be an advantage to bank performance. Next, we compared Chinese owned banks with two other groups namely: Hong Kong locally owned banks and foreign (other countries except China) owned banks. Finally, we ran a regression employing our enlarged sample of banks, which included the top 30 banks (nine Chinese owned banks, nine local owned banks, and eleven foreign owned banks) in Hong Kong (Table 3). To this regression, we added one more independent variable called Equity Multiplier (EM) defined as total assets divided by total equity.

Table 3 Top 30 banks in Hong Kong according to total assets.

Ranking	Bank name	Country/ Region	Latest total assets (Mil HKD)
1	Hong Kong and Shanghai Banking Corporation Limited	GB	5039918
2	Bank of China (Hong Kong) Limited	CN	1612194
3	Hang Seng Bank Ltd.	GB	916911
4	Standard Chartered Bank (Hong Kong) Limited	GB	758555
5	Bank of East Asia Ltd	HK	534193
6	Industrial and Commercial Bank of China (Asia) Limited	CN	266938.5
7	DBS Bank (Hong Kong) Limited	SG	247422.5
8	Nanyang Commercial Bank Ltd	CN	192175.2
9	Wing Hang Bank Ltd	HK	159296.5
10	CITIC Bank International Limited	CN	148208.9
11	Wing Lung Bank Ltd	CN	137074.6
12	Dah Sing Bank, Ltd	HK	130508.5
13	Citibank (Hong Kong) Limited	US	119299
14	Shanghai Commercial Bank Ltd	TW	118641.7
15	China Construction Bank (Asia) Corporation Limited	CN	102728.1
16	Chong Hing Bank Limited	HK	74289
17	Fubon Bank (Hong Kong) Limited	TW	61779.6
18	Hong Kong Mortgage Corporation Limited	HK	55033
19	Chiyu Banking Corporation Ltd.	CN	41066.6
20	Public Bank (Hong Kong) Limited	BM	36848
21	China Everbright Limited	HK	33941.7
22	Sun Hung Kai & Co. Limited	HK	20151.3
23	BOCI Securities Limited	CN	11501.7
24	Daiwa Capital Markets Investments Asia	HK	1481.1
25	China Construction Bank (Asia) Finance Limited	CN	6175.3
26	China Merchants Securities (HK) Co. Ltd	CN	5011.07
27	Kookmin Bank Hong Kong Limited	KR	608.1
28	Standard Bank Asia Limited	ZA	456.9
29	Sun Hung Kai Investment Services Limited	HK	3340.1
30	Orix Asia Limited	JP	408.577

Source: BankScope database.

The basic regression model takes the form:

$$\text{Bank Performance Measure} = \text{Constant} + \beta_1 \times \text{MARGIN} + \beta_2 \times \text{NIE} + \beta_3 \times \text{NPL} + \text{epsilon}.$$

$$\text{Bank Performance Measure} = \text{Constant} + \beta_1 \times \text{MARGIN} + \beta_2 \times \text{NIE} + \beta_3 \times \text{NPL} + \beta_4 \times \text{AE} + \text{epsilon}.$$

The variables specified are as the following:

Dependent variables

ROA = profits after tax/total average assets.

ROE = profits after tax/total average equity.

Independent variables

MARGIN = (interest income − interest payment)/interest-earning assets.

NIE = non-interest expense/total average assets.

NPL = impaired loans(NPLs)/gross loans.

EM = total assets/total equity.

In this study, all regression equations were estimated using pooled time series cross-section analysis (TSCS).

5. EMPIRICAL RESULTS

Table 4 presents the regression results for the major seven Chinese owned banks operating in Hong Kong from 2004 to 2010. Rows (1–7) provide an indication of the effect of net interest margin on ROA and ROE for each bank. For example, in Row 1 (CITIC) banks results from the regression of net interest margin on ROA and ROE are provided. These results indicate that ROA and ROE are positively related to MARGIN but only significant for Wing Lung Bank (WL) and Nanyang Commercial Bank (NY). Interestingly, Row 7 (NIE) indicates the relationship between non-interest expense and ROA and ROE. The result here indicates that in almost 100% of cases, WL's NIE reduces its return on assets, while non-interest expenses are also highly significant and negatively related to the bank's return on equity. However, for other banks this effect is insignificant and positive (except Nanyang Commercial Bank which showed a negative relation). The last seven rows indicate that negative and significant relationship appears for impaired loans and ROA in the case of WL, and negative and significant in the case of CITIC bank.

When we examine the results from Table 5, we mainly find the results for MARGIN indicate that net interest margin has a significant and positive relationship with ROA and ROE for two banks. Our results suggest that licensed banks are more profitable than unlicensed banks. For example, when net interest margin increases by 1%, licensed banks can increase (ROA) by 0.53305% and (ROE) by 15.0740%, while for unlicensed banks the returns are 0.21412% (ROA), and 2.3734% (ROE), respectively. We also found a positive relationship between NIE and profitability (ROA and ROE), but the results are only significant for ROE in the case of licensed banks. For NPL and ROA, the results are significant and positive for unlicensed banks (0.9989). Related to ROA, an increase of 1% in NPL will cause ROE to decline by 2.0610% for licensed banks and 1.001196% for unlicensed banks.

When we examine the results from Table 5, we conclude the following: overall the results for MARGIN indicate that margin has a significant and positive relationship

Table 4 Top 7 Chinese owned banks performance in Hong Kong, 2004–2010.

Independent variables	Dependent variable	ROA	ROE
Margin	CITIC	0.789763	11.68895
		(0.5026)	(0.3398)
	WL	2.155831	14.86588
		(0.0024)***	(0.0323)**
	CCB	0.405504	2.060298
		(0.2150)	(0.5369)
	BOCH	0.214121	2.522788
		(0.7858)	(0.7569)
	BOC	0.894061	10.75756
		(0.5431)	(0.4798)
	NY	0.964440	7.582789
		(0.0161)**	(0.0601)*
	ICBC	0.515843	7.747985
		(0.4993)	(0.3292)
NIE	CITIC	1.040611	13.19317
		(0.3904)	(0.2943)
	WL	−3.362110	−23.60442
		(0.0024)***	(0.0093)**
	CCB	0.177811	1.290475
		(0.8058)	(0.8630)
	BOCH	0.872433	12.91793
		(0.5165)	(0.3553)
	BOC	3.249124	43.59143
		(0.3304)	(0.2100)
	NY	−0.714374	−5.803179
		(0.3586)	(0.4691)
	ICBC	0.075847	1.965366
		(0.9750)	(0.9374)
NPL	CITIC	−0.362462	−5.722973
		(0.3502)	(0.0591)*
	WL	−1.331741	12.90126
		(0.0442)**	(0.1700)
	CCB	−0.091242	0.527238
		(0.9661)	(0.9810)
	BOCH	0.003200	−6.618514
		(0.9987)	(0.7499)
	BOC	1.350908	8.845383
		(0.3912)	(0.5852)
	NY	0.245330	2.533016
		(0.5532)	(0.5537)
	ICBC	0.185415	2.558332
		(0.8682)	(0.8248)
R^2		0.611503	0.592413

Notes:
*Significance at 10% level.
**Significance at 5% level.
***Significance at 1% level.

Table 5 Licensed Chinese owned banks and unlicensed Chinese owned banks performance in Hong Kong, 2004–2010.

Independent variables	Dependent variable	ROA	ROE
MARGIN	Licensed	0.533053	15.07401
		(0.0978)*	(0.0800)
	Unlicensed	0.214121	2.373465
		(0.0819)*	(0.0922)*
NIE	Licensed	0.215984	1.706929
		(0.8362)	(0.0254)**
	Unlicensed	0.872433	1.230153
		(0.5934)	(0.8413)
NPL	Licensed	0.209627	−2.061082
		(0.0799)*	(0.0355)**
	Unlicensed	0.9989	−1.001196
		(0.0032)***	(0.0524)*
R^2		0.566299	0.702646

Notes:
*Significance at 10% level.
**Significance at 5% level.
***Significance at 1% level.

with ROA and ROE for two banks. Our results suggest that licensed banks are more profitable than unlicensed banks. For example, when margin increases by 1%, licensed banks can increase (ROA) by 0.533053% and (ROE) by 15.07401%, while unlicensed banks returns are 0.214121% (ROA) and 2.373465% (ROE), respectively. We also found a positive relationship between NIE and profitability (ROA and ROE), but the results are only significant for ROE in the case of licensed banks. For NPL and ROA, the results are significant and positive for unlicensed banks (0.9989). Related to ROA, an increase of 1% in NPL will cause ROE to decline by 2.061082% for licensed banks and 1.001196% for unlicensed banks.

The statistics in Table 6 indicates the results for HK's top 15 banks over period 2004–2010. In terms of the relationship between net interest margin and profitability, the results appear to be mixed across Chinese owned banks. MARGIN on Bank of China (Hong Kong) and CITIC bank is associated with a negative sign but shows an insignificant relationship for ROA and ROE, while for the other two bank groups this effect is positive. As regards NIE and profitability, we found the results to be ambiguous. For example, the highly significant and negative relationship appears for NIE and ROA in the case of Wing Lung Bank (−3.3572) and Bank of East Asia (−1.7503), while for Hong Kong and Shanghai Banking Corporation this relationship is significantly positive (1.242263).

As regards the results for NIE and ROE, we only found evidence for five significant results including two for Chinese owned banks (BOC and WLU), two for Hong Kong

Table 6 Top 15 banks performance in Hong Kong, 2004–2010.

Independent variables		Dependent variable	ROA	ROE
MARGIN	Chinese-owned banks	BOC	−0.894061	−10.75756
			(0.4037)	(0.3466)
		ICBC	0.515843	7.747985
			(0.3535)	(0.1933)
		NY	0.964440	7.582789
			(0.0009)***	(0.0117)**
		CITIC	−0.789763	−11.68895
			(0.3571)	(0.2031)
		WLU	2.152847	14.83528
			(0.0000)***	(0.0041)***
		CCB	0.405504	2.060298
			(0.0880)*	(0.4108)
	Hong Kong local banks	BOEA	1.583841	16.67085
			(0.0697)*	(0.0733)*
		WLA	2.287652	30.64399
			(0.0218)**	(0.0045)***
		DS	0.639456	7.308102
			(0.4257)	(0.3936)
	Foreign-owned banks	HKSH	0.310197	10.16891
			(0.6563)	(0.1751)
		HS	1.612816	21.82092
			(0.1606)	(0.0769)*
		SC	0.945729	8.742491
			(0.0435)**	(0.0785)*
		DBS	0.720075	6.835456
			(0.1323)	(0.1793)
		CITI	4.551043	4.234877
			(0.1253)	(0.0001)***
		SCB	0.648829	4.828662
			(0.3288)	(0.4945)
NIE	Chinese-owned banks	BOC	3.249124	1.707784
			(0.1809)	(0.0941)*
		ICBC	0.075847	−1.965366
			(0.9657)	(0.9168)
		NY	−0.714374	−5.803179
			(0.2070)	(0.3348)
		CITIC	1.040611	13.19317
			(0.2379)	(0.1618)

(*Continued*)

Table 6 (Continued)

Independent variables		Dependent variable	ROA	ROE
		WLU	−3.357284 (0.0000)***	−23.55725 (0.0034)***
		CCB	0.177811 (0.7358)	1.290475 (0.8184)
	Hong Kong local banks	BOEA	−1.750362 (0.0427)**	−16.82504 (0.1856)
		WLA	−2.862145 (0.0826)*	−39.68585 (0.0255)**
		DS	0.008683 (0.9950)	0.039009 (0.9979)
	Foreign-owned banks	HKSH	1.242263 (0.1993)*	5.530305 (0.7241)
		HS	−0.623514 (0.0998)*	−6.886503 (0.7928)
		SC	−0.352015 (0.0514)*	1.316591 (0.8132)
		DBS	−0.044082 (0.0642)*	1.235044 (0.9062)
		CITI	−8.029151 (0.0615)*	4.942662 (0.0000)***
		SCB	1.172952 (0.5099)	7.375564 (0.6972)
NPL	Chinese-owned banks	BOC	−1.350908 (0.0387)**	8.845383 (0.4674)
		ICBC	0.185415 (0.8199)	2.558332 (0.7683)
		NY	0.245330 (0.4154)	2.533016 (0.4304)
		CITIC	−0.362462 (0.0992)*	−5.722973 (0.0599)*
		WLU	−1.334513 (0.0438)**	−12.92733 (0.0661)*
		CCB	−0.091242 (0.9535)	0.527238 (0.9748)
	Hong Kong local banks	BOEA	0.467813 (0.4459)	2.258221 (0.7295)
		WLA	−0.358646 (0.0611)*	−4.018856 (0.5828)

(Continued)

Table 6 (Continued)

Independent variables	**Dependent variable**	**ROA**	**ROE**
	DS	−0.611951 (0.0822)*	−6.645590 (0.0769)*
Foreign-owned banks	HKSH	−0.738506 (0.0183)**	−6.559722 (0.4998)
	HS	−1.071641 (0.0454)**	−12.38169 (0.1154)
	SC	−0.287842 (0.0551)*	−1.326421 (0.7729)
	DBS	−0.200391 (0.6298)	−1.771156 (0.6894)
	CITI	−2.071532 (0.0826)*	−62.87232 (0.0000)***
	SCB	−0.454543 (0.1850)	−2.935596 (0.4194)
R^2		0.811509	0.910842

Notes:
*Significance at 10% level.
**Significance at 5% level.
***Significance at 1% level

local banks (BOEA and WLA) and one for a foreign owned bank (CITIC). In conclusion for these five banks, we find the return on equity to increase along with non-interest expense for Bank of China and CITI bank; therefore, BOC and CITI are less efficient than the other three banks due to higher ROE used and higher NIE. For example when we examine the results of CITI and WLA banks, we find that a rise in non-interest expense by 1% causes ROE to increase by 4.9426%, while for WLA ROE increases by 39.6858% if NIE decreases 1%. The last 15 rows suggest that a negative relationship exists between NPL and profitability.

Table 7 examines the relationship between the top banks (30) performance indicators in HK against the profitability measures ROA and ROE. Rows (1–3) indicate that foreign owned banks will be more profitable on assets than Chinese owned banks if they charge the same percentage of net interest margin. Unfortunately, we cannot provide any indication of the effect of MARGIN on ROE in terms of insignificant results. Based on the results for NIE which indicate that non-interest expense has a negative and significant relationship with ROE in local owned banks (−11.1892) and foreign owned banks (−3.3588), overall only one bank group here showed a significant result. As regards the results for bank equity multiplier and ROE, we find a positive and significant relationship

Table 7 Top 30 banks performance in Hong Kong by groups, 2004–2010.

Independent variables	Dependent variable	ROA	ROE
MARGIN	Chinese-owned banks	0.751079	5.516343
		(0.0676)*	(0.3565)
	Hong Kong local banks	−0.163194	0.614732
		(0.8510)	(0.8603)
	Foreign-owned banks	1.817346	1.947733
		(0.0765)*	(0.9255)
NIE	Chinese-owned banks	−0.008661	−0.686199
		(0.9904)	(0.8134)
	Hong Kong local banks	1.164322	−11.18927
		(0.4573)	(0.0964)*
	Foreign-owned banks	−0.596159	−3.358825
		(0.5559)	(0.0436)**
NPL	Chinese-owned banks	−0.058759	−1.174420
		(0.0920)*	(0.7654)
	Hong Kong local banks	0.157672	−15.12383
		(0.8955)	(0.0104)
	Foreign-owned banks	−0.098403	−2.139432
		(0.9421)	(0.6958)
EM	Chinese-owned banks	−0.001910	0.395811
		(0.9954)	(0.0674)*
	Hong Kong local banks	0.022145	3.049135
		(0.8511)	(0.0001) ***
	Foreign-owned banks	−0.085822	1.868586
		(0.9390)	(0.0801)*
R^2		0.569363	0.901379

Notes:
*Significance at 10% level.
**Significance at 5% level.
***Significance at 1% level.

between EM and ROE in all cases for Chinese owned banks, and for Hong Kong owned banks and foreign owned banks.

6. CONCLUSION

In this study, we constructed a model of the profitability of Chinese owned banks in Hong Kong. Generally, the model proposed performs well for net interest margin, non-interest expense, and impaired loans ratio and equity multiplier. The purpose of this study was to evaluate how banking profitability in Hong Kong has been affected by these measures. Based on four regressions with annual data for the period from 2003 to 2010, our empirical results provide some interesting outcomes. The results indicate that for the top seven Chinese owned banks, Wing Lung Bank has recorded superior profits in terms of returns on assets and return on equity compared with other Chinese owned banks.

It is interesting to note that licensed Chinese owned banks will make more profits than unlicensed Chinese owned banks where both have similar net interest margin, management efficiency (non-interest expense), and asset's risk (impaired loans ratio). Comparing the top 15 banks across our groupings (Chinese, HKSAR, and Foreign), we found that in general Chinese banks tend to perform poorly in terms of MARGIN while profitability is ranked average in terms of non-interest expense and impaired loans. When we applied the equity multiplier indicator, the results support claims that Chinese owned banks are the least profitable among foreign owned and local owned banks.

The choices for China's banks future are therefore to continue expansion via merger and acquisition with overseas banks in Hong Kong. This is happening to a degree with European banks at present. The apparent advantages in terms of transferring technical and managerial efficiency gains to China's banks involved in M&A with foreign banks appear to be the major advantage of such activities. In addition, foreign banks operating in Hong Kong have added to their overall performance in their foreign operations in the fastest growing banking markets globally.

REFERENCES

Berger, A.N., Udell, G.F., 2006. A more complete conceptual framework for SME finance. Journal of Banking and Finance 30 (11), 2945–2966

Bourke, P., 1989. Concentration and other determinants of bank profitability in Europe, North America and Australia. Journal of Banking and Finance 13 (1), 65–79

Davis, K., Lewis, M., 1982. Foreign banks and the financial system, Australian Financial System Inquiry. Commissioned Studies and Selected Papers. Part 1: Macroeconomic Policy: Internal Policy. Australian Government Publishing Service, Canberra

Federal Reserve Bank of New York 1973, 70-71.

Guru, B.K., Vaithilingam, S., Ismail, N., 2000. Electronic banking in Malaysia: a note on evolution of services and consumer reactions. Journal of Internet Banking and Commerce 5 (1), 234–256

Guttentag, J., Herring, R., 1986. Disclosure policy and international banking. Journal of Banking and Finance 10 (1), 75–97

Herring, R.J., 1999. Credit risk and financial instability. Oxford Review of Economic Policy 15 (3), 63–79

Molyneux, P., Lloyd-Williams, D.M., Thornton, J., 1994. Competitive conditions in European banking. Journal of Banking and Finance 18 (3), 445–459

Petersen, M.A., Rajan, R.G., 1994. The effect of credit market competition on lending relationships. NBER Working Papers 4921, National Bureau of Economic Research.

Rhoades, S., 1998. The efficiency effects of bank mergers: an overview of case studies in nine mergers. Journal of Banking and Finance 22 (3), 273–291

Ruckes, M., 2004. Bank competition and credit standards. Review of Financial Studies 17 (4), 1073–1102

Salas, V., Saurina, J., 2002. Credit risk in two institutional regimes: Spanish commercial and savings banks. Journal of Financial Services Research 22 (3), 203–224

Samad, A., Hassan, M.K., 2000. The performance of Malaysian Islamic bank during 1984–1997: an exploratory study. Thoughts on Economics 10 (1–2), 7–26

Short, B.K., 1978. The relation between commercial bank profit rates and banking concentration in Canada, Western Europe, and Japan. Journal of Banking and Finance 3 (3), 209–219

CHAPTER 4

Determinants of the Real Rate of Return: Evidence from Cross-Country Panel Data*

Marcelo Sánchez
European Central Bank, Frankfurt, Germany

1. INTRODUCTION

The main object of the present chapter is to analyze the determinants of the real rate of return using a cross-country panel data approach. The methodology used here follows Mishkin's (1981) seminal paper, which estimates regressions of the *ex post* real rate for three month US treasury bills on past values of some plausible explanatory variables.[1] The present study extends Mishkin's work by assessing the behavior of two alternative measures of the real rate of return, namely, the return on bank deposits and that on equity. This allows one to compare the behavior of an asset (such as bank deposits) whose nominal rate of return is known by the time of the financial contract with that of an asset (such as stocks) whose nominal rate of return is unknown. A second way in which I extend the current literature is that I use a cross-country panel data set that includes data for bank deposit rates in up to 153 countries and data for equity yields in up to 53 countries.

In addition to the analysis of the behavior of the real rate of return in terms of past information, in the case of equity—whose nominal yield is unknown by the time the asset is purchased—it makes sense to examine the impact of *current* inflation on the real return, after controlling for other sources of real rate variability. This second object of the present analysis extends the existing literature on the effect of inflation on financial variables, and in particular that focusing on real rates of return.[2] Among the latter studies,

* This paper updates results previously contained in my PhD thesis, 'Effects of Inflation on Financial and Real Activity', UC Berkeley, Chapter 2, which benefited from David Romer's criticism, comments, and encouragement. From a very early stage, Maurice Obstfeld made very useful comments on that chapter, which also benefited from discussions with Roger Craine, Brad DeLong, Dwight Jaffee, and James Wilcox.

[1] Other papers using the same methodology are Mishkin (1988) and Romer (1992).

[2] Other studies concentrate on the effect of inflation on financial activity. For example, Boyd et al. (2001) find substantial evidence that financial development is negatively correlated with inflation. In addition, they find that the relation between financial development and inflation exhibits significant nonlinearities. In particular, economies with average rates of inflation exceeding certain thresholds have significantly less well-developed financial systems than do economies with inflation rates below these thresholds. Boyd et al.'s paper is more comprehensive than that of English (1999), who finds that the size of a nation's financial services sector is positively affected by its inflation rate.

Emerging Markets and the Global Economy
http://dx.doi.org/10.1016/B978-0-12-411549-1.00004-1

Choi et al. (1996), Boyd et al. (2001), and Barnes et al. (1999) present regressions for some countries that support a negative correlation between inflation and real returns to equity. The latter two studies are more complete in that they include some high inflation countries. They conclude that inflation reduces real rates of return in low-to-moderate inflation countries, while in high inflation countries nominal rates of return adjust to provide considerably better hedge against inflation. In an environment of high inflation (like the one experienced in some Latin American countries), financial disintermediation may arise, even though financial instruments could in principle be designed in order to compensate for investors' potential inflation losses (see, e.g., Gonzalez-Astudillo and Orus, 2004).

As a first approximation, I run some "basic" regressions under the assumption that agents know the rate of inflation up to the middle of the last month of the quarter before the real returns are determined. As a refinement, I then consider an alternative measure of the latest quarterly inflation in the available information set, which does not incorporate the last month of inflation in the former definition. The second ("refined") characterization is a more reasonable one if one believes that agents have trouble figuring out the inflation rate during the last month of a given quarter because the latest public information on CPI inflation refers to the middle of previous month.

Some additional remarks are in order here. First, the use of a Fisher equation framework relies on the notion that nominal interest rates move in tandem with (expected) inflation. However, in a deflationary context this comovement might not be possible, given that nominal interest rates cannot be negative; see, e.g., Gavin (2010) and Glasner (2011) for a discussion of this point. In our sample, however, there is no visible evidence of such deflationary episodes. Second, the literature has discussed whether expected inflation is the right argument to be used in the Fisher equation. For instance, Geanakoplos et al. (2004) argue that, in a context of real uncertainty in which the central bank sets the nominal rate of interest, the rate of inflation in the Fisher equation should be replaced by the harmonic mean of the growth rate of money. In turn, Rhodes (2007) advocates the use of what the author calls the expected appreciation of money; this is defined as the rate of change in the inverse of the price level, and is not equivalent to expected inflation, due to Jensen's inequality. The present paper does not consider these candidate substitutes for expected inflation, but it does include money supply indicators as controls in a number of regressions.

The remainder of this chapter proceeds as follows. Section 2 describes the data employed. Section 3 discusses the methodology used. Sections 4 and 5 present my findings when I assess the effect of unexpected inflation on real rate variability. Section 6 briefly concludes.

2. THE DATA

The main purpose of this chapter is to explain the behavior of the real rate of return based on past information. Information on bank deposit rates and stock returns are available in nominal terms. While equity yields are calculated between the end of the previous quarter and the end of the current one, interest rates are measured as the ones prevailing at the end of the period.[3] The inflation rate is used to convert these nominal yields into real returns. A list of countries and sample dates for rates of return on bank deposits and stocks appears in the Appendix, where I distinguish between developed and emerging and developing countries (on the basis of IMF's classification).

Since a cross-country panel data set is involved here, I will denote observation units by subscript i and periods by subscript t, where $i = 1, \ldots, n$ and $t = 1, \ldots, T_i$ (which allows for unbalanced panels).[4] Many RHS variables are defined as rates of change. In the case of some variables (CPI, international commodity prices, and output), the quarterly rates of change are calculated from monthly average indices. This means that the rates of change used here are calculated between the middle of the last month of a given quarter and the middle of the last month of the next quarter. In the remaining case of money supply growth, quarterly rates of change are computed between the end of two periods.

In all cases of rate-of-change variables, which are the relevant two periods between which they are computed depends on the following consideration. The end of the last period must be such that by then agents get to know the value of the variable in question. That is, the variable must be in the information set of agents. Among the RHS variables that are not rates of change, there are series for world interest rates. As indicated below, world interest rates are measured as the ones prevailing at the end of the period.

I employ quarterly data on the variables listed below:

Bank deposit rates ($i_{i,t+1}$): This is the nominal rate offered by banks to resident customers for demand, time or savings deposits (IFS line 60l). Moreover, this rate is measured at the end of the period.

Nominal equity returns (s_{it}): They are proxied by the rates of change in an index of nominal stock prices (IFS line 62).

Inflation (π_{it}): For the inflation rate I use the quarterly rate of change in each country's CPI, expressed as a percentage. The CPI data are from IFS line 64.

Money supply growth: Two measures of the money supply are available from IFS. First, there is an M_1 measure including currency and demand deposits ("money," IFS line

[3] Since the length of bank deposits is roughly one quarter, it is assumed that the interest rate at the end of period t prevails during period $t + 1$.

[4] The expression "observation units" is used synonymous with "countries." Concerning the use of unbalanced panels, the econometric techniques used here allow one to make an efficient use of the information available. Naturally, the specific results reported here would have been different if more data had been available for some countries.

14). This is the preferred measure since it is more homogeneous across countries. The corresponding growth rate is denoted by μ_{it}. Second, a broader measure ("quasi-money," IFS line 15) including time deposits and savings is considered.[5]

Rate of change in commodity prices: I employ the rate of change in the indices of the international prices of food (P_{1t}), crude oil (P_{2t}), metals (P_{3t}), and agricultural raw materials (P_{4t}). Data on these indices are from IFS lines 176ex, 176aa, 176ay, and 176bx, respectively.

World interest rates: These are London Interbank Offer rates (LIBOR) on US deposits. Data on LIBOR deposits are from IFS lines 60ldd, 60lde, and 60ldf, where the corresponding term to maturity is 3 months, 6 months, or 12 months, respectively. In practice, all of these three series imply the same substantive results, so I only report below findings obtained using the three-month rate, which is labeled i^*_{3t}. In order to capture the idea that changes in world interest rates can have different effects on borrower and lender countries, I construct a dummy variable, DEV_{it}, for developed countries ($DEV_{it} = 1$ if country i is developed according to the IMF definition, 0 otherwise) which I use as a proxy for lender countries. I then define $i^*_{DEVit} \equiv DEV_{it} * i^*_{3t}$ to be equal to the world interest rate i^*_{3t} if country i is developed, 0 otherwise. Similarly, $i^*_{NDEV_{it}} \equiv (1 - DEV_{it}) * i^*_{3t}$ is defined to be equal to the world interest rate i^*_{3t} if i is an emerging or developing country, 0 otherwise. In practice, the estimated coefficients are found not to be significantly affected by distinguishing developed from emerging and developing countries. However, the effects of a given variable might exhibit differences across these two country groupings, as will be illustrated below for some robust results.

Real growth (g_{it})*:* This is the rate of change in an industrial production index (IFS line 66).

The variables of interest in this study are the real rates of return on bank deposits and stocks. I generically denote by $r_{i,t+1}$ the *ex post* real rate of return for observation unit i from holding an asset from period t to $t+1$. In the case of bank deposit rates, it will be given by the real interest rate, that is, $rb_{i,t+1} = i_{i,t+1} - \pi_{i,t+1}$, where $i_{i,t+1}$ is the nominal interest rate set at t for period $t+1$ and $\pi_{i,t+1}$ is the rate of inflation from t to $t+1$. In the case of equity returns, the real rate of return is denoted by $rs_{i,t+1} = S_{i,t+1} - \pi_{i,t+1}$, where $s_{i,t+1}$ is the nominal rate of return to stocks.[6] The main difference between the two cases is that while $i_{i,t+1}$ is known as of t, $s_{i,t+1}$ is not.

For concreteness, Table 1 reports the cross-sectional correlations (for all countries) of selected variables, which include the variables of interest as well as some explanatory variables. Foreign variables and lags of all variables are not considered in Table 1. The real deposit rate exhibits a slightly negative correlation (−0.009) with inflation as well as

[5] In this study, however, I only report regression results using the first measure since those obtained the "quasi-money" alternative were found to be remarkably similar.

[6] The definitions in the text are for purposes of presentation and correspond to the continuous time case. Since I deal with discrete time data, the operational measures of the real rate of return are $rb_{i,t+1} = (i_{i,t+1} - \pi_{i,t+1})/(1 + \pi_{i,t+1})$ and $rs_{i,t+1} = (s_{i,t+1} - \pi_{i,t+1})/(1 + \pi_{i,t+1})$.

Table 1 Cross-sectional correlations (all countries).

	rb_{t+1}	rs_{t+1}	i_{t+1}	s_t	π_t	μ_t	g_t
rb_{t+1}	1						
rs_{t+1}	−0.089	1					
i_{t+1}	−0.962	−0.127	1				
s_t	−0.106	0.994	−0.124	1			
π_t	0.009	0.092	0.020	0.096	1		
μ_t	−0.036	−0.162	−0.015	−0.157	−0.100	1	
g_t	−0.233	−0.245	−0.247	0.244	0.049	−0.030	1

low negative correlations with the rates of change in money and output. The real return on stocks shows a very low correlation with inflation.[7] It also displays little association with other candidate explanatory variables such as deposit rates and the rates of change in money and output. Other variables as well as lags of all variables in the data set will also be considered in order to explain the behavior of both measures of the rate of return.

3. THE METHODOLOGY

As explained above, $r_{i,t+1}$ denotes the *ex post* real rate of return for observation unit i from holding an asset from period t to $t+1$. Let $R_{i,t+1}$ be the generic *ex ante* real rate of return, or simply the real rate. One can then write for the ith observation unit in quarter t:

$$r_{i,t+1} = R_{i,t+1} + \varepsilon_{i,t+1}, \tag{1}$$

where $\varepsilon_{i,t+1}$ is a forecast error. This error is simply the inflation forecast error in the case of bank deposits. In the case of equity returns, however, $\varepsilon_{i,t+1}$ also includes the error made in forecasting the nominal rate of return to stocks, $s_{i,t+1}$.

Following Mishkin (1981), the approach used here to analyzing the behavior of the real rate, $R_{i,t+1}$, involves regressions using the *ex post* real rate of return, $r_{i,t+1}$. The underlying assumption behind this analysis is the rationality of expectations in the asset markets, which plies the following condition:

$$E[\varepsilon_{i,t+1}|\mathbf{\Phi}_{it}] = 0, \tag{2}$$

where $\mathbf{\Phi}_{it}$ is the available information set. Equation (2) says that the forecast error in (1) must be uncorrelated with past available information.

If the *ex ante* real rate, $R_{i,t+1}$, is correlated with vector of variables, $\mathbf{X}_{it}$, which are elements of the available information set $\mathbf{\Phi}_{it}$, then:

$$R_{i,t+1} = \alpha_i + \mathbf{X}_{it}'\mathbf{B} + u_{it}, \tag{3}$$

[7] Given the weak correlation between both real rates of return and inflation, Table 1 also shows that there is a very high correlation between each real rate of return and the corresponding nominal rate of return.

where u_{it} are the individual (country) effects and $\mathbf{B}$ is the vector of coefficients associated with regressors $\mathbf{X}_{it}$. Note that the error term, u_{it}, is determined at t. Substituting (1) into (3) yields:

$$\begin{aligned} r_{i,t+1} &= \alpha_i + \mathbf{X}_{it}'\mathbf{B} + u_{it} + \varepsilon_{i,t+1} \\ &= \alpha_i + \sum_{l=1}^{L} \delta_l \, r_{i,t+1-l} + \mathbf{x}_{it}'\boldsymbol{\beta} + u_{it} + \varepsilon_{i,t+1}, \end{aligned} \tag{4}$$

$$r_{i,t+1} - r_{it} = \sum_{l=1}^{L} \delta_l \, (r_{i,t+1-l} - r_{i,t-l}) + (\mathbf{x}_{it} - \mathbf{x}_{i,t-1})'\boldsymbol{\beta} + u_{it} - u_{i,t-1} + \varepsilon_{i,t+1} - \varepsilon_{it},$$

where the second line decomposes the matrix of explanatory variables (other than the individual effects) into lags of the dependent variable and other regressors, that is, $\mathbf{X}_{it} = [r_{it} \; r_{i,t-1} \ldots r_{i,t+1-L} \; \mathbf{x}_{it}]$. Similarly, the vector of coefficients (other than α_i) can be written as $\mathbf{B} = [\delta_1 \; \delta_2 \ldots \delta_L \; \boldsymbol{\beta}]$.

Data on the *ex post* real rate, $r_{i,t+1}$, are observable, in contrast with data on the *ex ante* real rate. Therefore, equation (4) can be estimated. In this chapter (4) is run for both bank deposit rates and stock returns as dependent variables. In my regressions I include in $\mathbf{x}_{it}$ variables such as inflation, money growth, real growth, and measures of foreign variables. Lags of all these variables, as well as seasonal dummies, are also employed. In the case of the bank deposit rate regressions, the nominal interest rate set at the end of t, $i_{i,t+1}$, is an additional explanatory variable.

It is crucial to make sure that the RHS variables are actually known at t, and thus are elements of the information set, $\boldsymbol{\Phi}_{it}$. Many of the RHS variables are rates of change which are in general calculated over the quarter elapsed between (the end or the middle of) the last month in quarter $t-1$ and (the end or the middle of) the last month in quarter t. Among the RHS that are not rates of change one finds world interest rates and dummy variables. The former will be measured between the middle of the last month in quarter $t-1$ and the middle of the last month in quarter t.

Among the RHS variables that are also a rate of change, the only exception to the general rule regarding timing described in the preceding paragraph is given by an alternative definition for the level of inflation. Inflation between (the middle of the last month in) quarter $t-1$ and (the middle of the last month in) quarter t will be used. This is a reasonable definition under the assumption that agents get to know the behavior of the general level of prices up to (the middle of the last month in) period t. However, one may believe that, as of (the middle of the last month in) period t, agents have trouble figuring out the inflation rate during the last monthly period because the latest public information on CPI inflation refers to the middle of previous month. Under that assumption, it would be more reasonable to define the latest quarterly inflation rate in the information set of agents to be that between the month previous to the end of quarter $t-1$ and the month previous to the end of quarter t. For completeness, I consider this alternative definition of inflation as a refinement to the basic methodology employed here. I denote the former measure simply as the already defined $\pi_{i,t}$ and the latter as π_{it}^{LU}, where LU stands for "last (monthly inflation rate) unknown."

The general estimation procedure is given by cross-country panel data regressions. As a result of inference analysis, out of the different possible specifications of the model only two were found to be relevant, namely, the fixed effects model and random effects model.

The former assumes that there are common slopes, but that each cross-section unit has its own intercept, which may or may not be correlated with the regressors. The random effects model resembles the former model, but it assumes that the intercepts are drawn from a common distribution with given mean and variance. Unlike the fixed effects model the estimates for this model will not be consistent if the individual intercepts are correlated with the independent variables. Because of this it is important to test for correlation. The tables below report the Hausman test statistic for the difference between the fixed effects and random effects estimates, along with its p-value.

Working with a classical regression framework, Mishkin (1981) demonstrated a few propositions that carry over to the present panel data context. The most important proposition can be restated as saying that the OLS estimates from the *ex ante* real rate regression (3) and the *ex post* real rate regression (4) are equal in expectation for the nonstochastic $\mathbf{X}_{it}$ case. Furthermore, with an appropriate assumption,[8] those OLS estimates will be equal in probability limit in the stochastic $\mathbf{X}_{it}$ case. This proposition holds without an assumption on the properties of u. In particular, it is valid even if the estimate of $\mathbf{B}$ is biased (or inconsistent).

This desirable statistical property notwithstanding, there are two good reasons why the OLS technique may fail to yield unbiased estimates.[9] The first reason has to do with a complication that arises in estimation of dynamic panel data models such as (4), where lagged values of the dependent variable appear as RHS variables. In this case, the absence of full independence between the disturbances and the lagged dependent variables leads to a finite sample bias of the OLS estimator. If the composite error in (4) is assumed to be independently and identically distributed, the OLS estimators will still be consistent and asymptotically normally distributed. The existence of a finite sample bias does not seem to be much of a problem in the case of bank deposit rates (given the large number of observation units available), but it could be a real complication in the analysis of equity return data.

The second problem with the OLS estimator is the presence of correlation of the composite error term $u+\varepsilon$ across t as well as i. This second source of bias is more severe in that it causes the estimator to be inconsistent. In this case, the bias does not depend

[8] I.e. plim $\frac{X'X}{n}$ exists.

[9] As Mishkin correctly points out, another problem with the present methodology results from the variance-covariance matrix of the estimates from (4) being larger than that from (3). Thus statistical tests will have lower power. It is important to keep this problem in mind when interpreting the results, but there is no clear method of remedying it.

on the sample size and thus would affect the OLS regressions no matter whether equity or bank deposit data were used. With regard to the correlation of $u + \varepsilon$ across t (serial correlation), it is a real possibility because the assumption of rationality does not rule out correlation of the forecast errors $\varepsilon_{i,t+1}$ with future values of variables such as u_{it}.[10] Furthermore, there is no denying that in the present context there is a potential danger of correlation of the errors across i, that is, across cross-sectional units. For example, the recent literature on international capital flows supports the idea that returns on assets such as equity are subject to common shocks. This would make the u_{it}'s dependent across i.

An estimation technique that permits to achieve consistent estimates is the generalized method of moments (GMM) applied to the first-differenced version of model (4). In either the fixed and random effects settings, the heterogeneity can be swept from the model by taking first differences, which yields:

$$r_{i,t+1} - r_{it} = \sum_{l=1}^{L} \delta_l \left(r_{i,t+1-l} - r_{i,t-l}\right) + (\mathbf{x}_{it} - \mathbf{x}_{i,t-1})'\boldsymbol{\beta} + u_{it} - u_{i,t-1} + \varepsilon_{i,t+1} - \varepsilon_{it}. \quad (5)$$

A consistent estimator can be obtained by using, among possible instruments, the first differences of the dependent variable starting from $(r_{i,t+1-L} - r_{i,t-L})$ backwards. Unless there is evidence in favor of their endogeneity, the other RHS variables in (5) can serve as their own instruments.[11] Some empirical studies have favored the use of a cointegration approach, which is a possible dynamic approach that differs from the one followed here. For instance, Westerlund (2008) tested the Fisher effect in a cointegrated panel of 20 OECD countries with quarterly data for the period 1980–2004 and could not reject the Fisher hypothesis. While panels tend to add power to cointegration tests due to the added cross-sectional dimension, they also impose restrictions, particularly on the cross-sectional dependencies, that may not hold in the data. The cointegration framework requires that inflation be characterized by an I(1) process, while Jensen (2009) finds that inflation follows a mean-reverting, fractionally integrated, long-memory process.

A case that deserves a special discussion is that when it is assumed that agents are not aware of changes in prices that occur during the last month of the quarter. In this case, regression (5) is run without any lags of the dependent variable. Among the regressors I include current and lagged first differences of the nominal rate of return and the relevant definition of inflation, π_{it}^{LU}.

This completes my description of the methodology employed to study the determinants of *ex ante* real returns. However, as I said in the Introduction, in the case of stocks it is also worth analyzing whether current inflation has an impact on the *ex post* real rate of return or whether, alternatively, equity markets provide a good hedge against inflation.

[10] This point has been raised by Cumby et al. (1983).

[11] The validity of the instruments used can be assessed in terms of the Sargan test of overidentifying restrictions, which is computed if the degrees of freedom are positive.

Before describing the methodology employed to assessing the effect of inflation on *ex post* real rate variability, I wish to make clear the differences between the two problems analyzed in this chapter. The first problem is that of understanding the behavior of the *ex ante* real rate of return. It is a fact that there is no information available on this variable. Therefore, I use *ex post* real rate regressions to estimate the impact of past values of some plausible variables on *ex ante* real returns.

The second problem is of a different nature. It corresponds to the analysis of the behavior of *ex post* real equity returns, and in particular the contribution of contemporary inflation, $\pi_{i,t+1}$. In order to examine this, I start by denoting by $es_{i,t+1}$ the part of the real rate of return on stocks that is not explained by past information. This can be computed as the residuals from an expression in levels such as (4), but using the coefficients estimated by running (5) by GMM.[12] Then I run regressions of es_{t+1} on contemporaneous inflation, $\pi_{i,t+1}$, controlling for other sources of *ex post* real rate variability. A detail of this specification is that, instead of using $\pi_{i,t+1}$ as such, I employ $\pi_{i,t+1}/(1+\pi_{i,t+1})$ because the latter is easier to interpret given the definition of the *ex post* real rate of return on stocks, $rs_{i,t+1}$ (see Footnote 8).

Since $\pi_{i,t+1}$ is not part of agents' information set, $\mathbf{\Phi}_{it}$, this step permits to evaluate the contribution of unexpected inflation to *ex post* real rate variability.[13] One could argue, however, that contemporaneous inflation can be predicted to some extent by agents based on past information. Thus, as a refinement of the procedure described in the previous paragraph, I must distinguish between the expected and unexpected components of current inflation and then assess whether such unexpected component has any impact on *ex post* real stock returns.

Therefore, in order to achieve this "refined" approach, I first run a forecasting regression to estimate the anticipations of $\pi_{i,t+1}$. Rational expectations imply that these anticipations will be formed optimally, using all available information. Let the vector $\mathbf{w}_{it}$ represent the relevant available information. Then the forecasting equation can be written as:

$$\pi_{i,t+1} = \Upsilon_i + \mathbf{w}_{it}'\omega + \nu_{i,t+1}, \tag{6}$$

[12] Note that in the tables below reporting regression results I use the notation $es_{ji,t+1}$, where the subscript j refers to different *ex post* real rate regressions (4), depending on whether all variables in data set but the real growth variable, g, or all variables in data set are used.

[13] An alternative approach would be to assess the relation between inflation uncertainty and real rate variability by constructing measures of the standard deviation of inflation and the real rates of return. For example, the standard deviation of inflation around its (say) quarterly mean can be calculated using the three monthly observations for that quarter. Inflation uncertainty can thus be measured as this standard deviation for overlapping quarters. This definition shares the idea of the one used by Judson and Orphanides (1996). Their annual measure of inflation variability is calculated from quarterly price indexes. It is different from other measures used in empirical studies on the relationship between inflation and growth, such as the standard deviation of the inflation rate around its decadal mean found in Barro (1995); or a time series estimate calculated as the standard deviation of the inflation rate around its mean for overlapping (say, decadal) periods, used by Fischer (1993). One interesting specification for an OLS regression of real rate variability on inflation volatility is the log one. This specification, as pointed out by Judson and Orphanides, has the advantage of nesting the ratio of the standard deviation of inflation to one plus the (say, quarterly) rate of inflation, which is the (relative) uncertainty specification suggested by some theoretical work (Davis and Kanago, 1992).

where Υ_i are the individual effects, $\boldsymbol{\omega}$ a coefficient vector, and $v_{i,t+1}$ an error term. The latter is assumed to be uncorrelated with any information available at t, which includes RHS variables and past values of $v_{i,t+1}$, and hence $v_{i,t+1}$ is serially uncorrelated. Estimation of (6) allows one to decompose $\pi_{i,t+1}$ into expected inflation, $\exp\pi_{i,t+1}$, which is an estimate of $\Upsilon_i + \mathbf{w}'_{it}\boldsymbol{\omega}$, and unexpected inflation, $e\pi_{i,t+1}$, which is an estimate of $v_{i,t+1}$.

Second, I need to estimate the impact of the two separate elements of inflation on the unexpected component of *ex post* real stock returns, which I have denoted by $es_{i,t+1}$. As previously stated, a series for the latter is calculated as the residuals from an expression in levels such as (4), but using the coefficients estimated by running the first-differenced version (5) by GMM. Therefore, the equation of interest can be expressed as:

$$es_{i,t+1} = \xi_i + \phi(\pi_{i,t+1} - \Upsilon_i - \mathbf{w}'_{it}\boldsymbol{\omega}) + \psi(\Upsilon_i + \mathbf{w}'_{it}\boldsymbol{\omega}) + \mathbf{t}'_{it}\varsigma + \eta_{i,t+1}, \quad (7)$$

where ξ_i are the individual effects; ϕ and ψ coefficients, ς a coefficient vector; $\mathbf{t}_{it}$ a vector of controlling variables; and $\eta_{i,t+1}$ an error term. The latter is assumed to be uncorrelated with the RHS variables. The second term on the RHS of (7) captures the effect of unexpected inflation, while the third one measures the impact of the expected component of $\pi_{i,t+1}$.

The easiest way to estimate equations (6) and (7) is to use a two-step procedure. First, one could estimate equation (6) by OLS, which allows one to decompose inflation into its expected and unexpected components.[14] Second, using the estimates of these two components, one can obtain estimates of ξ_i, ϕ, ψ, and ς by running equation (7) by OLS.

One desirable property of this two-step procedure is that it yields consistent estimates of all the coefficients. It must be borne in mind, however, that this method does not generate valid F statistics (Mishkin, 1983). The procedure implicitly assumes that there is no uncertainty in the estimation of ξ_i and $\boldsymbol{\omega}$. This results in inconsistent estimates of the standard errors of the parameters and hence test statistics that do not have the assumed F distribution.

4. DETERMINANTS OF ASSET RETURNS: SOME BASIC RESULTS

In this section, I analyze the determinants of the real rate of return on both bank deposits and equity. Among the RHS variables here considered, I use the first definition of inflation, π_{it}, measured between (the middle of the last month in) quarter $t-1$ and (the middle of the last month in) quarter t. For completeness, the alternative definition of inflation described in the last section is considered in Section 5 as a refinement to the basic methodology employed in the present section.

In the case of stocks, I also run a regression of the unexplained component of the real return on contemporaneous inflation, controlling for other sources of real rate variability.

[14] Given that OLS estimates might suffer from endogeneity, I estimate (6) by GMM on the first-differenced version of the model.

The decomposition of inflation into its expected and unexpected components is left as an additional refinement for Section 5.

4.1. Bank Deposit Rates

Table 2 reports the regression results obtained from explaining the behavior of the real rate of interest on bank deposits in terms of past information. This information is represented by the levels of inflation, money supply growth, international prices, world interest rates, and production growth.[15] The current level of the nominal interest rate, $i_{i,t+1}$, which is an element of the available information set, is included among the explanatory variables. Lags of the dependent variable are also considered in order to test for the presence of inertia in the behavior of real interest rates.

Table 2 presents two different sets of *ex post* real rate regression results, which correspond to the inclusion of different variables—and thus of different groups of countries—in the sample. The first column corresponds to the case when all variables in the data set but (current and lagged values of) industrial production growth, g_t, are considered, while the second column reports regression results obtained using all available variables.[16]

Past information appears to explain about 35–40% of the variation in the real rate of interest on bank deposits. The results reported in both columns of Table 2 have many points in common. In both, the nominal interest rate has a positive but insignificant effect on the real rate. In both cases, too, the first and second lags of the inflation variable $\pi_{it}/(1+\pi_{it})$ show a significantly positive influence, while the same variable is not significant at time t in either column of Table 2. Both columns indicate that the lagged dependent variable and past information on money growth do not enter significantly. Concerning foreign variables, the only one that enters significantly is the rate of change in the international price of crude oil (lagged one period in the first column, and contemporaneously in the second column). Finally, information on output growth (which is only considered in the second column) fails to enter significantly.

In sum, up to one fourth of the behavior of the real *ex post* bank deposit rate can be predicted by information currently available. Past information on the inflation rate variable (more precisely, its first two lags) has a significantly positive effect on the real interest rate. Oil prices appear to be the only significant foreign variable. Other variables, such as the lagged dependent variable and past information on the rate of growth of the money supply and output, do not enter significantly.

[15] Data on nominal equity returns are not used here because that would lead to a reduction in the number of observations. In the next subsection, I use data on bank deposit rates in the real stock returns regressions reported since the reduction in the number of observations that occurs is not considerable.

[16] In practice, this means that the number of observations considered in the second column shrinks compared with those available for the regressions reported in the first column.

Table 2 Panel data regressions[a].

Dependent variable: Real interest rate on bank deposits (rb_{t+1}) Method: GMM on first-differenced version of model		
	(1)	**(2)**
i_{t+1}	0.771 (1.030)	0.297 (0.253)
rb_t	−0.029 (−0.055)	0.683 (0.811)
$\pi_t/(1+\pi_t)$	0.744 (1.250)	1.538 (1.664)
$\pi_{t-1}/(1+\pi_{t-1})$	0.455 (3.671)	0.449 (3.613)
$\pi_{t-2}/(1+\pi_{t-2})$	0.254 (3.734)	0.252 (3.236)
μ_t	0.001 (1.215)	0.001 (0.821)
μ_{t-1}	0.001 (1.045)	0.001 (0.643)
P_{2t}		0.097 (2.677)
$P_{2,t-1}$	−0.046 (−2.104)	
$i^*_{3,t-1}$	−0.209 (−1.104)	0.444 (1.630)
g_t		0.040 (0.999)
g_{t-1}		−0.213 (−0.876)
Sargan	1.29	0.38
p-value	0.86	0.54
d.f.	4	3
R^2	0.371	0.356
Regression F	269.67	155.31
p-value	0.00	0.00
No. obs.	5042	3667
No. units	59	49

Instruments for (1): First differences of $i_t, i_{t-1}, rb_{t-1}, rb_{t-2}, \pi_t/(1+\pi_t), \pi_{t-1}/(1+\pi_{t-1}), \pi_{t-2}/(1+\pi_{t-2}), \mu_t, \mu_{t-1}, P_{2,t-2}, P_{3t}, P_{3,t-1}, i^*_{3,t-1}$, and seasonals.

Instruments for (2): First differences of $i_t, i_{t-1}, rb_{t-1}, rb_{t-2}, \pi_t/(1+\pi_t), \pi_{t-1}/(1+\pi_{t-1}), \pi_{t-2}/(1+\pi_{t-2}), \pi_{t-3}/(1+\pi_{t-3}), \mu_t, \mu_{t-1}, P_{1,t-1}, P_{2,t-1}, i^*_{3,t-1}, g_t, g_{t-1}$, and seasonals.

(1) All variables in data set but g;

(2) All variables in data set.

[a] Estimated coefficients of the seasonals are not reported. t-statistics for the parameters are given in parentheses (corresponding to standard errors computed from heteroskedastic-consistent matrix). Sargan statistic refers to the test of overidentifying restrictions.

4.2. Stock Returns

Tables 3 and 4 show the basic regression results using stock returns. Table 3 presents the results obtained from running a regression of the real stock returns on past information. The latter is represented by the levels of the bank deposit rate (current and lagged), inflation, money supply growth, international prices, world interest rates, and production growth. As with bank deposit rates, lags of the dependent variable are also considered in order to test for the presence of inertia in the behavior of real interest rates. The current

Table 3 Panel data regressions[a].

Dependent variable: Real rate of return on stocks (rs_{t+1})
Method: GMM on first-differenced version of model

	(1)	(2)
rs_t	−0.658 (−2.140)	−0.854 (−1.251)
rs_{t-1}	0.086 (1.015)	0.202 (1.151)
$\pi_t/(1+\pi_t)$	0.067 (1.410)	0.030 (0.342)
$\pi_{t-1}/(1+\pi_{t-1})$	0.015 (3.322)	0.019 (2.693)
$\pi_{t-2}/(1+\pi_{t-2})$	0.056 (1.696)	0.010 (1.733)
i_{t+1}	0.114 (2.665)	0.165 (2.244)
i_t	−0.099 (−2.753)	−0.156 (−2.254)
i_{t-1}	−0.046 (−1.158)	−0.046 (−0.899)
μ_t	−0.006 (−2.189)	−0.007 (−1.543)
μ_{t-1}	−0.007 (−2.495)	−0.001 (−2.052)
P_{1t}	0.004 (0.545)	
$P_{1,t-1}$		0.007 (0.686)
P_{2t}	0.030 (3.053)	0.005 (2.854)
$P_{3,t-1}$	−0.011 (−4.071)	−0.007 (−1.460)
$P_{4,t-1}$	−0.002 (−0.276)	0.006 (0.325)
g_t		0.025 (1.905)
g_{t-1}		0.015 (0.813)
Sargan	0.38	0.004
p-value	0.54	0.83
d.f.	1	1
R^2	0.197	0.176
Regression *F*	26.90	9.61
p-value	0.00	0.00
No. obs.	1771	843
No. units	21	11

Instruments for (1): First differences of rs_{t-2}, rs_{t-3}, i_{t+1}, i_t, i_{t-1}, $\pi_t/(1+\pi_t)$, $\pi_{t-1}/(1+\pi_{t-1})$, $\pi_{t-2}/(1+\pi_{t-2})$, $\pi_{t-3}/(1+\pi_{t-3})$, μ_t, μ_{t-1}, $P_{1,t-1}$, P_{2t}, $P_{3,t-1}$, $P_{4,t-1}$, and seasonals.
Instruments for (2): First differences of rs_{t-2}, rs_{t-3}, i_{t+1}, i_t, i_{t-1}, $\pi_t/(1+\pi_t)$, $\pi_{t-1}/(1+\pi_{t-1})$, $\pi_{t-2}/(1+\pi_{t-2})$, $\pi_{t-3}/(1+\pi_{t-3})$, μ_t, μ_{t-1}, $P_{1,t-1}$, P_{2t}, $P_{3,t-1}$, $P_{4,t-1}$, g_t, g_{t-1}, and seasonals.
(1) All variables in data set but *g*;
(2) All variables in data set.
[a]Estimated coefficients of the seasonals are not reported. *t*-statistics for the parameters are given in parentheses (corresponding to standard errors computed from heteroskedastic-consistent matrix). Sargan statistic refers to the test of overidentifying restrictions.

level of nominal returns, s_{t+1}, which is not in the available information set, is not included among the explanatory variables.

Table 3 summarizes two different *ex post* real rate regression results, which correspond to the inclusion of different variables—and thus of different groups of countries—in the

Table 4 Panel data regressions[a].

Dependent variables: Residuals from Table 3 ($es_{1,t+1}$ and $es_{2,t+1}$)		
	(1)	(2)
$\pi_{t+1}/(1+\pi_{t+1})$	−6.810 (−1.209)	−2.672 (−0.380)
$P_{1,t+1}$	−9.062 (−8.178)	−10.475 (−5.770)
$P_{2,t+1}$	4.703 (3.813)	4.996 (2.680)
$P_{3,t+1}$	3.894 (9.454)	3.678 (5.400)
$P_{4,t+1}$	−0.532 (−0.692)	0.752 (0.623)
$i^*_{3,t+1}$	−16.804 (−2.263)	−15.036 (−1.222)
g_{t+1}		0.685 (0.520)
Hausman χ^2	20.34	3.84
p-value	0.02	0.95
Technique	fixed effects	random effects
R^2	0.115	0.114
Adjusted R^2	0.100	0.104
No. obs.	1811	843
No. units	21	11

(1) All variables in data set but g;
(2) All variables in data set.
[a]Estimated coefficients of the seasonals are not reported. t-statistics for the parameters are given in parentheses. Hausman χ^2 statistic refers to the test for correlated effects (random effects is the null hypothesis).

sample. The first column corresponds to the case when all variables in the data set but production growth are considered, while the second column reports regression results obtained using all available variables.[17]

In either regression, past information explains almost one fifth of the variation in the real return on stocks. Of the two lags of the dependent variable only the first lag in column 1 is significant (and negative). Both columns report a significantly positive coefficient for the second lag of the inflation variable, $\pi_{i,t-1}/(1+\pi_{i,t-1})$. The other inflation terms also have a positive effect, but one that does not appear to be significant. In both columns, current information on the nominal interest rate ($i_{i,t+1}$) enters with a significantly positive coefficient, while the corresponding first lag (i_{it}) enters with a significantly negative coefficient.[18] Past information on the rate of growth of the money supply has a significantly negative effect, except for current money supply growth in the regressions that include $\boldsymbol{g}_t$. Past information on foreign variables is found to be relevant for

[17] As a result, the number of observations considered in the second column is reduced compared with those available for the regressions reported in the first column.
[18] In none of the two columns is the second lag of this variable ($i_{i,t-1}$) significant.

the calculation of real stock returns. Changes in the international price of crude oil have a significantly positive effect on the dependent variable, as do changes in the international prices of metals in column 1. Finally, past information on other foreign variables (such as international interest rates and prices of food and agricultural raw materials) and domestic output do not enter significantly.

While Table 3 reports results on the impact of past available information on equity returns, Table 4 assesses whether current inflation is responsible for the unexplained component of those returns, after controlling for other sources of real rate variability. The dependent variables of the regressions presented in Table 4 are the residuals from the two different regressions presented in Table 3, $es_{1,t+1}$ and $es_{2,t+1}$.

The overall performance of these second-step regressions is rather modest, with values of the R^2 slightly above 10% (Table 4). The results reported in both columns are fairly similar. The contemporaneous inflation coefficient is negative but not significant. This means that equity provides a good hedge against changes in the general level of prices. Three foreign variables enter significantly in both columns of Table 4. In fact, contemporaneous changes in the international prices of food have a significantly negative effect on the dependent variable, while current changes in the international price of crude oil and metals enter with a significantly positive coefficient. The world interest rate has a significantly negative effect only in the first column. Finally, prices of agricultural raw materials and domestic output are not significant.

5. DETERMINANTS OF ASSET RETURNS: SOME REFINEMENTS

The previous section presents results where the *ex post* real rate regressions (3) use a definition of inflation, π_{it}, that is measured between the middle of the last month of quarter $t-1$ to the middle of the last month of quarter t. In this section, I analyze whether and how regression results for either bank deposits or stocks change if a different measure of inflation is considered to be part of agents' available information set. This alternative definition, which was defined as π_{it}^{LU} in Section 3, is measured between the month previous to the end of quarter $t-1$ and the month previous to the end of quarter t. This would be the right variable if one believes that, as of (the middle of the last month in) period t, agents have trouble figuring out the inflation rate during the last monthly period because the last public information on CPI inflation refers to the middle of previous month.

In addition to this refinement in the analysis of the determinants of real returns, I consider a second refinement in the study of the effects of current inflation on the unexpected component of equity yields. As was described in Section 3, this alternative specification starts by decomposing contemporaneous inflation into its expected and unexpected components. The final step consists of a regression of the component of stock returns that is not explained by past information on both the expected and unexpected components of current inflation. The basic idea behind this procedure is to determine which, if any, of the two components of inflation is responsible for *ex post* variability in the real rate of return.

5.1. Bank Deposit Rates

Table 5 shows the "refined" regression results for bank deposit rates using the alternative definition of inflation, π_{it}^{LU}, measured between the month previous to the end of quarter $t-1$ and the month previous to the end of quarter t. In addition to this variable, past information is represented here by the levels of the nominal interest rate (current and lagged), money supply growth, international prices, and world interest rates.[19]

The overall performance of these second-step regressions is quite poor. Yet, as indicated by the value of the regression F statistic, it is possible to reject the hypothesis that the RHS variables are not jointly significant. The only inflation term to enter significantly (with a negative coefficient) is the first lag of π_{it}^{LU}. Unlike Table 2, the current nominal interest rate has a significantly positive influence on the real rate it helps determine. In all cases, the point estimate is positive. Focusing on the significant coefficient in Table 5, it is worth reporting that the quarterly contribution of the current nominal interest rate to real bank deposit rates differs across country groupings, being of some 1% among developed countries and about 10% for emerging and developing economies. Past information on money growth have a negative effect, but fails to enter significantly. Foreign variables are not significant, with the exception of changes in the international price of raw materials, which exhibit a significantly positive coefficient in the second column.

I now summarize the results obtained using the two alternative definitions of inflation. As was mentioned before, there is one important difference between the two cases. When the traditional measure, π_{it}, is used (results in Table 2), the first and second lags of the inflation variable, $\pi_{it}/(1+\pi_{it})$, show a significantly positive influence (the level of that variable at time t is not significant, though). In contrast, using the alternative definition π_{it}^{LU} (results in Table 5), past information of this variable is either not found to be significant, or it enters with a significantly negative coefficient (as is the case for the first lag of this variable). In addition, contemporaneous bank deposit rates enter significantly in Table 5, whereas past information of this variable plays no significant role when the traditional inflation measure is used. Past information on money growth fails to enter significantly. Furthermore, it is possible to detect a moderate role of foreign variables, with no significant role in particular for the world interest rate. Among the international prices, crude oil prices are the only ones that enter significantly in Table 3, while prices of raw materials are the only ones that enter significantly in

[19] Results obtained using data on (current and lagged values of) industrial production growth, g_t, were considered, but are not reported because the number of available observations then drops to 561 (for only 10 countries).

Table 5 Panel data regressions[a].

Dependent variable: Real interest rate on deposits (rb_{t+1}) **Method: GMM on first-differenced version of model**	
i_{t+1}	0.640 (2.091)
i_t	0.431 (1.387)
π_t^{LU}	−0.044 (−1.058)
π_{t-1}^{LU}	−0.011 (−2.337)
π_{t-2}^{LU}	−0.054 (−1.336)
μ_t	−0.009 (−0.582)
μ_{t-1}	−0.005 (−0.287)
P_{1t}	−0.084 (−1.680)
P_{2t}	−0.019 (−0.371)
P_{3t}	0.001 (0.033)
P_{4t}	0.094 (2.439)
i_{3t}^*	−0.019 (−0.371)
Sargan	2.95
p-value	0.40
d.f.	3
R^2	0.017
Regression F	1.84
p-value	0.03
No. obs.	1499
No. units	20

Instruments: First differences of rb_{t-2}, i_t, i_{t-1}, π_t^{LU}, π_{t-1}^{LU}, π_{t-2}^{LU}, π_{t-3}^{LU}, μ_t, μ_{t-1}, P_{1t}, P_{2t}, P_{3t}, P_{4t}, i_{3t}^*, and seasonals.

[a]Estimated coefficients of the seasonals are not reported. t-statistics for the parameters are given in parentheses (corresponding to standard errors computed from heteroskedastic-consistent matrix). Sargan statistic refers to the test of overidentifying restrictions.

Table 5. Finally, in the case of the traditional measure, π_{it}, output growth is found to be insignificant.

5.2. Stock Returns

Tables 6 through 8 report the "refined" regression results using equity yields. Table 6 shows the results obtained from running a regression of the real rate of return on stocks. This time, past information is represented by the levels of the nominal interest rate (current and lagged), nominal equity returns, money supply growth, international prices, and world interest rates.[20] As in the previous subsection, π_{it} is not included as a RHS variable, but past information on the alternative definition, π_{it}^{LU}, is.

[20] Once more, output growth is not included among the regressors. The reason is that the number of available observations otherwise drops to 366 (for only six countries).

Table 6 Panel data regressions[a].

Dependent variable: Real rate of return on stocks (rs_{t+1}) Method: GMM on first-differenced version of model	
s_t	−0.034 (−1.874)
s_{t-1}	−0.096 (−1.536)
i_{t+1}	−0.021 (−0.580)
i_t	−0.053 (−1.525)
i_{t-1}	0.029 (0.781)
π_t^{LU}	−0.001 (−0.162)
π_{t-1}^{LU}	−0.006 (−1.162)
π_{t-2}^{LU}	−0.002 (−0.378)
μ_t	−0.002 (−1.524)
μ_{t-1}	−0.001 (−0.933)
$P_{1,t-1}$	0.021 (3.175)
$P_{3,t-1}$	−0.003 (−1.451)
$P_{4,t-1}$	0.029 (7.217)
Sargan	1.27
p-value	0.26
d.f.	1
R^2	0.322
Regression F	38.11
p-value	0.00
No. obs.	1209
No. units	16

Instruments : First differences of rs_{t-3}, rs_{t-4}, i_{t+1}, i_t, i_{t-1}, π_t^{LU}, π_{t-1}^{LU}, π_{t-2}^{LU}, π_{t-3}^{LU}, μ_t, μ_{t-1}, P_{1t}, P_{3t}, P_{4t}, and seasonals.

[a]Estimated coefficients of the seasonals are not reported. t-statistics for the parameters are given in parentheses (corresponding to standard errors computed from heteroskedastic-consistent matrix). Sargan statistic refers to the test of overidentifying restrictions.

The results in Table 6 are not entirely consistent with those obtained using the other measure of inflation, π_{it}, in Table 3. Table 6 shows that past information on nominal stock yields is found to reduce real stock returns but the coefficient is not significant. This result is in line with Table 3 when the regression controls for output growth, but differs from the presence of a significantly negative lagged dependent variable in column 1 in Table 3 (where output growth is not included as a RHS variable). Given the estimated coefficients, the quarterly contribution of past stock returns is estimated to be different across country groupings. Focusing on the significant coefficient in column 1 in Table 3, past stock returns contribute negatively with some 1.5% among developed countries and about 5% for emerging and developing economies.

Other differences are the lack of significance in variables such as the nominal bank deposit rate, inflation, and money growth in Table 6, which stands in contrast with the statistical significance detected in Table 3 for $i_{i,t+1}$, i_{it}, and $\pi_{i,t-1}$,[21] as well as for most terms considered to capture money growth (with the exception of contemporaneous money growth when the regression controls for output growth). Concerning foreign variables, the results in Tables 3 and 6 are coincident in that world interest rates are not significant and international prices play a moderate role. Even here, the two sets of results differ in the specific international prices involved, with prices for crude oil and metals entering significantly in Table 3 and prices for food and raw materials being significant in Table 6.

While Table 6 reports results on the impact of past available information on equity returns, Tables 7 and 8 permit one to examine whether current inflation affects the unexplained component of those returns, after controlling for other sources of *ex post* real rate variability. As was explained in Section 3, the second refinement that I introduce here is a decomposition of the inflation rate into its expected and unexpected components.

The method used in Tables 7 and 8 consists of a two-step procedure. Table 7 shows the results from estimating (as a first step) a forecasting equation for the inflation rate, which corresponds to equation (6) in Section 3. The estimation of this regression is based on data on the conventional measure of inflation, π_{it}, which is the dependent variable and whose lags feature in the RHS of the regression.[22] Table 8 reports (as a second step) the regression results for equation (7), which expresses the unexplained component of equity returns as a function of both the expected and unexpected components of inflation, together with some controlling variables. More concretely, the dependent variable in Table 8 is the part of the real rate of return on stocks that is not explained by past information. Generically, this component is labeled as $es_{i,t+1}$.[23] In Table 8, these residuals are denoted by $es_{1i,t+1}$ and $es_{2i,t+1}$, which also are the dependent variables in Table 4. They are derived from the estimates in the *ex post* real stock return regressions reported in the two different columns of Table 3. Among the RHS variables of Table 8 are the expected and unexpected components of the current inflation rate. More precisely, the latter, expressed as $\pi_{i,t+1}/(1+\pi_{i,t+1})$, is decomposed into an expected component $\exp\pi_{i,t+1}/(1+\pi_{i,t+1})$, and an unexpected one, $e\pi_{i,t+1}/(1+\pi_{i,t+1})$, by means of the estimates reported in Table 7. All the regressions in Table 8 control for other sources of *ex post* real rate variability.

[21] Note that, when it comes to stock returns and inflation terms as explanatory variables, the comparison must take into account the fact that Table 3 differs from Table 6 in that stock returns are deflated by using consumer prices.

[22] Tables 9 and 10 report the corresponding results from this same two-step procedure when the alternative measure of inflation, π_{it}^{LU}, is used.

[23] Section 3 explained the exact method of computing these residuals from an expression in levels such as (4), but using the coefficients estimated by running (5) by GMM.

Table 7 Panel data regressions: the inflation rate[a].

Dependent variable: π_{t+1} **Method: GMM on first-differenced version of model**		
	(1)	**(2)**
π_t	−0.809 (−14.076)	−0.807 (−11.493)
π_{t-1}	−0.517 (−9.760)	−0.519 (−7.552)
π_{t-2}	−0.250 (−6.026)	−0.263 (−4.620)
i_{t+1}	0.258 (0.731)	0.517 (0.633)
i_t	−0.046 (−0.096)	−0.496 (−0.370)
s_t	0.027 (0.815)	0.034 (0.346)
s_{t-1}	−0.029 (−0.420)	0.047 (0.360)
μ_t	−0.072 (−2.127)	−0.099 (−1.606)
μ_{t-1}	−0.010 (−0.348)	−0.023 (−0.270)
P_{1t}	−0.017 (−0.725)	−0.059 (−0.083)
$P_{2,t-1}$	−0.065 (−1.091)	−0.016 (−1.419)
$P_{3,t-1}$	−0.007 (−0.380)	−0.049 (−0.353)
$P_{4,t-1}$	0.055 (1.033)	0.038 (0.256)
$i^*_{3,t-1}$	1.754 (0.853)	0.975 (0.199)
g_t		0.080 (0.893)
g_{t-1}		−0.025 (−0.872)
Sargan	0.01	0.58
p-value	0.90	0.46
d.f.	1	1
R^2	0.278	0.382
Regression F	42.66	27.93
p-value	0.00	0.00
No. obs.	1781	832
No. units	21	11

Instruments for (1): First differences of $i_t, i_{t-1}, s_{t-3}, s_{t-4}, \pi_{t-1}, \pi_{t-2}, \pi_{t-3}, \mu_t, \mu_{t-1}, P_{1t}, P_{2,t-1}, P_{3,t-1}, P_{4,t-1}, i^*_{3,t-1}$, and seasonals.
Instruments for (2): First differences of $i_t, i_{t-1}, s_{t-3}, s_{t-4}, \pi_{t-1}, \pi_{t-2}, \pi_{t-3}, \mu_t, \mu_{t-1}, P_{1t}, P_{2,t-1}, P_{3,t-1}, P_{4,t-1}, i^*_{3,t-1}, g_t, g_{t-1}$, and seasonals.
(1) All variables in data set but g;
(2) All variables in data set.
[a]Estimated coefficients of the seasonals are not reported. t-statistics for the parameters are given in parentheses; they are based on standard errors computed from quadratic form of analytic first derivatives.

This methodology yields consistent parameter estimates. Given that it does not provide valid test statistics,[24] the results reported in the rest of this paragraph concentrate on comparing between the signs of the coefficients in Table 4 with those obtained in Table 8

[24] One good statistical property of the GMM estimates in Table 7 is that the inflation regressions use instrumental variables in order to control for the possible endogeneity of the model.

Table 8 Panel data regressions[a].

Dependent variables: Residuals from Table 3 ($es_{1,t+1}$ and $es_{2,t+1}$)		
	(1)	(2)
$e\pi_{t+1}/(1+\pi_{t+1})$	−7.233 (−1.274)	−1.952 (−0.282)
$\exp\pi_{t+1}/(1+\pi_{t+1})$	−5.032 (−0.689)	8.645 (0.906)
$P_{1,t+1}$	−9.040 (−8.089)	−10.443 (−5.701)
$P_{2,t+1}$	4.725 (3.819)	4.175 (2.641)
$P_{3,t+1}$	3.860 (9.437)	3.744 (5.417)
$P_{4,t+1}$	−0.682 (−0.829)	0.228 (0.183)
$i^*_{3,t+1}$	−20.279 (−2.111)	−23.911 (−1.719)
g_{t+1}		0.762 (0.581)
Hausman χ^2	20.68	10.18
p-value	0.02	0.54
Technique	fixed effects	random effects
R^2	0.104	0.117
Adjusted R^2	0.099	0.106
No. obs.	1800	842
No. units	21	11

(1) All variables in data set but g;
(2) All variables in data set.
[a]Estimated coefficients of the seasonals are not reported. t-statistics for the parameters are given in parentheses; they are based on standard errors computed from quadratic form of analytic first derivatives.

(with a focus on parameters found to be significant in Table 4). In Table 4, it was found that the contemporaneous inflation coefficient is negative but not significant. This means that equity provides a good hedge against changes in the general level of prices. Moreover, three parameters were significant in Table 4, namely, those relating to the contemporaneous changes in the international prices of food, crude oil, and metals. The world interest rate coefficient was found to be significantly negative only in the first column of Table 4. Table 8 only partially confirms the signs of the coefficients that were significant in Table 4. This is the case for food prices and the world interest rate in column 1 (negative signs for both foreign variables). Instead, the results from Table 8 reverse the positive sign found in Table 4 for the current changes in the international price of crude oil and metals.

Tables 9 and 10 report the results from the corresponding two-step procedure when the lags of the alternative measure of inflation, π_{it}^{LU}, are used as RHS variables to forecast the traditional measure of actual inflation. While actual inflation is the dependent variable in Table 9, in Table 10 the LHS variable is given by the residuals denoted by $es_{3i,t+1}$. Let us now focus on reporting the results corresponding to comparisons between the signs of the significant coefficients in Table 4 and the point estimates in Table 10. Table 10

Table 9 Panel data regression: the inflation rate[a].

Dependent variable: π_{t+1}	
Method: GMM on first-differenced version of model	
π_t^{LU}	0.047 (1.180)
π_{t-1}^{LU}	0.079 (1.744)
π_{t-2}^{LU}	0.049 (1.285)
i_{t+1}	0.294 (1.158)
i_t	−0.427 (−1.593)
s_t	−0.046 (−1.684)
s_{t-1}	−0.027 (−1.123)
μ_t	−0.008 (−0.522)
μ_{t-1}	0.008 (0.552)
$P_{1,t-1}$	0.010 (2.130)
P_{2t}	−0.058 (−1.299)
$P_{4,t-1}$	−0.095 (−2.860)
Sargan	1.79
p-value	0.62
d.f.	3
R^2	0.019
Regression F	1.72
p-value	0.04
No. obs.	1227
No. units	16

Instruments: First differences of i_{t+1}, i_t, i_{t-1}, s_{t-1}, s_{t-2}, s_{t-3}, s_{t-4}, π_{t-1}^{LU}, π_{t-2}^{LU}, π_{t-3}^{LU}, μ_t, μ_{t-1}, $P_{1,t-1}$, P_{2t}, $P_{4,t-1}$, and seasonals.

[a]Estimated coefficients of the seasonals are not reported. t-statistics for the parameters are given in parentheses. Hausman χ^2 statistic refers to the test for correlated effects (random effects is the null hypothesis).

is only available for the case when output growth is not included as a regressor. None of the signs for the three significant international price coefficients from Table 4 (i.e., those corresponding to for prices of food, crude oil, and metals) is confirmed in Table 10. Moreover, the sign for the world interest rate is not confirmed either.

In sum, Table 4 shows that the contemporaneous inflation coefficient is negative but not significant. This means that equity provides a good hedge against changes in the general level of prices. Three parameters are significant in Table 4, namely, those relating to the contemporaneous changes in the international prices of food, crude oil, and metals. The world interest rate coefficient is significantly negative only when output growth is not included among the regressors. Table 8 only partially confirms the signs of the coefficients that were significant in Table 4. This is the case for food prices and the world interest

Table 10 Panel data regressions[a].

Dependent variables: Residuals from Table 6 ($es_{3,t+1}$)	
$e\pi_{t+1}/(1+\pi_{t+1})$	−0.072 (−1.686)
$\exp\pi_{t+1}/(1+\pi_{t+1})$	−0.111 (−8.594)
$P_{1,t+}$	0.027 (4.074)
$P_{2,t+1}$	−0.009 (−1.186)
$P_{3,t+1}$	−0.007 (−3.175)
$P_{4,t+1}$	0.009 (1.960)
$i^*_{3,t+1}$	0.052 (8.785)
R^2	0.111
Adjusted R^2	0.104
Hausman χ^2	16.20
p-value	0.09
Technique	random effects
No. obs.	1211
No. units	16

[a]Estimated coefficients of the seasonals are not reported. t-statistics for the parameters are given in parentheses. Hausman χ^2 statistic refers to the test for correlated effects (random effects is the null hypothesis).

rate when the regression does not control for output growth (negative signs for both foreign variables). Instead, the positive sign found in Table 4 for the current changes in the international price of crude oil and metals is reversed in Table 8. Finally, the signs of the significant coefficients in Table 4 are compared with those reported in Table 10 (obtained when the lags of the alternative measure of inflation, π_{it}^{LU}, are used to predict actual inflation and the regression does not control for output growth). None of the signs for the coefficients related to the foreign variables in Table 4 is confirmed in Table 10.

6. CONCLUSIONS

This study analyzes the determinants of the real rate of return using a cross-country panel data approach. The behavior of the real rate of return is examined in terms of two alternative measures, namely, bank deposit rates and equity yields.

As a first approximation, I have run some "basic" regressions under the assumption that agents know the rate of inflation up to the middle of the last month of the quarter before the real returns are determined. As a refinement, I then consider an alternative measure of the latest quarterly inflation in the available information set, which does not incorporate the last month of inflation in the former definition. The second ("refined") characterization is a more reasonable one if one believes that agents have trouble figuring out the inflation rate during the last month of a given quarter because the latest public information on CPI inflation refers to the middle of previous month.

Moreover, I have considered two sets of regressions for either the "basic" and the "refined" specification, depending on whether a measure of output growth (which is not available for many countries) is included in the data set or not. Although the estimated coefficients are found not to be significantly affected by distinguishing developed from emerging and developing countries, this study has illustrated that the effects of a given variable display differences across these two country groupings for some robust results.

In the case of bank deposit rates, for the "basic" regressions it is found that up to one fourth of the behavior of the real *ex post* interest rates can be predicted by information currently available. Past information on the inflation rate variable (more precisely, its first two lags) has a significantly positive effect on the real interest rate. Oil prices appear to be the only significant foreign variable. Other variables, such as the lagged dependent variable and past information on the rate of growth of the money supply and output, do not enter significantly. There is one important difference between the "basic" and the "refined" specifications, as in the latter case it is found that past information on inflation is either not found to be significant, or it enters with a significantly negative coefficient (as is the case for the first lag of this variable). In addition, contemporaneous bank deposit rates enter significantly in the "refined" regression, whereas past information of this variable plays no significant role when the traditional inflation measure is used.

Among the robust results, one finds that the current nominal interest rate has a significantly positive effect on the real rate it contributes to determine. Past information on money growth fails to enter significantly. Overall, foreign variables seem not to make a significant contribution in the regressions that do not include output growth, while changes in the international price of raw materials and (in the "basic" regression) the world interest rate both show a significantly negative coefficient when one controls for output growth. Furthermore, it is possible to detect a moderate role of foreign variables, with no role in particular for the world interest rate. Among the international prices, crude oil prices are the only ones that enter significantly in the "basic" regression, while prices of raw materials are the only ones that enter significantly when the alternative inflation measure is used. Finally, in the case of the traditional inflation measure, output growth is found to be insignificant.

With regard to equity yields, when the "basic" regression is run past information explains almost one fifth of the variation in the real return on stocks. Of the two lags of the dependent variable only the first lag is significant (and negative) in the regressions that do not include output growth as a regressor. A significantly positive coefficient is found for the second lag of the inflation variable. The other inflation terms also have a positive effect, but one that does not appear to be significant. Current information on the nominal interest rate enters with a significantly positive coefficient, while the corresponding first lag enters with a significantly negative coefficient. Past information on the rate of growth of the money supply has a significantly negative effect, except for current money supply growth when output growth is included among the RHS variables. Past information on foreign variables is found to be relevant for the calculation of real stock returns. Changes in the international price of crude oil have a significantly positive effect on the dependent variable, as do changes in the international prices of metals when the regression does not control for output growth. Finally, past information on other foreign variables (such as international interest rates and prices of food and agricultural raw materials) and domestic output do not enter significantly.

The results from the "refined" regressions for stock returns are not entirely consistent with those obtained using the traditional measure of inflation. For the "refined" regressions, past information on nominal stock yields is found to reduce real stock returns but the coefficient is not significant. This result is in line with the "basic" regression when the model controls for output growth, but differs from the "basic" regression that includes output growth as a RHS variable in which case the lagged dependent variable enters with a significantly negative coefficient. Other differences are the lack of significance of variables such as the nominal bank deposit rate, inflation, and money growth in the "refined" regression, which stands in contrast with the statistical significance detected in the "basic" specification. Concerning foreign variables, the results are coincident between the two specifications, with the world interest rate being insignificant and international prices playing a moderate role in both cases. Even here, the two sets of results differ in the specific prices involved, with evidence that prices for crude oil, and metals enter significantly in the "basic" regression and prices for food and raw materials being significant in the "refined" regression.

In addition to the analysis of the impact of past available information on equity returns, I have examined whether current inflation is responsible for the unexplained component of those returns, after controlling for other sources of *ex post* real rate variability. The focus is on the analysis of a model where the unexplained component of equity returns is regressed on current inflation. It is found that the contemporaneous inflation coefficient is negative but not significant. This indicates that equity provides a good hedge against changes in the general level of prices. Three foreign variables enter significantly: contemporaneous changes in the international prices of food have a significantly negative effect on the dependent variable, while current changes in the international price of crude oil and metals enter with a significantly positive coefficient. The world interest rate has a significantly negative effect only when output growth is not included as a regressor. Finally, prices of agricultural raw materials and domestic output are not significant. The signs of the regressors found to be significant are then compared with two sets of robustness checks. These robustness checks have in common the fact that inflation is decomposed into its expected and unexpected components. They differ in whether the inflation regressions used to obtain this decomposition include as regressors the lags of the traditional inflation measure or the lags of the alternative inflation variable. Let us start with the case of the inflation decompositions derived employing the lags of the traditional inflation measure as RHS variables. In this case, the signs of the coefficients found to be significant in the regression of unexplained stock returns (namely, international prices of food, crude oil, and metals, as well as—when output growth is not included as a regressor—the world interest rate) are only partially confirmed. The signs are confirmed for food prices and the world interest rate when the regression does not control for output growth (negative signs for these two foreign variables). Instead, the positive sign for the current changes in the international price of crude oil and metals is reversed when inflation is decomposed using past information about the traditional inflation measure. Finally, let us turn to the comparison between the signs of the significant coefficients in question and those estimated when the inflation decomposition is obtained employing the lags of the alternative inflation variable. In this case, none of the signs for the three significant international price coefficients is confirmed, nor is the sign for the world interest rate (obtained when the models control for output growth).

Appendix List of Countries

(A). Bank Deposit Interest Rate

The quarterly periods that accompany the names of the countries are those for which the IMF's publication *International Financial Statistics* permits one to construct a series for the nominal rate of interest on bank deposits, i_{t+1}.[25]

Developed economies	
United States	63:1–12:4
United Kingdom	57:1–99:2
Austria	80:4–01:1
Belgium	57:3–04:1
Denmark	80:4–90:2
France	66:2–12:4
Germany	77:3–03:3
Italy	83:2–04:2
Luxembourg	85:3–99:3
Netherlands	78:1–12:4
Norway	86:3–10:2
Sweden	66:2–06:4
Switzerland	81:2–12:4
Canada	71:2–12:4
Japan	57:2–12:4

[25] The symbol * means that the country was not considered in the regressions due to the lack of data on the rate of change of the money supply.

Finland	85:2–05:4
Greece	61:1–06:2
Iceland	76:2–05:2
Ireland	62:2–06:4
Malta	77:2–07:4
Portugal	76:1–12:4
Spain	82:2–03:2
Cyprus	71:1–08:3
Israel	83:4–12:4
Kuwait	80:2–12:4
Hong Kong	94:2–12:4
Singapore	77:2–12:4
Czech Republic	93:2–12:4
Slovak Republic	93:2–09:1
Estonia	93:2–12:4
Slovenia	92:1–09:4
Emerging and developing economies	
Turkey	79:1–12:4
South Africa	78:1–12:4
Argentina	77:2–12:4
Bolivia	81:1–12:4
Brazil	83:1–12:4
Chile	77:2–12:4
Colombia	86:2–12:4
Costa Rica	82:2–12:4
Dominican Republic	95:1–12:4
Ecuador	83:2–12:4
Guatemala	78:2–12:4
Haiti	95:1–12:4
Honduras	85:2–12:4
Mexico	76:2–12:4
Nicaragua	88:2–12:4
Panama	86:2–12:4
Paraguay	90:1–12:4
Peru	88:2–12:4
Uruguay	76:4–12:4
Venezuela	84:2–12:4
Bahamas	85:2–12:4
Aruba	86:2–12:4
Barbados	81:1–12:4
Dominica	82:1–12:4
Grenada	81:1–12:4
Guyana	81:2–12:4
Belize	79:1–12:4
Jamaica	76:2–12:4

Netherlands Antilles	84:2–10:4
St. Kitts and Nevis	81:1–12:4
St. Lucia	82:1–12:4
St. Vincent & Grenadines	83:1–12:4
Suriname	91:1–12:4
Trinidad & Tobago	85:2–12:2
Bahrain	75:2–12:4
Iran	04:1–12:3
Iraq	05:1–12:3
Jordan	92:1–12:4
Lebanon	82:2–12:4
Oman	86:1–12:4
Qatar	04:4–12:4
Syrian Arab Republic	79:1–11:3
Egypt	76:2–12:4
Yemen	96:1–12:4
Bangladesh	76:2–12:3
Bhutan	83:1–12:4
Brunei	03:2–12:3
Myanmar	75:3–12:4
Cambodia	94:3–12:4
Sri Lanka	78:2–12:3
Indonesia	74:3–12:4
Timor Leste	03:1–12:4
Maldives	96:1–12:4
Pakistan	04:2–12:4
Vietnam	97:2–12:4
Djibouti	95:4–12:3
Argelia	80:2–12:4
Angola	95:2–12:4
Botswana	80:2–12:4
Burundi	85:2–12:4
Cameroon	79:2–12:4
Cape Verde	85:2–12:4
Central African Republic	79:2–12:4
Chad	79:2–12:4
Congo, Republic of	79:1–12:4
Congo, Democratic Republic of	07:2–12:4
Benin	70:2–12:4
Equatorial Guinea	85:2–12:4
Ethiopia	93:1–09:1
Gabon	79:2–12:4
Gambia	85:3–12:4
Ghana	91:2–12:4
Guinea-Bissau	88:2–12:4

Guinea	87:2–12:4
Côte d'Ivoire	70:2–12:4
Kenya	95:1–12:4
Lybia	68:2–12:3
Madagascar	91:1–12:4
Malawi	80:1–12:4
Mali	70:2–12:4
Mauritania	80:2–12:4
Mauritius	80:3–12:4
Morocco	98:1–12:4
Niger	70:2–12:4
Nigeria	70:2–12:4
Rwanda	78:2–11:4
Seychelles	81:2–12:4
Senegal	70:2–12:4
Sierra Leone	77:2–12:4
Namibia	91:2–12:4
Swaziland	74:1–12:4
Tanzania	74:2–12:4
Togo	70:2–12:4
Tunisia	77:4–12:4
Uganda	81:1–12:4
Burkina Faso	70:2–12:4
Zambia	78:2–12:4
Solomon Islands	81:2–12:4
Fiji	93:1–12:4
Samoa	02:1–12:4
Tonga	81:1–12:4
Armenia	95:3–12:4
Albania	92:2–12:4
Georgia	95:4–12:3
Kyrgyz Republic	96:2–12:4
Bulgaria	91:2–12:4
Moldova	95:4–12:4
Russia	95:2–12:4
Ukraine	93:1–12:4
Latvia	93:4–12:4
Hungary	71:1–12:4
Mongolia	87:1–12:4
Lithuania	93:1–11:1
Croatia	93:1–12:4
Macedonia	94:2–12:4
Bosnia & Herzegovina	98:4–12:4
Poland	07:4–07:1
Romania	94:1–12:4

(B). Rate of return on stocks

The dates that accompany the names of the countries are the quarterly periods for which a series for the nominal rate of return on stocks, s_{t+1}, can be constructed using data from IMF's publication *International Financial Statistics*.

Developed economies	
United States	57:2–12:4
United Kingdom	63:2–12:4
Austria	57:2–12:4
Belgium	57:2–12:4
Denmark	96:2–12:4
France	88:2–12:4
Germany	70:2–12:4
Italy	57:2–12:4
Luxembourg	80:2–99:3
Netherlands	57:2–12:4
Norway	57:2–12:4
Sweden	57:2–12:4
Canada	84:2–12:4
Japan	57:2–12:4
Finland	57:2–12:4
Greece	94:1–12:4
Iceland	02:3–12:4
Ireland	57:2–12:4
Portugal	88:2–12:4
Spain	61:2–12:4
Israel	57:2–12:4
Hong Kong	96:2–12:4
Singapore	89:4–12:4
Czech Republic	97:4–12:4
Slovak Republic	00:2–12:4
Estonia	96:3–12:4
Slovenia	94:3–12:4

Emerging and developing economies	
Turkey	86:2–12:4
South Africa	60:2–12:4
Argentina	91:2–12:4
Bolivia	91:2–12:4
Brazil	94:1–12:4
Chile	90:2–12:3

Mexico	98:2–12:4
Iran	91:3–11:2
Bangladesh	88:2–12:4
India	57:2–12:4
Maldives	02:3–12:4
Kenya	97:2–12:4
Mauritius	89:4–12:4
Zambia	97:2–12:4
West African Economic and Monetary Union	98:4–12:4
Fiji	00:2–12:4
Bulgaria	01:1–12:4
Russia	97:4–12:4
Ukraine	98:1–12:4
Latvia	96:3–12:4
Hungary	00:2–12:4
Lithuania	01:2–12:4
Croatia	97:4–12:4
Poland	93:2–12:4

REFERENCES

Barnes, M., Boyd, J., Smith, B., 1999. Inflation and asset returns. European Economic Review 43, 737–754
Barro, R., 1995. Inflation and economic growth. NBER Working Paper No. 5226, October.
Boyd, J., Levine, R., Smith, B., 2001. Inflation and financial market performance. Journal of Monetary Economics 47, 221–248
Choi, S., Smith, B., Boyd, J., 1996. Inflation, financial markets, and capital formation. Federal Reserve Bank of St. Louis Review 78, 9–30
Cumby, R., Huizinga, J., Obstfeld, M., 1983. Two-step two-stage least squares estimation in models with rational expectations. Journal of Econometrics 21, 333–355
Davis, G., Kanago, B., 1992. Misspecification bias in models of the effect of inflation uncertainty. Economics Letters 38, 325–329
English, W., 1999. Inflation and financial sector size. Journal of Monetary Economics 44, 379–400
Fischer, S., 1993. The role of macroeconomic factors in growth. Journal of Monetary Economics 32, 485–512
Gavin, W., 2010. Deflation and the Fisher equation. Economic Synopses No. 27, St. Louis Federal Reserve Bank.
Geanakoplos, J., Karatzas, I., Shubik, M., Sudderth, W., 2004. The harmonic Fisher equation and the inflationary bias of real uncertainty. Yale School of Management Working Papers No. 388.
Glasner, D., 2011. The Fisher Effect Under Deflationary Expectations, January 26. Available at SSRN: <http://ssrn.com/abstract=1749062 or http://dx.doi.org/10.2139/ssrn.1749062>.
Gonzalez-Astudillo, M., Orus, J., 2004. Inflation-proof credits and financial instruments. Making the Fisher Hypothesis a Reality. Presented at the Ninth Annual Meeting of LACEA, Costa Rica, November 4–6.
Jensen, M., 2009. The long-run Fisher effect: can it be tested? Journal of Money, Credit, and Banking 41, 221–231
Judson, R., Orphanides, A., 1996. Inflation, Volatility and Growth, Finance and Economics Discussion Series, 96-16, Board of Governors of the Federal Reserve System, May.

Mishkin, F., 1981. The real interest rate: an empirical investigation. Carnegie-Rochester Conference Series in Public Policy 15, 151–200
Mishkin, F., 1983. A Rational Expectations Approach to Macroeconomics. University of Chicago Press, Chicago and London
Mishkin, F., 1988. Understanding real interest rates. American Journal of Agricultural Economics 70, 1064–1075
Rhodes, J., 2007. Devolution of the Fisher equation: rational appreciation to money illusion. GRIPS Discussion Papers 07–05, National Graduate Institute for Policy Studies.
Romer, C., 1992. What ended the great depression? Journal of Economic History 52, 757–784
Westerlund, J., 2008. Panel cointegration tests of the Fisher effect. Journal of Applied Econometrics 23, 193–233

CHAPTER 5

Understanding the Relationship Between Liquidity and Inflation in the Post Crisis Period in India: from Bank Dealers' Perspectives

Rituparna Das[*] and Michael C.S. Wong[†]

[*]Centre of Risk Management and Derivatives, National Law University, Jodhpur, India
[†]Department of Economics and Finance, College of Business, City University of Hong Kong, China

1. INTRODUCTION

The Reserve Bank of India (RBI) hiked the repo rate more than a dozen times starting from the end of the fourth quarter of the financial year (FY) 2009–2010 and continuing till the beginning of the third quarter of the FY 2010–2011 (Ninnan, 2011). In this context, the link between inflation and liquidity management received special emphasis in research from the academia, the central banks, and the banking industry in the Indian context.

Practitioners like Mohan (2006) viewed liquidity as the volume of bank reserves, the price of which is set as some short-term rate of interest in terms of overnight inter-bank borrowing and lending rates, either secured or unsecured, which affect the reserves that the banks (henceforth the term "bank" would imply "commercial bank") keep. In this context, liquidity means monetary base. Thus the demand for liquidity has two components—(a) one depends on the public's demand for currency arising out of transaction needs and opportunity cost of holding money and (b) the other depends on the banks' demand for reserves arising out of the need for meeting obligations. The RBI, viewed here to be the sole supplier of liquidity, modulates the same in order to set the short-term rate in a manner such that the volatility of short rates does not disrupt the real productive investments of the economy. In these circumstances, the RBI targets the overnight call money rate to bring about the equilibrium level of liquidity. Foreign capital inflow is considered not to be influencing this equilibrium unless the same exceeds the current account deficit in an emerging market developing economy (EDE) like India.

Academia like Dash and Bhole (2011) viewed the aforesaid process of influencing the real short-term rates as reflection of the short-term monetary policy, though in the long run the nominal interest rate equals the equilibrium real rate plus an adjustment factor for inflation. In order to estimate the natural rate of interest for India, they researched on the

Emerging Markets and the Global Economy
http://dx.doi.org/10.1016/B978-0-12-411549-1.00005-3

above real short-term interest rate which, when consistent with long-run output and a stable inflation rate, they term as "the natural or real rate of interest." A global perspective of the same is available in Canzoneri et al. (2012). The trio, however, accepted the difficulty in estimating the unobserved natural rate of interest, given the source of uncertainty. The intuition mentioned in Canzoneri et al. (2012) that "when an increase in aggregate demand, or a decrease in productivity, pushes inflation above its target, the policy rate should be raised above its natural rate for a period of time, raising the real rate of interest to curb the rise in inflation" is common with that given in Dash and Bhole (2011).

Keeping in view that a bank needs to maintain certain stock of liquidity in fulfillment of the SLR (statutory liquidity ratio) norm imposed by the RBI, it is imperative for the treasurer or the chief dealer of the bank to consider different options in procuring security at the time of need. The chief dealer may delegate the responsibility to the following dealers of four different products—money market products, government securities (G-secs), foreign exchange, and gold (i.e. commodity). Essentially it is a game where we can apply the alternative frameworks of imperfect competition and real option analysis and detect the solutions in terms of Nash equilibrium and various strategies.

2. THE SCENARIO

The global and domestic liquidity scenarios relevant to banks and financial institutions in India are reflected in the Economic Survey of the Ministry of Finance of the Government of India, quarterly and mid-quarter reviews of the RBI, and the reports of the credit rating agencies like CRISIL and the business solution providers like Dun and Bradstreet. As per the Ministry of Finance (2013), the post-financial-crisis stimulus led to stronger growth in 2009–2010 and 2010–2011 and the consequent boost to consumption, coupled with supply-side constraints, led to higher inflation. In the mid-quarter monetary policy review in March 2013, the Reserve Bank of India (2013a) decided to reduce the repo rate in view of an improved liquidity condition since the third quarter review in January 2013. At the same time, the RBI accepted that the inflationary potential is not conducive to growth. In the third quarter review, the Reserve Bank of India (2013b) decided to reduce the cash reserve ratio in order to inject primary liquidity. Here, the RBI Governor admitted that there was a softening of inflation that may not continue for long owing to expected hikes in administrative prices. In the beginning of the third quarter of the FY 2012–2013, CRISIL (2012) noted an increase in the wholesale price index (*WPI*) following a revision in the electricity prices, which was expected to lead to hikes in administered prices. The information about inflation in the above-mentioned report was concerned with the hikes in the prices of diesel, and chemical and food products, emanating from deficiencies in rainfall in the North-West India, which is supposed to be the largest contributor to food grain production of all regions. In this context, the Ministry of Finance (2013) opined that given the higher weightage to food in the consumer price indices (CPI), the

CPI inflation has remained close to double digits and there was a pressing need to cut government spending. For the G-sec dealers in the banks and the financial institutions, Dun and Bradstreet (2013) wrote that in the near term yields in the G-sec market are expected to remain stable with an upward bias as cash deficit in the banking system was likely to increase following the outgo of advance taxes and due to low government spending during the last month of the FY 2011–2012 with a view to curbing fiscal deficit on part of the government.

The above information motivates a dealer to consider two alternative situations of downside risk—(i) *status quo* inflation rate and (ii) increasing inflation rate. Accordingly the structure of the game would vary. In what follows after a brief overview of the literature on economic games, we shall look into the strategies of a G-sec dealer in a bank in a scenario similar to the above.

3. THE EXISTING LITERATURE ON ECONOMIC GAMES

The developments in the literature on Game Theory in Economics range from Pindyck (2013) to Neuman and Morgenstern (1944). In between the above, notable works are a few doctoral theses published by the Universities in the USA and Europe like Maredia (2010), Nayyar (2009), and Pimienta (2007); textbooks like Cooter and Ulen (2004), Gibbons (1992), Allen and Morris (1998), Shy (1995), and Pindyck (2012), and journal papers like Basu (1992, 1987). The economic application of Game Theory in most of the aforesaid literature includes an analysis of topics such as the cost of new entry and the topics in financial economics such as pricing of new investment options and analysis of political and market institutions.

4. FEATURES OF THE GAME IN DECISION MAKING OF A DEALER IN THE GOVERNMENT SECURITY DESK

4.1. Zero-Sum Game

A game is called a zero-sum game if the total pay-off is constant, i.e. one player can increase its pay-off only at the equivalent cost of the other. In this case, the total pay-off of the game remains constant. If both the players can increase their pay-offs, the total pay-off of the game increases. Then it is called a positive sum game. If one player increases its pay-off by causing more than equivalent loss to the other, the total pay-off comes down. It is called a negative sum game. The assumption of non-cooperation applies throughout the game here.

Let us consider a duopolistic market structure where there are only two banks. One is a composite public sector undertaking (PSU) bank assuming that all PSU banks merged into a single entity denoted by "CPSUB." The other is a composite private sector bank denoted by "CPrSB," with an assumption similar to the above. This assumption

Table 1 Pay-off (billion INR).

CPSUB		CPrSB	
		Disinvestment	Buy and sell
	Disinvestment	5, 2	3, 4
	Buy and sell	4, 3	2, 5

is plausible because the Indian banking industry has experienced a series of mergers between the PSU banks and between private sector banks. Ghose (2013) has reported on the Ministry of Finance encouraging mergers between PSU banks in order to create stronger PSU banks via consolidation, but in the entire industry the merger between the private sector bank the Centurion Bank of Punjab and the HDFC Bank in 2008 is the biggest till date.

When the chief dealer of the CPSUB asks the G-sec dealer to procure liquidity under inflationary circumstance, there may be the following four outcomes under the assumption of non-cooperation which are described in Table 1.

For a G-sec dealer, there are two alternatives to procure liquidity—(i) disinvesting or liquidating some of the existing dated securities and (ii) buying some profitable issues for selling at a higher price and making capital gain. The G-sec portfolio of a typical bank in India has three components—(i) held for trading (HFT), (ii) available for sale (AFS), and (iii) held to maturity (HTM). If opportunities are available for disinvesting out of either or both of HFT or AFS categories, there is no need to buy and sell. But in the absence of such opportunities, there may be an occasion for disinvesting a HTM security. In that case, the G-sec dealer is required to replenish the HTM portfolio and hence buy and sell. It is because the HTM portfolio consists of long-term securities with high coupon rates with a maximum permissible holding period before selling, i.e. 90 days (Reserve Bank of India, 2012). If there is a sound forecast about future liquidity requirements of the bank, the G-sec dealer may avail of any opportunity to ride the yield curve, given the opportunities of selling out of the HTM portfolio. In Table 1, there are four alternative outcomes with a constant aggregate pay-off equal to 7. This is called the zero-sum game.

4.2. Pure Strategy and Nash Equilibrium

Nash equilibrium with pure strategy means a player sticks to one of the alternative strategies, not any mix or combination thereof, wherefrom she does not have any incentive to deviate. Such a strategy is called the pure strategy with Nash equilibrium (Pindyck and Rubinfeld, 1995) because playing with Nash equilibrium is a rational strategy as a one-shot action in the non-cooperation frame (Risee, 2000). In Table 1, the top-left cell is Nash equilibrium for the CPSUB and the bottom-right cell is Nash equilibrium for the CPrSB.

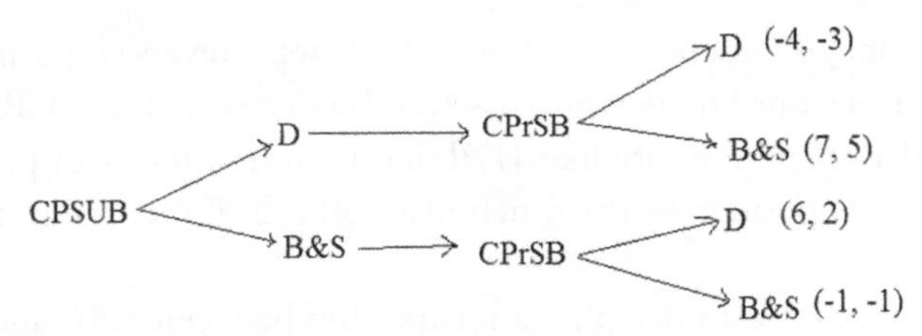

Figure 1 The Pay-off Tree.

4.3. Decision Tree and Sequential Game

The use of decision tree and sequential game is suitable in a non-cooperation setup where the CPSUB assumes that taking the first move is beneficial to itself, provided the CPrSB does the best and vice versa. There are two alternative moves that are available to each player—(i) D, i.e. disinvesting and (ii) B&S, i.e. buying and selling. Each move maximizes the pay-off of whosoever chooses it first. If the CPSUB chooses D first, then the CPrSB should instantly choose B&S in order to maximize its pay-off and vice versa. Keeping in view this specific sequence, the game is also called sequential game. If the sequence is altered, i.e. the CPrSB chooses D in response to choosing D by the CPSUB, the CPrSB causes loss to itself as well as to the competitor and vice versa. This is explained in Figure 1.

The numbers in parentheses in Figure 1 denote the pay-offs of the CPSUB and the CPrSB, respectively. This application of the decision tree was inspired by Hull (2009).

5. FORECASTING LIQUIDITY

In forecasting liquidity, there are two views. One view is forecasting liquidity in the macroeconomic system. This is related to bank reserves which in turn are related to some measure of money supply. The other view is forecasting liquidity of certain financial instruments or securities in a financial market.

As regards the macroeconomic liquidity view, we note that central banks across the countries forecast the liquidity for their economic systems as a whole. The conceptual frames are similar to what is described in Mitra and Abhilasha (2012). They opined that the range of quantitative measures of macroeconomic liquidity varies from the day-to-day liquidity provided by the central bank at one end of the spectrum to the broadest measure of monetary and liquidity aggregates at the other. For practical purposes, they described the key indicator of macroeconomic liquidity to be the liquidity adjustment facility (*LAF*) on a day-to-day basis. It may be remembered that in 1998 the Third Working Group of the RBI introduced liquidity as measures of money supply and now RBI is periodically publishing the liquidity aggregates. They divided the drivers of liquidity into two categories—autonomous factors and discretionary factors. Autonomous factors include transactions with authorized dealers, government's cash balances with the RBI, and demand for money. Discretionary factors include repo, reverse repo, market stabilization scheme operations, open market purchases, and cash reserve ratio (CRR). Here some macroeconomic drivers of liquidity like *WPI* and industrial index of production (*IIP*), etc., may be included considering the functional position of the dealer on a day-to-day basis.

In this context, we tried to decipher a relationship between *LAF* and *WPI* in India on monthly frequency because *WPI* is measured primarily on this monthly frequency. Because of the nil values of *LAF* from October 2009 to February 2010, we sliced the time series data into two samples—Sample 1: the period close to but after the crisis from June 2010 to February 2013 and Sample 2: the period during and close to the crisis from November 2007 to September 2009. We observed that there is a meager negative correlation between the two around −9% in Sample 1 and around −8% in Sample 2. The negative correlation becomes stronger to an extent of around −49% between squared *WPI* and *LAF* in Sample 1, whereas in Sample 2 it was as meager as −9%. This indicates the development of awareness on the part of the regulator about liquidity management in the phase of inflation illustrated in Figures 2 and 3. The parabolic shapes of the *LAF* in Figure 2 suggest a function of relationship of second degree. Further, since in Sample 1 all *LAF* figures are positive, we take their square roots and then we find that the negative correlation looked further up to around −73%. Thus the nature of correlation between macroeconomic liquidity and inflation depends on the nature of function.

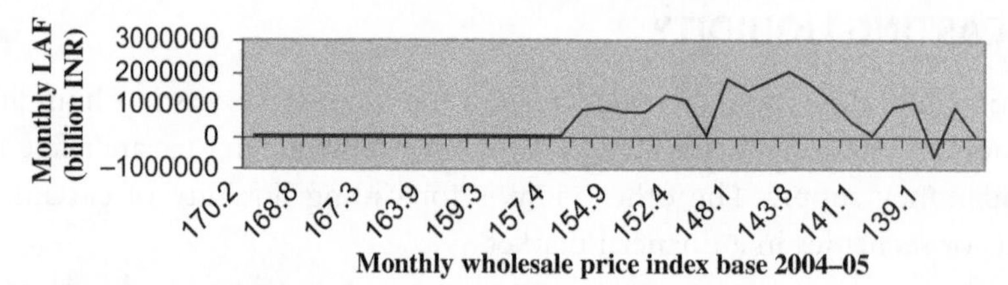

Figure 2 Bank liquidity and inflation from June 2010 to February 2013.

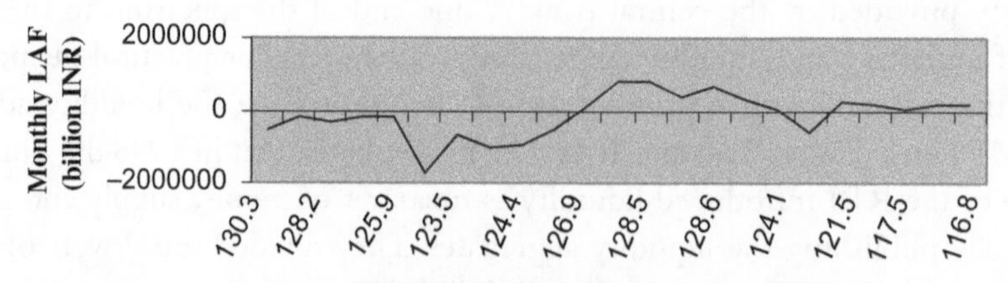

Figure 3 Bank liquidity and inflation from November 2007 to September 2009.

Figure 3 depicts a mean-reversal movement of *LAF*, as if there is no systemic liquidity stress, while Figure 2 reveals a strong response of the systemic liquidity managers to inflation. We suggest the readers carry out a similar analysis involving *IIP*.

The methods of macroeconomic liquidity forecasts may vary, e.g., the description of forecasting liquidity in the Bank of England, put forth by Gray (2008), is different than that of the Reserve Bank of India (2002). While the former takes a balancesheet approach, the latter, by way of financial and econometric modeling, produces a number of determinant relationships whereby the relevant variables like net liquidity inflows/outflows and excess liquidity reserves may be predicted. The approach of Gray (2008) resembles that of Bjerve (1957). A more recent work of Bhattacharya and Sahoo (2011) connects systemic liquidity to monetary policy. They identified the liquidity management task of the central bank to be the one of identifying the optimum monetary policy instrument. In the process they developed a simple model of liquidity management using the framework of partitioning liquidity into autonomous and discretionary factors. Given that the central banks are following an inherent rule of offsetting autonomous liquidity conditions through discretionary measures, they derived combinations of optimal policy mix and a robust sufficient condition for stabilization of market interest rates. They noted that while the aforesaid partitioning approach has been used by many EDEs in the past, its recent adoption by several advanced economies is in focus, particularly in the wake of global crisis because it demonstrated the efficacy of both the quantum channel and the rate channel in managing liquidity. They developed a model of the market for bank reserves in which the central bank uses different instruments at its disposal for stabilizing the price of liquidity. A contemporary work is Fadare (2011). Employing a linear least square model and time series data from 1980 to 2009, he studied the determinants of banking sector liquidity in Nigeria and assessed the extent to which the recent financial crises affected liquidity in deposit money banks in the country. His findings are as follows—(i) only liquidity ratio, monetary policy rate, and lagged loan-to-deposit ratio are significant for predicting the liquidity in the banking sector, (ii) decreases in monetary policy rates, liquidity ratios, volatility of output in relation to trend output, and the demand for cash, lead to increases in current loan-to-deposit ratios, and (iii) decreases in currency in circulation in proportion to banking sector deposits, and lagged loan-to-deposit ratios lead to declines in current loan-to-deposit ratios. His result suggests that during periods of economic or financial crises, banks are significantly illiquid relative to benchmarks, and at the juncture getting the right monetary policy is crucial in ensuring the survival of the banking sector. However, it may not sound unscrupulous to comment that the concern for systemic liquidity revolves around the liquidity with the banks.

Regarding the market-specific liquidity, Thomas (2006) in the Indian context maintained that liquidity of security markets reflects on the impact cost and resilience. Lower the impact cost and higher the resilience, more liquid is the security market. She found that in the Indian equity market, liquidity was robust to negative price shocks, whereas in the Indian bond market liquidity appeared to be fragile when faced with negative price shocks. National Stock Exchange (2012) explained lucidly the concept of impact cost with vivid examples. Recently Kane et al. (2011) analyzed threadbare the concept of limit order book in this context. Thomas and Shah (2006) explained the concept of security market resilience with the example of Colombo Stock Exchange. Wyss (2004) worked upon the stocks of the Swiss Market Index. Wuyts (2007) analyzed the economic forces that drive liquidity in stock markets. He investigated the impact of inter-market competition on liquidity. He considered competition between stock exchanges and included alternative trading systems. He argued that liquidity comprises several interacting dimensions: spread, depth, resiliency, and immediacy. He discussed these dimensions for a quote driven and an order driven market. He also investigated other design elements of trading system, such as transparency, anonymity, and the presence of a trading floor. Subsequently he shifted the focus from one market to the impact of inter-market competition on liquidity. In bringing together some main conclusions from the analysis, he focused on the following four beneficiaries of liquidity: traders, stock exchanges (or alternative trading systems), listed issuers, and the stability of the financial system.

Hence, what follows is discussed under varying circumstances in the stock market as to how a equality dealer of a commercial bank takes decision regarding investment.

6. DECISION MAKING OF A DEALER IN THE EQUITY DESK

The decision taker is the equity dealer belonging to non-SLR equity desk of the bank (henceforth "the dealer"). Her choice variable is how much to invest in the stocks specified by the Investment Committee headed by the treasurer. For example, the variable may be denoted by $x = x(NDTL, \sigma, w)$, x is an endogenous variable, while the net demand and time liabilities of the bank, i.e. aggregate demand and time deposits minus inter-bank deposits denoted by "*NDTL*," are determined by the economic system. Volatility of the Nifty 50 index may be denoted by σ as an environmental parameter considered to be determined outside the banking system. The ratio of the growth rate of *WPI* to the growth rate of *IIP* denoted by w is also considered to be an environmental parameter determined outside the banking system. These growth rates are published periodically by the Office of the Economic Advisor (2013). The quantum of x varies inversely with each of the above environmental parameters and directly with *NDTL*.[1] Approximately 25% of the *NDTL* in a bank is required by the Reserve Bank of India (2012) to be invested in the products approved by the RBI. These products are risk-free and considered to be the reservoirs of liquidity because of their quick convertibility into cash. These products include treasury bills, central and state government securities, gold, and cash.

[1] Hence, a plausible form of $x = \frac{kNDTL}{\sigma * w}$, where "$k$" is a the market risk appetitive parameter and can take a value from zero to 75% depending on the market risk policy of the bank, which in turn depends on the risk appetite of the bank.

The basic treatment of choice under uncertainty is given in Pindyck and Rubinfeld (1995). In a bit advanced level, in line with Gravel and Rees (1992) we suppose that the bank operates over two consecutive business days. On the day 1, the values of σ and w are known to the dealer. The dealer plans on the day 1 for the value of x on the day 2 based on her expectations about the values of σ and w on the day 2. The vector of the environmental variables $E = \sigma w$ can take a finite number of values, say n, and hence may be denoted by '$E_j' = (\sigma_j, w_j)$ for all $\forall j = 1, \ldots.., n$.[2] A combination of a specific set of the values is called a state of the system denoted by "s" since all E_js are finite the number of states is also finite. Corresponding to every "E_j" there is a unique s_j. From the dealer's viewpoint, these states are exhaustive, mutually exclusive in terms of the values of σ and w, and outside her control. This dealer may be assumed to represent all equity dealers in all banks, to distinguish between the day 1 and the day 2, and to assign a probability on the day 1 to a particular state or combination of σ and w to occur on the day 2. These probabilities may vary across the dealers but their properties like being a fraction for the occurrence of a state and zero for the simultaneous occurrence of multiple states remain the same. Since the dealers continuously interact with their peers in other banks through chatting apps on the desktop screen, smart phones and professional networks, our dealer may further be assumed to know others' state-contingent plans of choices on the day 1 for the alternative possible states on the day 2 and to not necessarily coincide her state-contingent plans with others'. For every s_j there is a unique contingent value of x, denoted by x_s and corresponding to every x_s, $\exists$ a unique probability, denoted by p_s such that the combination of p_s and x_s for some s_j may be called an outcome denoted by $\Xi = (p, x)$.[3] So preferences between alternative quanta of non-SLR equity investments imply the same between alternative outcomes. As an example we can consider a set of four alternative states $\{s_{hh}, s_{ll}, s_{hl}, s_{lh}\}$:

s_{hh}: High volatility and high inflation growth relative to industrial output growth.
s_{ll}: Low volatility and low inflation growth relative to industrial output growth.
s_{hl}: High volatility and low inflation growth relative to industrial output growth.
s_{lh}: Low volatility and high inflation growth relative to industrial output growth.

If we denote the terms "is preferred over" by the sign "$>$," for a risk-lover (and optimistic) dealer $s_{hh} > s_{hl} > s_{lh} > s_{ll}$, i.e. the investment amount would be the maximum for s_{hh}. Similarly for a risk-averse (and pessimistic) dealer the preferences may be opposite such that $s_{ll} > s_{lh} > s_{hl} > s_{hh}$. For every different state the investment quanta are different and hence outcomes are also different.

Next we shall introduce four self-validating axioms and from them we shall derive three corollaries, one lemma, and one theorem.

[2] The notation "$\forall$" means "for all."

[3] The notation "$\exists$" means "there exist" or "there exists."

6.1. Axiom I

A dealer can always prefer one macroeconomic environmental state to another or may be indifferent between two macroeconomic environmental states. The investment amounts in each state may be ordered in an ascending order such that they can be described to abound between the lowest amount denoted by x_L and the highest amount denoted by x_H, such that $\exists$ an interval $I = [x_L, x_H]$. If we define a special outcome denoted by $\Xi^{\#}$ as the choice of either the highest amount with some probability of the choice say, p_1, implying the probability of the choice of the lowest amount $1 - p_1$, the associated special outcome may be denoted by $\Xi^{\#}{}_1 = \{p_1, I\}$. Similarly for a different probability p_2, the associated outcome is, $\Xi^{\#}{}_2 = \{p_2, I\}$.

6.2. Axiom II

If p_i increases the preference for the associate outcome, $\Xi^{\#}{}_i = \{p_i, I\}$,it increases for a risk-lover equity dealer and decreases the preference for a risk-averse equity dealer. Hence the dealer is able rationally to order the outcomes in accordance with the associated probabilities and at the same she would seek the highest probability of a particular value of x_H.

6.3. Corollary I

Axiom II means $\exists$ a utility function of the dealer $u = u(p)$ with $u' > 0$. This is true if the states s_{hh}, s_{hl}, s_{lh}, and s_{ll} are complete, reflexive, transitive, continuous, and strongly monotonic, $\exists$ a continuous utility function of the dealer for all outcomes involving these sets in line with Varian (1992). If we like to theorize the utility of the dealer in line with Gravel and Rees (1992), we can consider the investment amounts on SLR and non-SLR products, respectively, as two goods and here "u" is an indirect utility function of the same subject to *NDTL* budget constraint. In order to decide the choice of the dealer, the reader may apply Roy's identity, Slutsky equation, and constrained maximization, a naive example of which is provided in the "Appendix" at the end of the chapter.

6.4. Axiom III

For any certain value of investment x_j between x_L and $x_{H,}$, $\exists$ a unique probability p_j corresponding to the outcome, $\Xi^{\#}{}_j = \{p_j, I\}$ such that the dealer is indifferent between x_j and, $\Xi^{\#}{}_j$. From this, we may derive Corollary II and a theorem.

6.5. Corollary II

It may be derived from Axiom III that for every value of x within the interval I, there exists a probability p, which we may denote as the probability function $p(x)$, where $p^1 > 0$ for a risk-lover investor and $p^1 < 0$ for a risk-averse investor.

6.6. Theorem

There should be a sizeable *NDTL* in the concerned bank which may be parked with non-SLR securities.

Proof of the Theorem

Let us consider two certain values of investments x_j and x_k and their corresponding equivalent outcomes $\Xi^{\#}{}_j$ and $\Xi^{\#}{}_j$. This means a 60% chance of occurrence of each of above certain values of investments implies a 60% chance of occurrence of each of the corresponding equivalent outcomes. Since these outcomes come with some probability, accordingly there should be a sizeable *NDTL* for the concerned bank which may be parked with non-SLR securities. This is an application from an axiom of well-behaved preference ordering in Varian (1992), if $x_j \sim x_k$ then $\rho \text{ o } x_j + (1 - \rho) \text{ o y} \sim \rho \text{ o } x_k + (1 - \rho)\text{o y}$. Now $\rho \text{ o } \Xi^{\#}{}_j + (1 - \rho) \text{ o y} \sim \rho \text{ o } \Xi^{\#}{}_k + (1 - \rho) \text{ o y}$ since $\Xi^{\#}{}_j \Leftrightarrow x_j$ and $\Xi^{\#}{}_k \Leftrightarrow x_k$., where "$\rho$" is any arbitrary probability.[4] From this, we can derive the following "Lemma."

6.7. Lemma

An equity dealer is indifferent between a certain outcome and a double outcome formed by replacing each value of investment by its equivalent special outcome.

Proof of the Lemma

As an example we may cite two situations—a dealer is indifferent between investments worth (i) $50 on the one hand and $60 or $70 with 60/40 probability on the other hand and (ii) $80 on the one hand and $160 or $50 with 65/35 probability on the other hand. Now if there is 70/30 probability of $50 or $80, she will be indifferent between it and 70–30 probability of one of the following two - (i) $60 or $70 with 60/40 probability and (ii) $160 or $50 with 65/35 probability.

6.8. Axiom IV

A risk-lover equity dealer may take double risk. Let us suppose in a certain state she invests an amount x_g in the first round and expects a capital gain g_1 where $g_1 > 0$, if her expectation is fulfilled she likes to invest further an amount equal to the portfolio value $x_g + g_1$ in the second round. Every round of investment is associated with a unique outcome. The outcome of the fist round investment is either fulfillment of expectation, i.e. $g_1 > 0$ with a probability p_{g1} or no fulfillment with the probability $1 - p_{g1}$. If her expectation is fulfilled in the first round, in the second round she would invest $x_g + g_1$ with a further expectation of capital gain $g_2 > 0$ with probability p_{g2} in order to invest $x_g + g_1 + g_2$ in the third round. This outcome associated with the second round of

[4] The symbol "o" means "multiplied by."

investment may be denoted by $\Xi^2 = (p_{g2}, x_g + g_1 - g_2)$, while the outcome associated with the above kind of double risk taking is called double outcome. It may be described as $\Xi^c = (p_{g1}, x_g - g_1, \Xi^2)$. Alternatively if we denote the probability of her positive capital gain $g > 0$ in the first round of her investment as q, the double outcome may be denoted as $\Xi^d = (q, x + g)$ because capital gain in the first round of investment means $x + g$ investment in the second round, and no gain or capital loss $g \leq 0$ in the first round means portfolio value $x - g$ with probability $(1 - q)$. Here Ξ^c may be considered to equal Ξ^d. If $\exists n$ different values of p for different values of "g" which may be defined as outcomes Ξ_h with, where $h = 1, \ldots, n$, accordingly $\exists$ probabilities θ_h's such that the average probability of getting a particular value of g is $\overline{p} = \sum_{h=1}^{n} \theta_h p_h$.

6.9. Corollary III

It may be derived from Axiom IV that the joint probability of capital gain in successive two rounds of investments is $p_{g1}p_{g2}$ because these associated outcomes are independent.

7. CONCLUSION

This chapter discussed the links between bank liquidity and inflation from the viewpoint of a government security dealer as well as an equity dealer in the front office of the treasury at a commercial bank. This chapter begins with the existing literature in the context of the background. Given the prevailing scenario, it throws light on different strategies of the G-sec dealer in the SLR desk from the game-theoretic perspective. Against the backdrop of varying macroeconomic state variables such as stock index volatility and inflation, this chapter analyzed the preferences of an equity dealer in the non-SLR desk using a number of self-validating axioms and derived therefrom three corollaries, one lemma, and one theorem. In short, the findings are (i) if there is sound forecast about future liquidity requirements of the bank, the government security dealer may have the opportunity, if any, of riding the yield curve given the choice of selling out of the HTM portfolio in the period of 90 days prescribed by the regulator; (ii) in a non-cooperative game between public sector banks merged together as a composite entity and its private sector counterpart under the above regulation as to the HTM portfolio, when the chief dealer of the composite public sector bank asks the G-sec dealer to procure liquidity under inflationary circumstance, the Nash equilibrium may consist of disinvesting in the case of composite public sector bank and, buying and selling in the case of its private sector counterpart; (iii) the decision tree and sequential game can apply to the analysis of the pay-offs in a non-cooperation game—where the composite public sector bank finds taking the first move to be beneficial to itself in response to choosing the best strategy by the rival, i.e. its private sector counterpart and vice versa; (iv) the utility function of an equity dealer in a bank is an indirect function of macroeconomic environmental state variables such as opportunity cost of holding and value at risk; (v) the probability of occurrence of some specific investment amount in equity increases with the amount for a risk-lover dealer and decreases with a risk-averse dealer; (vi) there should be a sizeable chunk of net demand and time liabilities for a bank, which may be parked with non-SLR securities because of varying probabilities of the quanta of investment conducive to variation in the macroeconomic environmental states; (vii) the joint probability of capitals gains in successive two rounds of equity investment is the product of their individual probabilities; and (viii) there is stronger liquidity management on part of the regulator in the post crisis period compared to the crisis period.

APPENDIX

The utility function of a risk-lover equity dealer is $u = u(p)$, where "p" is the probability of choice of the maximum investment amount "x." Hence $p = p(x)$. In discussing the nature of "x," let us define it in a different way more conducive to utility maximization analysis than what is already done. Let us define "x" as a function of two goods—logarithmic return and risk associated with a stock approved by the investment board of the bank. The risk of a stock is measured by volatility of the stock. The price of logarithmic return "l" is the opportunity cost or the best alternative risk-free return "R" foregone because of investment in this stock. The price of volatility "ω" is the value at risk (V) equivalent to which the market risk capital need to be maintained. The aggregate of the opportunity cost and market risk capital should not exceed the equity portion, "E" of the Tier I capital of the bank. Hence $x = x(l, \omega)$ and the budget constraint is $l \circ R + \omega \circ V \leq E$. Applying the concept of indirect utility function here it may be shown that "x" is an indirect function of "R," "V," and "E" because the choices of "l" and "ω" depend on these parameters and therefore $p = p(x)$ is also an indirect function of the same. Thus $u = u(p)$ is an indirect function of "R," "V," and "E."

REFERENCES

Allen, F., Morris, S., 1998. Finance Applications of Game Theory. Wharton Financial Institutions Centre. <http://fic.wharton.upenn.edu/fic/papers/98/9823.pdf>.

Basu, K., 1987. Modeling finitely-repeated games with uncertain termination. Economics Letters 23, 147–151

Basu, K., 1992. Collusion in finitely repeated oligopolies. International Journal of Industrial Organization 10, 595–609

Bhattacharya, I., Sahoo, S., 2011. Comparative statics of central bank liquidity management: some insights. Economics Research International 2011, 1–7. Article ID 930672. <http://www.hindawi.com/journals/econ/2011/930672/>

Bjerve, P.J., 1957. Forecasting Bank Liquidity. Income and Wealth 6, 52–77. <http://www.roiw.org/6/4.pdf>

Canzoneri, M.B., Cumby, R.E., Diba, B., 2012. Monetary policy and the natural rate of interest. Bank for International Settlement Paper No. 65. <http://www.bis.org/publ/bppdf/bispap65g_rh.pdf>.

Cooter, R., Ulen, T., 2004. Law and Economics. Pearson Education, New Delhi

CRISIL, 2012. Inflation:WPI inflation gains pace with electricity price revision. CISIL Economy First Cut. <http://crisil.com/pdf/economy/eco-insight-inflation_sept12.pdf>.

Dash, P., Bhole, L.M., 2011. Measuring the natural rate of interest for India. The Indian Economic Journal 59, 39–55

Dun and Bradstreet, 2013. RBI to cut the repo rate by 25 bps. Dun & Bradstreet's Economy Forecast, March 2013. <http://www.dnb.co.in/News_Press.asp?mid=294>.

Fadare, S., 2011. Banking sector liquidity and financial crisis in Nigeria. International Journal of Economics and Finance 3, 3–11 <www.ccsenet.org/journal/index.php/ijef/article/download/12313/8622>

Ghose, J., 2013. PSU Bank Merger Urgency. The Telegraph. <http://www.telegraphindia.com/1130107/jsp/business/story_16410477.jsp#.UVReLxdkMzM>.

Gibbons, R., 1992. Game Theory for Applied Economists. Princeton University Press, New Jersey

Gravel, H., Rees, R., 1992. Microeconomics. Prentice Hall, London

Gray, S., 2008. Liquidity Forecasting. Bank of England. <http://www.bankofengland.co.uk/education/Documents/ccbs/handbooks/pdf/ccbshb27.pdf>.

Hull, J., 2009. Options, Futures and Other Derivatives. Pearson Prentice Hall, London

Kane, D., Lieu, A., Nguyen, K., 2011. Analyzing an electronic limit order book. The R Journal 3, 64–68 <http://journal.r-project.org/archive/2011-1/RJournal_2011-1_Kane~et~al.pdf>

Maredia, K., 2010. A Study in Decision Analysis using Decision Trees and Game Theory. University of Houston-Downtown, Houston, Texas. <http://cms.uhd.edu/faculty/redlt/kizzieseniorproject.pdf>

Ministry of Finance, 2013. State of the economy and prospects. Economic Survey 2012–13. <http://indiabudget.nic.in/es2012-13/echap-01.pdf>.

Mitra, A.K., Abhilasha, 2012. Determinants of Liquidity and the Relationship Between Liquidity and Money: A Primer. Reserve Bank of India. <http://www.rbi.org.in/scripts/PublicationsView.aspx?id=14331>.

Mohan, R., 2006. Coping with Liquidity Management in India: a Practitioner's View. <http://rbidocs.rbi.org.in/rdocs/Speeches/PDFs/69613.pdf>.

National Stock Exchange, 2012. Impact Cost. <http://www.nseindia.com/products/content/equities/indices/impact_cost.htm>.

Nayyar, S., 2009. Essays on Repeated Games. Princeton University <http://www.princeton.edu/~smorris/pdfs/PhD/Nayyar.pdf>

Neuman, J., Morgenstern, O., 1944. Theory of Games and Economic Behaviour. Princeton University Press, New Jersey

Ninnan, O., 2011. RBI Increase Repo Rate, Loans to be Costlier, 25 October. The Hindu. <http://www.thehindu.com/business/Economy/rbi-increases-repo-rate-loans-to-be-costlier/article2570210.ece>.

Office of the Economic Advisor, 2013. Key Economic Indicators. <http://www.eaindustry.nic.in/Key_Economic_Indicators/Key_Economic_Indicators.pdf>.

Pimienta, J., 2007. Three Essays on Game Theory. Universidad Carlos Iii De Madrid. <http://e-archivo.uc3m.es/bitstream/10016/2532/1/tesis_gonzalez_pimienta_eng.pdf>.

Pindyck, R., 2012. Lecture Notes on Entry and Reactions to Entry. <http://web.mit.edu/rpindyck/www/Courses/ERE.pdf>.

Pindyck, R., 2013. Lecture Notes on Real Options. <http://web.mit.edu/rpindyck/www/courses.htm>.

Pindyck, R., Rubinfeld, D., 1995. Microeconomics. Prentice Hall, New Jersey

Reserve Bank of India, 2002. A Short Term Liquidity Forecasting Model for India. <http://www.rbi.org.in/scripts/PublicationReportDetails.aspx?UrlPage=&ID=287>.

Reserve Bank of India, 2012. Master Circular – Cash Reserve Ratio (CRR) and Statutory Liquidity Ratio (SLR). <http://www.rbi.org.in/scripts/BS_ViewMasCirculardetails.aspx?id=7340#2>.

Reserve Bank of India, 2013a. Mid-quarter Monetary Policy Review: March 2013. <http://www.rbi.org.in/Scripts/BS_PressReleaseDisplay.aspx?prid=28335>.

Reserve Bank of India, 2013b. Third Quarter Review of Monetary Policy 2012–13. <http://rbi.org.in/scripts/BS_PressReleaseDisplay.aspx?prid=28038>.

Risee, M., 2000. What is rational about Nash equilibrium. Synthesis 124, 361–384

Shy, O., 1995. Industrial Organization. MIT Press, Cambridge

Thomas, S., 2006. Resilience of liquidity in Indian securities markets. Economic and Political Weekly 41, 3452–3454

Thomas, S., Shah, A., 2006. Measuring Liquidity. www.cse.lk/270808/pdf/6_measuring_liquidity.pdf.

Varian, H., 1992. Microeconomic Analysis. Norton and Company, New York

Wuyts, G., 2007. Stock market liquidity: determinants and implications. Tijdschrift voor Economie en Management 52, 279–316. <https://lirias.kuleuven.be/bitstream/123456789/203006/1/PUBLISHED-VERSION-TEM_2-07_05_Wuyts.pdf>

Wyss, R., 2004. Measuring and Predicting Liquidity in the Stock Market. <ttp://www1.unisg.ch/www/edis.nsf/SysLkpByIdentifier/2899/$FILE/dis2899.pdf>.

CHAPTER 6

Demographic Transition and Savings Behavior in Mauritius

Rafael Munozmoreno*, Verena Tandrayen-Ragoobur†, Boopendra Seetanah‡, and Raja Vinesh Sannassee‡

*World Bank, Mauritius
†Department of Economics and Statistics, Faculty of Social Studies and Humanities, University of Mauritius, Reduit, Mauritius
‡Department of Finance and Accounting, Faculty of Law and Management, University of Mauritius, Reduit, Mauritius

1. INTRODUCTION

Over the last three decades, the world has witnessed a large and increasing divergence in saving rates. World saving rates have been falling since the early 1970s and the gap between industrial-country and developing-country saving rates has widened further. Within the developing world, the saving divergence has been dramatic as saving rates have doubled in East Asia, stagnated in Latin America, and collapsed in Sub-Saharan Africa (Schmidt-Hebbel and Serven, 1997). These saving disparities have been closely reflected in the respective growth performance across world regions.

Addressing the distortions that are at the root of undersaving is the key to higher long-run growth and welfare (Schmidt-Hebbel and Serven, 1997). The age composition of a country's population may be associated with its saving rate, and may therefore have consequences for its economic growth (Schultz, 2002). One explanation for such an association is that the savings rate tends to be relatively high for a birth cohort when it experiences its peak earnings, and relatively low when a cohort anticipates relatively low earnings, like during retirement. Variations in the age composition of a population thus determine variations in national savings rates, over time, holding other things equal.

Population aging has two direct effects on savings: first, aging is traditionally believed to reduce aggregate saving rates because the fraction of people that are "prime" savers will decrease and the dis-saving fraction will increase as implied by the life cycle hypothesis (LCH) by Modigliani (1966, 1970), Modigliani and Brumberg (1954a,b). This effect will lead to lower economic growth (Solow, 1956; Lee, 1994; Lee and Mason, 2007; Weil, 1997). Second, increasing life expectancy is the other important component of population aging and will lead to a higher saving rate as people anticipate a longer retirement period to be financed partly by private savings (Jorgensen and Jensen, 2010). These two effects consequently have an offsetting impact on saving and ultimately on growth. In addition, there are many possible indirect effects of aging on savings. For instance, when fewer workers must finance a growing number of elderly receiving public pensions, tax rates

Emerging Markets and the Global Economy
http://dx.doi.org/10.1016/B978-0-12-411549-1.00006-5

create distortions that lead to lower demand for leisure and, thus, positive endogenous effects on the intensity of labor supply. Alternatively, the intensity of labor supply falls when retirement ages are increased (Jorgensen, 2011).

While demographic change is occurring in almost all countries, its extent and timing differ substantially. Europe and some Asian countries have almost passed the closing stages of the demographic transition process, while Latin America and Africa are only at the beginning stages (Bloom and Williamson, 1998; UN Population Division, 2001). Mauritius is no exception to the problem of low savings and an increasingly aging population.

The Mauritian economy is one of the fastest growing economies in Sub-Saharan Africa and is classified by the World Bank as an upper-middle income country. Mauritius is thereby striving to diversify its "four-pillar" economy namely sugar, textiles, tourism, and financial services, to make it more resilient to shocks and support growth and job creation. The Mauritian government has been focusing on rebalancing growth, boosting productivity, consolidating social development and social justice, and promoting environmental protection. Real gross domestic product (GDP) grew by 4.1% in 2010, up from 3.1% in 2009 but lower than the 5.5% in 2008. Despite challenges at home and abroad, the government has maintained a steady growth path. In 2011, GDP growth remained around 4%. The standard of living in Mauritius is currently among the highest in the African region with a present real Gross National Income per capita of around USD 13,400. The Gini Coefficient stands presently at 0.39 and the poverty rate is a low 8%. Moreover, Mauritius leads Sub-Saharan Africa in economic freedom and is ranked 12th worldwide, according to the 2010 Index of Economic Freedom[1] (Heritage Foundation, 2011). For the third consecutive year, the World Bank's 2011 Doing Business report ranks Mauritius first among African economies (20th worldwide, out of the 183 economies) in terms of overall ease of doing business.

However, the low domestic savings rate remains an immense challenge and the key policy question for Mauritius is how to finance its growing economy in the medium term, especially when it is facing an aging population with very high life expectancy and low fertility rates. We first examine the macroeconomic implications of population aging on savings in Mauritius. The second contribution of the chapter is a microeconomic analysis to analyze the age-specific private saving rates in the small island economy.

The chapter is structured as follows. Section 2 reviews the literature on savings and existing work on the population-savings nexus. Section 3 provides an analysis of savings behavior in Mauritius. Section 4 sets out the two methodologies applied to analyze the macroeconomic implications of aging by constructing a macroeconomic and microeconomic model of savings. Section 5 presents new econometric evidence for Mauritius on the aging-saving relationship. Section 6 builds on the microeconomic analysis using household budget survey data and we conclude in Section 7.

[1] The Index measures economic openness, regulatory efficiency, rule of law, and competitiveness.

2. LITERATURE SURVEY

The major determinants of savings are the demographics of the particular country, the income ratios, production level of the economy, consumerism, and the increasing borrowing opportunities. Other factors relate to the price difference between the domestic goods and the foreign goods, public finance, real interest rates, and the inflation rates among others. Demographics represent an important element influencing the savings rate in developing countries. Demographic processes are determined by a demographic transition characterized by falling mortality rates followed by a decline in birth rates, resulting in population aging and a fall in the population growth rate. From a macroeconomic perspective, population aging will change the balance between capital and labor. Labor supply will become relatively scarce, whereas capital will become relatively abundant. This will drive up wages relative to the rate of return to capital, reducing households' incentives to save (if the interest elasticity of saving is positive). In addition, a decreasing labor supply reduces the demand for investment goods since less capital is needed to achieve any given capital-labor ratio.

From a microeconomic perspective, the theoretical link between demography and savings comes from the life cycle hypothesis (LCH) according to which the main motive for saving is accumulation for retirement. Standard life cycle models (Modigliani, 1966, 1970; Modigliani and Brumberg, 1954a,b) generate a strong link between the age composition of the population and private savings. The LCH assumes that individuals maximize lifetime utility by allocating lifetime discounted income to consumption in various periods of the life cycle. Similarly, Friedman's (1957) permanent income hypothesis emphasizes smoothing of consumption from a "transitory variation" in realized income. From the life cycle permanent income hypothesis, private consumption is driven by permanent income where a permanent increase in wealth boosts consumption due to its impact on expected lifetime income. An increase in consumption is predicted in each period over the remaining lifetime. The marginal propensity to consume should be equal to one in the long run, if consumers are rational and forward-looking. Young people save and old people dis-save, so that changes in the age structure of the population alter aggregate saving rates. Further, young couples may save little or dis-save when they are bringing up children, only saving in middle age for their retirement, so that aggregate savings depend not only on the balance between young and old, but on the fractions of children, of working-age adults and of the elderly (Deaton and Paxson, 2004).

The life cycle scheme has further been modified with the inclusion of an early life cycle stage of dependency, which depresses public as well as private savings. Both childhood and retirement are likely to affect savings. The demographic transition of a country is such that mortality and fertility rates' decline affects promptly the fraction of children in the population, but impacts substantially the fraction of elderly after a time, because much of the early decline in mortality occurs as infants and children survive in greater numbers

(Coale and Hoover, 1958). This framework is called the "demographic dividend," a rapid demographic transition facilitates a large increase in the rate of national savings after a decade or two, followed by a gradual peaking in savings and then an expected decline in the rate of saving after four or more decades, as an increasing share of the population retires (Higgins and Williamson, 1996; Bloom and Williamson, 1998; Mason, 2001; Birdsall et al., 2001).

In addition, children are seen as an intertemporal investment, or a mechanism for transferring resources over the life cycle of parents from a period of relatively high adult productivity to a period of relatively low productivity in old age. Samuelson (1958) concluded that parents are motivated to have children in part by the expectation that their children will help support and care for them in old age. This essential function of the family has given rise to an extensive literature of overlapping generations models of savings, intergenerational transfers, and growth. An "exogenous" reduction in fertility would motivate parents to substitute more of their resources into savings and wealth accumulation in other forms for their old age support. Becker (1981) further hypothesized on the quantity of children and the quality of children. If the quantity and quality of children are indeed substitutes, this would help to account for a negative covariation between fertility and the savings of parents allocated to investment in human capital per child (Schultz, 2002).

There are three competing hypotheses which try to explain the impact of additional children on aggregate savings (Prskawetz et al., 2007). The redistribution effect, where changes in the composition of a household, leads to a redistribution of consumption among household members, leaving both the total consumption and the rate of consumption unaffected. Second, the level effect which models an increase in the number of household members causing an increase only in the level of household consumption (Prskawetz et al., 2007). Last, the intertemporal substitution or timing effect where an increase in the number of household members results in intertemporal substitution, that is, a currently increased level of consumption is compensated by reduced consumption during other periods of time. According to the redistribution hypothesis, there is no influence of childbearing on aggregate savings. The level hypothesis implies that a decline in childbearing results in an increase in aggregate savings. Finally, the timing effect states that lower fertility reduces current consumption and increases savings to pay for future consumption. The timing effect corresponds with the life cycle model (Prskawetz et al., 2007).

Life cycle savings allow households to shift income between time periods to adapt to the path of desired expenditures. In periods when earnings exceed desired expenditures, households will save and vice versa. Consequently, savings will be highest in the middle of a person's life when saving for retirement takes place. Aggregate savings, being among the major sources of investment, depend on savings of currently working households and the dis-saving of currently retired households. According to life cycle savings, decreasing fertility influences savings for two reasons. A reduced burden of childrearing leads to less consumption and an increase of savings at the household level. This is called the dependency effect. On the other hand, reduced fertility causes population aging and, in turn, the relative number of older households increases. Since older households on average have a lower rate of saving, this again reduces savings.

A growing population, on the other hand, means that the young and saving households outnumber the old and dis-saving households, consequently a growing population leads to an increase in aggregate savings. Therefore, this second effect is called the rate of growth effect. While the dependency effect implies a negative relation between rapid population growth and savings, the growth effect implies a positive relation. Not all saving that takes place is actually due to life cycle saving. Households also conduct estate savings, which are savings for the purpose of a permanent increase in wealth. Estate savings always result in increased aggregate savings, which is not the case for life cycle savings. If a fertility decline stimulates households to allocate a higher share of their income to estate savings, then aggregate savings will increase. Within the life cycle savings framework, a decline in the number of children will increase savings according to the growth rate of aggregate income. Moreover, a lower rate of population growth results in a lower number of households engaged in life cycle savings relative to the number of households engaged in life cycle dis-savings.

The dependency effect and the rate of growth effect are both based upon the life cycle hypothesis which is fundamentally a microeconomic theory. On the macrolevel, changes in the age structure affect savings because an increase of younger age groups, for instance, increases consumption relative to production and vice versa.

The empirical relationship between age and savings has been studied using a variety of approaches with macro data for countries and microdata for households. Leff (1969) finds across 74 countries in 1964 that the log of gross savings rates is inversely related to the fraction of the population under the age of 15, and the fraction over the age of 64, while controlling for log GDP per capita, and log growth of GDP per capita in the previous 5 years. Kelley and Schmidt (1996) use the same approach for 89 countries for three decades of the 1960s, 1970s, and 1980s. They find savings rates are higher in countries with higher GDP per capita, and not significantly related to the fraction of youth and elderly in 1960s or the 1970s. However, by the 1980s the fraction of youth and elderly was negatively related to the savings rate, as predicted by the LCH model. Estimates of this model for the pooled three cross-sections reveal no relation between savings and the relative size of the two dependent age groups in the population, whereas when changes over time within country are estimated by including both country fixed effects and decade-shifters, the youth fraction is unexpectedly associated with higher savings.

Also, cross-country econometric studies using aggregate time-series data reveal correlations between saving rates and demographic structure broadly confirming LCH predictions; countries with more elderly populations tend to have lower saving rates (Graham, 1987; Koskela and Virén, 1992, and Miles, 1999). The international evidence on whether savings follow the LCH is mixed if low- and middle-income countries are also considered and highly dependent on how income is estimated. Fry and Mason (1982) propose an aggregate LC savings model that includes an interaction effect between the fraction of dependent youth and growth in income, which is expected to depress savings (Mason, 1987). Kelley and Schmidt (1996) incorporate this feature in their second set of regressions by including growth in income, the youth dependency share, and the interaction of the youth share and growth variables. The estimated savings effect of the interaction of income growth and youth dependency is negative in the cross-section regression for the 1960s, 1970s, and 1980s, and in the pooled and country fixed-effect model specifications. When they restrict their sample to low-income countries (56 out of 89 countries), the youth dependency fraction interacted with income growth is negatively associated with savings only in the 1980s, and in the pooled and fixed-effect specifications.

Microeconometric tests of the predictive power of the life cycle framework in accounting for savings behavior at the household level had even less success. The correlation of consumption and income is high in household surveys across groups of households whose head has the same age, and even within a birth cohort followed statistically over time in repeated independently drawn cross-sectional surveys. In other words, average consumption does not deviate much from average income across ages. This micro-empirical regularity is difficult to account for, because the life cycle savings framework anticipated consumption is displaced from periods of expected high income to those with expected low income (Lee and Lapkoff, 1988; Carroll and Summers, 1991; Paxson, 1996; Deaton, 1997; Schultz, 1998). As a consequence, other motivations for savings are often advanced to explain household savings data, such as precautionary or buffer-stock savings to insure against risks and the uncertainty of the individual's lifetime, and the desire of the elderly to leave a bequest to heirs (Browning and Lusardi, 1996; Deaton, 1997).

A possible explanation for the small magnitude of micro-empirical estimates of life cycle savings is because age is measured by the age of the head of household, and individuals who are not heads (or spouse of heads) are not the focus of analyses of life cycle savings behavior. If the young and old who are most likely to be dis-saving are not observed to be household heads because they live in their parents' or children's household, respectively, the convexity of the savings rate profile with respect to age may be underestimated. Although the likelihood of being a head of household may be close to one from age 30 to 50, it will be far below one among younger and older persons on whom any test of the life cycle savings hypothesis critically depends (Schultz, 1999). In conclusion, the microhousehold studies of savings have not found evidence consistent with the large negative aggregate association reported between the share of youth and elderly in a nation and the national savings rate (Mason, 2001).

Despite an extensive literature on saving behavior, several empirical issues have not been resolved conclusively, including the effects of real interest rates, demographic factors, and per capita income on private saving; the relationship between growth and saving; and the extent to which private saving offsets movements in public (dis-)saving (Aghevli et al., 1990).

3. SAVINGS TRENDS

3.1. Savings Trends for Mauritius

The early 1970s saw a rise in the average savings rate, which culminated in a peak of 34.1% in 1974. This was primarily the result of an improvement in terms of trade as sugar prices more than trebled between 1972 and 1975. The significant rise in domestic savings arising from the sugar boom provided a major source of finance for the development of EPZ and Tourism. By 1976, the uptrend in world sugar prices was reversed and in the face of serious economic difficulties in the latter half of the 1970s the average savings rate experienced a constant decline. Thus, in 1980, the average savings rate reached a historic low at 10.4%.

Two devaluations in 1979 and 1981 combined with the adoption of Structural Adjustment Programme helped ease the economic difficulties in the 1980s. It contributed to improving the savings rate, which attained 28.6% in 1986. A number of reforms in the financial sector after 1987 helped maintain the relatively high savings rate at the time. These included the liberalization of interest rates through the abolition of the minimum deposit rate and the maximum loan rate guideline; issuing of two Bank of Mauritius savings bonds to non-financial institutions; the introduction of the tax-free savings bonds by Mauritius Housing Corporation and the creation of the Stock Exchange of Mauritius.

The average savings rate fluctuated within the range of 23% and 29% during the 1990s, averaging a respectable 26.4% between the years 1990 and 2000. However, it has been in decline in recent years, falling to 24.6% in the period 2001–2005. This is comparable to the low savings levels of the early 1970s and 1980s and can be linked to the deterioration of economic conditions and the rise in consumption driven by household debt and changing consumption patterns. Also, because the savings rate is below the investment rate, this exerts demand pressures on prices and has an adverse impact on the balance of payments' current account. Table 1 below shows a decomposition of savings for the Mauritian economy across non-financial corporations, financial corporations, general government, and households from 2002 to 2007.[2] We can observe a decline in household savings and even dis-savings over these years. Savings rate has been increasing for both non-financial and financial corporations while public savings have also improved over this period.

[2] This breakdown of savings is effected by Statistics Mauritius only as from 2002 and recent data are available only until 2007.

Table 1 Breakdown on savings as a share of GDP in Mauritius from 2002 to 2007.

%	2002	2003	2004	2005	2007
Breakdown on savings as a share of GDP					
Non-financial corporations	15.02	17.88	18.98	17.51	20.89
Financial corporations	2.71	1.43	2.02	2.33	3.28
General government	0.92	−0.37	0.13	0.62	1.71
Household savings	3.15	2.40	−0.88	−4.25	−1.88

Source: Statistics Mauritius.

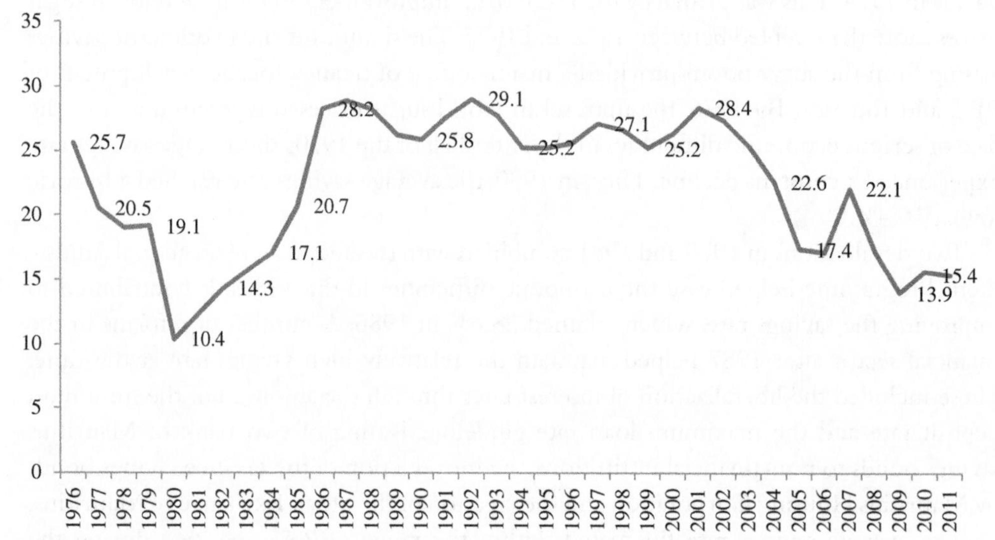

Figure 1 Gross national savings as a share of GDP (%).
Source: Statistics Mauritius.

Further, Figure 1 shows the trend in savings rate from 1976 to 2011.

It can be observed that national savings go down from the high rates of above 25%, nearing 30% in the early 1990s, and have kept declining consistently. In 2001, savings rate stood at 28.4% and has since then been on a declining trend. Savings rate was 15.4% in 2011, which is only marginally lower than the 15.5% share in 2010. Despite being far from the 20.7% figure obtained in 2007, the rate is still better than the low point experienced in 2009, when it stood at 13.6%.

As the growth of the Mauritian economy is consumption-driven, savings rate has to increase; otherwise Mauritius will face more indebtedness. Final consumption expenditure increased by 8.7% in 2011, which is higher than the 5.3% growth registered in 2010. In 2011, the figure amounted to Rs 284.6 billion, while in 2010 it stood at Rs 261.9 billion. Households' share of final consumption expenditure has been hovering

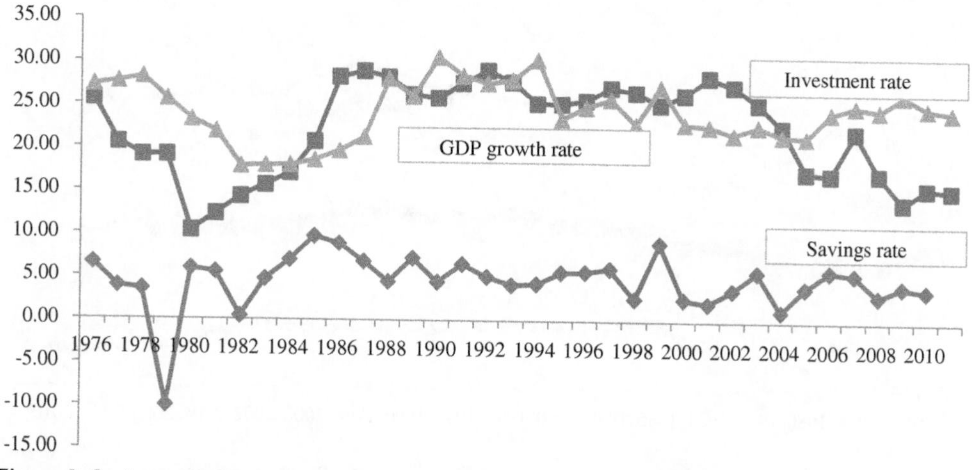

Figure 2 Savings rate, investment rate and GDP growth rate in Mauritius (1976–2011).
Source: Statistics Mauritius.

around the 85% figure, standing at 84.5% in 2011, up by 0.4 percentage point from 2010. In 2011, it stood at Rs 240.6 billion, increasing by 9.2%, while in 2010 it only managed a 5.5% increase. Expenditure in fact increased by more than compensation of employees (7.6%), implying that households are increasing their indebtedness to maintain their purchasing power. Government consumption expenditure increased, on the other hand by 5.8%, to stand at Rs 44.0 billion.

The mirror image of the declining savings rate is also a declining investment rate. Gross Domestic Fixed Capital Formation (GDFCF) has been going down and the distribution of GDFCF between public and private is a cause for concern. The resource gap, which is the difference between GDFCF and GNS, has stabilized at Rs 27.7 billion in 2011, from Rs 27.9 billion in 2010. This is, nevertheless, far from the Rs 8.8 billion gap of 2007. The resource gap is further illustrated in Figure 2.

3.2. Saving Rates for Mauritius and Comparators

From Figure 3, we note that the savings rate for Mauritius is below those of Singapore and Malaysia but even below the average of all Sub-Saharan African economies. Singapore, Malaysia as well as Mauritius benefited from a rise in savings around 2007 but then declining savings rate, may be due to unfavorable economic conditions worldwide.

4. METHODOLOGY

4.1. Macroeconomic Modeling

While the bi-variate relationships discussed above reveal important insights into the interaction between saving rate and various macroeconomic variables, it is important to bring

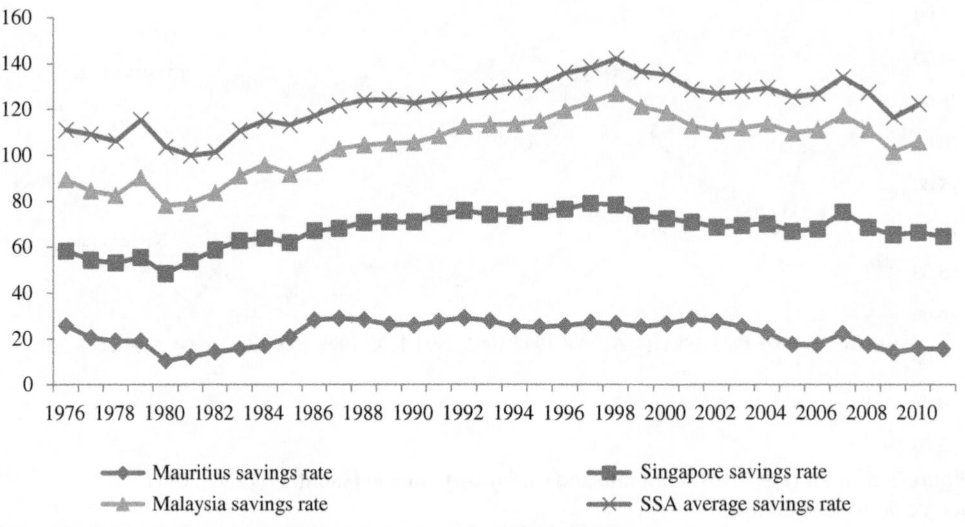

Figure 3 Comparative savings rates across countries (1976–2011).

these variables together to estimate the saving function for Mauritius with particular emphasis on the demographic situation. Higgins and Williamson (1996, 1997) estimate the relationship between a country's age composition and savings rate. Their study provides an explanation for the "East Asian Miracle," and suggests policies that facilitate the demographic transition by lowering fertility rates. These were responsible for opening a "window of economic opportunity" and yielding a "demographic dividend" driven by the changing age composition of the population, which is causally related to increasing savings rates and economic growth rates (Bloom and Williamson, 1998; Birdsall et al., 2001; Mason, 2001).

4.1.1. Model Specification

We here, assume that saving depends on four types of variables, which include income, financial development, fiscal position, and demographics. The objective is to provide a framework to address how changes in the independent variables have affected savings over the last decades in Mauritius, which will be the basis for policy interventions to boost the savings rate in the future.

The structure of the model is as follows:

$$S_t = \gamma S_{(t-1)} + \beta X_t + U_t, \tag{1}$$

where S_t is the saving rate in year t; $S_{(t-1)}$ captures the extent to which past year saving rate affect the current year saving rate; X_t is a matrix of explanatory variables in year t; and U_t is the error term. The core economic determinants of saving, X_t, include the annual rate of growth of gross domestic product, age-dependency ratio, the share of urban population in total population, the ratio of domestic credit to the private sector to GDP, and the share of government expenditure to GDP. The estimation results are based on ordinary least square regressions and the VAR approach.

4.1.2. Data Source and Variable Definition

Data Source

Data are collected from the World Bank Development Indicators, 2012 and Statistics Mauritius. Equation (1) above is estimated using time-series data annual data for 1975–2011 for Mauritius. The estimation period was determined largely by the availability of adequate data on all variables.

Variable Definition

Income Growth There is strong empirical evidence about the positive association between saving and growth across countries and time. However, the issue of the direction of causality between the two is unsettled. On the one hand, observers suggest that high growth rates tend to drive high saving rates. The basic argument is that rapid per capita growth triggers saving as income rises faster than consumption. Modigliani (1970), using the life cycle hypothesis, argues that a higher growth rate would, with no changes in the saving rate, increase aggregate saving because it would increase the aggregate income of those working relative to those who do not. On the other hand, growth is a function of investment in physical and human capital, and since investment is financed from postponed consumption (i.e., saving), then saving engenders growth (Levine, 1997).

Put differently, saving provides the capital needed for investment in human and physical infrastructure and thus itself (through increased capital accumulation) fuels growth. Neoclassical models such as Solow (1956) suggest that increase in saving generates higher growth only in the short run, while in the long run economic growth is only a function of technological progress and growth of the labor force. Rodrik (2000) empirically examines this issue of causality and its short-versus long-run implications, and finds that while growth transitions (arising from improved terms of trade) increase domestic investment and result in permanent increases in saving, saving spurts affect positively growth only temporarily. Regardless of the direction of causality, saving and growth feed in each other, resulting in multiple growth-saving equilibria.

In line with Lahiri (1989) for East Asian countries and Muhleisen (1996), among others, we expect economic growth to lead to both higher public and private saving rates.

Past Savings Saving rates show inertia, that is current and past rates of saving are serially correlated even when controlling for other factors. The inclusion of a lagged dependent variable, in this case the savings rate from the previous year, S_{t-1}. Savings rates for individuals are expected to gradually adapt to new prevailing conditions, and may not achieve new equilibrium values in precisely a year. The temporal spilling over into the next time period of these adjustments implies that whatever "errors" are present in the savings equation in one year will not be independent of the error in savings in the prior (or following) years.

Demography Demographics present another group of factors that impact savings decisions. Size, age, and composition of households influence saving behaviors. Models based on Modigliani's life-cycle hypothesis predict that saving follows an inverted U-shaped pattern, i.e., saving rate is high at middle age, and low at young and old ages. Societies during the peak of demographic transitions (when the proportion of prime age workers is the highest) will save more than societies with a larger dependency ratio Modigliani (1970). Empirical evidence at international and single country level confirms the hypothesis that high dependency ratios have a negative effect on private saving rates (Loayza et al., 2000). This finding suggests that countries in a process of demographic transition may experience strong short-term shifts in saving rates. The age-dependency ratio (the fraction of the population under the age of 16 and over the age of 64) is used as a determinant of saving and in line with other studies like Lahiri (1989) and Muhleisen (1996), among others; we expect the usual negative relationship between the two variables. In our regression for Mauritius, we use the age-dependency ratio (percentage of working-age population) to account for demographics.

Urban population that is the share of urban population to the total population of the Mauritian economy is also used. The urbanization ratio bears significant influence on saving rates. This suggests that urban centers not only offer access to jobs and higher incomes, but also attract people with higher propensity to save in conventional ways. Moreover, capturing the informal saving in rural areas, channeling it into conventional forms, and consequently, productive investment, would increase the rate of return for the individual saver.

Level of Financial Development Economic theory suggests that financial development may influence saving behaviors in ambiguous ways (Bandiera et al., 2000). The ambiguity comes from the net effect of several simultaneous channels through which financial development could affect saving. For example, it is well established in the literature that financial repression through its below market (repressed) interest rates would exert negative impact on the intermediation of financial resources and consequently affect negatively the economy, including the saving rate (McKinnon, 1973 and Shaw, 1973). However, financial liberalization (via raising interest rates in the absence of financial repression) could encourage consumer and housing lending, and suppressed saving by allowing individuals to access more resources and consume at a higher level than they would otherwise. At the same time, financial liberalization (again via increase in interest rates) can increase the level of saving as it makes saving returns more attractive than current consumption. Financial development also enriches the availability of instruments for saving which could ultimately influence savings in a positive way, too.

Similarly, interest rate fluctuations can impact saving through two separate channels (the income channel and the substitution channel), with opposite effects on agents' saving behaviors. The net impact on saving will depend on the relative size of each of the effects. The former works its way as follows: a real interest rate increase makes individuals more prone to consume than save, as it would positively affect the individual disposable income. The latter, however, suggests that higher effective interest rates would increase saving if the individuals are willing to postpone current consumption for high returns, and thus would provide the incentive to save. If the real interest rate affects saving negatively, the income effect will be exerting more influence than the substitution effect, and vice versa. Financial sector variables in our analysis are proxied by either the share of domestic credit to the private sector in GDP or the real interest rate on deposits.

Government Expenditure Saving decisions are affected by changes in government spending on public goods or the level of taxes as such changes affect the demand for the economy's output of goods and services. In turn, the effect of changes in the supply of public goods on saving decisions depends on the degree of substitutability between private and public goods. Theoretically, a permanent rise in government saving will be fully offset by a corresponding reduction in private saving, leaving national saving unchanged, that is the Ricardian equivalence. Empirically, however, the hypothesis does not hold, finding that the offset is often only partial (Lopez et al., 2000). Hence, fiscal instruments can influence the direction of saving rates.

We use the share of government expenditure to GDP as a proxy for the government sector. The higher the government expenditure, the lower the level of public savings in the economy, thus postulating a negative relationship.

4.2. Microeconomic Modeling

4.2.1. Survey Data

We use data from Household Budget Survey (HBS) conducted in 2 years 2001/2002 and 2006/2007. The HBS 2001/02 covers a sample of 6720 households, out of an estimated 300,000 private households in the country. Similarly the HBS 2006/07 surveys a sample of 6720 households, out of an estimated total 335,000 households. Each sample was selected to be representative of all households in the country through a stratified two-stage design with probability proportional to size. The survey questionnaire covers information about the household and household member characteristics such as demographics, education; family size, occupation, expenditures; assets and housing conditions among others. We use the Ordinary Least Squares estimation technique for our empirical analysis.

4.2.2. Methodology

We use a measure of household saving built on the information on income and expenditure flows provided by the HBS database. We compare the average monthly income of households and their consumption expenditures, and evaluate the part of their income that households can save. In order to identify which factors explain household saving, we estimate different models. A reduced-form approach is adopted, taking into account a variety of saving determinants identified in the literature (Edwards, 1996; Loayza et al., 2000; Schmidt-Hebbel and Servén, 2000). The estimations are undertaken using Ordinary Least Squares after some robustness checks.

Model Specification

Our specification includes as dependent variable savings as a share of income. The econometric equation is as follows:

$$\ln\left(\text{savincome}_i\right) = \alpha + \beta_1 HH_i' + \beta_2 X_i' + \varepsilon_i, \tag{2}$$

where the dependent variable $\ln\left(\text{savincome}_i\right)$ is savings behavior of the head of household (that is the ratio of savings to income), HH_i' denotes a vector of dummies for different types of households and X_i' is a vector including the characteristics of the household and the profile of the head of household. ε_i is a random error assumed to be independent and identically distributed. Multiple regression analysis is carried out to find determinants of household savings.

The list of determinants is the monthly household income of the household head; the gender of the household head; age and age-squared of the household head, the household size; the activity status of the household that is whether the household is employed, unemployed, self-employed, or retired and the location of the household that is district dummies.

4.2.3. Data Analysis

In this section, we analyze the income distribution and consumption pattern of all households.

Income Pattern A comparison with poor households is also given (as per the definition of Statistics Mauritius). The income used in our analysis refers to the total household resources which comprises mainly income from employment, transfers, property, and imputed rent that is, an equivalent rental value of non-renting households. It should also be pointed out that the income refers to the income at current prices at both 2001/02 and 2006/07 HBS. In order to allow comparison over time, we have adjusted for price increase from 2001/02 to 2006/07.

In 2006/07, the majority (around 87%) of poor households derived a monthly income less than Rs 10,000 compared with 17% for all households. Comparison over time shows that the percentage of poor households deriving an income higher than Rs 7,500 increased from 11% in 2001/02 to 45% in 2006/07 (see Table 2).

In 2006/07, the average monthly household income of poor households stood at Rs 7,055, compared with Rs 22,242[3] for all households, thus showing that the income

[3] Average exchange rate is 1 USD= Rs 30.

Table 2 Distribution (%) of all households by income class, HBS 2001/02 and 2006/07.

Monthly household disposable income (Rs)	2001/02		2006/07	
	Households (%)	Total income (%)	Households (%)	Total income (%)
Under 3,000	3.5	0.5	2.1	0.2
3,000 to <4,000	3.2	0.8	1.7	0.3
4,000 to <5,000	3.5	1.1	2.7	0.6
5,000 to <6,000	5.0	1.9	2.8	0.8
6,000 to <7,000	6.6	3.0	3.9	1.3
7,000 to <8,000	6.8	3.5	3.9	1.5
8,000 to <9,000	7.3	4.4	4.7	2.1
9,000 to <10,000	6.7	4.5	5.1	2.5
10,000 to <12,000	11.8	9.0	10.7	6.1
12,000 to <14,000	9.2	8.4	9.7	6.6
14,000 to <16,000	7.3	7.6	9.1	7.2
16,000 to <20,000	9.8	12.2	12.1	11.3
20,000 to <25,000	7.6	11.8	10.5	12.3
25,000 to <30,000	4.4	8.5	6.5	9.4
30,000 to <35,000	2.5	5.7	3.8	6.4
35,000 to <40,000	1.5	3.9	3.0	5.8
40,000 & over	3.3	13.2	7.7	25.5
Total	**100.0**	**100.0**	**100.0**	**100.0**

Source: Statistics Mauritius, 2007.

Table 3 Average monthly household income (Rs) of poor households and all households, HBS 2001/02 and 2006/07.

	Average monthly household income		Percentage increase 2001/02 to 2006/07	
	2001/02	2006/07	%	%
Poor households	5,078	7,055	38.9	3.5
All households	16,642	22,242	33.6	−0.5

Source: Statistics Mauritius, 2007.

for all households was more than three times higher than that for poor households. A similar situation is observed in 2001/02. However, comparison of data from 2001/02 to 2006/07 shows that the average monthly household income of poor households grew by 38.9% against 33.6% for all households. Removing the effect of change in prices over the five-year period, the income of poor households grew by 3.5% while that of all households dropped by 0.5% (see Table 3).

Table 4 Average monthly household income (Rs) of poor households and all households by source of income, HBS 2001/02 and 2006/07.

	2001/02		2006/07	
	Poor households	**All households**	**Poor households**	**All households**
Paid employment	2,152	10,258	2,906	13,463
Self-employment	886	2,592	1,140	2,928
Transfers	1,100	1,562	1,698	2,630
Other income*	977	2,693	1,342	3,603
Average monthly gross household income	5,115	17,105	7,086	22,624
Deductions	37	463	31	382
Average monthly household income	5,078	16,642	7,055	22,242

Source: Statistics Mauritius, 2007.
*Income includes property income, imputed rent for non-renting households, and income from own produced goods and services.

Income from paid employment represented the main source of income for both poor and all households (see Table 4). The share of income from paid employment over total gross income stood at 41.0% for poor households and 59.5% for all households. After removing the effect of price changes during the five-year period, income from paid employment grew by 0.6% for poor households but dropped by 2.2% for all households.

Transfers (income from social security benefits, pension from employer, alimony, allowances from parents and relatives, etc.) constituted the second main source of income for the poor. The share of transfer income over total income represented 24.0% for poor households against 11.6% for all households. Removing the effect of price changes over the five-year period, transfer income grew by 15% for poor households against 25% for all households. On average, female-headed poor household earned less income than male-headed household in both 2001/02 and 2006/07. Between 2001/02 and 2006/07, income of male-headed and female-headed household increased by around 37% and 40%, respectively.

Expenditure Pattern In 2006/07, 41.7% of the poor households spent less than Rs 5000 per month compared with 9.8% for all households. On the other hand, only 12.0% of the poor households spent Rs 10,000 or more per month compared with 56.5% for all households. Comparison over time shows that the percentage of poor households spending at least Rs 5000 increased from 31.8% in 2001/02 to 58.3% in 2006/07. The corresponding percentage for all households increased from 79.3% to 90.2%. It should

Table 5 Distribution (%) of poor households and all households by consumption expenditure class, HBS 2001/02 and 2006/07.

Consumption expenditure class (Rs)	2001/02		2006/07	
	Poor households	All households	Poor households	All households
Below 2,500	22.8	3.8	7.3	1.3
2,500 to <5,000	45.4	16.9	34.4	8.5
5,000 to <7,500	20.5	23.7	31.1	15.6
7,500 to <10,000	7.5	19.2	15.2	18.1
10,000 to <12,500		12.8	5.5	15.2
12,500 to <15,000	3.8	7.9	6.5	10.3
15,000 and above		15.7		31.0
Total	100.0	100.0	100.0	100.0
Average monthly* household consumption expenditure	4,384	10,220	6,500	14,300

Source: Statistics Mauritius, 2007.
*The expenditure figures for 2001/02 have not been adjusted for infrequently purchased items such as air-tickets, household appliances, etc., while for 2006/07 an adjustment has been made.

be also pointed out that the proportion of poor households spending Rs 10,000 or more increased from 3.8% to 12.0% while for all households, the corresponding percentage increased from 36.4% to 56.5% (see Table 5).

In 2006/07, 41.7% of the poor households spent less than Rs 5,000 per month compared to 9.8% for all households. On the other hand, only 12.0% of the poor households spent Rs 10,000 or more per month compared with 56.5% for all households. Comparison over time shows that the percentage of poor households spending at least Rs 5,000 increased from 31.8% in 2001/02 to 58.3% in 2006/07. The corresponding percentage for all households increased from 79.3% to 90.2%. It should be also pointed out that the proportion of poor households spending Rs 10,000 or more increased from 3.8% to 12.0% while for all households, the corresponding percentage increased from 36.4% to 56.5%.

From Table 6 below, we note that expenditure of households is mainly concentrated in food items and non-alcoholic beverages. Transport is the next expenditure item of Mauritian households (15.2% in 2006/07 compared with 13.9% in 2001/02). This may have declined over the years with free transport facilities provided to students and the elderly. Housing water, electricity, and gas also have a high expenditure share.

On average, all households spent 50% more on food than poor households (Rs 4,500 against Rs 3,000). Also, the expenditure of all households on clothing and footwear, health,

Table 6 Adjusted average monthly household consumption expenditure by COICOP division—2001/02 and 2006/07 HBS.

Division	2001/02		2006/07	
	Rs	%	Rs	%
1. Food and non-alcoholic beverages	3,401	29.9	4,504	29.7
2. Alcoholic beverages and tobacco	979	8.6	1,448	9.5
3. Clothing and footwear	686	6.0	803	5.3
4. Housing, water, electricity, gas, and other fuels	1,094	9.6	1,492	9.8
5. Furnishing, household equipment, and routine household maintenance	909	8.0	1,015	6.7
6. Health	321	2.8	466	3.1
7. Transport	1,583	13.9	2,312	15.2
8. Communication	359	3.1	568	3.7
9. Recreation and culture	607	5.3	759	5.0
10. Education	273	2.4	510	3.4
11. Restaurants and hotels	567	5.0	680	4.5
12. Miscellaneous goods and services	610	5.4	631	4.2
Total	11,390	100.0	15,188	100.0

Source: Statistics Mauritius, 2007.

education, and transport was around 3–5 times that of poor households. Compared with all households, poor households had larger shares of their expenditure on "food and non-alcoholic beverages" (46% against 32%) and "housing, water, electricity, gas, and other fuels" (15% against 11%) in 2006/07.

Household Debt In 2006/07, the percentage of indebted households, that is households having made at least one loan repayment, is estimated at 46% for all households against 20% for poor households. On the average, poor indebted households disbursed Rs 1,401 per month on loan repayment against Rs 4,353 for all households. The highest loan repayment for the poor households was on housing (Rs 2,491), whereas for all households the highest loan repayment was on motor vehicle (Rs 4,036) (see Table 7).

5. FINDINGS—MACROECONOMIC MODELING

5.1.1. OLS Regression

Table 8 presents the results of the estimated savings function for Mauritius. The results fit the expected direction of relationship.

The estimation results suggest that demography plays a very important role in gross savings for Mauritius. Models based on Modigliani's life cycle hypothesis predict that saving follows an inverted U-shape pattern, i.e., saving rate is high at middle age, and low

Table 7 Average monthly loan repayment for poor indebted households and all indebted households by selected item of debt, HBS 2006/07.

Item of debt	Poor households		All households	
	Percentage of indebted poor households	**Average household debt (Rs)**	**Percentage of indebted poor households**	**Average household debt (Rs)**
Housing	26.1	2,491	54.7	3,891
Furniture	25.9	670	14.8	1,214
Audio and household appliances	40.9	633	27.9	1,133
Motor/vehicles	0.0	0	11.6	4,036
Other loan	29.8	923	40.0	2,757

Source: Statistics Mauritius, 2007.

at young and old ages. Societies during the peak of demographic transitions (when the proportion of prime age workers is the highest) will save more than societies with a larger dependency ratio. Empirical evidence at international and single country level confirms the hypothesis that high dependency ratios have a negative effect on private saving rates (Loayza et al., 2000). Our finding in column (1) is in line with Modigliani's life cycle hypothesis, which suggests that a one percentage point rise in dependency ratio reduces savings by 0.40 percentage point.

We also use the share of urban population in total as a proxy of these demographic changes. The variable is statistically significant showing that a one percentage point increase in the share of urban population would result in 0.015 percentage point increase in savings as a share of GDP, all other variables held constant. It is interesting to note that urbanization carries a positive and statistically significant sign for Mauritius (similar result found by Vincelette, 2006 for Pakistan; Lopez et al., 2000). The explanation may be related to income and wealth as people move to the cities for jobs and enhanced earning opportunities. A complementary explanation could rest on the higher propensity of the rural population to save in informal non-financial instruments, left out of the formal financial system. In addition, access to saving instruments may be larger in urban centers than in rural areas.

To test for persistence, we use the lagged saving as an independent variable. The coefficients are positive and highly significant. This implies that previous period saving influences current period saving in Mauritius. Further, GDP growth is found to be positive and statistically significant determinant of savings, holding all other variables constant. A 1% increase in the annual growth rate is expected to add 0.35% to savings as a share of GDP (column (1) in Table 8). In addition, the financial sector variable (proxied by the share of domestic credit to the private sector in GDP) affects the savings rate in Mauritius in a statistically significant way. An increase in the share of private sector credit

Table 8 OLS regression of savings function for Mauritius from 1975 to 2011.

	(1)	(2)
Dependent variable	**Gross savings as a share GDP (%)**	
Independent variables	**Coefficient**	**Coefficient**
Age-dependency ratio (% of working-age population)	−0.40	–
	(1.65)*	–
Urban population as a share of total population	–	0.015
	–	(3.27)***
GDP growth (%)	0.35	0.33
	(1.90)*	(2.03)*
Real rate of interest (%)	0.31	0.24
	(2.87)***	(2.36)**
Domestic credit to public sector as a share of GDP (%)	−0.15	−0.32
	(2.46)**	(3.86)***
Government expenditure as a share of GDP (%)	−1.19	−1.63
	(2.37)**	(3.75)***
Lagged gross savings as a share of GDP (%)	0.67	0.59
	(8.39) ***	(8.08)***
Constant	46.41	−29.89
	(2.91)***	(1.75)*
R-squared	0.91	0.93
Number of observations	30	30

Absolute *t*-ratios are in brackets.
*Significant at 10%.
**Significant at 5%.
***Significant at 1%.

in output is associated with a decrease in domestic saving as a share GDP, all other things held constant. A percentage point increase in domestic credit to the private sector would lead to around 0.32 percentage point decrease in the domestic savings, all other things being equal. This result is particularly important for Mauritius, given the rising corporate credit expansion and the rapid asset price appreciation that have created a downward pressure on saving.

The sign of deposit real interest rate elasticity of saving is positive, implying that the substitution effect is stronger than the income effect. There is a statistically significant relationship between the two variables, suggesting that households and corporations react rationally to movements of the interest rates. Lastly, government expenditure as a share of GDP is negative and statistically significant, showing that increased spending by the state leads to declining public savings.

5.1.2. A VAR Approach

In fact, the static single equation framework often adopted by an overwhelming number of studies fails to take into account the presence of dynamic feedback among relevant variables. Accordingly, we opted to use a VAR approach to study the relationship between transport capital and poverty reduction. Such an approach does not impose an a priori restriction on the dynamic relations among the different variables. It resembles simultaneous-equation modeling in that several endogenous variables are considered together.

However, before that we tested for the time-series properties of our data series. The Augmented Dickey-Fuller (ADF) (1979) and Phillips-Perron (PP) (1988) unit-root tests reveal that our variables are all integrated of order 1($I(1)$) and are thus stationary in first difference. Analysis of cointegration among the six variables was then undertaken using the Johansen Maximum Likelihood procedure and is based on a VAR of order 2, suggested by the Schwarz Bayesian criterion (SBC). Both the Maximum Eigenvalue test and the Trace test reveal the presence of one cointegrating vector. The estimated cointegrating vector, normalized on output, and the estimated adjustment parameters are presented in Table 9 below.

The VAR results are as a prior expectation and are along the same line as the results based on the OLS estimation technique. In addition, to capture short-run determinants of savings, a Vector Error Correction model was formulated, in the presence of cointegration. The results are overall similar to those of the long run in terms of significance and sign, although lower coefficients are observed. This may be explained by the fact that determinants of savings may take some time to have their full effects. Moreover, the significant error correction term obtained implies the presence of dynamism in savings modeling. (Full set of results can be obtained upon request.)

6. FINDINGS—MICROECONOMIC MODELING

Table 10 indicates the results for household saving behavior. In 2006/07, income plays an important role in determining household saving as the desire and ability to save depends on having more than the resources dedicated basic needs (Carpenter and Robert, 2002). Further, household size is considered as an important determinant of household saving behavior at the microeconomic level. On one hand, having more children can induce parents to save more as a way to finance their future education, for instance. On the other hand, it can constrain parents to decrease their saving because of higher household consumption. We find that the household size positively affects saving. An additional member in the household significantly induces household saving.

In addition, gender is identified as an important variable in the saving household behavior. Our results show that female heads of households tend to save more than their male counterparts. By gender analysis this is relevant because women usually save more

Table 9 Long-run estimates of the VAR model savings function for Mauritius from 1975–2011.

	(1)	(2)
Dependent variable	**Gross savings as a share GDP (%)**	
Independent variables	**Coefficient**	**Coefficient**
Age-dependency ratio (% of working-age population)	−0.65	–
	(1.69)**	–
Urban population as a share of total population	–	0.012
	–	(3.12)***
GDP growth (%)	0.39	0.27
	(1.96)*	(2.01)*
Real rate of interest (%)	0.24	0.28
	(2.36)***	(2.21)**
Domestic credit to public sector as a share of GDP (%)	−0.18	−0.25
	(2.27)**	(3.22)***
Government expenditure as a share of GDP (%)	−1.01	−1.35
	(2.28)**	(3.16)***
Lagged gross savings as a share of GDP (%)	0.59	0.47
	(5.45) ***	(5.23)***
Constant	34.34	−7.11
	(2.34)**	(1.88)*
Number of observations	30	30

Absolute t-ratios are in brackets.
*Significant at 10%.
**Significant at 5%.
***Significant at 1%.

than men (with their children's education in mind) and manage their saving more actively: "the savings strategies of men and women are very different; women (…) manage their saving at any time between consumption needs, social needs and economic activity" (Goldstein and Barro, 1999). Following the life cycle hypothesis, we assume age will have consequences on the household saving behavior. Age and age-squared are included to test this hypothesis. Saving exhibits a hump-shaped relationship with respect to age but the results are not significant.

7. CONCLUSION

An aging population is an inevitable consequence of the demographic transition. Economic behavior and macroeconomic outcomes change both systematically and endogenously with aging. Therefore, aging countries are bound to experience pressure on fiscal sustainability, while saving and investment are risking falling short of what is needed

Table 10 Determinants of household savings for HBS 2001/02 and 2006/07.

	(1) HBS 2001/02	**(2) HBS 2006/07**
Dependent variable	**Savings as a ratio of income**	
Independent variables	**Coefficient**	**Coefficient**
Age	0.002	−0.012
	(0.21)	(1.68)
Age^2	0.0001	0.0001
	(0.52)	(1.19)
Male	−0.028	−0.141
	(0.29)	(2.37)*
ln income	0.009	0.667
	(0.31)	(15.97)**
Married	−0.217	−0.108
	(2.84)**	(2.31)*
Widowed	−0.204	−0.028
	(1.67)	(0.33)
Divorced	−0.085	0.035
	(0.76)	(0.45)
Family size	0.082	−0.058
	(4.62)**	(5.51)**
Employed	−0.025	−0.126
	(0.22)	(1.96)
Self-employed	0.124	−0.814
	(1.06)	(9.54)**
Retired	−0.026	−0.342
	(0.20)	(4.78)**
Port Louis	0.029	−0.045
	(0.41)	(0.55)
Pamplemousses	−0.210	−0.079
	(2.78)**	(1.10)
Riviere Du Rempart	−0.236	−0.042
	(3.03)**	(0.55)
Flacq	−0.144	0.016
	(2.01)**	(0.23)
Grand Port	−0.231	0.008
	(3.13)**	(0.11)
Savanne	−0.242	0.003
	(2.16)*	(0.04)
Plaine Wilhems	−0.243	−0.154
	(3.66)**	(2.34)*

(Continued)

Table 10 (Continued)

	(1) HBS 2001/02	(2) HBS 2006/07
Dependent variable	**Savings as a ratio of income**	
Independent variables	**Coefficient**	**Coefficient**
Moka	−0.261	−0.048
	(2.03)*	(0.60)
Black River	−0.174	0.046
	(1.99)*	(0.67)
Constant	0.078	−5.410
	(0.25)	(16.55)**
R^2	0.02	0.29
N	6717	4888

Robust standard errors are in brackets.
*significant at 5%;
**significant at 1%.

to keep capital accumulation, wealth, and welfare at desirable levels. Sufficient saving is important for an economy in order to generate a high income per capita. Our macroeconomic findings reveal that high dependency ratios have a negative effect on saving rates. Our macroeconomic results are in line with Modigliani's life cycle hypothesis, which suggests that a one percentage point rise in dependency ratio reduces savings by 0.40 percentage point. We also observe a positive influence of lagged savings and GDP growth on current savings. A good economic performance and past savings behavior influence positively present savings. In addition, the financial sector variable affects the saving rate in Mauritius in a statistically significant way. An increase in the share of private sector credit in output is associated with a decrease in domestic saving as a share GDP, all other things held constant. This result is particularly important for Mauritius, given the rising corporate credit expansion and the rapid asset price appreciation that have created a downward pressure on saving.

Further, household savings are a crucial determinant of the supply of funds for investment. For low-income countries, financial development is likely to have important implications for economic growth. By using an original survey, this chapter presents a micro econometric analysis of the saving determinants in Mauritius. The results obtained are mostly in accordance with previous findings in the empirical literature on saving in developing economies. In line with Gibson and Scobie (2001), we find that income significantly explains the cross-sectional variation of the saving behavior of households in Mauritius. Indeed, income happens to be among the prevalent determinants of saving behavior, but alone it is unlikely to explain the time trend in the macroeconomic picture of household saving. In regard to the household size, an additional member increases the saving level in the household. To test the life cycle hypothesis, we have considered the age but the results are not significant. Our findings also indicate that Mauritian female-headed households save more than male-headed households.

REFERENCES

Bijan, A., Boughton, J., Montiel, P., Villanueva, V., Woglom, G., 1990. The role of national saving in the world economy: recent trends and prospects. IMF Occasional Paper No 67.

Bandiera, O., Caprio, G., Honohan, P., Schiantarelli, F., 2000. Does financial reform raise or reduce saving? Review of Economics and Statistics 82 (2), 239–263

Becker, G.S., 1981. A Treatise on the Family. Harvard University Press, Cambridge MA

Birdsall, N., Kelley, A.C., Sinding, S.W., 2001. Population Matters. Oxford University Press, Oxford

Bloom, D.E., Williamson, J.G., 1998. Demographic transition and economic miracles in emerging Asia. World Bank Economic Review 12 (3), 419–455

Browning, M., Lusardi, A., 1996. Household savings: micro theories and micro facts. Journal of Economic Literature 34 (4), 1797–1855

Carpenter, S.B., Robert, T.J., 2002. Household participation in formal and informal savings mechanisms: evidence from Pakistan. Review of Development Economics 6 (3), 314–328

Carroll, C.D., Summers, L.J., 1991. Consumption growth parallels income growth. In: Bernheim, B.D., Shoven, J.B. (Eds.), National Savings and Economic Performance. University of Chicago Press, Chicago, pp. 305–343

Coale, A.J., Hoover, E.M., 1958. Population Growth and Economic Development in Low Income Countries. Princeton University Press, Princeton, NJ

Deaton, A., 1997. The Analysis of Household Surveys, Baltimore. Johns Hopkins University Press, MD

Deaton, A.S., Paxson, C., 2004. Mortality, income, and income inequality over time in britain and the United States. NBER chapters. In: Perspectives on the Economics of Aging. National Bureau of Economic Research Inc., pp. 247–286

Dickey, D.A., Fuller, W.A., 1979. Distribution of the estimators for autoregressive time series with a unit root. Journal of the American Statistical Association 74, 427–431

Edwards, S., 1996. Why are Latin America's savings rates so low? An International Comparative Analysis, Journal of Development Economics 51 (1), 5–44

Friedman, M., 1957. A Theory of the Consumption Function. Princeton University Press, Princeton NJ

Fry, M.J., Mason, A., 1982. The variable rate of growth effect of the life cycle savings model. Economic Enquiry 20, 426–442

Gibson J., Scobie G., 2001. Household Saving Behaviour in New Zealand: A Cohort Analysis, Working Paper 01–18, New Zealand Treasury.

Goldstein, G., Barro, I., 1999. Etude sur le rôle et l'impact des services et produits d'épargne du secteur informel et des institutions de microfinance en Afrique de l'Ouest, PNUD-FENU, Unité Spéciale pour la Microfinance (SUM), MicroSave-Africa, mimeo.

Graham, J.W., 1987. International differences in saving rates and the life cycle hypothesis. European Economic Review 31 (8), 1509–1529

Heritage Foundation, 2011. Index of Economic Freedom, Promoting Economic Opportunity and Prosperity. The Wall Street Journal: New York

Higgins, M., Williamson, J.G., 1996. Asian demography and foreign capital dependence. NBER Working Paper No. 5560. National Bureau of Economic Research, Cambridge, MA.

Higgins, M., Williamson, J.G., 1997. Age structure dynamics in Asia and dependence on foreign capital. Population and Development Review 23 (2), 261–293

Jorgensen, O.H., 2011. Macroeconomic and policy implications of population aging in Brazil. World Bank Policy Research Working Paper 5519.

Jorgensen, O.H., Jensen, S.E.H., 2010. Labor supply and retirement policy in an overlapping generations model with stochastic fertility. World Bank Policy Research Working Paper No. 5382.

Kelley, A.C., Schmidt, R.M., 1996. Saving, dependency and development. Journal of Population Economics 9 (4), 365–386
Koskela, E., Virén, M., 1992. Inflation, capital markets and household saving in the Nordic countries. Scandinavian Journal of Economics 94 (2), 215–227
Lahiri, A., 1989. Dynamics of Asian savings: the role of growth and age structure. IMF Staff Papers 36, 228–261
Lee, R.D., 1994. The formal demography of population aging, transfers, and the economic life cycle. In: Martin, L.G., Preston, Samuel H. (Eds.), Demography of Aging, Committee on Population, Commission on Behavioral and Social Sciences and Education, National Research Council. National Academy Press, Washington, D.C
Lee, R.D., Mason, A., 2007. Consumption, saving and capital accumulation as age distributions change. Research Paper, Demography and Economics, University of California at Berkley and Department of Economics, University of Hawaii at Manoa.
Lee, R.D., Lapkoff, S., 1988. Intergenerational flows of time and goods: consequences of slowing population growth. Journal of Political Economy 96 (3), 618–651
Leff, N.H., 1969. Dependency rates and savings rates. American Economic Review 59 (5), 886–896
Levine, R., 1997. Financial development and economic growth: views and agenda. JEL 35, 688–726
Loayza, N., Schchmidt-Hebbel, K., Serven, L., 2000. What drives private saving across the world? Review of Economics and Statistics. 82 (2), 165–181
Lopez, J.H., Schchmidt-Hebbel, K., Serven, L., 2000. How effective is fiscal policy in raising national saving? Review of Economics and Statistics 82 (2), 226–238
Mason, A., 1987. National savings rates and population growth. In: Johnson, D.G., Lee, R.D. (Eds.), Population Growth and Economic Development. University of Wisconsin Press, Madison, WI
Mason, A., 2001. Population Change and Economic Development in East Asia. Stanford University Press, Stanford, CA
McKinnon, R.I., 1973. Money and Capital in Economic Development. Brookings Institution, Washington, D.C.
Miles, D., 1999. Modelling the impact of demographic change upon the economy. Economic Journal 109 (452), 1–36
Modigliani, F., 1966. The life-cycle hypothesis of saving, the demand for wealth, and the supply of capital. Social Research 33 (2), 160–217
Modigliani, F., Brumberg, R.H., 1954. Utility analysis and the consumption function: an interpretation of the cross-section data. In: Kurihara, Kenneth K. (Ed.), Post-Keynesian Economics. Rutgers University Press, New Brunswick, pp. 388–436
Modigliani, F., Brumberg, R.H., 1954. Utility analysis and aggregate consumption functions: an attempt at integration. In: Abel, A. (Ed.), The Collected Papers of Franco Modigliani. The Life-Cycle Theory of Saving, Vol. 2. MIT Press, Cambridge, MA, pp. 128–197
Modigliani, F., 1970. The life cycle hypothesis of savings and the intercountry differences in the savings ratio. In: Eltis, W.A., Scott, M.F.G., Wolfe, J.N. (Eds.), Induction, Growth and Trade: Essays in Honor of Sir Roy Harrod. Clarendon Press, Oxford
Muhleisen, M., 1996. India—Policies to Increase Domestic Saving. International Monetary Fund, Washington, DC (Processed)
Paxson, C., 1996. Savings and growth: evidence from microdata. European Economic Review 40, 255–288
Phillips, P.C.B., Perron, P., 1988. Testing for a unit root in time series regression. Biometrika 75, 335–346
Prskawetz, A., Fent, T., Barthel, W., Crespo-Cuaresma, J., Lindh, T., Malmberg, B., Halvarsson, M., 2007. The relationship between demographic change and economic growth in the EU. EU Research, Report 32.
Rodrik, Dani, 2000. Institutions for high-quality growth: what they are and how to acquire them. CEPR Discussion Papers 2370.
Samuelson, P.A., 1958. An exact consumption loan model of interest with or without the contrivance of money. Journal of Political Economy 66 (6), 467–482
Schmidt-Hebbel, K., Serven, L., 1997. Saving across the world. World Bank Discussion Paper No. 354, World Bank.

Schultz, T.P., 1998. Life cycle savings, choice of family composition and the demographic transition. Paper presented at the European Society for Population Economics meetings, June 3–5, 1998, Amsterdam.

Schultz, T.P., 1999. Who is a household head? Paper presented at European Society for Population Economics Meetings, Turin, Italy, June 16.

Schultz, T.P., 2002. Fertility transition: economic explanations. In: Smelser, N.J., Baltes, P.B. (Eds.), International Encyclopedia of the Social and Behavioral Sciences. Pergamon Press, Oxford, UK, pp. 5578–5584

Shaw, E.S., 1973. Financial Deepening in Economic Development. Oxford University Press, New York

Solow, R.M., 1956. A Contribution to the theory of economic growth. Quarterly Journal of Economics 70 (1), 65–94 (MIT Press)

UN Population Division, 2001. World Population Prospects: the 2000 Revision, United Nations, New York.

Vincelette A.G., 2006. Determinants of Saving in Pakistan, World Bank PREM Working Paper Series No. SASPR 10

Weil, D.N., 1997. The economics of population aging. In: Rosenzweig, M.R., Stark, O. (Eds.), Handbook of Population and Family Economics. Elsevier Science

CHAPTER 7

An Investigation of the Deviation from the Market Efficiency and its Implications for Capital Market Development: The DSE Evidence

A.S.M. Sohel Azad, Amirul Ahsan, and Victor Fang
School of Accounting, Economics and Finance, Faculty of Business and Law, Deakin University, Melbourne, Australia

1. INTRODUCTION

The study of whether an equity market follows a random walk and hence constitutes an evidence of market efficiency has been extensively researched by both the finance practitioners and economists (for a survey of literature, see Azad et al. (2014) and Azad (2009a,b)). The premise of the random walk and efficiency hypothesis is that a market is said to be efficient if the price fully and correctly reflects all available information (Malkiel and Fama, 1970; Malkiel, 1992). In an informationally efficient market, it is not likely to generate profits consistently over time through speculation by the market players based on the publicly available information set. If the market players can make profits consistently from that market, then we can say that the market is not efficient with respect to the information. Market efficiency is divided into three forms by Malkiel and Fama (1970), such as weak, semi-strong, and strong form of efficiency. This division is classified based on the market's ability to reflect available information on share prices. The empirical studies, however, reveal that the markets in developing and less developed countries are not efficient in semi-strong or strong form. Emerging and developing markets in Asia, Latin America, and Africa are found to be inefficient in weak form (see, for instance, Azad et al., 2014; Azad, 2009a,b; Ojah and Karemera, 1999; Olowe, 1999). Evidences suggest that such inefficiencies in developing markets have arisen due to several factors, namely the size of the markets, thinness of trading, information disclosure procedure, speculation, and manipulation (Azad et al., 2014; Azad, 2009a,b; Keane, 1983; Mlambo et al., 2003). Of the several types of manipulation, trade-induced or volume-driven manipulation is found to be one of the significant reasons of market inefficiency or non-randomness in South Asian markets including Bangladesh. A recent study by Azad et al. (2014) shows that if the policy makers fail to control (trade-induced) manipulation through exemplary punishments, then the market efficiency could not be

Emerging Markets and the Global Economy
http://dx.doi.org/10.1016/B978-0-12-411549-1.00007-7

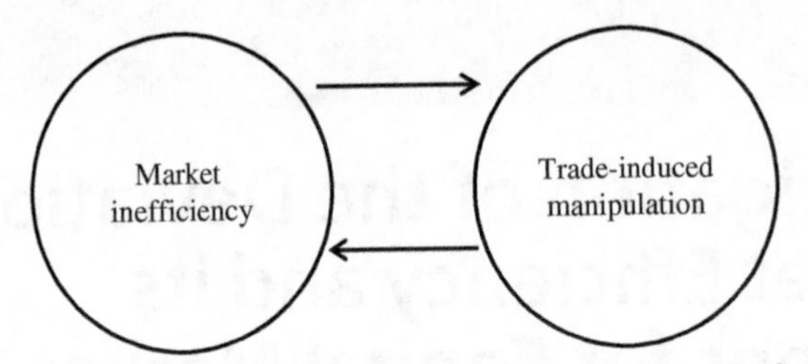

Figure 1 Causal link between market inefficiency and trade-induced manipulation.
Source: Azad et al., 2014.

improved in emerging markets such as DSE. For instance, Azad et al. (2014) argue that lack of strict regulatory framework in emerging markets causes a vicious circle of manipulation-led market inefficiency and a persistent causal link of market inefficiency and manipulation (see Figure 1). Figure 1 implies that there is a causal link between trade-induced manipulation and market inefficiency.

While there is a vast literature on both emerging and developed markets, there are only a few studies on the random walk and market efficiency tests on the small emerging markets such as the Dhaka Stock Exchange. Basher et al. (2007) apply the univariate GARCH approach to examine the volatility and efficiency of the Dhaka Stock Exchange and find that the DSE stock market is inefficient. Cooray and Wickremasinghe (2007) and Islam and Khaled (2005) also study the stock market efficiency of the south Asian stock markets including the DSE. Cooray and Wickremasinghe (2007) find that the DSE does not follow random walk, while Islam and Khaled (2005) find that the DSE follows the random walk behavior following the market crash. Islam and Khaled (2005) apply the Lo and MacKinlay (1988) variance-ratio tests. But none of them apply the Ng and Perron (hereafter, NP, 2001) unit root tests and the variance-ratio tests of Wright (2000) to examine the random walk behavior of the stock markets of Bangladesh.

To fill the above research gap, this chapter re-examines the random walk hypothesis to test for weak-form market efficiency in DSE. There are two implications of the random walk test: (i) an identification of the unit root component and (ii) an identification of the uncorrelated increments (i.e., *iid*/*mds* property). This chapter examines both these properties of the random walk in DSE. Several econometric techniques are applied to test both these properties of the random walk and market efficiency hypothesis of a financial time series. The widely used tools are unit root tests, autocorrelation tests, and variance-ratio tests. However, among these methods, the unit root tests and the variance-ratio tests are more popular since these tests capture two major properties of the random walk hypothesis (RWH). While the unit root component is identified through the unit root tests, the uncorrelated increments are identified by the variance-ratio tests. Therefore, the variance-ratio tests and the unit root tests are not directly competing with each other but rather complementing each other in testing the random walk hypothesis. However, if the results are conflicting between the unit root and the variance-ratio tests, it is recommended to rely on the variance-ratio tests to draw inferences. This is because the unit root process can have predictable elements, but a random walk indicates that returns must be uncorrelated (i.e., the series has a martingale property).

The variance-ratio test is a nonparametric test that considers both homoskedastic and heteroskedastic components in the model. The variance-ratio test is originally proposed by Lo and MacKinlay (1988). Using Monte Carlo experiments, Lo and MacKinlay (1989) demonstrate that the variance-ratio statistic is more powerful than unit root based tests or the autocorrelations based tests. Recently, Wright (2000) modifies the variance-ratio tests to examine the null that the series is a martingale difference sequence (*mds*). Wright (2000) applies his new tests to five exchange rate return series and finds that these tests are capable of detecting violations of the martingale hypothesis for all five series. Wright (2000) argues that of the several variance-ratio tests, ranks and signs based tests have better power than the conventional variance-ratio tests. Therefore, this chapter also compares the inferential outcomes between the two variance-ratio tests (of Lo and MacKinlay and Wright).

While this study is similar in spirit to that of Azad et al. (2014), unlike Azad et al. (2014), we divide the full sample into different sub-samples to investigate whether the market efficiency behavior is different during the normal period and pre- and post-crash period. Using long history of daily data and different econometric methodologies like unit root and variance-ratio tests, we provide the conclusive evidence that the DSE does not follow random walk and hence constitutes weak-form market inefficiency. This finding is consistent with the large-scale prior studies on emerging markets and a recent work by Azad et al. (2014) on South Asia.

The remainder of the chapter is organized as follows. Section 2 discusses the background of DSE. Section 3 explains the methodologies and simulation of critical values for the Wright's rank and sign based tests. Section 4 describes the type and source of data, the econometric packages used, and the summary statistics on the DSE. Section 5 presents empirical results and analysis followed by a conclusion and policy implications in Section 6.

2. BACKGROUND OF DSE

Stock trading in Bangladesh started in 1956, although its major stock exchange, the Dhaka Stock Exchange (DSE), was not registered as a Public Limited Company until 1969. Although DSE was established more than five decades ago, it is still regarded an emerging market because of thin trading and market size. The Chittagong Stock Exchange (CSE), the country's second largest stock exchange, began its journey on October 10, 1995. The market capitalization in early 1990s was USD 20 million, which reached nearly USD

9 billion in 2006–2007 and USD 24 billion in 2013. In the 1990s, the market had gone through series of development phases. It is governed by Company Act 1994, Security and Exchange Commission Act 1993, Security and Exchange Commission Regulation 1994, and Security Exchange (Inside Trading) regulation 1994.

The Bangladeshi stock market is characterized by both speculative and manipulative practices. The market participants in the 1990s had very little knowledge about stock markets. In the early 1990s, some executives from both DSE and CSE used to visit different organizations including universities to educate people about the stock market, thereby motivating investors to invest in the share market. Being motivated by them, many ill-fated investors invested and traded (mid-1990s onward), albeit, rarely on fundamentals. Investors rarely looked at financial statements, annual reports, and/or relevant news of the companies they invested. Most players withdrew money from other investments and banks in order to invest in the share markets. Even Bangladeshi residents who were working in the Middle East and other countries fuelled the market with their remittances. The result was obvious. Trading on misleading information (noise, rumors, absence of fundamentals) opened enough room for manipulators and speculators to manipulate the prices and gain abnormal returns. The market experienced its first (manipulation-led) bubble, followed by an immediate burst, in late 1996, as can be seen from Figure 2.

Figure 2 shows that while the market was flourishing slowly, it came under speculative attack in late 1996. The price index increased from nearly 800 (in January 1996) to 3627 on November 15, 1996, by almost 450% in just 1 year before the major market crash that happened in December 1996. That is, a manipulator who bought a share at Taka 800 sold at Taka 3627 making 350% profit (roughly) from the sale of a share, thereby causing huge loss (on a game theory perspective it is −350%) to the ill-fated investors.

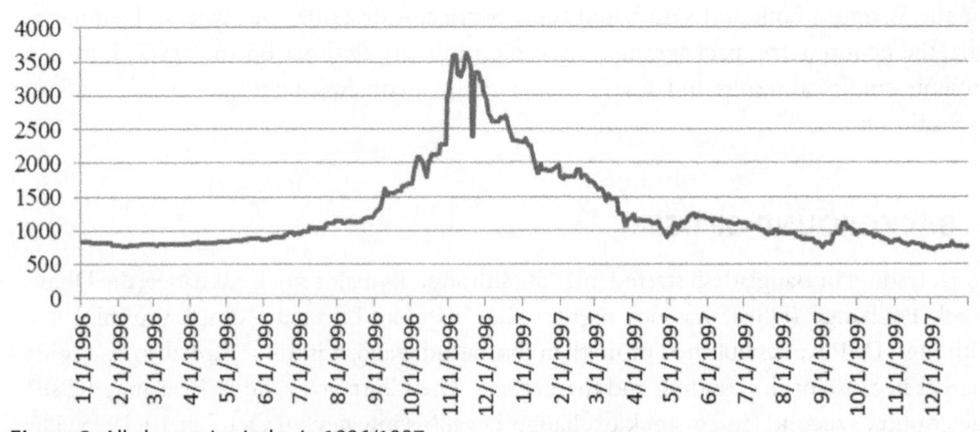

Figure 2 All-share price index in 1996/1997.
This figure shows the daily share price index since January 1, 1996 to December 31, 1997. The figure is based on the data collected from DataStream.

During 1996 manipulation, manipulators pumped up (excessive buying with high prices to mislead the general investors) the market before crashing it. One striking observation would amaze anyone. There was a large-scale repatriation of foreign investments, which actually inflated the market before the crash happened. According to a statistics released by the Bangladesh Bank, during the period 1992–1995, the purchase of shares by foreign investors exceeded the amount of shares sold. The statistics also indicate that there was a massive outflow (more than Taka 6 billion a year) of foreign investment during the period 1996–1997, compared with Taka 0.6 billion of investments by foreign investors during the corresponding period, which caused the market to crash. The Securities and Exchange Commission (SEC) investigated the crash, as it suspected that brokerage houses (both domestic and foreign) and individual investors had deliberately manipulated the market (*Financial Times*, April 23, 1999). On April 2, 1997, the Bangladeshi court ordered the arrest of 36 brokers, dealers, and company executives, for causing the market crash of December 1996 (*Reuters*, April 3, 1997).

In an effort to regain public confidence and improve transparency, an Automated Trading System (ATS) was introduced in 1998, which effectively started in 2001. Under the ATS, there are four classifications: (a) public market (market lots), (b) spot market (24-h settlement), (c) block market (bulk quantity), and (d) odd lot market (odd lot scripts). Then a Central Securities Depository System was initiated on January 24, 2004. Even after all these efforts, DSE is generally considered to be very vulnerable to speculative attacks and inside trading due to lack of strict implementation of the regulations. In addition, the market suffers from low depth and liquidity with high level of volatility and market concentration.

The evidence of several cases of pumping and dumping also suggests that exemplary punishments were not enforced by the regulators. Brokers were found to use the pump and dump scheme in the shares of DSE several times. According to a news of *United News of Bangladesh* (April 18 and May 5, 2005), in March 2005, this pump and dump manipulation caused the index to decline by 23% in a matter of few days.

The DSE has even bitter experience in recent years. Figure 3 shows that the index rose to 9000 on 3rd December 3, 2010 from nearly 2000 in early 2009. In just 2 years, the index increased by 450% before it crashed down to almost 2009 level again. These basic figures and characteristics of DSE lead us to consider weak-form efficiency for this study. The next section discusses the methodologies used to carry out that empirical investigation.

Another feature of the DSE is the thin trading. Figure 4 shows the daily trading volume is very low. Hoque et al. (2007) argue that thin trading aggravates the market inefficiency in the emerging markets like DSE. Azad et al. (2014) also report some interesting results relating to DSE trading volume and returns. They find that trading volume increases during the manipulation period and declines during the post-manipulation period. They also find positive price-volume relationship in DSE, which indicates that the manipulation ceases the market efficiency in this market.

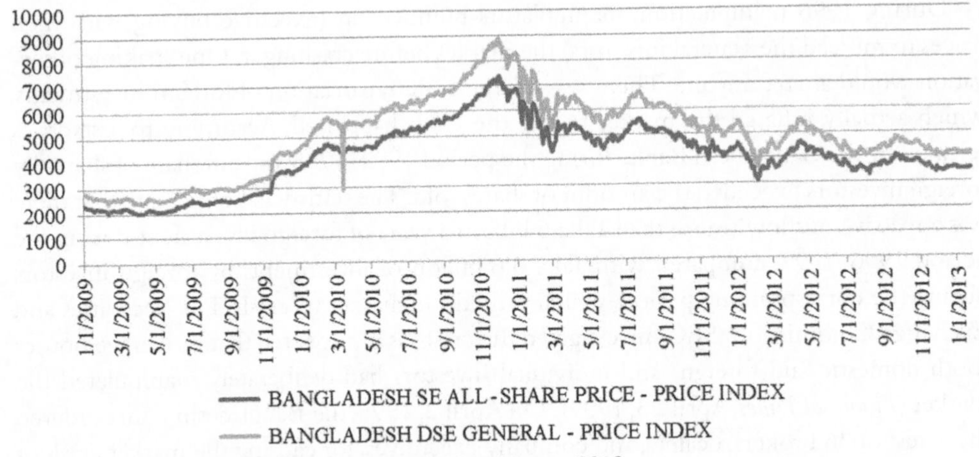

Figure 3 Share price indices from January 2009 to January 2013.
This figure shows the daily share price indices since January 1, 2009 to January 31, 2013. The figure is based on the data collected from DataStream.

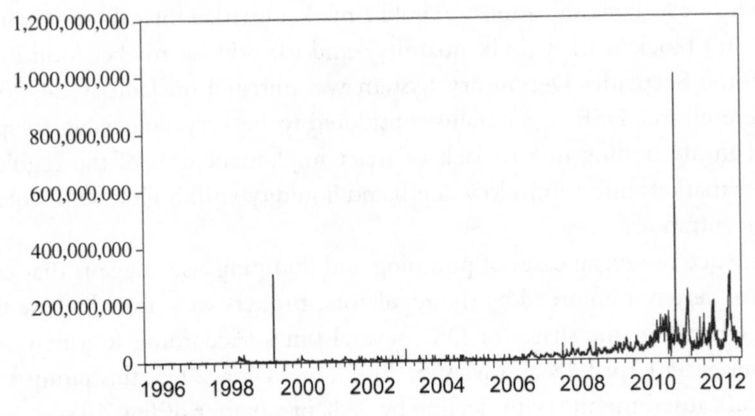

Figure 4 DSE daily trading volume.
This figure shows the daily DSE daily trading volume since January 1, 1996 to January 25, 2013. The figure is based on the data collected from DataStream.

3. TESTING METHODOLOGIES

In this section, we discuss the unit root tests proposed by Ng and Perron (2001), the variance-ratio tests of Lo and MacKinlay (1988) and Wright (2000), and the simulated critical values for Wright's rank and sign based tests.

3.1. Unit Root Tests

The unit root test is a common procedure to determine whether a financial variable follows a random walk. If the existence of a unit root for a series cannot be rejected, then the series is said to follow a random walk. Among the several unit root tests, we choose the Ng and Perron (2001) tests because the modified information criteria (MIC) coupled with the GLS-detrended data provide the tests with desirable size and predictive power properties. Ng and Perron (2001) construct four test statistics as follows:

$$MZ_{\alpha}^{d} = \left(T^{-1}\left(y_T^d\right)^2 - f_0\right)\Big/2\kappa \quad \text{where,} \quad \kappa = \sum_{t=2}^{T}\left(y_{t-1}^d\right)^2\Big/T^2, \tag{1}$$

$$MZ_t^d = MZ_{\alpha} \times MSB, \tag{2}$$

$$MSB^d = \left(k/f_O\right)^{1/2}, \tag{3}$$

$$MP_T^d = \begin{cases} (\bar{c}^2k - \bar{c}T^{-1}(y_T^d)^2)/f_0 \\ (\bar{c}^2k + (1-\bar{c})T^{-1}(y_T^d)^2)/f_0 \end{cases} \text{if} \quad \begin{matrix} x_t = \{1\}, \\ x_t = \{1, t\}. \end{matrix} \tag{4}$$

where $\bar{c} = \begin{cases} -7 \\ -13.5 \end{cases} \text{if} \begin{matrix} x_t = \{1\} \\ x_t = \{1, t\} \end{matrix}$ and x_t are optional exogenous regressors, which may consist of constant, or a constant and trend.

3.2. Variance-Ratio Tests

According to Lo and MacKinlay (1988), if y_t is a time series of stock returns with a sample of size T, the variance-ratio to test the hypothesis that y_t is *iid* or that it is an *mds* is defined as:

$$\text{Variance-ratio} = \left\{\frac{1}{Tk}\sum_{t=k+1}^{T}(y_t + y_{t-1} + \cdots + y_{t-k} - k\hat{\mu})^2\right\} \div \left\{\frac{1}{T}\sum_{t=1}^{T}(y_t - \hat{\mu})^2\right\}, \tag{6}$$

where $\hat{\mu} = T^{-1}\sum_{t=1}^{T} y_t$. The numerator of variance-ratio is $1/k$ times the variance of y_t after aggregation by a factor of k. This statistic should be close to 1 if y_t is *iid* but not if it is serially correlated. Lo and MacKinlay (1988) show that if y_t is *iid* then:

$$T^{1/2}(VR - 1) \rightarrow_d N\left(0, \frac{2(2k-1)(k-1)}{3k}\right).$$

So, the test statistics are:

$$M_1 = (VR - 1)\left(\frac{2(2k-1)(k-1)}{3kT}\right)^{-1/2}, \tag{7}$$

$$M_2 = (VR - 1)\left(\sum_{j=1}^{k-1}\left[\frac{2(k-j)}{k}\right]^2 \delta_j\right)^{-1/2}, \tag{8}$$

where $\delta_j = \left\{\sum_{t=j+1}^{T} (y_t - \hat{\mu})^2 (y_{t-j} - \hat{\mu})^2\right\} \div \left\{\left[\sum_{t=1}^{T} (y_t - \hat{\mu})^2\right]^2\right\}$. M_1 is asymptotically standard normal under the *iid* null (homoskedasticity), while M_2 is a robust test statistic that accounts for conditional heteroskedasticity.

Wright (2000) modifies the above tests and proposes ranks (R_1 and R_2) and signs (S_1 and S_2)[1] as alternatives to M_1 and M_2. Wright (2000) argues that the new tests are capable of decisively rejecting the martingale model of stock returns when M_1 and M_2 tests give ambiguous results. Wright (2000) proposes the following rank and sign tests:

$$R_1 = \left(\frac{\frac{1}{Tk} \sum_{t=k+1}^{T} (r_{1t} + r_{1t-1} + \cdots + r_{1t-k})^2}{\frac{1}{T} \sum_{t=1}^{T} r_{1t}^2} - 1 \right) \times \left(\frac{2(2k-1)(k-1)}{3kT} \right)^{-1/2}, \tag{10}$$

$$R_2 = \left(\frac{\frac{1}{Tk} \sum_{t=k+1}^{T} (r_{2t} + r_{2t-1} + \cdots + r_{2t-k})^2}{\frac{1}{T} \sum_{t=1}^{T} r_{2t}^2} - 1 \right) \times \left(\frac{2(2k-1)(k-1)}{3kT} \right)^{-1/2}, \tag{11}$$

$$S_1 = \left(\frac{\frac{1}{Tk} \sum_{t=k+1}^{T} (s_t + s_{t-1} + \cdots + s_{t-k})^2}{\frac{1}{T} \sum_{t=1}^{T} s_t^2} - 1 \right) \times \left(\frac{2(2k-1)(k-1)}{3kT} \right)^{-1/2}, \tag{12}$$

where $r_{1t} = r(y_t) - \frac{T+1}{2} \Big/ \sqrt{\frac{(T-1)(T+1)}{12}}$ and $r_{2t} = \Phi^{-1}\left(r(y_t)/(T+1)\right)$. Φ is the standard normal cumulative distribution function. $\{s_t\}_{t=1}^{T}$ is an *iid/mds* sequence, each element of which is 1 with probability 0.5 and -1 otherwise.

We obtain the critical values for R_1, R_2, and S_1 by simulating their exact sampling distributions. Table 1 shows the critical values for R_1, R_2, and S_1 test statistics associated with the sample sizes ($T = 1500$, $T = 2500$, and $T = 4000$) and holding periods.

The variance-ratio tests are examined for several values of k considering our samples. The random walk or martingale hypothesis can be strongly rejected when the test statistics are rejected for all k. However, for the decision rule to make the testing procedure operationally easier, one can also reject the hypothesis if there are more than two rejections (see, Azad, 2009a,b).

4. DATA, ECONOMETRIC PACKAGES, AND DESCRIPTIVE STATISTICS

The study takes the daily DSE closing price indices, all vis-à-vis US dollar, on 5 days a week basis from January 1990 to July 2006. These 17 years cover the most crucial periods of DSE. Real development of the market started since early 1990s, however, it was interrupted in 1996–1997 when the market crashed due to excessive speculative

[1] The sign based test S_2 is not considered because in Monte Carlo simulation, Wright (2000) finds that the size and power properties of S_2 are inferior to those of S_1.

Table 1 Critical values for Wright's (2000) R_1, R_2, and S_1 tests.
The critical values were simulated with 10,000 replications in each case. For each entry, the numbers in column 2, 4, and 6 give the 2.5 percentile of the distribution of the test statistics (for specified values of T and k) and the numbers in column 3, 5, and 7 give 97.5 percentile of that distribution.

k	T = 1500		T = 2500		T = 4000	
R1						
2	−2.025	1.945	−1.970	1.915	−1.973	1.959
5	−1.970	1.933	−1.997	1.919	−2.003	1.901
10	−1.990	1.914	−1.950	1.928	−1.975	1.912
20	−1.959	1.839	−1.979	1.888	−1.997	1.933
30	−1.957	1.805	−1.972	1.837	−1.991	1.902
40	−1.942	1.808	−1.975	1.807	−1.986	1.896
R2						
2	−1.997	1.917	−1.965	1.919	−1.965	1.935
5	−1.993	1.912	−2.025	1.933	−2.010	1.902
10	−1.997	1.911	−1.965	1.913	−2.009	1.912
20	−1.969	1.841	−1.974	1.852	−1.994	1.925
30	−1.952	1.787	−1.975	1.848	−2.007	1.894
40	−1.933	1.777	−1.950	1.828	−2.018	1.864
S1						
2	−2.014	1.911	−1.920	1.960	−1.961	1.961
5	−1.914	1.933	−1.950	1.980	−1.980	1.946
10	−1.915	1.982	−1.910	1.995	−1.928	1.943
20	−1.893	2.039	−1.883	2.015	−1.944	1.949
30	−1.843	2.049	−1.876	1.999	−1.943	1.950
40	−1.810	2.034	−1.866	2.011	−1.916	1.965

attacks. Over the following 10 years (1997–2006), the government and the regulators brought in many improvements and changes in the market to regain public confidence, improve governance, and increase transparency in the system. So over these 17 years of sample period, a total of 4046 observations of the closing price index data are collected from the Global Financial Data. The whole sample period is split into pre- and post-stock market crash period to distinguish between inferential outcomes, if any. The return series is constructed as the first difference of logarithms of the closing price indices. To test for the robustness of the results, we compare the results from the unit root tests with those of the variance-ratio tests. Data are analyzed using the following econometric packages: E-Views, RATS, and R.

Table 2 presents summary statistics for the DSE price indices. The return indices indicate almost the similar statistical properties to those of the price indices. Basher et al. (2007) also report the statistical properties of the DSE stock returns. Therefore, to conserve

Table 2 Summary statistics of the DSE all-share index.
This table shows the summary statistics of the DSE all-share price index in natural logarithm. This index is a capitalization-weighted price index with an original base of 1985 = 100 and a revised base of November 24, 2001 = 817.62.

	Whole sample	Pre-crash	Post-crash
Period	1/1/1990–30/7/2006	1/1/1990–31/12/1996	1/1/1997–30/7/2006
N	4046	1525	2521
Mean	2.887	2.864	2.9003
Variance	0.1476	0.2197	0.10359
Skewness	1.4035	1.434	1.2977
Kurtosis	2.8816	2.5609	1.5483
Q (up to lag = 30)	105379.0689***	43924.2105***	72683.5803***
JB	2729.6924***	939.4337***	960.146***
LM (lag)	4037.264 (22)***	1514.285 (11)***	2494.761 (20) ***

***Significance at the 1% level. LM = Breusch-Godfrey Serial Correlation Lagrange Multiplier (LM) test for conditional heteroskedasticity (ARCH). Analysis is based on the data from Global Financial Data. The data were collected while the first author was conducting a research in Ritsumeikan Asia Pacific University.

the space, the summary statistics of the return indices are not shown here. The results can be obtained from authors on request.

It is evident from the Jarque-Bera test for normality that the returns are non-normal, while the Lagrange multiplier (LM) test for the presence of the ARCH effect indicates clearly that prices at different samples show strong conditional heteroskedasticity. Figure 5 presents the time plots of different samples in natural logarithm. The shaded area in the first panel of Figure 1 shows the crash period. Not surprisingly, the DSE shows distinctive downward spikes in the late 1996, corresponding to the timing of the market crash. To isolate the effect of the market crash on the outcomes of both the unit root and the variance-ratio tests, we divide the data into two sub-periods in the Results and Analysis section. The first sub-period covers the period from January 1990 to December 1996 with 1525 observations, while the second sub-period covers from January 1997 to July 2006 with 2521 observations. The tests are applied to the whole sample (4046 observations) as well as to these two sub-periods.

5. RESULTS AND ANALYSIS

5.1. Results from the Unit Root Tests

The NP tests examine the null of a unit root or non-stationarity. We cannot reject the null hypothesis of a unit root if the test statistic is greater than the critical value. This means that the series has a unit root and thus meets the first requirement of the random

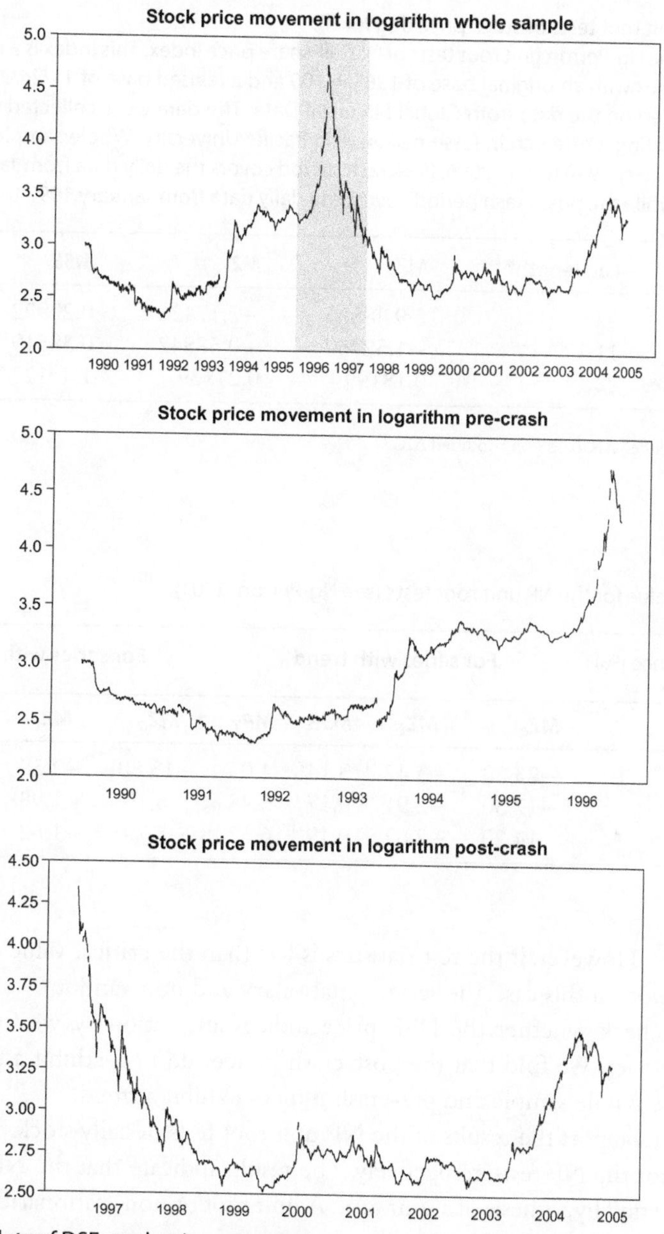

Figure 5 Time plots of DSE stock price movement.
This figure indicates the daily stock price movement (in logarithm). Panel 1 indicates the whole sample period (January 1990 to July 2006), panel 2 indicates the pre-crash period (January 1990 to December 1996), and panel 3 indicates the post-crash period (January 1997 to July 2006).

Table 3 The NP unit root tests of stock price (log level).
This table shows the Ng-Perron unit root tests of DSE all-share price index. This index is a capitalization-weighted price index with an original base of 1985 = 100 and a revised base of 11/24/2001 = 817.62. The analysis is based on the data from Global Financial Data. The data were collected while the first author was conducting a research in Ritsumeikan Asia Pacific University. Whole sample includes the daily data from January 1990 to July 2006. Pre-crash period covers the daily data from January 1990 to December 1996, while the post-crash period covers the daily data from January 1997 to July 2006.

Data coverage	Lag length**	MZ_α	MZ_t	MSB	MP_T
Whole sample*	22	−9.48566	−2.17426	0.22922	9.62251
Pre-crash*	11	−1.52760	−0.58842	0.38519	34.9629
Post-crash*	22	0.18199	0.27139	1.49123	121.625

*Indicates no trend.
**Spectral GLS-detrended AR based on modified AIC.

Table 4 Critical value for the NP unit root tests (see Ng-Perron, 2001).

Level of significance (%)	For series with trend				For series with no trend			
	MZ_α	MZ_t	MSB	MP_T	MZ_α	MZ_t	MSB	MP_T
1	−23.80	−3.42	0.14	4.03	−13.80	−2.58	0.17	1.78
5	−17.30	−2.91	0.17	5.48	−8.10	−1.98	0.23	3.17
10	−14.20	−2.62	0.19	6.67	−5.70	−1.62	0.28	4.45

walk hypothesis. However, if the test statistics is less than the critical value we reject the null of a unit root. In this case, the series is stationary and non-random.

Before we check whether the DSE price indices are stationary, we first check the trend of these series. We find that the post-crash indices do not exhibit a trend in their levels, while the whole sample and pre-crash indices exhibit a trend.

Tables 3 and 4 report the results of the NP unit root tests of daily stock prices and the critical values for the NP tests, respectively. The results indicate that the NP tests largely fail to reject the null hypothesis of a unit root. A unit root or non-stationarity in the series indicates that the stock returns have a time-varying mean or a time-varying variance or both. The returns are not correlated and the investors cannot forecast the returns using the available market information. Thus, the unit root tests provide the evidence of the random walk behavior of the DSE for all series namely, the whole sample, pre-market crash, and the post-market crash period.

5.2. Results from the Variance-Ratio Tests

Table 5 shows the variance-ratio test statistics for whole sample (Panel A), before market crash (Panel B) and after market crash (Panel C) of the daily stock returns. While $M1$ and $M2$ are the variance-ratio test statistics of Lo and MacKinlay, $R1$, $R2$, and $S1$ are the variance-ratio test statistics of Wright.

The results from the conventional variance-ratio tests (of Lo and MacKinlay) are mixed in different sub-samples. The L-M tests fail to reject the *iid/mds* null hypothesis for whole sample as well as after market crash if the heteroskedastic increments are not considered. Thus, both the series (full sample and after market crash) exhibit market efficiency at all lags under the conditions of heteroskedasticity. However, under the conditions of homoskedasticity, the L-M tests strongly reject the *iid/mds* null for all series at all lags (all

Table 5 The variance-ratio test statistics for the stock returns.
This table shows the variance-ratio test statistics ($M1$, $M2$, $R1$, $R2$, and $S1$) of DSE all-share price index returns. This index is a capitalization-weighted price index with an original base of 1985 = 100 and a revised base of 11/24/2001 = 817.62. Analysis is based on the data from Global Financial Data. The data were collected while the first author was conducting a research in Ritsumeikan Asia Pacific University. $M1$ and $M2$, two test statistics of Lo and MacKinlay, are asymptotically distributed standard normal. $R1$, $R2$, and $S1$ are three test statistics of Wright.

k	M1	M2	R1	R2	S1
Panel A: whole sample					
2	9.84*	0.56	8.75*	8.24*	8.33*
5	−6.61*	−0.51	8.91*	8.15*	9.52*
10	−4.63*	−0.49	9.94*	9.39*	10.32*
30	−0.78	−0.14	11.19*	10.88*	10.78*
Panel B: pre-market crash					
2	5.34*	2.03*	37.51*	35.25*	4.41*
5	5.82*	1.92	64.31*	61.35*	6.07*
10	6.59*	2.28*	91.97*	86.66*	6.19*
30	7.40*	2.91*	157.51*	148.71*	5.97*
Panel C: post-market crash					
2	3.26*	1.33	21.38*	19.17*	7.05*
5	3.05*	1.33	33.40*	31.15*	7.29*
10	3.78*	1.72	46.49*	42.33*	8.13*
30	3.41*	1.74	75.18*	69.89*	8.65

*Indicates the rejections of *iid/mds* null at 1% level of significance. Whole sample includes the daily data from January 1990 to July 2006. Pre-crash period covers the daily data from January 1990 to December 1996, while the post-crash period covers the daily data from January 1997 to July 2006.

k) with the exception of whole sample at $k = 30$. These mixed findings are consistent with Islam and Khaled (2005).

Islam and Khaled (2005), however, have not used rank and sign based tests of Wright. As noted earlier, these tests have better power properties than those of Lo and MacKinlay. As we can see, the rank and sign based tests ($R1$, $R2$, and $S1$) of Wright give much consistent results throughout different sub-samples than those of conventional variance-ratio tests in terms of *iid*/*mds* null rejections, meaning that the Wright's tests yield exact tests and confirm better power than the Lo and MacKinlay variance-ratio tests. All rejections are at the right tail tests for both conventional and alternative variance-ratio tests except for the whole sample at $k > 2$ for $M1$ and $M2$, the rejections are at the left tail tests.

The inferential outcomes with regard to the random walk and efficiency hypothesis differ between the variance-ratio tests and the unit root tests. It is to note that an identification of unit root is one of the conditions of RWH but it is rather weak. For a market to be informationally efficient, it also needs to satisfy the *iid*/*mds* null property of the RWH. The results show that although the first property of the RWH is fulfilled by the unit root tests, the second property of the RWH (i.e., the series is an *iid* or an *mds*) is strongly rejected for whole sample as well as for pre- and post-crash samples. Thus, we can firmly state that the DSE does not follow a random walk. Nonetheless, this inference is consistent with those of Azad et al. (2014).

6. CONCLUSION AND POLICY IMPLICATIONS

This chapter sheds light on two major properties of the RWH/market efficiency: the unit root component and the martingale null behavior of the Dhaka Stock Exchange (DSE) to address their policy implications. While the NP tests are used to test for the evidence of a unit root component in the series, the variance-ratio tests are applied to examine the martingale behavior of that series. Although the NP tests fail to reject the unit root null, the variance-ratio tests strongly reject the *iid*/*mds* null. Since the later variance-ratio tests have better predictive power properties, we conclude that RWH is rejected for the stock market of Bangladesh. Our conclusion, nonetheless, corroborates the suggestion put forward by Cecchetti and Lam (1994) and . They suggest that when the inferential outcomes differ between the unit root tests and the variance-ratio tests, the conclusion should be based on variance-ratio test. This makes the decision rule operationally easier.

It is crucial to determine the correct form of efficiency to identify appropriate policy implications. Findings of this chapter remove any confusion over the true form of market efficiency present in DSE. The rejection of the *iid*/*mds* null for the DSE may be attributed to several anomalies and inconsistencies in the market that (i) there could be frequent unchecked manipulations as detected by Azad et al. (2014); (ii) there is an information asymmetry among the investors with regard to price changes (see, for example,

Grossman and Stiglitz, 1980; Ito and Lapavitsas, 1998); (iii) the markets are characterized by excessive speculation; (v) investors/traders are naïve and lack understanding of market mechanism; and (vi) there is excessive deregulation in the DSE.

Future policies should address all these shortcomings in DSE and take appropriate measures of improvement. Understanding the anomalies and inconsistencies is essential to map out proper policy prescriptions. Unchecked manipulations could cause recurrent trade-induced manipulations (for example, pumping and dumping, trade- or action-induced manipulation), continuity of market inefficiency and development of capital market. Such manipulations are evident in emerging and developing markets including DSE. It is alleged that speculators and foreign investors manipulated share prices in DSE during 1996. In the hope of making gains from the price increase, the uninformed trader enters the market and reinforces the trend. This gives the manipulator the opportunity to gradually sell her/his stocks and exit the market. When there is not enough momentum left, the manipulator crashes the market by selling excessively. This causes fear and rumors among the investors to sell and salvage from whatever they can. As a consequence, a plummeting price gives the manipulator the option to buy back her/his stocks and keep the original ownership undiluted. The whole exercise allows the informed trader having market power to make supernormal profits without losing ownership of their stock portfolios. Given the small size of DSE, it was easier for the speculators and foreign investors to control the market and then to make considerable gains.

DSE needs to improve its transparency and information dissemination procedure. Since 2001, the market has adopted automated trading, the chances for price mismatch have been reduced but not completely eliminated. In one of the recent studies, Ahkam and Mostafa (2013) examined the companies listed at DSE and tested the speed of adjustment of market prices to released information. They found that the adjustment is not immediate, and it takes about 15 days for the market to fully absorb and reflect such information. This delay in adjustment can actually lead to an undue profitable strategy for investors and speculators.

While the investors are recommended not to ignore the small emerging markets, they should be cautious in forecasting the returns. The investors in these markets always try to exploit the opportunity of intertemporal inefficiency. This gives the speculators a further incentive to manipulate/float the prices much higher than the rational growth. The weak/small market players become misguided and wrongly estimate the returns from these markets. Taking advantage of such situations, the speculators manipulated DSE in 1996–1997 and caused the market to crash.

Throughout the 1990s, the noise trading had more influence than the information in the stock markets of Bangladesh. During the period, investors mostly traded on rumors and rarely traded on fundamentals. There was a trend and tendency among many investors to liquidate their deposits and/or sell their valuables to invest in the stock markets. Those investors did not behave rationally using fundamental analysis of the markets rather relied on sentiments and/or noises. Further, the unplanned and misleading promotional activities of the stock exchanges in 1990s increased the number of irrational arbitragers. Consequently, the markets had more liquidity than the desired and optimal level. Eventually, the markets had experienced both the bubble and burst in the late 1996.

Excessive or pre-mature deregulation was a case for Bangladesh during the mid-1990s. During the period, the policies were aimed to encourage foreign investors to participate in the DSE. However, the foreign investors manipulated the prices and caused the markets to collapse.

This study draws the regulators' attention to the need for appropriate reforms in order to improve the level of efficiency. Inefficiencies encourage manipulations and discourage both domestic and foreign investments. As a result it could do more long-term harm to these emerging markets. These practices are extremely unethical as they result in corruption and unfair wealth redistribution from the uninformed trader to the informed manipulator. Exemplary punishments against the manipulators need to be implemented to protect small and weak players in the market. In the absence of these practices, the emerging markets, such as DSE, would operate in an environment of fair exchange and experience higher efficiency.

ACKNOWLEDGMENTS

For helpful comments and suggestions, we would like to thank Dipendra Sinha (deceased) and Suzuki Yasushi (both from Ritsumeikan Asia Pacific University, Japan). All errors and omissions are solely our responsibility.

REFERENCES

Ahkam, S.N., Mostafa, T., 2013. Studying market reaction to right share offers in Bangladesh. In: Proceedings of Third Global Accounting, Finance and Economics Conference 5–7 May, Rydges Melbourne

Azad, A.S., 2009a. Random walk and efficiency tests in the Asia-Pacific foreign exchange markets: evidence from the post-Asian currency crisis data. Research in International Business and Finance 23, 322–338

Azad, A.S., 2009b. Efficiency, cointegration and contagion in equity markets: evidence from China, Japan and South Korea. Asian Economic Journal 23, 93–118

Azad, A., Azmat, S., Fang, V., Edirisuriya, P., 2014. Unchecked manipulations, price-volume relationship and market efficiency: evidence from emerging markets. Research in International Business and Finance 30, 51–71

Basher, S.A., Hassan, M.K., Islam, A.M., 2007. Time-varying volatility and equity returns in Bangladesh stock market. Applied Financial Economics 17, 1393–1407

Cecchetti, S.G., Lam, P.-S., 1994. Variance-ratio tests: small sample properties with an application to international output data. Journal of Business and Economic Statistics 12, 177–186

Cooray, A., Wickremasinghe, G., 2007. The efficiency of emerging stock markets: empirical evidence from the South Asian region. Journal of Developing Areas 41, 171–184

Gilmore, C.G., McManus, G.M., 2003. Random-walk and efficiency tests of central European equity markets. Managerial Finance 29 (4), 42–61

Grossman, S.J., Stiglitz, J.E., 1980. On the impossibility of informationally efficient market. American Economic Review 70, 393–408

Hoque, H., Kim, J., Pyun, C., 2007. A comparison of variance ratio tests of random walk: a case of asian emerging stock markets. International Review of Economics and Finance 16 (4), 488–502

Islam, A., Khaled, M., 2005. Tests of weak-form efficiency of the Dhaka Stock Exchange. Journal of Business Finance & Accounting 32, 1613–1624

Ito, M., Lapavitsas, C., 1998. Political Economy of Money and Finance. Macmillan, London

Keane, S.M., 1983. Stock Market Efficiency: Theory, Evidence, Implications. Philip Alan Publishers, Bath

Lo, A., MacKinlay, A.C., 1988. Stock market prices do not follow random walks: evidence from a sample specification test. Review of Financial Studies 1, 41–66

Lo, A., MacKinlay, A.C., 1989. The size and power of the variance-ratio test in finite samples: a Monte Carlo investigation. Journal of Econometrics 40, 203–238

Malkiel, B., 1992. Efficient market hypothesis. In: Newman, P., Milgate, M., Eatwell, J. (Eds.), New Palgrave Dictionary of Money and Finance. Macmillan, London

Malkiel, B.G., Fama, E.F., 1970. Efficient capital markets: A review of theory and empirical work. Journal of Finance 25 (2), 383–417

Mlambo, C., Biekpe, N., Smit, E.M., 2003. Testing the random walk hypothesis on thinly-traded markets: the case of four African stock markets. African Journal of Finance 5 (1), 16–35

Ng, S., Perron, P., 2001. Lag length selection and the construction of unit root tests with good size and power. Econometrica 69, 1519–1554

Ojah, K., Karemera, D., 1999. Random walks and market efficiency tests of Latin American emerging equity markets: a revisit. Financial Review 34 (2), 57–72

Olowe, R.A., 1999. Weak form efficiency of the Nigerian stock market: further evidence. African Development Review 11 (1), 54–68

Wright, J.H., 2000. Alternative variance-ratio tests using ranks and signs. Journal of Business and Economic Statistics 18, 1–9

CHAPTER 8

An Econometric Analysis of the Impact of Oil Prices on Stock Markets in Gulf Cooperation Countries

Mohamed El Hedi Arouri* **and Christophe Rault**†
*CRCGM, University of Auvergne, Clermont-Ferrand, France
†Toulouse Business School, France

1. INTRODUCTION

Numerous recent works establish that oil price fluctuations have significant effects on economic activity in many developed and emerging countries (Cunado and Perez de Garcia, 2005; Balaz and Londarev, 2006; Gronwald, 2008; Cologni and Manera, 2008; Kilian, 2008). However, there is less evidence on the effects of oil price shocks on stock markets. And the bulk of what little work has been done has focused on the stock markets in developed countries. Very few studies have looked at the stock markets in emerging economies. These studies focus largely on the short-term interaction of energy price shocks and stock markets for net oil-importing countries. Using recent data and new panel unit root and cointegration tests, this paper investigates the long-term relationship between oil price shocks and stock markets in the Gulf Cooperation Council (GCC) countries.

GCC countries are interesting for several reasons. First, as they are the major suppliers of oil in world energy markets, their stock markets are likely to be susceptible to changes in oil prices. Second, GCC markets differ from those of developed and from other emerging countries in that they are only weakly integrated within international markets and are overly sensitive to regional political events. Finally, GCC markets are very promising areas for international portfolio diversification and several reforms have been made recently in order to attract global investors. Studying the influence of oil price shocks on GCC stock market returns can help GCC and foreign investors make necessary investment decisions and may be of use to policy-makers who regulate stock markets. For these reasons, a study centered on GCC countries should be of great interest.

The pioneering paper by Jones and Kaul (1996) tests the reaction of international stock markets to oil price shocks. They find that for the US and Canada this reaction can be accounted for entirely by the impact of the oil shocks on cash flows. The results for Japan and the UK were inconclusive. By contrast, using an unrestricted vector autoregressive

Emerging Markets and the Global Economy
http://dx.doi.org/10.1016/B978-0-12-411549-1.00008-9

(VAR), Huang et al. (1996) find no evidence of a relationship between oil prices and market indices such as the S&P 500. However, Sadorsky (1999) applies an unrestricted VAR with GARCH effects to American monthly data and shows a significant relationship between oil price changes and aggregate stock returns. More recently, Park and Ratti (2008) show that oil prices have negative impacts on stock returns in the US and 12 European countries, while Norway, as an oil exporter country, shows a positive response of stock market to oil price rises. Finally, some papers have investigated the case of sector returns in developed oil-exporting countries. For instance, Boyer and Filion (2007) show that oil price increases affect positively stock returns of Canadian oil and gas companies. El-Sharif et al. (2005) and Arouri (2012) reach the same conclusion for oil and gas returns in UK and in Europe, respectively.

Some recent papers focus on major European, Asian, and Latin American emerging markets. The results of these studies show a significant short-term link between oil price changes and emerging stock markets (Papapetrou, 2001; Basher and Sadorsky, 2006). However, less attention has been paid to smaller emerging markets, especially in the GCC countries where share dealing is a relatively recent phenomenon. Using VAR models and cointegration tests, Hammoudeh and Eleisa (2004) show that there is a bidirectional relationship between Saudi stock returns and oil price changes. Bashar (2006) uses VAR analysis to study the effect of oil price changes on GCC stock markets and shows that only the Saudi and Omani markets have predictive power of oil price increase. More recently, Hammoudeh and Choi (2006) examined the long-term relationship of the GCC stock markets in the presence of the US oil market, the S&P 500 index, and the US Treasury bill rate. They find that the T-bill rate has a direct impact on these markets, while oil prices and the S&P 500 have indirect effects. Finally, using different econometric techniques Arouri et al. (2012) show that the reaction of GCC stock markets to oil price shocks presents some asymmetry.

As can be seen, the results of the few available works on GCC countries are too heterogeneous. These results are puzzling because the GCC countries are heavily reliant on oil export (and thus sensitive to changes in oil prices) and have similar economic structures. The aim of this article is to add to the current literature on the subject by examining the long-term links between oil price changes and stock markets in GCC countries using two different complementary datasets (weekly obtained from the MSCI database and monthly sourced from the Arab Monetary Fund (AMF) database), respectively, from June 7, 2005 to October 21, 2008, and from January 1996 to December 2007. There are two main reasons for using these two datasets. Firstly, our weekly dataset, the MSCI dataset, which deals with all the six GCC countries, only includes less than four years of data, which can be considered as too short to attempt to fit a cointegrating relationship. Indeed, cointegration is a long-term concept and long-span data are therefore required to insulate the results from particular short-term factors that may have been influencing the relationship. Secondly, our monthly database, the AMF dataset, which covers 12 years of data, only includes four GCC countries out of six and does not permit us to draw any conclusion about Qatar and United Arab Emirates which are absent from the database. In addition, despite the shortness of our weekly data we think that they may capture the interaction of oil and stock prices in the region better than monthly data. Thus, we choose to apply recent econometric techniques to the two datasets and to compare the results we obtain.

We take advantage of non-stationary panel data econometric techniques and seemingly unrelated regression (SUR) methods. More precisely, we use the recently developed bootstrap panel unit root test of Smith et al. (2004), which uses a sieve-sampling scheme to account for both the time series and the cross-sectional dependencies of the data. In addition, we use the bootstrap second-generation panel cointegration test proposed by Westerlund and Edgerton (2007), which makes it possible to accommodate both within and between the individual cross-sectional units. To the best of our knowledge, such an analysis has not been done to study the links between oil prices and stock markets. On the other hand, and since the influence of oil prices on stock markets certainly needs to be tackled country by country, a country wide assessment is also necessary; it is therefore useful to have as many time series observations as possible. In this context, the SUR approach (another way of addressing cross-sectional dependence) provides additional country-specific results complementing the panel data.

The remainder of this paper is organized as follows. Section 2 describes the GCC markets and the role of oil. Section 3 briefly discusses some transmission channels of oil price fluctuations to stock prices in GCC markets. Section 4 presents the data and discusses the results of the empirical analysis, which includes second-generation panel unit root tests, panel, cointegration, and SUR analysis, while Section 5 provides some policy implications and Section 6 concludes the paper.

2. GCC STOCK MARKETS AND OIL

Table 1 presents some key financial indicators for the stock markets in GCC countries. The GCC was established in 1981 and it includes six countries: Bahrain, Oman, Kuwait, Qatar, Saudi Arabia, and the United Arab Emirates (UAE). The GCC countries have several patterns in common. Together, they account for about 20% of global oil production, they control 36% of global oil exports, and they have 47% of proven global reserves. The contributions of oil to GDP range from 22% in Bahrain to 44% in Saudi Arabia. Moreover, as Table 1 shows, the stock market liquidity indicator of the three largest GCC economies (Saudi Arabia, the UAE, and Kuwait) is positively associated with the oil importance indicator.

Saudi Arabia leads the region in terms of market capitalization. However, by percentage of GDP, Qatar is the leader. Stock market capitalization exceeded GDP for all counties except Oman. Kuwait has the largest number of listed companies, followed

Table 1 Stock markets in GCC countries in 2007.

Market	Number of companies*	Market capitalization ($ billion)	Market capitalization (% GDP)*	Oil (% GDP)+
Bahrain	50	21.22	158	22
Kuwait	175	193.50	190	35
Oman	119	22.70	40	41
Qatar	40	95.50	222	42
UAE	99	240.80	177	32
S. Arabia	81	522.70	202	44

Source: Arouri and Nguyen (2010).
*Numbers in 2006.

by Oman. Overall, GCC stock markets are limited by several structural and regulatory weaknesses: relatively small numbers of listed firms, large institutional holdings, low sectoral diversification, and several other deficiencies. In recent years, however, a broad range of legal, regulatory, and supervisory changes have increased market transparency. More interestingly, GCC markets are beginning to improve their liquidity and open their operations to foreign investors. In March 2006, the Saudi authorities lifted the restriction that limited foreign residents to dealing only in mutual investment funds; the other markets have followed the Saudi lead.[1]

Finally, although GCC countries have several economic and political characteristics in common, they depend on oil to differing degrees; likewise, efforts to diversify and liberalize the economy differ from country to country. The UAE and Bahrain, for example, are less reliant on oil than Saudi Arabia and Qatar (Figure 1). Furthermore, the composition of stock market and the concentration degree considerably differ across GCC stock markets. Besides, we have to mention that several other institutional differences remain between GCC stock markets. For instance, unlike other GCC stock markets, the Saudi market is highly dominated by State entities that are not active traders. In fact in Saudi Arabia, state-controlled companies dominate the listing. The stock market capitalization thereby heavily concentrates on banks, telecoms, and materials. Moreover, the perception of insider trading is widespread. These elements are likely to undermine normal market operations such as arbitrage and speculation in the Saudi stock market. Thus, the comparison of GCC stock markets makes for an interesting subject and we expect stock prices in these markets to have different responses to oil price fluctuations. The panel data econometric tools we use in this paper have the advantages to take into account these different features.

[1] For interested readers, further information about and discussion of the market characteristics and financial sector development of these countries can be found in Creane et al. (2004), Neaime (2005), and Naceur and Ghazouani (2007).

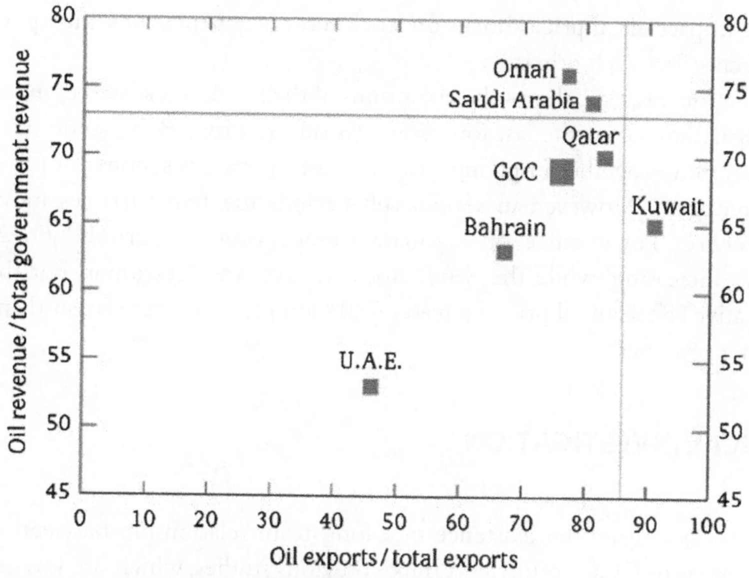

Figure 1 Dependence on oil of GCC countries.
Source: Fasano and Iqbal (2003), International Monetary Fund.

3. TRANSMISSION CHANNELS

In the financial theory, the value of stock is equal to the discounted sum of expected future cash flows. On the basis of this definition, various transmission channels exist through which oil price fluctuations can affect stock prices in GCC countries. First, in most GCC countries oil exports largely determine earnings, government budget revenues and expenditures, and aggregate demand. The latter impact corporate input and income, which may affect company future cash flows and thus stock prices. Second, oil prices may have an indirect effect on stock prices. In fact, the effect of oil prices on the aggregate demand influences the expected inflation and money supply, which in turn affect the discount rate and therefore stock prices in GGC countries. Furthermore, GCC countries are importers of manufactured goods from developed and emerging countries. So oil price fluctuations can indirectly impact GCC markets through their influence on the prices of imports, and increases in oil prices are often indicative of inflationary pressure in GCC economies; inflationary pressures, in turn, could dictate the future of interest rates and of investment in securities.

Thus, given the large influence of oil on GCC economies, it is interesting to investigate the link between oil price fluctuations and the performance of stock markets in the region. In fact, unlike most net oil-importing countries, where the expected link between oil prices and stock markets is negative, GCC countries may be subject to other phenomena: the transmission mechanism of oil price shocks to stock market returns is ambiguous and the total impact of oil price shocks on stock returns depends on which positive and negative effects offset each other.

For illustration, Figure 2 shows the evolutions of the Saudi stock market index and oil prices (in logarithms) over the last four years. As one can remark, in some sub-periods, the two series move together implying that oil price increase is synonym of Saudi stock market appreciation. However, in several sub-periods the two variables move in the opposite direction. For instance, during many months over the period 2006–2007, the oil price was increasing, while the Saudi stock market was decreasing. For these sub-periods, negative effects of oil price increases (inflation pressure) were larger than positive effects (higher revenues).

4. EMPIRICAL INVESTIGATION

4.1. Data

Our goal is to investigate the existence of a long-term relationship between oil prices and stock markets in GCC countries. Unlike previous studies, which use low-frequency data (yearly, quarterly, or monthly), our study uses both weekly and monthly data for the reasons discussed in the Introduction of this paper.

Weekly data are obtained from MSCI and covered the six GCC members. We think that weekly data may more adequately capture the interaction of oil and stock prices in the region than low-frequency data. We do not use weekly data in order to avoid time difference problems with international markets. In fact, the equity markets are generally closed on Thursdays and Fridays in GCC countries, while the developed and international oil markets close for trading on Saturdays and Sundays. Furthermore, for the common open days, the GCC markets close just before US stocks and commodity markets open. Accordingly, we opt to use weekly data and choose Tuesday as the weekday for all variables because this day lies in the middle of the three common trading days for all markets. Specifically, our sample period goes from June 7, 2005 to October 21, 2008 for the six GCC members.

As for our second dataset, we use monthly data obtained from Arab Monetary Fund (AMF) over the period January 1996–December 2007. Note that stock exchanges in UAE and Qatar are newly established and did not participate in the AMF database when it began in 2002. Thus, the AMF data we use include only four of the six GCC stock markets: Bahrain, Kuwait, Oman, and Saudi Arabia.[2]

For oil, we use the weekly and monthly OPEC spot prices. These prices are weighted by estimated export volume and are obtained from the Energy Information Administration (EIA).[3] All prices are in American dollars.

[2] Data for 2008 are not available in the AMF database. Furthermore, weekly data are not available.

[3] Very similar results are obtained with West Texas Intermediate and Brent spot prices. Oil prices are in US dollars per barrel. Note also that GCC currencies have been officially pegged to the US dollar since 2003. However, Kuwait has recently moved back to pegging its currency to a basket currency.

4.2. Bootstrap Panel Unit Root Analysis

The body of literature on panel unit root and panel cointegration testing has grown considerably in recent years and now distinguishes between the first-generation tests (Maddala and Wu, 1999; Levin et al., 2002; Im et al., 2003) developed on the assumption of the cross-sectional independence of panel units (except for common time effects), the second-generation tests (Bai and Ng, 2004; Smith et al., 2004; Moon and Perron, 2004; Choi, 2006; Pesaran, 2007) allowing for a variety of dependence across the different units, and panel data unit root tests that make it possible to accommodate structural breaks (Im and Lee, 2001). In addition, in recent years it has become more widely recognized that the advantages of panel data methods within the macro-panel setting include the use of data for which the spans of individual time series data are insufficient for the study of many hypotheses of interest.

Cross-sectional dependence can arise due to a variety of factors, such as omitted observed common factors, spatial spillover effects, for example via regional integrated financial markets, unobserved common factors, or general residual interdependence, all of which could remain even when all observed and unobserved common effects have been taken into account. In the GCC context, some possible cross-country dependence can be envisaged in the presence of similar regulations in various fields (such as economy, finance, trade, customs, tourism, legislation, and administration), high economic, fiscal and political corporation, and increasing financial integration. To test for the presence of such cross-sectional dependence in our data, we have implemented the simple test of Pesaran (2004) and have computed the CD statistic. This test is based on the average of pairwise correlation coefficients of the OLS residuals obtained from standard augmented Dickey-Fuller regressions for each individual. Its null hypothesis is cross-sectional independence and is asymptotically distributed as a two-tailed standard normal distribution. Results available upon request indicate that the null hypothesis is always rejected regardless of the number of lags included in the augmented DF auxiliary regression (up to five lags) at the five percent level of significance. This confirms that the GCC countries are, as expected, cross-sectionally correlated.

Then, to determine the degree of integration of our series of interest (oil price index and stock market indices) in our panel of GCC countries, we employ the bootstrap tests of Smith et al. (2004), which use a sieve-sampling scheme to account for both the time series and cross-sectional dependencies of the data[4]. The tests that we consider are denoted $\bar{t}$, $\overline{LM}$, $\overline{\max}$, and $\overline{\min}$. All four tests are constructed with a unit root under the null hypothesis and heterogeneous autoregressive roots under the alternative, which indicates that a rejection should be taken as evidence in favor of stationarity for at least

[4] Notice that Bootstrap methods can sometimes be sensitive to the sample size, smoothness, and the assumption made for re-sampling.

one country.[5] The results, shown in Tables 2a and 2b (associated respectively to our weekly and monthly datasets), suggest that for all the series (taken in logarithms) the unit root null cannot be rejected at any conventional significance level for the four tests.[6] We therefore conclude that the variables are non-stationary[7] in our country panel.[8]

4.3. Panel Cointegration

The series of oil price index and stock market indices being integrated of order one, we now use the bootstrap panel cointegration test proposed by Westerlund and Edgerton (2007) to test for the existence of the cointegration of oil prices and GCC stock markets (in conjecture with equation (1)):

$$Lstock_{it} = \alpha + \beta \; Loil_{it} + \varepsilon_{it}, \tag{1}$$

where $i(i = 1, \ldots, N)$ is the country, $t(t = 1, \ldots, T)$ is the period, *Lstock* is the stock index price in logarithm, and *Loil* is the oil price in logarithm.[9] This test relies on the popular Lagrange multiplier test of McCoskey and Kao (1998), and makes it possible to accommodate correlation both within and between the individual cross-sectional units. In addition, this bootstrap test is based on the sieve-sampling scheme and has the advantage of significantly reducing the distortions of the asymptotic test. Note that this test has the appealing advantage that its joint null hypothesis is that all countries in the panel are cointegrated. Therefore, in case of non-rejection of the null, we can assume that there is cointegration of oil prices and stock markets for the whole set of GCC countries.

The panel cointegration results shown in Tables 3a and 3b for a model including either a constant term or a linear trend clearly indicate the absence of a cointegrating relationship between oil prices and stock markets for our panel of six and four GCC countries

[5] The $\bar{t}$ test can be regarded as a bootstrap version of the well-known panel unit root test of Im et al. (2003). The other tests are modifications of this test. For further details on the construction of the four tests, we refer the reader to Smith et al. (2004).

[6] The order of the sieve is permitted to increase with the number of time series observations at the rate $T^{1/3}$, while the lag length of the individual unit root test regressions is determined using the Campbell and Perron (1991) procedure. Each test regression is fitted with a constant term only.

[7] We also show in Appendix 1 the results of the well-known time series Kwiatkovski-Phillips-Schmidt-Shin (KPSS, 1992) test. However, as recently stressed by Carrion-i-Silvestre and Sanso (2006), the main drawback of stationarity tests is the difficulty entailed by the estimation of the long-run variance needed to compute them. To deal with this issue we therefore follow their recommendations and apply the KPSS test using the procedure developed by Sul-Phillips-Choi (SPC, 2005) to estimate the long-run variance. This strategy involves less size distortion than that of the LMC test, while preserving reasonable power. The results obtained in a country-by-country approach are in accordance with those of the panel data tests in the sense that all series are found to be integrated of order one for all GCC countries and for the oil price in our two (weekly and monthly) datasets.

[8] We have of course also checked using the bootstrap tests of Smith et al. (2004) that the first difference of the series is stationary, hence confirming that the series expressed in level are integrated of order one.

[9] Note that we have also considered a larger system including GCC stock markets, oil prices, and other external variables (such as money supply, industrial production, interest rates) and have obtained very similar results to those reported here.

Table 2a Panel unit root tests for oil price index and stock price series (weekly dataset on the 6 GCC countries).*

	Oil price index				Stock price indices			
Test	Statistic (a)	Bootstrap *p*-value*	Statistic (b)	Bootstrap *p*-value*	Statistic (a)	Bootstrap *p*-value*	Statistic (b)	Bootstrap *p*-value*
$\overline{t}$	−1.668	0.452	−1.693	0.745	−1.375	0.650	−1.641	0.928
$\overline{LM}$	2.916	0.454	3.021	0.745	2.005	0.816	2.931	0.959
$\overline{\max}$	−1.290	0.387	−1.725	0.567	−1.183	0.379	−1.511	0.824
$\overline{\min}$	1.756	0.400	3.021	0.573	1.627	0.556	2.437	0.898

Notes: (a)- model includes a constant.
(b)- model includes both a constant and a time trend.
*Test based on Smith et al. (2004). Rejection of the null hypothesis indicates stationarity at least in one country. All tests are based on 5,000 bootstrap replications to compute the *p*-values.

Table 2b Panel unit root tests for oil price index and stock price series (monthly dataset on 4 GCC countries).*

	Oil price index				Stock price indices			
Test	Statistic (a)	Bootstrap *p*-value*	Statistic (b)	Bootstrap *p*-value*	Statistic (a)	Bootstrap *p*-value*	Statistic (b)	Bootstrap *p*-value*
$\overline{t}$	1.588	0.998	−0.703	0.967	−1.195	0.880	−1.852	0.874
$\overline{LM}$	2.602	0.474	0.522	0.968	1.795	0.832	2.751	0.964
$\overline{\max}$	2.602	0.259	0.517	0.940	−1.684	0.321	−1.741	0.784
$\overline{\min}$	1.184	0.994	−0.576	0.967	1.821	0.521	2.337	0.983

Notes: (a)- model includes a constant.
(b)- model includes both a constant and a time trend.
*Test based on Smith et al. (2004). Rejection of the null hypothesis indicates stationarity at least in one country. All tests are based on 5,000 bootstrap replications to compute the *p*-values.

Table 3a Panel cointegration test results between oil price index and stock index series (weekly dataset on the 6 GCC countries).#

	LM-stat	Asymptotic *p*-value	Bootstrap *p*-value
Model with a constant term	40.539	0.000	0.250
Model including a time trend	41.300	0.000	0.104

Notes:
The bootstrap is based on 2000 replications and the null hypothesis of the tests is cointegration of current Oil Price Index and Stock Index series.
#Test based on Westerlund and Edgerton (2007).

Table 3b Panel cointegration test results between oil price index and stock index series (monthly dataset on 4 GCC countries).#

	LM-stat	Asymptotic *p*-value	Bootstrap *p*-value
Model with a constant term	10.813	0.000	0.773
Model including a time trend	38.596	0.000	0.161

Notes:
The bootstrap is based on 2000 replications and the null hypothesis of the tests is cointegration of current Oil Price Index and Stock Index series.
#Test based on Westerlund and Edgerton (2007).

(according to the database considered). This result, however, is based on conventional asymptotic critical values that are calculated on the assumption of cross-sectional independence of countries, an assumption that is probably absent for the oil price and stock market indices time series for GCC countries for which strong economic links exist (see Section 2).

Therefore, it seems more reasonable to use bootstrap critical values (which are valid if there is some dependence among individuals). In this case, the conclusions of the tests are now much more straightforward, and retaining a 10% level of significance, we conclude that there is a long-run relationship between oil prices and stock markets for our panel of six and four GCC countries included, respectively, in our two (weekly and monthly) datasets, whatever the specification of the deterministic component. This implies in particular that over the longer term oil prices and stock market indices move together in GCC countries. The forces that move markets in GCC countries are basically the forces that move oil prices, mainly OPEC intervention policy, global economic growth, changes in oil inventories, and other global, regional, and domestic political and economic events.

The estimated coefficients of equation (1) are shown in Tables 4a and 4b.

Panel estimates show, as expected, significant positive coefficient β. The elasticity of stock prices to oil prices is less than 1, but the stock price effect of oil changes is great: a 10% increase in oil prices leads to an average appreciation of the stock markets in GCC

Table 4a Estimated coefficients for the GCC panel (weekly dataset on the 6 GCC countries, average relation).

Coefficients α, β in equation (1)		*t*-statistic	Probability
α	3.312	25.267	0.000
β	0.308	10.021	0.000

Note: balanced system, total observations: 1062.

Table 4b Estimated coefficients for the GCC panel (monthly dataset on 4 GCC countries, average relation).

Coefficients α, β in equation (1)		*t*-statistic	Probability
α	2.918	25.821	0.000
β	0.629	19.054	0.000

Note: balanced system, total observations: 575.

countries by 3.08% if the reference period is the week, and of 6.29% if the reference period is the month.[10]

4.4. SUR Estimates

As a cointegrating relationship exists for our panel of six GCC countries, we now estimate the system:

$$Lstock_{it} = \alpha_i + \beta_i \; Loil_{it} + \varepsilon_{it}, \quad i = 1, \ldots, N; \quad t = 1, \ldots, T, \tag{2}$$

by the Zellner (1962) approach to handle cross-sectional dependence among countries using the SUR estimator. This way of proceeding enables us to estimate the individual coefficients β_i in a panel framework and hence to investigate the influence of oil prices on the stock market for each country taken individually. The SUR estimation results are shown in Tables 5a and 5b.

On a country-by-country basis, oil price increases have a positive impact on stock prices, except for Saudi Arabia. Several economic and institutional differences between the Saudi market and the other GCC markets could explain this result. In fact, the Saudi stock market is highly concentrated and largely dominated by the financial industry. This lack of diversification may explain the negative relationships observed over some sub-periods, as shown by Figure 2, between oil price and the Saudi market index. Furthermore, Saudi Arabia is the largest GCC market, but its economy is overly dependent on oil-importing countries and suffers more than other GCC countries from imported inflation

[10] Panel causality tests, not reported here, show that oil price changes significantly affect stock prices in GCC countries.

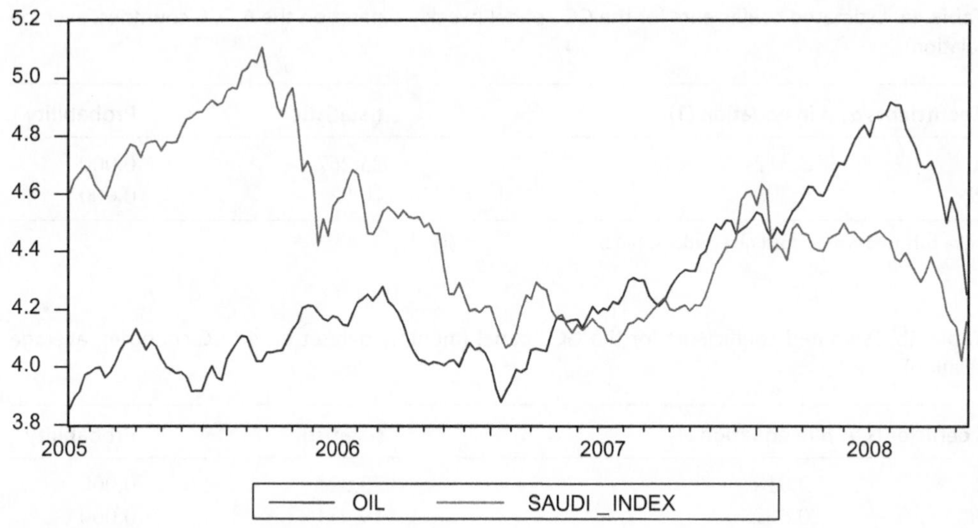

Figure 2 Oil prices and the Saudi stock market.

Table 5a SUR estimation for the GCC panel (weekly dataset on the 6 GCC countries).

Country	Coefficients α_i, β_i in equation (2)		t-statistic	Probability
Bahrain	α_1	2.728	25.398	0.000
	β_1	0.419	16.638	0.000
Kuwait	α_2	2.503	16.964	0.000
	β_2	0.585	16.908	0.000
Oman	α_3	1.761	11.194	0.000
	β_3	0.680	18.443	0.000
Saudi Arabia	α_4	5.593	18.466	0.000
	β_4	−0.262	−3.7005	0.000
Qatar	α_5	2.741	10.757	0.000
	β_5	0.443	7.4218	0.000
United Arab Emirates	α_6	4.548	18.275	0.000
	β_6	0.201	3.1251	0.000

Notes: Seemingly unrelated regression, linear estimation after one-step weighting matrix. Balanced system, total observations: 1062.

and economic pressures. Moreover, the annual turnover in Saudi Arabia is low and the Saudi stock market is considered shallow when compared with other emerging markets. There are two main reasons behind this low trading volume. First, unlike other GCC markets, the Saudi governments still hold a large chunk of listed firms that they rarely trade. Second, strategic shareholders hold another large chunk. This makes shares available for trading very limited in the Saudi's stock market, causing investors to shy away from

Table 5b SUR estimation for the GCC panel (monthly dataset on 4 GCC countries).

Country	Coefficients α_i, β_i in equation (2)		*t*-statistic	Probability
Bahrain	α_1	3.776	27.46	0.000
	β_1	0.322	8.023	0.000
Kuwait	α_2	2.405	16.79	0.000
	β_2	0.827	19.76	0.000
Oman	α_3	4.183	20.94	0.000
	β_3	0.195	3.346	0.000
Saudi Arabia	α_4	1.311	7.139	0.000
	β_4	−0.384	−21.83	0.000

Notes: Seemingly unrelated regression, linear estimation after one-step weighting matrix.
Balanced system, total observations: 575.

these companies. These elements are likely to undermine normal market operations such as arbitrage and speculation in Saudi Arabia.

Finally, we also use a Wald test, which may in principle be useful to uncover any common behavior for some country sub-groups, to test the homogeneity of β_i across countries. For instance, one could consider that it is more likely to pair countries with smaller estimated β_i, and countries with higher estimated β_i coefficients. The results of these tests are shown in Tables 6a and 6b.

While the null hypothesis of homogeneity (as well as of a unit coefficient) in the cointegration relationship is always rejected for the overall panel set of GCC countries in our two (weekly and monthly) datasets, it holds for some specific country pairings. For instance, it is possible to see that the null of homogeneity for β_i, that is the similarity in the responses of GCC stock markets to changes in oil prices, is not rejected jointly for Bahrain, and Qatar or for Kuwait, and Oman in the weekly and monthly datasets. Thus, despite the several similarities and economic links between GCC countries, their stock markets do not have similar sensitivities to oil price changes. Finally, our results suggest that GCC markets have the potential to yield different stock returns and are therefore candidates for regional portfolio diversification.

5. POLICY DISCUSSION

Theoretically, oil price changes affect stock prices through their effects on both expected earnings and discount rate. In the last decade, researchers and market participants have attempted to find a practical framework that identifies how oil prices affect stock prices. However, they do not reach any general consensus. Using robust new econometric techniques, our results show the existence of strong significant long-run relationships between oil prices and stock markets in GCC countries and that oil price increases have a positive

Table 6a Testing the homogeneity of β across countries (weekly dataset on the 6 GCC countries).

Panel/country group	Chi-square statistic	Probability
$\beta_i = 1$ for all GCC countries	1550.83	0.0000
$\beta_i = \beta$ for all GCC countries	1008.61	0.0000
$\beta_i = 1$ for all GCC countries except Saudi Arabia	1831.55	0.0000
$\beta_i = \beta$ for all GCC countries except Saudi Arabia	1002.16	0.0000
$\beta_1 = \beta_5$ and $\beta_2 = \beta_3$	4.59	0.1003

Table 6b Testing the homogeneity of β across countries (monthly dataset on 4 GCC countries).

Panel/country group	Chi-square statistic	Probability
$\beta_i = 1$ for all GCC countries	501.06	0.0000
$\beta_i = \beta$ for all GCC countries	238.17	0.0000
$\beta_i = 1$ for all GCC countries except Saudi Arabia	490.647	0.0000
$\beta_i = \beta$ for all GCC countries except Saudi Arabia	107.79	0.0000
$\beta_1 = \beta_5$ and $\beta_2 = \beta_3$	3.46	0.1609

impact on stock prices in most GCC countries. This finding is not unexpected given the fact that GCC countries are heavily reliant on oil export (and thus sensitive to changes in oil prices) and have similar economic structures. Our results have important implications for researchers and market participants.

First, our findings suggest that international diversification benefits can be achieved by including assets from both net oil-importing countries (such as most developed countries) and net oil-exporting countries (such as GCC countries). In fact, a portfolio constituted of assets with both positive and negative sensitivities to oil is weakly affected by oil price shocks. Alternatively, global investors may consider hedging for oil price shocks using oil-based derivatives.

Second, the existence of a long-term stable relationship between oil prices and stock prices in GCC countries suggests, from the perspective of investments, that oil and stock market can be considered integrated rather segmented markets implying that expected benefits from diversification within the GCC region by holding assets in both the oil and stock markets are decreasing. Thus, investors in the region should search abroad for new investment opportunities in order to hold diversified portfolios. However, global investors from developed and emerging markets can invest a part of their wealth in GCC countries if they want to reduce the effects of oil price rises on their profitability.

Third, the significant relationship between oil prices and stock markets implies some degree of predictability in the GCC stock markets. On the base of demand and supply expectations in oil and oil-related products markets, one may expect the evolution of oil prices and then their effects on stock market prices in GCC countries. Thus, profitable speculation and arbitrage strategies can be built based on our results.

Finally, our results show that oil price changes affect significantly stock markets in GCC countries. Stock markets are the barometer of economic activity and are strongly related to both consumer and investors' confidence. Thus, GCC countries as major OPEC policy-makers should pay attention to how their actions impact oil prices and to the effects of oil price fluctuations on their own economies and stock markets.

6. CONCLUSION

This paper uses recent bootstrap panel cointegration techniques and seemingly unrelated regression methods, which, to the best of our knowledge, have never been used in this context, to look into the existence of long-term relationships between oil prices and GCC stock markets. Since GCC countries are major oil producers and exporters, their stock markets are likely to be susceptible to oil price shocks. Based on two different (weekly and monthly) datasets covering respectively the periods from June 7, 2005 to October 21, 2008, and from January 1996 to December 2007, our results show that there is evidence for cointegration of oil prices and stock markets in GCC countries. Our findings should be of interest to researchers, regulators, and market participants. In particular, GCC countries as OPEC policy-makers should keep an eye on the effects of oil price fluctuations on their own economies and stock markets. For investors, the significant relationship between oil prices and stock markets implies some degree of predictability in the GCC stock markets.

There are several avenues for future research. First, the long-run link between oil and stock markets in GCC countries can be expected to vary from one economic industry to another. A sectoral analysis of this long-run link would be informative and an investigation of asymmetric reactions of sectoral indices to oil price changes should be relevant. Second, the panel unit root and panel cointegration models applied in this article could be used to examine the effects of other energy products, such as natural gas. Third, further research could examine the links of causality binding oil and stock markets in GCC countries and other oil-exporting countries.

Appendix 1—Individual Stationarity Tests for Series (in Logarithm)

See Tables A1 and A2.

Table A1 Results for the weekly dataset on 6 GCC countries.[a]

Series	KPSS with constant[b]	KPSS with time trend[b]
Oil Price Index	1.302	0.252
Bahrain Stock Index	0.948	0.259
Kuwait Stock Index	1.396	0.299
Oman Stock Index	0.843	0.339
Saudi Arabia Stock Index	0.899	0.245
Qatar Stock Index	0.798	0.364
United Arab Emirates Stock Index	0.899	0.245
	Critical values	Critical values
cv (1%)	0.741	0.217
cv (5%)	0.463	0.148
cv (10%)	0.348	0.120

Note that the null hypothesis of the Kwiatkowski-Phillips-Schmidt-Shin test is stationarity around a constant, or around a (linear) time trend.

[a]We follow here the recommendations given by Carrion-i-Silvestre and Sanso (2006) and apply the KPSS test using the procedure developed by Sul et al. (2005) to estimate the long-run variance.

[b]We have used the Akaike Information Criterion (AIC) to select the order of the autoregressive correction with pmax = $\text{int}[12(T/100)^{(1/4)}]$. Regarding the critical values, we report the finite sample critical values drawn from the response surfaces in Sephton (1995).

Table A2 Results for the monthly dataset on 4 GCC countries.[a]

Series	KPSS with constant[b]	KPSS with time trend[b]
Oil Price Index	1.190	0.307
Bahrain Stock Index	1.001	0.313
Kuwait Stock Index	0.985	0.286
Oman Stock Index	0.841	0.486
Saudi Arabia Stock Index	0.871	0.256
	Critical values	Critical values
cv (1%)	0.741	0.217
cv (5%)	0.463	0.148
cv (10%)	0.348	0.120

Note that the null hypothesis of the Kwiatkowski-Phillips-Schmidt-Shin test is stationarity around a constant, or around a (linear) time trend.

[a]We follow here the recommendations given by Carrion-i-Silvestre and Sanso (2006) and apply the KPSS test using the procedure developed by Sul et al. (2005) to estimate the long-run variance.

[b]We have used the Akaike Information Criterion (AIC) to select the order of the autoregressive correction with pmax=$\text{int}[12(T/100)^{(1/4)}]$. Regarding the critical values, we report the finite sample critical values drawn from the response surfaces in Sephton (1995).

ACKNOWLEDGMENT

We are very grateful to an anonymous referee for his useful comments and suggestions. The usual disclaimer applies.

REFERENCES

Arouri, M., 2012. Stock returns and oil price changes in Europe: a sector analysis. Manchester School 80 (2), 237–267

Arouri, M., Jouini, J., Nguyen, D.K., 2012. On the relationships between world oil prices and GCC stock markets. Journal of Quantitative Economics 10 (1), 98–120

Arouri, M., Nguyen, D.K., 2010. Stock returns and oil price fluctuations: short and long-run analysis in the GCC context. International Journal of Global Energy Issues 33 (3–4), 121–138

Bai, J., Ng, S., 2004. A PANIC attack on unit roots and cointegration. Econometrica 72 (4), 1127–1177

Balaz, P., Londarev, A., 2006. Oil and its position in the process of globalization of the world economy. Politicka Ekonomie 54 (4), 508–528

Bashar, Z., 2006. Wild oil prices, but brave stock markets! The Case of Gulf Cooperation Council (GCC) Stock Markets, Middle East Economic Association Conference, Dubai.

Basher, S.A., Sadorsky, P., 2006. Oil price risk and emerging stock markets. Global Finance Journal 17, 224–251

Boyer, M.M., Filion, D., 2007. Common and fundmental factors in stock returns of canadian oil and gas companies. Energy Economics 29 (3), 428–453

Carrion-i-Silvestre, J., Sanso, A., 2006. A guide to the computation of stationarity tests. Empirical Economics 31, 433–448

Choi, I., 2006. Combination unit root tests for cross-sectionally correlated panels. In: Corbae, D., Durlauf, S., Hansen, B. (Eds.), Econometric Theory and Practice: frontiers of Analysis and Applied Research, Essays in Honor of Peter C.B. Phillips. Cambridge University Press, Cambridge

Cologni, A., Manera, M., 2008. Oil prices, inflation and interest rates in a structural cointegrated VAR model for the G-7 countries. Energy Economics 30, 856–888

Creane, S., Goyal, R., Mobarak, A.M., Sab, R., 2004. Financial sector development in the Middle East and North Africa. Working Paper No. 04/102. IMF, Washington, DC.

Cunado, J., Perez de Garcia, F., 2005. Oil prices, economic activity and inflation: evidence for some Asian countries. The Quarterly Review of Economics and Finance 45 (1), 65–83

El-Sharif, I., Brown, D., Burton, B., Nixon, B., Russel, A., 2005. Evidence on the nature and extent of the relationship between oil and equity value in UK. Energy Economics 27 (6), 819–830

Fasano, U., Iqbal, Z., 2003. GCC countries: from oil dependence to diversification. International Monetary Fund, Washington DC.

Gronwald, M., 2008. Large oil shocks and the US economy: infrequent incidents with large effects. Energy Journal 29, 151–171

Hammoudeh, S., Aleisa, E., 2004. Dynamic relationship among GCC stock markets and NYMEX oil futures. Contemporary Economic Policy 22, 250–269

Hammoudeh, S., Choi, K., 2006. Behavior of GCC stock markets and impacts of US oil and financial markets. Research in International Business and Finance 20 (1), 22–44

Huang, R.D., Masulis, R.W., Stoll, H.R., 1996. Energy shocks and financial markets. Journal of Futures Markets 16, 1–27

Im, K., Lee, J., 2001. Panel LM unit root test with level shifts. Discussion paper, Department of Economics, University of Central Florida.

Im, K., Pesaran, M., Shin, Y., 2003. Testing for unit roots in heterogeneous panels. Journal of Econometrics 115 (1), 53–74

Jones, C.M., Kaul, G., 1996. Oil and the stock markets. Journal of Finance 51 (2), 463–491

Kilian, L., 2008. Exogenous oil supply shocks: how big are they and how much do they matter for the US economy? Review of Economics and Statistics 90, 216–240

Kwiatkowski, D., Phillips, P., Shin, Y., 1992. Testing for the null hypothesis of stationarity against the alternative of a unit root. Journal of Econometrics 54, 159–178

Levin, A., Lin, C.-F., Chu, C.-S., 2002. Unit root tests in panel data: asymptotic and finite sample properties. Journal of Econometrics 108 (1), 1–24

Maddala, G., Wu, S., 1999. A comparative study of unit root tests and a new simple test. Oxford Bulletin of Economics and Statistics 61 (1), 631–652

McCoskey, S., Kao, C., 1998. A residual-based test of the null of cointegration in panel data. Econometric Reviews 17 (1), 57–84

Moon, H., Perron, B., 2004. Testing for a unit root in panels with dynamic factors. Journal of Econometrics 122 (1), 8–126

Naceur, S.B., Ghazouani, S., 2007. Stock markets, banks, and economic growth: empirical evidence from MENA region. Research in International Business and Finance 21, 297–315

Neaime, S., 2005. Financial market integration and macroeconomic volatility in the MENA region: an empirical investigation. Review of Middle East Economics and Finance 3, 231–253

Papapetrou, E., 2001. Oil price shocks, stock market, economic activity and employment in Greece. Energy Economics 23, 511–532

Park, J., Ratti, R.A., 2008. Oil price shocks and stock markets in the US and 13 European countries. Energy Economics 30, 2587–2608

Pesaran, M., 2004. General diagnostic tests for cross section dependence in panels. Cambridge Working Papers in Economics, No 435, University of Cambridge.

Pesaran, M., 2007. A simple panel unit root test in the presence of cross section dependence. Journal of Applied Econometrics 22 (2), 265–312

Sadorsky, P., 1999. Oil price shocks and stock market activity. Energy Economics 2, 449–469

Sephton, P.S., 1995. Response surface estimates of the KPSS stationarity test'. Economics Letters 47, 255–261

Smith, V., Leybourne, S., Kim, T.-H., 2004. More powerful panel unit root tests with an application to the mean reversion in real exchange rates. Journal of Applied Econometrics 19, 147–170

Sul, D., Phillips, P., Choi, C., 2005. Prewhitening bias in HAC estimatio. Oxford Bulletin of Economics and Statistics 67, 517–546

Westerlund, J., Edgerton, D., 2007. A panel bootstrap cointegration test. Economics Letters 97, 185–190

Zellner, A., 1962. An efficient method of estimating seemingly unrelated regressions and tests of aggregation bias. Journal of the American Statistical Association 57, 348–368

Trading Intensity and Informed Trading in the Tunis Stock Exchange

Rabaa Karaa[*,†], **Skander Slim**[‡], **and Dorra Mezzez Hmaied**[*]
[*]Institute of Higher Commercial Studies of Carthage, University of Carthage, Tunisia
[†]Higher Institute of Transport and Logistics of Sousse, University of Sousse, Tunisia
[‡]Institute of High Commercial Studies of Sousse, University of Sousse, Tunisia

1. INTRODUCTION

The concept of asymmetric information plays a crucial role in the market microstructure theory involving the fact that market participants may have different information. According to asymmetric information models, there are two types of traders. Informed traders who act strategically or hide their identity to benefit from their informational advantage and uninformed investors (or liquidity traders) who trade for liquidity needs or portfolio rebalancing. Traders can learn from observing market information, such as prices and trades. Glosten and Milgrom (1985) and Kyle (1985) examine the informational content of prices in an asymmetric information environment. Easley and O'Hara (1987) postulate that the trade size is also informative and suggest that informed agents may be identified by their large quantities. Previous microstructure models consider that the timing of trades is irrelevant and exogenous to price process. Diamond and Verrecchia (1987) and Easley and O'Hara (1992) are the first to give theoretical evidence for the relevance of time between trades. Diamond and Verrecchia (1987) argue that periods of absence of trade are indicative of bad news. In the model of Easley and O'Hara (1992), the lack of trade reveals a signal of no new information (either good or bad) on the market. Clearly, economic agents may infer information from trade characteristics and thus adjust their intensity of trading.

Theoretical literature based on asymmetric information gives ambiguous predictions about the relationship between trading intensity and the interaction of informed and uninformed investors. Easley and O'Hara (1992) associate fast trading to the occurrence of information event and a high proportion of informed agents. Admati and Pfleiderer (1988) suggest that the risk-neutral informed traders prefer to trade when the market is thick, especially during periods of high volume from uninformed traders. They report that when information acquisition is endogenous, the increase of competition between informed traders may improve the terms of trade for liquidity traders and thus involve a concentration of uninformed trading. Foster and Viswanathan (1990) assume that the presence of informed investors drives out liquidity traders from trading.

Emerging Markets and the Global Economy
http://dx.doi.org/10.1016/B978-0-12-411549-1.00009-0

Over the past 15 years, the analysis of trading intensity has been the focus of many empirical studies in finance based on ultra-high frequency data. The time between trades is usually used as an indicator of trading intensity (Spierdijk, 2004; Bauwens and Veredas, 2004; Engle, 2000). Empirical microstructure models attempt to describe the impact of trade features like trading volume, volatility, and spread on trade duration. Grammig and Wellner (2002) investigate the influence of volatility on trading intensity. Their results indicate that both expected volatility, and volatility shocks have a negative (positive) impact on trading intensity (trade duration). Dufour and Engle (2000) investigate the role of trade duration in the price formation process. They point out that high trading activity is related to greater price impact of trades and faster price adjustment to trade-related information (i.e. lower market liquidity), suggesting an increased presence of informed traders on the NYSE. The study of Spierdijk (2004) based on five frequently traded stocks listed on the NYSE reveals that the impact of small absolute returns, large trades on trading intensity is positive. Manganelli (2005) shows that price movement and volume affect negatively the trade duration only for liquid stocks. He concludes that the NYSE is characterized by a high presence of informed trading only for frequently traded stocks. Wu (2004) argues that infrequently traded NASDAQ stocks have higher informed trading intensity than frequently traded stocks. Brockman and Chung (2000) investigate the trading behavior of informed and uniformed traders in the Hong Kong Stock Exchange. They find that large, actively traded firms attract more informed and uninformed traders compared with small, inactively traded firms. In the model of Easley et al. (1996), infrequently traded stocks tend to have higher probability of informed trading and lower arrival rates of uninformed traders than active ones. Unlike Manganelli (2005), Wong et al. (2009) reveal the presence of informed trading in illiquid stocks listed on the Shanghai Stock Exchange. They claim that if volume is low, the presence of uninformed traders can explain the higher trading intensity. But at high volume, a short duration signals the presence of informed agents who deter liquidity traders from trading, only for liquid stocks. The authors also posit that large spread may deter uninformed liquidity traders from trading and encourage informed investors to trade more quickly, thereby increasing duration in the former case and reducing duration in the latter case. Biais et al.'s (1995) empirical analysis of the Paris Stock Exchange reveals that the time interval between trades is low when the spread is large. The competing traders, who control the market, quickly submit (limit) order within the quotes to supply liquidity and gain time priority. Hmaied et al. (2006) point out that on the Tunis Stock Exchange (TSE), the spread has a positive impact on volatility because large relative spread leads eager traders to place aggressive orders inside the spread inducing mid-quote variations. Ma et al. (2007) estimate the probability of informed trading in the order-driven Taiwan OTC market and argue that high liquidity does not attract informed trading.

Despite the abundant literature on the relationship between duration and trade features, few papers have focused on trading intensity in emerging purely order-driven market. The small number of empirical studies which describe trading activity and liquidity on the TSE is based on the analysis of low frequency time series or equally spaced intraday data. However, the choice of fixed time interval data involves a loss of information about market microstructure. It is thus interesting to study the dynamics of trading activity on the TSE, using tick-by-tick data.

This chapter examines the issue of informed trading via trading intensity and investigates the impact of trading volume and liquidity on the proportion of informed traders. Our contribution is to analyze the relationship between trade duration, trading volume, volatility, and relative spread for stocks listed on the TSE, using a mixed-Weibull Log Autoregressive Conditional Duration (LACD) model. Beyond, their superior fit to transaction data (De Luca and Gallo, 2009; De Luca and Zuccolotto, 2003) the rationale for mixture distribution models is that the trading process may arise as a result of the interaction of possibly heterogeneous subpopulations of market participants, i.e. informed and uninformed traders with different trading intensity. One may infer from the differences in arrival rates the likelihood of informed or uninformed trading. Unlike the exponential mixture used in De Luca and Gallo (2009) in which the hazard rate is completely monotone, the mixed-Weibull distribution provides a flexible model as it generates a wide variety of shapes of the conditional hazard function and is also able to depict non-monotonic hazard rates. To check whether high trading activity in the TSE coincides with an increased informed trading for both liquid and illiquid stocks, we estimate a fixed weight mixture LACD model that distinguishes between the two types of investors. A time-varying version of our model, in which the proportion of informed and uninformed traders varies with the information flow, is also designed to test if large trading volume and high liquidity attract more informed trading. The econometric models proposed in this study are applied to a sample of 16 stocks traded on the TSE. The stocks are divided into two groups according to their trading intensity to investigate whether frequently and infrequently traded stocks are characterized by different information transmission mechanisms.

Our findings reveal that high trading intensity is associated with large trading volume, high volatility, and narrow relative spread only for actively traded stocks, suggesting that the exogeneity of the trade arrival process may be a relevant hypothesis for illiquid stocks (Dufour and Engle, 2000; Glosten and Milgrom, 1985; Kyle, 1985). We also find that the proportion of informed traders on the TSE is high for both liquid and illiquid stocks. Our study indicates that uninformed arrival rate, for active stocks, is lower than it is for inactive stocks. Inconsistent with Admati and Pfleiderer (1988), we find that high informed trading follows low liquidity. Thus, large relative spread attracts informed traders to provide liquidity submitting less aggressive limit orders, especially for frequently traded stocks. In addition, low trading volume induces more informed trading. This result suggests that total trading volume would be a poor proxy for information arrival on the TSE.

The remainder of the chapter is organized as follows. Section 2 provides the institutional features of the Tunis Stock Exchange. Section 3 details the econometric models. Section 4 describes data pre-processing and presents the empirical results. Finally, Section 5 concludes.

2. INSTITUTIONAL FEATURES OF THE TUNIS STOCK EXCHANGE

The Tunis Stock Exchange (TSE) is a purely order-driven market in which short-selling is absolutely prohibited. Shares are traded on a screen-based electronic system called NSC V900. The TSE is relatively small and thin by international standards. It is exclusively dominated by the presence of brokerage firms. The potential for insider trading is significant because no mechanism exists to prevent insiders from buying and selling company shares based on inside information.

Traders can submit market or limit orders according to their preferences and the probability of order execution. They use limit orders to provide liquidity and submit market orders to demand liquidity. Unlike limit orders, market orders offer an immediate and certain execution.

The TSE is open from Monday to Friday from 10:00 am to 2:00 pm. The pre-opening session takes place from 9:00 am to 10:00 am. During this period, orders are accumulated, modified, or cancelled without occurring transaction. A theoretical opening price is calculated and updated when new orders entered into limit order book. The opening of market starts by a call auction at 10:00 am. Investors cannot modify or cancel previous orders. These orders are matched and all transactions are executed at the opening price, which is usually near the previous day's closing price. For the infrequently traded securities, there are two other fixed call auctions: the second call occurs at 11:30 am and the last fixing takes place at 1:00 pm. For the frequently traded securities, the opening phase is followed by a continuous trading session, which runs from 10:00 am to 2:00 pm. During normal trading period, the buy orders are matched with the sell orders using the trading priority rules. Consequently, one or more transactions are immediately executed. The trading system computes the closing price at 2:10 pm. It represents a benchmark price of the following day. Only, the best five bid and ask prices are revealed continuously to public investors. The limit order book is fully visible to brokers and regulatory authorities. The tick size (minimum price variation unit) ranges from 0.01 Dinars to 0.1 Dinars depending on the price level of the security. The TSE currently sets the daily price limits at ±3% of benchmark price. When a stock reaches its price limit, trading in this stock is halted for 30 min after which new limits (±1.5%) are applied without exceeding the maximum daily price variation of 6.09%.

3. ECONOMETRIC MODELS

3.1. The LACD Model

Since the seminal paper of Engle and Russell (1998), the Autoregressive Conditional Duration (ACD) model has become a benchmark tool in modeling the behavior of irregularly time-spaced transaction data. Bauwens and Giot (2000) introduced a logarithmic version of the ACD model (LACD), which is more convenient than the ACD model when conditioning variables are included in the model in order to test microstructure effects. The general class of LACD models may be written as follows:

$$x_i = \varphi_i \varepsilon_i, \tag{1}$$

$$\varphi_i = E(x_i|\Omega_{i-1}) = \exp\left\{\mu + \sum_{j=1}^{p} \alpha_j g(\varepsilon_{i-j}) + \sum_{j=1}^{q} \beta_j \varphi_{i-j}\right\}, \tag{2}$$

where x_i is the ith duration, φ_i is the conditional expectation of x_i given the information set Ω_{i-1} at the time $i-1$; μ, α_j, and β_j are coefficients; and $\{\varepsilon_i\}$ is a unit mean *iid* innovation process. The common distributional assumptions for ε_i are Exponential, Weibull, or Gamma. We consider an augmented LACD (1,1) model with $g(\varepsilon_{i-1}) = \varepsilon_{i-1}$. The functional form of φ_i is given by:

$$\varphi_i = \exp\left\{\mu + \alpha\varepsilon_{i-1} + \beta\varphi_{i-1} + \kappa S_{i-1} + \eta V_{i-1} + \xi|u_{i-1}|\right\}, \tag{3}$$

where S_{i-1} denotes the relative spread at time $i-1$, V_{i-1} is the lagged trading volume, and $|u_{i-1}|$ is the proxy for volatility. Unlike the earlier formulation of ACD-type models, such specification ensures positive expected duration without the need to impose non-negativity constraints on the parameters. The autoregressive structure in Eq. (3) allows the model to account for durations clustering and bears the economic motivation following from the clustering of news and financial events in the market. A low-order LACD model is often successful in removing the temporal dependence in durations. Moments and conditions for the LACD model are provided by Bauwens et al. (2008). One necessary condition for covariance stationarity is that $|\beta| < 1$. When the random variable ε_i follows a Weibull distribution with a scale parameter λ and a shape parameter γ, its density function is:

$$f_\varepsilon(\varepsilon_i; \lambda; \gamma) = \frac{\gamma}{\lambda}\varepsilon_i^{\gamma-1} \exp\left\{-\frac{\varepsilon_i^\gamma}{\lambda}\right\}. \tag{4}$$

The mean and variance are, respectively, given by:

$$\mathbb{E}(\varepsilon_i) = \lambda^{1/\gamma}\Gamma\left(1 + \frac{1}{\gamma}\right), \tag{5}$$

and

$$\sigma^2(\varepsilon_i) = \lambda^{2/\gamma}\left[\Gamma\left(1 + 2/\gamma\right) - \Gamma^2\left(1 + 1/\gamma\right)\right]. \tag{6}$$

Then the conditional density of x_i is given by:

$$f_X(x_i|\Omega_{i-1}) = \frac{\gamma}{x_i\lambda}\left(\frac{x_i}{\varphi_i}\right)^{\gamma} \exp\left\{-\frac{x_i^{\gamma}}{\varphi_i^{\gamma}\lambda}\right\}. \quad (7)$$

The Weibull distribution nests the exponential one and the hazard function can take many parametric shapes. The LACD formulation with Weibull innovations implies that the conditional hazard function might be either constant ($\gamma = 1$), monotonically increasing ($\gamma > 1$), or monotonically decreasing ($\gamma < 1$).

3.2. The Weibull Mixture LACD Model

Although the conditionally autoregressive structure of LACD model performs well in capturing the persistence in the duration process, the fit of distributions used in empirical studies tends to be poor. A number of recent studies suggest alternative distributional assumptions of the innovation process and associate the ACD model to different market participants. The microstructure literature supports the interaction of informed and uninformed traders through information-revealing price formation process. To the extent that two types of traders coexist in the market with different trading conditions, their actions are governed by two different innovation processes. This difference in behavior motivates the introduction of a mixture of two distributions, since the instantaneous rate of transaction can be viewed as being different across categories. In particular, De Luca and Gallo (2004) assume that the innovations to the duration process follow a mixture of two exponential distributions with a mixing parameter interpreted as the probability that a specific transaction is carried out by the informed type of trader, while Hujer and Vuletić (2007) propose a mixture of two Burr distributions. De Luca and Gallo (2009) introduce time-varying mixing weights in ACD model where the weights can be assumed to follow a logistic function, similar to the formulation of Markov Switching models with time-varying probabilities.

Based on the previous empirical literature, we develop a time-varying Weibull mixture LACD model that accounts for these two types of traders, in a way that they can be identified through their trading patterns. Hence, excess durations are assumed to be drawn from a mixture in scale and shape of two Weibull distributions $f_\varepsilon^1(\varepsilon_i; \lambda_{1i}; \gamma_1)$ and $f_\varepsilon^2(\varepsilon_i; \lambda_2; \gamma_2)$, labeled "I" and "U", respectively. The density function of the mixture is given by:

$$f(\varepsilon_i; \Theta_\varepsilon) = P_{1i}\frac{\gamma_1}{\lambda_{1i}}\varepsilon_i^{\gamma_1 - 1} \exp\left\{-\frac{\varepsilon_i^{\gamma_1}}{\lambda_{1i}}\right\} + P_{2i}\frac{\gamma_2}{\lambda_2}\varepsilon_i^{\gamma_2 - 1} \exp\left\{-\frac{\varepsilon_i^{\gamma_2}}{\lambda_2}\right\}, \quad (8)$$

where $\Theta_\varepsilon = (\gamma_1, \lambda_{1i}, \gamma_2, \lambda_2)$ is the parameter set of the innovations densities and $0 < P_{1i} < 1$ is the mixing weight at time i, with $P_{1i} + P_{2i} = 1$. The inverse of arrival rates of informed and uninformed traders are, respectively, given by:

$$\mathcal{E}_{1i} = \lambda_{1i}^{1/\gamma_1}\Gamma\left(1 + \frac{1}{\gamma_1}\right), \tag{9}$$

and

$$\mathcal{E}_2 = \lambda_2^{1/\gamma_2}\Gamma\left(1 + \frac{1}{\gamma_2}\right). \tag{10}$$

In order to obtain a unit mean innovations, we impose the following constraint:

$$\mathbb{E}(\varepsilon_i) = P_{1i}\mathcal{E}_{1i} + (1 - P_{1i})\mathcal{E}_2 = 1. \tag{11}$$

Then the time-varying scale parameter λ_{1i}, which involves a link between the arrival rates of the two components, is restricted to:

$$\lambda_{1i} = \left[\frac{1}{P_{1i}\Gamma\left(1 + \frac{1}{\gamma_1}\right)}\left(1 - (1 - P_{1i})\lambda_2^{\frac{1}{\gamma_2}}\Gamma\left(1 + \frac{1}{\gamma_2}\right)\right)\right]^{\gamma_1}. \tag{12}$$

Hence, one may distinguish between the two types of traders throughout their arrival rates. We suggest a higher arrival rate of uninformed traders[1] relative to informed ones. Besides, the proportions of informed and uninformed traders vary as information arrives on the market. With a non-constant arrival of news, the arrival rate of informed traders, $1/\mathcal{E}_{1i}$, is allowed to vary over time while the arrival rate of uninformed traders is kept constant.

A general approach is to relate the weights of the components to observed market variables, at time $i - 1$, via logistic response function. In particular, the weights depend on the lagged spread, volume, and past estimates of P_{1i}:

$$P_{1i} = \frac{\exp\{c + c_P P_{1i-1} + c_S S_{i-1} + c_V V_{i-1}\}}{1 + \exp\{c + c_P P_{1i-1} + c_S S_{i-1} + c_V V_{i-1}\}}. \tag{13}$$

The motivation for this specification is to investigate the interaction between liquidity and traded volume with the weight attributed to informed traders. It is worth noting that, from the unit mean restriction in (11), the time-varying arrival rate of informed traders, $1/\varepsilon_{1i}$, is increasing with respect to P_{1i} when the constant arrival rate of uninformed traders, $1/\varepsilon_2$, is greater than one, and decreasing when $1/\varepsilon_2$ is smaller than one. The relevant case, at least in our empirical application, is that $1/\varepsilon_2 > 1$. The relationship between P_{1i} and the arrival rate of informed traders $1/\varepsilon_{1i}$ shares the same properties with the exponential mixture model of De Luca and Gallo (2009) so that, at the limit when

[1] It is generally assumed that uninformed investors trade for liquidity reasons or portfolio rebalancing and their trading decision are usually independent of the existence of any information (e.g., Easley and O'Hara, 1992).

$P_{1i} \to 0$, $1/\varepsilon_{1i} \to 0$ and $1/\varepsilon_{1i} \to 1$ when $P_{1i} \to 1$. The baseline hazard function for the Weibull mixture is:

$$h_{\varepsilon_i}(t) = \frac{P_{1i}\frac{\gamma_1}{\lambda_{1i}}t^{\gamma_1-1}\exp\left\{-\frac{t^{\gamma_1}}{\lambda_{1i}}\right\} + P_{2i}\frac{\gamma_2}{\lambda_2}t^{\gamma_2-1}\exp\left\{-\frac{t^{\gamma_2}}{\lambda_2}\right\}}{P_{1i}\exp\left\{-\frac{t^{\gamma_1}}{\lambda_{1i}}\right\} + P_{2i}\exp\left\{-\frac{t^{\gamma_2}}{\lambda_2}\right\}}. \tag{14}$$

The mixture of Weibull distributions provides a rather flexible model to be fitted to data, and it is also able to depict non-monotonic hazard rates. The use of non-monotonic hazard functions for transaction durations is advocated by Grammig and Maurer (2000) and Bauwens and Veredas (2004). Monte Carlo evidence presented by Grammig and Maurer (2000) shows that imposing monotonic conditional hazard functions when the true data generating process requires non-monotonic hazard functions can have severe consequences for predicting expected durations because estimators of exponential and Weibull ACD models tend to be biased and inefficient. The Weibull mixture model generates a wide variety of shapes of the conditional hazard function. Figure 1 illustrates the diversity of hazard functions of Weibull mixtures in scale and/or shape. A mixture in scale has a decreasing hazard rate when its common shape parameter does not exceed one, which is illustrated by Figure 1a. Non-monotonic hazard rates arise when the common shape parameter is greater than one (Figure 1b) as well as

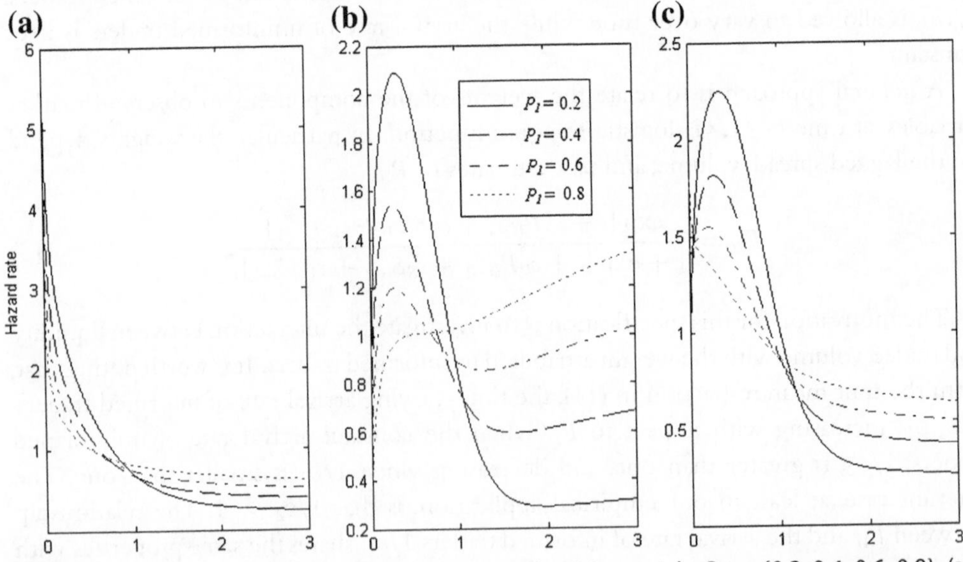

Figure 1 Hazard rates of several Weibull mixtures, with mixing weight $P_1 \in \{0.2, 0.4, 0.6, 0.8\}$. (a) Mixture in scale, $\gamma_1 = \gamma_2 = 0.8$, $\lambda_2 = 0.3$, and $\lambda_1 \in \{2.73, 1.65, 1.25, 1.03\}$ calculated from the unit mean restriction in (11). (b) Mixture in scale, $\gamma_1 = \gamma_2 = 1.3$, $\lambda_2 = 0.3$, and $\lambda_1 \in \{5.72, 2.64, 1.75, 1.34\}$. (c) Mixture in scale and shape, $\gamma_1 = 0.8$, $\gamma_2 = 1.3$, $\lambda_2 = 0.3$, and $\lambda_1 \in \{2.48, 1.54, 1.19, 1.01\}$.

when the mixed distributions have both different scale and shape parameters, as shown in Figure 1c.

The Weibull mixture model is therefore richer than the exponential mixture suggested by De Luca and Gallo (2009) model in terms of the class of conditional, and therefore unconditional, hazard functions it can produce. It is also noteworthy that, as a byproduct, the variance of the mixture of distributions is inversely related to the proportion of informed traders, that is:

$$\sigma^2(\varepsilon_i|\Omega_{i-1}) = P_{1i}\left[\lambda_{1i}^{\frac{2}{\gamma_1}}\Gamma\left(1+\frac{2}{\gamma_1}\right) - 2\varepsilon_{1i}+1\right] + (1-P_{1i}) \times \left[\lambda_2^{\frac{2}{\gamma_2}}\Gamma\left(1+\frac{2}{\gamma_2}\right) - 2\varepsilon_2+1\right]. \quad (15)$$

When the mixture of two Weibull distributions is applied to the augmented LACD model in (3), the conditional density of trade duration is:

$$f_X(x_i|\Omega_{i-1};\Theta) = P_{1i}f_X^1(x_i|\Omega_{i-1};\lambda_{1i};\gamma_1) + (1-P_{1i})f_X^2(x_i|\Omega_{i-1};\lambda_2;\gamma_2). \quad (16)$$

The model parameters are estimated by maximum likelihood. The associated log-likelihood function is given by:

$$\mathcal{L}(x,\Theta) = \sum_{i=1}^{N} \log\left[f_X(x_i|\Omega_{i-1};\Theta)\right], \quad (17)$$

where N is the number of observations and $\Theta = (\mu, \alpha, \beta, \gamma_1, \gamma_2, c, c_P, c_S, c_V, \lambda_2, \kappa, \eta, \xi)$ is the vector of parameters. For the empirical analysis, we estimate the time-varying Weibull mixture model (TVMLACD) as well as the fixed weight version of the model (MLACD) in which the parameter set is reduced to $\Theta = (\mu, \alpha, \beta, \gamma_1, \gamma_2, P_1, \lambda_2, \kappa, \eta, \xi)$.

4. EMPIRICAL ANALYSIS

4.1. Data

We use irregularly time-spaced high-frequency data obtained from the TSE. The initial sample contains 34 stocks listed continuously on the TSE from September 01, 2008 to December 31, 2009.[2] We select eight frequently traded stocks and eight infrequently traded stocks according to the number of trades during the sample period. The dataset gives information about the time stamp of transaction, transaction price, traded volume,[3] and bid-ask quotes.

[2] Since October 2008, the regular trading hours have been extended to 5 h and 10 min to provide more opportunities for investors. The dataset collected from the TSE covers this sample period that is sufficient to our empirical study.

[3] Like Wong et al. (2009), the trading volume refers to the number of shares traded in each interval.

To build our database, we employ two types of files, from which block trades are removed. The first is the trade dataset which contains the date, the transaction time, the security code, the transaction price, and the traded volume. The second file is the quote dataset which includes the security code, the date, the time, the bid (ask) price, the number of buy (sell) orders, and the buy (sell) orders quantity. Some information about the sample stocks used in our analysis is presented in Table 1. We note that there is a notable difference in both the number of observations and the market capitalization between the two groups of stocks. We determine for every transaction the bid and ask prices that appear at the time of transaction (Engle, 2000; Zhang et al., 2001). The observations without quotes on one or two sides of the limit order book are excluded. We also eliminate all transactions that were not carried out during the continuous trading session. Recall that the continuous trading runs from 10:00 am to 2:00 pm from Monday to Friday. For July, August, and Ramadan months, we drop the transactions that occurred before the opening time 9:30 am and after the closing time 12:00 pm because the trading hours change.

According to Engle and Russell (1998) and Manganelli (2005), trade durations are defined as time intervals between consecutive transactions. The transactions recorded at the same time (i.e. zero duration) are considered as one single transaction. For these transactions, we aggregate the volume (Manganelli, 2005). From Table 1, the multiple transactions occurring within a given second are approximately 42.70% and 33.90% of the number of trade observations, respectively, for liquid and illiquid stocks. Instead of using transaction price, we use the average of the bid and ask quotes. This price measure reduces the problem of bid-ask bounce and price discreteness, as advanced by Engle (2000), Hmaied et al. (2006), and Manganelli (2005). The mid-quote return is measured by the difference of log mid-quote prices. Estimates of volatility series are obtained from the residuals of an *ARMA (1,1)* process, $r_i = \omega + \theta r_{i-1} + \rho u_{i-1} + u_i$. So that our instantaneous volatility proxy $|u_i|$ is the residual series after removing the microstructure effect of the original mid-quote return series. The relative spread defined by absolute bid-ask spread (i.e. ask price minus bid price) divided by the bid-ask midpoint is used in our empirical work as an inverse proxy for liquidity (Hmaied et al., 2006; Chai et al., 2010; Brockman and Chung, 2000).

As it is well documented in the literature, there is a strong intraday periodicity in transaction data. In order to account for the time-of-the day effects, the time series of duration, volume, volatility, and relative spread are diurnally adjusted. This is achieved by first averaging raw observations over 30-min intervals for each day, setting the average durations of the mid-points of these intervals to the resulting averaged values, and then fitting a cubic spline over the course of the day, using these midpoints as fixed. The raw series are then diurnally adjusted by dividing each data point by the corresponding diurnal factor. From Table 1, we note that raw trade durations exhibit strong dependence using the Ljung-Box test. The Ljung-Box statistics of the diurnally adjusted data are slightly decreased but indicate a significant autocorrelation.

Table 1 Sample stocks.

Company name (ticker)	Industry sector	N^*	Zeros	MC	N	LB raw	N adjusted
Liquid stocks							
TPR	Basic materials	28158	12396	82362	12658	2010	1942
ATTIJARI BANK (TJARI)	Finance	23678	9834	317087	11127	1959	1790
TUNISAIR (TAIR)	Consumer services	23631	11030	68415	7792	1554	1449
SOMOCER (SOMOC)	Industry	22831	10341	43382	8562	1145	1118
ASSAD	Consumer goods	20174	8263	57403	9184	1140	1045
ADWYA	Health	20139	8684	48020	9071	1149	992.4
STB	Finance	17355	7001	101134	8099	3225	2868
STAR	Finance	16816	6675	101542	7569	1627	1441
Illiquid stocks							
SOTRAPIL (STPIL)	Oil and gas	6477	2364	9774	2804	255.9	143.8
EL WIFACK LEASING (WIFAK)	Finance	5287	2018	20739	2429	279.4	191.9
SPDIT-SICAF (SPDIT)	Finance	4421	1393	17649	1803	195.0	189.2
TUNINVEST-SICAR (TINV)	Finance	3840	1311	7817	1789	136.5	117.3
SIPHAT (SIPHA)	Health	3611	1165	7465	1688	193.7	180.7
ELECTROSTAR (LSTR)	Consumer goods	3575	1167	5375	1558	53.22	41.88
SIMPAR (SIMPA)	Industry	2882	951	9775	1133	124.22	37.81
ESSOUKNA (SOKNA)	Industry	2577	859	3922	1180	102.8	49.06

This table gives information on the name, ticker (in parentheses) of the sampled stocks used in this study. A sample of 16 stocks listed continuously on the Tunis Stock Exchange, from September 01, 2008 to December 31, 2009, is classified into eight liquid and eight illiquid stocks according to the number of trades. Market capitalization (MC), in thousand Dinars, the number of transaction observations (N^*) before filtering, the number of trade durations (N) excluding the opening period of each day, from 10:00 am to 10:30 am, are presented for each stock. Zero observations (Zeros) refer to simultaneous transaction in the data. Ten lags are used in calculating the Ljung-Box statistics (LB) for raw and diurnally adjusted durations.

4.2. Fixed Weight Mixture LACD Estimates

To investigate the impact of volatility, trading volume, and relative spread on trade duration, we estimate the augmented MLACD (1,1) model with fixed mixing weights by maximum likelihood. Table 2 provides the estimation results of the model given by (3). The coefficient, α, is always significantly positive indicating that shorter lagged excess durations imply shorter conditional expected trade durations. Estimates of the autoregressive coefficient, β, show a high persistence in the dynamic of the duration process. This result sheds light on the possibility that clustering of transactions may be occurring at certain time periods of a trading day. Infrequently traded stocks have higher estimated

Table 2 Parameters estimates of the mixture model (MLACD).

Ticker	μ	α	β	γ_1	γ_2	P_1	ε_2	κ	η	ξ	$\mathcal{L}$	*LB*	*VAR*
Liquid stocks													
TPR	**−0.119**	**0.107**	**0.945**	**0.868**	**1.098**	**0.577**	**0.291**	**0.016**	**−0.006**	**−0.007**	−9917.5	**31.083**	1.735
	(0.000)	(0.000)	(0.000)	(0.000)	(0.000)	(0.000)	(0.000)	(0.000)	(0.000)	(0.006)		(0.000)	
TJARI	**−0.090**	**0.088**	**0.941**	**0.824**	**1.142**	**0.660**	**0.206**	**0.013**	**−0.015**	**−0.009**	−8190.6	**31.775**	1.922
	(0.000)	(0.000)	(0.000)	(0.000)	(0.000)	(0.000)	(0.000)	(0.000)	(0.000)	(0.000)		(0.000)	
TAIR	**−0.092**	**0.080**	**0.943**	**0.799**	**1.223**	**0.717**	**0.152**	**0.032**	**−0.024**	**−0.010**	−5320.5	14.958	2.044
	(0.000)	(0.000)	(0.000)	(0.000)	(0.000)	(0.000)	(0.000)	(0.000)	(0.000)	(0.000)		(0.133)	
SOMOC	**−0.075**	**0.104**	**0.909**	**0.781**	**1.063**	**0.552**	**0.237**	**0.038**	**−0.059**	**−0.032**	−5294.5	10.901	2.111
	(0.000)	(0.000)	(0.000)	(0.000)	(0.000)	(0.000)	(0.000)	(0.000)	(0.000)	(0.000)		(0.365)	
ASSAD	**−0.113**	**0.111**	**0.876**	**0.804**	**1.109**	**0.663**	**0.188**	**0.163**	**−0.033**	**−0.016**	−6893.1	11.501	2.054
	(0.000)	(0.000)	(0.000)	(0.000)	(0.000)	(0.000)	(0.000)	(0.000)	(0.000)	(0.000)		(0.319)	
ADWYA	**−0.067**	**0.078**	**0.937**	**0.784**	**1.105**	**0.620**	**0.181**	**0.015**	**−0.028**	**−0.011**	−6308.2	13.138	2.200
	(0.000)	(0.000)	(0.000)	(0.000)	(0.000)	(0.000)	(0.000)	(0.001)	(0.000)	(0.014)		(0.216)	
STB	**−0.131**	**0.101**	**0.931**	**0.759**	**1.177**	**0.631**	**0.159**	**0.025**	**−0.011**	−0.005	−3785.9	17.352	2.298
	(0.000)	(0.000)	(0.000)	(0.000)	(0.000)	(0.000)	(0.000)	(0.000)	(0.000)	(0.208)		(0.066)	
STAR	**−0.126**	**0.107**	**0.896**	**0.777**	**1.056**	**0.563**	**0.211**	**0.039**	**−0.021**	**−0.019**	−5095	12.558	2.219
	(0.000)	(0.000)	(0.000)	(0.000)	(0.000)	(0.000)	(0.000)	(0.000)	(0.000)	(0.000)		(0.249)	

(*Continued*)

Table 2 (Continued)

Ticker	μ	α	β	γ_1	γ_2	P_1	ε_2	κ	η	ξ	$\mathcal{L}$	*LB*	*VAR*
Illiquid stocks													
STPIL	**−0.082**	**0.095**	**0.915**	**0.863**	**1.147**	**0.690**	**0.103**	0.008	−0.014	−0.010	−2253.4	7.024	2.308
	(0.000)	(0.000)	(0.000)	(0.000)	(0.000)	(0.000)	(0.000)	(0.417)	(0.051)	(0.266)		(0.723)	
WIFAK	**−0.122**	**0.096**	**0.845**	**0.841**	**1.105**	**0.655**	**0.127**	**0.056**	−0.001	−0.028	−2017.1	8.722	2.318
	(0.000)	(0.000)	(0.000)	(0.000)	(0.000)	(0.000)	(0.000)	(0.020)	(0.836)	(0.050)		(0.558)	
SPDIT	**−0.069**	**0.059**	**0.907**	**0.869**	**1.195**	**0.661**	**0.066**	0.015	0.009	−0.015	−1251.4	14.353	2.872
	(0.000)	(0.000)	(0.000)	(0.000)	(0.000)	(0.000)	(0.000)	(0.236)	(0.125)	(0.136)		(0.157)	
TINV	**−0.078**	**0.093**	**0.905**	**0.809**	**0.969**	**0.648**	**0.129**	0.033	**−0.044**	−0.012	−1311.9	13.680	2.549
	(0.000)	(0.000)	(0.000)	(0.000)	(0.000)	(0.000)	(0.000)	(0.124)	(0.001)	(0.470)		(0.188)	
SIPHA	**−0.154**	**0.110**	**0.771**	**0.923**	**1.038**	**0.595**	**0.113**	**0.083**	−0.023	−0.008	−1322.2	4.411	2.863
	(0.002)	(0.000)	(0.000)	(0.000)	(0.000)	(0.000)	(0.000)	(0.019)	(0.062)	(0.551)		(0.926)	
LSTR	**−0.087**	**0.081**	**0.851**	**0.890**	**1.066**	**0.729**	**0.095**	0.036	−0.005	−0.024	−1348.8	5.567	2.203
	(0.029)	(0.000)	(0.000)	(0.000)	(0.000)	(0.000)	(0.000)	(0.265)	(0.451)	(0.226)		(0.850)	
SIMPA	**−0.205**	**0.159**	**0.633**	**1.011**	**1.053**	**0.591**	**0.115**	0.072	0.003	−0.022	−910.1	9.992	2.418
	(0.003)	(0.000)	(0.000)	(0.000)	(0.000)	(0.000)	(0.000)	(0.092)	(0.293)	(0.378)		(0.441)	
SOKNA	**−0.253**	**0.163**	**0.492**	**0.896**	**0.893**	**0.600**	**0.114**	0.063	−0.002	0.049	−916.6	17.001	2.826
	(0.000)	(0.000)	(0.000)	(0.000)	(0.000)	(0.000)	(0.000)	(0.225)	(0.881)	(0.126)		(0.067)	

Entries report the maximum likelihood estimates of the model parameters, the Ljung-Box statistics of order 10 (*LB*) of the estimated residuals, *p*-values (in parentheses), the variance of excess duration (*VAR*), and the maximized log-likelihood value ($\mathcal{L}$). The inverse of arrival rate of uninformed traders, ε_2, is calculated by Eq. (10) using the estimated model parameters λ_2 and γ_2. Bold format denotes significance at the 5% level.

residuals' variance than frequently traded stocks, dictating that there is more uncertainty around the expected durations. At a lag of 10, the Ljung-box statistics for residuals are significant, at 5% level, for 2 out of 16 stocks. Manganelli (2005) and Wong et al. (2009) also face similar data-fitting problems, although their time series are extremely long compared with those used in our empirical study.

The lagged volatility coefficient, ξ, is negative but strongly significant for frequently traded stocks. Thus, high trading periods on the TSE seem to coincide with a higher fraction of informed traders when the stock is liquid. This finding is consistent with existing theoretical and empirical predictions, such as Easley and O'Hara (1992) and Manganelli (2005). From Table 2, the fixed weight attributed to the distribution I, P_1, is clearly significant for all stocks, revealing the existence of two types of traders, informed and uninformed (liquidity) traders. For the liquid stocks, the value of P_1 ranges from 55.2% to 71.7%, whereas in the case of illiquid stocks it ranges from 59.1% to 72.9%. Illiquid stocks seem to be subject to more informed trading than liquid stocks, a result consistent with Easley et al. (1996) and Wu (2004). Our finding of high proportion of traders possessing private information for the two groups of stocks reflects that our model predicts the presence of informed trading for both large and small stocks, as suggested by Wong et al. (2009). This result corroborates the hypothesis of higher asymmetric information in emerging markets than in developed ones due to the lack of appropriate market regulation on financial reporting as well as the low level of information disclosure.

The arrival rate for distribution U, $1/\varepsilon_2$, associated to frequently traded stocks tends to be slightly lower than that for infrequently traded stocks. Even though inactive stocks have a great proportion of informed traders, they are weakly riskier than active stocks due to the high uninformed arrival rate.

For both groups, the estimated shape parameter, γ_1, is smaller than one while the estimated mixing parameter, γ_2, is greater than unity in most cases. Therefore, the downward sloping hazard rate, associated to the distribution I, is in line with the trading pattern of informed traders who act immediately upon the arrival of private information. The increasing hazard rate, associated to the distribution U, is consistent with the trading pattern of uninformed traders who adopt a lagged behavior that is conditional on the order flow created by informed traders. Hence, our results provide further insight into the identification of regime-specific hazard functions that accommodate the trading behavior of two types of traders.

The impact of lagged volume, η, on the expected conditional duration is significant and negative for 9 out of 16 stocks. For all liquid stocks, large trading volume tends to be followed by high trading intensity. Manganelli (2005) and Spierdijk (2004) provide similar findings, especially when the stocks are frequently traded. The trading volume is used as a proxy of the information arrival into the market (Andersen, 1996; Lamoureux and Lastrapes, 1990; Bohl and Henke, 2003). The result for trading volume suggests that significant information flow intensifies the trading activity. The lagged relative spread coefficient, κ, is significantly positive for the eight actively traded stocks. Short trade duration is associated with narrow relative spread. We find the same result for 2 out of 8 small stocks. The negative relation between trading intensity and relative spread can be explained by the fact that high liquidity encourages traders to consume liquidity and thus trade immediately submitting market order. Moreover, a decrease of transaction intensity due to the lack of liquidity may be related to investors who do not issue aggressive orders to quicken the execution like on the Paris Stock Exchange (Biais et al., 1995).

Our previous empirical results based on frequently traded stocks report that high volatility, large trading volume, and narrow relative spread imply short trade duration. When the analysis is extended to the infrequently traded stocks, the coefficients of lagged additional variables are not significant in most cases, consistent with Manganelli (2005). We conclude that the assumption of duration exogeneity, as suggested by Glosten and Milgrom (1985) and Kyle (1985), may be valid only when dealing with illiquid stocks.

4.3. Time-Varying Mixing Weights LACD Estimates

The previous model assumes constant weights in the mixture. Indeed, informed traders continually receive signals about the trading environment and consequently induce a varying trading intensity. In the following, we estimate LACD model with time-varying mixing weights (TVMLACD). The estimation results reported in Table 3 show that the Ljung-box statistics for residual autocorrelation are satisfactory, except for TPR and TJARI. The estimated variance of residuals reveals a decrease of the noise in excess duration for 14 out of 16 stocks. Such noise reduction is more pronounced in illiquid securities than in liquid ones. All stocks have significant likelihood ratio statistics, indicating that the TVMLACD model outperforms its counterpart with fixed mixing weights (MLACD). The impact of market-related variables like volatility, trading volume, and relative spread on conditional trading intensity is qualitatively similar to the MLACD estimates.

From Table 4, we can note that the average proportion of informed traders for each stock is higher than 0.5, which provides strong evidence supporting the presence of agents possessing private information (e.g., brokerage firms). We find that the variability of informed trading is low, except for STAR, SOKNA, and TINV.

To study the time variation of the mixing weights attributed to the distribution I, P_{1i}, we analyze the results of the logistic specification presented in (13). The autoregressive term, c_P, is significant and positive for 6 out of 8 liquid stocks, indicating a strong autocorrelation. Hence, the presence of informed traders is more likely to last long because their private information seem to be not quickly revealed. This prediction is in line with Kyle (1985) who claims that informed investor trades in such a way that his private information is gradually incorporated into prices. This persistence is, however, found to be significant for 1 out of 8 infrequently traded stocks, suggesting that informed agents tend to enter and leave the market quickly when the stock is illiquid. The estimated parameter, c_S, allows us to see how the presence of informed agents interacts with liquidity. The impact

Table 3 Parameters estimates of the time-varying mixture model (TVMLACD).

Ticker	μ	α	β	γ_1	γ_2	ε_2	c	c_P	c_S	c_V	κ	η	ξ	$\mathcal{L}$	LB	VAR
Liquid stocks																
TPR	**−0.117**	**0.110**	**0.943**	**0.878**	**1.092**	**0.293**	**−1.927**	**3.906**	−0.004	**−0.012**	**0.021**	**−0.010**	**−0.010**	**−9891.2**	**26.084**	1.759
	(0.000)	(0.000)	(0.000)	(0.000)	(0.000)	(0.000)	(0.000)	(0.000)	(0.075)	(0.000)	(0.000)	(0.000)	(0.000)	[52,6]	(0.003)	
TJARI	**−0.090**	**0.094**	**0.941**	**0.827**	**1.134**	**0.207**	**−1.384**	**3.165**	0.018	**−0.062**	**0.012**	**−0.014**	**−0.009**	**−8172.1**	**31.507**	1.908
	(0.000)	(0.000)	(0.000)	(0.000)	(0.000)	(0.000)	(0.000)	(0.000)	(0.220)	(0.000)	(0.000)	(0.000)	(0.000)	[37]	(0.000)	
TAIR	**−0.103**	**0.100**	**0.926**	**0.794**	**1.195**	**0.165**	**−1.642**	**3.482**	**0.119**	**−0.038**	**0.039**	**−0.035**	**−0.012**	**−5303**	8.220	2.046
	(0.000)	(0.000)	(0.000)	(0.000)	(0.000)	(0.000)	(0.000)	(0.000)	(0.043)	(0.000)	(0.000)	(0.000)	(0.011)	[35]	(0.607)	
SOMOC	**−0.093**	**0.120**	**0.893**	**0.774**	**1.065**	**0.231**	**−2.009**	**4.057**	**−0.005**	**−0.010**	**0.047**	**−0.056**	**−0.033**	**−5264.5**	6.471	2.034
	(0.000)	(0.000)	(0.000)	(0.000)	(0.000)	(0.000)	(0.000)	(0.000)	(0.000)	(0.000)	(0.000)	(0.000)	(0.000)	[60]	(0.774)	
ASSAD	**−0.111**	**0.121**	**0.870**	**0.807**	**1.105**	**0.192**	**−0.955**	**2.527**	0.020	**−0.074**	**0.031**	**−0.036**	**−0.016**	**−6877.4**	11.751	2.049
	(0.000)	(0.000)	(0.000)	(0.000)	(0.000)	(0.000)	(0.011)	(0.000)	(0.473)	(0.000)	(0.000)	(0.000)	(0.003)	[31.4]	(0.302)	
ADWYA	**−0.076**	**0.082**	**0.941**	**0.785**	**1.104**	**0.182**	**−1.325**	**3.100**	−0.020	**−0.087**	**0.014**	**−0.016**	**−0.009**	**−6289.3**	15.027	2.175
	(0.000)	(0.000)	(0.000)	(0.000)	(0.000)	(0.000)	(0.000)	(0.000)	(0.109)	(0.000)	(0.006)	(0.000)	(0.035)	[37.8]	(0.131)	
STB	**−0.131**	**0.105**	**0.927**	**0.754**	**1.172**	**0.161**	0.089	0.490	**0.152**	**−0.021**	**0.025**	**−0.013**	−0.006	**−3777.3**	17.063	2.254
	(0.000)	(0.000)	(0.000)	(0.000)	(0.000)	(0.000)	(0.707)	(0.225)	(0.003)	(0.035)	(0.000)	(0.000)	(0.179)	[17.2]	(0.073)	
STAR	**−0.111**	**0.122**	**0.905**	**0.729**	**1.032**	**0.214**	**−0.527**	−0.244	**1.603**	**−0.109**	**0.024**	**−0.012**	**−0.015**	**−5049.6**	13.699	1.890
	(0.000)	(0.000)	(0.000)	(0.000)	(0.000)	(0.000)	(0.009)	(0.431)	(0.000)	(0.000)	(0.000)	(0.000)	(0.000)	[90.8]	(0.187)	

(Continued)

Table 3 (Continued)

Ticker	μ	α	β	γ_1	γ_2	ε_2	c	c_P	c_S	c_V	κ	η	ξ	$\mathcal{L}$	*LB*	*VAR*
Illiquid stocks																
STPIL	**−0.079**	**0.101**	**0.912**	**0.852**	**1.159**	**0.100**	0.105	0.949	**0.157**	**−0.070**	0.003	**−0.016**	−0.007	**−2246.7**	6.570	2.266
	(0.000)	(0.000)	(0.000)	(0.000)	(0.000)	(0.000)	(0.831)	(0.196)	(0.033)	(0.025)	(0.680)	(0.039)	(0.379)	[13.4]	(0.765)	
WIFAK	**−0.103**	**0.094**	**0.861**	**0.877**	**1.053**	**0.137**	−0.611	1.556	**0.197**	**0.063**	0.039	0.002	−0.024	**−2009.3**	8.388	2.269
	(0.000)	(0.000)	(0.000)	(0.000)	(0.000)	(0.000)	(0.228)	(0.062)	(0.021)	(0.008)	(0.054)	(0.371)	(0.055)	[15.6]	(0.590)	
SPDIT	**−0.072**	**0.061**	**0.902**	**0.875**	**1.187**	**0.066**	−0.442	**1.662**	0.077	**−0.076**	0.015	**0.011**	−0.015	**−1245.4**	14.584	2.793
	(0.000)	(0.000)	(0.000)	(0.000)	(0.000)	(0.000)	(0.360)	(0.029)	(0.169)	(0.004)	(0.254)	(0.026)	(0.159)	[12]	(0.148)	
TINV	**−0.061**	**0.083**	**0.936**	**0.809**	**0.976**	**0.124**	0.772	−1.070	**0.870**	**−0.173**	0.012	**−0.025**	−0.003	**−1291.9**	14.052	2.377
	(0.001)	(0.000)	(0.000)	(0.000)	(0.000)	(0.000)	(0.266)	(0.264)	(0.001)	(0.002)	(0.362)	(0.010)	(0.755)	[40]	(0.170)	
SIPHA	**−0.122**	**0.097**	**0.832**	**0.940**	**1.022**	**0.114**	0.208	−0.206	**0.355**	−0.067	**0.062**	−0.019	−0.008	**−1312.6**	4.003	2.494
	(0.002)	(0.000)	(0.000)	(0.000)	(0.000)	(0.000)	(0.649)	(0.790)	(0.002)	(0.051)	(0.015)	(0.107)	(0.496)	[19.2]	(0.947)	
LSTR	**−0.066**	**0.078**	**0.881**	**0.872**	**1.079**	**0.093**	**4.296**	**−4.748**	**0.349**	−0.011	0.025	−0.008	−0.024	**−1342.9**	4.814	2.174
	(0.026)	(0.000)	(0.000)	(0.000)	(0.000)	(0.000)	(0.000)	(0.000)	(0.028)	(0.284)	(0.277)	(0.229)	(0.175)	[11.8]	(0.903)	
SIMPA	**−0.234**	**0.163**	**0.571**	**1.067**	**1.013**	**0.130**	−0.942	1.696	**0.316**	**−0.073**	**0.094**	**0.019**	−0.025	**−899.2**	11.415	2.321
	(0.000)	(0.000)	(0.000)	(0.000)	(0.000)	(0.000)	(0.115)	(0.181)	(0.037)	(0.025)	(0.003)	(0.000)	(0.356)	[21.81]	(0.326)	
SOKNA	**−0.188**	**0.178**	**0.554**	**0.886**	**0.871**	**0.113**	−0.402	0.101	**1.119**	**−0.101**	−0.003	0.007	**0.060**	**−893.7**	14.388	2.543
	(0.000)	(0.000)	(0.000)	(0.000)	(0.000)	(0.000)	(0.261)	(0.874)	(0.000)	(0.016)	(0.901)	(0.536)	(0.016)	[45.87]	(0.156)	

Entries report the maximum likelihood estimates of the TVMLACD model parameters, coefficients estimates of the logistic specification for the time-varying mixing weights in (13), the Ljung-Box statistics of order 10 (*LB*) of the estimated residuals, the variance of excess duration (*VAR*), and the maximized log-likelihood value ($\mathcal{L}$). Given model parameters λ_2 and γ_2, we report the estimated values of the constant inverse of arrival rate of uninformed traders. The arrival rate of informed traders is time-varying. The values in parentheses are *p*-values of the estimated parameters, whereas the values in square brackets are the likelihood ratio test (LR) statistics for the TVMLACD model over the nested MLACD specification. Under the null hypothesis, the LR statistics are distributed as chi-square with three degrees of freedom with 7.81 as 5% critical value. Bold format denotes significance at the 5% level.

of relative spread on the proportion of informed traders is significantly positive for 10 out of 16 stocks. This effect is more pronounced for infrequently traded stocks than for the frequently traded ones. Similar to Ma et al. (2007), we find that higher liquidity does not lead to more informed traders. Our finding suggests that, narrow relative spread attracts rather uninformed traders to quickly consume liquidity. Meanwhile, low liquidity incites informed traders to act as liquidity providers submitting less aggressive limit order in the market, especially when the stocks are actively traded. In this case, trade durations for frequently traded stocks seem to be long. Furthermore, the incentive of informed traders to trade may also depend on other factors such as the quality of their information and their degree of risk aversion. Indeed, Admati and Pfleiderer (1988) argue that risk-neutral informed traders want to trade when the market is thick and their number increases during the periods of concentrated liquidity trading. Nevertheless, this prediction may not be valid when the informed agents are risk-averse (Subrahmanyam, 1991). We find that surprisingly, for 13 out of 16 stocks, the proportion of informed traders responds negatively to past trading volume. This result indicates that news arrival attracts less informed trading. Hence, our conjecture is not consistent with Easley and O'Hara's (1992) prediction that informed investors trade only when there is new information on the market. Thus, the total trading volume would be a poor proxy for information flow on the TSE.

Figure 2 presents the time series graph for the proportion of agents possessing private information and variance of the residuals in (15). It shows that data attributes a higher weight to the distribution I when the variance of the residuals is low, while a high variance of excess duration has the effect of increasing the weight of the distribution U (e.g., the highest spikes in the residual's variance are associated with a proportion of informed trading close to zero). Our results reveal that large trading volume induces less weight to the distribution I and thus high noise in excess durations. Following De Luca and Gallo (2009), we suggest that the presence of uninformed traders makes prediction of future expected durations less precise.

5. CONCLUSION

This chapter examines the relationship between volatility, trading volume, relative spread, and trade duration. It also studies the impact of trading volume and liquidity on the presence of informed trading in the Tunis Stock Exchange (TSE). We estimate a fixed mixing weight LACD model for 16 stocks classified into two groups according to their trade intensity. We extend this model by assuming that the proportion of informed traders is time-varying. Consistent with the results of Manganelli (2005), we find that high trading intensity is related to high volatility, large trading volume, and narrow relative spread only for liquid stocks. This result indicates that intensive trading activity coincides with the involvement of informed traders who choose to exploit their information advantage in

Table 4 Summary statistics of the time-varying weight attributed to informed trading.

Ticker	Mean	SD	Auto.	Min.	Median	Max.
Liquid stocks						
TPR	0.568	0.057	0.975	0.021	0.587	0.623
TJARI	0.654	0.048	0.832	0.003	0.666	0.850
TAIR	0.707	0.058	0.897	0.037	0.701	0.989
SOMOC	0.569	0.099	0.998	0.208	0.622	0.663
ASSAD	0.656	0.042	0.707	0.018	0.667	0.769
ADWYA	0.614	0.069	0.871	0.060	0.634	0.696
STB	0.626	0.046	0.630	0.024	0.614	0.980
STAR	0.597	0.205	0.659	0.000	0.559	1.000
Illiquid stocks						
STPIL	0.699	0.048	0.566	0.139	0.694	0.955
WIFAK	0.616	0.061	0.612	0.000	0.611	0.951
SPDIT	0.655	0.047	0.579	0.035	0.659	0.801
TINV	0.649	0.130	0.237	0.023	0.627	0.999
SIPHA	0.589	0.073	0.447	0.301	0.574	0.989
LSTR	0.743	0.071	−0.608	0.425	0.744	0.997
SIMPA	0.552	0.104	0.751	0.000	0.537	0.983
SOKNA	0.608	0.166	0.496	0.028	0.559	1.000

Entries report the summary statistics of the time-varying weight attributed to informed trading, P_{1i}. SD and Auto., denote the standard deviation and the first-order autocorrelation, respectively.

the frequently traded stocks. Infrequently traded stocks, however, seem to have different information transmission mechanisms.

Our results reveal the existence of two types of agents, informed and uninformed traders. In line with the empirical findings of Wong et al. (2009) who use nonlinear LACD model, our mixture LACD models do not exclude the presence of informed traders from trading in illiquid stocks. Although the Tunis Stock Exchange is known to be smaller and less liquid than developed stock markets, the proportion of informed trading is found to be higher in both large and small stocks, suggesting low quality of information disclosure into the market. Frequently traded stocks are characterized by high persistence of informed trading and low uninformed arrival rate compared with infrequently traded stocks. Our findings suggest that an informed investor trades in a gradual manner when the stock is liquid. Similar to Ma et al. (2007), we find that high liquidity does not attract more informed trading. It seems that low relative spread encourages uninformed agents to consume liquidity. However, informed traders tend to act as liquidity providers during periods of increased relative spread. We also find that the proportion of informed traders is decreasing with trading volume. Consequently, high presence of informed trading can result from low information arrival. This result does not support the assumption of

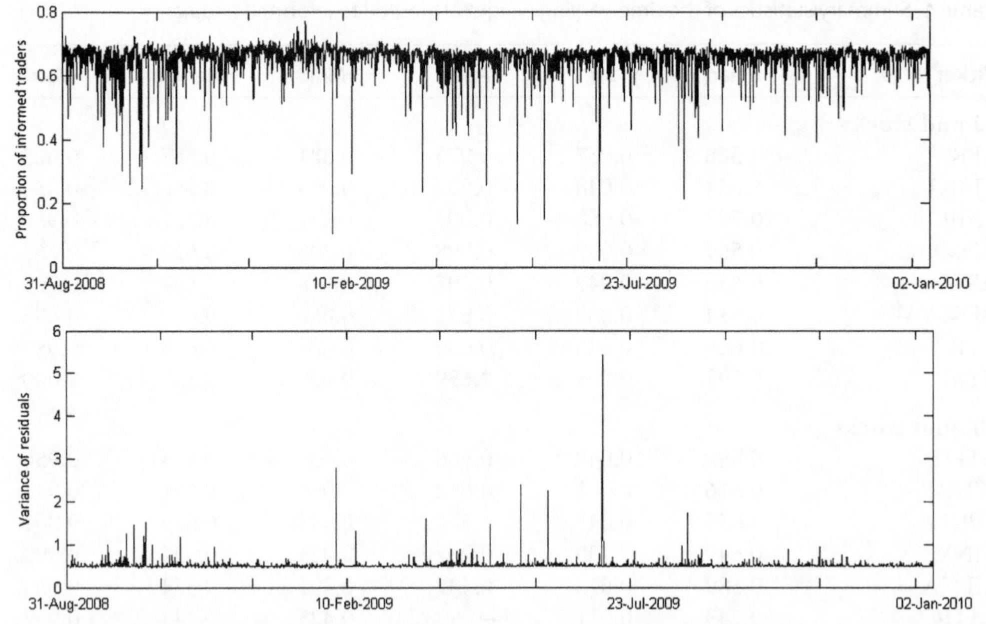

Figure 2 Time series plot of the proportion of informed trading (top panel) and the conditional variance of residuals (down panel) for ASSAD. Time-varying variance of residuals, drawn on a log scale, is obtained from (15) using estimated model parameters in Table 3.

Easley and O'Hara (1992) that informed agents only trade on the existence of new information. Therefore, the total trading volume appears to be a poor proxy for information flow.

Unlike Wong et al. (2009), we show that linear LACD model does not appear to be a model misspecification when we adopt a mixture of distribution approach. Our findings could inform policymakers about initiatives and new strategies to improve the transparency of trading mechanism and the liquidity of the stock market. A policy implication that follows from our analysis is that a stricter regulation should be imposed to brokerage firms in order to reduce information asymmetry between traders.

ACKNOWLEDGMENTS

The authors would like to thank members of the Tunis Stock Exchange, especially, Abderraouf Boudabous and Lilia Achich Touzri from the communication department and Hatem Zribi from the market promotion direction for providing the dataset. We are also grateful to Hedi Kasraoui from "*Compagnie Générale D'investissement*" (a Brokerage firm) for helpful discussions about data and market activity.

REFERENCES

Admati, A.R., Pfleiderer, P., 1988. A theory of intraday patterns: volume and price variability. Review of Financial Studies 1, 3–40

Andersen, T.G., 1996. Return volatility and trading volume: an information flow interpretation of stochastic volatility. Journal of Finance 51, 169–204

Bauwens, L., Giot, P., 2000. The logarithmic ACD model: an application to the bid-ask quote process of three NYSE stocks. Annales d'Economie et de Statistique 60, 117–149

Bauwens, L., Veredas, D., 2004. The stochastic conditional duration model: a latent variable model for the analysis of financial durations. Journal of Econometrics 119, 381–412

Bauwens, L., Galli, F., Giot, P., 2008. The moments of log-ACD models. Quantitative and Qualitative Analysis in Social Sciences 2, 1–28

Biais, B., Hillion, B., Spatt, C., 1995. An empirical analysis of the order book and order flow in the Paris Bourse. Journal of Finance 50, 1655–1689

Bohl, M.T., Henke, H., 2003. Trading volume and stock market volatility: the Polish case. International Review of Financial Analysis 12, 513–525

Brockman, P., Chung, D.Y., 2000. Informed and uninformed trading in an electronic, order-driven environment. Financial Review 35, 125–146

Chai, D., Faff, R., Gharghori, P., 2010. New evidence on the relation between stock liquidity and measures of trading activity. International Review of Financial Analysis 19, 181–192

De Luca, G., Gallo, G.M., 2004. Mixture processes for intradaily financial durations. Studies in Nonlinear Dynamics and Econometrics 8,

De Luca, G., Gallo, G.M., 2009. Time-varying mixing weights in mixture autoregressive conditional duration models. Econometric Reviews 28, 102–120

De Luca, G., Zuccolotto, P., 2003. Finite and infinite mixtures for financial durations. Metron 61, 431–455

Diamond, D.W., Verrecchia, R.E., 1987. Constraints on short-selling and asset price adjustments to private information. Journal of Financial Economics 18, 277–311

Dufour, A., Engle, R.F., 2000. Time and the price impact of a trade. Journal of Finance 55, 2467–2498

Easley, D., O'Hara, M., 1987. Price, trade size and information in securities markets. Journal of Financial Economics 19, 69–90

Easley, D., O'Hara, M., 1992. Time and the process of security price adjustment. Journal of Finance 47, 577–606

Easley, D., Kiefer, N.M., O'Hara, M., Paperman, J.B., 1996. Liquidity, information, and infrequently traded stocks. Journal of Finance 55, 1405–1436

Engle, R.F., 2000. The econometrics of ultra-high frequency data. Econometrica 68, 1–22

Engle, R.F., Russell, J.R., 1998. Autoregressive conditional duration: a new model for irregularly spaced transaction data. Econometrica 66, 1127–1162

Foster, F.D., Viswanathan, S., 1990. A theory of the intraday variations in volume, variance, and trading costs in securities markets. Review of Financial Studies 3, 593–624

Glosten, L.R., Milgrom, P.R., 1985. Bid, ask and transaction prices in a specialist market with heterogeneously informed traders. Journal of Financial Economics 14, 71–100

Grammig, J., Maurer, K.O., 2000. Non-monotonic hazard functions and the autoregressive conditional duration model. Econometrics Journal 3, 16–38

Grammig, J., Wellner, M., 2002. Modeling the interdependence of volatility and inter-transaction duration processes. Journal of Econometrics 106, 369–400

Hmaied, D., Grar, A., Sioud, O., 2006. Dynamics of market liquidity of Tunisian stocks: an analysis of market resiliency. Electronic Market 16, 140–153

Hujer, R., Vuletić, S., 2007. Econometric analysis of financial trade processes by discrete mixture duration models. Journal of Economic Dynamics and Control 31, 635–667

Kyle, A.S., 1985. Continuous auctions and insider trading. Econometrica 53, 1315–1335

Lamoureux, C.G., Lastrapes, W.D., 1990. Heteroscedasticity in stock return data: volume versus GARCH-effects. Journal of Finance 45, 221–229

Manganelli, S., 2005. Duration, volume and volatility impact of trades. Journal of Financial Markets 8, 377–399

Ma, T., Hsieh, M.H., Chen, J.H., 2007. The probability of informed trading and the performance of stock in an order-driven market. Asia-Pacific Journal of Financial Studies 36, 871–896

Spierdijk, L., 2004. An empirical analysis of the role of the trading intensity in information dissemination on the NYSE. Journal of Empirical Finance 11, 163–184

Subrahmanyam, A., 1991. Risk aversion, market liquidity, and price efficiency. Review of Financial Studies 4, 417–441

Wong, W.K., Tan, D., Tian, Y., 2009. Informed trading and liquidity in the Shanghai stock exchange. International Review of Financial Analysis 18, 66–73

Wu, C., 2004. Information flow volatility and spreads of infrequently traded Nasdaq stocks. Quarterly Review of Economics and Finance 44, 20–43

Zhang, M.Y., Russell, J.R., Tsay, R.S., 2001. A nonlinear autoregressive conditional duration model with applications to financial transaction data. Journal of Econometrics 104, 179–207

CHAPTER 10

Energy Sector Companies of the BRICS: Systematic and Specific Financial Risks and Value at Risk

Marcelo Bianconi* **and Joe A. Yoshino†**

*Department of Economics, Tufts University, Medford, MA, USA
†Department of Economics, FEA, University of Sao Paulo, Brazil

1. INTRODUCTION

This chapter studies how common factors and specific factors affect equity returns for publicly traded nonrenewable energy sector and their effect on value at risk for those companies. Our sample is in the realm of the group of emerging markets consisting of Brazil, Russia, India, China, and South Africa, known as the BRICS. We set out to measure and analyze the exposure of the nominal equity returns of a company denominated in the currency of the stock exchange of the country of origin. Those nominal returns may or may not be exposed to company specific factors and common factors as well as other sources of risks.

In the tradition of the Arrow-Debreu framework of general equilibrium under uncertainty, if we assume complete global financial markets, the conditional CAPM implies that specific idiosyncratic factors are fully diversified away and only global risk is priced. A diametrically opposed situation is the other extreme of full absence of international risk sharing where specific idiosyncratic risk is fully priced and non-diversified. The potential for an in-between case of partial risk sharing is plausible under the common assumptions of information asymmetries. In this case, equity returns are exposed to both global risks and specific risks and our main objective is to measure and to price those risks in the narrow context of the BRICS oil and gas companies.

We cover 16 companies from the oil and gas sector from four countries using daily data from July 15, 2003 to August 14, 2012. Our choice of a recent period benefits from the inclusion of the end of the great moderation as well as the housing crisis and the financial crisis emanating from the US economy. While the energy market can be regarded as a sector that supports the entire economy, our focus is on the systematic risk faced by companies in the nonrenewable energy sector.[1] In addition, for the BRICS

[1] In the case of the US, Ferson and Harvey (1994) study the sources of risk and expected returns in global equity markets, see also Karolyi and Stulz (2003) for a survey. Alternatively, Pierret (2012) studies the systemic risk that emanates from energy markets. Hamilton (1983) is the classic reference on the broad effects of oil on the macroeconomy in the US.

Emerging Markets and the Global Economy
http://dx.doi.org/10.1016/B978-0-12-411549-1.00010-7

those companies are of utmost importance, both from an economic and from a security perspective.

Our measurements indicate that the specific factors are not robustly priced factors for BRICS companies.[2] In the space of common factors, the market premium of the US Dow Jones industrials, the price of West Texas Intermediate (WTI) oil, and the exchange rates relative to the US dollar of the Euro, Brazilian real, and South African rand are robustly priced common factors.

There is a vast literature on the effect of oil prices on energy markets but little has been done on the BRICS oil and gas companies. Besides, our main focus includes oil prices as one potential factor among many others. In this chapter, first we use methods of OLS, panel fixed effects, panel GMM (Generalized Method of Moments), and panel with threshold ARCH (TARCH) effects. We extend the empirical analysis to multivariate GARCH models with dynamic conditional correlations (DCC) methods on a company by company basis.

We also compute the one-day horizon value at risk based on the model's estimated first and second moments and evaluate the performance of value at risk with a back-testing procedure.

One key result is that the companies in the oil and gas sector of the BRICS have significant heterogeneity in response to specific factors and common factors. Firms from the BRICS in this sector are relatively sensitive to credit concerns and the Euro-US dollar exchange rate impacts negatively on the returns across all quantiles, and the change in the crude oil price impacts positively across all quantiles. The Euro effect indicates that as the currency devalues, the rate of change increases relative to the US dollar, company stock returns decline showing particular exposure to the Euro-US dollar exchange risk. The change in the crude oil price shows robust exposure to the price of oil, with higher oil prices increasing stock returns in the sector.

The per company average estimates of the one-day horizon 5% value at risk range from 2.1% value at risk for the lowest 10th quantile to 4.6% value at risk at the 90th quantile, while the median is at 3.9% one-day horizon value at risk. The two companies on or below the 10th quantile are potential benchmarks for risk in the sector, and they are PetroChina Company Limited of China and Oil India Limited of India. The two companies clearly on or above the 90th quantile value at risk in the sample are riskier relative to the benchmark. They are both from Brazil, HRT Holdings and OGX Petroleo.

The results show that raw volatility of returns of BRICS companies is very large relative to model-based volatility. Volatility is smoother when exposure is taken into account, and the early period in the sample of 2003–2004 is the period of largest volatility under no exposure, consistent with the US wars in the Middle East. The dynamic conditional correlations (DCC) between returns and the market premium show that the model-based

[2] For example, for a general group of firms, Haushalter (2000) shows that the extent of hedging is related to financing costs for oil and gas industry firms and finds that companies with greater financial leverage manage price risks more extensively. This is not the case for BRICS companies.

DCC in the absence of exposure is very smooth and shows a critical period of burst during the financial crisis from 2008 to early 2009. However, under exposure the DCC becomes larger in magnitudes and with more significant range after the financial crisis of 2008. In particular, under exposure some companies emerge as clear hedges against the market risk with significant negative DCC from the crisis period onwards.

Finally, we show that a naïve calculation based on raw data would overestimate the value at risk considerably over the sample period relative to the value at risk accounting for exposure. The econometric calculation without taking into account exposure is slightly less volatile relative to the case of exposure. In accounting for the exposure to all factors, we note that for the BRICS, value at risk increased only mildly during the financial crisis and remained stable in magnitude over the whole period.

The rest of the chapter is organized as follows. Section 2 presents a literature review while Section 3 discusses the role of oil and gas in the BRICS. Section 4 presents the data sample and Section 5 discusses the econometric methods and models. Section 6 presents the empirical evidence and Section 7 concludes and discusses potential avenues for future research. The appendix provides the description of the firms in the sample.

2. LITERATURE REVIEW

The literature on oil and gas companies of the BRICS is limited. Here, we review some of the main contributions in the general area of the oil and gas companies worldwide.[3] The authors in Giovannini et al. (2004) investigate the correlations of volatilities in the stock price returns and their determinants for the most important integrated oil companies, and find low to high/extreme interdependence between the volatilities of companies' stock returns and the relevant stock market indexes or crude oil prices. We do include the crude oil prices in our econometric evaluations of the BRICS oil and gas companies.

More generally, for the US market returns, Chiou and Lee (2009) study the relationship of the S&P 500 and crude oil transactions and find that high fluctuations in oil prices have asymmetric unexpected impacts on S&P 500 returns. Elyasiani et al. (2011) examine the impact of changes in the oil returns and oil return volatility on US industries excess stock returns and return volatilities and find evidence that oil price fluctuations constitute a systematic asset price risk at the industry level.

Mohanty and Nandha (2011) estimate oil price risk exposures of the US oil and gas sector using the Fama-French (1992, 1995) framework. They show that the market, book-to-market, and size factors, as well as momentum characteristics of stocks and changes in oil prices are significant determinants of returns for the sector. Lombardi and Ravazzoloz (2012) find that joint modeling of oil and equity prices produces more accurate point and density forecasts for oil prices. In addition, several authors study the exposure of

[3] The reader is also referred to Bianconi and Yoshino (2012b and 2013) for additional review of related issues in the broad commodities sector from a worldwide perspective.

Canadian oil and gas companies to risk factors including Boyer and Filion (2007) and Sadorsky (2001).

Ramos and Veiga (2011) analyze the exposure of the oil and gas industry of 34 countries to oil prices. They use a panel dataset and find that oil price is a globally priced factor for the oil industry. Sadorsky (2008) investigates the impact that global oil market risk factors have on the oil price risk of oil company stock prices. Results indicate that oil prices and market risk are both positive and statistically significant priced risk factors. Oil price risk is negatively impacted by increases in oil reserves. Oil price risk is positively impacted by increases in oil production. Oil price risk is more sensitive to changes in production rates than to changes in reserve additions rates.

Our analysis of the exposure of returns to nominal exchange rates in the BRICS is also found in the general literature. De Santis and Gerard (1998) study the size of the premium for currency risk and find strong support for models that includes both market and foreign exchange risk. However, Roache (2008) assesses the macro risk exposure offered by commodity futures and test whether these risks are priced. He finds that, although some commodities are also a hedge against US dollar depreciation, this risk is not priced. We find robust evidence that exchange rate risk is priced in the BRICS.

3. THE ROLE OF GAS AND OIL IN THE BRICS

National Oil and Gas Companies in the BRICS are of utmost importance. In some cases, such as Brazil, the companies must fulfill some non-commercial objectives imposed by the Government. Broadly speaking, one general objective is to ensure the energy security of their country. In effect, energy security among the BRICS should include cooperation in oil exploration and refining and in natural gas supply through pipelines and liquefied natural gas terminals.[4]

In terms of macroeconomic outcomes, the BRICS have had different growth experiences and strategies. In China, the export economy is the main driving force for its overall economic dynamic. China's fast growth has meant that it became a net importer of oil and gas. The oil and gas sector reforms started in the 1980s with production sharing agreements introduced to attract foreign investments. In terms of security, China's problem is due to the fact that oil reserves, while robust, are insufficient for the growing consumption. China is the world's second-largest consumer of oil behind the United States, and the second-largest net importer of oil as of 2009. Although natural gas use is rapidly increasing in China, the fuel comprised less than 4% of the country's total primary energy consumption in 2009. China's natural gas production and demand have risen substantially in the past decade. China became a net natural gas importer in 2007 and imports have increased dramatically in the past few years alongside China's rapidly developing infrastructure.

[4] See The BRICS Report, 2012, Oxford University Press for The World Bank.

Russia has a leading role in energy markets; its oil production was the second most important after Saudi Arabia in 2011 and its proved oil reserves place it on the eighth place. The key to Russia's economy is that it is the world's largest energy producer. Russia's exports of oil and natural gas represent 75% of its total exports. Russia's economy is not much diversified and the Russian government depends on oil and gas receipts.

India's economic growth is largely supported by strong capital imports. India created a Directorate of Oil and Natural Gas, with limited administrative and financial functions and after several changes, this Directorate became a limited company in 1994, Oil and Gas Company (ONGC). After 1999, foreign and private companies had the right to participate in call of tenders and foreign direct investment was allowed even at 100%. But, India doesn't allow oil and gas exports. The Indian government controls the ONGC company by imposing restrictions, audits by governments' agencies and it also nominates members in the board of directors and the managing director. Also, the ONGC has to follow the government's standards for the remuneration of its employees. India was the fourth largest consumer of oil and petroleum products in the world in 2011, after the United States, China, and Japan. The country depends heavily on imported crude oil, mostly from the Middle East. The high degree of dependence on imported crude oil has led Indian energy companies to attempt to diversify their supply sources. India's oil supply security profile is distinctive. The country doesn't have many reserves, so it buys assets overseas in countries like Nigeria, Sudan, or Angola. This strategy helps the country to reduce the dependency on spot markets and to be less vulnerable to volatility in oil prices.

In India, natural gas serves as a substitute for coal for electricity generation. The country began importing liquefied natural gas (LNG) from Qatar in 2004 and increasingly relies on imports to meet domestic natural gas needs. Indian companies use both long-term supply contracts and more expensive spot LNG contracts. Indian companies have attempted to secure new longer-term deals with suppliers such as Russia's Gazprom.

One of Brazil's main engines of growth is its strong domestic demand and it also has become an important net exporter of commodities. Brazil might become an important producer and exporter of oil in the next decade, thanks to the new pre-salt reserves discovered in 2006. The United States Energy Information Administration considers that these reserves could increase Brazil's reserves significantly. According to the Oil and Gas Journal (OGJ), Brazil has the second-largest oil reserves in South America after Venezuela. The offshore Campos and Santos Basins hold the vast majority of Brazil's proven reserves. Despite Brazil's substantial natural gas reserves, natural gas production has grown slowly in recent years, mainly due to a lack of domestic transportation capacity and low domestic prices. Natural gas consumption is a small part of the country's overall energy mix, constituting only 7% of total energy consumption in 2010.

South Africa is the major economy of Africa and a main source of growth has been regional integration. In 2010, about 70% of South Africa's total energy supply came from coal, followed by oil representing 19%.[5] South Africa's energy balance also includes relatively small shares of natural gas and its dependence on hydrocarbons, particularly coal, has led the country to become the leading carbon dioxide emitter in Africa. It has a very limited upstream oil and gas sector, and the sector is highly regulated. South Africa is the sole importer of natural gas from Mozambique via pipeline. It has very limited and declining conventional natural gas reserves, but potentially large shale gas resources.[6]

Figure 1a shows the Oil reserves of the BRIC, and African nations including South Africa. Russia has the largest reserves. India and China have been very stable in the last 30 years with China above India consistently. Recently, there have been some significant discoveries in Africa, but South Africa has significantly less oil reserves. The key to this group is Brazil. Brazil has consistently shown constant growth in discoveries culminating with the recent Pre-Salt which put is in the same level as China.

Figure 1b shows the Gas reserves of the BRIC, and African nations including South Africa. Russia by far has the largest reserves. In this resource, all other nations have been increasing their level of reserves. China, Africa (including South Africa), and India have

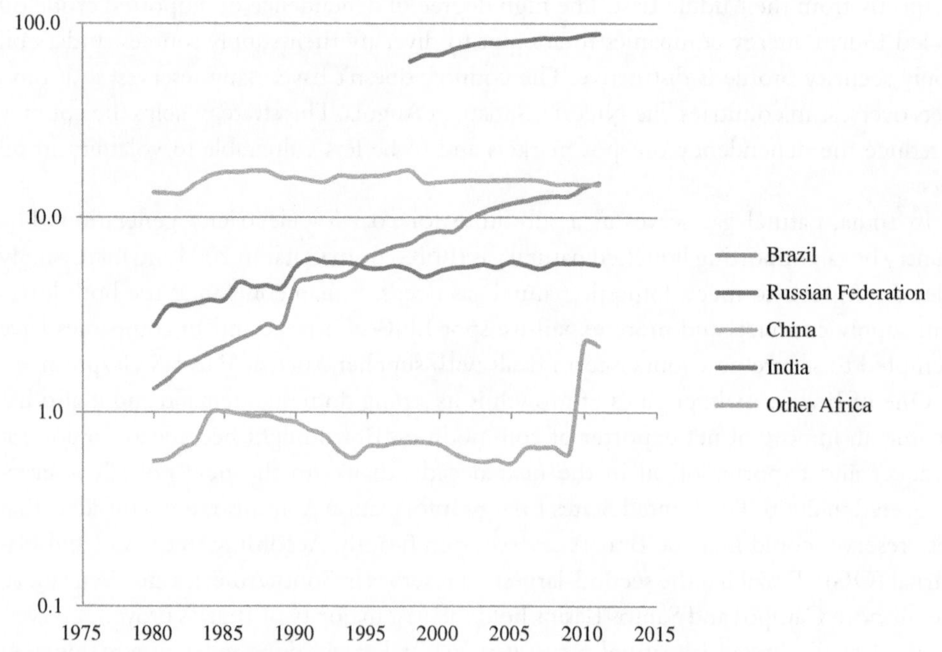

Figure 1a Oil resources of BRICS.
Notes: Logarithmic Scale.
Source: Statistical Review of World Energy.

[5] United States Energy Information Administration.

[6] The United States Energy Information Administration estimates that the countries with the largest shale gas reserves are China (1,275 trillion cubic feet), Argentina (774), Mexico (681), South Africa (485), the USA (482), Australia (396), Canada (388), Libya (290), Algeria (231), Brazil (226), and France (180).

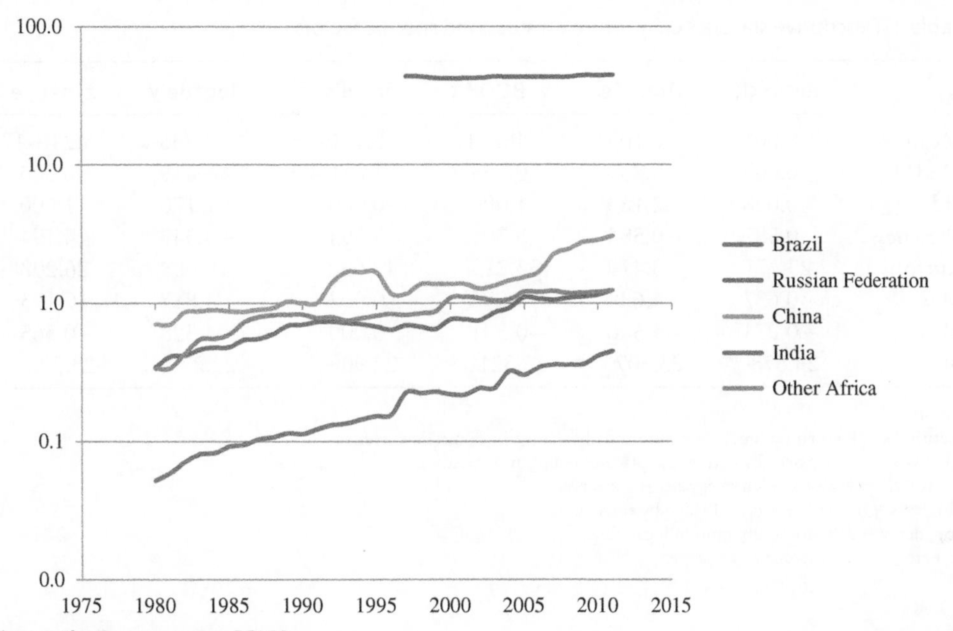

Figure 1b Gas resources BRICS.
Notes: Logarithmic Scale.
Source: Statistical Review of World Energy.

significant gas reserves and have grown steadily. Brazil is the last in this category but shows a slightly steeper rate of discoveries in the period.

4. DATA

The focus of this chapter is on oil and gas companies of the nonrenewable energy sector, publicly traded in exchange markets from the BRICS. We have a sample of 16 companies and daily observations from July 15, 2003 to August 14, 2012, when assets are traded. The source of the data for the companies is Bloomberg data services. Table A1 in the Appendix lists the companies in the sample. We have companies from five countries, namely Brazil, Russia, China, India, and South Africa.

The main variables in the analysis are as follows.[7] The return on stock is calculated as the continuous daily change in the price of the stock denominated in the currency of the traded stock. Table 1 shows the descriptive statistics of the daily returns in the sample. The returns are severely leptokurtic in the panel. Figure 2a shows the evolution of the returns over time and the cumulative sum of returns by company in the sample. Most companies show a healthy cumulative sum of returns in the period; however, some are much less successful.

Table 1 also presents descriptive statistics of the firm specific factors in the sample. The first two specific factors are the well-known Fama and French (1992, 1995) factors.

[7] The company data are from Bloomberg unless otherwise noted.

Table 1 Descriptive statistics daily return on stock and specific factors.

	Retur˜ck	lTotAs˜e	z_BOOK˜t	fin_le˜s	log_de˜y	z_net_˜e
Mean	0.001	−0.105	2.46E-17	8.12E-05	3.236	5.24E-17
Med	0.000	−0.250	−0.235	1.61E-05	3.419	−0.383
Std	0.028	2.133	1.000	0.000	1.170	1.000
Skewness	0.587	−0.583	5.305	5.594	−3.347	4.194
Kurtosis	23.771	3.419	34.213	42.692	18.088	26.208
Max	0.637	4.639	9.996	0.003	4.817	10.193
Min	−0.274	−5.576	−0.301	0.000	−4.328	−0.565
N	24,578	23,307	23,321	22,908	22,277	23,323

Legend:
Retur~ck = Return on Stock, continuous daily change in domestic currency.
lTotAs~e = Total assets divided by the price of equity in logarithms.
z_BOOK~t = Book-to-market ratio as a z-score.
fin_le~s = financial leverage divided by total assets.
log_de~y = debt-to-equity ratio in logarithms.
z_net~_e = net income as a z-score.

As a proxy for size, we have the total assets scaled by the price of equity in logarithms (lTotAs~e). The proxy for value is the book value scaled by the market value of equity normalized to mean zero and variance one, i.e., as a z-score (z_BOOK~t). As measures of leverage we have financial leverage scaled by total assets (fin_le~s); and financial policy of the company we have the debt-to-equity ratio in logarithms (log_de~y); and gauging revenues we have net income normalized to mean zero and variance one, i.e., as a z-score (z_net~_e).

Table 2 presents descriptive statistics for the common factors. First, the variable premium_mkt is the daily continuous return of the US Dow Jones Industrials minus the daily yield of the 3-month US Treasury bill rate all denominated in US$ dollars.[8] The variable ch_VIX is the continuous daily change of the VIX options volatility index from the Chicago Board of Exchange, measuring the volatility of options in the market, known as the "fear" index. We include several nominal exchange rates to account for exchange risk. The variable ch_euro_x is the continuous daily change of the Euro/US$ dollar exchange rate; ch_china_x is the continuous daily change of the Chinese yuan versus the US dollar exchange rate; ch_india_x is the continuous daily change of the Indian rupee versus the US dollar exchange rate; ch_japan_x is the continuous daily change of the Japanese yen versus the US dollar exchange rate; ch_uk_x is the continuous daily change of the UK Pound$/US$ dollar exchange rate; ch_russia_x is the continuous daily change of the Russian ruble versus the US dollar exchange rate, ch_brl_x is the continuous daily change of the Brazilian real versus the US dollar exchange rate, and

[8] We choose the US Dow Jones industrials, as opposed to the broader S&P500, for the purpose of measuring international exposure to the systematic risk from a narrow, but widely covered market.

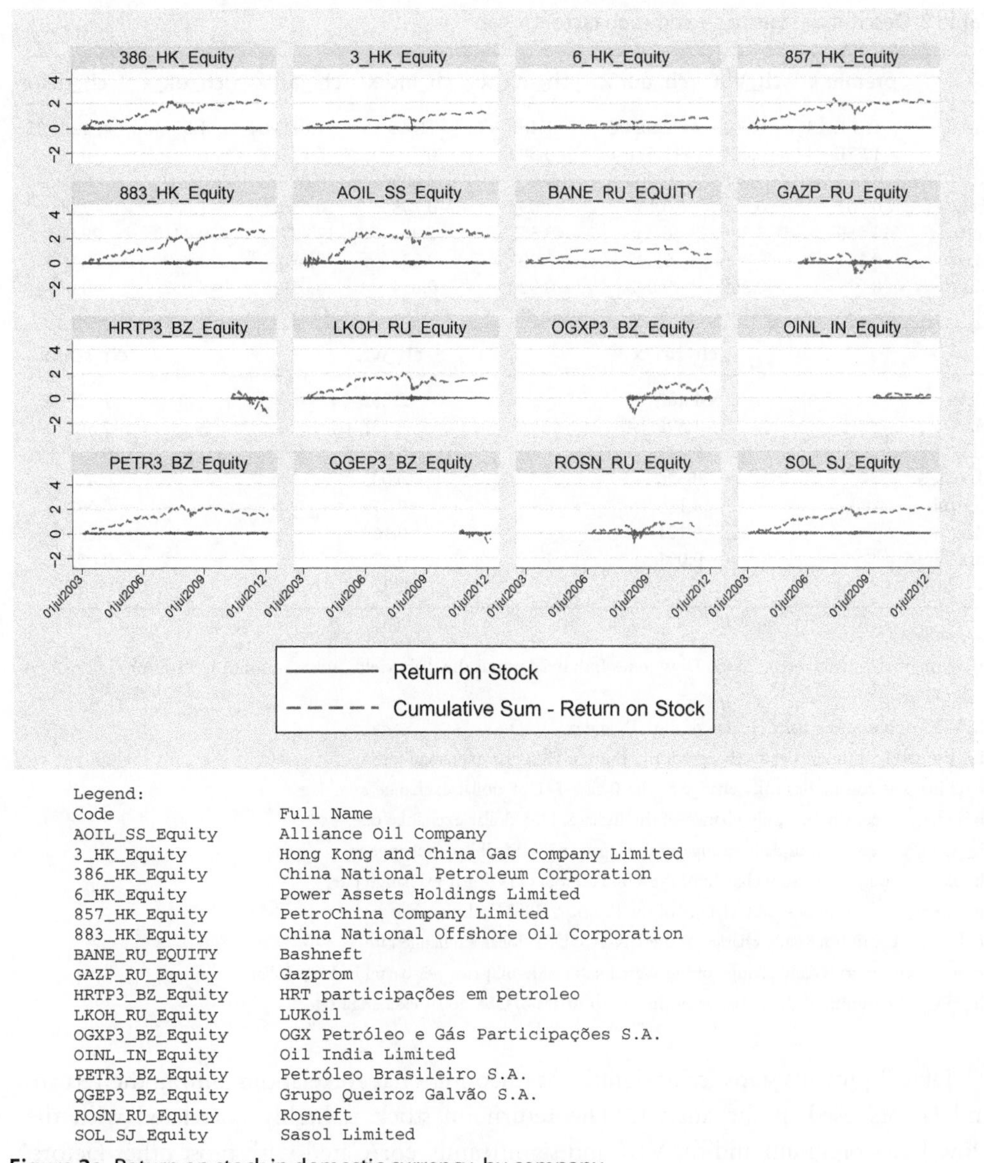

Legend:

Code	Full Name
AOIL_SS_Equity	Alliance Oil Company
3_HK_Equity	Hong Kong and China Gas Company Limited
386_HK_Equity	China National Petroleum Corporation
6_HK_Equity	Power Assets Holdings Limited
857_HK_Equity	PetroChina Company Limited
883_HK_Equity	China National Offshore Oil Corporation
BANE_RU_EQUITY	Bashneft
GAZP_RU_Equity	Gazprom
HRTP3_BZ_Equity	HRT participações em petroleo
LKOH_RU_Equity	LUKoil
OGXP3_BZ_Equity	OGX Petróleo e Gás Participações S.A.
OINL_IN_Equity	Oil India Limited
PETR3_BZ_Equity	Petróleo Brasileiro S.A.
QGEP3_BZ_Equity	Grupo Queiroz Galvão S.A.
ROSN_RU_Equity	Rosneft
SOL_SJ_Equity	Sasol Limited

Figure 2a Return on stock in domestic currency, by company.

ch_sou~x is the continuous daily change of the South African rand versus the US dollar. The variable ch_wti is the continuous daily change of the West Texas Intermediate oil price per barrel in US dollars. The data are shown to be leptokurtic as well and in the group of exchange rates, the Brazilian real has the highest variability in the sample, while the Chinese yuan has the lowest. The change in the VIX, followed by the crude oil price, has the highest variability of all common factors in the sample.

Table 2 Descriptive statistics—common factors.

	premiu˜t	ch_VIX	ch_eur˜x	ch_˜na_x	ch_ind˜x	ch_jap˜x	ch_uk_x	ch_rus˜x
Mean	1.10E-04	−0.001	−2.2E-05	−1.18E-04	−7E-05	1.62E-04	1.55E-06	−1.2E-05
med	1.77E-04	−0.007	−1.59E-04	0.000	0	0	0	0
Sd	0.012	0.068	0.007	0.001	0.005	0.007	0.007	0.006
skewness	0.067	0.696	0.150	−2.092	−0.248	0.950	−1.006	−2.000
kurtosis	13.589	7.504	6.230	49.535	12.903	17.477	20.441	29.865
Max	0.111	0.496	0.047	0.007	0.033	0.080	0.058	0.043
Min	−0.079	−0.369	−0.040	−0.020	−0.054	−0.059	−0.082	−0.077
N	24426	23310	24578	24578	24578	24578	24578	24578

	ch_brl_x	ch_wti	ch_sou˜x
Mean	−1.40E-04	2.23E-04	7.22E-05
Med	−1.69E-04	9.13E-04	−2.89E-04
Sd	0.011	0.025	0.012
Skewness	0.526	−0.005	0.475
Kurtosis	14.186	7.379	6.092
Max	0.121	0.164	0.085
Min	−0.091	−0.128	−0.053
N	23546	23892	24578

Legend:
premium_mkt = daily return of the Dow Jones Industrial minus the daily yield of the 3-month US Treasury bill rate (in US$ Dollars).
ch_VIX = continuous daily change of the VIX index.
ch_euro_x = continuous daily change of the Euro/US$ dollar exchange rate.
ch_china_x = continuous daily change of the China-$/US$ dollar exchange rate.
ch_india_x = continuous daily change of the India-$/US$ dollar exchange rate.
ch_japan_x = continuous daily change of the Japan-Y$/US$ dollar exchange rate.
ch_uk_x = continuous daily change of the UK Pound$/US$ dollar exchange rate.
ch_russia_x = continuous daily change of the Russia-$/US$ dollar exchange rate.
ch_brl_x = continuous daily change of the BR-R$/US$ dollar exchange rate.
ch_wti = continuous daily change of the West Texas crude oil price per barrel in US$ dollar.
ch_sou_x = continuous daily change of the South Africa $/US$ dollar exchange rate.

Table 3 presents statistically significant unconditional correlations among the returns and factors used in the analysis. The return on stock is highly correlated with the Dow Jones premium and the VIX and significantly correlated with most other factors. The Dow Jones premium is significantly correlated with all other common factors, but not with firm specific factors. In particular, the premium and the VIX have the largest correlation in magnitude (shaded cell). Most exchange rates are significantly correlated with one another as well. The WTI oil price is significantly correlated with firm's net income, with the return on stock and with all other common factors.

Figure 2b shows unconditional average returns and standard deviation of returns by company, with linear fits for positive average returns. For positive average returns, the

Table 3 Unconditional correlation matrix of returns, common factors, and specific factors (significant at 5% or less only).

	Retur˜ck	lTotAs˜e	z_BOOK˜t	fin_le˜s	log_de˜y	z_net_˜e	premiu˜t
Return_Stock	1						
lTotAsset_˜e		1					
z_BOOK_to_˜t	−0.0128	0.457	1				
fin_lev_to˜s		−0.2011	−0.086	1			
log_debt_e˜y	0.0145	0.1404	0.0665	−0.2026	1		
z_net_income		0.5192	0.6396	−0.1707		1	
premium_mkt	0.2284						1
ch_VIX	−0.1958						−0.7333
ch_euro_x	−0.1933						−0.1476
ch_china_x	−0.0439						
ch_india_x							0.0366
ch_japan_x	0.0133						
ch_uk_x							−0.0219
ch_russia_x							
ch_brl_x	−0.1837						−0.1969
ch_wti	0.2265						0.2727
ch_southaf˜x	−0.2644					−0.1768	0.1617

(*continued*)

Table 3 Continued

	ch_VIX	ch_eur˜x	ch_˜na_x	ch_ind˜x	ch_jap˜x	ch_uk_x	ch_rus˜x	ch_brl_x	ch_wti
ch_VIX	1								
ch_euro_x	0.1316	1							
ch_china_x		0.2334	1						
ch_india_x	−0.0237			1					
ch_japan_x	−0.016	0.02	0.0326	−0.0536	1				
ch_uk_x	0.0156	0.0252	−0.0236	0.3153	0.0449	1			
ch_russia_x	0.0139			0.3659		0.3826	1		
ch_brl_x	0.2188	0.2145	0.0434				0.015	1	
ch_wti	−0.2181	−0.2023	−0.0769		0.0257	−0.0237		−0.1545	1
ch_southaf˜x	0.1617	0.5319	0.1021	0.0169	−0.0228	0.3526			−0.2187

See Tables 1 and 2.

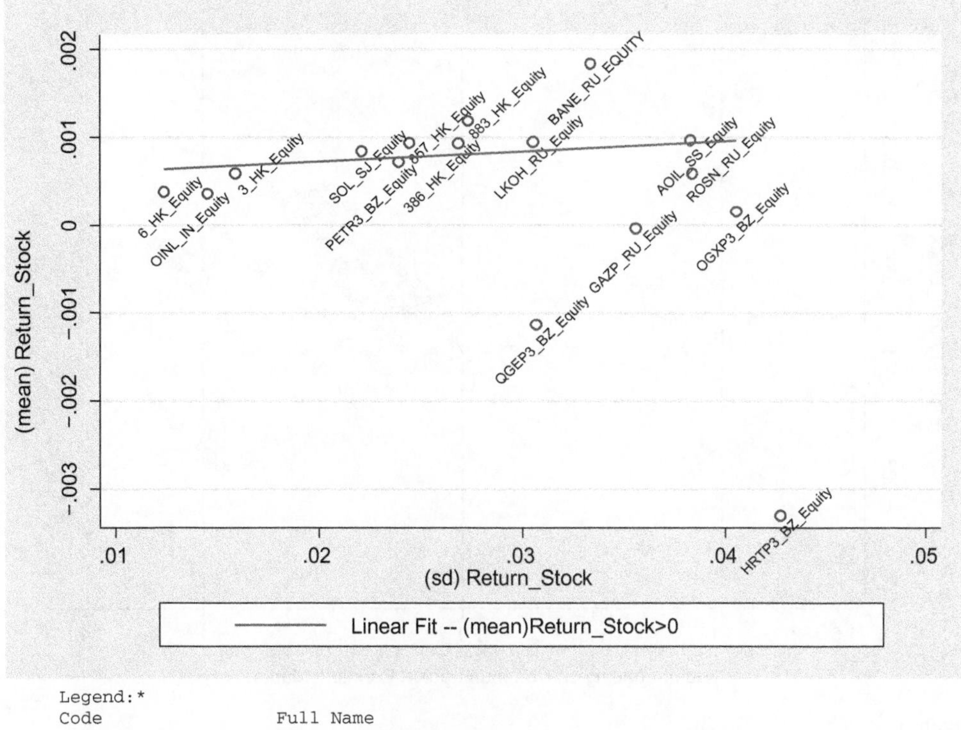

Legend:*

Code	Full Name
AOIL_SS_Equity	Alliance Oil Company
3_HK_Equity	Hong Kong and China Gas Company Limited
386_HK_Equity	China National Petroleum Corporation
6_HK_Equity	Power Assets Holdings Limited
857_HK_Equity	PetroChina Company Limited
883_HK_Equity	China National Offshore Oil Corporation
BANE_RU_EQUITY	Bashneft
GAZP_RU_Equity	Gazprom
HRTP3_BZ_Equity	HRT Holdings in Petroleum
LKOH_RU_Equity	LUKoil
OGXP3_BZ_Equity	OGX Petróleo e Gás Participações S.A.
OINL_IN_Equity	Oil India Limited
PETR3_BZ_Equity	Petróleo Brasileiro S.A. (Petrobras)
QGEP3_BZ_Equity	Grupo Queiroz Galvão S.A.
ROSN_RU_Equity	Rosneft
SOL_SJ_Equity	Sasol Limited

Figure 2b Average daily return on stock and mean square root of return on stock squared by company.

linear fit is positively sloped indicating higher expected returns at higher risk; however, the slope is small indicating that the risk reward is small.

Figures 3a–3e, show the exposure of the return on stock in domestic currency to common factors.[9] Figure 3a shows the market premium factor. The betas are clearly negatively related to the average returns thus indicating a non-standard security market

[9] The data for Figures 3a–e, are obtained using Fama and MacBeth (1973) procedure of estimating a time series OLS regression of the returns on stock for each company on the premium of the market and relating the average return on stock of each company to the factor loading of each regression.

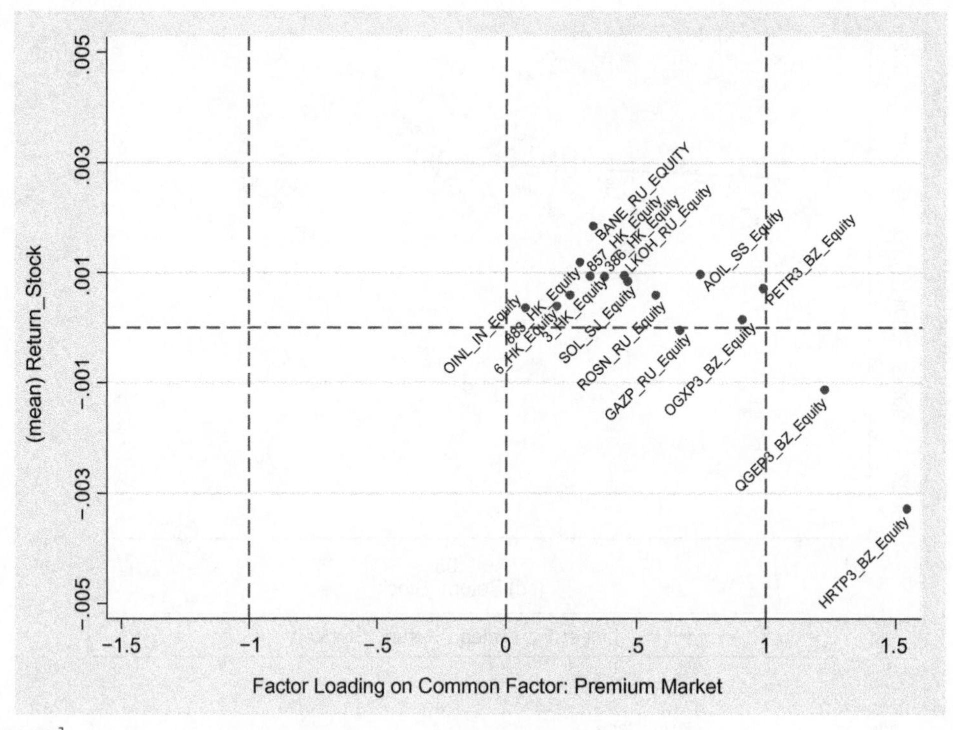

Legend:

Code	Full Name
AOIL_SS_Equity	Alliance Oil Company
3_HK_Equity	Hong Kong and China Gas Company Limited
386_HK_Equity	China National Petroleum Corporation
6_HK_Equity	Power Assets Holdings Limited
857_HK_Equity	PetroChina Company Limited
883_HK_Equity	China National Offshore Oil Corporation
BANE_RU_EQUITY	Bashneft
GAZP_RU_Equity	Gazprom
HRTP3_BZ_Equity	HRT Holdings in Petroleum
LKOH_RU_Equity	LUKoil
OGXP3_BZ_Equity	OGX Petróleo e Gás Participações S.A.
OINL_IN_Equity	Oil India Limited
PETR3_BZ_Equity	Petróleo Brasileiro S.A. (Petrobras)
QGEP3_BZ_Equity	Grupo Queiroz Galvão S.A.
ROSN_RU_Equity	Rosneft
SOL_SJ_Equity	Sasol Limited

Figure 3a Exposure of return on stock in domestic currency to common factor: Dow Jones industrials market premium in US dollars.

line for this sample.[10] Only two companies in the sample have betas greater than one in this case. Figure 3b shows the loadings on the crude oil price. Most companies are clouded together with loadings between zero and 1/2, except for the two mild

[10] A negatively sloped security market line may indicate that equity holders are risk loving.

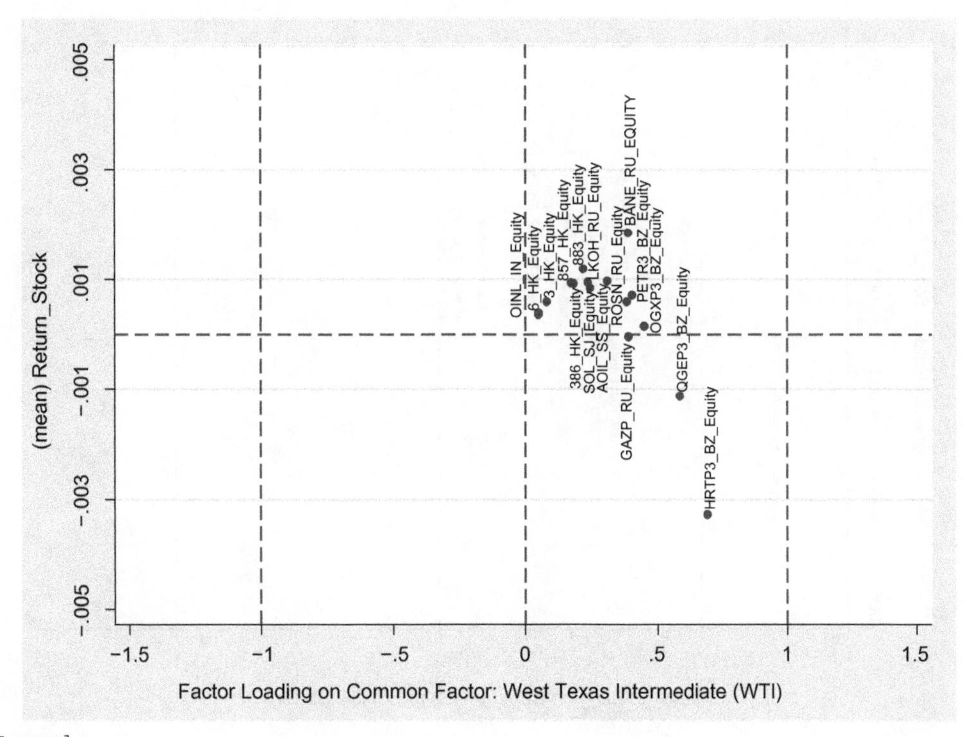

Legend:

Code	Full Name
AOIL_SS_Equity	Alliance Oil Company
3_HK_Equity	Hong Kong and China Gas Company Limited
386_HK_Equity	China National Petroleum Corporation
6_HK_Equity	Power Assets Holdings Limited
857_HK_Equity	PetroChina Company Limited
883_HK_Equity	China National Offshore Oil Corporation
BANE_RU_EQUITY	Bashneft
GAZP_RU_Equity	Gazprom
HRTP3_BZ_Equity	HRT Holdings in Petroleum
LKOH_RU_Equity	LUKoil
OGXP3_BZ_Equity	OGX Petróleo e Gás Participações S.A.
OINL_IN_Equity	Oil India Limited
PETR3_BZ_Equity	Petróleo Brasileiro S.A. (Petrobras)
QGEP3_BZ_Equity	Grupo Queiroz Galvão S.A.
ROSN_RU_Equity	Rosneft
SOL_SJ_Equity	Sasol Limited

Figure 3b Exposure of return on stock in domestic currency to common factor: West Texas Intermediate (WTI) price change.

outliers. Figures 3c–3e, show loadings on the Brazil/US nominal exchange rate, the South Africa/US nominal exchange rate and the Euro/US nominal exchange rate respectively, and all are negative indicating that returns for the companies in the BRICS increase as the US dollar appreciates.

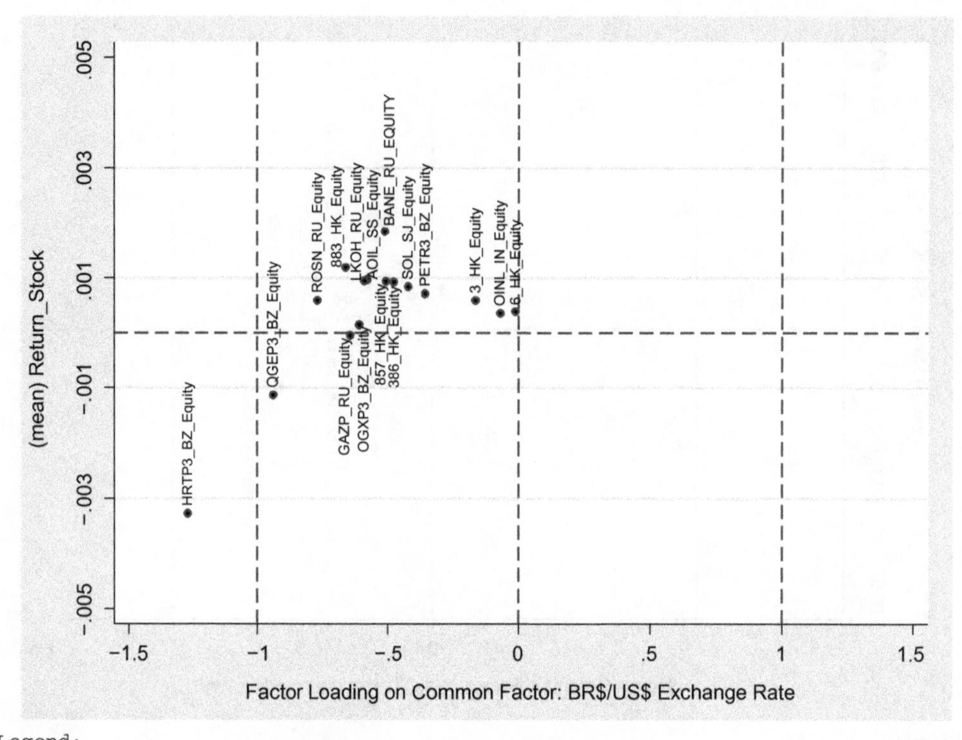

Legend:

Code	Full Name
AOIL_SS_Equity	Alliance Oil Company
3_HK_Equity	Hong Kong and China Gas Company Limited
386_HK_Equity	China National Petroleum Corporation
6_HK_Equity	Power Assets Holdings Limited
857_HK_Equity	PetroChina Company Limited
883_HK_Equity	China National Offshore Oil Corporation
BANE_RU_EQUITY	Bashneft
GAZP_RU_Equity	Gazprom
HRTP3_BZ_Equity	HRT Holdings in Petroleum
LKOH_RU_Equity	LUKoil
OGXP3_BZ_Equity	OGX Petróleo e Gás Participações S.A.
OINL_IN_Equity	Oil India Limited
PETR3_BZ_Equity	Petróleo Brasileiro S.A. (Petrobras)
QGEP3_BZ_Equity	Grupo Queiroz Galvão S.A.
ROSN_RU_Equity	Rosneft
SOL_SJ_Equity	Sasol Limited

Figure 3c Exposure of return on stock in domestic currency to common factor: Brazil Real versus US dollars change in exchange rate.

5. ECONOMETRIC MODELS

The core of our methodology is to measure the effect of systematic risk on the returns of the nonrenewable energy sector with a sample of oil and gas companies. We use panel methods and conditional heteroskedasticity methods applied to the panel, and multivariate conditional heteroskedastic and dynamic conditional correlation methods applied to each company.

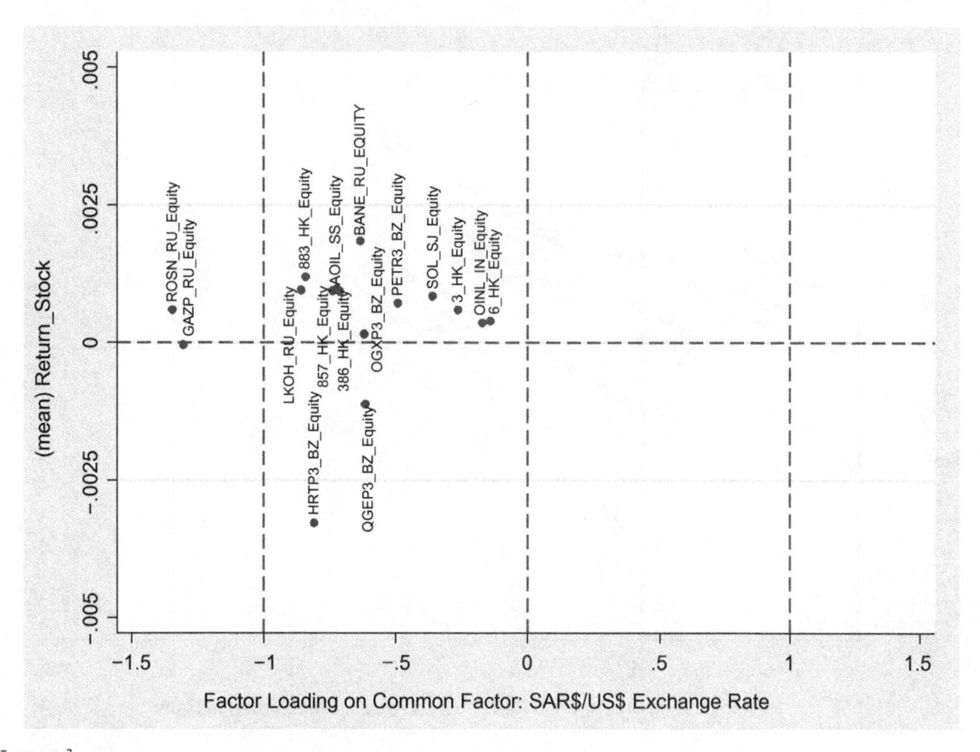

Legend:

Code	Full Name
AOIL_SS_Equity	Alliance Oil Company
3_HK_Equity	Hong Kong and China Gas Company Limited
386_HK_Equity	China National Petroleum Corporation
6_HK_Equity	Power Assets Holdings Limited
857_HK_Equity	PetroChina Company Limited
883_HK_Equity	China National Offshore Oil Corporation
BANE_RU_EQUITY	Bashneft
GAZP_RU_Equity	Gazprom
HRTP3_BZ_Equity	HRT Holdings in Petroleum
LKOH_RU_Equity	LUKoil
OGXP3_BZ_Equity	OGX Petróleo e Gás Participações S.A.
OINL_IN_Equity	Oil India Limited
PETR3_BZ_Equity	Petróleo Brasileiro S.A. (Petrobras)
QGEP3_BZ_Equity	Grupo Queiroz Galvão S.A.
ROSN_RU_Equity	Rosneft
SOL_SJ_Equity	Sasol Limited

Figure 3d Exposure of return on stock in domestic currency to common factor: South Africa Rand versus US dollar change in the exchange rate.

5.1. Systematic and Specific Risks with Panel Methods

First, the OLS and panel estimation is for the general model

$$Return\_Stock_{i,t} = \beta_0 + \boldsymbol{\alpha}'\ Specific\_Factors_{i,t} + \boldsymbol{\beta}'\ Common\_Factors_t + \gamma_i + \delta_t + u_{i,t} \quad (1)$$

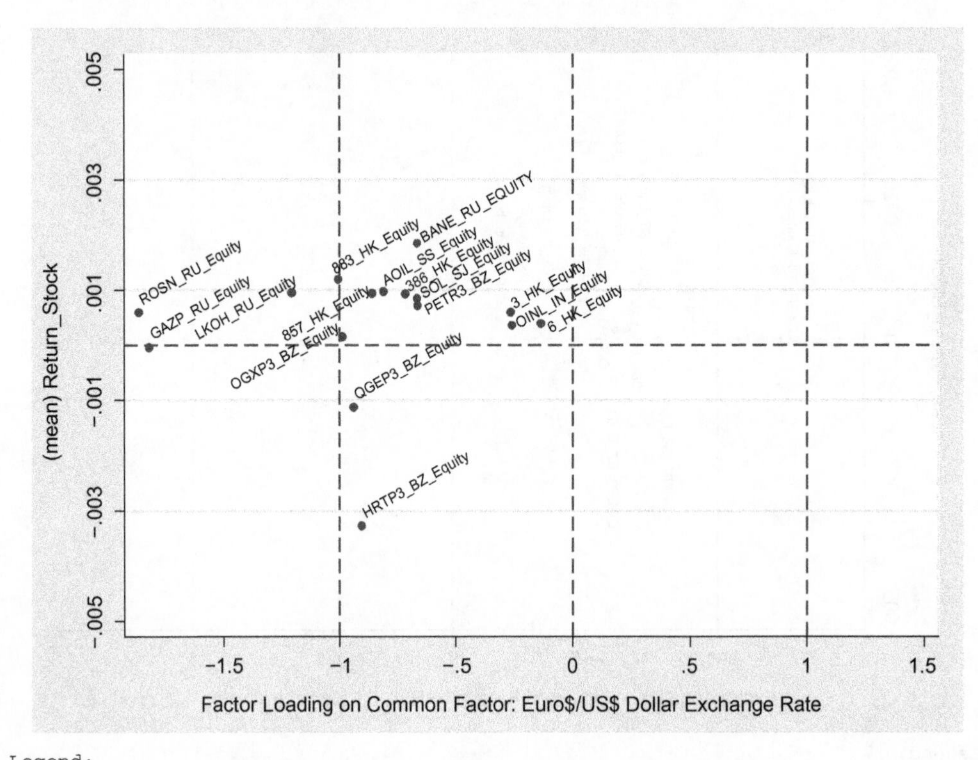

Legend:

Code	Full Name
AOIL_SS_Equity	Alliance Oil Company
3_HK_Equity	Hong Kong and China Gas Company Limited
386_HK_Equity	China National Petroleum Corporation
6_HK_Equity	Power Assets Holdings Limited
857_HK_Equity	PetroChina Company Limited
883_HK_Equity	China National Offshore Oil Corporation
BANE_RU_EQUITY	Bashneft
GAZP_RU_Equity	Gazprom
HRTP3_BZ_Equity	HRT Holdings in Petroleum
LKOH_RU_Equity	LUKoil
OGXP3_BZ_Equity	OGX Petróleo e Gás Participações S.A.
OINL_IN_Equity	Oil India Limited
PETR3_BZ_Equity	Petróleo Brasileiro S.A. (Petrobras)
QGEP3_BZ_Equity	Grupo Queiroz Galvão S.A.
ROSN_RU_Equity	Rosneft
SOL_SJ_Equity	Sasol Limited

Figure 3e Exposure of return on stock in domestic currency to common factor: Euro versus US dollar change in the exchange rate.

where γ_i is a vector of company fixed effects, δ_t is a vector of time fixed effects, and $u_{i,t}$ is a random error term. We estimate four models imposing restrictions on the parameter space of (1).

The GMM formulation includes a dynamic component for the lagged dependent variable instrumented by the second lag of the dependent variable[11]:

$$\begin{aligned} E\Big[Return_{Stock\,i,t} - \beta_0 - \beta_1 E\left[Return\_Stock_{i,t-1} \mid .\right] - \boldsymbol{\alpha}'\ Specific\_Factors_{i,t} \\ -\boldsymbol{\beta}'\ Common\_Factors_t - \gamma_i - \delta_t\Big] = 0 \end{aligned} \tag{2}$$

where, similarly, we estimate four models imposing restrictions on the parameter space of (2).

The conditional heteroskedasticity family includes the threshold ARCH or TARCH formulation for conditional heteroskedasticity,[12] and autoregressive and moving average components for the mean equation with the whole panel. It is of the form:

$$\begin{aligned} Return\_Stock_{i,t} = \beta_0 + \beta_1 Return\_Stock_{i,t-1} + \boldsymbol{\alpha}'\ Specific\_Factors_{i,t} \\ + \boldsymbol{\beta}'\ Common\_Factors_t + \gamma_i + \delta_t + u_{i,t} + \theta_1\ u_{i,t-1} \end{aligned} \tag{3a}$$

$$h_{i,t} = \pi_0 + \pi_1 h_{i,t-1} + \pi_2 u^2_{i,t-1} + \pi_3 I^+_{i,t-1} u^2_{i,t-1} \tag{3b}$$

where $h_{i,t}$ is the variance of $u_{i,t}$, e.g., the heteroskedastic function, and $I^+_{i,t} = u_{i,t} > 0$. This specification has the ability to capture the potential tendency of volatility to asymmetrically change more with news. In the case where $\pi_3 < 0$, volatility increases more with negative news as opposed to positive ones.

5.2. Multivariate GARCH, Dynamic Conditional Correlation, and Value at Risk

In the multivariate GARCH framework with dynamic conditional correlation, we follow the procedure of estimating the model for each company in the panel separately, e.g., Engle (2002), and Brownlees and Engle (2011). For each company labeled i, we estimate a bivariate GARCH(1,1) model with dynamic conditional correlation between the return on stock and the premium on the market using a Student's t distribution for the errors with endogenous degrees of freedom.[13] The full model is given by the expressions:

$$\begin{aligned} Return\_Stock_{t,each\ i} = \beta_0 + \beta_1 Return\_Stock_{t-1,each\ i} + \boldsymbol{\alpha}'\ Specific\_Factors_{t,each\ i} \\ + \boldsymbol{\beta}'\ Common\_Factors_t + u_t \end{aligned} \tag{4a}$$

$$Premium\_mkt_{t,each\ i} = \delta_0 + e_t \tag{4b}$$

$$\varepsilon_{t,each\ i} = \left(u_t e_t\right)' = H_t^{1/2} z_t \tag{4c}$$

$$H_{t,each\ i} = E\left[\varepsilon_t \varepsilon_t' \mid .\right] \tag{4d}$$

[11] The GMM (Generalized Method of Moments) estimation is used to mitigate the excess kurtosis found in the data throughout and generally common in finance data, e.g., Cochrane (2005).

[12] The TARCH model is exposed in Rabemananjara and Zakoian (1993), Glosten et al. (1993) and Zakoian (1994).

[13] This is again to mitigate the excess kurtosis found in the data.

where u_t and e_t are random error terms, H_t is the conditional covariance matrix, and z_t is a vector of i.i.d. innovations.[14]

The one-day horizon value at risk (VaR) is then calculated based on the predictions of the model 4a–4d.[15] Using the one-step ahead forecasts of the estimated mean and conditional variances, we estimate the $1-\alpha\%$ value at risk for each company i as:

$$VaR_{t+1,each\ i} = E\left[\mu_{t+1} + t_{\alpha} H_{t+1}^{1/2} \mid .\right] \tag{5a}$$

where μ_{t+1} is the mean forecast and t_{α} is the corresponding quantile for the Student's t distribution adjusted by the estimated degrees of freedom.

We proceed with the back-testing for the VaR using the likelihood ratio test via the Kupiec (1995) approach. The null hypothesis of the failure probability $\pi*$ is tested against the alternative that the failure probability differs from a given $\pi*_0$. The likelihood function can be written as:

$$LR = -2\log\left((1-\pi*)^{n0-n1}\pi*^{n1}\right) + 2\log\left((1-\hat{\pi}*)^{n0-n1}\hat{\pi}*^{n1}\right) \sim \chi^2(1) \tag{5b}$$

which has a chi-square distribution with one degree of freedom under the null hypothesis; where $\hat{\pi}*$ is the estimated probability of failure.

We apply models (4–5) to three alternative cases. First, we use the raw data for the daily return on stock as a measure of the mean component and the daily return on stock squared as a measure of the daily variance of the return on stock. Second, we impose the restriction of no exposure to any factors by estimating (4–5) with the restriction $\beta_1 = \boldsymbol{\alpha}'_1 = \boldsymbol{\beta}' = 0$ and no dynamic conditional correlation. Third, we estimate the full unrestricted model (4–5).

6. EMPIRICAL RESULTS

We estimate models from Section 5 and find the following results.

6.1. Systematic and specific risks with panel methods

Table 4 presents four alternative OLS estimations of the basic model in expression (1). Model 1 includes only specific factors and model 2 includes only common factors. Model 3 includes both common and specific factors. The key result is that the specific factors are not statistically significant in all cases. The common factors play a more important role with the market premium, the crude oil price change, the Brazil/US, South Africa/US, and Euro/US nominal exchange rates presenting significant effects. The financial crisis of 2008 is also significant.

[14] See, e.g., Khalfaoui and Boutahar (2012) for similar class of models.

[15] We use the negative of the return on stock for the VaR calculation since it refers to a long position.

Table 4 OLS estimation.

	(1) Return stock	(2) Return stock	(3) Return stock
lTotAsset_~e	−0.0000755		−0.000126
z_BOOK_to_~t	−0.000323		−0.000378
fin_lev_to~s	−0.655		−0.573
log_debt_e~y	0.000402		0.000427*
z_net_income	0.0000220		0.000213
premium_mkt		0.281***	0.277***
ch_VIX		−0.0123*	−0.00793
ch_wti		0.154***	0.144***
ch_brl		−0.163***	−0.167***
ch_china_x		0.00738	−0.0878
ch_india_x		−0.0168	−0.0157
ch_russia_x		0.00242	−0.0146
ch_southaf~x		−0.378***	−0.395***
ch_uk_x		0.0335	0.0319
ch_euro_x		−0.177***	−0.206***
ch_japan_x		0.0231	0.0182
fincrisis		−0.00115**	−0.000894**
Year			
Month			
Day of Week			
Company			
_cons	−0.000757	0.00102***	−0.000613
N	21850	22382	19870
adj. R-sq	0.000	0.127	0.146

Notes:
Return stock = daily continuous return on equity.
lTotAs~e = Total assets divided by the price of equity in logarithms.
z_BOOK~t = Book to market ratio as a z-score.
fin_le~s = financial leverage divided by total assets.
log_de~y = debt-to-equity ratio in logarithms.
z_net_income = z_net_~e = net income for company as a z-score.
premium_mkt = daily return of the Dow Jones Industrial minus the daily yield of the 3-month US Treasury bill rate (in US$ Dollars).
ch_VIX = continuous daily change of the VIX index.
ch_euro_x = continuous daily change of the Euro/US$ dollar exchange rate.
ch_china_x = continuous daily change of the China-$/US$ dollar exchange rate.
ch_india_x = continuous daily change of the India-$/US$ dollar exchange rate.
ch_japan_x = continuous daily change of the Japan-Y$/US$ dollar exchange rate.
ch_uk_x = continuous daily change of the UK Pound$/US$ dollar exchange rate.
ch_sou_x = continuous daily change of the South Africa rand $/US$ dollar exchange rate.
ch_russia_x = continuous daily change of the Russia-$/US$ dollar exchange rate.
ch_brl_x = continuous daily change of the BR-R$/US$ dollar exchange rate.
ch_wti = continuous daily change of the West Texas crude oil price per barrel in US$ dollar.
Year, Month, Day of Week, Company fixed effects.
Fincrisis = 1 if after September 15, 2008 (Lehman Brothers failure).
Year, Month, Day of Week, Company fixed effects.
*$p < 0.05$.
**$p < 0.01$.
***$p < 0.001$.

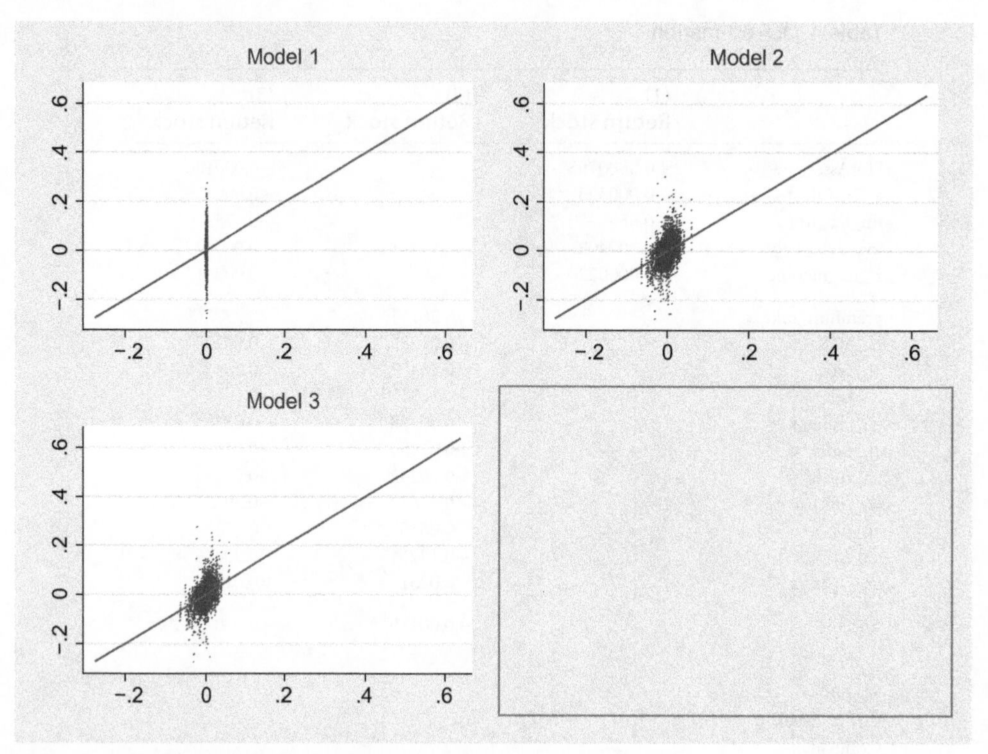

Figure 4 Return on stock versus predicted return on stock OLS estimation.

Figure 4 shows the actual versus the model predicted return on stock where the line represents the 45° angle. Models 1, 2, and 3 refer to columns labeled 1, 2, and 3 in Table 4. The predictive power of the models is shown to be small and, in particular, the specific factors of model 1 are shown to be orthogonal to the returns on stock for BRICS companies in the sample.[16]

Table 5 presents four alternative panel fixed effects estimations of the basic model in expression (1). All models include company fixed effects. Model 1 includes only specific factors, model 2 includes only common factors. Model 3 includes both common and specific factors and model 4 includes the additional time effects. All specific factors are statistically significant except for book-to-market ratios. The common factors continue to play a significant role with the market premium, the crude oil price change, the Brazil/US, South Africa/US, and Euro/US nominal exchange rates presenting significant effects. The financial crisis of 2008 is only marginally significant, but becomes insignificant when time fixed effects are included.

[16] Cochrane (2005) refers to the comparison of actual versus predictive returns as "back-tests." Diebold and Mariano (1995) provide a simple test for predictive accuracy as well.

Table 5 Panel fixed effects.

	(1) Return stock	(2) Return stock	(3) Return stock	(4) Return stock
lTotAsset_~e	−0.00466***		−0.00547***	−0.00707***
z_BOOK_to_~t	0.000618		0.000451	0.000566
fin_lev_to~s	2.591**		2.769**	3.241***
log_debt_e~y	0.000779*		0.000905**	0.000945
z_net_income	−0.00103***		−0.000793***	−0.000602**
premium_mkt		0.281***	0.277***	0.275***
ch_VIX		−0.0124	−0.00830	−0.00868
ch_brl		−0.163***	−0.164***	−0.164***
ch_china_x		0.00723	−0.0177	−0.112
ch_india_x		−0.0171	−0.0201	−0.00758
ch_russia_x		0.00228	−0.0186	−0.0220
ch_southaf~x		−0.378***	−0.396***	−0.394***
ch_uk_x		0.0338	0.0343*	0.0271
ch_euro_x		−0.177*	−0.203**	−0.204**
ch_japan_x		0.0239	0.0188	0.0197
ch_wti		0.154***	0.143***	0.141***
fincrisis		−0.000951*	0.000994*	0.00162
Year				Y
Month				Y
Day of Week				Y
Company	Y	Y	Y	Y
_cons	−0.00243*	0.000926***	−0.00355**	−0.000933
N	21850	22382	19870	19870
adj. R-sq	0.003	0.127	0.149	0.150

Notes: see Table 4.
*$p < 0.05$.
**$p < 0.01$.
***$p < 0.001$.

Figure 5 shows the actual versus the model predicted return on stock where the line represents the 45° angle. Models 1, 2, 3, and 4 refer to columns labeled 1, 2, 3, and 4 in Table 5. The predictive power of the models improves relative to the OLS case, but in the case of model 1 continues to be small.

Table 6 presents four alternative estimations of the model in expression (2) via GMM and instrumentation of the lagged endogenous variable. The specific factors do not play an important role in this case. Only in model 4, the size and debt-to-equity factors are significant. The common factors continue to play a significant role with the market

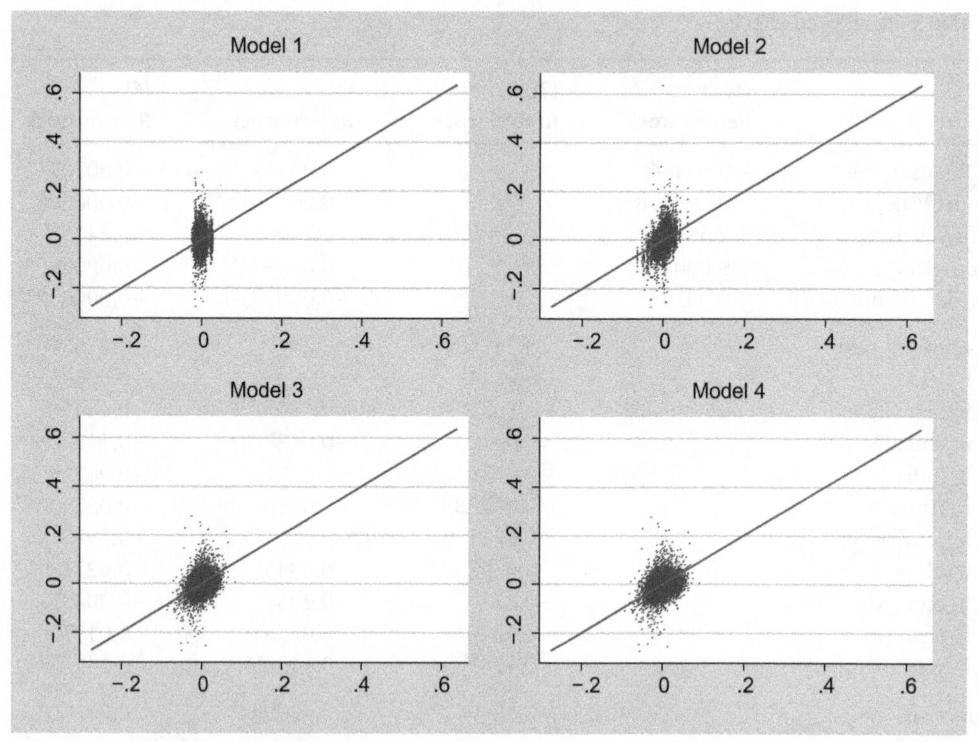

Figure 5 Return on stock versus predicted return on stock panel fixed effects estimation.

premium, the crude oil price change, the Brazil/US, South Africa/US, and Euro/US nominal exchange rates presenting significant effects. The financial crisis of 2008 is only marginally significant, but becomes insignificant when time fixed effects are included.

Figure 6 shows the actual versus the model predicted return on stock where the line represents the 45° angle. Models 1, 2, 3, and 4 refer to columns labeled 1, 2, 3, and 4 in Table 6. The predictive power improves under the GMM estimation, in particular model 1 is less orthogonal and models 3 and 4 are plausible.

Table 7 presents four alternative estimations of the model in expressions (3a and b) using the threshold ARCH approach. In model 4 only, the size and debt-to-equity factors are significant. The common factors continue to play a significant role with the market premium, the crude oil price change, the Brazil/US, South Africa/US, and Euro/US nominal exchange rates presenting significant effects. The financial crisis of 2008 becomes insignificant when time fixed effects are included. All ARMA components of the mean equation are robust and significant across specifications. The ARCH parameters in the heteroskedastic function are robust and significant for all specifications as well. In particular, the GARCH parameter for own autocorrelation of variances is larger in magnitude than the ARCH innovations parameter. The TARCH asymmetry parameter is negative

Table 6 GMM estimation.

	(1) Return stock	(2) Return stock	(3) Return stock	(4) Return stock
L.Return_~ck	−1.095	−0.433	−0.404	−0.689
lTotAsset_~e	−0.000168		−0.000175	−0.0123**
z_BOOK_to_~t	−0.000682		−0.000535	0.00109
fin_lev_to~s	−1.352		−0.710	6.359
log_debt_e~y	0.000808		0.000581	0.00162*
z_net_income	0.0000621		0.000255	−0.000950
premium_mkt		0.250***	0.260***	0.235***
ch_VIX		−0.00375	0.00115	0.00479
ch_wti		0.147***	0.140***	0.131***
ch_brl		−0.339*	−0.335*	−0.447*
ch_china_x		−0.313	−0.377	−0.623
ch_india_x		−0.0428	−0.0415	−0.0401
ch_russia_x		0.0429	0.0352	0.0596
ch_southaf~x		−0.368***	−0.376***	−0.356***
ch_uk_x		0.0294	0.0289	0.0189
ch_euro_x		−0.200***	−0.220***	−0.227***
ch_japan_x		0.0585	0.0558	0.0844
fincrisis		−0.00161**	−0.00124*	0.00115
Year				Y
Month				Y
Day of Week				Y
Company				Y
_cons	−0.00147	0.00132***	−0.000911	−0.0615**
N	21830	22352	19852	19852

Notes: see Table 4.
*$p < 0.05$.
**$p < 0.01$.
***$p < 0.001$.

for all specifications showing that volatility increases more with negative innovations in this sample period.[17] Figure 7 shows the actual versus the model predicted return on stock where the line represents the 45° angle. Models 1, 2, 3, and 4 refer to columns labeled 1, 2, 3, and 4 in Table 7. The predictive power of the models shows worst adherence relative to the GMM estimation though.

[17] This is a common feature of models that cover the financial crisis period, see, e.g., Brownlees and Engle (2011).

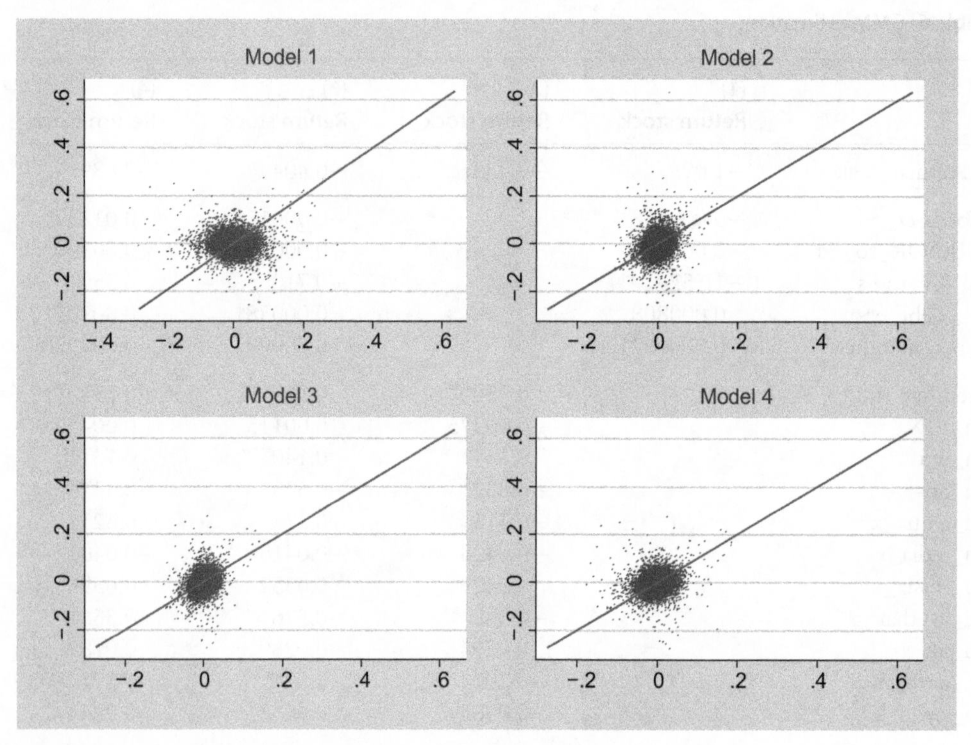

Figure 6 Return on stock versus predicted return on stock GMM estimation.

In summary, the empirical evidence presented from panel regressions is that the GMM models are relatively a better fit, but there is evidence of arbitrage opportunities given that the constant term is significant except in model 3. In the class of TARCH models, specification 3 indicates lack of arbitrage opportunities from the zero constant term, but shows significant positive autocorrelation in daily returns. In the group of common factors, exposure to the US Dow Jones market premium is statistically significant. The FX group of factors shows that the Brazil/US, South Africa/US, and Euro/US nominal exchange rates present significant negative effects indicating that when any of those currencies devalues, or the rate of change increases relative to the US dollar, company stock returns decline in the domestic currency showing exposure to currency risk and potential effects on company costs. The key result is that the specific factors are not relatively important in the BRICS sample.

6.2. Multivariate GARCH, Dynamic Conditional Correlation, and Value at Risk

Tables 8a–8d present selected quantiles of the parameter estimates of the full model 4a–4d. The results indicate considerable heterogeneity among firms in the sector in response to specific and common factors and conditional volatility and correlation estimates.

Table 7 TARCH estimation.

	(1) Return stock	(2) Return stock	(3) Return stock	(4) Return stock
lTotAsset_~e	−0.0000283		−0.0000590	−0.00379***
z_BOOK_to_~t	−0.000311		−0.000377	0.000727
fin_lev_to~s	0.395		0.500	−0.835
log_debt_e~y	0.0000659		0.000119	0.000471*
z_net_income	0.000436		0.000518*	−0.0000336
premium_mkt		0.225***	0.230***	0.221***
ch_VIX		0.00132	0.00412	0.00343
ch_wti		0.0984***	0.0944***	0.0925***
ch_brl		−0.143***	−0.143***	−0.145***
ch_china_x		−0.219	−0.262	−0.247
ch_india_x		−0.00703	−0.0256	−0.0235
ch_russia_x		0.0155	0.0156	0.0183
ch_southaf~x		−0.260***	−0.267***	−0.265***
ch_uk_x		0.0140	0.0115	0.00766
ch_euro_x		−0.0584*	−0.0478	−0.0474
ch_japan_x		−0.0181	−0.0277	−0.0185
fincrisis		−0.000793**	−0.000780**	−0.000774
Year				Y
Month				Y
Day of Week				Y
Company				Y
_cons	0.000261	0.000731***	0.000266	0.0118***
ARMA				
L.ar	−0.944***	0.854***	0.845***	0.868***
L.ma	0.956***	−0.885***	−0.878***	−0.900***
ARCH				
L.ARCH	0.0958***	0.219***	0.204***	0.206***
L.TARCH	−0.0335***	−0.0680***	−0.0756***	−0.0769***
L.GARCH	0.923***	0.816***	0.829***	0.830***
_cons	0.00000172***	0.00000995***	0.00000872***	0.00000768***
N	21850	22382	19870	19870

Notes: see Table 4 and ARCH = autocorrelation parameter estimate for the innovations in the conditional heteroskedasticity of returns on stock. TARCH = autocorrelation parameter estimate for the positive innovations in the conditional heteroskedasticity of returns on stock. GARCH = autocorrelation parameter estimate for the conditional heteroskedasticity of returns on stock.

*$p < 0.05$.

**$p < 0.01$.

***$p < 0.001$.

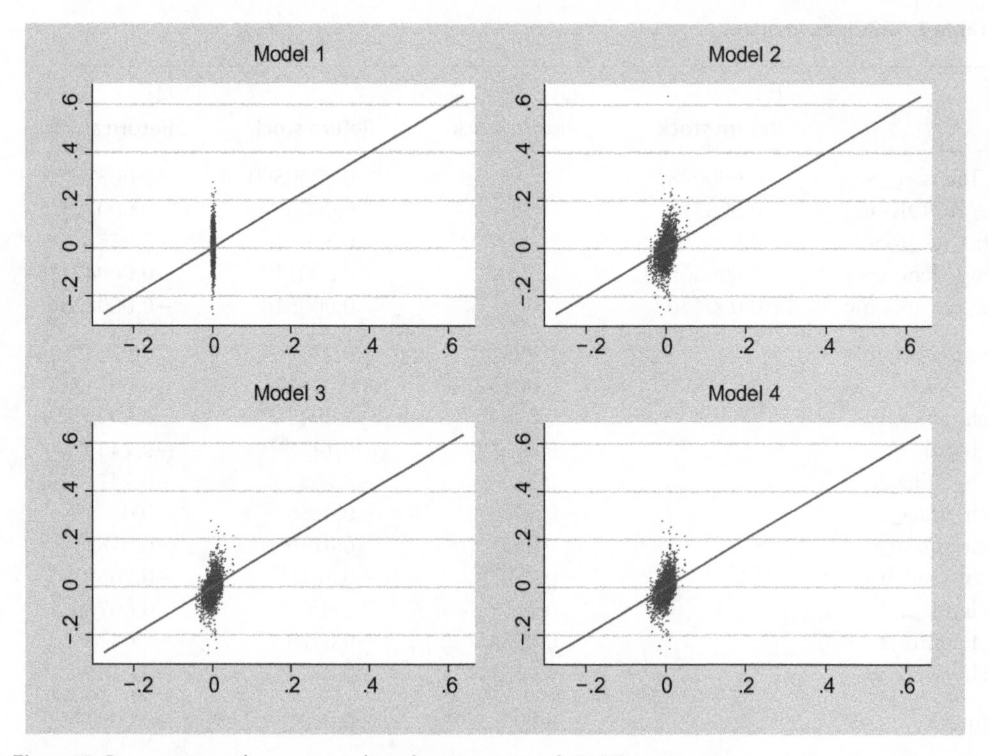

Figure 7 Return on stock versus predicted return on stock TARCH estimation.

Table 8a Parameter estimates for specific factors.

	ltotas˜e	z_book˜t	fin_le˜s	log_de˜y	z_net_˜e
10th quantile	−0.0523	−2.9789	−246.6696	−0.0105	−48.1212
25th quantile	−0.0094	−1.2895	−50.3365	−0.0034	−1.4475
Median	−0.0004	−0.2066	50.5921	−0.0008	−0.0062
75% quantile	0.0081	0.0925	198.4214	0.0003	0.0186
90th quantile	0.0399	1.4883	3679.7230	0.0058	0.1446

lTotas~e = Total assets divided by the price of equity in logarithms.
z_book~t = Book to market ratio as a z-score.
fin_le~s = financial leverage divided by total assets.
log_de~y = debt to equity ratio in logarithms.
z_net_income = net income for company as a z-score.

First, Table 8a shows specific factor parameters. Size and value factor parameters are negative in the lower quantiles and median but become mildly positive at the upper quantiles. The debt-to-equity factor is the one that has the smallest range across the quantiles and is also negative in the lower quantiles and median but become mildly

Table 8b Parameter estimates for common factors I.

	premiu˜t	ch_VIX	ch_eur˜x	ch_chi˜x	ch_ind˜x	ch_jap˜x
10th quantile	−0.0629	−0.0506	−0.6274	−1.2539	−0.1260	−0.1124
25th quantile	0.0768	−0.0201	−0.4554	−0.8885	−0.0396	−0.0605
Median	0.3713	−0.0053	−0.1693	−0.1952	−0.0088	−0.0012
75% quantile	0.6244	0.0105	−0.0484	0.1073	0.0651	0.1121
90th quantile	0.9280	0.0202	0.0371	0.6824	0.1403	0.5643

Notes:
premium_mkt = daily return of the Dow Jones Industrial minus the daily yield of the 3-month US Treasury bill rate (in US$ Dollars).
ch_VIX = continuous daily change of the VIX index.
ch_euro_x = continuous daily change of the Euro/US$ dollar exchange rate.
ch_china_x = continuous daily change of the China-$/US$ dollar exchange rate.
ch_india_x = continuous daily change of the India-$/US$ dollar exchange rate.
ch_japan_x = continuous daily change of the Japan-Y$/US$ dollar exchange rate.

Table 8c Parameter estimates for common factors II.

	ch_uk_x	ch_rus˜x	ch_brl_x	ch_wti	ch_sou˜x
10th quantile	−0.1432	−1.4564	−0.3297	0.0202	−0.6760
25th quantile	−0.0915	−0.2109	−0.2450	0.0267	−0.4949
Median	−0.0050	−0.0051	−0.1096	0.1396	−0.2556
75% quantile	0.0554	0.0468	−0.0449	0.2059	−0.0223
90th quantile	0.0650	0.1499	0.0030	0.2655	0.1864

Notes:
ch_uk_x = continuous daily change of the UK Pound$/US$ dollar exchange rate.
ch_russia_x = continuous daily change of the Russia-$/US$ dollar exchange rate.
ch_brl_x = continuous daily change of the BR-R$/US$ dollar exchange rate.
ch_wti = continuous daily change of the West Texas crude oil price per barrel in US$ dollar.
ch_sou_x = continuous daily change of the South Africa rand $/US$ dollar exchange rate.

Table 8d Parameter estimates for conditional heteroskedasticity and conditional correlations.

	ARCH	GARCH	DCC	λ_1	λ_2
10th quantile	0.0833	−0.0088	−0.2558	0.0016	0.2327
25th quantile	0.1353	0.1180	−0.1199	0.0136	0.5246
Median	0.1666	0.6884	−0.0079	0.0298	0.7145
75% quantile	0.1889	0.8264	0.0661	0.0600	0.8192
90th quantile	0.2324	0.8555	0.1488	0.0814	0.8768

Notes:
ARCH = autocorrelation parameter estimate for the innovations in the conditional heteroskedasticity of returns on stock.
GARCH = autocorrelation parameter estimate for the conditional heteroskedasticity of returns on stock.
DCC = Conditional correlation estimate between return on stock and market premium factor.
λ_1 = conditional correlation innovations parameter estimate.
λ_2 = autocorrelation of conditional correlations parameter estimate.

positive at the upper quantiles. The net income factor has a wide range with a negligible median but a large negative effect at the lower 10th quantile. The financial leverage specific factor has a large magnitude across quantiles in the sample indicating that firms in this sector are relatively sensitive to credit concerns. However, the effects of value and net income are of large magnitude in the lower quantiles.

Tables 8b and 8c show the common factor parameter estimates. The VIX volatility factor has the smallest range of impact. The effect of the VIX is mostly negative, but becomes positive at the upper quantiles. The market premium factor ranges from negligible lower quantiles to 1.26 at the 90th quantile with a sizable negative effect at the lower 10th quantile. The price of crude oil in the last column shows a uniformly positive impact with potentially large responses at the upper 90th quantile as expected. The nominal exchange rates vis-à-vis the US dollar have distinct patterns. The Chinese yuan and the Russian ruble exchange rates have the largest ranges across quantiles with positive effects at the upper quantiles. This is not surprising since China is a sizable trading partner with nations worldwide and Russia is a key player in energy markets. The Euro exchange rate has uniformly negative impact on stock returns. The Indian rupee, Japanese yen, UK pound, and South African rand have similar patterns across quantiles with a range across quantiles from the negative to the positive spectrum. Lastly, the Brazilian real exchange rate has a larger negative impact at the lower quantiles and a small positive effect at the 90th quantile only. The qualitative results at the median are roughly consistent with the panel estimates of Section 3.1 above where the Russian ruble and Indian rupee are not statistically significant.

Table 8d shows the multivariate conditional heteroskedasticity and dynamic conditional correlation parameter estimates as well as the parameters of the error correction for the dynamic conditional correlations, λ_1, λ_2 In particular, λ_1 is the news parameter which captures the deviations of the standardized residuals from the unconditional correlation, while is the decay adjustment parameter that captures λ_2 the autocorrelation of the dynamic conditional correlations themselves, e.g., Engle (2002). Both the ARCH innovations effects and the innovations in conditional correlations are uniformly positive but small in magnitude across quantiles. On the other hand, the autocorrelation of variances (GARCH) and the autocorrelation of the correlations (λ_2) are larger in magnitude and uniformly positive. The correlations between the company return on stock and the market premium common factor show significant heterogeneity among firms in this sample. While the median is negligible, it can be as low as −25% at the 10th quantile to 14% at the upper 90th quantile.

The key result of Tables 8a–8d is that the companies in the oil and gas sector of the BRICS have significant heterogeneity in response to specific factors and common factors. The debt-to-equity specific factor has a small impact across quantiles in the sample, but the financial leverage variable has a much wider range of impact. Thus, firms from the BRICS in this sector are relatively sensitive to credit concerns. The only two common factors that show robust qualitative effects across quantiles are the Euro-US dollar rate, which is negative across all quantiles, and the change in the crude oil price which is positive across all quantiles. The Euro effect indicates that as the currency devalues, the rate of change increases relative to the US dollar, company stock returns decline showing particular exposure to the Euro-US dollar exchange risk. The change in the crude oil price shows robust exposure to the price of oil with higher oil prices increasing stock returns in the sector. Also, the autocorrelations of variances and correlations are significantly larger in magnitude than innovations in variances and autocorrelations.

Table 9a shows the selected quantiles of the per company average estimates of the one-day horizon 5% value at risk from expression (5a). The estimates range from 2.1% value at risk for the lowest 10th quantile to 4.6% value at risk at the 90th quantile while the median is at 3.9% one-day horizon value at risk. Figure 8 shows the estimated average one-day horizon 5% value at risk per company in the sample with the dashed lines representing the respective quantiles of Table 9a. The companies that are above the 90th quantile are clearly riskier, while the companies below the 10th quantile face much less value at risk. The two companies on or below the 10th quantile are potential benchmarks for risk in the sector, they are PetroChina Company Limited and Oil India Limited. The two companies clearly on or above the 90th quantile value at risk in the sample are riskier relative to the benchmark: HRT Holdings and OGX Petroleo, both of Brazil. In particular, HRT shows extreme average value at risk in the period.

Table 9b presents the back-testing for the one-day horizon 5% value at risk estimates using expression (5b). The model performance gives 69% probability within the estimated 5% VaR range, and 31% probability outside the estimated 5% VaR range with 10% significance level.

Next, Figures 9, 10, 11 present comparisons of heteroskedasticity, dynamic conditional correlation, and value at risk for the raw data, the GARCH(1,1) model without any exposure nor dynamic conditional correlations, the GARCH(1,1) model without any exposure in the returns equation but with dynamic conditional correlations with the market premium common factor, and the full model 4a–4d with dynamic conditional correlations with the market premium common factor. Figure 9, panel a.

Table 9a Value at risk $\alpha = 0.95$, 5% value at risk.

	95% VaR
10th quantile	0.0209
25th quantile	0.0298
Median	0.0386
75% quantile	0.0417
90th quantile	0.0459

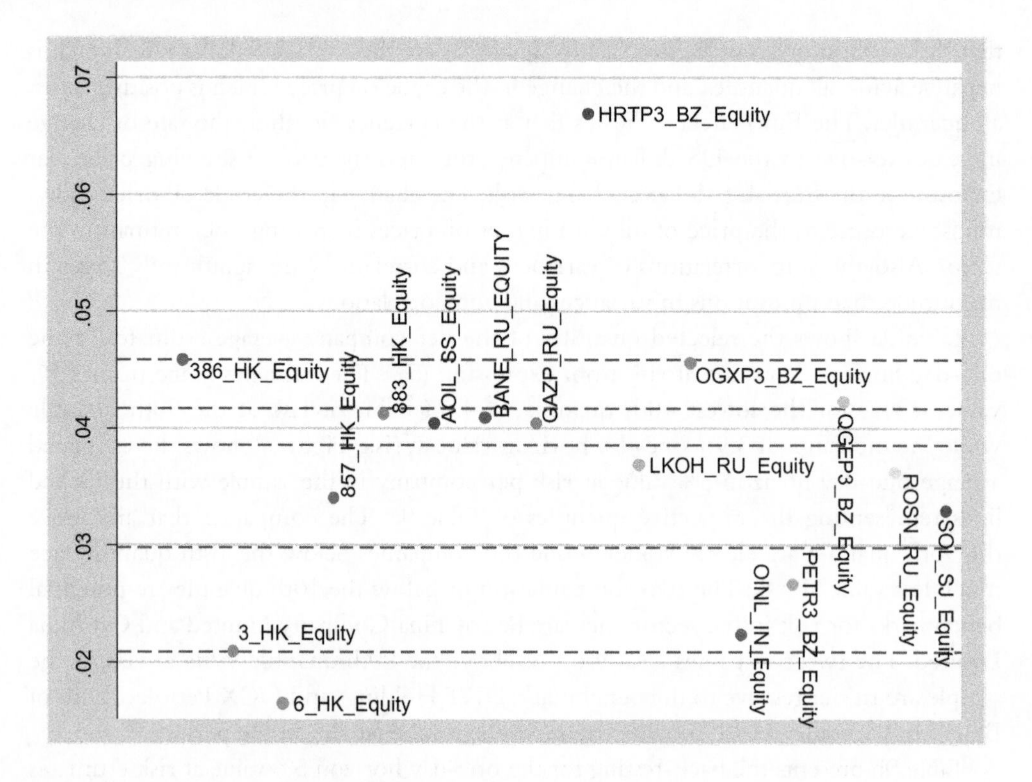

Code	Full Name
AOIL_SS_Equity	Alliance Oil Company
3_HK_Equity	Hong Kong and China Gas Company Limited
386_HK_Equity	China National Petroleum Corporation
6_HK_Equity	Power Assets Holdings Limited
857_HK_Equity	PetroChina Company Limited
883_HK_Equity	China National Offshore Oil Corporation
BANE_RU_EQUITY	Bashneft
GAZP_RU_Equity	Gazprom
HRTP3_BZ_Equity	HRT Holdings in Petroleum
LKOH_RU_Equity	LUKoil
OGXP3_BZ_Equity	OGX Petróleo e Gás Participações S.A.
OINL_IN_Equity	Oil India Limited
PETR3_BZ_Equity	Petróleo Brasileiro S.A. (Petrobras)
QGEP3_BZ_Equity	Grupo Queiroz Galvão S.A.
ROSN_RU_Equity	Rosneft
SOL_SJ_Equity	Sasol Limited

Figure 8 95% VaR—average by company.
Note: dashed lines: 10th, 25th, 50th, 75th, 90th quantiles from Table 9a.

shows the absolute value of the daily returns, a measure of the unconditional volatility of stock returns. Panel b. shows the standard deviation of conditional variance of stock returns without exposure to any factor and panel c. shows the same variable estimated with exposure to all factors. The results show that raw volatility is very large relative to

Table 9b Value at risk $\alpha = 0.95$, 5% value at risk—back-testing.

Number of companies in the sample	Number of companies in the sample (% of total)	Back-test outcome
5	31.25%	Reject null of 95% VaR
11	68.75%	Do not reject null of 95% VaR
16	–	Total companies in the sample

model-based volatility. Volatility is smoother when exposure is taken into account, and panel b. shows that the early period in the sample of 2003–2004 is the period of largest volatility under no exposure, consistent with the US wars in the Middle East.

Figure 10 shows dynamic conditional correlations (DCC) between returns and the market premium in two alternative cases. Panel a. shows the DCC in the M-GARCH(1,1) model without any exposure in the returns equation but with dynamic conditional correlations with the market premium common factor and Panel b. shows the full model with exposure in the returns equation. The model-based DCC in the absence of exposure is very smooth and shows a critical period of burst during the financial crisis from 2008 to early 2009. However, under exposure the DCC becomes larger in magnitudes and with more significant range after the financial crisis of 2008. In particular, under exposure some companies emerge as clear hedges against the market risk with significant negative DCC from the crisis period onwards.

Figure 11 shows the one-day horizon 5% value at risk estimations for each of the cases. Panel a. shows value at risk based on raw data. Panel b. shows value at risk without exposure to any factor and panel c. shows the same variable estimated with exposure to all factors. Panel a. shows that a naïve calculation based on raw data would overestimate the value at risk considerably over the sample period relative to the value at risk accounting for exposure in panel c. The calculation without taking into account exposure in panel b. is slightly less thick (volatile) relative to the case of exposure. In accounting for the exposure to all factors, panel c. shows that value at risk increases mildly during the financial crisis and remains stable in magnitude over the whole period.

7. CONCLUSIONS AND FUTURE RESEARCH

Our measurements indicate that in the space of common factors, the market premium of the US Dow Jones industrials, the price of West Texas Intermediate (WTI) oil, and the exchange rates relative to the US dollar of the Euro, Brazilian real, and South African rand are robustly priced common factors. However, we find that specific factors are not robustly priced factors for BRICS companies. One potential reason may be that BRICS oil and gas companies are more integrated with world oil and gas

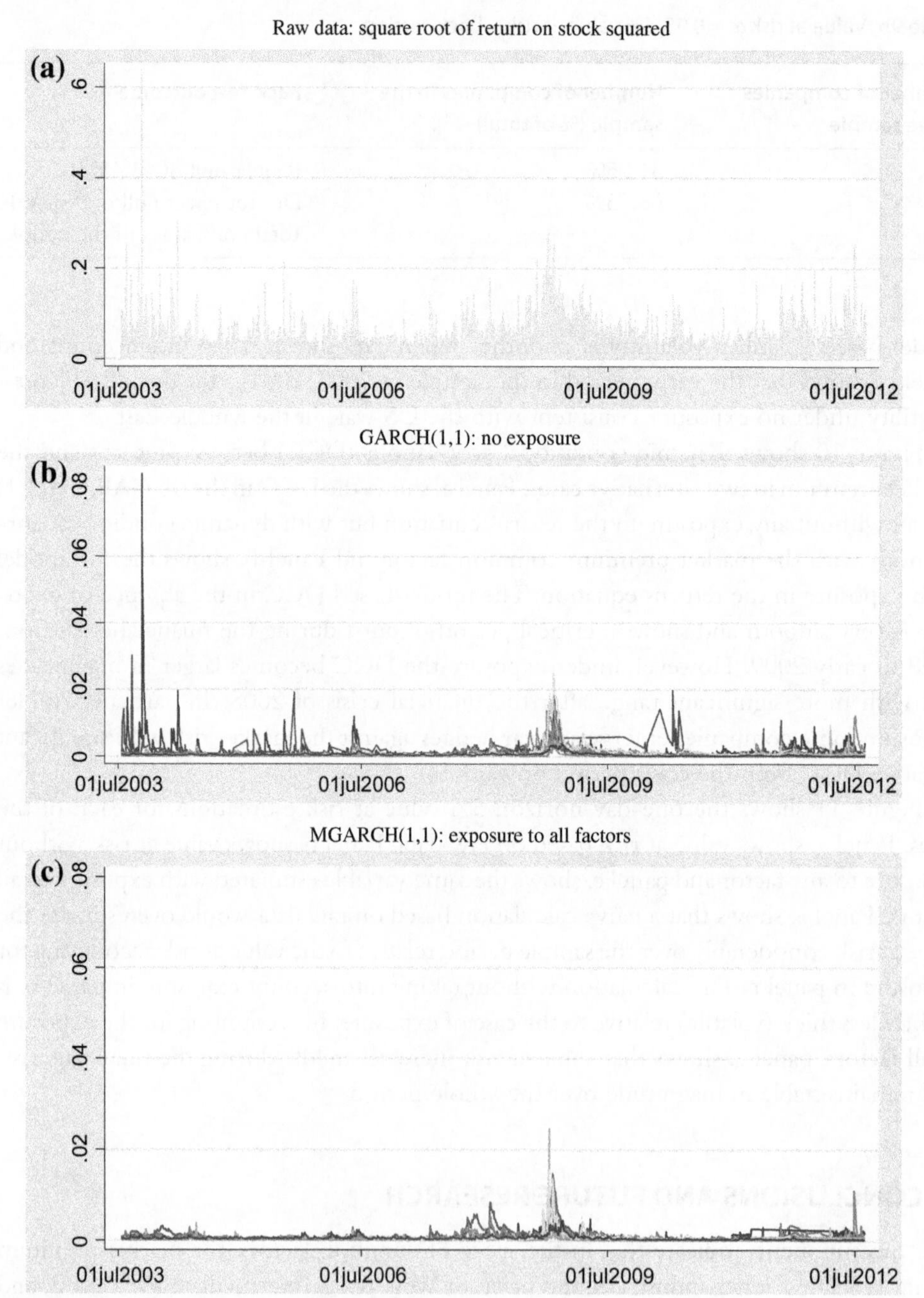

Figure 9 Unconditional and conditional heteroskedasticity: exposure comparisons.

international markets and company idiosyncratic risks may be more diversified in this sector.

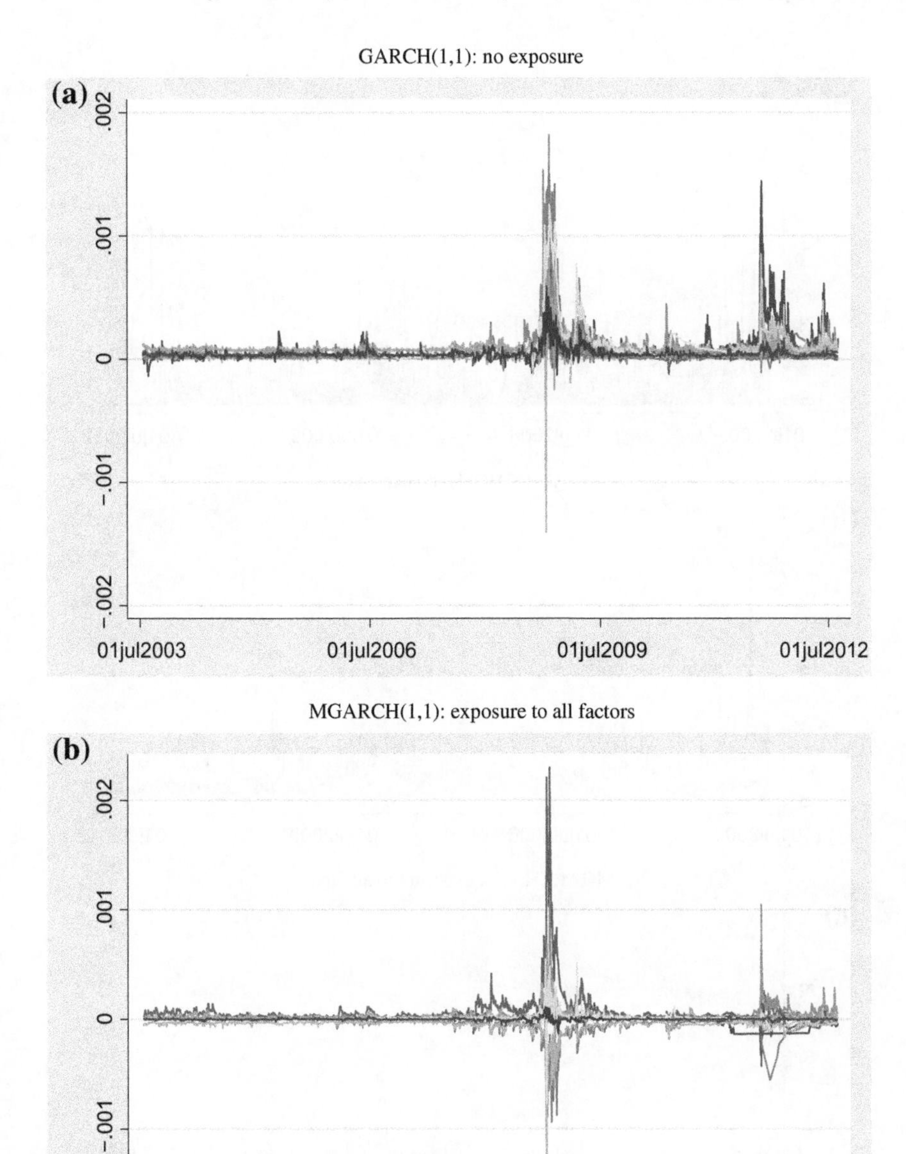

Figure 10 Dynamic conditional correlations: exposure comparisons.

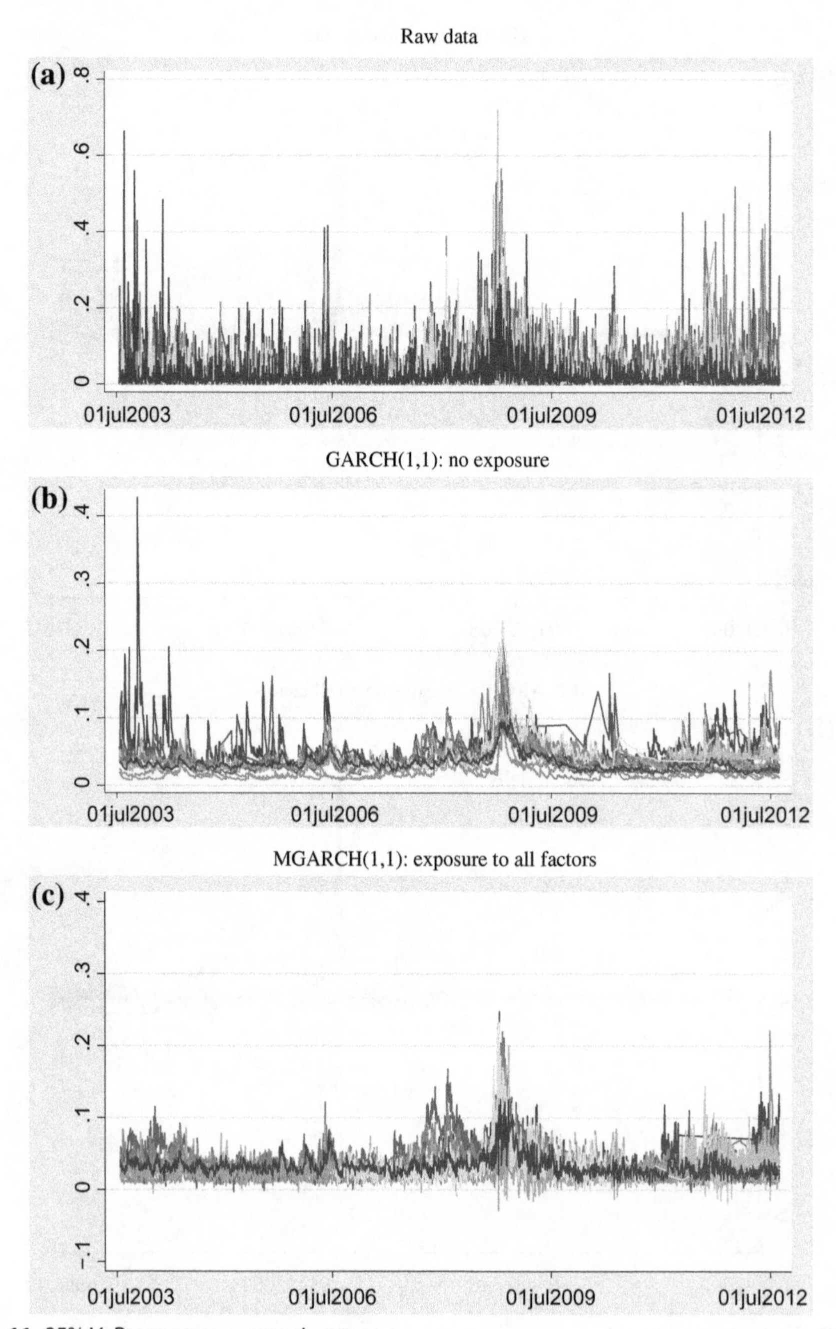

Figure 11 95% VaR: exposure comparisons.

The companies in the oil and gas sector of the BRICS have significant heterogeneity in response to both specific factors and common factors. Firms from the BRICS in this sector are relatively sensitive to credit concerns and the Euro-US dollar exchange rate impacts negatively on the returns across all quantiles, and the change in the crude oil price impacts positively across all quantiles. The per company average estimates of the one-day horizon 5% value at risk range from 2.1% value at risk for the lowest 10th quantile to 4.6% value at risk at the 90th quantile while the median is at 3.9% one-day horizon value at risk. The two companies on or below the 10th quantile are potential benchmarks for risk in the sector, and they are PetroChina Company Limited of China and Oil India Limited of India. The two companies clearly on or above the 90th quantile value at risk in the sample are riskier relative to the benchmark. They are both from Brazil, HRT Holdings and OGX Petroleo.

The results show that raw volatility of returns of BRICS companies is very large relative to model-based volatility. Volatility is smoother when exposure is taken into account, and the early period in the sample of 2003–2004 is the period of largest volatility under no exposure, consistent with the US wars in the Middle East. The dynamic conditional correlations (DCC) between returns and the market premium shows that the model-based DCC in the absence of exposure is very smooth and show a critical period of burst during the financial crisis from 2008 to early 2009. However, under exposure the DCC becomes larger in magnitudes and with more significant range after the financial crisis of 2008. In particular, under exposure some companies emerge as clear hedges against the market risk with significant negative DCC from the crisis period onwards. Finally, we show that a naïve calculation based on raw data would overestimate the value at risk considerably over the sample period relative to the value at risk accounting for exposure. The econometric calculation without taking into account exposure is slightly less volatile relative to the case of exposure. In accounting for the exposure to all factors, we note that for the BRICS, value at risk increased only mildly during the financial crisis and remained stable in magnitude over the whole period.

We find the methods used in this analysis useful for a variety of other measurements of the exposure of companies to alternative sources of risk. In this application, we focused on the specific and systematic components as applied to a narrow sector in the group of BRICS nations. The analysis can be extended to account for systemic sources of risk from one group to another and/or from one sector to another with reference to the conditional value at risk framework of Adrian and Brunnermeier (2011). For example, Bianconi and Yoshino (2012a) find evidence of conditional premium persistence and conditional volatility persistence in the national real estate sector of Brazil recently. The national real estate sector can be interacted with the oil and gas sector for potential measurements of systemic risk and contagion.

APPENDIX

Table A1 Companies from BRICS in the sample.

Short name	Code	Full name	Country	Description
Alliance_ Oil_CO	AOIL_SS_ Equity	Alliance Oil Company	Russia	Extraction, refining, transportation, and sale of petroleum
Hong_Kong_ China_Gas_Co	3_HK_ Equity	Hong Kong and China Gas Company Limited	China	Gas and water distribution
China_ Petroleum	386_HK_ Equity	China National Petroleum Corporation	China	Extraction, refining, transportation, and sale of oil and gas
Power_Assets_ Holdings	6_HK_ Equity	Power Assets Holdings Limited	China	Power and gas distribution
Petrochina	857_HK_ Equity	PetroChina Company Limited	China	Oil and gas extraction
CNOOC	883_HK_ Equity	China National Offshore Oil Corporation	China	Oil and gas extraction
Bashneft_ OAO	BANE_RU_ Equity	Bashneft	Russia	Oil and gas extraction
Gazprom_ OAO	GAZP_RU_ Equity	Gazprom	Russia	Oil and gas extraction
HRT	HRTP3_BZ_ Equity	HRT participações em petroleo	Brazil	Oil and gas extraction
Lukoil	LKOH_RU_ Equity	LUKoil	Russia	Oil and gas extraction
OGX	OGXP3_BZ_ Equity	OGX Petróleo e Gás Participações S.A.	Brazil	Oil and gas extraction
Oil_India	OINL_IN_ Equity	Oil India Limited	India	Oil and gas extraction
Petrobras	PETR3_BZ_ Equity	Petróleo Brasileiro S.A.	Brazil	Oil and gas extraction
Queiroz_ Galvao	QGEP3_BZ_ Equity	Grupo Queiroz Galvão S.A.	Brazil	Construction, oil gas, food, iron production, and public utilicades
Rosneft	ROSN_RU_ Equity	Rosneft	Russia	Oil and gas extraction
SASOL	SOL_SJ_ Equity	Sasol Limited	South Africa	Oil and gas extraction, mining, chemistry

ACKNOWLEDGMENT

We thank the useful comments and suggestions of the editors. We thank Raphael Lolis for able research assistance in collecting and organizing the data from Bloomberg, and Bruno Huang and Allan Pio for able research assistance. Any errors are our own.

REFERENCES

Adrian, T., Brunnermeier, M., 2011. CoVaR. Working Paper, Department of Economics Princeton University and FRB of New York.

Bianconi, M., Yoshino, J.A., 2012a. Firm market performance and volatility in a national real estate sector. International Review of Economics and Finance 22, 230–253

Bianconi, M., Yoshino, J.A., 2012b. Worldwide commodities sector market-to-book and return on equity valuation. Working Paper, Tufts University and FEA-Economics-USP (October).

Bianconi, M., Yoshino, J.A., 2013. Risk factors and value at risk in publicly traded companies of the nonrenewable energy sector. Working Paper, Tufts University and FEA-Economics-USP (January).

Boyer, M.M., Filion, D., 2007. Common and fundamental factors in stock returns of Canadian oil and gas companies. Energy Economics 29, 428–453

Brownlees, C.T., Engle, R.F., 2011. Volatility. New York University Working Paper, Correlations and Tails for Systemic Risk Measurement (June).

Chiou, J.-S., Lee, Y.-H., 2009. Jump dynamics and volatility: Oil and the stock markets. Energy 34, 788–796

Cochrane, J.H., 2005. Asset Pricing, revised ed. Princeton University Press, NJ

De Santis, G., Gerard, B., 1998. How big is the premium for currency risk? Journal of Financial Economics 49, 375–412

Diebold, F., Mariano, R., 1995. Comparing predictive accuracy. Journal of Business and Economic Statistic 13, 253–263

Elyasiani, E.I.Mansur, Odusami, B., 2011. Oil price shocks and industry returns. Energy Economics 33, 966–974

Engle, R.F., 2002. Dynamic conditional correlation: a simple class of multivariate generalized autoregressive conditional heteroskedasticity models. Journal of Business & Economic Statistics 20, 339–350

Fama, E.F., MacBeth, J.D., 1973. Risk, return, and equilibrium: empirical tests. Journal of Political Economy 81 (3), 607–636 (May - Jun)

Fama, E.F., French, K., 1992. The cross-section of expected stock returns. Journal of Finance, 427–465 (June)

Fama, E.F., French, K., 1995. Size and book-to-market factors in earnings and returns. Journal of Finance 50 (1), 131–155 (Mar)

Ferson, W., Harvey, C., 1994. Sources of risk and expected returns in global equity markets. Journal of Banking and Finance 18, 1625–1665

Giovannini, M.M., Grasso, Lanza, A., Manera, M., 2004. Conditional correlations in the returns on oil companies stock prices and their determinants. IEM – International Energy Markets Working Paper (April).

Glosten, L.R., Jagannathan, R., Runkle, D.E., 1993. On the relation between the expected value and the volatility of the nominal excess return on stocks. Journal of Finance 48, 1779–1801

Hamilton, J., 1983. Oil and the macroeconomy since World War II. Journal of Political Economy 91, 228–248

Haushalter, D.G., 2000. Financing Policy, Basis Risk, and Corporate Hedging: Evidence from Oil and Gas Producers. Journal of Finance LV (1)

Karolyi, A., Stulz, R., 2003. Are financial assets priced locally or globally? In: Constantinides, M.H.D., Stulz, R. (Eds.), Handbook of the Economics of Finance. North-Holland, Amsterdam

Khalfaoui, R., Boutahar, M., 2012. Portfolio risk evaluation: An approach based on dynamic conditional correlations models and wavelet multiresolution analysis. MPRA Paper No. 41624 (September).

Kupiec, P., 1995. Techniques for verifying the accuracy of risk management models. Journal of Derivatives 3, 73–84

Lombardi, M.J., Ravazzoloz, F., 2012. Oil price density forecasts: Exploring the linkages with stock markets CAMP Working Paper Series No 3/2012. Norwegian Business School, December.

Mohanty, S.N., Nandha, M., 2011. Oil risk exposure: the case of the U.S. oil and gas sector. Financial Review 46, 165–191

Pierret, D., 2012. The systemic risk of energy markets. Université Catholique de Louvain, Working Paper (July).

Rabemananjara, R., Zakoian, J.M., 1993. Threshold ARCH models and asymmetries in volatility. Journal of Applied Econometrics 8 (1), 31–49

Ramos, S.B., Veiga, H., 2011. Risk factors in oil and gas industry returns: international evidence. Energy Economics 33, 525–542

Roache, S.K., 2008. Commodities and the Market Price of Risk. International Monetary Fund WP/08/221 (September).

Sadorsky, P., 2001. Risk factors in stock returns of canadian oil and gas companies. Energy Economics 23, 17–28

Sadorsky, P., 2008. The oil price exposure of global oil companies. Applied Financial Economics Letters 4 (2), 93–96

Zakoian, J.M., 1994. Threshold heteroskedastic models. Journal of Economic Dynamics and Control 18, 931–955

CHAPTER 11

Developed and Emerging Equity Market Tail Risk: Is it Constant?

Stefan Straetmans and Bertrand Candelon
School of Business and Economics, Maastricht University, Maastricht, The Netherlands

1. INTRODUCTION

Financial market turmoil like the 1997 Asian crisis, the LTCM debacle, the Mexican "Tequila" crisis, the Russian debt crisis, or the recent subprime credit crunch has increased the awareness of both academics and practitioners on the importance of accurately assessing the likelihoods of such extreme events. However, the academic interest into large tail events is far from new, see, e.g., Mandelbrot (1963) as a seminal reference. This constitutes one of the first studies to acknowledge that overnight financial market turbulence cannot well be described by the normal distribution paradigm. More specifically, tail probabilities seem to exhibit a polynomial tail decay ("heavy" tails) in contrast to the exponential tail decays of so-called "thin-tailed" models like the normal df. This "heavy tail" characteristic has been detected for most financial asset classes. Numerous empirical studies subsequently focused on identifying the degree of probability mass in the tail by estimating the so-called tail index α.[1] Loosely speaking, this parameter reflects the number of bounded distributional moments that are still finite.

Much less attention has been paid to the possibility and consequences of nonconstant tail behavior, i.e., a time varying α.[2] Stochastic Volatility models such as the ARCH- and GARCH-type class reconcile a stationary unconditional df (constant α) with clusters of high and low volatility in the conditional df. However, the question arises whether it is realistic to assume that the tail of the unconditional df (and thus measures of long-run risk like unconditional quantiles) stays invariant over very long time periods; or,

[1] Jansen and de Vries (1991), Longin (1996), Lux (1996), and Hartmann et al. (2004) investigated the probability mass in the tails of stock market returns; whereas fat tails in foreign exchange returns have been considered, inter alia, by Koedijk et al. (1990, 1992), Hols and de Vries (1991), and Hartmann et al. (2003). Bond extremes have been rather neglected in the empirical literature; de Haan et al. (1994) and Hartmann et al. (2004) constitute two notable exceptions. More recent applications on extreme value analysis mainly focus on stock market tails and include, inter alia, Bollerslev and Todorov (2011), Bollerslev et al. (2013), or Chollette et al. (2012).

[2] Exceptions constitute Phillips and Loretan (1990), Koedijk et al. (1990, 1992), Jansen and de Vries (1991), Pagan and Schwert (1990), and more recently Straetmans et al. (2008) and Straetmans and Chaudhry (2013). These studies all perform "exogenous" tests of breakpoint detection in the tail index by imposing the candidate-breakpoint.

Emerging Markets and the Global Economy
http://dx.doi.org/10.1016/B978-0-12-411549-1.00011-9

alternatively, whether there may be a trendwise increase in α and accompanying long-run risk). Otherwise stated, can highly volatile periods like the Asian crisis or the Mexican Tequila crisis and periods of market quiescence be explained by the same stationary distributional model or do crisis periods induce structural breaks in tail behavior, i.e., shifts in α?

Testing for structural change in the tail behavior of the unconditional distribution is important from both a statistical and policy perspective. First, whether Extreme Value Theory (EVT) or the cited ARCH and GARCH models of the conditional df are applicable or not depends on the stationarity assumption for the unconditional tail. Also, a nonconstant α implies a violation of covariance stationarity which invalidates standard statistical inference based on regression analysis. From a policy perspective, quantifying the correct level of the tail index is of potential importance to risk managers and financial regulators because it is a necessary ingredient to calculating the unconditional Value-at-Risk (VaR) very far into the distributional tail, e.g., the sake of stress testing. For example, if a decrease in α (and thus a rise in the magnitude and frequency of extreme events) is not properly recognized by risk managers and regulators, unconditional VaR quantiles will most probably be underestimated resulting in insufficient capital buffers. This can ultimately jeopardize the stability of the financial system.

The scant empirical literature on the constancy issue mainly focuses on testing for a single known (i.e., exogenously selected) breakpoint in α.[3] To the best of our knowledge, Quintos et al. (2001) constitute the only stability study on detecting single breakpoints in α that also proposes estimators for break *dates* in α.[4] Our study extends and refines the previous breakpoint analyses in several directions. First, we select the number of extreme returns to estimate α by minimizing its Asymptotic Mean Squared Error (AMSE) instead of conditioning on a fixed fraction of the total sample. The former approach constitutes common practice in EVT, whereas taking a fixed percentage of extremes leads to a degenerate asymptotic limiting df for the α-estimator and accompanying stability tests. Second, our simulation study of the stability tests' finite sample properties is much more general than previous studies because we also use data generating processes (DGPs) that consider higher order tail behavior or empirical stylized facts like, e.g., volatility clustering in returns. Last but not least, we apply stability tests to the tails of a large cross-section of developed and emerging equity market index returns. Emerging stock markets may be seen as a "control" sample because breaks in the tail index α—if present—may be

[3] The breakpoint literature includes Koedijk et al. (1990, 1992), Jansen and de Vries (1991), Pagan and Schwert (1990), and Straetmans et al. (2008). One can distinguish tests for structural change in α from cross-sectional equality tests (see, e.g., Koedijk et al., 1990, on exchange rates or Jondeau and Rockinger, 2003, on stock markets) or asymmetry tests between left and right tails of the same series (see, e.g., Jansen and de Vries, 1991 on stock index tail asymmetries).

[4] Werner and Upper (2002), Galbraith and Zernov (2004), Candelon and Straetmans (2006), and Hartmann et al. (2006) already apply the Quintos et al. (2001) methodology. However, they all use the Quintos et al. (2001) asymptotic critical values. We argue in this paper that these critical values do not take into account the bias in the Hill estimator and lead to overrejection of the null hypothesis of tail index constancy.

expected to occur more often in a context of high political risk, recurring exchange rate regime shifts, or underdeveloped governance and supervision.

Anticipating our results, we find that size, (size-corrected) power, and the ability to detect breaks in finite samples vary considerably with the assumed DGP. That is the reason why we propose to bootstrap the critical values in empirical applications for each data set separately. Moreover, the outcomes of our experiments on size-corrected power and the ability to detect breaks suggest that a "recursive" version of the stability test is to be preferred provided the sample is sufficiently large ($n \geq 2000$). Upon applying a bootstrap-based version of this test to our cross-section of developed and emerging equity returns, we mainly detect breaks in the tail behavior of emerging currencies.

The rest of the paper is organized as follows. Section 2 is devoted to the statistical theory on the measurement of heavy tails and the accompanying endogenous stability tests. Section 3 reports a Monte Carlo investigation of the endogenous breakpoint tests' size, power, and the ability to date breaks. Section 4 provides an empirical application. Conclusions are comprised in Section 5.

2. TESTING STRUCTURAL CHANGE IN TAIL BEHAVIOR: THEORY

A short digression on the theory and estimation of the index of regular variation is provided in Section 2.1 followed by a short review of the Quintos et al. (2001) stability tests for the tail index α in Section 2.2.

2.1. Regular Variation

We start from the empirical stylized fact that sharp fluctuations in financial market prices are poorly described by exponentially declining tails, i.e., financial returns exhibit fat tails, see, e.g., Mandelbrot (1963) for early references or the more recent monograph by Embrechts et al. (1997). Without loss of generality (and for the sake of notational convenience), we adopt the convention to take the negative of a return such that all presented estimation and testing procedures are expressed in terms of the right tail, i.e., the survivor function $P\{X \geq x\} := 1 - F(x)$. Under fairly general conditions the survivor function of heavy tailed (or "regularly varying") distributions can be approximated by the second order Taylor expansion for large x:

$$1 - F(x) = ax^{-\alpha}(1 + bx^{-\beta} + o(x^{-\beta})), \tag{1}$$

with $a > 0$, $b \in \Re$, $\beta > 0$, see, e.g., de Haan and Stadtmüller (1996). The parameters β and b that govern the second order behavior in (1) reflect the deviation from pure Pareto behavior in the tail. As will be argued later on, those parameters also strongly influence the small sample properties of the Hill statistic and stability tests. The case $\beta = 0$ corresponds to the expansion $P\{X \geq x\} \simeq ax^{-\alpha}[1 + b\ln x]$. If $b = 0$, the tail specializes to an exact Pareto.

The regular variation property implies that the upper extremal returns (appropriately scaled) lie in the (maximum) domain of attraction of the Type-II extreme value ("Fréchet") distribution. The tail index α reflects the speed at which the tail probability in (1) decays if x is increased. Clearly, the lower α the slower the probability decay and the higher the probability mass in the tail of X, *ceteris paribus* the level of x. The regular variation property, *inter alia*, implies that all distributional moments higher than α, i.e., $E[X^r], r > \alpha$, are unbounded, signifying the "fat tail property". Models of the unconditional distribution like the Student-t, symmetric stable, Burr, and Fréchet dfs as well as Stochastic Volatility models of the conditional distribution like the GARCH class all exhibit heavy tails.[5] As for the tail of the standard normal distribution, a popular tail approximation expresses the survivor function $1 - \Phi(\cdot)$ in terms of the density $\phi(x)$:

$$\begin{aligned} 1 - \Phi(x) &\simeq \frac{\phi(x)}{x}, \ x \text{ large} \\ &= (2\pi x)^{-1} \exp\left(-\frac{1}{2}x^2\right), \end{aligned}$$

which clearly describes an exponentially declining tail, see Feller (1971,VII.1). Distributions with this type of tail decay are classified as "thin tailed" because the tail probabilities $1 - \Phi(x)$ decline much faster to zero as in (1); but these distributions possess all moments, and hence do not capture what is observed in financial data.

The focus of the paper will be on the small sample properties of temporal stability tests for α-estimators. The investigated test statistics use Hill's (1975) estimator for α as an input. Let $X_{1,n} \leq X_{2,n} \leq \cdots \leq X_{n,n}$ represent the ascending order statistics that correspond with the return series X for a sample of size n. Then Hill's estimator boils down to:

$$\widehat{\alpha} = \left(\frac{1}{m}\sum_{j=0}^{m-1} \ln\left(\frac{X_{n-j,n}}{X_{n-m,n}}\right)\right)^{-1}, \tag{2}$$

with m the number of highest order statistics used in the estimation. The convergence in distribution of the Hill statistic critically depends on the rate at which the nuisance parameter m grows with the total sample size n. The main convergence in distribution result for $\widehat{\alpha}$ is summarized in the following theorem:

[5] Note that Hall (1982) imposes the more stringent condition $\alpha = \beta$ on the tail expansion. This covers certain distributions like the stable laws and the Type-II extreme value distribution (Fréchet). But it does not apply to, e.g., the Student-t or the Burr df. For the Student-t df the tail expansion (1) holds, though, with α equal to the degrees of freedom ($\alpha = \nu$) and $\beta = 2$. As for the Burr, the second order parameter can be freely chosen. The value of β is unknown for the GARCH class. All the mentioned distributional models together with some temporally dependent variants will be put at work in the Monte Carlo section.

Theorem 1 (Convergence in distribution). *Assume that* $1 - F(x)$ *obeys (1). If* $m, n \longrightarrow \infty$ *we distinguish two cases:*

(A) If $m = o\left(n^{2\beta/2\beta+\alpha}\right)$ *then* $\sqrt{m}\left(\widehat{\alpha} - \alpha\right) \xrightarrow{d} N\left(0, \eta\alpha^2\right)$.

(B) If $m = cn^{2\beta/2\beta+\alpha}$ *then* $\sqrt{m}\left(\widehat{\alpha} - \alpha\right) \xrightarrow{d} N\left(\varphi\alpha, \eta\alpha^2\right)$ *for strictly positive and finite* $c = \left(\frac{a^{2\beta/\alpha}(\alpha+\beta)^2\alpha}{2b^2\beta^3}\right)^{\frac{\alpha}{2\beta+\alpha}}$ *and* $\varphi = sign(b)(2\beta/\alpha)^{-1/2}$.

Asymptotic normality for the Hill statistic was initially established by, e.g., Hall (1982) and Haeusler and Teugels (1985) for the i.i.d. case ($\eta = 1$). Convergence in distribution has also been derived in the presence of temporal dependencies ($\eta \neq 1$).[6]

Loosely speaking, Theorem 1 implies that convergence requires m to rise with n at a "sufficiently slow" pace, i.e., $m, n \rightarrow \infty$ but $m/n \rightarrow 0$. Selecting a fixed fraction of extremes $\kappa = m/n$ (as under Dumouchel's (1983) rule), however, does not guarantee proper convergence because both (A) and (B) in Theorem 1 are violated. Previous studies—including Quintos et al. (2001)—have argued that this simple rule-of-thumb performs well in small samples but its lack of asymptotic justification constitutes a major problem. We will, therefore, renege from using this criterion. Notice that condition (B) of the convergence theorem provides an alternative way to selecting the nuisance parameter. It can be easily shown that the expression for the nuisance parameter m under (B) minimizes the Asymptotic Mean Squared Error (AMSE) for $\widehat{\alpha}$, see, e.g., Danielsson and de Vries (1997). The AMSE minimization principle is applied in virtually all empirical EVT studies and we will therefore use this criterion in the rest of the paper. Notice, however, that Theorem 1 also makes clear that applying the AMSE criterion also induces a bias in the Hill statistic, i.e., $E(\widehat{\alpha} - \alpha) \sim m^{-1/2}\varphi\alpha$. We will thoroughly document the small sample consequences of this bias effect on the accompanying stability tests in the Monte Carlo simulation section.

2.2. Structural Change in Tail Behavior

Quintos et al. (2001) propose a recursive, rolling, and sequential procedure for detecting single unknown breaks in the Hill statistic $\widehat{\alpha}$. Let t denote the endpoint of a subsample of size $w_t < n$. The recursive estimator uses subsamples $[1; t] \subset [1; n]$ and boils down to:

$$\widehat{\alpha}_t = \left(\frac{1}{m_t}\sum_{j=0}^{m_t-1} \ln\left(\frac{X_{t-j,t}}{X_{t-m_t,t}}\right)\right)^{-1}, \tag{3}$$

with $m_t = ct^{\frac{2\beta}{(2\beta+\alpha)}}$. The rolling estimator is conditioned on a fixed subsample size $w^* < n$; the tail index is estimated by rolling over the subsample, i.e., the subsample is shifted

[6] Quintos et al. (2001) derive convergence in distribution of the Hill statistic under stationary GARCH processes with conditionally normal innovations. Drees (2003) derives convergence in distribution for stationary time series processes exhibiting general forms of linear and nonlinear dependence. All these studies conclude that the asymptotic variance for dependent data differs from the i.d.d. variance α^2. This explains the $\eta-$ factor in Theorem 1.

through the full sample by eliminating past observations and adding future observations while keeping the subsample size constant at w^*:

$$\widehat{\alpha}_t^* = \left(\frac{1}{m_{w^*}} \sum_{j=0}^{m_{w^*}-1} \ln\left(\frac{X_{w^*-j,w^*}}{X_{w^*-m_{w^*},w^*}} \right) \right)^{-1}, \tag{4}$$

with $m_{w^*} = c(w^*)^{\frac{2\beta}{(2\beta+\alpha)}}$.[7] Finally, the sequential estimator (denoted by $\widehat{\alpha}_{2t}$) is identical to the recursive estimator in (3) but calculated in reverse calendar time, i.e., using the more recent observations first.

The three tests can now be constructed using the sequences:

$$Y_n^2(r) = \left(\frac{tm_t}{n} \right) \left(\frac{\widehat{\alpha}_t}{\widehat{\alpha}_n} - 1 \right)^2, \tag{5}$$

$$V_n^2(r) = \left(\frac{w^* m_{w^*}}{n} \right) \left(\frac{\widehat{\alpha}_t^*}{\widehat{\alpha}_n} - 1 \right)^2, \tag{6}$$

$$Z_n^2(r) = \left(\frac{tm_t}{n} \right) \left(\frac{\widehat{\alpha}_t}{\widehat{\alpha}_{2t}} - 1 \right)^2, \tag{7}$$

with $r = t/n$. Expressions (5) and (6) measure the fluctuation in the recursive and rolling values of the Hill statistic relative to their full sample counterpart $\widehat{\alpha}_n$ whereas the sequential test uses (7) to compare the fluctuations of the recursive with the reverse recursive estimator. The null hypothesis of interest is that the tail index α does not exhibit any temporal changes. The null hypothesis of constancy then takes the form:

$$H_0 : \alpha_{[nr]} = \alpha, \quad \forall r \in R_\varepsilon = [\varepsilon; 1-\varepsilon] \subset [0; 1], \tag{8}$$

with $[nr]$ representing the integer value of nr. Without prior knowledge about the direction of a break, one is interested in testing the null against the two-sided alternative hypothesis $H_A{:}\,\alpha_{[nr]} \neq \alpha$. For practical reasons the above test is calculated over compact subsets of $[0; 1]$, i.e., t equals the integer part of nr for $r \in R_\varepsilon = [\varepsilon; 1-\varepsilon]$ and for small $\varepsilon > 0$. Sets like R_ε are often used in the construction of parameter constancy tests (see, e.g., Andrews, 1993).[8] In line with Quandt's (1960) pioneering work on endogenous breakpoint determination in linear time series models, the candidate break date r is

[7] Notice that the number of upper order extremes is increasing in the subsample size for the recursive estimator but is constant for the rolling estimator.

[8] The restricted choice of r implies that $\varepsilon n \leq t \leq (1-\varepsilon)n$. When the lower bound would be violated, the recursive estimates might become too unstable and inefficient because of too small subsample sizes. On the other hand, the test will never find a break for t equal or very close to n, because the test value (5) is close to zero in that latter case. Thus, for computational efficiency one might stop calculating the tests beyond the upper bound of $(1-\varepsilon)n < n$. Conform with Andrews (1993), we set $\varepsilon = 0.15$.

selected where the testing sequences (5)–(7) reach their supremum which renders the most likely time point for the constancy hypothesis to be violated.

Quintos et al. (2001) also establish asymptotic distribution theory for the three stability tests under the two cases (A) and (B) from Theorem 1. We are interested in the asymptotic behavior under outcome (B) as this corresponds with the standard practice of minimizing the AMSE of $\widehat{\alpha}$ with respect to m. Upon denoting Q, Q^*, and $Q^\#$ as the recursive, rolling, and sequential test statistics, the corresponding limiting distributions boil down to:

$$Q = \sup \eta_Y^{-1} Y_n^2(r) \to^d \sup \left[\bar{W}(r) + \varphi r^{1/2}\left(1 - r^{1/2}\right)\right]^2,$$

$$Q^* = \sup \eta_V^{-1} V_n^2(r) \to^d \sup \left[\bar{W}(r, \gamma_0) + \varphi \gamma_0^{1/2}\left(1 - \gamma_0^{1/2}\right)\right]^2,$$

$$Q^\# = \sup \eta_Z^{-1} Z_n^2(r) \to^d \sup \left[\bar{W}^\#(r) + \varphi r^{1/2}\left(1 - \left(r/(1-r)\right)^{1/2}\right)\right]^2,$$

$$r \in [0.15, 0.85], \qquad \varphi = sign(b)(2\beta/\alpha)^{-1/2},$$

with $\bar{W}(r) = W(r) - rW(1)$, $\bar{W}(r, \gamma_0) = W(r, \gamma_0) - (r-s)W(1, 1)$, $\bar{W}^\#(r) = W(r) - (r/(1-r))W(1-r)$ and where $W(r)$ is a standard Wiener process. The scaling factors η_Y^{-1}, η_V^{-1}, and η_Z^{-1} correct for possible nonlinear dependence in the data; but estimators for these correction factors are only known for the GARCH class. We will implement these correction factors in the empirical application.

Nonsurprisingly, the parameter φ that governed the Hill statistic's asymptotic bias reappears in the limiting distributions of the stability tests. The bias term suggests that "globally valid" asymptotic critical values that can be applied to all financial return tails do not apply. In the next section, we investigate the impact of this bias term on the critical values, power and ability to date breaks in finite samples. Whereas the asymptotic distributions across different DGPs can only differ due to differences in $\varphi = sign(b)(2\beta/\alpha)^{-1/2}$, the small sample outcomes for critical values, power and break datation are also potentially depending on the sample size n, the optimal nuisance parameter m^*, and the scaling factor a.

3. MONTE CARLO EXPERIMENTS

We investigate the small sample behavior of the recursive, rolling, and sequential test for a variety of stochastic models—both for the conditional and the unconditional df—used in the modeling of financial time series. Each model exhibits regularly varying tails and obeys the asymptotic second order expansion in (1). The number of upper order extremes for the Hill statistic is chosen to minimize the Asymptotic Mean Squared Error of the Hill estimator. We calculate (size-corrected) small sample power against a variety of realistic break scenarios as alternative hypotheses. Last but not least, we report simulated break estimates averaged over the statistically significant breaks at the 95% significance level.

A short description of the main data generating processes is provided in Section 3.1. The analytic derivation of the nuisance parameters for these DGPs is discussed in Section 3.2. The outcomes of our Monte Carlo experiments (small sample size, power, location of break dates) are summarized in Section 3.3.

3.1. Data Generating Processes

We choose regularly varying data generating processes such as to get a sufficiently large heterogeneity in parameter values (a, b, α, β). Monte Carlo simulations are reported for the symmetric stable df, Student-t, Fréchet (Type-II extreme value), i.e., $P\{X > x\} = \exp\left(-x^{-\alpha}\right)$, Burr, i.e., $P\{X > x\} = \left(1 + x^{\beta}\right)^{-\alpha/\beta}$, AR(1) with stable innovations, GARCH(1,1) with conditionally normal errors and a Stochastic Volatility model. Thus, we distinguish between i.i.d. draws and dependent draws.

For the sake of comparison with the Quintos et al. (2001) Monte Carlo results we generate symmetric stable draws using the algorithm proposed by Samorodnitsky and Taqqu (1994):

$$X_{\text{stable}} = \frac{\sin \alpha \gamma}{(\cos \gamma)^{1/\alpha}} \left(\frac{\cos (1 - \alpha)\gamma}{W} \right), \tag{9}$$

where $0 < \alpha < 2$ represents the tail index. For $\alpha = 2$, the stable df coincides with the normal df, which implies that α is not interpretable as the tail index in this case. The parameter γ is drawn uniformly on $[-\pi/2; \pi/2]$ whereas W is exponentially distributed with mean 1.[9] The tail index of the Student-t, Fréchet, and Burr is varied between 2 and 4, which is the range one typically observes for stock market tails, see also Jansen and de Vries (1991) or Hartmann et al. (2004) for previous studies on stock market tail behavior.

We also allow for models that exhibit linear and nonlinear dependence because the i.i.d. assumption is too restrictive for financial return data. First order serial correlation (linear dependence) is generated by means of an AR(1) process with first order auto-correlation $\theta = 0.1$ and with symmetric stable innovations.[10] The choice for stable

[9] Mandelbrot (1963) was arguably the first proponent of using this distribution class for modeling financial returns. He mainly based his choice on the property that the stable distribution is preserved under addition *over the full distributional support* (up to a location and scale adjustment). However, Feller (1971, Chapter VIII.8) has proven that the additivity property only holds for the *tail area* of regularly varying dfs (the class of stable dfs constituting a notable exception). This suggests that the stable model might be overly restrictive. Also, one can argue that less heavy tailed models are to be preferred because the class of stable dfs fails to have a finite second moment. Finally, notice that the normal df can act as a "local alternative" for the stable model. Indeed, let α stand for the tail index as defined earlier. For $\alpha < 2$, α determines the maximal number of bounded moments up to α but when $\alpha = 2$ (the case of the normal df in (9)) all moments exist and α is not interpretable as the tail index. Thus, stable processes with α close to 2 can only be distinguished from a normal df on the basis of α-estimates in very large samples.

[10] At low return frequencies (daily, weekly) empirical studies typically do not find a statistically and economically significant autocorrelation in financial return series, which is consistent with the weak version of the market efficiency hypothesis. On the contrary, market microstructure effects in high frequency data might induce statistically significant (but economically minor) first order serial correlations, see, e.g., Andersen and Bollerslev (1997).

innovations is motivated by their invariance property under addition.[11] In order to generate persistence in volatility, we use two distinct models. First, we implement a model from Danielsson et al. (2001):

$$Y_t = U_t \sqrt{\frac{v}{\chi^2(v)}} H_t,$$
$$H_t = \beta Q_t + \theta H_{t-1}, \tag{10}$$

with $P\{U_t = -1\} = P\{U_t = 1\} = 0.5, \beta = 0.1, \theta = 0.9$ and where Q is standard normally distributed. The unconditional df is Student-t with $\alpha = v$ degrees of freedom. The multiplicative factor U_t guarantees the fair game property $E_{t-1}Y_t = 0$ (without this factor, the model both exhibits dependence in the first and the second moment). Finally, we also simulate from a GARCH(1,1) model with conditionally normal innovations. The sum of the GARCH volatility parameters $\theta = \beta_0 + \beta_1$ is chosen such that the tail index of the corresponding unconditional df equals 4, see Appendix A for details on the relation between the GARCH parameters and the tail index.

3.2. Choice of Optimal Number of Extremes

Tail index estimators like the Hill statistic imply a bias/variance trade-off, i.e., the more data used from the distributional center the smaller will be the variance of the estimator but the more bias will be introduced. Goldie and Smith (1987) therefore proposed to select m in (2) such as to minimize the asymptotic Mean Squared Error (AMSE) of the Hill statistic. Using the second order expansion for regularly varying dfs in (1), Danielsson and de Vries (1997) derived an expression of the AMSE of $\widehat{\alpha}_{\text{HILL}}$ in terms of the second order expansion parameters:

$$\text{AMSE}(\widehat{\alpha}_{\text{HILL}}, m) = a^{-2\beta/\alpha} \frac{1}{\alpha^2} \frac{\beta^2 b^2}{(\alpha+\beta)^2} \left(\frac{m}{n}\right)^{\frac{2\beta}{\alpha}} + \frac{1}{\alpha^2 m}, \tag{11}$$

where the first part is the squared bias and the second part is the variance. The above expression shows that the second order parameters b and β are responsible for the bias in the Hill statistic, i.e., if either b or β equals zero, the bias term disappears and the distributional tail in (1) specializes to an exact Pareto.

Minimizing (11) with respect to m renders the optimal number m^* of highest order statistics:

$$m^* = cn^{2\beta/2\beta+\alpha}, \quad c = \left(\frac{\alpha(\alpha+\beta)^2}{2\beta^3 b^2} a^{2\beta/\alpha}\right), \tag{12}$$

[11] An AR(1) process $X_t = \theta X_{t-1} + u_t$ with first order serial correlation $0 < \theta < 1$ is equivalent to the MA (∞) process $X_t = \sum_{i=0}^{\infty} \theta^i u_{t-i}$. If the innovations u_{t-i} are i.i.d. symmetric stable, it follows from Feller (1971, Chapter VIII.8) that $X_t \stackrel{d}{=} \left(1 + \theta^{\phi} + \theta^{2\phi} + \cdots\right) u_t = \left(\frac{1}{1-\theta^{\phi}}\right)^{\frac{1}{\phi}} u_t$. Thus the AR(1) dependent stable draws and the i.i.d. stable innovations exhibit the same distribution upon some scaling constant.

Table 1 Tail expansion parameters and corresponding optimal nuisance parameters for selected data generating processes.

	Tail expansion parameters				**Opt. m^***
	a	b	β	$\rho = -\frac{\beta}{\alpha}$	
Stable	$\pi^{-1}\Gamma(\alpha)\sin\frac{\alpha\pi}{2}$	$-\frac{\Gamma(2\alpha)\sin\alpha\pi}{2\Gamma(\alpha)\sin\frac{\alpha\pi}{2}} > 0$	α	-1	$2^{1/3}\left(\frac{a}{b}n\right)^{2/3}$
Student	$\frac{\Gamma\left(\frac{\alpha+1}{2}\right)}{\Gamma\left(\frac{\alpha}{2}\right)\sqrt{\pi\alpha}}\alpha^{\frac{\alpha-1}{2}}$	$-\frac{\alpha^2(\alpha+1)}{2(\alpha+2)} < 0$	2	$-\frac{2}{\alpha}$	$\left(\frac{\alpha(\alpha+2)^2 a^{4/\alpha}}{16b^2}\right)^{\frac{\alpha}{4+\alpha}} n^{\frac{4}{4+\alpha}}$
Fréchet	1	$-1/2 < 0$	α	-1	$2n^{2/3}$
Burr	1	$-\rho^{-1} < 0$	nonrestricted		$\left(-\frac{(1-\rho)^2}{2\rho}\right)^{\frac{1}{1-2\rho}} n^{-\frac{2\rho}{1-2\rho}}$

which is the same expression as under condition (B) of Theorem 1. The optimal threshold path implies that smaller fractions of upper order extremes m/n will be selected when the sample size n grows large.[12]

Table 1 reports the parameter vectors (a, b, α, β) for the tail expansions of all considered DGPs.

The optimal nuisance parameter m^* to be used in the Monte Carlo simulation is also included. Further details on the tail expansion derivations are provided in Appendix A. A number of interesting observations can be made from this table. First, the table reveals that the condition $\alpha = \beta$ employed in a number of previous studies (Quintos et al., 2001; Hall, 1982) only holds for the Type-II extreme value df (Fréchet) and the symmetric stable class but not for the other considered models. The second order parameter β for the Student-t equals 2 regardless of the degrees of freedom parameter. As for the Burr df, β can be varied and chosen independent from α and is therefore suited as a vehicle to study the impact of changing higher order tail behavior in (1). The table also reveals that b can both be positive and negative which implies that the sign of the asymptotic Hill bias, *sign*(b), differs across different models. In the next subsection, the relation between the bias and the sign of this parameter will further be clarified when discussing the simulation results.

The Monte Carlo study for small sample critical values will be performed using the analytic expressions for m^* in Table 1.[13] However, for the Monte Carlo study of power and ability to date breaks, as well as for the empirical application, we shall minimize a

[12] It can be easily shown that for $m = m^*$ the bias part and the variance part of the AMSE vanish at the same rate $(n^{-2\beta/(2\beta+\alpha)})$. If either the bias or the variance part is converging at a higher rate, then the other part converges more slowly than $n^{-2\beta/(2\beta+\alpha)}$, and hence the whole AMSE converges more slowly.

[13] The tail expansion parameters of a GARCH(1,1) model are unknown and we therefore resort to the Beirlant et al. (1999) criterion in order to determine m.

sample equivalent of the Asymptotic Mean Squared Error (AMSE) along the lines of Beirlant et al. (1999) in order to select the optimal m^*.[14] These authors derived an exponential regression model for the log-spacings of upper order statistics from regularly varying tails:

$$j\left(\ln X_{n-j+1,n} - \ln X_{n-j,n}\right) \sim \left(\gamma + d_{n,m}\left(\frac{j}{m+1}\right)^{-\rho}\right) f_j, \tag{13}$$

with $1 \leq j \leq m$. Moreover, $\gamma = 1/\alpha$, $\rho = -\beta/\alpha$, $(f_1 f_2, \ldots, f_m)$ is a vector of independent standard exponential random variables, and $d_{n,m}$ stands for $d\left(\frac{n+1}{m+1}\right)$, $3 \leq m \leq n/3$. The asymptotic variance and the asymptotic bias for the inverse of the Hill statistic $\widehat{\gamma} = 1/\widehat{\alpha}$ can be approximated by $\sigma^2(\widehat{\gamma}) \sim \gamma^2/m$ and $E(\widehat{\gamma} - \gamma) \sim \frac{d_{n,m}}{1-\rho}$. The Asymptotic Mean Squared Error (AMSE) for the Hill statistic $\widehat{\gamma}$ can now be estimated for different values of m:

$$\text{AMSE}(\widehat{\gamma}) = \left(\frac{d_{n,m,LS}}{1 - \rho_{LS}}\right)^2 + \frac{\gamma_{LS}^2}{m},$$

which is typically U-shaped as a function of m due to the bias/variance trade-off. The estimators γ_{LS}, ρ_{LS} and $d_{n,m,LS}$ refer to Ordinary Least Squares estimators of the corresponding parameters in the nonlinear model (13). The optimal sample fraction m^* is then estimated as the one where AMSE reaches its minimum, i.e., $m^* = \arg\min_m[\text{AMSE}(\widehat{\gamma})]$.

For the sake of convenience, we make two additional assumptions when implementing the Beirlant et al. (1999) criterion. First, we impose the restriction $\alpha = \beta(\rho = -1)$ on the parameters of the tail expansions; this circumvents the need of separate β-estimation. Simulations have shown that the Beirlant criterion still performs well under the restriction $\alpha = \beta$ even when this restriction does not hold. Second, we did not apply the Beirlant optimization criterion on each recursive, rolling, or sequential subsample considered in (5)–(7) separately. Instead, we determined the full sample $\widehat{m}$ which implies that the full sample scaling constant c in (11) equals $\widehat{c} = \widehat{m}/n^{2/3}$. Upon extrapolating the optimal path for m to the subsamples defined by the stability tests, we obtain $\widehat{m}_t = \widehat{c}t^{2/3}$ for the recursive and sequential tests and $\widehat{m}_{w^*} = \widehat{c}\left(w^*\right)^{2/3}$ for the rolling test, respectively. Thus, for the sake of simplicity we assume that c does not change across subsamples and that it can be set equal to its full sample value.[15]

[14] Subsample bootstrap algorithms (see, e.g., Danielsson et al., 2001) to select m^* by means of AMSE minimization constitute an alternative route; but these are only applicable for sample sizes that are larger than the ones we employ in the Monte Carlo section and the empirical application.

[15] When $\alpha = \beta$, it follows from (11) that $m^* = 2^{1/3}(a/b)^{1/3}n^{2/3}$. Thus, the temporal constancy requirement for $c = 2^{1/3}(a/b)^{1/3}$ imposes the same requirement on a and b.

3.3. Monte Carlo Results

As a benchmark for comparison with the rest of the simulations, we start by shortly reconsidering the small sample behavior of the Hill estimator. From Theorem 1 we recapitulate that the Hill statistic—when applied on regularly varying tails and conditioned on a nuisance parameter m that minimizes AMSE—exhibits small sample bias and standard deviation:

$$E(\widehat{\alpha}) - \alpha \simeq m^{-1/2} sign(b) \alpha^{3/2} (2\beta)^{-1/2}, \tag{14}$$

with s.e.$(\widehat{\alpha}) \simeq m^{-1/2}\widehat{\alpha}$ and $m = f(a, b, \alpha, \beta, n)$. Clearly the bias depends on the parameters of the tail expansion (1) as well as the sample size n.[16] We would like to know to what extent these bias and variance properties transmit to the small sample critical values and power properties of the considered stability tests for $\widehat{\alpha}$. We also want to establish whether the bias problem erodes the ability of the tests to accurately locate break dates. To that aim, we simulate from the set of models that have been introduced in the previous section. The optimal number of highest order statistics m^* is chosen analytically by minimizing the Asymptotic Mean Squared Error (AMSE) provided the tail expansion (1) is known. For GARCH(1,1) models, the parameters a, b, and β stay unknown and we resort to choosing m by using the Beirlant et al. (1999) algorithm.

Table 2 reports simulated means and standard deviations of the Hill statistic for samples of size $n = 500, 2000$. Averages and standard deviations are calculated over 20,000 replications.

The table is divided into a left/right panel and an upper/lower panel. The left panel contains Hill estimates for "optimal" m in minimal AMSE sense, whereas the right panel conditions the Hill statistic on a fixed percentage of tail observations (i.e., Dumouchel's rule). We further distinguish between models that either generate dependent or independent draws (lower and upper panel, respectively). In the upper panel, we let α and β vary; in the lower panel, the degree of serial correlation or volatility clustering is manipulated *ceteris paribus* α and β.

First and foremost, one can see that deviations from unbiasedness $|E(\widehat{\alpha}) - \alpha|$ decrease with increasing sample size n when m^* is chosen "optimally" in the sense that AMSE is minimized. Indeed, the right-hand side (RHS) panel estimates ($m = 0.1n$) diverge away from the true underlying value of α when the sample size is increased. This should not surprise us given that Dumouchel's rule does not guarantee proper convergence in distribution of the Hill statistic (see Theorem 1). The optimal m^* results in the left panel still show a large heterogeneity in small sample bias and estimation accuracy across different distributions. As predicted by the theoretical bias expression (14), the sign of the bias corresponds with the sign of b. Indeed, from Table 1, we know that b is only positive for the stable class which explains the positive Hill bias in Table 2 for stable draws and

[16] From the optimal path in (12), it can be easily seen that an increase in the scaling constant a—or, alternatively, a decrease in the second order parameter b—reduces the bias and standard deviation of the Hill statistic via an increase in m^*. The effects of varying α and β on bias and estimation risk are less straightforward to determine and will therefore be derived via Monte Carlo simulation.

Table 2 Hill statistic: small sample bias and estimation risk models.

	$\widehat{\alpha}$ (s.e.)			
	$m = m^*$		$m = 0.1n$	
	$n = 500$	$n = 2000$	$n = 500$	$n = 2000$
Panel A: I.I.D. models				
Stable (α)				
1.2	1.23 (0.16)	1.24 (0.10)	1.25 (0.18)	1.23 (0.09)
1.5	1.79 (0.44)	1.66 (0.25)	1.77 (0.27)	1.74 (0.13)
Student (α)				
2	1.79 (0.28)	1.87 (0.19)	1.72 (0.23)	1.70 (0.11)
4	3.16 (0.74)	3.40 (0.56)	2.43 (0.31)	2.41 (0.15)
Fréchet (α)				
2	1.88 (0.16)	1.92 (0.10)	1.98 (0.28)	1.96 (0.14)
4	3.75 (0.32)	3.84 (0.21)	3.97 (0.57)	3.91 (0.28)
Burr ($\alpha, -\rho$)				
(2, −0.5)	1.68 (0.28)	1.77 (0.21)	1.59 (0.21)	1.57 (0.10)
(2, −5)	1.97 (0.11)	1.98 (0.06)	2.04 (0.29)	2.01 (0.14)
(4, −0.5)	3.37 (0.56)	3.56 (0.42)	3.18 (0.43)	3.14 (0.21)
(4, −5)	3.93 (0.22)	3.96 (0.12)	4.08 (0.59)	4.02 (0.29)
Panel B: time dependence (first or second moment)				
AR (α, θ)				
(1.5, 0.2)	1.82 (0.48)	1.68 (0.27)	1.78 (0.29)	1.74 (0.14)
(1.5, 0.4)	1.87 (0.55)	1.70 (0.32)	1.80 (0.34)	1.75 (0.17)
SVSTU (α, θ)				
(4, 0.85)	3.21 (0.76)	3.42 (0.57)	2.45 (0.33)	2.41 (0.16)
(4, 0.95)	3.27 (0.77)	3.43 (0.56)	2.52 (0.37)	2.43 (0.19)
GARCH (α, θ)				
(4, 0.85)	4.38 (1.77)	3.75 (0.82)	2.82 (0.45)	2.66 (0.23)
(4, 0.95)	4.74(1.99)	3.88 (0.92)	2.81 (0.50)	2.62 (0.27)

Note: simulated average values and standard deviations are reported for the Hill statistic (20,000 replications) and for different sample sizes. The Hill statistic is conditioned on both a fixed fraction of extremes and the fraction that minimizes the asymptotic mean squared error. Parameters α and $\rho = -\beta/\alpha$ refer to the tail index and the ratio of the second order parameter to the tail index, respectively. The first order serial correlation of an AR(1) or the volatility persistence parameter in GARCH(1,1) models or stochastic volatility models with Student-t innovations (SVSTU) are denoted by θ.

the negative bias for all other classes of dfs. One also observes that the deviation from unbiasedness as well as the corresponding standard deviation of the Hill statistic is smaller for heavier tails (lower values of α). The intuition behind this result is that lighter tails are closer to a thin tailed local alternative like the normal distribution that does not satisfy (1). This decreases the accuracy—both in terms of bias and standard deviation—of tail estimation techniques that assume regular variation as a starting point. It is also worth noticing what happens when the second order parameter β changes for given values of α. Only in the Burr distribution case, we can let β evolve independently from α. The Burr outcomes reveal that the bias and standard error of $\widehat{\alpha}$ decrease for higher values of β, i.e., the closer the tail expansion (1) approximates a pure Pareto tail the smaller will be the bias and estimation risk. The lower table panel reports the impact of temporal dependence on bias and variance properties of the Hill statistic. Both higher serial correlation in the AR(1) processes as well as a higher persistence in volatility clustering (Stochastic Volatility and GARCH model class) seem to increase the deviation from unbiasedness as well as the standard deviation.

Next we investigate to what extent the Hill bias tranfers into the size and power properties of the stability tests as well as their ability to accurately identify break dates, i.e., are the stability test properties very different for the high bias/variance cases as compared with the low bias/variance cases? Tables 3 and 4 report simulated critical values for i.i.d. models and models that exhibit temporal dependence, respectively. Each table is further split into three panels containing the small sample distributional quantiles for the recursive, rolling, and sequential tests presented in (5)–(7). The quantiles of the test statistics are calculated as follows. For samples of size $n = 500$ and 2000 we generate 20,000 simulation replications to obtain estimates of the 90th, 95th, and 99th percentile of the stability tests' small sample distribution.

The heterogeneity in the small sample critical values across different DGP's is nearly one-to-one with the preceding table results on bias and estimation risk for the Hill estimator: critical values and their estimation risk are higher for those cases that exhibit a higher bias in the Hill estimator. More specifically, higher values of the tail index α and the persistence parameter θ (either standing for serial correlation or volatility persistence) increase the critical values, whereas higher values of the second order parameter β (cf. Burr df) decrease the critical values. Thus, the tables provide convincing evidence that the bias in the Hill estimator is transferred into the critical values as predicted already by Theorem 2. The critical values for $\rho = -5$ actually come close to the asymptotic critical values reported in Quintos et al. (2001). This should not surprise us given the fact that the Burr tail is very close to a pure Pareto in the latter case (Hill estimators do not exhibit asymptotic bias for pure Pareto data). But the table also convincingly shows that using asymptotically unbiased critical values leads to huge size distortions in tests of parameter constancy when the true critical values are upward biased due to the asymptotic Hill bias.

Next, Tables 5 and 6 report small sample power and estimates of the breakpoints for the recursive, rolling, and sequential stability test, respectively. We consider sudden upward and downward jumps in α of different magnitudes and at different points in time ($r = 0.25, 0.50, 0.75$). The power is based on 20,000 replications and is size-adjusted by means of the small sample critical values in the previous table. The breakpoint estimates are also based on 20,000 replications but the reported average breakpoint estimates are

Table 3 Small sample critical values for recursive, rolling, and sequential tests: i.i.d. models.

DGP	*n* = 500			*n* = 2000		
	0.90	**0.95**	**0.99**	**0.90**	**0.95**	**0.99**
Panel A: recursive test						
Stable (α)						
1.2	1.97 (0.04)	2.78 (0.08)	5.22 (0.20)	2.00 (0.02)	2.67 (0.03)	4.64 (0.19)
1.5	5.12 (0.13)	8.39 (0.19)	20.37 (1.27)	3.41 (0.10)	4.97 (0.20)	9.61 (0.63)
Student (α)						
2	1.99 (0.05)	2.85 (0.06)	5.80 (0.26)	1.84 (0.02)	2.43 (0.04)	4.24 (0.15)
4	2.42 (0.08)	3.87 (0.21)	9.20 (0.81)	2.18 (0.04)	3.17 (0.08)	6.33 (0.34)
Burr (α, ρ)						
(2, −1)	1.81 (0.03)	2.43 (0.03)	4.35 (0.19)	1.80 (0.02)	2.29 (0.03)	3.69 (0.12)
(2, −5)	1.54 (0.03)	1.95 (0.04)	3.07 (0.09)	1.56 (0.01)	1.93 (0.01)	2.84 (0.07)
Panel B: rolling test ($\gamma = 0.2$)						
Stable (α)						
1.2	2.40 (0.07)	3.33 (0.08)	5.98 (0.22)	2.33 (0.05)	3.00 (0.10)	4.82 (0.18)
1.5	14.20 (0.54)	22.44 (1.18)	54.82 (4.69)	6.12 (0.13)	8.33 (0.26)	14.84 (0.79)
Student (α)						
2	2.87 (0.04)	4.10 (0.11)	7.97 (0.44)	2.15 (0.05)	2.87 (0.08)	4.84 (0.22)
4	4.81 (0.19)	7.46 (0.31)	17.66 (1.10)	3.06 (0.07)	4.38 (0.15)	8.40 (0.34)
Burr (α, ρ)						
(2, −1)	1.95 (0.01)	2.64 (0.03)	4.64 (0.16)	1.73 (0.02)	2.22 (0.04)	3.51 (0.06)
(2, −5)	1.66 (0.01)	2.10 (0.03)	3.25 (0.09)	1.53 (0.01)	1.82 (0.02)	2.55 (0.05)
Panel C: sequential test						
Stable (α)						
1.2	21.67 (0.53)	31.73 (0.86)	59.01 (1.89)	16.21 (0.45)	22.54 (0.96)	40.38 (1.98)
1.5	24.33 (0.73)	39.03 (1.53)	87.89 (3.10)	16.51 (0.40)	24.13 (1.12)	48.81 (2.29)
Student (α)						
2	21.49 (0.34)	31.54 (1.04)	60.26 (3.62)	17.86 (0.43)	25.18 (0.80)	45.70 (1.22)
4	25.05 (0.47)	38.41 (0.77)	77.96 (3.55)	19.04 (0.67)	28.16 (1.06)	53.39 (2.55)
Burr (α, ρ)						
(2, −1)	19.03 (0.33)	27.13 (0.48)	49.78 (1.60)	16.80 (0.31)	23.09 (0.61)	39.84 (1.17)
(2, −5)	20.14 (0.24)	27.72 (0.59)	49.08 (1.21)	19.75 (0.21)	26.37 (0.42)	43.87 (0.88)

Note: critical values are reported for varying sample sizes (n), and different levels of statistical significance. Critical values are based on 20,000 Monte Carlo replications. Corresponding standard errors for the critical values are reported between brackets (s.e.). The parameters α and $\rho = -\beta/\alpha$ refer to the tail index and the second order parameter, respectively.
Source: Table 3 in Straetmans and Candelon (2013).

Table 4 Small sample critical values for recursive, rolling, and sequential tests: dependent models.

DGP	$n = 500$			$n = 2000$		
	0.90	**0.95**	**0.99**	**0.90**	**0.95**	**0.99**
Panel A: recursive test						
ARSTA (α, θ)						
(1.2, 0.2)	2.65 (0.07)	4.04 (0.13)	8.73 (0.71)	2.65 (0.05)	3.74 (0.07)	6.97 (0.27)
(1.2, 0.4)	4.01 (0.10)	6.43 (0.23)	15.05 (1.02)	4.01 (0.08)	5.97 (0.13)	11.79 (0.64)
SVSTU (α, θ)						
(2, 0.85)	2.25 (0.04)	3.27 (0.08)	6.67 (0.36)	1.92 (0.04)	2.56 (0.05)	4.59 (0.18)
(2, 0.95)	2.56 (0.06)	3.82 (0.12)	7.96 (0.47)	2.05 (0.05)	2.78 (0.06)	4.95 (0.23)
GARCH (α, θ)						
(4, 0.85)	3.41 (0.15)	6.08 (0.31)	20.46 (1.68)	2.63 (0.03)	3.42 (0.06)	7.25 (0.71)
(4, 0.95)	4.14 (0.14)	7.67 (0.30)	26.20 (2.50)	3.33 (0.07)	5.05 (0.21)	15.30 (1.63)
Panel B: rolling test						
ARSTA (α, θ)						
(1.2, 0.2)	3.16 (0.05)	4.40 (0.11)	8.26 (0.49)	3.12 (0.08)	4.07 (0.08)	6.54 (0.24)
(1.2, 0.4)	4.64 (0.07)	6.63 (0.15)	12.70 (0.46)	4.75 (0.08)	6.26 (0.09)	10.53 (0.34)
SVSTU (α, θ)						
(2, 0.85)	3.24 (0.10)	4.54 (0.20)	8.97 (0.42)	2.27 (0.04)	3.04 (0.05)	5.05 (0.24)
(2, 0.95)	3.73 (0.08)	5.22 (0.13)	9.87 (0.43)	2.46 (0.05)	3.25 (0.09)	5.48 (0.16)
GARCH (α, θ)						
(4, 0.85)	4.86 (0.08)	8.31 (0.26)	25.80 (1.84)	2.05 (0.03)	2.71 (0.06)	5.66 (0.26)
(4, 0.95)	5.75 (0.10)	9.81 (0.34)	29.06 (2.28)	2.89 (0.08)	4.31 (0.14)	10.31 (0.61)
Panel C: sequential test						
ARSTA (α, θ)						
(1.2, 0.2)	26.86 (0.78)	40.68 (1.30)	85.68 (2.97)	21.41 (0.42)	31.06 (0.99)	60.6 (3.97)
(1.2, 0.4)	35.98 (0.64)	56.60 (2.13)	133.09 (5.63)	30.33 (0.45)	46.62 (0.77)	100.18 (4.54)
SVSTU (α, θ)						
SV (2, 0.85)	21.24 (0.68)	31.60 (0.95)	61.84 (2.80)	17.84 (0.33)	25.34 (0.63)	45.50 (2.34)
SV (2, 0.95)	21.25 (0.59)	31.54 (0.95)	60.88 (2.34)	17.72 (0.33)	25.15 (0.58)	45.62 (2.17)
GARCH (α, θ)						
(4, 0.85)	38.55 (1.11)	59.42 (2.31)	123.01 (3.55)	38.11 (0.88)	57.20 (1.01)	117.21 (4.69)
(4, 0.95)	36.76 (0.97)	57.25 (1.92)	119.74 (6.98)	214.97 (0.90)	264.68 (1.05)	396.78 (6.50)

Note: critical values are reported for varying sample sizes (n), and different levels of significance. Critical values are based on 20,000 Monte Carlo replications. Corresponding standard errors for the critical values are reported between brackets (s.e.). The first order serial correlation of an autoregressive process with stable innovations (ARSTA), the volatility persistence parameter in GARCH(1,1) models and in stochastic volatility models with Student-t innovations (SVSTU) is always denoted by θ.
Source: Table 4 in Straetmans and Candelon (2013).

only based on "candidate"-breaks $\hat{r}$ that are statistically significant according to the 95% small sample critical values from Tables 3 and 4.[17]

[17] For break scenarios (α_1, α_2) we calculate the power and break estimates using the 95% small sample critical value that corresponds with min (α_1, α_2). Quintos et al. (2001), on the contrary, calculated the power properties by conditioning on the 95% asymptotic critical values. Moreover, they evaluated the ability to date breaks by averaging over all "candidate"-breakpoints (both statistically significant and insignificant ones).

Table 5 Size-corrected finite sample power for recursive, rolling, and sequential tests.

DGP ($\alpha_1; \alpha_2$)	$n = 500$			$n = 2000$		
	$r = 0.25$	$r = 0.5$	$r = 0.75$	$r = 0.25$	$r = 0.50$	$r = 0.75$
Stable (1.5, 1.2)						
- rec	22	32	25	53	71	55
- rol	7	8	5	32	38	22
- seq	14	28	42	15	45	69
Stable (1.2, 1.5)						
- rec	1.18	1.36	1.5	1.96	2.66	1.1
- rol	5	9	7	22	37	30
- seq	6	3	1	10	4	2
Student (4, 2)						
- rec	21	32	24	49	73	62
- rol	6	6	4	27	32	15
- seq	10	21	35	12	41	71
Student (2, 4)						
- rec	0.5	0.7	2	2.54	0.94	1.18
- rol	4	6	5	15	31	27
- seq	3	1	0.4	0.6	0.1	0.6
Burr (4, 2)						
$\rho = -1$						
- rec	31	37	26	52	66	53
- rol	19	22	15	35	45	30
- seq	17	41	57	14	45	68
Burr (2, 4)						
$\rho = -1$						
- rec	1.16	0.5	1.3	0.3	0.22	1.76
- rol	15	21	19	32	46	36
- seq	1	0.2	0.08	0.28	0.02	0.1
SVSTU (4, 2)						
$\theta = 0.95$						
- rec	20	31	23	49	71	59
- rol	12	22	16	43	66	55
- seq	10	22	36	12	43	71
SVSTU (2, 4)						
$\theta = 0.95$						
- rec	0.56	0.70	1.80	3.16	1.84	1.16
- rol	0.2	0.26	0.66	1.28	0.74	0.8
- seq	1.82	1.1	1.98	0.34	0.20	0.64

(*Continued*)

Table 5 (Continued)

DGP (α_1; α_2)	$n = 500$			$n = 2000$		
	$r = 0.25$	$r = 0.5$	$r = 0.75$	$r = 0.25$	$r = 0.50$	$r = 0.75$
ARCH (4,2)						
- rec	6.2	16.74	22.18	17.42	31.54	22.56
- rol	2.7	3.62	4.16	7.94	15.86	22.16
- seq	6.72	10	14.88	9.14	20.24	40.6
ARCH (2,4)						
- rec	0.34	2.86	2.7	0.06	0.36	0.94
- rol	2.82	1.8	1.2	5.4	3.44	2.06
- seq	1.30	0.90	1.74	0.32	0.08	0.54

Note: the power is reported for different sample sizes ($n = 500, 2000$), different locations of the (true) breakpoints ($r = 0.25, 0.50, 0.75$) and different jump scenarios (α_1, α_2) for the tail index. The power is size-corrected using finite sample critical values and is calculated as the rejection frequency under the null hypothesis of parameter constancy using 20,000 Monte Carlo replications. The parameters α and $\rho = -\beta/\alpha$ refer to the tail index and the second order parameter, respectively. The volatility persistence parameter in the stochastic volatility models with Student-t innovations (SVSTU) is denoted by θ.
Source: Table 5 in Straetmans and Candelon (2013).

Just as in the Quintos et al. (2001) analysis, the direction of change in α seems to be the crucial factor. The recursive and rolling tests both exhibit satisfactory power if α decreases; however, the power of the rolling test is larger in detecting an increase in α. The latter result can be understood by observing that Eq. (2) is based on the m largest observations, so that extremal returns that occur in the initial recursive sample will partly remain in the selection of the m highest order statistics when the sample size is increased. This initial extremes' dominance when $\alpha_1 < \alpha_2$ does not occur for the rolling test because the influence on $\widehat{\alpha}$ of extremal behavior that occurs in the initial sample gradually drops out when the rolling window is shifted through the total sample. The sequential test seems to perform poorly, although the power differs quite a lot depending on the location of the break and the direction of the change in α. As regards the ability to date breaks, the recursive test clearly outperforms the other two tests for most considered DGPs provided the break scenario implies an increase in the tail fatness ($\alpha_1 > \alpha_2$).[18] However, the recursive test's inability to detect breaks when $\alpha_1 < \alpha_2$ is more apparent than real, see Candelon and Straetmans (2006). Indeed, if one lacks prior knowledge on the direction of the jump in the tail index (as is the case in most empirical applications), the recursive test can be performed both in calendar time ("forward" recursive test) as well as by inverting the sample ("backward" or "reverse" recursive test). A decrease in the tail index—if present in the data—should then be signaled by the forward version of the recursive test, whereas

[18] The power and break date results show that satisfactory power is not a sufficient condition for accurate breakpoint detection. The rolling test for $\alpha_1 < \alpha_2$ provides a nice illustration.

Table 6 Breakpoint estimates for recursive, rolling, and sequential tests.

DGP (α_1; α_2)	$n = 500$			$n = 2000$		
	$r = 0.25$	$r = 0.5$	$r = 0.75$	$r = 0.25$	$r = 0.50$	$r = 0.75$
Stable (1.5, 1.2)						
- rec	0.42 (0.17)	0.53 (0.13)	0.64 (0.16)	0.33 (0.12)	0.50 (0.10)	0.66 (0.14)
- rol	0.37 (0.22)	0.39 (0.14)	0.51 (0.18)	0.65 (0.10)	0.36 (0.11)	0.48 (0.18)
- seq	0.81 (0.08)	0.79 (0.09)	0.81 (0.04)	0.76 (0.14)	0.70 (0.13)	0.80 (0.05)
Stable (1.2, 1.5)						
- rec	0.62 (0.11)	0.55 (0.15)	0.48 (0.17)	0.48 (0.13)	0.48 (0.08)	0.48 (0.16)
- rol	0.68 (0.17)	0.81 (0.14)	0.86 (0.20)	0.72 (0.17)	0.84 (0.11)	0.95 (0.09)
- seq	0.83 (0.03)	0.83 (0.05)	0.84 (0.01)	0.83 (0.02)	0.82 (0.03)	0.82 (0.03)
Student (4, 2)						
- rec	0.40 (0.17)	0.53 (0.13)	0.67 (0.15)	0.33 (0.13)	0.51 (0.10)	0.70 (0.11)
- rol	0.37 (0.22)	0.39 (0.14)	0.49 (0.17)	0.26 (0.10)	0.37 (0.11)	0.49 (0.18)
- seq	0.80 (0.09)	0.78 (0.10)	0.81 (0.04)	0.78 (0.11)	0.71 (0.13)	0.80 (0.04)
Student (2, 4)						
- rec	0.58 (0.20)	0.42 (0.22)	0.41 (0.17)	0.53 (0.11)	0.51 (0.12)	0.39 (0.15)
- rol	0.71 (0.18)	0.81 (0.14)	0.85 (0.20)	0.72 (0.17)	0.83 (0.11)	0.95 (0.08)
- seq	0.58 (0.20)	0.42 (0.22)	0.41 (0.17)	0.53 (0.11)	0.51 (0.12)	0.39 (0.15)
Burr (4, 2)						
$\rho = -1$						
- rec	0.38 (0.16)	0.51 (0.16)	0.61 (0.19)	0.30 (0.09)	0.50 (0.08)	0.70 (0.10)
- rol	0.28 (0.13)	0.37 (0.13)	0.48 (0.18)	0.26 (0.10)	0.37 (0.11)	0.48 (0.18)
- seq	0.73 (0.17)	0.74 (0.12)	0.81 (0.05)	0.63 (0.22)	0.66 (0.15)	0.79 (0.06)
Burr (2, 4)						
$\rho = -1$						
- rec	0.62 (0.16)	0.47 (0.22)	0.40 (0.19)	0.65 (0.16)	0.31 (0.19)	0.37 (0.14)
- rol	0.71 (0.18)	0.82 (0.12)	0.92 (0.12)	0.71 (0.17)	0.83 (0.11)	0.94 (0.10)
- seq	0.82 (0.04)	0.82 (0.04)	0.69 (0.16)	0.67 (0.17)	0.70 (0.14)	0.75 (0.12)
SVSTU (4, 2)						
$\theta = 0.95$						
- rec	0.40 (0.17)	0.52 (0.14)	0.64 (0.17)	0.35 (0.14)	0.51 (0.11)	0.56 (0.17)
- rol	0.33 (0.19)	0.40 (0.14)	0.49 (0.19)	0.26 (0.10)	0.37 (0.11)	0.48 (0.17)
- seq	0.77 (0.12)	0.75 (0.11)	0.80 (0.06)	0.78 (0.10)	0.70 (0.13)	0.79 (0.06)
SVSTU (2, 4)						
$\theta = 0.95$						
- rec	0.63 (0.16)	0.43 (0.21)	0.46 (0.19)	0.58 (0.14)	0.58 (0.13)	0.58 (0.17)
- rol	0.72 (0.18)	0.79 (0.15)	0.87 (0.18)	0.70 (0.17)	0.83 (0.11)	0.95 (0.08)
- seq	0.81 (0.04)	0.82 (0.04)	0.75 (0.11)	0.83 (0.02)	0.84 (0.01)	0.82 (0.03)

(Continued)

Table 6 (Continued)

DGP (α_1; α_2)	$n = 500$			$n = 2000$		
	$r = 0.25$	$r = 0.5$	$r = 0.75$	$r = 0.25$	$r = 0.50$	$r = 0.75$
ARCH (4,2)						
- rec	0.41 (0.18)	0.52 (0.15)	0.65 (0.19)	0.37 (0.15)	0.60 (0.14)	0.75 (0.09)
- rol	0.49 (0.27)	0.49 (0.23)	0.54 (0.21)	0.31 (0.17)	0.39 (0.15)	0.49 (0.19)
- seq	0.71 (0.19)	0.73 (0.14)	0.78 (0.10)	0.77 (0.13)	0.73 (0.12)	0.81 (0.05)
ARCH (2,4)						
- rec	0.35 (0.23)	0.71 (0.20)	0.67 (0.21)	0.71 (0.15)	0.82 (0.05)	0.82 (0.06)
- rol	0.70 (0.20)	0.70 (0.21)	0.62 (0.27)	0.71 (0.17)	0.78 (0.16)	0.88 (0.19)
- seq	0.77 (0.17)	0.64 (0.24)	0.63 (0.18)	0.84 (0.07)	0.54 (0.26)	0.61 (0.12)

Note: estimated break dates are reported for different sample sizes ($n = 500, 2000$), different locations of the (true) breakpoints ($r = 0.25, 0.50, 0.75$), and different jump scenarios (α_1, α_2) for the tail index. "Candidate" break dates are calculated over 20,000 Monte Carlo replications. Average break date estimates are obtained by averaging over the statistically significant "candidate" breaks using the finite sample critical values. The parameters α and $\rho = -\beta/\alpha$ refer to the tail index and the second order parameter, respectively. The volatility persistence parameter in stochastic volatility models with Student-t innovations (SVSTU) is denoted by θ.
Source: Table 6 in Straetmans and Candelon (2013).

an increase should be detected by the backward version of the recursive test. This will also be our strategy in the empirical application.

So far the general discussion has focused on power and break date ability. One can also often observe large differences in power results and breakpoint detection across different DGPs. This heterogeneity can again be explained by the determinants of the Hill bias. More specifically, higher values of the persistence parameter θ (either standing for serial correlation or volatility persistence) increase the Hill bias and the bias in the estimated break dates but decrease the power. On the other hand, higher values of the second order parameter β (cf. Burr df) decrease the Hill bias and the bias in the estimated break dates but increase the power. Thus, the tables provide convincing evidence that the bias in the Hill estimator is also influencing the stability tests' power and ability to date breaks. Indeed, the power for the Burr case with $\rho = -5$ lies close to 100%, even in small samples, whereas bias and estimation risk for $\widehat{r}$ are negligibly small in that pareto-type case.

4. EMPIRICAL APPLICATION

We perform stability tests for a large cross-section of 21 developed and emerging stock markets. Daily price indices (excluding dividends) denominated in local currency were obtained from Datastream Inc.[19] Returns are calculated as log first differences and our

[19] Stock prices decline at ex-dividend date but these price declines rarely enter the return tails. In other words, working with clean price indices or total return indices does not seem to matter much for the analysis of extreme values.

sample ranges from January 1, 1988 until August 13, 2007, which amounts to 5117 daily prices.[20] If breaks occur in the tail index of equity market returns, one expects more frequent breaks in emerging stock market tails, which makes it interesting to distinguish between developed and emerging stock markets. First, emerging stock markets historically exhibit a higher degree of instability and volatility (i.e., a higher incidence of financial crises). Moreover, the institutional framework (government regulation and supervision, corporate governance culture, etc.) in which traders of financial assets have to operate is still in development, changing frequently and not always free of corruption. Also, emerging banking and financial systems are typically less developed than their Western counterparts and central banks are far from independent. Finally, most developing countries are characterized by higher political and country risks (probability of regime changes), which also potentially impact stock markets.

Given the poor properties of the rolling and sequential test in terms of power and ability to detect breaks, we focus on the recursive test in the empirical application. From the Monte Carlo investigation, we know that small sample critical values can differ considerably depending on the fat tailed model assumed for the tail. This is because the severity of the Hill bias and its resulting influence on the small sample critical values of stability tests largely differs across different parametrizations. In order to avoid this "model risk" related to a Monte Carlo simulation or a parametric bootstrap, we opted for a bootstrap-based semi-parametric approach toward determining the critical values of the test. The previous simulation section has also illustrated that temporal dependence in the data increases the critical values of the considered stability tests. Upon assuming that GARCH-type volatility clustering constitutes the main source of temporal dependence, we implement a GARCH-corrected version of the recursive test:

$$Q_{r \in R_\tau} = \sup \widehat{\eta}_t^{-1} Y_n^2(t), \tag{15}$$

where $\widehat{\eta}_t$ is the estimate of the time-varying scaling factor, see Quintos et al. (2001, p. 643). Subsequently, small sample critical values are bootstrapped (CV_B) at the 90%, 95%, and 99% levels.[21] As the scaling factor already corrects the test for any temporal dependence, the bootstrap does not have to take account of this data feature and we can resort to a "wild" version of the bootstrap instead of a block bootstrap.[22] We

[20] In a twin paper, we also employed the same stability testing framework to a variety of asset classes (including stock indices) that encompass the 2007–2009 financial crisis. This does not fundamentally change the testing results for equity markets, i.e., breaks remain scarce, see Straetmans and Candelon (2013).

[21] Davidson and Flachaire (2007) argue that the asymptotic properties of the bootstrap in an EVT context may be hampered when time series do not possess a finite second moment ($\alpha < 2$). An example constitutes the class of symmetric stable distributions. However, the vast majority of empirical studies on the magnitude of the tail index for stock markets find that $\widehat{\alpha}$ hoovers around 3 and is significantly above 2, see e.g., Jansen and de Vries (1991) or Longin (1996).

[22] A bootstrap in blocks would be appropriate in case one would not have corrected the recursive test for temporal dependence effects like volatility clusters. However, to the best of our knowledge, there is no rule-of-thumb available yet for choosing the optimal block length in an Extreme Value Theory (EVT) framework. That is why we first scaled the test such that we are allowed to randomly reshuffle the data afterwards.

run the recursive test both in calendar time (forward test) and in reverse calendar time (backward test) in order to detect potential falls and rises in the tail index, respectively.

Results of the stability tests are contained in Table 7 for 21 mature and emerging stock market indices. For the sake of comparison, we also calculate stability tests for the Quintos et al. (2001) sample (this subsample is situated around the Asian crisis from January 2, 1995 until October 16, 1998). Testing results for that subsample are summarized in Table 8. The number of upper order extremes m^* (first table column) used in estimating the test statistic and the bootstrap-based critical values are determined using the Beirlant et al. (1999) method. The maximum values for the forward and backward version of test (15) are included in the columns labeled Q_F and Q_B, respectively. Evidently, bootstrapped critical values are identical for the forward and backward test. The null of parameter constancy is rejected if the sup-value calculated according to (15) exceeds the bootstrap-based critical values, e.g., $Q > CV(p)$ with $p = 5\%$ or 1%. Statistically significant break dates are reported between brackets beneath the testing values (dd/mm/yy).

The tables only provide minor evidence for time variation in the tail behavior. The subsample results for Hong Kong, Italy, Indonesia, and South Korea provide evidence for a decrease in α over the short sample period, whereas the full sample results for Taiwan and Hong Kong suggest an increase in α over the extended sample. The subsample break dates are suggestive of a relation between the outbreak of the Asian crisis and the decrease in α (an increase in tail probability mass), whereas the full sample breaks suggest an opposite movement in α, maybe due to a stabilization in the market brought by institutional reform and liberalization in the aftermath of the crisis. However, only the full sample result for Taiwan and the subsample result for South Korea are statistically significant at the 1% significance level. That the (scant) empirical evidence for structural change in α is mainly generated by emerging market data is not too surprising given the degree of institutional reform, liberalization experiments, regime changes in monetary and exchange rate policies and last but not least the vehement financial turmoil that has frequently hit these markets. On the other hand, notice that even emerging markets exhibit stationary tail behavior in a majority of cases. Finally, upon comparing our subsample outcomes with those of Quintos et al. (2001), we were unable to find a break for Indonesia and Malaysia. The different testing outcomes may be due to the fact that asymptotically unbiased critical values can lead to overrejection of the null of parameter stability.

The empirical application leaves us with the conviction that heavy tails are quite constant over time and that the tail index α constitutes a structural characteristic of financial series useful for the assessment of long-run risk, stress testing, and financial stability.

Table 7 Forward and backward recursive testing outcomes (Full sample: 01/01/1988–13/08/2007).

Country	*m*	Recursive test		Bootstrapped critical values		
		Q_F	Q_B	*CV* (90%)	*CV* (95%)	*CV* (99%)
Argentina	122	0.324	0.807	2.170	2.649	3.914
Australia	116	0.199	0.941	2.307	2.866	4.420
Austria	72	0.381	0.649	2.366	2.953	4.569
Britain	57	0.481	0.715	2.449	3.025	4.294
Canada	129	2.581	0.541	2.656	3.242	4.507
Chile	98	0.067	0.898	2.012	2.499	3.904
France	125	0.432	0.362	1.929	2.324	3.250
Germany	180	0.936	0.793	2.323	2.755	3.725
Hong Kong	165	1.583	2.911*	1.951	2.374	3.433
(break date)		(3/6/98)				
India	56	1.845	0.229	2.033	2.581	3.975
Indonesia	85	1.484	1.211	2.025	2.631	4.393
Italy	194	0.939	1.591	2.613	3.130	4.068
Japan	74	0.412	0.619	2.122	2.925	5.512
Korea	126	1.853	0.726	1.960	2.362	3.445
Malaysia	127	0.642	1.284	2.971	4.196	7.474
Mexico	92	0.452	0.515	2.440	3.156	5.105
Philippines	66	1.191	1.009	2.834	3.486	4.867
Spain	113	1.864	1.731	2.306	2.774	3.954
Taiwan	50	1.194	6.211**	1.989	2.412	3.424
(break date)		(2/6/1991)				
Thailand	176	1.564	0.943	5.134	6.066	8.005
US	151	0.714	0.564	3.146	3.786	5.100

Note: the forward and backward version of the recursive test are denoted by Q_F and Q_B, respectively. Critical values are based on 20,000 bootstrapped sample replications. Statistically significant break dates are indicated below the critical values (dd/mm/yy).
*Statistically significant rejections of the null hypothesis of tail index constancy at the 5% significance level.
**Statistically significant rejections of the null hypothesis of tail index constancy at the 1% significance level.

5. CONCLUSIONS

This paper provided a thorough study of the small sample behavior of some popular tests for detecting time variation in the tail index of equity returns. The tests are "endogeneous" in the sense that they produce an estimate of the breakpoint location upon detection of a statistically significant break. Our Monte Carlo experiments determined critical values, size-corrected power and the ability to date breaks for a myriad of data generating

Table 8 Structural change tests (Full sample 02/01/1995–16/10/1998).

Country	*m*	Recursive test		Bootstrapped critical values		
		Q_F	Q_B	*CV* (90%)	*CV* (95%)	*CV* (99%)
Argentina	52	0.418	2.164	2.401	2.908	4.232
Australia	83	0.399	0.378	2.544	3.040	4.166
Austria	39	0.982	0.291	2.601	3.229	5.024
Britain	61	1.283	0.208	2.489	3.026	4.297
Canada	43	1.147	0.109	2.111	2.737	4.880
Chile	118	0.62	0.673	1.922	2.334	3.441
France	50	1.097	0.262	2.138	2.616	3.849
Germany	75	0.399	0.206	2.549	3.037	4.137
Hong Kong	49	3.691*	0.177	3.181	3.859	5.293
(break date)		(21/1/98)				
India	88	0.699	1.210	2.697	3.263	4.493
Indonesia	31	3.283**	0.574	2.554	3.235	5.648
		(28/1/98)				
Italy	66	2.982**	0.856	1.858	2.366	3.920
(break date)		30/9/97				
Japan	65	2.115	0.198	3.550	4.241	5.588
Korea	94	7.802***	0.261	2.398	2.854	3.763
(break date)		(28/8/97)				
Malaysia	67	0.733	0.408	2.252	2.758	4.093
Mexico	74	3.113	0.221	3.754	4.423	5.848
Philippines	58	1.126	0.149	2.497	3.045	4.218
Spain	52	1.64	0.304	2.113	2.672	4.219
Taiwan	29	0.756	0.835	2.592	3.364	6.326
Thailand	55	1.191	0.269	2.481	3.044	4.311
US	43	0.512	0.39	2.082	2.732	4.348

Note: the forward and backward version of the recursive test are denoted by Q_F and Q_B, respectively. Critical values are based on 20,000 bootstrapped sample replications. Statistically significant break dates are indicated below the critical values (dd/mm/yy).
*Statistically significant rejections of the null hypothesis of tail index constancy at the 10% significance level.
**Statistically significant rejections of the null hypothesis of tail index constancy at the 5% significance level.
***Statistically significant rejections of the null hypothesis of tail index constancy at the 1% significance level.

processes (DGPs). The tests all use the Hill estimator for the tail index as an input. Conform to the preceding empirical literature, the number of upper order extremes is selected by minimizing the sample Mean Squared error of the Hill statistic. The DGPs were chosen to mimic some popular empirical stylized facts of financial data like volatility clustering and serial dependence. We find that the small sample critical values differ a lot across different distributional models and sample sizes. More specifically, critical values are higher when the bias in the Hill estimator is more severe. Moreover, the bias in the Hill estimator and the critical values persists in large samples and removing it can be shown to be notoriously difficult. We therefore propose a bootstrap-based procedure to determine the critical values of the stability test when using real-life data. Using simulation-based or bootstrap-based small sample critical values, (recursive) stability tests were found to exhibit satisfactory power and were also able to detect breaks quite well. Applying the test on a large set of emerging and developed stock market data, we were hardly able to detect breaks in the tail behavior. Otherwise stated, the tails of the unconditional distribution of stock market returns seem to be relatively unchanged over time. For those series with breaks in the tail behavior, it is advisable to base tail risk measures like VaR or expected shortfall on the post-break sample. A related application constitutes the calculation of trading limits for investment banks, see, e.g., Danielsson and de Vries (1997). They propose to use an extreme VaR quantile as basis for calculating trading limits. In the presence of breaks in the tail index, however, full sample trading limits will be biased and it is advisable to consider post-break estimates of the trading limit estimator for sake of internal risk management.

APPENDIX A. CALIBRATION OF GARCH(1, 1) PARAMETERS

In order to generate the clusters of volatility feature for the conditional df, we simulated, inter alia, from a GARCH(1,1) process with conditionally normal disturbances. Let X_t follow a GARCH(1,1) process, then:

$$X_t = \sigma_t Z_t,$$
$$\sigma_t^2 = \beta_0 + \beta_1 \sigma_{t-1}^2 + \lambda X_{t-1}^2,$$
$$Z_t \sim \text{i.i.d. } N(0,1).$$

It can be shown that the GARCH scheme also induces the fat tail property on the unconditional distribution of the returns, see, e.g., Embrechts et al. (1997). Also, the tail index α is a function of the parameters of the model. Given the normality of Z_t and provided $\beta_1 + \lambda < 1$, one can show that α is related to the parameters of the conditional df:

$$E\left(\lambda Z^2 + \beta_1\right)^{\alpha/2} = 1, \tag{16}$$

see, e.g., Mikosch and Starica (2000). Empirical evidence suggests that $2 < \alpha < 4$ and we therefore used these boundary values in the Monte Carlo simulations. When $\alpha = 2$, Eq. (16) implies that $\lambda + \beta_1 = 1$. This still leaves an infinite number of possible parameter combinations. As for the upper bound value $\alpha = 4$, Eq. (16) boils down to:

$$3\lambda^2 + 2\beta\lambda + \beta^2 - 1 = 0. \tag{17}$$

Upon substituting $\beta_1 = c - \lambda$ $(c < 1)$ into (17), one obtains a quadratic equation in λ:

$$2\lambda^2 = 1 - c^2.$$

It follows that for a given value of c, the clusters of volatility parameters in the GARCH(1,1) model are uniquely identified, i.e., $(\lambda, \beta_1) = \left(\sqrt{\frac{1-c^2}{2}}, c - \sqrt{\frac{1-c^2}{2}}\right)$. In empirical studies one often encounters $\beta_1 + \lambda$ close to 1. We therefore set c equal to 0.75, 0.85, or 0.95 in the Monte Carlo section to investigate the impact of different degrees of volatility persistence on the test statistics. The intercept β_0 is set to 10^{-6}, which is in line with previous simulations, see, e.g., Danielsson and de Vries (1997).

APPENDIX B. DERIVATIONS OF SECOND ORDER EXPANSION PARAMETERS

In Theorem 1, we argued that $m = cn^{2\beta/(2\beta+\alpha)}$ is the optimal nuisance parameter for the Hill statistic that minimizes the AMSE $(\widehat{\alpha})$. The scaling constant c in turn depends on the parameters (a, b, α, β) of the second order tail expansion (1). Thus, the parameters and the resulting m^* are uniquely determined upon knowledge of this tail expansion. To simplify their derivation it is instructive to re-express the tail expansion (1) for $p = x^{-1}$ close to zero:

$$1 - G(p) = ap^{\alpha}\left(1 + bp^{\beta} + o(p^{\beta})\right), \tag{18}$$

with $a > 0$, $b \in \Re$, $\beta > 0$, and $F(x) = G(p)$. In the Monte Carlo section, we show that biases in the Hill estimator, the stability tests' critical values, and the breakpoint estimates are critically determined by the level of b and β. The pure Pareto model ($b = 0$ and/or $\beta \sim \infty$) provides the benchmark case because it renders unbiased Hill estimates, test statistics, and breakpoint estimates.

The parameters a, b, and β easily follow by either expanding the cumulative distribution $G(p)$ (c.d.f.) (if it exists in closed form) or the accompanying density around $p = 0$. The Fréchet and Burr dfs have c.d.f.s in closed form, which implies that their respective second order Taylor expansions for p small (x large) straightforwardly follow as:

$$\begin{aligned} 1 - G_{\text{FRECHET}}(p) &= 1 - \exp\left(-p^{\alpha}\right) \\ &\simeq p^{\alpha}\left(1 - \frac{1}{2}p^{\alpha}\right), \quad p \text{ small} \\ &= x^{-\alpha}\left(1 - \frac{1}{2}x^{-\alpha}\right), \quad x \text{ large} \end{aligned}$$

and

$$(a, b, \beta)_{\text{FRECHET}} = (1, -1/2, \alpha)$$

As for the Burr distribution, the second order expansion for the c.d.f. reads:

$$\begin{aligned} 1 - G_{\text{BURR}}(p) &= \left(1 + p^{-\beta}\right)^{-\alpha/\beta} \\ &\simeq p^{\alpha}\left(1 - \frac{\alpha}{\beta}p^{\beta}\right), \quad p \text{ small} \\ &= x^{-\alpha}\left(1 - \frac{\alpha}{\beta}x^{-\beta}\right), \quad x \text{ large} \end{aligned}$$

which implies:

$$(a, b)_{\text{BURR}} = (1, -\alpha/\beta)$$

Clearly, whereas first order and higher order behavior are related ($\beta = \alpha$) in the Fréchet case, the second order parameter can be freely chosen for the Burr model. This implies that the Burr distribution becomes indistinguishable from a pure Pareto distribution for large β.

The other DGPs do not exhibit explicit dfs in closed form, which may somewhat complicate the derivation of the second order parameters. For the symmetric stable class, neither the c.d.f. nor the density exists in closed form but we can exploit an existing tail expansion (Ibragimov and Linnik, 1971, Chapter 2) in order to determine the parameters in (18):

$$1 - F(x) = \pi^{-1}\sum_{i=1}^{\infty}(-1)^{i}\frac{\Gamma(i\alpha)}{i!x^{i\alpha}}\sin\left(\frac{i\alpha\pi}{2}\right), \quad x \text{ large}$$

Only considering the expansion's first two terms renders the second order approximation:

$$1 - F(x) \simeq \frac{1}{\pi}\Gamma(\alpha)\sin\left(\frac{\alpha\pi}{2}\right)x^{-\alpha}\left(1 - \frac{\Gamma(2\alpha)\sin(\alpha\pi)}{2\Gamma(\alpha)\sin\left(\frac{\alpha\pi}{2}\right)}x^{-\alpha}\right).$$

Thus the parameter vector that we need for determining m^* boils down to:

$$(a; b; \beta)_{\text{STABLE}} = \left(\frac{1}{\pi}\Gamma(\alpha)\sin\left(\frac{\alpha\pi}{2}\right); -\frac{\Gamma(2\alpha)\sin(\alpha\pi)}{2\Gamma(\alpha)\sin\left(\frac{\alpha\pi}{2}\right)}; \alpha\right)$$

It follows from the second order term that the restriction $\alpha = \beta$ holds for the symmetric stable class.[23]

In order to determine the tail expansion parameters for the Student-t, we need to expand the tail density $g(p)$ because the c.d.f. does not exist in closed form. The asymptotic expansion for the class of regularly varying densities easily follows from (18):

$$\begin{aligned} G'(p) = g(p) &\simeq a\alpha p^{\alpha+1} + ab(\alpha+\beta)p^{\alpha+\beta+1} \\ &= ax^{-\alpha-1}\left(\alpha + b(\alpha+\beta)x^{-\beta-1}\right), \end{aligned} \tag{19}$$

[23] This restriction also holds for the Fréchet model because it falls within the symmetric stable class of distributions.

with p small (x large). Upon rewriting the second order Taylor expansion of the Student-t density for large x (small p) in the above format, we obtain:

$$\begin{aligned} f(x) &= \frac{\Gamma\left(\frac{\alpha+1}{2}\right)}{\Gamma\left(\frac{\alpha}{2}\right)\sqrt{\pi\alpha}}\left(1+\frac{x^2}{\alpha}\right)^{-\frac{\alpha+1}{2}} \\ &\simeq \frac{\Gamma\left(\frac{\alpha+1}{2}\right)}{\Gamma\left(\frac{\alpha}{2}\right)\sqrt{\pi\alpha}}\alpha^{\frac{\alpha-1}{2}}\alpha x^{-\alpha-1}\left[\alpha-\frac{\alpha^2(\alpha+1)}{2(\alpha+2)}(\alpha+2)x^{-3}\right], \end{aligned}$$

with x large. This directly renders the parameter vector:

$$(a, b, \beta)_{\text{STUDENT}} = \left(\frac{\Gamma\left(\frac{\alpha+1}{2}\right)}{\Gamma\left(\frac{\alpha}{2}\right)\sqrt{\pi\alpha}}\alpha^{\frac{\alpha-1}{2}}; -\frac{\alpha^2(\alpha+1)}{2(\alpha+2)}, 2\right)$$

It follows from the second order term between brackets that the restriction $\beta = 2$ holds for the symmetric stable class.

Finally, it can be easily shown that the serially correlated stable draws (denoted by ARSTA in the tables) and the Student-t draws that exhibit dependence in the second moment (SVSTU) in Eq. (10) exhibit the same optimal m^* as their I.I.D. stable and Student-t counterparts. The additivity property under addition for the symmetric stable df ensures that the serially dependent stable draws exhibit the same distribution as the I.I.D. symmetric stable upon some scaling constant. The Student-t draws that exhibit dependence in the second moment are also identically distributed to I.I.D. Student-t draws upon some scaling constant. In general, a linear transform $\widetilde{X} = tX$ that changes the scaling constant leaves the tail index and the optimal value of upper order extremes invariant. This directly follows from the tail expansion for $\widetilde{X}$:

$$\begin{aligned} P\{\widetilde{X} > x\} &= P\{X > t^{-1}x\} \\ &\simeq at^{\alpha}x^{-\alpha}\left(1 + bt^{\beta}x^{-\beta}\right), \end{aligned}$$

which implies that $\widetilde{a} = at^{\alpha}$ and $\widetilde{b} = bt^{\beta}$. The parameters α and β are left unchanged by the linear transform. Substituting $\widetilde{a}$ and $\widetilde{b}$ into $c = \left(\frac{\alpha(\alpha+\beta)^2}{2\beta^3 b^2}a^{2\beta/\alpha}\right)$ leaves the value of $m^* = cn^{\frac{2\beta}{2\beta+\alpha}}$ invariant.

ACKNOWLEDGMENT

We benefited from suggestions and comments by participants at the Netherlands Econometrics Study Group (NESG) in Tilburg and seminar participants at IESE (Barcelona) and the Université d'Orléans.

REFERENCES

Andersen, T.G., Bollerslev, T., 1997. Intraday periodicity and volatility persistence in financial markets. Journal of Empirical Finance 4, 115–158

Andrews, D., 1993. Tests for parameter stability and structural change with unknown change point. Econometrica 59, 817–858

Beirlant, J., Dierckx, G., Goegebeur, Y., Matthys, G., 1999. Tail index estimation and an exponential regression model. Extremes 2, 177–200

Bollerslev, T., Todorov, V., 2011. Tails, fears, and risk premia. Journal of Finance 66, 2165–2211

Bollerslev, T., Todorov, V., Li, S.Z., 2013. Jump tails, extreme dependencies, and the distribution of stock returns. Journal of Econometrics 172, 307–324

Candelon, B., Straetmans, S., 2006. Testing for multiple regimes in the tail behavior of emerging currency returns. Journal of International Money and Finance 25, 1187–1205

Chollette, L., de la Pena, V., Lu, C., 2012. International diversification: an extreme value approach. Journal of Banking and Finance 36, 871–885

Danielsson, J., de Vries, C.G., 1997. Tail index and quantile estimation with very high frequency data. Journal of Empirical Finance 4, 241–257

Danielsson, J., de Haan, L., Peng, L., de Vries, C.G., 2001. Using a bootstrap method to choose the sample fraction in tail index estimation. Journal of Multivariate Analysis 76, 226–248

Davidson, R., Flachaire, E., 2007. Asymptotic and bootstrap inference for inequality and poverty measures. Journal of Econometrics 141, 141–166

de Haan, L., Stadtmüller, U., 1996. Generalized regular variation of second order. Journal of the Australian Mathematical Society (Series A) 61, 381–395

de Haan, L., Jansen, D.W., Koedijk, K.G., de Vries, C.G., 1994. Safety first portfolio selection, extreme value theory and long run asset risks. In: Galambos, J. (Ed.), Proceedings from a Conference on Extreme Value Theory and Applications. Kluwer Press, pp. 471–487

Drees, H., 2003. Extreme quantile estimation for dependent data with applications to finance. Bernoulli 9, 617–657

Dumouchel, W.H., 1983. Estimating the stable index α in order to measure tail thickness: a critique. Annals of Statistics 11, 1019–1031

Embrechts, P., Klüppelberg, C., Mikosch, T., 1997. Modelling Extremal Events. Springer, Berlin

Feller, W., 1971. An Introduction to Probability Theory and its Applications, vol. I, third ed. Wiley, New York

Galbraith, J.W., Zernov, S., 2004. Circuit breakers and the tail index of equity returns. Journal of Financial Econometrics 2, 109–129

Goldie, C.M., Smith, R., 1987. Slow variation with remainder: theory and applications. Quarterly Journal of Mathematics 38, 45–71

Haeusler, E., Teugels, J., 1985. On asymptotic normality of Hill's estimator for the exponent of regular variation. Annals of Statistics 13, 743–756

Hall, P., 1982. On some simple estimates of an exponent of regular variation. Journal of the Royal Statistical Society (Series B) 42, 37–42

Hartmann, P., Straetmans, S., de Vries, C.G., 2003. A global perspective on extreme currency linkages. In: Hunter, W.C., Kaufman, G.G., Pomerleano, M. (Eds.), Asset Price Bubbles: Implications for Monetary, Regulatory and International Policies. MIT Press, Cambridge, MA, pp. 361–383

Hartmann, P., Straetmans, S., de Vries, C.G., 2004. Asset market linkages in crisis periods. Review of Economics and Statistics 86, 313–326

Hartmann, P., Straetmans, S., de Vries, C.G., 2006. Banking system stability: a cross-atlantic perspective. In: Carey, M., Stulz, R.M. (Eds.), The Risk of Financial Institutions. The University of Chicago Press, Chicago and London, pp. 133–193

Hill, B.M., 1975. A simple general approach to inference about the tail of a distribution. The Annals of Statistics 3, 1163–1173

Hols, M., de Vries, C.G., 1991. The limiting distribution of extremal exchange rate returns. Journal of Applied Econometrics 6, 287–302

Ibragimov, I.A., Linnik, Y.V., 1971. Independent and Stationary Sequences of Random Variables. Wolters-Noordhof, Groningen

Jansen, D.W., de Vries, C.G., 1991. On the frequency of large stock returns: putting booms and busts into perspective. Review of Economics and Statistics 73, 19–24

Jondeau, E., Rockinger, M., 2003. Testing for differences in the tails of stock-market returns. Journal of Empirical Finance 10, 559–581

Koedijk, K.G., Schafgans, M.M.A., de Vries, C.G., 1990. The tail index of exchange rate returns. Journal of International Economics 29, 93–108

Koedijk, K.G., Stork, P.A., de Vries, C.G., 1992. Foreign exchange rate regime differences viewed from the tails. Journal of International Money and Finance 11, 462–473

Longin, F.M., 1996. The asymptotic distribution of extreme stock market returns. Journal of Business 69, 383–408

Lux, T., 1996. The stable Paretian Hypothesis and the frequency of large returns: an examination of major German stocks. Applied Financial Economics 6, 463–475

Mandelbrot, B., 1963. The variation of certain speculative prices. Journal of Business 36, 394–419

Mikosch, T., Starica, C., 2000. Limit theory for the sample autocorrelations and extremes of a GARCH(1, 1) process. Annals of Statistics 28, 1427–1451

Pagan, A.R., Schwert, G.W., 1990. Testing for covariance stationarity in stock market data. Economics Letters 33, 165–170

Phillips, P.C.B., Loretan, M., 1990. Testing covariance stationarity under moment condition failure with an application to common stock returns. Cowles Foundation Discussion Paper No. 947.

Quandt, R., 1960. Test of the hypothesis that a linear regression obeys two separate regimes. Journal of the American Statistical Association 55, 324–330

Quintos, C., Fan, Z., Phillips, P., 2001. Structural change tests in tail behaviour and the Asian crisis. Review of Economic Studies 68, 633–663

Ross, S.A., Westerfield, R.W., Jaffe, J., 2005. Corporate Finance, seventh ed. McGraw-Hill

Samorodnitsky, G., Taqqu, M., 1994. Stable Non-Gaussian Random Processes. Chapman and Hall, New York

Straetmans, S., Candelon, B., 2013. Long-term asset tail risks in developed and emerging markets. Journal of Banking and Finance 37, 1832–1844

Straetmans, S., Chaudhry, S., 2013. Tail risk and systemic risk for U.S. and Eurozone financial institutions in the wake of the global financial crisis. SSRN Working Paper.

Straetmans, S., Verschoor, W., Wolff, C., 2008. Extreme U.S. stock market fluctuations in the wake of 9/11. Journal of Applied Econometrics 23, 17–42

Werner, T., Upper, C., 2002. Time variation in the tail behaviour of Bund futures returns. Journal of Futures Markets 24, 387–398

CHAPTER 12

Measuring Systemic Risk in Emerging Markets Using CoVaR

Anastassios A. Drakos[*] **and Georgios P. Kouretas**[*]
[*]Department of Business Administration, Athens University of Economics and Business, Athens, Greece

1. INTRODUCTION

The global financial crisis of 2007–2009 illustrated how distress can spread quickly through the financial system and threaten financial stability. Furthermore, Brunnermeier and Pedersen (2009) argue that the degree to which international financial institutions are linked depends on the level of market liquidity. Banks play a crucial role in the proper functioning of an economy because they provide the necessary liquidity to the markets and help to promote economic growth (Levine, 1997). Ill-functioning of the banking sector dramatically increases the costs in the real economy and historically has been a major source of financial crises, like the recent one, in both developed and emerging economies (Barth and Caprio, 2006; Demirguc-Kunt et al., 2009; Reinhart and Rogoff, 2009). Since October 1987, financial and banking regulation has focused on monitoring and regulating the banking industry.

The recent financial crisis revealed that the micro-prudential regulatory framework is not sufficient to prevent worldwide contagion as a result of bank failures initially in the US and subsequently in Europe and elsewhere. The micro-prudential regulatory framework is based on the provisions of the Basle I and II agreements which imposed minimum capital requirements on the banks as a measure of prevention against unexpected losses (Pillar I). Within this framework, the Basle II agreement led to the development of internal systems for the measurement of market risk and such a regulation looked at the soundness of individual financial institutions. However, such provisions based only on capital adequacy ignored factors such as size, degree of leverage, and interrelationships with the rest of the system. Stein (2010, p. 50) argued that "the overarching goal of financial reform must not be only to fortify a set of large institutions, but rather to reduce the fragility of our *entire system* of credit creation."

Thus, there is now a shift in macro-prudential regulation, which implies that we observe the operation of the banking system as a whole (see Borio and Lowe, 2002; Borio and Drehmann, 2009; Gauthier et al., 2012). The Bassle III agreement which is still under formation is expected to address most of the issues related to systemic risk and develop the appropriate framework for regulation and supervision of the financial

Emerging Markets and the Global Economy
http://dx.doi.org/10.1016/B978-0-12-411549-1.00012-0

markets based on recent experience. Therefore, for Central Banks and financial regulators, it is of great value to be able to quantify the risks that can threaten the financial system, not only at the national level but also globally. Early works on this front by Lehar (2005), Goodhart et al. (2005, 2006), and Goodhart (2006) proposed alternative measures of financial fragility which can be implemented at both the individual and the aggregate levels. Additionally, the Financial Sector Assessment Program (a joint IMF and World Bank initiative) was set up with the purpose of increasing the effectiveness of plans to promote the soundness of financial systems in their member countries.

Interdependence among financial institutions becomes particularly important during periods of distress, when losses tend to spread across institutions and the whole financial system becomes vulnerable. In this respect, systemic risk is defined as multiple simultaneous defaults of large financial institutions. A systemic crisis that disrupts the stability of the financial system can have serious consequences and large costs for the whole economy and the society. During financial crises, episodes of contagion among financial institutions occur very often and therefore regulators need to take them into consideration when assessing the health of the financial system. Central banks are responsible for promoting financial stability in the domestic economy and hence it is a central component of the central banks' activities to follow and analyze systemic risk. The financial crisis of 2007–2009 has put increased emphasis on analyzing systemic risk and developing systemic risk indicators that can be used by central banks and others as a monitoring tool. In order to evaluate the stability of the banking system, a crucial element is the measurement of the systemic risk of a financial system. According to the Group of Ten (2001, p.126):

> *Systemic financial risk is the risk that an event will trigger a loss of economic value or confidence in, and attendant increases in uncertainly [sic] about, a substantial portion of the financial system that is serious enough to quite probably have significant adverse effects on the real economy. Systemic risk events can be sudden and unexpected, or the likelihood of their occurrence can build up through time in the absence of appropriate policy responses. The adverse real economic effects from systemic problems are generally seen as arising from disruptions to the payment system, to credit flows, and from the destruction of asset values.*

Arnold et al. (2012) also argue that key aspects of recent regulatory reforms which are under way through the Basle III agreement include measuring and regulating systemic risk and designing and implementing macro-prudential policies in an appropriate way. To this end the EU has established the European Systemic Risk Board and the US the Financial Stability Oversight Council in order to focus on the issue of systemic risk not only in those two regions but also at the global level. The collapse of numerous financial institutions over the last 5 years has imposed significant negative spillovers on governments and the economy as a whole. Therefore, in measuring systemic risk we need to consider the degree of risk of financial institutions and to allocate risks and costs across them so that we take into account the negative spillovers associated with financial instability. Although the issue of stability of the banking sector is very important, there are only a few studies that examine the impact of bank regulation and supervision on banking risk, some of which find that it has little effect on minimizing banking risk. Thus, Demirguc-Kunt and Detragiache (2011), using a sample of 3000 banks from 86 countries, reject the hypothesis that better regulation and supervision results in a sounder banking system. In contrast, Klomp and de Haan (2012) also examine the issue of the effectiveness of bank regulation and supervision and find evidence in favor of its effectiveness for high-risk banks. However, when they consider low-risk banks then they find no support in favor of the effectiveness of the regulatory framework.

The most commonly used measure of market risk is the Value-at-Risk (VaR) which calculates the monetary loss an institution may experience within a given confidence level. The problem with such a measure is that it does not consider the institution as part of a system which might itself experience instability and spread new sources of economic risk. Furthermore, it is noted that traditional measures have focused on banks' balance sheet information, including non-performing loans ratios, earnings and profitability, liquidity and capital adequacy measures which are not appropriate to evaluate the soundness of a financial system (see Huang et al., 2009; Sylvain et al., 2012).

Recently, Adrian and Brunnermeier (2011) developed CoVaR as a measure of systemic risk. CoVaR measures the contribution of a financial institution to systemic risk and its contribution to the risk of other financial institutions. CoVaR stands for Conditional Value-at-Risk, and indicates the Value-at-Risk (VaR) of financial institution i, conditional on financial institution j being in distress. Adrian and Brunnermeier (2011) argue that this is a more complete measure of risk since it is able to capture alternative sources of risk which affect institution i even though they are not generated by it. Furthermore, if we consider that institution i is the whole financial system, then ΔCoVaR is defined as the difference between the CoVaR and the unconditional VaR and it captures the marginal non-causal contribution of a particular institution to the overall systemic risk.

In this chapter, we build on the CoVaR methodology which allows us to generate time-varying estimates of the systemic risk contribution of three specific sectors of the financial industry subject to different regulation and supervisory framework: banks, insurances, and financial services. We employ weekly data from December 1995 to February 2013 for selected countries from a group of emerging economies from Latin America, Central and Eastern Europe, and Southeast Asia which have been seriously affected by the recent financial crisis. Furthermore, the purpose of the analysis is to examine whether the contribution of the different financial sectors has changed following the failure of Lehman Brothers in September 2008. Applying the CoVaR analysis we want to measure risk spillovers and model the conditional second moments of the financial sectors on the whole economy.

There are several important findings that stem from our analysis. First, the estimations of 1% and 50% quantile regressions show that equity returns are a key determinant in triggering systemic risk episodes. There is also evidence that volatility of the general index ex financials (system variable), liquidity spread, the three-month rate change, and yield spread have an effect, although weaker. Second, we show that for Mexico, the Czech Republic, Hungary, Romania, Hong Kong, Indonesia, the Philippines, and Thailand it is the banking sector that contributes mostly to the systemic risk. In Malaysia, the insurance industry contributes most to the systemic risk, whereas in Poland, Turkey, Korea, Malaysia, and Singapore the highest percentage contribution to systemic risk is due to the other financial services. Finally, based on the results of ΔCoVaR estimates before and after 2008, it is observed that for all emerging markets the contribution of each financial industry to systemic risk increased after the unfolding of the crisis.

The structure of the chapter is as follows: Section 2 presents and discusses the recent literature on CoVaR modeling. Section 3 discusses the CoVaR modeling approach to estimate systemic risk. Section 4 presents the data and empirical results while a summary and Section 5 gives the concluding remarks.

2. REVIEW OF THE LITERATURE

Achieving macroeconomic stability requires the identification of systemic risk in the financial system and the factors driving it. Although there is no consensus on the definition and measurement of systemic risk, we review the recent literature on the topic in this section (for a complete survey, see Bisias et al., 2012).

The recent literature has followed two main channels to analyze systemic risk. First, several studies examine the channels through which risk is transmitted from one financial institution to another. Pritsker (2000) and Forbes and Rigobon (2001) were among the first studies to explain the transmission of disturbances from one market to another over time, identifying two transmission channels which take the form either of interdependence or contagion. Within this framework we also observed the development of research on early warning indicators for both developed and emerging economies in an attempt to forecast systemic events (see, for example, Borio and Lowe, 2002; Alessi and Detken, 2009; Alfaro and Drehmann, 2009, Borio and Drehmann, 2009; Giesecke and Kim, 2011; Huang et al., 2009; Khandani et al., 2010; Borio et al., forthcoming). A second approach of measuring systemic risk using either macroeconomic data or balance sheet data has also been employed but suffers from two shortcomings. Thus, Cerutti et al. (2011) emphasize the problem that researchers face with the lack of useful and consistent data and suggest the creation of a common reporting template for globally systematically important financial institutions. A second shortcoming of this approach lies in the static modeling of institutional behavior and therefore models with low-frequency data are not appropriate for studying the effects of the regulatory and supervisory framework.

The second strand of literature on measuring systemic risk uses high-frequency time series data. Several approaches have been proposed. Segoviano and Goodhart (2009) and Moreno and Peña (2013) argue that CDS spreads are good estimators of systemic risk. The problem with this approach is that it captures only credit risk and not market risk, which is the issue under examination in the present paper. Another approach focuses on individual measures of systemic risk, which seek to predict how much the stocks of financial institutions fall in a major market downturn. Essentially, this approach provides a framework to evaluate the co-dependence of financial institutions on a given system when a distress event occurs. The theoretical foundations of this approach were developed in Acharya and Richardson (2009), Acharya et al. (2010), and Acharya et al. (2012). Acharya et al. (2010) define the systemic expected shortfall as the propensity of a financial institution to be undercapitalized when the system as a whole is undercapitalized. In addition, Acharya et al. (2012) show that when this negative event occurs, the government usually wants to minimize the resulting cost to the taxpayer. Furthermore, it is shown that this cost is a function of size, leverage, and expected equity losses during a crisis. Brownlees and Engle (2012) propose a bivariate GARCH model for volatility as well as an asymmetric DCC model to capture correlation. Furthermore, they construct short- and long-run Marginal Expected Shortfall forecasts and propose the SRISK index, which is also a distress measure.

Adrian and Brunnermeier (2011) propose the CoVaR methodology in order to evaluate the impact of financial units which are in distress on the whole financial system. Therefore, this approach is useful in measuring risk transmission from a financial institution to the financial system. For their empirical application they use quantile regressions to estimate the conditional models using data for 1266 US financial institutions which are distinguished into four groups: commercial banks, broker-dealers (including the investment banks), insurance companies, and real estate. They conclude that systemic risk depends significantly on size, leverage, and maturity mismatch. This methodology has been applied in several recent studies. Van Oordt and Zhou (2010) extended CoVaR to analyze situations at an extremely low probability level. Their analysis is based on 46 equally weighted industry portfolios including NYSE, AMEX, and NASDAQ firms. Wong and Fong (2010) examine the interrelationships among 11 Asia-Pacific economies by estimating CoVaR for the CDS of their banks. Their main finding is that CoVaR measurements are higher than the respective unconditional VaR measure. Chan-Lau (2008) using a similar approach, studied the existence of spillover effects using the CDS spreads of a sample of 25 financial institutions in Europe, Japan, and the United States.

Recently, Agrippino (2009) proposed the implementation of CoVaR analysis of five US commercial banks using daily data in order to distinguish between interdependence and spillovers among financial institutions. The analysis concludes that CoVaR provides superior measurement of risk compared with the estimated with the traditional VaR model, particularly in case of financial instability when negative effects are spread across institutions. Roengpitya and Rungcharoenkitkul (2011) employ panel data from six major banks of Thailand in order to examine risk spillover effects among these financial institutions. Girardi and Ergun (2013) modified the CoVaR model. They change the definition of financial distress from a financial institution *i* to a financial institution *j* as being higher, instead of being equal, than its VaR estimate. They estimate the systemic risk contributions of four financial industry groups consisting of a large number of institutions. Lopez-Espinoza et al. (2012a) analyze the banking system responses to positive and negative shocks to the market-value balance sheets of individual banks. Lopez-Espinoza et al. (2012b) employ an asymmetric CoVaR methodology to deal with a representative sample of 54 international banks and to address the asymmetric patterns that may underlie tail dependence. Bjarnadottir (2012) studies the contribution of four major Swedish banks to the systemic risk of the Swedish financial system. Finally, Bernal et al. (2012) depart from the above-mentioned papers since they study systemic risk by analyzing how financial sectors of an economy that operate under different regulation systems contribute to systemic risk. Therefore, they examine the existence of interrelationships between the financial sector and the whole, instead of focusing on individual institutions. They estimate the respective CoVaR model using daily data for the banking, insurance, and other financial services industries of the US and the Eurozone, and they find that the insurance sector contributes relatively more to the systemic risk in periods of distress compared with the banking and other financial services industries.

This chapter adopts the approach suggested by Bernal et al. (2012) in evaluating the contribution to systemic risk by different aggregated components of the financial system including the banking, insurance, and other financial services industries. The argument that Bernal et al. (2012) make is that the evaluation of the impact of shocks affecting one of these different financial industries on the whole system is important in designing an appropriate regulation. We employ CoVaR analysis to study the impact of these three financial sectors on the whole system for a selected group of emerging markets from three regions: Latin America, Central and Eastern Europe, and Southeast Europe.

To the best of our knowledge, this is the first study that provides an analysis of assessing systemic risk for the case of emerging markets, since all aforementioned studies focused exclusively on developed economies. This is due to the fact that the recent crisis is one of the few if not the first one whose source is the developed economies and not the emerging economies. Therefore, the propagation mechanism is from the US and the Eurozone to the emerging markets. The recent banking crisis in Cyprus (a member country of the Eurozone) came with a possible 5-year delay from the initial shock. It was partly caused by the Eurozone debt crisis and more specifically as an outcome of the Greek debt crisis since the "haircut" on the Greek long-term sovereign bonds that took place in March 2012 imposed a loss of 4.5 billion euros on the banking system of Cyprus. The emerging economies suffered substantial losses since the credit crunch of 2007–2008 and the collapse of Lehman Brothers in September 2008. These negative effects have not been symmetric to the different groups of emerging markets. In particular, the economies of the Central and Eastern European countries had to undergo major adjustment in their financial sectors and their real economies as a whole because of the recent financial and debt crisis. Countries like Hungary and Estonia almost went bankrupt and had to devalue their currency up to 30%. The Czech Republic, Poland, and Romania also faced similar adjustments. Latin America countries were also hit by the credit crunch which was evident, for example, in Argentina where the long adjustment process to return to financial markets following the 2001 collapse has deteriorated once again. The Southeast Asian countries were also affected, although in a milder way, particularly with the experience of increased volatility in their stock markets.

3. ECONOMETRIC METHODOLOGY

During the last 15 years there has been a voluminous literature on measuring approaches on market risk and propagation channels and causes of risk contagion effects. However, it has been shown that these traditional approaches have several modeling limitations, as well as strong assumptions with respect to the returns distribution and thus their application was proven problematic. Following the Basle II agreement, the Value-at-Risk measure became very popular to measure market risk because of its simplicity since the calculation of a single number was considered to be sufficient to quantify the minimum capital adequacy requirements for a financial institution. Intuitively, the VaR(α) is the worst loss over a target horizon that will not be exceeded with a given level of confidence $1 - \alpha$ (Jorion, 2007). Statistically, the VaR(α) defined for a confidence level $1 - \alpha$ corresponds to the α-quantile of the projected distribution of gains and losses over the target horizon.

This was the main approach used within the context of micro-prudential regulation as proposed by the Basle I and Basle II agreements. First, VaR models only estimate their own minimum loss if tail takes place under several alternative error distribution specifications. However, these models do not bring to the surface the potential loss of systemic risk transmitted from other sectors of either the domestic economy or the global economy. A stylized fact of these models is that the error terms of the dynamic correlation model or the autoregressive conditional heteroskedasticity model are assumed to have a specific distribution which leads to a bias toward the coefficients' estimation. Second, the extreme value theory and the derived models for estimating VaR do not take into consideration the full set of observations of the sample, leading to an underestimation of the respective risk measure, whereas there is also a small sample bias (see, for example, Wong and Fong, 2010). A final critical issue on modeling interrelationships between different sectors of the economy refers to time lag.

Given these criticisms regarding the ability of the traditional VaR model to capture systemic risk, we employ the CoVaR model (Adrian and Brunnermeier, 2011). The CoVaR model is particularly useful for measuring systemic risk by the VaR of an institution conditional on other institutions being in distress. During the 2007–2009 global financial crisis, the emerging economies faced severe credit risk and major financial problems. Therefore, the CoVaR model is appropriate to study risk spillovers and therefore is also a convenient measure of systemic risk.

Following Adrian and Brunnermeier (2011) we define $\text{CoVaR}_q^{j|i}$, which implies that the VaR_q^j of an institution j (or of the financial institution) conditional on institution i's event $C(R^i)$ which is realized by the returns for this institution (R^i) being equal to its level of VaR for a qth quantile $R^i = \text{VaR}_q^i$. $\text{CoVaR}_q^{j|i}$ is then the qth quantile of the conditional probability distribution of returns of j:

$$P(R^j \leq \text{CoVaR}_q^{j|C(R^i)} | C(R^i)) = q. \tag{1}$$

Adrian and Brunnermeier (2011) define ΔCoVaR as the difference between the CoVaR of the financial institution j conditional on the distress of another institution i and CoVaR of institution j conditional on the normal state of institution i. Therefore, this CoVaR measurement calculates how much an institution contributes to another institution's risk:

$$\Delta\text{CoVaR}_q^{j|i} = \text{CoVaR}_q^{j|X^i=\text{VaR}_q^i} - \text{CoVaR}_q^{j|X^i=\text{Median}^i}, \tag{2}$$

where $\Delta\text{CoVaR}_q^{j|i}$ denotes the VaR of institution j's asset returns when institution i's returns are at its normal state of their distribution (e.g. 50% percentile), and $\Delta\text{CoVaR}_q^{j|i}$ is institution j's VaR when institution i's returns are in a distressed or extremely bad condition like the one experienced during the recent financial crisis. It can also be taken as the additional VaR caused by outside influences, which is above the ordinary interdependencies.

We further calculate ΔCoVaR for each institution as follows:

$$\Delta\text{CoVar}_t^{j|i}(q) = \text{CoVaR}_t^{j|i}(q) - \text{CoVaR}_t^{j|i}(50\%) = \hat{\beta}^{j|i}[\text{VaR}_t^i(q) - \text{VaR}_t^i(50\%)]. \tag{3}$$

Adrian and Brunnermeier (2011) estimate the related $\text{VaR}_q^{j|i}$ and their $\Delta\text{CoVaR}_q^{j|i}$ with the use of the growth rates of market-valued total assets for an individual institution and define them as a function of a constant, lagged state variables, and error term. In order to assess the link between a set of independent variables and the quantiles of the dependent variable, they employ the quantile regressions methodology developed by Koenker and Basset (1978) and Koenker (2005).

In this chapter, we depart from Adrian and Brunnermeier (2011), who focus on the financial system, and we consider the real economy as the system variable. Recently, Bernal et al. (2012) defined systemic risk as the impact that a group of financial institutions may have on the whole economy. In this context, systemic risk is measured with the estimation of ΔCoVaR. Based on equations (1) and (2) we define $\text{CoVaR}_q^{\text{system}|i}$ as the $\text{VaR}_q^{\text{system}}$ of the whole system conditional on an event $C(R^i)$ affecting a financial sector i being equal to its level of VaR for a qth quantile. This is given by the following probability:

$$P(R^{\text{system}} \leq \text{CoVaR}_q^{\text{system}C(R^i)}|C(R^i) = q. \tag{4}$$

Therefore,

$$\Delta\text{CoVaR}_q^{\text{system}|i} = \text{CoVaR}_q^{\text{system}|X^i=\text{VaR}_q^i} - \text{CoVaR}_q^{\text{system}|X^i=\text{Median}^i}. \tag{5}$$

Following Bernal et al. (2012) we use this modeling approach to assess risk transmission from a given financial sector to the whole economy in selected emerging economies of Latin America, Central and Eastern Europe, and South East Asia. The econometric approach is implemented in five stages.

The first stage deals with modeling the returns R^i as a function of a set of state variables:

$$R_t^i = \alpha^i + \gamma^i M_t + \varepsilon_t^i, \tag{6}$$

where α^i is the constant, M_t represents a vector of contemporaneous control variables, and ε_t^i is a white noise error term. We then estimate the 1% quantile of market return based on the quantile regressions.

The second step involves the computation of the predicted 1% VaR for each segment of the financial system using only the statistically significant variables that were identified in the first stage. Given that the VaR(α) defined for a confidence level $1 - \alpha$ is the quantile of the distribution of gains and losses over the target horizon, the forecast will be obtained as follows:

$$\hat{\text{VaR}} = \hat{\alpha}^i + \hat{\gamma}^i M_t, \tag{7}$$

where $\hat{\alpha}^i$ and $\hat{\gamma}^i$ are the coefficient estimates from equation (6).

We then move to third stage of our analysis in which we estimate the system's returns using the following equation:

$$R_t^{\text{system}} = \alpha^{\text{system}|i} + \beta^{\text{system}|i} R_t^i + \gamma^{\text{system}|i} M_t + \varepsilon_t^{\text{system}|i}, \tag{8}$$

where $\alpha^{\text{system}|i}$ is the constant, β gives the contribution of the return R_t^i of each financial sector to the real economy, M_t is a set of contemporaneous control variables, and $\varepsilon_t^{\text{system}|i}$ is a white noise error term. Again the 1% quantile of returns is obtained from the quantile regression.

In the next stage, we compute the CoVaR of the system which is the VaR of the system conditional with a situation of distress within either one of the individual financial sectors, represented by the 1% quantiles computed in the previous stages. Therefore, the estimation of CoVaR requires the use of the computed VaR (1%) from equation (7), given all the significant control variables obtained from equation (8):

$$\hat{\text{CoVaR}}_t^i = \hat{\alpha}^{\text{sytem}|i} + \hat{\beta}^{\text{systemi}}\,\hat{\text{VaR}}_t^i + \hat{\gamma}^{\text{system}|i} M_t, \tag{9}$$

where $\hat{\alpha}^{\text{system}|i}$, $\hat{\beta}^{\text{system}|i}$ and $\hat{\gamma}^{\text{system}|i}$ are derived from equation (8).

The fifth and final stage of the estimation process involves the computation of ΔCoVaR which, as we explained above, is the difference between the CoVaR at the 1% quantile and the CoVaR at the 50% quantile. The calculation of CoVaR at the 50% quantile is made using the same approach, with the only difference being that we take 50% of the returns at each step. This CoVaR at the 50% quantile describes a conditional event at a median state given in formulation (5) which is required in order to compute the systemic risk measure. ΔCoVaR is the marginal contribution of each financial sector to systemic risk, i.e.:

$$\Delta\hat{\text{CoVaR}}_t^i(q) = \hat{\text{CoVaR}}_t^i(1\%) - \hat{\text{CoVaR}}_t^i(50\%). \tag{10}$$

During a financial crisis, portfolio returns of all financial institutions are at their VaR level. Therefore, the CoVaR model is particularly appropriate for capturing risk contagion from a systemic crisis. Because the credit risk faced by financial institutions is more severe when there is a dramatic fall in prices and therefore returns, we focus on the downside risk of the changes in prices and thus, $\Delta\hat{\text{CoVaR}}$ takes negative values because it is computed from the 1% returns of each financial industry. Within this framework, we consider that the financial sector with the larger absolute $\Delta\hat{\text{CoVaR}}$ is the sector that contributes the most to systemic risk in periods of distress.

4. DATA AND EMPIRICAL RESULTS

We analyze the effect that three segments of the financial industry, namely banking, insurance, and financial services sectors, have on the whole economy. It is interesting to note that these three sectors are subject to different regulatory frameworks. We employ our analysis for three groups of emerging markets: in Latin America, South East Asia, and Central and Eastern Europe. We use weekly data from December 29, 1995 to March 1, 2013. We will thus be able to provide evidence as to whether there is a shift in the evidence before and after 2008, which will indicate whether or not systemic risk increased after the financial crisis.[1]

The first set of variables (R_t^i s) consists of the returns of the three financial sectors and of the system. Specifically, for each country we employ the Banks index, the Insurances

[1] Due to data availability the countries used in the present analysis are: Mexico, the Czech Republic, Hungary, Poland Romania, Turkey, Hong Kong, Indonesia, Korea, Malaysia, the Philippines, Singapore, and Thailand. The same holds for the sample used in the estimations. The number of observations used also depends on data availability. We use high-frequency weekly data in order to obtain a reactive measure of systemic risk. Alternatively, we could use daily data but the problem is that the bond markets in these emerging economies are not very liquid and we would unable to capture substantial reaction and volatility of the stock market indices.

index and the Financial Services index, whereas the system variable is proxied by the general stock returns index excluding the Financials index.[2]

In order to estimate the time-varying CoVaR_t and VaR_t, we include a set of control variables M_t. These variables are taken to capture time variation in conditional moments of asset returns and at the same time are liquid and tradable. These control variables M_t are given as follows: (1) *Liquidity spread*, which measures short-term liquidity risk, is defined as the difference between the three-month repo rate and the three-month treasury bill rate. (2) *three-month treasury bill spread variation* is defined as the difference between the three-month bond rate in time t and the three-month bond rate in time $t-1$. Following Adrian and Brunnermeier (2011) we use the change in the three-month treasury bill, because the change and not the level is considered to be more significant in explaining the tails of financial sector market-valued asset returns. (3) *Yield spread change* is defined as the difference between the 10-year or 5-year government bond rate (depending on the availability of data) and the three-month treasury bill rate. This measure captures the change in the slope of the yield curve. (4) *Equity return* is calculated using the general price index. Finally, we use a volatility measure to capture volatility of the system variable, since implied volatility measures are only available for the US and the Eurozone but not for any of the emerging markets under consideration. To construct a proxy of volatility, we run a rolling regression for the returns of the general stock returns index excluding the Financials index with a window of 13 weeks. The estimated series of standard deviations are used to measure volatility. All data are in national currency. The spreads and the spread changes are expressed in basis points and the returns are expressed in percent. The series were taken from *Datastream* and *Bloomberg*.[3]

4.1. Quantile Regressions

Table 1 reports quantile regressions results for the 1% and 50% quantile returns of the banking, insurance, and other financial services industries of the 13 emerging markets. Furthermore, Table 1 reports estimates for the system's returns in which the General stock market index excluding financial services is used to proxy each country's real economy. Table 1 also reports the pseudo-R^2 in order to assess the goodness-of-fit of quantile regressions. This measure has a similar interpretation as the standard R^2. The pseudo-R^2 is derived using the distances from data points to estimates in each quantile regression at each point along the R_t^i—distribution. The estimated pseudo-R^2 obtained values imply that our estimated models have the appropriate specification.

[2] The insurance index is not available for the Czech Republic, Hungary, Poland, Romania, Indonesia, or the Philippines. For these economies we consider only the banking and other financial services industries.

[3] Adrian and Brunnermeier (2011) and Bernal et al. (2012) employ an additional control variable to capture the time variation in the tails of asset returns, the change in *credit spread* which is defined as the difference between the 10-year Macrobond BBB corporate bonds rate and the 10-year bond rate. However, this data is not available for any emerging economies and therefore we did not include it in our estimations.

Table 1 Quantile regressions.

Mexico: banks

Variable	Quantile regression 1%		Quantile regression 50%	
	R_t^i	R_t^{system}	R_t^i	R_t^{system}
Volatility	−0.2966	−0.0126	−0.2051	0.0143*
	(1.6262)	(0.0964)	(0.2558)	(0.0068)
Liquidity spread	0.3532	0.1594*	0.4127	0.0062
	(0.5677)	(0.0543)	(0.2473)	(0.0089)
Three-month rate change	−0.5391	−0.0456	−0.1891	0.0086
	(1.0722)	(0.1339)	(0.8211)	(0.0419)
Yield spread change	−0.4450	−0.0970*	−0.1960*	−0.0001
	(0.9396)	(0.0416)	(0.0858)	(0.0027)
Equity return	0.7625***	1.0729***	0.8168***	1.0941***
	(0.1745)	(0.0164)	(0.0765)	(0.0033)
R_t^i		−0.0777***		−0.0818***
		(0.0089)		(0.0026)
Pseudo-R^2	0.3882	0.9577	0.2669	0.9625

Notes: the R_t^i and the R_t^{system} are respectively the weekly market returns of the banks index and the weekly market returns of the general index excluding the financial index.
*Significance at the 10% critical level.
**Significance at the 5% critical level.
***Significance at the 1% critical level.

Mexico: insurance companies

Variable	Quantile regression 1%		Quantile regression 50%	
	R_t^i	R_t^{system}	R_t^i	R_t^{system}
Volatility	1.9518	−0.0005	−0.0115	0.0261
	(2.1089)	(0.2284)	(0.0432)	(0.0334)
Liquidity spread	3.6105	−0.0699	0.0005	−0.0063
	(3.3281)	(0.1010)	(0.0203)	(0.0213)
Three-month rate change	−1.9659	−0.0309	0.5076	−0.0838
	(2.6027)	(0.1198)	(0.3921)	(0.0529)
Yield spread change	−1.3405	0.0585	−0.0016	0.0004
	(1.2115)	(0.0636)	(0.0169)	(0.0093)
Equity return	0.4465	1.0133***	0.0165	1.0234***
	(0.3026)	(0.0137)	(0.0147)	(0.0055)
R_t^i		0.0138		0.0059
		(0.0193)		(0.0045)
Pseudo-R^2	0.0935	0.9355	0.2500	0.922

Notes: the R_t^i and the R_t^{system} are respectively the weekly market returns of the insurances index and the weekly market returns of the general index excluding the financial index.
*Significance at the 10% critical level.
**Significance at the 5% critical level.
***Significance at the 1% critical level.

Table 1 (Continued)

Mexico: financial services

Variable	Quantile regression 1% R_t^i	Quantile regression 1% R_t^{system}	Quantile regression 50% R_t^i	Quantile regression 50% R_t^{system}
Volatility	−0.1950	0.0782	−0.2650	0.0032
	(1.2309)	(0.0726)	(0.2729)	
Liquidity spread	0.2866	−0.0567	0.0005	0.0004
	(0.5577)	(0.0323)	(0.1712)	
Three-month rate change	−0.3866	0.0483	0.5282	−0.0097
	(1.4056)	(0.0636)	(0.3741)	
Yield spread change	0.0124	0.0275	−0.0717	0.0006
	(0.4426)	(0.0310)	(0.0894)	
Equity return	0.7742***	1.1230***	0.7800***	1.1108***
	(0.1917)	(0.0110)	(0.0588)	(0.0012)
R_t^i		−0.1168***		−0.1110***
		(0.0062)		(0.0012)
Pseudo-R^2	0.4663	0.9785	0.3405	0.9807

Notes: the R_t^i and the R_t^{system} are respectively the weekly market returns of the financial services index and the weekly market returns of the general index excluding the financial index.
*Significance at the 10% critical level.
**Significance at the 5% critical level.
***Significance at the 1% critical level.

Czech Republic: banks

Variable	Quantile regression 1% R_t^i	Quantile regression 1% R_t^{system}	Quantile regression 50% R_t^i	Quantile regression 50% R_t^{system}
Volatility	−5.8501***	−0.0223	0.0036	0.0475
	(1.9607)	(0.3235)	(0.6347)	(0.0255)
Liquidity spread	1.9368	1.4582	0.1806	0.0365
	(3.4615)	(0.7674)	(1.6295)	(0.1107)
Three-month rate change	−14.6919***	2.1009	−0.2650	0.0386
	(3.8920)	(1.2612)	(1.5385)	(0.0780)
Yield spread change	−1.1872	0.3350***	0.0464	0.0222
	(0.8069)	(0.1281)	(0.2226)	(0.0114)
Equity return	1.5970***	1.2104***	0.9701***	1.2029***
	(0.2162)	(0.0262)	(0.0780)	(0.0516)
R_t^i		−0.1909***		−0.1923***
		(0.0195)		(0.0041)
Pseudo-R^2	0.5186	0.9251	0.2179	0.9256

Notes: the R_t^i and the R_t^{system} are respectively the weekly market returns of the banks index and the weekly market returns of the general index excluding the financial index.
*Significance at the 10% critical level.
**Significance at the 5% critical level.
***Significance at the 1% critical level.

Table 1 (Continued)

Czech Republic: financial services

	Quantile regression 1%		Quantile regression 50%	
Variable	R_t^i	R_t^{system}	R_t^i	R_t^{system}
Volatility	−5.5203***	−0.2075	−0.1094	0.0444
	(1.5439)	(0.2862)	(0.5936)	(0.0233)
Liquidity spread	−1.0939	0.6498	0.8666	0.0306
	(4.6569)	(0.4293)	(1.6452)	(0.1343)
Three-month rate change	−13.9268**	1.0989	−1.2100	0.1195
	(4.8530)	(1.1885)	(1.4743)	(0.0882)
Yield spread change	−0.4681	0.1839	−0.0169	0.0244*
	(0.6755)	(0.1271)	(0.2532)	(0.0101)
Equity return	1.5445***	1.2310***	0.9655***	1.1979***
	(0.2535)	(0.0257)	(0.0641)	(0.0064)
R_t^i		−0.2204***		−0.1966***
		(0.0226)		(0.0049)
Pseudo-R^2	0.5254	0.9261	0.2150	0.9246

Notes: the R_t^i and the R_t^{system} are respectively the weekly market returns of the financial services index and the weekly market returns of the general index excluding the financial index.
*Significance at the 10% critical level.
**Significance at the 5% critical level.
***Significance at the 1% critical level.

Hungary: banks

	Quantile regression 1%		Quantile regression 50%	
Variable	R_t^i	R_t^{system}	R_t^i	R_t^{system}
Volatility	−3.1705*	−1.0626**	0.0456	0.0501
	(1.3976)	(0.3612)	(0.4189)	(0.0436)
Liquidity spread	−0.5483	0.2519	−0.0735	−0.0179
	(1.1452)	(0.1653)	(0.6613)	(0.0510)
Three-month rate change	−5.0844***	−0.4281	−1.1520	−0.0119
	(1.3626)	(0.2986)	(0.7928)	(0.0359)
Yield spread change	−0.8306**	0.1934***	−0.0718	0.0003
	(0.2837)	(0.0413)	(0.0680)	(0.0058)
Equity return	1.3542***	1.3826***	1.2896***	1.3078***
	(0.1272)	(0.0326)	(0.0658)	(0.0079)
R_t^i		−0.3380**		−0.3016**
		(0.0192)		(0.0064)
Pseudo-R^2	0.6646	0.9074	0.4206	0.9040

Notes: the R_t^i and the R_t^{system} are respectively the weekly market returns of the banks index and the weekly market returns of the general index excluding the financial index.
*Significance at the 10% critical level.
**Significance at the 5% critical level.
***Significance at the 1% critical level.

Table 1 (Continued)

Hungary: financial services

Variable	Quantile regression 1% R_t^i	Quantile regression 1% R_t^{system}	Quantile regression 50% R_t^i	Quantile regression 50% R_t^{system}
Volatility	−2.3062*	−1.0564**	0.0655	0.0312
	(0.9273)	(0.3504)	(0.4236)	(0.0362)
Liquidity spread	−0.0564	0.2182	−0.1577	−0.0027
	(1.1198)	(0.1831)	(0.5518)	(0.0235)
Three-month rate change	−4.8104***	−0.4428	−0.9210	−0.0277
	(1.2297)	(0.3441)	(0.6408)	(0.0236)
Yield spread change	−0.6927**	0.2075***	−0.0685	−0.0051
	(0.2264)	(0.0468)	(0.0732)	(0.0047)
Equity return	1.2871***	1.3787***	1.2561***	1.3249***
	0.1043)	(0.0382)	(0.0613)	(0.0063)
R_t^i		−0.3548***		−0.3281***
		(0.0207)		(0.0064)
Pseudo-R^2	0.6714	0.9066	0.4206	0.9040

Notes: the R_t^i and the R_t^{system} are respectively the weekly market returns of the financial services index and the weekly market returns of the general index excluding the financial index.
*Significance at the 10% critical level.
**Significance at the 5% critical level.
***Significance at the 1% critical level.

Poland: banks

Variable	Quantile regression 1% R_t^i	Quantile regression 1% R_t^{system}	Quantile regression 50% R_t^i	Quantile regression 50% R_t^{system}
Volatility	−1.2853	−0.2600	0.2062	−0.1166
	(1.2868)	(0.4101)	(0.2884)	(0.0859)
Liquidity spread	−0.5227	−0.0073	0.0075	0.0265
	(0.3872)	(0.1033)	(0.0977)	(0.0234)
Three-month rate change	0.6493	0.0868	−0.0874	−0.1389
	(0.9271)	(0.3243)	(0.2030)	(0.0747)
Yield spread change	0.4940***	−0.0048	−0.0638	−0.0190*
	(0.1468)	(0.0567)	(0.0376)	(0.0092)
Equity return	1.2544***	1.6175***	1.0712***	1.6004*
	(0.1220)	(0.0598)	(0.0286)	(0.0239)
R_t^i		−0.5941***		−0.6181***
		(0.0400)		(0.0233)
Pseudo-R^2	0.6570	0.8759	0.5645	0.8572

Notes: the R_t^i and the R_t^{system} are respectively the weekly market returns of the banks index and the weekly market returns of the general index excluding the financial index.
*Significance at the 10% critical level.
**Significance at the 5% critical level.
***Significance at the 1% critical level.

Table 1 (Continued)

Poland: financial services

	Quantile regression 1%		Quantile regression 50%	
Variable	R_t^i	R_t^{system}	R_t^i	R_t^{system}
Volatility	−1.6784	−0.5244*	0.0468	0.0008
	(1.1358)	(0.2440)	(0.2013)	(0.0260)
Liquidity spread	−0.3985	−0.1169	0.0441	0.0312
	(0.2802)	(0.0707)	(0.1044)	(0.0201)
Three-month rate change	0.7467	−0.0656	0.0864	−0.0330
	(0.8109)	(0.1889)	(0.1945)	(0.0271)
Yield spread change	0.5197***	0.0960*	−0.0607	−0.0173
	(0.1418)	(0.0373)	(0.0419)	(0.0090)
Equity return	1.1911***	1.7164***	1.0153***	1.7947***
	(0.1360)	(0.0470)	(0.0270)	(0.0173)
R_t^i		−0.7526***		−0.8123***
		(0.0411)		(0.0161)
Pseudo-R^2	0.6948	0.9157	0.5876	0.9178

Notes: the R_t^i and the R_t^{system} are respectively the weekly market returns of the financial services index and the weekly market returns of the general index excluding the financial index.
*Significance at the 10% critical level.
**Significance at the 5% critical level.
***Significance at the 1% critical level.

Romania: banks

	Quantile regression 1%		Quantile regression 50%	
Variable	R_t^i	R_t^{system}	R_t^i	R_t^{system}
Volatility	−1.4403	0.3458	−0.6337	0.0361
	(1.2755)	(0.8352)	(0.3294)	(0.1310)
Liquidity spread	−1.8808	0.1307	0.0493	−0.0341
	(1.0993)	(0.3029)	(0.3197)	(0.0517)
Three-month rate change	−1.5584	0.0477	−0.0567	−0.0368
	(1.8411)	(0.3561)	(0.4360)	(0.0769)
Yield spread change	1.1922**	−0.0019	−0.1094	0.0217
	(0.3895)	(0.1768)	(0.1112)	(0.231)
Equity return	1.0925***	1.5570***	0.9175***	1.3678***
		(0.1103)	(0.0786)	(0.0211)
R_t^i		−0.5201***		−0.3889***
		(0.0815)		(0.0172)
Pseudo-R^2	0.6615	0.9271	0.4423	0.8572

Notes: the R_t^i and the R_t^{system} are respectively the weekly market returns of the banks index and the weekly market returns of the general index excluding the financial index.
*Significance at the 10% critical level.
**Significance at the 5% critical level.
***Significance at the 1% critical level.

Table 1 (Continued)

Romania: financial services

Variable	Quantile regression 1%		Quantile regression 50%	
	R_t^i	R_t^{system}	R_t^i	R_t^{system}
Volatility	−1.9274	−0.3478	−0.2637	0.0055
	(1.1703)	(0.2174)	(0.3707)	(0.0125)
Liquidity spread	−0.5855	−0.0976	−0.1592	0.0158
	(0.9897)	(0.0614)	(0.2865)	(0.0093)
Three-month rate change	−2.3288	−0.1111	−0.2578	0.0043
	(1.9277)	(0.1164)	(0.2589)	(0.0155)
Yield spread change	0.8933*	−0.0207	−0.0131	0.0010
	(0.3653)	(0.0319)	(0.0988)	(0.0034)
Equity return	1.2687***	1.5055***	0.9516***	1.5834***
	(0.1963)	(0.0329)	(0.0434)	(0.0124)
R_t^i		−0.4939***		−0.5792***
		(0.0300)		(0.0129)
Pseudo-R^2	0.7551	0.9784	0.5511	0.9578

Notes: the R_t^i and the R_t^{system} are respectively the weekly market returns of the financial services index and the weekly market returns of the general index excluding the financial index.
*Significance at the 10% critical level.
**Significance at the 5% critical level.
***Significance at the 1% critical level.

Turkey: banks

Variable	Quantile regression 1%		Quantile regression 50%	
	R_t^i	R_t^{system}	R_t^i	R_t^{system}
Volatility	−3.8876	−0.5620	0.7080	−0.1331
	(2.5255)	(0.8940)	(0.7637)	(0.3242)
Liquidity spread	0.0985	0.3736	0.4507	0.0461
	(0.5678)	(0.3204)	(0.3704)	(0.0933)
Three-month rate change	−0.1054	0.2031	0.5937	0.0374
	(0.8660)	0.3790)	(0.4975)	(0.1180)
Yield spread change	−0.0525	−0.1306	−0.0927	0.0052
	(0.3369)	(0.0940)	(0.1737)	(0.0394)
Equity return	1.3065***	1.8485***	1.2452***	1.7585***
	(0.1299)	(0.1595)	(0.0647)	(0.0478)
R_t^i		−0.9109***		−0.8017***
		(0.1172)		(0.0385)
Pseudo-R^2	0.7881	0.8982	0.6994	0.8538

Notes: the R_t^i and the R_t^{system} are respectively the weekly market returns of the banks index and the weekly market returns of the general index excluding the financial index.
*Significance at the 10% critical level.
**Significance at the 5% critical level.
***Significance at the 1% critical level.

Table 1 (Continued)

Turkey: insurance companies

Variable	Quantile regression 1%		Quantile regression 50%	
	R_t^i	R_t^{system}	R_t^i	R_t^{system}
Volatility	−8.3180*	−1.3265	−3.2190	0.0715
	(3.8619)	(1.5795)	(1.9185)	(0.8088)
Liquidity spread	−1.4839	0.6495	0.4576	−0.3037
	(1.6196)	(0.9220)	(0.6287)	(0.3212)
Three-month rate change	0.4649	−1.2836	0.8807	−0.6442
	(1.5596)	(0.7829)	(1.2879)	(0.4081)
Yield spread change	0.9536	−0.0904	0.0713	−0.0053
	(0.5683)	(0.2223)	(0.3438)	(0.1550)
Equity return	0.7338***	0.7746***	0.8917***	0.7011***
	(0.2062)	(0.1452)	(0.0824)	(0.0613)
R_t^i		0.0230		0.0396
		(0.0764)		(0.0462
Pseudo-R^2	0.6376	0.7468	0.2420	0.5963

Notes: the R_t^i and the R_t^{system} are respectively the weekly market returns of the insurances index and the weekly market returns of the general index excluding the financial index.
*Significance at the 10% critical level.
**Significance at the 5% critical level.
***Significance at the 1% critical level.

Turkey: financial services

Variable	Quantile regression 1%		Quantile regression 50%	
	R_t^i	R_t^{system}	R_t^i	R_t^{system}
Volatility	−3.3219	−0.8118*	−0.1035	−0.0120
	(2.0211)	(0.3303)	(0.8051)	(0.0596)
Liquidity spread	0.6936	0.0230	0.4031	0.0185
	(0.4364)	(0.1002)	(0.2901)	(0.0286)
Three-month rate change	0.5409	0.2051	0.5931	0.0060
	(0.6783)	(0.1280)	(0.3497)	(0.0227)
Yield spread change	0.2828	0.0835**	0.0833	0.0066
	(0.1912)	(0.0298)	(0.1266)	(0.0135)
Equity return	1.2325***	2.2176***	1.2195***	2.0792***
	(0.0885)	(0.0610)	(0.0486)	(0.0135)
R_t^i		−1.2002***		−1.0770***
		(0.0491)		(0.0124)
Pseudo-R^2	0.8425	0.9652	0.7528	0.9544

Notes: the R_t^i and the R_t^{system} are respectively the weekly market returns of the financial services index and the weekly market returns of the general index excluding the financial index.
*Significance at the 10% critical level.
**Significance at the 5% critical level.
***Significance at the 1% critical level.

Table 1 (Continued)

Honk Kong: banks

Variable	Quantile regression 1% R_t^i	Quantile regression 1% R_t^{system}	Quantile regression 50% R_t^i	Quantile regression 50% R_t^{system}
Volatility	−6.4697	0.0063	−1.2105	−0.2354
	(5.3042)	(1.0772)	(1.7889)	(1.0053)
Liquidity spread	−0.3221	−0.6134*	−0.9321	−0.0825
	(1.6357)	(0.2419)	(0.5022)	(0.04266)
Three-month rate change	−10.2197	3.2529	9.3180	3.4356
	(22.1665)	(6.4970)	(8.5954)	(4.9693)
Yield spread change	2.3856	−0.8598	−0.7804	0.0684
	(3.0190)	(0.4815)	(1.2976)	(0.6377)
Equity return	0.7047**	1.0348***	0.9624**	1.1181***
	(0.2373)	(0.0774)	(0.1222)	(0.0836)
R_t^i		−0.1527*		−0.1915*
		(0.0650)		(0.781)
Pseudo-R^2	0.6885	0.9131	0.5527	0.8125

Notes: the R_t^i and the R_t^{system} are respectively the weekly market returns of the banks index and the weekly market returns of the general index excluding the financial index.
*Significance at the 10% critical level.
**Significance at the 5% critical level.
***Significance at the 1% critical level.

Honk Kong: insurance companies

Variable	Quantile regression 1% R_t^i	Quantile regression 1% R_t^{system}	Quantile regression 50% R_t^i	Quantile regression 50% R_t^{system}
Volatility	7.1390	0.6249	6.9271	0.5473
	(7.7416)	(1.0574)	(4.0332)	(1.0892)
Liquidity spread	4.4245	−0.4020	0.3860	0.0562
	(3.5962)	(0.4112)	(1.4467)	(0.3890)
Three-month rate change	−14.7512	−8.2801	−38.1728*	3.0200
	(36.0537)	(7.8816)	(16.5155)	(5.1442)
Yield spread change	0.7080	−1.2734	−0.5889	0.1453
	(4.7174)	(0.7259)	(2.8018)	(0.6054)
Equity return	1.3910***	0.9199***	0.8995***	0.9984**
	(0.3490)	(0.0699)	(0.2452)	(0.0692)
R_t^i		−0.0207		−0.0557
		(0.0440)		(0.0660)
Pseudo-R^2	0.4611	0.8983	0.3685	0.7890

Notes: the R_t^i and the R_t^{system} are respectively the weekly market returns of the insurances index and the weekly market returns of the general index excluding the financial index.
*Significance at the 10% critical level.
**Significance at the 5% critical level.
***Significance at the 1% critical level.

Table 1 (Continued)

Honk Kong: financial services

Variable	Quantile regression 1% R_t^i	Quantile regression 1% R_t^{system}	Quantile regression 50% R_t^i	Quantile regression 50% R_t^{system}
Volatility	−5.5107	−0.1013	−0.4319	−0.0073
	(3.3442)	(0.0672)	(1.9190)	(0.0519)
Liquidity spread	1.0699	−0.0083	0.0454	−0.0010
	(1.2435)	(0.0321)	(0.6133)	(0.0222)
Three-month rate change	−0.0742	−0.1692	−7.6256	−0.0580
	(8.8936)	(0.3755)	(7.7663)	(0.2857)
Yield spread change	0.6623	0.0767	0.2261	0.0340
	(1.7609)	(0.0440)	(1.1742)	(0.0397)
Equity return	1.0069***	1.5387***	1.0832***	1.5465***
	(0.1402)	(0.0180)	(0.0867)	(0.0146)
R_t^i		−0.5413***		−0.5456***
		(0.0156)		(0.0148)
Pseudo-R^2	0.7615	0.9936	0.6996	0.9859

Notes: the R_t^i and the R_t^{system} are respectively the weekly market returns of the financial services index and the weekly market returns of the general index excluding the financial index.
*Significance at the 10% critical level.
**Significance at the 5% critical level.
***Significance at the 1% critical level.

Indonesia: banks

Variable	Quantile regression 1% R_t^i	Quantile regression 1% R_t^{system}	Quantile regression 50% R_t^i	Quantile regression 50% R_t^{system}
Volatility	−3.2923**	−0.2489	0.4656	0.0062
	(1.2000)	(0.1444)	(0.2754)	(0.105)
Liquidity spread	0.4887	0.0336	−0.0232	0.0047
	(0.3760)	(0.0437)	(0.0994)	(0.0066)
Three-month rate change	0.3704	−0.1826	−0.8251	−0.0154
	(1.6461)	(0.1548)	(0.9483)	(0.0300)
Yield spread change	−0.2493	−0.0126	−0.0146	0.0060*
	(0.2059)	(0.0290)	(0.0511)	(0.0028)
Equity return	0.9975***	1.3322***	1.0564***	1.3838***
	(0.011)	(0.0279)	(0.0286)	(0.0066)
R_t^i		−0.3565***		−0.3760***
		(0.0168)		(0.0058)
Pseudo-R^2	0.6578	0.9728	0.5336	0.9637

Notes: the R_t^i and the R_t^{system} are respectively the weekly market returns of the banks index and the weekly market returns of the general index excluding the financial index.
*Significance at the 10% critical level.
**Significance at the 5% critical level.
***Significance at the 1% critical level.

Table 1 (Continued)

Indonesia: financial services

Variable	Quantile regression 1%		Quantile regression 50%	
	R_t^i	R_t^{system}	R_t^i	R_t^{system}
Volatility	−3.2244**	−0.1314	0.3926	0.0056
	(1.0480)	(0.1109)	(0.2370)	(0.0039)
Liquidity spread	0.1384	0.0665**	−0.0099	0.0005
	(0.3664)	(0.0254)	(0.0967)	(0.0038)
Three-month rate change	0.2979	−0.1401	−0.8276	−0.0057
	(1.6392)	(0.0863)	(0.0509)	(0.0219)
Yield spread change	−0.0576	−0.0257	−0.0149	0.0008
	(0.1835)	(0.0183)	(0.0486)	(0.0008)
Equity return	0.9703***	1.3796***	1.0304***	1.4050***
	(0.0881)	(0.0160)	(0.0266)	(0.0019)
R_t^i		−0.3826***		−0.4051***
		(0.0110)		(0.0019)
Pseudo-R^2	0.6724	0.9811	0.5436	0.9792

Notes: The R_t^i and the R_t^{system} are respectively the weekly market returns of the financial services index and the weekly market returns of the general index excluding the financial index.
*Significance at the 10% critical level.
**Significance at the 5% critical level.
***Significance at the 1% critical level.

Korea: banks

Variable	Quantile regression 1%		Quantile regression 50%	
	R_t^i	R_t^{system}	R_t^i	R_t^{system}
Volatility	−4.2649***	−0.0725	−0.3687	−0.0689
	(1.2408)	(0.1636)	(0.4145)	(0.0410)
Liquidity spread	−10.1465***	0.0598	−0.9035	0.1287
	(1.9950)	(0.2721)	(1.1486)	(0.0067)
Three-month rate change	2.7933	0.3784	3.3108	0.1232
	(5.6895)	(0.7271)	(0.4319)	(0.2402)
Yield spread change	0.8920*	0.0444	0.3624	−0.0023
	(0.4357)	(0.0825)	(0.2454)	(0.0140)
Equity return	0.8214***	1.1502***	1.0683***	1.1384***
	(1.1298)	(0.0160)	(0.1017)	(0.0065)
R_t^i		−0.1536***		−0.1413***
		(0.0110)		(0.0062)
Pseudo-R^2	0.5797	0.9610	0.3132	0.9349

Notes: the R_t^i and the R_t^{system} are respectively the weekly market returns of the banks index and the weekly market returns of the general index excluding the financial index.
*Significance at the 10% critical level.
**Significance at the 5% critical level.
***Significance at the 1% critical level.

Table 1 (Continued)

Korea: insurance companies

Variable	Quantile regression 1%		Quantile regression 50%	
	R_t^i	R_t^{system}	R_t^i	R_t^{system}
Volatility	1.7094	−0.6666	0.3917	0.0381
	(2.4170)	(0.3524)	(0.7364)	(0.0563)
Liquidity spread	−1.8349	−0.0824	−2.4150	0.0722
	(4.5279)	(0.3308)	(1.6430)	(0.1544)
Three-month rate change	7.3084	−1.0449	1.3844	−0.2523
	(7.0853)	(1.1396)	(3.9024)	(0.3798)
Yield spread change	1.0504	0.0381	0.2667	−0.0264
	(1.4071)	(0.0972)	(0.2748)	(0.0317)
Equity return	1.1320***	1.0156***	0.7525***	1.0244***
	(1.4071)	(0.0272)	(0.0662)	(0.0131)
R_t^i		−0.0573***		−0.0500***
		(0.0231)		(0.0073)
Pseudo-R^2	0.4840	0.9152		0.2324

Notes: the R_t^i and the R_t^{system} are respectively the weekly market returns of the financial services index and the weekly market returns of the general index excluding the financial index.
*Significance at the 10% critical level.
**Significance at the 5% critical level.
***Significance at the 1% critical level.

Korea: financial services

Variable	Quantile regression 1%		Quantile regression 50%	
	R_t^i	R_t^{system}	R_t^i	R_t^{system}
Volatility	−4.4326*	0.1269	0.1283	−0.0012
	(2.0750)	(0.0650)	(0.3841)	(0.0071)
Liquidity spread	0.9476	−0.3003	−0.2612	0.0155
	(2.7630)	(0.2117)	(0.8166)	(0.0140)
Three-month rate change	12.8915	−0.1132	3.1132	0.0816**
	(11.1145)	(0.3144)	(2.1022)	(0.0303)
Yield spread change	−1.0793*	0.0168	0.0736	−0.0013
	(0.5259)	(0.0392)	(0.1461)	(0.0034)
Equity return	0.8221***	1.2099**	1.0387***	1.2033***
	(0.1560)	(0.0089)	(0.529)	(0.0035)
R_t^i		−0.2165***		−0.2033***
		(0.0106)		(0.0034)
Pseudo-R^2	0.6058	0.9823	0.4305	0.9798

Notes: the R_t^i and the R_t^{system} are respectively the weekly market returns of the banks index and the weekly market returns of the general index excluding the financial index.
*Significance at the 10% critical level.
**Significance at the 5% critical level.
***Significance at the 1% critical level.

Table 1 (Continued)

Malaysia: banks

	Quantile regression 1%		Quantile regression 50%	
Variable	R_t^i	R_t^{system}	R_t^i	R_t^{system}
Volatility	−2.2497*	−0.2664***	0.0831	0.0085
	(0.9671)	(0.0773)	(0.2538)	(0.0234)
Liquidity spread	−0.9803	0.0217	0.0543	−0.0081
	(0.5182)	(0.0452)	(0.1297)	(0.0123)
Three-month rate change	2.5564	0.3685	0.3916	0.1021
	(1.6235)	(0.2200)	(0.6910)	(0.0878)
Yield spread change	0.1223	−0.0524	0.1034	0.0112
	(0.5612)	(0.0317)	(0.0968)	(0.0104)
Equity return	1.0876***	1.2730***	1.0047***	1.2638***
	(0.1172)	(0.0117)	(0.0362)	(0.0075)
R_t^i		−0.3016***		−0.2867***
		(0.0100)		(0.0061)
Pseudo-R^2	0.6848	0.9702	0.5161	0.9482

Notes: the R_t^i and the R_t^{system} are respectively the weekly market returns of the banks index and the weekly market returns of the general index excluding the financial index.
*Significance at the 10% critical level.
**Significance at the 5% critical level.
***Significance at the 1% critical level.

Malaysia: insurance companies

	Quantile regression 1%		Quantile regression 50%	
Variable	R_t^i	R_t^{system}	R_t^i	R_t^{system}
Volatility	−11.3252***	−0.9666***	0.0472	−0.0461
	(3.9085)	(0.2894)	(0.4699)	(0.1323)
Liquidity spread	1.2972	−0.1772*	0.2092	−0.0100
	(1.7761)	(0.0853)	(0.2984)	(0.0418)
Three-month rate change	6.9709	−0.9004	−0.5689	0.0334
	(9.5411)	(0.6551)	(1.7372)	(0.2633)
Yield spread change	−1.0521	−0.2167*	−0.0502	−0.0313
	(1.0338)	(0.1031)	(0.2231)	(0.0377)
Equity return	0.8019*	0.9673***	0.6289***	0.9585***
	(0.4018)	(0.0249)	(0.0972)	(0.0142)
R_t^i		−0.0582***		0.0068
		(0.0172)		(0.0104)
Pseudo-R^2	0.2640	0.9098	0.1263	0.8239

Notes: the R_t^i and the R_t^{system} are respectively the weekly market returns of the insurances index and the weekly market returns of the general index excluding the financial index.
*Significance at the 10% critical level.
**Significance at the 5% critical level.
***Significance at the 1% critical level.

Table 1 (Continued)

Malaysia: financial services

	Quantile regression 1%		Quantile regression 50%	
Variable	R_t^i	R_t^{system}	R_t^i	R_t^{system}
Volatility	−1.2280	−0.0249	0.0009	0.0020
	(0.9452)	(0.0301)	(0.2953)	(0.0031)
Liquidity spread	−0.6430	−0.0147	0.0602	−0.0007
	(0.4447)	(0.0116)	(0.1147)	(0.0012)
Three-month rate change	1.9435	−0.0912	0.0413	−0.0038
	(2.0258)	(0.0565)	(0.5670)	(0.0094)
Yield spread change	0.3457	−0.0093	0.0821	0.0000
	(0.4210)	(0.0087)	(0.1072)	(0.0010)
Equity return	1.2681***	1.3351***	1.0936***	1.3547***
	(0.1248)	(0.0072)	(0.0240)	(0.034)
R_t^i		−0.3365***		−0.3548***
		(0.0062)		(0.0034)
Pseudo-R^2	0.7323	0.9930	0.5879	0.9911

Notes: the R_t^i and the R_t^{system} are respectively the weekly market returns of the financial services index and the weekly market returns of the general index excluding the financial index.
*Significance at the 10% critical level.
**Significance at the 5% critical level.
***Significance at the 1% critical level.

Philippines: banks

	Quantile regression 1%		Quantile regression 50%	
Variable	R_t^i	R_t^{system}	R_t^i	R_t^{system}
Volatility	−2.8536*	0.0330	−0.3156	−0.0716
	(1.2027)	(0.3819)	(0/2731)	(0.0563)
Liquidity spread	0.1106	−0.0381	−0.0161	−0.0250
	(0.2020)	(0.0621)	(0.0715)	(0.0186)
Three-month rate change	−0.9939	0.1973	−0.1596	−0.0173
	(0.5172)	(0.2682)	(0.3305)	(0.0440)
Yield spread change	−0.0411	−0.0964*	−0.0843	−0.0142
	(0.1129)	(0.0435)	(0.0479)	(0.0124)
Equity return	0.8156***	1.2403***	0.9278***	1.2280***
	(0.1129)	(0.0544)	(0.0317)	(0.0151)
R_t^i		−0.3201***		−0.2814***
		(0.0499)		(0.0141)
Pseudo-R^2	0.6245	0.8835	0.4605	0.8321

Notes: the R_t^i and the R_t^{system} are respectively the weekly market returns of the banks index and the weekly market returns of the general index excluding the financial index.
*Significance at the 10% critical level.
**Significance at the 5% critical level.
***Significance at the 1% critical level.

Table 1 (Continued)

Philippines: financial services

Variable	Quantile regression 1% R_t^i	Quantile regression 1% R_t^{system}	Quantile regression 50% R_t^i	Quantile regression 50% R_t^{system}
Volatility	−1.7896	−0.1513	−0.0743	0.0011
	(1.1239)	(0.1286)	(0.2459)	(0.0176)
Liquidity spread	0.5203***	0.0311	−0.0072	0.0063
	(0.1414)	(0.0446)	(0.0467)	(0.0053)
Three-month rate change	−0.9265	−0.0778	0.0446	−0.0079
	(0.8356)	(0.0720)	(0.2432)	(0.0261)
Yield spread change	0.1463	−0.0896**	−0.0016	0.0040
	(0.0904)	(0.0289)	(0.0428)	(0.0043)
Equity return	0.9154***	1.4566***	1.0753***	1.4828***
	(0.0745)	(0.0225)	(0.0307)	(0.0225)
R_t^i		−0.4879***		−0.4840***
		(0.0263)		(0.0221)
Pseudo-R^2	0.7094	0.9491	0.5920	0.9419

Notes: the R_t^i and the R_t^{system} are respectively the weekly market returns of the financial services index and the weekly market returns of the general index excluding the financial index.
*Significance at the 10% critical level.
**Significance at the 5% critical level.
***Significance at the 1% critical level.

Singapore: banks

Variable	Quantile regression 1% R_t^i	Quantile regression 1% R_t^{system}	Quantile regression 50% R_t^i	Quantile regression 50% R_t^{system}
Volatility	−5.6314***	−1.1196**	0.5068	0.2346***
	(1.3706)	(0.2838)	(0.3116)	(0.0707)
Liquidity spread	−3.4250	0.0489	0.0791	−0.0041
	(1.9306)	(0.2368)	(0.2528)	(0.0594)
Three-month rate change	−0.6569	−0.2836	−1.6337	0.2474
	(2.5854)	(0.6978)	(0.9175)	(0.2248)
Yield spread change	0.8717*	0.0202	0.0656	0.0210
	(0.3481)	(0.0983)	(0.0676)	(0.0186)
Equity return	1.4728*	1.2406***	1.1272***	1.2935***
	(0.1460)	(0.0335)	(0.0469)	(0.0192)
R_t^i		−0.3135***		−0.3203***
		(0.0231)		(0.0175)
Pseudo-R^2	0.6262	0.8732	0.4706	0.8339

Notes: the R_t^i and the R_t^{system} are respectively the weekly market returns of the banks index and the weekly market returns of the general index excluding the financial index.
*Significance at the 10% critical level.
**Significance at the 5% critical level.
***Significance at the 1% critical level.

Table 1 (Continued)

Singapore: insurance companies

	Quantile regression 1%		Quantile regression 50%	
Variable	R_t^i	R_t^{system}	R_t^i	R_t^{system}
Volatility	−9.6197**	−2.5613**	−0.0483	0.0680
	(3.6951)	(0.7753)	(0.4554)	(0.0799)
Liquidity spread	1.6195	−0.1287	−0.4837	0.0530
	(1.2065)	(0.5499)	(0.3491)	(0.0721)
Three-month rate change	6.7470	−1.1680	0.7206	0.7253**
	(4.0473)	(0.8008)	(1.1381)	(0.2621)
Yield spread change	−0.5644	−0.0406	0.0874	−0.0325
	(0.5392)	(0.1594)	(0.1016)	(0.0282)
Equity return	0.2743	0.9620***	0.3989***	0.9472***
	(0.3033)	(0.0576)	(0.0578)	(0.0161)
R_t^i		−0.0793*		−0.0336**
		(0.0332)		(0.0116)
Pseudo-R^2	0.3160	0.7606	0.0757	0.7224

Notes: the R_t^i and the R_t^{system} are respectively the weekly market returns of the insurances index and the weekly market returns of the general index excluding the financial index.
*Significance at the 10% critical level.
**Significance at the 5% critical level.
***Significance at the 1% critical level.

Singapore: financial services

	Quantile regression 1%		Quantile regression 50%	
Variable	R_t^i	R_t^{system}	R_t^i	R_t^{system}
Volatility	−5.0329*	−0.8242***	−0.1750	−0.0002
	(2.1215)	(0.2304)	(0.1800)	(0.0090)
Liquidity spread	−3.6533*	−0.7685	−0.0495	−0.0079
	(1.8492)	(0.4114)	(0.1110)	(0.0113)
Three-month rate change	−1.6315	−0.5365	−1.4013*	−0.0600
	(2.4357)	(0.4904)	(0.6557)	(0.0321)
Yield spread change	0.5336	−0.0016	0.0446	0.0033
	(0.3390)	(0.0406)	(0.5465)	(0.0021)
Equity return	1.2696***	1.5332***	1.1139***	1.5856***
	(0.1125)	(0.0618)	(0.0287)	(0.0082)
R_t^i		−0.5348***		−0.5850***
		(0.0581)		(0.0085)
Pseudo-R^2	0.6654	0.9225	0.6163	0.9563

Notes: the R_t^i and the R_t^{system} are respectively the weekly market returns of the financial services index and the weekly market returns of the general index excluding the financial index.
*Significance at the 10% critical level.
**Significance at the 5% critical level.
***Significance at the 1% critical level.

Table 1 (Continued)

Thailand: banks

	Quantile regression 1%		**Quantile regression 50%**	
Variable	R_t^i	R_t^{system}	R_t^i	R_t^{system}
Volatility	−0.4978	0.0789*	0.2956	0.0181
	(1.1203)	(0.0401)	(0.3679)	(0.0173)
Liquidity spread	2.6328*	0.1177	−0.5904	−0.0009
	(1.1124)	(0.0780)	(0.5078)	(0.0356)
Three-month rate change	0.6211	0.2862	1.1425	0.0270
	(4.2454)	(0.1505)	(2.0214)	(0.0605)
Yield spread change	0.3933	−0.0008	−0.0329	0.0122
	(0.2505)	(0.0147)	(0.1025)	(0.0067)
Equity return	1.0958***	1.3149***	1.0352***	1.3082***
	(0.1402)	(0.0103)	(0.0305)	(0.0058)
R_t^i		−0.3149***		−0.3067***
		(0.0099)		(0.0046)
Pseudo-R^2	0.7052	0.9819	0.5491	0.9646

Notes: the R_t^i and the R_t^{system} are respectively the weekly market returns of the banks index and the weekly market returns of the general index excluding the financial index.
*Significance at the 10% critical level.
**Significance at the 5% critical level.
***Significance at the 1% critical level.

Thailand: insurance companies

	Quantile regression 1%		**Quantile regression 50%**	
Variable	R_t^i	R_t^{system}	R_t^i	R_t^{system}
Volatility	−3.2089	−0.6079	−0.0301	0.0768
	(2.6942)	(0.3370)	(0.5916)	(0.1163)
Liquidity spread	−10.1392**	0.6455	−0.3401	0.2406
	(3.8848)	(0.4466)	(0.5176)	(0.1736)
Three-month rate change	−21.1113*	−1.2609	0.8836	−0.7231
	(9.2554)	(−1.5294)	(1.8312)	(0.5840)
Yield spread change	1.8403*	0.0261	0.1847	−0.0071
	(0.8385)	(0.1041)	(0.1147)	(0.0335)
Equity return	0.6952***	0.8895***	0.2132	0.9803***
	(0.2022)	(0.0470)	(0.1134)	(0.0131)
R_t^i		0.0138		0.0018
		(0.0144)		(0.0069)
Pseudo-R^2	0.4416	0.8977	0.0127	0.8215

Notes: the R_t^i and the R_t^{system} are respectively the weekly market returns of the insurances index and the weekly market returns of the general index excluding the financial index.
*Significance at the 10% critical level.
**Significance at the 5% critical level.
***Significance at the 1% critical level.

Table 1 (Continued)

Thailand: financial services

	Quantile regression 1%		Quantile regression 50%	
Variable	R_t^i	R_t^{system}	R_t^i	R_t^{system}
Volatility	−0.7821	−0.0604	−0.0618	0.0027
	(0.8500)	(0.0561)	(0.3406)	(0.0032)
Liquidity spread	0.9903	0.0372	−0.7055	0.0153
	(1.0879)	(0.0804)	(0.4923)	(0.0083)
Three-month rate change	−0.5807	−0.0700	2.5191	0.0045
	(4.0308)	(0.1839)	(1.7136)	(0.0217)
Yield spread change	0.2186	−0.0161	0.0214	0.0004
	(0.2491)	(0.0218)	(0.1423)	(0.0015)
Equity return	1.1214***	1.3569***	1.0626***	1.3297***
	(0.1282)	(0.0140)	(0.0347)	(0.7921)
R_t^i		−0.3470***		−0.3299***
		(0.0101)		(0.0034)
Pseudo-R^2	0.7495	0.9856	0.5662	0.9801

Notes: the R_t^i and the R_t^{system} are respectively the weekly market returns of the financial services index and the weekly market returns of the general index excluding the financial index.
*Significance at the 10% critical level.
**Significance at the 5% critical level.
***Significance at the 1% critical level.

Results for the Mexican banking industry show that equity returns have a positive impact on the 1% quantile returns of the banking index. With respect to the banking index at 50% (normal state), we observe that equity returns still influence its return but in addition volatility also has a positive effect. Turning now to the General Index ex Financials 1% quantile returns, we note that liquidity spread and equity returns are statistically significant with a positive sign, whereas yield spread change and bank index total return are statistically significant with a negative sign. With respect to the 50% quantile returns for the General Index ex Financials, volatility and equity returns have a positive influence and bank index total return has a negative impact. The situation of the Mexican insurance industry is somehow weaker since the only statistically significant control variable is the equity return for the 1% and 50% quantile returns for the General Index ex Financials. Finally, our estimates for other financial services in Mexico show that both 1% and 50% quantile returns are positively impacted by equity returns for the General Index ex Financials, whereas the insurance index total return has no statistically significant impact on the system variable.

The evidence for the four Central and Eastern European countries relies only on the banking industry and the other financial services industry since no insurance index is available. Looking at the banking industry of the Czech Republic, we see that the 1% quantile returns of the banking index are influenced positively by the three-month rate change and the equity returns and negatively by volatility. In the case of the banking index at the 50% quantile returns, only the equity return has a statistically significant impact. For the case of the 1% and 50% quantile returns of the General Index ex Financials, the yield spread change and equity returns enter positively and the bank index total returns negatively and equity returns positively and bank index returns negatively, respectively. The banking index of Hungary, Poland, and Romania exhibits very similar patterns with respect to the variables that influence the banking index and the General Index ex Financials at the 1% and 50% quantile returns, although in the case of Poland and Romania the three-month rate change is not statistically significant.

Looking at the financial services industry for the Czech Republic, our results indicate that the financial services 1% quantile returns are negatively related to volatility and the three-month rate change and positively to equity returns. The 50% quantile returns are only positively related to equity returns. The General Index ex Financials 1% and 50% are positively influenced by equity returns and negatively by the financial index total return, whereas in addition the 50% quantile returns are influenced by the yield spread change. Hungary's 1% and 50% quantile returns for the financial services index are similar to those of the Czech Republic, but in addition volatility is also statistical by significant with a negative sign. The same holds for the 1% and 50% for the General Index ex Financials. Poland and Romania exhibit minor differences from the results obtained for the Czech Republic and Hungary since the volatility variable has no influence on the 1% and 50% for the financial services index. The results for the 1% and 50% quantile returns of the General Index ex Financials show no significant statistically significant results.

Results for the Turkish banking industry indicate that only equity returns positively influence the bank index at the 1% and 50% quantile returns and the same evidence holds for both estimated quantiles for the General Index ex Financials. Turning our attention to the insurance industry, we observe that at the 1% quantile returns of the insurance index, volatility enters significantly with a negative sign and the equity returns affect this index positively. In the 50% quantile returns, only the equity returns have a positive impact. In the case of the General Index ex Financials, the equity returns are the only variable that influences in a positive way at both the 1% and 50% quantile returns. Finally, our estimates for the other financial services in Turkey indicate that both the 1% and 50% quantile returns for the financial services index are negatively influenced by the equity returns. Concerning the General Index ex Financials, the volatility and the financial services total returns negatively influence and yield spread change and equity returns positively influence at the 1% quantile returns, whereas at the 50% quantile returns, equity returns have a positive impact and the financial services total returns influence in a negative manner.

Finally, we discuss the evidence from Southeast Asia. For the case of Indonesia and the Philippines, we only consider the effects of the banking and other financial services industries. For the case of the banking sector in Hong Kong, we observe that for both the

1% and 50% quantile returns the equity returns positively influence the banking index. For both the 1% and the 50% of the General Index ex Financials, the equity returns have a positive impact and the liquidity spread and the banking sector total return have a negative impact. In addition for the 1% quantile returns there is a negative effect by liquidity spread. Similar results were obtained for Indonesia, Korea, Malaysia, the Philippines, Singapore, and Thailand. Furthermore, in these markets the liquidity spread change and volatility also play an important role.

The results for the insurance industry are summarized as follows. In Hong Kong, for both the 1% and 50% quantile returns, equity returns positively affect the insurance index and for the latter case, the index is also influenced negatively by the three-month rate change. For the 1% and 50% quantile returns for the General Index ex Financials index, only the equity returns positively affect the insurance index. The results for the insurance industry in Korea, Malaysia, Singapore, and Thailand are similar. In Korea, Malaysia, and Singapore, the insurance index total return enters significantly in the 1% and 50% quantile returns of the General Index ex Financials.

Finally, our estimates for other financial services in Hong Kong at the 1% and 50% quantile returns of the insurance index are influenced positively by the equity returns. For the General Index ex Financials both at the 1% and 50% quantile returns, the equity returns have a positive impact and the financial services total return has a negative effect. Similar results hold for Malaysia and Thailand. In addition, for the case of Indonesia, Korea, the Philippines, and Singapore, the liquidity spread has a positive impact at the 1% quantile returns, whereas the coefficient of volatility is negative and statistically significant.

4.2. ΔCôVaR Estimates

In this section, we present and discuss the ΔCôVaR estimates based on our presentation in Section 3. We define that a ΔCôVaR with a value of zero implies that none of the three financial industries contributes to the systemic risk. Therefore, if the value is different from zero, we then consider the case that the financial industry which has the larger absolute estimate of ΔCôVaR is taken to be the sector that contributes relatively the most to systemic risk in periods of distress.

In Table 2, we report descriptive statistics of the estimated ΔCôVaR. We observe that for Mexico, the Czech Republic, Hungary, Romania, Hong Kong, Indonesia, the Philippines, and Thailand, the absolute value of the estimated ΔCôVaR conditional to the banking sector is larger than the corresponding values for the insurance and other financial services industries. This finding suggests that when a distress situation occurred in the banking industry, it will increase the value of the VaR in those emerging markets as a whole compared with the normal state. Looking at the cases of Poland, Turkey, Korea, and Singapore, it is documented that the estimated ΔCôVaR conditional to the financial services industry has the larger absolute value and therefore it is the segment of

Table 2 ΔCôVaR estimates.

Mexico

	1996–2013		1996–2007		2008–2013	
	Mean	Standard deviation	Mean	Standard deviation	Mean	Standard deviation
ΔCoVaR banks	−0.227	0.137	0.005	0.093	−0.165	0.192
ΔCoVaR insurances	−0.003	0.030	0.006	0.080	−0.014	0.120
ΔCoVaR financial services	0.002	0.025	−0.033	0.107	0.065	0.218

Czech Republic

	1999–2013		1999–2007		2008–2013	
	Mean	Standard deviation	Mean	Standard deviation	Mean	Standard deviation
ΔCoVaR banks	1.390	0.602	−0.024	0.223	1.155	0.882
ΔCoVaR financial services	0.838	0.691	0.619	0.296	1.208	0.854

Hungary

	1999–2013		1999–2007		2008–2013	
	Mean	Standard deviation	Mean	Standard deviation	Mean	Standard deviation
ΔCoVaR banks	−0.814	1.028	−0.498	0.372	−2.038	0.773
ΔCoVaR financial services	−0.610	0.988	−0.231	0.354	−1.583	0.563

Poland

	1999–2013		1999–2007		2008–2013	
	Mean	Standard deviation	Mean	Standard deviation	Mean	Standard deviation
ΔCoVaR banks	0.084	0.857	0.201	0.471	0.020	0.525
ΔCoVaR financial services	−0.343	0.949	0.371	0.939	0.984	1.512

Table 2 (Continued)

Romania

	1996–2013		1996–2007		2008–2013	
	Mean	Standard deviation	Mean	Standard deviation	Mean	Standard deviation
ΔCoVaR banks	2.429	1.543	0.044	0.444	2.523	1.593
ΔCoVaR financial services	1.767	1.332	0.084	0.849	1.605	1.143

Turkey

	1996–2013		1996–2007		2008–2013	
	Mean	Standard deviation	Mean	Standard deviation	Mean	Standard deviation
ΔCoVaR banks	−0.060	0.575	−0.091	0.631	−0.012	0.403
ΔCoVaR insurances	0.043	0.415	0.020	0.432	0.008	0.291
ΔCoVaR financial services	−0.431	0.147	−0.139	0.061	−0.415	0.147

Hong Kong

	1996–2013		1996–2007		2008–2013	
	Mean	Standard deviation	Mean	Standard deviation	Mean	Standard deviation
ΔCoVaR banks	−1.695	0.247	−1.203	0.401	−1.895	0.247
ΔCoVaR insurances	−0.008	0.268	−0.032	0.135	0.005	0.273
ΔCoVaR financial services	0.004	0.130	0.015	0.090	1.543	1.145

Indonesia

	1998–2013		1998–2007		2008–2013	
	Mean	Standard deviation	Mean	Standard deviation	Mean	Standard deviation
ΔCoVaR banks	2.065	0.533	−0.405	0.368	1.499	0.942
ΔCoVaR financial services	1.197	0.537	−0.191	0.364	1.334	0.807

Table 2 (Continued)

Korea

	1996–2013		1996–2007		2008–2013	
	Mean	**Standard deviation**	**Mean**	**Standard deviation**	**Mean**	**Standard deviation**
ΔCoVaR banks	0.774	0.574	−0.638	0.360	0.376	0.365
ΔCoVaR insurances	−0.005	0.159	0.006	0.151	−0.905	0.441
ΔCoVaR financial services	1.163	0.472	0.800	0.527	1.294	0.538

Malaysia

	1996–2013		1996–2007		2008–2013	
	Mean	**Standard deviation**	**Mean**	**Standard deviation**	**Mean**	**Standard deviation**
ΔCoVaR banks	0.259	0.215	0.003	0.164	0.677	0.369
ΔCoVaR insurances	−0.766	0.213	−0.308	0.381	−2.019	0.332
ΔCoVaR financial services	−0.004	0.172	0.004	0.192	−0.0004	0.017

Philippines

	1998–2013		1998–2007		2008–2013	
	Mean	**Standard deviation**	**Mean**	**Standard deviation**	**Mean**	**Standard deviation**
ΔCoVaR banks	0.633	0.334	−0.509	0.165	1.184	0.278
ΔCoVaR financial services	−0.482	0.352	1.050	0.454	−0.123	0.185

Singapore

	1998–2013		1998–2007		2008–2013	
	Mean	**Standard deviation**	**Mean**	**Standard deviation**	**Mean**	**Standard deviation**
ΔCoVaR banks	−0.256	0.517	1.240	0.704	1.517	0.600
ΔCoVaR insurances	−1.184	0.590	−2.222	0.964	1.449	0.683
ΔCoVaR financial services	2.159	1.995	1.444	1.189	2.271	0.730

Table 2 (Continued)

Thailand

	1996–2013		1996–2007		2008–2013	
	Mean	**Standard deviation**	**Mean**	**Standard deviation**	**Mean**	**Standard deviation**
ΔCoVaR banks	−0.221	0.189	−0.207	0.201	0.181	0.281
ΔCoVaR insurances	−0.003	0.388	0.002	0.202	0.0057	0.098
ΔCoVaR financial services	−0.000	0.0491	−0.105	0.090	0.008	0.154

Notes: all the figures above are in percentages.

the financial sector that contributes most to the systemic risk in these emerging markets. Finally, in Malaysia, the absolute value of the estimated ΔCôVaR conditional to the insurance industry has the larger absolute value which means that when this industry is in distress will contribute most to the systemic risk.

An additional interesting result we can derive from the results in Table 2 is that when we split the full sample into two periods, before and after the financial crisis with the year 2008 as the break point, then we note that the absolute values of the estimated ΔCôVaR for all cases in the period prior to the financial crisis are smaller compared with those obtained for the post-crisis period. This finding provides further evidence that the banking, insurance, and other financial services, when in distress, contribute more to the systemic risk as the financial crisis moves into full swing.

5. SUMMARY AND CONCLUDING REMARKS

The recent financial crisis led to the understanding that financial intermediary distress documented in extreme (tail) events tend to spill over to financial institutions, financial industries and through them to the whole economy. It was also made clear that such spillovers are the results of an increase in the risk-appetite of banks, insurances, and other financial services, either individually or at the industry level. Another important aspect of these negative effects is the need for a new regulatory framework that is currently under development within the context of Basle III in order to embody the main factors of systemic risk. Following the failure of the micro-prudential regulatory framework, there is now a shift to the development of macro-prudential regulations.

In this chapter, we adopt ΔCoVaR, a recent econometric methodology developed by Adrian and Brunnermeier (2011). This is a parsimonious measure of systemic risk that complements measures designed for individual financial institutions and extends risk measurement to allow for a macro-prudential approach. We implement this new measure of systemic risk on selected countries from three regions of emerging markets, namely, Latin America, Central and Eastern Europe, and Southeast Asia. Although recent studies investigate many aspects of the financial crisis in relation to developed economies, less research has been done with respect to emerging economies. Following Bernal et al. (2012), we do not study systemic risk in the context of individual financial institutions. We consider the contribution of the banking, insurance, and other financial services industries that may be in distress to the systemic risk. The ΔCoVaR analysis allows us to investigate the additional level of risk that the economy as a whole faces when at least one of the financial sectors is in distress.

We use weekly data for the period December 1995–February 2013 for Mexico, the Czech Republic, Hungary, Poland, Romania, Turkey, Hong Kong, Indonesia, Korea, Malaysia, the Philippines, Singapore, and Thailand. The main findings, based on estimation of 1% and 50% quantile regressions, show that equity returns are a key determinant in triggering systemic risk episodes. There is also evidence that volatility of the general index ex financials (system variable), liquidity spread, the three-month rate change, and yield spread have an effect although weaker. Furthermore, we show that for Mexico, the Czech Republic, Hungary, Romania, Hong Kong, Indonesia, the Philippines, and Thailand, it is the banking sector that contributes mostly to the systemic risk. In Malaysia, the insurance industry contributes most to the systemic risk, whereas in Poland, Turkey, Korea, and Singapore the highest percentage contribution to systemic risk is due to the other financial services. Finally, based on the results of ΔCoVaR estimates before and after 2008, it is observed for all emerging markets that the contribution of each financial industry to systemic risk increased after the unfolding of the crisis.

Our results are of interest to regulators since it is shown that the different financial industries have an important and negative impact on the economy as a whole. It is emphasized that regulatory authorities should be able to identify the different segments of the financial sector of the economy which represent different risks for the system. Therefore, there is a need for regulatory provisions to reduce the risk on the whole economy emanating from these financial industries being in distress.

ACKNOWLEDGMENTS

Kouretas acknowledges financial support from a Marie Curie Transfer of Knowledge Fellowship of the European Community's Sixth Framework Programme under Contract No. MTKD-CT-014288, as well as from the Research Committee of the University of Crete under Research Grant #2257. We thank Stelios Bekiros, Manthos Delis, Dimitris Georgoutsos Jean-Yves Gnabo, and Christos Tsoumas for many helpful comments and discussions. Theodoros Bratis, Elpianna Emmanouilidi, and Evangelos Salachas provided superb research assistance. We also thank Marcus Brunnermeier and Jean-Yves Gnabo for providing us with the STATA codes for estimating CoVaR. The usual caveat applies.

REFERENCES

Acharya, V.V., Richardson, M., 2009. Restoring Financial Stability: how to Repair a Failed System. John Wiley and Sons, New York

Acharya, V.V., Pedersen, L.H., Philippon, T., Richardson, M.P., 2010. Measuring systemic risk. New York University, Working Paper.

Acharya, V.V., Engle, R., Richardson, M., 2012. Capital shortfall: a new approach to ranking and regulating systemic risk. American Economic Review 102, 59–64

Adrian, T., Brunnermeier, M.K., 2011. CoVaR, NBER Working Paper No, 17454.

Agrippino, S.M., 2009. Measuring risk contagion and interdependence, Bocconi University, Department of Economics, Working Paper.

Alessi, L., Detken, C., 2009. Real time early warning indicators for costly asset price boom/bust cycles: a role for global liquidity, European Central Bank Working Paper 1039.

Alfaro, R., Drehmann, M., 2009. Macro stress tests and crises: what can we learn? BIS Quarterly Review, 29–41 December

Arnold, B., Borio, C., Ellis, L., Moshirian, F., 2012. Systemic risk, macroprudential policy frameworks, monitoring financial systems and the evolution of capital adequacy. Journal of Banking and Finance 36, 3125–3132

Barth, J., Caprio, G., 2006. Rethinking Bank Regulation: Till Angels Govern. Cambridge University Press, Cambridge

Bernal, O., Guilmin, G., Gnabo, J-Y., 2012. Assessing the Contribution of Banks, Insurances and Other Financial Services to Systemic Risk, Mimeo.

Bisias, D., Flood, M., Lo, A.W., Valavanis, S., 2012. A survey of systemic risk analytics. U.S., Department of Treasury, Office of Financial Research, Working Paper No 1.

Bjarnadottir, F., 2012. Implementation of CoVaR. A measure for systemic risk. KTH Royal Institute of Technology, Working Paper.

Borio, C., Drehmann, M., 2009. Assessing the risk of banking crisis-revisited. BIS Quartely Review, 29–46

Borio, C., Drehmann, M., Tsatsaronis, K., forthcoming. Stress-testing, macro-stress tests: does it live up to expectations? Journal of Financial Stability.

Borio, C., Lowe, P., 2002. Assessing the risk of banking crisis. BIS Quartely Review, 43–54

Brownlees, C.T., Engle, R.F., 2012. Volatility, correlation and tails for systemic risk measurement. New York University, Working Paper.

Brunnermeier, M., Pedersen, L.H., 2009. Market liquidity and funding liquidity. Review of Financial Studies 22, 2201–2238

Cerutti, E., Claessens, S., McGuire, P., 2011. Systemic risks in global banking: what available data can tell us and what more data are needed? IMF Working Paper 11/222.

Chan-Lau, J.A., 2008. Default risk codependence in the global financial system: was the bear stearns bailout justified? IMF and Tufts University, Working Paper.

Demirguc-Kunt, A., Kane, E., Laeven, L., 2009. Deposit Insurance Around the World: issues of Design and Implementation. MIT Press, Cambridge Mass

Demirguc-Kunt, A., Detragiache, E., 2011. Basel core principles and bank soundness: does compliance matter? Journal of Financial Stability 7, 179–190

Forbes, K., Rigobon, R., 2001. Measuring contagion: conceptual and empirical issues. In: Claasens, S., Forbes, K. (Eds.), International Financial Contagion. Kluwer Academic Publishers, Boston, pp. 43–66

Gauthier, C., Lehar, A., Souissi, M., 2012. Macroprudential capital requirements and systemic risk. Journal of Financial Intermediation 21, 594–618

Giesecke, K., Kim, B., 2011. Risk analysis of collateralized debt obligations. Operation Research 59, 32–49

Girardi, G., Ergün, T., 2013. Systemic risk measurement: multivariate GARCH estimation of CoVaR. Journal of Banking and Finance 37, 3169–3180

Goodhart, C., 2006. A framework for assessing financial stability? Journal of Banking and Finance 30, 3415–3422

Goodhart, C., Sunirand, P., Tsomocos, D., 2005. A risk assessment model for banks. Annals of Finance 1, 197–224

Goodhart, C., Sunirand, P., Tsomocos, D., 2006. A model to analyze financial fragility. Economic Theory 27, 107–142

Group of Ten, 2001. Report on consolidation in the financial sector. Bank for International Settlements, Basel, Switzerland.

Huang, X., Zhou, H., Zhu, H., 2009. A framework for assessing the systemic risk of major financial institutions. Journal of Banking and Finance 33, 2036–2049

Jorion, P., 2007. Value at Risk: the New Benchmark for Managing Financial Risk, 3rd ed. McGraw-Hill, New York

Khandani, A.E., Kim, A.J., Lo, A.W., 2010. Consumer credit risk models via machine-learning algorithms. Journal of Banking and Finance 34, 2767–2787

Klomp, J., de Haan, J., 2012. Banking risk and regulation: does one size fit all? Journal of Banking and Finance 36, 3197–3212

Koenker, R., 2005. Quantile Regression. Cambridge University Press, Cambridge

Koenker, R., Basset, G.W., 1978. Regression quantiles. Econometrica 46, 33–50

Lehar, A., 2005. Measuring systemic risk: a risk management approach. Journal of Banking and Finance 29, 2577–2603

Levine, R., 1997. Financial development and economic growth: views and agenda. Journal of Economic Literature 32, 668–726

Lopez-Espinoza, G., Moreno, A., Rubia, A., Valderrama, L., 2012a. Systemic risk and asymmetric responses in the financial industry, IMF Working Paper.

Lopez-Espinoza, G., Moreno, A., Rubia, A., Valderrama, L., 2012. Short-term wholesale funding and systemic risk: a global CoVaR approach. Journal of Banking and Finance 36, 3150–3162

Moreno, M.R., Peña, J.J., 2013. Systemic risk measures: the simpler the better? Journal of Banking and Finance 37, 1817–1831

Pritsker, M., 2000. The channels for financial contagion. In: Claessens, S., Forbes, K. (Eds.), International Financial Contagion. Kluwer Academic Publishers, Boston

Reinhart, C.M., Rogoff, K.S., 2009. This Time is Different: Eight Centuries of Financial Folly. Princeton University Press, Princeton

Roengpitya, R., Rungcharoenkitkul, P., 2011. Measuring systemic risk and financial linkages in the Thai banking system, Bank of Thailand Working Paper.

Segoviano, M.A., Goodhart, C., 2009. Banking stability measures, IMF Working Paper.

Stein, J.C., 2010. Securitization, shadow banking and financial fragility. Dedalus 139, 41–51

Sylvain, B., Colletaz, G., Hurlin, C., Pérignon, C., 2012. A theoretical and empirical comparison of systemic risk measures, Mimeo.

Wong, A., Fong, T., 2010. An analysis of the interconnectivity among the Asia-Pacific economies, Hong Kong Monetary Authority Working Paper.

Van Oordt, M., Zhou, C., 2010. Systematic risk under adverse conditions. De Nederlandsche Bank, Working Paper.

CHAPTER 13

An Empirical Study on Mutual Funds Performance Persistence in China

Dawei Chen, Christopher Gan, and Baiding Hu
Department of Accounting, Economics and Finance, Lincoln University, Canterbury, New Zealand

1. INTRODUCTION

Mutual funds, as one professionally managed investment vehicle, are becoming more and more important in the global capital market. They are generally managed by investment companies and large financial institutions to utilize the notion of pooled contributions (Elton and Gruber, 1995; Bodie et al., 2004). According to Jensen (1968), evaluating the "performance" of portfolios of risky investments has always been a central problem in finance. By investigating the portfolios' performance, the abilities of the portfolio manager to increase returns by correctly predicting the future and the abilities to minimize portfolios risk could be observed (Jensen, 1968). With the increasing importance of mutual funds in financial markets, the debate on the measurement of mutual fund performance persistence has been an ongoing issue since the 1960s.

The test of mutual fund performance persistence examines whether past winners could continuously outperform and past losers continuously have unfavorable performance. Hendricks et al. (1993) find the "hot hands" of mutual fund managers continuously generate superior performance. The phenomenon of performance persistence was confirmed by Goetzmann and Ibbotson (1994) and Brown and Goetzmann (1995) using contingency tables as a non-parametric methodology. Recently, Abdel-Kader and Kuang (2007) examine the performance of mutual funds in the Hong Kong market during the period from 1995 to 2005 based on two-year intervals. The authors confirm that mutual funds in the Hong Kong financial market could only perform persistently for both the winners and losers within a short time period.

On the other hand, Kahn and Rudd (1995) investigate performance persistence for equity funds managers that are publicly available in the US market from 1983 to 1993, and find no evidence of performance persistence among equity mutual funds. The results from Kahn and Rudd (1995) are consistent with Jensen (1968), Kritzman (1983), Dunn and Theisen (1983), and Elton et al. (1990). The authors suggest that persistence could be influenced more by managers rather than funds. Active managers could perform persistently with their good ideas, however, as the ideas become well known in the

Emerging Markets and the Global Economy
http://dx.doi.org/10.1016/B978-0-12-411549-1.00013-2

market, active managers could no longer beat the market to maintain their persistence. The conclusion from Kahn and Rudd (1995) is further confirmed by Rhodes (2000).

Previous studies have attempted to evaluate mutual fund performance persistence based on different market, using a variety of performance measurement techniques and adjustments for risk. The results are mixed. Most of the researches in mutual fund performance persistence focus on the US and UK stock markets, such as Goetzmann and Ibbotson (1994) and Allen and Tan (1999). However, no such similar study was conducted in the Chinese stock market, despite several studies having been conducted in terms of the application of capital assets pricing models and the Fama-French models. This study provides an overview of mutual funds performance persistence in China and investigates whether the performance persistence phenomenon exists in the Chinese mutual funds industry in both short term and long term. This study employs Goetzmann and Ibbotson's (1994) model and the research period covers January 2002 to December 2010. All open-end equity mutual funds are included in the sample, which is also free of survivorship bias. Equity open-end funds, which are terminated or merged into other funds before the end of 2010, are eliminated from the original sample. The main findings of this study are consistent with the previous results documented for the US stock market, and demonstrate that equity mutual funds in China could perform persistently in the short term but not in the long term.

This paper is organized as follows. Section 2 reviews existing literatures on mutual funds performance persistence. Section 3 discusses the data and research methodology. Section 4 presents the empirical finding and Section 5 concludes the study.

2. LITERATURE REVIEW

2.1. Persistence of Mutual Funds Performance

Early studies of persistence performance begin with Sharpe (1966) who compares the mutual fund performance in terms of the reward-to-volatility ratio (Sharpe ratio) between 1944 and 1953 and 1954 to 1963. The author ranks mutual funds using the Sharpe ratio and finds a correlation of 0.36 between the two periods with a *t*-ratio of 1.88. Sharpe (1966) also ranks the mutual fund performance in terms of Treynor's (1966) ratio for the same two decades. The volatility of a fund in Sharpe ratio, which measures its own risk, is replaced by the total volatility. The correlation between the two periods based on the Treynor ratio is 0.4008 with a *t*-ratio of 2.47. The difference in mutual fund performance in the continuous period can be predicted by both methods. The author concludes the phenomenon of mutual fund performance persistence might exist.

Goetzmann and Ibbotson (1994) use a sample of 276 mutual funds from 1976 to 1988 to examine whether past performance of mutual funds predicts future performance based on monthly returns. The authors argue that survivorship bias may exist but will not impact the results because the goal of the research is to compare surviving mutual funds to other survivors' performance rather than to measure whether funds outperform the indices. Based on the results, the authors suggest that at least 60% of winners repeat the superior performance in the next period by either one-year or two-year intervals. For the monthly persistence test, the authors adopt the bootstrap method. The results indicate the monthly returns are significantly predictable both in the short and long term. The authors conclude that investors can use past ranking of mutual fund performance to earn excess returns.

Brown and Goetzmann (1995) analyze the performance persistence of mutual funds using a sample of monthly data of 372 funds in 1976 and 829 funds in 1988. Brown and Goetzmann (1995) extend Goetzmann and Ibbotson's (1994) method to create contingency tables as a nonparametric methodology. In order to avoid the survivorship bias, Brown and Goetzmann (1995) modify the contingency tables which include data of disappearance,[1] new funds established, and missing data in each year. The cross-product ratio, which is the ratio of the number of repeat performers to the number in the rest of the sample, is the indicator of performance persistence. The results indicate mutual fund performance persistence exists; the performance pattern depends on the time period observed. The authors conclude the persistence phenomenon is a useful indicator for mutual funds investors, but the evidence of earning excess returns remains weak.

Malkiel (1995) follows Goetzmann and Ibbotson (1994) to analyze mutual fund performance persistence by constructing two-way contingency tables. Malkiel (1995) uses Jensen (1968) alpha as the measurement for equity funds performance. The author ranked the mutual funds every year from 1971 to 1991 using the funds' quarterly returns. Malkiel defined winners as the funds that achieve higher returns than the median of all funds' returns in a calendar year. Malkiel concludes that about 65.1% of mutual funds in the sample repeat their superior performance in the 1970s and 51.7% of winners remain strong in the 1980s. The phenomenon of performance persistence is also confirmed by either using one-quarter period or two-year period, where winners are defined as funds having positive alphas. On the other hand, the "hot hand" phenomenon did not exist significantly from 1980 to 1991, which is consistent with the results of Brown and Goetzmann's (1995) study.

Bollen and Busse (2005) employ the Carhart (1997) four-factor model and extend Treynor and Mazuy (1966) and Henriksson and Merton's (1981) market timing models with three additional explanatory variables (Book-to-Market, High-minus-Low, and Momentum) to compute the risk-adjusted returns (alphas) in the US market for 230 mutual funds from 1985 to 1995 on a daily basis. All funds in the sample are quarterly ranked by alphas into deciles and then an estimate of the performance of each decile is obtained in the subsequent periods. The results indicate that the successful mutual funds could continuously provide positive excess returns and mutual funds with

[1] "Disappearance" refers to mutual funds that have been delisted or merged into other mutual funds during or at the end of the research period (Brown and Goetzmann, 1995).

underperforming records might persistently produce unfavorable results. The authors then increase the evaluation period from one quarter to 1 year. The quarterly average excess returns of the top decile in the post-ranking quarter drop to 9 basis points, and the statistically insignificant result suggests no evidence of performance persistence could be found in the long term (Bollen and Busse, 2005). Similar results are obtained where mutual funds are ranked by returns instead of risk-adjusted returns. The authors argue that superior performance appears in short term only where some managers might be able to exploit information on advantages. The authors conclude the phenomenon of performance persistence exists and is a short-lived phenomenon after controlling for the momentum anomaly.

Benos and Jochec (2011) test mutual fund performance persistence in the short term using 448 US mutual funds from 1999 to 2007. The results indicate that only the top performing mutual funds and the poor performance mutual funds exhibit performance persistence. The authors argue that "winner-picking" strategy requires rebalancing quarterly, thus the abnormal returns earned by small investors would be offset by sales charges. On the other hand, by investing class-A fund shares, large investors might make profits since they are usually excused from fees if they hold the fund share for at least 1 year with a total amount of investment over one million dollars.

2.2. Non-Persistence of Mutual Funds Performance

Phelps and Detzel (1997) follow Goetzmann and Ibbotson's (1994) methodology to analyze performance persistence from 1983 to 1994 in the US stock market. Both nonparametric (two-way contingency table) and parametric (regression) methods are employed to test persistency for subsequent periods of equal length. Phelps and Detzel (1997) find performance persistence disappears if mutual funds' returns are adjusted for size and style characteristics. The authors argue that positive performance persistence is the result of persistence in broad equity classes (macro persistence) rather than sustainable managerial ability (micro persistence), and the macro persistence phenomenon in the 1980s and 1990s is the reason that leads to the general conclusion of performance persistence in other studies.

Brown et al. (1992) and Malkiel (1995) argue the results of mutual funds' superior performance and performance persistence might be due to survivorship bias in which merged or ceased operation funds are excluded in the research. Brown and Goetzmann (1995) find further evidence that the phenomenon of performance persistence would be partly attributed to mutual funds with poor performance. Quigley and Sinquefield's (2000) study in the UK market and Bauer et al. (2006) in the New Zealand market provide more evidence to suggest that performance persistence is driven by "icy hands" (poor performers) rather than "hot hands" (top performers).

Rhodes (2000) examines whether past investment performance repeats for UK unit trusts from 1981 to 1998. The author reports that small groups of funds may show performance persistence in the short term, especially for poorly performing funds, however, the general results suggest that there is no strong evidence for performance persistence in recent times (after 1987). The author explained that the reason funds managers could earn high return is that they can access information not widely spread and use the information better and faster than others. As a result, if the market is getting more efficient, which means the market can adjust to new information quickly and accurately reflect the true value, it gets more difficult for funds managers to persistently beat the market. Therefore, weak evidence of performance persistence was found in earlier times and no evidence of performance persistence in more recent times.

Bessler et al. (2010) investigate the factors impacting non-persistent performance of mutual funds by examining 3946 US equity mutual funds from 1992 to 2007. The authors find mutual funds that outperform the market could continuously perform well only if there are no high inflows or changes in the management structure, while mutual funds that underperform the market could significantly improve their performance where outflows occur and the manager is replaced. Bessler et al. (2010) argue that the past performance might be the only conditional indicator of future performance, and investors should pay more attention to fund flows and changes in the management structure in mutual funds.

2.3. Mixed Results of Performance Persistence

Allen and Tan (1999) test UK mutual fund performance persistence with a sample of weekly returns of 131 funds from 1989 to 1995. The UK fund managers return index is used as the benchmark. The authors employ Goetzmann and Ibbotson's (1994) two-way contingency tables to test persistence in the long run (over one-year or two-year intervals). The results indicate 56% of the funds repeat their above average performance measured by raw returns, and 59% of winners continuously perform well when performance is measured by risk-adjusted returns. In the short run (semi-annually and monthly), however, the evidence appears to reverse. In addition, three empirical tests, OLS regression of risk-adjusted excess returns and independent SRCC calculations, all provide little evidence to confirm the results.

Fletcher and Forbes (2002) examine the persistence in UK unit trust (open-end mutual funds) performance from 1982 to 1996. The sample contains monthly returns of 724 trusts and all selected trusts are equity objective. The Financial Times All Shares (FTA) index is used as the benchmark. The authors follow Jensen (1968), Carhart (1997), and Connor and Korajczyk (1991) methods to measure trust performance. The authors also follow Brown and Goetzmann's (1995) method to set up a two-way contingency table and calculate the log-odds ratio to test for performance persistence. Their results indicate significant performance persistence of trusts when performance is measured by the Capital Asset Pricing Model (CAPM) or Arbitrage Pricing Model (APT), but performance persistence is eliminated when performance is measured by the Carhart (1997) method. The authors argue that the performance persistence of UK trusts is not due to superior stock selection ability, but can be explained by factors that are known to capture cross-sectional differences in stock returns.

Busse et al. (2010) examine mutual fund performance persistence by investigating 4617 US equity funds from 1991 to 2008. The authors used Fama and French (1993) three-factor model and Carhart (1997) four-factor model, and their results reveal that the average excess returns are statistically insignificant from zero. For the performance persistence of mutual fund, the authors argue that the evidences of performance persistence are sensitive to the model selections. Further, modest evidence of performance persistence based on the three-factor model is found, but the result based on the four-factor model, conditional four-factor model, and seven-factor model shows little evidence of performance persistence.

3. METHODOLOGY

The equity mutual funds data for this study are obtained from CCER (China Centre for Economic Research at Beijing University) database. The CCER database provides a comprehensive coverage of the Chinese economy and capital markets' information and commits itself to be the world-leading Chinese financial information provider and analyst.[2] The dataset includes all open-end mutual funds from 2002 to 2010. Since the first open-end equity mutual fund was established in November 2001, this research covers the period from January 2002 to December 2010. No mutual funds have ceased operations or merged with other mutual funds during the study period. Qualified Foreign Institutional Investors (QFII), Exchange Traded Funds (ETF), Listed Open-end Funds (LOF), and index funds are excluded from the sample. The market index used in this research is S&P/CITIC indices, which is the only overall market index available in China. The S&P/CITIC indices cover both Shanghai and Shenzhen A-share markets (market capitalization-weighted indices) and consider other factors such as non-tradable shares, dividend reinvestment, large/small capitalization, and value/growth stock classifications. Following Drew et al. (2003) study, the one-year fixed deposit rate in the first month of each year is used as the risk-free rate. The fixed one-year deposit rates were obtained from the People's Bank of China.

This study follows Morningstar's (2007) method to calculate monthly returns of the mutual funds. Dividends are assumed to be paid and reinvested at dividend payment date for each fund. According to Bodie et al. (2004), a share split takes place when a corporation issues a given number of shares in exchange for the current number of shares held by investors. Following a share split, the number of shares outstanding increases and the price (net asset value) decreases. In order to calculate the monthly returns of funds accurately, share splits are also considered. Using monthly returns to estimate a single-index alpha

[2] See http://www.ccerdata.com/eng/AboutUs/About_Us.htm for more details.

(Jensen, 1968) has two distinct advantages. According to Mains (1977), the systematic risk coefficients can be estimated more efficiently and the bias of reinvestment can be reduced. Grinblatt and Titman (1989), Goetzmann and Ibbotson (1994), and Wermers (2000) use monthly returns to estimate the single-index alpha.

According to Jensen (1968) and Bodie et al. (2004), the monthly raw returns for each fund can be calculated using equation (1), where the funds' shares are not split:

$$R_{it} = \log_e \left(\frac{NAV_{it} + D}{NAV_{it-1}} \right), \tag{1}$$

where R_{it} represents the raw returns of fund i in month t, NAV_{it} is the net asset value at the end of month t, NAV_{it-1} is the net asset value at the end of month $t - 1$, D is the dividend and capital distribution of fund i in month t, under the assumption of zero fees and expenses.

Mains (1977) argues that annual mutual fund returns calculated by Jensen (1968) might be biased and lead to underestimate the funds' returns since mutual funds pay dividends quarterly. Mains assumes that dividends paid by mutual funds are reinvested at the end of the month. This might also be biased and underestimate the funds' returns. In order to accurately calculate monthly net returns of mutual funds, *NAV* at the end of the month, *NAV* at the end of the previous month, dividend payout ratio, and the *NAV* in which dividends are reinvested are taken into account. The formula provided by Morningstar (2007) is given as follows:

$$R_{it} = \log_e \left[\frac{NAV_{it}}{NAV_{it-1}} \times \prod_{j=1}^{m} \text{Ratio}_j \times \prod_{i=1}^{n} \left(1 + \frac{D_i}{N_i} \right) \right], \tag{2}$$

where R_{it} represents the monthly net returns of fund i in month t, NAV_{it} is the net asset value at the end of month t, NAV_{it-1} is the net asset value at the end of month $t - 1$, m is the number of times shares are split within a month, Ratio_j is the split ratio on the jth share split, n is the number of times cash dividend is paid out, D_i is the cash dividend paid out ratio on the ith cash dividend payout, and N_i is the net asset value in which dividends are reinvested, under the assumption of zero fees and expenses.[3]

[3] Most studies use quarterly or monthly return data for mutual funds in the US from CDA, Lipper, and Morningstar. Researchers calculate monthly returns for mutual funds only if the data source is provided by Wiesenberger. (For example, Bollen and Busse (2005), Elton et al. (1996), and Cai et al. (1997) describe the process of calculating monthly returns but did not provide the formula.)

Equation (2) is obtained from Morningstar (2007) mutual fund performance calculation. Unlike equation (1) it assumes dividends are reinvested at the end of the month, equation (2) assumes dividends are reinvested at *NAV* on the same day when dividends are paid out. It might be more accurate if a fund pays out dividends several times in a month. It also considers the effect of share splitting. Many funds split shares and pay out a dividend at the same time, and then the *NAV* is adjusted.

Jensen single-index alpha (Jensen, 1968) is employed to measure mutual fund performance as shown in equation (3):

$$R_{it} - R_{ft} = \alpha_i + \beta_i(R_{mt} - R_{ft}) + \varepsilon_{it}, \tag{3}$$

where R_{it} is the net return (gross return) of fund i in month t calculated from equations (2) and (3), R_{ft} is the risk-free rate in month t, R_{mt} is the return on the local equity benchmark in month t from A-Share composite index, α_i is the intercept term; and ε_{it} is the error term.

The single-index alpha (Jensen, 1968) is the intercept term in equation (3). It represents superior (inferior) performance of fund i if the alpha is greater (less) than zero. The regression assumes that the error terms are independently and normally distributed with a zero mean and constant variance for all observations. The single-index alpha for each fund is generated from equation (3). The research period for each of the funds starts from the month the fund was established until December 2010.

Elton et al. (1996) four-index model is also employed to measure mutual funds' performance. Elton et al. argue that since mutual funds might have specific investment objectives in stocks-specific characteristics such as growth or value, big-capitalization or small-capitalization, the risk-adjusted alpha would be more accurate after introducing more indexes to account for the markets' performance. The four-index model is shown in equation (4):

$$R_{it} - R_{ft} = \alpha_i + \beta_{iSP}(R_{mt} - R_{ft}) + \beta_s SMB_t + \beta_{gv} HML_t + \beta_b(R_{bt} - R_{ft}) + \varepsilon_{it}, \tag{4}$$

where α_i is a factor-adjusted alpha for fund i, R_{mt} is the return of S&P/CITIC Composite A-Share index in the month t, SMB_t is the return of the small-large index in the month t, and HML_t is the difference between returns of growth index and value index. The small-large index is formed by large-cap index subtracting small-cap index. Growth index is formed by averaging the large-cap, mid-cap, and small-cap stock growth indexes and subtracting the average of the large-cap, mid-cap, and small-cap stock value indexes, R_{bt} is the return of bond market index in the month t; and R_{ft} is the risk-free rate.

3.1. Non-Parametric Persistence Test Model

Mutual fund performance, for either a one-year (applied for short-term persistence test) or two-year interval (applied for long-term persistence test), is measured in both raw returns (net returns) and risk-adjusted returns. Monthly raw returns for each fund are compounded to create one-year or two-year cumulative returns as shown in equation (5), under the assumption of monthly reinvestment of income (Goetzmann and Ibbotson, 1994):

$$AR_{ip} = \prod_{t=1}^{t}(1 + R_{it}) - 1. \tag{5}$$

The risk-adjusted returns for one-year and two-year intervals are generated from equations (3) and (4). The risk-adjusted returns avoid the problem of differential expected returns between high-risk versus low-risk funds.

All funds are ranked by their prior interval performance (raw returns or risk-adjusted returns) from high to low. The "winners" are defined as funds that performed better than the median. The "losers," on the other hand, are defined as funds that are below the median performance. In the subsequent intervals, the same funds are ranked again by performance and winners/losers are defined by the same criterion. Only funds established before the test interval could be ranked and compared (Goetzmann and Ibbotson, 1994). In a non-parametric test, two-way contingency tables introduced by Goetzmann and Ibbotson (1994) are used to examine the performance persistence in different intervals. Four categories are included in the two-way contingency tables: winners/winners (*WW*), winners/losers (*WL*), losers/winners (*LW*), and losers/losers (*LL*). According to Goetzmann and Ibbotson (1994), the cross-product ratio (*CPR*) is the odd ratio of the number of repeat performers to the number of those that do not repeat shown in equation (6):

$$CPR = (WW * LL)/(WL * LW). \tag{6}$$

The repeat performers represent funds performing persistently from the prior interval to the subsequent interval; reverse performers do not continuously remain in the same category in different interval. Repeat performers are more than the reverse performers if the *CPR* is greater than 1, and vice versa. If the *CPR* is equal to 1, it indicates no phenomenon of performance persistence exists (Goetzmann and Ibbotson, 1994).

In order to test the significance of *CPR*, a log-odds ratio test is applied in this study. The *CPR* assumed the natural log form and is divided by the standard error, as shown in equations (7) and (8). According to Brown and Goetzmann (1995), large samples with independent observations, the standard error of the natural log of the odds ratio is approximated by equation (9):

$$LOR = \ln(CPR). \tag{7}$$

$$Z\text{-statistic} = \frac{LOR}{\sigma_{LOR}}. \tag{8}$$

$$\text{Standard error in odds ratio } (\sigma_{LOR}) = \sqrt{\frac{1}{WW} + \frac{1}{WL} + \frac{1}{LW} + \frac{1}{LL}}. \tag{9}$$

3.2. Parametric Persistence Test Model

According to Grinblatt and Titman (1992), Brown et al. (1992), and Goetzmann and Ibbotson (1994), parametric test is used to analyze the robustness of the results for both short-term and long-term tests, since the two-way contingency table test (winner-loser test) is a non-parametric test as shown in equation (10):

$$R_{bi} = \alpha_1 + \alpha_2 R_{ai} + \varepsilon_i, \tag{10}$$

where R_{ai} is the risk-adjusted return of the fund i (single-index alpha or four-index alpha) from prior interval, R_{bi} is the risk-adjusted return of the fund i (single-index alpha or four-index alpha) from subsequent interval, α_1 is the intercept term, and α_2 is the slope coefficient. A positive α_2 indicates positive persistence, a negative α_2 indicates negative persistence, and a zero α_2 indicates non-persistence. The non-parametric test only indicates either persistence or non-persistence mutual funds performance, whereas the parametric test indicates the trend of mutual funds performance persistence (Goetzmann and Ibbotson, 1994).

4. RESEARCH FINDINGS

4.1. Equity Mutual Funds Performance Persistence in Short Term

4.1.1. Non-Parametric Test

For non-parametric test based on raw returns, the number of repeat performers is greater than reversal performers in the first three one-year intervals. The total number of repeat performers is also more than the reversal performers. In addition, 50.83% of the funds (122 out of 240 observations) in the sample performed persistently. Table 1 shows that the Cross-Product Ratios (CPR) in the entire observation period is greater than one. The results are consistent with Goetzmann and Ibbotson's (1994), and indicate that equity mutual funds in China could perform persistently in the short term. Due to the small sample size and the absence of extreme numbers of repeat performers during the study period, the result from the one-year interval based on the raw returns is not statistically significant.

According to the non-parametric test based on the single-index alpha, the number of repeat performers is also greater than the number of reversal performers in the first four one-year intervals (from 2005 to 2010) and in the entire observation period. In the sample, 54.17% of the mutual funds perform consistently on a yearly basis. Table 1 shows the CPR for each one-year interval from 2005 to 2009 and the entire observation period is greater than one. The Z-value of CPR for the entire observation period is statistically significant at 10% level. The non-parametric test results in the short term based on the single-index alpha are consistent with Malkiel's (1995) study. According to Malkiel (1995), although the results of performance persistence in each one-year interval are mixed (CPR is less than one in only one of five one-year intervals), the overall CPR for the entire period is greater than one, which indicates performance persistence might exist in the short term in China.

Mutual funds performance is also measured by the four-index alpha in this study. The results are generated by employing Elton et al. (1996) model. Based on the four-index

Table 1 Mutual funds performance persistence in the short term (2005–2010).

	Non-parametric test (CPR)			Parametric test on α_2	
	Raw returns	Single-index alpha	Four-index alpha	Single-index alpha	Four-index alpha
2005–2006	–	–	–	0.737[c]	−0.312[d]
2006–2007	2.222[a]	2.222[a]	2.222[a]	0.211[c]	0.122[c]
2007–2008	1.190[a]	1.690[a]	1.190[a]	0.179[c]*	0.123[c]*
2008–2009	0.640[b]	2.469[a]*	1.249[a]	0.357[c]**	0.372[c]**
2009–2010	1.166[a]	0.735[b]	1.166[a]	−0.050[d]	0.193[c]***
Entire Period	1.069[a]	1.396[a]*	1.306[a]	0.046[c]	0.129[c]**

[a]CPR is greater than one in non-parametric test.
[b]CPR is less than one in non-parametric test.
[c]Slope is greater than zero in non-parametric test.
[d]Slope is less than zero in non-parametric test.
*Significant at 10% level
**Significant at 5% level.
***Significant at 1% level.

alpha results, the number of repeat performers is more than the number of reversal performers in each of the five one-year intervals and in the entire observation period. The result shows 53.33% of the mutual funds in the sample perform persistently and the CPRs are greater than one in each one-year interval and for the entire observation period (see Table 1). The result of the non-parametric test based on the four-index alpha is consistent with Fletcher (1999) and Dahlquist et al. (2000) findings. The values of the CPRs are larger than one, which suggests the phenomenon of mutual funds performance persistence might exist in the short term in China. The results also confirm the findings of performance persistence in the raw returns and single-index alpha.

4.1.2. Parametric Test

Based on Goetzmann and Ibbotson's (1994) study, both the single-index and four-index alphas are employed in this study for the parametric test of mutual funds performance persistence. Table 1 shows the slopes of the regressions in each one-year interval and for the entire observation period when the mutual funds performance is measured by the single-index alpha and four-index alpha. The result based on the single-index alpha indicates that mutual funds could perform persistently in four out of five one-year intervals and for the entire observation period. The performance persistence phenomenon exists from 2006 to 2009, but the α_2 value is statistically significant only at the 5% level in the period 2008–2009. Compared with the non-parametric test based on the single-index alpha at one-year intervals, the results from the parametric test are consistent with results described in Section 4.1.1.

The results of the one-year interval parametric test where the mutual funds performance is measured by the four-index alpha, the slopes are positive in four out of five one-year intervals and for the entire observation period. The performance persistence results are statistically significant at the 5% level in the one-year intervals of 2008–2009, 2009–2010 and for the entire observation period. The positive significant results of α_2 from the parametric test based on the four-index alpha indicate that the mutual funds could perform persistently in the short term and the strong evidence of performance persistence is obtained in two one-year intervals and for the entire observation period. The results from the parametric test based on the four-index alpha are consistent with the parametric test based on the single-index alpha and the results from the non-parametric tests for the short term.

4.2. Equity Mutual Funds Performance Persistence in Long Term

According to Goetzmann and Ibbotson (1994), a two-year interval is the most appropriate observation period for a long-term test of performance persistence. As a result, in the non-parametric test, mutual funds in the sample are first ranked by their past performance in the previous two-year intervals, and then ranked again in a subsequent two-year interval. The research period for this study is from 2004 to 2010, and only mutual funds that existed for at least 2 years are selected to test mutual funds performance persistence in the long-term. Thus, 64 mutual funds are selected in the final sample for the long-term tests in three two-year intervals (2005–2006 to 2007–2008, 2006–2007 to 2008–2009, and 2007–2008 to 2009–2010).

4.2.1. Non-Parametric Test

For non-parametric test in the long term, the results on the mutual funds performance measured by raw returns indicate that the number of repeat performers is less than the number of reversal performers in two of the three two-year intervals and for the entire observation period. In addition, the CPR is greater than one in only one of three two-year intervals and the CPR is less than one for the entire observation period (see Table 2). The results are not statistically significant for any two-year intervals and/or the entire observation period, which further suggests that there is no evidence of performance persistence for mutual funds in the Chinese financial market.

In order to further analyze the mutual funds performance persistence in the long term, the single-index alpha is used as a measurement of mutual funds performance. The single-index alpha results confirmed the results obtained using raw returns, but they are not statistically significant for any two-year intervals or the entire observation period (see Table 2). These results further confirm that there is no evidence of performance persistence for mutual funds in the long term in the Chinese financial market.

The mutual funds performance persistence in the long term is further tested using the four-index alpha including size, BTM, and bond market effects. The result shows no

Table 2 Summary of the results of the mutual funds performance persistence in the long term (2005–2010).

	Non-parametric test (CPR)			Parametric test on α_2	
	Raw returns	Single-index alpha	Four-index alpha	Single-index alpha	Four-index alpha
2005/2006–2007/2008	–	–	–	-1.257^{b}	-1.126^{b}
2006/2007–2008/2009	2.222^{a}	2.222^{a}	2.222^{a}	0.233^{a*}	0.148^{a}
2007/2008–2009/2010	0.592^{b}	0.592^{b}	1.690^{a}	-0.114^{b}	0.049^{a}
Entire Period	0.775^{b}	0.775^{b}	1.648^{a}	0.054^{a}	0.027^{a}

[a] CPR is greater than one in non-parametric test.
[b] Slope is greater than zero in non-parametric test.
*Significant at 10% level.

evidence of performance persistence in the long term. As shown in Table 2, the CRPs are greater than one for two of three two-year intervals and for the entire observation period. The Z-values indicate the performance persistence results are statistically insignificant.

The non-parametric tests of performance persistence in the long term based on the four-index alpha are consistent with the results from the raw returns and the single-index alpha. This suggests that size, BTM, and bond market effects do not impact performance persistence in the long term in the Chinese financial market.

The results from the non-parametric test for the mutual funds performance persistence in the long term based on raw returns, single-index alpha, and four-index alpha are consistent with Kahn and Rudd's (1995) study. The results are statistically insignificant, which suggests there is no evidence of performance persistence for mutual funds in the long-term in the Chinese financial market. Moreover, the results based on raw returns and the single-index alpha are closer to negative where the number of repeat performers is less than the number of reversal performers, which further suggests the non-persistence of mutual funds performance in the Chinese financial market. According to Goetzmann and Ibbotson (1994), changes in mutual funds management structure might be a reason for long-term non-persistence performance. In addition, non-persistence of mutual funds performance can also be a consequence of the unstable Chinese stock market from 2008 to 2009. According to the Morningstar database (2010), the Chinese stock market fluctuated dramatically from 2009 and therefore it is quite difficult for mutual fund managers to retain their persistent performance in such unstable market conditions. In addition, the 60–90 criteria from the Securities Association of China make it even harder for mutual fund managers to adjust their investment portfolios properly according to the unstable market.

Consistent with Phelps and Detzel's (1997) study, the mutual funds performance persistence results in the long term based on raw returns, single-index alpha and four-index alpha are statistically insignificant. Changes in management structure might be a possible reason that the results are statistically insignificant. Selective ability and the investment strategy are likely to change due to changes in management structure (Goetzmann and Ibbotson, 1994). Another possible reason for the insignificant result might be the small sample size. The sample size in this study for the long-term performance persistence test is only 64, which is far less than the number of mutual funds tested in Goetzmann and Ibbotson's study (1994). According to Kahn and Rudd (1995), an insufficient number of funds and the short length of the observation period of our study might be the possible reason leading to the insignificant results.

4.2.2. Parametric Test

The performance persistence parametric test of the mutual funds in the long term is tested by regressing the mutual funds performance in the current observation period on the mutual funds performance in the previous period of two-year intervals. The mutual funds performance is measured by the single-index alpha and four-index alpha. A total of 64 funds are selected from 2005 to 2010 for the parametric test.

Based on the single-index alpha results, the slopes (α_2) of the regressions are negative in the first and third two-year intervals and positive for the second two-year interval and for the entire period (see Table 2). Except for the second two-year interval, all results for α_2 are statistically insignificant, and the α_2 for the second two-year interval is statistically significant only at the 10% level of significance. Therefore, consistent with the results from the non-parametric test in Section 4.2.1, the results suggest that there is no evidence of performance persistence for mutual funds in the Chinese financial market in the long term.

Similar to the non-parametric test for the long term, the four-index alpha is used to measure mutual funds performance which includes size, BTM, and bonds effects. The slopes (α_2) of the regressions are positive for the second and third two-year intervals and for the entire observation period. The first two-year interval, which includes three funds, exhibits a negative slope value (see Table 2). However, consistent with the results from the non-parametric test and the parametric test based on the single-index alpha, none of the results is statistically significant.

Consistent with Kahn and Rudd (1995) and Dahlquist et al. (2000) studies, the results from parametric test further confirm that there is no evidence of performance persistence for mutual funds in the Chinese financial market in the long term. Similar with the non-parametric test in the long term, the Chinese stock market was unstable from 2008 to 2009[4] (Jiang et al., 2010) and the possible changes in management structure could be

[4] According to Jiang et al. (2010), the SSEC (Shanghai Stock Exchange Composite Index) and SZSC (Shenzhen Stock Exchange Component Index) indices experienced more than 70% drop from the historical high during the period from October 2007 to October 2008. From November 2008 until the end of July 2009, the Chinese stock markets had been rising dramatically.

the reason for the non-persistence performance of the mutual funds in China. Moreover, the relatively small sample size compared with the larger sample size in Goetzmann and Ibbotson (1994) study produces insignificant result (Kahn and Rudd, 1995).

5. CONCLUSIONS

The non-parametric and parametric test results demonstrate that equity mutual funds in China could perform persistently in the short term but not in the long term. The results show mutual funds that could perform persistently in the short term imply that the "repeat-performer" pattern appears to be a guide to beat the market over the short term. The evidence of supporting performance persistence in the short term can help investors to avoid potential losses in their investment portfolios. By looking at the historical ranking of mutual funds annually and investing in the funds with good performance records in previous year, investors can improve their chance of earning abnormal profits in the next year. However, the persistent performance pattern for mutual funds in China is inconsistent over the long term. As a result, if investors invest in the mutual fund which has better performance than the median which ranked mutual fund based on their performance in the last 2 years, excess return cannot be guaranteed in the next 2 years.

There are certain limitations in this study. The first limitation is the relatively small sample size and short research period compared to studies documented in the US. Since mutual funds are new to the market in China, the first open-end fund was issued in 2001 and the first equity mutual fund was established in 2004. The second limitation is the scope of this study, which focuses only on equity mutual funds in China. Due to the difficulties of obtaining data and constructing appropriate benchmark indices, other types of funds, such as balanced funds and debt funds in China, are not included in this study. Therefore, the empirical methods in this study are applied only to test performance persistence for equity mutual funds, and the conclusions reached in this study cannot be applied to the entire mutual funds industry in China.

Another limitation of this study is the benchmark indices selection. The benchmark applied in this research is the S&P/CITIC indices, however, not all mutual fund managers use the S&P/CITIC indices as the benchmark. This is because there is no official overall market index available for both Shanghai and Shenzhen A share markets in China. The market index used in this research is S&P/CITIC indices, which may not be widely applied by mutual fund managers in China and mutual fund managers have other market indices available to choose from. However, S&P/CITIC is the best benchmark for this study since it is the only overall market index available in China. If an overall official market index is available in China in the future, mutual fund managers, who currently choose official indices (Shanghai A-share market index, Shenzhen A-share market index, and Shanghai-Shenzhen 300 market index) or S&P/CITIC, might switch their current benchmarks to the overall official market index. As a result, the overall official market index might be a better benchmark to evaluate mutual funds performance in China since all mutual fund managers will use the same market index as the benchmark.

Future research could conduct tests performance persistence for other types of funds, such as debt funds, balanced funds, index funds, and QFIIs. Testing performance persistence of all types of mutual funds could provide a better overview of mutual fund industry in China. Moreover, future research could investigate whether changes in management structure can impact mutual fund performance persistence in China financial market. According to Goetzmann and Ibbotson (1994), changes in management structure might impact mutual fund performance persistence. The reason for non-persistence mutual fund performance could be due to either mutual fund managers do not have selective ability or experience changes in management structure in the funds. Since there are no data available for management structure changes in mutual funds this test cannot be conducted for this study.

REFERENCES

Abdel-Kader, M., Kuang, Y., 2007. Risk-adjusted performance, selectivity, timing ability and performance persistence of Hong Kong mutual funds. Journal of Asia-Pacific Business 8 (2), 25–58

Allen, D.E., Tan, M.L., 1999. A test of the persistence in the performance of U.K. managed funds. Journal of Business Finance and Accounting 26, 559–595

Bauer, R., Otten, R., Rad, A.T., 2006. New Zealand mutual funds: measuring performance and persistence in performance. Accounting and Finance 46, 1–17

Benos, E., Jochec, M., 2011. Short term persistence in mutual fund market timing and stock selection abilities. Annals of Finance 7 (2), 221–246

Bessler, W., Blake, D., Lückoff, P., Tonks, I., 2010. Why does mutual fund performance not persist? The impact and interaction of fund flows and manager changes, MPRA Paper 34185.

Bodie, Z., Kane, A., Marcus, A.J., 2004. Investment, sixth ed.. McGraw-Hill, Irwin

Bollen, N.P.B., Busse, J.A., 2005. Short-term persistence in mutual fund performance. Review of Financial Studies 18 (2), 569–597

Brown, S., Goetzmann, W., 1995. Performance persistence. Journal of Finance 50, 679–698

Brown, S.J., Goetzmann, W., Ibbotson, R.G., Ross, S.A., 1992. Survivorship bias in performance studies. Review of Financial Studies 5, 553–580

Busse, J.A., Goyal, A., Wahal, S., 2010. Performance and persistence in institutional investment management. Journal of Finance 65, 765–790

Cai, J., Chan, K.C., Yamada, T., 1997. The performance of Japanese mutual funds. Review of Financial Studies 10 (2), 237–274

Carhart, M., 1997. On persistence in mutual fund performance. Journal of Finance 52 (1), 157–182

Connor, G., Korajczyk, R.A., 1991. The attributes, behaviour, and performance of U.S. mutual funds. Review of Quantitative Finance and Accounting 1 (1), 5–26

Dahlquist, M., Engstrom, S., Soderlind, P., 2000. Performance and characteristics of Swedish mutual funds. Journal of Financial and Quantitative Analysis 25 (3), 409–423

Drew, M.E., Naughton, T., Veeraraghavan, M., 2003. Firm size, book-to-market equity and security returns: evidence from the Shanghai stock exchange. Australian Journal of Management 28 (2), 119–139

Dunn, P.C., Theisen, R.D., 1983. How consistently do active managers win? Journal of Portfolio Management 9, 47–51

Elton, E.J., Gruber, M.J., 1995. Modern Portfolio Theory and Investment Analysis, fifth ed. John Wiley & Sons Inc., United States

Elton, E.J., Gruber, M.J., Rentzler, J., 1990. The performance of publicly offered commodity funds. Financial Analysts Journal 46 (4), 23–30

Elton, E.J., Gruber, M.J., Blake, C.R., 1996. The persistence of risk-adjusted mutual fund performance. Journal of Business 69 (2), 133–157
Fama, E.F., French, K.R., 1993. Common risk factors in the returns on stocks and bonds. Journal of Financial Economics 33, 3–56
Fletcher, J., 1999. The evaluation of the performance of U.K. American unit trusts. International Review of Economics & Finance 8 (4), 455–466
Fletcher, J., Forbes, D., 2002. An exploration of the persistence of U.K. unit trust performance. Journal of Empirical Finance 9 (5), 475–493
Goetzmann, W., Ibbotson, R., 1994. Do winners repeat? Patterns in mutual fund performance. Journal of Portfolio Management 20, 9–18
Grinblatt, M., Titman, S., 1989. Mutual fund performance: an analysis of quarterly portfolio holdings. Journal of Business 62, 393–416
Grinblatt, M., Titman, S., 1992. The persistence of mutual funds performance. Journal of Finance 47, 1977–1984
Hendricks, D., Patel, J., Zeckhauser, R., 1993. Hot hands in mutual funds: short-run persistence of performance, 1974–1988. Journal of Finance 48, 93–130
Henriksson, R., Merton, R., 1981. On market timing and investment performance. II. Statistical procedures for evaluating forecasting skills. Journal of Business 54 (4), 513–533
Jensen, M.C., 1968. The performance of mutual funds in the period 1945–1964. Journal of Finance 23, 389–416
Jiang, Z.Q., Zhou, W.X., Sornette, D., Woodard, R., Bastiaensen, K., Cauwels, P., 2010. Bubble diagnosis and prediction of the 2005–2007 and 2008–2009 Chinese stock market bubbles. Journal of Economic Behavior and Organization 74 (3), 149–162
Kahn, R.N., Rudd, A., 1995. Does historical performance predict future performance? Financial Analysts Journal 51 (6), 43–52
Kritzman, M., 1983. Can bond manager perform consistently? Journal of Portfolio Management 9, 54–56
Mains, N.E., 1977. Risk, the pricing of capital assets, and the evaluation of investment portfolios: comment. Chicago Journal 50 (3), 381–384
Malkiel, B.G., 1995. Returns from investing in equity funds: 1971–1991. Journal of Finance 50, 549–572
Morningstar, 2007. Morningstar mutual fund performance evaluation methodology. Morningstar China Research Centre, June 8. <http://cn.morningstar.com/article/AR00000902>.
Morningstar Database, 2010. Morningstar Investment Research Center. <http://cn.morningstar.com/main/default.aspx>.
Phelps, S., Detzel, L., 1997. The non persistence of mutual fund performance. Quarterly Journal of Business and Economics 36, 55–69
Quigley, G., Sinquefield, R., 2000. Performance of U.K. equity unit trusts. Journal of Asset Management 1 (1), 72–92
Rhodes, M., 2000. Past imperfect? The performance of U.K. equity managed funds, Financial Services Authority Occasional Paper No. 9.
Sharpe, W., 1966. Mutual fund performance. Journal of Business 39, 119–138
Treynor, J.L., 1966. How to rate management investment funds. Harvard Business Review 43, 63–75
Treynor, J.L., Mazuy, K.K., 1966. Can mutual funds outguess the market?, 131–136
Wermers, R., 2000. Mutual fund performance: an empirical decomposition into stock-picking talent, style, transactions costs, and expenses. Journal of Finance 55 (4), 1655–1703

CHAPTER 14

Cultural Behavioral Finance in Emerging Markets

Brian M. Lucey[*,†,‡] **and Michael Dowling**[§]
[*]School of Business Studies and Institute for International Integration Studies, Trinity College Dublin, Ireland
[†]Glasgow Business School, Glasgow Caledonian University, Glasgow, UK
[‡]Faculty of Economics, University of Ljubljana Kardeljeva, Ljubljana, Slovenia
[§]DCU Business School, Dublin City University, Ireland

1. INTRODUCTION

This chapter provides a comprehensive review of the role of investor psychology and culture in emerging markets. A key conclusion is that an understanding of behavioral influences on investors in emerging markets must be driven by an acknowledgment of the mediating role of culture in decision making. Further, we conclude that this mediating role for culture varies according to behavioral principle, with some behaviors varying predictably according to cultural differences, some applying more to particular cultural groups, and some behaviors are best viewed as innate and static across cultures. A mediating role for culture is something which we find to be generally lacking in prior behavioral finance studies in emerging markets, with the majority of cross-country studies assuming universal behavioral principles.

We take the MSCI Emerging Markets constituent index as our reference point for defining emerging markets, thus we include Asian, Latin American, African, and Eastern European country studies in the review. However, the vast majority of studies reviewed are concentrated on Asian markets due to the preponderance of research in these markets. This does not necessarily hamper the review, rather the suggested predictable mediating role for culture proffers fruitful theoretical avenues for future behavioral finance research in these neglected regions.

The structure adopted is that Section 2 analyzes the mediating role culture is likely to play, and has been shown to play, in investor financial decision-making approaches across countries. Section 3 reviews the key findings on behavioral finance in emerging markets analyzed within an overarching behavioral finance framework and with reference to developed economy studies of the behavioral principles. The review of cultural influences in Section 2 is applied to understand differences between emerging market and developed economy findings. Finally, Section 4 summarizes the key findings on culture and behavioral finance, and proposes directions, based on this, for future behavioral finance studies in emerging markets which is cognisant of the likely role of culture in investment decision making.

Emerging Markets and the Global Economy
http://dx.doi.org/10.1016/B978-0-12-411549-1.00014-4

2. CULTURE AND FINANCIAL DECISION MAKING

National culture is an area that has only in recent years begun to penetrate into the research agenda of finance and economics. This is surprising given the prominence it has achieved in cognate areas, notably international business. National culture has been shown in Kirkman et al. (2006) to impact on literally hundreds of international business and management research papers on foreign direct investment, mergers and acquisitions, the modality of market entry, managerial control, capital structure, and on the structure of corporate and national financial systems. This section outlines some aspects of national culture and then looks at such research as is on how this impacts on emerging markets.

2.1. Conceptualizing National Culture and its Interaction with Finance

Cultural factors can and do have a significant impact on financial decision making. Financial decisions are driven by information costs and asymmetry, agency costs, moral hazard, and incomplete contracts. In order to mitigate some of the effects of these imperfections, economists and researchers argue that agents develop contracts that better align the interests of the various economic agents involved within the legal framework in a given jurisdiction. This approach underlies the burgeoning law and economics literature, however all such contracts are necessarily incomplete as specifying all contingencies is impossible in practice. Contracting parties are thus forced to depend on the interaction of relative ethics, social mores, and customary business practices—all these are collectively part of what we commonly term culture. Thus, from first principles we can see that cultural and other soft measurements of the nature of social and business interactions are important determinants of economic and financial decisions.

Consequently, financial scholars have become increasingly aware of the extent to which disciplines such as genetics (Maddox et al., 1984); anthropology, geography, history, and philosophy (House et al., 2002); and psychology (O'Grady and Lane, 1996) contribute to our understanding of the determinants of national culture. National culture in turn has been found to impact major elements of financial decision making. We see research that links culture or variations in national culture to the structure of financial systems (Aggarwal and Goodell, 2009a,b); intra-firm valuation of subsidiaries (Antia et al., 2007); compensation practices (Schuler and Rogovsky, 1998); dividend payout patterns (Fidrmuc and Jacob, 2010); corporate governance (Bushman et al., 2004; Breuer and Salzmann, 2012); foreign portfolio investment (Aggarwal et al., 2012); and corporate cash holdings (Ramírez and Tadesse, 2009). All of this evidence indicates that culture significantly impacts financial decision making (Kirkman et al., 2006).

Culture is neither conceptually nor empirically easy to measure. Taras et al. (2009) provide an extensive authoritative overview of 121 approaches to measuring culture. Culture is a complex, multilevel construct that has basic assumptions and values at its core, and is buttressed by practices, symbols, and artifacts. The most commonly used measures are by Hofstede (2001) who describes four essential but orthogonal dimensions of national culture: individualism, power distance, uncertainty avoidance, and masculinity. More recently, researchers using the Hofstede approach have added a fifth, long-term orientation. Each of these dimensions, and combinations of them, has potential effects on financial decision making. While there are alternative frameworks of measuring national culture and psychic distance, such as Schwartz and Sagiv (1995) and House et al. (2002), most finance researchers who have examined national culture have used Hofstede's measures, with smaller numbers using the World Values Survey (Inglehart and Welzel, 2005).

A society's degree of individualism refers to the extent that its members tend to be loosely connected and responsible for their own wellbeing, rather than being closely connected within cohesive groups that offer protection in return for loyalty which occurs in collectivist societies. High individualism societies tend to emphasize the importance of individual motivation and individual rather than group decision making, and with compensation based on the individual's contribution rather than on the group's performance. A recent work by Gorodnichenko and Roland (2010) suggests that countries that demonstrate higher levels of individuality grow faster and are wealthier. All things being equal therefore a greater distance in individuality would correspond to greater wealth disparity and greater investment opportunities. Also, suggested, by this research is a greater role for individual cognitive biases in highly individualistic societies (this is explored further in Section 3.1).

The degree of masculinity in national culture refers to the extent that societies emphasize and reward the male characteristics, these are taken to be assertiveness, competition, and success counterpoised to female characteristics of nurturance and support, and it also embodies the extent to which societal members are expected to manifest and perform these roles. Societies that score high on masculinity tend to exhibit behavior toward achievement rather than solidarity, confrontation rather than cooperation, and intellectual independence rather than moral obligation. Although the degree of masculinity does not correlate with the other dimensions (except uncertainty avoidance, with a statistically significant positive value in wealthier countries and a marginally significant negative value in poorer countries), this is perhaps the least accepted of the four because it is more difficult to distinguish its implied behavioral traits.

The concept of power distance was developed by Mulder (1977) and built upon by Hofstede (2001) to refer to the differential weights that societies assign to inequality in power, status, and wealth, and the extent to which society expects that power should be shared unequally among its individual members. House et al. (2002) in their development of the project GLOBE trace the roots of this cultural dimension to Plato's argument for the merits of an elite ruling class in the 4th century BC, to Confucian and Hindu philosophy that respects tradition and seniority, to the Hobbesian 17th century recognition of the need for checks on individual greed and ambition. Low power distance cultures tend to disseminate information broadly, to provide broad access to education and resources for personal development, to exhibit substantial social mobility, and to encourage participation in discussion and critique during corporate decision making. By contrast, high power distance cultures tend to exhibit localized information, unequal access to education and resources, and to corporate decision making by those in positions of seniority with limited input from subordinates, and limited social mobility. Confucianism, Hinduism, Catholicism, and Islam tend to be high in power distance, while Buddhism and Protestantism tend to be low in power distance.

The concept of uncertainty avoidance is familiar to financial analysts and researchers, particularly given the many tools that have been designed to manage risk and to financially engineer preferred combinations of risk and reward. Initiated by Cyert and March (1953), the uncertainty avoidance dimension in national culture was developed by Hofstede (2001) to capture the anxiety that people feel when exposed to ambiguity and uncertainty. Societies construct mechanisms to cope with uncertainty that fall under three main headings: technology (which helps us cope with uncertainties of nature), law (which helps us cope with uncertainties caused by the behavior of other people), and religion (which helps us cope with uncertainties we cannot otherwise defend against). High uncertainty avoidance societies tend to exhibit more complete accounting disclosures, less risk-taking, lower ambition for personal advancement, greater resistance to change, and higher average age in senior positions.

Long-term orientation is a metric of thrift, of persistence. It relates to tradition in that long-term orientation also involves conservatism in relation to actions. Countries with high long-term orientation emphasize hard work, high savings, and family orientation. It may be difficult to effect change in these societies but when change is so effected it is incorporated into the traditional set and becomes embodied. Not all countries have been measured with regard to long-term orientation and as a consequence it is frequently not incorporated in research.

As noted there are other conceptualizations of culture. Chui and Kwok (2009) use the project GLOBE cultural measures to examine the determinants of life assurance. Shao et al. (2009) examine the determinants of national dividend policy using the Schwartz measures (Schwartz and Sagiv, 1995). However, the World Value Survey data appears to be rarely used as correlates, in finance research, of national differences. An exception is Georgarakos and Pasini (2009) on stock market participation in Europe. The Schwartz measures have been used by Breuer and Salzmann (2012) in the evaluation of corporate governance issues.

2.2. National Culture and Emerging Markets

What then do we find when we examine the interaction of national culture and emerging markets finance? It is difficult to identify papers that make such an explicit split. This suggests that heretofore this issue, of the potential differential effects of national culture on emerging versus developed markets, was not identified. It should be noted that the emerging versus developed markets split is not particularly useful from a cultural perspective. A prediction of difference is not driven by this division, but rather that the diverse cultural groups within the emerging market group are likely to display differing financial behaviors compared to the relatively culturally homogenous group of developed countries. With that proviso in mind, there have been a limited number of studies that have examined cultural variances in financial behavior incorporating a range of emerging markets in the investigation.

Aggarwal and Goodell (2009b) suggest that uncertainty avoidance is an important element in the depth of equity markets. Examining corporate valuation Antia et al. (2007) include emerging markets but unfortunately do not separate out these findings from the general findings of a negative relationship between cultural distance and valuation.

Examining corporate governance, via a combination of the Schwartz and Hofstede approach (but focusing mainly on Schwartz), Breuer and Salzmann (2012) find compelling evidence of a relationship. They find for emerging regions that single cultural attributes strongly correlate with governance. Mastery, similar to power distance, emerges as the main cultural attribute, which affects corporate governance in Africa and Middle East countries. A similar, albeit firm level, analysis was undertaken using Hofstede measures by Jiatao and Harrison (2008) who did not separate the data along emerging/developed market lines.

Gorodnichenko and Roland (2010) do provide some evidence along regional lines, with the Hofstede measure of individualism (and Schwartz analogs of same) being more impactful on wealth measures in Africa, having nearly double the impact than it does on OECD countries. Investigating corporate cash holdings, neither Chang and Noorbakhsh (2009) nor Ramírez and Tadesse (2009) explicitly look at the developing/emerged split but in the case of Ramirez and Tadesse they segment by political risk scores. Given that emerging markets tend to have higher such scores, the finding that after controlling for Hofstede measures, political risk is no longer an important determinant of cash holdings, implying cultural variation is the cause.

While the overview above suggests cultural influence in emerging markets, it merely highlights the cultural differences without attempting to explain the decision-making process that might be causing the differences. This is not particularly useful in terms of generalizability to other areas of financial decision making. What is required is a confluence of the cultural and behavioral finance literatures, given that the latter focuses on explaining the psychological decision-making processes that influence financial decision makers. The next section addresses this absence in the literature.

3. BEHAVIORAL FINANCE IN EMERGING MARKETS: A CULTURAL PERSPECTIVE

This section reviews the key prior research investigating the ability of behavioral finance theories to explain emerging market investor behavior and asset pricing. The cultural influences highlighted in Section 2 are applied to understand differences between emerging market and developed economy behavioral finance findings.

The behavioral finance framework followed for this review is that of Hirshleifer (2001) who proposes four categories of behavioral biases that influence investors:

- *Heuristic Simplification:* Because of limits to cognitive processing abilities and the presence of excessive information required to be processed for complex decisions, investors rely on cognitive heuristics, or "rules of thumb," to guide them in their decision making. This is generally an efficient information processing approach, but a number of biases also emanate from these heuristics, which can be priced in aggregate asset prices.
- *Self-Deception:* People are naturally overconfident through evolutionary development. Positive self-image can be self-fulfilling; for example, it can help people to persuade others of their ability and their viewpoint. However, self-deception can also lead to an excessive belief in one's own ability and powers of analysis to the detriment of perhaps ignoring the (possibly superior) information, advice, and actions of others.
- *Emotions:* The emotions experienced throughout the decision-making process, and emotions felt toward possible outcomes, influence the eventual decision, especially in complex investment decisions.
- *Social Dynamics:* Given the social nature of human society, it is argued that investor's views and opinions are molded, in part, by the views and opinions of those people within the social set of the person. Some biases emanate from this social interaction, especially concerning conformist thinking.

Each subsection briefly addresses the main theory for the category of behavioral bias argued to influence investors, overviews the leading empirical studies of the theory, and then evaluates the application of the theory in an emerging market context. A focus for the emerging market analysis is the differences observed from the main studies of developed markets, and the influence that culture might have in driving these findings. We start with a brief discussion of which psychological behaviors are likely to be mediated by culture.

3.1. Cultural Variances in Psychology

Markus and Kitayama's (1991) highly influential work on culture and the self suggests paths with which culture might interact with psychology. They characterize Western cultures (particularly the USA) as being characterized by an independent self, while other cultures, including in Asia and Africa, are best characterized as interdependent selves. An independent self is internally, personally focused and thus likely primarily driven by the psychological theories that are the focus of modern investor psychology. An interdependent self, on the other hand, will be driven by these same behaviors, but there will be a greater role for culture to mediate the behaviors. The groupings behind this argument are related to the Hofstede cultural dimension of individualism versus collectivism.

A key decision-making difference is that interdependent selves tend to approach decision making in a holistic manner—seeking overall meaning of systems of organization—while the Western analytic approach tends to focus more on context-driven formal logic processes (Nisbett et al., 2001). Holistic cognition is characterized less by the rule and object-based approach followed in the Western analytic cognition process, and instead relies on a more generalist assessment with influence from one's social network. With formal logic processes playing less of a role in holistic decision making, many of the cognitive biases that derive from heuristic simplification (as discussed in the following section) will have less of an ability to influence decision making in cultures characterized by this form of decision making. Instead, culture and behavioral biases not explicitly linked to formal logic processes, such as social dynamics, are likely to play a greater decision-influencing role in these cultures.

An important issue to additionally consider in terms of interpreting current empirical studies of emerging markets versus developed markets is the role of experience. Experience can determine the influence of biases on financial decision making, with lower experience leading to greater reliance on heuristics (Feng and Seasholes, 2005; Nicolosi et al., 2009). Thus traders in developing markets where there is possibly lower knowledge of trading behavior and optimum financial decision are likely to default to reliance on heuristic simplifications to guide behavior. This immediate driver of behavior should presumably counteract any longer-term broadly experienced tendency of a culture toward lesser reliance on cognitive biases.

This suggests a broad hypothesis that heuristic simplification (as it is currently understood in the behavioral finance literature) will influence both developed and emerging markets but for different reasons: developed markets due to higher reliance on formal logic processes; emerging markets due to inexperience. We further expect that emerging markets, due to the background of collectivist cultures, will display a greater influence from social dynamics due to higher reliance on social networks and social feedback.

Further research presented in the remainder of this section argues that self-deception is strongly culturally mediated by individualism versus collectivism. We also argue that emotional bias is best viewed as a universal influence at this early stage in the development of emotion research in finance; but that there are some cultural distinctions within types of emotions that could be explored further in future research.

3.2. Heuristic Simplification

Given that investing in equity markets involves highly complex decision making, it is argued that this leads to the use of cognitive heuristic simplification rules to guide decision making. These heuristic rules are commonly divided into three groups: representativeness and conservatism; framing; and salience and availability.

3.2.1. Representativeness and Conservatism

Representativeness refers to how people judge the probability of a hypothesis matching a dataset or an event matching a class of events based on the similarity between the hypothesis and dataset or based on how typical the event is of the class of events (Kahneman et al., 1982). Biases include base-rate underweighting (overweighting the conditional probability and underweighting the unconditional probability) and sample size neglect (attaching too great a weight to small samples of a population and too little weight to large samples of a population).

While base-rate underweighting has largely been subsumed into a noise trader literature (e.g., Cutler et al., 1990) which is no longer in favor, significant advances have been made in recent years in understanding the influence of sample size neglect in investment decision making. Rabin and Vayanos (2010) summarize the investment implications primarily as excessively extrapolating short-term investment performance including the recent past performance of mutual funds in what is described as the "hot hand effect." Thus investors have been shown to switch in to mutual funds with good recent performance despite a general lack of persistence to these performances and the cost of switching (Cashman et al., 2012). Similar overreaction to short-run performance is found in the classic papers of De Bondt and Thaler for equity prices (1985) and security analysts (1990).

An important potential difference for Asian emerging markets is highlighted in Ji et al. (2008) who document how Chinese investors are more likely than Canadian investors to predict a reversal in a price trend (Canadians in the study tended to assume a short-term trend would continue in the same direction). However, Chen et al. (2007) find that individual Chinese investor trading accounts do show evidence of buying equities which have had a positive four-month prior performance, suggesting a universality of trend following. They do note though that in culturally collectivist countries, like China, there should be less of a regret aversion motivation for trend extrapolation trading compared to individualistic cultures. There is also some evidence to suggest that extrapolating excessively from small samples is a universal human behavior, with the effect documented in remote tribes (Shuar hunter-horticulturalists in the Amazon) as well as in developed countries (Wilke and Barrett, 2009) thus representativeness might be a behavioral bias which is relatively immune to cultural influence.

Under the heuristic of conservatism, people are argued to overweight base rates and underweight new information, for example, people are slow to adjust base rates when new information arises (Edwards, 1968). A similar heuristic is proposed by Lord et al. (1979), who find that people are slow to change their beliefs even if evidence suggests that they should. Griffin and Tversky (1992) argue that investors excessively react to extreme, high salience, information, and underreact to numerical base-rate information; this drives both representativeness with respect to high salience information, and leads to conservatism through underreaction to base-rate information.

Consistent with conservatism, investors appear to underreact to certain types of news events, including stock splits, earnings announcements, and mergers and acquisitions (see Ikenberry and Ramnath (2002) for a review and application to stock splits). This conservatism is also present in emerging markets with trading on conservative reactions to earnings announcements profitable across 32 emerging markets (Van der Hart et al., 2003). Combining both representativeness and conservatism in financial markets, Griffin et al. (2010) find no evidence that these behaviors vary across developed and emerging markets. This suggests that these behavioral influences are currently best viewed as universal.

3.2.2. Framing

Tversky and Kahneman (1981) find a framing effect in how people make decisions; namely that how a problem is presented can significantly affect the choices made. Specifically, people tended to frame choices "narrowly"; that is a set of choices are assessed in isolation, rather than as being choices that can be placed in a universe of choices, or as choices with a multitude of implications (Hirshleifer, 2001). A major framing bias is "anchoring," which, as developed by Tversky and Kahneman (1974), refers to how people make a decision by starting at a specific reference point and then adjusting away from that reference point as new information is added. An application of anchoring is "loss aversion", where people are argued to assess the performance of a selected choice relative to the initial value of that choice (or the value at the time of the last performance assessment), i.e., the initial value of the choice is the anchoring point. This leads to decisions being assessed in terms of gains and losses (or break-even). Kahneman and Tversky's (1979) "prospect theory" is primarily based on loss aversion.

Benartzi and Thaler (1995) address the issue of the equity premium puzzle using prospect theory. They argue that the premium could be due to the framing effect of investors re-evaluating their portfolios on a regular basis. For example, if an investor re-evaluates their portfolio every month, it is almost equally likely that the performance over the past month will be negative or positive. If an investor re-evaluates performance every five years it is highly likely that the performance will be positive. Given investor's loss aversion, Benartzi and Thaler conjecture that the equity risk premium could be due to regular investor portfolio re-evaluation. Their study shows that if investors evaluate their portfolios on a (intuitively appealing) yearly basis, this could explain the equity premium. Prospect theory has also been linked to a tendency on the part of investors to hold on to losing stocks too long ignoring the tax benefits of selling (Grinblatt and Han, 2005). More generally, loss aversion is shown to be a significant feature of investment decision making among market participants (Hwang and Satchell, 2010) and finance professionals (Eriksen and Kvaloy, 2009).

Some evidence exists that prospect theory and loss aversion are particularly pronounced in emerging markets. For example, Estrada (2002) finds an applicability for a D-CAPM model which emphasizes downside risk in expected return across emerging markets, and suggests this is more pertinent to emerging markets than developed markets. Chen et al. (2007) also find a reluctance to sell loser stocks using Chinese household data. Research on how culture might influence financial decision framing is generally absent, hampering a generalized view of the interaction between framing and culture in emerging markets, however it is commonly noted that framing effects should be culturally determined without providing specifics for any particular country or cultural region (Elliott and Hayward, 1998; Van Gorp, 2007).

3.2.3. Salience and Availability

The salience or availability of information relevant to a decision influences probability assessment (Bordalo et al., 2012). Information that is recalled with greater ease is assigned a greater weight in probability assessment. This includes recently received information being weighted greater than older information (Hogarth and Einhorn, 1992) and vivid images and personally salient information being weighted greater than abstract information (Kahneman and Tversky, 1973). Biases related to salience and availability include: hindsight bias (past events remembered as more predictable than they actually were), and the familiarity bias (being familiar with something leading to judgements of less riskiness).

Hindsight bias has primarily been investigated in financial markets by means of experimental studies as the nature of the bias creates difficulty in designing tests for aggregate financial data. The area is relatively understudied. An example of the testing approach is seen in a recent experimental study by Biais and Weber (2009) which tests for the presence of hindsight bias among German and UK investment bankers, and generally finds the presence of the bias when participants are questioned about the volatility of past economic and financial events. Greater perceived predictability and lower volatility of past events is reported than was actually the historic situation.

Given the paucity of studies on hindsight bias in financial decision making in general it is unsurprising that the bias has not been directly studied among emerging markets investors. However, psychological research suggests that the presence of hindsight bias should be more pronounced in certain emerging markets compared to studies of European or US investors. Yama et al. (2010) argue that hindsight bias is more pronounced in Asian countries compared to Western countries due to a prevalence of holistic cognition decision making processes in these countries.

The familiarity bias is widely studied through assessment of investor portfolio diversification. The main findings are that investors tend to invest in the equity of companies that are situated close to where they live, and the level of investment is in excess of what is suggested for a properly diversified portfolio (Grinblatt and Keloharju, 2001; Huberman, 2001; Massa and Simonov, 2006). This appears to be driven by investors feeling more comfortable investing in local companies that they think they understand, although analysis of investor portfolios of local equity holdings shows that these investments have no ability to outperform the market (Seasholes and Zhu, 2010). Coval and Moskowitz

(1999) draw a general link between local bias and the overall home bias that investors exhibit of excessive allocation of investment to their own country's equities, which is not explainable purely by rational factors such as transaction costs and regulations.

With regard to emerging markets and familiarity bias Chiou (2008) demonstrates that emerging market investors (primarily in Asia and Latin America countries) stand to gain the most from international portfolio diversification compared to developed economy investors. Thus the presence of familiarity bias in emerging market investor decision making would be particularly damaging to investment performance. Despite this, emerging market countries are generally strongly home biased in terms of investment; Fidora et al. (2007), using 2003 International Monetary Fund statistics, report that emerging market country investors allocate just 3.3% of their portfolios to developed markets, which constitute 83.1% of world market capitalization. Some partial explanations for this underdiversification are not behavioral; including transaction costs and barriers (Warnock, 2002), information asymmetries and local information advantages (Coval and Moskowitz, 2001; Dvorak, 2005). However, recent explanations have focused on explicitly cultural explanations for portfolio diversification patterns: namely, patriotism, and cultural familiarity.

Morse and Shive (2011) find that home bias is strongly related to level of patriotism, with a 1 standard deviation lowering of patriotism associated with 3–5% increase in investment in foreign markets. Contrasting the emerging markets groups, we can see that Latin American and African countries usually display high patriotism and therefore low external diversification. Asian countries are underrepresented in the study due to sampling issues, for example China is not included. Russian and Eastern European emerging market countries are outliers in the study; displaying very low levels of patriotism but still not diversifying overseas, perhaps due to institutional issues.

The direction of foreign investment in a portfolio also appears to be driven by cultural familiarity. Chan et al. (2005) find that common language helps determine foreign investment destination, something of relevance in the emerging market subgroupings. Aggarwal et al. (2012) explicitly test whether cultural familiarity, using a gravity model and Hofstede cultural dimensions, drives foreign investment choice on the part of investors, and confirm a significant role for culture. These results include all the emerging market countries, which are observed to cluster together in terms of the individualism and power distance cultural dimensions.

The research reviewed above on familiarity bias prompts an addition to the framework for understanding cultural behavioral finance in emerging markets. The familiarity bias is explicitly culturally rather than psychologically driven, yet it is commonly included in the family of investor psychology biases. This suggests that the investor psychology literature has tended to conflate psychological and cultural variations in behavior, which contributes to poor understanding of the drivers. This is also observed in the review of social dynamics influences in emerging market financial decision making.

3.3. Self-Deception

People are naturally overconfident through evolutionary development. Positive self-image can be self-fulfilling; it can also help people to persuade others of their ability and their viewpoint. However, self-deception can also lead to an excessive belief in one's own ability to the detriment of perhaps ignoring the (possibly superior) information, advice, and actions of others (Goleman, 1997). An important feature of overconfidence is an excessive belief in one's abilities (Kruger, 1999).

There is widespread evidence that people, especially men, are overconfident. Studies of probability judgements (calibration studies) find that people demonstrate excessively optimistic confidence that their estimates are correct (Alpert and Raiffa, 1982). For example, Alpert and Raiffa find in an experimental study that when people claim they are 98% confident in the accuracy of an estimate, they should only be 60% confident.

Overconfidence is partially due to biased self-attribution. Under biased self-attribution, people attribute successful outcomes to their own actions, and unsuccessful outcomes to the actions of others or bad luck (Langer and Roth, 1975). Another contribution toward overconfidence is hindsight bias, where past events seem more predictable than they actually were. People also tend to seek out information that confirms their beliefs rather than disproves them (confirmation bias), and this reinforces overconfidence (Isenberg, 1986).

In financial market studies, overconfident traders have been shown to trade too frequently (Barber and Odean, 2001), which has been linked to sensation-seeking on the part of investors (Grinblatt and Keloharju, 2009) and biased self-attribution (Statman et al., 2006). Overconfidence has been particularly studied in terms of corporate financial decision making, with overconfident CEOs associated with higher levels of mergers and acquisitions (Malmendier and Tate, 2005), increased financing reliance on retained earnings (Deshmukh et al., 2013), but also with increased levels of firm innovation through higher risk-taking willingness (Hirshleifer et al., 2012).

Overconfidence has proven particularly fruitful in terms of understanding emerging market investment behavior. This is driven by Hofstede's individualism measure where countries high in individualism display higher levels of overconfidence through higher biased self-attribution and cultural upbringing (Heine et al., 1999). Thus, Chui et al. (2010) find that the profitability of momentum strategies, linked to investors excessively attributing the profitability of short-term trend trading to their own decisions, is primarily a feature of markets in countries high in individualism and is largely not a feature of collectivist cultures such as East Asian countries. Studies of CEO overconfidence in emerging markets are confounded by a lack of simultaneous cross-country studies. For example, Huang et al. (2011) find that overconfident CEOs make investment decisions based on overconfident projections of future cash flows; but we do not know the extent to which the prevalence of overconfident CEOs in China differs from overconfident CEOs in, e.g., the USA. A recent study by Graham et al., (2013) does suggest there is a different prevalence of overconfidence. They survey US CEO and CFOs to determine confidence levels and optimism and compare this to similar responses from non-US executives in Europe and Asia. US executives are found to display significantly more confidence, optimism, and risk tolerance, suggesting a similar lack of generalizability across cultures to CEO overconfidence studies, as seen for investor overconfidence. In particular, a country's individualism vs collectivism score is an important mediating determinant that must be considered.

3.4. Emotions

There is persuasive evidence that emotions, feelings, and mood states influence decision making, this is particularly true when the decision involves conditions of risk and uncertainty (Loewenstein et al., 2001; Schwarz and Clore, 2003; Slovic et al., 2002). The general finding is that people in good moods are more optimistic in their assessments of future probabilities, benefits, and risks, while people in bad moods are more pessimistic (Wright and Bower, 1992). People can misattribute the source of their mood state and allow it to influence other decisions they make (Schwarz and Clore, 1983).

Research in behavioral finance has investigated whether investors might misattribute mood states linked to widely experienced mood influencers, such as weather and biorhythm variables, and allow them to influence their investment decisions (for a summary of this literature, see Lucey and Dowling, 2005). However, this can best be described as a nascent literature.

Hirshleifer and Shumway (2003) find a relationship between bright sunshine days (linked to positive mood states) and positive equity returns, while Kamstra et al. (2003) find a pattern in equity returns that mirrors the pattern in mood variation linked to Seasonal Affective Disorder. Dowling and Lucey (2008) find a pattern of temporal mood influence across 37 country stock markets, including a number of emerging markets and find a broad similarity to the extent of the influence of emotions.

Another approach to understanding how emotions influence investment is based on the work of Paul Slovic and colleagues. They particularly concentrate on "affect," or emotions toward a risky activity, with a key finding being that affect appears to direct both the perceived benefit and the perceived risk of the activity (Finucane et al., 2000).

> *If an activity was "liked", people tended to judge its risks as low and its benefits as high. If the activity was "disliked", the judgements were the opposite – high risk and low benefit. (Finucane et al., 2000, p. 4)*

This affect heuristic appears to influence investment. MacGregor et al. (2000) collected affect ratings of various industries from a sample of participants for 20 industries. In addition to finding the affect rating associated with each industry, participants were also asked to estimate the performance of the industry in the previous financial year, the performance of the industry over the coming year, and to say whether they would be willing to buy into an IPO from a company in the industry. Findings suggested that liking an industry led to it being judged as low risk and potentially high return, while disliking an industry (such as tobacco) led to judgment of high risk and low return.

It is likely that emotional reaction does not vary significantly across culture, although this is an underresearched area. Emotions do differ in some aspects across cultures, but the "basic" fundamental emotions are generally considered universal (Mesquita and Haire, 2004), further emotions are argued to be primary, often preceding rational thought, suggesting their fundamental influence in behavior (Zajonc, 1980; LeDoux, 1996). Given the lack of wider research on emotions in finance, and the evidence pointing to a universality of major emotions, it is suggested that emotions in behavioral finance are best treated as common across cultures. One note for further research though is that there is a difference in cultural influence between broadly experienced emotions, and ego-driven emotions such as those characterized by the affect heuristic, with ego-driven emotions being culturally mediated (Markus and Kitayama, 1991). This proffers the possibility that the affect heuristic, being typically viewed as ego-driven, can fruitfully be investigated across countries using cultural mediators to explain cross-country differences in behavior.

3.5. Social Dynamics

Social psychology provides evidence of social dynamics impacting on perception, cognition, attitudes, prejudice, and aggression (among other areas). However, while this suggests a potential influence on financial decision making, the theories of social psychology do not lend themselves to hypothesis development and testing in finance as easily as the theories in cognitive and emotional psychology.

Research applying social psychology theories in behavioral finance has concentrated primarily on the theory of conformity. Conformity is the tendency for individuals in a group to adopt similar attitudes; it has been linked to cultural formation, fashion fads, herd behavior, and a wide variety of social norms (Baron and Byrne, 2004). The theory of conformity is said to originate with Asch's (1955; see Baron et al., 1996, for a comprehensive review) experiments where participants in an experiment were persuaded to give wrong answers to a straightforward question when they had to give their answer after a number of "pretend" participants all gave the wrong answer.

In behavioral finance studies, links have been drawn between the social interaction of groups of people and their tendency to invest. Shiller and Pound (1989) find that the decision to buy a particular equity is influenced by someone the investor knows directly telling them about it. Shiller (2000) also noted the importance of social interaction in the internet stock pricing bubble driven by herding behavior. Hong et al. (2004) find that factors such as church attendance (as a proxy for social interaction) were a determinant of likelihood to invest. While Duflo and Saez (2002) found that employees' tendency to invest in a pension scheme seems to depend on social norms in that workplace. More recently, Kaustia and Knüpfer (2012) show that the decision to enter financial markets is partially determined by the past success of peers, further suggestive of herding behavior.

Other research, such as Nofsinger (2005), draws a plausible link between social mood and overconfidence.

In emerging markets, Ahmed et al. (2010) document evidence of price bubbles in nearly all MSCI emerging markets at some point between 1995 and 2005 (start date for a country dependent on data availability), but do not explore whether the frequency of such bubbles differs from developed markets. Chang et al. (2000) document a greater presence of herding behavior in the emerging markets of South Korea and Taiwan compared to developed markets. More recent research by Chiang and Zheng (2010) documents herding as being more prevalent in the culturally collectivist Asian countries compared to the relatively individualistic Latin American countries. In other emerging markets (and less-developed markets), Białkowski et al. (2012) find that for Muslim-majority countries stock markets tend to rise predictably during the socially (and, of course, religiously) important month of Ramadan, perhaps suggestive of herding in these markets in that period. Chen et al. (2007) further claim that herding should be more prevalent in collectivist cultures in their study of emerging markets and behavioral finance. This is suggestive of a greater role for social dynamics in collectivist emerging markets, but clearly the literature is very limited and in need of further expansion.

4. THE FUTURE OF CULTURAL BEHAVIORAL FINANCE RESEARCH IN EMERGING MARKETS

By way of concluding the chapter, we now extract the key findings from our review of culture and behavioral finance in emerging markets with a focus on how this might inform future studies. The findings can be summarized as follows:

1. Behavioral finance approaches are generally underapplied in terms of understanding emerging market financial behavior. This is particularly the case for the cultural clusters outside of Asia.
2. Culture should be an important factor in the applicability of behavioral finance theories to cross-country studies. There are multiple instances of psychological theories not being uniformly present across countries and this appears to be driven by cultural differences. There appears to be a tendency in cross-market studies to apply the same behavioral principle without regard to these cultural differences. At the very least, cultural dimensions should be included as controls in such studies.
3. Given the cultural differences within emerging market countries, these are best not studied as a uniform group in financial markets' research. This suggests extension studies to existing emerging markets studies that divide countries by cultural groupings.
4. The area of social dynamics is likely to be of greatest relevance in emerging markets characterized by holistic approaches to decision making. Emotional influences on financial behavior are best characterized as universal. Cognitive bias influences are confounded by the opposite influences of culture and relative inexperience.

5. A particularly important cultural dimension is collectivism versus individualism (although the importance of this dimension is partially driven by it being the most applied cultural variable). Given that emerging markets have a greater prevalence of collectivist countries compared to developed markets, this is of particular relevance to emerging market studies. One issue is controlling for differences across emerging markets in terms of investor sophistication, as lack of investor sophistication might introduce cognitive biases through this route. Emerging markets could be differentiated along sophistication lines using measures such as extent of foreign investor participants in markets, with an expectation being that collectivist countries with sophisticated investors showing a greater influence from culture on the presence of cognitive biases.

REFERENCES

Aggarwal, R., Goodell, J.W., 2009a. Markets and institutions in financial intermediation: national characteristics as determinants. Journal of Banking and Finance 33, 1770–1780

Aggarwal, R., Goodell, J.W., 2009b. Markets versus institutions in developing countries: national attributes as determinants. Emerging Markets Review 10, 51–66

Aggarwal, R., Kearney, C., Lucey, B., 2012. Gravity and culture in foreign portfolio investment. Journal of Banking and Finance 36, 525–538

Ahmed, E., Rosser, J., Uppal, J., 2010. Emerging markets and stock market bubbles: nonlinear speculation? Emerging Markets Finance and Trade 46, 23–40

Alpert, M., Raiffa, H., 1982. A progress report on the training of probability assessors. In: Kahneman, D., Slovic, P., Tversky, A. (Eds.), Judgement under Uncertainty: Heuristics and Biases. Cambridge University Press, Cambridge

Antia, M., Lin, J.B., Pantzalis, C., 2007. Cultural distance and valuation of multinational corporations. Journal of Multinational Financial Management 17, 365–383

Asch, S., 1995. Opinions and social pressure. Scientific American 193, 31–35

Barber, B.M., Odean, T., 2001. Boys will be boys: gender, overconfidence, and common stock investment. Quarterly Journal of Economics 116, 261–292

Baron, R.A., Byrne, D., 2004. Social Psychology: International Edition. Pearson, Boston

Baron, R.S., Vandello, U., Brunsman, B., 1996. The forgotten variable in conformity research: impact of task importance on social influence. Journal of Personality and Social Psychology 71, 915–927

Benartzi, S., Thaler, R., 1995. Myopic loss aversion and the equity premium puzzle. Quarterly Journal of Economics 110, 73–92

Biais, B., Weber, M., 2009. Hindsight bias, risk perception, and investment performance. Management Science 55, 1018–1029

Białkowski, J., Etebari, A., Wisniewski, T., 2012. Fast profits: investor sentiment and stock returns during Ramadan. Journal of Banking and Finance 36, 835–845

Bordalo, P., Gennaioli, N., Shleifer, A., 2012. Salience theory of choice under risk. Quarterly Journal of Economics 127, 1243–1285

Breuer, W., Salzmann, A., 2012. National culture and corporate governance. In: Boubaker, S., Nguyen, B.D., Nguyen, D.K. (Eds.), Corporate Governance: Recent Developments and New Trends. Springer-Verlag, Berlin

Bushman, R.M., Piotroski, J.D., Smith, A.J., 2004. What determines corporate transparency? Journal of Accounting Research 42, 207–252

Cashman, G.D., Deli, D.N., Nardari, F., Villupuram, S., 2012. Investors do respond to poor mutual fund performance: evidence from inflows and outflows. Financial Review 47, 719–739

Chan, K., Covrig, V., Ng, L., 2005. What determines the domestic bias and foreign bias? Evidence from mutual fund equity allocations worldwide. Journal of Finance 60, 1495–1534
Chang, E.C., Cheng, J.W., Khorana, A., 2000. An examination of herd behavior in equity markets: an international perspective. Journal of Banking and Finance 24, 1651–1679
Chang, K., Noorbakhsh, A., 2009. Does national culture affect international corporate cash holdings? Journal of Multinational Financial Management 19, 323–342
Chen, G., Kim, K.A., Nofsinger, J.R., Rui, O., 2007. Trading performance, disposition effect, overconfidence, representativeness bias, and experience of emerging market investors. Journal of Behavioral Decision Making 20, 425–451
Chiang, T.C., Zheng, D., 2010. An empirical analysis of herd behavior in global stock markets. Journal of Banking and Finance 34, 1911–1921
Chiou, W., 2008. Who benefits more from international diversification? Journal of International Financial Markets, Institutions and Money 18, 466–482
Chui, A., Kwok, C., 2009. Cultural practices and life insurance consumption: an international analysis using GLOBE scores. Journal of Multinational Financial Management 19, 273–290
Chui, A., Titman, S., Wei, K.C., 2010. Individualism and momentum around the world. Journal of Finance 65, 361–392
Coval, J.D., Moskowitz, T., 1999. Home bias at home: local equity preference in domestic portfolios. Journal of Finance 54, 2045–2073
Coval, J.D., Moskowitz, T.J., 2001. The geography of investment: informed trading and asset prices. Journal of Political Economy 109, 811–841
Cutler, D., Poterba, J., Summers, L.H., 1990. Speculative dynamics and the role of feedback traders. American Economic Review 80, 63–68
Cyert, R., March, J., 1953. A Behavioral Theory of the Firm. Prentice Hall, New Jersey
De Bondt, W., Thaler, R., 1990. Do security analysts overreact? American Economic Review 80, 52–57
De Bondt, W., Thaler, R., 1985. Does the stock market overreact? Journal of Finance 40, 793–805
Deshmukh, S., Goel, A.M., Howe, K., 2013. CEO overconfidence and dividend policy. Journal of Financial Intermediation 22, 440–463
Dowling, M., Lucey, B.M., 2008. Robust global mood influences in equity pricing. Journal of Multinational Financial Management 18, 145–164
Duflo, E., Saez, E., 2002. Participation and investment decisions in a retirement plan: the influence of colleagues' choices. Journal of Public Economics 85, 121–148
Dvorak, T., 2005. Do domestic investors have an information advantage? Evidence from Indonesia. Journal of Finance 60, 817–839
Edwards, W., 1968. Conservatism in human information processing. In: Kleinmutz, B. (Ed.), Formal Representation of Human Judgment. John Wiley and Sons, New York
Eriksen, K.W., Kvaloy, O., 2009. Do financial advisors exhibit myopic loss aversion? Financial Markets and Portfolio Management 24, 159–170
Elliott, C.S., Hayward, D.M., 1998. The expanding definition of framing and its particular impact on economic experimentation. Journal of Socio-Economics 27, 229–243
Estrada, J., 2002. Systematic risk in emerging markets: the D-CAPM. Emerging Markets Review 3, 365–379
Feng, L., Seasholes, M., 2005. Do Investor sophistication and trading experience eliminate behavioral biases in financial markets? Review of Finance 9, 305–351
Fidora, M., Fratzscher, M., Thimann, C., 2007. Home bias in global bond and equity markets: the role of real exchange rate volatility. Journal of International Money and Finance 26, 631–655
Fidrmuc, J.P., Jacob, M., 2010. Culture, agency costs, and dividends. Journal of Comparative Economics 38, 321–339
Finucane, M.L., Alhakami, A., Slovic, P., Johnson, S.M., 2000. The affect heuristic in judgments of risks and benefits. Journal of Behavioral Decision Making 13, 1–17
Georgarakos, D., Pasini, G., 2009. Trust, sociability and stock market participation. Netspar Discussion Paper No 04/2009-015.
Goleman, D., 1997. Vital Lies, Simple Truths: The Psychology of Self-Deception. Simon & Schuster, New York
Gorodnichenko, Y., Roland, G., 2010. Culture, institutions and the wealth of nations. NBER Working Paper No 16368.

Graham, J.R., Harvey, C., Puri, M., 2013. Managerial attitudes and corporate actions. Journal of Financial Economics 109, 103–121
Griffin, D., Tversky, A., 1992. The weighting of evidence and the determinants of overconfidence. Cognitive Psychology 24, 411–435
Griffin, J.M., Kelly, P.J., Nardari, F., 2010. Do market efficiency measures yield correct inferences? A comparison of developed and emerging markets. Review of Financial Studies 23, 3225–3277
Grinblatt, M., Han, B., 2005. Prospect theory, mental accounting, and momentum. Journal of Financial Economics 78, 311–339
Grinblatt, M., Keloharju, M., 2001. How distance, language and culture influence stockholdings and trades. Journal of Finance 56, 1053–1073
Grinblatt, M., Keloharju, M., 2009. Sensation seeking, overconfidence, and trading activity. Journal of Finance 64, 549–578
Heine, S.J., Lehman, D., Markus, H., Kitayama, S., 1999. Is there a universal need for positive self-regard? Psychological Review 106, 766–794
Hirshleifer, D., 2001. Investor psychology and asset pricing. Journal of Finance 56, 1533–1597
Hirshleifer, D., Low, A., Teoh, S.H., 2012. Are overconfident CEOs better innovators? Journal of Finance 67, 1457–1498
Hirshleifer, D., Shumway, T., 2003. Good day sunshine: stock returns and the weather. Journal of Finance 58, 1009–1032
Hofstede, G., 2001. Culture's Consequences: Comparing Values, Behaviors, Institutions and Organizations across Nations. Sage, Thousand Oaks
Hogarth, R.M., Einhorn, H.J., 1992. Order effects in belief updating: the belief-adjustment model. Cognitive Psychology 24, 1–55
Hong, H., Kubik, J.D., Stein, J.C., 2004. Social interaction and stock-market participation. Journal of Finance 59, 137–163
House, R., Javidan, M., Hanges, P., Dorfman, P., 2002. Understanding cultures and implicit leadership theories across the globe: an introduction to project GLOBE. Journal of World Business 37, 3–10
Huang, W., Jiang, F., Liu, Z., Zhang, M., 2011. Agency cost, top executives' overconfidence, and investment-cash flow sensitivity—evidence from listed companies in China. Pacific-Basin Finance Journal 19, 261–277
Huberman, G., 2001. Familiarity breeds investment. Review of Financial Studies 14, 659–680
Hwang, S., Satchell, S.E., 2010. How loss averse are investors in financial markets? Journal of Banking and Finance 34, 2425–2438
Ikenberry, D.L., Ramnath, S., 2002. Underreaction to self-selected news events: the case of stock splits. Review of Financial Studies 15, 489–526
Inglehart, R., Welzel, C., 2005. Modernization, Cultural Change, and Democracy: The Human Development Sequence. Cambridge University Press, Cambridge
Isenberg, D., 1986. Group polarization: a critical review and meta-analysis. Journal of Personality and Social Psychology 50, 1141–1151
Ji, L., Zhang, Z., Guo, T., 2008. To buy or to sell: cultural differences in stock market decisions based on price trends. Journal of Behavioral Decision Making 21, 399–413
Jiatao, L., Harrison, J.R., 2008. Corporate governance and national culture: a multi-country study. Corporate Governance 8, 607–621
Kahneman, D., Slovic, P., Tversky, A., 1982. Judgement Under Uncertainty: Heuristics and Biases. Cambridge University Press, Cambridge
Kahneman, D., Tversky, A., 1973. On the psychology of prediction. Psychological Review 80, 237–251
Kahneman, D., Tversky, A., 1979. Prospect theory: an analysis of decision under risk. Econometrica 47, 263–291
Kamstra, M.J., Kramer, L., Levi, M., 2003. Winter blues: A SAD stock market cycle. American Economic Review 93, 324–343
Kaustia, M., Knüpfer, S., 2012. Peer performance and stock market entry. Journal of Financial Economics 104, 321–338

Kirkman, B.L., Lowe, K.B., Gibson, C.B., 2006. A quarter century of culture's consequences: a review of empirical research incorporating Hofstede's cultural values framework. Journal of International Business Studies 37, 285–320

Kruger, J., 1999. Lake Wobegon Be gone! The 'below-average effect' and the egocentric nature of comparative ability judgments. Journal of Personality and Social Psychology 77, 221–232

Langer, E., Roth, J., 1975. Heads I win, tails it's chance: the illusion of control as a function of the sequence of outcomes in a purely chance game. Journal of Personality and Social Psychology 32, 951–955

LeDoux, J.E., 1996. The Emotional Brain. Simon and Schuster, New York

Loewenstein, G., Weber, E., Hsee, C.K., Welch, N., 2001. Risk as feelings. Psychological Bulletin 127, 267–286

Lord, C., Ross, L., Lepper, M., 1979. Biased assimilation and attitude polarization: the effects of prior theories on subsequently considered evidence. Journal of Personality and Social Psychology 37, 2098–2109

Lucey, B.M., Dowling, M., 2005. The role of feelings in investor decision-making. Journal of Economic Surveys 19, 211–237

MacGregor, D.G., Slovic, P., Dreman, D., Berry, M., 2000. Imagery, affect, and financial judgment. Journal of Psychology and Financial Markets 1, 104–110

Maddox, J., Wilson, E., Quintan, A., Turner, J., Bowker, J., 1984. Genes, minds and culture. Zygon 19, 213–232

Malmendier, U., Tate, G., 2005. CEO overconfidence and corporate investment. Journal of Finance 60, 2661–2700

Markus, H.R., Kitayama, S., 1991. Culture and the self: implications for cognition, emotion, and motivation. Psychological review 98, 224–253

Massa, M., Simonov, A., 2006. Hedging, familiarity and portfolio choice. Review of Financial Studies 19, 633–685

Mesquita, B., Haire, A., 2004. Emotion and culture. Encyclopedia of Applied Psychology, 731–737

Morse, A., Shive, S., 2011. Patriotism in your portfolio. Journal of Financial Markets 14, 411–440

Mulder, M., 1977. The Daily Power Game. Martinus Nijhoff, Amsterdam

O'Grady, S., Lane, H.W., 1996. The psychic distance paradox. Journal of International Business Studies 27, 309–333

Nicolosi, G., Peng, L., Zhu, N., 2009. Do individual investors learn from their trading experience? Journal of Financial Markets 12, 317–336

Nisbett, R.E., Peng, K., Choi, I., Norenzayan, A., 2001. Culture and systems of thought: holistic versus analytic cognition. Psychological Review 108, 291–310

Nofsinger, J.R., 2005. Social mood and financial economics. Journal of Behavioral Finance 6, 144–160

Rabin, M., Vayanos, D., 2010. The Gambler's and hot-hand fallacies: theory and applications. Review of Economic Studies 77, 730–778

Ramírez, A., Tadesse, S., 2009. Corporate cash holdings, uncertainty avoidance, and the multinationality of firms. International Business Review 18, 387–403

Schuler, R.S., Rogovsky, N., 1998. Understanding compensation practice variations across firms: the impact of national culture. Journal of International Business Studies 29, 159–177

Schwarz, N., Clore, G.L., 1983. Mood, misattribution, and judgments of well-being: informative and directive functions of affective states. Journal of Personality and Social Psychology 45, 513–523

Schwarz, N., Clore, G.L., 2003. Mood as information: 20 years later. Psychological Inquiry 14, 296–303

Schwartz, S.H., Sagiv, L., 1995. Identifying culture-specifics in the content and structure of values. Journal of Cross-Cultural Psychology 26, 92–116

Seasholes, M., Zhu, N., 2010. Individual investors and local bias. Journal of Finance 65, 1987–2010

Shao, L., Kwok, C., Guedhami, O., 2009. National culture and dividend policy. Journal of International Business Studies 41, 1391–1414

Shiller, R.J., 2000. Conversation, information, and herd behavior. American Economic Review 85, 181–185

Shiller, R.J., Pound, J., 1989. Survey evidence on diffusion of interest and information among investors. Journal of Economic Behavior and Organization 12 (1), Elsevier

Slovic, P., Finucane, M.L., Peters, E., MacGregor, D.G., 2002. The affect heuristic. In: Gilovich, T., Griffin, D., Kahneman, D. (Eds.), Heuristics and Biases: The Psychology of Intuitive Judgment. Cambridge University Press, Cambridge

Statman, M., Thorley, S., Vorkink, K., 2006. Investor overconfidence and trading volume. Review of Financial Studies 19, 1531–1565

Taras, V., Rowney, J., Steel, P., 2009. Half a century of measuring culture: review of approaches, challenges, and limitations based on the analysis of 121 instruments for quantifying culture. Journal of International Management 15, 357–373

Tversky, A., Kahneman, D., 1974. Judgement under uncertainty: heuristics and biases. Science 185, 1124–1131

Tversky, A., Kahneman, D., 1981. The framing of decisions and the psychology of choice. Science 211, 453–458

Van der Hart, J., Slagter, E., Van Dijk, D., 2003. Stock selection strategies in emerging markets. Journal of Empirical Finance 10, 105–132

Van Gorp, B., 2007. The constructionist approach to framing: bringing culture back in. Journal of Communication 57, 60–78

Warnock, F.E., 2002. Home bias and high turnover reconsidered. Journal of International Money and Finance 21, 795–805

Wilke, A., Barrett, H.C., 2009. The hot hand phenomenon as a cognitive adaptation to clumped resources. Evolution and Human Behavior 30, 161–169

Wright, W.F., Bower, G.H., 1992. Mood effects on subjective probability assessment. Organizational Behavior and Human Decision Processes 52, 276–291

Yama, H., Manktelow, K., Mercier, H., Henst, J.B.V., Soo Do, K., Kawasaki, Y., Adachi, K., 2010. A cross-cultural study of hindsight bias and conditional probabilistic reasoning. Thinking and Reasoning 16, 346–371

Zajonc, R.B., 1980. Feeling and thinking: preferences need no inference. American Psychologist 35, 151–175

CHAPTER 15

Early Warning System for Financial Crisis: Statistical Classification Approach

Young Min Kim*, Kyong Joo Oh*, and Tae Yoon Kim†

*Department of Information and Industrial Engineering, Yonsei University, Seoul, South Korea
†Department of Statistics, Keimyung University, Daegu, South Korea

1. INTRODUCTION

The financial crisis triggered by the downfall of Thailand's Baht in the late 1990s caused tremendous social and economic damage in several Asian countries. This financial tsunami led many researchers to analyze—and to attempt to forecast—financial crises. Landmark findings (see, e.g., Frankel and Rose, 1996) have resulted from these collective efforts; many of these results were found by studying financial crises in the context of crisis-related financial and economic variables. Financial crisis studies have conventionally focused on fundamental economic conditions. In the 1990s, however, new theories emerged that identified self-fulfilling market processes or contagion theory as a reliable alternative explanation for the crises. Since the emergence of these theories, many studies of financial crises have focused their analyses on stock markets—particularly on emerging stock markets—because of the pivotal role they play in the self-fulfilling process or contagion theory.

Over the last 10 years, emerging stock markets in Korea, Hong Kong, Singapore, and Taiwan have been incorporated into the world financial market (Ghysels and Seon, 2005). Globalization and the removal of local market regulations make global institutional investors (GII) major influences in local markets. As a result, the movements of GII may actually control local markets, particularly when severe external or internal shocks hit them. For example, by May 2004, GII occupied almost half of Korean stocks in terms of total market capitalization; in cases of external or internal shock, such as in the Asian financial crisis in 1997, the Russian moratorium in 1998, the liquidity crises of the Daewoo group in June–December 1999 and the Hyundai group in June–December 1999, and the 9/11 terrorists attack in 2001, abnormal pullouts of GII have led the Korean stock market to near collapse (Kim and Wei, 1999). Such an abnormal pullout tends to ignite the self-fulfilling process or contagion theory in emerging markets. To combat such a devastating situation, a proper early warning system (EWS) that detects or

Emerging Markets and the Global Economy
http://dx.doi.org/10.1016/B978-0-12-411549-1.00015-6

predicts the abnormal pullout of GII (and particularly of global hedge funds) is strongly desired in local markets.

One of the most significant procedures in developing EWS for GII (EWSGII) is a procedure proposed by Oh et al. (2006) that employs a statistical classification approach in establishing EWS for financial markets. In formulating EWS as a classification problem, they introduce a "gray zone" that is characterized by abrupt reversals of market sentiments or sudden changes of market volatility. The gray zone is uniquely important for this type of EWS because it is regarded as a transition period (i.e., having gone through the gray zone, the market may proceed either to crisis or stability), and the EWS issues a warning signal whenever a financial market enters the gray zone. For establishing EWSGII in this study, we mainly follow Oh et al. (2006). Technically, the EWSGII issues a warning by forecasting the future condition of the market that will be classified later. Thus, the core of the procedure is defining the oracle rule that determines future market conditions and tracing the oracle rule (the equivalent of lag-l forecasting) with a trained machine learning algorithm.

There are various EWS's, which are designed to monitor economic or financial condition, e.g., Eichengreen et al. (1996), Frankel and Rose (1996), Goldsten (1996), Kaminsky and Reinhart (1999), Goldstein et al. (2000), and Edison (2000). Most of them are developed under the hypothesis that crisis is an eventual result of long-term deterioration of economic fundamentals (Krugman, 1979; Obestfed, 1986; Eichengreen et al., 1995) and focus on the economic long-term variables. Our work developed EWS under different hypothesis that crisis may result from short-term financial market instability without a significant deterioration of long-term economic fundamentals (Velasco, 1987; Ozkan and Sutherland, 1995). Thus, we focus on short-term variables such as daily movement of financial market indexes and, as a result, our EWS is expected to behave in a more time-varying fashion, compared to the existing EWS's.

In the subsequent sections, these subjects are discussed in detail and the EWSGII for the Korean stock market is established as an empirical case study. Indeed, Section 2 provides the entire procedure description and then Sections 3–5, respectively, handle the oracle classifier, the lag-l forecasting classifier, and linking various classifiers. In Section 6, the empirical example and the related experimental results are illustrated.

2. PROCEDURE DESCRIPTION

Let us assume that there is the oracle lag-zero rule:

$$f_0 : \mathbf{Z} \rightarrow Y \tag{1}$$

that maps the oracle predictor $Z = (Z_1, \ldots, Z_q) \in \mathbf{Z}$ onto its classification label. Consider the problem of forecasting $y_{t+l} (l > 0)$ at time t by the predictor variable $\mathbf{x}_t$, which may be different from $\mathbf{z}_{t+l}$. For this problem, we introduce the lag-l forecasting or classification model, which may be defined as:

$$Y_{t+l} = f_l(X_{1t}, \ldots, X_{pt}), \tag{2}$$

where f_l is a lag-l classifier with a set of predictor variables, $X = (X_{1t}, \ldots, X_{pt})$, and a discrete (or categorical) response variable, $y_{t+l} = f_0(z_{1(t+l)}, \ldots, z_{q(t+l)})$, from Equation (1). For the model described in Equation (2), the training data set of size n may be expressed as:

$$\Xi_n = \{(x_{11}, \ldots, x_{p1}, y_{1+l}), \ldots, (x_{1n}, \ldots, x_{pn}, y_{n+l})\}. \tag{3}$$

The training data set Ξ_n then produces the lag-l forecasting classifier:

$$\hat{f}_l : \mathbf{X} \rightarrow Y \tag{4}$$

that maps $\{\mathbf{x}_t = (x_{11}, \ldots, x_{p1}) : t = 1, \ldots, n\}$ onto its classification label $\{(y_{1+l}, \ldots, y_{n+l})\}$. After the $\hat{f}_l$s are successfully established, they are linked to produce the final *EWSGII* via Bayesian approach as follows:

Let us suppose that there are q forecasters, $\hat{f}_{l_1}, \ldots, \hat{f}_{l_q}$, that are to be linked and that each of them classifies the future condition S_F into one of p classes (i.e., $\Omega_p = \{1, \ldots, p\}$). It is assumed that the desired forecaster has the following form:

$$b(t) = \sum_{i=1}^{q} w(i)\hat{f}_{l_i}(t),$$

where $b(t)$ is the final forecasting result at time t, $w(i)$ is the weight given to the classifier $\hat{f}_{l_i}$, and $\hat{f}_{l_i}(t)$ is the forecasting result of $\hat{f}_{l_i}$ at time t. Thus, $w(i)$ above must be found that satisfies the following condition:

$$\sum_{i=1}^{q} w(i) = 1.$$

Please refer to Figure 1 for a simple illustration of constructing EWSGII.

To successfully implement the lag-l forecasting classifier, the following various technical subjects must be taken up such as: (i) selecting predictor variables and training data for the oracle classifier; (ii) selecting predictor variables and training data for the lag-l forecasting classifier; (iii) choice of parameter l; (iv) selection of specific type classifiers (e.g., case-based reasoning); and (v) integration of various classifiers into one classifier for better lag-l forecasting. In the subsequent sections, these subjects are discussed and the EWSGII for the Korean stock market is established as an empirical case study.

3. ORACLE CLASSIFIER

3.1. Definition

The oracle classifier f_0 is required because the trained classifier f_l is designed to predict (or trace) the future market condition that is predetermined by the oracle classifier f_0. The oracle model in Equation (1) assumes that the unknown rule f_0 defines $Y \in \mathrm{Y}$ in terms

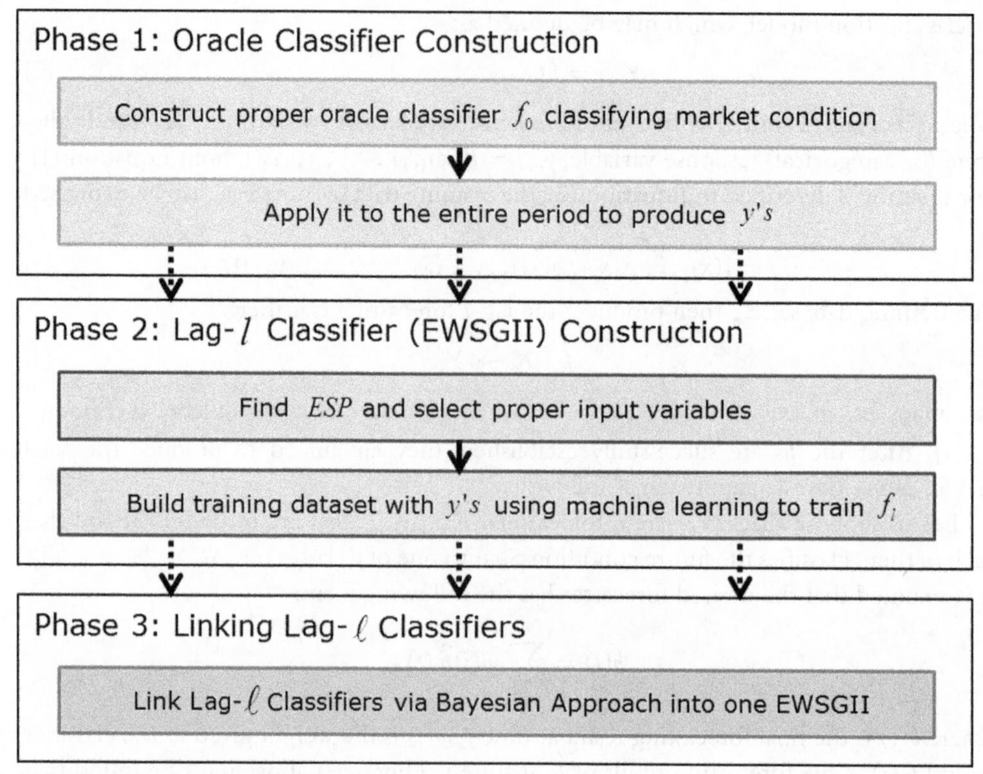

Figure 1 Architecture of the EWSGII construction procedure.

of the predictor $Z \in \mathbf{Z}$ "without lag". Thus, to determine the value of y_t for a given value of t, it is necessary to wait until time t and obtain the value of $\mathbf{Z}_t = (Z_{1t}, \ldots, Z_{qt})$ (sometimes simply to determine Z). For instance, in the example of rise and fall forecasting of the stock market, $Z(= Y)$ may equal one or zero depending on whether the price of stocks has risen or fallen, whereas X might be the stock price and the trading volume from the previous day. However, Z is typically difficult to determine, particularly for early warning forecasters.

In building the oracle classifier f_0, there must be a postulated template with which f_0 is supposed to work. One possible template is to define or classify the market condition as a stable period (SP), a transition period (TP or the gray zone), or a crisis period (CP) exclusively. Here we may define CP as the period during which the GII sells enormous stocks with a contingency plan and TP as the period during which GII shifts from a net long position (buying trend) to a net short position (selling trend) to initiate the contingency plan. Another possible template consists of "before the unstable period (BP)", "the unstable period (UP)", and "after the unstable period (AP)". UP is the period in which GII turns from a net long position (or buying trend) to a net short position (or selling trend) to initiate a contingency plan. AP is the period during which the GII sells an enormous quantity of stocks with a contingency plan. BP is the period that belongs to neither AP nor UP. By using terminology BP, UP, and AP in this context, we implicitly assume that an abnormal pullout by GII will be made in the time order of BP, UP, and AP. Hereinafter, $Y = \{1, 2, 3\}$ implies either {SP, TP, CP} or {BP, UP, AP} as the range of the oracle response.

3.2. Predictor Variables

In obtaining predictor variables $\mathbf{Z}_t = (Z_{1t}, \ldots, Z_{qt})$, it is notable that these variables are selected for defining either {SP, TP, CP} or {BP, UP, AP} efficiently. For defining {SP, TP, CP}:

$$(z_1, z_2, z_3, z_4) = \{\text{quarterly, monthly, weekly, and daily net sales of GII}\} \quad (5)$$

are appropriate because they reflect a selling trend with a contingency plan fairly well. In fact, these quantities are monitored by the Financial Supervisory Service in Korea, which has its own rules of thumb in using quantities for detecting abnormal massive selling of GII. Refer to Table 1.

For defining BP, UP, and AP quantitatively, the net buying position of the GII (NPG) might be considered, where NPG(r) represents the buying (long) position of the GII minus the selling (short) position of the GII during the period r. A positive NPG corresponds to the situation in which the volume of stock purchases by the GII exceeds stock sales, whereas a negative NPG corresponds to a situation in which stock sales by the GII exceed stock purchases. To consider market capitalization, NPG is scaled as follows:

$$NPGR_t(r) = \frac{NPG_t(r)}{MC_t}, \quad (6)$$

where MC_t implies market capitalization of the stock market at time t. As discussed above, we implicitly assume that an abnormal pullout by GII will be made in the time order of BP, UP, and AP. Thus, the definitions of BP, UP, and AP using Equation (6) are given such that the scaled NPG monitoring behavior of GII deteriorates in the order of BP, UP, and AP (refer to Table 2 below). This indicates that BP, UP, and AP might technically have been forecasted independently of time order but the order of occurrence BP-UP-AP is expected to hold while the scaled NPG moves continuously. This type of continuity assumption among class indices justifies the use of linear sums as solution statistics (refer to Equation (10) later). For a more concrete quantification of (BP, UP, AP) or (SP, TP, CP), an enormous selling period (ESP) by GII in the past should be focused upon, which may be obtained by examining selling trends by GII in a statistical analysis. A formal definition of ESP would be of great help, if available.

The following facts are known with respect to ESP. First, ESP with the market trend may not provide as efficient feature vectors as ESP against the market trend; this appears

Table 1 Oracle classification rules for CP, TP, and SP.

	Classification rule
$f_O(1)$	**If** Quarterly net sales more than 2.4* (or) monthly net sales more than 1.6* (or) weekly net sales more than 0.8* (or) daily net sales more than 0.4*, **Then** $Y = 3$ **(CP)** **Else If** Quarterly net sales more than 1.2* (or) monthly net sales more than 0.8* (or) weekly net sales more than 0.4* (or) daily net sales more than 0.15*, **Then** $Y = 2$ **(TP)** **Else** $Y = 1$ **(SP)**
$f_O(2)$	**If** Quarterly net sales more than 3.0* (or) monthly net sales more than 2.0* (or) weekly net sales more than 1.0* (or) daily net sales more than 0.5*, **Then** $Y = 3$ **(CP)** **Else If** Quarterly net sales more than 1.5* (or) monthly net sales more than 1.0* (or) weekly net sales more than 0.5* (or) daily net sales more than 0.2*, **Then** $Y = 2$ **(TP)** **Else** $Y = 1$ **(SP)**
$f_O(3)$	**If** Quarterly net sales more than 4.0* (or) monthly net sales more than 3.0* (or) weekly net sales more than 1.5* (or) daily net sales more than 0.7*, **Then** $Y = 3$ **(CP)** **Else If** Quarterly net sales more than 2.0* (or) monthly net sales more than 1.5* (or) weekly net sales more than 0.8* (or) daily net sales more than 0.4*, **Then** $Y = 2$ **(TP)** **Else** $Y = 1$ **(SP)**

*Unit: 1 billion won.

to be related to the fact that an ESP with the market trend is hard to detect. Second, a more sensitive oracle classifier for the ESP should be used with the market trend. Here ESP against (with) the market trend indicates that enormous selling is done while market is in a buy (sell) position.

Table 2 Oracle classification rules for BP, UP, and AP.

Classification rule
If NPGR(1) <= −0.05
(or) NPGR(6) <= −0.2
(or) NPGR(17) <= −0.5
(or) NPGR(60) <= −1.4
Then $Y = 3$ **(AP)**
Else If −0.05 < NPGR(1) <= −0.025
(or) −0.2 < NPGR(6) <= −0.1
(or) −0.5 < NPGR(17) <= −0.25
(or) −1.4 < NPGR(60) <= −0.7
Then $Y = 2$ **(UP)**
Else $Y = 1$ **(BP)**

4. LAG-l FORECASTING CLASSIFIER

4.1. Definition

As discussed in Section 1, we assume that there is the oracle lag-zero rule:

$$f_0 : \mathbf{Z} \rightarrow \mathrm{Y} = \{1, 2, 3\} \tag{7}$$

that maps the oracle predictor $Z = (Z_1, \ldots, Z_q) \in \mathbf{Z}$ onto its classification label $Y \in \mathrm{Y} = \{1, 2, 3\}$. By using the predictor variable $\mathbf{x}_t$, one may forecast $y_{t+l} (l > 0)$ at time t. Indeed, the lag-ℓ forecasting or classification model f_l given by Equation (2) and the training data set Ξ_n given by Equation (3) are employed to produce the lag-ℓ forecasting classifier $\hat{f}_l$ given by Equation (4). The f_l of Equation (2) assumes that forecasting $y_{t+\ell} (\ell > 0)$ at time t is possible via $\mathbf{x}_t = (x_{1t}, \ldots, x_{pt})$ and hence is based on a stationarity assumption of f_ℓ.

For the predictor variables $X_1, X_2, \ldots, X_p$, financial variables that are likely to reflect the movement of the GII are selected. For obtaining proper $X_1, X_2, \ldots, X_p$, transformation or expert opinions should be taken into account. For example, in addition to NPG, the net long position of index futures by GII (NPI), the stock price index (SPI), the foreign exchange rate (FER), and the Dow-Jones index (DJI) might be considered with their own derivative variables based on moving average and moving variance. Here, NPI represents the daily long position of index futures by GII minus the daily short position of index futures by GII. These variables must be selected such that f_l may efficiently reflect the trend, and the volatility of market and the desired fitting level to Ξ_n may be achieved. It may be desirable for each f_l to have different predictors, depending on l. A detailed discussion about the selection of l will be given later with respect to machine learning tools in Section 4.3.

Table 3 Input variables considered.

Variable name	Numerical formula	Description
IND	x_t	Index or rate
MA(m)	$\overline{p}_{m,t} = \sum_{i=t-(m-1)}^{t} x_t/m$	m -day moving average
MV(m)	$s_{m,t}^2 = \sum_{i=t-(m-1)}^{t} (x_i - \overline{p}_{m,t})^2/m$	m -day moving variance

4.2. Training Data Set

Because the accuracy of f_l as a forecaster depends mainly on the training data set Ξ_n (or $\hat{f}_l$, equivalently), building desirable Ξ_n is critical. As with oracle classifier f_0, ESP by GII in the past should be focused by examining daily, weekly, monthly, or quarterly selling trends by GII, and the formal definition of ESP, if available, might be helpful at this juncture. In addition, moving average and moving variances of weekly, monthly, and quarterly NPG data (refer to the numerical formulae from Table 3) are sometimes helpful in finding ESP.

With respect to the stationarity issue of f_l, certain technical tips with training data Ξ_n may be provided. First, because $\hat{f}_\ell$ is trained using Ξ_n such that it can accurately forecast the label of Y defined by f_0 after lag-ℓ, it might be necessary to include the variables as predictors that mimic the oracle predictor Z. Second, the normalization or transformation of predictor X (e.g., the linear transformation of the predictor variable from the training data to [0, 1]) may be effective in preventing extremely large or extremely small values of the predictor variables from affecting $\hat{f}_\ell$ significantly. It is accepted that transformation within a specific range helps reduce forecasting error by inducing a stationary relationship between $(X_{1t}, \ldots, X_{pt})$ and $Y_{t+\ell}$ (Lapedes et al., 1998).

Finally, performance of $\hat{f}_l$ (or Ξ_n, equivalently) depends on the assigned oracle rule f_0 and ESP (enormous selling period). For Ξ_n based on the ESP against the market trend, a conservative oracle classifier appears to be desirable, whereas for Ξ_n based on the ESP with the market trend, a sensitive oracle classifier appears to be useful. Here, a conservative (sensitive) oracle classifier indicates the rule that tends to produce less (more) CP or UP, and the ESP against (with) market trend indicates ESP when market is in a buy (sell) position.

4.3. Machine Learning Tools

For efficient training of $\hat{f}_\ell$, one may consider the following four popularly used classification methods: artificial neural network (ANN), multinomial logistic regression (MLR), decision tree (DT), and case-based reasoning (CBR). Our discussions with these machine learning algorithms address certain technical matters, including the selection of l. Among these four algorithms listed above, MLR is parametric, whereas the remaining three are nonparametric. Out of the three nonparametric algorithms, DT is the closest to a parametric algorithm. Ahn et al. (2011) found that CBR performs better overall than other machine learning algorithms. Below, we summarize their findings about the selection of machine learning.

(i) MLR and DT exhibit certain limitations for a (relatively) large value of l. MLR assumes the parametric model given by:

$$P(Y_{t+\ell} = 0) = 1/\left[1 + \sum_{j=1}^{J} \exp(X_t\beta_j)\right], \tag{8}$$

$$P(Y_{t+\ell} = j) = \exp(X_t\beta_j)/\left[1 + \sum_{j=1}^{J} \exp(X_t\beta_j)\right]. \tag{9}$$

Note that Equations (8) and (9) reduce to $P(Y_{t+\ell} = j) = 1/(1 + J)$ for $j = 0, 1, \ldots, J$, if $\beta_j = 0$, and that $\beta_j = 0$ implies independence between the response and predictor variables. Such independence is expected with large values of l. Therefore, as the value of l increases, the distribution of Y in the MLR model approaches a uniform distribution. Thus, the MLR model may fail for large values of l unless the real values of Y follow the exactly same uniform distribution. DT appears to exhibit a similar limitation because it produces a decision tree with a structure that determines a specific distribution of Y when independence is assumed between the response and predictor variables (Breiman et al., 1984). As a result, a parametric machine learning algorithm such as MLR and DT may be more effective for short-term forecasting (or for small values of l), whereas a nonparametric machine learning algorithm such as ANN or CBR may be more effective for long-term forecasting (or for large values of l).

(ii) Ahn et al. (2011) found that CBR performs better than other machine learning algorithms across different values of l. This may be because CBR is useful when knowledge of the sample conditions is incomplete or when the sample is sparse (Kolodner, 1991). Sparse sampling is intrinsic to crisis-related data because crisis is uncommon. In this sense, CBR appears to be desirable in building early warning systems to predict rare crises. Recently, the sample-sparseness aspect of crisis has been resolved by minutely examining the rare occurrence of crisis from several different aspects, which inevitably increases the number of available inputs or predictor variables. In fact, this type of problem is known as a high-dimension low sample-size (HDLSS) classification problem (Hall et al., 2005).

5. LINKING VARIOUS CLASSIFIERS

In this section, the Bayesian forecaster is presented, which links together all the available forecasters using case-based optimization. See Ahn et al. (2012) for its detail.

5.1. Bayesian Forecaster and Case-Based Optimization

Let us suppose that there are q forecasters, $\hat{f}_1, \ldots, \hat{f}_q$, that are to be linked and that each of them classifies the future condition S_F into one of p classes (i.e., $\Omega_p = \{1, \ldots, p\}$). It is assumed that the desired forecaster has the following form:

$$b(t) = \sum_{i=1}^{q} w(i)\hat{f}_i(t), \tag{10}$$

where $b(t)$ is the final forecasting result at time t, $w(i)$ is the weight given to the classifier $\hat{f}_i$, and $\hat{f}_i(t)$ is the forecasting result of $\hat{f}_i$ at time t. Thus, $w(i)$ of Equation (10) must be found that satisfies the following condition:

$$\sum_{i=1}^{q} w(i) = 1. \tag{11}$$

If $w(i)$ is to be decided by the conditional accuracy of each forecaster $\hat{f}_i$, $w(i)$ can be obtained through our Bayesian approach. For the implementation of the Bayesian approach to be successful, a proper posterior distribution must be found, given a future realization. Its expectation serves as a solution to the Bayesian approach. Based on this idea, we describe the procedure to find $\{w(i) : i = 1, \ldots, q\}$.

Let $\Delta_{T,q} = \{\hat{f}_i(t) : i = 1, \ldots, q;$ and $t = 1, \ldots, T\} \in R^{q\times T}$, $k \in \Omega_p = \{1, \ldots, p\}$, $\mathbf{w} = \{w(1), \ldots, w(q)\}$, $\hat{\mathbf{f}}(t) = \{\hat{f}_1(t), \ldots, \hat{f}_q(t)\}$ for $t = 1, \ldots, T$, $\mathbf{W} = \{\mathbf{w}'\hat{\mathbf{f}}(1), \ldots, \mathbf{w}'\hat{\mathbf{f}}(T)\} \in R^T$, and $\mathbf{1} = \{1, \ldots, 1\} \in R^T$. We introduce an objective function $\lambda(w(1), \ldots, w(q))$ and find its minimizer $\hat{\mathbf{w}} = (\hat{w}(1), \ldots, \hat{w}(q))$ that satisfies the condition $\sum_{i=1}^{q} \hat{w}(i) = 1$ with $\hat{w}(i) \geq 0$, i.e.:

$$\arg\min_{w(1),\ldots,w(q)} \lambda(w(1), \ldots, w(q)) = \arg\min_{w(1),\ldots,w(q)} \sum_{k=1}^{p} ||\mathbf{W} - k\mathbf{1}||_T^2. \tag{12}$$

Note that Equation (12) may be rewritten as follows:

$$\arg\min_{w(1),\ldots,w(q)} \lambda(w(1), \ldots, w(q)) = \arg\min_{w(1),\ldots,w(q)} \sum_{k=1}^{p}\sum_{t=1}^{T}\left[\sum_{i=1}^{q} w(i)\hat{f}_i(t) - k\right]^2. \tag{13}$$

Thus, Equation (13) indicates that the solution $(\hat{w}(1), \ldots, \hat{w}(q))$ may be found by minimizing the quadratic distance between $\mathbf{w}'\hat{\mathbf{f}}(t)$ and k over $t = 1, \ldots, T$ and $k = 1, \ldots, p$. Because $||\mathbf{W} - k\mathbf{1}||_T^2$ measures the squared error of the linked forecasters when k is the future realization class, its distribution is clearly determined by the posterior distribution of $\Delta_{T,q}$, given the value of k. Thus, the Bayesian solution can be represented as follows:

$$\arg\min_{w(1),\ldots,w(q)} E_{\Delta_{T,q}}(||\mathbf{W} - k\mathbf{1}||_T^2 | k). \tag{14}$$

Further, if one can find the marginal distribution of $k \in \Omega_p$, the Bayesian solution becomes the following:

$$\arg\min_{w(1),\ldots,w(q)} E_k[E_{\Delta_{T,q}}(||\mathbf{W} - k\mathbf{1}||_T^2|k)], \tag{15}$$

which can be estimated by Equation (12) and hence by Equation (13). In Equation (12), the Bayesian solution assumes a non-informative marginal value for k. This may be improved by finding the proper marginal value for $k \in \Omega_p$ (from earlier data). In this instance, Equation (12) changes to the following:

$$\arg\min_{w(1),\ldots,w(q)} \lambda(w(1),\ldots,w(q)) = \arg\min_{w(1),\ldots,w(q)} \sum_{k=1}^{p} \alpha_k ||\mathbf{W} - k\mathbf{1}||_T^2, \tag{16}$$

where $\{\alpha_1,\ldots,\alpha_p : \sum_{k=1}^{p} \alpha_k = 1\}$ is a proper marginal distribution on a set of classes $\{1,\ldots,p\} \in \Omega_p$. It should be noted that, at Equation (10), categorical forecasters or responses are introduced in a linear combination, which results in a numerical number not in Ω_p. To resolve this, we propose to employ a method that rounds off the resulting value of $b(t)$ to its nearest class index. In fact, this method (which implicitly assumes continuity among class indices) is employed in our empirical study and experiment below.

There are certain technical matters to be resolved for our Bayesian approach, i.e., the selection of solution statistics, prior on the future classes, and the proper machine learning algorithm for finding optimal $\hat{\mathbf{w}} = (\hat{w}(1),\ldots,\hat{w}(q))$. The selection of solution statistics and the selection of prior are related to the questions of whether a linear sum at Equation (10) is appropriate as a tool combining forecasters and whether a non-informative marginal distribution on a set of classes $\{1,\ldots,p\} \in \Omega_p$ is valid, respectively. We believe that correct answers to these questions depend primarily on the type of problem at hand and that our approach that employs linear sums as solution statistics provides one general solution, particularly with respect to the case in which a continuity assumption among class indices is plausible. In principle, our Bayesian algorithm proceeds automatically, once that solution statistics and the marginal are fixed. For a proper machine learning optimizer, we recommend evolutionary algorithm (EA) or genetic algorithm (GA) because these algorithms might resolve local optimum problem efficiently. Recall that our Bayesian linking approach is subject to local optima. These matters are discussed in detail in the next section through empirical examples.

6. EMPIRICAL EXAMPLE AND EXPERIMENT

The main aim of this section is to develop an EWSGII in the Korean stock market and experiment with it with the objective of providing useful information about the construction of EWSGII. To achieve this, we have developed three forecasters to predict massive selling by the GII over different time horizons (daily, weekly, and monthly) and have then linked them through a single Bayesian forecaster. Of course, EWSGII is established by following the procedure described in the previous sections, i.e., the oracle classifier (f_0) and then the three lag-l classifiers ($\hat{f}_l$s) are derived first and then linked to form a single Bayesian forecaster. Note that the linking procedure is desirable because forecasting must be performed over several different time horizons and not merely in one particular instance of time.

For deriving the oracle classifier f_0 and the lag-l classifier $\hat{f}_l$, we employ a BP-UP-AP template that is defined via $NPGR_t(r)$ that is given in Equation (6). Figures 2 and 3 show

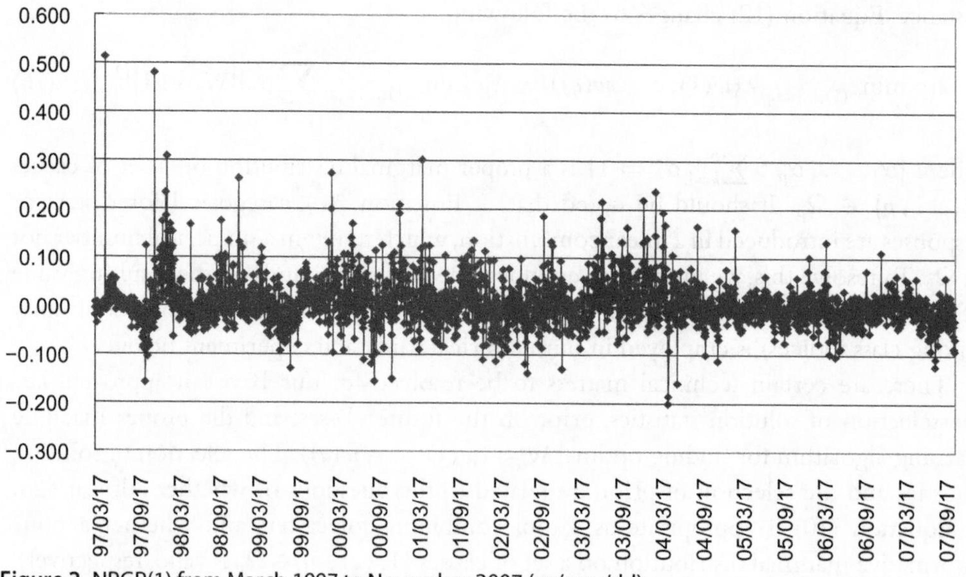

Figure 2 NPGR(1) from March 1997 to November 2007 (yy/mm/dd).

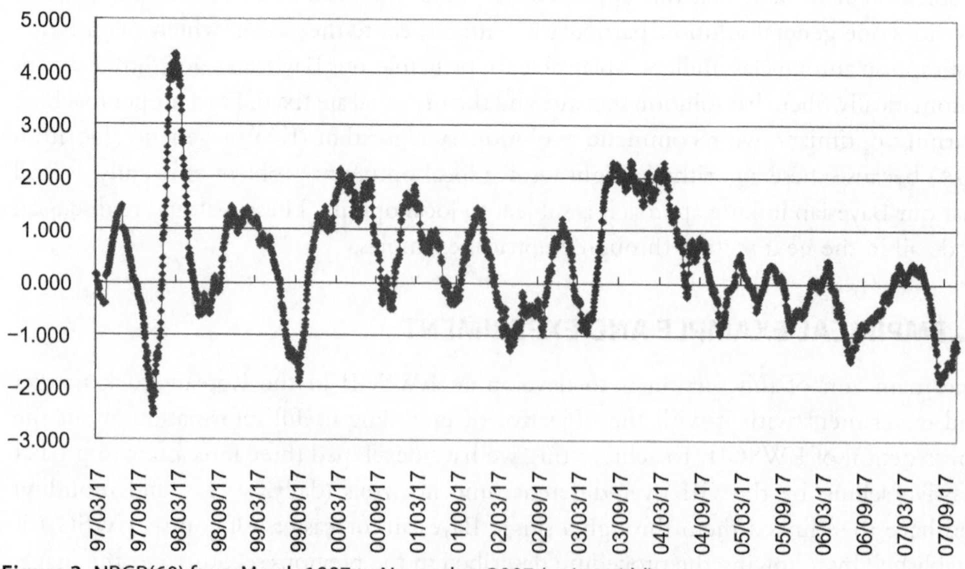

Figure 3 NPGR(60) from March 1997 to November 2007 (yy/mm/dd).

NPGR(1) and NPGR(60) for the Korean stock market index (SPI) from March 1997 to November 2007. We are assuming that the order of occurrence BP-UP-AP holds.

6.1. Phase 1: Oracle Classifier f_0 Construction

The f_0 defines BP, UP, and AP in terms of the quarterly, monthly, weekly, and daily NPGRs, i.e., NPGR(60), NPGR(17), NPGR(6), and NPGR(1), respectively. These four NPGRs, denoted by $z_1, \ldots, z_4$, are the oracle predictor variables, and y is the oracle response, which takes values of 1, 2, and 3 that correspond to BP, UP, and AP, respectively. Thus, at a given time t, the oracle classifier f_0 in Equation (1) is found. In our empirical example, the oracle classifier f_0 was established by expert opinion that was based on an empirical analysis of the behavior of the four NPGRs from March 1997 to November 2007 (shown in Table 2). Figure 4 shows the result of the oracle rule applied to several selected time periods.

6.2. Phase 2: Lag-l Classifier $\hat{f}_l$ Construction

To build a training data set, we defined an enormous selling period (ESP) by examining NPGR(60) for the GII in the past (see Figure 3). Three different ESPs that shocked the Korean stock market (10/1997–01/1998, 05/1999–10/1999, and 01/2002–08/2002) were selected based on the value of NPGR(60), which dipped to -1.0 in these three periods. The critical value of -1.0 was found by an empirical analysis of NPGR(60). The remaining ESPs satisfying this condition were treated as test periods. The three selected ESPs were known to have different characteristics. The first ESP (10/1997 – 01/1998) corresponded to the market crash of 1997. The second ESP (05/1999 – 10/1999) occurred in 1999 when the market was on the path to overheating. The third ESP (01/2002 – 08/2002) occurred in 2002 when the market experienced high fluctuations in its index over an extended period of time.

To build our lag-l forecaster, the response variable Y is assigned by applying the oracle classifier (see, e.g., Figure 4). We selected 18 predictors, $X_1, \ldots, X_{18}$, that are financial variables or their variations that are likely to reflect the movement of the GII properly. More specifically, the following predictors were employed in this study: NPG, the Korean Stock Price Index (SPI), the Korean won/US dollar exchange rate (FER), the Dow-Jones index (DJI), the net long position of index futures of the GII (NPI), and the transformations of each of these variables (see Tables 3 and 4). Here, NPI represents the difference of the daily long and short positions of the index futures of the GII.

Thus, the training data set for lag-l forecasting can now be expressed as follows:

$$(X_{11}, \ldots, X_{s1}, Y_{1+l}), \ldots, (X_{1n}, \ldots, X_{sn}, Y_{n+l}), \tag{17}$$

where $s = 18$, n is the size of training data, and $Y_{1+l}, \ldots, Y_{n+l}$ are obtained by applying the oracle classifier f_0. For our empirical study, we built 15 training data sets (or 15 $\hat{f}_l$s,

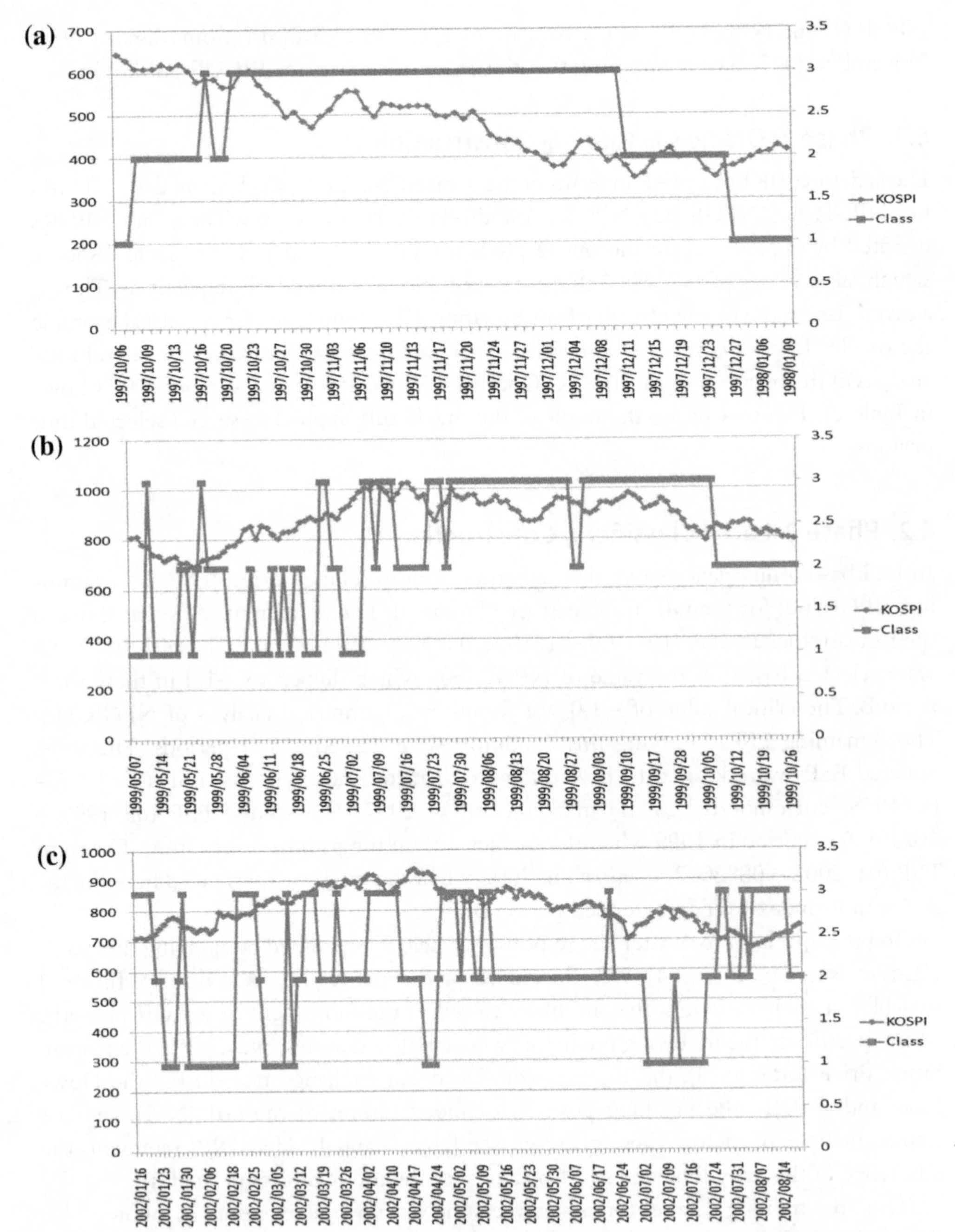

Figure 4 Oracle classification result for the three training periods. (a) 97/10/06 ~ 98/01/09 (ESP_{97}), (b) 99/05/07 ~ 99/10/27 (ESP_{99}), (c) 02/01/16 ~ 02/08/21 (ESP_{02}).

Table 4 List of predictor and response variables for the EWSIGII.

Variable names	Predictor variables*	Response variable
NPG	IND, MA(8), MA(17), MA(60), MV(17)	y (condition of market)
SPI	IND, MA(8), MA(17), MV(17)	
FER	IND, MA(17), MV(17)	
DJI	IND, MA(17), MV(17)	
NPI	IND, MA(8), MA(17)	

*Predictor variables consist of the total of 18 variables presented above. The response variable y denotes the condition of the market (1 = BP, 2 = UP, 3 = AP).

Table 5 Number of data for training and testing of classifiers from each *ESP*.

Data set	ESP_{97}	ESP_{99}	ESP_{02}	ESP_{97+99}	$ESP_{97+99+02}$
Training	90	129	147	219	366
Testing	2694	2655	2637	2565	2418
Total	2784	2784	2784	2784	2784

equivalently) in the following manner. First, we built five training data sets, i.e., ESP_{97} from the ESP in 1997, ESP_{99} from the ESP in 1999, and ESP_{02} from the ESP in 2002, following which two or three training data sets were combined to produce the two augmented training data sets ESP_{97+99} and $ESP_{97+99+02}$. Each training data set was built such that the cardinalities of BP, UP, and AP were equal. For instance, in Table 5, the training data from ESP_{97} consists of a total of 90 values, i.e., 30 BPs, 30 UPs, and 30 APs. This data set was used to justify the non-informative marginal on k in Equation (12). Second, each of the five training data sets yielded three lag-l classifiers with $l = 1, 5, 20$ as follows (refer to Equation (17)):

$$\hat{f}_l : X \to Y. \tag{18}$$

This produced a total of 15 forecasters or classifiers. As a machine learning algorithm for training f_l, the backpropagation neural networks (BPN) were employed here as artificial neural networks (ANN). More precisely, the number of hidden layers of BPN ranged from 2 to 10 and the logistic function was employed as an activation function with learning rate, momentum, and initial weight given by 0.1, 0.1, and 0.3, respectively. Furthermore, all predictor variables were scaled from 0 to 1 and the validation set was randomly assigned to 33% of the total training set. ANN is implemented by NeuroShell2 v4.0.

Table 6 Training and testing hit rates (%) of each EWSGII.

Training data	Rates	Daily ($\hat{f}_1$)	Weekly ($\hat{f}_5$)	Monthly ($\hat{f}_{20}$)
ESP_{97}	Training	97.7	95.6	95.8
	Testing	43.8	43.6	40.5
ESP_{99}	Training	96.1	99.2	96.9
	Testing	40.2	37.2	37.1
ESP_{02}	Training	95.9	95.2	95.9
	Testing	57.7	41.6	40.1
ESP_{97+99}	Training	95.9	96.3	96.3
	Testing	62.1	43.1	37.5
$ESP_{97+99+02}$	Training	95.4	94.3	95.1
	Testing	58.4	48.1	42.2

Remark 1. After training, each $\hat{f}_l$ was tested against its test data set to evaluate its performance. Here, the test data for $\hat{f}_l$ were defined by the data set given in Equation (17) for the entire time interval (03/1997 – 11/2007), except for the training period. Note that the number of the training data set (which varies in size from 90 to 366 cases) is small compared to that of the test data, as shown in Table 5. Hit rates for training and testing data were calculated as the number of correct forecasts divided by the number of total forecasts. Table 6 shows the results of these calculations for 15 classifiers. Table 6 contains several noteworthy facts about building EWSGIIs. First, unlike ESP_{97} and ESP_{02}, ESP_{99} fails to show proper performance. For example, $\hat{f}_l$ trained on ESP_{99} tends to register poor testing rates for all $l = 1, 5, 20$. This demonstrates that it is difficult to extend or generalize the ESP training data when they are against the market trend. Second, both daily and weekly forecasting perform reasonably well compared to monthly forecasting. This is not surprising because accurate forecasting of the distant future is typically difficult. Finally, the training data set seasoned with various types of ESPs tends to yield more reliable results; i.e., ESP_{97+99} and $ESP_{97+99+02}$ seem to outperform other training sets. As described earlier, ESP_{97} is a training data set that is consistent with the market trend, ESP_{99} is a training data set that is against the market trend, and ESP_{02} is a training data set from market trends with high fluctuations.

6.3. Phase 3: *b – EWSGII* Construction

After the $\hat{f}_l$s were successfully established, they were linked to produce the Bayesian forecaster $b - EWSGII$ as follows:

$$b - EWIGII(t, 1) = \sum_{i=1}^{3} \hat{w}(i)\hat{f}_{l_i}(t + 1 - l_i, l_i), \tag{19}$$

Table 7 Parameter range for preliminary GA experiments.

Parameter	Value
Population size	$50 \sim 200$
Crossover rate	$0.3 \sim 0.5$
Mutation rate	$0.05 \sim 0.06$

where $b - EWSGII(t, 1)$ denotes lag-one forecasting at time t made by the Bayesian forecaster and $\hat{f}_{l_i}(t + 1 - l_i, l_i)$ denotes lag-l_i forecasting at time $t + 1 - l_i$ made by the lag-l_i forecaster $\hat{f}_{l_i}$. Of course, $l_1 = 1, l_2 = 5, l_3 = 20$ and $\hat{w}(i)$ are weights found by:

$$(\hat{w}(1), \hat{w}(2), \hat{w}(3)) = \arg\min_{w(1),w(2),w(3)} \sum_{k=1}^{3} \sum_{t=1}^{T} \left[\sum_{i=1}^{3} w(i)\hat{f}_{l_i}(t+1-l_i, l_i) - k \right]^2 \tag{20}$$

on three training data sets, EWS_{97}, EWS_{97+99}, and $EWS_{97+99+02}$. These three training data sets were employed here because they registered a better performance than the other data sets (refer to Table 6). At this juncture, it should be stressed that $b - EWSGII$ is designed to forecast Y_{t+1} at given t, i.e., lag-one forecasting at given t, and thus, it links $\hat{f}_1(t, 1)$, $\hat{f}_5(t-4, 5)$, and $\hat{f}_{20}(t-19, 20)$ through a linear combination in an optimal manner. The Bayesian lag-l forecaster using all $\hat{f}_1, \hat{f}_5$, and $\hat{f}_{20}$ is not technically possible for $l > 1$.

To link these daily, weekly, and monthly EWSGIIs into $b - EWSGII$, a genetic algorithm (GA) was chosen as proper EA (see, e.g., Aci et al., 2010). Before GA optimization, small preliminary experiments were performed to obtain a proper parameter setting for the successful implementation of GA. Indeed, the experiments were conducted over the parameter range given in Table 7, and the best ones in terms of the fitness measure given by (12) were obtained. The number of generations was fixed at 500, and GA was designed to stop when improvement in terms of the fitness measure was less than 1% in 1000 consecutive trials. As a result, population size, crossover rate, and the mutation rate were obtained as 200, 0.5, and 0.06, respectively. Recall that GA operates the process of crossover and mutation on initial chromosomes and iterates until certain stopping conditions are satisfied. In addition, operators used for crossover and mutation are uniform crossover and static mutation, respectively, and that implementation of GA in this subsection has been undertaken via Evolver Ver. 4 by Palisade Co.

Remark 2. After the completion of this procedure, three Bayesian classifiers with ESP_{97}, ESP_{97+99}, and $ESP_{97+99+02}$ ($b_1 - EWSGII$, $b_2 - EWSGII$, and $b_3 - EWSGII$, respectively) were established. Table 8 presents the weights found by GA in the process of building the three Bayesian classifiers, which reveals that the lag-1 (daily) forecaster must be heavily weighted for $b_1 - EWSGII(ESP_{97})$, that lag-1 and lag-20 (daily and monthly)

Table 8 Weights for the Bayesian forecaster by GA.

Training data set	$\hat{w}(l)$	Weights
	$\hat{w}(1)$	0.9998
$b_1 - EWIGII(ESP_{97})$	$\hat{w}(5)$	0.0000
	$\hat{w}(20)$	0.0001
	$\hat{w}(1)$	0.4285
$b_2 - EWIGII(ESP_{97+99})$	$\hat{w}(5)$	0.0000
	$\hat{w}(20)$	0.5714
	$\hat{w}(1)$	0.3666
$b_3 - EWIGII(ESP_{97+99+02})$	$\hat{w}(5)$	0.3589
	$\hat{w}(20)$	0.2744

Table 9 Testing hit rates (%) for the Bayesian forecaster.

Training data set	Hit rates (%)
$b_1 - EWIGII(ESP_{97})$	45.5
$b_2 - EWIGII(ESP_{97+99})$	58.6
$b_3 - EWIGII(ESP_{97+99+02})$	58.4

forecasters play key roles for $b_2 - EWSGII(ESP_{97+99})$, and that lag-1, lag-5, and lag-20 (daily, weekly, and monthly, respectively) forecasters are almost equally important to $b_3 - EWSGII(ESP_{97+99+02})$. This explicitly indicates that, although the lag-1 forecaster exhibits the best performance (regardless of the type of training data), its importance (or weight) for the Bayesian forecaster decreases significantly as the training data set becomes seasoned with different types of data. This is significant because the Bayesian forecaster designed for lag-1 forecasting tends to value lag-5 and lag-20 highly as the training data set becomes seasoned with different types of data.

Remark 3. Table 9 shows the testing hit rates for each Bayesian forecaster. As shown in Tables 6 and 9, when the testing hit rates of the Bayesian forecasters are compared with those of the regular lag forecasters, the improvements made by the Bayesian forecasters appear to be somewhat limited because both testing hit rates are similar. A closer examination of the experimental results, however, reveals a different story. It is clear from Figures 5 and 6 that the Bayesian forecaster (lag-1 forecaster b_2 and b_3 in Figures 5 and 6) sufficiently smoothes the regular forecaster (lag-1 forecaster $\hat{f}_1$ in Figures 5 and 6) and and thereby achieves an equally high level of performance. One remarkable aspect of this smoothness of the Bayesian forecaster is that the equally high level of performance by

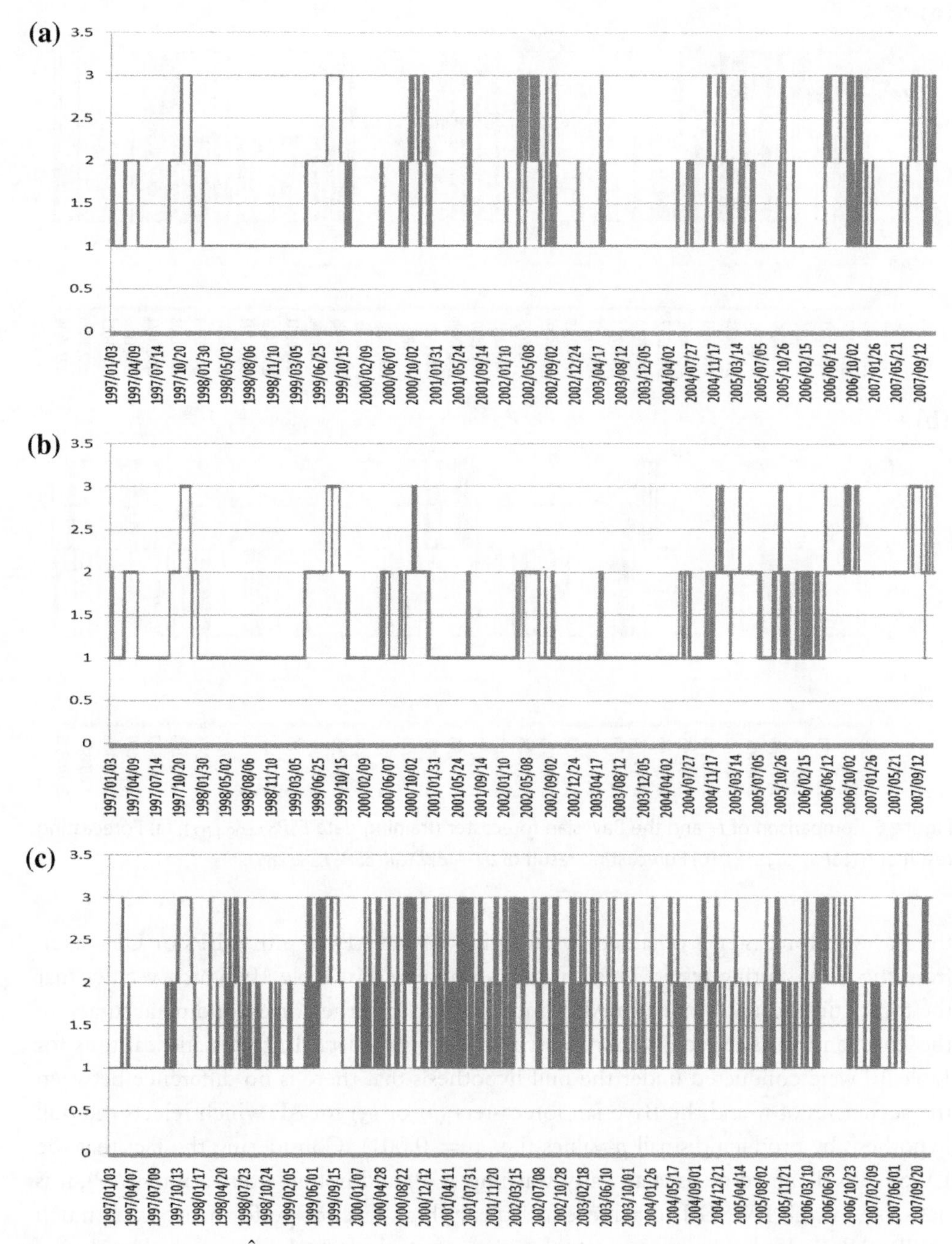

Figure 5 Comparison of $\hat{f}_1$ and the Bayesian forecaster (training data ESP_{97+99}). (a) Forecasting result of $\hat{f}_1(ESP_{97+99})$, (b) Forecasting result of $b_2 - EWIGII(ESP_{97+99})$, (c) Classification result of oracle classifier.

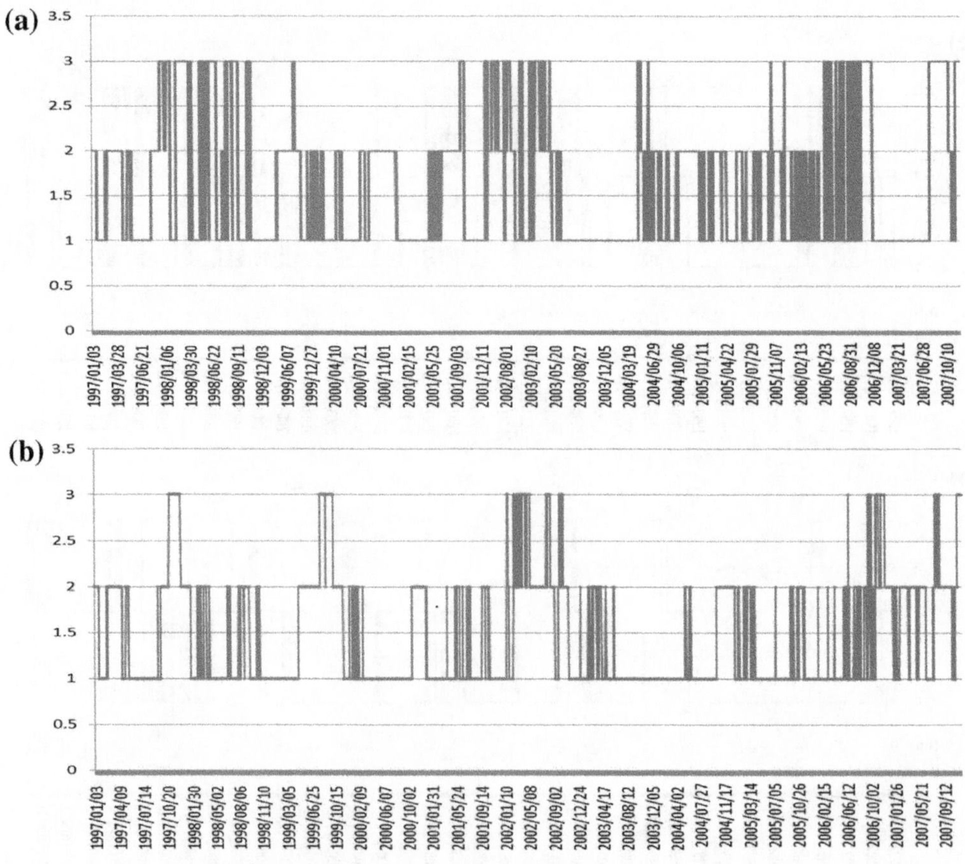

Figure 6 Comparison of $\hat{f}_1$ and the Bayesian forecaster (training data $ESP_{97+99+02}$). (a) Forecasting result of $\hat{f}_1\,(ESP_{97+99+02})$, (b) Forecasting result of $b_3 - EWXGII(ESP_{97+99+02})$.

the Bayesian forecaster is obtained by changing several APs to either BPs or UPs taken from the $\hat{f}_1$ forecasting result. This can be also observed in Table 10, which verifies that the forecasting accuracy of $\hat{f}_1$ for AP is much better than the corresponding accuracy of the Bayesian forecaster across the two types of training data. In fact, statistical tests for Table 10 were conducted under the null hypothesis that there is no difference between the accuracies of $\hat{f}_1$ and the Bayesian forecasters (b_2 or b_3) for AP, which rejects the null hypothesis by producing small p-values (i.e., $p = 0.001$). Considering the fact that the EWSGII is designed to issue an early warning (UP) and not an afterwarning (AP), it is desirable for the EWSGII to achieve an equally high level of performance with much smaller APs. To look more deeply into this issue, a statistical check was repeated by changing the test data to a more recent period (i.e., the period of 01/2007–12/2009 only), which reproduces a similar tendency with a related p-value close to zero. The numbers in parentheses of Table 10 help explain this result. In conclusion, all of these observations

Table 10 Class-wise comparison of $\hat{f}_1$ and the Bayesian forecaster.

Class	$\hat{f}_1$	$b_2 - EWIGII$
(a) Class-wise hit ratio of $\hat{f}_1$ and $b_2 - EWIGII$ when training data are ESP_{97+99}.		
BP	84% (99%)*	70% (98%)*
UP	23% (7%)*	51% (44%)*
AP	48% (69%)*	35% (1%)*
Overall	64.7% (68.9%)*	61.5% (55.3%)*
Class	$\hat{f}_1$	$b_3 - EWIGII$
(b) Class-wise hit ratio of $\hat{f}_1$ and $b_3 - EWIGII$ when training data are $ESP_{97+99+02}$.		
BP	69% (90%)*	74% (98%)*
UP	49% (5%)*	48% (27%)*
AP	61% (66%)*	39% (31%)*
Overall	63.2% (63.3%)*	63.0% (60.6%)*

*The number in parentheses denotes the hit ratio when testing period is changed to January 2007 December 2009.

Table 11 Weights for the Bayesian forecaster by CMA-ES.

Training data set	$\hat{w}(l)$	Weights
$b_1 - EWIGII(ESP_{97})$	$\hat{w}(1)$	1.0000
	$\hat{w}(5)$	0.0000
	$\hat{w}(20)$	0.0000
$b_2 - EWIGII(ESP_{97+99})$	$\hat{w}(1)$	0.4286
	$\hat{w}(5)$	0.0000
	$\hat{w}(20)$	0.5714
$b_3 - EWIGII(ESP_{97+99+02})$	$\hat{w}(1)$	0.3666
	$\hat{w}(5)$	0.3589
	$\hat{w}(20)$	0.2745

together strongly demonstrate the usefulness of the Bayesian forecaster in monitoring the status of the Korean stock market. This suggests that the Bayesian forecaster could efficiently adjust the distribution of the classes forecasted in a desirable fashion by using class-based optimization.

Remark 4. As a closing remark for this subsection, we report certain technical results regarding the justification of using EA (or equivalently GA) for the Bayesian classifier. As discussed previously, the main reasons behind the use of GA are the local optimum and non-differentiable optimization. To check these, we experimented with two techniques as alternatives (i.e., Mead simplex and generalized reduced gradient method (Mckinnon, 1999)), which are both known to suffer from local optimum problems. When we applied the reduced gradient method with absolute fitness function $\sum_{k=1}^{p}\sum_{t=1}^{T}|\sum_{i=1}^{q}w(i)f_i(t)-k|$ to obtain b_3-*EWSGII*, it appeared to suffer from local optima; i.e., the optimal weight found by the generalized reduced gradient was (0.0, 0.5, 0.5) with a given starting point and then moved to (0.5, 0.5, 0.0) with a different starting point. The optimal weight found by GA is (0.5, 0.5, 0.0) consistently. To compare GA with the other competitive EA algorithm, CMA-ES (covariance matrix adaptation-evolution strategy; Hansen and Ostermeier, 2001) is implemented. It produced exactly the same optimal weight as GA. Compare Table 8 with Table 11. Thus, it appears that most EAs could serve efficiently for the specific problem in this subsection.

7. CONCLUSION

Globalization and deregulation of local stock markets make GII major influences at the local markets. A problem with GII is that they may try to sell the stocks as much and fast as possible and leave the local stock market in the case that external shocks like Asia crisis arises since their main goal is to gain an absolute return for their customers. Therefore, an efficient and predictive EWS is strongly needed for monitoring or forecasting the movements of GII. To provide a feasible alternative to this, we propose a statistical classification approach which consists of oracle classifier, lag-*l* forecaster, and Bayesian linking procedure in this chapter. Our empirical experiments developing EWSGII for the Korean stock market demonstrate usefulness of this approach in the sense that they provide early warning with quality accuracy on various time lags and can be further improved by the Bayesian linking procedure.

ACKNOWLEDGMENTS

Parts of this Chapter are reprinted from Ahn et al. (2011) with permission from Elsevier, Ahn et al. (2012) with permission from Springer, and Son et al. (2009) with permission from John Wiley and Sons. We are grateful to all of them. This work was supported by the 2012 Bisa Scholar Grant of Keimyung University and the Basic Science Research Program through the National Research Foundation of Korea (NRF) funded by the Ministry of Education, Science and Technology (KRF-2011-0015936).

REFERENCES

Aci, M., Inan, C., Avci, M., 2010. A hybrid classification method of k nearest neighbor, Bayesian methods and genetic algorithm. Expert Systems Applications 37, 5061–5067

Ahn, J.J., Byun, H.W., Oh, K.J., Kim, T.Y., 2012. Bayesian forecaster using class-based optimization. Applied Intelligence 36, 553–563

Ahn, J.J., Son, I.S., Oh, K.J., Kim, T.Y., Song, G.M., 2011. Lag-l forecasting and machine learning algorithms. Expert Systems 28 (3), 269–282

Breiman, L., Friedman, J.H., Olshen, R.A., Charles, J.S., 1984. Classification and Regression Trees. Wadsworth, New York

Edison, H., 2000. Do indicators of financial crises work? An evaluation of an early warning system. International Finance Discussion Papers No. 675, Board of Governors of the Federal Reserve System.

Eichengreen, B., Rose, A., Wyplosz, C., 1996. Contagious currency crisis. Scandinavian Economic Review 98, 463–484

Eichengreen, B., Rose, A., Wyplosz, C., 1995. Exchange market mayhem: the antecedents and aftermath of speculative attacks. Economic Policy 21, 249–312

Frankel, J.A., Rose, A.K., 1996. Currency crashes in emerging markets: an empirical treatment. Journal of International Financial Markets 41, 351–366

Ghysels, E., Seon, J., 2005. The Asian financial crisis: the role of derivative securities trading and foreign investors in Korea. Journal of International Money and Finance 24, 607–630

Goldsten, M., 1996. The seven deadly sins – presumptive indicators of vulnerability to financial crises in emerging economies: origin and policy options. Economic Papers 46, Bank for International Settlements (BIS).

Goldstein, M., Kaminsky, G., Reinhart, C., 2000. Assessing Financial Vulnerability: An Early Warning System for Emerging Markets. Institute for International Economics, Washington, DC

Hall, P., Marron, J.S., Neeman, A., 2005. Geometric representation of high dimension, low sample size data. Journal of the Royal Statistical Society B67, 427–444

Hansen, N., Ostermeier, A., 2001. Completely derandomized self-adaptation in evolution strategies. Evolutionary Computation 9, 159–195

Kaminsky, G., Reinhart, C.M., 1999. The twin crises: the causes of banking and balance-of-payments problems. American Economic Review 89, 473–500

Kim, W., Wei, S., 1999. Foreign portfolio investors before and during a crisis. NBER Working Paper No. 6968, Cambridge, MA.

Kolodner, J., 1991. Improving human decision making through case-based decision aiding. AI Magazine 12, 52–68

Krugman, P., 1979. A model of balance-of-payment crises. International Journal of Money, Credit and Banking 11, 311–325

Lapedes, A., Farber, R., 1998. How neural nets work. In: Anderson, D.Z. (Ed.), Neural Information Processing Systems. American Institute of Physics, New York

Mckinnon, K.I.M., 1999. Convergence of the Nelder–Mead simplex method to a non-stationary point. SIAM Journal on Optimization 9, 148–158

Obestfed, M., 1986. Rational and self-fulfilling balance-of-payment crisis. American Economic Review 76, 72–81

Oh, K.J., Kim, T.Y., Kim, C., 2006. An early warning system for detection of financial crisis using financial market volatility. Expert Systems 23, 83–98

Ozkan, F.G., Sutherland, A., 1995. Policy measures to avoid a currency crisis. Economic Journal 105, 510–519

Son, I.S., Oh, K.J., Kim, T.Y., Kim, D.H., 2009. An early warning system for global institutional investors at emerging stock markets based on machine learning forecasting. Expert Systems with Application 36, 4951–4957

Velasco, A., 1987. Financial and balance of payments crises: a simple model of the southern cone experience. Journal of Development Economics 27, 263–283

CHAPTER 16

Comovements and Volatility Spillovers Between Oil Prices and Stock Markets: Further Evidence for Oil-Exporting and Oil-Importing Countries

Khaled Guesmi
IPAG Business School, IPAG—Lab & EconomiX, University of Paris West Nanterre La Défense, France

1. INTRODUCTION

This chapter explores models that provide evidence of volatility transmission between crude oil prices and stock markets. Our objective is to complement this line of research by addressing the dynamics of volatility transmission using multivariate GJR-GARCH-class models which can detect the volatility asymmetry and spillover.

There have already been a few attempts to address the aforementioned topic, but none of the existing papers has approached the issue within a multivariate framework. The recent literature on volatility transmission and measurement has been developed through models that link the oil and stock markets by investigating their comovements.[1] Hammoudeh et al. (2004) investigated spillover effects and dynamic relationships of five daily S&P oil sector stock indices and five daily oil prices for the US oil markets using cointegration techniques as well as ARCH-type models. They show evidence of some volatility spillover from the oil futures market and the stock returns of some oil sectors.

Chiou and Lee (2009) examined the asymmetric effects of daily WTI oil prices on S&P 500 stock returns. Using the Autoregressive Conditional Jump Intensity model with expected, unexpected, and negative unexpected oil price fluctuations, they found that high fluctuations in oil prices have unexpected asymmetric effects on stock returns. Malik and Ewing (2009) relied on bivariate GARCH models to estimate the volatility transmission between weekly WTI oil prices and equity sector returns and found evidence of spillover mechanisms.

[1] Most of this literature offers substantial evidence of the impact of oil on stock prices, suggesting a negative relationship between oil price and stock market returns. For instance, Jones and Kaul (1996) used a standard cash-flow dividend valuation model and found a significant negative impact of oil price shocks on US and Canadian quarterly stock prices in the post-war period. Models relying on some variants of Vector Autoregressive Analysis show similar findings (Park and Ratti, 2008; Sadorsky, 1999; Papapetrou, 2001).

Emerging Markets and the Global Economy
http://dx.doi.org/10.1016/B978-0-12-411549-1.00016-8

Choi and Hammoudeh (2010) extended the time-varying correlations analysis by considering the commodity prices of Brent oil, WTI oil, copper, gold and silver, and the S&P 500 index. They showed that commodity correlations have increased since 2003, limiting hedging substitutability in portfolios. More recently, Arouri and Nguyen (2010) examined the relationship between oil prices and 12 stock sectors in European countries. The authors showed that the reaction of sector returns to changes in oil prices differs considerably across sectors and that the inclusion of oil assets in a portfolio of sector stocks helps to improve the portfolio's risk-return characteristics. Choi and Hammoudeh (2010) extended the time-varying correlations analysis by considering the commodity prices of Brent oil, WTI oil, copper, gold and silver, and the S&P 500 index. They showed that commodity correlations have increased since 2003, limiting hedging substitutability in portfolios.

Filis et al. (2011) investigated time-varying correlations between Brent oil prices and stock markets on both oil-importing and oil-exporting countries. Using a multivariate asymmetric DCC-GARCH approach, they found that the conditional variance of oil and stock prices remains the same for oil-importing and oil-exporting economies. However, time-varying correlations depend on the origin of the oil shocks: the response from aggregate demand-related shocks is much greater than the response from supply-related shocks originating from OPEC's production cuts.

Awartani and Maghyereh (2013) investigated return and volatility spillover effects between the oil market and the Gulf Cooperation Council (GCC) countries stock markets using indices proposed by Diebold and Yilmaz (2009, 2012), and revealed transmission in both directions between 2004 and 2012. They identified a significant flow of information from oil returns and volatilities to the GCC stock exchanges, while the flow in the opposite direction was found to be marginal. Moreover, the oil market appears to give other markets more than it receives in terms of both returns and volatilities. The empirical evidence from the sample is consistent with a system in which oil plays the dominant role in the information transmission mechanism between oil and equities in the GCC countries.

Our study also looks at models on volatility transmission and thus contagion among stock markets of oil-exporting and oil-importing countries. The first empirical paper on financial contagion was the simple comparative analysis of Pearson's correlation coefficients between stock markets in periods of calm and periods of crisis. Contagion is found when significant increases in correlations occur in crisis periods. King and Wadhwani (1990), and Lee and Kim (1993) used the correlation coefficient between stock returns to test for the impact of the 1987 US stock crash on the equity markets of several countries. The empirical findings show that the correlation coefficients between several markets increased significantly during the crash. Hamao et al. (1990) found statistically significant correlations across stock markets during the 1987 crisis by estimating conditional variance under a GARCH model. Using a switching ARCH model,

Edwards and Susmel (2001) found that many Latin American equity markets are significantly correlated during times of high market volatility, which proves contagion effects. Forbes (2004) studied the impact of the Asian and Russian crises on stock returns for a sample of over 10,000 companies worldwide, arguing that trade linkages are a vector of volatility transmission.

However, evidence on financial contagion is not really conclusive. Bordo and Murshid (2001) found that after accounting for heteroskedasticity, there was no significant increase in correlation between asset returns in pairs of crisis-hit countries. They concluded that there was no contagion but only interdependence. This is somewhat in contrast with Corsetti et al. (2005) who tested for financial contagion on a single-factor model and found some contagion and some interdependence. Further, focusing on different transmission channels, Froot et al. (2001) confirmed the existence of contagion effect. Guesmi et al. (2013) investigated the comovements between monthly US stock markets and those of the other 16 OECD countries over the period 2002–2009 in order to study the contagion effect in the case of the recent global financial crisis. Using a multivariate DCC-GARCH, their results show the presence of shift-contagion effects arising from the financial crisis to most of the OECD stock markets, apart from Germany, Italy, the UK and, to a certain extent, Japan, where only interdependencies were detected. The other OECD stock markets were significantly impacted by shift contagion during the financial crisis (2007–2009).

Our current work extends the method that is used to measure the volatility spillover between oil and stock markets by applying multivariate GJR-DCC-GARCH models. Our study thus differs from the previous ones in at least two respects. First of all, it identifies two main findings. Oil price shocks in periods of global turmoil or during global business cycle fluctuations (downturn or expansion) appear to have a significant impact on the relationship between oil and stock market prices, both in oil-importing and oil-exporting countries. In exporting countries, our analysis unveils higher and multiple peaks that coincide with major events (such as the 2008 oil price crisis). In the case of importing countries, the pattern of interaction is far smoother when compared with exporting countries. Other oil price shocks originating from events, such as OPEC's production cuts, hurricanes, and so on, do not seem to have a significant impact on the correlation between oil and stock markets in importing countries.

The rest of the chapter is organized as follows. Section 2 describes the data and methodology model. Section 3 reports the empirical results. Section 4 concludes.

2. DATA AND METHODOLOGY

2.1. Data Description

In this study, we use monthly data for oil prices and stock market indices. The sample consists of oil-importing (US, Italy, Germany, Netherlands, and France) and -exporting

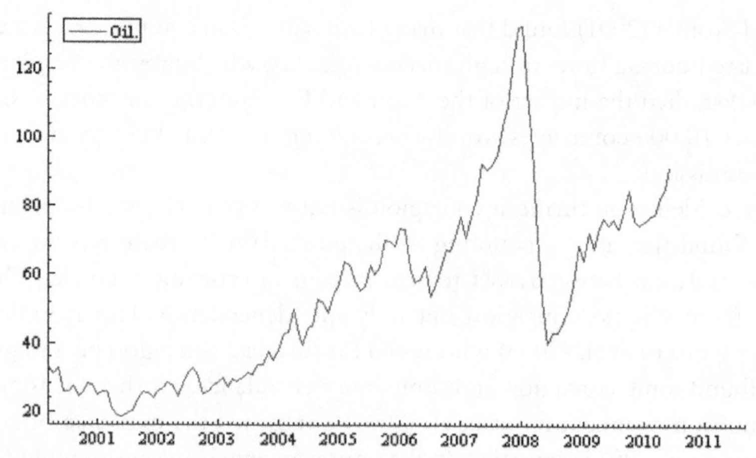

Figure 1 Brent crude oil price, in dollars, from 2000 to 2010.

countries (United Arab Emirates, Kuwait, Saudi Arabia, and Venezuela). The following criteria had to be satisfied for inclusion in the sample: (i) the countries studied need to have a well-established stock market and (ii) the selected countries have to be in the top 20 oil-importing and -exporting countries.

The Brent crude oil index was used as it accounts for 65% of the global daily oil production (IMF, 2010). The data range from 03/09/2000 to 03/12/2010 and were extracted from the Federal Reserve Bank of Saint Louis and Datastream International database. The study period is selected on the basis of data availability and intends to cover the major economic and political events over recent years such as the last global financial crisis, the September 11 terrorist attack in the US, the second Gulf War, the Russian economic crisis, and the different monetary and financial crises in the Asian, Latin American, and Middle East regions. The choice of this study period thus enables us to come to robust conclusions on the link between the oil price dynamics and the financial market returns.

Figure 1 presents the Brent crude oil prices in dollars, from September 2000 to October 2010.

Oil price movements show some significant peaks and troughs during the study period. The main peaks are observed between 2007 and 2008. Another peak is observed in June 2009, when prices increased by more than 60% from their January 2009 price levels. All these changes are linked to aggregate demand-related oil price shocks. The first θ such demand related oil price shock occurred during the Asian economic crisis, the second took place in 2000, when interest rates decreased significantly creating a bust in the housing market and construction industries. The third took place in the period 2006–2007, a result of the rising demand for oil in China, while the fourth demand-related oil price shock occurred during the global financial crisis of 2008.

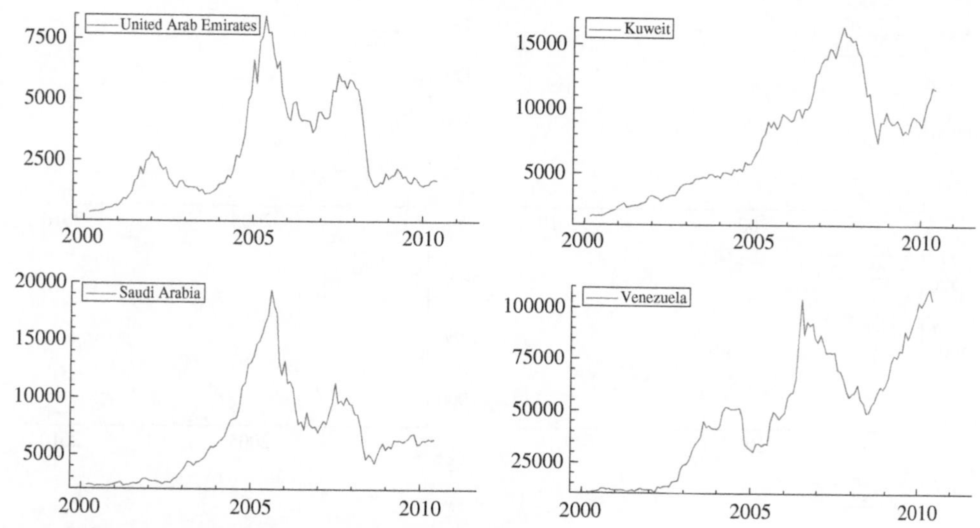

Figure 2 Stock market indices of oil-exporting countries.

Figures 2 and 3 describe stock market indices during the period under analysis respectively for oil-exporting and -importing countries. Taking into account the peaks and troughs of oil prices and the events that took place during our period of study, the relations between oil and stock market indices exhibit some noteworthy aspects.

First, in exporting countries (Figure 2), we observe the same oil price fluctuation movement in stock markets in the sub-period 2000–2005, with periods of increasing oil prices and stock market prices. However, for the sub-period 2005–2010, oil prices rose consistently. In addition, the period 2005 until mid-2007 is characterized by a continuous oil price increase, as well as increased stock market prices. During mid-2006 until early 2007, when we observe an oil price trough, the stock markets also fell. Moreover, from 2007 until 2009, both oil prices and stock indices were bullish. Finally, after the sub-period 2008–2009, both oil and stock market prices experienced a bearish performance. Venezuela exhibited a slightly different pattern, given the weaker development of its financial markets.

As a preliminary result, we note that the visual inspection of the series does not provide a clear distinction between stock market performance and oil prices in oil-exporting and -importing countries. However, we observe that the stock indices of importing countries (Figure 3) do not follow the same trend as oil prices. For example, during the sub-period 2000–2003, oil prices exhibited an increase, whereas the majority of the stock markets showed a decrease. For the sub-period 2007–2008, stock prices decreased while oil prices rose steadily.

Table 1 reports the main statistics of return series for stock market, real exchange rate, and Brent crude oil indices for the five stock markets considered.

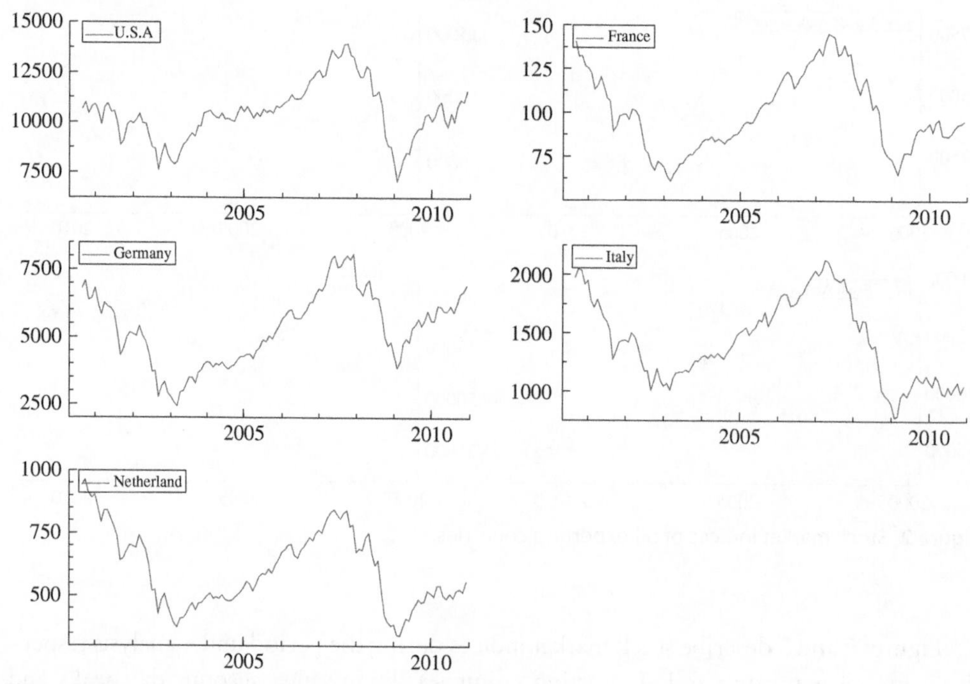

Figure 3 Stock market indices of oil-importing countries.

Table 1 Descriptive statistics of return series.

	Mean	Std dev.	Skewness	Kurtosis	ARCH (1)
United Arab Emirates	0.013107	0.126709	0.118074	3.354331	17.145++
Kuwait	0.015864	0.059667	−0.284409	3.587228	24.044+++
Saudi Arabia	0.008233	0.083340	−0.822876	4.298505	23.696+++
Venezuela	0.018655	0.083850	0.449107	6.660345	17.174+++
USA	0.003945	0.061376	−0.867876	7.874304	20.294+++
France	0.004031	0.005572	−0.998552	3.529250	28.966+++
Germany	0.003945	0.005591	−0.695120	3.597867	27.126+++
Italy	0.001543	0.064840	0.706611	3.592523	33.158+++
Netherlands	0.003876	0.056325	−1.290798	6.326385	26.221+++

Notes: ARCH(1) are the empirical statistics of the Engle (1982) test for the first order of ARCH effects. +, ++, and +++ indicate that the null hypothesis of no ARCH effects is rejected at the 10%, 5%, and 1% levels, respectively.

The average exchange rate returns range from −0.001% (Italy) to 0.18% (Venezuela). All of the series depart from normality conditions and conditional heteroskedasticity. The United Arab Emirates market was the most volatile during the period under study in terms of standard deviation (12.67%), while France was the least volatile (0.055%).

The skewness coefficients are positive for the United Arab Emirates, Venezuela, and Italy. They are significantly different from zero for almost all markets, indicating the presence of asymmetry in the return distribution. In addition, all the return series are characterized by a statistically significant and greater than 3 kurtosis coefficient, and thus have fatter tails than those of a normal distribution. Engle (1982)'s test for the first order of conditional heteroskedasticity is also performed and we cannot reject the hypothesis of no ARCH effects for all the return series considered. This result motivates our choice of a GARCH modeling approach for conditional variance processes.

2.2. Estimation of Dynamic Correlations

In this study, we apply the time-varying correlation coefficients estimated from a multivariate DCC-GARCH model intruded by Engle (2002). By allowing conditional correlations to vary over time, his specification is viewed as a generalization of the Constant Conditional Correlation GARCH model of Bollerslev (1990). To illustrate the dynamic conditional correlation model for our purposes, let x_t be a (11×1) vector containing the return, volume, and implied volatility series in a conditional mean equation as:

$$x_t = \mu_t + \varepsilon_t \quad \text{with} \quad \varepsilon_t \,|\psi_{t-1} \sim N(0, H_t), \tag{1}$$

where $\mu_t = E\left[x_t \| \Pi_{t-1}\right]$ is the conditional expectation of x_t given the past information Π_{t-1}, and ε_t is a vector of errors in autoregression AR(1). H_t is the variance-covariance matrix of returns at time t.

Under the assumption that the return, volume, and implied volatility series x_t are determined by the information set available at time $t-1$, the model may be estimated using maximum likelihood methods, subject to the requirement that the conditional covariance matrix H_t be positive and definite for all values of ε_t in the sample. We also assume that μ_t is formed as follows:

$$\mu_{i,t} = \Phi_0 + \Phi_1 x_{i,t-1}, \quad \forall \text{i}, \tag{2}$$

where Φ_1 measures the ARCH effect in the data series. In the traditional multivariate GARCH framework, the conditional variance-covariance matrix can be written as:

$$H_t = D_t R_t D_t', \tag{3}$$

where H_t is the variance-covariance matrix of returns at time t. R_t is the (11×11) symmetric matrix of dynamic conditional correlations (five oil-exporting countries, four oil-importing countries, world market, and oil market). D_t is a diagonal matrix of conditional standard deviations for each of the return series, obtained from estimating a univariate GJR-GARCH[2] process developed by Glosten et al. (1993) in the equation of

[2] This model gives a better statistical result than DCC-GARCH.

variance expressed as:

$$h_{ii,t} = w_i + \alpha_i \varepsilon^2_{ii,t-1} + \beta_i h_{ii,t-1} + \gamma_i I_{i,t} \varepsilon^2_{ii,t-1}, \quad (4)$$

where persistence is measured by the coefficients β_i, and the indicator variables $I_{i,t}$ capture asymmetry in the estimate of coefficients γ_i. A negative value of γ_i implies that negative residuals increase the variance more than positive residuals.

Therefore, for a pair of markets i and j, their conditional correlation at time t can be written as:

$$\rho_{ijt} = (1 - \theta_1 - \theta_2)\rho_{ij} + \theta_2 \rho_{ij,t-1} + \theta_1 \frac{\sum_{m=1}^{M} u_{i,t-m}, u_{j,t-m}}{\sqrt{\left(\sum_{m=1}^{M} u^2_{i,t-m}\right)\left(\sum_{m=1}^{M} u^2_{j,t-m}\right)}}, \quad (5)$$

where $u_{it} = \frac{\varepsilon_{it}}{\sqrt{h_{iit}}}$.

The estimation of the vector of unknown parameters (θ) is carried out by the quasi-maximum likelihood estimation (QMLE) method that is robust to departures from normality of return series under regular conditions (see Bollerslev and Wooldridge, 1992). The log-likelihood function to be maximized is expressed as:

$$L = -\frac{1}{2} \sum_{t=1}^{T} (k \log(2\pi) + 2 \log |D_t| + \log |R_t| + \mu_t' R_t^{-1} \mu_t), \quad (6)$$

where μ_t is the standardized residual derived from the first stage univariate GARCH estimation, which is assumed to be i.i.d with a mean zero and a variance of R_t.

3. EMPIRICAL RESULTS

The graphs from time-varying correlation coefficients as computed from equation (5) between each stock market index and the crude oil prices are presented in Figures 4 and 5.

In 2003, there was a relatively lower dynamic correlation in the case of exporting countries (Dubai, Kuwait, and South Africa). This result is explained by the war in Iraq in March 2003 and the strike movement in Venezuela. We observe a breakdown in dynamic correlation for all exporting countries in 2006. We explain this decrease in interdependence between oil prices and the stock market index by a military attack in Nigeria, which caused the shutdown of more than 600,000 billion barrels a day.

Another period of interest is that spanning from 2006 until mid-2008, characterized by high oil prices due to rising demand, mainly from China. The level of correlation shows an increasing and positive pattern for all countries. This aggregate demand-related oil price shock had a positive impact on stock markets (both in oil-importing and oil-exporting

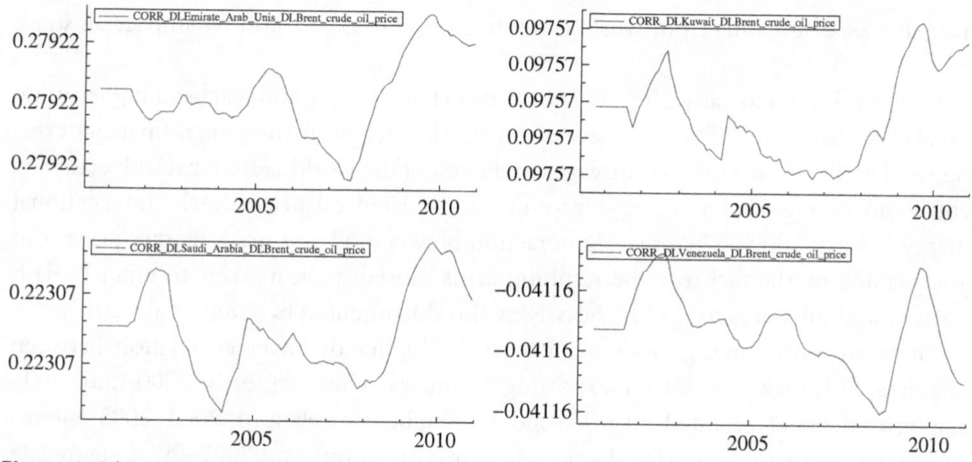

Figure 4 Oil-exporting countries.

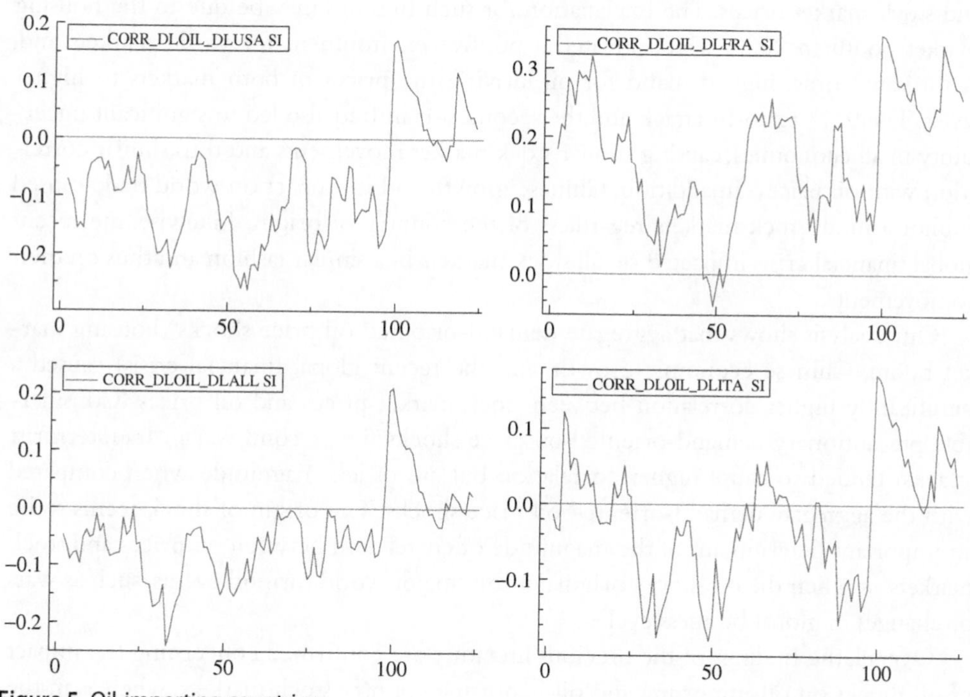

Figure 5 Oil-importing countries.

countries) as it signaled an increase in world trade. These findings are in line with Hamilton (2009) and Kilian and Park (2009), who suggest that aggregate demand-related oil price shocks, originating from world economic growth, have a positive impact on stock prices.

From mid-2006 to early 2009, the correlation rises sharply and reaches a higher value (except for Venezuela). The main event during this period is the global financial crisis triggered by the export of US mortgages to the rest of the world as asset-backed securities, which can be regarded as an aggregate demand-related oil price shock (International Energy Agency 2009). The greater interaction between oil and stock market prices can be explained by the fact that the resulting crisis caused stock markets to enter bearish territory and oil prices to decline heavily, as also documented by Creti et al. (2013).

There are only three periods of noteworthy higher or lower correlation between oil prices and stock markets for exporting countries. These are early 2000 until 2001 (aggregate demand-oriented oil price shocks—higher correlation), 2003–2005 (aggregate demand-oriented oil price shocks—higher correlation), and 2007–2008 (aggregate demand-oriented oil price shock—positive correlation).

The years 2003–2005 (Figure 5) represent the sole period showing little difference between importing and exporting countries in terms of the correlation pattern of oil and stock market prices. The explanation for such findings may be due to the housing market boom in 2000, which created a positive environment for world markets and, at the same time, high demand for oil, driving the prices of both markets to higher levels. The 9/11 terrorist attack and the second war in Iraq also led to significant uncertainty in all economies, causing similar stock market movements and thus similar correlation with oil prices. In addition, Chinese growth and its impact on world trade caused euphoria in all stock markets regardless of the country of origin. Likewise, the recent global financial crisis impacted on all stock markets in a similar fashion and thus on their comovements.

Our analysis shows that aggregate demand-oriented oil price shocks (housing market boom, Chinese economic growth, and the recent global financial crisis) caused a significantly higher correlation between stock market prices and oil prices. Considerable precautionary demand-oriented oil price shocks (i.e., second war in Iraq, terrorist attacks) tended to cause higher correlation but are of less magnitude when compared with the aggregate demand-oriented oil price shocks. The origin of shock seems to be an important determinant of the magnitude of correlation between oil prices and stock markets, as when the oil shocks originate from major world turmoil events, such as wars or changes in global business cycles.

Overall, the findings of the previous literature are confirmed concerning the impact of oil shocks on oil-importing and oil-exporting country stock markets, whereas in the case of supply shocks, our findings show some aspects that have been neglected to date. In particular, we highlight the role of crisis periods in oil prices as drivers of the comovements between oil and stock markets.

4. CONCLUSION

This chapter investigates the issue of oil and stock market interdependence in oil-exporting and -importing countries by measuring the interaction between oil price and stock market indices using the asymmetric DCC-GARCH approach. This process is applied to the stock market indices of oil-exporting countries: the United Arab Emirates, Kuwait, Saudi Arabia, and Venezuela, and oil-importing countries: the USA, Italy, Germany, the Netherlands, and France.

Apart from the Venezuelan stock market, our analysis shows that high oil prices driven by demand-related shocks move in line with stock prices, especially in exporting countries. Supply shocks cause higher correlation only in exporting countries. Therefore, in terms of potential diversification, oil is not always countercyclical with respect to stock markets, as generally predicted by the previous literature. Oil can have this role in importing countries, when high oil prices originate from supply shocks. On the other hand, if the shock originates from demand, oil prices and stock markets tend to move together with varying degrees of strength in both importing and exporting countries, depending on the origin of the shock.

REFERENCES

Arouri, M.E.H., Nguyen, D.K., 2010. Oil prices, stock markets and portfolio investment: evidence from sector analysis in Europe over the last decade. Energy Policy 38, 4528–4539

Awartani, B., Maghyereh, A., 2013. Dynamic spillovers between oil and stock markets in the Gulf cooperation council countries. Energy Economics 36 (1), 28–42

Bollerslev, T., 1990. Modelling the coherence in short-run nominal exchange rates: a multivariate generalized ARCH model. Review of Economics and Statistics 72, 498–505

Bollerslev, T., Wooldridge, J.M., 1992. Quasi-maximum likelihood estimation and inference in dynamic models with time-varying covariances. Econometric Reviews 1, 143–173

Bordo, M.D., Murshid, A.P., 2001. Are financial crises becoming increasingly more contagious? What is the historical evidence on contagion?. In: Claessens, S., Forbes, K.J. (Eds.), International Financial Contagion. Kluwer Academic, Boston, pp. 367–403 (Chapter 14)

Chiou, J.S., Lee, Y.H., 2009. Jump dynamics and volatility: oil and the stock markets. Energy 34 (6), 788–796

Choi, K., Hammoudeh, S., 2010. Volatility behavior of oil, industrial commodity and stock markets in a regime-switching environment. Energy Policy 38 (8), 4388–4399

Corsetti, G., Pericoli, M., Sbracia, M., 2005. Some contagion, some interdependence: more pitfalls in tests of financial contagion. Journal of International Money and Finance 24, 1177–1199

Creti, A., Joets, M., Mignon, V., 2013. On the links between stock and commodity markets' volatility. Energy Economics 37, 16–28

Diebold, F.X., Yilmaz, K., 2009. Measuring financial asset return and volatility spillovers, with application to global equity markets. Economic Journal 119, 158–171

Edwards, S., Susmel, R., 2001. Volatility dependence and contagion in emerging equity markets. Journal of Development Economics 66 (2), 505–532

Engle, R., 1982. Autoregressive conditional heteroskedasticity with estimates of the variance of UK inflation. Econometrica 50, 987–1008

Engle, R., 2002. Dynamic conditional correlation: a simple class of multivariate generalized autoregressive conditional heteroskedasticity models. Journal of Business and Statistics 20 (3), 339–350

Filis, G., Degiannakis, S., Floros, C., 2011. Dynamic correlation between stock market and oil prices: the case of oil-importing and oil-exporting countries. International Review of Financial Analysis 20 (3), 152–164

Forbes, K., 2004. The Asian flue and Russian virus: the international transmission of crisis in firm-level data. Journal of International Economics 63, 59–92

Froot, K.A., O'Connell, P.G.J., Seasholes, M.S., 2001. The portfolio flows of international investors. Journal of Financial Economics 59, 151–194

Glosten, L., Jagannathan, R., Runkle, D., 1993. On the relationship between the expected value and the volatility of the nominal excess returns on stocks. Journal of Finance 48, 1779–1801

Guesmi, K., Kaabia, O., Kazi, I.A., 2013. Does shift contagion exist between OECD stock markets during the financial crisis. Journal of Applied Business Research 29 (2), 469–484

Hamao, Y.R., Masulis, R.W., Ng, V.K., 1990. Correlations in price changes and volatility across international stock markets. Review of Financial Studies 3, 281–307

Hamilton, D.J., 2009. Understanding crude oil prices. Energy Journal 30 (2), 179–206

Hammoudeh, S., Dibooglu, S., Aleisa, E., 2004. Relationships among U.S. oil prices and oil industry equity indices. International Review of Economics and Finance 13 (4), 427–453

IMF, 2010. People's Republic of China: 2010 Article IV Consultation—Staff Report; Staff Statement; Public Information Notice on the Executive Board Discussion, IMF Staff Country Report No. 10/238, Washington.

Jones, C.M., Kaul, G., 1996. Oil and the stock markets. Journal of Finance 51 (2), 463–491

Kilian, L., Park, C., 2009. The impact of oil price shocks on the U.S market. International Economic Review 50, 1267–1287

King, M.A., Wadhwani, S., 1990. Transmission of volatility between stock markets. Review of Financial Studies 3, 5–33

Lee, S.B., Kim, K.J., 1993. Does the October 1987 crash strengthen the co-movements among national stocks markets? Review of Financial Economics 3, 89–102

Malik, F., Ewing, B.T., 2009. Volatility transmission between oil prices and equity sector returns. International Review of Financial Analysis 18, 95–100

Papapetrou, E., 2001. Oil price, shocks stock, market economic activity and employment in Greece. Energy Economics 23 (5), 511–532

Park, J., Ratti, R.A., 2008. Oil price shocks and stock markets in the U.S. and 13 European countries. Energy Economics 30, 2587–2608

Sadorsky, P., 1999. Oil price shocks and stock market activity. Energy Economics 2, 449–469

CHAPTER 17

Collateral in Emerging Economies*

Elmas Yaldız Hanedar*, Eleonora Broccardo*,†, and Flavio Bazzana*

*Department of Economics and Management, University of Trento, Via Inama, Trento, Italy
†Cefin (Centro Studi Banca e Finanza), Modena, Italy

1. INTRODUCTION

Financing difficulties can have a strong influence on the survival and growth of businesses. Most theoretical and empirical models have shown that the pledging of collateral is a necessary condition for access to finance and that it is even more important for small- and medium-size enterprises (SMEs) in the more underdeveloped financial economies. In this chapter, we will focus on collateral requirements in emerging countries.

Collateral requirements are stringent in emerging countries because of more severe information asymmetry and weaker enforcement processes. Most of the empirical studies on collateralization have been conducted in a single country and have largely focused on developed countries; few studies have examined collateral requirements in emerging economies. We close this gap by analyzing the role of collateral with data compiled from a cross-country sample of emerging markets found in the Business Environment Survey (WBES). The WBES dataset, compiled by the World Bank, consolidates internationally comparable indicators that allow us to perceive changes in the business environment over time, which fosters an objective comparison of firm constraints and the business environment. This dataset allows us to obtain deep and detailed information about firm characteristics and about the perceptions of these firms regarding the business environment in which they operate. We investigate the role of collateral—both at the firm- and country-specific levels—by analyzing its presence and the degree of collateralization by employing the collateral-to-loan-value ratio. We also provide a robustness analysis on a subsample of SMEs.

Our main results indicate that country-specific variables are more important than firm-specific variables in determining both the presence and degree of collateralization for a loan. Accordingly, we find that not all firm characteristics explain collateral requirements. Collateral requirements appear to be a tool for resolving the problem of asymmetric information with respect to a firm. These results have significant policy implications.

The remainder of the chapter is organized as follows. Section 2 reviews the theoretical and empirical literature on collateral in both developed and emerging countries. Section 3

* Sections 3.1, 3.2, 3.3, and 4 are attributable to Elmas Yaldız Hanedar; Sections 1, 2, and 3.4 are attributable to Eleonora Broccardo; Sections 5 and 6 are attributable to Flavio Bazzana.

Emerging Markets and the Global Economy
http://dx.doi.org/10.1016/B978-0-12-411549-1.00017-X

refers to the empirical analysis of this study. Section 4 presents robustness checks. Section 5 discusses the policy implications, and Section 6 concludes.

2. LITERATURE ON COLLATERAL

In this section, we review the literature on collateral with regard to both developed and emerging countries. Within the wider literature on collateral in developed countries, we are selective in our coverage and concentrate only on those studies that are most related to our analysis. Therefore, we focus on the role of collateral with respect to (i) risk related to the borrower, (ii) the asymmetric information problem, and (iii) bank competition. Because there is only scarce literature on these topics about emerging countries, we do not concentrate on selective issues. Accordingly, we first discuss the theoretical and empirical literature chronologically; then, we examine those cross-country studies that are more closely related to our analysis.

2.1. Studies on Developed Countries

2.1.1. Collateral and Risk Related to the Borrower

The theoretical literature indicates that the pledging of collateral is an efficient solution for the problems of information asymmetry about the quality of borrowers with no ex-ante adverse-selection or ex-post moral hazard problems. In a hidden-information scenario, the borrower's willingness to post collateral may mitigate the lender's adverse-selection problems (Stiglitz and Weiss, 1981; Hart and Moore, 1984; Bester, 1987; Besanko and Thakor, 1987b; Chan and Thakor, 1987). In a perfectly competitive market, banks choose collateral requirements and interest rates to sort borrowers into risk classes. The adverse-selection hypothesis predicts that unobservable lower-risk (higher-quality) borrowers will pledge more and better collateral than higher-risk (lower-quality) borrowers because lower-risk borrowers have a lower likelihood of losing the collateral and pledging the collateral is less costly. However, conventional wisdom suggests that when risk is observable, higher collateral requirements are most often associated with higher-risk borrowers. Indeed, in a hidden-action scenario, collateral may help prevent riskier borrowers from taking ex-post unobservable risk-shifting behavior that adversely affects the project payoff (Boot et al., 1991). The credible threat of losing collateral incentivizes the borrower to exert greater effort and thus reduces the risk of the borrower's default. The observed-risk hypothesis predicts that observable higher-risk (lower-quality) borrowers will more likely pledge collateral.

2.1.2. Collateral and Information Asymmetry

Empirical research has mostly tested the observed-risk hypothesis, whereas there is a lack of substantial empirical support for the adverse-selection hypothesis. Within this stream of literature, most studies have investigated whether a reduction in asymmetric information affects collateral requirements. By using ex-post default as a measure of ex-ante adverse private information, Jimenez et al. (2006) find that the likelihood of pledging collateral among young borrowers who cope with information asymmetries is positively associated with their credit quality. Berger et al. (2011b) show that a technological innovation in loan evaluation techniques leads to a reduction in information gaps and, therefore, to reduced collateral requirements. The strength of the lender-borrower relationship is often used as an inverse proxy for the degree of asymmetric information (for an overview, see, e.g., Boot, 2000). The theoretical assumption is that the stronger the relation, the more reliable the borrower's risk information and the more favorable the terms of the contract (Boot and Thakor, 1994; Petersen and Rajan, 1995).[1] Empirical research has shown that the variables employed as proxies for the strength of the relationship—such as the length, breadth, or intensity of the relationship—can affect the empirical results. Although several studies find either no significant or positive correlation between the lending relationship and the pledging of collateral (Machauer and Weber, 1998; Hernández-Cánovas and Martínez-Solano, 2006; Voordeckers and Steijvers, 2006; Ono and Uesugi, 2009; Uchida, 2011), most of the research shows a negative relationship (Berger and Udell, 1995; Harhoff and Körting, 1998; Degryse and Van, 2000; Chakraborty and Hu, 2006; Jimenez et al., 2006; Brick and Palia, 2007). Within this debate, certain authors have attempted to test both the adverse-selection and the observed-risk hypotheses (Berger et al., 2011a; Godlewski and Weill, 2011). The main results show that, when there is strong information asymmetry, the borrower uses collateral to signal its quality, whereas when there is low information asymmetry, the bank detects the risk related to the borrower and requires appropriate collateral. In addressing how the borrower's observed risk is related to collateral requirements, many different aspects of the lending relationship have been analyzed. Because of the wide availability of data, empirical research in the developed countries has focused on various factors, including the type and size of the lender (Jimenez and Saurina, 2004; Uchida, 2011), the type of the loan (Chakraborty and Hu, 2006), lender-borrower physical distance (Inderst and Mueller, 2007; Jimenez et al., 2009), and lending characteristics (Berger and Udell, 1995; Voordeckers and Steijvers, 2006; Brick and Palia, 2007).[2] More recent literature investigates how risk assessment and collateral requirement are affected by the expected value of collateral (Benmelech and Bergman, 2009; Grunert and Weber, 2009; Niinimäki, 2011).

[1] However, it is notable that access to private information by the lender can lead to conflicting predictions about collateral required because the information on the borrower's quality may be favorable or unfavorable.

[2] The literature on collateral is extensive and widespread and addresses many different issues related to collateral requirements, such as credit rationing (Bester, 1985; Besanko and Thakor, 1987a; Coco, 1999; Berger et al., 2011b), enforcement rights (Porta et al., 1997), credit access (Jimenez and Saurina, 2004), and lender monitoring (Rajan and Winton, 1995; Repullo and Suarez, 1998; Park, 2000; Manove et al., 2001; Ono and Uesugi, 2009; Cerqueiro et al., 2011).

2.1.3. Collateral and Bank Competition

Theoretical studies on the role of collateral and bank competition are mostly included in the broader stream of literature on relationship banking. One theoretical view argues that, as bank competition increases, the bank's incentive to invest in information collection may decrease because borrowers may be tempted to switch to other banks (Besanko and Thakor, 1987a; Petersen and Rajan, 1995). As a consequence, the use of collateral would be more likely in competitive loan markets. Thus, assuming a negative relationship between competition and concentration, the use of collateral is expected to be empirically less likely in more concentrated (less competitive) lender markets. A negative relationship between the use of collateral and loan market concentration suggests that collateral and a bank's market power are substitutes for one another (Jimenez et al., 2011). A second theoretical view asserts that competition may induce banks to focus even more deeply on relationship lending (Boot and Thakor, 2000; Berlin and Butler, 2002) because only client-driven lending helps a bank to distinguish itself from competitors. Increased banking competition is expected to decrease collateral requirements. A positive relationship between the use of collateral and loan market concentration suggests that collateral and a bank's market power might be complementary (Voordeckers and Steijvers, 2006; Hainz et al., 2008).

2.2. Studies in Emerging Countries

Thus far, the theoretical literature has not specifically focused on the role of collateral in emerging markets. Those models addressing the collateral issue typically refer to financially developed economies, and their empirical verifications primarily use data from firms and banks in developed countries. Because of the more serious information asymmetry in emerging economies, these studies only suggest that an investigation of collateral requirements in these countries might provide support for the adverse-selection hypothesis and reveal a negative relationship between collateral and loan spread. Instead, Caballero and Krishnamurthy (2001) are the first—as far as we know—to specifically develop a theoretical model for collateral in emerging countries. However, their contribution is specific to the context of crisis. Because limited international collateral seems to be an important constraint in emerging economies, the authors aim to provide new insights into emerging markets' crises by analyzing how both domestic and international collateral constraints affect financial and real variables. In their model, limited international collateral, i.e., export revenues that can be seized in the event of a loan default, determines the amount of financing that foreign investors extend to firms, whereas domestic collateral—real estate—determines the amount of financing they can obtain from one another. These two types of collateral constraints interact with one another to produce even more severe interaction effects in emerging economies. The model shows that firms in countries with limited domestic collateral and binding international collateral constraints systematically undervalue international collateral by taking actions that lead them to reduced international collateral during crises, which exacerbates the effects of adverse shocks.

The studies addressing the role of collateral in emerging countries are primarily empirical in nature. Nonetheless, the scant availability of both firm and loan data in emerging countries explains the scarceness of the empirical research on collateral in these economies compared with the research in developed economies. Information on the value and type of collateral pledged by the borrower, in addition to firm-level data, is not commonly available in a country's database. As discussed below, most of the empirical research is single-country analysis, and data are mostly collected through surveys.

Feder et al. (1988) analyze the use of collateral, particularly land collateral, in institutional and non-institutional lending markets in developing rural markets and find that, in rural financial markets in developing countries, some concern may arise with regard to the effectiveness of the use of collateral. Indeed, political, legal, and social issues might influence the enforcement of land pledged as collateral and affect the lending transaction. Within this context, the paper aims to investigate both the use of collateral and the availability of credit in three developing rural countries. The number of observations and the analyzed period vary considerably. They investigate 316 borrowing transactions in Thailand (during the 1985–1986 period) and 100 borrowing transactions in India (during the 1979–1980 period). Transaction data in Korea are available only as percentages of the total volume of loans extended in 1968. The results show that, where it is legal—in Thailand and in India—an extensive and predominant use of land collateral among institutional lenders emerges because it reduces creditworthiness assessment costs. In 1968, the prohibition in Korea to use land as collateral, which was aimed at protecting farmers against pauperization, led institutional lenders to require third-party guarantees, whereas non-institutional lenders more often used land collateral (obtained through *ad hoc* sales contract). The limitation on the use of collateral, however, causes a loss of efficiency because lenders must spend more time and resources in assessing the credit of borrowers. The authors attempt to understand whether collateral requirements are also associated with higher credit availability. Because of the number of observations, they can perform the analysis only on the Thai data, where land foreclosure is allowed, but is not common. The results indicate that pledging land collateral increases the amount of institutional credit offered by more than 40% compared with loans without security. The threat of losing the land makes collateral useful in accessing financing.

Within the literature that analyzes the consequences of financial reform on both investment and credit allocation, Gelos and Werner (2002) consider an emerging market in testing whether and how the liberalization of the Mexican financial sector in late 1988 affected firm constraints and capital expenditure. Their empirical approach was an innovation with respect to the previous methodology, which typically tested whether cash flow in the investment equation explains capital expenditures. Indeed, these authors add the value of a firm's real estate, used as a proxy for collateralizable assets, to explore cash flow relevance after financial liberalization. The authors use a sample of 1046 manufacturing establishments. Data were compiled from a survey conducted from 1984 to 1994.

The observed period allows for investigation of the years preceding and following the 1988 financial reform. Consistent with other studies, the results show that cash flow is significantly correlated with investment before and after financial reform. After the financial liberalization, the financial constraints were eased only for smaller firms. Moreover, the value of collateral is strongly correlated with investment during the entire period studied. The effect of collateral on capital expenditures is even more significant than that of cash flow, and it appears to have become more important after 1989. The authors suggest that the primary effect of financial liberalization is not to lower the cost of credit but to increase its availability. The number of firms seeking financing increased after the reform, but banks appear to have continued to rely heavily on collateral in their lending because of persistent informational and enforcement problems. In fact, the reform of the financial sector did not instantly improve banks' credit analysis techniques and monitoring. Credit continued to be extended primarily against collateral. Therefore, firms must be able to pledge proper collateral to obtain financing. In this collateral-based lending, the authors show the potential for future financial instability. In fact, a decline in a firm's net worth might reduce investment and lead to a sharp decline in asset prices, which might reduce the future availability of funds reduce capital expenditures even further.

There is significant debate in the literature over the effectiveness of relationship lending in transition and emerging economies. Because of expected higher asymmetry of information, banks in developing economies may be prone to extract rent from lending by collateralization. As far as we know, the effect of the lending relationship on collateral requirements in emerging economies was first investigated by La Porta et al. (2003) with regard to Mexico. In their analysis, so-called related borrowers consist of a bank's shareholders, associates, family, and firms controlled by banks. The authors aim to assess if related lending is efficient (exploiting quality assessment and monitoring) or detrimental (enabling insiders to divert resources from depositors or minority shareholders to themselves). The authors find that strong relationship-oriented loan transactions show a lower level of collateral. However, related borrowers also show higher default rates and lower recovery rates than unrelated borrowers. Relating lending in Mexico appears to be consistent with the pessimistic assessment—the so-called looting view—of related lending.

Conversely, with regard to a Thai bank sample, Menkhoff et al. (2006) find a positive relation between collateralization and relationship banking. Their paper is the first to explore the determinants of collateral and has the specific aim of verifying systematic differences between emerging and developed markets. By analyzing a dataset of 560 credit transactions engaged in by nine commercial Thai banks during the 1992–1996 period, the authors find support for significant diversity of collateral determinants. Thai banks require higher collateral more often than analogous banks in developed countries. Collateral is used in reducing the risk level of lending to smaller and younger firms (who are typically more informationally opaque) instead of mitigating information asymmetry.

In their analysis, the bank variable is positive and highly significant. Relationship-oriented house-banks appear more likely to be affected by a hold-up problem than by a reverse looting problem, as found by La Porta et al. (2003) in Mexico. Moreover, larger banks require more collateral from smaller firms, which contrasts with evidence for US banks. The authors suggest that this might be caused by large banks with bargaining power that are able to lock in smaller borrowers to both higher interest rates and higher collateral requirements.

In a subsequent paper, Menkhoff et al. (2012) focus on householders in north-eastern Thailand to study possible substitutes for collateral. These authors argue that borrowers in emerging markets that most require financing are those upon whom higher collateral requirements are imposed and those less likely to hold pledgeable assets. To solve this puzzle, they offer evidence of useful substitutes that allow smaller firms to access collateral-free financing. The data are from a survey conducted in 2007 in 2186 rural households. They find that only 11% households are credit-constrained and, furthermore, most of the householders borrow without pledging collateral. Indeed, the share of collateralized loans is consistently small and does not exceed 25%. It is notable that even low-income households (surprisingly) possess assets, typically land, that might serve as collateral. However, the slow marketability process and the complex legal system have rendered the enforcement on this type of collateral ineffective. This helps to explain the high number of loan with collateral substitutes. The regression analysis confirms that the use of third-party guarantees decreases the probability of collateral requirement by a factor of 0.54–0.57, whereas relationship lending decreases the probability by only 0.07–0.10. The two substitutes work independently, although guarantees are relatively more important at formal financial institutions. This empirical research is important because it addresses the collateral issue from a broader perspective. In fact, Menkhoff et al. (2012) are the first (as far as we know) to recognize that, where collateral is not widely used, research must account for several substitutes to fully understand the determinants of collateral.

Thus, empirical research on emerging countries is often narrow in its coverage with respect to the selected country, and most of them analyze a single market. Cross-country analyzes on the role of collateral in emerging markets are scarce. Three recent papers address this issue. Although important results are shown for the role of collateral in emerging markets, we argue that these studies present limitations with regard to their observed sample. Hainz et al. (2008) investigate the relation between collateral and bank competition in 70 countries, of which fewer than half are emerging countries. Liberti and Mian (2010) analyze a sample of loans extended to firms in emerging countries. However, these loans are extended by a single multinational bank. Godlewski and Weill (2011) investigate how collateral mitigates adverse selection. However, their cross-country sample is not composed exclusively of emerging countries but includes developed economies.

Hainz et al. (2008) argue that to investigate the role of bank competition in access to credit, collateral use must be investigated because collateral requirements are consistently considered to be a major financing obstacle. To our knowledge, this is the first paper that investigates the effect of bank competition on collateral in a cross-country analysis that considers emerging markets. In a theoretical model, the authors show that firms that are located nearby a bank are best financed by screening contracts, whereas distant borrowers are required to pledge collateral. As bank competition increases, the proportion of firms financed by screening contracts increases, and the use of collateral consequently decreases. These predictions are empirically tested in a cross-country analysis on a sample of 4931 bank loans from 70 countries composed of both developed and emerging economies. The bank competition variable presents a significant positive value, which shows that collateral is more likely when the level of bank competition is lower.

Liberti and Mian (2010) investigate how financial development affects collateral requirements using an original sample of loans extended in 15 countries to small and medium enterprises. Because the moral hazard concern is more severe in financially underdeveloped economies, the authors estimate the cost of financial underdevelopment in terms of its effect on collateral spreads (instead of interest rate spreads). The country's collateral spread is measured as the difference in collateralization rates between high- and low-risk loans within the same economy. Their results show that the average collateral spread is large; a 1% increase in the probability of default increases the rate of collateralization by 2.1%. Moreover, declines in collateral spreads are explained by fundamental institutional differences across countries; a one-standard deviation improvement in financial development reduces a country's collateral spread by almost one-half. The authors exploit a wide (and rare) availability of data concerning the value and type of collateral pledged for each loan and concerning banks' ex-ante and ex-post assessments of the risk related to borrowers. However, it must be noted that the data come from a single multinational bank, and its specific lending policies might affect the results. Nevertheless, as noted by the authors, the constant nature of the lending allows for a more reliable comparison of the borrowers. The most relevant result in this paper is in collecting and analyzing the collateral value and type, which are objective measures of firm risk and which enable the investigation of how collateral requirements differ with firm risk and across countries.

Godlewski and Weill (2011) contribute to the debate between the adverse-selection and the observed-risk hypotheses. They argue that, with strong information asymmetry, the borrower has an incentive to signal its quality by pledging higher collateral; with low information asymmetry, the bank recognizes the quality of the borrower and requires only commensurate collateral. They aim to test whether the degree of information asymmetry affects the link between collateral and the loan spread. By using the Dealscan dataset, they perform a cross-country analysis over a sample of 4940 large-bank loans from 31 countries; almost half of these are developed countries. The degree of asymmetric information between the bank and the borrower before loan approval is captured by a set of proxies that control for financial information, trust, and economic and financial development in each country. Their results validate both adverse-selection and observed-risk hypotheses based on the degree of information asymmetries in a country. They find a positive relationship between the presence of collateral and the loan spread. They also observe that this relationship may be (barely) negative in countries with strong information asymmetries, but this result is observed only in developing countries. As they suggest (p. 64), further investigation is required on a sample composed only of emerging markets in which information asymmetries may be severe. Moreover, a limitation of the analysis is that large loans are less likely to be exposed to the issue of information asymmetry. However, this results from the absence of a cross-country database available for small loans in their cross-country analysis.

By studying collateral in emerging markets, we argue that a limitation of Godlewski and Weill (2011) is that less than half of their sample consists of emerging countries. Thus, we contribute to the literature by (i) constructing a cross-country sample consisting solely of emerging market economies, (ii) collecting deep and wide data at both the firm- and loan-levels, and (iii) performing a robustness analysis on a subsample of small and medium enterprises. We are not aware of a previous cross-country study on collateral determinants based solely on a sample of emerging markets.

3. EMPIRICAL ANALYSIS

In this section, we aim to investigate the determinants of collateral with a set of 16 countries that represent the majority of emerging countries, as defined by S&P and MSCI classifications of emerging markets. Our aim is to determine whether collateral requirements in emerging countries depend more on firm-specific or country-specific variables.

3.1. Data

The data are based on the World Business Environment Survey (WBES), which is repeatedly conducted by the World Bank Group in a roughly standardized form in 80 countries throughout the world. The purpose of these surveys is to provide uniform evaluation methodology in assessing the conditions for private investments in developing economies, by focusing on broader aspects of business environments, such as services to business, economic policy, financial barriers, corruption, and governance. Through personal interviews, the structured questionnaires allow the collection of firm-level information at the managerial level. Although the questionnaires have changed over time (different countries often required country-specific questions), these surveys are extremely important to make regional comparisons of constraints affecting the business environment. Paying attention to what business say about the environment they face has been confirmed to be a useful way to understand what is really necessary to improve business growth (Stone, 1992).

Table 1 Sample (2002–2006).

Countries	All firms	SMEs	Large firms
Brazil	375	205	170
Chile	672	512	160
China	1228	507	721
Colombia	337	303	34
Czech Republic	181	126	55
Hungary	399	309	90
India	1327	987	340
Indonesia	308	116	192
Korea	168	142	26
Malaysia	692	473	219
Mexico	100	62	38
Poland	510	394	116
Russia	305	206	99
South Africa	250	136	114
Thailand	1296	553	743
Turkey	544	402	142
Total	8692	5433	3259

The WBES provides two standardized datasets in which country data are matched to a standard set of questions.[3] The primary data come from the Productivity and the Investment Climate Private Enterprise Survey. (PICS), conducted by the World Bank with the intention of measuring the quality of the "investment climate."[4] This survey is based on a representative sample of 26,852 firms and was collected from 2002 to 2006 over a wide range of emerging countries. We designed our sample by selecting those surveys in which information on both the presence of collateral and the collateral-to-loan-value ratio was available. Of the 26,852 firms, 12,748 firms answered whether the most recent loan includes collateral (our *COLL1* variable), and 8692 firms provided the collateral-to-loan-value ratio (our *COLL2* variable). This left us with a final sample of 8692 observations covering the emerging countries reported in Table 1.

3.2. The Model

Because we aim to investigate collateral requirements both in terms of the presence and the amount of pledged collateral, we specify two types of dependent variables. First, we utilize a dummy variable equal to one if the most recent loan required collateral and zero

[3] This format allows cross-country comparisons and analysis but sacrifices those country-specific survey questions that cannot be matched.

[4] https://www.enterprisesurveys.org/portal/elibrary.aspx?libid=14.

otherwise (*COLL1*), which is estimated via the first of the two equations below. The second dependent variable is a continuous variable, which is the percentage of collateral-to-loan value (*COLL2*), which is estimated via OLS, as in the second equation below. Thus, we estimate the following two equations:

$$
\begin{aligned}
Prob\left(COLL1_{imkjt} = 1\right) \\
&= F\left(b_0 + b_1 SIZE_{imkjt} + b_2 AGE_{imkjt} + b_3 BUSI_{ASSOC\,imkjt} + b_4 AUDIT_{imkjt}\right. \\
&\quad + b_5 CAPACITY_{imkjt} + b_6 INTEREST_{LOAN_{imkjt}} + b_7 DURATION_{LOAN_{imkjt}} \\
&\quad + b_8 CREDITINFO_{imkjt} + b_9 BRKM_{imkjt} + b_{10} BRPC_{imkjt} + b_{11} LGDPPC_{imkjt} + d_k + t_t \\
&\quad \left. + l_m + e_{imkjt}\right).
\end{aligned}
$$

$$
\begin{aligned}
COLL2_{imkjt} \\
&= \beta_0 + b_1 SIZE_{imkjt} + \beta_2 AGE_{imkjt} + \beta_3 BUSI_{ASSOC\,imkjt} + \beta_4 AUDIT_{imkjt} \\
&\quad + \beta_5 CAPACITY_{imkjt} + \beta_6 INTEREST_{LOAN\,imkjt} + \beta_7 DURATION_{LOAN\,imkjt} \\
&\quad + \beta_8 CREDITINFO_{imkjt} + \beta_9 BRKM_{imkjt} + \beta_{10} RPC_{imkjt} + \beta_{11} LGDPPC_{imkjt} + \delta_k + \tau_t \\
&\quad + \lambda_m + e_{imkjt}.
\end{aligned}
$$

where i, m, k, j, and t represent firms, location of the firms, sector, country, and year, respectively, and β's are regression coefficients to be estimated. We model these firm-level dependent variables as a function of firm-loan specific and country-specific variables that are listed in Table 2. For the logit regressions, the $F(\cdot)$ is the logit function and "Prob" refers to probability; δ_k, τ_t, λ_m are the sector, year, and location fixed effects, respectively, e_{imkjt} and represents the error term.

The set of firm-specific variables refers to both firm and loan characteristics. To account for firm characteristics, we use several dependent variables. We employ the logarithm of the average number of permanent workers (*SIZE*) as a measure of firm size. Because larger firms may be considered more reputable, we might expect the larger firms to obtain loans with less stringent conditions, i.e., to have a negative coefficient estimate. Conversely, smaller firms are less likely to hold collateralizable assets and are thus less likely to apply for and obtain loans that require collateral. However, if they agree upon a loan that requires collateral (i.e., *COLL1* = 1), they might be more likely to have higher collateral-to-loan-value ratios. We also used the number of years that the firm has been operating (*AGE*). Older firms are more likely to have longer relationship with lenders, as shown by Berger and Udell (1995); thus, these more established firms can obtain loans with better conditions, i.e., lower interest rates and less collateral. Thus, we expect to observe a negative coefficient estimate for *AGE*. Conversely, according to the adverse-selection hypothesis, older firms may want to signal their quality. Accordingly, their loan contracts may present higher collateralization. Given that the opacity of firm's financial information can affect the information asymmetry problem and influence collateral requirements, we aim to capture the level and quality of financial information through two variables. We use first a dummy variable that equals one if the firm is a

Table 2 Variable definition and sources (2002–2006 and 2006–2010).

Variables		Source	Exp. sign
COLL1	Dummy variable = 1 if the most recent loan or overdraft requires col lateral or deposit, zero otherwise.	PICS	
COLL2	The approximate value of collateral required as percentage of the loan value (excludes zeroes).	PICS	
Firm characteristics			
SIZE	Logarithm of the average number of permanent workers.	PICS	+/−
AGE	The number of years that the firm has been operating.	PICS	+/−
BUSI_ASSOC	Dummy variable equals one if the firm member of a business association, zero otherwise.	PICS	+/−
AUDIT	Dummy variable that equals one if annual financial statements of the firm are reviewed by external auditor, zero otherwise.	PICS	+/−
CAPACITY	Average capacity utilization over the last year (%).	PICS	+/−
QUALITY	Dummy variable equals one if the firm has a quality certification (ISO), zero otherwise.	PICS	+/−
Loan characteristics			
INTEREST_LOAN	Approximate annual cost/rate of interest of loan (%).	PICS	−
DURATION_LOAN	Duration (term) of the loan (months).	PICS	+
LAMOUNT_LOAN	Logarithm of the loan amount (in $US).	PICS	+
Loan market characteristics			
CREDITINFO	Credit information index.	WB	−
CONCENTRATION	Assets of three largest banks as a share of assets of all commercial banks (%).	WB	+/−
BRKM	Number of branches per 1000 km^2.	WB	+/−
BRPC	Number of branches per 100,000 people.	WB	+/−
Macroeconomics environment			
LGDPPC	Logarithm of the GDP per capita (US$).	WB	−

member of a business association and zero otherwise (*BUSI_ASSOC*). Second, we use a dummy variable that equals one if annual financial statements of the firm are reviewed by an external auditor and zero otherwise (*AUDIT*). Because being a member in a business association and being externally audited helps firms become more transparent and provide more reliable financial reports, we expect to observe both positive and negative effects on collateralization. We might expect that firms with higher capacity utilization (*CAPACITY*) to have higher repayment capability and thus be less likely to have collateralized loans, which indicates a negative relationship between collateralization and *CAPACITY*. Conversely, such firms also might want to signal their quality by pledging collateral and agreeing on higher collateral-to-loan-value ratios, which indicates a positive association between *CAPACITY* and collateralization.

Loan characteristics are captured by two variables. We include the approximate annual interest of the loan (*INTEREST_LOAN*) and the duration (maturity) of the loan expressed in months (*DURATION_LOAN*). According to the insight provided by Godlewski and Weill (2011), because of more severe information asymmetry, we expect that firms in emerging countries attempt to signal their quality by pledging more collateral and obtaining lower interest rates on loans. Therefore, we expect a negative sign on the *INTEREST_LOAN* variable. Another standard means to reduce information asymmetry is to shorten the duration of the loan and disincentivize the firm from engaging in risk-shifting behavior. Thus, we expect short-term loans and collateral to be substitutes for one another; the coefficient estimation of *LLOAN_DURATION* variable is thus expected to be positive.

The set of country-specific independent variables refers to both information asymmetry and loan market characteristics. With regard to information asymmetry, we include the credit depth of information index (*CREDITINFO*). This index takes into account rules affecting the scope, accessibility, and quality of credit information. The source of information can be either a public registry or a private bureau. The index scores range from 0 to 6, with higher values indicating the availability of more information on firms. The availability of information on firms is important to reduce informational asymmetries and eventually decrease adverse-selection problems. In countries with weaker information-sharing mechanisms, lenders are more likely to experience difficulties in credit-risk measurement and offer loans with stricter conditions. Therefore, we expect a negative association between *CREDITINFO* and collateralization. To measure concentration in the lending market, we use the *CONCENTRATION* variable, i.e., the share of all commercial bank assets that are owned by the three largest commercial banks. To account for branch penetration, we use the number of commercial branches per 1000 km^2 (*BRKM*) and per 100,000 adults (*BRPC*). Competition in loan markets (lower concentration and higher penetration of banking services) might lead lenders to focus more deeply on client-driven lending to become the preferred lenders. As a consequence, competition may induce banks to relax contract terms, i.e., lower their collateral ratios

(Boot and Thakor, 2000; Berlin and Butler, 2002). Thus, loan contracts might become less stringent as competition increases. However, another branch of literature (Petersen and Rajan, 1995) suggests that banks would maintain the incentive to invest in information collection and, therefore, require lower collateral only in concentrated lending markets. Thus, we might expect less collateralization in concentrated lending markets (lower penetration of banking services) as banks possess an informational advantage over firms in these markets. This advantage would produce less stringent collateral requirements.

To control for the unobserved fixed effects in sector (δ_k), year (τ_t), and location level (λ_m), we include the relevant dummy variables in all regressions. Our sample is composed of firms from 27 subgroups of industry, in both goods and services. To control for differences in collateralization of loan contracts extended in locations of different sizes, we employ a set of dummy variables that account for the location of the establishment. Because of the existence of transaction (for firms) and enforcement costs (for banks), the location of firms is important for determining the cost of loans and the various terms of the loan contract, such as collateral. We include in regression λ_m a set of *location* dummies (1 = Capital City; 2 = Other city with a population over 1 million; 3 = City with a population of 250,000–1 million; 4 = City with a population of 50,000–250,000; 5 = Town or location with a population of less than 50,000).

3.3. Descriptive Statistics

Table 3 reports the summary statistics of the variables used in the analysis, which is based on 16 emerging countries. Because certain countries are surveyed in multiple years, we have 26 observations for country-level variables. In our sample, both the presence of collateral and the collateral-to-loan-value ratio is high. The mean value of *COLL1* indicates that 70% of loans are secured by collateral. The average collateral-to-loan-value ratio is clearly above 100%, with an average standard deviation of 79.7%, as observed by Menkhoff et al. (2012). Of the loan contracts that include collateral, 35% required an amount of collateral that exceeded the value of the loan (that is, *COLL2* > 100).

Table 4 presents the mean values of *COLL1* and *COLL2* at the country level. The lowest mean value for the presence of collateral is in Colombia, in which approximately only one-half of commercial loans are secured by collateral. Hungary shows the highest collateralization; 91% of business loans were secured by collateral. Hungary is also first with respect to the degree of collateral at an average collateral-to-loan-value ratio (*COLL2*) of 169.4%; Malaysia has the lowest mean value of collateral-to-loan-value ratio at 85.5%.

Table 5 reports statistics for collateralization in different countries, divided by income categories.[5] No major differences emerge among country groups with respect to the

[5] The countries are grouped into income categories (according to the survey year) defined by the WB in the survey. The lowest income country in the survey is India. Lower middle-income countries are Brazil, China, Colombia, Indonesia, Russia (2002), South Africa, Turkey (2002), and Thailand. The upper middle-income countries are Chile, Czech Republic, Hungary, Malaysia, Mexico, Poland, Russia (2005), Turkey (2004 and 2005). The highest income OECD country is South Korea.

Table 3 Summary statistics (2002–2006).

Variables	# obs.	Mean	Std dev.	Min.	Max.
COLL1	12,748	0.70	0.46	0	1
COLL2	8692	112.95	79.67	0.17	1000
Firm characteristics					
SIZE	12,465	3.98	1.80	0	11.121
AGE	11,676	18.48	16.83	0	202
BUSI_ASSOC	10,203	0.63	0.48	0	1
AUDIT	11,881	0.69	0.46	0	1
CAPACITY	11,203	75.82	20.27	0	103.6
Loan characteristics					
INTEREST_LOAN	6506	11.66	10.29	0	171
DURATION_LOAN	7016	30.94	35.59	0	540
Loan market characteristics					
CREDITINFO	26	3.74	1.76	0	6
CONCENTRATION	26	61.05	19.46	33.26	99.20
BRKM	26	11.66	13.95	0.19	65.02
BRPC	26	9.35	6.45	1.33	28.25
Macroeconomic environment					
LGDPPC	26	7.73	0.83	6.33	9.44

mean values of collateralization on loans. Collateral (*COLL1*) is slightly more likely in lower income groups than in higher ones. The degree of collateral (*COLL2*) follows a different pattern because it is higher for higher income groups. In general, SMEs are less likely than large firms to include collateral. However, once collateral is included in the loan contracts, SMEs have higher collateral-to-loan-value ratios compared with large firms.

Table 6 shows the percentage of collateral types included in loan contracts. Land and buildings appear to be the most-preferred type of collateral and constitute nearly 40% of the collateral pledged. Machinery and equipment are a secondary choice. These results are consistent with the observation of Niinimäki (2009) that real estate is the most common and dominant form of collateral.

3.4. Results

Table 7 reports the estimation results. To account for the unobserved fixed effects for industry, year, and location, we include the relevant dummy variables in all regressions. We do not control for country-fixed effects in the regressions in Table 7 resulting from multicollinearity because we use country-level variables, i.e., *CREDITINFO,*

Table 4 Collateralization by country (2002–2006).

Countries	*COLL1*	*COLL2*
Hungary	0.91	169.41
Indonesia	0.87	116.32
Czech Republic	0.84	128.01
Thailand	0.83	88.49
Russia	0.82	146.97
India	0.79	112.96
Poland	0.77	148.93
Korea	0.69	134.61
Brazil	0.67	125.19
China	0.67	85.94
Mexico	0.65	169.00
Malaysia	0.63	85.46
South Africa	0.61	142.44
Chile	0.58	117.96
Turkey	0.57	110.66
Colombia	0.51	129.46
Total	0.70	112.95

Countries are ordered by decreasing *COLL1*.

CONCENTRATION, BRKM, BRPC, and *LGDPPC*. The 3rd and 6th columns of Table 7 do not include the loan characteristic variables of *INTEREST_LOAN* and *DURATION_LOAN* to allow for a higher number of observations. A higher number of observations create significant changes neither in the significance nor in the point estimates of the coefficients.

The effect of firm characteristics on the presence of collateral as measured by *COLL1* shows that larger and older firms are both more likely to have collateral in their loan contracts. However, these relationships are not valid for the collateral-to-loan-value ratios as measured by *COLL2*. The estimation results provide strong evidence in favor of a negative relationship between capacity utilization and collateralization measured by both the presence of collateral in loan contracts and the collateral-to-loan-value ratios. Because *CAPACITY* may be a proxy for creditworthiness, this finding suggests that firms of higher quality obtain loans under more favorable conditions in terms of collateral requirements.

As for loan characteristics, the negative coefficient estimates for *INTEREST_LOAN* indicate a substitution relationship between high interest rates and high collateralization. This result provides important support for Godlewski and Weill (2011) results and, by considering only emerging countries, is consistent with their recommendation for further investigation. However, this relationship is only statistically significant at a 10% level

Table 5 Collaterization by income country groups (2002–2006).

Var.	Income	All firms			SMEs			Large firms		
		Mean	Std dev.	# obs.	Mean	Std dev.	# obs.	Mean	Std dev.	# obs.
COLL1	low	0.79	0.40	1774	0.78	0.42	1340	0.85	0.36	434
	Lower-middle	0.70	0.46	5876	0.65	0.48	3150	0.76	0.43	2726
	Upper-middle	0.67	0.47	4805	0.69	0.46	3397	0.63	0.48	1408
	High-OECD	0.69	0.46	293	0.71	0.46	230	0.60	0.49	63
	Total	0.70	0.46	12,748	0.69	0.46	8117	0.72	0.45	4631
COLL2	Low	112.96	92.77	1327	113.93	98.99	987	110.15	71.78	340
	Lower-middle	101.02	71.48	4045	103.53	81.09	2001	98.57	60.54	2044
	Upper-middle	127.11	82.97	3152	131.84	88.10	2303	114.28	65.48	849
	High-OECD	134.61	25.15	168	135.35	24.26	142	130.58	29.74	26
	Total	112.95	79.67	8692	118.25	87.60	5433	104.12	63.35	3259

Table 6 Percentage of collateral types (2002–2006).

Forms of collateral	# obs.	Mean	Std dev.	Min.	Max.
Land and buildings	2994	39.12	43.48	0	100
Machinery	2401	16.39	31.25	0	100
Intangible assets (accounts receiv., inventory)	2401	7.95	23.45	0	100
Personal assets of owner/manager (e.g., house)	2400	9.97	27.02	0	100

This table shows the summary statistics for types of collateral as a share of collateral pledged in the loan contracts and as percentage of total collateral.

in regression (4) and is statistically insignificant in the remaining regressions. The positive and statistically significant coefficient estimates for *DURATION_LOAN* along the regressions show that longer-term loan contracts are more likely to include collateral (as measured by *COLL1*) and require higher collateral (as measured by *COLL2*) compared with short-term loan contracts.

As a country-level variable, the coefficient estimates of *CREDITINFO* yield both theoretically and statistically significant results. This strong finding indicates that, as the depth of credit information index increases (i.e., higher values indicate that more credit information is available to facilitate lending decisions from either a public registry or a private bureau), both the probability for the presence of collateral in loan contracts and the collateral-to-loan-value ratios decrease significantly. The coefficient estimates for *CONCENTRATION* indicate that the presence of collateral in business loan contracts is more likely in countries that have more concentrated banking sectors. However, this relationship is only significant at a 10% level in the first and second columns of Table 7, whereas it yields statistically insignificant estimates in the rest of the regressions. As for the penetration of banking services, as the number of banks per 100,000 people (*BRPC*) increases, both the likelihood of collateral and the collateral-to-loan-value ratios increase in each regression. Conversely, we observe a negative relationship between the number of banks per 1000 km^2 (*BRKM*) and collateral-to-loan-value ratios (*COLL2*).

For the effect of macroeconomic conditions, we observe that as *LGDPPC* increases, the likelihood of collateral in business loan contracts decreases. However, once collateral is included, the collateral-to-loan-value ratios increase as *LGDPPC* increases.

4. ROBUSTNESS CHECKS

To check whether our results are robust to subsamples, we group the firms with respect to their size, i.e., small versus large firm. Moreover, we perform separate regressions for a second sample of firms, over a different period (2006–2010).

Table 7 Collateral requirements (2002–2006).

Variables	(1) *COLL1*	(2) *COLL1*	(3) *COLL1*	(4) *COLL2*	(5) *COLL2*	(6) *COLL2*
Firm characteristics						
SIZE	0.057*	0.057*	0.051**	−0.439	−0.318	0.108
	(0.017)	(0.017)	(0.008)	(0.583)	(0.691)	(0.867)
AGE	−0.005*	−0.005*	−0.005**	−0.132	−0.112	−0.029
	(0.024)	(0.032)	(0.004)	(0.057)	(0.107)	(0.602)
BUSI_ASSOC	0.171	0.161	0.209**	−1.930	−2.811	−2.854
	(0.053)	(0.066)	(0.001)	(0.476)	(0.298)	(0.156)
AUDIT	0.015	0.019	0.090	−4.812	−4.432	−5.074*
	(0.866)	(0.839)	(0.215)	(0.088)	(0.116)	(0.030)
CAPACITY	−0.009***	−0.009***	−0.007***	−0.160**	−0.156**	−0.158***
	(0.000)	(0.000)	(0.000)	(0.006)	(0.008)	(0.001)
Loan characteristics						
INTEREST_LOAN	−0.001	−0.001		−0.252	−0.140	
	(0.731)	(0.890)		(0.062)	(0.284)	
DURATION_LOAN	0.003	0.003*		0.074	0.095*	
	(0.051)	(0.034)		(0.064)	(0.016)	
Loan market characteristics						
CREDITINFO	−0.230***	−0.208***	−0.195***	−11.41***	−9.991***	−7.99***
	(0.000)	(0.000)	(0.000)	(0.000)	(0.000)	(0.000)
CONCENTRATION	0.008	0.007	0.001	−0.002	−0.086	−0.075
	(0.052)	(0.079)	(0.812)	(0.983)	(0.456)	(0.399)
BRKM	−0.004			−0.472**		
	(0.327)			(0.001)		
BRPC	0.071***	0.066***	0.052***	1.791***	1.293***	0.970***
	(0.000)	(0.000)	(0.000)	(0.000)	(0.000)	(0.000)
Macroeconomic environment						
LGDPPC	−0.277	−0.357*	−0.180	40.49***	33.54***	39.23***
	(0.091)	(0.012)	(0.104)	(0.000)	(0.000)	(0.000)
R^2	0.05	0.05	0.06	0.18	0.18	0.17
# obs.	4167	4167	6683	3073	3073	4891

All regressions include constant terms, year, industry, and location fixed effects. The *p*-values corresponding to robust standard errors are reported in parentheses. In none of the regressions does the average variance inflation factor exceed 2.71, which indicates the absence of multicollinearity. First three models are logit, and the second three models are OLS regressions. Pseudo and adjusted R^2s are reported for the logit and OLS regressions, respectively. The countries that are included in the regressions (1), (2), (4), and (5) are Brazil 2003; Chile 2004; China 2003; Czech 2002, 2005; Hungary 2002, 2005; Poland 2002, 2003, 2005; Russia 2002, 2005; South Africa 2003; South Korea 2005; Turkey 2002, 2004. The (3)rd and (6)th regressions include all countries.

*Significance at the 10% level.

**Significance at the 5% level.

***Significance at the 1% level.

Table 8 Collateral requirements in SMEs (2002–2006).

Variables	(1) *COLL1*	(2) *COLL1*	(3) *COLL1*	(4) *COLL2*	(5) *COLL2*	(6) *COLL2*
Firm characteristics						
SIZE	0.183***	0.184***	0.144***	0.842	1.471	2.057
	(0.000)	(0.000)	(0.000)	(0.542)	(0.285)	(0.097)
AGE	−0.004	−0.003	−0.004	−0.023	0.044	0.115
	(0.357)	(0.380)	(0.222)	(0.853)	(0.721)	(0.276)
BUSI_ASSOC	−0.015	−0.020	0.095	0.561	−0.970	−2.715
	(0.892)	(0.855)	(0.241)	(0.870)	(0.776)	(0.322)
AUDIT	0.018	0.020	0.092	−9.858*	−9.047**	−9.069**
	(0.868)	(0.852)	(0.287)	(0.005)	(0.010)	(0.003)
CAPACITY	−0.008***	−0.008***	−0.006	−0.226**	−0.219**	−0.233***
	(0.001)	(0.001)	(0.005)	(0.004)	(0.005)	0.000
Loan characteristics						
INTEREST_LOAN	−0.002	−0.002		−0.318	−0.164	
	(0.688)	(0.735)		(0.062)	(0.323)	
DURATION_LOAN	0.006**	0.006**		0.025	0.061	
	(0.001)	(0.001)		(0.649)	(0.260)	
Loan market characteristics						
CREDITINFO	−0.292***	−0.281***	−0.254***	−15.50***	−13.05***	−11.02***
	(0.000)	(0.000)	(0.000)	(0.000)	(0.000)	(0.000)
CONCENTRATION	0.015**	0.014**	0.006	0.018	−0.131	−0.101
	(0.003)	(0.003)	(0.063)	(0.912)	(0.401)	(0.405)
BRKM	−0.002			−0.731***		
	(0.718)			(0.000)		
BRPC	0.080***	0.077***	0.065***	2.574***	1.828***	1.436***
	(0.000)	(0.000)	(0.000)	(0.000)	(0.000)	(0.000)
Macroeconomic environment						
LGDPPC	−0.402	−0.447**	−0.189	47.86***	34.32***	40.57***
	(0.056)	(0.009)	(0.157)	(0.000)	(0.000)	(0.000)
R^2	0.07	0.07	0.07	0.18	0.17	0.17
# obs.	2609	2609	3996	1925	1925	2830

*Significance at the 10% level.
**Significance at the 5% level.
***Significance at the 1% level.

As the first round of robustness checks, we run separate regressions for firms with less than 100 full-time employees (SMEs) and firms with more than 100 full-time employees. Regression results for SMEs (Table 8) confirm the baseline regression results, and only certain coefficient estimates lose statistical significance because of the drop in the number of observations.

Conversely, we observe that loans extended to larger firms (Table 9) are less likely to include collateral because the coefficient estimates for the *SIZE* variable are negative and statistically significant for the first three regressions. The regressions in which *COLL2* is the dependent variable also confirm this relationship because the coefficient estimate for the *SIZE* variable is significant at a 10% level for the fourth and fifth regressions. Consistent with Menkhoff et al. (2006), this result might be explained by the fact that banks possess more information about large firms—which is most likely obtained through long-term lending relationship—and are able to extend loans with lower collateral. Conversely, higher collateral requirements are imposed upon lesser-known small firms. In the large firm sample, *CREDITINFO* is statistically significant only at a 10% level in the third regression. This shows that the availability of information on a firm's credit history does not have the same significant effect it had for SMEs. Most likely, banks rely more on soft private information and firm's reputation when lending to larger firms instead of on hard information, as represented by the *CREDITINFO* variable. Notably, the negative coefficient estimates for *CONCENTRATION* show that the effect of banking concentration is found to be negative for the large firms, i.e., more concentrated banking environments lead to lower probability of observing collateral in business loans extended to large firms. Conversely, banking concentration positively affects the probability of collateral in business loans extended to SMEs. These results suggest that banking concentration eases loan conditions (i.e., lower probability for the presence of collateral) for large firms and makes it more difficult for the SMEs. When competition is low, banks can exploit their bargaining power and lock in smaller firms to higher collateral requirements.

The effect of the macroeconomic environment, as measured by *LGDPPC*, shows that loans to large firms are not affected from the declines in *LGDPPC*, whereas loans to SMEs are affected, i.e., SMEs are more vulnerable to changes in macroeconomic environment.

As a second round of robustness tests, we check whether our results are sensitive for another group of emerging markets. We design a second sample from WBES by collecting data over a different period, from 2006 to 2010. Unfortunately, because the questionnaires have changed over time, this sample does not contain the same firm-level information as our primary dataset of PICS. Accordingly, our firm-level independent variables are not identical to our baseline regressions. More specifically, in the regressions for firm characteristics we do not have *BUSI_ASSOC* variable, whereas for loan characteristics, we do not have *INTEREST_LOAN* variable. However, we are able to include the *QUALITY* variable (that approximates for firm quality) as a dummy variable that equals one if the firm has an internationally recognized quality certification such as ISO 9000, 9002, or 14,000 and zero otherwise. In addition, we are able to include *LAMOUNT_LOAN*, i.e., the logarithm of the loan amount (in $US), as an important variable of loan characteristics. In this sample, only 2104 firms provide information about loan duration. This reduces the number of observations significantly. Moreover, firms in the Philippines and Indonesia were not asked to provide information about collateral-to-loan-value ratios, which leads to a decrease in the number of observations of *COLL2*. This drop in the number of observations also reduces the statistical significance of the firm-level independent variables

Table 9 Collateral requirements in large firms (2002–2006).

Variables	(1) *COLL*1	(2) *COLL*1	(3) *COLL*1	(4) *COLL*2	(5) *COLL*2	(6) *COLL*2
Firm characteristics						
SIZE	−0.251***	−0.252***	−0.216***	−3.789	−3.817	−1.677
	(0.000)	(0.000)	(0.000)	(0.075)	(0.073)	(0.225)
AGE	−0.004	−0.004	−0.004*	−0.129	−0.126	−0.054
	(0.133)	(0.134)	(0.033)	(0.112)	(0.118)	(0.382)
BUSI_ASSOC	0.618***	0.616***	0.470***	−4.325	−4.473	−2.998
	(0.000)	(0.000)	(0.000)	(0.340)	(0.322)	(0.307)
AUDIT	0.127	0.126	0.157	8.586	8.404	7.209
	(0.511)	(0.515)	(0.317)	(0.094)	(0.100)	(0.066)
CAPACITY	−0.009**	−0.009	−0.009***	−0.053	−0.053	−0.045
	(0.006)	(0.006)	(0.001)	(0.551)	(0.552)	(0.480)
Loan characteristics						
INTEREST_LOAN	0.000	0.000		−0.116	−0.091	
	(0.955)	(0.972)		(0.611)	(0.681)	
DURATION_LOAN	−0.002	−0.002		0.107	0.111	
	(0.252)	(0.255)		(0.064)	(0.054)	
Loan market characteristics						
CREDITINFO	−0.110	−0.105	−0.130	−2.261	−1.977	−0.761
	(0.279)	(0.265)	(0.087)	(0.326)	(0.374)	(0.677)
CONCENTRATION	−0.004	−0.004	−0.011	0.010	−0.011	−0.023
	(0.587)	(0.562)	(0.043)	(0.958)	(0.949)	(0.861)
BRKM	−0.001			−0.133		
	(0.900)			(0.630)		
BRPC	0.037	0.035	0.028	0.116	−0.034	−0.140
	(0.255)	(0.244)	(0.216)	(0.861)	(0.953)	(0.763)
Macroeconomic environment						
LGDPPC	0.025	0.011	−0.087	28.46***	27.45***	32.59***
	(0.938)	(0.970)	(0.692)	(0.000)	(0.000)	(0.000)
R^2	0.08	0.08	0.07	0.13	0.13	0.13
# obs.	1544	1544	2680	1148	1148	2061

*Significance at the 10% level.
**Significance at the 5% level.
***Significance at the 1% level.

compared with our baseline estimation results. The summary statistics of the variables used in the regression analysis are shown in Table 10.

Table 11 presents information on the forms of collateral pledged in loan contracts. These results are consistent with the results of our baseline sample reported in Table 6.

Table 10 Summary statistics (2006–2010).

Variables	# obs.	Mean	Std dev.	Min.	Max.
COLL1	8070	0.59	0.49	0	1
COLL2	2627	111.17	88.80	1	900
Firm characteristics					
SIZE	8047	3.85	1.48	0	9.65
AGE	8040	22.16	18.09	0	210
AUDIT	8025	0.52	0.50	0	1
CAPACITY	5526	74.24	20.59	0.00	100.00
QUALITY	7791	0.30	0.46	0	1
Loan characteristics					
DURATION_LOAN	2104	30.76	30.68	1	288
LAMOUNT_LOAN	6943	11.92	2.49	2.936	21.53
Loan market characteristics					
CREDITINFO	16	5.09	0.68	3	6
BRPC	16	8.79	4.14	2.24	28.25
BRKM	16	4.91	5.89	0.19	31.04
CONCENTRATION	16	54.91	10.84	42.95	77.14
Macroeconomic environment					
LGD	16	7.91	0.51	6.88	9.03

Table 11 Forms of collateral (2006–2010).

Variables	# obs.	Mean	Std dev.	Min.	Max.
Land and buildings under ownership of establishment	4635	0.52	0.50	0	1
Machinery and equipment, including movables	4638	0.29	0.45	0	1
Accounts receivable and inventories	4624	0.17	0.38	0	1
Personal assets of owner (house, etc.)	4620	0.27	0.44	0	1
Collateral not included in categories above	4605	0.23	0.42	0	1

Note: table reports the summary statistics for the dummy variables for each type of collateral included in the loans.

With regard to collateral determinants, our results are reported in Table 12. As for firm characteristics, we do not observe significant effects for the *SIZE*, *AGE*, and *AUDIT* variables. We see that firms that operate close to full capacity (*CAPACITY*) are less likely to have collateral in their loan contracts, which confirms our baseline results from the

Table 12 Collateral requirements (2006–2010).

Variables	(1) *COLL1*	(2) *COLL1*	(3) *COLL1*	(4) *COLL1*	(5) *COLL2*	(6) *COLL2*	(7) *COLL2*	(8) *COLL2*
Firm characteristics								
SIZE	−0.061	−0.058	−0.057	−0.056	−5.155	−4.958	−5.145	−4.915
	(0.389)	(0.411)	(0.424)	(0.427)	(0.143)	(0.162)	(0.143)	(0.166)
AGE	−0.006	−0.006	−0.007	−0.007	0.188	0.167	0.165	0.155
	(0.132)	(0.110)	(0.075)	(0.087)	(0.392)	(0.451)	(0.450)	(0.483)
AUDIT	−0.206	−0.199	−0.220	−0.203	17.430	16.930	15.040	16.040
	(0.120)	(0.133)	(0.100)	(0.129)	(0.075)	(0.085)	(0.137)	(0.107)
CAPACITY	−0.006	−0.006	−0.005	−0.006	−0.043	−0.034	−0.018	−0.024
	(0.068)	(0.069)	(0.078)	(0.072)	(0.816)	(0.853)	(0.920)	(0.895)
QUALITY	−0.478**	−0.479**	−0.475**	−0.478**	13.120	13.290	13.360	13.410
	(0.005)	(0.005)	(0.005)	(0.005)	(0.307)	(0.300)	(0.293)	(0.294)
Loan characteristics								
DURATION_LOAN	0.011***	0.011	0.01	0.011	−0.020	−0.034	−0.045	−0.045
	(0.000)	(0.000)	(0.000)	(0.000)	(0.867)	(0.773)	(0.705)	(0.702)
LAMOUNT_LOAN	0.126**	0.123**	0.129**	0.124**	−4.853*	−4.686*	−4.022	−4.379*
	(0.006)	(0.007)	(0.006)	(0.007)	(0.025)	(0.030)	(0.063)	(0.042)
Loan market characteristics								
CREDITINFO	0.359*				7.437			
	(0.025)				(0.421)			
CONCENTRATION				0.009				−0.195
				(0.133)				(0.574)
BRKM			−0.044				4.863	
			(0.483)				(0.202)	
BRPC	−0.0725*				−0.394			
	(0.046)				(0.847)			
Macroeconomic environment								
LGDPPC	0.033	0.139	0.047	0.066	3.655	4.840	7.546	4.553
	(0.850)	(0.422)	(0.793)	(0.699)	(0.766)	(0.700)	(0.549)	(0.712)
R^2	0.066	0.065	0.063	0.064	0.062	0.061	0.064	0.062
# obs.	1248	1248	1248	1248	672	672	672	672

*Significance at the 10% level.
**Significance at the 5% level.
***Significance at the 1% level.

2002–2006 dataset.[6] We also observe that loan contracts extended to firms with internationally recognised quality certifications are less likely to include collateral compared with

[6] We also re-estimate the baseline regressions (2002–2006) for each regional subgroup, i.e., Latin America and the Caribbean, Eastern Europe and Central Asia, East Asia and Pacific. The coefficient estimates for *SIZE, AGE,* and *CAPACITY* remained similar to those in the baseline regression in terms of direction and statistical significance with only few exceptions, e.g., the coefficient estimates for *AGE* were not statistically significant for firms located in the East Asia and Pacific region. As the results for the firm-level variables mostly confirm the baseline regressions, the country-level variables mostly yield statistically insignificant coefficient estimates because countries located in the same regional groups have similar structures.

loan contracts extended to firms without internationally recognized quality certifications. However, operating close to full capacity and with an internationally recognized quality certification do not have a statistically significant impact on *COLL2*.

As for the effect of loan characteristics, loan contracts with longer terms (higher *DURATION_LOAN*) are more likely to be secured by collateral, although this effect is not valid for collateral-to-loan-value ratios. The positive coefficient estimates for *DURATION_LOAN* are consistent with our baseline results. A similar picture seems to be valid for *LAMOUNT_LOAN* variable. The probability of a loan contract to be secured by collateral is higher for larger business loans, whereas larger loans have smaller collateral-to-loan-value ratios (*COLL2*) than smaller business loans.

As for the country-level variables, our regression results do not seem to be consistent with the regression results from 2002 to 2006 because of the lower number of observations. The logit regressions of *COLL1* are based on 1248 observations from only four Latin American countries and South Africa. Because these countries are similar to one another in terms of our country-level independent variables, we fail to observe the expected relationships between our dependent and independent variables.[7] Because we run regressions only with firm size, industry, and legal status fixed effects, we obtain both economically and statistically more significant results for the *CREDITINFO* variable, in particular. In these regressions, the number of observations increases to 5414 (when controlled for firm size, industry and legal status fixed effects). As we run logit regressions for *COLL1* on *SIZE* and *CREDITINFO*, the number of observations increases to 8047, the coefficient estimate of *CREDITINFO* becomes −0.111 and statistically significant at 0.01%.[8] This strong evidence is consistent with that of the 2002–2006 dataset. Accordingly, we have more reasons to trust a negative relationship between *CREDITINFO* and collateralization, particularly when it is measured by *COLL1*. However, this negative relationship is not valid for the OLS regressions on *COLL2*.

The results in Table 12 also do not validate the negative and positive relationships of *LGDPPC* with *COLL1* and *COLL2*, respectively. However, as we run separate regressions that include only *SIZE* and *LGDPPC* as independent variables, we confirm the robustness of the estimation results that we obtained for the 2002–2006 dataset (i.e., we observe a negative relationship between *COLL1* and *LGDPPC*, whereas we observe a positive relationship between *COLL2* and *LGDPPC*) that result from the expansion of the number of observations. Because we run regressions only with *SIZE* and *CONCENTRATION*, however, we fail to confirm the estimation results that we obtained for the 2002–2006 dataset. This may be attributable to the debatable theoretical effects of concentration on collateralization.

[7] The *CREDITINFO* variable ranges from 5 (for Chile and Colombia) to 6 (for Mexico, Peru, South Africa) for these 5 countries.

[8] *CREDITINFO* ranges from 3 to 6 for the 16 country-level observations included in this regression (Brazil 2009; Chile 2006 and 2010; Colombia 2006 and 2010; Czech Republic 2009; Hungary 2009, Indonesia 2009; Mexico 2006; Peru 2006 and 2010; Philippines 2009; Poland 2009; Poland 2009; Russia 2009; South Africa 2007; Turkey 2008).

5. POLICY IMPLICATION

Our main findings suggest that the role of country-specific factors is more important in emerging economies than firm-specific factors for determining both the presence of and the degree of collateral required for a loan. However, these results are significantly different if we consider the dimension of the firms, which shows that country-level factors—information asymmetry—are more significant for SMEs, and firm factors—firm risk—are more important for large firms. These results seem to confirm the arguments of Godlewski and Weill (2011) that, in cases of higher information asymmetry, the borrower (in this case, SMEs) has an incentive to undertake higher collateralization of the loan to better signal their quality. In particular, we see that the level of credit information in a country has a positive effect (reducing the degree of collateralization) only for SMEs. By contrast, the size of the firm has a positive role in reducing the presence of collateral for large firms but a negative effect for SMEs. These results yield important policy implications for financial institutions and policy makers in emerging countries.

Regarding the implications for financial institutions, it appears to be critical to improve the process of collecting information about the borrower to improve the abilities of SMEs to access capital, both in terms of quality (how risk is evaluated) and in terms of the credibility of the information (who performs the analysis). Lending may benefit from financial institutions that are dedicated to the information collecting process, such as mutual guarantee societies (MGSs) and rating agencies.

As information-sharing institutions, MGSs can play an important role in improving access to credit for SMEs by offering guarantees that are consistent with Basel II guidelines. MGSs can reduce the degree of information asymmetry between banks and SMEs by processing credit information during the guaranty granting process. Thus, the bank can reduce the level of collateralization of the loan because of the presence of an external guarantee and because of increased credit information derived from the relationship between MGSs and SMEs.

Rating agencies can also enhance access to credit for SMEs if they specialized in SMEs with ratings that can be used by banks to compute Basel II capital requirements. In addition, if the rating procedure is validated by a central bank, the information asymmetry may be reduced, so that SMEs may possibly obtain reduced levels of collateralization.

The two information-sharing institutions, MGSs and rating agencies, may be subsidized by local governments and/or by supranational entities to reduce the costs of the guarantee and the costs of rating for SMEs. Reducing costs means it is possible to increase the potential users—normally SMEs—of such information services, but it can also better direct public funds to SMEs in a more efficient way. All these proposed policies may be an important way to indirectly reduce the observed differences in access to credit between SMEs and large firms in emerging economies.

6. CONCLUSIONS

In this chapter, we analyzed the role of collateral in loan contracts in emerging markets. We find that the degree of asymmetric information is an important factor in determining the overall level of collateralization, particularly for SMEs. In fact, we find that firm-specific variables are more significant for large firms, compared with country-specific variables. It seems that, in countries with higher levels of information asymmetry, the borrower has incentive to signal the quality of the borrower by pledging higher collateral, as indicated by Godlewski and Weill (2011); in countries with low information asymmetry, the bank can better measure the risk of the borrower and require the correct degree of collateralization. The policy implications that follow on that analysis are relatively simple, i.e., to foster information-sharing institutions, such as mutual guarantee societies and the rating agencies specialized in the SMEs sector, as subsidized by (local) government.

REFERENCES

Benmelech, E., Bergman, N.B., 2009. Collateral pricing. Journal of Financial Economics 91, 339–360

Berger, A.N., Frame, W.S., Ioannidou, V., 2011. Tests of ex ante versus ex post theories of collateral using private and public information. Journal of Financial Economics 100, 85–97

Berger, A.N., Espinosa-Vega, M.A., Frame, W.S., Miller, N.H., 2011. Why do borrowers pledge collateral? New empirical evidence on the role of asymmetric information. Journal of Financial Intermediation 20, 55–70

Berger, A.N., Udell, G.F., 1995. Relationship lending and lines of credit in small firm finance. Journal of Business 68, 351–381

Berlin, M., Butler, A.W., 2002. Collateral and Competition. Federal Reserve Bank of Philadelphia Working Paper 22.

Besanko, D., Thakor, A.V., 1987a. Collateral and rationing: sorting equilibria in monopolistic and competitive credit markets. International Economic Review 28, 671–689

Besanko, D., Thakor, A.V., 1987b. Competitive equilibria in the credit market under asymmetric information. Journal of Economic Theory 42, 167–182

Bester, H., 1985. Screening vs. rationing in credit markets with imperfect information. American Economic Review 75, 850–855

Bester, H., 1987. The role of collateral in credit markets with imperfect information. European Economic Review 31, 887–899

Boot, A.W.A., 2000. Relationship banking: What do we know? Journal of Financial Intermediation 9, 7–25

Boot, A.W.A., Thakor, A.V., 2000. Can relationship banking survive competition?. Journal of Finance 55, 679–713

Boot, A.W.A., Thakor, A.V., 1994. Moral hazard and secured lending in an infinitely repeated credit market game. International Economic Review 35, 899–920

Boot, A.W.A., Thakor, A.V., Udell, G.F., 1991. Secured lending and default risk: equilibrium analysis, policy implications and empirical results. Economic Journal 101, 458–472

Brick, I.E., Palia, D., 2007. Evidence of jointness in the terms of relationship lending. Journal of Financial Intermediation 16, 452–476

Caballero, R.J., Krishnamurthy, A., 2001. International and domestic collateral constraints in a model of emerging market crises. Journal of Monetary Economics 48, 513–548

Cerqueiro, G., Degryse, H., Ongena, S., 2011. Rules versus discretion in loan rate setting. Journal of Financial Intermediation 20, 503–529

Chakraborty, A., Hu, C.X., 2006. Lending relationships in line-of-credit and nonline-of-credit loans: evidence from collateral use in small business. Journal of Financial Intermediation 15, 86–107

Chan, Y.S., Thakor, A.V., 1987. Collateral and competitive equilibria with moral hazard and private information. Journal of Finance 42, 345–363

Coco, G., 1999. Collateral, heterogeneity in risk attitude and the credit market equilibrium. European Economic Review 43, 559–574

Degryse, H., Van Cayseele, P., 2000. Relationship lending within a bank-based system: evidence from European small business data. Journal of Financial Intermediation 9, 90–109

Feder, G., Tongroj, O., Tejaswi, R., 1988. Collateral, guaranties and rural credit in developing countries: Evidence from Asia. Agricultural Economics 2, 231–245

Gelos, G., Werner, A.M., 2002. Financial liberalization, credit constraints, and collateral: investment in the mexican manufacturing sector. Journal of Development Economics 67, 1–27

Godlewski, C.J., Weill, L., 2011. Does collateral help mitigate adverse selection? A cross-country analysis. Journal of Financial Services Research 40, 49–78

Grunert, J., Weber, M., 2009. Recovery rates of commercial lending: Empirical evidence for German companies. Journal of Banking and Finance 33, 505–513

Hainz, C., Weill, L., Godlewski, C.J., 2008. Bank competition and collateral: theory and evidence. Bank of Finland Research Discussion Paper 27.

Harhoff, D., Körting, T., 1998. Lending relationships in Germany – Empirical evidence from survey data. Journal of Banking and Finance 22, 1317–1353

Hart, O., Moore, J., 1984. A theory of debt based on the inalienability of human capital. Quarterly Journal of Economics 109, 841–879

Hernández-Cánovas, G., Martínez-Solano, P., 2006. Banking relationships: effects on debt terms for small Spanish firms. Journal of Small Business Management 44, 315–333

Inderst, R., Mueller, H.M., 2007. A lender-based theory of collateral. Journal of Financial Economics 84, 826–859

Jimenez, G., Salas, V., Saurina, J., 2006. Determinants of collateral. Journal of Financial Economics 81, 255–281

Jimenez, G., Salas, V., Saurina, J., 2009. Organizational distance and use of collateral for business loans. Journal of Banking and Finance 32, 234–243

Jimenez, G., Salas, V., Saurina, J., 2011. The effects of formal and informal contracting in credit availability. Journal of Money, Credit and Banking 43, 109–132

Jimenez, G., Saurina, J., 2004. Collateral, type of lender and relationship banking as determinants of credit risk. Journal of Banking and Finance 28, 2191–2212

La Porta, R., López-de-Silanes, F., Zamarripa, G., 2003. Related lending. Quarterly Journal of Economics 118, 231–268

La Porta, R., López-de-Silanes, F., Shleifer, A., Vishny, R., 1997. Legal determinants of external finance. Journal of Finance 52, 1131–1150

Liberti, J., Mian, A., 2010. Collateral spread and financial development. Journal of Finance 65, 147–177

Machauer, A., Weber, M., 1998. Bank behaviour based on internal credit ratings of borrowers. Journal of Banking and Finance 22, 1355–1383

Manove, M., Padilla, J., Pagano, M., 2001. Collateral versus project screening: a model of lazy banks. RAND Journal of Economics 32, 726–744

Menkhoff, L., Neuberger, D., Rungruxsirivorn, O., 2012. Collateral and its substitutes in emerging markets' lending. Journal of Banking and Finance 36, 817–834

Menkhoff, L., Neuberger, D., Suwanaporn, C., 2006. Collateral-based lending in emerging markets: evidence from Thailand. Journal of Banking and Finance 30, 1–21

Niinimäki, J.P., 2009. Does collateral fuel moral hazard in banking?. Journal of Banking and Finance 33, 514–521

Jimenez, G., Salas, V., Saurina, J., 2011. The effects of formal and informal contracting in credit availability. Journal of Money, Credit and Banking 43, 109–132

Jimenez, G., Salas, V., Saurina, J., 2009. Organizational distance and use of collateral for business loans. Journal of Banking and Finance 32, 234–243

Jimenez, G., Salas, V., Saurina, J., 2006. Determinants of collateral. Journal of Financial Economics 81, 255–281

Jimenez, G., Saurina, J., 2004. Collateral, type of lender and relationship banking as determinants of credit risk. Journal of Banking and Finance 28, 2191–2212
La Porta, R., López-de-Silanes, F., Zamarripa, G., 2003. Related Lending. Quarterly Journal of Economics 118, 231–268
La Porta, R., López-de-Silanes, F., Shleifer, A., Vishny, R., 1997. Legal determinants of external finance. Journal of Finance 52, 1131–1150
Liberti, J., Mian, A., 2010. Collateral spread and financial development. Journal of Finance 65, 147–177
Machauer, A., Weber, M., 1998. Bank behaviour based on internal credit ratings of borrowers. Journal of Banking and Finance 22, 1355–1383
Manove, M., Padilla, J., Pagano, M., 2001. Collateral versus project screening: a model of lazy banks. RAND Journal of Economics 32, 726–744
Menkhoff, L., Neuberger, D., Rungruxsirivorn, O., 2012. Collateral and its substitutes in emerging markets' lending. Journal of Banking and Finance 36, 817–834
Menkhoff, L., Neuberger, D., Suwanaporn, C., 2006. Collateral-based lending in emerging markets: evidence from Thailand. Journal of Banking and Finance 30, 1–21
Niinimäki, J.P., 2009. Does collateral fuel moral hazard in banking?. Journal of Banking and Finance 33, 514–521
Niinimäki, J.P., 2011. Nominal and true cost of loan collateral. Journal of Banking and Finance 35, 2782–2790
Ono, A., Uesugi, I., 2009. Role of collateral and personal guarantees in relationship lending: evidence from japan's loan market. Journal of Money, Credit and Banking 41, 936–960
Park, C., 2000. Monitoring and structure of debt contracts. Journal of Finance 55, 2157–2195
Petersen, M.A., Rajan, R.G., 1995. The effect of credit market competition on lending relationships. Quarterly Journal of Economics 110, 407–443
Rajan, R.G., Winton, A., 1995. Covenants and collateral as incentives to monitor. Journal of Finance 50, 1113–1146
Repullo, R., Suarez, J., 1998. Monitoring, liquidation, and security design. Review of Financial Studies 11, 163–187
Stiglitz, J.E., Weiss, A., 1981. Credit rationing in markets with imperfect information. American Economic Review 71, 393–410
Stone, A.H.W., 1992. Listening to firms: how to use firm-level surveys to assess constraints on private sector development. World Bank Policy Research Working Paper 923.
Uchida, H., 2011. What do banks evaluate when they screen borrowers? Soft information, hard information and collateral. Journal of Financial Services Research 40, 29–48
Voordeckers, W., Steijvers, T., 2006. Business collateral and personal commitments in SME lending. Journal of Banking and Finance 30, 3067–3086

CHAPTER 18

Tactical Risk Analysis in Emerging Markets in the Wake of the Credit Crunch and Ensuing Sub-prime Financial Crisis

Mazin A.M. Al Janabi
Department of Economics and Finance, College of Business and Economics, United Arab Emirates University, Al-Ain, United Arab Emirates

1. INTRODUCTION

To measure the risks involved in their daily trading operations, major financial institutions, and asset management entities are increasingly developing Value-at-Risk (VaR) models. Since financial markets and institutions differ in their individual characteristics, tailor-made internal risk models are more appropriate. Fortunately, and in line with Basel II and Basel III capital adequacy accords (Bank of International Settlements, 2009, 2013), financial institutions are allowed to develop and use their own internal risk models (such as VaR techniques, stress testing, and scenario analysis) for the purpose of providing for adequate risk measures. Furthermore, internal risk models can be used in the determination of economic-capital (or risk-capital) that banks and other financial service firms must hold to endorse their trading of securities.[1] The benefit of such an approach is that it takes into account the relationship between various asset types and can accurately assess the overall risk for a whole combination of financial trading assets (Al Janabi, 2010).

A number of Arab countries are voluntarily joining the implementation of modified versions of Basel II (and the forthcoming Basel III) capital adequacy accords. In fact, the Gulf Cooperation Council (GCC) financial markets, in general, are in progressive stages of implementing advanced risk management regulations and techniques. Moreover, in recent years remarkable progress has been done in cultivating the culture of risk management among local financial entities and regulatory institutions. In the Middle

[1] Economic-capital (or risk-capital) can be defined as the minimum amount of equity capital a financial entity needs to set aside to absorb worst losses over a given time horizon with a certain confidence level (Al Janabi, 2013a). This is with the objectives of sustaining its trading operations activities and without subjecting itself to insolvency matters. Economic-capital can be assessed with an internal method and modeling techniques such as parametric Liquidity-Adjusted Value-at-Risk (LVaR). Economic-capital differs somehow from regulatory-capital, which is necessary to comply with the requirements of Basel II committee on capital adequacy. However, building an internal market risk modeling techniques to assess economic-capital can significantly aid the financial entity in complying with Basel II (and the forthcoming Basel III) capital adequacy requirements (Al Janabi, 2013a).

Emerging Markets and the Global Economy
http://dx.doi.org/10.1016/B978-0-12-411549-1.00018-1

East, the majority of banking assets are expected to be covered by Basel II and Basel III regulations during 2010–2014 frameworks. By and large, capital ratios are fairly strong in the GCC, although they have fallen lately as banks have expanded their products and operations (Al Janabi, 2013a,b). Within the GCC, there have been negotiations for common application of Basel II and Basel III capital rules, albeit with different time frames of implementation. This is due to the fact that some GCC countries are more diverse, for instance, in terms of the presence of foreign banks than others (Al Janabi, 2011b, 2009a).

The financial industry in GCC countries is generally sound, and the six countries continue to develop their financial system to attract more foreign portfolio investors, and to expand the opening of its financial system to the exterior world (Al Janabi, 2013a,b). Consequently, several local financial institutions are in a consolidation route; and some others have already followed a process of convergence of their financial operations and have started the procedure of modernizing their internal risk management capabilities. By the standards of emerging market countries, the quality of banking supervision in the six GCC states is well above average (Al Janabi, 2011b, 2010). Despite the latest progress in the GCC financial markets to become Basel-compliant countries, it has recently been deemed necessary (by local regulatory authorities) to adopt proper internal risk models, and regulations that financial entities, regulators, and policymakers should consider in setting up their daily trading risk management objectives, particularly in light of the aftermath of the latest credit crunch and the resulting sub-prime global financial crisis.

Indeed, methods for measuring market (or trading) risk have been well developed and standardized in the academic as well as the banking world. Asset liquidity trading risk, on the other hand, has received less attention from researchers, perhaps because it is less significant in developed countries where most of the market risk methodologies had originated (Al Janabi, 2013a). In all but the most simple of circumstances, comprehensive metrics of liquidity trading risk management do not exist explicitly within the modern portfolio theory. Nonetheless, the combination of the recent rapid expansion of emerging markets' trading activities and the recurring turbulence in those markets, in the wake of the upshots of the latest sub-prime financial crisis, has propelled asset liquidity trading risk to the forefront of market risk management research and development (Al Janabi, 2011a).

Set against this background, equity risk assessment has become an important theme in emerging and illiquid markets, such as in the case of GCC financial markets. Accordingly, the goals of this work are to demonstrate the necessary analytical modeling steps and internal risk management simulation techniques that a market's participant (dealer or market-maker) will need in his day-to-day positions' taking. To this end, this chapter provides real-world and clear-cut risk assessment techniques and strategies that can be applied to equity trading portfolios in emerging markets, such as the GCC financial markets. This is with the objective of developing the basis of modeling tactics and global regulatory framework for the assessment of risk exposures in the day-to-day trading operations predominantly in view of the repercussions of the credit crunch and the ensuing sub-prime global financial crisis. As such, financial modeling procedures that are discussed in this work can aid financial markets' participants and regulatory institutions in founding sound and up-to-date modeling techniques to handle equity trading risk exposures under adverse and extreme market circumstances.

To this end, in this chapter the parameters required for the construction of appropriate and simplified parametric Liquidity-Adjusted Value-at-Risk (LVaR) and stress-testing methods are reviewed from previous works and adapted to the specific applications of these methods to emerging GCC financial markets. The theoretical mathematical algorithms and financial modeling structure applied herein are based on an advanced matrix-algebra approach. The latter tactic can simplify the financial modeling and programing process of algorithms. Likewise, it can aid in a straightforward integration of short-sales and long positions of assets in the daily equity trading process. Moreover, a simplified modeling technique for the incorporation of illiquid asset, in daily trading risk management practices, is defined and is appropriately integrated into parametric LVaR and stress-testing along with the development of a risk optimization process for the calculation of maximum authorized LVaR boundary risk limits.

In essence, this chapter provides pioneering tactical risk assessment and management techniques that can be applied to investment and trading portfolios in emerging financial markets, such as in the context of the GCC stock markets. In this work, key equity price risk assessment methods and modeling techniques that financial entities, and regulators should consider in developing their daily price risk management objectives are examined and tailored to the particular needs of emerging markets. This is with the intention of setting up the basis of a contemporary modeling technique for the measurement and management of tactical equity price exposures in the day-to-day financial trading operations. Indeed, while extensive literatures have reviewed the statistical and economic proposition of VaR models, this chapter provides clear-cut financial modeling techniques that can be applied to financial trading portfolios under the notion of illiquid and crisis-driven adverse financial market circumstances.

As such, our broad risk model can simultaneously handle parametric LVaR appraisal under normal and severe market conditions, besides it takes into account the effects of liquidity of traded equity securities under different crisis-driven correlation factors. In order to illustrate the proper use of parametric LVaR and stress-testing methods, real-world paradigms of trading risk assessment are presented for the GCC stock markets. To this end, structured simulation case studies are attained with the aspiration of bringing about a reasonable framework for the assessment and analysis of equity trading risk exposures under crisis-driven market conditions. The modeling techniques discussed in this chapter can assist financial institutions, regulators, and policymakers in the instigation of meticulous and up-to-date simulation algorithms to handle equity price risk exposure. The suggested analytical methods and procedures can be put into practice in virtually all emerging markets, if they are custom-made to be compatible to every market's initial level of complexity.

2. RELATED LITERATURE REVIEW AND PURPOSE OF PRESENT STUDY

Risk assessment and management have become of paramount importance in the financial industry and a major endeavor by academics, practitioners, and regulators; and a cornerstone of recent interest is a class of models called VaR techniques (Al Janabi, 2012). The concepts of VaR and other advanced risk management techniques are not new and are based—with some modifications—on the modern portfolio theory. Albeit VaR is one of many—both quantitative and qualitative—factors that should be integrated into a cohesive risk management approach, it is remarkably a vital one. In fact, VaR is not the maximum loss that will occur, but rather a loss level threshold that will be pierced some percentage of the time. The actual loss that occurs could be much higher than VaR estimations. As such, VaR should be used in conjunction with other risk measures such as stress-testing, scenario analysis, and other asset/business-specific risk measures (Al Janabi, 2012). The most common parametric VaR models estimate variance/covariance matrices of asset returns using historical time series, under the assumption that asset returns are normally distributed and that portfolio risk is a function of the risk of each asset and the correlation factors among the returns of all trading assets within the portfolio. The VaR is then calculated from the standard deviation of the portfolio, given the appropriate investment/liquidation horizon, and the specified confidence interval (Al Janabi, 2010).

In the 1950s, Markowitz (1959) describes the theoretical framework for modern portfolio theory and the creation of efficient portfolios. Markowitz's mean-variance portfolio optimization methodology is a landmark in the development of modern portfolio theory. The solution to the Markowitz theoretical models revolves around the portfolio weights, or the percentage of asset allocated to be invested in each financial instrument. In a similar vein, Sharpe (1963) develops the single-index model, which relates returns on each security to the returns on a common index—abroad market index of common stock returns such as S&P 500 is generally used for this purpose.

Despite many criticisms and limitations of the VaR method, it has proven to be a very useful measure of market risk and is widely used in financial and non-financial markets. The *RiskMetrics*^{TM} system (Morgan Guaranty Trust Company, 1994), developed and popularized by *J. P. Morgan*, has provided a tremendous impetus to the growth in the use of VaR concept and other modern risk management modeling techniques. Since then, the VaR concept is well known and scores of specific applications are adapted to credit risk management and mutual funds' investments. The general recognition and use of large-scale VaR models has initiated considerable literature including statistical descriptions of VaR and assessments of different modeling techniques. For a comprehensive survey, and the different VaR analysis and techniques, one can refer to Jorion (2001).

On another front, Berkowitz and O'Brien (2001) question how accurate VaR models are at commercial banks. Due to the fact that trading accounts at large commercial banks have considerably grown and become increasingly diverse and complex, the authors presented statistics on the trading revenues from such activities and on the associated VaR forecasts internally estimated by banks. Several other authors have attempted to tackle the issues of extreme events and fat-tails phenomena in the distribution of returns. Nonetheless, most of their approaches and techniques are good exercises for academic purposes, they do lack evidence of real-world applications with actual market portfolios.

On the other hand, Garcia et al. (2007) tackle a specific issue within the VaR and that is the subadditivity property required for the VaR to be a coherent measure of risk. The authors argue that, in the context of decentralized portfolio management, central management possesses only a fraction of information that belongs to each specialist (trader). In such a context, a distribution appears always thicker to the central unit than to the specialist. Therefore, because of a lack of information, VaR may appear fallaciously nonsubadditive to the central management unit. Despite evidence to the contrary, the authors show that decentralized portfolio management with a VaR allocation to each specialist will work, and furthermore VaR remains subadditive in many situations of practical interest.

Within the Liquidity-Adjusted Value-at-Risk (LVaR) framework, Bangia et al. (1999) approach the liquidity risk from another angle and provide a model of VaR adjusted for what they call exogenous liquidity—defined as common to all market players and unaffected by the actions of any one participant. It comprises such execution costs as order processing costs and adverse selection costs resulting in a given bid-ask spread faced by investors in the market. On the contrary, endogenous liquidity is specific to one's position in the market and depends on one's actions and varies across market participants. It is mainly driven by the size of the position: the larger the size, and the greater the endogenous illiquidity. They propose splitting the uncertainty in market value of an asset into two parts: a pure market risk component arises from asset returns and uncertainty due to liquidity risk (Al Janabi, 2013a). Their model consists of measuring exogenous liquidity risk, computed using the distribution of observed bid-ask spreads and then integrating it into a standard VaR framework. Indeed, their argument is based on treating liquidity risk and market risk jointly and thus they make the assumption that in adverse market environments extreme events in both returns and spreads arise concurrently. They argue that while the correlation between asset mid-price movements and bid-ask spreads is not perfect, it is strong enough during severe market conditions to persuade the handling of extreme movements in market and liquidity risk simultaneously. Accordingly, they incorporate both a 99th percentile movement in the underlying and a 99th percentile movement in the bid-ask spread and estimate for example that, in May 1997, asset liquidity risk accounted for over 17% of the market risk of a long position on USD/Thai Baht and for only 1.5% for liquid positions on USD/Yen.

Using a similar methodology, Le Saout (2002) applies the model developed by Bangia et al. (1999) to the French stock market (CAC-40) and states that neither exogenous liquidity risk (which accounts for about half of total market risk) nor endogenous liquidity risk (also a potentially significant component of market risk) should be overlooked by financial entities subject to market risk. In an attempt to consider the effect of liquidating large positions, Le Saout (2002) incorporates the weighted average spread into the LVaR measure. The author's results indicate that exogenous liquidity risk, for illiquid stocks, can represent more than a half of total market risk (up to 52% for certain securities). Furthermore, the author extends the model to incorporate endogenous liquidity risk and shows that it represents an important component of the overall liquidity risk (Al Janabi, 2011a).

In a relatively recent study, Angelidis and Benos (2006) loosen the conventional, yet idealistic, postulation of perfect, and frictionless financial markets (that is, traders can either buy or sell any amount of securities without triggering major price changes). To this end, Angelidis and Benos (2006) expand the earlier work of Madhavan et al. (1997) (who debated that traded volume can explicate security price movements) and exploit an LVaR model based on bid-ask spread components, following the earlier work of Bangia et al. (1999). The authors argue that under this structure, asset liquidity risk is decomposed into its endogenous and exogenous components, thereby allowing an estimation of the liquidation risk of a specific trading position. The authors then apply LVaR measures to the Athens Stock Exchange by incorporating bid-ask variation and the price effect of position liquidation. Their study focuses on the use of high-frequency transaction level data of stocks besides sorting out each stock according to their average transaction prices and capitalization. Furthermore, the results indicate that adverse selection increases with trade size while the cost component of the bid-ask spread decreases. Based on these findings, endogenous and exogenous liquidity risks are linked to spread components. For high-priced, high-capitalization stocks, it is found that a VaR correction for illiquidity is not necessary since liquidity risk represents only 3.40% of total market risk. On the other hand, for low-capitalization stocks, the percentage of risk due to illiquidity reaches as much as 11% of total market risk and hence it should not be neglected in the overall assessment of LVaR (Al Janabi, 2011a). As with other research on LVaR, this pertinent and thorough work does not attempt to address portfolio liquidity risk, the foremost motive of this chapter.

In a different vein, Almgren and Chriss (1999) present a concrete framework for deriving the optimal execution strategy using a mean-variance approach, and show a specific calculation method. Their approach has a high potential for practical application. They assume that price changes are caused by three factors: drift, volatility, and market impact. Their analysis leads to general insights into optimal portfolio trading, relating risk aversion to optimal trading strategy, and to several practical implications including the definition of LVaR. Unlike Almgren and Chriss (1999), Hisata and Yamai (2000) turn the sales period into an endogenous variable and propose a practical framework for the quantification of LVaR which incorporated the market liquidity of financial products. Their model incorporates the mechanism of market impact caused by the investor's own dealings through adjusting VaR according to the level of market liquidity and the scale of the investor's position. In addition, Hisata and Yamai (2000) propose a closed-form solution for calculating LVaR as well as a method of estimating portfolio LVaR.

On the other hand, Berkowitz (2000) argues that unless the likely loss arising from liquidity risk is quantified, the models of VaR would lack the power to explicate the embedded risk. In practice, operational definitions vary from volume-related measures to bid-ask spreads and to the elasticity of demand. The author asserts that elasticity-based measures are of most relevance since they incorporate the impact of the seller actions on prices. Moreover, under certain conditions the additional variance arising from seller impact can easily be quantified given observations on portfolio prices and net flows; and that it is possible to estimate the entire distribution of portfolio risk through standard numerical methods.

In a different tactic, Al Janabi (2010, 2011a, 2013a,b) establishes a practical framework for the measurement, management, and control of trading risk under illiquid and adverse market conditions. The effects of illiquid assets, that are dominant characteristics of emerging markets, are also incorporated in the risk models. Furthermore, his literature provides real-world risk management techniques and strategies that can be applied to trading portfolios in emerging markets. The intent of his research studies is to propose a simple approach for including liquidation trading risk in standard VaR analysis and to capture the liquidity risk arising due to illiquid trading positions by obtaining parametric LVaR estimation. The key methodological contribution is a different and less conservative liquidity scaling factor than the conventional root-time multiplier. The proposed add-on is a function of a predetermined liquidity threshold defined as the maximum position, which can be unwound without disturbing market prices during one trading day. In addition, the re-engineered model is quite simple to implement even by very large financial institutions with multiple assets and risk factors.

Set against this background, the objective of this research study is to provide practical and robust guidelines, modeling techniques, and empirical assessments of market risk for equity trading portfolios (frequently it can be called, trading, investment, or price risk) under extreme and crisis-driven conditions. As such, the aim is to create a pragmatic approach to assist in the establishment of sound risk assessment practices and within a prudential framework of global financial regulations, particularly in the wake of the credit crunch and ensuing global sub-prime financial crisis. To this end, the parameters required for the construction of appropriate and simplified parametric LVaR and stress-testing methods are reviewed from previous works and refined to the specific applications of these methods to equity trading portfolios of the GCC stock markets. Furthermore, a simplified approach for the incorporation of illiquid assets is defined and is appropriately integrated into parametric LVaR and stress-testing models. For this purpose, a parametric risk-engine algorithm has been developed to assess market and liquidity risk exposure under illiquid and adverse market conditions. Moreover, an optimization modeling algorithm is devised with the objective of setting maximum boundaries on LVaR trading limits. To this end, a number of parametric LVaR case studies are performed under varied market simulation scenarios and an optimum risk-budgeting perspective is selected among the different market settings.

The remainder of the chapter is organized as follows. The following section lays out the financial mathematical technique and the quantitative modeling infrastructure of parametric LVaR method, its limitations, and a model that incorporates the effects of illiquid assets in daily market risk assessment. Results of the empirical tests and simulations of LVaR boundary limits for the GCC financial markets are drawn in the fourth section. The final section provides a summary along with concluding remarks. Further details for the derivation of parametric LVaR modeling structure during the close-out period are illustrated in APPENDIX A.

3. METHODOLOGY AND RESEARCH DESIGN

Value-at-Risk is a method of assessing market risk that uses standard statistical techniques routinely used in other technical fields. Formally, VaR measures the worst expected loss over a given time interval under normal market conditions at a given confidence level. Assuming the return of a financial product follows a normal distribution, linear pay-off profile, and a direct relationship between the underlying product and the income, the VaR is to measure the standard deviation of the income for a certain confidence level. Although the method relies on many assumptions, it has gained wide acceptance for the quantification of financial risks. As a result of the generalization of this method, economic-capital allocations for trading and active investment activities tend to be calculated and adjusted with the VaR method.

So far, there is no industry consensus on the best method for calculating VaR. As with any statistical model, VaR depends on certain assumptions. The choice of which method of calculation is used is normally dictated by the user's aversion to unrealistic or oversimplistic assumptions. There are three popular methods: the parametric method (it is also known as the variance/covariance, correlation, and delta-neutral method), the historical simulation method, and the Monte-Carlo simulation method. Each of these methods has its own set of assumptions and each is a simplification of reality.

The parametric method is the simplest one in terms of application to financial practices and computer time consumption. This method assumes that the returns of the risk factors are normally distributed and the correlations between risk factors are constant. For risk assessment purposes using the normal distribution assumption is generally considered to be acceptable. Deviation from normality usually does not significantly alter the results of the VaR calculations under normal market conditions. Within this method a bell-shaped curve (Gaussian distribution) is essentially assumed and it also assumes that extreme price swings, such as market crashes, occur too rarely to contribute to an accurate picture of the likelihood of future events.

To calculate VaR using the parametric method, the volatility of each risk factor is extracted from a predefined historical observation period. The potential effect of each component of the portfolio on the overall portfolio value is then worked out. These effects are then aggregated across the whole portfolio using the correlations between the risk factors (which are, again, extracted from the historical observation period) to give the overall VaR value of the portfolio with a given confidence level.

In fact, many financial service institutions have chosen a confidence interval of 95% (or 97.5% if we only look at the loss side [one-tailed]) to calculate VaR. This means that once every 40 trading days a loss larger than indicated is expected to occur. Some entities use a 99% (one-tailed) confidence interval, which would theoretically lead to larger loss once every 100 trading days. Due to fat tails in the distribution of probability, such a loss will occur more often and can cause problems in calculating VaR at higher confidence levels. Some financial institutions feel that the use of a 99% confidence interval would place too much trust on the statistical model and, hence, some confidence level should be assigned to the "*art-side*" of the risk measurement process (Al Janabi, 2007).

Really, the choice of the confidence level also depends on its use. If the resulting VaRs are directly used for the choice of an economic-capital cushion, then the choice of the confidence level is crucial, as it should reflect the degree of risk aversion of the firm and the cost of a loss of exceeding the calculated VaR numbers. The higher the risk aversion or the greater the costs, implies that a big amount of economic-capital should be set aside to cover possible losses and this consequently will lead to a higher confidence level. In contrast, if VaR numbers are only used to provide a firmwide yardstick to compare risks among different portfolios and markets, then the choice of confidence level is not that relevant.

Set against this background, a simplified calculation process of the estimation of VaR risk factors (using the parametric method), for a single and multiple assets' positions, is illustrated as follows: From elementary statistics it is well known that for a normal distribution, 68% of the observations will lie within 1σ (standard deviation) from the expected value, 95% within 2σ, and 99% within 3σ from the expected value. As such, for a single trading asset position the absolute value of VaR can be defined in monetary terms as follows:

$$\text{VaR}_i = |\ (\mu_i - \alpha * \sigma_i)[Asset_i * Fx_i]\ | \approx |\ \alpha * \sigma_i[Asset_i * Fx_i]\ |, \tag{1}$$

where μ_i is the expected return of the single asset, α is the confidence level (or in other words, the standard normal variant at confidence level α), and σ_i is the forecasted standard deviation (or conditional volatility) of the return of the security that constitutes the single position. The $Asset_i$ is the mark-to-market value of the trading asset and indicates the monetary amount of equity position in asset i and Fx_i denotes the unit foreign exchange rate of asset i. Without a loss of generality, we can assume that the expected value of daily returns μ_i is close to zero. As such, although Eq. (1) includes some simplifying assumptions, it is routinely used by researchers and practitioners in the financial markets for the estimation of VaR for a single trading position (Al Janabi, 2011a).

Trading risk in the presence of multiple risk factors is determined by the combined effect of individual risks. The level of total risk is determined not only by the magnitudes of the individual risks but also by their correlations. Portfolio effects are crucial in risk management not only for large diversified portfolios but also for individual instruments that depends on several risk factors. For multiple assets or portfolio of assets, parametric VaR is a function of each individual security's risk and the correlation factor $[\rho_{i,j}]$ between the returns on the individual securities, detailed as follows:

$$\text{VaR}_P = \sqrt{\sum_{i=1}^{n}\sum_{j=1}^{n} \text{VaR}_i \, \text{VaR}_j \, \rho_{i,j}} = \sqrt{|\text{VaR}|^T \; | \rho \| \text{VaR} \, |}. \tag{2}$$

This formula is a general one for the calculation of parametric VaR for any portfolio regardless of the number of securities. It should be noted that the second term of this formula is presented in terms of matrix-algebra techniques—a useful form to avoid mathematical complexity, as more and more securities are added. This approach can simplify the algorithmic programing process and can permit a straightforward incorporation of short-sales positions in the market risk assessment process. As such, in order to calculate VaR (of a portfolio of any number of securities), one needs first to create a vector $|\text{VaR}|$ of the individual VaR positions—explicitly n rows and one column ($nx1$) matrix—a transpose vector $|\text{VaR}|^T$ of the individual VaR positions—an ($1xn$) vector, and hence the superscript "T" indicates transpose of the vector—and finally a matrix, $|\rho|$, of all correlation factors (ρ)—an (nxn) matrix. Consequently, as one multiplies the two vectors and correlation matrix and then takes the square root of result, one ends up with VaR_P of any portfolio with any n-number of securities. This simple number summarizes the portfolio's exposure to market risk. Investors and senior managers can then decide whether they feel comfortable with this level of risk. If the answer is no, then the process that led to the estimation of VaR can be used to decide where to reduce redundant risk. For instance, the riskiest securities can be sold, or one can use derivative securities such as futures and options to hedge undesirable risk.

Illiquid securities such as foreign exchange rates and equities are very common in emerging markets. Customarily these securities are traded infrequently (at very low volume). Their quoted prices should not be regarded as a representative of the traders' consensus vis-à-vis their real value but rather as the transaction price that was arrived at by two counterparties under special market conditions. This of course represents a real dilemma to anybody who seeks to measure the market risk of these securities with a methodology which is based on volatilities and correlation matrices. The main problem arises when the historical price series are not available for some securities or, when they are available, they are not fully reliable due to the lack of liquidity (Al Janabi, 2007).

Given that institutional investors usually have longer time horizons, the liquidity of their positions will be lower. The investment horizon of the investor as well as the liquidity characteristics of the mutual fund need to be integrated into the risk quantification process. For instance, portfolios with long investment horizons and/or low liquidity need distinct risk measures than those that have shorter horizons and are very liquid. The choice of time horizon or the number of days to liquidate (unwind) a position is a very important factor and has big impact on VaR numbers, and it depends upon the objectives of the portfolio, the liquidity of its positions, and the expected holding period. Typically for a bank's trading portfolio invested in highly liquid currencies, a one-day horizon may be acceptable. For an investment manager with a monthly re-balancing and reporting focus, a 30-day period may be more appropriate. Ideally, the holding period should correspond to the longest period for orderly portfolio liquidation (Al Janabi, 2007).

In fact, if returns are independent and they can have any elliptical multivariate distribution, then it is possible to convert the VaR horizon parameter from daily to any t-day horizon. The variance of a t-day return should be t times the variance of a 1-day return or $\sigma^2 = f(t)$. Thus, in terms of standard deviation (or volatility), $\sigma = f(\sqrt{t})$ and the daily VaR number [VaR (1-day)] can be adjusted for any t horizon to yield parametric LVaR estimation, such as:

$$\text{LVaR } (t\text{-day}) = \text{VaR } (1\text{-day})\sqrt{t}. \tag{3}$$

The above formula was proposed and used by *J.P. Morgan* in their earlier *RiskMetrics*^{TM} method (Morgan Guaranty Trust Company, 1994). This methodology implicitly assumes that liquidation occurs in one block sale at the end of the holding period and that there is one holding period for all assets, regardless of their inherent trading liquidity structure. Unfortunately, the latter approach does not consider real-life-trading situations, where traders can liquidate (or re-balance) small portions of their trading portfolios on a daily basis. Moreover, this could generate unreliable risk assessments and can lead to considerable overestimates of LVaR figures, especially for the purposes of economic-capital allocation between trading and/or investment units.

Indeed, the assumption of a given holding period for orderly liquidation inevitably implies that assets' liquidation occurs during the holding period. Accordingly, scaling the holding period to account for orderly liquidation can be justified if one allows the assets to be liquidated throughout the holding period. In order to perform the calculation of parametric LVaR under more realistic illiquid market conditions, we can define the following liquidation risk factor (or multiplier) throughout the close-out period[2]:

$$LVaR_{adj} = VaR\sqrt{\frac{(2t+1)(t+1)}{6t}}, \quad (4)$$

where t is the number of liquidation days (t-day to liquidate the entire asset fully), VaR = parametric Value-at-Risk under liquid market conditions (as presented formerly in Eq. (1)), and $LVaR_{adj}$ = parametric Value-at-Risk (or Liquidity-Adjusted VaR) under illiquid market conditions. The latter equation indicates that $LVaR_{adj} > VaR$, and for the special case when the number of days to liquidate the entire assets is one trading day, then we get $LVaR_{adj} = VaR$. Consequently, the difference between $LVaR_{adj}$ and VaR should be equal to the residual market risk due to the illiquidity of any asset under illiquid markets conditions. As a matter of fact, the number of liquidation days (t) necessary to liquidate the entire assets fully is related to the choice of the liquidity threshold; however, the size of this threshold is likely to change under severe market conditions (Al Janabi, 2011a). Indeed, the choice of the liquidation horizon can be estimated from the total trading position size and the daily trading volume that can be unwound into the market without significantly disrupting market prices.[3]

Essentially, parametric LVaR method is only one approach of measuring market risk and is mainly concerned with maximum expected losses under normal market conditions. In extreme situations, parametric LVaR models do not function very well. As a result, for prudent risk management and as an extra management tool, firms should boost parametric LVaR analysis with stress-testing and scenario procedures. From a risk management perspective, however, it is desirable to have an estimate for what potential losses could be under severely adverse conditions where statistical tools do not apply. As a result, stress-testing estimates the impact of unusual and severe events on the entity's value and should be reported on a daily basis as part of the risk reporting process. For emerging economies with extreme volatility, the use of stress-testing should be highly emphasized and full description of the process is to be included in any financial service entity's policy and procedure manual. In general terms, stress-testing usually takes the form of subjectively specifying scenarios of interest to assess changes in the value of a portfolio and it can involve examining the effect of past large market moves on today's portfolio.

The advantage of this method is that it may cover situations that are completely absent from historical data and therefore forces management to consider events that they might

[2] For further details on the mathematical derivation and the rational usefulness of the liquidation multiplier during the unwinding (close-out) period, one can refer to APPENDIX A.

[3] It is imperative to note that Eq. (4) can also be used to calculate parametric LVaR, for a single asset and/or portfolio of assets, and for any time horizon subject to the constraint that the overall LVaR figure should not exceed at any state of affairs the nominal exposure, or in other words the total trading volume. Indeed, the square root of time Eq. (3) suggested by *RiskMetrics*^{TM} method (Morgan Guaranty Trust Company, 1994) has similar characteristics in the sense that the total LVaR exposure can exceed nominal exposure as the close-out time tends to approach infinity.

have otherwise ignored. Albeit stress-testing may provide a better idea for potential losses under worst-case events, like the devaluation of an emerging market's currency, politically upheavals events, etc., it gives little indication of the prospect of such extreme events. It also handles correlations very flimsily, which can be an indispensable component of risk in a portfolio of securities. However, it can be a very robust tool when used to complement the statistical parametric LVaR analysis. Subsequent to exploring the bulk of value distribution through LVaR methodology, stress-testing might provide key insights by drawing a few situations from the furthest tails.

In this chapter, risk management procedure is developed to assess potential exposure due to an event risk (severe crisis) that is associated with large movements of the GCC stock market indices, under the assumption that certain GCC markets have typical 6% – 12% leap during periods of financial turmoil. The task here is to measure the potential trading risk exposure that is associated with a predefined leap and under the presumption of several crisis-driven correlation factors.

In essence, certain stocks and stock market indices in emerging markets are highly exposed to event risk. As such, event risk is used to describe the risk that the financial entity runs into under unusual situations and that is not captured by day-to-day risk management tools. In fact, event risk will be evident in situations where prices are heavily dependent on certain structural factors (e.g. a political restructuring) or where price behavior is manipulated due to the lack of reinforcement of adequate regulations. Moreover, event risk will usually coincide with relative illiquidity of financial markets.

For trading risk management, it is essential to draw a distinction between developed stock markets and emerging markets. In general, emerging-economies' stock markets are more susceptible to event risk, thus it is necessary to establish separate LVaR limit-setting for trading in these securities. Volume-based limits or a combination of LVaR limits and volume-based limits are applied in markets which are prone to event risk and where liquidity is not sufficient at all times.

In most professional trading and asset management units (such as commercial banks, foreign exchange dealers, institutional investors, etc.), LVaR limit-setting (or maximum risk-budgeting boundaries) is based on the concept of risk appetite. The risk appetite is defined as the maximum loss potential that management is willing to accept when an adverse move, in stocks or stock market indices, occurs within a specified time horizon. In general, risk appetite will be dependent upon (Al Janabi, 2009b):

- The performance track-record in trading/investing equity securities.
- The strategic importance of equity trading by the trading/investment unit in question.
- The quality of trading/investment unit's infrastructure in handling traded products.
- The overall exposure that trading/investment unit wants to have to proprietary trading and/or active investment risks in general and equity risks in particular.
- The volatilities of the stocks/indices (as determined by the risk manager) and the correlation factors between all assets within the trading portfolio.

- The forecasted liquidation horizons (unwinding, or close-out periods) of the equity assets.
- The forecasted unwinding period of the entire portfolio(s) that consists of VaRied equity assets.
- Local and/or global regulatory constraints for the operations of equity securities.

In general, LVaR limits are allocated to each trading desk and the head of a particular trading unit is responsible for the delegation of limits to individual traders and trading books within the overall guidelines as specified by the risk management unit. In general, global and main trading units (within commercial banks) should have a higher risk appetite percentage than local trading units in emerging countries. This will enable them to focus more on proprietary trading than solely on customer-driven businesses (Al Janabi, 2009b). In this chapter, a hands-on procedure is devised for the setting of optimum LVaR risk limits that can aid in the establishment of sound global financial regulations, predominantly in light of the credit crunch and the subsequent sub-prime global financial crisis.

4. RESULTS AND DISCUSSION OF FINDINGS

4.1. The Dataset

In this empirical research study, database of daily price returns of the GCC stock markets' main indicators (indices) is assembled, filtered, and adequately adapted for the development of relevant inputs for the calculation of all risk factors and optimization parameters. The total number of indices that are combined in this work is nine; seven local indices for the GCC region (including two indices for the UAE markets) and two benchmark indices, detailed as follows:

1. DFM General Index (United Arab Emirates, Dubai Financial Market General Index).
2. ADX Index (United Arab Emirates, Abu Dhabi Stock Market Index).
3. BA All Share Index (Bahrain, All Share Stock Market Index).
4. KSE General Index (Kuwait, Stock Exchange General Index).
5. MSM30 Index (Oman, Muscat Stock Market Index).
6. DSM20 Index (Qatar, Doha Stock Market General Index).
7. SE All Share Index (Saudi Arabia, All Share Stock Market Index).
8. Shuaa GCC Index (Shuaa Capital, GCC Stock Markets Benchmark Index).
9. Shuaa Arab Index (Shuaa Capital, Arab Stock Markets Benchmark Index).

For this particular study, we have chosen a confidence interval of 95% (or 97.5% with *"one-tailed"* loss side) and several liquidation time horizons to compute parametric LVaR. Historical database (of more than 6 years) of daily closing index levels, for the period 17/10/2004 to 22/05/2009, is assembled for the purpose of carrying out this research and further for the construction of market risk assessment parameters and optimization algorithms. The historical database of the settlement levels of daily indices is drawn from Reuters 3000 Xtra Hosted Terminal Platform and Thomson Reuters Datastream datasets. The analysis of data and discussions of relevant findings and empirical results of this research are structured and clarified in the following subsections, detailed as follows.

4.2. Statistical Inference of Non-Normality and Correlation Patterns

In this section, analysis of the particular risk of each index and a test of non-normality (asymmetry) are performed on the sample equity indices. To investigate the statistical properties of the data, we have computed the log returns of each series. As such, descriptive statistics for the analysis of maximum, minimum, mean, and arithmetic mean are presented in Table 1.[4] To take into account the distributional anomalies of asset returns, tests of non-normality are performed on the sample equity indices. In the first study, the measurements of skewness and kurtosis are achieved on the sample equity indices and the results are depicted in Table 1. It is seen that all indices have shown asymmetric behavior (between both positive and negative values). Moreover, kurtosis studies have shown similar patterns of abnormality (i.e. peaked distributions). At the upper extreme, the MSM30 Index has shown a big negative skewness (−0.57) which is combined with a very high Kurtosis—peakedness of (18.40). Some indices, such as the DSM20 Index, have shown less non-normality pattern (Skewness of −0.11 and kurtosis of 5.59). As evidenced in Table 1, the above results of general departure from normality are also confirmed with the Jarque-Bera (JB) test. The JB statistics is calculated as follows:

$$\mathrm{JB} = n/6 \left\lfloor S^2 + (K-3)^2/4 \right\rfloor \approx \chi^2(2) \tag{5}$$

where S is the skewness, K is the kurtosis, and n is the number of observations. The JB statistics reassembles approximately a Chi-squared distribution $[\chi^2(2)]$ with 2 degrees of freedom. The 95% and 99% percentage points of the Chi-squared distribution with 2 degrees of freedom are 5.99 and 9.21, respectively, thus, the lower the JB statistics, the more likely a distribution is normal. Nonetheless, the JB test shows an obvious general deviation from normality and, thus, rejects the hypothesis that GCC stock markets' time series returns are normally distributed. The appealing outcome of this study suggests the necessity of combining parametric LVaR calculations—which assumes normal distributions of returns—with other methods such as stress-testing and scenario analysis to get a detailed picture of the other remaining risks (fat tails in the probability distribution) that cannot be captured with the simple assumption of normality (Al Janabi, 2011b, 2013a,b).

On the other hand, three matrices of correlations are created in this study, namely $\rho = 1, 0$, and empirical correlations. The objectives here are to establish the necessary financial modeling infrastructure for cutting-edge risk assessment that will follow shortly. For the empirical correlation case, the assembled correlation matrix is depicted in Table 2

[4] Source: All tables included in this research study are developed by the author using historical dataset from 2004 to 2009.

Table 1 Risk simulation dataset: descriptive statistics and testing for non-normality.

Stock market indices	Maximum (%)	Minimum (%)	Median (%)	Arithmetic mean (%)	Skewness	Kurtosis	Jarque-Bera (JB) test
DFM General Index	9.9	−12.2	0.01	0.12	0.01	7.86	955**
ADX Index	6.6	−7.1	0.00	0.07	0.12	7.26	734**
BA All Share Index	3.6	−3.8	0.00	0.05	0.43	10.24	2142**
KSE General Index	5.0	−3.7	0.00	0.09	−0.18	8.38	1173**
MSM30 Index	5.2	−8.7	0.00	0.12	−0.57	18.40	9617**
DSM20 Index	6.2	−8.1	0.00	0.06	−0.11	5.59	273**
SE All Share Index	9.4	−11.0	0.07	0.03	−0.97	8.47	1361**
Shuaa GCC Index	11.1	−8.1	0.00	0.06	−0.66	14.00	4949**
Shuaa Arab Index	9.4	−7.6	0.00	0.07	−0.61	13.79	4758**

Notes:
** Denotes statistical significance at the 0.01 levels.

Table 2 Risk simulation dataset: correlation matrix of GCC stock markets indices.

	DFM General Index	ADX Index	BA All Share Index	KSE General Index	MSM30 Index	DSM20 Index	SE All Share Index	Shuaa GCC Index	Shuaa Arab Index
DFM General Index	100%								
ADX Index	56%	100%							
BA All Share Index	12%	8%	100%						
KSE General Index	17%	16%	12%	100%					
MSM30 Index	12%	17%	11%	11%	100%				
DSM20 Index	18%	23%	12%	12%	20%	100%			
SE All Share Index	20%	20%	7%	16%	11%	10%	100%		
Shuaa GCC Index	37%	35%	13%	19%	13%	26%	62%	100%	
Shuaa Arab Index	39%	36%	12%	24%	15%	26%	60%	93%	100%

for the nine GCC stock market indices. The latter correlation matrix is an essential element along with conditional volatility matrices for the simulation of parametric LVaR and stress-testing. Contrary to general belief, our analysis indicates that for the long-run period, in general, there are relatively small correlations (relationships) between the GCC stock markets. Nonetheless, in the short-run period (or on a daily crisis basis), however, we found that correlations tend to increase in value (although not on a large scale) and it could even switch signs under certain circumstances.

These long-run low correlation relationships are advantageous information for investors who would like to hold a diversified equity portfolio in GCC countries and particularly for medium/long investment horizon. On the whole, it seems that the Saudi market, with correlation factors of 62% and 60%, respectively, presides over the scenery of actions and therefore has the principal effect (and correlation relationship) on both the Shuaa GCC and Shuaa Arab indices. The Dubai and Abu Dhabi financial markets have indicated a relatively low relationship of 56%, albeit both markets are operating and regulated in the same country. Likewise, and in accordance with general expectation, the Shuaa GCC and Shuaa Arab indices have shown a strong relationship of 93%.

4.3. Risk Exposure for Structured Equity Portfolios Under Different Simulation Scenarios

To examine the relationship between stock market indices' expected returns and volatility, we implement a conditional volatility approach to determine the risk parameters that are needed for the parametric LVaR's engine and thereafter for the estimation of daily market risk exposure. To this end, a Generalized Autoregressive Conditional Heteroskedasticity (GARCH) in mean model [that is, GARCH-M (1,1) model] is used for the estimation

Table 3 Simulation of liquidity trading risk management and asset allocation (full case LVaR analysis).

Stock Market Indices	Market Value in AED	Asset Allocation	Liquidity Holding Horizon	Daily Volatility (Normal)	Daily Volatility (severe)	Sensitivity Factor	Expected Return	Undiversified LVaR in AED (Normal)	Undiversified LVaR in AED (Severe)
DFM General Index	$ 30,000,000	20.0%	1	1.81%	12.16%	0.58	0.14%	544,093	3,647,180
ADX Index	$ 20,000,000	13.3%	1	1.32%	7.08%	0.40	0.07%	264,942	1,415,107
BA All Share Index	$ 18,000,000	12.0%	1	0.58%	3.77%	0.06	0.04%	104,551	678,268
KSE General Index	$ 20,000,000	13.3%	1	0.71%	3.74%	0.14	0.08%	142,497	747,293
MSM30 Index	$ 15,000,000	10.0%	1	0.79%	8.70%	0.10	0.10%	118,901	1,304,848
DSM20 Index	$ 20,000,000	13.3%	1	1.48%	8.07%	0.31	0.07%	296,066	1,614,827
SE All Share Index	$ 27,000,000	18.0%	1	1.86%	11.03%	0.98	0.01%	501,571	2,978,882
Shuaa GCC Index	$ -	0.0%	1	1.30%	8.10%	1.05	0.08%	-	-
Shuaa Arab Index	$ -	0.0%	1	1.15%	7.57%	1.00	0.10%	-	-
Total Portfolio Value in AED	$ 150,000,000	100%					0.07%		

Expected Return and Risk-Adjusted Return	
Trading Portfolio Expected Return	0.07%
Risk-Adjusted Expected Return (Normal)	4.74%
Risk-Adjusted Expected Return (Severe)	0.76%

Daily Liquidity-Adjusted Value at Risk (LVaR) in AED [Normal Market Conditions]		
ρ = *Empirical*	ρ = *1*	ρ = *0*
2,337,945	3,945,243	1,733,013
1.56%	2.63%	1.16%

Diversification Benefits	
$ 1,607,297	68.75%

Daily Liquidity-Adjusted Value at Risk (LVaR) in AED [Severe (Crisis) Market Conditions]		
ρ = *Empirical*	ρ = *1*	ρ = *0*
14,565,598	24,772,810	10,864,064
9.71%	16.52%	7.24%

Diversification Benefits	
$ 10,207,212	70.08%

Overall Sensitivity Factor: Portfolio of Stock Indices
0.422

of expected return and conditional volatility for each of the time series variables.[5] As a result, Table 3 illustrates the daily conditional volatility and expected return of each of the sample indices under normal market and severe (crisis) market conditions.[6] In fact, crisis market volatilities are calculated by implementing an empirical distribution of past returns for all stock market indices' time series and, hence, the maximum negative returns (losses), which are observed in the historical time series, are selected for this purpose. This approach can aid in overcoming some of the limitations of normality assumption and can provide a better analysis of LVaR and particularly under severe and illiquid market circumstances.

In order to emphasize the importance of simulating different portfolios under varied market settings, two full case studies are performed on the GCC stock markets. This is with the intention of setting up a financial modeling tool for proactive daily equity risk taking practices and for assessing trading risk properly under extreme market circumstances. In the calculations reported herein, the effects of different combinations of structured portfolios, various liquidation periods (or unwinding horizons of assets holdings) are

[5] In this study, the following Generalized Autoregressive Conditional Heteroskedasticity in mean model [GARCH-M (1,1)] is used for the estimation of expected return and conditional volatility for each of the time series variables:

$$R_{it} = a_i + b_i \sigma_{it} + \varepsilon_{it},$$
$$\sigma_{it}^2 = c_i + \beta_{i1} \sigma_{it-1}^2 + \beta_{i2} \varepsilon_{it-1}^2,$$

where R_{it} is the continuous compounding return of time series i, σ_{it} is the conditional standard deviation as a measure of volatility, and ε_{it} is the error term return for time series i. The denotations a_i, b_i, c_i, β_{i1}, and β_{i2} represent parameters to be estimated. The parameters representing variance are assumed to undertake a positive value.

[6] In this chapter, severe or crisis market conditions refer to unexpected extreme adverse market situations at which losses could be severalfold larger than losses under normal market situation. Stress-testing technique is usually used to estimate the impact of unusual and severe events.

investigated. Furthermore, all risk modeling and analyses are performed at the one-tailed 97.5% level of confidence over different close-out periods.

The parametric LVaR outcomes are premeditated under normal and severe market conditions by taking into consideration different correlation factors (+1, 0, and empirical correlations between the various risk factors). Under correlation +1, one is supposing 100% positive associations between all risk factors (risk positions) all the times, whereas for the zero-correlation case, there are no relationships between risk positions at all times. The last correlation case takes into account the empirical correlation factors between all positions and is calculated via a variance/covariance (correlation) matrix as indicated in Table 2.

Table 3 illustrates an expedient simulation report for the modeling of trading risk assessment of a hypothetically structured equity portfolio of the GCC stock markets. Asset allocation and parametric LVaR analysis are performed under the assumption that local indices represent exact replicas of diversified portfolios of local stocks for each GCC stock market, respectively. In the first case study, total portfolio value is AED 150 million (UAE Dirham), with varied asset allocation ratios and with a liquidity horizon (unwinding or close-out period) of one trading day—that is, one day to unwind all equity trading positions. Furthermore, Table 3 demonstrates the effects of stress-testing (that is, LVaR under severe market conditions) and different correlation factors on daily parametric LVaR assessments. The LVaR simulation report also depicts the overnight conditional volatilities and expected returns calculated via the means of a GARCH-M (1,1) model, in addition to their respective sensitivity factors vis-à-vis the benchmark Shuaa Arab index.[7] Severe market daily volatilities are calculated and illustrated in the simulation report too. As discussed earlier, these daily volatilities, under severe and crisis-simulated market settings, represent the maximum negative returns (losses), which are perceived in the historical time series for all stock market indices. As a result, we can observe from Table 3 that the index with the highest volatility is SE All Share Index (under normal market condition), whereas the DFM General Index demonstrates the highest volatility under severe market situations. An interesting outcome of the study of beta factors for systematic risk is the manner in which the results are varied across the sample indices as indicated in Table 3. SE All Share Index appears to have the highest sensitivity factor (0.98) vis-à-vis the Shuaa Arab Index (that is the highest systematic risk) and the BA All Share Index seems to have the lowest beta factor (0.06). Likewise, and in accordance with general belief, Shuaa GCC Index (with a sensitivity factor of 1.05) is the best contender of the entire sample indices that appears to move very closely with respect to the benchmark Shuaa Arab Index (with a beta factor of 1.0).

Additionally, Table 3 points out the individual risk factors for each equity index in terms of AED and under the perception of normal and severe market specifications.

[7] The sensitivity factors are the common beta factors for the measurement of systematic risk. These factors assess the relationship of each GCC stock market index against the benchmark index (Shuaa Arab Index).

These individual risk factors are in fact a reflection of a non-diversified LVaR figures. As such, the parametric LVaR-engine's simulation report depicts the overnight conditional undiversified LVaRs (or undiversified risk factors) for each GCC stock market. These undiversified risk factors (under normal and severe market conditions) are calculated also with the aid of conditional volatilities estimated via a GARCH-M (1,1) model. Expected returns and risk-adjusted expected returns (under normal and severe market situations) are also included in the parametric LVaR's simulation report. Consequently, with 97.5% confidence, the actual equity trading portfolio should expect to realize no greater than AED 2,337,945 decrease in the value over a one-day time frame.[8] In other words, the loss of AED 2,337,945 is one that an equity portfolio should realize only 2.5% of the time. If the actual loss exceeds the parametric LVaR estimation, then this would be considered a violation of the assessment. From a risk management perspective, the LVaR estimate of AED 2,337,945 is a valuable piece of information. Since every equity trading business has different characteristics and tolerances toward risk, the trading risk manager must examine LVaR estimation relative to the overall position of the entire business. Simply put, can the firm tolerate or even survive such a rare event—a loss of AED 2,337,945 (or a 1.56% of total portfolio value)? This question is not only important to the equity trading unit, but also to financial institutions (or other funding units such as treasury unit within the same hierarchy and organizational structure of the trading unit) who lend money to these trading units. The inability of a trading unit to absorb large losses may jeopardize their ability to make principal and interest payments. Therefore, various risk management strategies could be examined in the context of how they might affect the LVaR estimation. Presumably, risk management strategies, such as the use of futures and options contracts in hedging possible fluctuation in equity prices, should reduce the LVaR appraisal. In other words, those extreme losses in equity trading, that would normally occur only 2.5% of the time, should be smaller with the incorporation of some type of risk management strategy.

Furthermore, the analysis of parametric LVaR under illiquid market conditions is performed with three different correlation factors: empirical, zero, and unity correlations, respectively. Indeed, it is essential to include different correlation factors in any parametric LVaR and stress-testing exercises. This is because existing trends in correlation factors may break down (or change signs) under adverse and severe market movements, caused by unforeseen financial or political crises. As one might expect, the case with correlation +1 gives the highest LVaR numbers (AED 3,945,243 and AED 24,772,810, respectively), owing to the fact that under these circumstances total LVaR is the weighted average of the individual LVaRs of each equity trading position. It is essential to include various

[8] It should be noted that under severe or crisis market conditions the actual equity trading portfolio can expect to realize greater decrease in value and major losses of approximately sixfold more than the normal market conditions simulation case. As depicted in the simulation report, the losses could amass to a total of AED 14,565,598 (9.71% of total portfolio value) over a one-day time horizon.

Table 4 Simulation of liquidity trading risk management and asset allocation (full case LVaR analysis).

Stock Market Indices	Market Value in AED	Asset Allocation	Liquidity Holding Horizon	Daily Volatility (Normal)	Daily Volatility (severe)	Sensitivity Factor	Expected Return	Undiversified LVaR in AED (Normal)	Undiversified LVaR in AED (Severe)
DFM General Index	$ 30,000,000	20.0%	2	1.81%	12.16%	0.58	0.14%	608,315	4,077,671
ADX Index	$ 20,000,000	13.3%	3	1.32%	7.08%	0.40	0.07%	330,440	1,764,949
BA All Share Index	$ 18,000,000	12.0%	4	0.58%	3.77%	0.06	0.04%	143,163	928,757
KSE General Index	$ 20,000,000	13.3%	7	0.71%	3.74%	0.14	0.08%	240,865	1,263,155
MSM30 Index	$ 15,000,000	10.0%	6	0.79%	8.70%	0.10	0.10%	189,040	2,074,576
DSM20 Index	$ 20,000,000	13.3%	4	1.48%	8.07%	0.31	0.07%	405,405	2,211,193
SE All Share Index	$ 27,000,000	18.0%	2	1.86%	11.03%	0.98	0.01%	560,773	3,330,491
Shuaa GCC Index	$ -	0.0%	1	1.30%	8.10%	1.05	0.08%	-	-
Shuaa Arab Index	$ -	0.0%	1	1.15%	7.57%	1.00	0.10%	-	-
Total Portfolio Value in AED	$ 150,000,000	100%					0.07%		

Expected Return and Risk-Adjusted Return	
Trading Portfolio Expected Return	0.07%
Risk-Adjusted Expected Return (Normal)	3.89%
Risk-Adjusted Expected Return (Severe)	0.62%

Daily Liquidity-Adjusted Value at Risk (LVaR) in AED [Normal Market Conditions]		
ρ = *Empirical*	$\rho = 1$	$\rho = 0$
2,847,556	4,956,002	2,071,043
1.90%	3.30%	1.38%
Diversification Benefits		
$ 2,108,446	74.04%	

Daily Liquidity-Adjusted Value at Risk (LVaR) in AED [Severe (Crisis) Market Conditions]		
ρ = *Empirical*	$\rho = 1$	$\rho = 0$
17,818,851	31,301,584	13,036,258
11.88%	20.87%	8.69%
Diversification Benefits		
$ 13,482,733	75.67%	

Overall Sensitivity Factor: Portfolio of Stock Indices
0.422

correlation factors in any stress-testing exercise, based on the fact that current trends in correlations may break down with severe market movements, caused by unexpected financial or political crises, such as the latest global sub-prime financial crunch. The degree of diversification of this hypothetical equity trading portfolio can also be displayed as the difference in value of the two greatest LVaRs, that is LVaR of correlation +1 case versus LVaR with empirical correlation (that is, AED 1,607,297 or 68.75% of diversification for the normal market conditions case). The overall sensitivity factor (beta factor) of this portfolio is also indicated in this report as 0.422, or in other words, the total equity portfolio value, with actual asset allocation percentage, moves distantly from the benchmark index (Shuaa Arab Index).

Finally, since the variations in daily parametric LVaR are mainly related to the ways in which trading assets are allocated in addition to the liquidation periods of each trading position, it is instructive to examine the way in which LVaR figures are influenced by changes in such parameters. All else equal, Table 4 illustrates the changes to LVaR figures when the liquidation periods (or holding horizons) of each trading position are increased discretionally from 1-day to 2-day, 3-day, 4-day, 6-day, and 7-day for all equity indices within the structured trading portfolio. As such, using empirical correlation, the LVaR figures increased to AED 2,847,556 (1.90%) and AED 17,818,851 (11.88%) under normal and severe markets conditions, respectively.

4.4. Algorithmic Optimization Technique for the Setting of Maximum LVaR Boundary

Optimum risk limits (or maximum risk-budgeting threshold) are an essential component for any trading/asset management risk unit and it should be defined clearly and used wisely to ensure control on the trading/investment unit's exposure to risk. All limit-setting and control, monitoring, and reporting should be performed by the risk management unit, independently from the front office's traders.

How should we set risk limits to safeguard against maximum loss amounts? These are some of the central questions risk managers must envisage. In this chapter, a simplified—however a real-world approach—is presented for the setting of optimum LVaR limits. To this end, a variety of case studies with different parametric LVaR calculations have been examined in order to set up measures for the development of optimum LVaR risk limits and to suggest adequate policies for handling situations in which trading/investment units are above the authorized LVaR-budgeting limits. The methodology and algorithm for the setting of maximum LVaR limits must be analyzed and approved by the board of directors of the concerned financial entity before any actual trading takes place. Ultimately, all trading/investment units need to have these approved maximum limits of LVaR as a strict trading policy and as hands-on guidelines for their daily risk takings. Any excess of LVaR beyond the ratified limits must be reported to top management by the risk management unit. Moreover, traders/asset managers need to give full and justified explanations of why their parametric LVaRs are beyond the approved maximum limits.

In order to ascertain coherent maximum LVaR trading limits, the mathematical formulation of the optimization process is set as follows:

From Eq. (4) we can define liquidation horizon factor (LHF_i) for each trading asset as:

$$LHF_i = \sqrt{\frac{(2t_i + 1)(t_i + 1)}{6t_i}}. \tag{6}$$

After substituting Eq. (6) into Eq. (2), we can compute the maximum authorized parametric portfolio $\text{LVaR}_{P_{adj}}$ trading limits by solving for the following quadratic nonlinear programing formulation under illiquid and adverse market settings, detailed along these lines:

$$Maximize : \text{LVaR}_{P_{adj}} = \sqrt{\sum_{i=1}^{n}\sum_{j=1}^{n} \text{LVaR}_{i_{adj}} \text{LVaR}_{j_{adj}} \rho_{i,j}} = \sqrt{|\,\text{LVaR}_{adj}\,|^{T} |\,\rho\,||\,\text{LVaR}_{adj}\,|}. \tag{7}$$

Subject to applying the following operational and financial budget constraints as specified by the trading risk manager and/or portfolio manager:

$$\sum_{i=1}^{n} x_i = 1.0; \; l_i \le x_i \le u_i \quad i = 1, 2, \ldots., n, \tag{8}$$

$$\sum_{i=1}^{n} V_i = V_P \quad i = 1, 2, \ldots., n, \tag{9}$$

$$|LHF| \geq 1.0; \forall_i \quad i = 1, 2, ..., n. \tag{10}$$

Here V_P denotes total portfolio volume, and x_i the weight or percentage asset allocation for each trading asset. The values l_i and u_i, $i = 1, 2, \ldots, n$ denote the lower and upper constraints for the portfolio weights x_i. If we choose $l_i = 0$, $i = 1, 2, \ldots, n$, then we have the situation where no short-sales are allowed. Moreover, $| LHF |$ indicates an $(nx1)$ liquidity risk factor vector for all $i = 1, 2, \ldots, n$.

Tables 5–8 represent four simulation case studies for the setting of realistic and optimum LVaR trading limits. In all four case studies, the effects of VaRious asset allocations (with or without short-sales) are investigated for the purpose of setting adequate LVaR boundary limits. In all case studies, the optimization is based on the definition of parametric LVaR as the maximum possible loss over a specified time horizon within a given confidence level. The optimization technique solves the problem by finding the market positions that maximize the loss, subject to the fact that all constraints are satisfied within their boundary values. Furthermore, in all cases the liquidation horizons varied from 2 to 5 trading days to unwind the constituents of the portfolio fully. For the sake of simplification of the optimization process and thereafter its analysis, a volume trading limit of AED 150,000,000 is assumed as a constraint on the optimization mathematical function—that is the financial entity (or trading unit) must keep a maximum overall market value of stocks of no more than AED 150,000,000 (between long-and short-sales positions).

While in Case Study 1 distinct asset allocation percentages are assumed, in Case Study 2 all equity trading position is concentrated in one market index that has, under severe market conditions, the highest daily return conditional volatility—that is, the Dubai Financial Market (DFM) General Index. Finally, in Case Study 3 and Case Study 4

Table 5 Simulation of liquidity trading risk management and asset allocation (LVaR boundary limits, Case Study 1).

Stock Market Indices	Market Value in AED	Asset Allocation	Liquidity Holding Horizon	Daily Volatility (Normal)	Daily Volatility (severe)	Sensitivity Factor	Expected Return	Undiversified LVaR in AED (Normal)	Undiversified LVaR in AED (Severe)
DFM General Index	$ 30,000,000	20.0%	2	1.81%	12.16%	0.58	0.14%	608,315	4,077,671
ADX Index	$ 25,000,000	16.7%	2	1.32%	7.08%	0.40	0.07%	370,267	1,977,673
BA All Share Index	$ 15,000,000	10.0%	3	0.58%	3.77%	0.06	0.04%	108,665	704,958
KSE General Index	$ 20,000,000	13.3%	4	0.71%	3.74%	0.14	0.08%	195,123	1,023,273
MSM30 Index	$ 15,000,000	10.0%	5	0.79%	8.70%	0.10	0.10%	176,359	1,935,403
DSM20 Index	$ 20,000,000	13.3%	3	1.48%	8.07%	0.31	0.07%	369,259	2,014,043
SE All Share Index	$ 25,000,000	16.7%	2	1.86%	11.03%	0.98	0.01%	519,235	3,083,788
Shuaa GCC Index	$ -	0.0%	1	1.30%	8.10%	1.05	0.08%	-	-
Shuaa Arab Index	$ -	0.0%	1	1.15%	7.57%	1.00	0.10%	-	-
Total Portfolio Value in AED	$ 150,000,000	100%					0.08%		

Expected Return and Risk-Adjusted Return	
Trading Portfolio Expected Return	0.08%
Risk-Adjusted Expected Return (Normal)	4.09%
Risk-Adjusted Expected Return (Severe)	0.65%

Daily Liquidity-Adjusted Value at Risk (LVaR) in AED [Normal Market Conditions]		
ρ = *Empirical*	ρ = *1*	ρ = *0*
2,754,405	4,694,444	1,994,076
1.84%	3.13%	1.33%

Diversification Benefits	
$ 1,940,039	70.43%

Daily Liquidity-Adjusted Value at Risk (LVaR) in AED [Severe (Crisis) Market Conditions]		
ρ = *Empirical*	ρ = *1*	ρ = *0*
17,214,462	29,633,615	12,553,014
11.48%	19.76%	8.37%

Diversification Benefits	
$ 12,419,153	72.14%

Overall Sensitivity Factor: Portfolio of Stock Indices
0.421

Table 6 Simulation of liquidity trading risk management and asset allocation (LVaR boundary limits, Case Study 2).

Stock Market Indices	Market Value in AED	Asset Allocation	Liquidity Holding Horizon	Daily Volatility (Normal)	Daily Volatility (severe)	Sensitivity Factor	Expected Return	Undiversified LVaR in AED (Normal)	Undiversified LVaR in AED (Severe)
DFM General Index	$150,000,000	100.0%	2	1.81%	12.16%	0.58	0.14%	3,041,574	20,388,354
ADX Index	$ -	0.0%	2	1.32%	7.08%	0.40	0.07%	-	-
BA All Share Index	$ -	0.0%	3	0.58%	3.77%	0.06	0.04%	-	-
KSE General Index	$ -	0.0%	4	0.71%	3.74%	0.14	0.08%	-	-
MSM30 Index	$ -	0.0%	5	0.79%	8.70%	0.10	0.10%	-	-
DSM20 Index	$ -	0.0%	3	1.48%	8.07%	0.31	0.07%	-	-
SE All Share Index	$ -	0.0%	2	1.86%	11.03%	0.98	0.01%	-	-
Shuaa GCC Index	$ -	0.0%	1	1.30%	8.10%	1.05	0.08%	-	-
Shuaa Arab Index	$ -	0.0%	1	1.15%	7.57%	1.00	0.10%	-	-
Total Portfolio Value in AED	$ 150,000,000	100%					0.14%		

Expected Return and Risk-Adjusted Return	
Trading Portfolio Expected Return	0.14%
Risk-Adjusted Expected Return (Normal)	3.43%
Risk-Adjusted Expected Return (Severe)	0.51%

Daily Liquidity-Adjusted Value at Risk (LVaR) in AED [Normal Market Conditions]		
ρ = *Empirical*	ρ = *1*	ρ = *0*
6,083,149	6,083,149	6,083,149
4.06%	4.06%	4.06%

Diversification Benefits	
$ -	0.00%

Daily Liquidity-Adjusted Value at Risk (LVaR) in AED [Severe (Crisis) Market Conditions]		
ρ = *Empirical*	ρ = *1*	ρ = *0*
40,776,709	40,776,709	40,776,709
27.18%	27.18%	27.18%

Diversification Benefits	
$ -	0.00%

Overall Sensitivity Factor: Portfolio of Stock Indices
0.580

Table 7 Simulation of liquidity trading risk management and asset allocation (LVaR boundary limits, Case Study 3).

Stock Market Indices	Market Value in AED	Asset Allocation	Liquidity Holding Horizon	Daily Volatility (Normal)	Daily Volatility (severe)	Sensitivity Factor	Expected Return	Undiversified LVaR in AED (Normal)	Undiversified LVaR in AED (Severe)
DFM General Index	$ 150,000,000	100.0%	2	1.81%	12.16%	0.58	0.14%	3,041,574	20,388,354
ADX Index	$ 50,000,000	33.3%	2	1.32%	7.08%	0.40	0.07%	740,534	3,955,345
BA All Share Index	$ (50,000,000)	-33.3%	3	0.58%	3.77%	0.06	0.04%	362,218	2,349,859
KSE General Index	$ 60,000,000	40.0%	4	0.71%	3.74%	0.14	0.08%	585,368	3,069,818
MSM30 Index	$ 30,000,000	20.0%	5	0.79%	8.70%	0.10	0.10%	352,717	3,870,805
DSM20 Index	$ 60,000,000	40.0%	3	1.48%	8.07%	0.31	0.07%	1,107,776	6,042,128
SE All Share Index	$ (150,000,000)	-100.0%	2	1.86%	11.03%	0.98	0.01%	3,115,407	18,502,728
Shuaa GCC Index	$ -	0.0%	1	1.30%	8.10%	1.05	0.08%	-	-
Shuaa Arab Index	$ -	0.0%	1	1.15%	7.57%	1.00	0.10%	-	-
Total Portfolio Value in AED	$ 150,000,000	100%					0.22%		

Expected Return and Risk-Adjusted Return	
Trading Portfolio Expected Return	0.22%
Risk-Adjusted Expected Return (Normal)	3.67%
Risk-Adjusted Expected Return (Severe)	0.58%

Daily Liquidity-Adjusted Value at Risk (LVaR) in AED [Normal Market Conditions]		
ρ = *Empirical*	ρ = *1*	ρ = *0*
9,016,331	4,700,688	9,237,048
6.01%	3.13%	6.16%

Diversification Benefits	
$ (4,315,643)	-47.86%

Daily Liquidity-Adjusted Value at Risk (LVaR) in AED [Severe (Crisis) Market Conditions]		
ρ = *Empirical*	ρ = *1*	ρ = *0*
56,582,509	32,947,727	57,969,536
37.72%	21.97%	38.65%

Diversification Benefits	
$ (23,634,781)	-41.77%

Overall Sensitivity Factor: Portfolio of Stock Indices
-0.079

the effect of short-sales of the sample stocks (or equity indices) is also contemplated by randomly short-selling some of the sample stocks. It should be noted that although current operational platform in the GCC financial markets does not permit short-sales of financial assets, accordingly in this chapter we relax this restriction on short-sales as we strive to determine asset market liquidity risk exposure. As such, our asset liquidity risk modeling includes both pure long trading positions and a combination of long/short-sales positions. A summary of parametric LVaR optimization results for the four case studies is illustrated in Tables 9 and 10 below.

Table 8 Simulation of liquidity trading risk management and asset allocation (LVaR boundary limits, Case Study 4).

Stock Market Indices	Market Value in AED	Asset Allocation	Liquidity Holding Horizon	Daily Volatility (Normal)	Daily Volatility (severe)	Sensitivity Factor	Expected Return	Undiversified LVaR in AED (Normal)	Undiversified LVaR in AED (Severe)
DFM General Index	$ 150,000,000	100.0%	2	1.81%	12.16%	0.58	0.14%	3,041,574	20,388,354
ADX Index	$ 70,000,000	46.7%	2	1.32%	7.08%	0.40	0.07%	1,036,748	5,537,483
BA All Share Index	$ (150,000,000)	-100.0%	3	0.58%	3.77%	0.06	0.04%	1,086,655	7,049,577
KSE General Index	$ 40,000,000	26.7%	4	0.71%	3.74%	0.14	0.08%	390,245	2,046,545
MSM30 Index	$ (150,000,000)	-100.0%	5	0.79%	8.70%	0.10	0.10%	1,763,585	19,354,025
DSM20 Index	$ 40,000,000	26.7%	3	1.48%	8.07%	0.31	0.07%	738,517	4,028,086
SE All Share Index	$ 150,000,000	100.0%	2	1.86%	11.03%	0.98	0.01%	3,115,407	18,502,728
Shuaa GCC Index	$ -	0.0%	1	1.30%	8.10%	1.05	0.08%	-	-
Shuaa Arab Index	$ -	0.0%	1	1.15%	7.57%	1.00	0.10%	-	-
Total Portfolio Value in AED	$ 150,000,000	100%					0.09%		

Expected Return and Risk-Adjusted Return	
Trading Portfolio Expected Return	0.09%
Risk-Adjusted Expected Return (Normal)	1.18%
Risk-Adjusted Expected Return (Severe)	0.18%

Daily Liquidity-Adjusted Value at Risk (LVaR) in AED [Normal Market Conditions]		
ρ = *Empirical*	ρ = *1*	ρ = *0*
11,150,368	10,944,504	10,004,106
7.43%	7.30%	6.67%
Diversification Benefits		
$ (205,864)	-1.85%	
Daily Liquidity-Adjusted Value at Risk (LVaR) in AED [Severe (Crisis) Market Conditions]		
ρ = *Empirical*	ρ = *1*	ρ = *0*
73,370,524	48,199,189	70,239,258
48.91%	32.13%	46.83%
Diversification Benefits		
$ (25,171,334)	-34.31%	
Overall Sensitivity Factor: Portfolio of Stock Indices		
1.707		

Table 9 Parametric LVaR maximum boundary limits in AED with various correlation factors (the case of normal market conditions).

LVaR maximum boundary limits (case studies)	ρ = empirical	$\rho = +1$	$\rho = 0$
LVaR case study [1]	2,754,405 (1.84%)	4,694,444 (3.13%)	1,994,076 (1.33%)
LVaR case study [2]	6,083,149 (4.06%)	6,083,149 (4.06%)	6,083,149 (4.06%)
LVaR case study [3]	9,016,331 (6.01%)	4,700,688 (3.13%)	9,237,048 (6.16%)
LVaR case study [4]	11,150,368 (7.43%)	10,944,504 (7.30%)	10,004,106 (6.67%)

Note: numbers in parentheses denote maximum parametric LVaR boundary limits as a percentage of total trading portfolio value of 150 million AED.

The principal effect of diversification on LVaR limits setting seems to be through Case Study 1; that is, with unequal asset allocation percentages. The highest LVaR numbers that are calculated so far are for Case Study 4, when the trading budget is allocated between long and short-sales equity trading positions. In fact, and in accordance with previous studies on other emerging financial markets, such as Mexico (see for instance, Al Janabi, 2007), the author found that short-selling usually decreases LVaR figures and, hence, lowers the maximum LVaR trading budget limits. Indeed, in the case of the GCC stock markets our empirical results contradict some of the previous studies on other emerging markets, such as that of Mexico. In essence, the above phenomena (of

Table 10 Parametric LVaR maximum boundary limits in AED with various correlation factors (the case of severe and crisis market conditions).

LVaR maximum boundary limits (case studies)	ρ = empirical	$\rho = +1$	$\rho = 0$
LVaR case study [1]	17,214,462 (11.48%)	29,633,615 (19.76%)	12,553,014 (8.37%)
LVaR case study [2]	40,776,709 (27.18%)	40,776,709 (27.18%)	40,776,709 (27.18%)
LVaR case study [3]	56,582,509 (37.72%)	32,947,727 (21.97%)	57,969,536 (38.65%)
LVaR case study [4]	73,370,524 (48.91%)	48,199,189 (32.13%)	70,239,258 (46.83%)

Note: numbers in parentheses denote maximum parametric LVaR boundary limits as a percentage of total trading portfolio value of 150 million AED.

high LVaR figures for long and short-sales positions) can be explained by the nature of the diminutive correlation factors that we have witnessed in the entire GCC stock markets. As such, these tiny correlation factors have led to grand diversification benefit for long equity trading positions and vice versa for short-sales positions. Furthermore, in contrast to previous research on other emerging financial markets, it is important to note here that in this work we have considered a more realistic model for the incorporation of daily conditional volatility under severe market condition, which takes into account the maximum negative returns (losses) that are identified in the historical time series for all nine stock market indices. Moreover, our risk-algorithm model is outfitted with additional features that can produce a clear-cut risk assessment and empirical simulation results under crisis-driven correlation factors that cannot be obtained with the plain assumption of normality.

As a conclusion of these four case studies, the board of directors of the financial trading/investment entity can set the maximum authorized daily LVaR limits (or optimum risk-budgeting threshold) for their equity trading portfolios as follows:

- Maximum approved daily LVaR budget limit under normal market conditions and under the supposition that empirical correlations will be sustained (that is, ρ = Empirical) = AED 11,150,368 (7.43% of total portfolio volume).
- Maximum approved daily LVaR budget limit under normal market conditions and under the supposition that correlations increase to unity (that is, $\rho = +1$ and empirical correlation will not be sustained) = AED 10,944,504 (7.30% of total portfolio volume).
- Maximum approved daily LVaR budget limit under normal market conditions and under the supposition of an absence of correlations (that is, $\rho = 0$ and empirical correlation will not be sustained) = AED 10,004,106 (6.67% of total portfolio volume).

- Maximum approved daily LVaR budget limit under severe or crisis market conditions and under the supposition that empirical correlations will be sustained throughout the crisis period (that is, ρ = Empirical) = AED 73,370,524 (48.91% of total portfolio volume).
- Maximum approved daily LVaR budget limit under severe or crisis market conditions and under the supposition that correlations increase to unity (that is, $\rho = +1$ and empirical correlation will not be sustained throughout the crisis period) = AED 48,199,189 (32.13% of total portfolio volume).
- Maximum approved daily LVaR budget limit under severe or crisis market conditions and under the supposition of an absence of correlations (that is, $\rho = 0$ and empirical correlation will not be sustained throughout the crisis period) = AED 70,239,258 (46.83% of total portfolio volume).
- Maximum approved daily volume limit = AED 150,000,000 (between long and short-sales trading positions).
- Minimum expected daily return of the trading portfolio = 0.09%.
- Maximum overall sensitivity (or beta) factor of the trading portfolio = 1.707.

It should be noted here that the above optimum approved LVaR trading budget limits are in their converted (or equivalent) UAE dirham (AED) values at the current or prevailing foreign exchange rates of other GCC countries versus the UAE dirham.

5. DISCUSSION AND CONCLUSION

There are many methods and ways to identify, to assess, and to control market risk, and trading risk managers have the task to ascertain the identity of the one that suits their needs. In fact, there is no right or wrong way to assess and manage trading risk; it all depends on each entity's objectives, lines of business, risk appetite, and the availability of funds for investment in trading risk management projects. Regardless of the methodology chosen, the most important factors to consider are the establishment of sound risk modeling techniques, standard policies & procedures, and the consistency in the implementation process across all lines of businesses and risks, particularly in the wake of the aftermaths of the latest credit crunch and the ensuing sub-prime global financial crisis.

Under special conditions when changes in market risk factors are normally distributed, the Liquidity-Adjusted Value-at-Risk (LVaR) can be calculated using a closed-form parametric approach. However, for emerging-economies environments, one needs to supplement the closed-form parametric approach with other analysis such as stress-testing and simulation analysis under adverse markets circumstances. This is done with the objective of estimating the impact of assumptions that are made under LVaR approach. Likewise, the effects of illiquidity of trading assets, in emerging economies, must be dealt with more wisely and should be brought into existence within the parametric LVaR framework.

Indeed, while extensive literatures have reviewed the statistical and economic proposition of Value-at-Risk (VaR) models, this chapter provides real-world modeling techniques that can be applied to financial trading portfolios under the notion of illiquid and adverse financial market circumstances. This chapter provides pioneering strategic risk assessment techniques that can be applied to investment and trading portfolios in emerging financial markets, such as in the context of the Gulf Cooperation Council (GCC) stock markets. In this research study, key equity price risk assessment methods and modeling techniques that financial entities, regulators, and policymakers should consider in developing their daily price risk management objectives are examined and tailored to the particular needs of emerging markets. This is with the intent of setting up the basis of a simulation algorithm and modeling technique for the assessment of tactical equity price exposures in the day-to-day financial trading operations under severe and crisis-driven circumstances.

In this document, a simplified and practical method for calculating stock markets risk exposure in emerging economies under crisis-driven circumstances is presented and empirically tested and analyzed. As such, the aim is to develop a pragmatic approach to assist in the establishment of sound risk assessment practices and within a prudential framework of global financial regulations, for the most part in light of the outcomes of the latest global credit crunch and the resultant sub-prime financial crisis. To this end, advanced matrix-algebra approach is used to derive the necessary mathematical modeling and quantitative market risk assessment methods. This tactic is a useful form to avoid mathematical complexity, as more and more securities are added to the portfolio of assets. Besides, it can simplify the financial modeling and programing process and can allow as well a clear-cut incorporation of short (sell) and long (buy) positions in the daily risk management process. In addition, the effects of illiquidity of trading assets are incorporated into our parametric LVaR quantitative approach. For that purpose, a simplified and practical model for the assessment of the effects of illiquid assets (unwinding of trading assets), in daily market risk management practices, is defined and is appropriately integrated into parametric LVaR and stress-testing models.

As such, our contemporary risk-engine modeling and simulation framework can simultaneously conduct LVaR appraisal under normal and adverse market conditions, besides it takes into account the effects of liquidity of the traded equity securities. In order to illustrate the proper use of parametric LVaR and stress-testing methods, real-world paradigms of trading risk assessment are presented for the GCC stock markets. To this end, several simulation case studies are attained with the aspiration of bringing about a reasonable framework for the measurement and analysis of equity trading risk exposures. The modeling techniques discussed in this chapter will aid financial institutions, financial regulators, and policymakers in the drawing-up of meticulous and up-to-date simulation algorithms to handle equity price risk exposure. The suggested analytical methods and procedures can be put into practice in virtually all emerging markets, if they are adapted to correspond to every market's preliminary level of intricacy.

For this particular research study, parametric LVaR simulations are assessed for normal and severe market conditions and under the notion of different crisis-driven correlation factors and unwinding periods. To this end, case studies are performed with different asset allocations and liquidation horizons with the aim of setting up a hands-on framework for the appraisal of market risk exposure of an equity trading unit. As such, a meaningful financial modeling procedure for constructing a structured risk engine with a robust simulation algorithm is developed. This is with the ultimate aim of instigating a no-nonsense approach for the estimation of parametric LVaR under varied market circumstances.

Trading risk management models, which are adopted in this work, are applied to the seven GCC stock markets. Thus, our analyses are carried out for main market indicators in the GCC stock markets, in addition to two benchmark GCC indices. To this end, databases of daily indices settlement levels are obtained, filtered, and matched. Two full simulation case studies are carried out with the objectives of calculating parametric LVaR under various scenarios and market conditions. The different scenarios are performed with distinct asset allocation percentages in addition to analyzing the effects of illiquidity of trading assets by imposing different unwinding horizons for each trading asset. All simulations and quantitative analyses are carried out under the assumption of normal and severe (crisis) market conditions. The appealing outcome of this study suggests the inevitability of combining parametric LVaR calculations with other methods such as stress-testing and scenario analysis to grasp a thorough picture of other remaining risks (such as fat tails in the probability distribution) that cannot be revealed with the plain assumption of normality. In conclusion, proper assessment of parametric LVaR is an important element for daily risk management process and for tactical risk-decision-making under adverse and illiquid market circumstances and particularly for emerging markets under crisis-driven conditions.

In a nutshell, the quantitative optimization techniques and modeling algorithms discussed in this chapter can aid financial institutions, regulators, and policymakers in the commencement of coherent market risk simulation tactic to tackle portfolio risk exposure in emerging economies. The proposed analytical techniques and optimization procedures can be put into practice in virtually all GCC and other emerging markets, if they are custom-made to be compatible to every market's initial level of complexity. Ultimately, this will help in offering a yardstick framework for compliance with Basel II accord and the forthcoming Basel III requirements on capital adequacy and regulatory supervision. As a matter of fact, the proposed risk methodology, optimization algorithms, and empirical results of this research study have imperative hands-on uses and applications for financial markets and institutions, financial regulators and policymakers, treasury and risk managers, and portfolio managers conducting financial operations in the GCC and other developing markets, and particularly in light of the most recent credit crunch and ensuing sub-prime financial meltdown.

APPENDIX A. DERIVATION OF LIQUIDITY-ADJUSTED VALUE-AT-RISK (LVAR) MATHEMATICAL STRUCTURE DURING THE CLOSE-OUT (UNWINDING) PERIOD

In this Appendix, we present a simple re-engineered modeling approach for calculating a closed-form parametric LVaR.[9] The proposed model and liquidity scaling factor is more realistic and less conservative than the conventional root-t multiplier. In essence the suggested multiplier is a function of a predetermined liquidity threshold defined as the maximum position which can be unwound without disturbing market prices during one trading day. The essence of the model relies on the assumption of a stochastic stationary process and some rules of thumb, which can be of crucial value for more accurate overall trading risk assessment during market stress periods when liquidity dries up. To this end, a practical framework of a modeling technique (within a simplified financial mathematical approach) is proposed below with the purpose of incorporating and calculating illiquid assets' daily LVaR, detailed as follows (Al Janabi, 2010, 2011a, 2013a).

The market risk of an illiquid trading position is larger than the risk of an otherwise identical liquid position. This is because unwinding the illiquid position takes longer than unwinding the liquid position, and, as a result, the illiquid position is more exposed to the volatility of the market for a longer period of time. In this approach, a trading position will be considered illiquid if its size surpasses a certain liquidity threshold. The threshold (which is determined by each trader) and defined as the maximum position which can be unwound, without disrupting market prices, in normal market conditions and during one trading day. Consequently, the size of the trading position relative to the threshold plays an important role in determining the number of days that are required to close the entire position. This effect can be translated into a liquidity increment (or an additional liquidity risk factor) that can be incorporated into parametric LVaR analysis. If for instance, the par value of a position is \$10,000 and the liquidity threshold is \$5000, then it will take 2 days to sell out the entire trading position. Therefore, the initial position will be exposed to market variation for 1 day, and the rest of the position (that is \$5000) is subject to market variation for an additional day. If it is assumed that daily changes of market values follow a stationary stochastic process, the risk exposure due to illiquidity effects is given by the following illustration, detailed along these lines.

In order to take into account the full illiquidity of assets (that is, the required unwinding period to liquidate an asset), we define the following:

t = number of liquidation days (t-days to liquidate the entire asset fully),

σ^2_{adj} = overnight (daily) variance of the illiquid position; and,

σ_{adj} = liquidity risk factor or overnight (daily) standard deviation of the illiquid position.

[9] The mathematical approach presented herein is largely drawn from Al Janabi (2010, 2011a, 2013a) research papers.

The proposed approach assumes that the trading position is closed out linearly over t-days and hence it uses the logical assumption that the losses due to illiquid trading positions over t-days are the sum of losses over the individual trading days. Moreover, we can assume with reasonable accuracy that asset returns and losses due to illiquid trading positions are independent and identically distributed (*iid*) and serially uncorrelated day-to-day along the liquidation horizon and that the variance of losses due to liquidity risk over t-days is the sum of the variance (σ_i^2, for all $i = 1, 2, \ldots, t$) of losses on the individual days, thus:

$$\sigma_{adj}^2 = \left(\sigma_1^2 + \sigma_2^2 + \sigma_3^2 + \cdots + \sigma_{t-2}^2 + \sigma_{t-1}^2 + \sigma_t^2\right). \tag{A.1}$$

In fact, the square root-t approach (Eq. (3)) is a simplified special case of Eq. (A.1) under the assumption that the daily variances of losses throughout the holding period are all the same as first day variance, σ_1^2, thus, $\sigma_{adj}^2 = \left(\sigma_1^2 + \sigma_1^2 + \sigma_1^2 + \cdots + \sigma_1^2\right) = t\sigma_1^2$. Basically, the square root-t equation overestimates asset liquidity risk since it does not consider that traders can liquidate small portions of their trading portfolios on a daily basis and then the whole trading position can be sold completely on the last trading day. Undeniably, in real financial markets operations, liquidation occurs during the holding period and thus scaling the holding period to account for orderly liquidation can be justified if one allows the assets to be liquidated throughout the holding period. As such, for this special linear liquidation case and under the assumption that the variance of losses of the first trading day decreases linearly each day (as a function of t) we can derive from Eq. (A.1) the following:

$$\sigma_{adj}^2 = \left(\left(\frac{t}{t}\right)^2 \sigma_1^2 + \left(\frac{t-1}{t}\right)^2 \sigma_1^2 + \left(\frac{t-2}{t}\right)^2 \sigma_1^2 + \cdots + \left(\frac{3}{t}\right)^2 \sigma_1^2 + \left(\frac{2}{t}\right)^2 \sigma_1^2 + \left(\frac{1}{t}\right)^2 \sigma_1^2\right). \tag{A.2}$$

Evidently, the additional liquidity risk factor depends only on the number of days needed to sell an illiquid equity position linearly. In the general case of t-days, the variance of the liquidity risk factor is given by the following mathematical functional expression of t:

$$\sigma_{adj}^2 = \sigma_1^2 \left(\left(\frac{t}{t}\right)^2 + \left(\frac{t-1}{t}\right)^2 + \left(\frac{t-2}{t}\right)^2 + \cdots + \left(\frac{3}{t}\right)^2 + \left(\frac{2}{t}\right)^2 + \left(\frac{1}{t}\right)^2\right). \tag{A.3}$$

To calculate the sum of the squares, it is convenient to use a short-cut approach. From mathematical series the following relationship can be obtained:

$$(t)^2 + (t-1)^2 + (t-2)^2 + \cdots + (3)^2 + (2)^2 + (1)^2 = \frac{t\,(t+1)\,(2t+1)}{6}. \tag{A.4}$$

Accordingly, from Eqs. (A.4) and (A.3), the liquidity risk factor can be expressed in terms of volatility (or standard deviation) as:

$$\sigma_{adj} = \sigma_1 \left(\sqrt{\frac{1}{t^2}[(t)^2 + (t-1)^2 + (t-2)^2 + \cdots + (3)^2 + (2)^2 + (1)^2]} \right),$$

$$\text{or } \sigma_{adj} = \sigma_1 \left(\sqrt{\frac{(2t+1)(t+1)}{6t}} \right). \tag{A.5}$$

The final result is of course a function of time and not the square root of time as employed by some financial market's participants based on the *RiskMetrics*^{TM} methodologies. The above approach can also be used to calculate parametric LVaR for any time horizon. In order to perform the calculation of LVaR under illiquid market conditions, the liquidity risk factor of Eq. (A.5) can be implemented in parametric LVaR modeling, hence, one can define the following:

$$\text{LVaR}_{adj} = \text{VaR}\sqrt{\frac{(2t+1)(t+1)}{6t}}, \tag{A.6}$$

where VaR = parametric Value-at-Risk under liquid market conditions (as presented formerly in Eq. (1)) and LVaR_{adj} = parametric Value-at-Risk under illiquid market conditions. The latter equation indicates that $\text{LVaR}_{adj} > \text{VaR}$, and for the special case when the number of days to liquidate the entire assets is one trading day, then we get $\text{LVaR}_{adj} = \text{VaR}$. Consequently, the difference between LVaR_{adj} and VaR should be equal to the residual market risk due to the illiquidity of any asset under illiquid markets conditions. As a matter of fact, the number of liquidation days (t) necessary to liquidate the entire assets fully is related to the choice of the liquidity threshold; however, the size of this threshold is likely to change under severe market conditions. Indeed, the choice of the liquidation horizon can be estimated from the total trading position size and the daily trading volume that can be unwound into the market without significantly disrupting market prices; and in actual practice it is generally estimated as:

$$t = \text{Total Trading Position Size of Equity } \textit{Asset}_i / \text{Daily Trading Volume of Equity } \textit{Asset}_i. \tag{A.7}$$

As such, the close-out time (t) is the time required to bring the positions to a state where the financial entity can make no further loss from the trading positions. It is the time taken to either sell the long positions or alternatively the time required to buy securities in case of short positions. In real practices, the daily trading volume of any trading asset is estimated as the average volume over some period of time, generally a month of trading activities. In effect, the daily trading volume of assets can be regarded as the average daily volume or the volume that can be unwound under a severe crisis period. The trading volume in a crisis period can be roughly approximated as the average daily trading volume less a number of standard deviations. Albeit this alternative approach is quite simple, it is still relatively objective. Moreover, it is reasonably easy to gather the required data to perform the necessary liquidation scenarios. In essence, the above liquidity scaling factor (or multiplier) is more realistic and less conservative than the conventional root-t multiplier and can aid financial entities in allocating reasonable and liquidity market-driven regulatory and economic-capital requirements.

Furthermore, the above mathematical formulas can be applied for the calculation of parametric LVaR for each trading position and for the entire portfolio. In order to calculate parametric LVaR for the full trading portfolio under illiquid market conditions ($\text{LVaR}_{P_{adj}}$), the above mathematical formulation can be extended, with the aid of Eq. (2), into a matrix-algebra form to yield the following:

$$\text{LVaR}_{P_{adj}} = \sqrt{\sum_{i=1}^{n}\sum_{j=1}^{n} \text{LVaR}_{i_{adj}} \text{LVaR}_{j_{adj}} \rho_{i,j}} = \sqrt{|\text{LVaR}_{adj}|^{T}|\rho||\text{LVaR}_{adj}|}. \tag{A.8}$$

The above mathematical structure (in the form of two vectors, $|\text{LVaR}_{adj}|$, $|\text{LVaR}_{adj}|^{T}$ and a correlation matrix, $|\rho|$) can facilitate the programing process so that the trading risk manager can specify different liquidation days for the whole portfolio and/or for each individual trading security according to the necessary number of days to liquidate the entire asset fully. The latter can be achieved by specifying an overall benchmark liquidation to liquidate the entire constituents of the portfolio fully. As a matter of fact, our modified liquidity risk factor approach, once compared with previously established liquidity risk models, could even lead to further reduction in the overall portfolio trading risk; and hence in the amount of regulatory-capital and/or economic-capital, as specified by Basel II (and the forthcoming Basel III) requirements on banking supervision and capital adequacy.

ACKNOWLEDGMENT

This work has benefited from the financial support of the College of Business and Economics (CBE), United Arab Emirates University, Al-Ain, UAE. The usual disclaimer applies.

REFERENCES

Al Janabi, M.A.M., 2007. Risk analysis, reporting and control of equity exposure: viable applications to the Mexican financial market. Journal of Derivatives and Hedge Funds 13 (1), 33–58

Al Janabi, M.A.M., 2009a. Market liquidity and strategic asset allocation: applications to GCC stock exchanges. Middle East Development Journal 1 (2), 227–254

Al Janabi, M.A.M., 2009b. Commodity price risk management: valuation of large trading portfolios under adverse and illiquid market settings. Journal of Derivatives and Hedge Funds 15 (1), 15–50

Al Janabi, M.A.M., 2010. Incorporating asset liquidity effects in risk-capital modeling. Review of Middle East Economics and Finance 6 (1), 1–30

Al Janabi, M.A.M., 2011a. A generalized theoretical modeling approach for the assessment of economic capital under asset market liquidity risk constraints. The Service Industries Journal 31 (13 & 14), 2193–2221

Al Janabi, M.A.M., 2011b. Economic capital allocation under coherent market liquidity constraints. Journal of Economic Research 16 (2), 147–186

Al Janabi, M.A.M., 2012. Risk management in trading and investment portfolios: an optimization algorithm for maximum risk-budgeting threshold. Journal of Emerging Market Finance 11 (2), 189–229

Al Janabi, M.A.M., 2013a. Optimal and coherent economic-capital structures: evidence from long and short-sales trading positions under illiquid market perspectives. Annals of Operations Research 205 (1), 109–139

Al Janabi, M.A.M., 2013b. GCC financial markets in the wake of recent global crisis. In: Peeters, M. (Ed.), Financial Integration—A Focus on the Mediterranean Region. Financial and Monetary Policy Studies, vol. 36. Springer, New York, USA, pp. 139–155

Almgren, R., Chriss, N., 1999. Optimal execution of portfolio transaction. Department of Mathematics, The University of Chicago, Working Paper.

Angelidis, T., Benos, A., 2006. Liquidity adjusted value-at-risk based on the components of the bid-ask spread. Applied Financial Economics 16 (11), 835–851

Bangia, A., Diebold, F., Schuermann, T., Stroughair, J., 1999. Modeling liquidity risk with implications for traditional market risk measurement and management. Working Paper, The Wharton School, University of Pennsylvania.

Bank of International Settlements, 2009. Enhancements to the basel II framework. Basel Committee on Banking Supervision, Basel, Switzerland. This publication is available on the BIS website (<www.bis.org>).

Bank of International Settlements, 2013. Basel III: The liquidity coverage ratio and liquidity risk monitoring tools. Basel Committee on Banking Supervision, Basel, Switzerland. This publication is available on the BIS website (<www.bis.org>).

Berkowitz, J., 2000. Incorporating liquidity risk into VaR models. Working Paper, Graduate School of Management, University of California, Irvine.

Berkowitz, J., O'Brien, J., 2001. How accurate are value-at-risk models at commercial banks? Working Paper, US Federal Reserve Board's Finance and Economic.

Garcia, R., Renault, E., Tsafack, G., 2007. Proper conditioning for coherent VaR in portfolio management. Management Science 53 (3), 483–494

Hisata, Y., Yamai, Y., 2000. Research toward the practical application of liquidity risk evaluation methods. Discussion Paper, Institute for Monetary and Economic Studies, Bank of Japan.

Jorion, P., 2001. Value-at-Risk: The New Benchmark for Controlling Market Risk. McGraw-Hill, Chicago

Le Saout, E., 2002. Incorporating liquidity risk in VAR models. Working Paper, Paris 1 University.

Madhavan, A., Richardson, M., Roomans, M., 1997. Why do security prices change? A transaction-level analysis of NYSE stocks. Review of Financial Studies 10 (4), 1035–1064

Markowitz, H., 1959. Portfolio Selection: Efficient Diversification of Investments. John Wiley, New York

Morgan Guaranty Trust Company, 1994. RiskMetrics-rechnical document. Morgan Guaranty Trust Company, Global Research, New York.

Reuters, 2009. 3000 Xtra Hosted Terminal Platform and Thomson Reuters Datastream datasets. <http://online.thomsonreuters.com/datastream/>

Sharpe, W., 1963. A simplified model for portfolio analysis. Management Science 9 (2), 277–293

PART *Two*

Dynamic Interactions With The Global Economy

CHAPTER 19

Volatility and Spillover Effects of Central and Eastern Europe: Impact of EU Enlargement

A. Golab[*], D.E. Allen[†,‡], R. Powell[*], and G. Yap[*]
[*]School of Accounting, Finance & Economics, Edith Cowan University, Joondalup, Australia
[†]Center for Applied Financial Studies, University of South Australia, Australia
[‡]School of Mathematics and Statistics, University of Sydney, Sydney, Australia

1. INTRODUCTION

The CEE stock markets have become of interest to many international financial researchers and policy-makers during the last decade. Former Eastern block economies became a source of investment attention to investors due to their better diversification opportunities. These markets have become more attractive and accessible for investors due to the unification of restrictions on transactions, a number of reforms in a European Union (EU) accession process, and an increase in financial transparency. Moreover, EU expansion creates a unique landscape for new financial investigation and analysis.

It could be argued that the CEE economies form a unique emerging markets structure, which typically offers attractive risk adjusted returns for international investors. Besides, both theoretical models and practical concerns motivate researchers toward focusing on volatility spillovers between financial markets. An accurate characterization of volatility spillovers has direct implications for portfolio management and asset allocation.

This chapter investigates a number of important aspects of portfolio selection and investment opportunities and their implications for CEE-based investors through modeling volatility spillovers and conditional correlations between more and less developed markets in periods before and after the date of the recent EU expansion. Specifically it deals with cross market relationships between the 12 emerging markets and does not attempt to include any developed markets.

The results show growing investment potential in these emerging equity markets, with a lowering of average risk post-joining the EU. This provides good opportunities for European investors as well as important indications for economic stability, growth, and integration of these markets in the post-EU period.

The remainder of the paper is organized as follows. Section 2 reviews the literature. Section 3 explains the data used in the empirical analysis and presents some summary statistics. Section 4 describes the methodology used in the study. The empirical results are analyzed in Section 5 followed by concluding remarks in Section 6.

Emerging Markets and the Global Economy
http://dx.doi.org/10.1016/B978-0-12-411549-1.00019-3

2. LITERATURE REVIEW

The transmission of volatility between markets and the comovements of stock markets has been extensively investigated in recent years. Globalization has brought about market integration, especially in stock markets, a fact which attracted the researchers' interest regarding the transmission of volatility among markets.

The investigation of the determinants of cross-country financial interdependence has been studied in a large empirical literature aimed at identifying the role of a set of factors of influence, such as trade intensity (Forbes and Chinn, 2004), financial development (Dellas and Hess, 2005), and business cycle synchronization (Walti, 2005). All of these papers concentrate on similar topics; however, their results and conclusions are slightly different. These concerns might be partly explained by the nature of the econometric approaches (cross-section vs. time-series), the measurement of market comovement and by the nature and the measurement of explanatory factors.

Volatility modeling has been one of the most active and successful areas of research in time series econometrics and economic forecasting in recent decades. The modeling of the risk-expected return relationship is of central importance in modern financial theory and of key practical importance to investors. Risk is typically characterized by uncertainty and measures such as the variance or volatility of a time series. Since 1982 when Engle introduced the Autoregressive Conditional Heteroskedasticity (ARCH) model, variants and developments from this model have been effectively applied to numerous economic and financial datasets in the modeling of financial time series. The original ARCH model generated a huge family of direct descendants in univariate and multivariate models' categories. As univariate GARCH models define the volatility of a given financial series and assume independence in the conditional variance across countries, they do not capture cross-market interdependent effects in volatility (or spillovers). This assumption may not be reasonable as researchers wish to know and investigate how shocks to variables can be correlated with each other and how those volatility shocks to one variable might affect the volatility of other related variables. To accommodate those spillover effects in conditional volatility, several models have been developed. Prominent multivariate GARCH models are: the Constant Conditional Correlation (CCC) models of Bollerslev (1990), the diagonal Baba-Engle-Kraft-Kroner (BEKK) model of Engle and Kroner (1995), the vector ARMA-GARCH (VARMA-GARCH) model proposed by Ling and McAleer (2003), and the vector ARMA-asymmetric GARCH (VARMA-AGARCH) model described by Chan et al. (2002). These models are the major focus of this study.

During the past few years a few empirical studies have been undertaken on four of the twelve mentioned CEE emerging markets: the Czech Republic, Hungary, Poland, and Slovakia. These studies mainly examine correlations in stock returns and their volatility in the Polish and Slovakian stock markets (Hranaiova, 1999), time-varying comovements while applying Engle's (2002) GARCH models between developed economies such as France, Germany and the UK and emerging ones; Czech Republic, Hungary, and Poland (Scheicher, 2001; Egert and Kocenda, 2007; Samitas and Kenourgios, 2011). Worthington and Higgs (2004) analyzed market efficiency using methods applying the serial correlation coefficient, ADF (Augmented Dickey-Fuller), PP (Phillips-Perron), and KPSS (Kwiatkowski, Phillips, Schmidt, and Shin) unit root tests and MVR (multiple variance ratio) tests. Another study constructed in a random walk framework is the paper by Cuaresma and Hlouskova (2005). An alternative issue to market efficiency is the issue of the degree of financial integration among the stock exchange markets in the Czech Republic, Hungary, Poland, and Slovakia in comparison with the euro zone market (Babetskii et al., 2007). The EMU equity market's volatility and correlation vs. US ones is also the subject of a study by Kearney and Poti (2008) and for global markets that of Capiello et al. (2006). Another approach, adopted by Bruggemann and Trenkler (2007), discusses the catching up process in the Czech Republic, Hungary, and Poland by investigating GDP behavior. The spillover effects of emerging markets have also been extensively investigated. Most studies focused on volatility spillovers within developed financial markets, so the relationship between the emerging markets of different regions remains relatively underexplored. For instance, Worthington et al. (2000) investigated price linkage in Asian equity markets, Kasch-Haroutounian and Price (2001) examined stock markets in Central Europe and Sola et al. (2002) analyzed volatility links between the stock markets of Thailand, South Korea, and Brazil. More recently, Li and Majerowska (2008), Fedorova and Vaihekoski (2009) studied the linkages between Eastern European markets and Russia. Saleem (2009) investigated the international linkages of the Russian markets. On the other hand, Christiansen (2010) investigated volatility spillovers from the US and aggregate asset markets into the European national asset markets. Harrison and Moore (2009) discussed the stock market indices' comovements and the cross market volatility of the 10 Eastern European countries. Some studies focused on stock market comovements in Central Europe (Hanousek and Kocenda, 2011; Kocenda and Egert, 2011), but yet again the studies have been limited to a few main countries.

Jorion and Goetzemann (1999) suggested that many emerging markets are actually re-emerging markets that for various reasons have gone through a period of relative decline. They pointed out that Poland, Romania, and Czechoslovakia had active equity markets in the 1920s prior to being subsumed in the Eastern block. This means that the attractive returns apparently offered by emerging markets may be a temporary phenomenon, an observation they backed up by simulations.

Overall, the majority of past studies of stock market comovements and integration have concentrated mainly on mature developed markets or advanced emerging markets such as the Czech Republic, Hungary, and Poland, while the behavior and inter-relationship of all others has been neglected. Little attention is given to the investment potential in CEE equity markets only. Thus the literature lacks a model which analyzes the interaction and integration of these markets at a regional and global level. The purpose of this study is an attempt to fill this gap.

This chapter examines the short and long-run behavior of the CEE emerging stock markets and assesses the impact of the EU on stock market linkages as revealed by the time series behavior of their stock market indices. This includes the application of multivariate VARMA GARCH models to test volatility spillovers and conditional correlations between markets. The models of CCC, BEKK, VARMA GARCH, and VARMA AGARCH are used to test for the existence of cross market effects, and in the case of the first two, to test for the conditional correlation.

3. DATA AND SUMMARY STATISTICS

The statistical data used in this study consist of the closing prices of the daily stock market indices in the 12 CEE stock markets[1] (Bulgaria, the Czech Republic, Cyprus, Estonia, Hungary, Latvia, Lithuania, Malta, Poland, Romania, Slovakia, and Slovenia). The data are obtained from DataStream for the period from January 1995 to May 2011. The 12 countries joined the EU during the latest two enlargements which took place on May 1, 2004 for the Czech Republic, Cyprus, Estonia, Hungary, Latvia, Lithuania, Malta, Poland, Slovakia, and Slovenia and January 1, 2007 for Bulgaria and Romania. Based on those two accession dates the sample period is divided into three phases: one pre-EU period (January 1995–April 2004) and two post-EU periods (May 2004–2012 for the first enlargement and January 2007–May 2012 for the second and final enlargement). One common currency, the euro, is used to express stock market prices in order to provide comparable findings (after Scheicher (2001) and Syriopoulos (2007)). The common currency is assumed for a euro-based investor, who does not hedge currency risk.

Table 1 provides descriptive statistics for the daily returns for the pre- and post-EU periods. Daily returns are defined as logarithmic price relatives: $R_t = ln\left(P_t/P_{t-1}\right) \times 100$. In every case, the return series has a mean value close to zero and a distribution characterized by non-normality (Jarque-Bera statistics). The highest mean of returns in the pre-EU period can be observed in Bulgaria (0.154) and Latvia (0.095) stock markets. A negative average return is observed in the Czech Republic (−0.006). In the post-EU period four countries, namely Bulgaria, Cyprus, Romania, and Slovenia, reported negative returns of −0.089, −0.009, −0.047, and −0.021, respectively. The highest mean return is assigned to Poland (0.049). If the data are normally distributed, then the mean and variance would completely describe the distribution of the data and the higher moments of skewness and kurtosis would provide no additional information about that distribution. However, the data contain positive skewness for two markets for the pre-EU period and on three occasions in the post-EU period. All other values for skewness are negative, which implies that the distribution has a long left tail, whereas the relevant Jarque-Bera statistics indicate rejection of the normality hypothesis. All markets generate kurtosis statistics of

[1] SOFIX (Bulgaria), SEPX (Czech Republic), CYSE (Cyprus), OMX Tallinn Stock Exchange (Estonia), BUX (Hungary), OMX Riga Stock Exchange (Latvia), OMX Vilnius Stock Exchange (Lithuania), MSE (Malta), WIG (Poland), BET (Romania), SAX (Slovakia), and SBI (Slovenia).

Table 1 Descriptive statistics of selected markets.

	Mean	Median	Max	Min	Std dev.	Skew	Kurtos	JarqueBera	Normality *p*-value
Pre-EU period									
Bulgaria	0.154	0.050	21.054	−20.893	1.856	−0.444	38.660	85624.18	0.000
Czech Rep	−0.006	0.000	5.930	−6.716	1.312	−0.238	5.299	603.6	0.000
Cyprus	N/A	N/A	N/A	N/A	N/A	N/A	N/A	N/A	N/A
Estonia	0.059	0.55	12.866	−21.576	1.981	−1.192	21.585	30196.4	0.000
Hungary	0.038	0.000	13.321	−19.483	1.797	−1.031	17.564	31348.1	0.000
Latvia	0.095	0.888	10.190	−14.720	1.863	−1.109	18.172	11061.1	0.000
Lithuania	0.070	0.035	4.580	−10.216	0.886	−1.176	21.143	15759.3	0.000
Malta	0.044	0.000	9.572	−7.589	0.793	2.571	34.716	93648.3	0.000
Poland	0.053	0.000	15.051	−17.714	2.283	−0.220	9.103	5309.1	0.000
Romania	0.028	0.001	11.863	−12.875	1.885	−0.159	9.135	3806.1	0.000
Slovakia	0.020	0.000	27.554	−12.452	1.720	2.232	41.320	171973.9	0.000
Slovenia	0.048	0.000	11.017	−11.344	1.255	−0.307	15.629	17951.9	0.000
Post-EU period									
Bulgaria	−0.089	0.000	7.289	−11.369	1.629	−0.894	10.056	2519.4	0.000
Czech Rep	0.039	0.068	14.469	−16.580	1.773	−0.412	16.497	13989.9	0.000
Cyprus	−0.009	0.000	12.123	−12.135	2.318	−0.017	6.388	835.5	0.000
Estonia	0.038	0.024	12.944	−7.045	1.251	0.300	12.598	7075.6	0.000
Hungary	0.036	0.134	15.402	−18.578	2.113	−0.164	11.212	5167.9	0.000
Latvia	0.005	0.000	10.053	−7.904	1.447	0.151	9.137	2888.2	0.000
Lithuania	0.027	0.000	11.865	−13.515	1.346	−0.020	22.386	28750.5	0.000
Malta	0.013	0.000	4.738	−4.536	0.795	0.197	9.085	2845.4	0.000
Poland	0.049	0.108	9.811	−11.126	1.719	−0.365	7.647	1692.8	0.000
Romania	−0.047	0.064	11.203	−14.399	2.281	−0.498	7.944	1209.6	0.000
Slovakia	0.015	0.000	11.880	−14.810	1.178	−1.693	31.193	61686.12	0.000
Slovenia	−0.021	0.000	7.681	−8.299	1.081	−0.742	14.805	9934.1	0.000

more than 3 (which is the benchmark for a normal distribution) which indicates the series is characterized by leptokurtosis. This means that the distribution of the data contains a greater number of observations in the tails than that found in a normal distribution. While it is possible to individually test the significance of the skewness and kurtosis, the more common approach is the joint test based on calculation of Jarque-Bera statistics with comparison to critical values, as shown in Table 1. Overall the skewness, kurtosis, and Jarque-Bera test values support the statement that the residuals are not normally distributed. Based on this statistical analysis the Quasi-Maximum Likelihood Estimator (QMLE), a sufficient condition for multivariate volatility models, will be applied for the purposes of further volatility GARCH model analysis.

3.1. Tests of the Normality of Sample Data

The first stage in the data analysis is to test whether the time series are stationary. In the data analysis of the series, we employ informal and formal tests of stationarity. The one informal test is classified as the preliminary visual (graphical) examination of the series. This allows the identification of any structural breaks and gives an idea of the trends evident in the dataset. Figure 1 shows that all variables become stationary with the first difference as fluctuations around mean zero are observable. Volatility, measured by the standard deviation of daily returns, shows that Polish and Estonian stock markets are the most volatile in pre-EU periods. For the post-EU period they are Cyprus, Romania, and Hungary. The market with the lowest volatility is Malta in both periods. The graph of the return series clearly shows volatility clustering, where large (small) changes tend to be followed by large (small) changes of either sign. The volatility clustering absorbs both good (positive variation) and bad (negative oscillation) news. This graph shows some common trends, which occur during certain periods of time, such as the 1998 Russian crisis, the late 1990s/early 2000s internet "bubble," the 9/11 terrorist attacks on the World Trade Centre, the 2007 global financial market turmoil, and the 2009 world financial downturn.

3.2. Non-Stationarity of the Time Series

A necessary condition in the time series analysis is to test each series for the presence of unit roots, which indicate whether the series are non-stationary and integrated of the same order. As we cannot do this based solely on the visual analysis of the series, as this is an informal test for stationarity, some formal tests should apply. Therefore, this study uses the Augmented Dickey-Fuller test (1981), which is a modified version of the pioneer work of Dickey and Fuller (1979) and the Phillips and Perron (1988) non-parametric test. Both ADF and PP tests examine the null hypothesis: the price series contains a unit root (i.e., testing the series as *I(0)* against a null of *I(1)*). Both tests were performed using the maximum lag length in every case.[2] The results from ADF and PP tests indicate that

[2] Akaike Information Criterion and Schwarz Bayesian Criterion were employed to select the appropriate lag length.

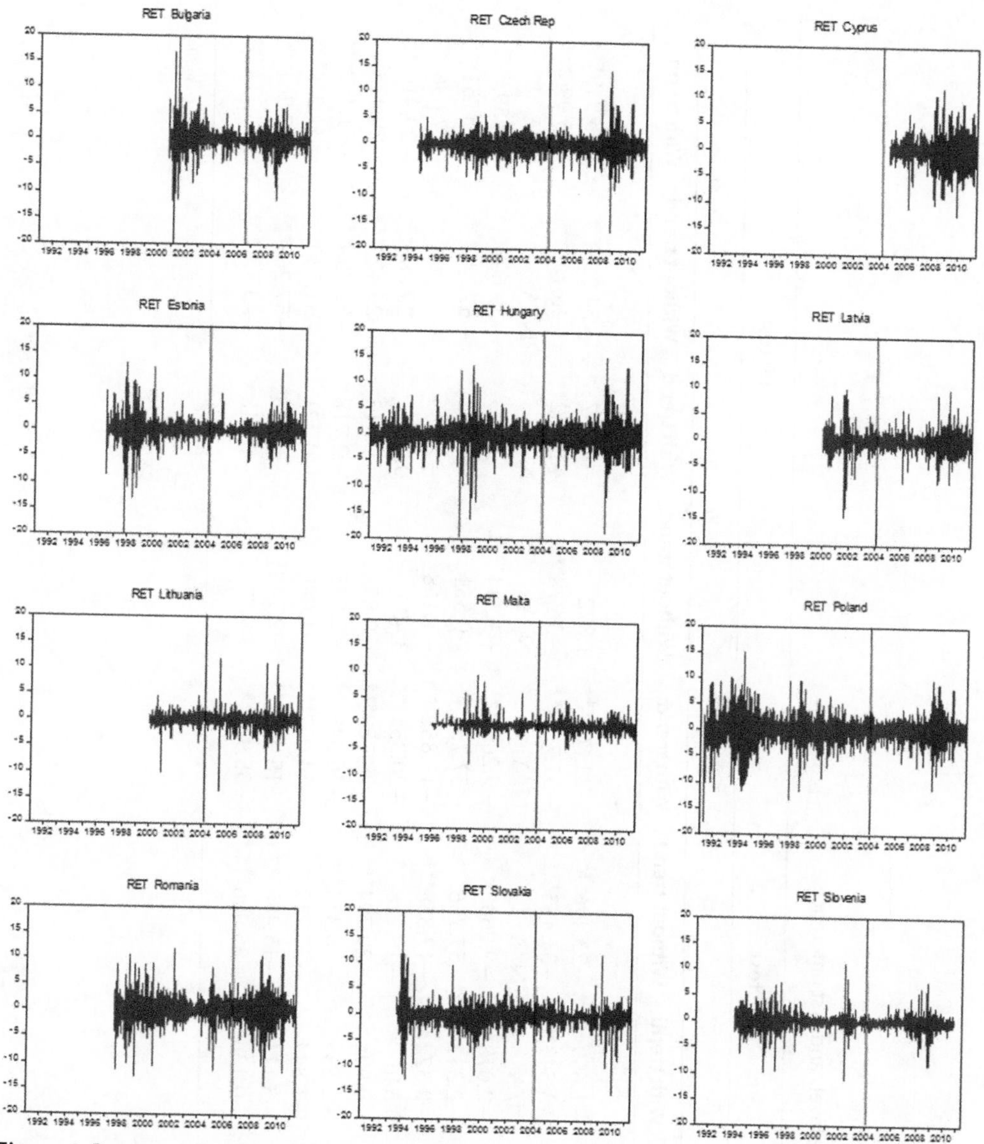

Figure 1 Return series dynamics of stock markets in the CEE. *Note:* Graphs have been divided by a vertical line into two phases showing pre- and post-EU periods.

the series are non-stationary in their levels. However, when all the variables in the series are differenced once, they become stationary.

The unit root test results in Table 2 show all the price series to be first-order integrated (*I(1)*) and the return series to be stationary at the 5% significance level. Moreover, this result is not sensitive to the presence of an intercept term and trend. Hence, the ADF

Table 2 Unit root tests on price levels and first difference.

	ADF test				PP test			
	v_t		Δv_t		v_t		Δv_t	
	Without trend	**With trend**	**Without trend**	**With trend**	**Without trend**	**With trend**	**Without trend**	**With trend**
Pre-EU period								
Bulgaria	1.991	−1.659	−23.496***	−23.663***	1.872	−1.697	−34.029***	−33.949***
Czech Rep	−3.185**	−3.549**	−31.483***	−31.757***	−3.278**	−3.582**	−46.196***	−45.996***
Cyprus	N/A	N/A	N/A	N/A	N/A	N/A	N/A	N/A
Estonia	−2.006	−2.078	−9.263***	−9.265***	−1.344	−1.445	−39.603***	−39593***
Hungary	−0.530	−2.347	−57.756***	−57.758***	−0.551	−2.402	−57.749***	−57.751***
Latvia	−0.951	−2.322	−17.858***	−17.852***	−1.168	−2.880	−27.706***	−27.696***
Lithuania	3.047	0.546	−19.778***	−20.351***	3.403	0.794	−29.886***	−29.910***
Malta	−0.956	−0.994	−29.794***	−29.789***	−0.898	−0.913	−29.429***	−29.423***
Poland	−2.137	−2.559	−36.354***	−36.349***	−2.235	−2.718	−51.499***	−51.492***
Romania	1.419	−1.844	−33.717***	−34.037***	−1.089	−0.721	−31.230***	−31.229***
Slovakia	−2.687*	−3.111	−15.488***	−15.485***	−2.748*	−3.148*	−57.267***	−57.261***
Slovenia	1.357	−0.136	−35.906***	−35.963***	0.977	−0.518	−43.736***	−43.714***

(Continued)

Table 2 (Continued)

	ADF test				PP test			
	v_t		Δv_t		v_t		Δv_t	
	Without trend	With trend	Without trend	With trend	Without trend	With trend	Without trend	With trend
Post-EU period								
Bulgaria	−0.793	−1.116	−10.762***	−10.759***	−0.796	−1.121	−30.653***	−30.638***
Czech Rep	−1.953	−1.803	−31.785***	−31.799***	−1.944	−1.790	−41.098***	−41.107***
Cyprus	−0.821	−1.199	−38.691***	−38.775***	−0.792	−1.189	−38.767***	−38.826***
Estonia	−1.402	−1.419	−20.710***	−20.717***	−1.490	−1.504	−38.983***	−38.968***
Hungary	−2.239	−2.174	−31.263***	−31.266***	−2.177	−2.107	−40.089***	−40.087***
Latvia	−0.963	−1.543	−43.902***	−43.923***	−1.065	−1.589	−44.191***	−44.189***
Lithuania	−1.504	−1.632	−14.988***	−15.022***	−1.584	−1.697	−39.602***	−39.577***
Malta	−1.327	−1.734	−23.189***	−23.311***	−1.370	−1.752	−30.839***	−30.908***
Poland	−1.554	−1.402	−40.453***	−40.452***	−1.590	−1.451	−40.539***	−40.537***
Romania	−1.109	−0.753	−31.159***	−31.166***	−1.089	−0.722	−31.230***	−31.229***
Slovakia	−1.480	−2.921	−42.040***	−42.238***	−1.562	−2.837	−42.614***	−42.596***
Slovenia	−0.421	−0.522	−28.747***	−28.822***	−0.288	−0.527	−30.469***	−30.540***

v_t: variable in levels; Δv_t: variable in first difference.
Critical values/without trend: −3.434 at the 1% level; −2.864 at the 5% level; −2.568 at 10% level.
Critical values/with trend: −3.962 at the 1% level; −3.412 at the 5% level; −3.128 at 10% level.
MacKinnon (1996) one-sided p-value.
Significance levels:
*0.10.
**0.05.
***0.01.

and PP tests clearly indicate that the price series are non-stationary, which concords with economic theory that most economic variables are not stationary at their levels.

3.3. Testing for Serial Correlation

Although there are several tests of autocorrelation, the Breusch-Godfrey (BG) test, also called the Lagrange multiplier (LM) test, has been chosen for the purpose of this study. As it is desirable to examine a joint test for autocorrelation, the BG test will allow examination of the relationship between residuals u_t and several of its lagged values at the same time (the regressed value may appear as an explanatory variable). Moreover, the BG test is a more general test for autocorrelation up to the rth order. As the BG test is sensitive to the lag length, lags have been specified in advance based on Akaike and Schwarz information criteria.

The results from LM and BG tests show that all the markets give enough statistical evidence to support the evidence of serial correlation hypothesis.[3]

3.4. Testing for an Autoregressive Conditional Heteroskedasticity

Prior to running the various models on the data, it is essential to test for evidence of autoregressive conditional heteroscedasticity in the residuals of the 12 time series regressions. This assessment is based on the LM test and this detects the kind of heteroscedasticity that invalidates the Ordinary Least Squares (OLS) statistics. As the actual error terms are unknown and are only estimated, the OLS residual, $\widehat{u}_t$ is an estimate of the error u_t for observation (Lee, 1991).

The heteroscedasticity tests results provide enough statistical evidence to show that the ARCH effect is present in all markets. As the test results are statistically significant, conditional volatility models should be used instead of an OLS regression.[4]

4. MULTIVARIATE GARCH MODELS

The purpose of the empirical analysis is to model the volatility spillovers, asymmetric effects, and conditional correlation across and within the 12 markets, using four multivariate GARCH models, namely CCC, the diagonal BEKK, VARMA-GARCH, and VARMA-AGARCH models. These four models that have been chosen and which are defined below are widely discussed and mathematically proven by McAleer (2005) and McAleer et al. (2008). For multivariate conditional volatility models, McAleer (2005) recommends use of the QMLE estimation technique. Additionally, for the purpose of model identification, fitting and validation of an Autoregressive Moving Average model is used.

[3] The results from LM and BG test are available upon request from authors.

[4] The tests undertaken for this diagnostic test are the ARCH LM test, the Breusch-Pagan-Godfrey test, and the White test (mostly as the decisive test where other two test results were inconclusive). All test results are available upon request from authors.

Let us consider the following specification for the conditional mean and conditional variance for the returns of the stock indices:

$$y_t = E(y_t|F_{t-1}) + \varepsilon_t,$$
$$\varepsilon_t = D_t\eta_t, \tag{1}$$

where y_t is the $n \times 1$ vector of returns, η_t is a sequence of iid random vectors, F_t is the past information available up to time t, $D_t = diag\left(\sqrt{h_{1t}}, \ldots, \sqrt{h_{mt}}\right)$ is a diagonal matrix of conditional variance on historical data (F_t), m is the number of market's index returns, and t is the number of observations for daily returns.

4.1. The Constant Conditional Correlation (CCC) Model

The CCC GARCH model was introduced by Bollerslev (1990). This model assumes that the conditional variance of the shocks to index return, $j, j = 1, \ldots, m$, follows a univariate GARCH (p, q) process defined as:

$$h_{jt} = \omega_j + \sum_{i=1}^{p} \alpha_{ji}\varepsilon_{t-i}^2 + \sum_{i=1}^{q} \beta_{ji}h_{t-i}, \tag{2}$$

where α_{ji} and β_{ji} represent the ARCH effects (the sort persistence of shocks to return j) and the GARCH effects (the contribution of shocks to long run persistence, namely $\sum_{i=1}^{p} \alpha_{ji} + \sum_{i=1}^{q} \beta_{ji}$) respectively. This model assumes the independence of conditional variances; therefore, there are no volatility spillovers except in the calculations of the conditional correlations. And this is because $\Gamma = \{\rho_{ji}\}$ is the matrix of constant conditional correlations given as:

$$\Gamma = D_t^{-1}Q_tD_t^{-1}, \tag{3}$$

where $\rho_{ji} = \rho_{ij}$ for $i, j = 1, \ldots, m$ and each conditional correlation coefficient is estimated from the standardized residuals in equations (1) and (2).[5]

4.2. The Diagonal BEKK

The BEKK model is a preliminary version of Engle and Kroner (1995). The main feature is that it does not need any restrictions on parameters to get positive definiteness of the H_t matrix, given its quadratic structure. In its first-order form, the models can be written as:

$$H_t = C'C + A'\varepsilon_{t-1}\varepsilon_{t-1}'A + B'H_{t-1}B, \tag{4}$$

where A, B, and C are $n \times n$ parameter matrices with C being lower triangle. The elements of matrix A measure the effect of shocks on the conditional variances. The matrix B shows how past conditional variances affect the current levels of conditional variances, so in other words, the degree of volatility persistence in conditional volatility among the markets.

[5] A relationship clarification between conditional correlations and conditional variances is provided in a paper by Engle (2002).

The diagonal BEKK is the simplified version of (4) in which A and B are diagonal matrices. This model trivially satisfies the equation $B = AD$ where D is a diagonal matrix. The elements of the covariance matrix H_t depend only on their own past values and past values of $\varepsilon_t \varepsilon_t'$, which means that the variances depend only on past own squared residuals, and the covariances depend only on past own gross products of residuals.

4.3. VARMA GARCH

To explain the relationship between the volatility across different markets, Ling and McAleer (2003) developed the vector ARMA GARCH model (VARMA GARCH). The authors claimed that h_{jt} should incorporate the interdependence of conditional variances across all markets. That is, h_{jt} should include all past information of ε_{jt} and ε_{it}, where $j \neq i$. Ling and McAleer define the vector specification for the multivariate conditional variance as:

$$H_t = W + \sum_{i=1}^{r} A_i \vec{\varepsilon}_{t-i} + \sum_{j=1}^{s} B_j H_{t-j}, \tag{5}$$

where $H_t = (h_{1t}, \ldots, h_{mt})'$, $\vec{\varepsilon} = (\varepsilon_{it}^2, \ldots, \varepsilon_{mt}^2)'$, and W, A_i and B_j are $m \times m$ matrices (for $i = 1, \ldots, r$ and $i = 1, \ldots, s$ elements, respectively, for matrix A_i and B_j) with typical elements of α_{ji} and β_{ji}. This model assumes that negative and positive shocks of the same magnitude have identical impact on the conditional variance.

4.4. VARMA AGARCH

As an extension of the VARMA GARCH model to accommodate asymmetric behavior of positive and negative shocks, Chan et al. (2002) proposed the following specification for the conditional variance, which is simply an extension of equation (5) to accommodate asymmetries with respect to ε_{it}:

$$H_t = W + \sum_{i=1}^{r} A_i \vec{\varepsilon}_{t-i} + \sum_{i=1}^{r} C_j I_{t-i} \vec{\varepsilon}_{t-i} + \sum_{j=1}^{s} B_j H_{t-j}, \tag{6}$$

where C_j are $m \times m$ matrices for $i = 1, \ldots, r$ and $I_t = diag(I_{1t}, \ldots, I_{mt})$. Moreover, the indicator variable of I_t is having the same sign as ε_t, and therefore takes the value of 1 if $\varepsilon_t < 0$ and 0 otherwise.

5. EMPIRICAL RESULTS

This section presents the results of models of the volatility and spillover effects of the 12 EU countries studied after applying multivariate GARCH methodology.

5.1. The Constant Conditional Correlation (CCC) Model

As was explained before, in the context of the CCC model the multivariate effects across the 12 data series are determined solely through the constant conditional correlation matrix.

The calculated constant conditional correlations among the 12 markets are summarized in Tables 3–5. The two entries for each pair of markets are their estimates and the Bollerslev-Wooldridge robust *t*-ratio. For the pre-EU period only a few pairs are significant at the 5% level, with the highest being 0.472 between Hungary and Poland. The other two high values of 0.455 and 0.416 are parameter estimates for the Czech Republic—Poland and the Czech Republic—Hungary respectively. All other significant values are less than 0.267. Please note that this highly significant relationship exists for the three main CEE studied countries of the Czech Republic, Hungary, and Poland. These three show that a relationship exists between the other markets of Estonia, Latvia, Lithuania, Romania, and Slovenia. Thus it is worth mentioning that the Estonian stock market shows a number of significant conditional correlations between itself and five other markets.

For the post-EU: 2004–2011 period the number of significant relationships increases, though the highest value belongs to the same pair of markets, namely: Hungary—Poland with a coefficient of 0.701. Very strong conditional correlations are recorded as well for the Czech Republic—Hungary (0.626) and the Czech Republic—Poland (0.671). It is also worth a mention that the Bulgarian, Cyprus, Estonian, and Romanian markets show a number of significant relationships between each other and other markets. Even though most of the markets report the existence of conditional correlations (cross-market relationships), Malta and Slovakia stay isolated from the others as well as from each other.

There are plenty of similarities between both post-EU periods, with the only difference being that the estimated parameters for post-EU: 2007–2011 are even higher, so the relationships in conditional correlations are even stronger. The other difference is that Cyprus takes a prime role between the Czech Republic, Hungary, and Poland with correlation coefficients of 0.525, 0.456, and 0.529, respectively. Next to Cyprus, the Romanian stock markets show a very strong relationship with Cyprus (0.425), the Czech Republic (0.539), Hungary (0.491), and Poland (0.522).

The second panel of Tables 3–5 show the CCC GARCH parameters' estimates. Here it is observable that ARCH and GARCH effects are significant for most of the 12 countries with only a few exceptions. These are: the parameters of β for Slovenia in pre-EU period and α and β for Slovakia in both post-EU periods. These results are very similar to the GARCH (1,1) model, which was described earlier in this chapter. This is the GARCH effect which is taking the major role in the modeling of volatility spillover effects among the stock markets.

5.2. The Diagonal BEKK

To circumvent the restrictive assumption of a constant correlation between the conditional volatilities, the diagonal BEKK model is estimated. With the diagonal BEKK model we examine results of the time-varying variance-covariance equation (4) in the system of the 12 markets. The values reported in the tables below illustrate the relationship in terms of shocks and volatility spillovers lying on diagonal (elements of α and β), and conditional covariance via the off diagonal elements.

Table 3 Multivariate regression analysis results for CCC GARCH (1, 1) model; pre-EU: 1995–2004.

	Bulgaria	Czech Rep.	Estonia	Hungary	Latvia	Lithuania	Malta	Poland	Romania	Slovakia	Slovenia
Panel A: constant conditional correlation matrix											
Bulgaria	1										
Czech Rep	0.011	1									
	(0.312)										
Estonia	**0.072**	**0.267**	1								
	(2.101)	**(8.417)**									
Hungary	0.013	**0.455**	**0.245**	1							
	(0.386)	**(16.143)**	**(7.511)**								
Latvia	0.043	**0.121**	**0.094**	**0.112**	1						
	(1.241)	**(3.439)**	**(2.567)**	**(3.397)**							
Lithuania	0.013	**0.079**	**0.206**	0.045	0.033	1					
	(0.414)	**(2.405)**	**(6.736)**	(1.413)	(0.902)						
Malta	0.043	0.024	0.057	**0.064**	0.022	0.007	1				
	(1.627)	(0.756)	(1.599)	**(1.973)**	(0.683)	(0.245)					
Poland	−0.026	**0.416**	**0.233**	**0.472**	**0.134**	**0.068**	0.050	1			
	(−0.838)	**(13.753)**	**(7.064)**	**(16.919)**	**(3.177)**	**(2.068)**	(1.597)				
Romania	−0.041	**0.123**	0.064	**0.180**	**0.097**	0.036	0.025	**0.181**	1		
	(−1.231)	**(3.820)**	(1.851)	**(5.805)**	**(3.118)**	(0.923)	(0.830)	**(5.122)**			
Slovakia	0.003	−0.028	−0.043	−0.024	0.000	−0.041	0.007	0.026	−0.012	1	
	(0.099)	(−0.759)	(−1.483)	(−0.755)	(0.009)	(−1.240)	(0.245)	(0.718)	(−0.385)		
Slovenia	0.040	**0.078**	**0.071**	**0.111**	0.025	−0.031	0.021	0.037	0.037	0.043	1
	(1.448)	**(2.885)**	**(2.326)**	**(3.957)**	(0.820)	(−1.272)	(0.684)	(1.247)	(1.152)	(0.840)	

(Continued)

Table 3 (Continued)

	Bulgaria	Czech Rep.	Estonia	Hungary	Latvia	Lithuania	Malta	Poland	Romania	Slovakia	Slovenia
Panel B: CCC GARCH model estimates											
ω	0.066	**0.084**	**0.080**	0.292	**0.117**	0.370	**0.078**	0.299	0.021	0.278	**0.168**
	(1.618)	**(2.573)**	**(2.885)**	(1.845)	**(2.740)**	(1.866)	**(3.572)**	(1.872)	(1.686)	(1.919)	**(1.999)**
α	**0.122**	**0.064**	**0.126**	**0.072**	**0.212**	**0.193**	**0.157**	**0.078**	**0.081**	**0.149**	**1.245**
	(2.941)	**(3.349)**	**(3.648)**	**(2.520)**	**(3.083)**	**(2.150)**	**(3.418)**	**(2.322)**	**(2.327)**	**(2.323)**	**(2.059)**
β	**0.884**	**0.886**	**0.803**	**0.791**	**0.747**	**0.368**	**0.667**	**0.789**	**0.915**	**0.678**	0.194
	(32.641)	**(26.540)**	**(17.356)**	**(8.646)**	**(10.958)**	**(2.550)**	**(10.478)**	**(8.347)**	**(31.107)**	**(5.285)**	(1.270)

Note: the two entries corresponding to each parameter are their estimates and Bollerslev-Wooldridge (1992) robust *t*-ratios in parentheses. Bold denotes significance at 5% level.

Table 4 Multivariate regression analysis results for CCC GARCH (1, 1) model; post-EU: 2004–2011.

	Bulgaria	Cyprus	Czech Rep.	Estonia	Hungary	Latvia	Lithuania	Malta	Poland	Romania	Slovakia	Slovenia
Panel A: constant conditional correlation matrix												
Bulgaria	1											
Cyprus	**0.154**	1										
	(5.862)											
Czech Rep	**0.186**	**0.405**	1									
	(7.549)	**(16.842)**										
Estonia	**0.216**	**0.197**	**0.275**	1								
	(7.935)	**(7.383)**	**(10.118)**									
Hungary	**0.118**	**0.350**	**0.626**	**0.230**	1							
	(4.855)	**(14.103)**	**(35.693)**	**(8.088)**								
Latvia	**0.155**	**0.123**	**0.145**	**0.253**	**0.110**	1						
	(6.007)	**(4.803)**	**(5.798)**	**(8.854)**	**(4.245)**							
Lithuania	**0.225**	**0.176**	**0.289**	**0.379**	**0.240**	**0.222**	1					
	(9.229)	**(6.259)**	**(9.630)**	**(9.197)**	**(9.012)**	**(7.382)**						
Malta	0.035	0.023	0.016	0.025	0.035	0.043	**0.055**	1				
	(1.347)	(0.854)	(0.599)	(1.252)	(1.323)	(1.715)	**(2.283)**					
Poland	**0.174**	**0.396**	**0.671**	**0.247**	**0.701**	**0.119**	**0.248**	0.037	1			
	(6.979)	**(15.826)**	**(39.194)**	**(8.966)**	**(45.596)**	**(4.517)**	**(8.767)**	(1.495)				
Romania	**0.224**	**0.324**	**0.412**	**0.257**	**0.363**	**0.016**	**0.246**	0.036	**0.400**	1		
	(8.390)	**(12.588)**	**(16.572)**	**(10.073)**	**(15.154)**	**(6.872)**	**(7.394)**	(1.280)	**(15.999)**			
Slovakia	0.051	0.031	0.048	**0.084**	0.045	0.017	**0.063**	−0.014	0.008	0.048	1	
	(1.577)	(0.935)	(1.334)	(2.710)	(1.503)	(0.551)	(2.315)	(−0.490)	(0.241)	(1.566)		
Slovenia	**0.201**	**0.163**	**0.175**	**0.192**	**0.119**	**0.027**	**0.186**	0.026	**0.162**	**0.238**	0.009	1
	(7.227)	**(6.591)**	**(6.732)**	**(8.069)**	**(4.477)**	**(4.574)**	**(7.014)**	(0.908)	**(6.011)**	**(7.669)**	(0.361)	

(Continued)

Table 4 (Continued)

	Bulgaria	Cyprus	Czech Rep.	Estonia	Hungary	Latvia	Lithuania	Malta	Poland	Romania	Slovakia	Slovenia
Panel B: CCC GARCH model estimates												
ω	**0.053**	**0.043**	**0.095**	**0.017**	**0.105**	**0.035**	**0.110**	**0.101**	**0.073**	**0.379**	**1.174**	**0.041**
	(4.507)	**(3.226)**	**(5.029)**	**(2.880)**	**(3.472)**	**(2.204)**	**(2.531)**	**(3.807)**	**(3.950)**	**(3.446)**	**(4.585)**	**(3.601)**
α	**0.280**	**0.073**	**0.094**	**0.090**	**0.075**	**0.091**	**0.175**	**0.278**	**0.046**	**0.180**	0.130	**0.224**
	(7.431)	**(5.482)**	**(5.116)**	**(4.578)**	**(4.721)**	**(4.014)**	**(5.336)**	**(5.420)**	**(4.457)**	**(3.650)**	(1.906)	**(5.420)**
β	**0.727**	**0.918**	**0.859**	**0.902**	**0.894**	**0.896**	**0.756**	**0.582**	**0.924**	**0.730**	−0.040	**0.738**
	(24.057)	**(67.187)**	**(42.830)**	**(44.139)**	**(43.897)**	**(34.605)**	**(10.764)**	**(8.644)**	**(63.497)**	**(11.907)**	(−1.578)	**(19.310)**

Note: the two entries corresponding to each parameter are their estimates and Bollerslev-Wooldridge (1992) robust *t*-ratios in parentheses. Bold denotes significance at 5% level.

Table 5 Multivariate regression analysis results for CCC GARCH (1, 1) model; post-EU: 2007–2011.

	Bulgaria	Cyprus	Czech Rep.	Estonia	Hungary	Latvia	Lithuania	Malta	Poland	Romania	Slovakia	Slovenia
Panel A: constant conditional correlation matrix												
Bulgaria	1											
Cyprus	**0.199**	1										
	(5.987)											
Czech Rep	**0.268**	**0.525**	1									
	(8.779)	**(19.345)**										
Estonia	**0.308**	**0.245**	**0.366**	1								
	(10.792)	**(7.732)**	**(12.388)**									
Hungary	**0.193**	**0.456**	**0.660**	**0.294**	1							
	(6.482)	**(15.899)**	**(31.346)**	**(8.705)**								
Latvia	**0.229**	**0.156**	**0.192**	**0.309**	**0.129**	1						
	(7.007)	**(4.693)**	**(5.999)**	**(10.169)**	**(3.780)**							
Lithuania	**0.317**	**0.253**	**0.381**	**0.541**	**0.317**	**0.325**	1					
	(10.789)	**(7.993)**	**(12.181)**	**(13.882)**	**(9.710)**	**(10.853)**						
Malta	0.056	0.012	0.041	0.069	0.055	0.053	**0.084**	1				
	(1.633)	(0.342)	(1.221)	(1.856)	(1.623)	(1.498)	**(2.562)**					
Poland	**0.243**	**0.529**	**0.736**	**0.313**	**0.724**	**0.134**	**0.339**	**0.069**	1			
	(7.754)	**(19.752)**	**(43.383)**	**(10.197)**	**(39.609)**	**(3.863)**	**(10.772)**	**(2.286)**				
Romania	**0.295**	**0.452**	**0.539**	**0.331**	**0.491**	**0.233**	**0.382**	0.063	**0.522**	1		
	(9.306)	**(14.846)**	**(19.975)**	**(10.291)**	**(18.871)**	**(7.329)**	**(11.514)**	(1.752)	**(18.976)**			
Slovakia	0.032	−0.005	0.018	**0.076**	0.014	0.010	0.044	−0.034	0.007	0.053	1	
	(0.951)	(−0.143)	(0.465)	**(2.346)**	(0.412)	(0.289)	(1.566)	(−1.093)	(0.190)	(1.525)		
Slovenia	**0.283**	**0.188**	**0.210**	**0.270**	**0.168**	**0.202**	**0.270**	**0.069**	**0.192**	**0.302**	0.020	1
	(8.967)	**(5.763)**	**(6.485)**	**(9.566)**	**(5.188)**	**(5.792)**	**(8.564)**	**(2.093)**	**(5.757)**	**(7.757)**	(0.547)	

(*Continued*)

Table 5 (Continued)

	Bulgaria	Cyprus	Czech Rep.	Estonia	Hungary	Latvia	Lithuania	Malta	Poland	Romania	Slovakia	Slovenia
Panel B: CCC GARCH model estimates												
ω	**0.105**	**0.032**	**0.084**	**0.052**	**0.091**	0.011	**0.082**	**0.145**	**0.072**	**0.397**	0.006	**0.077**
	(3.440)	**(2.270)**	**(4.398)**	**(2.895)**	**(2.763)**	(1.360)	**(2.866)**	**(3.736)**	**(3.053)**	**(2.143)**	(1.367)	**(3.364)**
α	**0.270**	**0.047**	**0.095**	**0.083**	**0.086**	**0.065**	**0.149**	**0.301**	**0.056**	**0.140**	0.027	**0.215**
	(5.439)	**(4.676)**	**(4.630)**	**(3.645)**	**(4.342)**	**(3.497)**	**(5.349)**	**(4.082)**	**(4.611)**	**(2.203)**	(1.843)	**(4.895)**
β	**0.709**	**0.950**	**0.875**	**0.896**	**0.895**	**0.934**	**0.805**	**0.423**	**0.923**	**0.778**	**0.974**	**0.733**
	(14.877)	**(102.728)**	**(46.328)**	**(36.480)**	**(41.977)**	**(49.120)**	**(19.062)**	**(4.159)**	**(60.763)**	**(9.018)**	**(76.432)**	**(16.496)**

Note: the two entries corresponding to each parameter are their estimates and Bollerslev-Wooldridge (1992) robust *t*-ratios in parentheses. Bold denotes significance at 5% level.

Table 6 Multivariate regression analysis results for diagonal BEKK model; pre-EU: 1995–2004.

	Bulgaria	Czech Rep.	Estonia	Hungary	Latvia	Lithuania	Malta	Poland	Romania	Slovakia	Slovenia
Panel A: covariance matrix											
Bulgaria	–										
Czech Rep	0.007										
	(1.352)	–									
Estonia	0.007	**0.053**									
	(1.183)	**(4.060)**	–								
Hungary	0.003	**0.069**	**0.045**								
	(0.889)	**(2.404)**	**(4.239)**	–							
Latvia	0.002	**0.020**	**0.011**	**0.021**							
	(0.746)	**(2.728)**	**(2.121)**	**(3.126)**	–						
Lithuania	0.008	**0.034**	**0.048**	0.018	0.006						
	(0.476)	**(1.969)**	**(2.944)**	(1.323)	(0.608)	–					
Malta	0.005	0.007	0.006	0.015	0.006	0.000					
	(0.588)	(0.925)	(0.905)	(1.691)	(0.781)	(0.052)	–				
Poland	−0.001	**0.084**	**0.057**	**0.098**	**0.035**	0.029	0.014				
	(−0.251)	**(2.693)**	**(4.038)**	**(2.861)**	**(3.169)**	(1.618)	(1.626)	–			
Romania	−0.001	**0.017**	0.005	**0.023**	0.002	0.008	0.001	**0.036**			
	(−0.593)	**(2.543)**	(1.072)	**(2.929)**	(0.606)	(0.566)	(0.098)	**(2.844)**	–		
Slovakia	0.007	−0.005	−0.009	−0.003	−0.002	−0.016	0.003	0.009	0.000		
	(1.042)	(−0.576)	(−1.394)	(−0.421)	(−0.313)	(−1.101)	(0.457)	(0.807)	(−0.058)	–	
Slovenia	0.226	**0.102**	**0.073**	**0.157**	0.079	−0.009	0.009	0.057	0.063	0.054	
	(0.560)	**(2.745)**	**(0.011)**	**(3.374)**	(1.583)	(−0.377)	(0.431)	(1.341)	(1.836)	(1.054)	–

(Continued)

Table 6 (Continued)

	Bulgaria	Czech Rep.	Estonia	Hungary	Latvia	Lithuania	Malta	Poland	Romania	Slovakia	Slovenia
Panel B: BEKK model estimates											
ω	0.008	0.146	**0.094**	**0.143**	**0.064**	**0.369**	**0.131**	**0.248**	**0.021**	0.210	**0.486**
	(0.817)	(1.950)	**(3.432)**	**(2.130)**	**(2.411)**	**(2.900)**	**(4.420)**	**(2.256)**	**(2.014)**	(1.870)	**(2.582)**
α	**0.148**	**−0.096**	**0.253**	**−0.065**	**0.258**	**0.281**	**0.381**	**−0.152**	**0.196**	**0.228**	**0.598**
	(4.725)	**(−3.751)**	**(7.523)**	**(−2.753)**	**(5.126)**	**(3.886)**	**(6.970)**	**(−4.365)**	**(4.356)**	**(4.389)**	**(5.672)**
β	**0.988**	**0.953**	**0.921**	**0.964**	**0.950**	**0.686**	**0.742**	**0.931**	**0.978**	**0.902**	**−0.241**
	(251.622)	**(40.518)**	**(47.970)**	**(58.811)**	**(63.237)**	**(7.358)**	**(13.481)**	**(31.345)**	**(113.667)**	**(19.181)**	**(−2.435)**

Note: the two entries corresponding to each parameter are their estimates and Bollerslev-Wooldridge (1992) robust *t*-ratios in parentheses. Bold denotes significance at 5% level.

Table 7 Multivariate regression analysis results for diagonal BEKK model; post-EU: 2004–2011.

	Bulgaria	Cyprus	Czech Rep.	Estonia	Hungary	Latvia	Lithuania	Malta	Poland	Romania	Slovakia	Slovenia
Panel A: covariance matrix												
Bulgaria	–											
Cyprus	−0.001											
	−(0.433)	–										
Czech Rep	−0.001	**0.012**										
	(−0.425)	**(4.158)**	–									
Estonia	0.001	0.001	**0.004**									
	(0.940)	(1.002)	**(1.986)**	–								
Hungary	−0.002	**0.008**	**0.025**	**0.004**								
	(−0.913)	**(3.041)**	**(5.168)**	**(2.257)**	–							
Latvia	0.001	0.002	0.002	**0.003**	0.001							
	(0.767)	(1.093)	(1.227)	**(2.217)**	(0.714)	–						
Lithuania	**0.005**	**0.007**	**0.011**	**0.013**	**0.017**	**0.009**						
	(2.026)	**(2.042)**	**(2.893)**	**(4.413)**	**(3.472)**	**(3.034)**	–					
Malta	0.005	0.009	0.006	0.004	0.019	0.012	0.005					
	(0.633)	(0.735)	(0.650)	(0.559)	(1.469)	(1.414)	(0.695)	–				
Poland	0.001	**0.007**	**0.021**	**0.004**	**0.025**	0.002	**0.011**	0.014				
	(0.422)	**(3.263)**	**(5.347)**	**(2.419)**	**(4.813)**	(1.095)	**(3.121)**	(1.337)	–			
Romania	0.002	**0.010**	**0.013**	**0.006**	**0.016**	0.005	**0.013**	0.006	**0.014**			
	(0.786)	**(2.513)**	**(3.346)**	**(2.466)**	**(3.444)**	(1.719)	**(2.493)**	(0.417)	**(3.546)**	–		
Slovakia	**0.003**	0.000	0.001	**0.004**	0.001	−0.001	**0.005**	0.004	−0.001	0.002		
	(3.022)	(0.561)	(0.820)	**(3.499)**	(0.682)	(−0.797)	**(2.703)**	(0.493)	−(0.657)	(1.678)	–	
Slovenia	0.001	0.003	0.002	0.002	0.000	0.001	0.001	−0.004	0.003	**0.007**	0.000	
	(0.404)	(1.510)	(0.944)	(1.209)	(−0.125)	(0.510)	(0.475)	(−0.560)	(1.516)	**(2.171)**	(−0.224)	–

(Continued)

Table 7 (Continued)

	Bulgaria	Cyprus	Czech Rep.	Estonia	Hungary	Latvia	Lithuania	Malta	Poland	Romania	Slovakia	Slovenia
Panel B: BEKK model estimates												
ω	**0.014**	**0.017**	**0.038**	**0.018**	**0.046**	**0.025**	**0.078**	**0.242**	**0.032**	**0.082**	0.003	**0.022**
	(4.368)	**(3.705)**	**(5.559)**	**(5.074)**	**(4.081)**	**(3.205)**	**(6.887)**	**(6.509)**	**(4.730)**	**(4.543)**	(0.927)	**(4.727)**
α	**0.220**	**0.142**	**0.197**	**0.196**	**0.148**	**0.193**	**0.280**	**0.537**	**0.145**	**0.179**	**− 0.108**	**0.327**
	(12.342)	**(11.165)**	**(10.118)**	**(9.717)**	**(7.907)**	**(9.044)**	**(8.664)**	**(9.541)**	**(8.892)**	**(8.974)**	**(−5.464)**	**(13.907)**
β	**0.974**	**0.988**	**0.973**	**0.975**	**0.983**	**0.976**	**0.934**	**0.594**	**0.984**	**0.974**	**0.994**	**0.937**
	(279.155)	**(567.603)**	**(293.065)**	**(279.514)**	**(308.753)**	**(203.441)**	**(111.873)**	**(8.917)**	**(360.749)**	**(186.818)**	**(365.879)**	**(132.965)**

Note: the two entries corresponding to each parameter are their estimates and Bollerslev-Wooldridge (1992) robust *t*-ratios in parentheses. Bold denotes significance at 5% level.

Table 8 Multivariate regression analysis results for diagonal BEKK model; post-EU: 2007–2011.

	Bulgaria	Cyprus	Czech Rep.	Estonia	Hungary	Latvia	Lithuania	Malta	Poland	Romania	Slovakia	Slovenia
Panel A: covariance matrix												
Bulgaria	–											
Cyprus	0.000	–										
	(0.014)											
Czech Rep	0.003	**0.032**	–									
	(1.117)	**(5.769)**										
Estonia	**0.010**	**0.014**	**0.021**	–								
	(3.034)	**(2.659)**	**(4.266)**									
Hungary	0.002	**0.026**	**0.036**	**0.020**	–							
	(0.439)	**(4.739)**	**(6.060)**	**(3.932)**								
Latvia	0.003	0.003	0.002	**0.013**	0.002	–						
	(1.421)	(0.981)	(0.777)	**(3.587)**	(0.488)							
Lithuania	**0.010**	**0.014**	**0.016**	**0.034**	**0.019**	**0.012**	–					
	(3.037)	**(2.218)**	**(3.942)**	**(7.073)**	**(3.845)**	**(3.514)**						
Malta	0.017	0.010	0.017	0.018	0.024	0.017	0.014	–				
	(1.742)	(0.605)	(1.263)	(1.705)	(1.572)	(1.591)	(1.431)					
Poland	0.005	**0.026**	**0.039**	**0.019**	**0.044**	0.002	**0.017**	0.027	–			
	(1.717)	**(4.852)**	**(6.094)**	**(4.148)**	**(6.001)**	(0.613)	**(4.049)**	(1.876)				
Romania	**0.022**	**0.101**	**0.072**	**0.041**	**0.081**	**0.020**	**0.036**	0.014	**0.085**	–		
	(2.620)	**(5.946)**	**(6.155)**	**(4.182)**	**(5.206)**	**(2.354)**	**(4.200)**	(0.786)	**(6.395)**			
Slovakia	0.001	0.001	0.002	0.003	0.001	0.000	0.002	−0.005	0.000	0.005	–	
	(1.034)	(0.454)	(1.060)	(1.340)	(0.474)	(−0.383)	(1.129)	(−0.498)	(0.257)	(0.917)		
Slovenia	**0.018**	0.019	0.012	**0.027**	0.008	0.011	**0.012**	0.006	0.014	**0.039**	0.004	–
	(2.707)	(1.933)	(1.690)	**(3.509)**	(0.891)	(1.906)	**(2.158)**	(0.625)	(1.787)	**(3.469)**	(1.277)	

(*Continued*)

Table 8 (Continued)

	Bulgaria	Cyprus	Czech Rep.	Estonia	Hungary	Latvia	Lithuania	Malta	Poland	Romania	Slovakia	Slovenia
Panel B: BEKK model estimates												
ω	**0.019**	**0.055**	**0.055**	**0.078**	**0.066**	**0.016**	**0.061**	**0.188**	**0.058**	**0.336**	**0.005**	**0.105**
	(4.513)	**(4.577)**	**(6.431)**	**(6.505)**	**(6.477)**	**(4.123)**	**(7.441)**	**(10.985)**	**(5.293)**	**(7.904)**	**(21.352)**	**(6.635)**
α	**0.194**	**0.131**	**0.208**	**0.160**	**0.184**	**0.174**	**0.224**	**0.451**	**0.157**	**0.257**	−0.014	**0.406**
	(20.211)	**(15.626)**	**(27.009)**	**(16.045)**	**(23.831)**	**(18.226)**	**(23.537)**	**(15.145)**	**(18.955)**	**(18.257)**	−(1.058)	**(18.144)**
β	**0.977**	**0.990**	**0.970**	**0.968**	**0.977**	**0.983**	**0.955**	**0.650**	**0.980**	**0.929**	**0.999**	**0.875**
	(468.162)	**(813.010)**	**(413.091)**	**(244.928)**	**(532.163)**	**(547.273)**	**(248.508)**	**(20.118)**	**(420.521)**	**(119.918)**	**(5460.578)**	**(69.430)**

Note: the two entries corresponding to each parameter are their estimates and Bollerslev-Wooldridge (1992) robust t-ratios in parentheses. Bold denotes significance at 5% level.

The diagonal elements of α capture the ARCH effects, while the diagonal elements of β measure the GARCH effect. As shown in Tables 6–8, the estimated parameters are all statistically significant with only one exception of the α parameter for Slovakia. The significance of those parameters indicates a strong GARCH (1,1) process which is driving the conditional variance of the 12 markets. In other words, the conditional variance is affected by its own past shocks and volatility.

The off diagonal elements capture cross market effects in the covariance matrix. In Table 6, we find evidence of the pre-EU relationship between markets. The two entries for each pair of markets are their estimated parameters and the Bollerslev-Wooldridge robust *t*-ratio. As in the previous model for the pre-EU period, only a few pairs of markets show significance at the 5% level. This mainly relates to the stock markets of the Czech Republic, Estonia, Hungary, and Poland. In the both post-EU periods, the covariance matrix shows that the cross market relationship exists between markets of the Czech Republic, Cyprus, Estonia, Hungary, Lithuania, Poland, and Romania. The isolated markets of Malta and Slovakia do not interfere with any other markets. The cross market affiliation is limited for Bulgaria, Slovakia, and Latvia.

In the next two sections, multivariate VARMA models will be used to test for the spillover effects of volatility. This will be done using data for eight markets. The decrease in parameters is due to computational problems. In their paper, McAleer et al. (2008, p. 1556) point out that a large number of parameters can cause numerical problems. Moreover "... *not all multivariate GARCH models are able to accommodate convenient two-step estimation methods.*" Unfortunately that was an issue in this analysis, therefore the four markets of Latvia, Lithuania, Malta, and Slovakia are not part of the further analysis.[6] Additionally, the preliminary analysis of the multivariate model has shown that the pre-EU period is going to be calculated from 2000, and not as previously from 1995. This is due to the different commencement dates for the various stock markets' data availability. Even though the pre-EU period becomes shorter by 5 years, there is a large enough number of observations to provide unbiased conclusion for this multivariate analysis.

5.3. VARMA GARCH

Using the data on the eight markets, namely Bulgaria, the Czech Republic, Cyprus, Estonia, Hungary, Poland, Romania, and Slovenia, the volatility spillover effects between markets and direction of the flow of the volatility from one market to another can affect the stock market returns for those countries.

The conditional mean is modeled in each case based on an ARMA (r, s) process. This conditional mean equation gives an aggregate measure of relative risk aversion. The results from this analysis show insignificance autocorrelation in almost every case. For the pre-EU period only Romania seems to show significance in the mean equation, for post-EU:

[6] The elimination process of the four markets is based on the previous volatility modeling of univariate and multivariate GARCH and of cointegration analysis. This is documented that those markets are not cointegrated with others and drifting away from the entire group.

2004–2011 period this is the Polish and Slovenian stock markets, and for post-EU: 2007–2011 period only the Slovenian. In the next step, the conditional volatility is estimated through the two VARMA models of VARMA GARCH and VARMA AGARCH.

In the pre-EU period, the conditional variance is generally affected by its own previous short run (α) and long run (β) shocks. There are a few cross market effects which confirm that volatility spillovers are observed (Table 9). As such, the Czech Republic is affected by previous short run and long run shocks from Hungary; Hungary only affects the Czech Republic through its previous long run behavior. Moreover, the Hungarian stock market is affected by β shocks from Romania and α shocks from Poland. Of all the markets analyzed the Polish one is mainly affected by previous short and/or long shocks in several countries, namely Bulgaria, the Czech Republic, Hungary, Romania, and Slovenia. The least affected are the markets of Estonia and Romania. All in all for the pre-EU period the markets appear to stand in a stronger independent position, showing only minimal cross markets interdependence.

Table 9 Summary of volatility spillovers between pairs of returns series, pre-EU: 1995–2004.

			Number of volatility spillovers			
			VARMA GARCH		VARMA AGARCH	
No.	Returns		ARCH effect	GARCH effect	ARCH effect	GARCH effect
1	Bulgaria	Czech Rep.				
2	Bulgaria	Estonia	1 →		1 →	
3	Bulgaria	Hungary				
4	Bulgaria	Poland	1 ←	1 ←	1 ←	1 ←
5	Bulgaria	Romania				
6	Bulgaria	Slovenia	2 ↔	2 ↔	2 ↔	2 ↔
7	Czech Rep.	Estonia				
8	Czech Rep.	Hungary	1 →	2 ↔		
9	Czech Rep.	Poland		1 ←		1 ←
10	Czech Rep.	Romania				
11	Czech Rep.	Slovenia	1 ←	1 →	1 ←	1 →
12	Estonia	Hungary			1 ←	
13	Estonia	Poland				
14	Estonia	Romania				
15	Estonia	Slovenia	1 →		1 →	1 ←
16	Hungary	Poland	1 →	1 ←	2 ↔	1 ←
17	Hungary	Romania		1 →	1 ←	1 ←
18	Hungary	Slovenia			1 →	
19	Poland	Romania		2 ↔		1 →
20	Poland	Slovenia	1 →		1 →	1 →
21	Romania	Slovenia		1 →		

Note: the symbol → (←) indicates the direction of volatility spillovers from A returns to B returns (B returns to A returns), ↔ means they are interdependent, if left blank means there are no volatility spillovers between pairs of returns.

The post-EU: 2004–2011 period evidence suggests we can observe slightly different relationships between markets. The least affected markets are the Czech Republic and Poland. The first one is affected by α shocks from Bulgaria and β shocks from Hungary and Poland. The other is influenced by α shocks from Bulgaria and Slovenia and β shocks in Slovenia. The most highly affected is the Slovenian stock market, which is influenced by previous short run and/or long run shocks from almost all the studied countries. There

Table 10 Summary of volatility spillovers between pairs of returns series, post-EU: 2004–2011.

			Number of volatility spillovers			
			VARMA GARCH		VARMA AGARCH	
No.	Returns		ARCH effect	GARCH effect	ARCH effect	GARCH effect
1	Bulgaria	Czech Rep.	1 ←	1 →		
2	Bulgaria	Cyprus				
3	Bulgaria	Estonia	1 ←	1 ←	1 →	
4	Bulgaria	Hungary	2 ↔	1 →		
5	Bulgaria	Poland	1 ←		1 ←	1 ←
6	Bulgaria	Romania	1 ←	1 →	1 ←	
7	Bulgaria	Slovenia	1 ←	1 ←		
8	Cyprus	Czech Rep.	1 →	1 →		
9	Cyprus	Estonia	2 ↔	1 →		1 ←
10	Cyprus	Hungary		1 ←		2 ↔
11	Cyprus	Poland				
12	Cyprus	Romania	2 ↔	1 →	2 ↔	1 →
13	Cyprus	Slovenia	1 ←	1 ←	1 ←	2 ↔
14	Czech Rep.	Estonia	1 ←	1 ←	1 →	1 →
15	Czech Rep.	Hungary		2 ↔		1 ←
16	Czech Rep.	Poland		2 ↔	1 ←	
17	Czech Rep.	Romania				
18	Czech Rep.	Slovenia				
19	Estonia	Hungary				
20	Estonia	Poland				1 →
21	Estonia	Romania	1 →			
22	Estonia	Slovenia		1 ←	2 ↔	2 ↔
23	Hungary	Poland		1 →		1 ←
24	Hungary	Romania	1 →		1 →	1 →
25	Hungary	Slovenia		2 ↔		1 ←
26	Poland	Romania	1 ←	1 ←		
27	Poland	Slovenia	1 →	2 ↔	1 →	2 ↔
28	Romania	Slovenia	1 ←	1 ←		

Note: the symbol → (←) indicates the direction of volatility spillovers from A returns to B returns (B returns to A returns), ↔ means they are interdependent, if left blank means there are no volatility spillovers between pairs of returns.

are three market pairs which appear to be affecting each other. They are: Bulgaria—Slovenia, the Czech Republic—Hungary and Poland—Romania. In summary, all the eight markets are generally affected by their own previous short run and long run shocks, plus volatility spillovers are observable.

The other post-EU: 2007–2011 period again shows different results to the previous two periods (Table 11). Thus it is observable that there are no spillover effects between

Table 11 Summary of volatility spillovers between pairs of returns series, post-EU: 2007–2011.

			Number of volatility spillovers			
			VARMA GARCH		VARMA AGARCH	
No.	Returns		ARCH effect	GARCH effect	ARCH effect	GARCH effect
1	Bulgaria	Czech Rep.				
2	Bulgaria	Cyprus				1 ←
3	Bulgaria	Estonia	1 →	1 →		
4	Bulgaria	Hungary	1 ←	1 ←		1 ←
5	Bulgaria	Poland				
6	Bulgaria	Romania	1 ←	1 ←		
7	Bulgaria	Slovenia				
8	Cyprus	Czech Rep.	1 ←		1 →	
9	Cyprus	Estonia	1 ←			
10	Cyprus	Hungary		1 ←	1 ←	1 ←
11	Cyprus	Poland	1 ←		1 ←	
12	Cyprus	Romania	1 ←			1 →
13	Cyprus	Slovenia	1 ←		1 ←	1 →
14	Czech Rep.	Estonia	1 ←	2 ↔	1 ←	1 ←
15	Czech Rep.	Hungary		1 ←		1 ←
16	Czech Rep.	Poland	1 ←	1 ←		
17	Czech Rep.	Romania	1 ←	2 ↔		1 ←
18	Czech Rep.	Slovenia		2 ↔		1 ←
19	Estonia	Hungary				
20	Estonia	Poland				
21	Estonia	Romania	1 →	2 ↔	2 ↔	1 ←
22	Estonia	Slovenia		1 ←		1 ←
23	Hungary	Poland	1 →	1 ←		
24	Hungary	Romania	2 ↔	1 ←	1 ←	1 ←
25	Hungary	Slovenia		2 ↔		2 ↔
26	Poland	Romania	1 ←	1 ←		1 ←
27	Poland	Slovenia	1 ←	1 →		
28	Romania	Slovenia		1 ←	2 ↔	1 ←

Note: the symbol → (←) indicates the direction of volatility spillovers from A returns to B returns (B returns to A returns), ↔ means they are interdependent, if left blank means there are no volatility spillovers between pairs of returns.

Cyprus and any other market. Cyprus is affected only by its own previous short run and long run shocks. There are a few spillover effects between the others, and as such Bulgaria is affected only by one country—Estonia. The Czech Republic is affected by previous past long run shocks from Bulgaria, Romania, and Slovenia. Poland is mostly affected by both α and β from Poland. The most affected is the Hungarian stock market with short and long run past shocks from all but Slovenia.

These different results from both post-EU periods could be related to differences in sample size. The second time frame contains daily observations from a period of 4 years in comparison to 7 years in the first one. This could violate the properties of QMLE for the Multivariate GARCH model in regard to the sample size. Therefore, it would have greater confidence in the results from the post-EU: 2004–2011 period.

5.4. VARMA AGARCH

The estimated results of the VARMA AGARCH model are presented in Tables 9–11. Similar to the previous model, the significant autocorrelation for the conditional mean equation is limited to Slovenia in both post-EU periods and Hungary in the post-EU: 2007–2011 period. The estimates of the conditional variances show significant positive asymmetric effects on the conditional volatility in the one case of Hungary in the pre-EU period, Cyprus, Hungary, Romania, and Slovakia in both post-EU periods, plus Poland in the post-EU: 2004–2011 period.

In terms of multivariate spillover effects on the conditional variance, for the pre-EU period, the markets are mostly affected by their long run shocks (β). The Estonian and Romanian stock markets are also affected by their own short run shocks (α). There is a demonstrable existence of spillover effects between the markets, and as such the most limited influence is on the Czech Republic and Estonia. The first contains long run shocks and the other short run shocks from Slovenia. Interestingly, Hungary is affected by previous short run shocks only from Estonia, Poland, and Slovenia. The most affected one is the Polish stock market and the spillover effects are recorded from previous short run shocks from Bulgaria, Hungary, and Slovenia, and the long run shocks from Bulgaria, the Czech Republic, Hungary, Romania, and Slovenia.

For the post-EU: 2004–2011 period spillover effects exist, but the interdependence is different. As such the least affected this time is Bulgaria, which is influenced only by the previous short run shocks from Estonia. In comparison with the previous time frame, the Czech Republic is no longer affected by Slovenia but by the previous shocks from Cyprus and Estonia. Moreover, the Estonian stock market is not only affected by Slovenia but also by the previous long run shocks from Poland. Similarly the most affected market is Poland and this cross market effect is between this country and five others; namely Bulgaria, the Czech Republic, Hungary, Romania, and Slovenia. The same relationship is observable for the stock market pairs of Bulgaria—Estonia and Bulgaria and Poland (Table 10).

The post-EU: 2007–2011 period is again differentiated from the previous post-EU: 2004–2011 period due to the same reason as defined previously. We can see that the stock markets of Bulgaria and the Czech Republic are affected only by their own previous α (Bulgaria only) and β (both markets) shocks, and no spillover effects are observable. In the previous two time frames, Poland was the most affected of markets, however this time all parameters are not significant, neither for its owns effects nor for the cross market ones. Therefore for the VARMA AGARCH model, the conclusion is made only on the first two time frames.

6. CONCLUSION

In summary, this chapter analyzed the changes in relationships in terms of volatility and spillover effects across the 12 CEE markets. More specifically, four multivariate GARCH models of the conditional variance of CCC, the diagonal BEKK, VARMA-GARCH, and VARMA-AGARCH were examined.

Multivariate VARMA-GARCH models show that spillover effects exist between countries. For each time frame discussed, there is evidence of interdependence between the Czech Republic, Hungary, and Poland and the others. In the multivariate framework, the conditional correlations were estimated showing the interaction among the volatility of market returns. This estimation was calculated via the CCC and the diagonal BEKK models. Overall, the correlation values are high and positive, showing dominance of the three markets of the Czech Republic, Hungary, and Poland; however, the Cyprus, Estonian, Romanian, and Slovenian markets are grouped between those countries that are interdependent between each other and the others.

It is not a surprise that the significant role of the Czech Republic, Hungarian, and Polish markets was evident. This confirms finding in the Campos and Horvath (2012) and Horvath and Petrovski (2013) publications of successful and strong European integration after the fall of communism. Authors agree that these countries are experiencing solid growth and slowly but consistently creating a market-oriented economy. As a result these markets have already been recognized by the FTSE and MSCI groups as advanced emerging markets. Furthermore, Estonia has developed into a strong international player through its membership in the EU. On the other hand, the Maltese and Slovakian stock markets appear to display more self-directed independent behavior than their peers.

As the majority of past studies on stock market comovements and integration have concentrated on mature developed markets or advanced emerging markets, this chapter tested the behavior and inter-relationship of all the CEE emerging markets only. The results show growing investment potential in those equity markets and that they provide good opportunities for European investors as well as important indications for economic stability, growth, and integration of the CEE markets in the post-EU period. No dramatic shocks during the accession phase in the post-EU period have been detected. This could be explained by the fact that those macroeconomic policies have been subject to an adjustment process for a long period of time. Throughout the process of preparing for admission to the EU, these equity markets have been propelled along similar paths (via the joining procedures) to those in developed market economies. Moreover, regional integration among the 12 countries was documented. Given this information, EU-based investors may observe stock market behavior in one group of markets as one investment opportunity instead of single separate classes of assets. Ideally, an investor based in the more developed markets of the EU would like to be able to invest in these Euro-denominated "emerging markets" and benefit from risk diversification. Paradoxically, the diversification benefits appear to be reduced in terms of the findings of increased cointegration. On the other hand, there is also evidence of a lowering of average risk, in terms of variance-based measures post-joining the EU.

These emerging markets are progressing very rapidly in their reforms and stability in domestic economies while in the process of becoming members of the EU. It is to be borne in mind that the aim and the greatest achievement of the creation of the EU is the development of a single market through a standardized system of laws which apply in all member states. Thus restrictions between member countries on trade and free competition have gradually been eliminated. As an outcome of those reforms and expansion, the EU has more influence on the world stage when it speaks with a single voice in international affairs.

A future extension of this study could consider the effects of developed markets on our cointegration analysis with the objective of verifying the assumption that the relationships between emerging EU markets would be broadly preserved.

REFERENCES

Babetski, I., Komarek, L., Komarkowa, Z., 2007. Financial integration of stock markets among new EU member states and the Euro area. Czech Journal of Economics and Finance 57 (7–8), 341–362

Bollerslev, T., 1990. Modelling the coherence in short-run nominal exchange rates: a multivariate generalized ARCH approach. Review of Economics and Statistics 72, 498–505

Bollerslev, T., Wooldridge, J.M., 1992. Quasi-maximum likelihood estimation and inference in dynamic models with time varying covariances. Econometric Reviews 11 (2), 143–172

Bruggemann, R., Trenkler, C., 2007. Are Eastern European countries catching up? Time series evidence for Czech Republic, Hungary and Poland. Applied Economics Letters 14, 245–249

Campos, N., Horvath, R., 2012. Reform redux: measurement, determinants and reversals. European Journal of Political Economy 28, 227–237

Capiello, L., Engle, R.F., Sheppard, K., 2006. Asymmetric dynamics in the correlations of global equity and bond returns. Journal of Financial Econometrics 4 (4), 537–572

Chan, F., Hoti, S., McAleer, M., 2002. Structure and asymptotic theory for multivariate asymmetric volatility: empirical evidence for country risk ratings. Paper Presented to the 2002 Australasian Meeting of the Econometric Society, Brisbane, Australia, July 2002.

Christiansen, C., 2010. Decomposing European bond and equity volatility. International Journal of Finance and Economics 15 (2), 105–122

Cuaresma, J.C., Hlouskova, J., 2005. Beating the random walk in Central and Eastern Europe. Journal of Forecasting 24, 189–201

Dellas, H., Hess, M., 2005. Financial development and stock returns: a cross-country analysis. Journal of International Money and Finance 24, 891–912
Dickey, D.A., Fuller, W.A., 1979. Distribution of the estimators for autoregressive time series with a unit root. Journal of the American Statistical Association 74, 427–431
Dickey, D.A., Fuller, W.A., 1981. Likelihood ratio statistics for autoregressive time series with unit root. Econometrica 49, 1057–1072
Egert, B., Kocenda, E., 2007. Time-varying comovements in developed and emerging European stock markets: evidence from intraday data. William Davidson Institute Working Paper, WP 861, March.
Engle, R., 1982. Autoregressive conditional heteroscedasticity with estimates of variance of UK inflation. Econometrica 50, 987–1008
Engle, R., 2002. Dynamic conditional correlation: a simple class of multivariate generalized autoregressive heteroscedasticity models. Journal of Business and Economic Statistics 20, 229–350
Engle, R.F., Kroner, K.F., 1995. Multivariate simultaneous generalized ARCH. Econometric Theory 11, 122–150
Fedorova, E., Vaihekoski, M., 2009. Global and local source of risk in Eastern Europe emerging stock markets. Czech Journal of Economics and Finance 59, 2–19
Forbes, K.J., Chinn, M.D., 2004. A decomposition of global linkages in financial markets. The Review of Economics and Statistics 86 (3), 705–722
Hanousek, J., Kocenda, E., 2011. Foreign news and spillovers in emerging European stock markets. Review of International Economics 19, 170–188
Harrison, B., Moore, W., 2009. Spillover effects from London and Frankfurt to Central and Eastern European stock markets. Applied Financial Economics 19, 1509–1521
Horvath, R., Petrovski, D., 2013. International stock market integrations: Central and South Eastern Europe compared. Economic Systems 37 (1), 81–91
Hranaiova, J., 1999. Price behaviour in emerging stock markets. Working Paper Series, WP, 9–17.
Jorion, P., Goetzemann, W., 1999. Re-emerging markets. Journal of Financial and Quantitative Analysis 34 (1), 1–32
Kasch-Haroutounian, M., Price, S., 2001. Volatility in the transition markets of Central. Applied Financial Economics 11, 93–105
Kearney, C., Poti, V., 2008. Have European stock becomes more volatile? An empirical investigation of volatilities and correlation in EMU equity markets at the firm, industry and market level. European Financial Management 14, 1–35
Kocenda, E., Egert, R., 2011. Time-varying synchronization of European stock markets. Empirical Economics 40, 393–407
Lee, J.H., 1991. A Lagrange multiplier test for GARCH models. Economics Letters 37, 265–271
Li, H., Majerowska, E., 2008. Testing stock market linkages from Poland and Hungary: a multivariate GARCH approach. Research in International Business and Finance 22, 247–266
Ling, S., McAleer, M., 2003. Asymptotic theory for a vector ARMA-GARCH model. Econometric Theory 19, 280–310
MacKinnon, J., 1996. Numerical distribution functions for unit root and cointegration tests. Journal of Applied Econometrics 11, 601–618
McAleer, M., 2005. Automated inference and learning in modeling financial volatility. Econometric Theory 21, 232–261
McAleer, M., Chan, F., Hoti, S., Lieberman, O., 2008. Generalized autoregressive conditional correlation. Econometric Theory 24, 1554–1583
Phillips, P., Perron, P., 1988. Testing for a unit root in time series regression. Biometrica 75, 335–346
Saleem, K., 2009. International linkages of the Russian market and the Russian financial crisis: a multivariate GARCH analysis. Research in International Business and Finance 23, 243–256
Samitas, A., Kenourgios, D., 2011. Equity market integration in emerging Balkan markets. Research in International Business and Finance 25, 296–307
Scheicher, M., 2001. The comovements of stock markets in Hungary, Poland and the Czech Republic. International Journal of Finance and Economics 6, 27–39
Sola, M., Spagnolo, F., Spagnolo, N., 2002. A test for volatility spillovers. Economics Letters 76, 77–84

Syriopoulos, T., 2007. Dynamic linkages between emerging European and developed stock markets: has the EMU any impact? International Review of Financial Analysis 16, 41–60
Walti, K., 2005. The macroeconomic determinants of stock market synchronisation. Working Paper, Trinity College, Department of Economics, Trinity College, Dublin.
Worthington, A., Higgs, H., 2004. Transmission of equity returns and volatility in Asian developed and emerging markets: a multivariate GARCH analysis. International Journal of Finance and Economics 9, 71–80
Worthington, A., Higgs, H., Katsuura, M., 2000. Price linkages in Asian equity markets and the Asian economic, currency and financial crises. School of Economics and Finance Discussion Paper and Working Paper Series 007. School of Economics and Finance, Queensland University of Technology.

CHAPTER 20

Price Jump Behavior During Financial Distress: Intuition, Analysis, and a Regulatory Perspective

Jan Novotný[*] and Jan Hanousek[†,‡,§]

[*]Centre for Econometric Analysis, Faculty of Finance, Cass Business School, City University London, London, UK
[†]CERGE-EI, Charles University and the Economics Institute of the Academy of Sciences of the Czech Republic Prague, Czech Republic
[‡]The William Davidson Institute, Michigan, USA
[§]CEPR, London, UK

1. INTRODUCTION

The financial literature considers a broad variety of ways to classify market volatility. In the context of this chapter, the most important aspect is the decomposition of volatility into regular noise (the Gaussian-like component) and price jumps.[1] A price jump is understood as an abrupt price change over a very short time, and is related to a broad range of market phenomena that cannot be connected to a noisy Gaussian distribution. The literature supports two main explanations of the source of price jumps. First, Bouchaud et al. (2006) and Joulin et al. (2008) advocate that jumps are mainly caused by a local lack of liquidity on the market, or what they call "relative liquidity." In addition, an inefficient provision of liquidity caused by an imbalanced market micro-structure can cause extreme price movements (see the survey in Madhavan, 2000). Second, price jumps can reflect the market reaction to unexpected information, see Lee and Mykland (2008) and Lahaye et al. (2011), who conclude that news announcements are the primary source of price jumps.[2]

Therefore, price jumps can serve as a proxy for information arrival and be utilized as tools for studying market efficiency (Fama, 1970) or phenomena like information-driven trading, see, e.g., Cornell and Sirri (1992) or Kennedy et al. (2006). Also, a good knowledge of price jump distribution would be useful for financial regulators to implement the most optimal policies, see Becketti and Roberts (1990) or Tiniç (1995). Finally, the non-Gaussian price movements influence the models and indicators employed in

[1] This separation can be seen in the first pioneering papers dealing with price jumps (see, e.g., Merton, 1976 or a summary in Gatheral, 2006). Recently, the division of the Gaussian-like component and price jumps was used by Giot et al. (2010). Although the original motivation for this decomposition was purely of a mathematical nature, it can be advocated by practitioners as well.

[2] They also show a connection between macroeconomic announcements and price jumps on developed markets.

Emerging Markets and the Global Economy
http://dx.doi.org/10.1016/B978-0-12-411549-1.00020-X

finance, such as value-at-risk or the performance of various financial vehicles (Heston, 1993; Bates, 1996; Scott, 1997; Gatheral, 2006).

In this chapter, we analyze how the recent financial crisis influenced the distribution and dynamics of price jumps. In particular, we aim to study to what extent one can observe similarities and transfers of price jumps from developed capital markets to emerging Central and Eastern European (CEE) markets. The choice of studying emerging capital markets in a new EU country is natural. First, compared with other emerging stock exchanges, they do not suffer so much from potential economic and political instability. Second, they are obviously under the strong influence of developed (EU and the US) markets, so causality is clearly one-directional. We will demonstrate some of the general features on the level of the market indexes of the Czech Republic, Hungary, and Poland, and a more detailed analysis will be conducted for the Czech Republic (the Prague Stock Exchange, i.e., PSE).

We choose to pair the New York Stock Exchange (NYSE) with the Prague Stock Exchange (PSE) for multiple reasons: (1) the PSE's overall liquidity and number of traded stocks are rather small, (2) the price formation mechanism at the PSE is under the strong influence of foreign news originating in mature EU and US markets, (3) despite its small size and relative isolation, the share of foreign investors in the PSE overall trading volume is substantial (Hanousek and Kočenda, 2011), and (4) there is no external regulation forcing local pension funds to hold a certain share of local equities in their portfolios. Last but not least, one can also see the selected pair of stock markets from the information-flow point of view: the NYSE is the original source of the financial crisis, while the PSE represents a small CEE emerging market that is under the substantial influence of global markets (e.g., Hanousek et al., 2009). In addition, Dungey et al. (2005) suggest that the opposite direction, i.e., the impact of other markets on the US, is rather non-existent or very weak.

The proper understanding of price jump dynamics and mutual correlation across markets has serious regulatory consequences. The new Basel Accords explicitly stress the importance of the proper correlation modeling of a portfolio during financial distress. On the other hand, the regulatory proposals suggest studying extreme price jump-like events in a case-by-case manner. The correlation structure between extreme events, or drops in the portfolio, may or may not necessarily be connected to the overall correlation structure. A proper understanding of price jump dynamics provides potential insight and could show the way to properly tackle the correlation of markets with respect to extreme events.

It is widely accepted that periods of financial turbulence cause higher volatility on markets as investors tend to overreact to bad signals (Anderson et al., 2007). However, it is still not well described or tested empirically whether and how distributions of price jumps change during a crisis and whether we observe a different pattern on mature/liquid financial markets compared with small emerging markets with relatively low liquidity.

The selected pair of capital markets allows us to study changes in price jump distribution: differences between the markets and differences before and after the crisis. We aim to study not only the behavior of the market indexes, but also the distribution of jumps of selected stocks representing important components of these indexes, all along with possible regulatory consequences.

The chapter is structured as follows. First, as a motivation we employ the market indexes to show that there is a sound reason for potential price jump transfers and overall dynamics between jumps originating in the US that are transferred to the Prague Stock Exchange. Then we analyze the price jump patterns of leading stocks traded on both markets. We analyze whether an overall increase in market volatility during the recent financial crisis occurred. Then, we focus on the price jumps and analyze how the behavior of price jumps changed during the recent financial crisis, particularly the aftermath of the Lehman Brothers collapse. We explicitly test for the temporary and permanent impact of this event on price jump behavior. Finally, we relate the results to a regulatory perspective and compare the change in price jump behavior with those of CDS. Then, a conclusion follows.

2. PRICE JUMPS AND FINANCIAL CRISIS

In this section, we provide a model of log-price dynamics and formalize the effect of financial distress due to the collapse of Lehman Brothers in a model of the volatility and in particular of price jumps. Consequently, the identification of price jumps is elaborated in detail.

2.1. Motivation for Price Jumps

Generally, a price jump is understood as an abrupt price movement that is very large when compared with the current market situation. The advantage of this definition is that it is model-independent: it does not require any specific underlying price-generating process. On the other hand, this definition is too general and rather vague and hence not useful for any statistical inference or testing. Therefore, we will formalize the general approach by assuming that the log-price $Y = \{Y_t\}_{0 \leq t \leq 1}$ is defined on the probability space $(\Omega, \mathscr{F}, (\mathscr{F}_t)_{t \geq 0}, \mathbb{P})$ over the time interval $[0, 1]$. The log-price process is a semi-martingale and its dynamics in continuous time can be specified by the stochastic differential equation:

$$dS_t = \mu_t dt + \sigma_t dW_t + d\mathscr{J}_t, \tag{1}$$

where μ_t and σ_t are processes driving the drift and volatility, dW_t is a standard Brownian motion, and the term $d\mathscr{J}_t$ represents the pure jump Levy process, see, for example, Merton (1976) or Jacod and Shiryaev (1987). In the following, we consider finite activity jumps (Aït-Sahalia and Jacod, 2011) and factorize the Levy processes as $Y_t dJ_t$. The first component corresponds to a random process driving the magnitude of price jumps, while the latter one drives the arrival.

In summary, the term $\sigma_t dW_t$ corresponds to the regular noise component, while the term $Y_t dJ_t$ corresponds to a price jump process. Both terms together form the volatility of the market. Based on this assumption for the underlying process, one can construct price jump indicators, i.e., a statistics used to identify the price jumps and theoretically assess their efficiency. The intuition behind the large body of price jump indicators lies in the difference between Quadratic Variation and Integrated Variation; see the discussion in Dumitru and Urga (2012) and references therein. Quadratic Variation is defined as:

$$QV_t = \int_0^t \sigma_s^2 ds + \sum_{i=1}^{N_t} c_i^2, \tag{2}$$

which estimates the overall volatility in the log-price process over a time interval $[0, t]$, i.e., both the contribution from the continuous-time volatility given by integration over σ_t^2 and N_t price jumps, whose individual sizes are given by c_i.

Integrated Variation, on the other hand, is defined over a time interval $[0, t]$ as:

$$IV_t = \int_0^t \sigma_s^2 ds, \tag{3}$$

where Integrated Variation disregards the contribution of price jumps.

While Quadratic Variation is estimated well by the Realized Variance, conveniently defined for time interval $[0, t]$ sampled into N returns as:

$$RV_t = \sum_{i=1}^{N} r_i^2, \tag{4}$$

the estimation of Integrated Variation is more difficult since one has to disregard all price jumps that are not known a priori. The literature provides several possible ways to treat this problem; see Barndorff-Nielsen and Shephard (2004), Barndorff-Nielsen and Shephard (2006), Andersen et al. (2012), or Mancini (2009). In this study, we employ bipower variance, introduced by Barndorff-Nielsen and Shephard (2004), which is defined for a time interval $[0, t]$ sampled into N equidistant steps as:

$$BV_t = \mu_1^{-2} \sum_{i=2}^{N} |r_i|\,|r_{i-1}|, \tag{5}$$

where $\mu_1 = E(|z|)$, with $z \sim N(0, 1)$. As shown, bipower variance is asymptotically equal to Integrated Variation.

Having in hand the proper methods to estimate Quadratic and Integrated Variation, we may analyze the contribution of price jumps to the total Variation of the price process.

The asymptotic properties of the estimators even allow us to construct explicit statistical tests. Among others, Barndorff-Nielsen and Shephard (2006) and Huang and Tauchen (2005) constructed tests of the difference between Realized and Quadratic Variations, while Lee and Mykland (2008) and Lee and Hannig (2010) used returns normalized by local IntegratedVariation and, together with the results of extreme value theory, estimated excessive returns.

Large price jumps and increased overall volatility typically appear together and the key issue is how to separate these two processes. As shown and discussed later, the distribution of returns and bipower variance could serve as very good identification techniques for detecting price jumps.

2.2. Financial Distress: The Case of Lehman Brothers

In this study, we explicitly focus on the events in the aftermath of the Lehman Brothers collapse. Lehman Brothers filed for bankruptcy on Monday, September 15, 2008. This event is in general considered as the moment when the financial crisis started and was a trigger for further financial problems. See McDonald and Robinson (2009) for more reasons behind the failure. More importantly, this event was not by its nature preceded by a drop in capital markets. We therefore consider this event as an exogenous trigger of the global financial collapse of capital markets.

To understand the impact of a financial event like this, we consider two different periods following the collapse of Lehman Brothers capturing the temporary and permanent effects of the collapse. We thus define the distressed period as a structural break in the sample and use two schemes:

- **Permanent Break (PB):** from September 9, 2008 until the end of the sample, July 31, 2009.
- **Temporary Break (TB):** 30 trading days from September 9, 2008 through October 20, 2008.

Let us note that this definition considers the start of the collapse a week before the filed bankruptcy. This reflects the fact that the bankruptcy itself was preceded by a series of events and consultations that could already have had an impact on financial markets. For robustness we also analyze different definitions of the time frame, but all results carry very similar results.

The PB scheme is intuitive and considers the Lehman Brothers event as a trigger of a deep and long-lasting crisis, which started as a financial crisis and further evolved into an economic crisis. The effect of the collapse is thus permanently present on financial markets at least until the end of July 2009. The TB scheme, however, focuses solely on the most problematic days following the plunge of the markets. The period of 30 working days was chosen based on the news and the behavior of financial markets. The two schemes thus provide different pictures. The PB approach answers the question about a permanent change in the behavior of financial markets, while the TB scheme rather focuses on the immediate panic that spread through the financial markets and affected the trading habits of market participants.

To capture the financial distress formally, i.e., following the data-generating process assumed in equation (1), we define the indicator (dummy) variable F_t, the risk factor indicator that takes a value of one during financial distress—either in the form of Temporary or Permanent Break—and zero otherwise.

First, the stylized facts suggest that the spot volatility σ_t will be a function of F_t, with the following effect:

$$\sigma_t = \sigma_t\left(F_t\right), \quad \text{with} \quad E\left[\sigma_t\left(F_t\right)|F_{t-} = 1\right] > E\left[\sigma_t\left(F_t\right)|F_{t-} = 0\right], \tag{6}$$

which in plain English means that the expected spot volatility during the distress period is strictly bigger than during usual market conditions.

Secondly, the distress period will have an effect on the price jump term as well. There are two possible impacts of distress on $Y_t dJ_t$:

$$\begin{aligned} Y_t = Y_t\left(F_t\right) \quad &\text{with} \quad E\left[\left|Y_t\left(F_t\right)\right| |F_{t-} = 1\right] > E\left[\left|Y_t\left(F_t\right)\right| |F_{t-} = 0\right], \\ dJ_t = dJ_t\left(\lambda_t\left(F_t\right)\right) \quad &\text{with} \quad E\left[\lambda_t\left(F_t\right)|F_{t-} = 1\right] > E\left[\lambda_t\left(F_t\right)|F_{t-} = 0\right], \end{aligned} \tag{7}$$

where the first line means that the magnitude of price jumps increases during distress, while the second line tells us that rate of price jumps increases during distress without influencing anything about the magnitude. The effect of financial distress expressed in (6) and (7) reflects the obvious intuition: financial distress increases market volatility as well as the rate and significance of rare price movements.

In this chapter, we employ the definition of the log-price process (7) and aim to verify the intuition related to the price jump term; in particular, the different arrival rate (distributions) of price jumps during financial distress. For that purpose, we need to define the distress period exogenously and hence we use the collapse of Lehman Brothers as an exogenous factor defining the distressed period. Later, we will use (6) and (7) to statistically analyze to what extent we identify significant differences in the volatility and jump process of (1).

The dependence of the diffusive and price jump terms on the risk factor F_t allows us to analyze the response of the price process across different markets. Our distress model does not contain any explicit correlation across markets since we do not aim to model the immediate response of price jumps in one market to another as was done by Aït-Sahalia et al. (2010). Rather, we use high-frequency data to describe the change in market regimes due to financial distress, where the driver of the distress is believed to be exogenous to the markets and any correlation is therefore realized through the distress factor.

It is worth noting that this provide methodology can be reverted to identify the distress period. Thus, by assuming that the distress period is defined as a regime with increased volatility and increased price jump arrival, or, alternatively, an increased contribution of

Table 1 Price jump indicators: a short overview.

Description/contribution of the test	Source
Bipower variance (BV)-based test statistics	Barndorff-Nielsen and Shephard (2004)
Improved asymptotic properties of tests using delta-method and BV	Huang and Tauchen (2005)
Returns normalized by BV combined with EVT	Lee and Mykland (2008)
Threshold realized variance (TRV)-based test statistics	Mancini (2009)
Improved test based on TRV	Corsi et al. (2010)
Returns normalized by TRV and small price jump detection	Lee and Hannig (2010)
Ratio of realized variances with two sampling frequencies	Aït-Sahalia and Jacod (2009)
Swap-variance-based test statistics	Jiang and Oomen (2008)
Statistical finance-based methods using the scaling behavior of tails	Joulin et al. (2008)
MinRV- and MedRV-based test statistics	Andersen et al. (2012)
Extension of tests to incorporate intraweek volatility periodicity	Boudt et al. (2011)

price jumps to the overall market volatility, we may devise an algorithm to search for a period where these conditions are significantly satisfied. For the purpose of this chapter, however, we work with the exogenously given distress period.

2.3. Identification of Price Jumps

The literature provides a number of different identification techniques to identify the occurrence of price jumps. Table 1 provides an overview of the existing papers with price jump indicators and briefly summarizes the basic principle or contribution of the paper.

In this study, we build on the results of Hanousek et al. (2012), which compares 14 different price jump indicators using an extensive Monte Carlo simulation study. In particular, the study analyzes how well price jump indicators can predict a "real" price jump. Let us note that in any price jump prediction we can make two types of errors: (1) we fail to identify a jump and (2) we incorrectly identify a jump.

The first case—when we fail to identify an existing jump—is similar to the Type-I error in testing. We can rate and compare price jump indicators with respect to their Type-I error, i.e., maximizing the number of correctly identified price jumps, with no penalty for false identification. In the framework of price jumps, this criterion is referred to as optimization with respect to the power of the test; in diagnostic analysis it is usually called the optimization of the false negative probability.

The second case—when we identify a price jump but it does not occur—is similar to the Type-II error in testing. In a comparison of jump indicators we can, therefore, select and use the indicator that minimizes the Type-II error, i.e., the indicator minimizing the false identification of non-occurring price jumps. Let us note that in the literature, this criterion is usually presented as optimality with respect to the size of the test, while in diagnostic analysis it is typically called the optimization of the false positive probability.

Type-I Error-Optimal Price Jump Indicators. In the simulation study Hanousek et al. (2012) shows that the best Type-I error indicator is based on centiles, i.e., price jumps are defined in a similar way as outliers in cross-sectional data. The identification of price jumps is based on Aït-Sahalia and Jacod (2009) and Mancini (2009). The price process is assumed to be decomposed into the Gaussian component, corresponding to normal (white) noise, and the non-homogenous Poisson component, corresponding to price jumps, as follows: $\Delta S = \sigma \Delta X + \Delta J$, where the price increment means $\Delta S = S_t - S_{t-\Delta t}$. We further assume that we observe the realization of price increments in equidistant price steps Δt. In this definition, X corresponds to the Brownian motion and J to a β-stable process. The increments of the two components can be expressed as $\Delta X = (\Delta t)^{1/2} X_1$ and $\Delta J = (\Delta t)^{1/\beta} J_1$ with equalities in distribution.

The different magnitudes of the two components can be used to discriminate between the noise component and big price jumps coming solely from the J-process. Big price jumps cause $\Delta S = \Delta J$ (in distribution) with X having a negligible effect, while in the presence of no big price jumps, which is most of the time, $\Delta S = \sigma(\Delta t)^{1/2} X_1$. Therefore, we can, for a given Δt, choose a threshold value equal to $\alpha(\Delta t)^{\gamma}$, with $\alpha > 0$ and $\gamma \in (0, 1/2)$, such that if $\Delta S > \alpha(\Delta t)^{\gamma}$ then ΔS is at a given moment dominated by J with a certain probability.

This argument can be reversed: assuming a knowledge of the rate of the arrival of big jumps, we can imply a corresponding threshold using centiles. Centiles, therefore, serve as a prior to form a threshold for discriminating price jumps from noise. The overall price volatility changes over the day, therefore we may eventually divide the trading day into blocks, and then form thresholds over the same blocks from different trading days. As we indicated earlier, the "optimal" price jump indicator that minimizes the Type-I error is easy to construct. Jumps are identified when returns are below the $(\alpha/2)$th centile or above the $(1 - \alpha/2)$th centile (centiles are calculated for the entire sample). Let us note that this indicator dominated in nearly all simulation cases.

Type-II Error-Optimal Price Jump Indicators. In the simulation study of Hanousek et al. (2012), the best Type-II error indicators are based on bipower variance, introduced by Barndorff-Nielsen and Shephard (2004), who discuss the role of standard variance, or the second centered moment, in models where the underlying process follows equation (1). In such a case, the standard realized variance captures the contribution from both the noise and the price jump process. In addition, the authors show that there exists a definition for the variance that does not take into account the term with price jumps and call it realized bipower variance.

Bipower variance can be used to define the proper statistics for the identification of price jumps one-by-one. This means testing every time step for the presence of a price jump as defined in equation (1). First, remember the definition of instantaneous quadratic variance calculated based on T preceding observations

$$\sigma_t^2 = \frac{1}{T-1} \sum_{\tau=t-T}^{t-1} r_\tau^2, \tag{8}$$

where returns during a moving window of length T are assumed to be centralized, and the instantaneous bipower variance is defined, according to Barndorff-Nielsen and Shephard (2004), as:

$$\tilde{\sigma}_t^2 = \frac{1}{T-2} \sum_{\tau=t-T+2}^{t-1} |r_\tau| \, |r_{\tau-1}| , \tag{9}$$

where the additional normalization factor of μ_1^{-2} is incorporated in the definitions of C_n and S_n below. We use a notation different from (4) and (5) to stress that we deal with spot quantities based on a moving window.

Let us define the statistics $\mathscr{L}_t$ introduced by Anderson et al. (2007) and further developed by Lee and Mykland (2008) as:

$$\mathscr{L}_t = r_t / \tilde{\sigma}_t. \tag{10}$$

Following Lee and Mykland (2008), for the identification of price jumps we use the variable ξ, which is defined as:

$$\frac{\max_{\tau \in A_n} |\mathscr{L}_\tau| - C_n}{S_n} \to \xi, \tag{11}$$

where A_n is the tested region with n observations and the employed parameters are:

$$C_n = \frac{(2 \ln n)^{1/2}}{c} - \frac{\ln \pi + \ln (\ln n)}{2c(2 \ln n)^{1/2}}, \quad S_n = \frac{1}{c(2 \ln n)^{1/2}}, \quad \text{and } c = \sqrt{2}/\sqrt{\pi}.$$

The variable ξ has in the presence of no price jumps the cumulative distribution function $P(\xi \leq x) = \exp\left(e^{-x}\right)$. The knowledge of the underlying distribution can be used to determine the critical value ξ_{CV} at a given significance level. Whenever ξ is higher than the critical value ξ_{CV}, the hypothesis of no price jump is rejected, and such a price movement is identified as a price jump. In contrast, when ξ is below the critical value, we cannot reject the null hypothesis of no price jump. Such a price movement is then treated as a noisy price movement. These statistics can be used to construct a counting operator for the number of price jumps in a given sample.

In the simulation study of Hanousek et al. (2012), the best Type-II error indicator utilizes ξ-statistics with a 99% confidence interval and $n = 120$. Let us note that this indicator again is dominant in nearly all simulation cases.

3. METHODOLOGY

In this section, we describe how to test the impact of the Lehman Brothers collapse on the price-generating process with a special focus on price jumps. In particular, we identify the price jump using the techniques optimal with respect to Type-I and Type-II errors and test to what extent we observe statistically significant differences for distress and non-distress periods. To be precise, we will use the concept of the binary distress factor F_t, which describes either a Permanent Break or a Temporary Break in the market operation regime due to financial distress, with the number of identified price jumps. The change in the market regime is a low-frequency process—in our case, we assume it happens once or twice in the entire sample. The effect of the particular regime, however, is observable and measurable at a high-frequency level since it affects the dynamics of the log-price process. The provided testing procedures have to reflect the requirement to employ high-frequency data to assess the presence of a regime switch.

First, we employ high-frequency data to estimate the daily distribution of price jumps. For the identification of price jumps we use the two "best" price jump estimators (Type-I error- and Type-II error-optimal) described in Section 2.3. Then we use the binary distress factor F_t, which describes either a Permanent Break or Temporary Break, to answer the following two questions:

Question 1. Does the fall of Lehman Brothers cause a temporary/permanent change in the number of price jumps on financial markets?

Question 2. Does the fall of Lehman Brothers cause a temporary/permanent change in the homogeneity of financial markets with respect to price jump arrivals?

The first question is based on the intuition that an extreme event such as the fall of Lehman Brothers would cause an increase in the overall volatility as well as an increase in the number of extreme price movements. In the second question, we explicitly ask whether the fall of Lehman Brothers caused a change in the distribution of price jumps, for example a higher variability in the arrival rate of price jumps. This means that during financial distress, we are likely to observe days when the rate of price jump arrivals will be extremely high, while there can be days that are rather calm.

To answer the above-mentioned questions we use corresponding statistically testable hypotheses. First, we divide the sample of trading days into two sub-samples according to the Permanent Break and Temporary Break schemes. These two sub-samples correspond to a period of financial distress and standard market conditions. Then, we use the daily figures of arrived price jumps and form the following two hypotheses.

Hypothesis A. H_0: The mean number of price jumps for the two sub-samples, i.e., during and not during distress, is the same.

The main scope of this test is to compare whether the estimated number of price jumps changes during the crisis.

Test. We employ the two-sample Wilcoxon test, which is a non-parametric test comparing whether two observed samples come from the same distribution (Mann and Whitney, 1947; Wilcoxon, 1945). Here we test whether the estimated price jump measures for the two sub-samples come from the same distribution. The observations in each of the two sub-samples are combined into one sample and then ranked. The z-statistics is composed based on the mutual comparison of ranks between the two samples. The z-statistics follows, for large samples,[3] a standard normal distribution. The null hypothesis of the test states that both observed samples come from the same distribution, or there is no significant asymmetry in the rankings for the two groups. When the calculated z-statistics exceeds the critical value, we reject the null hypothesis. In addition, the sign of the z-statistics can suggest the position of the medians of the two compared samples.

Hypothesis B. H_0: The variance in the number of jumps of the two sub-samples, i.e., during and not during distress, is unchanged.

This test asks the question whether the trading days in either of the two sub-samples were on average more heterogeneous. In other words, this procedure tests the heterogeneity of the trading days between the sub-samples.

Test. We employ the standard F-test and compare whether the variance of the estimated price jump measures changed during the crisis. The F-test is defined as:

$$\frac{S_C^2}{S_{No-C}^2} \sim F_{(N_C-1, N_{No-C}-1)}, \tag{12}$$

where S^2 is the standard deviation of the characteristic coefficient calculated during the crisis "C" and not during the crisis "$No - C$." N_C is the number of days the crisis lasts and N_{No-C} is the complement to the total number of days in the sample.

We aim to test these two hypotheses for different markets and segments (market indexes, ETF and/or selected stocks). In particular, we plan to analyze how price jumps in a developed capital market compare with a Central and Eastern European (CEE) market, and how price jumps transfer from one to the other. For a more detailed analysis we choose the Prague Stock Exchange (PSE) in the Czech Republic and the NYSE in the US. There are several reasons why we opt to pair the NYSE and the PSE. First, in terms of information flow, the NYSE is the original source of financial crisis, while the PSE is a small CEE emerging market under the influence of global markets (Hanousek and Kočenda, 2011). Second, the PSE is under the strong influence of developed markets,

[3] Usually above 20 is sufficient, see Mann and Whitney (1947) and Wilcoxon (1945).

so the direction of possible causality must be one-directional. Third, the Czech Republic (and the PSE), representing here a new EU market, does not suffer so much from potential economic and political instability compared with other emerging stock countries and exchanges.

Focusing on the NYSE and PSE allows us to study such changes in the price jump distribution: we can see the differences between these markets and compare the states of each market both before and after the crisis. Our aim is to study the behavior of the market indexes in addition to the distribution of jumps of selected stocks, which are important components of these two indexes.

4. DATA DESCRIPTION

We employ high-frequency data of realized prices for the market indexes and selected stocks from two different stock exchanges: the Prague Stock Exchange (PSE) and the New York Stock Exchange (NYSE). We summarize the selected stocks and descriptive statistics first for PSE stocks and then for NYSE stocks. Data from both stock exchanges cover the period from January 1, 2008 to July 31, 2009 and thus cover a sufficiently long enough period before and after the collapse of Lehman Brothers.

The general picture of volatility and extreme price movements can be visualized using different measures of the variation of the main market indexes. Figure 1 depicts the daily levels in Quadratic Variation during the two sub-samples, financial distress and the standard market period for the PX Index (the left panel) and the S&P 500 Index (the right panel). In addition, both Quadratic and Integrated Variation responded in the same manner, which does not allow us to easily draw conclusions about price jumps without employing more subtle techniques. For illustratory purposes, we accompany the pictures for Quadratic Variation with a difference between the Quadratic and Integrated Variations for both markets, which provides an intuition (but not a reliable statistic) about price jump behavior. In the following, we will in particular focus on the level of the individual assets and estimate the rate of price jumps. From the provided graphics, it is clearly visible that following the collapse of Lehman Brothers the markets became more volatile. The response of the volatility to the distress is a significant increase in levels for the entire stock market index. Further, the response of the US market was much higher compared with the Czech stock market. The US markets reacted more abruptly and the effect of the distress was rather permanent. Clearly, Lehman Brothers was a trigger of a volatile period; however, the crisis gradually worsened as the highest increase in volatility was at the end of the Temporary Break we use in this study. Consequently, the financial distress transmitted into the real economy and economic crisis emerged.

In the following, we focus on the market micro-structure level and employ realized prices for stocks from the PSE and the NYSE.

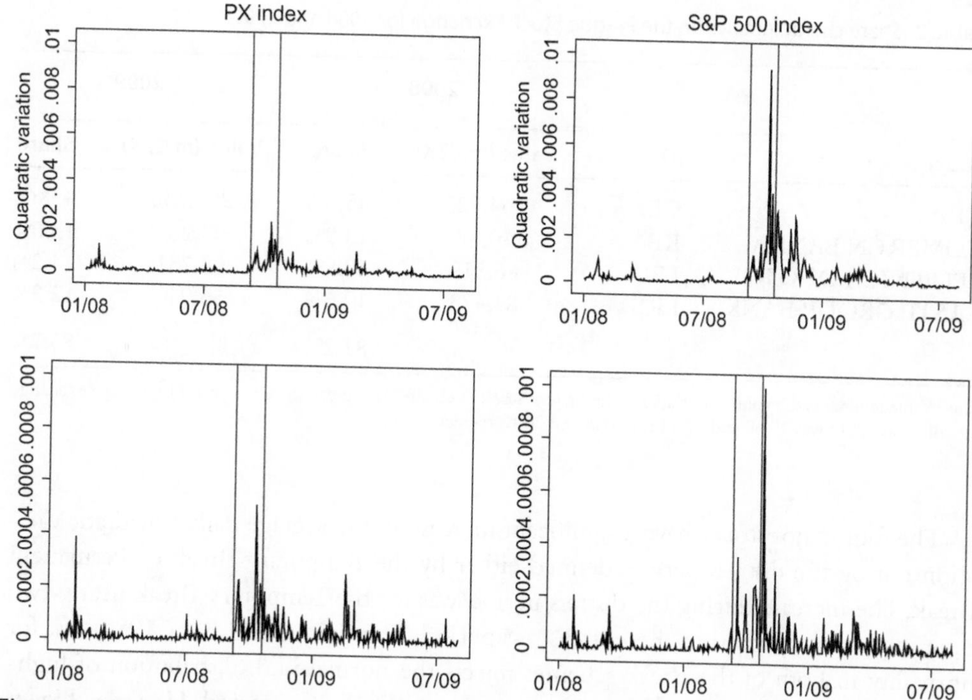

Figure 1 Quadratic variation and the difference between quadratic and integrated variations for the PX index and the S&P 500 index.
Note: the upper panel contains the quadratic variation, which is estimated by realized variance. The lower panel depicts the difference between quadratic and integrated variation, which is estimated by bipower variance; figures are in daily levels. The first vertical line corresponds to September 9, 2008, and the second vertical line corresponds to October 20, 2008. These two dates define the permanent and temporary breaks.

4.1. Prague Stock Exchange

Data for the PSE (analyzed at a 5-minute frequency) shows in the vast majority of cases that realized skewness is negative, which means that the distribution of returns has a fatter left tail, or in other words, that extreme movements down tend to be more likely. Kurtosis is clearly higher than 3, which means that distributions of returns are fat-tailed. The null hypothesis stating that returns are i.i.d. following the normal distribution (Jarque-Bera statistics) implies a rejection of the null hypothesis at a very high confidence level, where the p-value does not exceed 0.0001 in any case.

Given the small number of stocks traded, we employ four of the most capitalized stocks from the Prague Stock Exchange, which represent about 80% of the traded volume of market capitalization. Table 2 contains the characteristics of the four traded companies on the Prague Stock Exchange for years 2008 and 2009. The cumulative share clearly shows that the four stocks included in this analysis capture the majority of the market. Similar to the index data, we will analyze these four stocks at a 5-minute frequency.

Table 2 Share characteristics on the Prague Stock Exchange for 2008 and 2009.

		2008		2009	
Issuer	**ID**	**Value (m.CZK)**	**Share**	**Value (m.CZK)**	**Share**
ČEZ	CEZ	364,225	45.8%	202,358	43.6%
KOMERČN BANKA	KB	110,544	13.9%	63,262	13.6%
TELEFNICA O2 C.R.	TEL	86,519	10.9%	65,731	14.2%
ERSTE GROUP BANK	ERSTE	84,473	10.6%	56,940	12.3%
			81.2%		83.7%

Note: Value represents the volume of trades at the Prague Stock Exchange for a given share per year. The average exchange rate of CZK-USD was 19.49 and 17.84 for 2008 and 2009, respectively.

The four major stocks have a significant increase in the average daily Quadratic Variation during the distress period, defined either by the Temporary Break or Permanent Break. The increase during the distress period was for the Temporary Break nearly two times higher as opposed to the not-distress period. The (Jarque and Bera, 1980) test for normality in both of the Break schemes rejects the normal i.i.d. distribution of high-frequency returns irrespective of being in or out of the distress period. However, bigger discrepancies were observed during the financial crisis, which suggests that a period of distress makes the markets more Gaussian but with higher overall Quadratic Variation (i.e., less jumps).

4.2. New York Stock Exchange

The NYSE market micro-structure is captured by employing a set of 16 stocks and one ETF from the Trade and Quote database (TAQ), reported in Table 3.

The stocks used for this analysis were chosen according to several criteria. First, all the stocks are internationally recognized and heavily traded with a large intraday stock flow. This allows us to sample them even at a 1-minute frequency and capture high-frequency phenomena. In addition, we have also included an Exchange Traded Fund (ETF), which tracks the performance of the S&P 500 index.[4] This ETF serves as a popular vehicle for those who want to be exposed to the S&P 500 index performance as a whole and it represents a benchmark for the performance of the US economy. Finally, the SPY ETF reflects overall trends on the market since any excess movement by a single stock is smoothed out by other stocks.

[4] The ETF does not track the S&P 500 index precisely since the value of the ETF is less maintenance fees.

Table 3 Companies and ETF for NYSE.

Company		ID
Bank of America Corp.	Financials	BAC
Citigroup, Inc.	Financials	C
Wells Fargo & Co.	Financials	WFC
Pfizer	Health Care	PFE
Johnson & Johnson	Health Care	JNJ
General Electric Co.	Conglomerate	GE
Chevron Corp.	Energy	CVX
Exxon Mobil Corp.	Energy	XOM
Apple Inc.	Information Technology	APPL
Microsoft Corp.	Information Technology	MSFT
Google Inc.	Information Technology	GOOG
Hewlett-Packard	Information Technology	HPQ
Intl. Business Machines Corp.	Information Technology	IBM
Coca-Cola Company	Consumer Staples	KO
Procter & Gamble	Consumer Staples	PG
AT&T Inc.	Telecommunication Services	T
S&P 500 ETF		SPY

5. RESULTS

As we indicated in Section 3 we want to analyze the effect of the financial distress period—defined as a Permanent Break (PB) or as a Temporary Break (TB). In particular we aim to test two hypotheses about jump distribution. Hypothesis A compares the mean number of jumps, and hypothesis B evaluates the variance of the number of price jumps during a period of financial distress. Following the discussion in Section 2.3, for the detection of jumps we use the following price jump indicators:

- Type-I Error-Optimal—We define a price jump as those returns that are below/above the 2.5%/97.5% centile level.
- Type-II Error-Optimal—We employ a bipower variance approach, in particular ξ-statistics with a 95% CL and $n = 120$.

Since we primarily focus on an emerging market (the Prague Stock Exchange) we will present the results for the PSE first. For a different perspective we provide the results for selected stocks from the NYSE in another sub-section.

5.1. The Prague Stock Exchange

The results of our pair of tests for four stocks from the Prague Stock Exchange are presented in Table 4.

For testing the difference in the average number of jumps (Hypothesis A) we employ the Wilcoxon sign test. Let us reiterate that negative (and significant) values here mean that the number of jumps is higher during the period of financial distress. For Type-I Error-Optimal identification we see a clear pattern indicating that we observe far more jumps during the financial crisis with TB or PB. The situation is reversed when we employ the Type-II Error-Optimal indicator for the detection of price jumps. As we see for PB we find a significant result only for KB (a commercial bank), while TB was significant for all stocks. The main difference is that when we minimize the probability of incorrect jump identification (Type-II error), we see that the number of "predicted" jumps was actually lower during the period of financial distress. This discrepancy could be caused by an overall increase in market volatility without an unnecessary increase in the rate of price jumps. Because jump prediction minimizing the Type-I error uses centiles (i.e., is based on outliers), such a method could incorrectly identify a lot of false jumps during the volatile period. For testing if the identified number of jumps has the same variance during both periods we use a standard *F*-test. The figures for Hypothesis B confirm the previous findings; namely that if the Type-I Error-Optimal indicator is used for the identification of price jumps, we see very significant results supporting the hypothesis that during the period of financial distress the variance of price jumps is also higher. However, when we switch to the Type-II Error-Optimal indicator, we cannot see the difference with the exception of PB for Erste Bank. We can speculate and explain these

Table 4 Hypothesis A and B—Type-I and Type-II error-optimal price jump indicators.

	Type-I error-optimal				Type-II error-optimal			
	Hypothesis A		Hypothesis B		Hypothesis A		Hypothesis B	
	PB	TB	PB	TB	PB	TB	PB	TB
CEZ	−7.51[a]	−7.20[a]	3.41[a]	3.05[a]	1.13	2.69[a]	0.97	0.48
ERSTE	−11.53[a]	−5.20[a]	7.00[a]	2.13[a]	−1.20	1.70[c]	1.23[c]	0.44
KB	−9.36[a]	−4.91[a]	3.57[a]	1.54[b]	3.34[a]	2.65[a]	0.59	0.44
TEL	−6.27[a]	−5.92[a]	1.29[b]	3.21[a]	−1.12	3.14[a]	1.09	0.53

Notes:
Hypothesis A: reported is z-statistics for the Wilcoxon test. Negative/positive z-values suggest that the mean of the number of identified price jumps (using Type-I and Type-II Error-Optimal indicators) tends to be lower/higher in the non-crisis period when compared with the period of crisis.

Hypothesis B: reported is the F-test which is asymptotically equal to $\sim F_{(223,174)}$ for the Permanent Break scheme, and $\sim F_{(29,368)}$ for the Temporary Break scheme. The null hypothesis states that there is no change in the variance of the number of price jumps for both sub-periods. The letters denote at what confidence level we can reject the null hypothesis: 90% (*c*), 95% (*b*), and 99% (*a*).

particular results by the dual listing of the stock (the primary market is the Vienna Stock Exchange) and by the bank's involvement in Iceland, Greece, and Spain lending.

Overall, the result of the test clearly indicates that there was a significant increase in the price jumps and their variance due to the distress as measured by the Type-I Error-Optimal price jump indicator. On the other hand, the Type-II Error-Optimal price jump indicator suggests that immediately after the fall of Lehman Brothers, the number of price jumps per day either dropped or remained the same. Since the numbers of price jumps estimated by the Type-I price jump indicator carry information about the overall quadratic variance, we may conclude that following the fall of Lehman Brothers, the overall volatility at Prague Stock Exchange rocketed; the stock market was more volatile but with less price jumps. In the next section, we compare the results with the US market.

5.2. The New York Stock Exchange and Comparisons

We report the results of our testing procedures in Table 5. We analyze 16 stocks and one actively traded ETF from the New York Stock Exchange. In order to capture higher volumes and the importance of the stocks we perform a similar analysis at a 1-minute frequency.

Similarly as for the PSE, we observe that the Type-I Error-Optimal identification leads to the conclusion that we observe significantly more jumps with higher variation during the period of financial distress. It is interesting that Type-II Error-Optimal identification—in contrast to the small emerging market (i.e., the PSE)—shows more significant results. What is more interesting is that for some stocks we see more identified jumps during the financial distress and for some stocks just the opposite. The response is clearly company/sector-specific. One can speculate that banking experienced a lower mean number of jumps with a higher variation; international firms in consumer staples show a higher number of jumps during the financial distress period with a potential shift to a higher variation, etc. For a detailed (sectoral) analysis we would need more stocks to be analyzed, which is beyond the scope of this chapter. We want to demonstrate the differences in testing results for PB and TP in the NYSE; for some cases we observe positive/negative values indicating a lower/higher number of jumps (different variation) during financial distress period(s). Virtually none of these phenomena were observed in the case of the PSE. For the US market we observe that the short period immediately after the Lehman Brothers collapse was dominated by an enormous increase in volatility and the number of price jumps. In addition, we also observe a change in the number of price jumps over a long-time horizon. The results suggest that the period following the fall of Lehman Brothers was characterized by enormous volatility and a higher level of uncertainty, which remains present even long after the initial signal of distress.

The comparison of the NYSE and the PSE displays interesting differences. First, in a mature market changes in price jump distribution during the financial distress are

Table 5 Hypothesis A and B—Type-I and Type-II error-optimal price jump indicators.

	Type-I error-optimal				Type-II error-optimal			
	Hypothesis A		Hypothesis B		Hypothesis A		Hypothesis B	
	PB	TB	PB	TB	PB	TB	PB	TB
BAC	−11.94[a]	−5.13[a]	21.77[a]	1.47	5.42[a]	0.30	1.00	2.25[a]
C	−11.22[a]	−5.42[a]	40.84[a]	1.71[b]	3.31[a]	−1.45	0.89	1.62[b]
WFC	−9.87[a]	−5.59[a]	12.992[a]	1.65[b]	4.79[a]	0.03	1.03	1.17
PFE	−14.04[a]	−6.22[a]	28.62[a]	3.17[a]	1.67[c]	0.28	0.91	1.23
JNJ	−13.09[a]	−4.68[a]	31.91[a]	3.64[a]	−1.34	−0.57	1.03	1.05
GE	−15.19	−6.10[a]	144.30[a]	2.19[a]	6.08[a]	0.57	1.05	1.21
CVX	−7.42[a]	−7.13[a]	20.10[a]	6.67[a]	0.00	−0.05	0.77[c]	0.70
XOM	−5.87[a]	−7.21[a]	18.90[a]	6.67[a]	2.31[b]	−0.85	1.11	0.74
APPL	−2.66[a]	−7.83[a]	4.18[a]	7.72[a]	−0.14	−0.16	1.28[c]	1.86[b]
MSFT	−10.97[a]	−6.07[a]	22.60[a]	5.24[a]	−0.41	−0.70	0.83	1.09
GOOG	−3.87[a]	−6.70[a]	6.62[a]	4.57[a]	−2.64[a]	2.02[b]	0.93	0.90
HPQ	−9.59[a]	−5.81[a]	16.86[a]	3.84[a]	2.14[b]	−1.99[b]	1.08	1.56[c]
IBM	−8.62[a]	−7.07[a]	22.61[a]	4.27[a]	1.66[c]	−1.42	1.05	1.51[c]
KO	−9.41[a]	−5.78[a]	19.58[a]	4.22[a]	−1.87[c]	1.95[c]	0.98	1.51[c]
PG	−12.63[a]	−4.95[a]	24.47[a]	3.71[a]	−2.67[a]	−2.29[b]	1.04	1.10
T	−6.76[a]	−6.35[a]	9.21[a]	2.93[a]	0.24	−2.19[b]	0.76[c]	1.11
SPY	−11.57[a]	−6.10[a]	31.91[a]	4.72[a]	−0.13	−0.78	0.95	1.51[c]

Notes:
Hypothesis A: reported is z-statistics for the Wilcoxon test. Negative/positive z-values suggest that the mean of the number of identified price jumps (using Type-I and Type-II Error-Optimal indicators) tends to be lower/higher in the non-crisis period when compared with a period of crisis.

Hypothesis B: reported is the F-test which is asymptotically equal to $\sim F_{(225,172)}$ for the Permanent Break scheme, and $\sim F_{(29,368)}$ for the Temporary Break scheme. The null hypothesis states that there is no change in the variance of the number of price jumps for both sub-periods. The letters denote at what confidence level we can reject the null hypothesis: 90% (c), 95% (b), and 99% (a).

company/sector specific, in some cases indicating a permanent change.[5] The overall reactions reflect an increase of uncertainty resulting in a change in volatility structure. Sector- and company-specific reactions enforce a link between the stock market and the real economy, see for example Cooper and Priestley (2013) for discussion of the link between asset pricing and economic and financial variables. On the other hand, the PSE shows relatively marginal reactions. We find an overall increase in volatility, however,

[5] For further research it would be interesting to compare different reactions across industrial sectors, comparing for example cyclical versus counter-cyclical industries and global versus local players.

changes in jump arrival and volatility structure are almost not detectable in the long run. Temporarily, however, all the companies from the PSE reveal a significant decrease in price jump arrival. This suggests that in the long-run perspective, the PSE (unlike the NYSE) had the entire price process scaled up without a direct effect on extreme price movement arrival. Therefore, we may conclude that volatility on both markets has significantly increased after the fall of Lehman Brothers, but at the PSE (representing a small CEE emerging market) we do not observe in the long run as many changes in the volatility structure or in the distribution of abrupt price changes (jumps).

6. REGULATORY CONSEQUENCES

The previous section concludes that responses to the financial distress of emerging and mature markets can be quite different. The usual wisdom is that emerging markets reveal both higher volatility (e.g., Schwert, 2011) and more frequent arrival of price jumps. However, we see when an emerging market is small, then the reaction to financial distress could lead to a sizable drop in value, along with an increase in volatility; however, the adjustment may not be abrupt in nature. One can speculate that the corresponding changes in market returns could be relatively gradual, reflecting a declining participation of foreign investors and/or a lack of demand from local (institutional) investors. Let us explore the obtained results from the regulatory perspective and stress testing in particular. We believe that the provided results could shed light on market risk management, especially in the context of a small emerging market.

The recent financial regulation placed large emphasis on different sources of risk and their proper evaluation; this can be seen in the most recent Basel III Accords. The need for better risk management emerged after the recent financial crisis, where many to-date reliable counterparties disappeared. In particular, the collapse of Lehman Brothers represents one of the prominent examples how a trustworthy and triple-A-rated primary dealer can disappear within a few days. In addition, abrupt and unexpected market drops are connected to (dramatic) losses of the market value of a company, which may in an extreme case result in (sudden) default. Therefore, we believe that there exists an intuitive connection between counterparty credit risk and market risk associated with price jumps. In particular, market risk connected with unexpected rapid market changes should be reflected in good financial regulations.

In the following, we discuss the empirical relation between the market risk insight we acquired in our quantitative analysis of price jumps for mature and emerging markets and the counterparty credit risk as defined in the Basel documents. Since this issue is very broad, we narrow the topic to the stress testing procedure and to the recently released Basel III document. Counterparty credit risk is modeled using CDS spreads, where high spreads correspond to an increased probability of default in the economy. When modeling the stress scenarios for the counterparty credit risk, the regulatory text states that "the

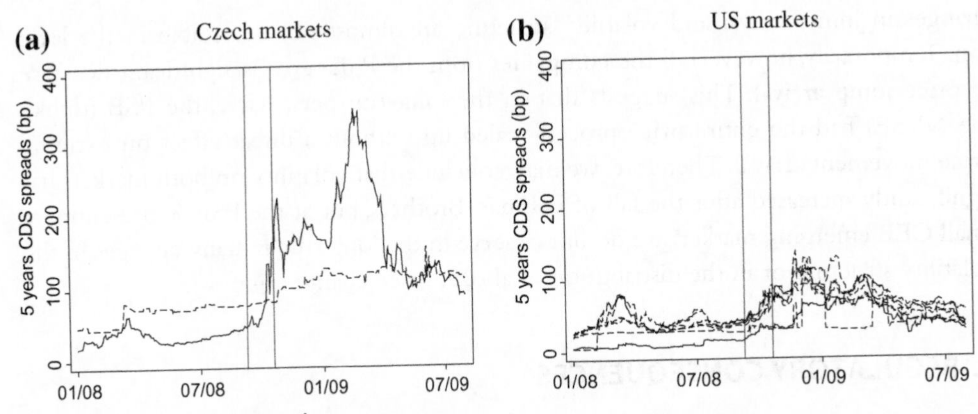

Figure 2 Five-year CDS spreads.
Note: the full line represents government bonds. The dashed line corresponds to a panel of companies that have a full history of 5-year CDS rates over the studied period. For the Czech market, we use CEZ, for US markets, we use AT&T, Coca-Cola, Hewlett-Packard, IBM, Chevron, and Microsoft. Data comes from Bloomberg.

bank must demonstrate, at least quarterly, that the stress period coincides with a period of increased CDS or other credit spreads" (p. 30, Paragraph 98–61).

Figure 2 depicts the 5-year CDS rates for the Czech and US markets covering stocks used in this study, for which the Bloomberg database contained the full history over the covered period. In the case of the Czech Republic, we plot CEZ, while for the US market, we plot AT&T, Coca-Cola, Hewlett-Packard, IBM, Chevron, and Microsoft. In addition, by a solid line we plot the CDS spreads for Czech and US government bonds.

Clearly, taking the Permanent Break as a definition of the financial distress period, the behavior of the CDS spreads confirms some of the previous findings. In particular, after the collapse of Lehman Brothers they significantly rose above the preceding levels, for the Czech economy with a notable delay and certain inconsistencies. Surprisingly, the spread of the Czech governmental bonds during the quite long period of financial distress was a multiple of the CDS spread of CEZ (a utility company, one of the largest CEE electricity producers and distributors). Despite relatively low debt and overall stability, the Czech governmental bonds are bundled with other rather exotic bonds and this fact could explain the observed externality. Besides, the Czech government is a majority owner of the publicly traded shares of CEZ; one can expect a bailout from the government if CEZ has problems. Finally, given the market position and strong fundamentals, there is no reason for a dramatic response of CEZ CDS spreads. Nevertheless, the described externality shows the limitations of the Basel rules applied in the framework of a small emerging market.

In the case of the US market, Permanent Break marks a period of increased spreads, which started to rise with the collapse of Lehman Brothers and were continually growing until the first quarter of 2009. The Temporary Break, on the other hand, represents a period of an initial increase in spreads, which could be interpreted as a period of growing market nervousness. Clearly, the levels of spreads are significantly lower than those for the Czech market. A different story would be the spreads of the big banks that got into significant financial difficulties during the financial crisis. Those banks, however, are a different story, and have to be treated on a case-by-case basis.

The Permanent Break also suggests for both countries a significant increase in the overall quadratic variance. Thus, the increased levels of the CDS spreads go hand-in-hand with the increased level of volatility. Considering the CDS as a distress indicator reflects, in the scope of our paper, both the increased market risk as well as counterparty credit risk.

However, what does this imply for price jump behavior? Do the increased CDS spreads really imply an increased level of price jumps since the drops in the firms' values are intuitively connected to possible defaults and/or a high and hedgeable variance of derivative contracts? Our results do not confirm this intuition since the rate of price jumps (using the Type-II Error-Optimal indicator controlling for increase in volatility) remains unchanged for the PSE and shows company/sector-specific behavior for the US market. As we mentioned earlier, for a small emerging market, the logic is reversed since immediately after the crisis, the rate of price jumps in the Prague Stock Exchange dropped. Therefore, we cannot clearly relate the CDS spreads to the price jumps, especially for small emerging markets.

To illustrate the possible consequences, let us imagine a US investor, who has a portfolio with a majority of US equities and with a small exposure to the emerging market.[6] The investor will be interested in stress testing her portfolio for behavior during distress like the fall of a large investment bank. Such a period corresponds to the Basel III requirements of increased CDS spreads and, in addition, it also reflects increased market risk. However, the structure of the market risk for developed and emerging markets is different, see Avramov et al. (2012). In addition, as we see from our results, the market responses are also very distinct. Applying the same patterns and rules for both types of markets does not correspond to a real market response and may lead to inaccurate stress-test scenarios. The investor, therefore, has to treat emerging and mature markets in a different manner and adequately account for their individual dynamics, which may be different. In addition, our result clearly shows that an "increase in the rate of price jumps" does not correspond to the real market response during a distress period.

6.1. Specific Features of Emerging Markets

The fact that our example of the PSE has a different response to (global) financial distress could have several reasons and consequences. First of all, small emerging markets, here

[6] In reality, CEZ, who plays a significant role on the Central and European energy market, is an attractive opportunity for large institutional investors.

represented by the PSE, do not reflect the underlying real economy. Second, the PSE is characterized by relatively small market capitalization, a very limited number of traded stocks, low turnover, a negligible number of IPOs, and little new capital raised. Third, the strong position of market makers allows strategic trading and potential price manipulation, including information-driven trading (see Hanousek and Kopřiva, 2011; Hanousek and Kopřiva, forthcoming).[7] From the regulatory perspective, volatility and high spreads could capture behavior during financial distress quite well, because stocks are not primarily reflecting immediate signals or firm fundamentals. Their price formation process is under the strong influence of local players interacting with a dramatically decreasing number (and interest) of foreign investors.

7. CONCLUSION

In this chapter, we analyzed the impact of the Lehman Brothers collapse on the volatility and especially the rate of price jumps at the Prague Stock Exchange (PSE) and the New York Stock Exchange (NYSE). We employed four stocks from the PSE, which represent about 80% of its turnover and market capitalization and sixteen shares from NYSE along with one ETF tracking the S&P 500. For the analysis we use high-frequency data from January 2008 until the end of July 2009; we use different jump price identifications to analyze the responses to financial distress of the NYSE and PSE.

It is rather obvious that even *ex-post* identification of the price jumps would depend on the actual method used, i.e., on the employed price jump indicator. Therefore, one can conclude that any analysis of the jump distributions during financial distress would be method-dependent. We use this apparent disadvantage in a potentially useful way—to distinguish between a significant volatility increase and a change in price jump arrival. In order to do so, we suggest using different identifications of price jumps, characterizing two extreme cases: (1) a Type-I Error-Optimal indicator, which maximizes the identification of true price jumps and (2) a Type-II Error-Optimal indicator, which minimizes incorrect price jump identification.[8] In this setting, Type-I error identification would capture both price jumps and the volatility structure, while Type-II error identification would target primarily the price jumps.

[7] The observed mismanagement of those small CEE capital markets is severe. In the Czech Republic, Hungary, and Slovakia, there are almost no local institutional investors. Poland, on the other hand, because of mandatory regulations to hold 15% of assets in shares (and 90% of them through the Warsaw Stock Exchange), creates another dangerous externality. Another dimension is related to investor protection. It is standard that during problematic periods (related to trading, information release, suspicion for information asymmetries, etc.) markets with good investor protection suspend stock trading. This happened for example on December 11, 2012 for KITD at NASDAQ, while the same stock dual-listed at the PSE was freely traded.

[8] In the literature, the Type-I error criterion is known as optimization with respect to the power of the test; in diagnostic analysis it is usually called the optimization of the positive negative probability. Similarly, Type-II error optimality is usually presented as optimality with respect to the size of the test, while in diagnostic analysis it is typically called the optimization of the false negative probability.

Using Type-I Error-Optimal and Type-II Error-Optimal price jump indicators we tested two hypotheses for the effect of the Lehman Brothers collapse on price jump distributions. The first hypothesis states that there was no permanent/temporary effect on the mean number of jumps. The second hypothesis states there was no permanent/temporary effect on the variance of the estimated price jump figures. These hypotheses were tested for the NYSE and PSE, as typical representatives of a mature, developed capital market and an emerging Central European stock exchange, respectively.

Our analysis suggests that the Type-I Error-Optimal price jump indicator, which captures both price jumps and volatility, rejects the null hypothesis and thus both the mature and emerging markets show increased levels of volatility during financial distress. In addition, we found interesting differences between the NYSE and the PSE using the Type-II Error-Optimal price jump indicator, which focus more on the price jumps. First, the mature market reveals company/sector-specific changes in price jump behavior, where there is evidence of the permanent effect of financial distress for some companies. The specific reactions of different sectors reveal the true link between the capital market and the real economy. On the contrary, companies listed at the PSE suggest a minor long-run reaction of price jumps to financial distress. Overall, we may conclude that volatility on both markets was significantly increased after the fall of Lehman Brothers, but at the PSE we do not observe in the long run as many changes in the volatility structure and in the distribution of abrupt price changes (jumps).

The regulatory consequences of the provided results are illustrated on the Basel approach by comparing price jump behavior with the characteristics of 5-year CDS spreads. Our results suggest that despite the obvious intuition, the rate of the arrival of price jumps is not uniformly increasing with the rise of CDS spreads, whose high level defines from the regulatory perspective financial distress. For the PSE, there is no clear correspondence between CDS rates and price jumps, while for the US market, the response is company/sector-specific, possibly with different signs. In conclusion, investors have to model emerging and mature markets differently to properly reflect their individual dynamics. Our results show that the expected "increasing rate of price jumps during financial distress" does not correspond to the real market behavior during a crisis.

REFERENCES

Aït-Sahalia, Y., Jacod, J., 2009. Testing for jumps in a discretely observed process. Annals of Statistics 37 (1), 184–222

Aït-Sahalia, Y., Jacod, J., 2011. Testing whether jumps have finite or infinite activity. Annals of Statistics 39 (3), 1689–1719

Aït-Sahalia, Y., Cacho-Diaz, J., Laeven, R.J., 2010. Modeling financial contagion using mutually exciting jump processes. Technical Report National Bureau of Economic Research.

Andersen, T., Dobrev, D., Schaumburg, E., 2012. Jump-robust volatility estimation using nearest neighbor truncation. Journal of Econometrics 169 (1), 75–93

Anderson, T., Bollerslev, T., Diebold, F., Vega, C., 2007. Real-time price discovery in global stock, bond and foreign exchange markets. Journal of International Economics 73 (2), 251–277

Avramov, D., Chordia, T., Jostova, G., Philipov, A., 2012. The world price of credit risk. Review of Asset Pricing Studies 2 (2), 112–152
Barndorff-Nielsen, O., Shephard, N., 2004. Power and bipower variation with stochastic volatility and jumps. Journal of Financial Econometrics 2 (1), 1–37
Barndorff-Nielsen, O., Shephard, N., 2006. Econometrics of testing for jumps in financial economics using bipower variation. Journal of Financial Econometrics 4 (1), 1–30
Bates, D., 1996. Jumps and stochastic volatility: exchange rate processes implicit in Deutsche mark options. Review of Financial Studies 9 (1), 69–107
Becketti, S., Roberts, D., 1990. Will increased regulation of stock index futures reduce stock market volatility? Economic Review 75 (6), 33–46
Bouchaud, J., Kockelkoren, J., Potters, M., 2006. Random walks, liquidity molasses and critical response in financial markets. Quantitative Finance 6 (02), 115–123
Boudt, K., Croux, C., Laurent, S., 2011. Robust estimation of intraweek periodicity in volatility and jump detection. Journal of Empirical Finance 18 (2), 353–367
Cooper, I., Priestley, R., 2013. The world business cycle and expected returns. Review of Finance, 1–36
Cornell, B., Sirri, E., 1992. The reaction of investors and stock prices to insider trading. Journal of Finance, 1031–1059
Corsi, F., Pirino, D., Renò, R., 2010. Threshold bipower variation and the impact of jumps on volatility forecasting. Journal of Econometrics 159 (2), 276–288
Dumitru, A.-M., Urga, G., 2012. Identifying jumps in financial assets: a comparison between nonparametric jump tests. Journal of Business & Economic Statistics 30 (2), 242–255
Dungey, M., Fry, R., González-Hermosillo, B., Martin, V., 2005. Empirical modelling of contagion: a review of methodologies. Quantitative Finance 5 (1), 9–24
Fama, E., 1970. Efficient capital markets: a review of theory and empirical work. Journal of Finance 25 (2), 383–417
Gatheral, J., 2006. The Volatility Surface: A Practitioner's Guide, vol. 357. Wiley
Giot, P., Laurent, S., Petitjean, M., 2010. Trading activity, realized volatility and jumps. Journal of Empirical Finance 17 (1), 168–175
Hanousek, J., Kočenda, E., 2011. Foreign news and spillovers in emerging European stock markets. Review of International Economics 19 (1), 170–188
Hanousek, J., Kopřiva, F., 2011. Detecting information-driven trading in a dealers market. Czech Journal of Economics and Finance (Finance a uver) 61 (3), 204–229
Hanousek, J., Kopřiva, F., forthcoming. Do broker/analyst conflicts matter? Detecting evidence from internet trading platforms. International Review of Financial Analysis, 28, 86–92.
Hanousek, J., Kočenda, E., Kutan, A., 2009. The reaction of asset prices to macroeconomic announcements in new EU markets: evidence from intraday data. Journal of Financial Stability 5 (2), 199–219
Hanousek, J., Kočenda, E., Novotný, J., 2012. The identification of price jumps. Monte Carlo Methods and Applications 18 (1), 53–77
Heston, S., 1993. A closed-form solution for options with stochastic volatility with applications to bond and currency options. Review of Financial Studies 6 (2), 327–343
Huang, X., Tauchen, G., 2005. The relative contribution of jumps to total price variance. Journal of Financial Econometrics 3 (4), 456–499
Jacod, J., Shiryaev, A., 1987. Limit Theorems for Stochastic Processes, vol. 288. Springer-Verlag, Berlin
Jarque, C., Bera, A., 1980. Efficient tests for normality, homoscedasticity and serial independence of regression residuals. Economics Letters 6 (3), 255–259
Jiang, G., Oomen, R., 2008. Testing for jumps when asset prices are observed with noise: a swap variance approach. Journal of Econometrics 144 (2), 352–370
Joulin, A., Lefevre, A., Grunberg, D., Bouchaud, J., 2008. Stock price jumps: news and volume play a minor role. Wilmott Magazine, 1–7
Kennedy, D., Sivakumar, R., Vetzal, K., 2006. The implications of IPO underpricing for the firm and insiders: tests of asymmetric information theories. Journal of Empirical Finance 13 (1), 49–78
Lahaye, J., Laurent, S., Neely, C., 2011. Jumps, cojumps and macro announcements. Journal of Applied Econometrics 26 (6), 893–921

Lee, S., Hannig, J., 2010. Detecting jumps from Lévy jump diffusion processes. Journal of Financial Economics 96 (2), 271–290
Lee, S., Mykland, P., 2008. Jumps in financial markets: a new nonparametric test and jump dynamics. Review of Financial studies 21 (6), 2535–2563
Madhavan, A., 2000. Market microstructure: a survey. Journal of Financial Markets 3 (3), 205–258
Mancini, C., 2009. Non-parametric threshold estimation for models with stochastic diffusion coefficient and jumps. Scandinavian Journal of Statistics 36 (2), 270–296
Mann, H., Whitney, D., 1947. On a test of whether one of two random variables is stochastically larger than the other. Annals of Mathematical Statistics 18 (1), 50–60
McDonald, L., Robinson, P., 2009. A Colossal Failure of Common Sense: The Inside Story of the Collapse of Lehman Brothers. Crown Business
Merton, R., 1976. Option pricing when underlying stock returns are discontinuous. Journal of Financial Economics 3 (1–2), 125–144
Schwert, G., 2011. Stock volatility during the recent financial crisis. European Financial Management 17 (5), 789–805
Scott, L., 1997. Pricing stock options in a jump-diffusion model with stochastic volatility and interest rates: applications of Fourier inversion methods. Mathematical Finance 7 (4), 413–426
Tiniç, S., 1995. Derivatives and stock market volatility: is additional government regulation necessary? Journal of Financial Services Research 9 (3), 351–362
Wilcoxon, F., 1945. Individual comparisons by ranking methods. Biometrics Bulletin 1 (6), 80–83

CHAPTER 21

Are Emerging Markets Exposed to Contagion from the United States: Evidence from Stock and Sovereign Bond Markets

Hakimzadi Wagan[*] and Zulfiqar Ali[†]
[*]University of Paris, Panthéon Sorbonne, France
[†]Department of Business Administration, University of Sindh Jamshoro, Pakistan

1. INTRODUCTION

Global financial crisis that broke out in the United States henceforth US, during 2008–2009, resulted in sharp declines in asset prices, stock markets, and skyrocketing of risk premiums on interbank loans. It also disrupted the country's financial system and threatened real economy with huge contractions. At the onset of crisis, there was the talk of decoupling in emerging markets; however in addition to its severe recessionary effects inside US, the crisis penalized emerging markets (EMs). Our interest in this topic concentrates mainly on the question how stock market downturn in US contributed to virulent volatility and contagion in emerging financial markets.

Our focus on these markets is motivated by several facts. First, the volatility in stock prices is generally considered as a gauge of financial stress for different segments of financial markets. Second, over the last couple of years, volatility in the LAC and EU region has become a key factor for determining the risk-taking behavior among international investors, mainly the rebalancing of portfolios between different securities (shift from sovereign bonds to government bonds). Third, as volatility tends to rise, it encourages write-offs and discourages position taking, increases risk budgets, and influences leverage conditions.

In order to understand the so-called contagion effect of financial crisis, it is necessary to answer some fundamental questions: is the level of interdependence between US and emerging financial markets constant or changing over time? Equally important is how the rising level of volatility in US stock market in the aftermath of 2008–2009 crisis and global risk aversion affects the correlation dynamics of emerging countries' stock and sovereign bond markets? Can the rising level of volatility and interdependence of emerging financial markets be partly attributed to rise in bilateral trade or integration between the countries

http://dx.doi.org/10.1016/B978-0-12-411549-1.00021-1

or regions? Which emerging national and regional financial markets saw the highest co-movements during the recent crisis?

Answering all these questions is important as international investors are interested in understanding the forces behind the co-movement between US stock market and emerging stock and sovereign bond markets to identify potential risks and rewards and reap the benefits of global diversification. Regulators and economic policy makers are interested in forces behind the interdependence of these markets to determine the level of financial liberalization and sovereign risk as from their point of view contagion means irrational capital outflows and deterioration of countries economic and fiscal balance.

This study is an attempt to answer the above questions surrounding the emerging LAC and EU stock and sovereign bond markets at country and regional level. Literature has also tried to amplify the issues related to financial contagion during the recent crisis (Shamiri and Isa, 2009; Yiu et al., 2010). Most of these studies focused on linkages between US and Asian markets; however, it seems that there is considerable gap in financial literature on the subject of contagion from US to emerging LAC and EU region. A relatively small strand of literature has touched this issue on the country level. In this regard, on the one hand the literature has claimed that LAC's banking sector showed strong resilience to the crisis (Powell et al., 2008; Valadao and Gico, 2010), on the other hand one cannot deny the growing influence of US financial market on this region given the higher degree of integration (González-Hermosillo and Hesse, 2011). Dooley and Hutchison (2009) also find dramatic reemergence of financial linkages post-Lehman failure resulting in rising credit default swap spreads on sovereign bonds and equity market volatility in LAC and EU countries.

This chapter is an attempt to bridge this gap by building our research on the above subject. First, we apply the concept of contagion from US to EMs during the recent crisis period to better understand how these toxic segments of the market infected entire EMs. Second, unlike previous studies we include emerging stock and sovereign bond markets to see how the fortunes of these markets rise and fall together with financial conditions in US. Third, we cover a sample of five emerging countries and two regions namely: emerging EU and LAC region which offers a reasonable basis for comparisons at country and regional market level, most of the earlier studies comparatively focus on few countries only in one region.

We do not examine in this paper the question as to whether the financial stress in the US during the global financial crisis propagated to the LAC and EU through real or financial channels. We rather concentrate on the financial linkages and examine empirically the link between the US stock market and the correlation dynamics of LAC and Europe stock and sovereign bond markets.

Different models have been used in the literature to examine the coupling and decoupling of financial markets with US during the recent crisis (Dooley and Hutchison, 2009; Rose and Spiegel, 2010; Berglöf et al., 2010). Most of them have used VAR or time-varying factor models. We use the Asymmetric DCC-Multivariate GARCH

(MGARCH) model proposed by Cappiello et al. (2006) over the other traditional MGARCH models such as the BEKK model of Engle and Kroner (1995) and the DCC model of Engle (2002). Compared to the BEKK model this model is less greedy in parameters and therefore it is more easily estimable, whereas the application of the ADCC model is more useful than the DCC model for modeling asymmetric effect of negative news on equity returns in our data set. Moreover, in the study of world-wide linkages in the dynamics of volatility and correlations of bonds and equity markets, Cappiello et al. (2006) showed that there were strong asymmetries in conditional volatility of equity index returns while bond index returns have little evidence of this behavior. Asymmetric effect occurs when unexpected downward movements in the price of an asset raise the conditional volatility of returns more than when there are unexpected upward movements (see Nelson, 1991; Engle and Ng, 1993). Hence the model has the advantage of being able to account for the asymmetric impact of negative shocks with respect to stock and bond markets. This econometric framework is carried out along with the application of Bai and Perron test (2003) for structural break to be sure about break in our series rather than relying on intuitions.

The rest of the paper is organized as follows: Section 2 provides some theoretical underpinnings on the subject. Section 3 provides background to the recent financial turmoil. Section 4 describes empirical methodology. Section 5 provides a first look at the data and descriptive statistics. Results are discussed in Section 6, what the findings of the study have to offer to regulators, policy makers, and investors in terms of policy implications and conclusion are provided in Section 7.

2. SOME THEORETICAL UNDERPINNINGS

In general, there are two main explanations as to why there is co-movement among different financial markets. The first explanation is based on the contagion effect, which is the part of financial markets' movement, which cannot be explained by the economic fundamentals. The second explanation relies on the economic integration, which means that the more the emerging economies are integrated to other economies in terms of trade and even in terms of co-movements in economic indicators such as inflation and interest rates, the more the interdependent financial markets would be.

2.1. Contagion

Generally, contagion can be defined as the spread of financial disturbances from one country to others. The research on financial contagion literally exploded since the thought-provoking paper by Forbes and Rigobon (2002). They describe contagion as "a significant increase in cross-market linkages after a shock to one country (or group of countries)," or else, a continued market correlation at high levels is considered to be "no contagion, only interdependence."

A great deal of theoretical and empirical exploration on this subject has identified two broad categories of research on this area, one based on informational factors and the other on institutional factors.

2.1.1. Informational Factors

Informational factors can be explained by the presence of soaring volatility in international capital flows in EMs where some market participants, particularly international investors, tend to disregard economic fundamentals and mimic what other investors do (Kaminsky et al., 2001; Zhou and Lai, 2009). The presence of such a herding behavior provides some explanations for rising volatility in equity (Chiang and Zheng, 2010) and bond markets and is more pronounced when selling the assets than buying. Such behavior on the part of international investors can have some serious consequences, as it has the potential to destabilize the prices and hinder the movement of capital flows. Herding behavior can be partly considered as departure from rationality on the grounds that it induces bouts of instability in financial markets. However, herding behavior does include elements of rationality. Rationalization includes reputation-based herding or principal agent problems. The main idea is that if a fund sponsor is not certain of money managers' (agents' or investors') ability to choose the right stock and separates luck from skill, conventionality with other money managers preserves the fog as money managers are evaluated against their peer groups. If the money manager takes the same choice as the market average, low returns carry little penalty compared to an ex post, unsuccessful pursuit of an unconventional strategy. Given the compensation structure, even the investors of superior quality may opt to hide in the herd rather than to pursue an ex ante which may dominate on risk return basis.

This thought advocates the insight of John Maynard Keynes that it is better to fail conventionally than to succeed unconventionally. In the case of EMs, this may lead to correlated withdrawals even if money managers are confident about economic fundamentals.

2.1.2. Institutional Factors

In the light of high volatility in international capital flows to most of the emerging countries, one may be tempted to conclude that the fickleness of institutions contributed to the bouts of instability and financial crises. According to one view, institutions destabilize financial asset prices; move the prices away from their fundamental values, thereby increasing long-run price volatility. This view is largely based on two assumptions. The first assumption is that swings in institutional demand have a larger impact on stock prices because of larger holdings than swings in individual demand, hence have larger trades. Correlated trading across large institutional investors can aggravate the conditions in financial markets. Fundamental strategies such as buying cheap high dividend yield stock take a long time to pay whereas managers can be fired after only a few quarters of bad performance, leads to our second assumption that agents may follow short-term investment plans based on feedback trading or technical analysis.

2.2. Economic Integration

Development in world economic environment and macroeconomic policies since 1990s has greatly influenced the structural architecture of financial markets through a confluence of different factors such as increased level of competition in financial services through changes in public policy, changes in banking sector, and macroeconomic changes (Vo and Daly, 2007). The growing level of integration in emerging financial markets can be ascribed to liberalization and reforms (Hedi Arouri and Foulquier, 2012).

In terms of liberalization, activities in financial sector led by offshore financial market activities have grown with a rapid pace as compared to real output growth in developed countries. Liberalization has given impetus to cross-border capital flows, innovation in financial instruments, portfolio diversification, and competition. Securitization has resulted in access to direct financing through international bond markets away from indirect financing through intermediaries. It is a universally accepted fact that all these developments have potential benefit, at the same time it has been identified that countries with highly open capital accounts are exposed to abrupt reversals in capital flows and risk of volatility. There are two broad measures to examine the extent of economic integration, the first one is direct and the other is indirect. The former is based on the equalization of rates of return, whereas the latter can be classified into two approaches (1) international financial market completeness and (2) sourcing domestic investment.

2.2.1. Equalization of Rates of Return

The first measure invokes the law of one price stating that assets with similar maturity and risk characteristics should earn similar rate of returns irrespective of political jurisdictions. However, utility of this approach is constrained by the search for those assets that share homogenous risk characteristics to allow for meaningful comparisons.

2.2.2. International Financial Market Completeness

According to this definition, financial integration is perfect when there exists complete set of international financial markets that permit economic agents and financial market players to ensure against the full set of expected states of nature.

2.2.3. Sourcing Domestic Investment

This definition assumes that perfect capital market integration means that for a small country operating in a large setup of financial markets, financing from abroad as a consequence of exogenous changes in national savings implies no change in the real interest rates. Literature has well documented and largely incorporated the definition given by Feldstein and Horioka (1980) that institutional rigidity gives rise to correlation between domestic investment and saving. Frankel (1992) later identified that the relationship between these variables does not hold implications for the degree of mobility of international capital flows.

3. SOME AMPLIFICATIONS ON RECENT CRISIS

Global financial crisis 2008–2009 that intensified in September 2008 originated from the subprime segment of the US financial market and infected the entire US and global financial system. Adoption of lax monetary policy and origin and distribution of the banking model laid the foundations for bank liquidity crisis (McGuire and Von Peter, 2009; Baba and Packer, 2009) and subsequent rising volatility paved the way for global risk aversion and emerging countries' sovereign risk problems.[1]

LIBOR and Overnight Index Swap (OIS) spread widened substantially in August 2007 and increased abruptly after the Lehman Brothers failure in September 2008, reflecting heightened funding and counterparty risk.[2] Interbank market became dysfunctional in developed markets in August 2007, providing the evidence of a run for quality among investors.[3] The immediate post-Lehman phase is marked by the unprecedented alignment of risks as the international investors' risk appetite decreased significantly over that period. The correlation between volatility in different asset classes such as VIX index which is a gauge of economic volatility embedded in stock price movements and LIBOR spreads also reemerged, clearly reflecting the view that a global downturn was now in train. Rising volatility fueled the margin requirements on hedge funds those holding asset-backed securities and other structured products. Consequently, liquidity in structured investments disappeared as these funds sell off the most liquid parts of their portfolios to respond to redemptions and to meet the margin calls.

Initially there were few spillovers to EMs, however, as the financial turmoil in US persisted, the spillovers became more evident in late 2008 in financial markets. There are mainly four spillovers that are evident across emerging financial markets: pressure on currencies, rise in global risk aversion along with rise in sovereign bond spreads, sell off in stock markets, and decline in external financing. Many emerging countries undertook monetary policy measures ranging from loosening monetary policy for easing stress in financial markets to more restrictive measures to resist currency depreciations leading to

[1] Under originate and distribute model funds are pooled, tranched, and resold through securitization (Brunnermeier, 2009).

[2] LIBOR and Overnight Index Swap (OIS) spread over the same duration shows the severity of liquidity problems in banks (Kwan, 2009).

[3] Flight-to-quality refers to a sudden shift in investment behaviors in a period of financial turmoil where investors try to sell assets perceived as risky and instead purchase safe assets. An important feature of flight-to-quality is an insufficient risk-taking behavior by investors. Though excessive risk taking can be a source of financial crisis, insufficient risk taking can severely dislocate credit and other financial markets during the financial crisis. These shifts in portfolio investments result in further negative shocks to financial sector. In accordance with this phenomenon, the demand for 10-year US Treasuries and gold increased during the recent financial turmoil.

some losses in foreign reserves. Lehman Brothers failure on 15 September 2008 resulted in sharp decline in global risk appetite because of rising concerns among international investors that looming recessionary pressures would impact emerging countries, particularly capital flows to emerging debt and stock markets turned negative.

In response to rising implied volatility, stock markets in EMs saw major declines. In addition, emerging countries' sovereign bond spreads increased substantially in different emerging market regions due to flight to safety and lack of confidence in financial markets. Emerging countries having substantial holdings of external debt denominated in foreign currency and large current account deficits observed difficulties in raising funds and have been most affected during the recent financial turmoil. Though rise in risk aversion was broad based, fall in risk appetite was more pronounced in equity markets than sovereign bond spreads across the regions.

4. METHODOLOGY

Our analytical framework is based on four steps. First we apply structural break test to identify the break date in our series. Traditionally, a break point is selected exogenously based upon some personal experience or some other phenomenon of interest and then its significance is tested (for example, the chow test). Instead of depending on our intuition we apply the structural break test suggested by Bai and Perron (1998, 2003) which allows identifying structural break dates without any prior knowledge. This methodology is considered more robust than the latter as it lets the data speak for itself. Bai and Perron (1998) suggest regressing the variable of interest on a constant and subsequently test the estimated parameters for structural changes. The model can be rewritten as:

$$P_t = \varphi_k + \varepsilon_t \quad t = T_{k-1} + 1, \ldots, T_k, \; k = 1, \ldots, m + 1,$$

where P_t is the stock market price index at time t, φ_k is the mean of the price in the kth regime and m represents the length of the time series, and ε_t represents the error term. In order to implement the procedure in Bai and Perron (2003), we need to specify the minimum number of observations between breaks and maximum number of possible breaks. Bai and Perron (1998) use three test statistics (supF test, the double maximum test, and the sequential test) to determine the significance of multiple structure breaks. As each of these tests has their own strengths and drawbacks, consequently Bai and Perron (2003) suggested to first check if any of the supF tests or double maximum tests was significant and then to proceed with the sequential test to determine the number of breaks. In-depth discussion of the tests is provided in Bai and Perron (2003). We first apply the Bai and Perron (1998, 2003) procedure with one structural break, i.e., two regimes to identify the crisis and the tranquil (before crisis) period. Most of the research articles using daily financial data find September 15, 2008 (see, for example, Blancheton et al., 2012) as the structural break date. Unfortunately September 15, 2008 does not fall in our data as we are using the weekly, Wednesday to Wednesday end of the day data. Using the Bai and Perron (2003) procedure we are able to discover the structural break on September 10, 2008 (it should be noted here that September 15, lies between the weekly dates of September 10, 17, 2008). The lower date on the 95% confidence interval is August 25, 2008, whereas the upper date on the 95% confidence interval is December 2, 2008.

Second, we use GARCH models to estimate conditional variances of each of the returns. For this purpose we estimate EGARCH(1,1) model instead of using GARCH(1,1) models as in Yiu et al. (2010). We estimate a mean equation to retrieve the residuals needed to model variance equation; hence, returns can be described by the following AR(p) process:

$$r_t = \Phi_0 + \sum_{i=1}^{k} \Phi_i r_{t-1} + \varepsilon_t,$$

$$\varepsilon_t \sim \text{idN}(0, \sigma_t^2),$$

where Φ_0 is a constant, Φ_i is the parameters, r_t is returns at time t, and ε_t is error term at time t.

Nelson (1991) introduced Exponential GARCH (EGARCH), which has advantage over GARCH as it permits good news and bad news to have a different impact on volatility by allowing bad news to have greater impact on volatility. The EGARCH model works in two steps, first it considers mean and then variance, it can be defined as:

$$\log(d_t) = \omega + \sum_{i=1}^{p} \left(\alpha_i \left| \frac{\varepsilon_{t-i}}{\sigma_{t-i}} \right| + \gamma_i \frac{\varepsilon_{t-i}}{\sigma_{t-i}} \right) + \sum_{i=1}^{q} \beta_i \log(d_{t-i}),$$

where ω, β, and γ are all parameters for estimating conditional variance. β_i shows the impact of last period measures on conditional variance. α_i is a coefficient that indicates the past standardized residuals' influence on current volatility. Finally γ_i explains asymmetry effect in variance. Third, we use asymmetric DCC model developed by Cappiello et al. (2006) to derive the time-varying conditional correlations. We denote the standardized regression mentioned above as:

$$\bar{\varepsilon}_t = \varepsilon_t \Big/ \sqrt{d_t}$$

To capture asymmetric impacts, the negative standardized residuals are defined by:

$$\bar{n}_t = \bar{\varepsilon}_t \text{ if } \bar{\varepsilon}_t < 0 \text{ and } \bar{n}_t = 0 \quad \text{otherwise.}$$

Then by depicting the dynamics of conditional correlation matrix denoted by P_t and unconditional correlation matrix between residuals denoted by $\bar{P}$ the asymmetric DCC(1,1) model is represented as:

$$P_t = Q_t^{*-1} Q_t Q_t^{*-1},$$

$$Q_t = (\bar{P} - a_1\,\bar{P} - b_1\,\bar{P} - g_1\,\bar{N}) + a_1\,\varepsilon_{t-1}\varepsilon'_{t-1} + g_1\,n_{t-1}n'_{t-1} + b_1\,Q_{t-1},$$

where a_1 and b_1 are scalars and Q_t is the conditional correlation matrix between standardized residuals. Q_t^* is a diagonal matrix with square root of ith diagonal element of conditional correlation matrix on its ith diagonal position. A necessary and sufficient condition to ensure that Q_t is positive definite for all realizations is that:

$$a^2 + b^2 + \delta g^2 < 1,$$

where δ represents maximum eigenvalue $\left[\overline{P}^{-1/2}\overline{NP}^{-1/2}\right]$.

Fourth, we model conditional correlations obtained from the third step by applying AR(1) models to check for the hypothesis that global financial crisis has significant impact on the dynamics of correlations between the US stock market and emerging stock and sovereign bond markets which is termed as evidence of contagion to these markets. We specify the dummy variable on the basis of Bai and Perron structural break test (2003) signifying the global financial crisis period (i.e., from September 17, 2008 to March 25, 2009) as under:

$$D\hat{C}C_t = \delta_0 + \delta_1 D\hat{C}C_{t-1} + \xi_1 Crisis_t + \nu_t.$$

5. DATA AND DESCRIPTIVE STATISTICS

This section details data employed and descriptive statistics.

5.1. Data

For our analysis we use weekly Wednesday to Wednesday data. The data set for EMs is comprised of five EMs (Argentina, Chile, Hungary, Russia, and Poland) and two geographical regions: emerging EU and LAC. Our choice of EMs is motivated by a number of factors. First, these markets are from two different regions, namely emerging LAC and Europe regions. This allows us to assess the evidence for contagion between the US stock market and the stock and sovereign bond markets in emerging EU and LAC region. Second, while the evidence for high stock market volatility and contagion during recent global financial crisis is well documented in the literature for Mexico (Walid et al., 2011) and Brazil (Samarakoon, 2011; Xu and Hamori, 2012), the systematic analysis of other countries in the respective regions such as Argentina and Russia allows us to gage the effect that US stock market has upon the relationship between the US stock and sovereign bond markets as these markets have the highest market capitalization weights of EMBI Global in the respective regions. Third, this study is intended to add to the literature on the integration between stock and sovereign bond markets in emerging and developed countries.

Fourth, as discussed below, our sample covers the period of global financial crisis. As reported in Frank and Hesse (2009) interlinkages between equity markets in advanced economies and emerging market financial indicators were highly correlated and have seen sharp increases during specific crisis moments.

This study covers two financial markets namely: equity and sovereign bond market. We use S&P 500 index for US and national benchmark stock market indices are used at country level. To depict the dynamics of emerging regional markets, we use emerging Morgan Stanley Capital International (MSCI) indices. We utilize weekly observations running from Wednesday to Wednesday to reduce the effects of the cross-country differences in weekend market closures. All the indices are taken in US dollars to account for the exchange rate fluctuations in our analysis when indices are expressed in local currency, part of the index's return volatility is influenced by changes in expected and actual inflation rate or monetary phenomenon. Some of the emerging countries particularly LAC's markets have been experiencing highest inflation rates leading to interpretation problems while using local currency denominated stock price indices.

During recent crisis, significant rise in spreads on sovereign bond segment contributed in fiscal and economic imbalances and resulted in rise in sovereign risk concerns. We use Morgan Emerging Market Bond Index Global Stripped Spread at local and regional level as proxy for EMs sovereign risk.[4] The time series for all the emerging local and regional markets starts from the first week of January 2004 and ends in third week of September 2011. Finally logarithmic returns are taken for each series.

5.2. Descriptive Statistics

Table 1 presents the detailed descriptive statistics of stock returns over pre-crisis period, crisis period, and post-crisis period. By applying the Bai and Perron (2003) structural break test, we identify September 17, 2009 as a break date in our data set. This date around the Lehman Brother's failure represents the beginning of global financial crisis in our data set. The last week of March 2009 is considered as the ending of crisis, as it is generally agreed that the global financial crisis itself ended in March 2009, though there have been aftershocks. Over the whole sample period, all the emerging LAC and EU countries including Emerging LAC and EU region experienced positive return in mean. While comparing the first two moments for the pre-crisis and post-crisis (tranquil) periods, the results reveal that weekly returns are usually higher in both tranquil periods, whereas the standard deviations remain larger during the crisis period. On the country level, the highest level of risk is observed for the Argentina and Russia's stock markets in LAC and EU region, respectively, whereas on regional level emerging EU remains most volatile market. Table 2 shows summary statistics for the returns for JPM EMBI Global Stripped Spreads. Over the entire sample returns remain positive for all the countries and regions except Argentina. It is noteworthy that the mean of the sovereign bond returns relatively increased during the crisis period, with Argentina and Hungary having the

[4] The Morgan EMBI Global (EMBIG) contains US-dollar-denominated Brady bonds, Eurobonds, traded loans, and local market debt instruments issued by sovereign and quasi-sovereign entities. The stripped spread shows the yield difference in basis points over US Treasuries of a JP Morgan emerging market bond index (EMBI) stripping out any credit enhancements such as principal and/or interest collateral.

Table 1 Summary of statistics on the stock index returns.

	US	Argentina	Chile	Hungary	Russia	Poland	LAM Reg.	EU Reg.
Whole sample: (January 14, 2004–September 21, 2011)								
Mean	0.00	0.10	0.27	0.07	0.23	0.17	0.27	0.12
Median	0.18	0.57	0.51	0.81	0.83	0.89	0.75	0.83
Maximum	9.63	23.34	10.96	22.35	25.34	14.69	10.83	20.71
Minimum	−16.45	−23.54	−27.83	−33.73	−44.54	−25.07	−40.32	−37.53
Std. Dev.	2.49	4.46	3.01	6.12	5.81	4.80	4.48	5.26
Skewness	−1.23	−0.77	−2.09	−1.23	−1.53	−1.22	−2.25	−1.60
Kurtosis	10.26	7.84	21.33	8.98	14.38	6.98	19.42	12.49
Jarque-Bera	985.45	434.07	5925.86	701.95	2329.55	365.74	4855.63	1681.87
Observations	402	402	402	402	402	402	402	402
Pre-crisis period: (January 14, 2004–September 10, 2008)								
Mean	0.03	0.10	0.26	0.36	0.33	0.41	0.43	0.27
Median	0.11	0.44	0.48	0.98	0.87	1.06	0.94	0.85
Maximum	3.99	9.20	10.48	9.85	12.31	8.64	10.83	7.00
Minimum	−6.25	−15.97	−9.21	−17.00	−17.47	−14.38	−13.67	−13.37
Std. Dev.	1.60	3.68	2.47	4.05	4.14	3.49	3.56	3.61
Skewness	−0.54	−0.96	−0.41	−1.07	−1.00	−0.93	−0.87	−1.13
Kurtosis	4.03	4.99	4.69	5.23	5.45	4.75	4.77	5.06
Jarque-Bera	22.76	78.03	36.03	97.95	102.91	66.76	63.02	95.48
Observations	244	244	244	244	244	244	244	244
Crisis period: (September 17, 2008–March 25, 2009)								
Mean	−1.48	−1.89	−0.52	−3.42	−2.10	−2.73	−1.40	−2.37
Median	−0.75	−2.76	0.18	−1.19	−1.66	0.00	0.53	0.81
Maximum	9.63	23.34	10.96	22.35	25.34	14.69	10.72	20.71
Minimum	−16.45	−23.54	−27.83	−33.73	−44.54	−25.07	−40.32	−37.53
Std. Dev.	5.85	9.80	6.71	13.96	15.08	10.16	10.55	13.43
Skewness	−0.32	0.09	−2.27	−0.53	−0.62	−0.50	−1.82	−0.58
Kurtosis	3.22	3.45	10.97	2.97	3.79	2.27	7.56	3.20
Jarque-Bera	0.55	0.27	98.21	1.33	2.53	1.82	39.81	1.62
Observations	28	28	28	28	28	28	28	28
Post-crisis period: (April 1, 2009–September 21, 2011)								
Mean	0.27	0.54	0.46	0.28	0.55	0.36	0.34	0.39
Median	0.55	0.81	0.80	0.31	0.66	0.71	0.33	0.79
Maximum	6.32	10.94	7.02	20.93	11.66	14.56	10.08	11.14
Minimum	−11.73	−16.50	−7.31	−20.21	−21.25	−20.70	−10.77	−21.48
Std. Dev.	2.60	3.89	2.67	6.47	4.88	5.01	3.82	4.71
Skewness	−0.84	−0.67	−0.31	−0.21	−0.51	−0.58	−0.20	−0.74
Kurtosis	5.60	5.23	3.12	3.81	5.07	4.84	3.17	5.79
Jarque-Bera	52.48	36.70	2.26	4.60	29.18	25.84	1.07	54.45
Observations	130	130	130	130	130	130	130	130

Table 2 Summary of statistics on the JPM EMBI Global spread returns.

	Argentina	Chile	Hungary	Russia	Poland	LAM Reg.	EU Reg.
Whole sample: (January 14, 2004–September 21, 2011)							
Mean	−0.42	0.17	0.69	0.08	0.31	0.00	0.12
Median	−0.14	−0.27	0.87	−0.19	0.02	−0.30	−0.44
Maximum	35.64	29.96	185.78	44.87	47.32	30.68	31.07
Minimum	−188.77	−16.29	−294.87	−34.86	−32.67	−25.32	−31.36
Std. Dev.	12.06	5.39	28.08	7.72	9.78	5.57	6.58
Skewness	−9.78	0.94	−1.60	0.72	0.33	0.88	0.47
Kurtosis	151.98	6.71	44.69	7.08	5.07	8.34	5.95
Jarque-Bera	378,192.0	291.56	29,291.97	314.64	79.74	530.84	161.55
Observations	402	402	402	402	402	402	402
Pre-crisis period: (January 14, 2004–September 10, 2008)							
Mean	−0.78	0.29	0.70	0.03	0.19	−0.09	0.11
Median	−0.02	−0.27	0.93	−0.08	−0.29	−0.56	−0.20
Maximum	34.05	21.59	185.78	19.18	34.94	15.38	17.77
Minimum	−188.77	−11.24	−294.87	−16.71	−30.44	−25.32	−14.07
Std. Dev.	14.29	4.38	35.02	6.11	9.53	4.87	5.38
Skewness	−9.73	1.16	−1.40	0.40	0.26	−0.02	0.36
Kurtosis	125.93	6.71	30.44	3.64	4.10	6.17	3.34
Jarque-Bera	157,499.1	195.48	7737.61	10.74	15.15	102.24	6.73
Observations	244	244	244	244	244	244	244
Crisis period: (September 17, 2008–March 25, 2009)							
Mean	3.46	1.78	4.48	3.02	3.35	2.16	2.55
Median	2.85	0.33	1.42	2.69	1.37	−0.11	−0.34
Maximum	35.64	29.96	77.27	44.87	47.32	30.68	31.07
Minimum	−13.34	−12.19	−20.68	−34.86	−13.12	−15.94	−31.36
Std. Dev.	10.98	8.97	17.59	15.66	11.45	11.06	12.96
Skewness	1.23	1.17	2.50	0.22	2.22	1.08	−0.02
Kurtosis	4.46	4.77	11.78	3.99	9.13	4.16	3.74
Jarque-Bera	9.61	10.09	119.36	1.38	67.01	7.04	0.64
Observations	28	28	28	28	28	28	28
Post-crisis period: (April 1, 2009–September 21, 2011)							
Mean	−0.58	−0.39	−0.12	−0.47	−0.11	−0.28	−0.37
Median	−0.77	−0.41	0.58	−1.18	0.21	−0.14	−1.10
Maximum	19.71	20.05	26.80	29.23	26.22	19.14	25.61
Minimum	−20.22	−16.29	−21.51	−17.44	−32.67	−10.58	−14.61
Std. Dev.	6.19	6.03	8.52	7.82	9.82	5.00	6.60
Skewness	−0.24	0.32	0.02	0.72	−0.21	0.35	0.47
Kurtosis	3.83	4.04	3.96	4.26	4.17	4.12	3.81
Jarque-Bera	5.02	8.10	5.07	19.99	8.48	9.49	8.49
Observations	130	130	130	130	130	130	130

highest mean and standard deviation in the LAC and EU region, respectively. In case of regional emerging market sovereign bond returns, maximum returns and risk is observed for the EU region.

6. EMPIRICAL RESULTS

6.1. EGARCH Specification

Our first step of DCC model building consists of fitting the univariate GARCH models to each of the stock and bond spreads return series. We chose EGARCH(1,1) models for all five countries and two regions. Tables 3 and 4 show the parameter estimates of univariate EGARCH(1,1), models of stock market, and sovereign bond spread returns of all the emerging countries and regions included in our data set. Most of the parameters of the variance equations are statistically significant. While parameters in mean equations for stock returns are significant at 1% for Chile and Russia and at 5% for emerging LAC region and for sovereign bond spread returns at 1% level for Argentina and emerging LAC region. As we are interested in analyzing dynamics of correlations between US stock returns and emerging stock and sovereign bond spread returns, these almost well-fitted variance equations provide sufficient grounds to believe that our EGARCH models fit the data plausibly well.

6.2. Estimation of Asymmetric DCC Models

In our second step, we derive the estimates of asymmetric DCC model proposed by Cappiello et al. (2006). Tables 5 and 6 present the estimates of asymmetric DCC(1,1) parameters estimates of stock index returns (US versus five countries and two region) and US stock index returns and emerging sovereign bond spread returns (five countries and two region) respectively. In Table 5, both the estimates on the parameter of standardized residuals (a_1) and the parameter of innovations in the dynamics of conditional correlation matrix (b_1) are statistically significant at 5% and 1%, respectively, for all the emerging countries and regions. However, the estimates on the parameter of the standardized negative residuals (g_1) are insignificant in all these models except emerging LAC region. This tends to indicate that conditional correlations of stock market returns between US and other countries and EU region will not be significantly influenced by bad news than the good news from US stock market. Our this finding is in line with the findings of Yiu et al. (2010) where they examine the dynamics of correlations between US stock market and 11 Asian stock markets during Asian crisis and global financial crisis using weekly data from February 1993 to March 2009.

In Table 6, it is interesting to note that both the estimates on the parameter of standardized residuals and the parameter of the standardized negative residuals are significant for Argentina, Chile and LAC region; this indicates that sovereign bond spread returns in these markets will be shocked both in the face of bad news and good news from US stock

Table 3 EGARCH models (stock index returns). Whole sample: (January 14, 2004–September 21, 2011).

	Model by country and region															
	US		Argentina		Chile		Hungary		Russia		Poland		LAM Reg.		EU Reg.	
Coefficient	EGARCH(1,1)		EGARCH(1,1)		EGARCH(1,1)		EGARCH(1,1)		EGARCH(1,1)		EGARCH(1,1)		EGARCH(1,1)		EGARCH(1,1)	
	Estimate	***SE***	***Estimate***	***SE***	***Estimate***	***SE***	***Estimate***	***SE***	***Estimate***	***SE***	***Estimate***	***SE***	***Estimate***	***SE***	***Estimate***	***SE***
Mean equation																
Mean	0.014	0.093	0.160	0.201	0.366***	0.131	0.361	0.230	0.578***	0.218	0.319*	0.175	0.404**	0.174	0.328*	0.197
Variance equation																
ω	0.039**	0.018	0.316***	0.104	0.359*	0.188	0.238***	0.068	0.414***	0.107	0.185***	0.055	0.131***	0.044	0.288***	0.079
α_1	0.014	0.061	0.020	0.050	0.030	0.043	0.146**	0.072	0.101	0.062	0.065	0.050	0.155**	0.073	0.136*	0.075
γ_1	0.440***	0.123	0.191**	0.081	0.143***	0.054	0.145*	0.080	0.341**	0.136	0.265***	0.085	0.211**	0.103	0.256**	0.121
β_1	0.707***	0.105	0.688***	0.086	0.858***	0.049	0.725***	0.053	0.576***	0.084	0.711***	0.056	0.692***	0.055	0.617***	0.068

*Statistical significance at 10% level.
**Statistical significance at 5% level.
***Statistical significance at 1% level.

Table 4 EGARCH models (sovereign bond spread returns). Whole sample: (January 14, 2004–September 21, 2011).

Coefficient	Model by country and region													
	Argentina EGARCH(1,1)		Chile EGARCH(1,1)		Hungary EGARCH(1,1)		Russia EGARCH(1,1)		Poland EGARCH(1,1)		LAM Reg. EGARCH(1,1)		EU Reg. EGARCH(1,1)	
	Estimate	***SE***	***Estimate***	***SE***	***Estimate***	***SE***	***Estimate***	***SE***	***Estimate***	***SE***	***Estimate***	***SE***	***Estimate***	***SE***
Mean equation														
Mean	−0.497***	0.160	−0.023	0.263	−0.110	0.554	−0.432	0.324	0.080	0.434	−0.040***	0.013	−0.180	0.294
Variance equation														
ω	0.816***	0.138	0.135***	0.045	0.110***	0.025	0.250***	0.086	0.137**	0.065	0.088***	0.029	0.207***	0.071
α_1	−0.094***	0.032	0.622***	0.241	0.039	0.029	0.721***	0.207	0.086	0.067	0.288***	0.110	0.586***	0.185
γ_1	0.187***	0.065	−0.519**	0.244	0.211***	0.078	−0.583***	0.222	0.040	0.081	−0.322***	0.113	−0.523***	0.182
β_1	0.409***	0.140	0.244**	0.113	0.815***	0.027	0.183	0.114	0.755***	0.097	0.583***	0.204	0.190	0.134

**Statistical significance at 5% level.
***Statistical significance at 1% level.

Table 5 Dynamic conditional correlation estimates of the stock index returns. (US versus five countries and two regions). Whole sample: (January 14, 2004–September 21, 2011).

Coefficient	Asymmetric DCC estimates by country and region (versus US)													
	Argentina		Chile		Hungary		Russia		Poland		LAM Reg.		EU Reg.	
	Estimate	*SE*	*Estimate*	*SE*	*Estimate*	*SE*	*Estimate*	*SE*	*Estimate*	*SE*	*Estimate*	*SE*	*Estimate*	*SE*
a_1	0.133**	0.066	0.234**	0.115	0.230**	0.098	0.246***	0.061	0.154***	0.040	0.200**	0.085	0.279***	0.056
b_1	0.970***	0.016	0.858***	0.066	0.930***	0.025	0.934***	0.042	0.979***	0.011	0.922***	0.027	0.930***	0.027
g_1	0.157	0.121	−0.149	0.328	−0.207	0.177	−0.196	0.207	−0.000	0.137	−0.237**	0.111	0.149	0.240

**Statistical significance at 5% level.
***Statistical significance at 1% level.

Table 6 Dynamic conditional correlation estimates of the S&P 500 returns and sovereign bond spread returns. **(US versus five countries and two regions)**. Whole sample: (January 14, 2004–September 21, 2011).

Coefficient	Asymmetric DCC estimates by country and region (versus US)													
	Argentina		Chile		Hungary		Russia		Poland		LAM Reg.		EU Reg.	
	Estimate	***SE***	***Estimate***	***SE***	***Estimate***	***SE***	***Estimate***	***SE***	***Estimate***	***SE***	***Estimate***	***SE***	***Estimate***	***SE***
a_1	0.479***	0.065	0.124***	0.041	0.082	0.111	0.221***	0.076	0.141**	0.056	0.275***	0.088	0.251***	0.059
b_1	0.846***	0.050	0.983***	0.011	0.978***	0.019	0.891***	0.110	0.983***	0.015	0.829***	0.168	0.895***	0.053
g_1	0.167***	0.053	0.132**	0.055	−0.104**	0.047	−0.000	0.132	0.043	0.290	−0.000***	0.000	−0.000	0.378

**Statistical significance at 5%.
***Statistical significance at 1%.

market. Hungary sovereign bond spread returns instead show that negative innovations to return do play a different role than positive innovations to returns or sovereign bond spread returns will be shocked more in the face of bad news than good news from US stock market. Sovereign bond spread returns of Russia, Poland, and EU region show a significant response to good news from US stock market. Table also presents that the estimates on the parameters of innovations in conditional correlation matrix are significant at 1% significance level for all EMs at country and regional level.

Figures 1 and 2 describe the evolution of time-varying conditional correlations between US stock market and stock markets of five emerging countries and two regions. Four key main findings can be highlighted from these graphs. First, US market correlations with EMs have moved in tandem with the highest spike in correlations in the fourth quarter of 2008. Emerging stock markets showed increased volatility and experienced strong fall in stock market returns in September 2008 after the Lehman Brothers failure. Our this finding is in line with the findings of Dooley and Hutchison (2009) and Naoui et al. (2010) where the former confirmed that correlations between percentage changes in US S&P 500 index and percentage changes in national equity market indices for selected emerging markets increased over this period and the latter identified contagion effects from US stock market to six developed and ten emerging countries' stock markets. Second, though failure of Lehman Brothers entailed a wave of stress in all these markets, however, show some peculiarities for instance in the case of Chile, we can notice that there is considerable surge in correlations in October 2008, however this rise in correlations is not long lasting, coming to the levels similar to those preceding 2008 after the first quarter of 2009 (this is in line with the findings of Dufrénot et al., 2011 who study the impact of worsening US financial environment on LAC's stock markets in the aftermath of the 2007/2008 crisis). Regarding other EMs patterns reveal certain differences with respect to Chile, all these markets experienced sudden increase in correlations after September 15, 2008, characterized by sharp fall in stock market returns followed by persistent high correlation thereafter with an exception in second quarter of 2009 where correlations fall for a while. This suggests that diversification opportunities between US and these markets decreased over that period. Third, after the inception of global financial crisis considerable peaks in correlations can be noticed from November 2009, mostly pronounced in emerging EU's stock markets. These spikes in correlations coincide with huge downturns in EU's stock markets because of the EU's sovereign debt crisis (see Tamakoshi et al., 2012).

Overall we find that the markets with high level of capital inflows, high ratios of equity holdings by US investors and mostly liquid showed greater co-movements with US.[5] A high intensity of sell-offs along with widening of emerging sovereign bond spreads after

[5] This is consistent with the view of margin calls where US investors experiencing huge losses in home withdraw their investments from foreign countries and for those investors who are exposed to US and are required to redeem their investments to make up US losses it is usual to exit in mostly liquid markets.

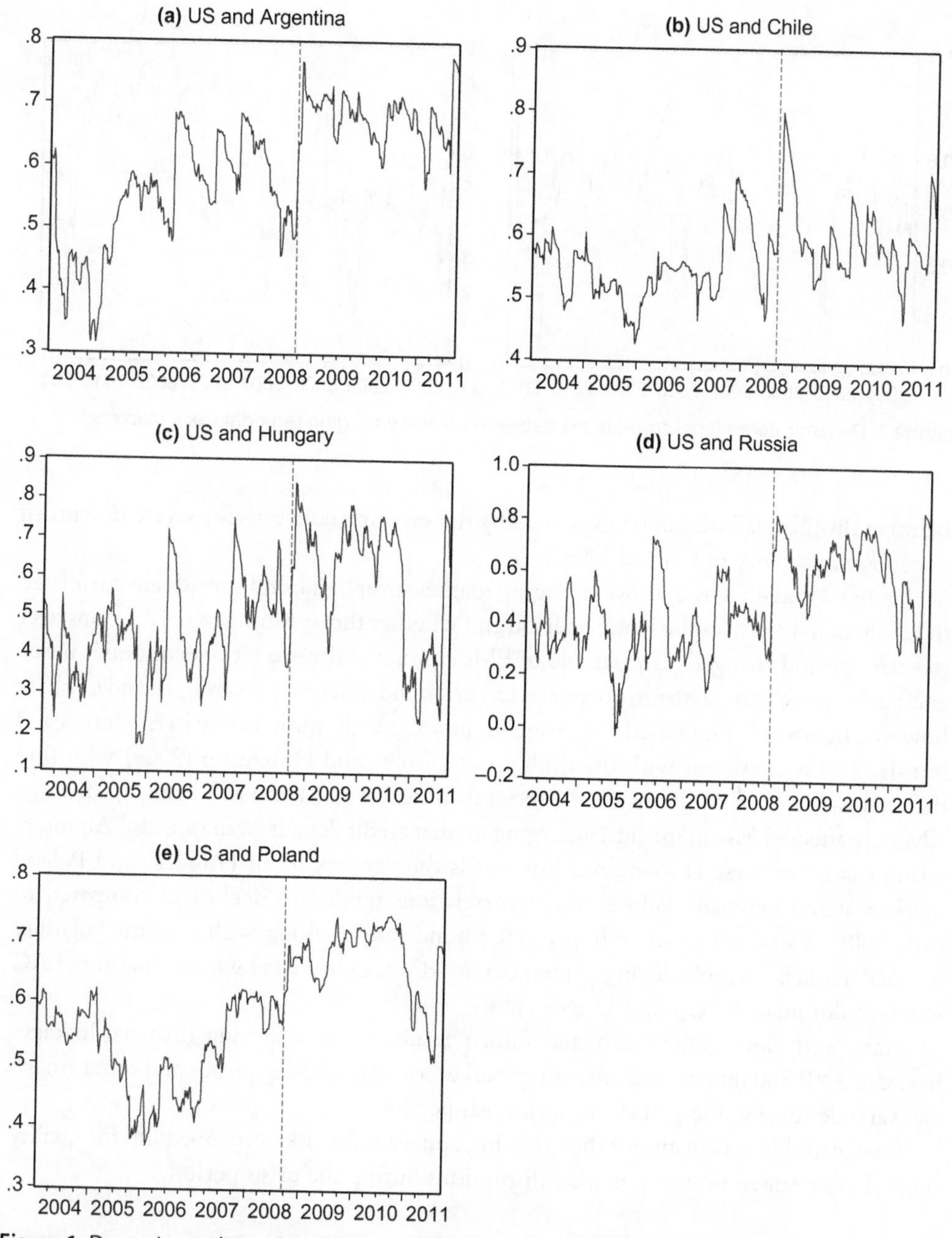

Figure 1 Dynamic conditional correlations between US and emerging stock markets. (*Note:* dotted lines in the figures indicate the beginning of the Global Financial Crisis as on September 17, 2008; as identified by structural break in S&P 500 index).

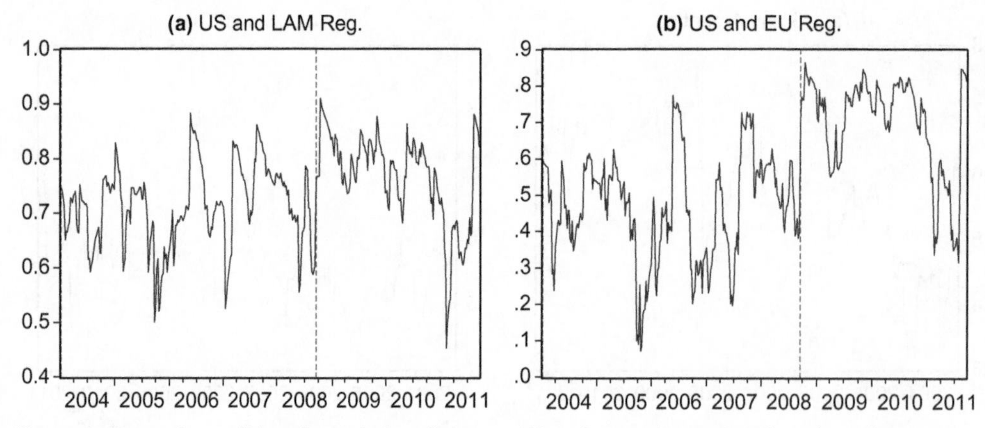

Figure 2 Dynamic conditional correlations between US and emerging regional stock markets.

Lehman Brothers failure can be explained by the growing concerns for severe downturn in economic activity in US and EMs.

Figures 3 and 4 focus on how emerging market sovereign bond spreads are correlated to US stock market over the sample period and whether the dynamics of correlations over the crisis period changed. Our sample of EMs consists of diverse set of economies influencing the correlation dynamics between US stock and emerging sovereign bond markets; however, Lehman failure raised the sovereign bond spreads immediately in Argentina and Russia. This is consistent with the findings of Dooley and Hutchison (2009) who find that write-downs of equity in US financial institutions and Lehman's bankruptcy news adversely affected (rise in spreads) emerging market credit default swap spreads.[6] An interesting feature of these cross-market linkages is the decoupling of Hungary and Poland markets at the Lehman's failure where correlations tended to decline as compared to early 2008. A spectacular surge in sovereign bond spreads along with extreme volatility in stock markets is visible during September 2008 at regional level where emerging LAC seems to dominate emerging EU region.

Frank and Hesse (2009) also find similar results while analyzing financial linkages between S&P 500 returns and emerging market sovereign bond spreads and other financial variables during the global financial crisis period.

One plausible explanation is that growing concerns for risk aversion, flight for quality might have resulted in strong market disruptions during the crisis period.

[6] A credit default swap (CDS) is a financial swap agreement that the seller of the CDS will pay off the buyer in the event of a loan default or other credit event. The buyer of the CDS makes a series of payments (the CDS "fee" or "spread") to the seller and in exchange receives a payoff if a borrower fails to adhere to its debt agreement.

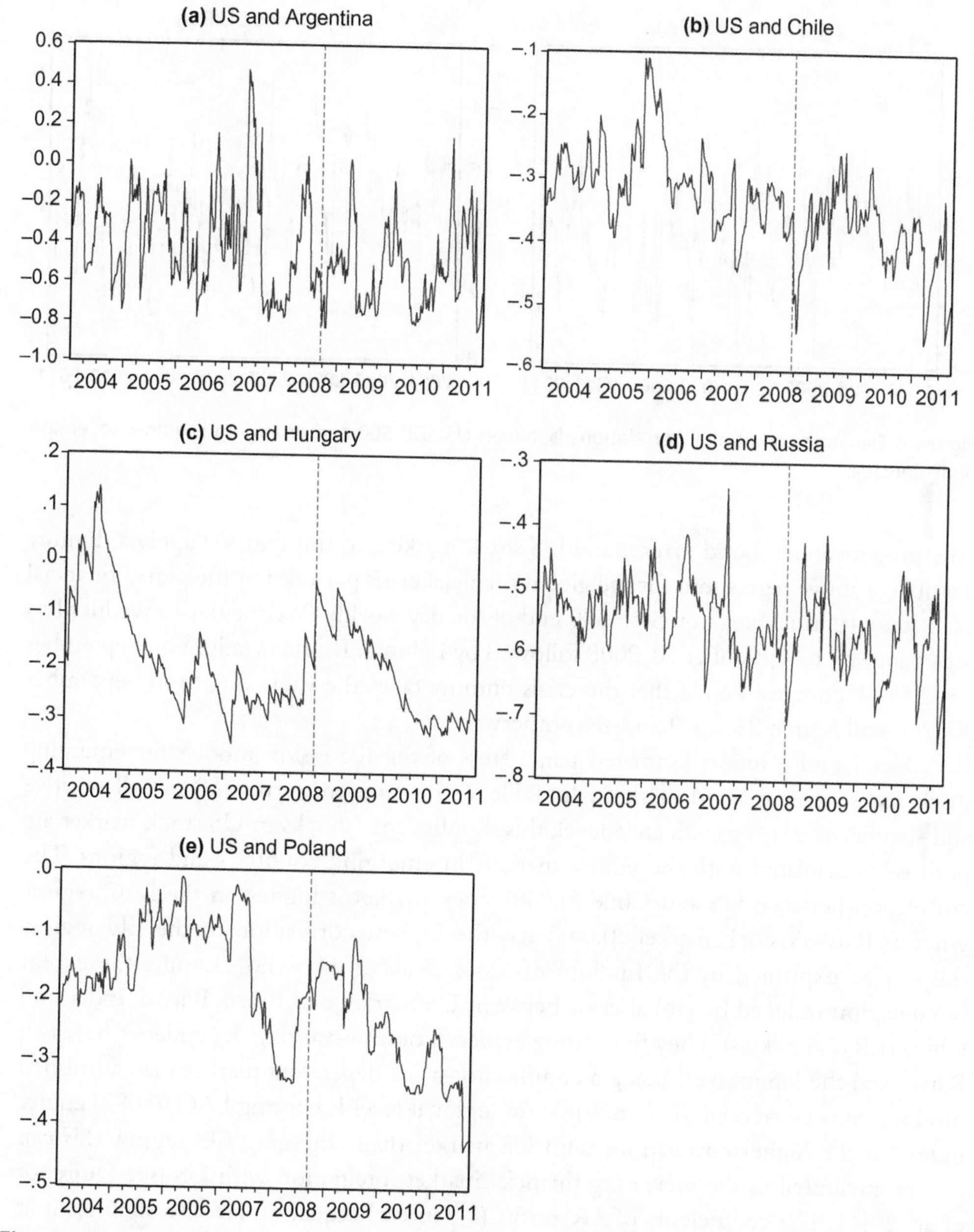

Figure 3 Dynamic conditional correlations between US S&P 500 and emerging market sovereign bond spreads.

6.3. AR Model for the Estimated Dynamic Conditional Correlations

Finally, we apply AR(1) models to analyze the impact of global financial crisis on the dynamics of the correlations between emerging stock markets and US stock market and

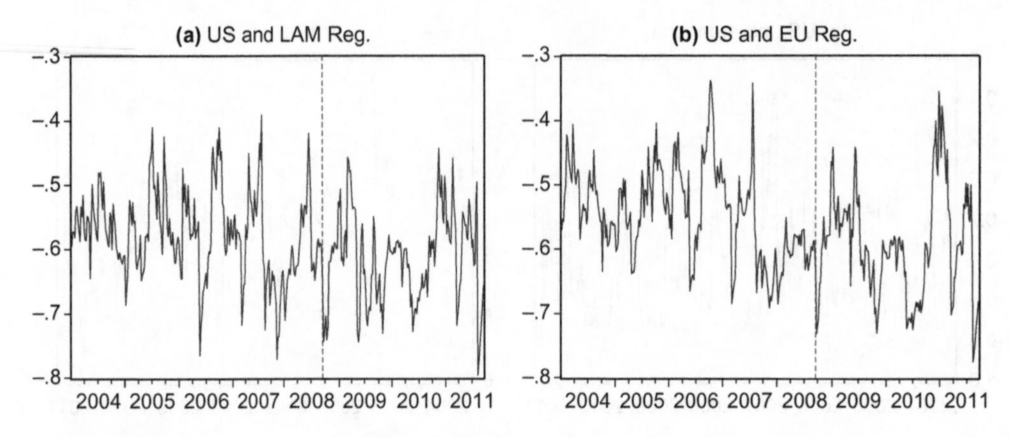

Figure 4 Dynamic conditional correlations between US S&P 500 and emerging regional sovereign bond spreads.

emerging sovereign bond market and US stock market. To this end, we apply a dummy variable in above regressions for the global financial crisis period. For the global financial crisis, the structural break on S&P 500 end of the day weekly (Wednesday to Wednesday) series appears at September 10, 2008 followed by Lehman Brothers failure on September 15, 2008. Hence we define that the crisis dummy takes the value one from September 17, 2008 till March 25, 2009 and zero otherwise.

Tables 7 and 8 report estimated parameters of the regression models for emerging stock and sovereign bond markets. In Table 7, the constant terms (δ_0) are all positive and significant at 1% significance level, this signifies that shocks in US stock market are positively correlated with the equity markets in emerging countries and regions. The correlation between US and Chile (0.049) stock market is highest in the LAC region, whereas Russia's stock market (0.043) has the highest correlation in the EU region; this can be explained by the findings of Aloui et al. (2011) who examine the extent of contagion induced by global crisis between US market and Brazil, Russia, India, and China (BRIC markets). They find strong evidence of time-varying dependence between Russia and the US markets being a commodity-price dependent market than a finished product export-oriented market. While on regional level Emerging LAC (0.082) equity index has the higher correlations with US market than emerging EU region, this can also be attributed to the increasing financial market integration with US (see Dufrénot et al., 2011). The coefficients of AR terms (δ_1) in each equation are also significant at 1% significance level for all markets with values less than unity thereby ensuring the stationarity of the model. A relatively high R^2 ranging from 0.81 to 0.96 ensures that

Table 7 AR(1) models for the estimated DCC coefficients for stock index returns. (US versus five countries and two regions). Whole sample: (January 14, 2004–September 21, 2011).

Coefficient	DCC estimates by country and region (versus US)													
	Argentina		Chile		Hungary		Russia		Poland		LAM Reg.		EU Reg.	
	Estimate	*SE*	*Estimate*	*SE*	*Estimate*	*SE*	*Estimate*	*SE*	*Estimate*	*SE*	*Estimate*	*SE*	*Estimate*	*SE*
δ_0	0.036***	0.009	0.049***	0.011	0.037***	0.009	0.043***	0.009	0.020***	0.007	0.082***	0.016	0.046***	0.010
δ_1	0.932***	0.017	0.912***	0.020	0.923***	0.018	0.882***	0.022	0.960***	0.013	0.885***	0.022	0.897***	0.021
ξ_1	0.011***	0.003	0.010**	0.004	0.024**	0.011	0.032***	0.008	0.006***	0.002	0.017**	0.007	0.027***	0.007
R^2	0.935		0.869		0.878		0.884		0.968		0.812		0.888	

**Statistical significance at 5% level.
***Statistical significance at 1% level.

Table 8 AR(1) models for the estimated DCC coefficients for sovereign bond spread returns. **(US S&P 500 versus emerging sovereign bond spread returns five countries and two regions).** Whole sample: (January 14, 2004–September 21, 2011).

Coefficient	DCC estimates by country and region (versus US)													
	Argentina		Chile		Hungary		Russia		Poland		LAM Reg.		EU Reg.	
	Estimate	*SE*	*Estimate*	*SE*	*Estimate*	*SE*	*Estimate*	*SE*	*Estimate*	*SE*	*Estimate*	*SE*	*Estimate*	*SE*
δ_0	−0.067***	0.013	−0.032***	0.007	−0.006**	0.002	−0.091***	0.015	−0.003*	0.002	−0.129***	0.018	−0.075***	0.014
δ_1	0.824***	0.028	0.891***	0.023	0.973***	0.011	0.829***	0.028	0.974***	0.012	0.775***	0.031	0.861***	0.025
ξ_1	−0.026*	0.014	−0.009***	0.003	0.008*	0.004	−0.007**	0.003	−0.004*	0.002	−0.008*	0.004	−0.007*	0.004
R^2	0.706		0.851		0.955		0.720		0.958		0.626		0.765	

*Statistical significance at 10% level.
**Statistical significance at 5% level.
***Statistical significance at 1% level.

the AR representation of each DCC equation is plausibly adequate. The coefficients of crisis dummies (ξ_1) are all positive and significant at least at the 5% for all markets. So, this suggests the contagion effects from US stock market to other emerging stock markets at country level and regional level during the global financial crisis period are evident.

In Table 8, the constant terms (δ_0) are all negative and statistically significant at least at 5% significance level except Poland. This reveals the fact that shocks in US stock market are negatively correlated with EMs sovereign bond spreads and signifies the fact that plunging stock prices in US cause increase in emerging countries' sovereign risk hence rise in risk premium or sovereign bond spreads.

Argentina's sovereign bond spreads have the higher correlation (−0.067) with US from LAC region and Russia's sovereign bond spreads maintain higher correlation with US (−0.091) from EU region. On regional level as part of global risk aversion because of the financial market downturn and process of widening spreads emerging LAC region has the higher correlation with US (−0.129) than EU region. The AR parameter (δ_1) in all equations is significant at 1% significance level. High level of R^2 ranging from 0.62 to 0.95 ensures the adequacy of AR(1) models. The global financial crisis dummies (ξ_1) are all negative (except Hungary) and significant at 5% significance level in Chile and Russia. These results confirm that during global financial crisis downturn in US stock market contributed significantly in rising sovereign bond spreads or sovereign risk in these EMs and resulted in contagion.

7. IMPLICATIONS AND CONCLUSION

Our findings hold several implications in the area of financial research on emerging countries, concentrating on equity and sovereign bond markets on substantive levels. A predominantly significant role has been played by the stress in US stock market on the volatility and changing correlation dynamics in financial markets in both regions. This is in line with Dooley and Hutchison (2009) where EMs reacted to host of bad news such as bankruptcy of Lehman and write down of equities resulting in the flight of capital and rising sovereign bond spreads in EMs due to the looming prospects for economic downturn.

There is strong evidence that rising concerns for risk aversion on behalf of investors resulted in decline in stock prices in EMs, particularly in LAC in the wake of recent crisis. Providing sufficient heterogeneity in macroeconomic fundamentals across countries and regions such correlations can be interpreted as sign of herding behavior and "bandwagon" effects on the part of investors.[7] Though the level of correlations following the crisis increased in all regions under consideration, the regional patterns vary, implying spillovers may be more regional than global. One possibility to counteract the contagion effects

[7] A form of group think, in which investor's probability of adopting any belief increases with the proportion who have already done so, hence investors do not discriminate among economic fundamentals across countries.

from the US financial markets would be to restore the intra-regional integration of capital markets and to implement risk sharing scheme between countries.

During the recent crisis, financial volatility has been termed as a more important determinant of spillover effects than fundamental indicators on EMs through its impact on global liquidity conditions and equity prices.

The conventional wisdom to come out of recent crises is the need for improving sovereign creditworthiness to regain the confidence of the international financial markets, sound and sustainable fiscal policies, reducing the level of domestic and external refinancing needs and lender of last resort considerations. All these can improve the economic prospects of the countries among international investors. A comprehensive approach is needed on national and international level to reassure financial markets and contain volatility in equity markets and sovereign bond markets.

Overall this paper focuses on the issue of contagion from US stock market to emerging equity and sovereign bond markets, an empirically elusive issue in financial research. To cope with such an issue, a comparative analysis was made using the Asymmetric DCC GARCH model introduced by Cappiello et al. (2006) for five countries and two regions namely emerging EU and LAC, first on country level and second on regional level. The paper unearths several important linkages on theoretical and empirical grounds and provides a number of interesting insights. In particular, it tends to indicate that rising volatility in US stock market does influence the dynamics of correlations with emerging countries' stock and sovereign bond markets and results in contagion in these markets at local and regional level during the crisis.

This tends to confirm that diversification opportunities decreased for international investors during the crisis period. We find abrupt increases in correlations post-Lehman Brothers failure in most local and regional EMs, theoretically this can be explained by the presence of herding behavior among international investors and correlated trading across large institutional investors in the face of rising uncertainty, resulted in contagion and exacerbated the conditions in emerging financial markets. Although during the recent financial crisis dislocations in these five regions were a global phenomenon, the strong disruptions in equity and sovereign bond spreads in emerging LAC region point toward an important finding that extent of economic integration with the US also contributed to volatility spillovers among these regions. Our empirical results highlight that the volatility in stock markets and agents' degree of risk aversion are the most significant factors in explaining the dynamics in emerging equities and sovereign spreads markets. This fall in risk appetite was more pronounced in emerging equity markets than sovereign bond spreads across the regions.

In the light of these results, further ramifications have also been addressed for the role of US financial market stress in EMs crisis, informational and institutional factors as conduit of contagion, importance of nonfundamental channels in spillovers to financial markets in emerging countries, domestic macro stabilization policies, and policy coordination at national and international level. Future research could attempt to model both the fundamental and financial market factors to better hone the impact of US spillovers (on short and long perspective) on these markets.

REFERENCES

Aloui, R., Ben, M.S., Nguyen, D.K., 2011. Global financial crisis, extreme interdependences, and contagion effects: the role of economic structure? Journal of Banking and Finance 35 (1), 130–141
Baba, N., Packer, F., 2009. Interpreting deviations from covered interest parity during the financial market turmoil of 2007–08. Journal of Banking and Finance 33 (11), 1953–1962
Bai, J., Perron, P., 1998. Estimating and testing linear models with multiple structural changes. Econometrica 66 (1), 47–78
Bai, J., Perron, P., 2003. Computation and analysis of multiple structural change models. Journal of Applied Econometrics 18 (1), 1–22
Berglöf, E., Korniyenko, Y., Plekhanov, A., Zettelmeyer, J., 2010. Understanding the crisis in emerging Europe. Public Policy Review Japan 6 (6),
Blancheton, B., Bordes, C., Maveyraud, S., Rous, P., 2012. Risk of liquidity and contagion of the crisis on the US, UK and Euro area money markets. International Journal of Finance and Economics, online first 10 mars 2011
Brunnermeier, M.K., 2009. Deciphering the liquidity and credit crunch. Journal of Economic Perspectives 23 (1), 77–100
Cappiello, L., Engle, R.F., Sheppard, K., 2006. Asymmetric dynamics in the correlations of global equity and bond returns. Journal of Financial Econometrics 4 (4), 537–572
Chiang, T.C., Zheng, D., 2010. An empirical analysis of herd behavior in global stock markets. Journal of Banking and Finance 34 (8), 1911–1921
Dooley, M., Hutchison, M.(NberEditors, Ed.), 2009. Transmission of the U.S. subprime crisis to emerging markets: evidence on the decoupling–recoupling hypothesis. Journal of International Money and Finance 28 (8), 1331–1349
Dufrénot, G., Mignon, V., Péguin-Feissolle, A., 2011. The effects of the subprime crisis on the latin american financial markets: an empirical assessment. Economic Modelling 28 (5), 2342–2357
Engle, R., 2002. Dynamic conditional correlation: a simple class of multivariate generalized autoregressive conditional heteroskedasticity models. Journal of Business and Economic Statistics 20 (3), 339–350
Engle, R.F., Kroner, K.F., 1995. Multivariate simultaneous generalized ARCH. Econometric Theory 11 (01), 122–150
Engle, R.F., Ng, V.K., 1993. Measuring and testing the impact of news on volatility. Journal of Finance 48 (5), 1749–1778
Feldstein, M., Horioka, C., 1980. Domestic saving and international capital flows. Economic Journal 90 (358), 314–329
Forbes, K.J., Rigobon, R., 2002. No contagion, only interdependence: measuring stock market comovements. Journal of Finance 57 (5), 2223–2261
Frank, N., Hesse, H., 2009. Financial spillovers to emerging markets during the global financial crisis. Czech Journal of Economics and Finance (Finance a uver) 59 (6), 507–521
Frank, N., Hesse, H., 2009. Financial spillovers to emerging markets during the global financial crisis. Quantitative Finance 59 (6), 507–521
Frankel, J., 1992. Measuring international capital mobility: a review. American Economic Review, 197–202
González-Hermosillo, B., Hesse, H., 2011. Global market conditions and systemic risk. Journal of Emerging Market Finance 10 (2), 227–252
Hedi Arouri, M.E., Foulquier, P., 2012. Financial market integration: theory and empirical results. Economic Modelling 29 (2), 382–394
Kaminsky, G., Lyons, R., Schmukler, S., 2001. Mutual fund investment in emerging markets: an overview. World Bank Economic Review 15 (2), 315–340
Kwan, S., 2009. Behavior of libor in the current financial crisis. FRBSF Economic Letter (January 23).

McGuire, P., Peter, G.V., 2009. The US dollar shortage in global banking. BIS, Quarterly Review, 47–63

Naoui, K., Universitaire, T.C., Economiques, S., Tel, T., El, T., Tel, M., 2010. A dynamic conditional correlation analysis of financial contagion: the case of the subprime credit crisis. Journal of Economics and Finance 2 (3), 85–96

Nelson, D.B., 1991. Conditional heteroskedasticity in asset returns: a new approach. Econometrica 59 (2), 347–370

Nelson, D.B., 1991. Conditional heteroskedasticity in asset returns: a new approach. Econometrica: Journal of the Econometric Society, 347–370

Valadao, M.A., Gico, I.T., 2010. The (Not So) great depression of the 21st century and its impacts on Brazil. Law and Business Review of the Americas 16 (1)

Powell, A., Martinez, J.F., 2008. On emerging economy sovereign spreads and ratings. Tech. rep., Working paper, Inter-American Development Bank, Research Department.

Rose, A.K., Spiegel, M.M., 2010. Cross-country causes and consequences of the 2008 crisis: international linkages and american exposure. Pacific Economic Review 15 (3), 340–363

Samarakoon, L.P., 2011. Stock market interdependence, contagion, and the U.S. financial crisis: the case of emerging and frontier markets. Journal of International Financial Markets, Institutions and Money 21 (5), 724–742

Shamiri, A., Isa, Z., 2009. The US crisis and the volatility spillover across south east asia stock markets. International Research Journal of Finance and Economics 34, 7–17

Tamakoshi, G., Toyoshima, Y., Hamori, S., 2012. A dynamic conditional correlation analysis of European stock markets from the perspective of the Greek sovereign debt crisis. Economics Bulletin 32 (1), 437–448

Vo, X.V., Daly, K.J., 2007. The determinants of international financial integration. Global Finance Journal 18 (2), 228–250

Walid, C., Chaker, A., Masood, O., Fry, J., 2011. Stock market volatility and exchange rates in emerging countries: a Markov-state switching approach. Emerging Markets Review 12 (3), 272–292

Xu, H., Hamori, S., 2012. Dynamic linkages of stock prices between the BRICs and the United States: effects of the 2008–2009 financial crisis. Journal of Asian Economics 23 (4), 344–352

Yiu, M.S., Ho, W.-Y.A., Choi, D.F., 2010. Dynamic correlation analysis of financial contagion in Asian markets in global financial turmoil. Applied Financial Economics 20 (4), 345–354

Zhou, R.T., Lai, R.N., 2009. Herding and information based trading. Journal of Empirical Finance 16 (3), 388–393

CHAPTER 22

Assessing the Effects of the Global Financial Crisis on the East Asian Equity Markets

Tran Phuong Thao[*,†], **Kevin Daly**[*], **and Craig Ellis**[*]

[*]School of Business, University of Western Sydney, Sydney, Australia
[†]Department of Banking, University of Economics, Ho Chi Minh City, Vietnam

1. INTRODUCTION

The Global Financial Crisis (GFC) is considered to have been the most severe crisis in history since the 1930s Great Depression. It was attributed to a series of severe market events such as the speculative bubble in the US housing market in 2006, the sub-prime mortgage crisis in the United States in early 2007, and the liquidity crunch in global credit markets in mid-2007. The crisis intensified in the second half of 2008 after the US State Bank and Government refused to rescue Lehman Brothers and confirmed the collapse of American International Group. These decisions partly caused panic among both investors and financial institutions around the world, leading to sharp declines in global equity market indices until the first quarter of 2009 (Bartram and Bodnar, 2009; Dooley and Hutchison, 2009). A comprehensive review of the history of the GFC can be found in a study by Arestis et al. (2011).

Prior research has documented the impacts of the GFC on the individual as well as regional and global markets (see, for example, Dooley and Hutchison, 2009; Markwat et al., 2009; Claessens et al., 2010; Allen and Carletti, 2010). Bartram and Bodnar (2009), for instance, and provides evidence of a sharp decline in global equity market indices of between 40 and 60% of their 2006 market values by the end of February 2009. In addition, several studies indicate that the GFC was more serious than previous crises. Gklezakou and Mylonakis (2010), for instance, show that while previous crises disturbed the financial systems in affected economies, the GFC penetrated practically every aspect of global economic activity. Recently, Guo et al. (2011) examined the impacts of the GFC on various markets such as stock, real estate, energy markets and credit default swap markets; their conclusion is that credit default swaps are non-existent in other crises.

Despite increasing concerns as regards the GFC, the issue of how the GFC was transmitted across global markets has not been widely developed in the literature. Several studies, such as those by Claessens et al. (2010) and Mishkin (2011), examine the transmission of the GFC to the global markets by visually describing the interactions of market

Emerging Markets and the Global Economy
http://dx.doi.org/10.1016/B978-0-12-411549-1.00022-3

movements during the crisis. Other studies explore the transmission empirically (see, for example, Gupta and Donleavy, 2009; Naoui et al., 2010; Marcal et al., 2011; Kenourgios et al., 2011), however, almost all of these studies focus on the impacts of the GFC on developed and major emerging markets that have strong links with the United States rather than other markets such as emerging and frontier markets. As such, the primary objective of this chapter is to empirically explore the extent to which the effects of the GFC were transmitted to different groups of equity markets around the globe.

In this chapter, we investigate the transmission mechanism of the shock caused by the GFC to equity markets in the East Asian region, including the developed markets (Hong Kong, Japan, Singapore), emerging markets (Malaysia, Thailand, Taiwan), and frontier market (Vietnam).[1] There are two main reasons for selecting these markets. *Firstly*, the East Asian region has consistently recorded some of the highest global growth rates in real GDP over the last two decades. *Secondly*, the region was severely affected by previous crises, particularly the 1997 Asian Financial Crisis, the area of interest, therefore, is how the equity markets of the East Asian region responded to the GFC. Our research employs panel data sourced from DataStream for the period from 1/7/2007 to 31/12/2010. The chapter is structured as follows: Section 2 presents the literature review on the crises along with a review of the transmission mechanisms of crises. Section 3 introduces data and research methodology, while Section 4 discusses empirical findings, the final Section 5 concludes the paper.

2. LITERATURE REVIEW

Over the recent decades, global markets have experienced a series of crises that originated in a specific market and rapidly transmitted to other markets. Such spread of financial turmoil across markets is often referred to as a "contagion effect" (Dornbusch et al., 2000; Forbes and Rigobon, 2002; Guo et al., 2011; Khalid and Kawai, 2003). A study by Claessens and Forbes (2001) indicates that the concept was first introduced in chemistry with reference to the spread of medical diseases; however, in the late 1990s, the concept was widely used in an economic context to describe a transmission of a shock across markets. There are several definitions of contagion in the existing literature. For instance, while Forbes and Rigobon (2002) define contagion as a significant increase in the correlation between equity markets during a crisis; Dornbusch et al. (2000) use the term contagion when describing an increase in a cross-market linkage after a shock to one country.

The World Bank classifies levels of contagion by proposing three definitions (Billio and Pelizzon, 2003; Claessens and Forbes, 2001). The first definition is very broad, defining contagion as the cross-country transmission of shocks or cross-country spillover

[1] The market classification is based on the 2012 MSCI global equity indices.

effects; however, this definition takes into consideration the transmission of shocks in both tranquil and crisis periods. The second definition is restrictive, stating that contagion is the transmission or co-movement of shocks in excess of what can be explained by economic fundamentals. This definition is claimed to be the most controversial one in order to identify the underlying fundamentals. The third definition is known to be of a very restrictive type emphasizing a transmission mechanism of a shock among countries during a period of crisis. This definition is similar to a "shift contagion" given by Forbes and Rigobon (2002) defining contagion as a significant increase in cross-market linkages after a shock to a specific market and is widely used in the literature (see, for example, Kuper and Lestano, 2007; Gupta and Donleavy, 2009; Yiu et al., 2010; Yu et al., 2010). In this paper, we utilize the definition of the shift contagion to examine the propagation of transmissions of the shock caused by the GFC to East Asian equity markets.

Contagion effects generally originate from two main sources. In early studies, international trade and financial linkages and common shocks are often used to provide thoughtful explanations for the transmission mechanism of contagion (Kearney, 2000; Phylaktis and Ravazzolo, 2002; Pretorius, 2002). These factors are known as fundamental-based factors. However, as many crises occurred more frequently in recent decades, empirical results find evidence of transmissions of a shock from one country to others that do not have close fundamental linkages to a host country. Khalid and Kawai (2003), for instance, document three sources of contagion, namely common shocks, financial linkages, and shifts, in investors' sentiments. Dornbusch et al. (2000) discuss two sources of contagion effect over turbulence periods. The first source is related to fundamental-based channels associated with real and financial linkages across borders, while the second is attributed to irrational behaviors of investors resulting from liquidity problems, imperfect information, and multiple equilibria. A similar viewpoint that employs investor behavior to explain the spillover of shocks across markets can be found in the studies by Claessens and Forbes (2001), Karolyi (2003), and Caramazza et al. (2004).

To explore whether contagion effects exist across global equity markets, several empirical models, which are based on different definitions and empirical tests, are suggested. For example, Claessens and Forbes (2001) discuss five categories of tests for contagion, namely correlation coefficient, conditional probabilities, volatility spillovers, movement of capital flows, and other tests. Dungey et al. (2005) present several empirical models of contagion including correlation tests and factor models. However, empirical findings reveal less consensus results among contagion tests. Using unconditional correlation tests, Forbes and Rigobon (2002) examine contagion effects in global markets during the three recent crises: the 1987 US stock market crisis, the 1994 Mexico crisis, and the 1987 East Asian crisis. The authors find evidence in favor of interdependence instead of contagion among the markets. In the meantime, Corsetti et al. (2005) reveal some contagion and some interdependence among global equity markets by employing a single-factor model. Ahlgren and Antell (2010) follow a co-breaking analysis based on the VAR model to test for contagion, and find evidence of contagion between developed markets, but not between emerging markets, or between emerging and developed markets during financial crises over the period 1980–2006. Another study by Yiu et al. (2010) uses the dynamics of correlations between 11 Asian stock markets and the US stock market, and finds an existence of contagion between the US and individual markets in Asia from the late 2007, but no such evidence is found during the Asian financial crisis. Therefore, we may conclude that despite a new concept in the financial discipline, contagion effect attracts increasing interest of researchers; however, empirical findings are not consistent across examined countries and crises.

3. DATA AND METHODOLOGY

3.1. Data Collection

In order to investigate the transmission of the GFC to the East Asian equity markets, this paper employs time series data consisting of the daily closing prices of seven market indices in the region including the Hang Seng Index for Hong Kong, the TSE Composite Index for Taiwan, the Strait Times Index for Singapore, the Nikkei 225 Stock Average for Japan, the KLSE Composite Index for Malaysia, the SET Index for Thailand, and the VN-Index for Vietnam. The S&P 500 Composite Index of the United States is employed to take into account the transmission of the GFC to the region. According to the market classification of the MSCI (2012), we separate the seven East Asian market indices in the sample into three groups. The developed market group includes Hong Kong, Japan, and Singapore. The emerging market group covers Malaysia, Taiwan, and Thailand, and the frontier market includes Vietnam. The data are sourced from the DataStream International for the period from 1/7/2007 to 31/12/2010. On non-trading days of the market indices, we assume it stays the same compared with the previous trading day. In addition, the market indices in local currency are used to capture influences of local economic policy and economic conditions on market linkages.

It is notable that the trading hours of Asian markets overlap while the United States equity markets lag one day behind the Asian markets. Hence, in this chapter, the equity market returns of the United States are lagged by one day compared with those of the other series data. The first differences of logarithms of market indices multiplied by 100 are constructed to measure market returns of the selected markets.

For capturing the transmission of the GFC to the selected markets, we separate the period of study into sub-periods according to the descriptions by Mishkin (2011) and Aït-Sahalia et al. (2012). In particular, the period of study is divided into three sub-periods. The pre-crisis period is from 1/7/2007 to 14/9/2008 comprising 315 observation of each series. The crisis period is from 15/9/2008 to 31/3/2009 comprising 142 observations of each series, and the post-crisis period starts on 1/4/2009 and ends on 31/12/2010 comprising 458 observations.

The descriptive statistics of the market returns over the sub-periods are shown in Table 1. In general, we can see some similar findings during the pre-crisis and crisis periods. More specifically, all the markets have negative average rate of returns over the two periods implying declines of the market levels of the entire markets. It can be explained by the severity and ample effects of the sub-prime crisis and the GFC on the regional markets. Interestingly, the Vietnam Index recorded the highest negative returns over the periods implying the strongest impacts of the crises on the frontier market compared with the other markets in the sample. In the meantime, the Hong Kong equity market experienced the highest standard deviation of market returns suggesting a high vulnerability of the market during the periods. It is notable that the higher standard

Table 1 Descriptive statistics of market returns.

	Mean	Std dev.	Skew	Kurtosis
Pre-crisis period (from 1/7/2007 to 14/8/2008)				
US	−0.06	1.29	−0.06	3.4
HK	−0.04	2.16	0.03	5.24
JP	−0.13	1.6	−0.26	3.82
SG	−0.1	1.55	0	4.34
ML	−0.08	1.2	−1.84	17.71
TW	−0.05	1.37	0.24	3.75
TL	−0.11	1.72	−0.29	3.93
VN	−0.24	1.8	0.02	3.21
Crisis period (from 15/9/2008 to 31/3/2009)				
US	−0.32	3.54	0.12	3.71
HK	−0.25	3.78	0.28	5.02
JP	−0.29	3.62	−0.14	4.94
SG	−0.29	2.69	0.06	3.83
ML	−0.13	1.23	0.14	4.57
TW	−0.29	2.59	−0.76	6.61
TL	−0.13	2.28	−0.17	3.42
VN	−0.37	2.33	0.09	2.38
Post-crisis period (from 1/4/2009 to 31/12/2010)				
US	0.1	1.19	−0.23	4.48
HK	0.12	1.46	0.33	4.66
JP	0.05	1.35	−0.01	3.47
SG	0.14	1.13	0.57	6.24
ML	0.12	0.62	0.31	4.63
TW	0.19	1.28	−0.27	4.91
TL	0.12	1.21	−0.06	6.38
VN	0.12	1.76	−0.08	3.41

deviations of developed markets, relative to those of the emerging and frontier markets during the crisis period, imply considerable influences of the GFC on the developed markets in the region.

During the post-crisis period, all the markets record positive average rates of return reflecting the recovery of the markets after the GFC; however, the pattern of recovery varies across the region. The highest return is for the Taiwan Index (0.19), while the lowest is for the Japan Index (0.05). It suggests a weak recovery of Japan compared with the other markets. It could be due to its high dependence on the export of advanced manufacturing products. In addition, the skewness reveals some negative but some positive values over the three periods, implying that market returns sometimes change from the long right tail to left right tail and vice versa over the sub-periods. The high kurtosis values suggest the peak distributions of market returns.

Table 2 shows the correlation coefficients of market returns between the equity markets. Overall, the table almost shows higher correlations among the markets during the crisis period compared with the pre- and post-crisis periods implying strong vulnerablity of the East Asian equity markets during the GFC.

During the pre-crisis period, the correlations between developed markets appear to be higher than those between emerging markets. The highest correlation is found between Singapore and Hong Kong (0.79) and the lowest correlation is between Singapore and Vietnam (−0.02). The strong relationship between Singapore and Hong Kong can be explained by their close trading linkages. In addition, the Vietnam equity market reveals the lowest correlations with both the emerging and developed markets in the sample suggesting quite an isolated relationship of the market toward the regional and global markets. The United States reveals the highest correlations with Japan (0.53) and Singapore (0.51), while the lowest correlation exists with Vietnam (0.07).

During the crisis, almost all correlations increased considerably, particularly the correlations between two equity markets in East Asia. The correlations between the advanced markets and emerging markets in the region span from 0.5 (Thailand and Taiwan) to 0.78 (Singapore and Hong Kong), implying that these markets move in similar patterns in this period. Notably, the correlations between the Vietnam and other markets under investigation considerably increase, particularly with the United States (0.55) and Japan (0.47). It implies strong influence of the GFC on the Vietnam equity market, which may enhance its linkages to global equity markets. Notably that among the East Asian markets, only Japan and Vietnam report impressively stronger correlations with the United States, while almost other markets reveal weaker interactions. The findings may suggest different influences of the shock to the United States on the East Asian equity markets.

During the post-crisis period, the correlations among the markets appear to slightly decline but only the Vietnam equity market reports the higher correlations with the other markets during the post-crisis period in comparison to those during the pre-crisis period. In addition, despite the slight decline, the United States maintains the highest

Table 2 Correlation coefficient of market returns.

	US	HK	JP	SG	ML	TL	TW	VN
Pre-crisis period (from 1/7/2007 to 14/8/2008)								
US	1							
HK	0.49	1						
JP	0.53	0.66	1					
SG	0.51	0.79	0.67	1				
ML	0.43	0.50	0.48	0.57	1			
TL	0.35	0.54	0.42	0.57	0.48	1		
TW	0.43	0.57	0.59	0.60	0.50	0.49	1	
VN	0.07	0.04	0.08	−0.02	0.00	0.00	0.00	1
Crisis period (from 15/9/2008 to 31/3/2009)								
US	1							
HK	0.37	1						
JP	0.65	0.68	1					
SG	0.30	0.78	0.60	1				
ML	0.37	0.54	0.56	0.67	1			
TL	0.26	0.69	0.56	0.70	0.59	1		
TW	0.45	0.63	0.65	0.58	0.60	0.50	1	
VN	0.55	0.24	0.47	0.22	0.34	0.36	0.36	1
Post-crisis period (from 1/4/2009 to 31/12/2010)								
US	1							
HK	0.38	1						
JP	0.55	0.57	1					
SG	0.33	0.75	0.49	1				
ML	0.42	0.55	0.46	0.57	1			
TL	0.23	0.55	0.37	0.54	0.43	1		
TW	0.38	0.60	0.53	0.60	0.50	0.36	1	
VN	0.33	0.18	0.21	0.15	0.18	0.10	0.16	1

correlations with Japan (0.55) compared with other markets in the region. It is notable that almost all the equity markets in the East Asian region reveal their highest correlations with Hong Kong and Singapore. It highlights considerable influences of the two markets in the region.

Plotting the movements of the daily market returns of the eight markets over the period of 2007–2010 allows us to visually inspect the market volatilities of the selected markets over time. In general, the markets are relatively stable before the crisis, but appear to be highly volatile during the crisis. From Figure 1 we observe that the United States, Hong Kong, and Japan are more volatile than the other markets because their volatilities span from −15 to +15; while those of other markets range from −10 to +10. In addition,

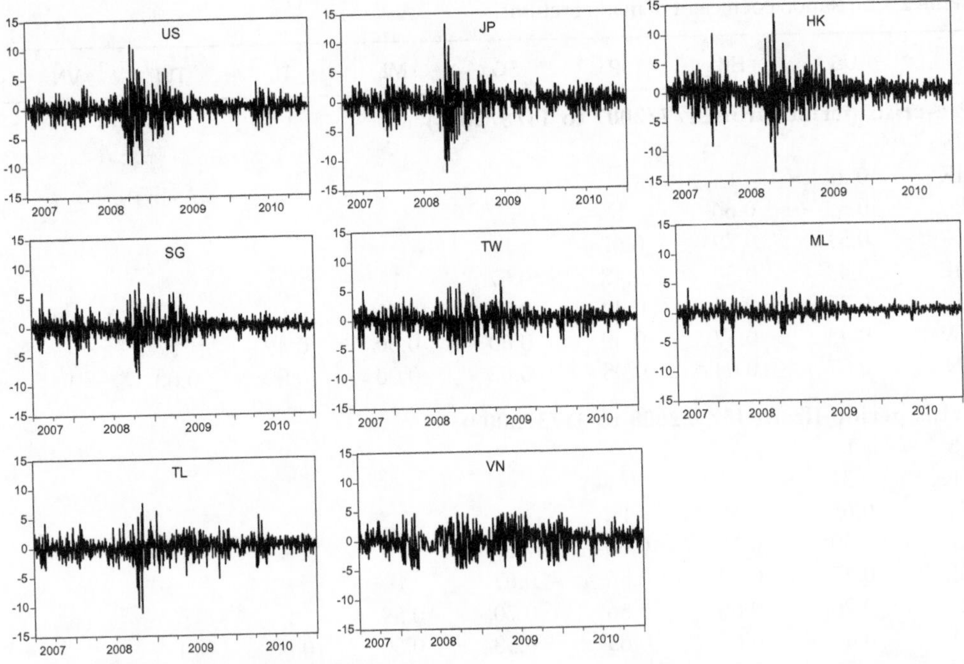

Figure 1 Movements of market returns.

Malaysia is likely to be less influenced by the GFC, except for a sharp drop in the first quarter of 2008 implying the quick response of the Malaysian government to overcome the crisis. Notably, although that there is no dramatic drop in the market volatilities of Vietnam, the market reveals a long involvement in the crisis. This could be explained by strict controls of the Vietnamese Governments on supervising and managing the market, such as a narrow daily price-limit change regulation and a maximum proportion of foreign ownership of listing firms in the market.

We conclude that due to differences in size and structure, the influences of the GFC on the East Asian equity markets are far from uniform. However, when and where the GFC transmitted to the markets in the region is not revealed by the above descriptive analysis. As such, other research approaches will be conducted to explore the transmission mechanism.

3.2. Research Methodology

In this paper, we investigate the transmission of a shock caused by the GFC to the East Asian markets by conducting empirical tests with regard to an existence of a contagion effect among the markets. As mentioned above, we follow the very strict definition of contagion as a significant increase in cross-market linkages after a shock or crisis. As such, we examine the contagion effect by measuring cross-market correlations. However, as discussed by Forbes and Rigobon (2002), a correlation between two markets is time-varying and conditional on market volatilities, particularly during a turbulent period because the correlation may be biased by increases of market volatilities. Hence, two models of time-varying correlations are used in the paper. The first model is the constant conditional correlation (CCC) suggested by Bollerslev (1990) and the second model is the time-varying dynamic conditional correlation (DCC) proposed by Engle (2002). These empirical methods estimate the dynamic of time-varying correlations tracking from multivariate generalized autoregressive conditional heteroskedasticity (MGARCH) model.

Specifically, to capture the time-varying variances of market returns, the univariate generalized autoregressive conditional heteroskedasticity model, GARCH(1,1) suggested by Bollerslev (1986), is firstly employed to estimate conditional return and conditional variance of individual market returns. The equations are given as follows:

$$\text{Returns equation} \qquad r_t = \mu + \varepsilon, \tag{1}$$

$$\text{Volatility equation} \qquad h_t = w_i + \alpha\varepsilon_{i,t-1}^2 + \beta h_{i,t-1}, \tag{2}$$

where $i = 1, 2\ldots$ m indicate the ith equation in the model. r_t is a linear regression of individual market returns equation including a constant term μ and the error term $\varepsilon_{i,t-1}$ of the ith equation. The conditional variance, $h_{i,t}$, is a function of lagged values of square residuals $\varepsilon_{i,t-1}^2$. α captures innovations of its past square residuals while β presents influences of lagged values of its conditional variance. w_i is a constant term of the volatility equation. The necessary conditions to equation (2) are both α and β are non-negative and $\alpha + \beta < 1$.

After estimating the volatilities of individual markets in the sample, we measure the CCC between pairs of the markets. The constant conditional correlation (ρ_t) is decomposed into a matrix of conditional variance (h_{ij}) and a diagonal matrix of the square root of the conditional variances ($h_{ii,t}^{-1/2}$) by using the following model:

$$\rho_t = h_{ii,t}^{-1/2} h_{ij,t} h_{jj,t}^{-1/2}. \tag{3}$$

The CCCs are estimated in the paper over the pre-crisis, crisis, and post-crisis periods. If the CCC significantly changes over the crisis and post-crisis periods compared with that over the pre-crisis period, it supports a hypothesis on a transmission of the GFC caused by the United States to the other market. If the CCC is not significant over the crisis and post-crisis periods compared with the pre-crisis period, we conclude that no transmission of a shock occurs in the markets. In case the CCC maintains the high values over the sub-period, a conclusion of interdependence between the markets is suggested.

Although the CCC model measures the conditional correlations of market volatilities, the correlations, however, are static over the period of study. As such, we further employ the DCC model that allows for time-varying conditional correlation. This model is also firstly based on the univariate GARCH(1,1) model of market returns of individual markets to estimate their conditional variances σ_t. Each univariate error process is then transformed to the standardized residuals by:

$$\delta_{t-1} = \frac{\varepsilon}{\sqrt{h_t}}. \tag{4}$$

The conditional variance is assumed to be time-varying by following the GARCH(1,1) model given by:

$$\sigma_{ij,t} = \left(1 - \theta_1 - \theta_2\right)\overline{\sigma}_{ij,t} + \theta_1\delta_{t-1}\delta'_{t-1} + \theta_2\sigma_{ij,t-1}, \tag{5}$$

where $\overline{\sigma}$ is the unconditional covariance of the standardized residuals (δ_t) resulting from the univariate GARCH, and θ_1 and θ_2 are parameters. Both θ_1 and θ_2 must be positive and $\theta_1 + \theta_2 < 1$. In other words, the DCC model includes the two GARCH(1,1) processes of stock returns and standardized residuals. The DCC is decomposed into a matrix of conditional variance (σ_{ij}) and a diagonal matrix of the square root of the conditional variances ($\sigma_{ij,t}^{-1/2}$) is given below:

$$\rho_t = \sigma_{ii,t}^{-1/2}\sigma_{ij,t}\sigma_{ii,t}^{-1/2}. \tag{6}$$

To measure the coefficients, Engle (2002) proposes to maximize the likelihood function in the following equation:

$$L_t = -\frac{1}{2}\sum_{t=1}^{T}\left[nlog(2\pi) + \log|D_t|^2 + \varepsilon_t' D_t^{-2}\varepsilon_t\right] - \frac{1}{2}\sum_{t=1}^{T}\left[\log|R_t| + \varepsilon_t' R_t^{-1}\varepsilon_t - \varepsilon_t'\varepsilon_t\right]. \tag{7}$$

The results of DCC tests are plotted in the seven graphs presenting the time-varying conditional correlations between the United States and other markets in the sample over the period from 1/7/2007 to 31/12/2010. The *MATLAB* package is used to perform these tests.

4. EMPIRICAL RESULTS

4.1. Volatilities of Individual Market

In order to estimate the conditional correlations of equity market volatilities, we firstly conduct the univariate GARCH(1,1) model for individual markets to estimate individual market volatility series. As it can be seen in Table 3, almost all of the parameters are statistically significant supporting the use of the CCC and DCC models to investigate the transmission of shock across the markets. In addition, the sum of parameters in the volatility equation nearly equals 1, implying that the market volatilities measure the behavior of each market. There are some parameters, however, insignificant during the crisis period. It can be explained by the shorter period of study of the crisis

Table 3 Results of the volatility equations of individual market returns.

Market	Coefficient	Pre-crisis (315 obs)	Crisis (142 obs)	Post-crisis (458 obs)
	ARCH	0.03**	0.08***	0.10**
US	GARCH	0.87	0.89***	0.89**
	constant	0.17	0.34	0.02**
	ARCH	0.16**	0.13***	0.03**
HK	GARCH	0.76***	0.83***	0.96**
	constant	0.40	0.57	0.01**
	ARCH	0.08**	0.19***	0.05**
JP	GARCH	0.86***	0.77***	0.91***
	constant	0.15***	0.56	0.07***
	ARCH	0.14**	0.08**	0.08**
SG	GARCH	0.78***	0.86***	0.90**
	constant	0.21	0.40	0.02**
	ARCH	0.24***	0.12***	0.18**
ML	GARCH	0.72***	0.76	0.68***
	constant	0.11***	0.18	0.05**
	ARCH	0.15***	0.06**	0.10**
TL	GARCH	0.79***	0.92**	0.87**
	constant	0.13***	0.04***	0.04**
	ARCH	0.10**	0.05***	0.07**
TW	GARCH	0.82***	0.16	0.91**
	constant	0.24	4.58	0.03**
	ARCH	0.31***	0.21	0.14**
VN	GARCH	0.62***	0.77	0.84**
	constant	0.28	0.16	0.07**

Notes:
**Statistical significance at 5%.
***Statistical significance at 10%.

period (142 observations) compared with the pre-crisis period (315 observations) and the post-crisis period (458 observations). It is notable that during the crisis period, the market volatilities of the Vietnam equity market cannot be measured by its own residuals and its lagged values because all the parameters are insignificant. Thus, we should show caution in interpreting empirical findings on the conditional correlations between the Vietnam and United States equity markets during the crisis period.

4.2. Constant Conditional Correlation

Table 4 presents the empirical estimations of the CCC-MGARCH(1,1) models. The results show the conditional correlation on market volatility of not only the relationships between the United States and other markets but also between the pairs of other markets.

Over the pre-crisis period, the market volatility of the United States reveals high correlations with the developed markets rather than the emerging and frontier markets, while the regional markets reveal the higher conditional correlations with both Hong Kong and Singapore. It implies significant roles of Hong Kong and Singapore in the region. The volatility of the Vietnam equity market is quite small suggesting for the less influences of the regional markets toward the Vietnam.

During the crisis, the United States reveals a significant increase in the conditional correlation with the Japan market, followed by Vietnam, Taiwan, and Hong Kong. It implies that Japan is likely to be the first market in the region affected by the crisis. However, it may be surprising that the CCCs between the United States equity markets and the East

Table 4 Constant conditional correlation of market volatilities.

	US	HK	JP	SG	ML	TL	TW	VN
Pre-crisis period (from 1/7/2007 to 14/8/2008)								
US	1							
HK	0.52	1						
JP	0.53	0.64	1					
SG	0.52	0.79	0.65	1				
ML	0.43	0.51	0.43	0.55	1			
TL	0.35	0.54	0.43	0.54	0.45	1		
TW	0.43	0.60	0.59	0.60	0.47	0.47	1	
VN	0.12	0.09	0.11	0.04	0.04	0.03	0.06	1
Crisis period (from 15/9/2008 to 31/3/2009)								
US	1							
HK	0.43	1						
JP	0.66	0.66	1					
SG	0.30	0.76	0.59	1				
ML	0.36	0.58	0.58	0.65	1			
TL	0.28	0.67	0.58	0.71	0.60	1		
TW	0.43	0.65	0.70	0.59	0.60	0.52	1	
VN	0.52	0.22	0.44	0.19	0.30	0.30	0.33	1
Post-crisis period (from 1/4/2009 to 31/12/2010)								
US	1							
HK	0.41	1						
JP	0.54	0.57	1					
SG	0.35	0.72	0.49	1				
ML	0.44	0.52	0.45	0.56	1			
TL	0.23	0.51	0.36	0.51	0.39	1		
TW	0.39	0.60	0.55	0.58	0.46	0.35	1	
VN	0.34	0.19	0.23	0.12	0.19	0.08	0.17	1

Asian equity markets do not increase, except for those of Japan and Vietnam. It is in line with our findings in the unconditional correlations among the markets. It may suggest that the contagion effect from the United States to the regional markets is not apparent. In addition, all the correlations of market volatility of the Vietnam market are reported to be significantly higher during the GFC than before the GFC, giving implications on a sensitive characterization of the frontier market toward the shock originated in the United States. Interestingly, our findings report that the Thailand equity market is less directly influenced by the GFC during the GFC as its conditional correlation of market volatility declines relative to that of the pre-crisis period. The fluctuation of the Thailand equity market over the crisis period may result from the volatilities of regional markets such as Hong Kong and Singapore.

Over the post-GFC, the conditional correlations of most markets turn back relative to the correlations during the pre-GFC. The market volatilities of both the Hong Kong and Singapore markets still prominently influence the other markets in the region. The volatilities of the Japan market reveal the highest close linkage to the volatilities of the United States market. Importantly, we find significant increases in the conditional correlations between the Vietnam and both the United States and regional markets. It gives implications on significant influences of the shock caused by the GFC on the frontier market.

In summary, we may conclude that the CCCs suggest that the markets of East Asia are closely connected during the crisis period. The transmission of the shock originated from the United States which quickly transferred to Japan and Vietnam rather than other countries. This suggests that the shock by the GFC originated from the United States may transmit to the East Asian equity market via Japan.

4.3. Dynamic Conditional Correlation

As indicated by Corsetti et al. (2005), a correlation between two market returns is not static but varies over time. As such, in the paper, we capture the time-varying correlations between the United States and the East Asian equity markets. Specifically, we employ the DCC-MGARCH model suggested by Engle (2002) to measure the time-varying conditional correlation coefficients between two markets. The results of the time-varying conditional correlation coefficients between the United States and the East Asian markets are plotted in Figure 2. In general, we can see that the highest volatility of the DCCs is found between the United States and Japan (spanning from 0.35 to 0.67), while the lowest volatility of the DCCs is found between the United States and Vietnam (spanning from 0.2 to 0.4).

During the pre-GFC, the graphs show a relatively high correlation in the dynamic path of several markets such as Hong Kong, Singapore, Malaysia, and Thailand, which can be explained by their significant influences on the sub-prime mortgage crisis in the United States. It is also notable that the time-varying conditional correlations of the United States and most markets decline significantly around January 2008, as some large

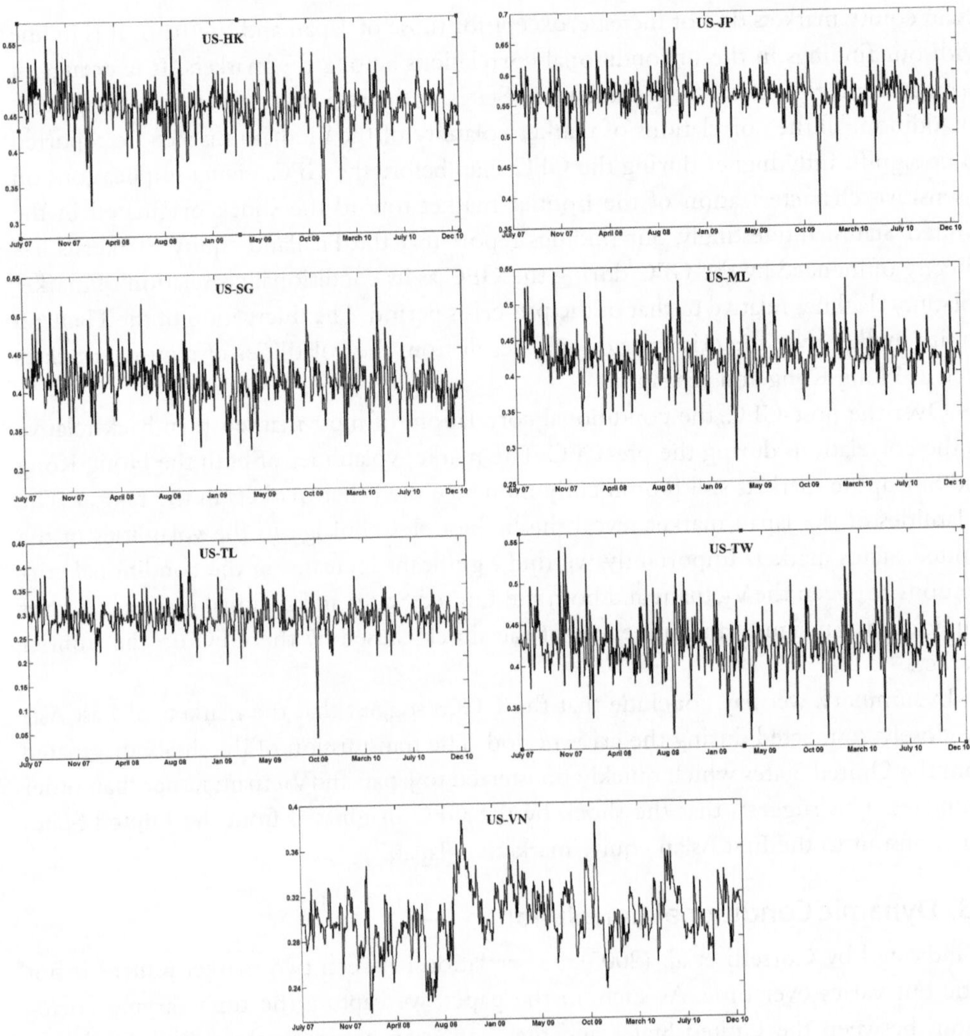

Figure 2 Time-varying dynamic conditional correlations of market volatilities.

U.S. international corporations reported losses in their performances in 2007. However, the DCCs then recover quickly, implying that the negative effects of the sub-prime mortgage crisis do not cause significant impacts on the East Asian equity markets.

Figure 2 also shows the high conditional correlation in the market volatilities of Japan, Hong Kong, Malaysia, Thailand, and Vietnam markets over the period from September 2008 to October 2008. It implies the transmission of the GFC to these markets particularly in September 2008 after the bankruptcy of the Lehman Brothers and the collapse of the AIG. Notably both the DCCs of Singapore and Taiwan do not significantly increase during this period in comparison to the DCC during the pre-crisis period. It can be explained by the fact that the United States is the largest importer of industrial products from Singapore and Taiwan. Hence, these countries are severely affected during the sub-prime mortgage crisis. As such, their responses over the GFC period are not sharp. Interestingly, the DCCs of the frontier market, Vietnam, significantly increase during the crisis period suggesting strong impacts of the market during the GFC.

It is noteworthy that the influences of the GFC toward the East Asian equity markets vary significantly. While many markets reveal the relatively low conditional correlations to the United States around March 2008, the correlation of Hong Kong remains moderate, and that of Vietnam is still high. These results imply for differences in the transmission of the shock from the United States and the East Asian equity markets during the crisis.

During the post-GFC, the time-varying conditional correlations between the developed and emerging markets in the East Asian region and the United States appear to decline slightly, implying less influence from the shock in the United States. However, the DCCs between the Vietnam and United States market maintain at relatively higher levels during the post-crisis period compared with those during the pre-crisis period implying stronger correlations between the Vietnam and the United States after the crisis.

To sum up, our findings suggest evidence of the transmissions of a shock from the United States to the East Asian market. It is partly in line with the results by Yiu et al. (2010) and Hwang (2012) who found a contagion effect from the United States to Hong Kong, Japan, and Singapore during the period from 9/2007 to 3/2009. However, our findings extend their results by showing that the contagion effect exists between the United States to both Hong Kong and Singapore during the sub-prime crisis, while between the United States and Japan during the global financial crisis. In addition, our results are consistent with a study by Gupta and Guidi (2012) who found evidence of a contagion effect from the United States to India market, as well as a study by Syllignakis and Kouretas (2011) who suggest a transmission of the shock in the United States to the CEE stock returns during the 2007–2009 financial crises.

5. CONCLUSION

This paper employs the constant and dynamic conditional correlation models based on the MGARCH(1,1) to investigate the transmission of the global financial crisis to the developed, emerging, and frontier markets in the East Asian region. The models allow us to trace for the time-varying correlation of market volatilities between the United States and each of the selected markets. By partitioning the period of study into the pre-crisis, crisis, and post-crisis periods, we can explore the transmission of the crisis to the East Asian equity market over time.

The empirical findings suggest that among the examined markets, Japan is the market most significantly influenced by the GFC due to its highest correlations found in the paper. In addition, both the Hong Kong and Singapore markets are more severely influenced by the sub-prime mortgage crisis in the United States in the middle of 2007 rather than the GFC. It can be explained by their close linkages in the international trades because the United States is the largest importer of industrial products from Hong Kong and Singapore. Furthermore, although the emerging markets in the region are influenced by the shock from the United States over the crisis period, they are more correlated to the developed markets in the region rather than the United States. In addition, the GFC is likely to transmit to the East Asian markets via Japan. Finally, the transmission of the GFC to the frontier market, Vietnam, is more significant than to the other markets in the region. The findings suggest that the GFC may lead to stronger linkages in the frontier market toward the global markets.

The results suggest some implications for policy makers and international fund managers. Firstly, an understanding of the transmission of a shock caused by one market to others may provide for policy makers a clear viewpoint on the linkages between the markets. In the paper, we not only find empirical evidences of the transmission of the shock caused by the United States to the East Asian markets, but also identify a certain period that the crisis transmitted to these markets. Thus, policy makers can understand the relationships between the volatilities of their equity markets and regional and global markets for better monitoring and supervising the markets. In addition, policy makers may consider international monetary policies to avoid negative impacts from a shock caused by another market. International fund managers also learn from the results of transmissions of the GFC to the East Asian markets to improve their portfolio diversification strategy toward equity markets in the region.

REFERENCES

Ahlgren, N., Antell, J., 2010. Stock market linkages and financial contagion: a cobreaking analysis. Quarterly Review of Economics and Finance 50 (2), 157–166

Aït-Sahalia, Y., Andritzky, J., Jobst, A., Nowak, S., Tamirisa, N., 2012. Market response to policy initiatives during the global financial crisis. Journal of International Economics 87 (1), 162–177. http://dx.doi.org/10.1016/j.jinteco.2011.12.001

Allen, F., Carletti, E., 2010. An overview of the crisis: causes, consequences, and solutions. International Review of Finance 10 (1), 1–26

Arestis, P., Sobreira, R.r., Oreiro, J.L.s., 2011. The Financial Crisis: Origins and Implications. Palgrave Macmillan

Bartram, S.M., Bodnar, G.M., 2009. No place to hide: the global crisis in equity markets in 2008/2009. Journal of International Money and Finance 28 (8), 1246–1292

Billio, M., Pelizzon, L., 2003. Contagion and interdependence in stock markets: have they been misdiagnosed?. Journal of Economics and Business 55 (5–6), 405–426. http://dx.doi.org/10.1016/S0148-6195(03)00048-1

Bollerslev, T., 1986. Generalized autoregressive conditional heteroskedasticity. Journal of Econometrics 31 (3), 307–327. http://dx.doi.org/10.1016/0304-4076(86)90063-1

Bollerslev, T., 1990. Modelling the coherence in short-run nominal exchange rates: a multivariate generalized arch model. Review of Economics and Statistics 72 (3), 498

Caramazza, F., Ricci, L., Salgado, R., 2004. International financial contagion in currency crises. Journal of International Money and Finance 23 (1), 51–70. http://dx.doi.org/10.1016/j.jimonfin.2003.10.001

Claessens, S., Forbes, K. (Eds.), 2001. International Financial Contagion. Kluwer Academic Publishers, Boston, London

Claessens, S., Dell'Ariccia, G., Igan, D., Laeven, L., 2010. Cross-country experiences and policy implications from the global financial crisis. Economic Policy 25 (62), 267–293

Corsetti, G., Pericoli, M., Sbracia, M., 2005. Some contagion, some interdependence: more pitfalls in tests of financial contagion. Journal of International Money and Finance 24 (8), 1177–1199. http://dx.doi.org/10.1016/j.jimonfin.2005.08.012

Dooley, M., Hutchison, M., 2009. Transmission of the U.S. subprime crisis to emerging markets: evidence on the decoupling–recoupling hypothesis. Journal of International Money and Finance 28 (8), 1331–1349

Dornbusch, R., Park, Y.C., Claessens, S., 2000. Contagion: understanding how it spreads. World Bank Research Observer 15 (2), 177–197

Dungey, M., Fry, R., Gonzalez-Hermosillo, B., Martin, V.L., 2005. Empirical modelling of contagion: a review of methodologies. Quantitative Finance 5 (1), 9–24

Engle, R., 2002. Dynamic conditional correlation: a simple class of multivariate generalized autoregressive conditional heteroskedasticity models. Journal of Business and Economic Statistics 20 (3), 339–350

Forbes, K.J., Rigobon, R., 2002. No contagion, only interdependence: measuring stock market comovements. Journal of Finance 57 (5), 2223–2261

Gklezakou, T., Mylonakis, J., 2010. Links and interdependence of developed stock markets under global economic crisis conditions. Journal of Financial Services Marketing 14 (4), 314–327

Guo, F., Chen, C.R., Huang, Y.S., 2011. Markets contagion during financial crisis: a regime-switching approach. International Review of Economics and Finance 20 (1), 95–109

Gupta, R., Donleavy, G.D., 2009. Benefits of diversifying investments into emerging markets with time-varying correlations: an Australian perspective. Journal of Multinational Financial Management 19 (2), 160–177. http://dx.doi.org/10.1016/j.mulfin.2008.10.001

Gupta, R., Guidi, F., 2012. Cointegration relationship and time varying co-movements among Indian and Asian developed stock markets. International Review of Financial Analysis 21, 10–22. http://dx.doi.org/10.1016/j.irfa.2011.09.001

Hwang, J.-K., 2012. Dynamic correlation analysis of Asian stock markets. International Advances in Economic Research 18 (2), 227–237

Karolyi, G.A., 2003. Does international financial contagion really exist? International Finance 6 (2), 179

Kearney, C., 2000. The determination and international transmission of stock market volatility. Global Finance Journal 11 (1–2), 31–52. http://dx.doi.org/10.1016/S1044-0283(00)00015-6

Kenourgios, D., Samitas, A., Paltalidis, N., 2011. Financial crises and stock market contagion in a multivariate time-varying asymmetric framework. Journal of International Financial Markets, Institutions and Money 21 (1), 92–106. http://dx.doi.org/10.1016/j.intfin.2010.08.005

Khalid, A.M., Kawai, M., 2003. Was financial market contagion the source of economic crisis in Asia? Evidence using a multivariate VAR model. Journal of Asian Economics 14 (1), 133

Kuper, G.H., Lestano, L., 2007. Dynamic conditional correlation analysis of financial market interdependence: an application to Thailand and Indonesia. Journal of Asian Economics 18 (4), 670–684. http://dx.doi.org/10.1016/j.asieco.2007.03.007

Marcal, E.F., Valls Pereira, P.L., Martin, D.M.L., Nakamura, W.T., 2011. Evaluation of contagion or interdependence in the financial crises of Asia and Latin America, considering the macroeconomic fundamentals. Applied Economics 43 (19), 2365–2379

Markwat, T., Kole, E., van Dijk, D., 2009. Contagion as a domino effect in global stock markets. Journal of Banking and Finance 33 (11), 1996–2012

Mishkin, F.S., 2011. Over the cliff: from the subprime to the global financial crisis. Journal of Economic Perspectives 25 (1), 49–70

MSCI, 2012. MSCI Frontier Markets Indices. <http://www.msci.com/products/indices/countryandregional/fm/>.

Naoui, K., Liouane, N., Brahim, S., 2010. A dynamic conditional correlation analysis of financial contagion: the case of the subprime credit crisis. International Journal of Economics and Finance 2 (3), 85–96

Phylaktis, K., Ravazzolo, F., 2002. Measuring financial and economic integration with equity prices in emerging markets. Journal of International Money and Finance 21 (6), 879–903. http://dx.doi.org/10.1016/S0261-5606(02)00027-X

Pretorius, E., 2002. Economic determinants of emerging stock market interdependence. Emerging Markets Review 3 (1), 84–105. http://dx.doi.org/10.1016/S1566-0141(01)00032-2

Syllignakis, M.N., Kouretas, G.P., 2011. Dynamic correlation analysis of financial contagion: evidence from the Central and Eastern European markets. International Review of Economics and Finance 20 (4), 717–732. http://dx.doi.org/10.1016/j.iref.2011.01.006

Yiu, M.S., Alex-Ho, W.-Y., Choi, D.F., 2010. Dynamic correlation analysis of financial contagion in Asian markets in global financial turmoil. Applied Financial Economics 20 (4), 345–354

Yu, I.-W., Fung, K.-P., Tam, C.-S., 2010. Assessing financial market integration in Asia - equity markets. Journal of Banking and Finance 34 (12), 2874–2885. http://dx.doi.org/10.1016/j.jbankfin.2010.02.010

CHAPTER 23

Contagion versus Interdependence: The Case of the BRIC Countries During the Subprime Crises

Mrabet Zouhair*, **Charfeddine Lanouar†,‡**, **and Ahdi Noomen Ajmi§**

*College of Business and Economics, Department of Finance and Economics, Qatar University, Qatar
†College of Administrative Sciences, Najran University, Najran, Saudi Arabia
‡Quantitatives Methods department, Institut Supérieur de Gestion de Gabès, Université de Gabès, Gabès, Tunisia
§College of Science and Humanities in Slayel, Business Administration Department, Salman bin Abdulaziz University, Saudi Arabia

1. INTRODUCTION

Global financial markets have become more closely related and interdependent over time due to market integration (see Lim, 2009). In this line, several studies have argued that financial integration plays an important role in accelerating financial crises, shocks transmission cross-countries correlations, and has important implications for international portfolio investment (see Lim, 2009; Kenourgios et al., 2011). In fact, the investigation of financial contagion is of great significance because of its damaging impacts on global economy in relation to the formulation of monetary and fiscal policy and financial risk management (see Forbes and Rigobón, 2002 among others).

Over the last three decades, several emerging and developing countries have implemented financial policies to accelerate their financial integration with international markets. The emerging countries that have initiated financial integration processes include the BRIC countries. Bhar and Nikolova (2009) find that the Indian market is the most integrated at the regional and global levels, followed by Brazil, Russia, and finally, China.

These countries' objective in initiating a financial integration process is to benefit from improved financial infrastructure, the use of new types of capital, and the reduction of problems such as adverse selection and moral hazard. Financial integration can also entail certain risks, primarily during the first years of openness. One well-known risk is that globalization can be related to financial crises. The crises in Asia and Russia in 1997–1998, Brazil in 1999, Ecuador in 2000, Turkey in 2001, Argentina in 2001, and Uruguay in 2002 are some examples that captured worldwide interest. During these crises, the interactions and linkages among financial markets'—played a crucial role, as the high degree of interaction among countries, and their financial markets, led to extreme volatility. This reduces the isolation of domestic markets and increases countries' abilities to

Emerging Markets and the Global Economy
http://dx.doi.org/10.1016/B978-0-12-411549-1.00023-5

promptly respond to news and shocks originating in the rest of the world. Consequently, if the proper financial infrastructure is not already in place or is not put in place during integration, liberalization followed by capital inflows can adversely affect the health of the local financial system.

Financial integration is currently associated with an increase in the vulnerability of domestic economies to international shocks and news, particularly to reversals in international capital movements. Moreover, international market imperfections can lead to crises and contagion, even in countries with strong economic fundamentals. As a consequence, -larger co-movements between asset prices across markets have been observed and stock markets seem to be highly correlated, particularly in crisis periods, see for example Bekaert and Harvey (1997), Loretan and English (2000), Longin and Solnik (2001), and Gagnon and Karolyi (2006).

Modeling co-movement and testing for the presence of financial contagion in emerging financial markets continue to be interesting subjects of debate in the empirical economic literature for two main raisons. First, most of the sizeable body of studies in this field is focused on developed countries, and few works have examined emerging markets; this is especially true for the BRICs (see for example Aloui et al., 2011). Second, the volatility of stock market returns is associated with unpredictability, uncertainty and has implications for risk. Generally, researchers tend to consider volatility a symptom of market disruption whereby securities are not priced fairly and the capital market is not functioning as well as it should. Thus, investigating the co-movement among stock markets in the BRIC countries before, during, and after subprime crises represents an interesting research subject. Such volatile co-movement can affect corporate capital budgeting decisions, investors' decisions, and business cycle variables in the BRICs.

Our study focuses on four major emerging stock markets, namely Brazil, Russia, India, and China (BRICs) and their links with the developed stock markets in the US Several reasons make the BRIC countries an interesting case study: (1) the BRIC countries pursue a policy of financial market liberalization, resulting in the internationalization of their financial markets, (2) these countries have also attracted increasing interest financial investors and economists because of their potential for economic growth, their resilience to financial crises, (3) the persistent volatility behavior characterizing these countries in conjunction with greater regional financial integration, (4) the Chinese and Indian economies are relatively closed and feature state-controlled capital markets, meaning that their development strategy is based on domestic industrialization catering to export markets. However, Brazilian and Russian economies are based on natural resources and are much more open and currently subject to relatively less state control.

In addition, we focus on the recent financial crisis that emerged in the wake of the 2007 US subprime mortgage crisis which produced chaotic effects throughout the international financial system. A major consequence of this crisis was significant damage to, investor confidence in numerous financial institutions and the resulting sharp decline in the share prices of investment banks in the fourth quarter of 2007 and first quarter of 2008 (see Morales and Gassie, 2011). Moreover, during the turbulent period from September 2008 to early March 2009, the US stock market fell by 43%, those in emerging markets fell by 50%, and frontier stock markets experienced a 60% decline (see Samarakoon, 2011).

In this study, we investigate stock market co-movements and financial contagion in these countries during the subprime financial crises using a class of Markov-switching models to distinguish among periods of high, medium, and low volatility to address the bias of the correlation approach caused by the time-varying behavior of unconditional volatility. The main feature of this approach is that one stock market is ex ante considered the originator of the crisis, and the correlation coefficient is made dependent on the state of this originating stock market. For this purpose, we combine the Switching-ARCH (SWARCH) model of Hamilton and Susmel (1994) and the adjusted correlation approach of Forbes and Rigobón (2002). The empirical results reveal the presence of a high degree of interdependence between the US and the BRIC countries, particularly in high volatility periods. Moreover, using probability smoothing, we show that periods of increased stock market volatility coincide across countries and are associated with certain historical events (i.e., political and financial crises).

The remainder of this chapter is organized as follows. Section 2 describes the BRIC countries. Section 3 provides an overview of the related literature. Section 4 presents the SWARCH—adjusted correlation approach methodology. Section 5 discusses the empirical results. Finally, Section 6 presents a summary and implications.

2. BRIC COUNTRIES

The BRIC countries are heterogenous. They differ in their structural characteristics, economic policies, and geopolitical importance. China and India are characterized by controlled capital markets and large shares of their populations residing in rural areas. Their development strategy is based on export activities, while Brazil and Russia are primarily natural resource-based economies and well-known commodity exporters. Their capital markets, while developed during very different periods and at different rates, are much more open and currently subject to relatively less state control. These countries are characterized by high growth rates relative to those observed in industrialized countries. Among the BRICs, China has experienced the most rapid economic growth in the current decade, followed by India. This growth has been affected by global economic crises, particularly the US subprime crisis. It is widely held that over the next few decades, growth in the largest developing countries, particularly the BRICs, could become a much more significant force in the world economy.

Among the BRICs, India and Brazil are relatively more domestic demand-driven economies. As a group, the BRICs experienced a more rapid economic recovery from the 2008 financial crisis than advanced and other emerging market economies. This

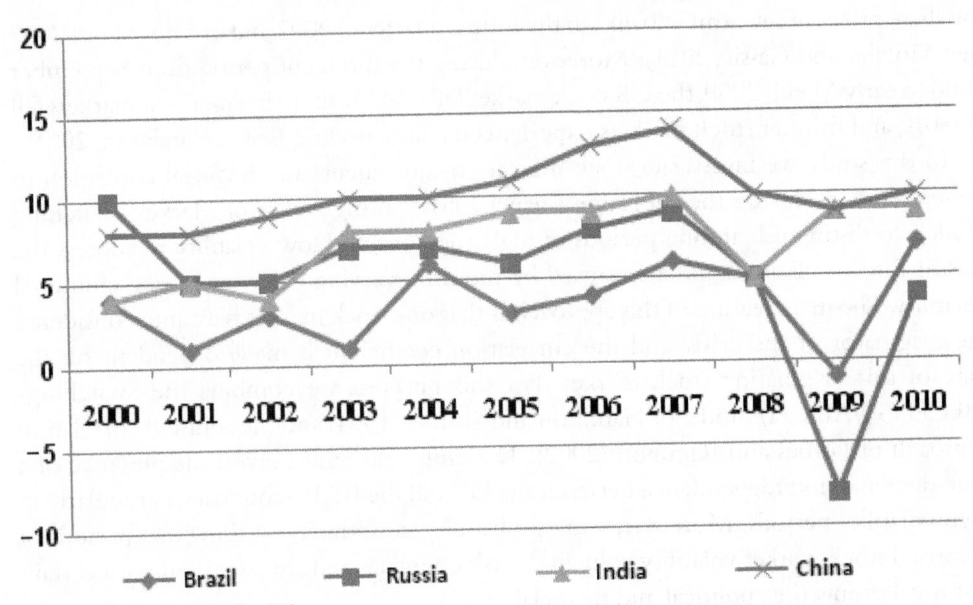

Figure 1 GDP growth rate (%).

means that the BRIC countries have the potential to account for 47% of global GDP by 2050. The inherent strength of the BRICs results from strong domestic demand-based economies in India and Brazil and the significant outward linkages of China and Russia. Regarding GDP growth, see Figure 1, Brazilian economy has the lowest growth rate, 3.5% on average, followed by Russia at an average of 5.5%. The other two countries, China and India, have higher average growth rates, 10% and 7.2%, respectively. Between 2000 and 2010, China's economy grew at an average of 10% per year. Similarly, India's economy grew at an average of 8% per year (see Figure 1).

The ratio of market capitalization to GDP is employed as an indicator of stock market development. The development of stock markets in BRIC economies, measured in terms of market capitalization to GDP, has progressively deepened over the years, see Figure 2. The ratio, which was as low as 35% for Brazil in 2000, reached a peak of 74% in 2010. The corresponding percentages for India in these years were 32% and 94%, respectively. China and Russia, both of which began with relatively shallower bases, rapidly caught up. In China, the market capitalization-to-GDP ratio in 2000 was 48%, which jumped to 80% in 2010. The corresponding ratios for Russia were 15% and 68%, respectively. Among the BRICs, India had the largest market capitalization relative to GDP in 2010.

While market capitalization divided by GDP may be a good overall indicator of stock market development, it may be interesting to consider more detailed structural characteristics of these stock markets. For instance, markets may be large, but relatively inefficient and/or illiquid. International investors are likely to avoid such markets. In addition, prices in inefficient markets may not be particularly informative, as various aspects—such as a

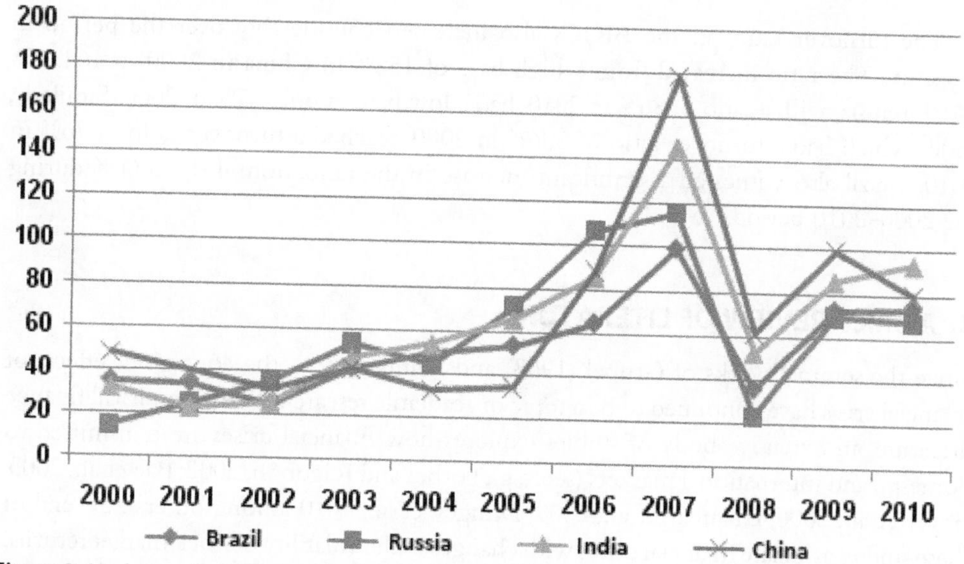

Figure 2 Market capitalization of listed companies (% of GDP).

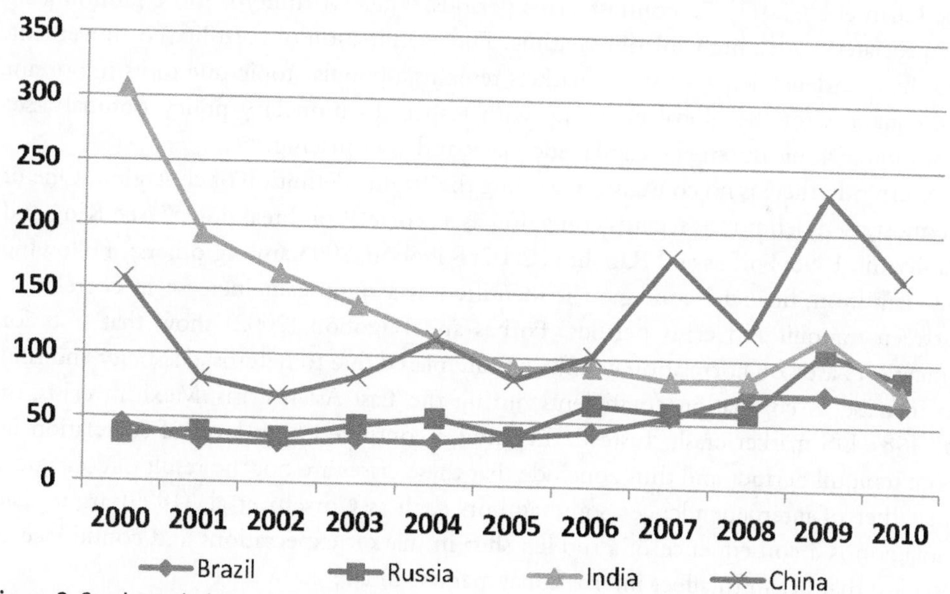

Figure 3 Stocks traded, turnover ratio (%).

lack of liquidity—prevent the rapid incorporation of new information into prices. We employ the stock market turnover ratio as a proxy for market liquidity, which is defined as the ratio of total value traded to total market capitalization, as a measure of stock market efficiency, see Figure 3.

The turnover ratios in the BRICs also increased considerably over the period in question. The ratio increased from a high base of 158% in China in 2000 to 164% in 2010. Russia, with a ratio of 86% in 2010, had a low base of only 37% in 2000. Similarly, India, which had a turnover ratio of 306% in 2000, reached a turnover ratio of 76% in 2010. Brazil also witnessed a significant increase in the ratio, from 45% to 66% during the 2000–2010 period.

3. A BRIEF REVIEW OF LITERATURE

Since the seminal works of Grubel (1968) and Solnik (1974), the contagious effects of financial crisis have continued to be a topic of academic research. In the empirical finance literature, an extensive body of studies explores how financial crises are transmitted to domestic and international markets (see, e.g., Forbes and Rigobón, 2002; Bae et al., 2003; Boyer et al., 2006; Chandar et al., 2009; Dungey et al., 2010 among others). Several of these studies associate financial crises with changes in the volatility of stock market returns. Generally, the periods before and after crises are characterized by low or medium volatility (see Chan et al., 2011). In contrast, crisis periods, where volatility is more pronounced, are associated with a high volatility regime. The examination of volatility, co-movement, and the interdependency of stock markets remains a popular topic due to its important consequences for the global economy with respect to monetary policy, optimal asset allocation, risk measurement, capital adequacy, and asset pricing.

Currently, there is no consensus regarding the "right" definition of contagion. One of the most used definitions regards contagion as a "correlation breakdown" (see King and Wadhwani, 1990; Forbes and Rigobón, 2002; Rigobón, 2003 among others). Following this definition, financial contagion is identified as a significant increase in correlation between tranquil and crisis periods. Forbes and Rigobón (2002) show that tests for contagion based on correlation coefficients are biased due to heteroskedasticity and find no increase in correlation coefficients during the East Asian crisis, Mexican crisis, or the 1987 US market crash. Instead, they find a continued high level of correlation in more tranquil periods and thus conclude that these crises are not the result of contagion but rather of interdependence. Some authors such as Corsetti et al. (1999) argue that contagion is a consequence of a sudden shift in market expectations and confidence, a situation that began to affect international markets in late 2007.

Considerable controversy appears to persist in the empirical literature, regarding testing for the presence of interdependence and contagion. Empirical results on this important issue seem to depend on the financial crises considered (ASIAN, BRICs, MENA, or national crises), the proxy (stock market returns, exchanges rates, etc...) used to test for contagion and the empirical methodology employed (correlation approach, ARCH model, switching models, Copula, etc...). For example, King and Wadhwani (1990),

Lee and Kim (1993) examined the correlation coefficient between stock returns to test for the impact of the 1987 US stock crash on stock markets in the UK, Japan, and several other countries. They found increased correlation coefficients between several markets during the crash. Longin and Solnik (1995) found that the correlation coefficient between stock returns in the US and seven OECD countries increased significantly over the period from 1960 to 1990.

Regarding the logit/probit approach, Eichengreen et al. (1996) employed a bivariate probit model to investigate the contagion effect of the currency crises experienced by France, Germany, the Netherlands, and other ERM nations. The empirical results demonstrated that a country that had experienced exogenous shocks was more likely to engage in opportunistic attacks against another country. Using the same methodology, De Gregorio and Valdes (2001) found that the Mexican crisis was the least contagious, while the Asian crisis was as contagious as the 1980s crisis. However, logit models define a financial crisis as a specific event at a given point in time, ignoring the independence of crises occurring in different periods. In a cointegration analysis framework, Sheng and Tu (2000) failed to observe cointegration among 12 Pacific nations, including Taiwan and the US, prior to the 1997 Asian financial crisis. Bonfiglioli and Favero (2005) found empirical evidence regarding the importance of contagion in the short-term interdependence between German and US stock markets using a structural vector error correction. The empirical results obtained by Raj and Dhal (2008) support the international integration of India's stock market when considering US dollars but not when using the local currency using the vector error correction and cointegration model (VECM). Lim (2009) found evidence of an increase in the level of integration and interdependence among ASEAN markets after the financial crisis and that the US market has a significant influence on all ASEAN markets using the Granger causality test and cointegration method. However, studies focusing on the long-term interdependence and causality among stock markets generally fail to address the contemporaneous structure of interdependence. In other words, the information might not be only be transmission across markets through returns but also through volatility (see Baele, 2005; Bessler and Yang, 2003 among others).

Another approach examines whether conditional variances are affected by additional information in the form of squared innovations occurring in other markets (see Engle et al., 1990). Engle et al. (1990) provide evidence that volatility spillovers occur between asset markets, suggesting that events in one market can be transmitted to others. This approach uses the ARCH family of models to measure the cross-market movements in the second moment of asset prices, see Engle (1982) and Bollerslev (1986). In this line, Christofi and Pericli (1999), Hong (2001), and Wang et al. (2005) examined volatility spillovers among developed and emerging European countries and the US, and most of these studies revealed the presence of an unidirectional volatility spillover from the US to the other countries. Wang and Thi (2006) and Chiang et al. (2007) used the DCC approach to investigate the presence of contagion during the Asian financial crisis, between Thailand and the Chinese Economic Area (CEA) markets over the period 1992–2000 and for nine Asian stock markets over the period from 1990 to 2003, respectively. Using the same approach, Kenourgios et al. (2007) and Yiu et al. (2010) found evidence of contagion, among BRIC emerging markets and US and UK markets and from the US to 11 Asian markets during the 2007 crisis, respectively. Their empirical results report no evidence of contagion between US and Asian markets during the period of the Asian crisis.

Using a framework that considers in both volatilities and regime switching, the Markov Switching ARCH model (SWARCH) of Hamilton and Susmel (1994), takes into account the possible presence of changes in regimes due to financial liberalization. The SWARCH model suggests that the unconditional volatility will alternate between low and high levels. This approach resolves a problem encountered when employing GARCH models, which are highly sensitive to regime changes; that is, the results obtained from these models might not be reliable during periods of low/high volatility. In the SWARCH model, the degree of stock market co-movement differs under high and low volatility regimes. Edwards and Susmel (2001) found evidence of volatility co-movement across Latin American markets during the crisis in the 1990s, but no volatility dependence between Hong Kong and Latin American markets using both univariate and multivariate techniques. Moreover, Boyer et al. (2006) demonstrated that there is greater co-movement during high volatility periods for numerous accessible and inaccessible stock indices using both regime switching models and extreme value theory. Baele (2005) found evidence of contagion spreading from the US to a number of European equity markets during periods of high global market volatility. Subsequently, Canarella and Pollard (2007) found that each high volatility episode appears to be associated with either a local or an international financial crisis by applying the SWARCH model to some Latin American countries. More recently, Diamandis (2008) suggested the existence of multiple volatility regimes and a significant increase in volatility during the Mexican, Brazilian, and Asian crises using a SWARCH-L model for four Latin American stock markets (Argentina, Brazil, Chile, and Mexico). Due to either subjective perceptions or the impact of possible structural breaks on the selected sample period, this methodology may lead to biased results (see Lamoureux and Lastrapes, 1990). To overcome this limitation observed in the existing literature, this chapter employs the Markov regime switching model, which is appropriate for modeling contagion effects because it allows the correlation between shocks to differ cross regimes. The Markov switching model has a further advantage in that the model parameters and regimes are jointly estimated.

4. THE EMPIRICAL METHODOLOGY

As our objective in this paper is to model co-movement in stock market returns and test for the presence of contagion among BRIC countries, we use the Markov switching

ARCH (SWARCH) model developed by Hamilton and Susmel (1994) to model time-varying volatility and the co-movement in stock market returns. Thereafter, we applied the adjusted correlation approach developed by Rigobón and Forbes (2001) to the different regimes identified using the SWARCH model and to each BRIC country and US stock market returns. Our empirical methodology will be organized in three steps. First, we begin by selecting the appropriate SWARCH model for each stock market return by testing for the presence of K states in the volatility of the stock market returns. Then, using probability smoothing, we classify the observations of the K regimes. Next, we use the adjusted correlation approach to investigate whether results reflect contagion or simply interdependence. As mentioned above, by combining these two approaches, we address certain limitations and criticisms of the adjusted correlation approach. The proposed approach resolves the difficulty of analyzing co-movement in a time varying context when the analysis is based on correlation coefficients.

4.1. SWARCH Models

Consider the following p-order Autoregression of BRIC's stock market returns:

$$y_t = \phi_0 + \phi_1 y_{t-1} + \cdots + \phi_p y_{t-p} + \varepsilon_t,$$

where $\varepsilon_t = \sqrt{g_{s_t}}\tilde{\varepsilon}_t$, $\tilde{\varepsilon}_t = h_t v_t$, and h_t follows an ARCH(q) process of the following form:

$$h_t = a_0 + a_1\tilde{\varepsilon}_{t-1}^2 + \cdots + a_1\tilde{\varepsilon}_{t-1}^2,$$

where v_t is a Gaussian distribution with a unit standard error, g_{s_t} are the scale changing regime parameters that capture the sizes of the volatilities in different regimes. They take the values of $\sqrt{g_1}, \sqrt{g_2}, \ldots, \sqrt{g_K}$, for $s_t = 1, s_t = 2, \ldots, s_t = K$, respectively, where s_t is an unobservable state variable taking the possible values of $1, 2, \ldots, k$.

The SWARCH model assumes that the unobservable realization of the states is governed by a discrete-time, discrete-state stochastic Markov process with fixed transition probabilities and state-dependent variances. The probability law that causes the economy to switch between (latent) regimes is then given by the (hidden) k-state, first-order Markov chain is as follows:

$$P(s_t = j\backslash s_{t-1} = i, s_{t-2} = k, \ldots, y_{t-1}, y_{t-2}, \ldots) = P(s_t = j\backslash s_{t-1} = i) = p_{ij},$$

for $i, j = 1, 2, \ldots, K$ and $\sum_{j=1}^{K} p_{ij} = 1$.

The transition probability parameter p_{ij} represents the transition probability of moving from state i to j. A large $p_{ij}(j = 1, 2, \ldots, K)$ means that the model tends to remain in state i for a longer period of time.

It is worth noting that u_t is a standard ARCH(q) setting. Moreover, when $s_t = 1(s_t = 2, s_t = 3)$, ε_t equals $\tilde{\varepsilon}_t$ multiplied by $\sqrt{g_1}(\sqrt{g_2}, \sqrt{g_3})$. Without loss of generality, we set $g_1 = 1$. This means that the volatility of state 2(3) is $g_2(g_3)$ times state 1. If the estimates of g_2 are significantly greater than the estimates of g_1 and significantly lower than the estimates of g_3, we can conclude that state 1(2, 3) is the low (medium, high) volatility state.

An important feature of the Markov switching model is its ability to more realistically capture sudden changes, and objectively date the states of the economy using the smoothed probabilities, $\Pr ob\,[S_t = j \backslash y_3, \ldots, y_T], j = 1, 2, \ldots, K$, where K is the number of states. As suggested by Hamilton and Susmel (1994), the variance regimes are identified using a classification scheme in which an observation belongs to regime i for $i = 1, 2, \ldots K$ if the smoothed probability is greater than 0.5. Moreover, the diagonal elements of the matrix of transition probabilities contain important information regarding the expected duration of a regime. The expected duration, $E(D)$, for regime i is equal to $1/(1 - p_{ii})$, where D denotes the duration.

4.2. Model Selection and Diagnostic Analysis

To select the SWARCH model that best depicts the evolution of the volatility in the return series of each BRIC country, we use different criteria as in Hamilton and Susmel (1994). Precisely, we use the Akiake and Bayesian information criteria (AIC and BIC). In addition to these two criteria, we use four standards criteria: (1) the Mean Square Error (MSE), (2) the Mean Absolute Error (MAE), (3) the ALE, and (4) the ALES. The decision rule is to retain the model that has the lower values of these criteria (information and standards criteria). In addition to these selection criteria, we use the regime classification measure (RCM) developed by Ang and Bekaert (2002) to assess the quality of the fitted Markov switching model. Baele (2005) standardized this measure for multiple states,

The RCM is given for $K > 0$ states by:

$$RCM(K) = 100* \left(1 - \frac{K}{K-1}\frac{1}{T}\sum_{t=1}^{T}\sum_{i=1}^{K}\left(p_{i,t} - \frac{1}{K}\right)^2\right),$$

where $p_{i,t} = \Pr[S_t = i | I_T]$ is the probability of being in regime i at time t. The constant, 100, serves to normalize the statistic between 0 and 100. The basic concept behind this measure is that under perfect regime classification the smoothed probabilities will be close to zero or one and the diagonal elements of the transition probabilities matrix will be also close to one. This causes the RCM close to be close to zero. In the alternative case, weak regime inference implies that the selected Markov switching model cannot successfully distinguish between regimes from the behavior of the data and may indicate misspecification. Then, the RCM statistic values will be close to 100.

5. EMPIRICALS RESULTS

5.1. Data and Descriptive Statistics

The data used in this study consist of time series of daily indexes, denominated in US dollars, for Brazil, China, India, Russia, and the US economies. The sample covers the period from 10 February 2005 to 09 February 2010, resulting in a total of 1304 observations. The data were taken from the Morgan Stanley Capital International data set. In Table 1, we present information on the mean, standard deviation, skewness coefficient, Kurtosis coefficient, the Jarque-Bera Normality test (JB), and Ljung-Box test (LB) for the level and squared series.

Table 1 reports summary statistics for the daily returns of the five countries under investigation.The mean returns range from −0.8% for the US to 7.9% for Brazil. As shown in the table, the daily indexes' returns exhibit substantial non-normality, as can be seen from the skewness, kurtosis, and JB statistics. The high kurtosis coefficient is also typical of high-frequency financial time series, and it is responsible for the rejection of normality. This is primarily a result of the excess kurtosis, indicating that short-term returns are more characterized by fat tails than asymmetry (skewness). To test for serial correlation in the level and squared level of the daily indexes, we applied the Ljung-Box (LB) test to both the returns series ($LB(q)$) and the square of the returns series ($LB^2(q)$). The results reveal significant autocorrelation except for the Chinese returns series. The autocorrelations of the squared returns series reveal strong volatility clustering. Moreover, the high level of dependence in the squared returns series indicates the presence of an ARCH effect.

To test for stationarity of the stock market returns time series, we performed the ADF, PP, and KPSS unit root tests.[1] The results are reported in Table 2 below. None of the indexes time series (level and difference) exhibit statistically significant trends or intercepts

Table 1 Returns descriptive statistics using the whole sample.

	USA	**Brazil**	**Russia**	**India**	**China**
Mean	−0.008	0.079	0.035	0.064	0.063
Median	0.059	0.253	0.128	0.091	0.044
Std. Dev.	1.493	2.740	2.962	2.171	2.217
Skweness	−0.260	−0.394	−0.460	0.100	−0.011
Kurtosis	13.375	10.039	16.822	10.27	8.738
Jarque-Bera	5859.7	2717.1	10419.2	2873.1	1787.3
ARCH LM(12)	427.20	489.66	257.41	97.69	351.32
$LB(12)$	52.593	23.832	54.672	41.521	15.872
$LB^2(12)$	1525.9	1508.1	670.56	199.64	1047.1
Observations	1303	1303	1303	1303	1303

[1] The Augmented Dickey Fuller (ADF) test (ADF, 1981) and the Phillips and Perron (1988) test are the most commonly used unit roots tests to test for the non-stationarity of time series. These two tests have the advantage of accounting for the presence of serial correlation and heteroskedasticity in the errors. The third test that we used in this chapter is the Kwiatkowski, Phillips, Schmidt, and Shin (KPSS, 1992) test. In contrast to the ADF and PP tests, the KPSS test uses the null hypothesis that the series is trend stationary. Again, this requires an estimate of the residual spectrum at frequency zero, and a set of exogenous regressors.

Table 2 ADF, PP, and KPSS unit root tests.

	Levels			First difference		
	ADF	PP	KPSS	ADF	PP	KPSS
USA	−1.10	−1.19	1.53	−30.32	−30.32	0.16
Bresil	−1.74	−1.72	2.26	−33.47	−34.47	0.14
Russia	−1.68	−1.655	0.75	−33.36	−33.36	0.25
India	−1.63	−1.68	1.36	−33.65	−33.65	0.14
China	−1.61	−1.61	2.26	−35.56	−35.56	0.17

Note: Critical values for the unit roots tests are −1.94 (ADF and PP) and 0.463 (KPSS), without intercept and trend for the ADF and PP tests and with intercept for the KPSS test.

when using the ADF and PP tests. The empirical results reported in Table 2 demonstrate that the stock market indexes series are not stationary in level, but they are stationary in first differences (returns series). This also means that all series have the same order of integration, I(1).

5.2. SWARCH Results

To overcome one of the limitations of the adjusted correlation approach, the presence of time varying volatility in stock market returns, we employ the SWARCH(K,q) process. This model is a modification of the ARCH(q) specification that accounts for structural changes in the data. For instance, if $K = 3$, we obtain a model with three volatility states, high, medium, and low. To select the most appropriate model, different SWARCH specifications have been estimated for the daily return indexes for the BRIC economies and the US with different lags ($p = 1, 2, 3$) and conditional distribution errors (Normal, GED, and Student). Moreover, we estimated different models for $K = 2$ to 4 states, and $q = 0$ to 3 for the ARCH terms.

As shown in Table 3, the estimated regime change parameters for the variances in regime 2(g_2) and regime 3(g_3) are significantly different from unity, suggesting that—stock market returns exhibit three different volatility states. In addition, g_2 and g_3 reveal volatility magnitude ratios indicating high and medium volatility regimes, respectively, relative to a low volatility regime. These ratios vary substantially across markets. For example, for the Indian stock market, the conditional variance in the high (moderate) volatility regime is on average 8.85 (2.75) times that in the low volatility regime. The corresponding ratios are 28.27 (5.81) for Russia. Thus, the relative strength of the high volatility and low volatility regimes in the Indian market is smaller than that in the Russian market. This implies that the Russian stock market is more volatile than that of India, and consequently, a high volatility regime has a larger impact on the Russian market than on the Indian market.

Table 3 Estimation results of the student-AR(1)-SWARCH(K,1) models.

Par.	USA			Brazil			Russia			India			China		
	M1	M2	M3	M1	M2	M3	M1	M2	M3	M1	M2	M3	M1	M2	M3
ϕ_0	0.07	0.07	0.06	0.25	0.22	0.20	0.18	0.17	0.17	0.23	0.22	0.20	0.15	0.16	0.16
	(3.55)	(3.38)	(3.74)	(4.04)	(3.96)	(3.17)	(3.81)	(3.86)	(3.54)	(5.10)	(5.45)	(4.90)	(3.27)	(4.04)	(3.94)
ϕ_1	−0.07	−0.08	−0.08	0.07	0.08	0.07	−0.01	−0.01	−0.02	0.11	0.06	0.08	0.04	0.03	0.02
	(−2.61)	(−3.05)	(−3.49)	(2.72)	(2.74)	(2.61)	(−0.44)	(−1.66)	(−0.30)	(2.60)	(2.03)	(2.84)	(1.43)	(1.25)	(0.70)
a_0	1.12	0.44	0.38	4.10	2.72	2.89	3.46	2.07	2.17	2.46	1.13	1.03	2.47	1.24	1.10
	(3.40)	(8.03)	(10.39)	(8.79)	(9.45)	(12.73)	(5.07)	(9.45)	(9.85)	(6.01)	(10.18)	(9.66)	(6.71)	(9.57)	(9.29)
a_1	0.343	0.048	0.003	0.138	0.039	0.016	0.500	−0.098	−0.037	0.467	0.057	0.047	0.245	−0.063	−0.0001
	(2.69)	(1.36)	(1.12)	(3.055)	(1.154)	(0.283)	(3.93)	(−2.095)	(−0.68)	(4.033)	(1.55)	(1.25)	(3.79)	(−1.95)	(−0.00)
a_2	0.803	−0.211	0.046	0.318	−0.149	0.060	0.577	−0.123	−0.084	0.383	−0.046	−0.047	0.412	−0.151	−0.081
	(3.041)	(−3.742)	(4.423)	(4.888)	(−3.233)	(1.318)	(3.796)	(−2.370)	(−1.622)	(3.649)	(−1.291)	(−6.752)	(4.351)	(−3.264)	(−2.019)
υ	2.637	4.177	6.617	4.309	7.815	11.617	2.957	4.871	5.453	3.190	7.075	7.968	3.613	5.641	10.358
	(9.602)	(3.718)	(4.823)	(6.971)	(2.814)	(1.722)	(9.343)	(4.038)	(3.570)	(8.597)	(3.644)	(2.459)	(6.917)	(3.589)	(1.637)
g_1	-	1	1	-	1	1	-	1	1	-	1	1	-	1	1
	-	-	-	-	-	-	-	-	-	-	-	-	-	-	-
g_2	-	6.969	4.208	-	4.890	2.780	-	8.001	5.810	-	6.992	2.749	-	5.502	3.707
	-	(6.830)	(6.781)	-	(5.649)	(8.214)	-	(7.350)	(7.366)	-	(9.645)	(3.058)	-	(7.999)	(8.085)
g_3	-	-	27.975	-	-	12.993	-	-	28.279	-	-	8.857	-	-	17.408
	-	-	(5.928)	-	-	(5.032)	-	-	(2.165)	-	-	(2.459)	-	-	(4.952)
p_{11}	-	0.995	0.993	-	0.986	0.993	-	0.995	0.994	-	0.987	0.991	-	0.992	0.990
	-	(2.933)	(3.657)	-	(5.050)	(3.491)	-	(3.494)	(4.047)	-	(5.379)	(2.947)	-	(4.109)	(4.365)

(Continued)

Table 3 (Continued)

Par.	USA			Brazil			Russia			India			China		
	M1	M2	M3	M1	M2	M3	M1	M2	M3	M1	M2	M3	M1	M2	M3
p_{12}	-	-	-	-	-	-	-	-	-	-	-	-	-	-	-
	-	-	-	-	-	-	-	-	-	-	-	-	-	-	-
p_{21}	-	-	0.001	-	-	0.002	-	-	0.003	-	-	0.001	-	-	0.002
	-	-	(5.613)	-	-	(4.785)	-	-	(6.745)	-	-	(7.245)	-	-	(8.965)
p_{22}	-	0.993	0.993	-	0.967	0.988	-	0.987	0.982	-	0.984	0.979	-	0.993	0.973
	-	(3.058)	(3.582)	-	(4.135)	(2.469)	-	(4.037)	(2.019)	-	(5.469)	(1.686)	-	(3.395)	(5.985)
p_{32}	-	-	0.008	-	-	0.049	-	-	0.017	-	-	0.012	-	-	0.024
	-	-	(2.483)	-	-	(1.819)	-	-	(1.729)	-	-	(2.449)	-	-	(3.769)
p_{33}	-	-	0.990	-	-	0.939	-	-	0.933	-	-	0.987	-	-	0.931
	-	-	5.920	-	-	5.389	-	-	3.936	-	-	4.324	-	-	2.927
LL	−1970.1	−1905.7	−1866.8	−2948.6	−2915.3	−2900.1	−2903.1	−2839.4	−2832.3	−2653.4	−2574.2	−2566.2	−2661.5	−2591.1	−2581.9
N. of Par.	6	9	14	6	9	14	6	9	14	6	9	14	6	9	14
LR(l/l + 1)	-	128.74	77.726	-	66.540	30.354	-	127.48	14.1	-	158.34	16.04	-	140.69	16.45
RCM(K)	-	10.922	4.355	-	22.055	13.379	-	9.280	9.309	-	13.528	19.896	-	10.526	17.112

Note: M1, M2, and M3 indicate the ARCH(2), SWARCH(2,2), and SWARCH(3,2) models, respectively.
Despite the fact that the Likelihood ratio (LR) cannot be used in this case because of its non-standard distribution, the LR statistic is equal, respectively, to 128.74 and 77.746 for the USA, to 140.69 and 16.45 for China, to 127.48 and 14.1 for Russia, to 158.34 and 16.04 for the India, and to 66.54 and 30.354 for Brazil when testing between linear model against the alternative of two regimes and between the null hypothesis of two states against the alternative of 3 regimes. Following empirical works of Hansen (1992, 1996), pa Garcia (1998), and Carrasco (2002), these empirical values are very much higher than the expected critical values, see also Hamilton and Susmel (1994). Then, one does not doubt on the rejection of the null hypothesis of two states against the alternative of three-state SWARCH model. This latter specification, SWARCH(3,1) model, is the convenient specification to describe the evolution of the BRIC countries stock market returns against the linear and two regime switching models.

The transition probabilities of the SWARCH model are also reported in Table 3. For all markets, we obtain values of p_{11}, p_{22}, and p_{33} that are close to one. This result implies that the volatility under each regime is highly persistent. More important, our results show that transition probability $p_{13} = 0$, while $p_{23} \neq 0$ for all markets. This suggests that the high volatility regime follows the medium volatility regime and the market cannot directly transition to the high volatility regime from the low volatility regime.

The empirical estimation results and residuals analysis of the preferred model, the ARCH(1) and SWARCH(K,1) for $K = 2$ and 3 using the Student distribution, are reported in Table 6. We note that all estimated parameters in the ARCH model are significant at the 5% level, but the residuals analysis indicates that there are remaining ARCH effects. Therefore, the observed high persistence of shocks is indicative of structural change in the statistical process (see Lamoureux and Lastrapes, 1990). From Table 3, results suggest that all parameters are statistically significant at the 5% level and a three-state SWARCH model is more appropriate than the ARCH(2) and SWARCH(2,2) specifications for all BRIC countries. Moreover, the AIC and BIC criteria and the ALE and ALES loss functions, (see Table 6) support the use of the three-state specifications. Ultimately, the three-state specifications are more convenient and better describe the evolution of stock market returns in the BRIC countries.

5.3. Smoothed Probabilities and Regime Classification

Table 7 summarizes the dates and durations of the low volatility and high volatility regimes obtained from the SWARCH(3,1) model for the USA and each BRIC country. For example, the quiet period (low volatility state) for the USA is from 10/02/2005 to 12/07/2007. The medium state corresponds to periods from 15/04/2009 to 09/02/2010 and from 13/07/2007 to 22/08/2008. Finally, the high volatility period corresponds to the periods from 23/08/2008 to 14/04/2009.

Figures 4–8 report the smoothed probabilities from the preferred SWARCH(3,1) model. The top panel plots the daily stock market returns for each BRIC country. The second panel plots the smoothed probability that the economy was in state 1 (low volatility) at time t; the third panel indicates that the economy was experiencing medium volatility at time t, and the fourth panel plots the periods of high volatility at time t. The observations are classified following Hamilton and Susmel (1994) proposed method for dating regime switches. Thus, they define an observation as belonging to regime i if the smoothed probability is greater than 0.5. Based on the smoothed probabilities we observe for the USA and all BRIC countries, each regime is highly persistent, as evinced by the large (and in general, highly significant) constant regime probabilities p_{11} and p_{22}, respectively.

In summary, the general pattern in the last line of Table 3 indicates that the SWARCH models deliver clear regime inferences, as the RCMs are far from 100. This

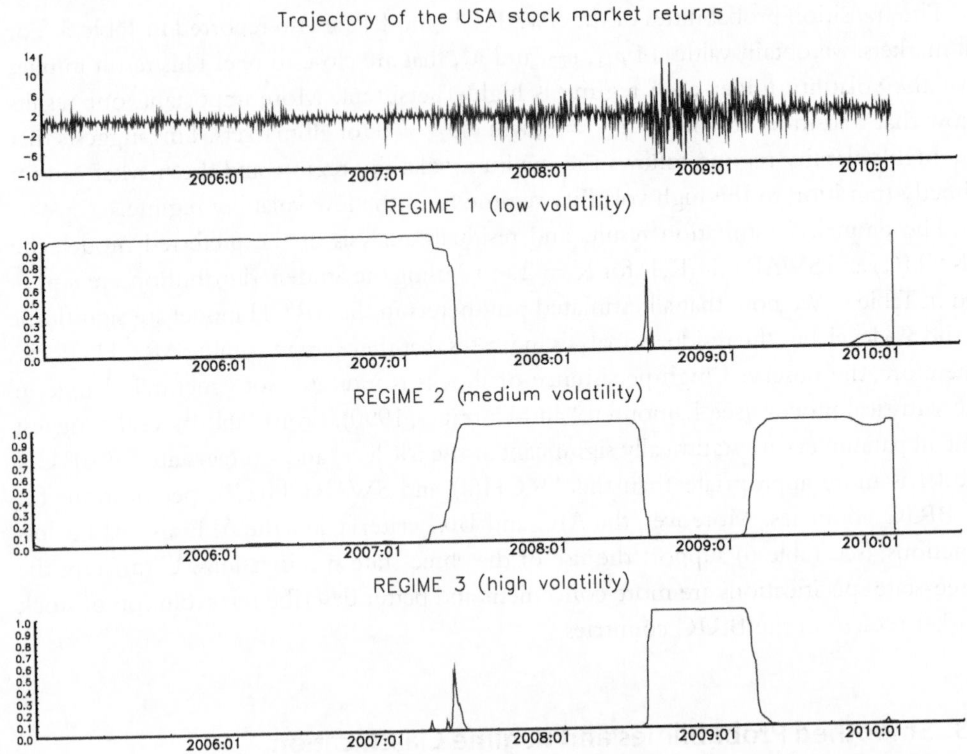

Figure 4 Smoothed probabilities of the SWARCH(3,1) model of the USA stock market returns.

means that these specifications are able to clearly identify the presence of three regimes in all periods considered.

According to Figures 4–8, stock market returns in the USA and BRIC countries most frequently switch between the low volatility state and the medium volatility state during the sample period. Thus, the high volatility regime is characterized by its brief duration. An interesting feature of the results in all figures is that the high volatility states correspond to the period of subprime crisis for the US and BRIC countries. The results may suggest that the BRIC countries were subject to some form of "volatility contagion" during the subprime crisis. We analyze this hypothesis in greater detail in Section 6.

6. INTERDEPENDENCE VERSUS CONTAGION

The objective of this section is to test for the presence of interdependence or contagion phenomena running from the US to the BRIC economies during the subprime crisis. To this end, we estimated the traditional correlation coefficient between each BRIC's stock market and the US stock market returns under the low, medium, and high variance regimes identified using the Hamilton and Susmel (1994) SWARCH model, see previous

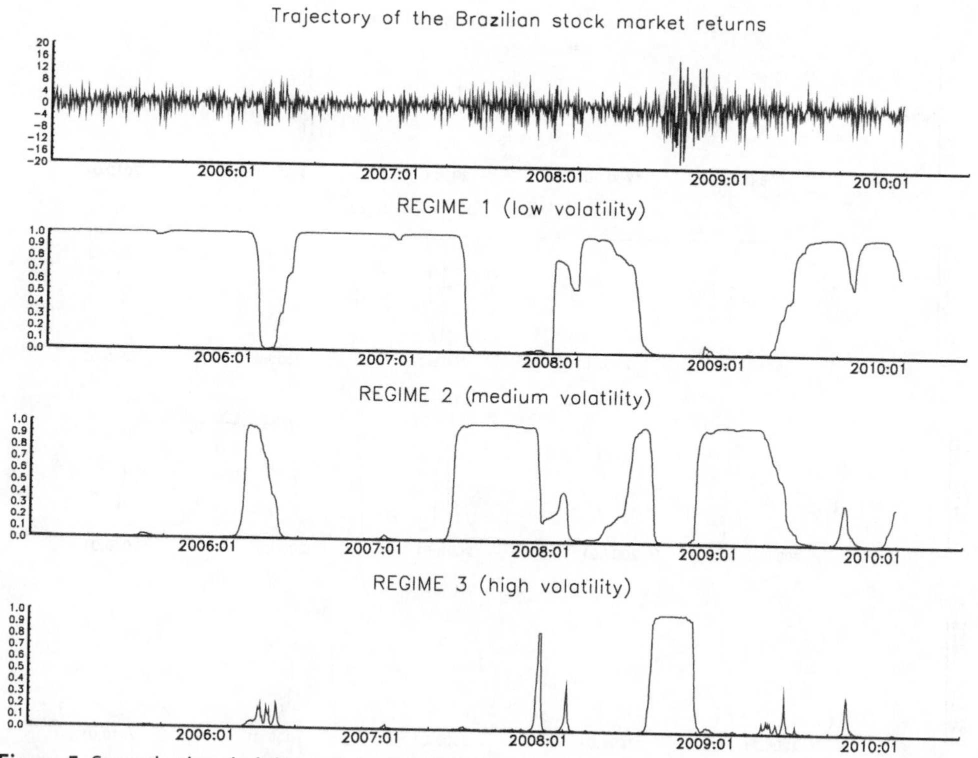

Figure 5 Smoothed probabilities of the SWARCH(3,1) model of the Brazilian stock market returns.

section. Then, we tested for significant increases in the adjusted correlation coefficients using the Rigobón and Forbes (2001) approach.

As noted above, testing for significant increases in correlations before and during crisis periods using the traditional correlation approach suffers from several limitations. First, there is a problem of heteroskedasticity when high-frequency data are used. Second, the omission of variables, such as those representing economic fundamentals, may also be a concern. Third, to identify contagion, there must be evidence of dynamic increases in the regressions, affecting at least the second moment correlations and covariances (see Kenourgios et al., 2011). To overcome the problem of heteroskedasticity, Forbes and Rigobón (2002) proposed an adjusted correlation approach, which is a modified version of the traditional correlation approach.

Let us now present the adjusted correlation approach developed by Rigobón and Forbes (2001) in greater detail. First, note that there are nine different sets of correlations that should be considered where: (1) US volatility is low and other countries volatilities are low, (2) US volatility is low and other countries volatilities are medium, (3) US volatility is low and other countries' volatilities are high, (4) US volatility is medium and other countries' volatilities are low, (5) US volatility is medium and other countries'

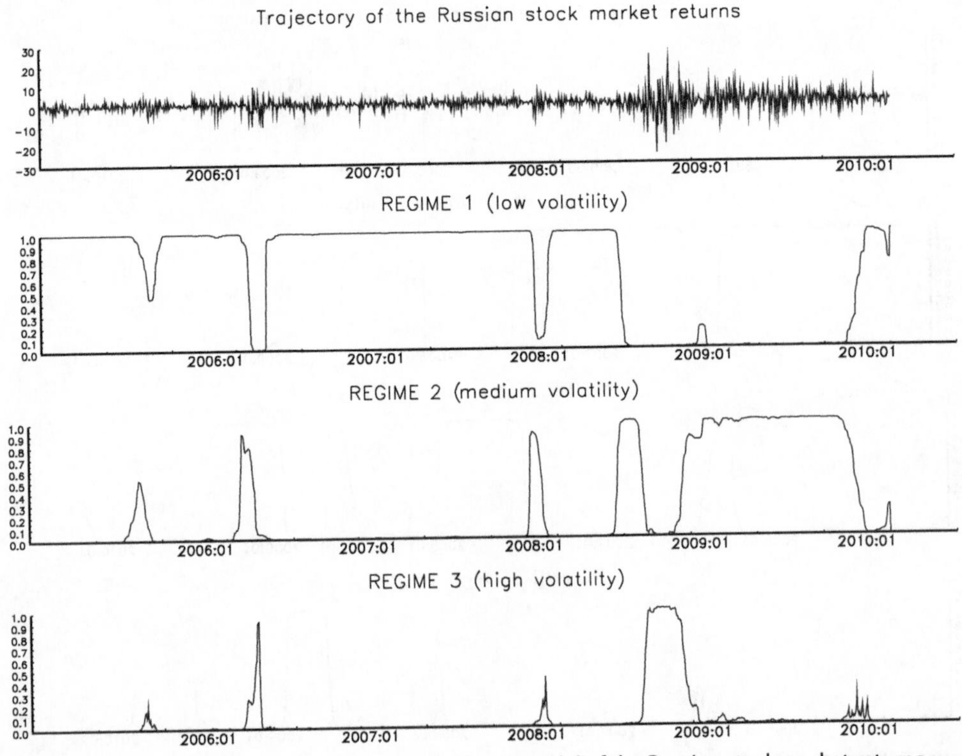

Figure 6 Smoothed probabilities of the SWARCH(3,1) model of the Russian stock market returns.

volatilities are medium, (6) US volatility is medium and other countries' volatilities are high, (7) US volatility is high and other countries' volatilities are low, (8) US volatility is high and other countries' volatilities are medium, and (9) US volatility is high and other countries' volatilities are high. We suppose that the pair-wise correlation coefficients during the low-low volatility regime (s = i) and the high-high volatility regime (s = j) are respectively:

$$\rho_i = \frac{Cov(r_{i,1}r_{i,2})}{\sqrt{Var(r_{i,1})\,Var(r_{i,2})}}$$

and

$$\rho_j = \frac{Cov(r_{j,1}r_{j,2})}{\sqrt{Var(r_{j,1})\,Var(r_{j,2})}}.$$

If there is an increase in the volatility in the returns of country 1, i.e., $\sigma_{j,1}^2 > \sigma_{i,1}^2$, then $\rho_j > \rho_i$, giving the false appearance of contagion. To adjust for this,

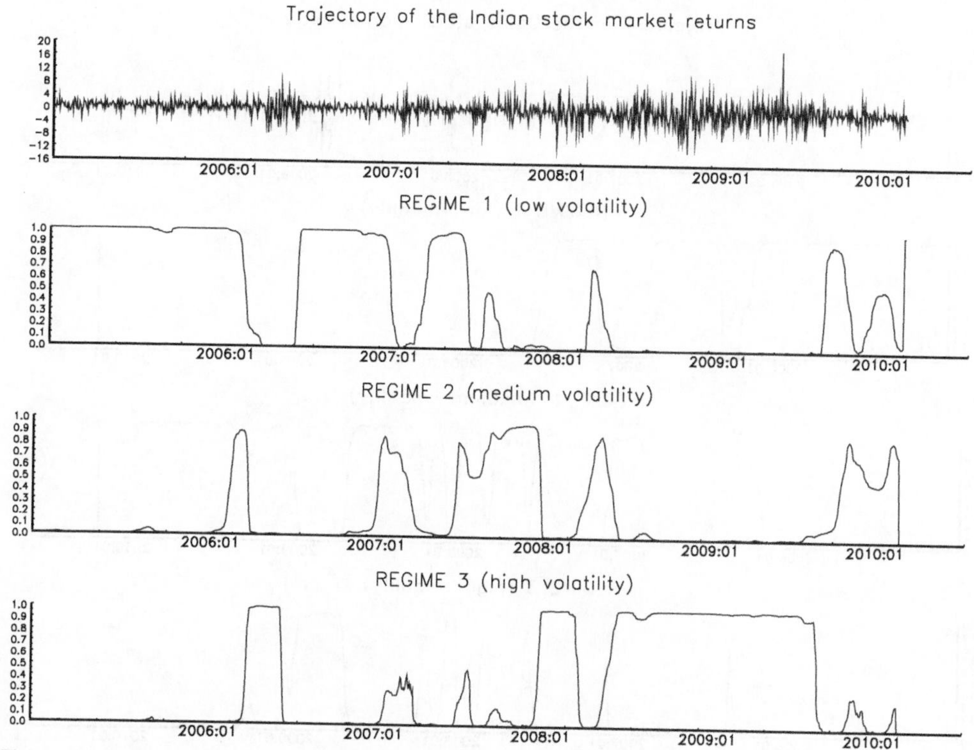

Figure 7 Smoothed probabilities of the SWARCH(3,1) model of the Indian stock market returns.

Forbes and Rigobón (2002) show that the adjusted (unconditional) correlation is given by:

$$\vartheta_j = \frac{\rho_j}{\sqrt{1 + \left(\frac{\sigma_{j,1}^2 - \sigma_{i,1}^2}{\sigma_{i,1}^2}\right)(1 - \rho_2)}}.$$

According to this equation, the unconditional correlation ϑ_2 is the conditional correlation (ρ_j) scaled by a non-linear function of the percentage change in the country's volatility $\frac{\sigma_{j,1}^2 - \sigma_{i,1}^2}{\sigma_{i,1}^2}$ in this case, over the high and low volatility periods.

Following Forbes and Rigobón (2002), if adjusted statistics are used and there is no evidence of a significant increase in the correlation coefficients during the subprime crisis, we can interpret the results as evidence of no contagion.

Table 4 reports the empirical results of the traditional correlation approach when the US is considered the "originator" of the crisis. This table shows that there is a dispersion of co-dependence of volatility regimes. Most of the coefficients are positive and statistically significant. This indicates that some countries exhibit significant return synchronization

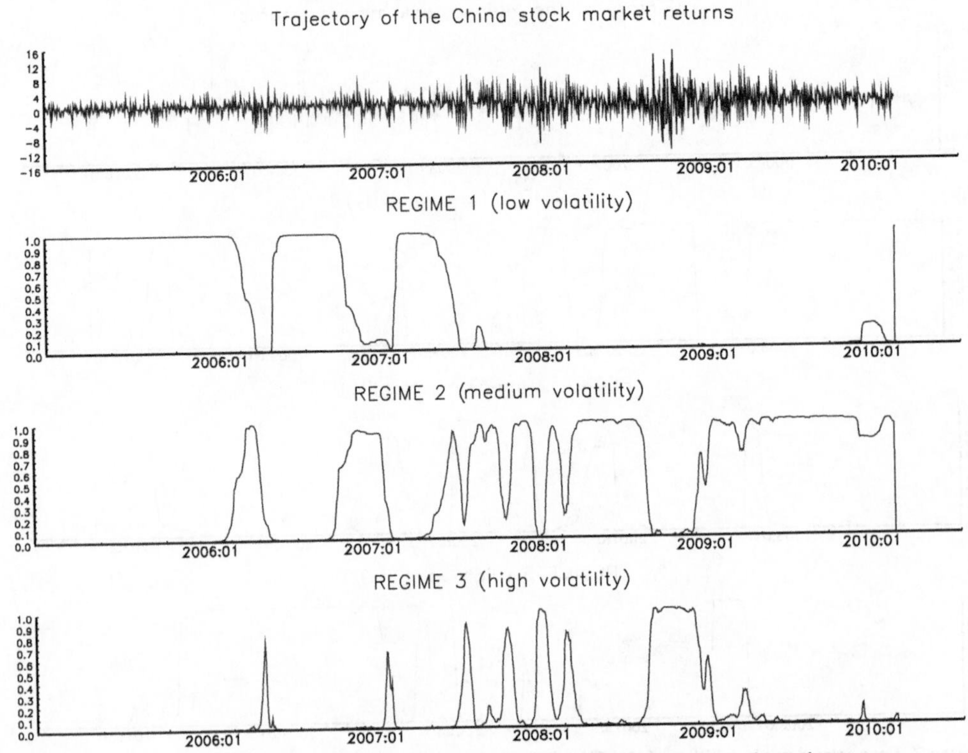

Figure 8 Smoothed probabilities of the SWARCH(3,1) model of the China stock market returns.

with the US market, i.e., shocks experienced in one market are transmitted to other markets. The correlation coefficients with the US market are more pronounced for all countries under the high-high volatility condition. This is explained by the increased strength of the links between the US and other countries' markets during the subprime crisis. However, the highest correlation coefficients are obtained for Brazil and Russia under certain correlation sets.

The question that arises at this level of analysis is whether this heterogeneity in the correlations between the individual BRIC countries and the US stock market can be considered contagion. The answer to this question will be affected by the definition of contagion considered. In this chapter, we adopted the definition proposed by Forbes and Rigobón (2002), which considers contagion to be a significant breakdown in the adjusted correlation coefficient.

Table 5 reports the estimated values of the adjusted correlation coefficients. From this table, it appears that the adjusted correlation coefficient is only significantly different from zero for Brazil. This result confirms that the increase in the co-movement is more pronounced for the Brazilian stock market during crisis periods than for the other

BRIC countries. This result also demonstrates that the Brazilian economy was subject to contagion during the subprime crisis of 2007.

In summary, the more efficient estimates displayed in Table 5 make it apparent that the high degree of co-movement between the US stock market and those of the BRIC countries is not homogenous. Moreover, contagion was only observed running from the US economy to the Brazilian economy.

7. SUMMARY AND IMPLICATIONS

In the last three decades, the BRIC countries underwent an important process of trade and financial liberalization to benefit from the advantages of market integration. As is commonly known, integrated financial markets allows, investors to allocate consumption risk more efficiently. This in turn decreases the costs of capital faced by firms and stimulates investment and economic growth. However, given the increase in the number of financial crises since the 1990s, several researchers have argued that increased financial integration has intensified contagion effects across markets, causing severe welfare losses for large geographical regions. Thus, integrating a national market with global financial markets may facilitate the transmission of international shocks to domestic stock markets. This will also have important implications for the decisions of investors', risk managers, and regulatory and monetary authorities and particular consequences for effective portfolio diversification. In this chapter, we combined the Markov switching ARCH model (SWARCH) and the adjusted correlation approach to account for time-varying volatility. Specifically, we address the issue of the effects of co-movement on stock market volatility by analyzing the common evolution of the return volatilities of the economies of the BRIC countries' and the US during the subprime crisis. To do so, we employ univariate switching ARCH models. We find that high volatility periods in the US and BRIC stock markets are short lived and tend to be associated with the international subprime crisis. Then, we examined the joint behavior of stock return in the US and BRIC countries. We find strong links between the US and BRIC countries' markets during the subprime crisis. Overall, we interpret our results as being more supportive of interdependence than of contagion, except for the case of Brazil, which presents evidence of contagion. Our empirical results also demonstrate that the estimated standard correlation coefficients between the BRICs' stock returns and US stock returns depend on different volatility regimes. Moreover, we note that there is an increase in the correlation coefficient of each country when moving from the low-low (stable period) to the high-high (more volatile and recession period) regime. In addition, the adjusted correlation results indicate that correlation coefficients are the most pronounced for Brazil, followed by India and then by China. These results can be interpreted as follows. First, the large correlation coefficients observed for Brazil before, during, and after the subprime crisis suggest that this economy is highly integrated with the US economy. In this respect, Brazil is followed by Russia,

Table 4 Pair-wise co-dependence of volatility regimes.

	USA vs Brazil			USA vs Russia			USA vs India			USA vs China		
	Corr	N. of obs.	Crit. val	Corr	N. of obs.	Crit. val	Corr	N. of obs.	Crit. val	Corr	N. of obs.	Crit. val
Low vs Low	0.577	590	0.082	0.13	491	0.090	0.091	507	0.089	0.115	631	0.079
Low vs Medium	0.641	37	0.329	-	-	-	0.101	112	0.189	-	-	-
Low vs High	-	-	-	-	-	-	-	-	-	-	-	-
Medium vs Low	0.583	303	0.115	0.45	36	0. 333	-	-	-	0.312	55	0.269
Medium vs Medium	0.641	203	0.141	0.35	168	0.154	-	-	-	0.059	451	0.094
Medium vs High	-	-	-	0.44	153	0.162	0.174	506	0.089	-	-	-
High vs Low	-	-	-	0.41	167	0.154	-	-	-	-	-	-
High vs Medium	0.702	99	0.201	-	-	-	0.407	85	0.217	0.227	108	0.192
High vs High	0.742	66	0.246	-	-	-	0.493	78	0.226	0.414	60	0.258

Table 5 Adjusted (unconditional) correlations.

	Adjusted unconditional correlations
USA - Brazil	0.1515
USA - Russia	–
USA - India	0.0843
USA - China	0.0659

India, and finally China. Second, it is well known that when the degree of integration of given economy with global financial markets is low, the possibility of portfolio diversification exists. This is the case for China and India which have small adjusted correlation coefficients relative to that of Brazil; see Table 5. These results are in keeping with several studies that found that the Indian and Brazilian markets have the highest level of integration among the BRIC countries, followed by Russia and China; see for instance (Aloui et al., 2011; Bianconi et al., 2013). Our results support those of Aloui et al. (2011), who found that financial dependence on the US during the 2007–2009 global financial crisis was much stronger for Brazil and Russia than for China and India, suggesting that countries with greater sensitivity to commodity-price changes tend to co-move closely with the US in both bull and bear markets. Our findings are also consistent with those of Bianconi et al. (2013), who reported that the effect of US financial stress on the Chinese stock market is negligible. The effects on stock returns in Brazil and Russia are negative and relatively larger than those on the Indian stock market. Fonseka et al. (2012) also obtain results similar to ours in the case of China, as the authors provide evidence that the increase in the correlation between the Chinese and US markets was small during the crisis. This finding is consistent with the fact that the Chinese stock market only declined by 13%, compared with a 39% drop in the US market, during the financial crisis. As suggested above, our empirical results have several implications for investment decisions, risk managers, and international portfolio diversification. The diversification sought by investing in multiple markets from different regional blocks is likely to be lower when it is most desirable (see Kenourgios et al., 2011). The presence of a high degree of co-dependence between the BRIC countries and the US on the one hand and the identification of contagion in the case of Brazil on the other are related to information processing. Domanski and Kremer (2000) suggest that if asset prices do not co-move in a very general sense, this can be interpreted as the result of information processing and market segmentation. The author quantifies three sources of market segmentation. First, the information relevant for price formation may differ between market segments. Second, even if the bases for the information are the same, the processing of information might differ systematically according to the different groups of investors that are most active in the respective markets. Third, even if information input and processing are congruent

Table 6 Residuals analysis.

	USA			Brazil			Russia			India			China		
	M1	M2	M3	M1	M2	M3	M1	M2	M3	M1	M2	M3	M1	M2	M3
Mean	−0.063	−0.074	−0.060	−0.059	−0.060	−0.050	−0.048	−0.052	−0.046	−0.059	−0.079	−0.069	−0.038	−0.043	−0.038
Std.dev	0.829	0.954	0.969	0.973	0.971	0.950	0.903	0.970	0.920	0.925	0.984	0.991	0.935	0.959	0.991
Skewness	−0.930	−0.572	−0.487	−0.195	−0.259	−0.382	−0.537	−0.386	−0.369	0.316	−0.116	−0.206	−0.100	−0.085	−0.014
E-Kurtosis	10.53	2.652	1.459	2.381	1.304	0.872	5.040	3.116	2.138	5.497	2.735	2.376	2.116	1.499	1.338
J-B	5114	451.57	166.6	315.73	106.69	72.717	1440.84	557.89	276.9	1661.1	407.8	314.78	245.05	123.13	97.02
Resid. Q(6)	5.959	6.723	5.682	5.9490	4.607	5.021	12.555	7.471	8.023	4.211	4.711	3.067	12.012	6.578	7.867
Resid. Q(12)	15.77	14.420	12.843	12.611	9.185	9.488	23.366	16.187	13.40	24.276	21.178	16.721	34.719	15.310	15.061
Sq. Resid Q(6)	15.60	45.927	8.649	109.51	31.174	10.233	56.979	26.032	11.99	29.533	10.143	10.107	102.98	45.420	20.646
Sq. Resid Q(12)	59.27	126.75	12.845	210.96	83.24	24.235	93.532	57.784	12.97	69.29	21.716	18.710	174.86	57.757	23.894
MSE	61.116	50.534	48.259	529.89	450.77	417.187	1240.36	1125.5	1054.1	201.72	189.94	187.12	185.93	157.61	155.28
MAE	2.999	2.474	2.405	9.253	8.137	8.153	11.653	10.067	10.55	5.872	5.141	5.125	6.098	5.357	5.333
ALES	14.075	10.544	9.966	10.213	8.790	8.756	11.892	9.076	9.338	9.575	8.181	7.521	10.716	8.418	8.666
ALE	2.849	2.349	2.248	2.327	2.092	2.088	2.618	2.169	2.207	2.363	2.052	2.006	2.478	2.149	2.129
N. of Par	6	9	14	6	9	12	6	9	14	6	9	14	6	9	14
AIC	3952.2	3829.5	3761.7	5909.1	5848.6	5828.2	5676.6	5696.7	5834.2	5318.8	5166.5	5164.4	5335.0	5200.3	5191.9
BIC	3983.3	3876.1	3834.17	5940.2	5895.2	5900.65	5707.6	5743.3	5936.65	53498	5213.0	5256.85	5366.1	5246.9	5264.44

Note: M1, M2, and M3 indicate the ARCH(2), SWARCH(2,2), and SWARCH(3,2) models, respectively.
$AIC = -2 \times LL + 2K$ and $BIC = -2 \times LL + k \times Ln(T)$, where K is the number of parameters under each model specification and T is the number of observations.
$MSE = \frac{1}{T}\sum_{i=1}^{T}\left(\hat{u}_t^2 - \sigma_t^2\right)^2$, $MAE = \frac{1}{T}\sum_{i=1}^{T}\left|\hat{u}_t^2 - \sigma_t^2\right|$, the $[LE]^2 = \frac{1}{T}\sum_{i=1}^{T}\left(\ln\left(\hat{u}_t^2\right) - \ln\left(\sigma_t^2\right)\right)^2$, and the $LE = \frac{1}{T}\sum_{i=1}^{T}\left|\ln\left(\hat{u}_t^2\right) - \ln\left(\sigma_t^2\right)\right|$.

Table 7 Periods of low, medium and high volatility states for each country (SWARCH(3,2) model).

	USA	Brazil	Russia	India	China
REGIME 1 Low volatility	10/2/05→12/07/07	10/2/05→02/05/06 24/06/06→12/07/07 18/01/08→14/07/08 09/06/09→09/02/10	10/02/05→20/03/06 20/07/06→01/02/07 18/04/07→17/07/07 18/08/09→01/10/09	10/02/05→13/04/06 14/06/06→20/11/06 06/03/07→05/07/07	10/02/05→12/07/07 25/11/09→09/02/10
REGIME 2 Medium volatility	13/07/07→22/08/08 15/04/09→09/02/10	03/05/06→23/06/06 13/07/07→17/01/08 15/07/08→02/09/08 04/12/08→08/06/09	18/07/07→07/01/08 01/04/08→30/05/08	14/04/06→06/06/06 21/11/06→23/02/07 05/07/07→28/08/08 17/12/08→09/02/10	13/07/07→01/09/08 25/11/08→19/11/09
REGIME 3 High volatility	23/08/08→14/04/09	03/09/08→03/12/08	08/01/08→31/03/08 02/10/09→09/02/10	29/08/08→16/12/08	02/09/08→24/11/08

across market segments, the price effect may differ owing to differing transaction costs or degrees of market liquidity. In our empirical application, this is the case for the Chinese and Russian economies. Regarding the Chinese economy, this may be due to the closed nature of its financial system, see for instance Bhar and Nikolova (2009). Regarding Brazil and India, their markets are highly integrated with the US market and the potential for portfolio diversification is less than that for China and Russia.

REFERENCES

Aloui, R., Ben Aissa, M.S., Nguyen, D.K., 2011. Global financial crisis, extreme interdependences, and contagion effects: the role of economic structure? Journal of Banking and Finance 35 (130), 141

Ang, A., Bekaert, G., 2002. Intentional asset allocation with regime shift. Review of Financial studies 15 (4), 1137–1187

Bae, K., Karolyi, A., Stulz, R., 2003. A new approach to measuring financial contagion. Review of Financial Studies 16, 717–763

Baele, L., 2005. Volatility spillover effects in European equity markets. Journal of Financial and Quantitative Analysis 40, 373–401

Bessler, D.A., Yang, J., 2003. The structure of interdependence in international stock markets. Journal of International Money and Finance 22, 261–287

Bekaert, G., Harvey, C.R., 1997. Emerging equity market volatility. Journal of Financial Economic 43, 29–78

Bhar, R., Nikolova, B., 2009. Return, volatility spillovers and dynamic correlation in the BRIC equity markets: an analysis using a bivariate EGARCH framework. Global Finance Journal 19 (3), 203–218

Bianconi, M., Yoshino, J.A., Machado de Sousa, M.O., 2013. BRIC and the U.S. financial crisis: an empirical investigation of stock and bond markets. Emerging Markets Review 14, 76–109

Bollerslev, T., 1986. Generalized autoregressive conditional heteroscedasticity. Journal of Econometrics 31, 307–327

Bonfiglioli, A., Favero, C.A., 2005. Explaining co-movements between stock markets: the case of US and Germany. Journal of International Money and Finance 24, 1299–1316

Boyer, B.H., Kumagai, T., Yuan, K., 2006. How do crises spread? Evidence from accessible in inaccessible stock indices. Journal of Finance 61, 957–1003

Canarella, G., Pollard, S.K., 2007. A switching ARCH (SWARCH) model of stock market volatility: some evidence from Latin America. International Review of Economics 54, 445–462

Carrasco, M., 2002. Misspecified structural change, threshold, and Markov-switching models. Journal of Econometrics 109, 237–239

Chan, K.F., Treepongkaruna, S., Brooks, R., Gray, S., 2011. Asset market linkages: evidence from financial, commodity and real estate assets. Journal of Banking and Finance 35, 1415–1426

Chandar, N., Patro, D.K., Yezegel, A., 2009. Crises, contagion and cross-listings. Journal of Banking and Finance 33, 1709–1729

Chiang, T.C., Jeon, B., Li, H., 2007. Dynamic correlation analysis of financial contagion: evidence from Asian markets. Journal of International Money and Finance 26, 1206–1228

Christofi, A., Pericli, A., 1999. Correlation in price changes and volatility of major Latin American stock markets. Journal of Multinational Financial Management 9, 79–93

Corsetti, G., Pesenti, P., Roubini, N., 1999. What caused the Asian currency and financial crisis? Japan and the World Economy 11, 305–373

De Gregorio, J., Valdes, R., 2001. Crisis transmission: evidence from the debt, tequila and Asian flu crises. The World Bank Economic Review 15 (2), 289–314

Diamandis, P.F., 2008. Financial liberalization and changes in the dynamic behaviour of emerging market volatility: evidence from four Latin American equity markets. Research in International Business and Finance 22, 362–377

Domanski, M., Kremer, M., 2000. The dynamics of international asset price linkages and their effects on German stock and bond markets. In: BIS Conference Papers, No 8. International Financial Markets and the Implications for Monetary and Financial Stability, March, pp. 134–158

Dungey, M., Milunovich, G., Thorp, S., 2010. Unobservable shocks as carriers of contagion. Journal of Banking and Finance 34, 1008–1021

Edwards, S., Susmel, R., 2001. Volatility dependence and contagion in emerging equity markets. Journal of Devevelopment Economy 66, 505–532

Eichengreen, B., Rose, A.K., Wyplosz, C., 1996. Contagious currency crises. Scandinavian Economics Review 98 (4), 463–484

Engle, R.F., 1982. Autoregressive conditional heteroskedasticity with estimates of the variance of U.K. inflation. Econometrica 50, 987–1008

Engle, R.F., Ito, T., Lin, W.L., 1990. A meteor showers or heat waves? Heteroskedastic intra-daily volatility in the foreign exchange market. Econometrica 58, 525–542

Fonseka, M.M., Samarakoon, L.P., Tian, G.L., 2012. Equity financing capacity and stock returns: evidence from China. Journal of International Financial Markets, Institutions & Money 22, 1277–1291

Forbes, K.J., Rigobón, R., 2002. No contagion, only interdependence: measuring stock market comovements. Journal of Finance 57, 2223–2261

Gagnon, L., Karolyi, G.A., 2006. Price and volatility transmission across borders. Financial Markets, Institutions and Instruments 5 (3), 107–158

Grubel, H.G., 1968. International diversified portfolios: welfare gains and capital flows. American Economic Review 58, 1299–1314

Hamilton, J.D., Susmel, R., 1994. Autoregressive conditional heteroscedasticity and changes in regime. Journal of Econometrics 64, 307–333

Hansen, B.E., 1992. The likelihood ratio test under nonstandard conditions: testing the Markov switching model of GNP. Journal of Applied Econometrics 7, S61–S82

Hansen, B.E., 1996. Inference when a Nuissance parameter is not identified under the null hypothesis. Econometrica 64, 413–430

Hong, Y., 2001. A test for volatility spillover with application to exchange rates. Journal of Econometrics 103, 183–224

Kenourgios, D., Aristeidis, S., Nikos, P., 2007. Financial crises and contagion: evidence for BRIC stock markets. Journal of International Financial Markets, Institutions and Money 21, 92–106

Kenourgios, D., Samitas, A., Paltalidis, N., 2011. Financial crises and stock market contagion in a multivariate time-varying asymmetric framework. Journal of International Financial Markets, Institutions & Money 21 (92), 106

King, M., Wadhwani, S., 1990. Transmission of volatility between stock markets. Review of Financial Studies 3, 5–33

Kwiatkowski, D., Phillips, P.C.B., Schmidt, P., Shi, Y., 1992. Testing the null hypothesis of stationarity against the alternative of a unit root: how sure are we that economic time series have a unit root? Journal of Econometrics 54, 159–178

Lamoureux, C., Lastrapes, W., 1990. Persistence in variance, structural change and the Garch model. Journal of Business Economic and Statistic 8, 225–234

Lee, S., Kim, K.J., 1993. Does the October 1987 crash strengthen the comovements among national stock markets? Review Financial Studies 3, 89–102

Lim, L.K., 2009. Convergence and interdependence between ASEAN-5 stock markets. Mathematics and Computers in Simulation 79, 2957–2966

Longin, F., Solnik, B., 1995. Is the correlation in international equity returns constant: 1960–1990. Journal of International Money and Finance 14, 13–26

Longin, F., Solnik, B., 2001. Extreme correlation in international equity markets. Journal of finance 56 (2), 649–676

Loretan, M., English, W.B., 2000. Evaluating correlation breakdowns during periods of market volatility. Intemationai Finance Discussion Papers, No. 658. Board of Governors of the Federal Reserve Board.

Morales, L., Gassie, E., 2011. Structural breaks and financial volatility: lessons from BRIC Countries. Dublin Institute of Technology, Dublin 1 Esmeralda Gassie, University of Limerick (May) pa Garcia, R., 1998. Asymptotic null distribution of the likelihood ratio test in Markov switching models. International Economic Review 39, 763–788

Phillips, P.C.B., Perron, P., 1988. Testing for a unit root in time series regression. Biometrika 75 (2), 335–346

Raj, J., Dhal, S., 2008. Integration of India's stock market with global and major regional markets. BIS Papers, No. 42.

Rigobón, R., 2003. On the measurement of the international propagation of shocks: is the transmission stable? Journal of International Economics 61 (2), 261–283

Rigobón, R., Forbes, K., 2001. Contagion in Latin America: definitions, measurement, and policy implications. Journal of LACEA Economia, LACEA—Latin American and the Caribbean Economic Association

Samarakoon, L.P., 2011. Stock market interdependence, contagion, and the U.S. financial crisis: the case of emerging and frontier markets. Journal of International Financial Markets, Institutions & Money. 21, 724–742

Sheng, H.C., Tu, A.H., 2000. A study of cointegration and variance decomposition among equity indices before and during the period of the Asian financial crisis. Journal of Multinational Financial Management 10, 345–365

Solnik, B., 1974. Why not diversify internationally rather than domestically. Financial Analysts Journal 30, 48–54

Wang, Y., Gunasekarage, A., Power, D.M., 2005. Return and volatility spillovers from developed to emerging capital markets: the case of South Asia. Contemporary Studies in Economic and Financial Analysis 86, 139–166

Wang, K.M., Thi, T.B.N., 2006. Does contagion effect exist between stock markets of Thailand and chinese economic area (CEA) during the Asian flu? Asian Journal of Management and Humanity Sciences 1 (1), 16–36

Yiu, M.S., Ho, W.A., Choi, D.F., 2010. Dynamic correlation analysis of financial contagion in Asian markets in global financial turmoil. Applied Financial Economics 20, 345–354

CHAPTER 24

On the Importance of Trend Gaps in Assessing Equity Market Correlations

Jarkko Peltomäki and Michael Graham
Stockholm University, School of Business, Sweden

1. INTRODUCTION

This chapter examines the use of trend gaps in assessing diversification benefits in global equity portfolios. The Nobel Laureate Professor Markowitz (1952), in his seminal paper, demonstrated the statistical benefits of asset diversification. The paper establishes that including assets with less than perfect correlations in a portfolio reduces its inherent diversifiable risk. Grubel (1968) confirms the Markowitz (1952) principles and finds that diversifying internationally yields higher rates of return or lower variances on a portfolio relative to a purely national diversification of assets. Successive studies by Levy and Sarnat (1970), Agmon (1972), and Grauer and Hakansson (1987) produce results supporting this conclusion and suggest that a rational portfolio choice must be a globally diversified portfolio. In a landmark study, Brinson et al. (1986) further emphasize the importance of asset allocation in portfolio returns and show that 94% of the variation of returns in a diversified portfolio can be explained by the asset allocation decision that determines the percentage of resources to be invested in different asset classes. Portfolio managers, unsurprisingly, pay close attention to asset class investing.

Markowitz (1952) also intuitively hypothesizes that in order to achieve a truly diversified portfolio, asset managers must effectively diversify within each asset class in their portfolio. In this context, examining the degree to which global stock markets co-move, thus, becomes an important issue given the implied consequences for equity allocation decisions and portfolio diversification. According to modern portfolio theory, internationally segmented equity markets (markets with no or low correlations) would enable portfolio managers to diversify and take advantage of the differences in the equity markets. Consequently, to reduce risk it is important to avoid equity securities or markets that are highly correlated with each other. This correlation can be measured in different ways, with some recent studies employing enhanced methodologies to provide best estimates.

Global equity market correlations, however, are not directly observable and tend to change over time. Hilliard (1979), in an early study, finds low co-movement of market returns between countries. The more recent literature generally indicates an increase in international co-movement of stock returns since the mid-1990s, with high

Emerging Markets and the Global Economy
http://dx.doi.org/10.1016/B978-0-12-411549-1.00024-7

co-movements between equity markets in developed regions. An increase in co-movement between developed stock markets and equity markets in some emerging regions has also been documented (see for example Brooks and Del Negro, 2004; Click and Plummer, 2005; Kizys and Pierdzioch, 2009; Rua and Nunes, 2009; Beirne et al., 2010; Graham and Nikkinen, 2011; Graham et al., 2012). Explanations offered in the literature for the increase in international co-movement of stock returns include growing global industry factors (Baca et al., 2000; Cavaglia et al., 2000), the stock market bubble of the late 1990s (Brooks and Del Negro, 2004), the increase in equity market integration in the 1990s (Ayuso and Blanco, 2001), an increase in bilateral trade flows (Pretorius, 2002), and geographical distance (Lucey and Zhang, 2009). The empirical literature on co-movement also reports evidence of asymmetry in the dependence in equity returns; that is, stock returns appear to be more highly correlated during market downturns than during market upturns (see for example Erb et al., 1994; Longin and Solnik, 2001; Ang and Bekaert, 2002; Ang and Chen, 2002; Das and Uppal, 2004; Patton, 2004; Garcia and Tsafack, 2011; Aloui et al., 2011). This has become a core part of the accepted wisdom among academics, practitioners, and the financial press. Estimating this variation in co-movement over time, nevertheless, needs an effective interpretation of what the correlation coefficient measures (Lhabitant, 2011).

Many studies have evaluated equity market co-movement through the correlation coefficient while investigating the evolving properties either through a rolling window correlation coefficient or by considering non-overlapping sample periods (see, e.g., King and Wadhwani, 1990; Lin et al., 1994; Brooks and Del Negro, 2004). Lhabitant (2011), however, suggests that investors and academics can misinterpret the meaning of correlation coefficient and that the interpretation given to the signs can be factually incorrect. That is, the direction of the deviations from the mean of two time series may be different from the tendency of two random variables to move either in the same direction or opposite direction. As he puts it, *a portfolio made of assets that all lose money at the same time, but with some deviations around their downward trend, should not be seen as very well diversified*. Therefore, when trends matter, the principle of including assets with no or low correlations in a portfolio (based on the standard correlation coefficient measurement) may be problematic and can present real and momentous challenges for equity portfolio managers. Trend gaps must, consequently, be taken into consideration when evaluating portfolio diversification.

Given the importance of the dependence structure for portfolio diversification, this chapter also focuses on equity market correlations. We take a practical approach to measuring equity market correlations and propose the use of trend gaps to assess diversification benefit in global equity markets. By using these trend gaps we re-examine the co-movement/correlation coefficient of emerging and developed market stock markets by considering trends of different international stock indexes. Ignoring trends raises the potential of constructing an internationally diversified equity portfolio with assets sharing the same trend. Any pair of stock indexes reflecting the similar trend would mean that diversification benefits are minimal even if correlations are negative or low for a long-run investor. In practical terms, global portfolio diversification strategies are not limited to developed equity markets and embrace emerging markets. As such there is always the need to examine emerging markets as part of the global market asset co-movement. Emerging equity markets have been shown to have market characteristics that are different from developed markets. There is also wide recognition in the literature that emerging market equities have vastly different characteristics than equities from developed capital markets including higher average returns, higher risk because of the additional risks they bear (e.g., political, economic, and currency), and low correlations with developed market returns (see e.g., Bekaert and Harvey, 1995; Graham et al., 2012). We relate upward and downward trends to bull and bear markets and re-estimate correlations between developed and emerging markets.

The results of the study suggest that market trends are more prevalent in emerging markets than developed markets. The relative characteristics have also changed over time as bull market trends have become more prevalent and bear market trends less prevalent across emerging markets. The results also show that the correlation of stock returns between emerging and developed markets is higher when bull markets are relatively more prevalent in emerging markets or bear markets are relatively more prevalent in developed markets.

The rest of this chapter is organized as follows: In Section 2, we present a brief overview of some of the approaches used to measure equity market correlations. Section 3 discusses the measurement of stock market trends. We also present our empirical approach and definitions for market trends here. Section 4 presents the data and descriptive statistics. In Section 5, we present the results and discuss the relevance of using the prevalence of market trends when assessing the benefits of global diversification and Section 6 concludes the chapter.

2. MEASURING MARKET CORRELATION

As has been reported elsewhere, Sir Galton (1886) is credited with introducing the well-known correlation coefficient, which he utilized to analyze the relationship between the average height of parents (both mothers and fathers) with those of their children to develop an evolutionary theory of heredity. Subsequent to this, Pearson (1896) published the first rigorous treatment of correlation, where he introduced the Pearson's product moment correlation coefficient to estimate the extent of a linear relationship between two random variables. The measure, given in equation (1), gives a standardized estimate of the extent to which two variables (time series) move together over time relative to their individual means:

$$\rho_{X,Y} = \frac{COV(X, Y)}{\sigma_X \sigma_Y}, \tag{1}$$

where ρ symbolizes the correlation between the two time series; *COV* is the covariance between the two variables; and σ_X and σ_Y are the standard deviation of the two time series, X and Y. The conditional correlation is defined as follows:

$$\rho_{X,Y} = \frac{E_{t-1}\left[COV(X, Y)\right]}{E_{t-1}(\sigma_X \sigma_Y)}, \tag{2}$$

where the conditional correlation is based on previously known information. The laws of probability necessitate that all correlations stated in this way must lie within the range [−1, 1].

The conditional correlations also meet this restriction for all possible realizations of previously known information. This seemingly makes the meaning of correlation easy and very convenient to convey to investors. The standard interpretation given to the correlation coefficient is that positive (negative) coefficients indicate the extent to which the variables move together in the same (opposite) direction. Placing this in the context of portfolio management, Markowitz (1952) shows that the variance of a portfolio's return equals the weighted average of the correlation coefficients of returns of the assets that make up the portfolio. Given that the asset weights are all positive, reducing portfolio risk necessitates the inclusion of assets that are less than perfectly positive correlation (+1), with a preference for uncorrelated or negatively correlated assets. This is crucial in the structure of portfolio construction.

A criticism of this conventional measure of asset dependence is that it represents only the average of deviations from the mean without making any distinction between large and small returns or negative and positive returns (Poon et al., 2004; Aloui et al., 2011). As a result the asymmetry in the dependence in equity returns bear and bull markets, documented in the literature, cannot be explained. Following this, a technical and extensive literature focusing on how best to estimate correlations and model their time-varying features over time and during market shocks have evolved. We briefly present the tenets of a few of these approaches here—wavelet coherency, the Dynamic Conditional Correlation GARCH model (DCC-GARCH), the extreme value and copulas models—and refer interested readers to the source of these models.

In the wavelet approach, the practical measure of dependency between two time series is obtained by calculating the wavelet squared coherency. This is done by squaring the cross wavelet power and dividing the result with the product of the two wavelet spectra as presented in equation (3). Torrence and Compo (1998), Ramsey and Lampart (1998), and Grinsted et al. (2004) provide excellent and detailed description of wavelet analysis.

$$R^2{}_n(s) = \frac{\left|S\left(s^{-1} W_n^{XY}(s)\right)\right|^2}{S\left(s^{-1}\left|W_n^X(s)\right|^2\right) \cdot S\left(s^{-1}\left|W_n^Y(s)\right|^2\right)}. \tag{3}$$

The numerator in equation (3) is the absolute value squared of the smoothed cross wavelet spectrum (where $W_n^{XY}(s) = W_n^X(s)W_n^Y(s)*$, W_n^X and W_n^Y are wavelet transforms of x_n and y_n). The denominator represents the smoothed wavelet power spectra. S denotes a smoothing operator in time and scale. Equation (3) is similar to squared correlation coefficient and gives a quantity between 0 and 1, with a high value showing strong correlations between two time series. Consequently the wavelet squared coherency function as a correlation coefficient around each moment in time and for each frequency. For that reason, it can be used to gauge the extent to which two time series move together over time, capturing time-varying features, and across frequencies which effectively separate short-term from long-term correlations.

Engle (2002) introduced one of the most practical and simple multivariate models, DCC-GARCH, that can be used to estimate time-varying correlations for a large class of assets. We briefly present the model here. Let r_t denote $nx1$ vector of return innovations at time t, which is assumed to be conditionally normal with a zero mean and a covariance matrix H_t:

$$r_t | \Phi_{t-1} \sim N(0, H_t), \tag{4}$$

where Φ_{t-1} is the information set at time $t-1$. The conditional covariance matrix H_t can be decomposed as follows:

$$H_t \equiv D_t R_t D_t, \tag{5}$$

where D_t is the $(n \times n)$ diagonal matrix of time-varying standard deviations from univariate GARCH models with $\sqrt{h_{it}}$ on the ith diagonal, $i = 1, 2, \ldots, n$. R_t is the $(n \times n)$ time-varying correlation matrix, containing conditional correlation. The DCC-GARCH model is estimated using a two-stage procedure. Initially, univariate GARCH models are fitted for each of the asset return series and residuals standardized by their estimated standard deviations are obtained. Subsequently, the standardized residuals are utilized to estimate the coefficients governing the dynamic correlations (see Engle, 2002 for more detailed description).

Extreme value theory and copula functions have also been used to capture asymmetric correlations. These deal with the extreme dependence structure of both negative and positive stock returns in a multivariate framework (see, e.g., Longin and Solnik, 2001; Pais and Stork, 2011). The extreme value theory involves two modeling features: the tails of the marginal distributions and the dependence structure of extreme observations. The theory demonstrates that the distribution of return exceedances can only converge toward a generalized Pareto distribution. Given a threshold, the distribution tail is characterized by three parameters: the tail probability, the dispersion parameter, and the tail index. The theory also illustrates that the distribution of extreme returns can only converge toward a distribution characterized by generalized Pareto marginal distributions and a dependence function, the shape of which is not well defined. Through the use of logistic function, Longin and Solnik (2001) model the dependence between extreme returns of different markets. They also discuss the estimation procedure of the correlation of extreme returns (see Longin and Solnik, 2001 for full details). Aloui et al. (2011) also combine conditional multivariate copula functions with extreme value theory as well as generalized autoregressive conditional heteroscedasticity process to model co-exceedances of stock returns above and below a given threshold.

We do not contend the usefulness of these approaches. In this chapter, we also take asymmetry into consideration and analyze the correlation between international stocks on the trend gap variables of global equity indexes. Unlike the technical models briefly presented above, we are particularly interested in trend gaps and how that can be used to enhance portfolio diversification. Thus, we do not analyze correlation on market returns or volatility, but the trend discrepancies between emerging and developed markets. Given that the direction of the deviations from the mean of two equity returns time series may be different from the tendency of two random variables to move either in the same direction or opposite direction, trend must be taken into consideration when analyzing market dependence using this measure (Lhabitant, 2011). This adds a practical extension to the literature.

3. DEFINING STOCK MARKET TRENDS

When considering stock market trends, one may relate upward (downward) market trend to bull market (bear market). Anecdotal evidence on bull and bear markets abounds in the literature (see for example Niermira and Klein, 1994; Rothchild, 1998). However, as it is often noted by both practitioners and academics, bull and bear markets do not have clear and formal definitions. Some practitioners, nevertheless, use different time intervals and return measures to define bull and bear markets. For example, the Vanguard Group note a generally accepted measure of a bear market, a 20% or more price decline of over a minimum of a two-month period.[1] Several academic studies use more technical approaches to define bull and bear markets. Pagan and Sossounov (2002), Gonzalez et al. (2005), and Maheu et al. (2012), for example, use algorithms to define and analyze bull and bear markets. Kole and Dijk (2010), on the other hand, make use of Markov regime-switching models to delineate bull and bear markets.

In this study, we follow an intuitive and practical approach in defining the bull and bear markets which we relate to stock market trends. Our definitions for bull and bear markets are based on the ratio between the index level and 44 trading days lagged value. For example, if a market index level at time t is 120 points and the level at time $t - 1$ (44 trading days ago) was 100, the ratio would be 120%. Following this approach we define a market to be in a bull market state when the ratio is 105% (5% price increases). Consequently, we define bear markets by using a cut-off ratio of 95% (5% price decline).

[1] https://retirementplans.vanguard.com/VGApp/pe/PubVgiNews?ArticleName=Stayingcalmbearmkt.

This approach is related to that pointed out by the Vanguard Group. However, we do not follow the more 20% price decline for the bear market because broad market indexes do not often increase or decrease 20% over a two-month period. Our 5% return cut-offs allow us to construct bull and bear market variables that exhibit sufficient amount of variation.

4. DATA AND DESCRIPTIVE STATISTICS

The stock price data utilized in this study is the Morgan Stanley Capital Indexes (MSCI) obtained from the Thomson Reuters Datastream database. We include three (3) developed market indexes (MSCI Europe[2]; MSCI Japan[3]; and MSCI USA[4]) and three (3) emerging market indexes (MSCI Emerging Asia[5]; MSCI Emerging Europe[6]; and MSCI Emerging Latin America[7]) in our sample. Our sample period is between January 1994 and December 2012. We utilize daily MSCI indexes and calculate returns as the first log difference of daily stock price indexes.

Table 1 presents descriptive statistics of returns for the indexes included in our sample. Generally the variations in daily returns are small and we detect that the MSCI Europe and MSCI USA indexes in our sample both recorded a 0.02% average returns between February 1993 and February 2013. The daily average return for MSCI Japan was 0% in the stated sample period. We also document average daily return of 0.02% and 0.03% for MSCI Latin America and MSCI Emerging Europe, respectively, during the same period. Both the largest daily return (18.6%) and the greatest daily loss (−19.93%) for the sample period were recorded in Emerging Europe. Table 1 also suggests that emerging markets are relatively more volatile than the developed markets. The return distribution for the market indexes seems to be non-normal and shows negative skewness (see Table 1 Panel A). We segment the data period into *bull* and *bear* markets and report some descriptive statistics on these in Panel B of Table 1. The average daily return for the *bull* (*bear*) period in our sample is 2.07% (1.41%), with a maximum daily return of 6% for both segments.

[2] The MSCI Europe Index is a free float-adjusted market capitalization weighted index constructed to measure the equity market performance of 16 developed markets in Europe. The index includes the following country indexes: Austria, Belgium, Denmark, Finland, France, Germany, Greece, Ireland, Italy, the Netherlands, Norway, Portugal, Spain, Sweden, Switzerland, and the United Kingdom.

[3] The MSCI Japan Index is a free float-adjusted market capitalization weighted index that is constructed to track the equity market performance of Japanese securities listed on four exchanges (Tokyo Stock Exchange, Osaka Stock Exchange, JASDAQ, and Nagoya Stock Exchange).

[4] The MSCI USA Index is a free float-adjusted market capitalization index constructed to measure large and midcap US equity market performance.

[5] The following countries are included in the index: Bangladesh, China, India, Indonesia, Korea, Malaysia, Pakistan, Philippines, Sri Lanka, Taiwan, Thailand, and Vietnam.

[6] MSCI Emerging Europe includes the Czech Republic, Hungary, Poland, Russia, and Turkey.

[7] This index includes the following countries: Brazil, Chile, Colombia, Mexico, and Peru.

Table 1 Descriptive statistics.
This table presents descriptive statistics for the returns of MSCI indexes and trend variables in our sample. The variable *BullMarkets105* defines the number bull markets across the indexes. The variable *BearMarkets95* defines the number bull markets across the indexes. The period is between January 1994 and December 2012. Panel A presents the statistics the returns of the indexes. Panel B presents the statistics for the *BearMarkets95* and *BullMarkets105* variables. The sample includes 4957 observations. All reported returns are in percentages (%).

Panel A

	Europe	Japan	USA	Emerging Asia	Emerging Europe	Latin America
Mean	0.02%	0.00%	0.02%	0.00%	0.02%	0.03%
Max.	10.70%	12.27%	11.04%	12.65%	18.60%	15.36%
Min.	−10.18%	−9.52%	−9.51%	−8.62%	−19.93%	−15.06%
Std. Dev.	1.31%	1.44%	1.22%	1.40%	1.88%	1.81%
Skewness	−0.14	0.08	0.25	−0.20	−0.51	−0.34
Kurtosis	10.30	7.59	11.33	8.14	13.36	12.49

Panel B

	BullMarkets105	BearMarkets95	BullMarkets105 − BearMarkets95
Mean	2.07	1.41	0.66
Max.	6.00	6.00	6.00
Min.	0.00	0.00	−6.00

5. RESULTS

5.1. Correlations

We present the pairwise return correlations for all pairs of indexes in our sample in Table 2. Of the six (6) stock index returns, the highest (lowest) correlation, 0.64 (0.04), is detected for that between MSCI Europe and MSCI Emerging Europe (MSCI Japan and MSCI USA). On average, Japan seems to have higher correlations with emerging countries relative to developed countries. Furthermore, developed countries exhibit relatively higher correlation with emerging regions that are relatively close in geographical proximity. As documented elsewhere in the literature, we detect a relatively high correlation between MSCI Europe and MSCI USA (0.51). Segmenting the period between pre- and post-2000, the correlation coefficients reported suggest an increase in the post-2000 period supporting the time-varying feature of correlation documented in the literature. Based on this, it may be suggested that combining Emerging Asia and Japan, Emerging Europe and Europe, Latin America and Emerging Europe, Latin America and Europe, as well as the US and Latin America in equity portfolios would exhibit reduced diversification gains.

Table 3 also documents an increase in correlation between the developed and emerging stock market indexes, from 0.24 to 0.41. Thus the correlation between the two aggregate markets has nearly doubled over the sample period. These are in general agreement with

Table 2 Correlation statistics.
The table presents the Pearson correlation coefficients of returns for the period January 1994 and December 2012. The full period is between January 1994 and December 2012. The correlations between emerging markets and developed markets are boldfaced. All correlation coefficients are statistically significant at the 5% level.

	Japan	EM Asia	EM Europe	Europe	Latin America	USA
Full sample						
Japan	1.00					
EM Asia	**0.47**	1.00				
EM Europe	**0.25**	0.44	1.00			
Europe	0.23	**0.39**	**0.64**	1.00		
Latin America	**0.14**	0.34	0.50	**0.59**	1.00	
USA	0.04	**0.17**	**0.33**	0.51	**0.61**	1.00
Prior 2001 (12/31/1993–12/29/2000)						
Japan	1.00					
EM Asia	**0.31**	1.00				
EM Europe	**0.24**	0.29	1.00			
Europe	0.26	**0.27**	**0.42**	1.00		
Latin America	**0.10**	0.17	0.20	**0.35**	1.00	
USA	0.02	**0.08**	**0.11**	0.35	**0.51**	1.00
After 2000 (1/01/2001–12/31/2012)						
Japan	1.00					
EM Asia	**0.56**	1.00				
EM Europe	**0.26**	0.51	1.00			
Europe	0.23	**0.44**	**0.70**	1.00		
Latin America	**0.16**	0.43	0.63	**0.69**	1.00	
USA	0.05	**0.21**	**0.41**	0.56	**0.66**	1.00

the literature reporting an increase in global market correlations (see, for example, Brooks and Del Negro, 2004; Click and Plummer, 2005; Kizys and Pierdzioch, 2009; Rua and Nunes, 2009; Beirne et al., 2010; Graham and Nikkinen, 2011). The result presented here, specifically, confirms that this increase in co-movement has also happened between emerging and developed stock markets.

As indicated above, when trends matter the direction of the deviations from the mean of two time series may be different from the tendency of two random variables to move either in the same direction or opposite direction. Consequently, it is important for market participants to consider trends in estimating correlations between any pair of markets.

Table 3 Average correlation statistics between emerging markets and developed markets. This table presents the averages of emerging-developed market correlations from Table 2. The full period is between January 1994 and December 2012.

	Full sample	Prior 2001 (12/31/1993–12/29/2000)	After 2000 (1/01/2001–12/31/2012)
Developed-emerging correlations	0.36	0.24	0.41

5.2. Trend Gaps

Table 4 presents information on the distribution of trend gaps for both emerging and developed markets. Trend gap for bull (bear) markets is the difference in the number of bull (bear) markets between emerging and developed markets. For both the full sample and subsamples the trend gap count variables are heavily distributed around zero. This implies that emerging market trends do not often deviate from developed market trends. Moreover, the variables are skewed to the left. For example, considering the full sample period, the trend gap variable for bull markets has 209 maximum observations against 9 minimum observations. The left-skewed characteristic of the trend gap variables implies that market trends are much more prevalent across different emerging stock markets. When bear markets are compared with bull markets, one can see that the trend gap variable for bull markets is even more heavily left-skewed than the trend gap variable for bear markets.

Table 5 shows comparisons of emerging market and developed markets trend gaps over different time periods. For the whole sample period, the results suggest that bull and bear trends are more prevalent in emerging markets than developed markets because the average values of the trend gap variables are positive. This result is sensible because emerging markets are considered to be more volatile (Bekaert and Harvey, 1995), and therefore market trends should be more prevalent in emerging markets. Nevertheless, the results in Table 5 indicate that higher volatility in emerging market stock returns apparently brings about more prevalent market trends.

The comparisons suggest that the characteristic of trend gaps between emerging and developed markets has substantially changed during the sample period of this study. Specifically, the average value *of Bear Markets Trend Gaps* has decreased from 0.54 to 0.04 during the sample period. The average value of *Bull Markets Trend Gaps* has, in turn, increased from 0.16 to 0.53. These statistics imply that bull market trends have become more prevalent and bear market trends less prevalent across emerging markets. Thus, the prevalence of bull market trends versus bear market trends may change over time. Gonzalez et al. (2005) also present evidence on the characteristics of bull and bear markets over different time periods. This evidence, for example, suggests that the average

Table 4 Distributions of the emerging and developed market trend gaps.
This table presents the distribution statistics for the emerging and developed market trend gaps. The variable *Bull Markets Trend Gaps (Bear Markets Trend Gaps)* is the difference in the number of bull (bear) markets between emerging markets and developed markets. The period is between January 1994 and December 2012.

	−3	−2	−1	0	1	2	3	−3	−2	−1	0	1	2	3
	Bull markets trend gaps (full sample)							**Bear market trend gaps (full sample)**						
Count	9	147	455	2562	1060	515	209	9	40	565	3115	771	348	109
Percent	0.18	2.97	9.18	51.68	21.38	10.39	4.22	0.18	0.81	11.4	62.84	15.55	7.02	2.2
	Bull markets trend gaps (12/31/1993–12/29/2000)							**Bear market trend gaps (12/31/1993–12/29/2000)**						
Count	1	100	299	910	304	142	70	0	7	172	872	454	241	80
Percent	0.05	5.48	16.37	49.84	16.65	7.78	3.83	0.00	0.38	9.42	47.75	24.86	13.2	4.38
	Bull markets trend gaps (1/01/2001–12/31/2012)							**Bear market trend (1/01/2001–12/31/2012)**						
Count	8	47	156	1652	756	373	139	9	33	393	2243	317	107	29
Percent	0.26	1.5	4.98	52.76	24.15	11.91	4.44	0.29	1.05	12.55	71.64	10.12	3.42	0.93

Table 5 Average emerging versus developed market trend gaps.
This table presents the averages of the *Bull Markets Trend Gaps* and *Bear Markets Trend Gaps* variables. The table also includes *t*-statistics for the differences in the means of *Bull Markets Trend Gaps* and *Bear Markets Trend Gaps* of each sample period.

	Means		
	Full sample	**Prior 2001**	**After 2000**
Bear markets trend gaps	0.23	0.54	0.04
Bull markets trend gaps	0.39	0.16	0.53
t-statistics	−8.60	11.02	−22.17

durations of bull and bear markets have changed over time. Our evidence, in turn, suggests that the cross-section of global market trends may change over time.

Table 6 presents the results of estimating correlating in different market states. It is shown that when bear market is prevalent in emerging markets, the Pearson correlation coefficient varies between 0.28 and 0.39 (also see Figure 2). The variations in the estimated correlation coefficients are more volatile when bear markets are prevalent in emerging regions. This may require more frequent rebalancing as global asset managers aim to maintain a level of diversification inherent in their portfolios.

The results in Table 6 also show a notable characteristic in correlations between developed and emerging markets when bull markets in emerging markets are more prevalent and bear markets in developed markets are more prevalent. Specifically, the extreme correlations are 0.39 for Bull Markets Trend Gaps and 0.53 for Bear Markets Trend Gaps. The results are also presented in Figure 1 that clearly show the distinguishing characteristic of the extreme trend gaps. The results imply that the correlations between developed and emerging markets increase when significant discrepancies between the trends of these two different sets of markets arise. In relation to Longin and Solnik (2001) that presents evidence for higher correlation between international stock markets in bear markets, this study presents evidence for higher correlation when the bear market trends do not collide.

Table 6 and Figure 1 also show results for the return correlations with the emerging and developed market groups. The results suggest that the extreme trend gaps between emerging markets are associated with unusual correlations. Specifically, the correlations within the developed market group go down when bear markets are relatively more prevalent (the value of the trend gap variables is 3) in emerging markets than developed markets. Also, the results suggest that the correlations within the emerging market group are significantly higher when bear markets are more prevalent (the value of the trend gap variable is −3) in developed markets than emerging markets. Overall, these results strongly suggest that the trend gaps between emerging and developed markets are important when assessing international portfolio diversification.

Table 6 Correlations on trend gaps.
This table presents the average correlations between different equity index returns on the *Bull Markets Trend Gaps* and *Bear Markets Trend Gaps* variables. Panel A presents emerging market—developed market correlations, panel B presents developed market—developed market correlations, and panel C presents emerging market—emerging market correlations.

Trend Gap	Correlations on bull market trend gaps	Correlations on bear market trend gaps
Panel A. Emerging market-developed market correlations		
3	0.39	0.18
2	0.31	0.32
1	0.31	0.37
0	0.38	0.37
−1	0.28	0.34
−2	0.30	0.29
−3	0.34	0.53
Panel B. Developed market-developed market correlations		
3	0.28	0.07
2	0.26	0.28
1	0.28	0.28
0	0.26	0.26
−1	0.21	0.23
−2	0.28	0.17
−3	0.33	0.36
Panel C. Emerging market-emerging market correlations		
3	0.13	0.07
2	0.11	0.10
1	0.10	0.12
0	0.14	0.14
−1	0.10	0.12
−2	0.11	0.07
−3	0.11	0.25

5.3. Global Trend Indicator

Using the same processes in identifying the trend gaps, we also develop a global trend indicator that can be used to analyze global market states. This trend indicator is a gauge of the prevalence of global market trends that should be relevant information beyond traditional market indexes. Investors have traditionally used major US and global indexes to characterize the state of different global markets. The problem with this traditional approach is that stock market indexes place more weight on the markets with highest market capitalization. As a result, stock market indexes may not provide a complete picture of the global market situation as they tell more about major stock markets. Therefore, the use of our global market trend indicator that weights different markets equally to

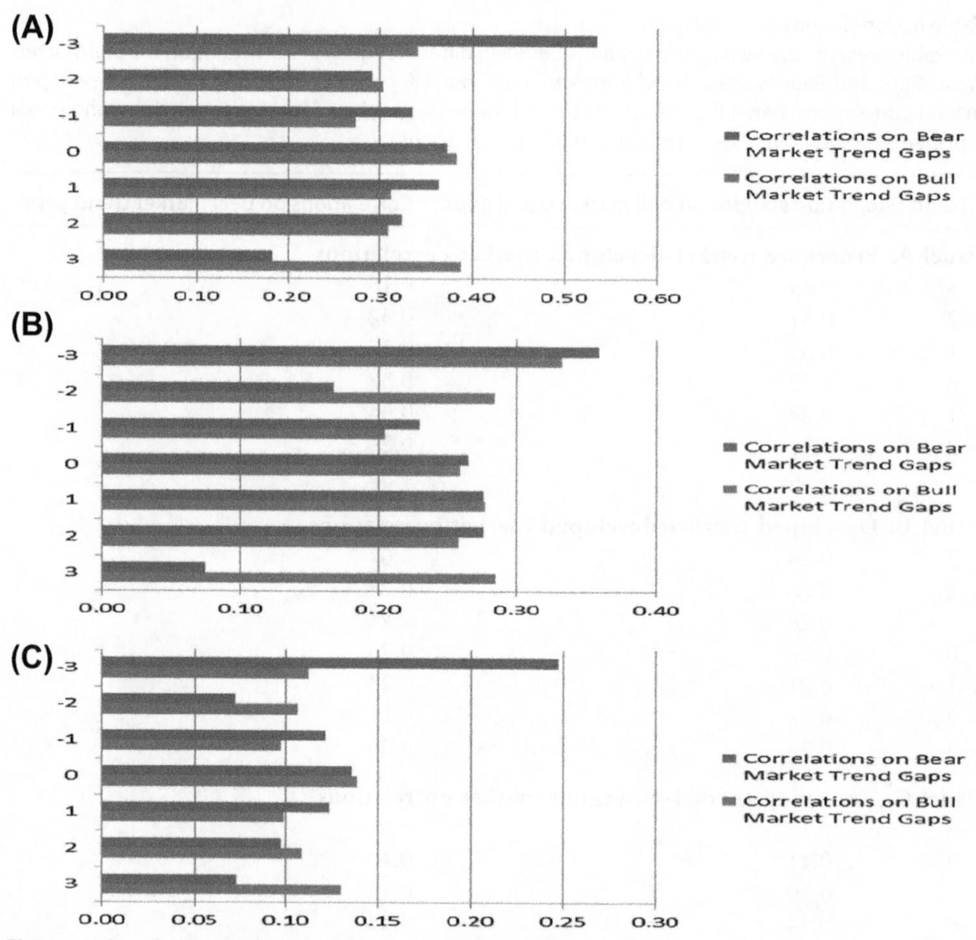

Figure 1 Correlations on Trend Gaps. This figure presents the averages of global stock market correlations between equity index returns on the bull market trend gap and bear market trend gap variables. Panel A presents emerging market—developed market correlations, panel B presents developed market—developed market correlations, and panel C presents emerging market—emerging market correlations.

gauge the state of global markets could be beneficial. Figure 2 presents our global trend indicator. The figure shows that the prevalence of the opposite market trends changes constantly, suggesting that market trends may change more often than is considered. These changes may have important implication for asset correlations as indicated in Table 6.

Given that market trends change from one extreme to another in Figure 2, it is reasonable to consider filtered values of the global trend indicator, thus excluding a cyclical component from the time series. Figure 3 presents smoothed values of the global trend indicator that are estimated using the Hodrick and Prescott (1997) filter. The figure shows that the most prevalent global bull market trends occurred in 2003 and 2009. The most prevalent bear market trend occurred in 2008. This shows that bull and bear market trends have become more prevalent after the dot-com bubble. Also, the statistics suggests that the bear and bull markets associated with the dot-com bubble were not global in nature. The stock market cycles related to the remaining sample period after the dot-com bubble seem to exhibit a more global effect.

Ignoring trends raises the potential of constructing an internationally diversified equity portfolio with assets sharing the same trend. Any pair of stock indexes reflecting the similar trend would mean that diversification benefits are minimal even if correlations are negative or low for a long-run investor. The results presented suggest that international stock market correlations depend on the trend gaps between emerging markets and developed markets. Specifically, the estimations imply that the diversification benefits in investing in different emerging markets worsen when emerging markets do not exhibit the bear market trends of developed markets. The gains from diversification by investing in different developed markets are higher when developed markets lack the bear market trends of emerging markets. All in all, the results imply portfolio managers look for diversification opportunities in developed countries when the trend gaps between the emerging and developed markets are wide.

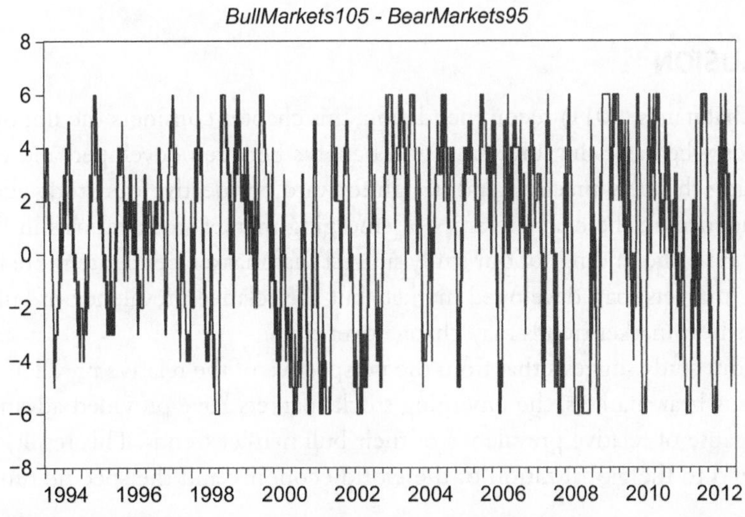

Figure 2 Global Trends. This figure presents global trends over the period January 1994 and December 2012. The global trend indicator is the difference in the averages of the *BullMarkets105* and *BearMarkets95* variables. The maximum (minimum) number of 6 (−6) indicates that all considered global stock markets are in a bull (bear) market state.

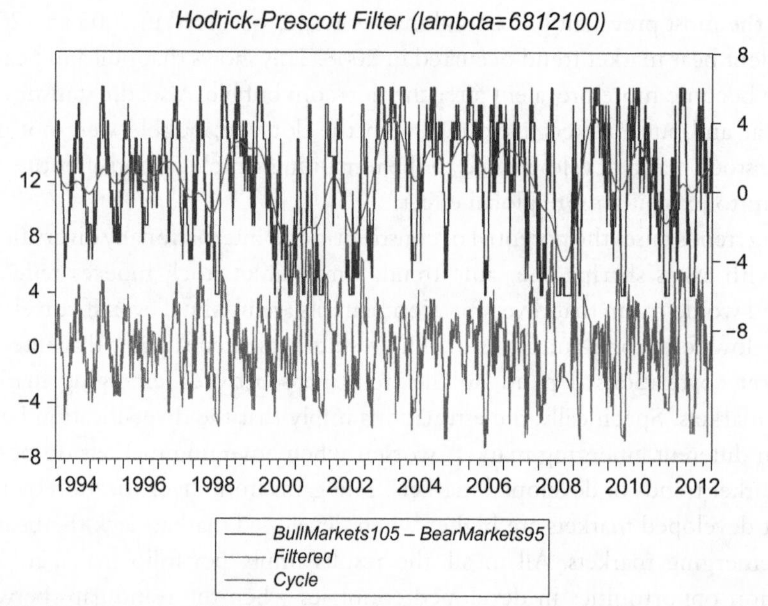

Figure 3 Global Trends Smoothed. This figure presents smoothed values of the global trend indicator presented in Figure 1. The Hodrick and Prescott (1997) filter is used to smooth the values of the global trend indicator. The filtered values are presented using red color and the residual values are presented using green color. (For interpretation of the references to color in this figure legend, the reader is referred to the web version of this book.)

6. CONCLUSION

Following Lhabitant's (2011) recommendation, this chapter considers the importance of market trends when assessing diversification benefits between developed and emerging markets. Using this new practical and straightforward perspective our study adds to the previous evidence on the characteristics of emerging market stock returns in three different ways. First, the findings of our study suggest that market trends are more prevalent in emerging markets than developed markets but the relative prevalence of bull market trends versus bear market trends may change over time.

Second, our study suggests that from the perspective of the relative prevalence of bull markets versus bear markets, the emerging stock markets have provided advantages for investors because of relative prevalence of their bull market trends. This result, however, may be related to the globalization of the world economy and the specific time period of this study.

Third, we also analyze global stock market and the average correlations between developed and emerging market returns on the bull market trend gap and bear market trend gap variables. The analysis suggests that the correlations are higher when bull markets are more prevalent in emerging markets than developed markets. For bear markets, however, the analysis suggests that the correlations are higher when bear markets are more prevalent in developed markets. To sum it up, the relative prevalence of bull markets in emerging markets and the relative prevalence of bear markets in developed markets tend to drive the correlations between emerging and developed market stock returns higher. As such, the study shows a new spot of high global market correlations that is not only related to extreme market movements but also trend gaps between different kinds of markets. Therefore, the results also challenge the orthodox view on correlations that they are likely to be higher when all the markets "move together."

This chapter also proposes the use of the prevalence of market trends to gauge the state of the global stock market. This utilizes the global trend indicator that is the difference in the number of bull markets and bear markets across different markets. The indicator provides a compact summary of global market trends. For practitioners, the ideas and applications in this study can be used to as simple gauges of global markets states. The main idea of the applications presented may be easily understood because the concepts of bull and bear market trends are widely acknowledged by investors even though they are not formally defined. Future studies could further exploit the avenue of analyzing market trends. The evidence presented in this chapter suggests that research should analyze the cross-section of the market trends of national stock market indexes. It would also be interesting to expand the number of different markets considered for the global trend indicator. Nevertheless, the main suggestion for future research arising from our study is that extreme trend gaps between different stock markets could be an interesting avenue for further research.

REFERENCES

Agmon, T., 1972. The relations among equity markets: a study of share price co-movements in the United States, United Kingdom, Germany and Japan. Journal of Finance 27, 839–855

Aloui, R., Ben Aissa, M.S., Nguyen, D.K., 2011. Global financial crisis, extreme interdependence, and contagion effects: the role of economic structure? Journal of Banking and Finance 35, 130–141

Ang, A., Bekaert, G., 2002. International asset allocation with regime shifts. Review of Financial Studies 15, 1137–1187

Ang, A., Chen, J., 2002. Asymmetric correlations of equity portfolios. Journal of Financial Economics 63, 443–494

Ayuso, J., Blanco, R., 2001. Has financial market integration increased during the nineties? Journal of International Financial Markets, Institutions and Money 11, 265–287

Baca, S., Garbe, B., Weiss, R., 2000. The rise of sector effects in major equity markets. Financial Analysts Journal, 34–40

Beirne, J., Caporale, G.M., Schulze-Ghattas, M., Spagnolo, N., 2010. Global and regional spillovers in emerging stock markets: a multivariate GARCH-in-mean analysis. Emerging Markets Review 11, 250–260

Bekaert, G., Harvey, C.R., 1995. Time-varying world market integration. Journal of Finance 50, 403–444

Brinson, G.P., Hood, L.P., Beebower, G.L., 1986. Determinants of portfolio performance. Financial Analysts Journal 42, 39–44

Brooks, R., Del Negro, M., 2004. The rise in comovement across national stock markets: market integration or IT bubble? Journal of Empirical Finance 11, 659–680

Cavaglia, S., Brightman, C., Aked, M., 2000. The increasing importance of industry factors. Financial Analysts Journal 26, 41–54

Click, R.W., Plummer, M.G., 2005. Stock market integration in ASEAN after the Asian financial crisis. Journal of Asian Economics 16, 5–28

Das, S., Uppal, R., 2004. Systemic risk and international portfolio choice. Journal of Finance 59, 2809–2834

Engle, R., 2002. Dynamic conditional correlation - a simple class of multivariate GARCH models. Journal of Business and Economic Statistics 20, 339–350

Erb, C.B., Harvey, C.R., Viskanta, T.E., 1994. Forecasting international equity correlations. Financial Analysts Journal 50, 32–45

Galton, F., 1886. Regression towards mediocrity in hereditary stature. Journal of the Anthropological Institute of Great Britain and Ireland 15, 246–263

Garcia, R., Tsafack, G., 2011. Dependence structure and extreme comovements in international equity and bond markets. Journal of Banking and Finance 35, 1954–1970

Gonzalez, L., Powell, J.G., Sihi, J., Wilson, A., 2005. Two centuries of bull and bear market cycles. International Review of Economics and Finance 14, 469–486

Graham, M., Nikkinen, J., 2011. Co-movement of the Finnish and international stock markets: a wavelet analysis. European Journal of Finance 17, 409–425

Graham, M., Kiviaho, J., Nikkinen, J., 2012. Integration of 22 emerging stock markets: a three-dimensional analysis. Global Finance Journal 23, 34–47

Grauer, R.R., Hakansson, N.H., 1987. Gains from international diversification: 1968–85 returns on portfolios of stocks and bonds. Journal of Finance 42, 721–739

Grinsted, A., Moore, J.C., Jevrejeva, S., 2004. Application of the cross wavelet transform and wavelet coherence to geophysical time series. Nonlinear Processes in Geophysics 11, 561–566

Grubel, H.G., 1968. Internationally diversified portfolios: welfare gains and capital flows. American Economic Review 58, 1299–1314

Hilliard, J.E., 1979. The relationship between equity indices on world exchanges. Journal of Finance 34, 103–114

Hodrick, R., Prescott, E.C., 1997. Postwar U.S. business cycles: an empirical investigation. Journal of Money, Credit, and Banking 29, 1–16

King, M., Wadhwani, S., 1990. Transmission of volatility between stock markets. Review of Financial Studies 3, 5–33

Kizys, R., Pierdzioch, C., 2009. Changes in the international comovement of stock returns and asymmetric macroeconomic shocks. Journal of International Financial Markets, Institutions and Money 19, 289–305

Kole, E., Dijk, D.J.C., 2010. How to identify and predict bull and bear markets? Working Paper, Erasmus School of Economics.

Levy, H., Sarnat, M., 1970. International diversification of investment portfolios. American Economic Review 60, 668–675

Lhabitant, F., 2011. Correlation vs. Trends in Portfolio Management: a Common Misinterpretation. Available at SSRN: <http://ssrn.com/abstract=1808267> or <http://dx.doi.org/10.2139/ssrn.1808267>.

Lin, W.-L., Engle, R., Ito, T., 1994. Do bulls and bears move across borders? International transmission of stock returns and volatility. Review of Financial Studies 7, 507–538

Longin, F., Solnik, B., 2001. Extreme correlation of international equity markets. Journal of Finance 56, 649–676

Lucey, B.M., Zhang, Q.-Y., 2009. Does cultural distance matter in international stock market comovement? Evidence from emerging economies around the world. Emerging Markets Review 11, 62–78

Maheu, J.M., McCardy, T.H., Song, Y., 2012. Components of bull and bear markets: bull corrections and bear rallies. Journal of Business and Economics Statistics 30, 391–403

Markowitz, H.M., 1952. Portfolio selection. Journal of Finance 7, 77–91

Niermira, M.P., Klein, P.A., 1994. Forecasting Financial and Economic Cycles. Wiley, New York

Pagan, A.R., Sossounov, K.A., 2002. A simple framework for analysing bull and bear markets. Journal of Applied Econometrics 18, 23–46

Pais, A., Stork, P.A., 2011. Contagion risk in the Australian banking and property sectors. Journal of Banking and Finance 35, 681–697

Patton, A., 2004. On the out-of-sample importance of skewness and asymmetric dependence for asset allocation. Journal of Financial Econometrics 2, 130–168
Pearson, K., 1896. Mathematical contributions to the theory of evolution, III. Regression, heredity and panmixia. Philosophical Transactions of the Royal Society of London 187, 253318
Poon, S.H., Rockinger, M., Tawn, J., 2004. Extreme-value dependence in financial markets: diagnostics, models and financial implications. Review of Financial Studies 17, 581–610
Pretorius, E., 2002. Economic determinants of emerging stock market interdependence. Emerging Markets Review 3, 84–105
Ramsey, J., Lampart, C., 1998. The decomposition of economic relationships by time scale using wavelets: expenditure and income. Studies in Nonlinear Dynamics and Econometrics 3, 23–42
Rothchild, J., 1998. The Bear Book. John Wiley and Sons, New York
Rua, A., Nunes, L.C., 2009. International comovement of stock returns: a wavelet analysis. Journal of Empirical Finance 11, 632–639
Torrence, C., Compo, G., 1998. A practical guide to wavelet analysis. Bulletin of American Meteorological Society 79, 61–78

CHAPTER 25

Stock Market Co-movement in ASEAN and China

Hooi Hooi Lean[*] and Russell Smyth[†]
[*]Economics Program, School of Social Sciences, Universiti Sains Malaysia, Malaysia
[†]Department of Economics, Monash University, Australia

1. INTRODUCTION

A large literature, which studies the level of integration between the world's stock markets, has emerged. The level of integration between the stock markets of the world is of importance for both investors and policy-makers. For investors, the level of financial integration determines the opportunities for international portfolio diversification. For policy-makers, co-movements between stock markets can result in contagion effects due to which the price changes, and potential errors, are transmitted across markets. Contagion effects have been magnified by the major events affecting stock markets such as the Global Financial Crisis (GFC).

As Burdekin and Siklos (2012, pp. 521–522) put it: "Not long ago developments in most Asian markets, other than Japan, were little more than an afterthought to western observers. [China] did not even have operating stock markets until December 1990 and most other Asian exchanges seemingly remained too limited in size to exert any meaningful influences on the United States or other major western financial centers". However, this situation changed with the onset of the Asian financial crisis, when the collapse of the Thai baht in July 1997 created contagion effects, which sent shockwaves around the world's stock markets.

More than 15 years after the Asian financial crisis, China and the 10 member states of the Association of Southeast Asian Nations (ASEAN) are becoming increasingly important on the World Economic Stage. This development reflects several factors. The first is the population base and the growing economic importance of China and ASEAN. China has a population of over 1.3 billion, while members of ASEAN have a combined population of 580 million (World Bank, 2012). China and the ASEAN members had a combined nominal Gross Domestic Product (GDP) of approximately $US 6 trillion in 2008 (Brown, 2010). ASEAN's economic importance has increased as Southeast Asia as a region has increased in economic importance. Establishment of the ASEAN in 1967 was primarily motivated by political and security considerations, but over time economic considerations have acquired more and more importance. Behind this, the ASEAN Free

Emerging Markets and the Global Economy
http://dx.doi.org/10.1016/B978-0-12-411549-1.00025-9

Trade Area (AFTA) was established in 1992 and the ASEAN Investment Area (AIA) followed in 1995. Regional economic cooperation has further intensified ever since the Asian financial crisis.

The second is the rapid growth of Asian equity markets. The Shanghai Stock Exchange is now the sixth largest in the world based on domestic market capitalization (WFE, 2013). While the ASEAN stock markets are much smaller, ASEAN is examining the potential for capital market integration, which, in the extreme, could involve the creation of a supranational stock market (Click and Plummer, 2005). The third is the growing influence of Chinese markets, which is related to the relaxation of its capital restriction on equity investment. The fourth is the emergence of China as a trading partner to the world. In 2006, the United States was the largest trading partner for 127 countries, while China was the largest trading partner for 70 countries. By 2011, they had switched places—China had become the largest trading partner for 124 countries, while the United States was the largest trading partner for 76 countries (McDonald and Lee, 2012).

The economies of China and ASEAN are also becoming increasingly interlinked. Between 1995 and 2008, bilateral trade between China and ASEAN increased more than 10-fold. The growth has been especially rapid since 2001 when China joined the World Trade Organization (WTO) and talks over the establishment of the ASEAN-China Free Trade Area (ACFTA) were initiated (Tong and Chong, 2010). ACFTA, which came into effect on January 1, 2010, has been a catalyst for further strengthening of economic ties between China and ASEAN. ACFTA is the largest free trade area in the world in terms of population covered and the third largest in terms of both nominal GDP and trade volume after the European Economic Area and the North American Free Trade Area (Gooch, 2009).

The objective of this chapter is to examine the level of integration between the Shanghai Stock Exchange and the stock exchanges of the ASEAN-6 (Malaysia, Singapore, Indonesia, Thailand, the Philippines, and Vietnam). To realize our objective, we employ daily data over the period January 2001–December 2012. The study extends the existing literature on financial integration in several directions. First, this is the only study to examine financial integration between China and the ASEAN-6. Second, this is one of the first studies to include the Ho Chi Minh City Stock Exchange, which was established in 2000. Most previous studies have focused on the stock markets of the ASEAN-5 (Malaysia, Singapore, Indonesia, Thailand, and the Philippines). The only other study, which we are aware, to consider the ASEAN-6 is Quang and Konya (2012). Third, this is the first study to examine financial integration in the post GFC period and the first study to examine financial integration since ACFTA came into operation. Fourth, from a methodological viewpoint, most existing studies of financial integration in ASEAN use either the Engle and Granger (1987) or Johansen (1988) cointegration methods, which fail to accommodate a structural break. By contrast, we employ the Gregory and Hansen (1996) cointegration method, which allows for a structural break, which is important given volatility in financial markets.

2. THEORETICAL UNDERPINNINGS OF STOCK MARKET LINKAGES

The main interest in financial integration of stock markets stems from its implications for international portfolio diversification. Testing whether stock market indices are cointegrated is a test of the level of arbitrage activity in the long run. If stock market indices are cointegrated, this implies that arbitrage brings those stock market indices together in the long run and that opportunities for making supranormal profits through international portfolio diversification are limited. However, if stock market indices are not cointegrated, arbitrage activities will not bring the indices together in the long run and the potential exists for acquiring long-run gains through international portfolio diversification (see, e.g., Narayan and Smyth, 2004, 2005 for statements to this effect). There are two provisos to this general observation (Masih and Masih, 1999). The first is that even if stock market indices are cointegrated, this does not preclude investors from making arbitrage profits through international portfolio diversification in the short run. Depending on the speed of adjustment, the short run can last for some time. Second, while opportunities to benefit from arbitrage in cointegrated markets are limited, they are unlikely to be completely eliminated, given that different securities vary in risk and different security cash flows co-vary less than perfectly across countries.

The implications of cointegration for the Market Efficiency Hypothesis (MEH) are debatable. On one side of the debate, Granger (1986) and Taylor and Tonks (1989) argued that cointegration implies that markets are inefficient. This argument is based on the premise that cointegration implies predictability in price movements, which, in turn, indicates, that traders in one market can use information in another market. Several studies have tested the MEH by testing for cointegration between stock markets (see, e.g., Guidi and Gupta, 2013; Sharma and Wongbangpo, 2002). The other side of the debate espouses that there is no general equivalence between cointegration and market efficiency (see, e.g., Dwyer and Wallace, 1992; Engel, 1996). Crowder (1996) suggests that while cointegration may imply that markets are inefficient, such a finding equally may imply that the markets are efficient, but that there exist some omitted factors, such as risk premia or regime shifts, that manifest themselves as cointegration. Thus, the preferable view is that cointegration implies prices are predictable, but does not necessarily imply anything about efficiency.

3. EXISTING LITERATURE ON STOCK MARKET LINKAGES

The seminal studies on stock market independence and portfolio diversification used correlation to examine short-run linkages (Grubel, 1968; Granger and Morgenstern, 1970; Levy and Sarnat, 1970). Most of these seminal studies found low correlation among stock markets, implying the potential for international portfolio diversification. Studies that have used cointegration to examine whether there are long-run benefits from international portfolio diversification stem from the 1990s, with Kasa (1992) being one of the earliest of such studies. The majority of these studies have examined linkages between the world's major equity markets or between the world's major equity markets and equity markets in emerging regions. One conclusion from these studies is that linkages between the major markets have increased over time. A second conclusion is that emerging markets are becoming more integrated with markets in the major financial centers, although the level of integration has not been as high as within the developed markets. The implication from both conclusions is that opportunities for international portfolio diversification have diminished over time.

There are a number of studies which examine stock market integration within ASEAN, focusing exclusively on the ASEAN-5 (Palac-McMiken, 1997; Roca et al., 1998; Azman-Saini et al., 2002; Sharma and Wongbangpo, 2002; Hee, 2002; Daly, 2003; Click and Plummer, 2005; Goh et al., 2005; Ibrahim, 2006; Chen et al., 2009; Lim, 2009; Majid et al., 2009). Several conclusions emerge from these studies. First, while the results are not conclusive, most of the studies find that the stock markets of the ASEAN-5 are cointegrated. Exceptions are Roca et al. (1998), Hee (2002), and Ibrahim (2006), which have found that the markets are not cointegrated. A few studies find partial evidence of cointegration. Sharma and Wongbangpo (2002) and Lim (2009) found that four of the markets were cointegrated, but the Philippines was segmented. Palac-McMiken (1997) found that four of the markets were cointegrated, but Indonesia was segmented. Second, some studies have found that the stock markets were not cointegrated during the Asian financial crisis (see, e.g., Goh et al., 2005). Third, the ASEAN-5 markets have become more integrated since the Asian financial crisis (Daly, 2003; Lim, 2009). Overall, existing studies suggest that opportunities for portfolio diversification within the ASEAN-5 are limited and that opportunities have decreased over time.

A second set of relevant studies consider financial integration between the ASEAN-5 (or ASEAN-6 in the case of Quang and Konya, 2012) and stock markets in Japan and the United States (Ibrahim, 2006; Majid et al., 2008; Ardliansyah, 2012; Quang and Konya, 2012). Majid et al. (2008) found that the ASEAN markets were cointegrated with Japan and the United States, while Ardliansyah (2012) found that the ASEAN markets were cointegrated with the United States. However, Ibrahim (2006) and Quang and Konya (2012) found that opportunities for international portfolio diversification exist between ASEAN markets and these major international financial centers. Thus, the jury is still out on the potential for portfolio diversification between ASEAN and the major markets. There is some evidence that convergence between the ASEAN markets and the United States has increased since the Asian financial crisis (Lim, 2009).

A third set of relevant studies focus on integration between China and other markets, such as the markets of the Asia-Pacific, Greater China, Japan, the United States, and the United Kingdom (Chan and Lo, 2000; Huang et al., 2000; Lean and Wong, 2004; Cheng and Glascock, 2005; Tian, 2007; Burdekin and Siklos, 2012; Jeong, 2012). The first finding from these studies is that there was either no evidence, or little evidence, of cointegration between China and regional and global markets before the Asian financial crisis (Chan and Lo, 2000; Huang et al., 2000; Lean and Wong, 2004). The second major finding is that financial integration between China and regional and global markets has increased over time, particularly since the Asian financial crisis (Lean and Wong, 2004; Burdekin and Siklos, 2012) and again in the period since the GFC (Jeong, 2012).

To summarize, there is no conclusive evidence on financial integration. However, the bulk of studies suggest that opportunities for portfolio diversification within ASEAN are limited and that opportunities for portfolio diversification between ASEAN, Japan, and the United States have declined over time. Moreover, the evidence suggests that the Chinese stock market has become more integrated with regional and global markets over time, restricting opportunities for international portfolio diversification between the Chinese market and other markets. This said, there are no studies which consider financial integration between China and the ASEAN-6 and this is a gap in the literature this study seeks to fill.

4. OVERVIEW OF THE MARKETS AND BILATERAL TRADE AND INVESTMENT

Table 1 provides an overview of the Shanghai and ASEAN-5 stock markets in 2011 with data on Vietnam unavailable. In terms of value of shares traded and domestic market capitalization, Shanghai is much larger than its ASEAN counterparts. In terms of both measures, Singapore is the largest of the ASEAN-5 and the Philippines is the smallest. Several of the markets exhibit high market concentration. This is consistent with previous research suggesting that corporate ownership is highly concentrated in Asia (La Porta et al., 1999). The main reasons for high ownership concentration are the prevalence of family control and the significant amount of state control in listed companies (Claessens et al., 2000).

It is expected that interdependence of stock markets across countries will reflect economic integration in the form of trade linkages and investment flows (Narayan and

Table 1 A comparison of the Shanghai and ASEAN-5 stock markets in 2011.

Stock exchange	No. of listed companies	Value of shares traded ($US million)	Market concentration of 5% most capitalized companies (%)	Domestic market capitalization ($US million)
Shanghai	931	3,670,155.7	59.8	2,357,423.3
Malaysia	940	135,524.1	74.1	395,623.8
Singapore	773	284,289.2	36.1	598,272.7
Indonesia	440	109,191.0	61.2	390,106.9
Thailand	545	222,111.9	68.8	268,488.8
Philippines	253	27,755.4	48.6	165,066.4

Notes: No statistics available for Vietnam.
Source: World Federation of Exchanges; http://www.world-exchanges.org/statistics/annual (accessed 25 January 2013).

Smyth, 2004). Overall, there is a high level of economic integration between China and ASEAN that has been increasing since the establishment of the ACFTA. This high level of economic integration is suggestive that we should expect to see stock market interdependence between ASEAN and China.

Trade in goods between the ASEAN-5 and China has increased markedly. As a share of ASEAN-5 GDP it has increased fivefold since the Asian financial crisis and in 2012 was worth $US 400 billion a year (Xu, 2013). In 2012, China was ASEAN's largest trading partner, while ASEAN, as a whole, was China's fourth largest trading partner (Xu, 2013). The ASEAN-China Centre predicts that ASEAN will become China's largest trading partner by 2015 (Xu, 2013).

Table 2 reports China's trade with the ASEAN-6 in 2010. The ASEAN-6 represented 10.1 per cent of China's trade with ASEAN, as a whole, constituting 10.3 per cent of China's trade. Malaysia was China's most important trading partner in ASEAN and China's seventh largest trading partner followed by Singapore, which was China's second most important trading partner in ASEAN and China's tenth most important trading partner overall. A common perception is that ASEAN is a big net exporter to China, but this is not necessarily the case with substantial export flows in both directions. Indonesia, Thailand, and Vietnam are, in fact, net importers from China and in Vietnam's case the trade deficit is quite substantial, running at about 11 per cent of GDP (Eskesen, 2013).

Stock market interdependence could also reflect the industrial structure of countries. Countries, which have similar industrial bases and export similar sorts of products, can be expected to have interdependent stock markets (Allen and MacDonald, 1995). China and ASEAN have similar industrial bases, which underlie a cross-border regional production network in Asia. Much of ASEAN-China trade is of the intra-industry type, reflected in the dominance of trade in materials, parts, and components. For example, exports of electrical machinery and apparatus accounted for 54 per cent of Malaysia's exports to

Table 2 China's trade with the ASEAN 6 in 2010.

	Rank	Million Euros	Percentage of China's total trade (%)
Malaysia	7	56,113.6	2.6
Singapore	10	42,999.7	2.0
Thailand	12	40,061.4	1.9
Indonesia	14	32,322.3	1.5
Vietnam	16	22,761.3	1.1
Philippines	18	21,016.6	1.0
Total ASEAN-6		215,274.9	10.1
Total ASEAN		221,255.6	10.3

Notes: Rankings treat European Union as a single entity, which is ranked first.
Source: http://trade.ec.europa.eu/doclib/docs/2006/September/tradoc_113366.pdf (accessed 25 January 2013).

Table 3 Inward and outward FDI between China and the ASEAN-6 in 2010.

	Chinese FDI in ASEAN-6			**ASEAN-6 FDI in China**		
	Amount ($US million)	**% of inward investment into host**	**Rank in inward investment into host**	**Amount ($US million)**	**% of inward investment into China**	**Rank in inward investment into China**
Singapore	N/A	N/A	N/A	5428.2	5.1	3rd
Malaysia	207.6	2.2	9th	294.3	0.3	18th
Indonesia	173.6	4.5	11th	76.8	0.07	26th
Philippines	125.4	3.8	9th	138.1	0.13	24th
Thailand	546.4	6.2	5th	51.3	0.05	29th
Vietnam	685	3.4	8th	N/A	N/A	N/A

Notes: N/A is not available.
Source: Japan-ASEAN Centre; http://www.asean.or.jp/en/asean/know/statistics/5.html (accessed 25 January 2013).

China in 2008, while electronic equipment and parts plus machinery appliances were responsible for 45 per cent of Malaysia's imports from China (Tong and Chong, 2010).

Table 3 reports inward and outward foreign direct investment between China and the ASEAN-6 in 2010. The main beneficiaries of Chinese foreign direct investment have been Malaysia, Thailand, and Vietnam. Generally China invests more in ASEAN, rather than the other way around with Malaysia and the Philippines being exceptions. While bilateral investment flows between ASEAN and China have increased, it constitutes only a relatively small proportion of the two regions' total foreign direct investment flow (Tong and Chong, 2010). China is still a relatively small investor in ASEAN, compared with investors from Japan, Singapore, and the United States. Similarly, with the exception of Singapore, which is the third largest investor in China, ASEAN investment in China is relatively small (Eskesen, 2013). However, investment flows between the two are expected to increase with a more harmonized region (Tong and Chong, 2010).

5. DATA

The sample consists of daily data from January 2001 to December 2012. The study will focus on the ASEAN-6 (Malaysia, Singapore, Indonesia, Thailand, the Philippines, and Vietnam) in addition to China. Daily stock indices from the main stock exchanges of these six ASEAN members and the Shanghai Stock Exchange in China were extracted from Datastream and Yahoo Finance. The indices were the Shanghai Stock Exchange Composite Index, IDX Composite Index, FTSE Bursa Malaysia KLCI, Philippines Stock Exchange Index (PSEI), Singapore Straits Times Index, Bangkok SET, and the Ho Chi Minh VN Index.

The time series plots of each stock index are presented in Figure 1. Each of the markets exhibits a peak prior to the GFC and then a trough in the GFC. The indices in Singapore, Indonesia, Malaysia, Philippines, and Thailand have rebounded since the GFC and in the case of Indonesia, Malaysia, Philippines, and Thailand, the indices were higher at the end of 2012 than prior to the GFC. The indices in China and Vietnam did not rebound following the GFC. Tables 4 and 5 present descriptive statistics for stock indices and stock returns respectively. Indonesia had the highest, and China had the lowest, mean daily

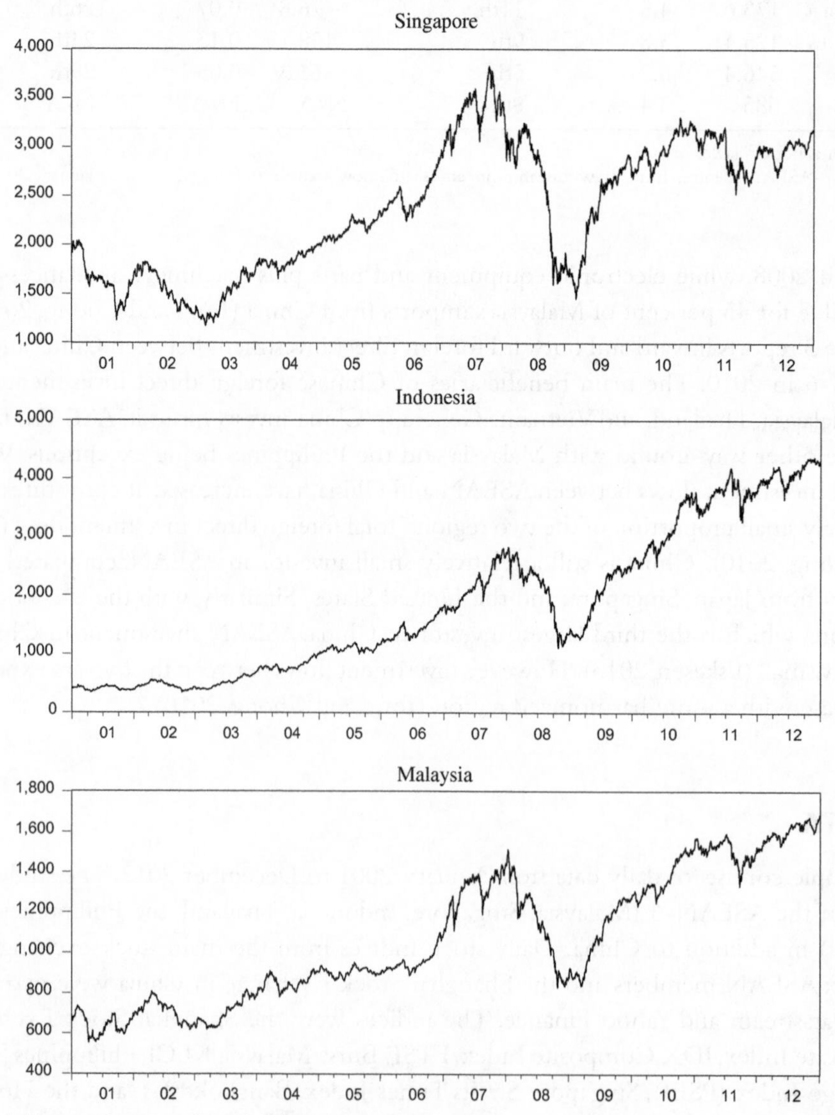

Figure 1 Time series plot of stock indices.

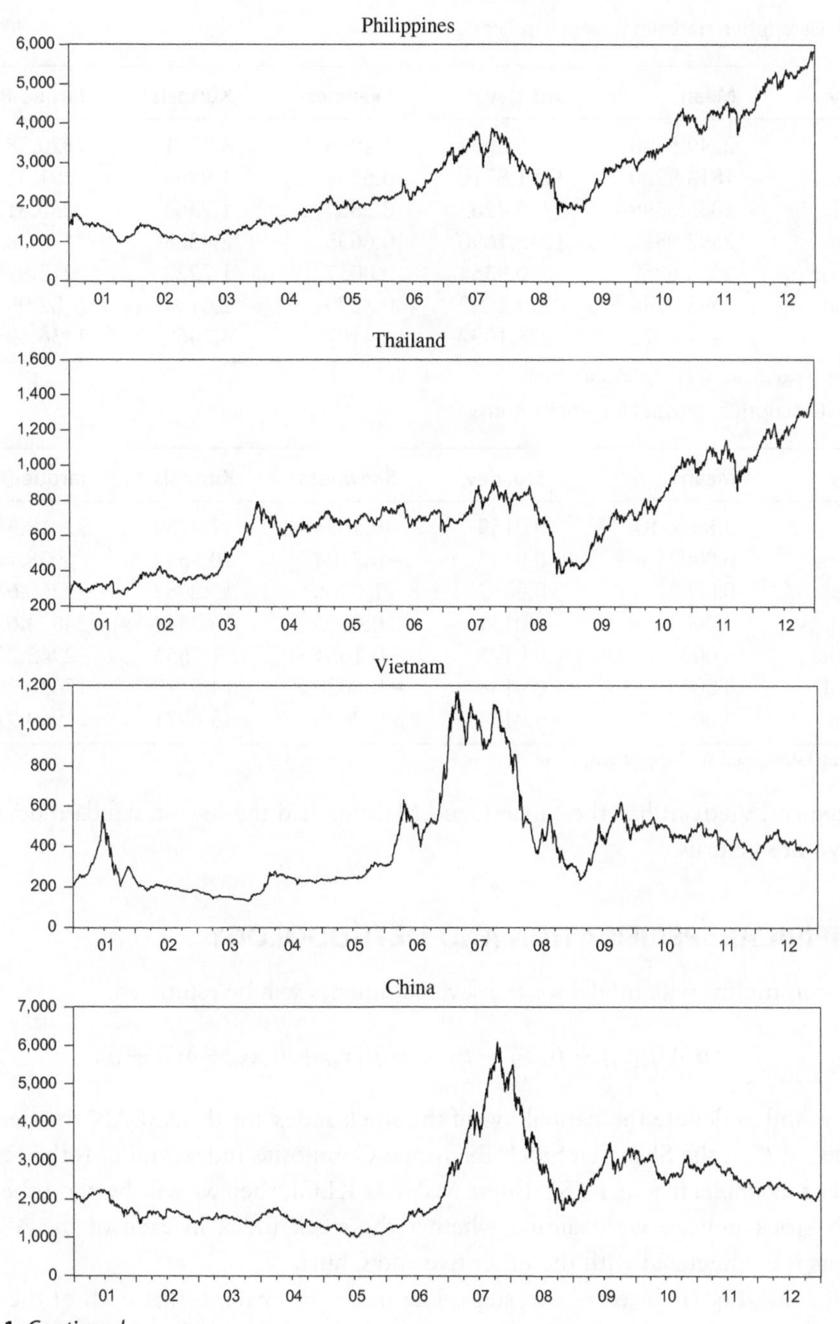

Figure 1 *Continued*

Table 4 Descriptive statistics for stock indices.

Country	Mean	Std. dev.	Skewness	Kurtosis	Jarque-Bera
China	2249.5520	965.8637	1.4006	5.1391	1620.5810***
Indonesia	1818.9220	1251.8710	0.5509	1.9904	291.3171***
Malaysia	1065.6590	323.7203	0.2853	1.7363	250.8108***
Philippines	2592.9820	1245.1690	0.6635	2.4388	270.7832***
Singapore	2365.6250	660.9354	0.0057	1.7227	212.8754***
Thailand	695.6744	259.4682	0.3479	2.6104	82.9514***
Vietnam	411.0872	228.1092	1.4107	4.7469	1436.5950***

***Statistical significant at 1% significance level.

Table 5 Descriptive statistics for stock returns.

Country	Mean	Std. dev.	Skewness	Kurtosis	Jarque-Bera
China	2.88×10^{-5}	0.0159	−0.1095	7.4754	2618.3500***
Indonesia	0.0007	0.0143	−0.7104	10.1544	6938.7560***
Malaysia	0.0003	0.0082	−1.0266	15.2957	20266.6400***
Philippines	0.0004	0.0131	0.0603	16.7544	24674.6300***
Singapore	0.0002	0.0123	−0.1634	7.7555	2963.2270***
Thailand	0.0005	0.0138	−0.8023	14.5179	17636.9600***
Vietnam	0.0002	0.0164	−0.2020	5.6971	969.9757***

***Statistical significant at 1% significance level.

stock returns. Vietnam had the highest, and Malaysia had the lowest, standard deviation of daily stock returns.

6. EMPIRICAL SPECIFICATION AND METHODOLOGY

A long-run multivariate model for the seven countries will be estimated:

$$y_t = \alpha + \beta_1 x_{1t} + \beta_2 x_{2t} + \beta_3 x_{3t} + \beta_4 x_{4t} + \beta_5 x_{5t} + \delta C_t + u_t, \quad (1)$$

where y_t and x_t denote the natural log of the stock index for the ASEAN six members respectively, C_t is the Shanghai Stock Exchange Composite Index, and u_t is the residual term. For example, if y_t is FTSE Bursa Malaysia KLCI, then x_t will be the other five ASEAN stock indices. We examine whether the stock index in each of the ASEAN members is cointegrated with the other five and China.

Estimating Eq. (1) involves two steps. The first is to establish that each of the stock price indices is non-stationary, which is a precondition to testing for cointegration using the Gregory and Hansen (1996) method. Hence, we begin by testing for a unit root in each of the indices. To do so we employ the Lee and Strazicich (2003) one break LM unit root test. The LM unit root test can be explained using the following data generating process (DGP):

$$y_t = \delta' Z_t + e_t, \quad e_t = \beta e_{t-1} + \varepsilon_t.$$

Here, *Zt* consists of exogenous variables and ε_t is an error term that follows the classical properties. The LM unit root test allows for structural breaks in the spirit of Perron (1989). We consider two models of structural change. Model A is known as the "crash" model and allows for a one-time change in intercept under the alternative hypothesis. Model A can be described by $Z_t = [1, t, D_t]'$, where $D_t = 1$ for $t \geq T_B + 1$, and zero otherwise, T_B is the time period of the structural break, and $\delta' = (\delta_1, \delta_2, \delta_3)$. Model C allows for a shift in intercept and change in trend slope under the alternative hypothesis and can be described by $Z_t = [1, t, D_t, DT_t]'$, where $DT_t = t - T_B$ for $t \geq T_B + 1$, and zero otherwise.

Second, having established the unit root properties of the indices, we proceed to estimate Eq. (1) using the Gregory and Hansen (1996) cointegration test, which consists of three models, each of which allows for one structural break in the cointegrating vector. The first contains a level shift (Model C):

$$y_t = \alpha_1 + \alpha_2 D_t^\tau + \beta_1 x_{1t} + \beta_2 x_{2t} + \beta_3 x_{3t} + \beta_4 x_{4t} + \beta_5 x_{5t} + \delta C_t + \mu_t, \quad t = 1, \ldots, n. \tag{2}$$

The second model contains a level shift and trend (Model C/T):

$$y_t = \alpha_1 + \alpha_2 D_t^\tau + \beta_0 t + \beta_1^\tau x_{1t} + \beta_2^\tau x_{2t} + \beta_3^\tau x_{3t} + \beta_4^\tau x_{4t} + \beta_5^\tau x_{5t} + \delta^\tau C_t + \mu_t, \quad t = 1, \ldots, n. \tag{3}$$

Here, $D_t^\tau = 0$ for $t < \tau$ and $D_t^\tau = 1$ for $t \geq \tau$. The intercept before the level shift is denoted as α_1, while α_2 is the change in intercept due to the level shift.

The third model allows for a regime shift (Model C/S):

$$\begin{aligned} y_t = {} & \alpha_1 + \alpha_2 D_t^\tau + \beta_0 t + \beta_1^\tau x_{1t} + \beta_2^\tau x_{2t} + \beta_3^\tau x_{3t} + \beta_4^\tau x_{4t} + \beta_5^\tau x_{5t} + \delta^\tau C_t + \phi_1^\tau x_{1t} D_t^\tau \\ & + \phi_2^\tau x_{2t} D_t^\tau + \phi_3^\tau x_{3t} D_t^\tau + \phi_4^\tau x_{4t} D_t^\tau + \phi_5^\tau x_{5t} D_t^\tau + \phi_6^\tau C_t D_t^\tau + \mu_t, \quad t = 1, \ldots, n. \end{aligned} \tag{4}$$

Here, α_1 and α_2 are as given in Equations (2) and (3). β_i^τ and δ^τ denote the cointegrating slope coefficients before the regime shift and ϕ_i^τ denotes the changes in the slope coefficient. Three statistics are used to ascertain whether cointegration exists:

$$\begin{aligned} ADF^* &= \inf_{\tau \in T} ADF(\tau), \\ Z_\alpha^* &= \inf_{\tau \in T} Z_\alpha(\tau), \\ Z_t^* &= \inf_{\tau \in T} Z_t(\tau). \end{aligned}$$

As the break point, τ, is unknown, the model is estimated recursively allowing the break point to vary between (0.15T, 0.85T), where T is the sample size. The null hypothesis of no cointegration is examined using the three statistics given above, with the smallest values across all break points required to reject the null hypothesis.

The cointegration test will ascertain whether or not there are long-run co-movements between ASEAN-6 and Chinese stock prices. However, stock prices may also react to each other in the short run. To ascertain this, we specify and estimate either a VAR or a VECM for each set of share prices and stimulate generalized impulse response functions and variance decompositions. From the generalized impulse response functions, we can trace whether ASEAN markets respond significantly to shocks in other ASEAN markets and the Chinese market. From the variance decompositions, we can assess whether own, regional, or Chinese shocks are more dominant in accounting for shocks in the ASEAN markets.

7. RESULTS

The results for the LM unit root test with one break in the intercept (Model A) are presented in Table 6 and the results for the LM unit root test with one break in the intercept and slope (Model C) are presented in Table 7. Both Model A and Model C suggest that each of the stock price indices contains a unit root. In Model A, each of the breaks occurs in either the GFC (2007–2008) or the financial bubble which preceded the GFC (2006). In Model C, four of the six breaks occur in the GFC or the financial

Table 6 Results of LM test with one break (Lee and Strazicich, 2003)—Model A.

Series	TB	k	S_{t-1}	B_t
China	01/12/2007	4	−0.0010 (−1.3158)	0.0445*** (2.7958)
Indonesia	10/03/2008	1	−0.0024 (−2.0412)	−0.1066*** (−7.5972)
Malaysia	03/07/2008	10	−0.0034 (−2.6062)	−0.0991*** (−12.5237)
Philippines	02/28/2007	3	−0.0024 (−2.0300)	0.0506*** (3.8694)
Singapore	06/15/2006	12	−0.0020 (−1.8327)	0.0302** (2.4647)
Thailand	12/18/2006	11	−0.0018 (−1.7899)	−0.1608*** (−12.0772)
Vietnam	05/10/2006	10	−0.0012 (−1.7864)	0.0577*** (3.6553)

Notes: critical values for the LM test at 10%, 5%, and 1% significant levels = −3.211, −3.566, −4.239.
**Statistical significance at the 5% level.
***Statistical significance at the 1% level.
Figures in parentheses are *t*-values.

Table 7 Results of LM test with one break (Lee and Strazicich, 2003)—Model C.

Series	TB	k	S_{t-1}	B_t	D_t
China	12/08/2006	4	−0.0026 (−2.1259)	0.0400** (2.5144)	0.0015* (1.6945)
Indonesia	11/15/2004	12	−0.0034 (−2.3594)	−0.0008 (−0.0532)	0.0009 (1.3295)
Malaysia	03/05/2007	10	−0.0034 (−2.6535)	0.0256*** (3.1363)	0.0001 (0.4775)
Philippines	01/09/2004	3	−0.0027 (−2.1450)	−0.0222* (−1.7031)	0.0010* (1.7006)
Singapore	02/14/2007	12	−0.0030 (−2.2603)	0.0219* (1.7839)	0.0003 (0.5336)
Thailand	08/07/2008	11	−0.0037 (−2.4451)	−0.0212 (−1.5535)	−0.0013* (−1.6490)
Vietnam	05/10/2006	10	−0.0020 (−2.4063)	0.0576*** (3.6495)	0.0001 (0.2078)

Critical values

location of break, λ	0.1	0.2	0.3	0.4	0.5
1% significant level	-5.11	-5.07	-5.15	-5.05	-5.11
5% significant level	-4.50	-4.47	-4.45	-4.50	-4.51
10% significant level	-4.21	-4.20	-4.18	-4.18	-4.17

Notes: the critical values are symmetric around λ and $(1 - \lambda)$.
*Statistical significance at the 10% level.
**Statistical significance at the 5% level.
***Statistical significance at the 1% level.
Figures in parentheses are *t*-values.

bubble which preceded it. The exceptions are Indonesia and the Philippines, in which the break occurred in 2004. The break in Indonesia is associated with the Boxing Day 2004 tsunami. Indonesia was the country most affected by the Boxing Day 2004 tsunami with 129,775 fatalities, 36,789 missing, and 504,518 displaced people (Ramiah, 2013). Meanwhile, the break in the Philippines is most likely associated with the 2004 fiscal crisis and bailout in that country.

The results of the Gregory and Hansen (1996) test as to whether the stock market for each of the ASEAN-6 is cointegrated with the other five ASEAN countries and China are presented in Table 8. There is evidence of cointegration for each of the ASEAN-6. The strongest evidence is for the stock markets of Indonesia, Malaysia, and Vietnam, for which all three Gregory and Hansen (1996) test statistics suggest each of Models C, C/S, and C/T is cointegrated. For the Philippines, Singapore, and Thailand, Model C/S is cointegrated based on all three test statistics, but there is mixed evidence of cointegration for Models C and C/T. The three test statistics suggest a different number of rejections of the null of no cointegration for the Philippines, Singapore, and Thailand. In these

Table 8 Gregory and Hansen test for cointegration with a structural break.

Series	Model	ADF*	k	TB	Z_t^*	TB	Z_α^*	TB
ID	C	−5.5225*	0	05/01/2006	−5.9484**	01/16/2006	−71.9559***	01/16/2006
	C/T	−5.5845*	3	05/18/2010	−6.1011**	05/05/2010	−74.4984**	05/05/2010
	C/S	−7.3298***	0	02/15/2006	−7.3444***	02/13/2006	−109.2485***	02/13/2006
MY	C	−5.7252**	3	02/27/2007	−5.5674**	12/07/2005	−61.1644**	12/29/2006
	C/T	−6.0736**	3	11/15/2005	−5.9790**	07/30/2007	−70.5640**	07/30/2007
	C/S	−7.6270***	0	01/12/2007	−7.6544***	01/15/2007	−114.1223***	01/18/2007
PH	C	−4.9290	3	11/07/2002	−5.4795*	11/05/2002	−59.0112*	11/05/2002
	C/T	−4.8915	3	11/07/2002	−5.4500	11/05/2002	−59.4503	04/10/2007
	C/S	−8.8150***	0	12/14/2006	−9.0135***	01/09/2008	−158.9767***	01/09/2008
SG	C	−5.1405	4	10/31/2008	−5.3136*	02/24/2005	−50.2940	02/24/2005
	C/T	−5.5486	2	02/23/2005	−5.8535**	02/21/2005	−64.1082*	02/21/2005
	C/S	−8.2473***	1	03/17/2008	−8.4737***	03/13/2008	−137.4762***	03/13/2008
TH	C	−5.0841	0	11/04/2002	−4.9928	11/05/2002	−46.2979	11/05/2002
	C/T	−5.6878*	0	07/09/2003	−5.6065*	07/08/2003	−59.4302	07/08/2003
	C/S	−6.9598***	0	04/26/2004	−7.0218***	11/11/2004	−95.6500***	07/20/2004
VN	C	−6.0449**	1	11/04/2002	−5.9494**	11/05/2002	−64.0896**	11/05/2002
	C/T	−7.3185***	4	06/27/2007	−7.0277***	07/31/2007	−93.6886***	07/31/2007
	C/S	−7.9342***	1	07/13/2006	−7.9552***	04/16/2007	−121.1682***	04/16/2007

Critical values with $m = 4$ (excluding intercept)

	ADF* and Z_t^*			Z_α^*		
Model	1%	5%	10%	1%	5%	10%
C	-6.05	-5.56	-5.31	-70.18	-59.40	-54.38
C/T	-6.36	-5.83	-5.59	-76.95	-65.44	-60.12
C/S	-6.92	-6.41	-6.17	-90.35	-78.52	-72.56

Notes:
*Statistical significance at the 10% level.
**Statistical significance at the 5% level.
***Statistical significance at the 1% level.

circumstances, Gregory and Hansen (1996) suggest that Z_t^* performs best in Monte Carlo simulations in terms of size and power. The Z_t^* test statistic suggests that all of the series are cointegrated, except Model C/T in the Philippines and Model C in Thailand, which, on balance, suggest that a reasonable conclusion is that all markets are cointegrated.

In most cases, for each model, for each country, the break take place in the same year across the three test statistics or, if not in the same year, is within a year or two. Across the three models and three test statistics, the majority of breaks fall into one of the three periods: namely, the recession of the early 2000s (14 breaks), the stock market boom in 2005–2006 (16 breaks), and the GFC in 2007–2008 (18 breaks). Exceptions are Model

C/T for Indonesia, in which the break occurs in 2010 in the recovery period from the GFC, and Model C/S for Thailand, in which the break occurs in 2004 and is linked to the 2004 Boxing Day tsunami.

We now turn to considering the short-run dynamics. Because each share price is I (1) and there is evidence of cointegration, we estimate a VECM with lag equal to four based on the AIC. Figure 2 presents the generalized impulse response functions generated from the VECM for a period of 25 days. Overall, we observe that shocks in specific share prices result in positive and permanent responses from other share prices. These results suggest that shocks to one market tend to spread quickly to other markets and that there are no benefits from portfolio diversification in the short run. This result is consistent with those of previous studies which have used generalized impulse response functions to analyze the short-run dynamics in ASEAN equity markets (see, e.g., Ibrahim, 2006).

To further analyze the relative importance of own shocks, shocks in other ASEAN markets, and shocks in the Chinese market, we compute variance decompositions up to 25 days. The results are reported in Table 9. Variations in the ASEAN markets are accounted for mainly by their own shocks followed by shocks in the Indonesian market. Among the ASEAN markets, Indonesia is most exogenous to shocks in other markets, while Thailand is the most responsive. Ibrahim (2006) also found that Indonesia had the most exogenous market in ASEAN. He suggests that this result reflects the dominance of domestic shocks affecting the Indonesian stock market, perhaps due to frequent political unrest in the country. After a 25-day horizon, variations in the Chinese market account for a small fraction of the forecast error variance in ASEAN markets, ranging from less than 1 per cent in Indonesia and Thailand, through to 3.3 per cent in Malaysia.

8. CONCLUSION

Linkages among stock markets have important implications for investors interested in the potential for portfolio diversification and policy-makers interested in closer regional financial integration and minimizing the adverse implications of contagion effects in times of financial crisis. There is a growing literature examining financial integration within ASEAN and between ASEAN members and stock markets in major financial centers. Given the growing importance of China in the Asian region, we extend this literature to examine financial integration between the ASEAN-6 and China in the short-and-long run.

Our results point to two general conclusions. The first is that the stock markets of the ASEAN-6 and Shanghai are cointegrated in the long run. This result is to be expected given the close economic linkages between ASEAN members and between ASEAN and China. It is consistent with the finding in most extant studies that stock markets within the ASEAN-5 are cointegrated. The second general conclusion is that shocks to one market are fast to reverberate to other markets in the region. The implication for investors is that

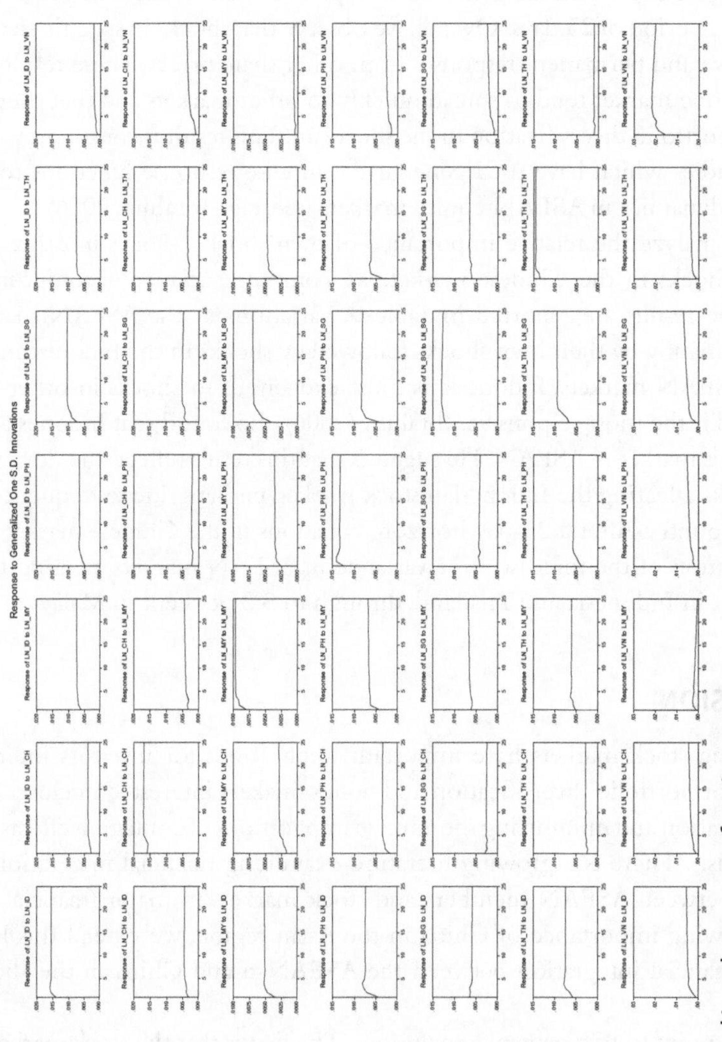

Figure 2 Generalized impulse response functions.

Table 9 Variance decompositions of individual ASEAN-6 and Chinese stock markets.

Period	ID	CH	MY	PH	SG	TH	VN
ID							
1	100.0000	0.000000	0.000000	0.000000	0.000000	0.000000	0.000000
5	98.72008	0.045704	0.052403	0.257218	0.866775	0.022753	0.035068
10	97.69456	0.132356	0.131803	0.414308	1.505205	0.012560	0.109204
15	97.34084	0.166388	0.159872	0.459150	1.711717	0.009735	0.152298
20	97.16380	0.183687	0.173747	0.481463	1.813386	0.008320	0.175600
25	97.05856	0.193972	0.182190	0.494600	1.873316	0.007476	0.189890
CH							
1	4.020662	95.97934	0.000000	0.000000	0.000000	0.000000	0.000000
5	5.755731	93.84012	0.014215	0.099273	0.070429	0.029609	0.190616
10	6.410799	92.62842	0.013405	0.114013	0.100508	0.036701	0.696158
15	6.610158	92.06765	0.024253	0.134217	0.086264	0.038849	1.038607
20	6.680387	91.71604	0.041588	0.159860	0.068174	0.039895	1.294052
25	6.700117	91.44259	0.063865	0.188745	0.054471	0.040513	1.509695
MY							
1	18.85003	1.462950	79.68702	0.000000	0.000000	0.000000	0.000000
5	26.65805	1.871879	69.54392	0.003667	1.793141	0.085551	0.043791
10	26.64518	2.719832	67.60371	0.002472	2.924217	0.072122	0.032467
15	26.69664	3.013747	66.87752	0.002433	3.314495	0.070337	0.024825
20	26.74059	3.163724	66.47951	0.002753	3.522301	0.069469	0.021648
25	26.77858	3.256517	66.21390	0.003195	3.658365	0.068963	0.020476
PH							
1	11.98650	0.567379	3.855543	83.59058	0.000000	0.000000	0.000000
5	26.06035	1.153645	4.745249	65.68477	2.059473	0.249347	0.047172
10	27.19051	1.630183	5.453803	62.63438	2.795799	0.200905	0.094421
15	27.65868	1.782465	5.812092	61.46372	2.940977	0.189867	0.152198
20	27.90223	1.846007	6.084196	60.82890	2.949170	0.184700	0.204790
25	28.05576	1.874007	6.318641	60.40633	2.908512	0.181909	0.254846
SG							
1	27.78530	1.955076	8.773466	0.920589	60.56557	0.000000	0.000000
5	23.99579	1.236604	8.536655	1.275117	64.83880	0.027026	0.090007
10	22.15823	1.248276	9.504259	1.279071	65.43687	0.064097	0.309191
15	21.65484	1.238153	10.05523	1.237811	65.26201	0.077255	0.474702
20	21.42830	1.218494	10.51978	1.186336	64.94858	0.084126	0.614393
25	21.30435	1.195572	10.94356	1.133695	64.59074	0.088530	0.743560

(Continued)

Table 9 (Continued)

Period	ID	CH	MY	PH	SG	TH	VN
TH							
1	17.85219	0.992717	4.319583	0.932332	5.900381	70.00280	0.000000
5	24.27980	0.645457	4.356022	2.136437	9.061303	59.49134	0.029642
10	24.92159	0.685648	4.308167	2.704741	11.31517	56.03183	0.032857
15	25.08809	0.702093	4.286567	2.882889	12.06795	54.94008	0.032328
20	25.17007	0.713252	4.254707	2.981918	12.47428	54.37191	0.033860
25	25.21846	0.721884	4.220985	3.048389	12.74129	54.01264	0.036345
VN							
1	0.407567	0.218308	0.069524	0.969420	0.103888	0.045273	98.18602
5	3.275989	0.611462	0.125530	0.520583	0.943617	0.055035	94.46779
10	3.968939	0.993498	0.095740	0.931566	1.341819	0.046042	92.62240
15	4.384897	1.239346	0.178131	1.253654	1.839190	0.042348	91.06243
20	4.717069	1.445855	0.317178	1.571889	2.416788	0.040708	89.49051
25	5.008682	1.635964	0.498553	1.895454	3.053356	0.039837	87.86815

opportunities for international portfolio diversification in the ASEAN-6 and Chinese markets are limited in the long-run and that the benefits of portfolio diversification are also restricted in the short run. A potential proviso to the conclusion that there are no benefits to portfolio diversification in the short run is that the Indonesian market appears relatively exogenous. However, this seems to stem from domestic political shocks and the political risk would need to be properly examined when considering whether to invest in Indonesia (Ibrahim, 2006).

REFERENCES

Allen, D.E., MacDonald, G., 1995. The long-run gains from international portfolio diversification: Australian evidence from cointegration tests. Applied Financial Economics 5, 33–42

Ardliansyah, R., 2012. Stock market integration and international portfolio diversification between US and AEAN equity markets. Thesis submitted in fulfillment of the MSc International Banking and Finance, Centre for Economic and Financial Studies, University of Glasgow.

Azman-Saini, W.N.M., Azali, M., Habibullah, M.S., Matthews, K.G., 2002. Financial integration and the ASEAN-5 equity markets. Applied Economics 34, 2283–2288

Burdekin, R.C.K., Siklos, P.L., 2012. Enter the dragon: interactions between Chinese, US and Asia-Pacific equity markets. Pacific Basin Finance Journal 20, 521–541

Brown, K., 2010. Biggest regional trade deal unveiled. Financial Times, January 1. <http://www.ft.com/intl/cms/s/0/823707e4-f6f1-11de-9fb5-00144feab49a.html#axzz2K48KSDXS> (accessed 06.02.13).

Chan, B., Lo, W., 2000. Financial market integration in the Greater China bloc: evidence from causality investigation of stock returns. Asia Pacific Journal of Finance 3, 53–69

Chen, C.W.S., Gerlach, R., Cheng, N.Y.P., Yang, Y.L., 2009. The impact of structural breaks on the integration of the ASEAN-5 stock markets. Mathematics and Computers in Simulation 79, 2654–2664

Cheng, H., Glascock, J.L., 2005. Dynamic linkages between the Greater China economic area stock markets – Mainland China, Hong Kong and Taiwan. Review of Quantitative Finance and Accounting 24, 343–357

Claessens, S., Djankov, S., Lang, L.H.P., 2000. The separation of ownership and control in East Asian corporations. Journal of Financial Economics 58, 81–102

Click, R.W., Plummer, M.G., 2005. Stock market integration in ASEAN after the Asian financial crisis. Journal of Asian Economics 16, 5–28

Crowder, W.J., 1996. A note on cointegration and international capital market efficiency: a reply. Journal of International Money and Finance 15, 661–664

Daly, K.J., 2003. Southeast Asian stock market linkages: evidence from pre-and-post-October 1997. ASEAN Economic Bulletin 20, 73–85

Dwyer, G., Wallace, M., 1992. Cointegration and market efficiency. Journal of International Money and Finance 11, 318–327

Engel, C., 1996. A note on cointegration and international capital market efficiency. Journal of International Money and Finance 15, 657–660

Engle, R., Granger, C.W.J., 1987. Cointegration and error-correction representation estimation and testing. Econometrica 55, 251–276

Eskesen, L., 2013. China and ASEAN – it cuts both ways. Financial Times blog, January 24. <http://blogs.ft.com/beyond-brics/2013/01/24/guest-post-china-and-asean-it-cuts-both-ways/#axzz2K4RQGTcZ> (accessed 06.02.13).

Goh, K.L., Wong, Y.C., Kok, K.L., 2005. Financial crisis and intertemporal linkages across the ASEAN-5 stock markets. Review of Quantitative Finance and Accounting 24, 359–377

Gooch, L., 2009. Asia free trade zone raises hopes and some fears about China. New York Times, December 31. <http://www.nytimes.com/2010/01/01/business/global/01trade.html?_r=0> (accessed 06.02.13).

Granger, C.W.J., 1986. Developments in the study of cointegrated economic variables. Oxford Bulletin of Economics and Statistics 48, 213–228

Granger, C.W.J., Morgenstern, O., 1970. Predictability of Stock Market Prices. Lexington Books, Massachusetts

Gregory, A.W., Hansen, B.E., 1996. Residual-based tests for cointegration in models with regime shifts. Journal of Econometrics 70, 99–126

Grubel, H., 1968. Internationally diversified portfolio: welfare gains and capital flows. American Economic Review 58, 89–94

Guidi, F., Gupta, R., 2013. Market efficiency in the ASEAN region: evidence from multivariate and cointegration tests. Applied Financial Economics 23, 265–274

Huang, B.N., Yang, C.W., Hu, J.W.S., 2000. Causality and cointegration of stock markets among the United States, Japan and South China growth triangle. International Review of Financial Analysis 9, 281–297

Hee, N.T., 2002. Stock market linkages in Southeast Asia. Asian Economic Journal 16, 353–377

Ibrahim, M., 2006. Financial integration and international portfolio diversification: US, Japan and ASEAN equity markets. Journal of Asia-Pacific Business 7, 5–23

Jeong, J., 2012. Dynamic Stock Market Integration and Financial Crisis: the Case of China, Japan and Korea. School of Business Administration, Korea University.

Johansen, S., 1988. Statistical analysis of cointegrating vectors. Journal of Economic Dynamics and Control 12, 231–254

Kasa, K., 1992. Common stochastic trends in international stock markets. Journal of Monetary Economics 29, 95–124

La Porta, R., Lopez-De-Silanes, F., Schleifer, A., 1999. Corporate ownership around the world. Journal of Finance 54, 471–517

Lean, H.H., Wong, W.K., 2004. Impact of other markets on China. China Journal of Finance 2, 81–108

Lee, J., Strazicich, M.C., 2003. Minimum Lagrange multiplier unit root test with two structural breaks. Review of Economics and Statistics 85, 1082–1089

Levy, H., Sarnat, M., 1970. International diversification of investment portfolios. American Economic Review 60, 668–675

Lim, L.K., 2009. Convergence and interdependence between ASEAN-5 stock markets. Mathematics and Computers in Simulation 79, 2957–2966

Majid, M.S.A., Meera, A.K.M., Omar, M.A., 2008. Interdependence of ASEAN-5 stock markets from the U.S. and Japan. Global Economic Review 37, 201–225

Majid, M.S.A., Meera, A.K.M., Omar, M.A., Aziz, H.A., 2009. Dynamic linkages among ASEAN-5 emerging stock markets. International Journal of Emerging Markets 4, 160–184

Masih, A.M.M., Masih, R., 1999. Are Asian stock market fluctuations due mainly to intra-regional contagion effects? Evidence based on Asian emerging stock markets. Pacific Basin Finance Journal 7, 251–282

McDonald, J., Lee, Y., 2012. China overtakes U.S. as trading partner. The Seattle, Times, December 2. <http://seattletimes.com/html/nationworld/2019816264_chinatrade03.html> (accessed 25.01.13).

Narayan, P.K., Smyth, R., 2004. Modelling the linkages between the Australian and G7 stock markets: common stochastic trends and regime shifts. Applied Financial Economics 14, 991–1004

Narayan, P.K., Smyth, R., 2005. Cointegration of stock markets between New Zealand, Australia and the G7 economies: searching for co-movement under structural change. Australian Economic Papers 44, 231–247

Palac-McMiken, E.D., 1997. An examination of ASEAN stock markets: a cointegration approach. ASEAN Economic Bulletin 13, 299–311

Perron, P., 1989. The great crash, the oil price shock and the unit root hypothesis. Econometrica 57, 1361–1401

Quang, H.D., Konya, L., 2012. Capital market integration and ASEAN countries. Manuscript, School of Economics. LaTrobe University, Australia.

Ramiah, V., 2013. Effects of the Boxing Day tsunami on the world capital markets. Review of Quantitative and Financial Accounting 40, 383–401

Roca, E., Selvanathan, E.A., Shepherd, W.F., 1998. Are the ASEAN equity markets interdependent? ASEAN Economic Bulletin 15, 109–120

Sharma, S.C., Wongbangpo, P., 2002. Long-term trends and cycles in ASEAN stock markets. Review of Financial Economics 11, 299–315

Taylor, M.P., Tonks, I., 1989. The internationalization of stock markets and the abolition of the UK exchange control. Review of Economics and Statistics 71, 332–336

Tian, G.G., 2007. Are Chinese stock markets increasing integration with other markets in the Greater China region and other major markets? Australian Economic Papers 46, 240–253

Tong, S.Y., Chong, S.K., 2010. China-ASEAN free trade area in 2010: a regional perspective. EAI Background Brief No. 519.

World Bank, 2012. World Development Indicators. World Bank, Washington DC

World Federation of Exchanges, 2013. <http://www.world-exchanges.org/statistics/annual> (accessed 25.02.13).

Xu, N., 2013. Partnership sees trade between ASEAN and China reach new high. China Daily, January 19. <http://www.nationmultimedia.com/opinion/Partnership-sees-trade-between-Asean-and-China-rea-30198195.html> (accessed 06.03.13).

CHAPTER 26

Stock and Bond Markets Co-movements in Selected MENA Countries: A Dynamic Coherence Function Approach

Jamel Boukhatem*,† and Zied Ftiti‡,§

*Faculty of Islamic Economics and Finance, Umm Al-Qura University, Mecca, Saudi Arabia
†URMOFIB, FSEG University of Tunis El Manar, Tunisia
‡IPAG Business School, IPAG lab, Paris, France
§University of Tunis, High Institute of Management, GEF-2A Laboratory, Tunis, Tunisia

1. INTRODUCTION

Many works have examined the relationship among financial markets and they have largely focused on the interactions between bonds and stocks. This is explained by the fact that stock-bond correlations are very important for risk management and are related to the optimal allocation of financial assets. Since the seminal work by Markowitz (1952, 1959), a common consensus showing the importance of stock-bond correlation in constructing the optimal portfolio emerged. The co-movements issue between stock and bond markets has been one of the most fundamental questions to the risk analysts, portfolio managers, and financial researchers, among others. In addition, co-movements in asset market returns provide indirect evidence on financial markets' expectations and their reaction to common information.

The literature on financial market linkages has evolved along two separate strands: the first one has focused on the stock markets and their determinants, and the second one has investigated the bond market linkages. Indeed, studying the co-movement between stock-bond markets is an important issue as their correlation plays a pivotal role in investors' diversification strategies and asset allocation decisions. This question—measuring co-movement between stock and bond markets—is still open and there is no general consensus among financial researchers. Results have shown that correlations between international equity markets vary strongly over time, and suggested two main explanations for this phenomenon. The first explanation is based on the belief that the transmission mechanism is stable, while the features of shocks (global versus idiosyncratic) are time varying. While the second explanation is based on the idea that periods of turbulence are characterized by the occurrence of abnormal shocks, which may come along with structural breaks in their transmission mechanism. Indeed, some authors, such as Keim and Stambaugh (1986), Campbell and Ammer (1993), and Kwan (1996), have

Emerging Markets and the Global Economy
http://dx.doi.org/10.1016/B978-0-12-411549-1.00026-0

empirically confirmed the theoretical evidence of positive correlation among stocks and bonds. Nevertheless, other works (Gulko, 2002; Connolly et al., 2005; Baur and Lucey, 2006) have proved the opposite; by supporting the phenomenon of "flight to quality" and "flight from quality."

In the literature, there are not abundant works that have attempted to check the nature of interdependence between stock and bond markets. The main existing studies have focused either on industrialized economies or on emerging Asia and Latin America but they have neglected the developing countries.

In this chapter, we deal with this limit and we focus on studying the co-movement between stock and bond markets in emerging market economies, especially in the context of MENA countries. Several reasons explain our interest in those kinds of markets. Firstly, the stock-bond co-movement is different from industrialized to emerging markets. In the literature, only a limited number of studies have analyzed this relationship in the case of emerging markets and to our acknowledgment there are no studies that focus on the MENA region. Secondly, emerging stock markets are characterized by high stock return volatility that may influence the bond market and then affect the portfolio diversification decisions. Thirdly, emerging bond markets, in the MENA region, are in the road of being developed. Fourthly, testing for evolving stock and bond markets in MENA region is particularly important because they have been subjected to a set of reforms in recent years with a view to improving performance and efficiency. In this direction, OECD (2005, p. 13) has observed, "*countries in the MENA region have been making significant attempts to strengthen their regulatory and institutional infrastructure for capital markets. Originally, many countries did not have institutions dedicated to capital market supervision. However, in the past few years, such institutions have been formed and efforts have been launched to enact necessary laws and regulations and to build human resources in the supervisory agencies.*" Due to limited published data on the bond markets in the MENA region, we only selected the three largest economies Egypt, Israel, and Turkey because they are the largest economies in the MENA region rather than oil producing countries.

Many econometric investigations are proposed to explore and measure market's interactions. Time-series analysis has started by the notion of rank reduction in order to measure co-movements between series (for more details, take a look at, Ahn and Reinsel, 1988). From this concept has arisen the cointegration approach (Engle and Granger, 1987): two processes are cointegrated if the spectral density has rank one, co-dependency (Gourieuroux and Peaucelle, 1992), which refers to linear combination of correlated process, has common features (Engle and Kozicki, 1993).

This class of concepts presents several problems. First, according to Quah (1993), Forni and Reichlin (1999) "*[...] high cross-correlation neither implies nor is implied by cointegration, common cycles or common features.*" Second, these measurements are binary. Finally, in order to test for rank reduction, we need to estimate the parameters of a VAR, which may be problematic when the number of time series is large. For all these reasons, and even if the notion of rank reduction is certainly interesting to characterize some aspects of the dynamic proprieties of multivariate time series, it is not the appropriate tool for the co-movement analysis.

If we define the co-movement as movement together, a second kind of empirical literature is proposed which consists of measuring the economic interaction according to a variety of correlation measurements (Forbes and Rigobon, 2002), such as: the dynamic correlation of Croux et al. (2001), and the concordance index of Harding and Pagan (2006). However, economic time series have many characteristics such as trends, cycles, seasonality, and serial correlation. A third kind of empirical literature employs a frequency approach in order to propose a relevant measure of co-movement. It is based on the coherence and cohesion function respectively for bivariate and multivariate processes. We propose in this chapter, similarly to Ftiti (2010) and Bouchouicha and Ftiti (2012), a frequency approach to measure the degree of dependence between stock and bond markets. The adopted methodology is based on the theory of evolutionary co-spectral analysis proposed by Priestley and Tong (1973).

In this research, we propose an original and a pioneer empirical methodology aiming to scrutinize the association between stock and bond markets, based on frequency approach. Indeed, we apply the evolutionary co-spectral analysis as defined by Priestley and Tong (1973) to measure the co-movement between stock and bond markets in our selected sample.

Contrary to classical approaches that apply either VAR model and/or cointegration technique, evolutionary co-spectral analysis does not depend on the assumption of the data. This approach proposed a valid spectral representation for the non-stationary process. Therefore, it does not show an "end-point problem": no future information is used, implied, or required as in band-pass or trend projection methods. The most important contribution with respect to traditional time-series analysis consists of the decomposition of series on two dimensions, that is frequency and time occurrence of the dependence. This allows studying time series according to different horizons, for instance short-term and medium term. Therefore, we aim at complementing the existing studies to uncover whether the results of the previous literature are robust to model specification, in particular in the dynamic dimension of the stock-bond market when selected MENA countries are accounted for.

The remainder of this chapter is organized as follows. Section 2 presents the related literature. Section 3 details the empirical methodology and data. Section 4 presents results and discussions. Finally Section 5 concludes the chapter.

2. RELATED LITERATURE

Two different strands of the literature on financial market linkages can be distinguished. The first one has focused on stock markets and their determinants and the second one has investigated the bond market linkages. Although there is a bulk of literature analyzing the stock market determinants in industrialized economies and in emerging Asia and Latin America, there is less attention to the question of bond market linkages especially in developing countries owing to the lack of data. In this chapter, we try to fill the gap in the literature by examining the MENA region stock markets and exploring the bond market linkages.

2.1. Stock Market Co-Movements

Since the seminal work of Grubel (1968), stock market co-movements have been the object of a series of studies that attempt to explain theoretically and empirically the linkages between stock markets and/or bond markets (with the macroeconomy), using different tools.

The literature focusing on the co-movement of international stock markets has grown rapidly such as: Granger and Morgenstern (1970), Eun and Shim (1989), Hamao et al. (1990), Richards (1995), Bekaert and Harvey (1995), Forbes and Rigobon (2002), Johnson and Soenen (2003), Bekaert et al. (2009), Gilmore et al. (2008), Syriopoulos (2007), Wang and Moore (2008), Syllignakis and Kouretas (2011), Egert and Kočenda (2011), Horvarth and Petroveski (2013), etc.

Without claiming completeness, we will concentrate on most referenced works. Granger and Morgenstern (1970) concluded that correlations between national stock market returns are surprisingly low. These results have been lately reversed by the empirical literature based on time-series analysis, aimed at identifying separately trend and cycle components in equity markets. According to Kasa (1992), the equity markets in US, Japan, England, Germany, and Canada between 1974 and 1990 share a single common stochastic trend, which reflects the existence of single common components in the structure of the dividend payments for all these markets. However, these results are controversial. Using daily data on US and main European stock markets, Kanas (1998) showed that US market is not pairwise cointegrated with any of the European equity markets. Consequently, there exist potential long-run benefits in risk reduction from diversifying in the US and European stocks.

Numerous empirical techniques have been used to measure co-movements between capital markets. King and Wadhwani (1990) and Bertero and Mayer (1990) used the Correlation between stock markets by presenting and discussing the evidence of changes in unconditional covariances and correlations between stock returns on high-frequency data around the crash of October 1987. Since then, many authors have been proposing different methods of modeling and testing the stability of correlations: ARCH and GARCH models (Longin and Solnik, 1995; Edwards and Susmel, 2000), cointegration (Kasa, 1992; Serletis and King, 1997), switching regimes (Hassler, 1995; Edwards and Susmel, 2000), etc. Those traditional approaches have been criticized by Forbes and Rigobon (2002). As a consequence, Rigobon (2003) proposed a new to test for contagion in the presence of interdependence. This type of research particularly focuses on the structural modeling of interdependence by adopting a limited information approach.

In order to extend this approach, Bonfiglioli and Favero (2005) tested the hypothesis of "no-contagion, only interdependence" through the full-information estimation of a small cointegrated structural model. This allows one to distinguish between long-run and short-run dynamics for equity prices on different markets.

In the context of European emerging market economies, Scheicher (2001) examined the co-movements between three markets: Czech Republic, Poland, and Hungary (CEE-3) in 1995–1997, using a VAR-CCC model. Scheicher (2001) presented evidence of both regional and global spillover in returns but only regional spillovers in volatilities. These results suggest that global shocks are transmitted to the Central European stock markets through return rather than volatility shocks.

Using a DCC model, Wang and Moore (2008) examined the interdependence between the same three emerging markets as in Scheicher (2001), vis-à-vis the aggregate euro area market. The results showed that the financial crisis and the enlargement of the European Union have a positive influence on the correlations between the CEE markets and the euro area market.

In the same context of the CEE markets and using the CCC and smooth transition CC(STCC) models, Savva and Aslanidis (2010) investigated, in the first step, the stock market integration for five countries (CEE-3, Slovakia, and Slovenia), and in the second step vis-à-vis the aggregate euro area market over the period 1997–2008. The largest CEE markets (namely, Czech Republic, Poland, and Hungary) reveal higher correlations vis-à-vis the euro area. Furthermore, the authors found increasing correlations among the CEE markets and between Polish, Slovenian, and Czech markets vis-à-vis the euro area.

Recently, the study of Horvarth and Petroveski (2013) analyzed both Central and South Eastern European (CEE-3, Croatia, Macedonia, and Serbia) stock markets and their correlations with Western Europe. The authors, using daily data from 2006 to 2011, analyzed the co-movements between the CEE and SEE stock markets vis-à-vis the euro area. The results issued from the estimation of a BEKK-GARCH model indicate a high integration degree between the CEE countries and the euro area and a low one between the SEE countries and the euro area. These results suggest the nonexistence of a significant change in the degree of stock markets correlations over the financial crisis.

Another strand of the literature attempts to analyze the co-movements between emerging and developed markets. For instance, Syllignakis and Kouretas (2011) employed a DCC model for weekly data from 1997 to 2009 in order to investigate the stock market correlations between CEE (CEE-3, Estonia, Romania, Slovakia, and Slovenia) vis-à-vis the US, Germany, and Russia. The results prove that correlations between stock markets increase over time, reducing consequently the diversification benefits in the CEE markets and can be mainly explained, according to the authors, by a greater degree of financial openness, followed by an increased presence of foreign investors in the region. Using the same econometric technique, Egert and Kočenda (2011) examined the co-movements between three developed (France, Germany, and United Kingdom) and three emerging stock markets (CEE-3). They suggested very low correlations among the emerging markets and between emerging and developed ones.

Finally, Gjika and Horvath (2012) examined the stock market co-movements among three major Central European markets (CEE-3) and between these markets and the aggregate euro area market. The authors found that asymmetric volatility is common in these stock markets. Therefore, asymmetries in the correlations are not as widespread as in the conditional variances. The results suggest also that the correlations have increased over time, and have been observed not only among all Central European stock markets but also between the Central European markets and the euro area. Similar results for the correlations among developed stock markets have been found by Cappiello et al. (2006) and Horvath and Poldauf (2012) in the context of US and Canadian stock markets.

In the context of emerging Latin American countries, equity markets co-movement has been investigated by several studies. Using cointegration tests and error correction models for a sample of six Latin American markets and the US market, Choudhry (1997) found evidence of cointegration relationship and significant causality among these markets. In the same order of idea, Chen et al. (2002) examined the interdependence between six stock markets in Latin America (Argentina, Brazil, Chile, Colombia, Mexico, and Venezuela) and showed evidence that there is a limited diversification benefit from investing in these markets. Authors explained their results according to the high-equity market co-movement in studied markets.

Johnson and Soenen (2003) examined the cross-country co-movement for the stock markets of Argentina, Brazil, Chile, Mexico, Colombia, Peru, Venezuela, and Canada with the US market and found a significant correlation linkage between these markets of the America and the US stock market. Fujii (2005) studied the intra- and inter-causal linkages among eight emerging stock markets in Asia and Latin America. Using standardized residuals estimated from an autoregressive process and a GARCH(1,1) model to calculate the residual correlation functions for the first and second moments of the stock returns, the author found the existence of significant causal linkages both within each region and across the two regions.

In a more recent paper, Arouri and Nguyen (2010), using a DCC-GARCH model, analyzed the time variations of conditional correlations between the markets of selected Latin American countries (Argentina, Brazil, Chile, Colombia, Mexico, and Venezuela). Arouri and Nguyen (2010) considered the correlations between these countries and the World stock market. The study showed that the degree of cross-market co-movements changed over time and has considerably increased since 1994.

Regarding the MENA region, there are only a handful of studies that focus on stock market co-movements. In an earlier study, Darrat et al. (2000) examined the interdependence of three emerging stock markets in the MENA region (Egypt, Morocco, and

Jordan) and global stock markets. Results support the important degree of segmentation of MENA markets from global markets and the existence of a high level of regional stock market co-movement. Otherwise, Neaime (2005), Gallegati (2005), Lagoarde-segot and Lucey (2007), and Cheng et al. (2010), found weak evidence of regional co-movement in the MENA region. They also found that MENA stock markets are largely segmented from global markets.

2.2. Stock-Bond Co-Movements

A common consensus emerged in economic literature on the importance to recognize the time-varying behavior of the correlation between stock and bond returns. There exists a very vast literature that presents different opinions regarding bond and stock relationship. This is because stock-bond correlations are very important for risk management and are related to the optimal allocation of financial assets.

Connolly et al. (2007), d'Addona and Kind (2006), and Kim et al. (2006) proved in their analysis that determining the nature of the time variation in the stock-bond correlation carries important implications for asset allocation and risk management. Much recent works have been made to explore various economic forces driving the time-varying stock-bond correlation. Connolly et al. (2007) showed that the future stock-bond correlation at higher daily frequency decreases with increasing stock market uncertainty in the US and several other major markets, arguably due to the flight-to-quality phenomenon. Kim et al. (2006), by studying many European markets, confirmed the similar role of stock market uncertainty. d'Addona and Kind (2006) showed that, although the volatility of real interest rates may increase the stock-bond correlation in G7 countries, the inflation volatility tends to reduce the correlation. However, Li (2002) showed that both the expected inflation uncertainty and the real interest rate uncertainty tend to increase the correlation between stock and bond returns.

De Pietri et al. (2009) analyzed the co-movements between bond markets in the Euro Area and the Eastern European Countries, in particular Poland and Hungary. They adopted the methodology developed in Rigobon (2003), to identify a structural VAR. The results shed light on the importance of two transmission channels between European emerging markets and Euro bond markets: "flight to quality" and "search for yield."

Lim et al. (1998), analyzing the relationship between bond markets and stock markets, found that bidirectional causality exists between the two markets. Previously, other scholars have investigated the same interrelationship, for both domestic markets (Shiller and Beltratti, 1992) and international markets (Solnik et al., 1996). These papers confirmed the stock-bond markets relationship. Indeed, they suggested that domestic stock prices tend to overreact to domestic bond yields, and the reaction could extend to foreign equity markets, due to the high degree of integration between major equity markets of the world. Maslov and Roehner (2004) considered the relationship between stock and bond prices both a natural and important one, and showed that there is a strong connection between stocks and bonds during crash-rebound episodes.

Our study joins the above literature by focusing on the stock and bond markets co-movements in order to deal with the lack of consensus on regional stock market co-movement for developing countries. It contributes to the existing literature by investigating the co-movement issue in the context of markets of the MENA region since they rank among the most mature markets within the universe of emerging countries. In addition, the MENA markets, actually, attract particular attention from global investors thanks to their great market openness.

3. EMPIRICAL ANALYSIS AND DATA

As mentioned in the Introduction, our objective is to measure the dynamic interaction between stock market and bond market for three selected MENA countries; Israel, Turkey, and Egypt. The interaction between these series is measured according to a frequency approach based on the theory of evolutionary co-spectral analysis of Priestley and Tong (1973). We measure the co-movement between series by the coherence function. We then propose a time-varying measure of this variable as Ftiti (2010).

3.1. Theory of the Evolutionary Co-Spectral (Priestley and Tong, 1973)

According to Priestley (1965), a non-stationary discrete[1] process or a continuous[2] process can be written as equation (1). Priestley and Tong (1973) extend the theory of the evolutionary spectral analysis of Priestley (1965, 1966), presented by Ftiti and Essaadi (2008), to the case of a bivariate non-stationary process. In this subsection, we summarize this theory.

Consider, for example, a bivariate continuous parameter process $\{X(t), Y(t)\}$ in which each component is an oscillatory process. Each component can be written as follows:

$$X(t) = \int_{-\infty}^{+\infty} A_{t,x}(w_1) e^{iwt} dZ_x(w_1), \tag{1}$$

$$Y(t) = \int_{-\infty}^{+\infty} A_{t,y}(w_2) e^{iwt} dZ_y(w_2), \tag{2}$$

where

$$\begin{aligned} E[dZ_x(w_1)dZ_x^*(w_2)] &= E[dZ_y(w_1)dZ_y^*(w_2)] \\ &= E[dZ_x(w_1)dZ_y^*(w_2)] = 0 \quad \text{for } w_1 = w_2, \end{aligned}$$
$$E[|dZ_x(w_1)|^2] = d\mu\ xx(w_1), \quad E[|dZ_y(w_1)|^2] = d\mu\ yy(w_1), \quad \text{and}$$

[1] A discrete process corresponds to a process of which the value of T is countable. Indeed, a time series is considered as a discrete process.

[2] A continuous process is a process used to describe the physical signal.

$$E[dZ_X(w_1)dZ_y^*(w_1)] = d\mu_{xy}(w)$$

with [.]* denoting the conjugate function of [.].

Let F_x, F_y denote respectively the families of oscillatory functions as:

$$\{\phi_{t,x}(w_1) \equiv A_{t,x}(w_1)e^{iwt}\}, \{\phi_{t,x}(w_1) \equiv A_{t,x}(w_1)e^{iwt}\}.$$

Priestley and Tong (1973) define the evolutionary power cross-spectrum at time t with respect to the families, F_x, F_y, $dH_{t,XY}(w)$ by:

$$dH_{t,XY}(w) = A_{t,X}(w)A_{t,Y}^*(w)d\mu_{XY}(w). \tag{3}$$

Further, if $\{X(t), Y(t)\}$ is a bivariate stationary process, so that F_x and F_y may be chosen to be the family of complex exponentials, namely, $F_x \equiv F_Y \equiv \{e^{iwt}\}$, $dH_{t,XY}(w)$, reduces to the classical definition of the cross-spectrum. Thus, for each t, we may write:

$$dH_{t,XY}(w) = E\left[A_{t,X}(w)dZ_X(w)A_{t,Y}^*(w)dZ_Y^*(w)\right]. \tag{4}$$

Priestley and Tong (1973) extend the above relation to the case of a non-stationary bivariate process where the amplitudes are time-dependent; correspondingly, the cross-spectrum is also time-dependent. Clearly, $dH_{t,XY}(w)$ is complex-valued, and, by virtue of the Cauchy-Schwarz equality, we have immediately that:

$$|dH_{t,XY}(w)|^2 \leq dH_{t,xx}(w)dH_{t,YY}(w), \quad \text{for each } t \text{ and } w. \tag{5}$$

If the measure $\mu_{XY}(w)$ is absolutely continuous with respect to the Lebesgue measure, we can write, for each t:

$$dH_{t,XY}(w) = h_{t,XY}(w)dw \tag{6}$$

and $h_{t,XY}(w)dw$ may then be termed the evolutionary cross-spectral density function.

3.2. Estimation of the Evolutionary Co-Spectral Density Function

The evolutionary cross-spectral density function estimation, which we develop here, is an extension of Priestley and Tong (1973) from the estimation of the evolutionary spectral density function in the univariate case, such as developed by Priestley (1965, 1966). In our analysis, we are interested in time series as discrete process.[3] We analyze two pairs of series-oil price series and stock market index of a country. Therefore, we detail the procedure to estimate the evolutionary cross-spectral density function.

Let a non-stationary discrete bivariate process $\{X(t), Y(t)\}$ have the Gramer representation for each $-\pi \prec w \prec \pi$:

$$X_t = \int_{-\pi}^{\pi} A_{t,X}(w)e^{iwt}dZ_X(w) \quad \text{and} \quad Y_t = \int_{-\pi}^{\pi} A_{t,Y}(w)e^{iwt}dZ_Y(w)$$

[3] For more details on continuous process, see Ftiti (2010).

with

$$E[dZ_x(w_1)dZ_x^*(w_2)] = E[dZ_y(w_1)dZ_y^*(w_2)]$$
$$= E[dZ_x(w_1)dZ_y^*(w_2)] = 0 \quad \text{for } w_1 = w_2,$$
$$E[|dZ_x(w_1)|^2] = d\mu\ xx(w_1), \quad E[|dZ_y(w_1)|^2] = d\mu\ yy(w_1), \quad \text{and}$$
$$E[dZ_X(w_1)dZ_y^*(w_1)] = d\mu_{xy}(w).$$

By virtue of the Cauchy-Schwarz inequality, we can write that:

$$|dH_{t,XY}(w)|^2 \leq dH_{t,xx}(w)dH_{t,YY}(w)$$

and

$$dH_{t,XY}(w) = h_{t,XY}(w)dw \quad \text{for each } t \text{ and } w,$$

where $h_{t,XY}(w)dw$ may then be termed the evolutionary cross-spectral density function.

The estimation of the evolutionary cross-spectral density function needs two filters. For the discrete univariate process, Priestley (1966) gives two relevant windows. These are relevant filters and they are tested by several works, such as Ahamada and Boutahar (2002), Ftiti and Essaadi (2008), Ftiti (2010), and Bouchouicha and Ftiti (2012). For the discrete bivariate process, Priestley and Tong (1973) adopt the same choice, that is:

$$g_u = \begin{cases} 1/(2\sqrt{h\pi})\ si|u| \geq h \\ 0 \qquad\qquad\quad si|u| \succ h \end{cases} \quad et \quad W_{T'v} = \begin{cases} 1/T'\ si|v| \leq T'/2, \\ 0 \qquad si|v| \succ T'/2. \end{cases} \tag{7}$$

Then, the estimation of the evolutionary cross-spectral density function is as follows:

$$\hat{h}_{t,XY}(w) = \sum_{v\in Z} W_{T'}(v)U_X(w, t-v)U_Y(w, t-v) \tag{8}$$

with

$$U_x(t, w) = \sum_{v\in Z} g(u)X(t-u)e^{-iw(t-v)}du, \tag{9}$$

$$U_Y(t, w) = \sum_{v\in Z} g(u)Y(t-u)e^{-iw(t-v)}du. \tag{10}$$

In this paper, we take $h = 7$ and $T' = 20$. We make the same choice[4] as Artis et al. (1992), Priestley (1965), Ahamada and Boutahar (2002), and Ftiti and Essaadi (2008).

According to Priestley (1988), if we have $E(\hat{h}(w)) \approx h_t(w)$, $\text{var}(\hat{h}(w))$, decreases when T' increases. $\forall(t_1, t_2)$, $\forall(w_1, w_2)$, $\text{cov}(\hat{h}_{t_1}(w_1), \hat{h}_{t_2}(w_2)) = 0$, if at least one of the following conditions (i) or (ii) is satisfied.

(i): *$|w \pm w'|$ are enough wide such as $||w_1 \pm w_2| \gg$ to the band width $|\Gamma(w)|^2|$.*
(ii): *$|S - t|$ is more broader than the function of $\{w(u)\}$.*

[4] This choice of values is justified by the fact that they respect the conditions (i) and (ii).

In order to respect conditions (i) and (ii), we choose $\{t_i\}$ and $\{w_j\}$ as follows:

$$t_i = \{18 + 20i\}_{i=1}^{I};$$

where $I = \left[\frac{T}{20}\right]$ and T the sample size:

$$w_j = \left\{\frac{\pi}{20}(1 + 3(j-1))\right\}_{j=1}^{7}.$$

To respect the (ii) condition, we inspect instability in these frequencies;

$$\frac{\pi}{20}, \frac{4\pi}{20}, \frac{7\pi}{20}, \frac{10\pi}{20}, \frac{13\pi}{20}, \frac{16\pi}{20}, \text{ and } \frac{\pi}{20}.$$

We finally have a co-spectral density function in 7 frequencies. However, we retain only two frequencies reflecting respectively short-term and medium-term. Indeed, the first frequency $\frac{\pi}{20}$ traduces the medium-term interdependence and the frequency $4\pi/20$ traduces the short-term one. The shift from the frequency domain to the time one takes place through the following formula: $\frac{2\pi}{\lambda}$, where λ is the studied frequency. For example, the frequency $\frac{\pi}{20}$ corresponds to $\frac{2\pi}{\frac{\pi}{20}}$ months = 3 years and one quarter, whereas $\frac{2\pi}{\frac{4\pi}{20}}$ refers to 10 month time frame.

3.2.1. Coherence Function

According to Priestley and Tong (1973), the evolutionary cross-spectral density function may be written as:

$$h_{t,XY}(w) = C_{t,XY}(w) - iQ_{t,XY}(w), \tag{11}$$

$$C_{t,XY}(w) = R\{h_{XY}(w_j, t)\},$$
$$Q_{t,XY}(w) = \text{Im}\{h_{XY}(w, t)\}, \tag{12}$$

and the real-valued functions $C_{t,XY}(w)$ and $Q_{t,XY}(w)$ termed the evolutionary co-spectrum and the evolutionary quadrature spectrum, respectively. If the measures $\mu_{XX}(w)$ and $\mu_{YY}(w)$ are absolutely continuous, Priestley and Tong (1973) similarly define the evolutionary auto-spectral density functions, $h_{XX}(w_j, t)$, $h_{YY}(w_j, t)$.[5] The coherency function is defined by the following expression:

$$C_{t,XY}(w) = \frac{|h_{t,XY}(w)|}{\{h_{t,XX}(w)\, h_{t,YY}(w)\}^{1/2}}$$
$$= \frac{|E[dZ_Y(w)dZ^*(w)]|}{\{E|dZ_x(w)|^2 E|dZ_Y(w)|^2\}^{1/2}}. \tag{13}$$

[5] For more details, see Ftiti (2010).

Priestley and Tong (1973) interpret $C_{t,XY}(w)$ as the modulus of the correlation coefficient between $dZ_X(w)$, $dZ_Y(w)$ or, more generally, as a measure of the linear relationship between corresponding components at frequency w in the processes $\{Y(t)\}$ and $\{Y(t)\}$.

The estimation of the coherency function is based on the estimation of the cross-spectral density function between two processes $\{Y(t)\}$ and $\{X(t)\}$ and the estimation of the auto-spectral density function of each process. So, the estimation coherency can be written as follows:

$$\hat{C}_{t,XY}(w) = \frac{|\hat{h}_{t,XY}(w)|}{\{\hat{h}_{t,XX}(w)\hat{h}_{t,YY}(w)\}^{1/2}}. \tag{14}$$

3.3. Data Description

In this study, we use daily data for bond and stock indices. All these indices are taken from DataStream Database from January 2000 to December 2012. To select the sample, we have adopted two criteria: (*i*) the most largely economies in the MENA region and (*ii*) the oil producing countries. Two kind of indices are used, the stock indices and the bond ones.

3.3.1. Stock Market Data

For the Tel-Aviv Stock Exchanges (TASE), we take the TA-100 index, which is one of the leading indices in the case of Israel.[6] For the Istanbul Stock Exchange (ISE), we use ISE national-100 index.[7] For Cairo and Alexandria Stock Exchanges (CASE), we employ the CASE 30 price index which includes the top 30 companies in terms of activities and liquidities.[8]

Indices from three markets of the MENA region are used to obtain returns. Continuously compounded rates of return, R_{it}, for each of the countries, were calculated as follows:

$$R_{it} = Ln\left(\frac{P_{it}}{P_{it-1}}\right),$$

where P_{it} is the closing price for each country index i at time t.

3.3.2. Bond Market Data

Concerning the bond returns, we use 10-year Treasury bond returns which express the yield on government bonds with a maturity of 10 years.

Note that for the evolutionary spectral estimation necessity, we lose 10 observations at the beginning and at the end.[9]

[6] This index consists of 100 stocks with the highest market capitalization that are included in TA-25 and TA-75 indices.

[7] This index contains the ISE national-50 and the ISE national-30 index companies.

[8] This index is weighted by market capitalization and adjusted by the free float.

[9] This interaction is measured by the dynamic coherence function developed by Ftiti (2010). The estimation of the coherence function was performed according to a code that we have developed with MATLAB software.

4. RESULTS AND DISCUSSIONS

Our analysis consists of measuring the degree of interaction between stock and bond markets. The major contribution of the study is to investigate the behavior of different stock-bond linkages for different horizons. We use co-spectral analysis in order to reveal the existence of a link between stock-bond markets. The coherence function allows us to identify the nature of the relationship and the convergence in each country.[10] Figures 1–3 show the co-movement respectively for the case of Israel, Turkey, and Egypt. We observe that the degree of co-movement between bond and stock markets is different across countries. Indeed, Figures 1 and 2 show that the coherence function is higher in the case of Israel than in the case of Turkey. However, relatively to Egypt, the dynamic coherence function remains high in the case of Turkey. In others words, bond and stock markets are more synchronized in the case of Israel than both Turkey and Egypt.

Let us analyze the pattern of the bond-stock markets interaction for each country separately. We start our analysis by studying the co-movement behavior between the stock and the bond markets in the case of Israel. We firstly observe the irregular evolution of their interdependence on the period 2000–2012. To test whether this interdependence is stronger during the expansion period or during the recession one, we consider evolutions in these different periods.

Figure 1 shows that, during the subprime crisis (2007–2009), the co-movement between stock and bond returns appears much weaker. This constitutes not only a weak argument in favor of diversification benefit from holding bonds with stocks but also rises challenges for asset allocation and risk management procedures. Hence, it is clear that

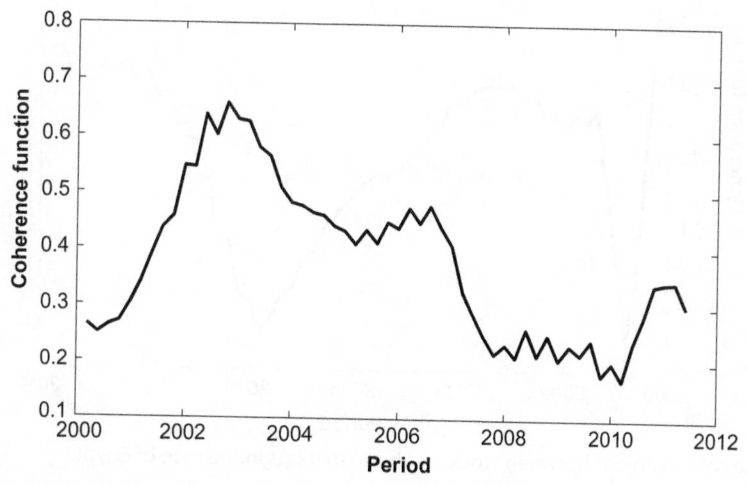

Figure 1 The co-movement between stock and bond markets in the case of Israel.

[10] The nature of dependence is short-run, medium-run or long-run.

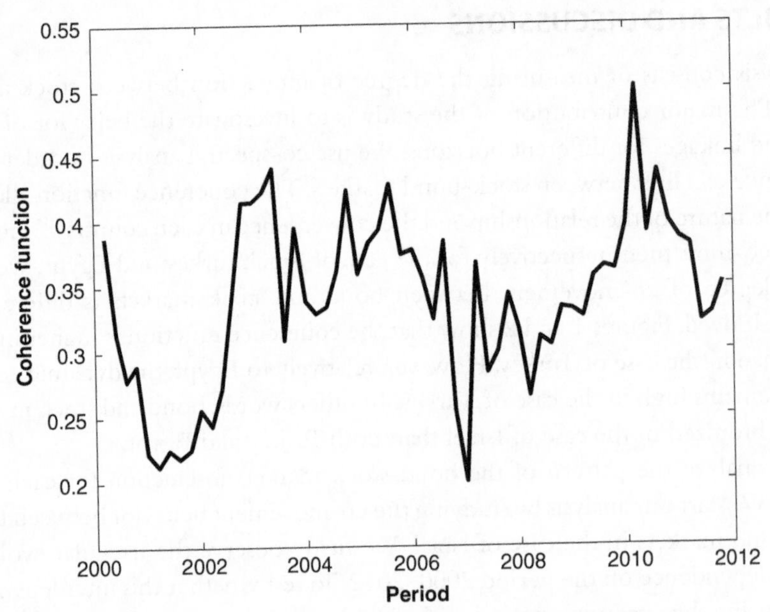

Figure 2 The co-movement between stock and bond markets in the case of Turkey.

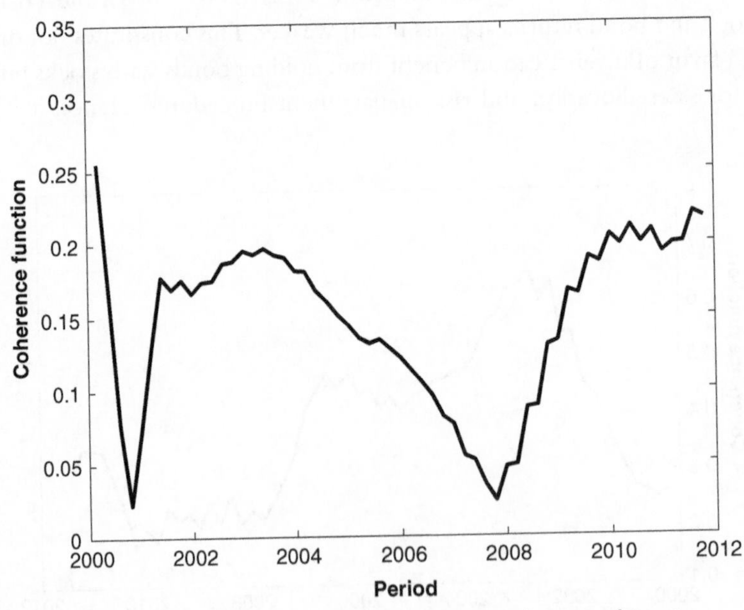

Figure 3 The co-movement between stock and bond markets in the case of Egypt.

the relation between bond and stock returns has been rather unstable over time. This constitutes evidence against constant correlation hypothesis.

Concerning the case of Turkey, Figure 2 shows some difference from the case of Israel. Indeed, the time-varying coherence function is less high in Turkey than in Israel and they have a different pattern. We can observe a high level of co-movement just before the 2001 Turkish crisis (Stock Market Crash). As a consequence, the relationship between stock and bond returns has fallen considerably in 2002.

From 2003 to the beginning of 2007, the degree of interdependence was still relatively stable with coherence mean value approximately equal to 0.35. Let us now focus on the impact of the subprime loans crisis. The results show that the relation between stock and bond returns has been very much lower during the subprime financial crisis. This result can be interpreted according to Hakan et al. (2010) who studied the impact of the Lehman Brothers bankruptcy on the volatility structure of Turkey price index (ISE-100). Therefore, the divergence in the co-movement in our analysis, during the subprime crisis, between bond and stock returns can be interpreted by the fact that investor panic at times of crisis is more intense than the enthusiasm expressed during growth periods. Unlike Forbes and Rigobon (2002), there is no significant co-movement under the financial crisis period.

Figure 3 presents the time-varying coherence function between bond and stock markets in the case of Egypt. The coherence function in the case of Egypt is different from those of Israel and Turkey. Indeed, the results show a high degree of divergence between bond and stock returns (coherence functions mean is approximately equal to 0.15, Table 1 in the Appendix).

Figure 3 shows a decrease in the level of co-movement since 2001 to the end of 2002 and under subprime crisis. At this level of study, the most outstanding result is that the degree of interdependence dropped drastically in 2010. In fact, this is an expected result since the European debt crisis coupled with the Arab spring exposed the fragility of Arab stock markets to absorb global shocks and to be under increasing pressure. Moreover, Egypt is one of the MENA countries which has high interaction levels with the European markets since around 23% of its non-oil exports go to the countries of the European Union.

Our analysis shows two main findings. Firstly, we show that bond and stock markets co-movement differs across countries in the MENA region. Indeed, there are different patterns in the selected countries. On the one hand, we show a higher degree of interdependence in the case of Israel than in the case of Turkey. On the other hand, there is no stock-bond co-movement in the case of Egypt. Secondly, financial crisis or business cycle fluctuations (downturn or expansion) seem to have a significant impact on the relationship between bond and stock returns, regardless of the status of the market (developed versus underdeveloped markets).

As economic implication these findings have many important facts. Co-movements in asset market returns provide indirect evidence on the expectations in financial markets and their reaction to common information. Indeed, there are two main channels through which information drives that relationship: (1) common sources of information influencing expectations in both stock and bond markets at the same time and (2) sources of information that only alter expectations in one market but spill over into the other market. It is very clear that, according to our results, the first channel is active; common sources of information influence expectations in both stock and bond markets. However, our contribution demonstrates that those markets have a divergent reaction to this information. The evolution of such co-movements provides some insights to policy makers on the interdependence between stock and bond markets in these economies, which may give rise to possible contagion risk during financial market turmoil.

In this work, we contribute to the literature of stock-bond co-movement in many points. Firstly, in our acknowledgment, this is the first study analyzing a selected MENA region. Previous analysis focuses more on stock markets co-movement and spillover effects. In addition, we propose in this chapter, a new time-varying measure of the interdependence degree between markets developed for the first time by Ftiti (2010) in other contexts. Finally, the co-movement behavior provides important information for portfolio diversification. Thus, any diversification benefits being required by the investor will depend crucially on the interdependence between stock and bond returns. Our findings show that the decline of the stock and bond markets co-movement in the turmoil periods (Turkish crisis, subprime crisis, and European debt crisis) can be explained by a more frequent rebalancing of portfolio investors due to the securities markets globalization and implied lower international diversification benefits.

5. CONCLUSION

The chapter investigates the issues of bond and stock markets interdependence in three selected MENA countries (Israel, Turkey, and Egypt) by measuring the co-movement between bond and stock returns according to the evolutionary co-spectral analysis as defined by Priestley and Tong (1973). The dataset consists of daily stock and bond returns from January 2000 to December 2012. Our analysis does not impose any kind of restriction or pre-treatment of the data (as it is the case of volatility analysis, for instance, which requires the series to be stationary or cointegration techniques, which can be only applied to time-series data integrated of order one). Moreover, no future information is used, implied, or required as in band-pass or trend projection methods. Finally, the evolutionary co-spectral analysis gives a robust frequency representation of non-stationary process.

Our analysis shows two main findings. Firstly, we point that stock-bond co-movement differs across countries in the MENA region, regardless of the status of the market (developed versus underdeveloped markets). Consequently, there is a higher degree of interdependence in the case of Israel than in the case of Turkey, but there is no co-movement between stock and bond markets in the case of Egypt. Secondly, financial crisis or fluctuations of the global business cycle seem to have a significant impact on the relationship between bond and stock returns.

These findings may have economic implications. Co-movements in asset market returns provide indirect evidence on the expectations in financial markets and their reaction to common information. According to our results, it is very obvious that a common source of information influences expectations in both stock and bond markets. However, our contribution consists in showing that those markets have a divergent reaction to this information. The evolution of such co-movements provides some insights to policy makers on the interdependence between stock and bond markets in these economies, which may give rise to possible contagion risk during financial market turmoil.

APPENDIX

Table 1 The mean of coherence function of the selected MENA countries.

Selected MENA countries	Mean of coherence function
Israel	0.401
Turkey	0.348
Egypt	0.126

REFERENCES

Ahamada, I., Boutahar, M., 2002. Tests for covariance stationarity and white noise, with application to Euro/US Dollar exchange rate. Economics Letters 77, 177–186

Ahn, S.K., Reinsel, G.C., 1988. Nested reduced-rank autoregressive models for multiple time series. Journal of The American Statistical Association 83, 849–856

Artis, M.J., Bladen-Hovell, R., Nachane, D.M., 1992. Instability of velocity of money, a new approach based on the evolutionary spectrum. CEPR Discussion Paper, n°735.

Arouri, M.E.-H., Nguyen, D.K., 2010. Time-varying characteristics of cross-market linkages with empirical application to Gulf stock markets. Managerial Finance 36, 57–70

Baur, D., Lucey, B.M., 2006. Flight-to-quality or contagion? An Empirical Analysis of Stock-bond Correlations. IIIS Discussion Paper Series 122.

Bekaert, G., Harvey, C.R., 1995. Time-varying world market integration. Journal of Finance 50, 403–444

Bekaert, G., Hodrick, R.J., Zhang, X., 2009. International stock return comovements. Journal of Finance 64, 2591–2626

Bertero, E., Mayer, C., 1990. Structure and performance: global interdependence of stock markets around the crash of October 1987. European Economic Review 34, 1155–1180

Bonfiglioli, A., Favero, C.A., 2005. Explaining co-movements between stock markets: the case of US and Germany. Journal of International Money and Finance 24, 1299–1316

Bouchouicha, R., Ftiti, Z., 2012. Real estate markets and the macroeconomy: a dynamic coherence framework. Economic Modelling 29, 1820–1829

Campbell, J.Y., Ammer, J., 1993. What moves the stock and bond markets? A variance decomposition for long term asset returns. Journal of Finance 48, 3–37

Cappiello, L., Gérard, B., Kadareja, A., Manganelli, S., 2006. Financial integration of new EU member states. European Central Bank Working Paper WP 683.
Chen, G.-M., Firth, M., Rui, O.M., 2002. Stock market linkages: evidence from Latin America. Journal of Banking and Finance 26, 1113–1141
Cheng, A.R., Jahan-Parvar, M.R., Rothman, P., 2010. An empirical investigation of stock market behavior in the Middle East and North Africa. Journal of Empirical Finance 17, 413–427
Choudhry, T., 1997. Stochastic trends in stock prices: evidence from Latin American markets. Journal of Macroeconomics 19, 285–304
Connolly, R., Stivers, C., Sun, L., 2005. Stock market uncertainty and the stock–bond return relation. Journal of Financial and Quantitative Analysis 40, 161–194
Connolly, R., Stivers, C., Sun, L., 2007. Commonality in the time-variation of stock–stock and stock–bond return comovements. Journal of Financial Markets 10, 192–218
Croux, C., Forni, M., Reichlin, L., 2001. A measure of co-movement for economic variables: theory and empirics. Review of Economics and Statistics 83, 232–241
d'Addona, S., Kind, A.H., 2006. International stock-bond correlations in a simple affine asset pricing model. Journal of Banking and Finance 30, 2747–2765
Darrat, A.F., Elkhal, K., Hakim, S.R., 2000. On the integration of emerging stock markets in the Middle East. Journal of Economic Development 25, 119–129
De Pietri, M., Sardena T., Zicchino, L., 2009. Co-movements between bond markets in euro area and Eastern European countries: an identification through heteroskedasticity. Paper Presented at the CICM Conference on 20 Years of Transition in Central and Eastern Europe: Money, Banking and Financial Markets, London Metropolitan Business School, London, 17–18 September 2009.
Edwards, S., Susmel, R., 2000. Interest Rate Volatility and Contagion in Emerging Markets: Evidence from the 1990s. University of California Los Angeles, mimeo.
Egert, B., Kočenda, E., 2011. Time-varying synchronization of the European stock markets. Empirical Economics 40, 393–407
Engle, R.F., Granger, C.W.J., 1987. Cointegration and error correction: representation and estimation and testing. Econometrica 55, 251–276
Engle, R.F., Kozicki, S., 1993. Testing for common features. Journal of Business and Economic Statistics 11, 369–380
Eun, C.S., Shim, S., 1989. International transmission of stock market movements. Journal of Financial and Quantitative Analysis 24, 241–256
Forbes, K., Rigobon, R., 2002. No contagion, only interdependence. Journal of Finance 57, 2223–2261
Forni, M., Reichlin, S., 1999. Dynamic common factors in large cross-section. Empirical Economics 21, 27–124
Ftiti, Z., 2010. The macroeconomic performance of the inflation targeting policy: an approach based on the evolutionary co-spectral analysis (extension for the case of a multivariate process). Economic Modelling 27, 468–476
Ftiti, Z., Essaadi, E., 2008. The inflation targeting effect on the inflation series: a new analysis approach of evolutionary spectral analysis. GATE Working Paper No. 08/32.
Fujii, E., 2005. Intra and inter regional causal linkages of emerging stock markets: evidence from Asia and Latin America in and out of crises. Journal of International Financial Markets, Institutions and Money 15, 315–342
Gallegati, M., 2005. Financial constraints and the balance sheet channel: a re-interpretation. Applied Economics 37, 1925–1933
Gilmore, C., Lucey, B., McManus, G., 2008. The dynamics of Central European equity market integration. Quarterly Review of Economics and Finance 48, 605–622
Gjika, D., Horvath, R., 2012. Stock market comovements in Central Europe: evidence from asymmetric DCC model. William Davidson Institute Working Papers Series WP1035.
Gourieuroux, C., Peaucelle, I., 1992. Série codépéndantes: Application à l'hypothèse de parité de pouvoir d'achat. Actualité Economique 68, 283–304
Granger, C.W.J., Morgenstern, O., 1970. Predictability of Stock Market Prices. Heath-Lexington Press, Lexington

Grubel, H.G., 1968. Internationally diversified portfolios: welfare gains and capital flows. American Economic Review 58, 1299–1314
Gulko, L., 2002. Decoupling. Journal of Portfolio Management 28, 59–67
Hakan, C., Soner, A., Yasemin, D.A., 2010. The impact of bankruptcy of Lehman brothers on the volatility structure of ISE-100 price index. Journal of Money, Investment and Banking 18, 1450–1488
Hamao, Y., Masulis, R., Ng, V., 1990. Correlations in price changes across international stock markets. Review of Financial Studies 3, 281–307
Harding, D., Pagan, A., 2006. Measurement of business cycles. Department of Economics Working Papers Series 966.
Hassler, J., 1995. Regime shifts and volatility spillovers on international stock markets. IIES Seminar Paper 603.
Horvarth, R., Petroveski, D., 2013. International stock market integration: Central and South Eastern Europe compared. Economics Systems 37, 81–91
Horvath, R., Poldauf, P., 2012. International stock market co-movements: what happened during the financial crisis? Global Economy Journal 12, 3
Johnson, R., Soenen, L., 2003. Economic integration and stock market comovement in the Americas. Journal of Multinational Financial Management 13, 85–100
Kanas, A., 1998. Volatility spillovers across equity markets: European evidence. Applied Financial Economics 8, 245–256
Kasa, K., 1992. Common stochastic trends in international stock markets. Journal of Monetary Economics 29, 95–124
Keim, D.B., Stambaugh, R.F., 1986. Predicting returns in the stock and bond markets. Journal of Financial Economics 17, 357–390
Kim, S.-J., Lucey, B.M., Wu, E., 2006. Dynamics of bond market integration between established and accession European union countries. International Finance Markets, Institutional and Money 16, 41–56
King, M., Wadhwani, S., 1990. Transmission of volatility between stock markets. Review of Financial Studies 3, 5–33
Kwan, S., 1996. Firm-specific information and the correlation between individual stocks and bonds. Journal of Financial Economics 40, 63–80
Lagoarde-Segot, T., Lucey, B.M., 2007. International portfolio: is there a role for the Middle East and North Africa? Journal of Multinational Financial Management 17, 401–410
Li, L., 2002. Macroeconomic factors and the correlation of stock and bond returns. Yale University Working Paper, 02-46.
Lim, E.S., Gallo, J.G., Swanson, P.E., 1998. The relationship between international bond markets and international stock markets. International Review of Financial Analysis 7, 181–190
Longin, F., Solnik, B., 1995. Is the correlation in international equity returns constant: 1960e1990? Journal of International Money and Finance 14, 3–26
Markowitz, H., 1952. Portfolio Selection. Journal of Finance 7, 77–91
Markowitz, H., 1959. Portfolio Selection, Efficient Diversification of Investments. John Wiley and Sons, New-York
Maslov, S., Roehner, B.M., 2004. The conundrum of stock versus bond prices. Physica A: Statistical Mechanics and its Applications 35, 164–182
Neaime, S., 2005. Portfolio diversification and financial integration of MENA stock markets. In: Neaime, Simon, Colton, Nora Ann (Eds.), Money and Finance in the Middle East: missed Opportunities or Future Prospects? Emerald Group Publishing Limited, pp. 3–20 (Research in Middle East Economics 6)
OECD, 2005. Challenges for Reform of Financial Markets in MENA Countries. <http://www.oecd.org/mena/investment/36086881.pdf>.
Priestley, M.B., 1965. Evolutionary spectra for non stationary process. Journal of Royal Statistic Society, Series B 27, 204–237
Priestley, M.B., 1966. Design relations for non stationary processes. Journal of Royal Statistic Society, Series B 28, 228–240
Priestley, M.B., 1988. Non-Linear and Non-Stationary Time Series Analysis. Academic Press, London
Priestley, M.B., Tong, H., 1973. On the analysis of bivariate non-stationary processes. Journal of Royal Statistic Society, Series B 35, 135–166

Quah, D., 1993. Comment. Journal of Business and Economics and Statistics 11
Richards, A.J., 1995. Comovements in national stock market returns: evidence of predictability, but not cointegration. Journal of Monetary Economics 36, 631–654
Rigobon, R., 2003. On the measurement of the international propagation of shocks: is the transmission stable? Journal of International Economics 61, 261–283
Savva, C.S., Aslanidis, C., 2010. Stock market integration between new EU member states and the eurozone. Empirical Economics 39, 337–351
Scheicher, M., 2001. The comovements of stock markets in Hungary, Poland and the Czech Republic. International Journal of Finance and Economics 6, 27–39
Serletis, A., King, M., 1997. Common stochastic trends and convergence of European union stock markets. The Manchester School 65, 44–57
Shiller, R., Beltratti, A., 1992. Stock prices and bond yields: can their co-movements be explained in terms of present value models? Journal of Monetary Economics 30, 25–46
Solnik, B., Boucrelle, C., Le Fur, Y., 1996. International market correlation and volatility. Financial Analysts Journal 52, 17–34
Syllignakis, M.N., Kouretas, G.P., 2011. Dynamic correlation analysis of financial contagion: evidence from the Central and Eastern European markets. International Review of Economics and Finance 20, 717–732
Syriopoulos, T., 2007. Dynamic linkages between emerging European and developed stock markets: has the EMU any impact? International Review of Financial Analysis 16, 41–60
Wang, P., Moore, T., 2008. Stock market integration for the transition economies: time-varying conditional correlation approach. The Manchester School 76, 116–133

CHAPTER 27

Equity Market Comovements Among Selected Emerging Countries from Long- and Short-Run Perspectives

Jamel Jouini*, Jihed Majdoub†, and Ines Ben Bouhouch‡

*Department of Economics, College of Business Administration, King Saud University, Saudi Arabia
†High School of Management of Tunis, University of Tunis, Tunisia
‡Faculty of Economics and Management of Nabeul, University of Carthage, Tunisia

1. INTRODUCTION

Since the pioneering work of Longin and Solnik (1974), researchers started to discover the advantages of diversification that allow drawing earnings when international equity markets are weakly correlated. The empirical studies are recently intensified by focusing on the effect of emerging equity market integration on the international diversification effectiveness. Within this context, Harvey (1995) outlines that US investors decrease their total portfolio risk when diversifying over emerging stock markets.[1] Jiang et al. (2010) point to the earnings drawn by Chinese investors by appending assets from emerging and Asian equity markets as well as the regional diversification effectiveness. The linkages between equity markets can induce contagion effects since investors incorporate price changes in other markets into their trading decisions. As a result, shocks can be transmitted to all markets especially in periods of high instability such as the stock market crash of 1987, the Asian financial crisis of 1997, and the recent global financial crisis of 2007–2009.

This chapter joins the empirical works of the literature in order to investigate the diversification opportunities in some emerging countries.[2] To that effect, we examine the international stock market integration by exploring the comovements among such countries because they are promising area for investors who want to reduce the portfolio risk. The study of comovements among equity markets also has important practical relevance for financial policy makers. This chapter also aims at checking the diversification effectiveness to foreign portfolio investors. We detect the comovements among markets of the same geographical region to examine the effect of geographical proximity, economic ties, and presence of similar investor groups and cross-listed companies on the

[1] The readers are also referred to Li et al. (2003), Phylaktis and Ravazzolo (2005) who reach similar conclusions in their analyses.

[2] Emerging countries are characterized by rapid economic growth and have investment opportunities.

Emerging Markets and the Global Economy
http://dx.doi.org/10.1016/B978-0-12-411549-1.00027-2

equity market linkages. We also deal with comovements among countries of different geographical regions to draw conclusions on the integration degree between them.

We also focus our attention on the comovements between the Chinese and other stock markets to depict the role played by China in the world integration. Such investigation is important for some reasons. First, the Chinese equity markets have recently opened to global investors and the domestic currency was liberalized. Second, China plays an important role in the region and for most emerging equity markets since it is considered as the most promising developing market. Third, the deregulation of the Chinese stock markets may increase their integration into international markets. This tells us more about the international diversification effectiveness based on emerging equity markets such as that of China. Finally, the Chinese Exchange's switch-over from a peg system to a managed float system enables us to investigated the stability of the Chinese stock market integration into international emerging equities.

Most of the previous empirical studies have investigated the international financial integration between markets using typically the cointegration approaches developed by Engle and Granger (1987), Johansen (1988), and Gregory and Hansen (1996). This chapter makes a methodological contribution to extend these techniques by examining the long-run comovements among equity markets based on the ARDL (Autoregressive Distributed Lags) bounds approach to cointegration of Pesaran et al. (2001).[3] This approach enables us to provide results with desirable properties leading to make reliable conclusions as shown by recent empirical studies on different areas. Moreover, we opt for the DCC-GARCH process of Engle (2002) to analyze the short-run comovements among stock markets. This approach offers the possibility of computing the conditional correlations in a time-varying framework in order to investigate the stock market integration degree among countries over time. The goal of combining these two approaches is to deal with comovements among equities from long- and short-run perspectives as the financial integration process between markets may differ over both long- and short-run.

The rest of the chapter is structured as follows. Section 2 reviews the major empirical works in the literature related to international equity market integration, and states the motivations for this chapter. Section 3 introduces the econometric methods employed to investigate the long- and short-run comovements among emerging equity markets. Section 4 presents a preliminary analysis of the data and discusses the results of stock market integration. The findings outline that the equity market integration between the selected emerging countries, in particular between China and the other countries, is quite high and has been affected by the recent global financial crisis. Moreover, the comovements between countries of the same geographical region appear to be important, which may be due to the similar political characteristics and economic ties. The obtained results are promising and have important implications for portfolio theory and diversification issues. Section 5 concludes the chapter.

[3] To the best of our knowledge, the ARDL approach was not used in the literature related to financial integration of equity markets.

2. INTEGRATION OF EQUITY MARKETS

Within the framework of stock market integration, investors generally seek to include in their portfolio assets characterized by weak correlation for potential diversification benefits. In the same context, Grubel (1968), and Levy and Sarnat (1970) outline that investing in international equity markets is motivated by the fact that correlation between assets is lower than that observed for domestic assets. Therefore, the low correlation between foreign equity markets is the key factor of international diversification, but this correlation is dynamic over time, which affects the concept of risk reduction. In the last decades, the globalization seems to contribute to rise the correlation between foreign equity markets. King et al. (1994) attempt to bring something to this, but their findings do not show evidence of increased correlations between equity assets. Solnik et al. (1996) reach similar conclusions by examining the links between foreign equities and the US stock market. Forbes and Rigobon (2002) outline that the links between international stock markets can be strong over tranquil periods as well as during crisis periods, which can lead to lose some diversification benefits.

The stock market integration between developed countries is strong and registers some increase. This has led investors to look at emerging equity markets hoping for weaker correlations between such markets and their developed counterparts. Various empirical works such as Driessen and Laeven (2007), Chang et al. (2008), and Gupta and Donleavy (2009) address the issue of investments into emerging stock markets for an investor from developed countries. Some empirical works outline that financial markets are less integrated, while others argue that financial integration has increased due to several factors. Voronkova (2004) examines empirically the existence of long-run linkages between emerging equity markets of Central Europe and developed stock markets of Europe and the United States. The results obtained from the application of the cointegration approach of Gregory and Hansen (1996) point out that emerging stock markets become more integrated with mature markets after controlling for breaks. Aggarwal and Kyaw (2005) investigate the financial integration of three equity markets (US, Canada, and Mexico) before and after the formation of the NAFTA area in 1993. Based on Johansen's (1988) cointegration tests, the authors show evidence of financial integration in the three markets only after the 1993 passage of NAFTA, which has important implications for policy makers and managers. In a related work, Arouri et al. (2013) investigate the short-run linkages and equity contagion among US and Latin American markets based on a DCC-GARCH model and a structural break analysis over the period 1988–2009. The results reveal time-varying comovements among markets and structural breaks in the correlation patterns over the study period. They do not also support the hypothesis of equity contagion for the crises of 1994, 1997, and 2007 in most cases.

Kenourgios and Samitas (2011) investigate the comovements between emerging Balkan stock markets, the United States, and mature markets of Europe over the period 2000–2009 based on usual cointegration methods and the Asymmetric DCC-GARCH model of Cappiello et al. (2006). The results reveal long-run links among the Balkan equity markets, and show high correlation between stock markets during the global financial crisis of 2008. The authors stress that their findings have important implications for international portfolio diversification. Recently, Horvath and Petrovski (2013) opt for a multivariate GARCH model to analyze the extent of short-run comovements between Western and South-Eastern European equity markets over the period 2006–2011. The results show evidence of high comovements among emerging countries and weak linkages between them and their developed counterparts, with the exception of Croatia which is integrated with Western Europe. An outstanding feature is that the global financial crisis of 2007–2009 does not exert any effect on the comovements among equity markets. In a related work, Gjika and Horvath (2013) examine the short-run linkages among Central Europe and euro area over the daily period from 2001 to 2011 based on a DCC-GARCH approach. Cross-market links are found to be strong and affected by the global financial crisis. There is also evidence of asymmetry in the conditional variances and correlations through stock markets. The results have important implications and stress that the diversification earnings of investors decrease disproportionally during instability periods.

Some empirical works have been conducted for the Asian region. Chelley-Steeley (2004) explores the empirical evidence of the stock market integration speed among developed and emerging Asia-Pacific countries. He finds that the equity market integration among emerging countries is faster than that between emerging and developed countries. Chi et al. (2006) show evidence of increased stock market integration of emerging Asian countries with Japan and the United States after the Asian financial crisis of 1997. In a related study, Singh et al. (2010) investigate the return and volatility transmission across North American and Asian equity markets. Kim et al. (2006) employ a gravity and a consumption risk-sharing models to show that the East Asian financial markets are relatively less integrated between them than to the global market. Jeon et al. (2006) indicate that the financial integration degree in East Asian countries increased recently. Guillaumin (2009) opts for a modified Feldstein-Horioka model to find evidence of high financial integration degree in East Asia. Yu et al. (2010) investigate financial integration of some Asian equity markets. They show that the integration degrees between developed and emerging equity markets are different, which may be due to the institutional, economic, and political dissimilarities across Asian countries. Most of these research works do not lead to reliable conclusions about the empirical evidence of the financial integration extent in the Asian region.

Most of studies on the issue of financial market integration in Asia suggest that Asian equity markets are only weakly integrated with the region compared with the integration with global markets. Nevertheless, the comovements between the Chinese equity market and other international stock markets were not extensively analyzed in the literature. The exception is the empirical work of Huang et al. (2000) who employ the cointegration approach of Gregory and Hansen (1996) to investigate the relationship between the equity markets of the United States, Japan, and the South China Growth Triangle. The results show evidence of long-run links between only the Shanghai and Shenzhen stock markets.

Most of empirical works in the literature therefore arrive at conflicting conclusions on the existence of long-run relationships between emerging equity markets. Moreover, these studies have not included the emerging countries from Africa in the analysis of comovements, despite the fact that their equity markets have experienced increased development and attract foreign investors. These shortcomings had motivated us to further investigate the comovements among emerging equity markets and their implications for potential diversification benefits by including an African country in the analysis. It is worthwhile at this stage to examine the stock market integration of China with other emerging countries. The resulting inference could yield interesting insights to practitioners, investors, and policy makers.

3. EMPIRICAL METHODS

We consider two econometric techniques to investigate empirically the comovements among selected emerging equity markets. Indeed, we first employ the ARDL approach to cointegration of Pesaran et al. (2001) to deal with long-run linkages. We then explore the short-run comovements based on the multivariate DCC-GARCH model of Engle (2002). The combination of these approaches allows distinguishing the comovements of the long-run from those of the short-run since, as we know, two equity markets may comove over the short-run and not over the long-run, and vice versa.

3.1. ARDL Approach to Cointegration

The ARDL approach developed by Pesaran et al. (2001) is a very useful tool to examine the long-run relationship between variables since it greatly improves the properties of the obtained estimates regardless of whether these variables are stationary or not. Unlike the usual cointegration techniques, the ARDL approach allows the lag length of the variables to differ.[4] The ARDL approach has also the advantage of being applied even for small samples. The analysis of cointegration between equity markets is then based on the following ARDL$(p,\ p_1,\ p_2, \ldots, p_n)$ model:

$$\Delta LY_t = \alpha+\beta t+\sum_{i=1}^{p} a_i \Delta LY_{t-i}+\sum_{k=1}^{n}\sum_{i=0}^{p_k} b_{ki}\Delta LX_{k,t-i}+\lambda LY_{t-1}+\sum_{k=1}^{n}\lambda_k LX_{k,t-1}+u_t, \quad (1)$$

where ΔLY and ΔLX_k are changes in the natural logarithm of the variables Y and X_k ($k = 1,\ 2,\ \ldots,\ n$), and n is the number of explanatory variables. a_i and b_{ki} are the short-run coefficients, and λ and λ_k are the long-run coefficients. The optimal lag lengths

[4] According to Pesaran et al. (2001), the lag length can be identical for all lagged variables without affecting the asymptotic theory.

$(\hat{p}, \hat{p}_1, \hat{p}_2, \ldots, \hat{p}_n)$ can be determined based on the Schwarz information criterion by estimating $(m+1)^{n+1}$ regression models given the maximum lag length m.

The null hypothesis of no cointegration between variables is formulated analytically as follows: $\lambda = \lambda_1 = \lambda_2 = \cdots = \lambda_n = 0$, which corresponds to the Fisher test of joint significance of the lagged variables. Under the null hypothesis, the asymptotic distribution of the test statistic is non-standard and, as a result, two sets of critical values for $I(0)$ and $I(1)$ variables are determined. In this context, the null hypothesis of no cointegration is rejected if the observed value of the test statistic is greater than the upper critical bound regardless of whether the variables are $I(0)$ or $I(1)$. On the other hand, we conclude in favor of no cointegration between the variables if the computed test statistic does not exceed the lower critical bound regardless of whether the variables are $I(0)$ or $I(1)$. The test is inconclusive when the empirical test statistic is between the lower and upper critical bounds regardless of whether the variables are $I(0)$ or $I(1)$.

For the variables where the null hypothesis of no cointegration is rejected, we estimate the long-run coefficients based on the following ARDL$(p, p_1, p_2, \ldots, p_n)$ model:

$$\Phi(L,p)\,Y_t = \alpha_0 + \sum_{i=1}^{n} \beta_i(L,p_i)\,X_{it} + \gamma' v_t + \varepsilon_t, \tag{2}$$

where $\Phi(L,p) = 1 - \phi_1 L - \phi_2 L^2 - \cdots - \phi_p L^p$, $\beta_i(L,p_i) = \beta_{i0} + \beta_{i1} L + \beta_{i2} L^2 + \cdots + \beta_{ip_i} L^{p_i}$ $(i = 1, 2, \ldots, n)$, Y_t is the dependent variable, X_{it} is the ith explanatory variable, v_t is the vector of deterministic variables, and ε_t is the disturbance term. After selecting the appropriate ARDL$(\hat{p}, \hat{p}_1, \hat{p}_2, \ldots, \hat{p}_n)$ model, the long-run coefficients are given by:

$$\hat{\mu}_i = \frac{\hat{\beta}_{i0} + \hat{\beta}_{i1} + \hat{\beta}_{i2} + \cdots + \hat{\beta}_{i\hat{p}_i}}{1 - \hat{\phi}_1 - \hat{\phi}_2 - \cdots - \hat{\phi}_{\hat{p}}}, \qquad i = 1, 2, \ldots, n. \tag{3}$$

To confirm the cointegration between variables, we estimate the following error correction model:[5]

$$\begin{aligned}\Delta Y_t = {} & -\left(1 - \hat{\phi}_1 - \hat{\phi}_2 - \cdots - \hat{\phi}_{\hat{p}}\right) ECM_{t-1} + \sum_{i=1}^{n} \beta_{i0}\Delta X_{it} + \gamma'\Delta v_t \\ & - \sum_{j=1}^{\hat{p}-1} \phi_j^* \Delta Y_{t-j} - \sum_{i=1}^{n}\sum_{j=1}^{\hat{p}_i-1} \beta_{ij}^* \Delta X_{i,t-j} + \varepsilon_t,\end{aligned} \tag{4}$$

where $ECM_t = Y_t - \sum_{i=1}^{n} \hat{\mu}_i X_{it} - \hat{\eta}' v_t$, $\hat{\eta}$ is the vector of the long-run coefficients of the deterministic variables, and ϕ_j^* and β_{ij}^* are the short-run coefficients.

[5] Note that the error correction model enables us to determine the dynamic adjustments of short-run deviations of the variables from their long-run equilibrium state.

3.2. DCC-GARCH Model

To assess the extent of short-run comovements among equity markets, we rely on dynamic conditional correlations obtained from the estimation of the following multivariate DCC-GARCH model of Engle (2002):

$$\begin{cases} R_t = \mu + \Phi R_{t-1} + \varepsilon_t \\ \varepsilon_t = H_t^{1/2} \eta_t \end{cases}, \tag{5}$$

where R_t is a $(l \times 1)$ vector of equity returns, μ is a $(l \times 1)$ vector of constant terms, $\Phi = diag\left(\phi_1, \phi_2, \ldots, \phi_l\right)$ is a $(l \times 1)$ diagonal matrix of coefficients, ε_t is a $(l \times 1)$ vector of the error terms of the conditional mean equations, and η_t is a sequence of *i.i.d.* random errors. The conditional variance-covariance matrix H_t is defined as follows:

$$H_t = D_t P_t D_t, \tag{6}$$

where $D_t = diag\left(\sqrt{h_t^1}, \sqrt{h_t^2}, \ldots, \sqrt{h_t^l}\right)$,[6] and P_t is the $(l \times l)$ conditional correlation matrix varying over time, i.e.,

$$P_t = \left(diag(Q_t)\right)^{-1/2} Q_t \left(diag(Q_t)\right)^{-1/2}, \tag{7}$$

where $Q_t = \left(1 - \alpha - \beta\right) \bar{Q} + \alpha \eta_{t-1} \eta_{t-1}' + \beta Q_{t-1}$ is the $(l \times l)$ symmetric positive definite matrix, $\bar{Q}$ is the $(l \times l)$ matrix of unconditional variances of the standardized errors η_t, and α and β are non-negative scalars such that the mean-reverting condition is satisfied, $\alpha + \beta < 1$. The conditional correlation coefficient between two equities, $\rho_{ij,t}$, is then given by

$$\rho_{ij,t} = \frac{\left(1 - \alpha - \beta\right) \bar{q}_{ij} + \alpha \eta_{i,t-1} \eta_{j,t-1} + \beta q_{ij,t-1}}{\left(\left(1 - \alpha - \beta\right) \bar{q}_{ii} + \alpha \eta_{i,t-1}^2 + \beta q_{ii,t-1}\right)^{1/2} \left(\left(1 - \alpha - \beta\right) \bar{q}_{jj} + \alpha \eta_{j,t-1}^2 + \beta q_{jj,t-1}\right)^{1/2}}, \tag{8}$$

where $q_{ij,t}$ is the element of the ith row and jth column of the matrix Q_t. The model is estimated by the maximum likelihood estimation method based on the optimization algorithm of Berndt-Hall-Hall-Hausman (BHHH).

4. DATA AND RESULTS

We consider equities of five emerging countries (Brazil, China, Mexico, South Africa, and Thailand) over the daily period from January 14, 2008 to January 14, 2013 (yielding thus 1306 observations).[7] The data are gathered from the Morgan Stanley Capital

[6] The conditional variances are specified as univariate GARCH (1,1) processes.

[7] The sample period is sufficiently recent and long enough to account for the last events that have occurred in the international stock markets and to allow better examination of the long-run relationship between equities based on the ARDL approach.

Table 1 Key indicators of emerging equity markets.

Market	Year launched	Market capitalization (US$ millions)	Number of companies	Index
Brazil	31/12/1988	487, 525.700	81	MSCI Brazil
China	7/9/2011	1, 635, 844.420	648	MSCI all China
Mexico	31/12/1987	204, 280.120	26	MSCI Mexico
South Africa	31/12/1995	275, 713.360	50	MSCI S. Africa
Thailand	31/12/1988	104, 483.840	25	MSCI Thailand

International (MSCI) database, and are expressed in US dollars to preserve homogeneity across equity markets and to avoid currency risk effects. Contrary to previous works on the stock market integration between emerging markets, our empirical investigation embodies countries from three different geographical regions, i.e., Africa, Asia, and Latin America. This enables us to further diversify the analysis of comovements among different countries and, therefore, to have more information on the process of international portfolio diversification. The analysis was conducted over the entire period and the post-crisis period from November 3, 2008 to January 14, 2013 in order to examine the financial integration process after the worsening of the global financial crisis with the collapse of equity markets in late 2008. Some empirical results are not reported in the chapter to preserve space, but are available upon request from the corresponding author.

Some key indicators about the emerging equity markets are reported in Table 1. The MSCI all China index captures large and mid-cap representation across all China securities listed in China, Hong Kong, the US, and Singapore. The MSCI index of the other countries allows measuring the performance of the large and mid-cap segments of the corresponding market of each country. The Brazilian, Mexican, and Thai equity markets were launched in late 1980s, the South African market was set up in the middle of the 1990s, and the Chinese market was however established in late 2011. Under these conditions, the data prior to the launch date of the Chinese market are backtested data. The Chinese equity market is the largest one in terms of market capitalization (1,635,844.420 US$ Millions) and listed firms (648). Another striking feature is that the equity markets with more listed companies have the highest market capitalization.

4.1. Data and Preliminary Analysis

The time-paths of the selected five emerging equities in levels and returns[8] are plotted in Figures 1 and 2. The level series indicate that the markets experience common time trending behavior throughout the study period, which is indicative of potential cointegration relationships between them. The equity markets in levels were heavily affected by the

[8] The returns are computed as the natural logarithm of the ratio between two successive prices.

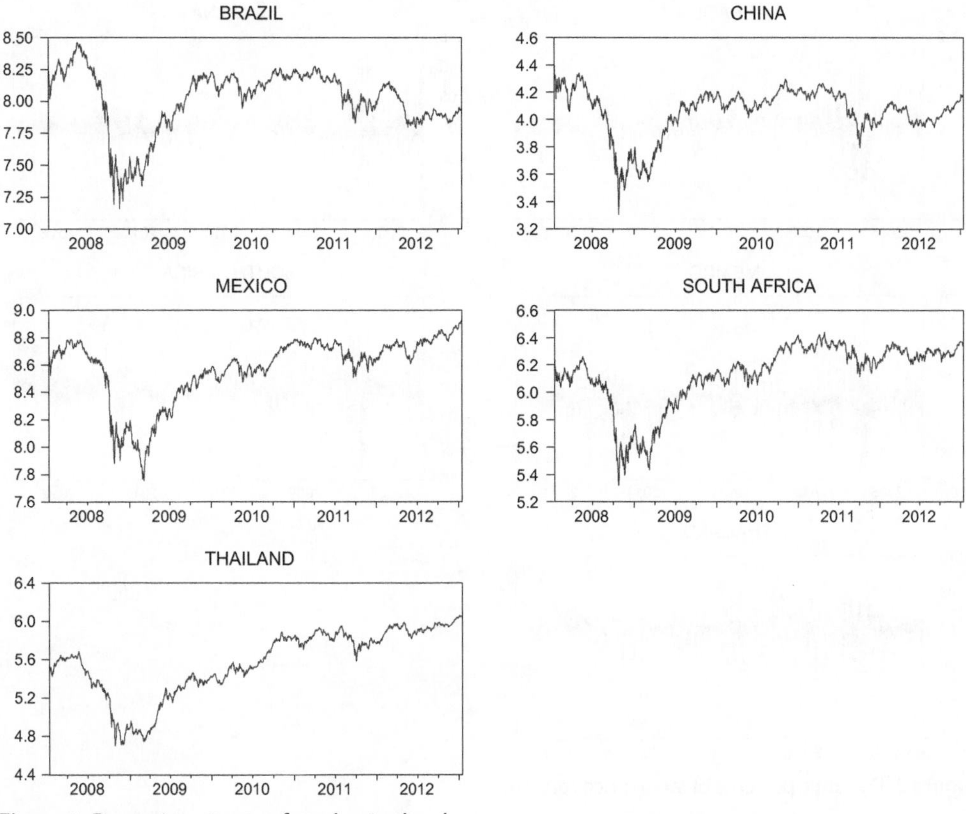

Figure 1 Dynamic patterns of stock price levels.

global financial crisis of 2008 since the values fell enormously compared with those before the crisis. Some recovery of the markets was observed for some time after the crisis. We also observed a turbulent period in late 2011 when the stock prices slightly decreased. The return series were unstable and more volatile during the global financial crisis of 2008 and in late 2011. Therefore, this first examination of the data tells us about potential comovements among equities.

Table 2 reports descriptive statistics and stochastic properties of the series over the whole sample. The Thai equity market is the most efficient since it displays the highest average returns. The Brazilian and Chinese stock markets experience negative average returns, which may be due to the global financial crisis. In addition to the best performance of the Thai market, it is the least volatile since its returns have lower risk than the other stock markets. This suggests that for investors, the Thai equity market may be attractive in terms of risk-return tradeoff. The skewness coefficient is negative in all cases, except for the Chinese returns, which may be indicative of extreme negative returns. The kurtosis coefficient exceeds three in all cases for the returns. For the stock prices in

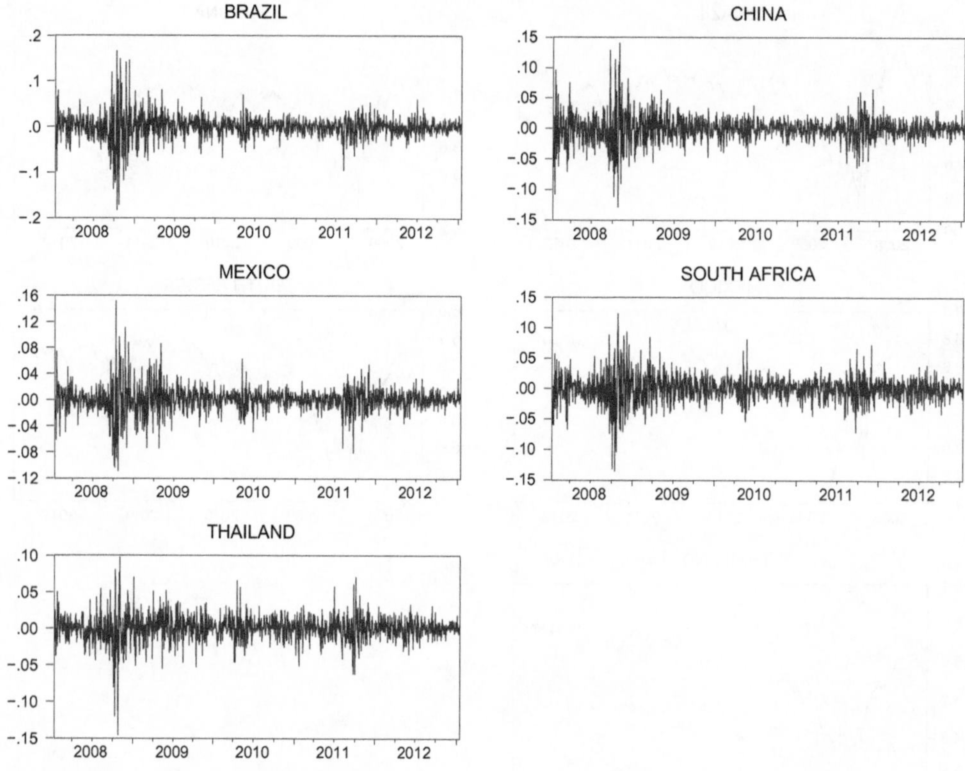

Figure 2 Dynamic patterns of stock price returns.

levels, the coefficient is less than three for the Thai market. These characteristics comply with the results of the Jarque-Bera test that strongly rejects the normal distribution of the level and return series. There is strong evidence of ARCH effects in all series. The Ljung-Box test reveals autocorrelation for all series.

The empirical unconditional correlations between equities depicted in Table 3 indicate that the emerging stock price levels are positively correlated between them. For the returns, the highest correlation is observed between Brazil and Mexico, which may be explained by the strong economic links between the two countries. However, the lowest correlation is between Brazil and Thailand (0.392), and Mexico and Thailand (0.393), which may support the view that international investors can still get important earnings from adding both financial assets of these three emerging countries into their international diversified portfolios. This correlation analysis gives us initial insights into the linkages between the selected emerging markets, but cannot be determinant. Therefore, an empirical issue on the relationship between such markets by employing powerful techniques is gainful to get reliable and final conclusions.

Table 2 Descriptive statistics and statistical properties of the series over the entire period.

	Mean	Std. dev.	Skew.	Kurt.	JB	ARCH	LB
Level series							
Brazil	8.010	0.247	−1.103	3.858	304.979*	1155.525*	14730*
China	4.056	0.175	−1.329	4.551	515.417*	1235.070*	14237*
Mexico	8.574	0.239	−1.343	4.054	453.080*	1265.649*	14902*
South Africa	6.130	0.229	−1.359	4.225	483.960*	1259.470*	14852*
Thailand	5.568	0.347	−0.769	2.676	134.578*	1279.731*	15310*
Returns							
Brazil	−2.29E-4	0.026	−0.319	11.955	4382.398*	669.945*	28.221*
China	−1.65E-4	0.022	0.040	9.202	2091.841*	395.324*	25.522**
Mexico	1.94E-4	0.020	−0.027	10.168	2794.098*	395.892*	26.691*
South Africa	7.60E-5	0.022	−0.213	7.379	1052.454*	339.572*	22.359**
Thailand	4.19E-4	0.018	−0.522	9.533	2380.024*	295.339*	21.707**

Notes: JB is the normality test of Jarque-Bera; ARCH refers to the test for conditional heteroskedasticity of order 12; LB is the Ljung-Box test for autocorrelation of order 12.
*Indicates the rejection of the null hypothesis of the associated tests at 1% level.
**Indicates the rejection of the null hypothesis of the associated tests at 5% level.

Table 3 Empirical unconditional correlations between equities over the entire period.

	Brazil	China	Mexico	S. Africa	Thailand
Level series					
Brazil	1.000	0.937	0.744	0.746	0.572
China		1.000	0.784	0.801	0.648
Mexico			1.000	0.942	0.929
South Africa				1.000	0.950
Thailand					1.000
Returns					
Brazil	1.000	0.447	0.818	0.663	0.392
China		1.000	0.422	0.509	0.613
Mexico			1.000	0.661	0.393
South Africa				1.000	0.420
Thailand					1.000

We now assess the degree of integration of level and return series by employing the unit root ADF (see Said and Dickey, 1984) and stationarity KPSS (see Kwiatkowski et al., 1992) tests. This exercise enables us to know whether we can apply the ARDL approach to cointegration or not since it is not valid for the case of series integrated of order two or more (see Ang, 2007). The results depicted in Table 4 suggest that the ADF test

Table 4 Unit root and stationarity tests over the entire period.

	ADF		KPSS		Zivot-Andrews	
	Intercept	Trend	Intercept	Trend	Break in trend	Break date
Level series						
Brazil	−2.010	−2.018	0.338	0.320*	−4.391	3/3/2009
China	−2.603***	−2.773	0.433***	0.290*	−4.702	9/3/2009
Mexico	−1.362	−2.220	1.824*	0.306*	−5.691*	9/3/2009
South Africa	−1.657	−2.785	2.397*	0.310*	−4.815	9/3/2009
Thailand	−0.446	−2.049	2.978*	0.339*	−4.310	9/3/2009
Returns						
Brazil	−34.596*	−34.584*	0.101	0.098	−12.949*	24/10/2008
China	−36.213*	−36.225*	0.168	0.096	−11.941*	24/10/2008
Mexico	−32.822*	−32.833*	0.179	0.082	−10.867*	23/10/2008
South Africa	−34.500*	−34.497*	0.134	0.097	−18.338*	23/10/2008
Thailand	−35.356*	−35.373*	0.221	0.125***	−10.950*	24/10/2008

*Indicates the rejection of the null hypothesis of the associated tests at 1% level.
***Indicates the rejection of the null hypothesis of the associated tests at 10% level.

generally concludes in favor of unit root for the stock price levels and stationarity for the returns at conventional significance levels. The KPSS test supports the conclusions of the ADF test for almost all series. We have also applied the unit root test developed by Zivot and Andrews (1992) that allows an unknown break in trend function.[9] Our motivation for this test is that the ADF and KPSS tests are not powerful when potential structural changes affect the variables since, as shown above in Figure 1, all stock prices registered sharp falls during the global financial crisis. The test produces results that comply with those of the ADF and KPSS tests (see Table 4). The detected break date may be due to the global financial crisis. Overall, the evidence in favor of stock prices integrated of order one, $I(1)$, is quite overwhelming and consequently, the analysis of cointegration between them can be conducted based on the ARDL approach. The tests lead to the same conclusions over the post-crisis period.

4.2. Long-Run Comovements

We first consider all possible specifications because there is no prior information about the long-run linkage directions between all equities. Indeed, there are five models to estimate: (i) **Model 1**: the Brazilian stock price is the dependent variable; (ii) **Model 2**: the Chinese stock price is the dependent variable; (iii) **Model 3**: the Mexican stock price

[9] The break in trend function is motivated by the time trending behavior of the series as shown above in Figure 1.

Table 5 *F*-statistic for cointegration for the multivariate setting.

	Model 1	Model 2	Model 3	Model 4	Model 5
Entire period	3.527	6.813*	1.497	13.122*	5.679**
Post-crisis period	5.302**	6.122*	3.269	14.504*	10.958*

Notes: the lower bound critical values are 3.03 (10%), 3.47 (5%), and 4.40 (1%), and the upper bound critical values are 4.06 (10%), 4.57 (5%), and 5.72 (1%) (see Pesaran et al., 2001).
*Indicates the rejection of the null hypothesis of no cointegration at 1% level.
**Indicates the rejection of the null hypothesis of no cointegration at 5% level.

is the dependent variable; (iv) **Model 4**: the South African stock price is the dependent variable; and (v) **Model 5**: the Thai stock price is the dependent variable. For all models, the remaining equities are considered as explanatory or forcing variables. We second focus on the integration of the Chinese equity market with each considered emerging market by testing for cointegration between four country pairs. Before conducting the cointegration test for each model, we have carried out diagnostic tests (Breusch-Godfrey LM test for autocorrelation of order 12, ARCH test of order 12, Jarque-Bera normality test, and Ramsey RESET test for the correct functional form) to check the validity of the above models. The results (not reported here) support the evidence of correctly specified models, which enables us to carry out the bounds test approach to test for cointegration between equity markets.

The multivariate test results presented in Table 5 indicate that the equity markets share long-run relationships over both the entire and post-crisis periods only when the Chinese, South African, and Thai equities are considered as dependent variables in the above specification (Models 2, 4, and 5).[10] The cointegration between all equity markets is also observed over the post-crisis period when the Brazilian stock index is the dependent variable. When including the Mexican stock market as dependent variable in the specification (Model 3), there is no cointegration between all markets over both the entire and post-crisis periods.

We now turn out to the results of the bivariate setting where the cointegration is tested between the Chinese market and each of the other equity markets. The results reported in Table 6 show evidence of cointegration relationships between the Chinese and the other equity market in both directions, with the exception of the China/Thailand pair over the entire period and the China/Brazil pair over the post-crisis period where we have a cointegrating link between the two equities in only one direction. Within this context, the long-run relationship is detected when the Thai (Chinese) equity market is set as dependent variable over the whole (post-crisis) period. These cointegration results may be explained by the fact that the links between China and the other equity markets have

[10] Finding a cointegration relationship suggests that the nexus between the equities is stable over the considered sample periods (see Tang, 2003).

Table 6 *F*-statistic for cointegration for the bivariate setting.

	China/Brazil	China/Mexico	China/S. Africa	China/Thailand
Entire period	12.636*	7.258***	9.221**	5.779
	10.840*	7.341**	15.648*	8.549**
Post-crisis period	7.888**	10.417*	8.107**	9.818*
	3.282	11.873*	15.634*	17.605*

Notes: for each country pair and period, the first value is for the case where the Chinese equity is the dependent variable and the second value is for the case where the other emerging equity is the dependent variable. The lower bound critical values are 5.59 (10%), 6.56 (5%), and 8.74 (1%), and the upper bound critical values are 6.26 (10%), 7.30 (5%), and 9.63 (1%) (see Pesaran et al., 2001).
*Indicates the rejection of the null hypothesis of no cointegration at 1% level.
**Indicates the rejection of the null hypothesis of no cointegration at 5% level.
***Indicates the rejection of the null hypothesis of no cointegration at 10% level.

surely been strengthened by the increasingly integrated economies. Overall, the results are globally satisfactory, and support the view that the selected emerging equity markets are interdependent and can be driven by international factors over the two periods. Moreover, they confirm the insights drawn from the above preliminary analysis.

We now estimate the coefficients of the detected long-run relationships between the Chinese equity market and the other markets over both the two considered periods in order to investigate the long-run causal links between the two markets and to examine the magnitude of the obtained coefficients over time. The ARDL long-run coefficients reported in Table 7 show evidence of positive bilateral causal linkage between the Chinese equity market and the other emerging markets since all coefficients are strongly

Table 7 Estimates of the long-run coefficients for the bivariate setting.

	China/Brazil	China/Mexico	China/S. Africa	China/Thailand
Entire period				
Other market	0.605*	0.478*	0.886*	–
	(0.051)	(0.163)	(0.077)	
China	1.373*	1.103*	0.944*	1.439*
	(0.106)	(0.164)	(0.056)	(0.183)
Post-crisis period				
Other market	0.597*	0.886*	0.905*	0.679*
	(0.064)	(0.124)	(0.097)	(0.172)
China	–	0.845*	0.885*	1.009*
		(0.063)	(0.054)	(0.083)

Notes: the values in parentheses are the standard errors.
*Indicates significance at 1% level.

significant over the two considered periods. The positivity of the coefficients implies that the two considered equity markets vary in the same sense. The results also indicate that the magnitude of the coefficients varies over the whole and post-crisis samples. As for the cointegration test results, the insights drawn here outline that the financial integration process between China and emerging countries is rather sensitive to the market situations since the findings slightly differ through the entire and post-crisis periods.

We complement the analysis of cointegration between equities by estimating the error correction term coefficients that serve as an additional exercise for the hypothesis of cointegration. To that effect, we estimate the error correction model given by (4) for the equities where the null hypothesis of no cointegration is rejected, and examine the statistical significance and sign of the error correction term coefficients. The results depicted in Tables 8 and 9 show evidence of significantly negative error correction term coefficients, which corroborates the cointegration of the considered emerging stock markets in the multivariate and bivariate settings. Therefore, there is evidence of a return to the long-run equilibrium state over both the entire and post-crisis periods.

Table 8 Estimates of the error correction terms for the multivariate setting.

	Model 1	Model 2	Model 3	Model 4	Model 5
Entire period	–	−0.044*	–	−0.104*	−0.029*
	–	(0.008)	–	(0.013)	(0.006)
Post-crisis period	−0.025*	−0.042*	–	−0.131*	−0.058*
	(0.007)	(0.009)	–	(0.015)	(0.009)

Notes: the values in parentheses are the standard errors.
*Indicates significance at 1% level.

Table 9 Estimates of the error correction terms for the bivariate setting.

	China/Brazil	China/Mexico	China/S. Africa	China/Thailand
Entire period	−0.039*	−0.017*	−0.037*	–
	(0.008)	(0.005)	(0.009)	–
	−0.034*	−0.018*	−0.053*	−0.014*
	(0.008)	(0.005)	(0.009)	(0.003)
Post-crisis period	−0.031*	−0.029*	−0.033*	−0.021*
	(0.009)	(0.008)	(0.009)	(0.007)
	–	−0.049*	−0.063*	−0.033*
	–	(0.010)	(0.011)	(0.007)

Notes: for each country pair and period, the first value is for the case where the Chinese equity is the dependent variable and the second value is for the case where the other emerging equity is the dependent variable. The values in parentheses are the standard errors.
*Indicates significance at 1% level.

4.3. Short-Run Comovements

The short-run comovements among emerging equity markets can be checked by the evolution of the fitted time-varying conditional correlation coefficients estimated from the DCC-GARCH model. To that effect, we have estimated the DCC-GARCH process over the entire and post-crisis periods by including the five equities in the model (multivariate setting). The mean-reverting condition is satisfied for all estimated DCC-GARCH models, which implies that the conditional volatility of the emerging equities slows to achieve the normal equilibrium state.

From the time-varying conditional correlations shown in Figures 3 and 4, some interesting conclusions can be drawn. Indeed, the emerging equity markets exhibit financial integration and significant comovements since the cross-market conditional correlations are all positive over the entire and post-crisis periods. The conditional correlation coefficients fluctuate throughout the study periods for all cases, and the average values differ across country pairs (see Table 10). The highest average value is observed for the Brazil/Mexico country pair (0.818 over the whole period, and 0.715 over the post-crisis period), suggesting thus strong linkage between these two markets. This conclusion contradicts that of Arouri et al. (2013) who find low dependence between these countries (0.378) based on monthly data observed over the period 1988–2009. These facts could support the view that the conclusions drawn from analyzing the comovements among

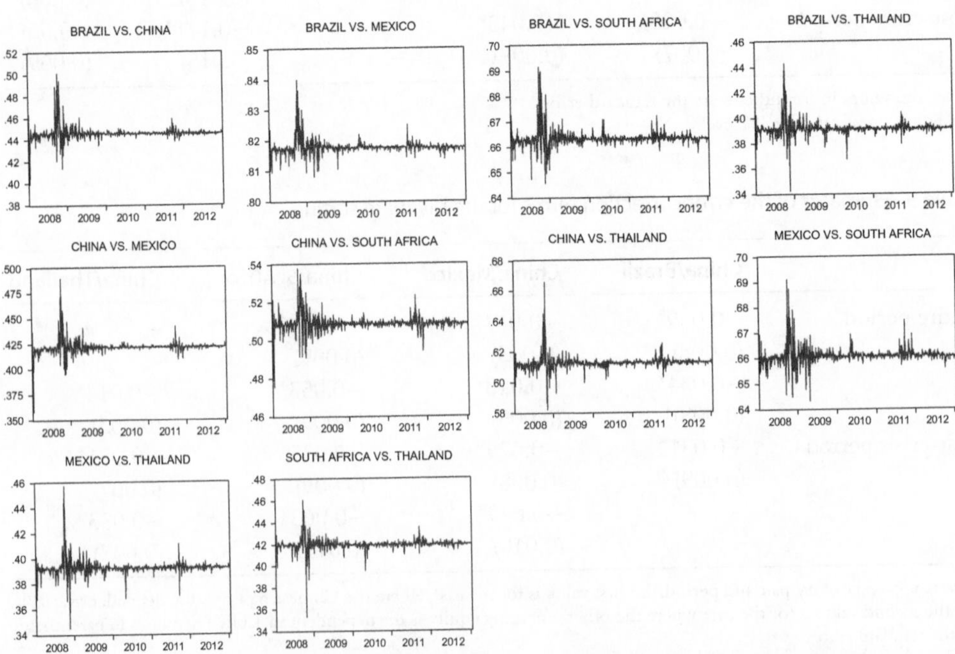

Figure 3 Time-varying correlations of equity returns in country pairs over the entire period.

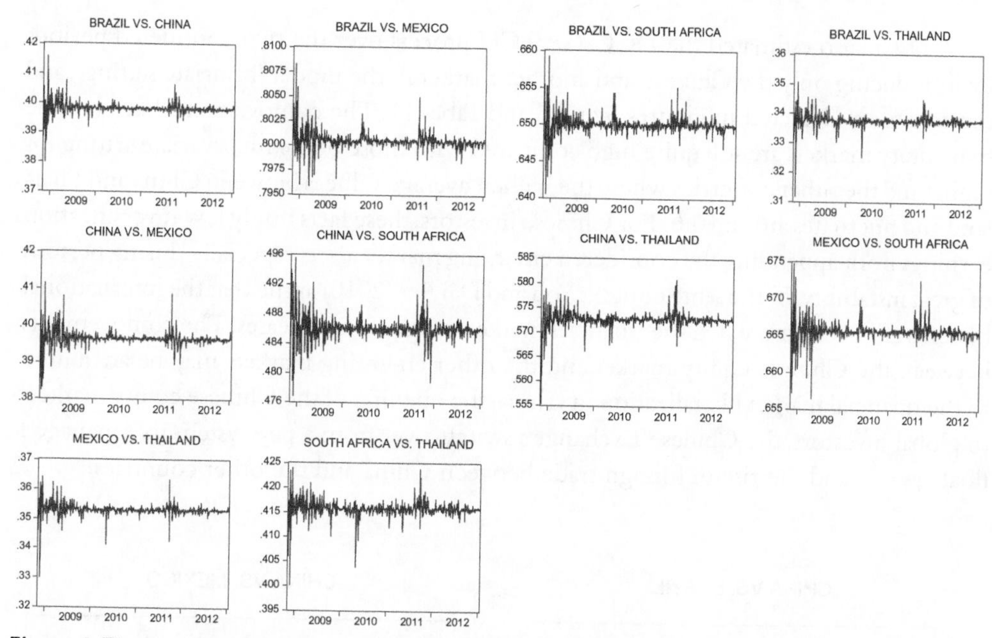

Figure 4 Time-varying correlations of equity returns in country pairs over the post-crisis period.

Table 10 Average correlations of equity returns in country pairs for the multivariate setting.

	Entire period	Post-crisis period
Brazil vs. China	0.446	0.359
Brazil vs. Mexico	0.818	0.715
Brazil vs. South Africa	0.663	0.635
Brazil vs. Thailand	0.391	0.310
China vs. Mexico	0.422	0.420
China vs. South Africa	0.509	0.478
China vs. Thailand	0.612	0.587
Mexico vs. South Africa	0.661	0.644
Mexico vs. Thailand	0.392	0.378
South Africa vs. Thailand	0.419	0.411

Note: all means are statistically significant.

markets may be misleading when using low-frequency data. The smallest average correlation is between Brazil and Thailand, and Mexico and Thailand, suggesting that the equity markets of Latin America are not highly integrated with the Thai equity market. For the other country pairs, the average values are quite high especially for countries of the same geographical region. All these facts contradict those observed in the literature mentioning that the emerging equity markets are weakly correlated.

We have also estimated the DCC-GARCH process over the two considered periods by introducing only the Chinese and another market in the model (bivariate setting), and the results are depicted in Figures 5 and 6 and Table 11. The comovements between the two equity markets are still quite high compared with those of the multivariate setting for China and the other countries where the highest average value is between China and Thailand and fluctuates around 0.6. For Chinese investors, these facts imply low diversification earnings from appending the considered emerging market assets especially during periods of great instability. In the same context, You and Daigler (2010) argue that the international benefits fall over time when the financial market integration increases. The comovements between the Chinese equity market and the other emerging markets may be attributed to the financial market liberalization in China, the opening of the Chinese equity markets to global investors, the Chinese Exchange's switch-over from a peg system to a managed float system, and the rise of foreign trade between China and the other countries.

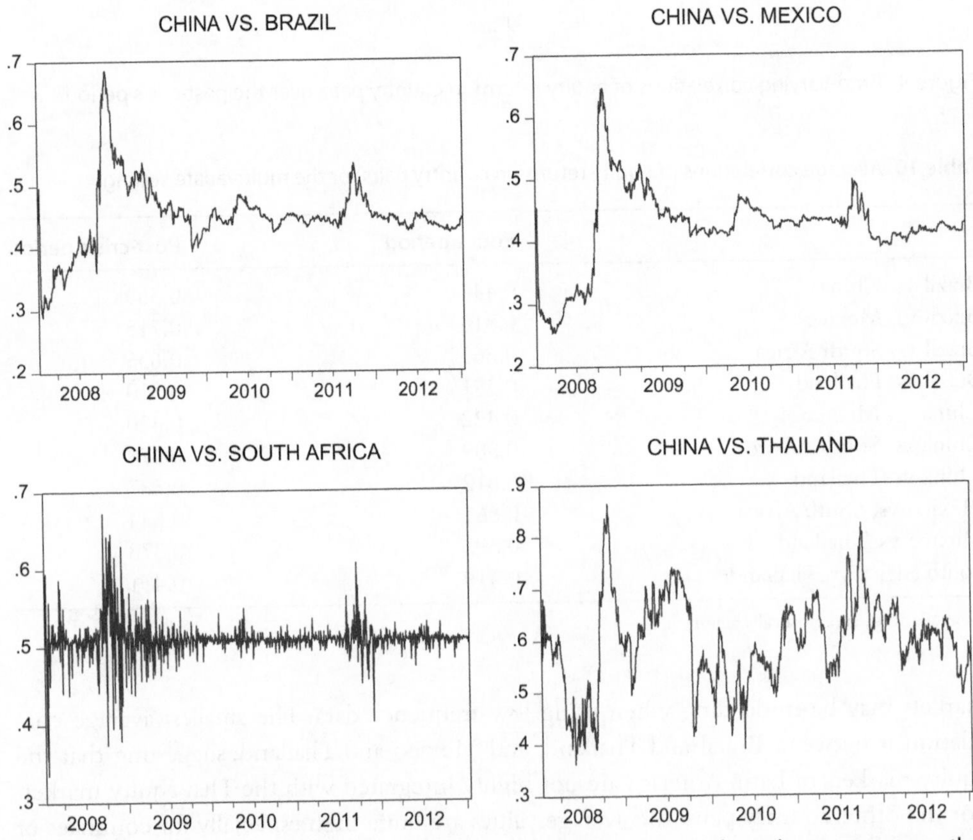

Figure 5 Time-varying correlations of equity returns between China and another country over the entire period.

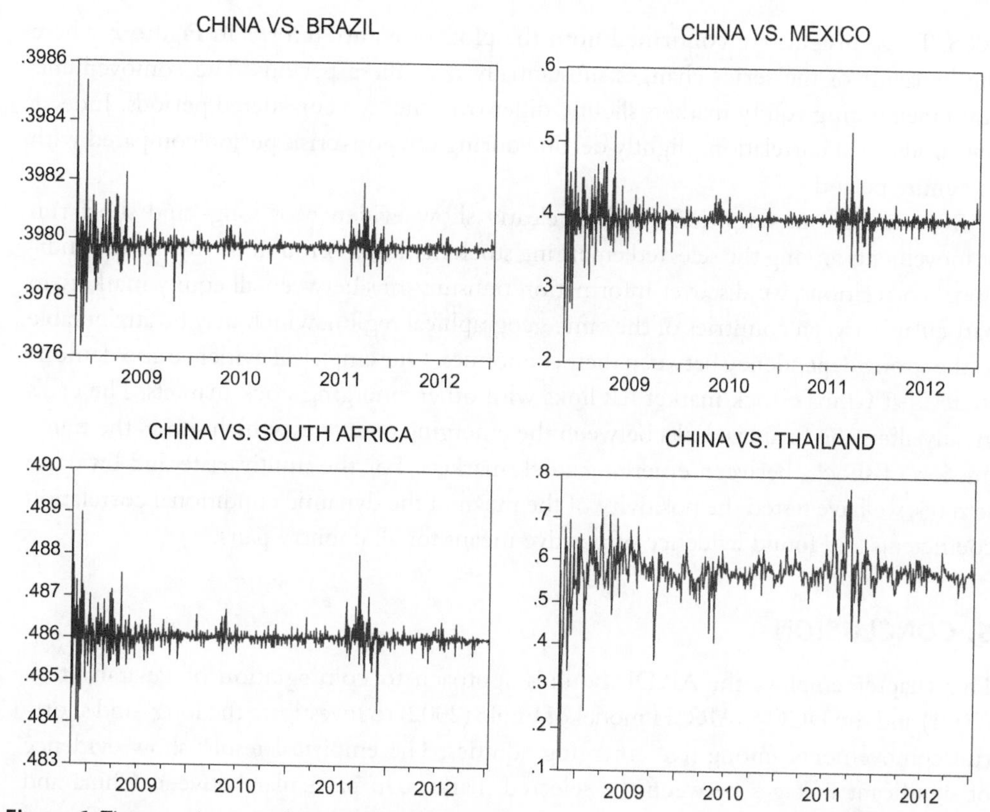

Figure 6 Time-varying correlations of equity returns between China and another country over the post-crisis period.

Table 11 Average correlations of equity returns between China and other countries for the bivariate setting.

	Entire period	**Post-crisis period**
China vs. Brazil	0.450	0.381
China vs. Mexico	0.423	0.446
China vs. South Africa	0.509	0.490
China vs. Thailand	0.594	0.582

Note: all means are statistically significant.

The conditional correlations between markets are greatly unstable and vary substantially during the global financial crisis period of 2008, showing thus the role of this crisis in the emerging equity integration. Another peak of equity market comovements is also observed in late 2011, but it is less important than that observed over the crisis of

2008. These insights are confirmed from the plots of equity returns in Figure 2 where the behavior of the series changes substantially over these periods. The comovements among emerging equity markets slightly differ over the two considered periods. Indeed, the conditional correlations slightly decline during the post-crisis period compared with the entire period.

To sum up, our empirical findings clearly show evidence of long- and short-run comovements among the selected emerging stock markets. Through the dynamic conditional correlations, we discover information transmissions between all equity markets, in particular between countries of the same geographical region, which may be attributable to the strong dependency between their economies. Our empirical evidence also demonstrates that China's stock market has links with other emerging stock markets. The crisis greatly alters the financial links between the emerging countries, which shows the transmission of shocks between emerging stock markets. For the multivariate and bivariate settings, we have tested the positivity of the mean of the dynamic conditional correlation coefficients and found evidence of positive means for all country pairs.

5. CONCLUSION

This chapter employs the ARDL bounds approach to cointegration of Pesaran et al. (2001) and the DCC-GARCH model of Engle (2002) to investigate the long- and short-run comovements among five emerging equities. The empirical results show evidence of significant linkages between the selected markets, in particular between China and the other countries over the long-run. The evolution of the time-varying conditional correlations reveals short-run comovements among markets especially those of the same geographical region, which may be explained by the strong economic ties. In this context, the Chinese equity market appears to be closer to the Thai equity market. Moreover, the results of the stock market integration are heavily affected by the global financial crisis.

Some future research works can also be conducted in the context addressed in this chapter. Indeed, one can incorporate other relevant exogenous variables into the model in order to shed some additional light on the comovements among emerging countries. One can also examine empirically the financial market causal relationships between emerging markets vis-à-vis developed markets and their links with global factors by employing techniques developed in the panel framework rather than approaches developed in time series analysis as done by most empirical works. Opting for panel methods enables us to embody country and time-specific effects to protect against unobserved factors that may be linked to the independent variables of the model.

REFERENCES

Aggarwal, R., Kyaw, N.A., 2005. Equity market integration in the NAFTA region: evidence from unit root and cointegration tests. International Review of Financial Analysis 14, 393–406

Ang, J.B., 2007. Are saving and investment cointegrated? The case of Malaysia (1965–2003). Applied Economics 39, 2167–2174

Arouri, M., Lahiani, A., Nguyen, D.K., 2013. Equity market comovements and financial contagion: a study of Latin America and the United States. Bankers, Markets and Investors 126, 17–29

Cappiello, L., Engle, R.F., Sheppard, K., 2006. Asymmetric dynamics in the correlations of global equity and bond returns. Journal of Financial Econometrics 25, 537–572

Chang, E., Chen, C., Chi, J., Young, M.R., 2008. IPO underpricing in China: new evidence from the primary and secondary markets. Emerging Markets Review 9, 1–16

Chelley-Steeley, P., 2004. Equity market integration in the Asia-Pacific region: a smooth transition analysis. International Review of Financial Analysis 13, 621–632

Chi, J., Li, K., Young, M.R., 2006. Financial integration in East Asian equity markets. Pacific Economic Review 11, 513–526

Driessen, J., Laeven, L., 2007. International portfolio diversification benefits: cross-country evidence from a local perspective. Journal of Banking and Finance 31, 1693–1712

Engle, R.F., 2002. Dynamic conditional correlation: a simple class of multivariate generalised autoregressive conditional heteroskedasticity models. Journal of Business and Economic Statistics 20, 339–350

Engle, R., Granger, C.W.J., 1987. Cointegration and error correction: representation, estimation and testing. Econometrica 55, 251–276

Forbes, K., Rigobon, R., 2002. No contagion, only interdependence: measuring stock market comovements. Journal of Finance 57, 2223–2261

Gjika, D., Horvath, R., 2013. Stock market comovements in Central Europe: evidence from the asymmetric DCC model. Economic Modelling 33, 55–64

Gregory, A.W., Hansen, B.E., 1996. Residual-based tests for cointegration in the models with regime shifts. Journal of Econometrics 70, 99–126

Grubel, H.G., 1968. Internationally diversified portfolios: welfare gains and capital flows. American Economic Review 58, 1299–1314

Guillaumin, C., 2009. Financial integration in East Asia: evidence from panel unit root and panel cointegration tests. Journal of Asian Economics 20, 314–326

Gupta, R., Donleavy, G.D., 2009. Benefits of diversifying investments into emerging markets with time-varying correlations: an Australian perspective. Journal of Multinational Financial Management 19, 160–177

Harvey, C.R., 1995. Predictable risk and returns in emerging markets. Review of Financial Studies 8, 773–816

Horvath, R., Petrovski, D., 2013. International stock market integration: Central and South Eastern Europe compared. Economic Systems 37, 81–91

Huang, B., Yang, C., Hu, J.W., 2000. Causality and cointegration of stock markets among the United States, Japan and the South China Growth Triangle. International Review of Financial Analysis 9, 281–297

Jeon, J., Oh, Y., Yang, D.Y., 2006. Financial market integration in East Asia: regional or global. Asian Economic Papers 5, 73–89

Jiang, J.X., Petroni, K.R., Wang, I.Y., 2010. CFOs and CEOs: who have the most influence on earnings management? Journal of Financial Economics 96, 513–526

Johansen, S., 1988. Statistical analysis of cointegration vectors. Journal of Economic Dynamics and Control 12, 231–254

Kenourgios, D., Samitas, A., 2011. Equity market integration in emerging Balkan markets. Research in International Business and Finance 25, 296–307

Kim, S., Kim, S.H., Wang, Y., 2006. Financial integration and consumption risk sharing in East Asia. Japan and the World Economy 18, 143–157

King, M., Sentana, E., Wadhwani, S., 1994. Volatility and links between national stock markets. Econometrica 62, 901–933

Kwiatkowski, D., Phillips, P.C.B., Schmidt, P., Shin, Y., 1992. Testing the null of stationarity against the alternative of a unit root: how sure are we that economic time series have a unit root? Journal of Econometrics 54, 159–178

Levy, H., Sarnat, M., 1970. International diversification of investment portfolios. American Economic Review 60, 668–675
Li, K., Sarkar, A., Wang, Z., 2003. Diversification benefits of emerging markets subject to portfolio constraints. Journal of Empirical Finance 10, 57–80
Longin, F., Solnik, B., 1974. Why not diversify internationally rather than domestically? Financial Analysts Journal 30, 48–54
Pesaran, M., Shin, Y., Smith, R., 2001. Bounds testing approaches to the analysis of level relationships. Journal of Applied Econometrics 16, 289–326
Phylaktis, K., Ravazzolo, F., 2005. Stock prices and exchange rate dynamics. Journal of International Money and Finance 24, 1031–1053
Said, E.S., Dickey, D.A., 1984. Testing for unit roots in autoregressive moving average models of unknown order. Biometrika 71, 599–607
Singh, P., Kumar, B., Pandey, A., 2010. Price and volatility spillovers across North American, European and Asian stock markets. International Review of Financial Analysis 19, 55–64
Solnik, B., Boucrelle, C., Le Fur, Y., 1996. International market correlation and volatility. Financial Analyst Journal 52, 17–34
Tang, T., 2003. Japanese aggregate import demand function: reassessment from the bounds testing approach. Japan and the World Economy 15, 419–436
Voronkova, S., 2004. Equity market integration in Central European emerging markets: a cointegration analysis with shifting regimes. International Review of Financial Analysis 13, 633–647
You, L., Daigler, R.T., 2010. Using four-moment tail risk to examine financial and commodity instrument diversification. Financial Review 45, 1101–1123
Yu, Ip-W, Fung, K.-P., Tam, C.-S., 2010. Assessing financial market integration in Asia – Equity markets. Journal of Banking and Finance 34, 2874–2885
Zivot, E., Andrews, D.W.K., 1992. Further evidence on the great crash, the oil-price shock, and the unit-root hypothesis. Journal of Business and Economic Statistics 10, 251–270

CHAPTER 28

Stock Market Volatility and Contagion Effects in the Financial Crisis: The Case of South-Eastern Europe

Theodore Syriopoulos
Department of Shipping, Trade and Transport, School of Business Studies, University of the Aegean, Chios, Greece
Audencia School of Management, Department of Finance, Nantes, France

1. INTRODUCTION

The South-Eastern European (SEE) countries constitute an interesting case study group that has not been adequately empirically researched. Most of the SEEs have become European Union (EU) Member States recently and are in a process of catching-up in economic growth with their developed European peers.

Prior to their EU accession, the SEEs had to undertake extensive structural reforms, stabilize macroeconomic conditions, privatize state-owned corporations, liberalize financial sectors and capital markets, and apply extrovert institutional adjustments in order to converge to and integrate with EU norms. For these reasons, during the 2000s, the SEEs exhibited impressive growth rates, were seen to attract significant international capital inflows and global portfolio investments and offer highly attractive stock market returns. Nevertheless, as in most emerging and developed economies, the 2008 global financial crisis led to fast deteriorated economic conditions in the SEE markets and resulted in a series of profound sovereign-debt events that infected, subsequently, the domestic financial sectors, leading, ultimately, to banking sector turmoil.

For international investors, a critical question remains whether fund allocation to the SEE stock markets can offer robust diversification benefits relative to developed stock markets, improving investors' risk-return potential and supporting efficient risk management. In this line, the identification of driving forces that shape asset returns, volatility behavior, and correlation dynamics turns out to be a core issue for successful international asset allocation and efficient portfolio management. Cross-market linkages, interactions, and spillovers are particularly relevant to optimal dynamic hedging strategies.

This Chapter provides a comprehensive empirical overview on these issues and its structure develops over three pillar sections. The first section summarizes recent economic developments in the SEE countries, paying attention to broader key macroeconomic factors and specific country short-term prospects. A brief assessment of country

Emerging Markets and the Global Economy
http://dx.doi.org/10.1016/B978-0-12-411549-1.00028-4

financial, economic, and political risks is also undertaken. The second section focuses on the SEE capital markets and presents their short modern history, critical stock market factors indicating growth potential and attractiveness to international investors. A concise literature review of empirical financial studies on the SEE stock market properties is also included. The third section contributes a dynamic empirical analysis into the SEE stock market risk and return properties, time-varying volatilities and correlations, and potential contagion and spillover effects. For that, the asymmetric dynamic conditional correlation (ADCC) model is incorporated, a flexible GARCH structure that allows for asymmetric effects in the variance functions. Particular attention is paid to the SEE stock market behavior before and after the global financial crisis. This empirical output is critical to efficient international asset allocation, portfolio diversification, and risk management decisions. To gain robust empirical insight into the SEE markets, a carefully selected sample includes new and old EU members (Romania, Bulgaria, Cyprus, and Greece) and potential prospective candidates (Turkey, Croatia), compared with and contrasted against leading benchmark international stock markets (Germany, USA). The final section concludes.

2. RECENT ECONOMIC DEVELOPMENTS IN THE SEE COUNTRIES

2.1. Key Macroeconomic Issues

Despite the sovereign-debt crisis in the Eurozone, EU continues to expand, predominantly toward SE Europe and the Western Balkans (Buttner and Hayo, 2011; Bechev, 2012). Following the fifth EU enlargement phase (January 2007) and the earlier accession of ten Member States (May 2004), Croatia became the EU Member State in July 2013. A number of countries have started negotiations to join the EU (including the Former Yugoslav Republic of Macedonia, Montenegro, Serbia, Turkey, and Iceland) or have been promised the prospect of joining when they are ready (Albania, Bosnia and Herzegovina, Kosovo).

Meanwhile, the economic environment has deteriorated due to the escalation of sovereign-debt crisis that turned into a banking sector crisis, mainly in a number of SEE economies. Integration is now perceived as a somewhat dubious process for the prospective members. During earlier phases of economic growth, the European core exported prosperity toward its SE periphery. In the current circumstances of deep crisis, however, it is exporting instability, shaping at the same time an overall different economic landscape (European Commission, 2013).

With fragile economic conditions and extensive austerity measures, financial recession in the euro area periphery is increasingly spilling into other economies in the region. Abrupt adjustments of internal and external imbalances and deleveraging have resulted in weaker domestic demand, although gradual recovery is expected by 2014. The recessionary spillovers led to GDP growth slowdown and fueled unemployment rates in

Table 1 Key economic forecasts: SEE and developed countries.

Country	Real GDP				Inflation				Unemployment rate			
	2011	2012	2013	2014	2011	2012	2013	2014	2011	2012	2013	2014
Romania	2.2	0.2	1.6	2.5	5.8	3.4	4.6	3.3	7.4	7.0	6.9	6.8
Bulgaria	1.7	0.8	1.4	2.0	3.4	2.4	2.6	2.7	11.3	12.2	12.2	11.9
Croatia	0.0	−1.9	−0.4	1.0	2.2	3.4	3.0	2.0	13.5	15.8	15.9	14.9
Cyprus	0.5	−2.3	−3.5	−1.3	3.5	3.1	1.5	1.4	7.9	12.1	13.7	14.2
Greece	−7.1	−6.4	−4.4	0.6	3.1	1.0	−0.8	−0.4	17.7	24.7	27.0	25.7
Turkey	8.5	3.0	3.5	5.0	6.5	8.7	6.5	5.0	9.8	9.4	9.9	9.0
Germany	3.0	0.7	0.5	2.0	2.5	2.1	1.8	1.7	5.9	5.5	5.7	5.6
USA	1.8	2.2	1.9	2.6	3.2	2.1	1.8	2.2	8.9	8.1	7.6	7.0
EU	1.5	−0.3	0.1	1.6	3.1	2.6	2.0	1.7	9.6	10.5	11.1	11.0

Source: European Commission (2013).

all SEE countries, though inflations remain under control and at a declining trend. Different factors affecting the European economies under study are responsible for substantial growth differentials. Currently, most SEE economies implement sizeable fiscal consolidation measures to contain deficits and structural imbalances. Table 1 summarizes key economic forecasts in emerging SEE and mature economies, including projections on real GDP, inflation, and unemployment rate.

The role of a flexible and smoothly operating financial system is critical in boosting domestic growth, enhancing macroeconomic stability, and supporting efficient economic integration of emerging and transitional economies with mature and developed economies. To this end, the following key factors of importance can be postulated (Bonetto et al., 2009):

- A developed financial sector exerts a positive impact on economic growth and output
- The stability of the financial sector is a prerequisite for establishing and preserving macroeconomic stability
- The growth and efficiency of financial sector intermediation further support the outcome of other reform measures, such as privatizations.

In spite of the global financial crisis, the financial institutions in most SEEs have managed to sufficiently absorb the external shocks (with the recent exception of the banking crisis in Cyprus). The banking sector in most SEEs was relatively unaffected because of its high degree of insulation and its impressive progress in recent years, especially since 2000 (Clausing and Dorobantu, 2005; Golubović and Golubović, 2005; Bonetto et al., 2009). In addition, prior to the financial crisis, the SEE stock markets (predominantly Romania) were seen to record highly attractive returns.

This reasonable reaction of the SEE economics to the adverse external conditions has been largely attributed to comprehensive economic policy reforms, regulatory and supervisory framework modernization, and convergence with EU norms. These developments, in turn, resulted in privatization of earlier state-owned banks, expansion of domestic presence of foreign banks, dramatic decline in bad loans, and intensified competition. In most SEE markets, extensive financial sector restructuring and bank privatization programs increased the market share of EU banks to up to 50–80% of domestic banking assets (Bonetto et al., 2009).

The SEE banking sectors continued exhibiting growth trends throughout the global financial crisis phase. Reasons for that include the low level of exposure to toxic financial assets, rather weak integration still with mature international markets, and the strong capitalization base of the international banks operating in many SEE markets. Despite serious risks and uncertainties in the heterogeneous SEE financial sectors, the contribution of domestic credit and the market capitalization are critical in speeding up economic convergence and further integration of the SEE countries.

Currently, the SEE financial markets remain fragile and financing conditions are seen constrained. The banking sector is under extensive restructuring as weaker banks attempt to strengthen their balance sheets and others struggle to regain access to market funding. As non-financial corporations and households are also deleveraging, weak bank lending reflects a combination of low credit demand and tight credit supply conditions. Uncertainty and downside risks still remain in the financial markets. A critical risk relates to potential aggravation of the sovereign-debt crisis that could lead in turn to renewed financial-markets turmoil. The effective implementation of recent policies undertaken to reinforce EMU attempts to contain this objective.

The issue of foreign direct investment (FDI) is a critical component for the SEE national financial accounts (Kekic, 2005). Foreign direct investment is investment of foreign assets into domestic structures, equipment, and organizations. It does not include foreign investment into the stock markets. Foreign direct investment is thought to be more useful to a country than investments in the equity of its companies because equity investments are potentially "hot money" which can leave at the first sign of trouble, whereas FDI is durable and generally useful whether the circumstances are favorable or adverse. FDI flows in emerging stock markets can be motivated by international investor expectations of higher returns and reduced portfolio risks (Middleton et al., 2008).

The increase in net inflows to SEEs during the 2000s is an indication of the attractive investment opportunities for international investors. However, this robust trend in FDIs is seen to have slowed down or to have reversed downwards, subsequent to the 2008 global financial crisis. According to UNCTAD (2013) estimates, FDI prospects continue to be fraught with risks and uncertainties. Standing at USD 1.5 trillion, global FDI flows exceeded pre-financial crisis levels in 2011 but the recovery is expected to level off in 2012 at an estimated USD 1.6 trillion. Transnational corporations have yet to convert available cash into new and sustained FDIs but this still remains a distant prospect, as global instability remains in international financial markets. In this setting, it is worth noting that half of global FDIs are directed to developing and transition economies, underlining the important development role that FDI can play.

In the SEE context, Romania and Bulgaria are predominantly seen to have capitalized on their robust economic growth prospects. These countries have managed to attract substantial FDI inflows, though at a declining pace after the financial crisis (Table 2).

2.2. Overview of the SE European Economies

A brief overview of the SEE economies under study now follows, including a summary of most recent critical developments in the national accounts balance sheet and core macroeconomic issues. The discussion draws extensively upon recent updated economic forecasts produced by the European Commission (2013) and the International Monetary Fund (IMF, 2005, 2012, 2013).

2.2.1. Romania

Romania is one of the least economically developed members of the European Union. Poverty rates are higher, education and healthcare spending are lower, and convergence with EU norms lags other emerging European countries. Romania is well endowed in natural and human resources to turn into one of the faster growing European economies and a leading investment destination.

Economic activity boomed in Romania in the run-up to the global crisis but contracted sharply thereafter. Romania's growth acceleration since 2000 was fueled mainly by improvements in total factor productivity and increasingly by a foreign financed credit and investment boom. Romania has strengthened its fiscal position considerably since the crisis, as it implemented one of the largest fiscal consolidations in the EU.

Although GDP growth was estimated to be flat at only 0.2% in 2012, economic forecasts for 2013 and 2014 indicate gradual recovery, with modest GDP growth at 1.6% in 2013 and acceleration to 2.5% in 2014. Domestic demand is anticipated to be the main growth driver. Investment is also a major contributor to growth, although at a slowing pace in comparison to 2012, due to weaker than expected economic activity in the rest of the EU. Net exports, however, are forecasted to contribute negatively due to a slower growth in export markets and stronger imports. A higher surplus in the balance of transfers and incomes is expected to support a significant improvement in the current account deficit at around 4.0% of GDP.

In the inflation front, rising food and energy prices are seen to have driven up inflation at around 5.4% in 2012, whereas wage pressures are likely to remain subdued, given the modest recovery of the economy. Annual inflation is projected to average 4.6% in 2013 and 3.3% in 2014. Although the labor market remains weak, affected by the difficult

Table 2 FDI flows by country: 2006–2011 (USD mln.).

Country	FDI inflows						FDI outflows					
	2006	2007	2008	2009	2010	2011	2006	2007	2008	2009	2010	2011
Romania	11,367	9921	13,909	4844	2940	2670	423	279	274	−88	−20	32
Bulgaria	7805	12,389	9855	3385	1601	1864	177	282	765	−95	229	190
Croatia	3468	4997	6180	3355	394	1494	261	296	1421	1234	−150	44
Greece	5355	2111	4499	2436	373	1823	4045	5246	2418	2055	979	1788
Cyprus	1834	2226	1415	3472	766	276	887	1240	2717	383	679	1828
Turkey	20,185	22,047	19,504	8411	9038	15,876	924	2106	2549	1553	1464	2464
Germany	55,626	80,208	8109	24,156	46,860	40,402	118,701	170,617	72,758	75,391	109,321	54,368
USA	237,136	215,952	306,366	143,604	197,905	226,937	224,220	393,518	308,296	266,955	304,399	396,656
EU	585,030	853,966	542,242	356,631	318,277	420,715	691,764	1,204,747	957,798	393,618	482,905	561,805

Source: UNCTAD (2013).

Table 3 Romania: country economic forecasts.

	2011 %GDP	Annual Δ% 1992–2008	2009	2010	2011	2012	2013	2014
GDP	–	2.9	−6.6	−1.1	2.2	0.2	1.6	2.5
Exports	40.0	10.9	−6.4	13.2	10.3	−3.5	0.9	2.6
Imports	45.4	13.4	−20.5	11.1	10.0	−1.9	2.4	3.6
Current account balance	–	–	−4.2	−4.4	−4.5	−3.8	−4.0	−3.9
General government debt	–	–	23.6	30.5	34.7	38.0	38.1	38.0

Source: European Commission (2013).

economic climate, unemployment was brought down to 7% in 2012 and is forecasted to remain around these levels in 2013 and 2014.

Fiscal consolidation is expected to continue supported by revenue measures. With government deficit below 3% of GDP in 2012, the budget targets a deficit of 2.4% and 2.2% of GDP in 2013 and 2014, respectively, benefiting from the expected acceleration in economic activity. Public debt is expected to stabilize at around 38% of GDP in 2013–2014 (see Table 3).

2.2.2. Bulgaria

Following a period of high economic growth and job creation linked to the income catching-up process, the Bulgarian economy has entered a hard phase, subsequent to the 2008 global financial crisis.

Conservative fiscal and financial supervisory policies have contributed to macroeconomic and financial stability in the Bulgarian economy, alas at sizeable job losses and a feeble recovery. Linkages with the Eurozone, substantial external debt, and rising nonperforming loans render the domestic economy vulnerable to external and internal factors. A key issue for Bulgaria is to succeed in restarting the growth and convergence process in order to mitigate the income and employment gap with the EU.

Bulgaria exhibited sluggish economic performance in 2012, based on indications of growth deceleration to below 1% per annum, down from 1.7% in 2011. The earlier pattern of economic recovery, driven by exports (though contracted demand) over 2010–2011, is seen to have reversed in 2012 (exports turned negative and domestic private demand strengthened). Public projects and modest FDI recovery (especially in the energy sector) supported investment stabilization in 2012, after a three-year contraction phase. As a result, GDP growth is projected to recover gradually to 1.4% in 2013 and further to 2.0% in 2014, with domestic demand leading the recovery and exports declining further. The

Table 4 Bulgaria: country economic forecasts.

	2011 %GDP	Annual Δ%						
		1992–2008	2009	2010	2011	2012	2013	2014
GDP	–	2.5	−5.5	0.4	1.7	0.8	1.4	2.0
Exports	66.5	–	−11.2	14.7	12.8	−0.1	3.1	4.5
Imports	65.8	–	−21.0	2.4	8.5	4.4	5.2	5.8
Current account balance	–	−7.3	−9.0	−0.4	1.7	−0.7	−1.6	−2.0
General government debt	–	–	14.6	16.2	16.3	18.9	17.1	17.3

Source: European Commission (2013).

current account is forecasted to slide into a deficit of 2% of GDP by 2014, predominantly due to increased imports (strengthened household consumption and investments).

The financial sector is expected to contribute positively to growth (modest credit multiplier) with both deposit and lending interest rates on a downward trend. The most significant downside risk is potential reversing of the positive household consumption trend, in relation to fragile domestic labor market conditions, affected by the broader Eurozone financial turbulence.

The general government fiscal deficit is seen to have improved significantly from 2% of GDP in 2011 to 1% of GDP in 2012 (related to strong VAT revenues) and is forecasted to weaken slightly to 1.3% in 2013 before improving back to 1% of GDP in 2014. The general government gross debt is forecasted to decline from 18.9% in 2012 and settle at 17.3% of GDP in 2014 (see Table 4).

2.2.3. Croatia

After 2 years of contraction, followed by stagnation in 2011, the Croatian economy is seen to struggle to restart growth after the 2009 recession, lagging behind most European economies. However, GDP is estimated to have contracted further by 1.9% in 2012, due to unfavorable external conditions and weakened domestic demand. Despite a significant narrowing of the current account deficit, the domestic economy remains highly vulnerable to external factors. In the short-term, further efforts are needed to return to fiscal sustainability.

Croatia continues to face both cyclical and structural economic rigidities, whereas the country's international competitiveness is seen to have remained weak. The annual real GDP growth has shrunk by 1.9% in 2012 with an anticipated further decline of 0.4% in 2013 and a reversing upturn of 1.0% in 2014. The earlier economic contraction (declining industrial production) has been partly compensated by robust tourism revenue.

Table 5 Croatia: country economic forecasts.

	2011 %GDP	Annual Δ%						
		1992–2008	2009	2010	2011	2012	2013	2014
GDP	–	–	−6.9	−1.4	0.0	−1.9	−0.4	1.0
Exports	41.8	–	−16.2	5.2	2.0	0.2	1.4	3.0
Imports	41.9	–	−21.4	−1.4	1.2	−1.8	1.5	3.8
Current account balance	–	–	−5.2	−1.1	−0.9	−0.5	−0.6	−1.5
General government debt	–	–	35.7	42.2	46.7	53.6	57.4	60.2

Source: European Commission (2013).

Nevertheless, consumer spending slowdown prevailed, as the labor market deteriorated further in 2012.

Credit conditions remain unfavorable, as households and companies are highly indebted and deleverage exerts an adverse impact on domestic demand. The banking system, largely foreign-owned, remains stable, well capitalized, and resistant to shocks, although high dependence on parent banks for funding remains critical.

Higher administered prices and rising energy and food prices (combined with increased VAT) resulted in significantly higher consumer price inflation, which is projected to remain at 3% in 2013 and to decline to around 2% in 2014. A long-standing current account deficit continued to narrow in 2012 (supported by tourism-related services exports). However, the current account deficit is expected to widen during 2013–2014, due to rising investments and consumption.

The fiscal policy has, to some extent, contained the negative budgetary consequences of the recession in 2012 and general government expenditure stabilized. The fiscal deficit of general government is projected to widen to 5% of GDP in 2013 but to narrow to 4.5% of GDP in 2014, due to an upturn of economic activity (mainly in energy and transport sectors). The general government debt increased significantly in 2012 (due to state-owned shipyards debt) and the debt ratio is projected to continue increase steadily at 60% of GDP in 2014 (see Table 5).

2.2.4. Greece

Following a strict economic reform program, backed up by international lenders, the economic situation in Greece showed some tentative signs of improvement in 2012. As market confidence is seen to gradually return after a phase of deep crisis, banks have experienced a reversal of deposit outflows and Greek market interest rates have been reduced significantly.

Table 6 Greece: country economic forecasts.

	2011 %GDP	Annual Δ% 1992–2008	2009	2010	2011	2012	2013	2014
GDP	–	2.9	−3.1	−4.9	−7.1	−6.4	−4.4	0.6
Exports	25.1	6.0	−19.4	5.2	0.3	−2.0	2.7	4.7
Imports	33.1	6.1	−20.2	−6.2	−7.3	−14.4	−5.9	−0.8
Current account balance	–	−7.8	−14.4	−12.8	−11.7	−7.7	−4.3	−3.3
General government debt	–	99.5	129.7	148.3	170.6	161.6	175.6	175.2

Source: European Commission (2013).

The heavy recessionary circumstances and the ongoing fiscal consolidation are projected to result in a further contraction of 4.4% of GDP in 2013. By 2014, however, initial signs of economic recovery, driven by positive supply-side developments, are expected to result in a positive 0.6% GDP growth. The bank recapitalization process and the overall economic stabilization are going to support a gradual domestic economic recovery.

Structural reforms lead to anticipated consumer price deflation of 0.8% and 0.4% in 2013 and 2014, respectively, improving competitiveness with favorable implications for exports growth. The current account deficit is expected to decrease from 7.7% of GDP in 2012 to 4.3% in 2013 and 3.3% in 2014. Since a large number of corporations face liquidity constraints, investment activity is anticipated to remain limited in the short-run. With contraction in demand, unemployment is forecasted to peak at 27.0% in 2013 and to remain still high at 25.7% in 2014.

Primary government balance followed by a primary surplus are targeted for 2013–2014, supported by a package of savings measures. Given interest payment reductions adopted by the Eurogroup, the overall government deficit in 2013 is expected to be at 4.6% of GDP. Gross public debt is estimated at 162% of GDP in 2012, increasing further up at 176% of GDP in 2013, before declining thereafter at an accelerated pace (see Table 6).

2.2.5. Cyprus

Following a profound bank sector restructuring recently, the economy of Cyprus is seen to run into prolonged recessionary and deleverage circumstances. Extremely tight credit conditions and a highly indebted corporate sector have hit investment activity severely. The strong contraction of the domestic economic activity has led to significantly weaker real GDP, down by 2.3% in 2012, driven by a significant decline of domestic demand (falling consumption and private investments). A long recessionary phase is projected to prevail beyond 2014.

Table 7 Cyprus: country economic forecasts.

	2011 %GDP	Annual Δ%						
		1992–2008	2009	2010	2011	2012	2013	2014
GDP	–	4.3	−1.9	1.3	0.5	−2.3	−3.5	−1.3
Exports	42.8	–	−10.7	3.8	3.3	3.1	1.6	1.9
Imports	45.9	–	−18.6	4.8	−4.1	−8.8	−8.0	−0.5
Current account balance	–	–	−10.7	−9.2	−4.2	−6.0	−1.7	0.1
General government debt	–	–	58.5	61.3	71.1	86.5	93.1	97.0

Source: European Commission (2013).

Fiscal consolidation implemented at the end of 2011, significant deterioration in the labor market, and high economic uncertainty have all affected domestic private consumption adversely. Despite trade balance improvements (mainly due to tourism revenue), the current account balance is projected to worsen, due to spillover effects on the domestic financial sector (partly associated with the financial crisis in Greece). The excessive government deficit is seen to persist, with stagnant revenues and expenditure lower than expected. Declining trends in consumer price inflation are projected for 2013–2014 (lower electricity and oil product prices as well as weaker domestic demand and lower disposable income). Labor market conditions are expected to worsen rapidly and unemployment rates to jump to historically high levels, due to extensive contraction in the banking sector and the overall economic activity.

A multi-annual reform program has been set recently into play to address the economic challenges (targeting the banking sector in particular), stabilize the financial system, achieve fiscal sustainability, and promote structural reforms, in order to support economic recovery. Downside risks remain critical, especially on the domestic credit front, due to the profound banking sector restructuring, worsening labor market conditions, house price declines, and prolonged economic uncertainty, with some consolidation potentially induced by higher investment activity in the energy sector (see Table 7).

2.2.6. Turkey

After 2 years of rapid growth, the Turkish economy has slowed down and imbalances have led to real GDP growth deceleration to 3.0% in 2012. Domestic demand weakened (driven by lower private consumption and investment), on the back of tighter macroeconomic policy and deteriorating external environment. However, short-term economic growth is expected to remain positive and balanced with forecasted real GDP to increase by 3.5% and 4.4% in 2013 and 2014, respectively. Net exports were seen as the main

Table 8 Turkey: country economic forecasts.

	2011 %GDP	Annual Δ% 1992–2008	2009	2010	2011	2012	2013	2014
GDP	–	–	−4.8	9.2	8.5	3.0	3.5	4.4
Exports	–	0.7	−1.3	0.9	1.6	4.0	2.0	1.1
Imports	–	1.2	4.0	−5.2	−3.0	−0.5	−2.1	−1.2
Current account balance	–	−5.2	−2.2	−6.4	−10.0	−7.5	−7.1	−7.9
General government debt	–	40.0	46.1	42.4	39.3	36.8	36.5	35.8

Source: European Commission (2013).

driver of growth (as imports declined and exports held up), despite weak demand in the traditional European markets.

A prompt policy response to the global financial crisis, normalization of global financial conditions, and the domestic economy's fundamentals (low public sector debt, low inflation, low unemployment, low interest rates, robust bank and private sectors, increasing economic openness) have contributed to a quick economic recovery and sizeable capital inflows. Nevertheless, Turkey remains vulnerable to capital flow reversal, due to its large external financing needs that could result in a hard landing.

The current account deficit has adjusted at a significant pace and inflation has decelerated at 8.7% in 2012 and is projected to decline further at 6.5% in 2013. Despite the earlier economic slowdown, unemployment fell below 9%, a ten-year low.

Whereas reducing imbalances further remains a key short-term priority, in the medium term Turkey must target higher savings (reduce dependence on external financing), better monetary, fiscal and macro-prudential policy integration, and maintenance of financial stability (see Table 8).

2.3. SEE Country Risk Assessment and Rating

A SEE country risk assessment and rating is now discussed, in order to provide useful insight into critical risk factors and shape a concise risk profile of the markets under study. This empirical output is based on the country risk assessment produced by the prestigious PRS Group (2013), founded in 1979 and located in New York, that consistently focuses on country risk analysis and compiles, tests, and publishes regularly the "International Country Risk Guide" (ICRG). The ICRG provides ratings for 140 countries on a monthly basis and for an additional 26 countries on an annual basis. Tables (9)–(12) summarize a combined set of weighted critical political, economic, and financial risk factors to subsequently produce SEE country risk ratings.

Table 9 Key financial risk factors by component.

Country	Total foreign debt as % of GDP (10)	Debt service as % of exports (10)	Current account % of exports (15)	International liquidity as months of import cover (5)	Exchange rate stability as % of change (10)	Financial risk rating 2011
Romania	4.0	7.5	11.0	3.5	9.5	**35.5**
Bulgaria	2.0	6.5	11.5	3.5	10.0	**33.5**
Croatia	2.5	5.5	11.5	3.5	10.0	**33.0**
Cyprus	1.0	9.0	11.0	0.0	10.0	**31.0**
Greece	0.5	8.0	10.0	0.0	10.0	**28.5**
Turkey	6.0	6.5	10.0	2.0	10.0	**34.5**
Germany	9.0	9.0	13.0	1.0	10.0	**42.0**
USA	5.0	10.0	12.0	0.0	10.0	**37.0**

Source: PRS Group (2013).

Table 10 Key economic risk factors by component.

Country	GDP per head of population (5)	Real annual GDP growth (10)	Annual inflation rate (10)	Budget balance as % of GDP (10)	Current account as % of GDP (15)	Economic risk rating 2011
Romania	2.0	5.0	8.0	4.0	10.0	**29.0**
Bulgaria	2.0	5.5	9.5	5.5	10.5	**33.0**
Croatia	3.0	5.0	10.0	5.0	10.0	**33.0**
Greece	4.0	0.5	8.5	3.5	10.0	**26.5**
Cyprus	4.0	6.0	9.5	4.5	9.0	**33.0**
Turkey	2.5	9.0	8.0	6.0	9.5	**35.0**
Germany	5.0	8.0	10.0	6.0	13.5	**42.5**
USA	5.0	7.5	10.0	3.0	10.0	**35.5**

Source: PRS Group (2013).

The ICRG rating system is based on a set of 22 components (variables) grouped into three major risk categories: political, financial, and economic risk, with political risk comprising 12 components (and 15 subcomponents), and financial and economic risk each comprising five components. Each component is assigned a maximum numerical value (risk points), with the highest number of points indicating the lowest potential risk for that component and the lowest number (0) indicating the highest potential risk. The maximum points able to be awarded to any particular risk component are pre-set within

Table 11 Key political risk factors by component.

Country	Government stability (5)	Socio-economic condi-tions (10)	Investment profile (10)	Internal conflict (10)	External conflict (15)	Political risk rating 2011
Romania	6.5	5.0	8.0	9.0	11.0	**66.5**
Bulgaria	6.0	5.5	9.5	10.0	9.0	**66.5**
Croatia	8.0	5.0	9.5	11.5	10.5	**75.5**
Greece	6.5	6.0	7.0	8.0	10.0	**68.0**
Cyprus	9.5	9.0	11.0	11.0	9.5	**80.5**
Turkey	8.5	5.5	7.5	7.5	7.5	**57.0**
Germany	6.5	9.0	11.5	10.0	10.5	**82.5**
USA	8.0	8.5	12.0	10.0	9.5	**81.5**

Source: PRS Group (2013).

Table 12 Actual vs. forecast composite risk factor ratings.

	Actual risk ratings 2011				Forecast risk ratings			
					1-year		5-years	
Country	Political risk	Financial risk	Economic risk	Actual composite risk rating	Worst case	Best case	Worst case	Best case
Romania	66.5	35.5	29.0	**65.5**	65.5	69.3	58.3	72.5
Bulgaria	66.5	33.5	33.0	**66.5**	61.0	69.3	56.0	72.8
Croatia	75.5	33.0	33.0	**70.8**	62.5	72.0	56.8	75.3
Greece	68.0	31.0	26.5	**61.5**	57.0	66.8	55.8	73.5
Cyprus	80.5	28.5	33.0	**72.3**	65.5	74.0	61.8	77.3
Turkey	57.0	34.5	35.0	**63.3**	57.8	67.5	53.8	71.5
Germany	82.5	42.0	42.5	**83.5**	77.5	85.5	74.0	88.5
USA	81.5	37.0	35.5	**77.0**	73.3	80.3	69.5	83.0

Source: PRS Group (2013).

the system and depend on the importance (weighting) of that component to the overall risk of a country.

A separate index is created for each of the subcategories; the "Political Risk" index is based on 100 points, the "Financial Risk" index on 50 points, and the "Economic Risk" index on 50 points. The total points from the three indices are divided by two to produce the weights for inclusion in the composite country risk score. The composite scores (ranging from 0 to 100) are then broken into categories from Very Low Risk (80–100 points) to Very High Risk (0 to 49.9 points). In other words, the lower the risk point total, the higher the risk; and the higher the risk point total, the lower the risk.

The financial risk rating takes into account five weighted variables, including: (1) total foreign debt as percentage of GDP; (2) debt service as percentage of exports of goods and services; (3) current account as percentage of exports of goods and services; (4) international liquidity as months of import cover; and (5) exchange rate stability as percentage of change (Table 9). The economic risk rating also incorporates five weighted variables, including: (1) GDP per head of population; (2) real annual GDP growth; (3) annual inflation rate; (4) budget balance as percentage of GDP; and (5) current account as percentage of GDP (Table 10). The political risk rating includes 12 weighted variables covering both political and social attributes: (1) government stability; (2) socio-economic conditions; (3) investment profile; (4) internal conflict; (5) external conflict; (6) corruption; (7) military in politics; (8) religious tensions; (9) law and order; (10) ethnic tensions; (11) democratic accountability; and (12) bureaucracy quality (Table 11).

As to short-term (one-year) and medium-term (five-year) forecasts, projections of future conditions are also produced, termed as "Best Case" and "Worst Case" scenarios (Table 12). This provides a probabilistic future country risk assessment that can support financial, economic, and political judgments and decision-making in relation to the underlying countries of interest.

Based on this approach of country risk rating assessment, the following key findings can be summarized for the SEE and developed countries under study (country selection with higher risk profiles):

- Financial risk: Greece, Cyprus, Croatia.
- Economic risk: Greece, Romania, Cyprus-Bulgaria-Croatia.
- Political risk: Turkey, Romania, Bulgaria.
- Composite risk: Greece, Turkey, Romania.
- 5-year forecast-best case scenario: Turkey, Romania, Bulgaria.

As a note of caution, these country risk rating assessments should be treated with due care. Recent adverse financial, economic, and political events in some of the countries under study (including predominantly the ailing Cypriot banking sector and the deeply recessionary Greek economy) are anticipated to have further contributed to deteriorated risk ratings and ranking.

3. SEE STOCK MARKET GROWTH AND PROSPECTS

3.1. Data and Descriptive Statistics

Most of the SEE stock markets have a relatively short active presence compared with major mature peer markets, such as Germany and the USA. A brief historical overview now follows to contribute useful insight into the growth path and attractive prospects of the SEE equity markets. For a start, the Bucharest Stock Exchange (BVB), Romania, was re-opened on April 1995; the BET Index (BET-C) was launched in 1997. The Bulgarian Stock Exchange (BSE) was established, as in its present form, in 1995, following the merger of nearly 20 regional exchanges; the BSE-Sofia Index (SOFIX) was launched in 2000. The Istanbul Stock Exchange (ISE), Turkey, was established in 1986; the ISE-National-100 Index (ISE-100) is the representative stock market index. The Zagreb Stock Exchange (ZSE), Croatia, was established in 1991; the CROBEX share index (CROBEX) was set in 1997. The Cyprus Stock Exchange (CSE) started its operation in March 1996; the Cyprus-General Index (CYP-GI) is the main stock market index. Finally, the Athens Stock Exchange (ASE), Greece, was officially established in September 1876; the ASE-General Index (ASE-GI) is the representative stock market index (Syriopoulos and Roumpis, 2009; Syriopoulos, 2011).

In order to better understand SEE stock market historical trends and growth prospects and compare them with developed markets, the following daily stock market index closing prices are collected: BET-C (Romania), SOFIX (Bulgaria), CROBEX (Croatia), ASE-GI (Greece), CYP-GI (Cyprus), and ISE-100 (Turkey) against DAX (Frankfurt Stock Exchange, Germany) and S&P500 (New York Stock Exchange, NYSE, USA) (Figure 1). The inclusion of Germany and the USA is important to compare and contrast emerging and leading mature stock markets with different growth paths and behavioral patterns. It would be useful to identify potential market interactions, spillovers, and contagion implications between these two distinctive stock market groups. Furthermore, the developed equity markets under study register significant international investment flows and transaction turnover and are anticipated to play a pivotal and influential role in international equity market comovements, volatility, and correlation effects. Table 13 summarizes key SEE and developed stock market figures, including listed company numbers, capitalization values, and market returns.

A daily frequency dataset was compiled from the Datastream base and was enriched with information collected from the official stock exchange bureaus. The full study period runs from January 1, 2000 to March 31, 2013 (Period 1). In order to gain useful insight into the risk-return profile and market reactions, time-varying volatility properties, linkages, and spillover effects between the sample equity markets, the full study period is subsequently split into two sub-periods (before and after the mid-2008 global financial crisis): Period 2, the pre-crisis period, runs from January 2000 to September 2008; and Period 3, the after-crisis period, runs from October 2008 to March 2013.

Compared with global developed markets, the SEE equity markets remain thin in terms of listed company numbers, market capitalization, and turnover value. According to all measurements and as anticipated, the NYSE and the Frankfurt Stock Exchange are the largest established equity stock markets whereas Cyprus, followed by Bulgaria, are the smallest SEE stock markets. Following the implementation of extensive economic

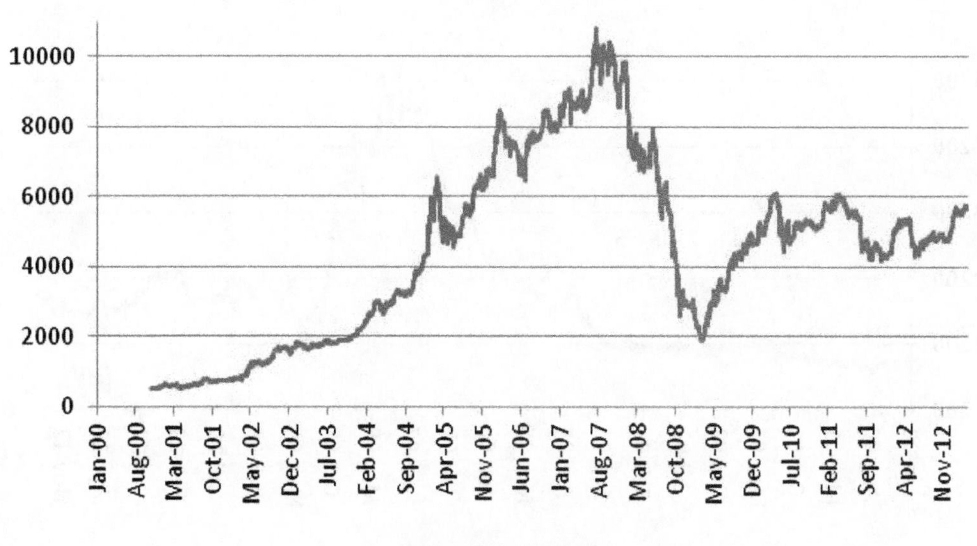

Bulgaria: SOFIX

Figure 1 SE European and mature stock markets.

reforms, the SEE economies have embarked upon a robust economic growth path over the last decade, which eventually led to their accession into the EU. This has improved the SEE economic environment, has attracted international investor funds at increasing numbers, and has produced exceptionally high, albeit volatile, cumulative equity portfolio returns during 2001–2007 (predominantly Romania followed by Bulgaria), materially surpassing the respective returns of the sample mature markets. These robust upward

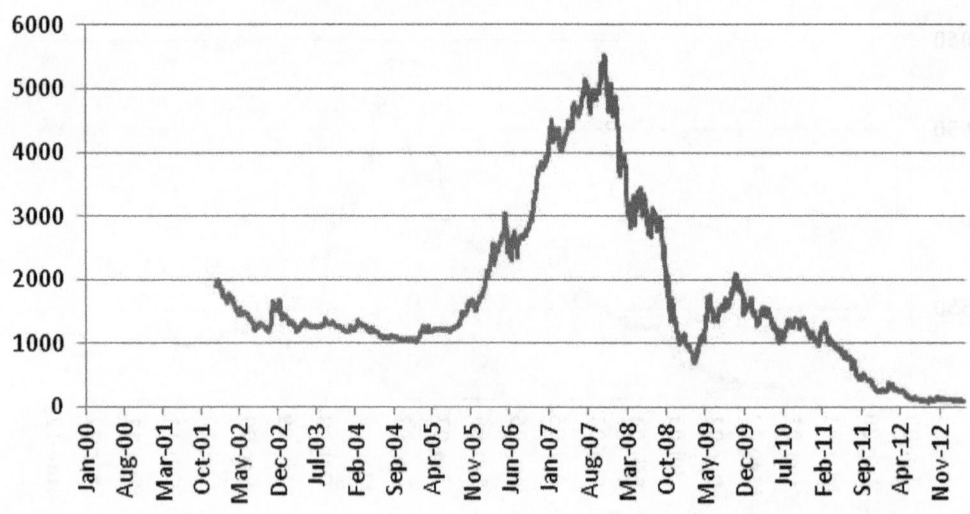

Figure 1 (*Continued*).

stock market trends were abruptly reversed in all of the markets under study with the escalation of the 2008 global financial crisis and the subsequent spillover implications of the EU sovereign debt and banking crisis.

Table 14 summarizes a set of key descriptive statistics and tests on the sample equity market returns. In Period 1 (full sample period), mean excess returns are found to be

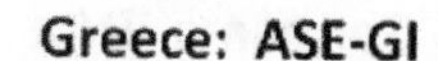

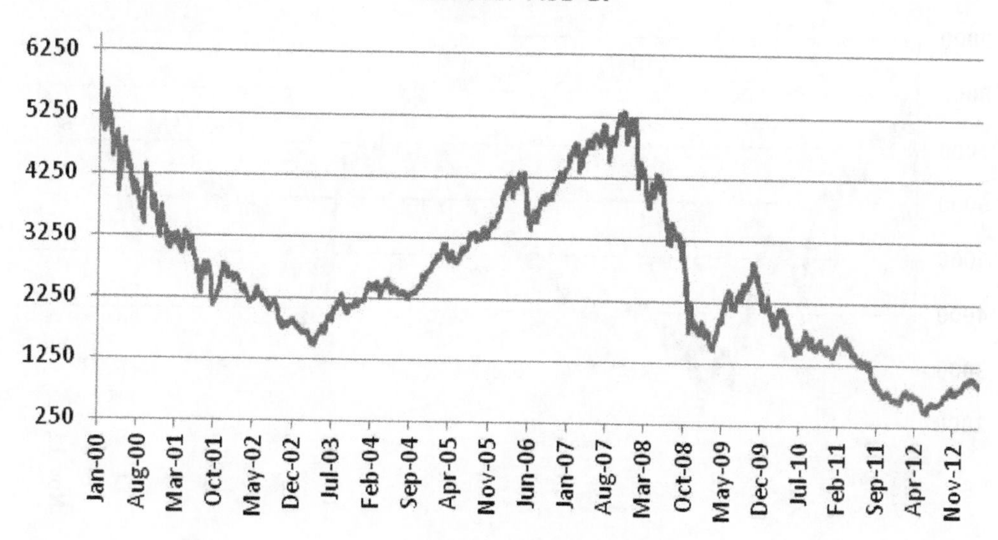

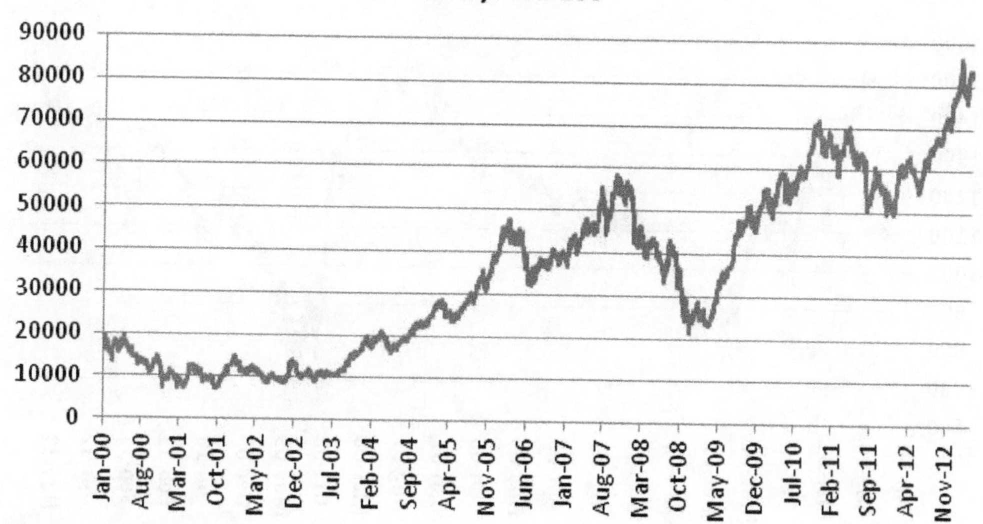

Figure 1 (*Continued*).

higher for Romania (BET-C), Bulgaria (SOFIX), and Turkey (ISE-100). In the after-crisis period (Period 3), apart from Romania and Turkey, Germany and the USA are also seen to deliver positive returns. The SEE markets are seen to exhibit relatively higher volatility, as indicated by larger standard deviation values, although the findings for emerging and mature markets are mixed over the after-crisis period, indicating broad sensitivity of risk

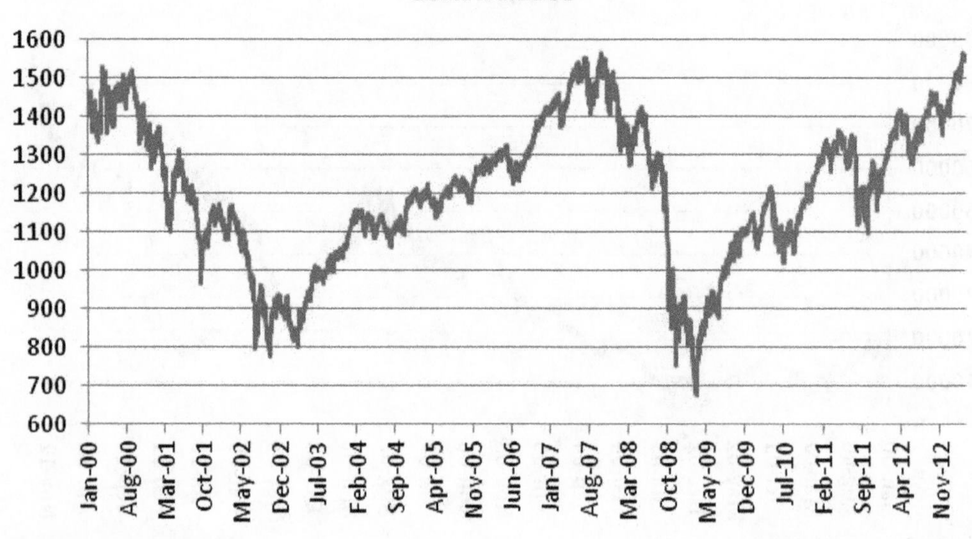

Figure 1 (*Continued*).

exposure to adverse events and crises. Most of the equity market series exhibit negative after-crisis skewness (except from Germany), whereas kurtosis statistics indicate fatter tails for all of the series compared with normal distribution. The Jarque-Bera test rejects normality in all cases.

Unconditional contemporaneous correlation coefficients in the sample equity markets depict pairwise correlations between emerging SE European and mature stock markets

Table 13 Key SEE stock market factors.

	2002	2004	2006	2008	2010	2012
Number of listed companies						
Romania	65	60	58	64	69	79
Bulgaria	356	332	357	399	390	387
Croatia	53	94	143	208	188	222
Greece	338	321	358	292	280	265
Cyprus	154	124	141	119	110	101
Turkey	262	275	291	250	264	271
Germany	934	819	760	832	765	747
USA	2366	2293	2280	1963	2317	2339
Market capitalization (mln. €)						
Romania	2686	8859	18,858	6474	9776	12,088
Bulgaria	0700	2062	7829	6371	5498	5025
Croatia	3764	8205	21,490	18,880	18,720	16,984
Greece	65,760	92,140	152,207	64,737	50,379	34,039
Cyprus	4505	3588	12,254	5733	5094	1514
Turkey	32,822	71,897	124,141	84,852	226,645	240,030
Germany	627,283	849,717	1,241,963	797,063	1,065,713	1,127,370
USA	6,848,000	9,911,950	12,028,511	7,182,969	10,447,384	10,987,036
Market return (%)						
Romania	126.95	103.50	22.2	−70.3	14.6	6.3
Bulgaria	42.47	32.50	48.20	−79.7	−15.13	7.3
Croatia	0.47	30.74	53.5	−61.7	−4.2	0.76
Greece	−32.50	23.10	19.93	−65.5	−35.6	33.4
Cyprus	−26.80	−9.96	128.80	−77.2	−33.9	−61.2
Turkey	−31.36	31.34	−1.65	−63.15	24.9	52.6
Germany	−41.00	6.30	21.30	−44.4	15.1	24.8
USA	−23.84	9.48	13.62	−37.60	11.00	11.68

Source: World Federation of Exchanges (2013); National Stock Exchanges. Figures as of respective year-end.

(Table 15). The following interesting findings can be summarized: (a) the SEE stock markets exhibit low or modest pairwise correlations with the leading mature equity markets but relatively robust ones with their peer SEE markets (e.g. Greece-Cyprus; Turkey-Cyprus; Romania-Bulgaria; Romania-Croatia); (b) the leading role of the German market is apparent, exhibiting high correlation with most SEE markets (predominantly Turkey, Romania, Greece, Croatia); (c) high correlation coefficients are found between the leading mature markets; (d) pairwise correlations are seen to increase in most cases in the

Table 14 SEE vs leading mature stock markets: descriptive statistics.

Statistics	BET-C	SOFIX	CROBEX	ASE-GI	CYP-GI	ISE-100	DAX	S&P500
Panel A—full sample period: January 2000–March 2013								
Mean	0.0007	0.0004	0.0002	−0.0005	0.0035	0.0004	0.00045	0.0019
Median	0.000	0.0002	0.0000	0.0000	0.0000	0.0009	0.0006	0.0002
Maximum	0.1457	0.0836	0.1477	0.1342	0.0180	0.1777	0.1079	0.1096
Minimum	−0.1198	−0.1135	−0.1076	−0.1021	−0.1465	−0.1997	−0.0743	−0.0947
Std. Dev.	0.0171	0.0140	0.0139	0.0176	0.0620	0.0230	0.0160	0.0133
Skewness	−0.1896	−0.4489	0.0302	0.0032	1.6452	−0.0458	0.0334	−0.1595
Kurtosis	11.8472	11.2292	15.4410	7.3464	13.5775	10.1203	6.9935	10.599
Jarque-Bera	10328.1	8248.9	21753	2655.07	2428.127	7126.55	2242.01	8131.5
(prob.)	(0.000)	(0.000)	(0.000)	(0.000)	(0.000)	(0.000)	(0.000)	(0.000)
Panel B—pre-crisis period: January 2000–September 2008								
Mean	0.0009	0.0004	0.0002	−0.0003	0.0027	0.0002	−0.0001	−0.0001
Median	0.0001	0.0002	0.0000	0.0000	0.0001	0.0000	0.0006	0.0008
Maximum	0.1457	0.0836	0.1477	0.08329	0.3720	0.1777	0.1078	0.1096
Minimum	−0.1182	−0.1135	−0.1076	−0.0961	−0.2395	−0.1997	−0.0743	−0.0922
Std. Dev.	0.01638	0.0140	0.0139	0.0140	0.0512	0.0257	0.0158	0.0121
Skewness	0.2157	−0.4489	0.0302	−0.0999	1.4604	−0.0092	−0.0231	−0.0180
Kurtosis	12.5021	11.2292	15.4410	7.9664	13.4768	9.2578	6.7114	10.1437
Jarque-Bera	7618.8	8248.9	21753	2298.6	2415.206	3643.5	1281.1	4748.3
(prob.)	(0.000)	(0.000)	(0.000)	(0.000)	(0.000)	(0.000)	(0.000)	(0.000)
Panel C—after-crisis period: October 2008–March 2013								
Mean	0.00004	−0.0003	−0.0002	−0.0009	−0.0005	0.0009	0.00038	0.0003
Median	0.0004	0.0000	0.0000	0.0000	0.0000	0.0009	0.0007	0.0005
Maximum	0.1284	0.0730	0.0855	0.1342	0.1233	0.9425	−0.1068	0.1024
Minimum	−0.1198	−0.1135	−0.0831	−0.1021	−0.1015	−0.0734	−0.0708	−0.0947
Std. Dev.	0.0187	0.0138	0.0142	0.0231	0.0246	0.0166	0.0164	0.0153
Skewness	−0.3809	−0.6935	−0.4060	−0.0768	−0.0649	−0.1699	0.1275	−0.3164
Kurtosis	11.8034	12.8951	11.193	5.2457	6.3762	6.5993	7.4190	10.004
Jarque-Bera	3712.1	4746.4	3222.9	240.89	314.76	621.42	931.50	2351.3
(prob.)	(0.000)	(0.000)	(0.000)	(0.000)	(0.000)	(0.000)	(0.000)	(0.000)

Notes: the table summarizes descriptive statistics on equity index returns of the following SEE and leading mature stock markets: Romania, BET-C; Bulgaria, SOFIX; Croatia, CROBEX; Greece, ASE-GI; Cyprus, CYP-GI; Turkey, ISE-100; Germany, DAX; USA, S&P500. Statistics include mean, median, maximum and minimum, standard deviation, skewness, kurtosis, and Jarque-Bera normality tests. Daily data frequency; Period 1 (full sample period): January 2000–March 2013; Period 2 (pre-crisis period): January 2000–September 2008; Period 3 (after-crisis period): October 2008–March 2013.

after-crisis period, in line with past empirical evidence that markets tend to comove closely at downward phases (Syriopoulos and Roumpis, 2009; Syriopoulos, 2011). As an initial reaction, correlation coefficients indicate that the SEE equity markets, especially the EU newcomers, exhibit weak short-term contemporaneous interactions with their mature counterparts; although correlations have broadly increased after the global financial crisis.

Table 15 SEE vs leading mature stock markets: unconditional correlation matrix (returns).

	BET-C	SOFIX	CROBEX	ASE-GI	CYP-GI	ISE-100	DAX	S&P500
BET-C								
Period 1	1.000							
Period 2	1.000							
Period 3	1.000							
SOFIX								
Period 1	0.257	1.000						
Period 2	0.088	1.000						
Period 3	0.431	1.000						
CROBEX								
Period 1	0.329	0.231	1.000					
Period 2	0.155	0.090	1.000					
Period 3	0.482	0.366	1.000					
ASE-GI								
Period 1	0.312	0.145	0.312	1.000				
Period 2	0.182	0.077	0.191	1.000				
Period 3	0.399	0.195	0.388	1.000				
CYP-GI								
Period 1	0.269	0.131	0.273	0.693	1.000			
Period 2	0.193	0.084	0.173	0.494	1.000			
Period 3	0.324	0.165	0.332	0.759	1.000			
ISE-100								
Period 1	0.259	0.136	0.272	0.361	0.270	1.000		
Period 2	0.189	0.079	0.160	0.393	0.299	1.000		
Period 3	0.367	0.229	0.434	0.397	0.303	1.000		
DAX								
Period 1	0.278	0.128	0.342	0.452	0.317	0.405	1.000	
Period 2	0.101	0.028	0.165	0.474	0.281	0.307	1.000	
Period 3	0.461	0.244	0.518	0.468	0.365	0.566	1.000	
S&P500								
Period 1	0.161	0.037	0.271	0.280	0.199	0.264	0.631	1.000
Period 2	0.016	0.014	0.053	0.229	0.125	0.146	0.585	1.000
Period 3	0.273	0.082	0.428	0.308	0.236	0.422	0.684	1.000

Notes: the table summarizes unconditional pairwise correlations of the sample equity markets. Market and index acronyms as in Notes of Table 14. Period 1 (full sample period): January 2000–March 2013; Period 2 (pre-crisis period): January 2000–September 2008; Period 3 (after-crisis period): October 2008–March 2013.

3.2. A Concise Empirical Literature Review

This section briefly reviews past empirical research on stock market dynamics, volatilities, and correlations with a focus on the SEE stock markets, as an introductory background to the empirical discussion of the next section. The majority of past studies have dealt predominantly with leading mature stock markets (e.g. Koutmos, 1996; Alexakis et al., 1997; Dickinson, 2000; Bessler and Yang, 2003; Ejara, 2009). The SEE markets, however, have not been analyzed extensively and empirical research remains thin on this topic

(Samitas et al., 2006; Syriopoulos and Roumpis, 2009; Kenourgios and Samitas, 2011; Syriopoulos, 2011). Only recently, during the 2000s, have these markets come into play, following their EU membership and profound domestic economic reforms undertaken (including liberalization of financial markets), leading to robust economic growth rates and upward stock market trends (Guidi and Ugur, 2013).

The empirical literature on the SEE capital markets typically employs either vector autoregression or vector error correction modeling to examine linkages, interactions, and comovements (Horvath and Petrovski, 2012). Alternative GARCH models have been also implemented to assess dynamic stock market risk-return properties, time-varying correlations and volatility transmissions. To explain stock market behavior, a diversity of factors have been investigated, including short- and long-run interdependencies, financial crises and external shock transmission, market deregulation, financial innovations, macroeconomic factors, regional cooperation and common economic policies, and bear-bull market behavior (e.g. Gelos and Sahay, 2001; Bessler and Yang, 2003; Yang et al., 2003; Athanassiou et al., 2006; Syriopoulos, 2004, 2006, 2007; Dvorak and Podpiera, 2006; Gilmore et al., 2008; Middleton et al., 2008; Fernández-Villaverde and Rubio-Ramirez, 2010; Kenc and Dibooglu, 2010). Tight market linkages indicate that a domestic capital market may not be efficiently insulated from external shocks, thus, international portfolio diversification benefits can be limited. In many cases, empirical evidence of long-run linkages, comovements, and spillover effects was concluded (Syriopoulos, 2004, 2006, 2007, 2011; Syriopoulos and Roumpis, 2009). Nevertheless, empirical findings have not been always consistent and converging.

A number of past studies indicate that emerging stock market behavior increasingly depends on mature stock market volatility swings (e.g. Phylaktis and Ravazzolo, 2002; Yang et al., 2003; Cappiello et al., 2006b; Egert and Kocenda, 2007; Syriopoulos, 2006, 2007, 2011; Beirne et al., 2010; Hanousek and Kocenda, 2011). If this is the case, then portfolio diversification and risk control may not be as efficient as anticipated. Given that correlations in international equity markets have increased over time (e.g. Marcelo et al., 2008), investors are interested in assessing the level of equity market linkages and interactions as well as the implications from increased volatility and correlations, in order to design well-diversified portfolio strategies.

A body of past literature attempts to quantify the implications of asymmetric dynamics on return volatility and correlation processes (e.g. Engle and Ng, 1993; Bekaert and Wu, 2000), as asymmetric volatility spillover effects have been indicated to be present in major financial markets (e.g. Kroner and Ng, 1998; Mazzotta, 2008). Similarly, the dynamic correlations between international capital markets also present asymmetric characteristics. Empirical evidence supports that correlations tend to increase in equity markets during turbulent periods of crises or downward markets (e.g. Kearney and Poti, 2006).

Of the few studies dealing with emerging European markets, Samitas et al. (2006) and Kenourgios and Samitas (2011) examine a number of Balkan stock markets (Romania,

Bulgaria, Serbia, FYROM, Turkey, Croatia, Albania) in relation to mature markets (USA, UK, Germany, Greece). Linear (error correction vector autoregressive model) and non-linear (switching regime error correction model) methods are employed to test for potential linkages between Balkans and developed stock markets. The empirical findings indicate that the Balkan markets display equilibrium relationships with their mature counterparts. The presence of interdependencies between emerging and developed markets may limit potential portfolio diversification benefits in the sample Balkan equity markets. Active rather than passive portfolio strategies are more efficient to attain attractive returns for international investors.

Syriopoulos and Roumpis (2009) investigate the presence of time-varying comovements, volatility implications, and dynamic correlations in major Balkan (Romania, Bulgaria, Croatia, Greece, Cyprus, Turkey) and mature equity markets (Germany, USA), to support efficient asset allocation decisions. Emphasis is placed on the constant and dynamic equity market correlations produced by alternative multivariate GARCH forms (the constant conditional correlation, CCC, the dynamic conditional correlation, DCC, and the asymmetric dynamic conditional correlation, ADCC, models). The Balkan stock markets are seen to exhibit dynamic correlations as a peer group but relatively low correlations with the mature markets.

Based on the same market sample as the previous study, Syriopoulos (2011) investigates the risk and return profile of international portfolios allocated by investors to major Balkan equity markets against Germany and the USA. An error correction vector autoregressive framework models financial integration and investigates causality effects and cointegration interrelationships, depicting short- and long-run dynamic linkages. The empirical findings support cointegration and indicate a stationary long-run relationship, shaped by both domestic and external forces. Long-run comovements imply that risk diversification and excess portfolio returns may be limited in these markets.

A recent comprehensive study by Guidi and Ugur (2013) investigates whether SEE stock markets (Romania, Bulgaria, Slovenia, Croatia, Greece, Turkey) have become more integrated with regional and global stock markets (Germany, UK, USA) during the 2000s. Using a variety of cointegration methodologies, the SEE stock markets are shown to have no long-run relationship with their mature counterparts, possibly indicating SEE market immunity to external shocks. A multivariate generalized autoregressive conditional heteroskedastic (MGARCH) model and the exponential weighted moving average (EWMA) model are incorporated to model time-varying correlations among these markets. The UK and USA market correlations with the SEE markets are found to shift over time, with increasing convergence being evident between the sample markets. The study also investigates whether the structure of correlations between returns of different markets changed in different phases of the 2007–2009 global financial crisis. Diversification benefits are concluded to be possible for investors diversifying their portfolios into the SEE markets.

To summarize, empirical research on the SEE stock market risk-return properties remains limited. The relevant empirical results appear to be somewhat mixed and sometimes conflicting and diverging. Many studies produce evidence of some interactions between emerging and mature stock markets in the short-term but the speed of volatility transmission is relatively gradual rather than fast. Some studies fail to find even any long-term relationship among the sample stock markets.

4. AN EMPIRICAL ANALYSIS OF THE SEE STOCK MARKETS

4.1. Modeling Dynamics in the Correlations

Past empirical research indicates that return volatilities of financial assets are not only time-varying but can also exhibit covariation over time, whereas evidence supports that international equity market correlations have increased recently (Syriopoulos, 2011). Investors are interested in assessing the degree of equity market linkages and volatility interactions, in order to construct well-diversified portfolios, evaluate risk-return tradeoffs, and implement efficient hedging strategies.

The class of multivariate GARCH models and their variants have proven to successfully capture dynamic return volatility properties and offer sophisticated parameterizations of the covariance structure. An interesting advantage of these models is their empirical insight into the interaction of conditional variances and covariances of the underlying asset returns (Cifarelli and Paladino, 2005; Savva et al., 2009; Skintzi and Refenes, 2006; Syriopoulos and Roumpis, 2009). However, the complex computational efforts required to fit these models into sample data are critical for the selection and estimation of a most appropriate functional form. The vectorized (VECH) model (Bollerslev et al., 1988) and the BEKK model (Engle and Kroner, 1995) have been among the early functional GARCH forms. The CCC model (Engle, 1982; Bollerslev, 1986; Bollerslev, 1990), the DCC model (Engle, 2002), and the ADCC model (Cappiello et al., 2006a) have been subsequently established as most popular multivariate GARCH models (Bauwens et al., 2006).

4.1.1. The CCC and DCC GARCH Models

Both the CCC and DCC models are a two-stage estimator of conditional variances and correlations. In the first stage, a univariate GARCH model is estimated; the univariate variance estimates are subsequently introduced as inputs in the second stage of the estimation process to obtain dynamic correlations (Bollerslev, 1986). The DCC model captures the dynamics of time-varying conditional correlations (relaxing the CCC model assumption of constant conditional correlations), with the covariance matrix, H_t, specified as (equation (1)):

$$H_t = D_t R_t D_t, \tag{1}$$

where $D_t = \text{diag}\left\{\sqrt{h_{i,t}}\right\}$ is a $m \times m$ diagonal matrix with the square roots of the conditional variances in the diagonal; and $R_t \equiv \{\rho_{ij}\}_t$ is the time-varying conditional correlations matrix. The first-order univariate GARCH process is (equation (2)):

$$h_{i,t} = \omega_i + \alpha_i \cdot \varepsilon_{i,t-1}^2 + \beta \cdot h_{i,t-1}, \tag{2}$$

where $i = 1, 2, \ldots, m$, indicates the ith equation in the VECM model and $h_{i,t}$ is the conditional variance of the error term, ε_{it}, of the ith equation, obtained from the first stage of the estimation procedure. In the second stage, the vector of the standardized residuals is employed to develop the DCC correlation specification as (equations (3) and (4)):

$$Q_t = (1 - \theta_1 - \theta_2)\bar{Q} + \theta_1 \eta_{t-1}\eta_{t-1}' + \theta_2 Q_{t-1} \tag{3}$$

and

$$R_t = Q_t^{*-1} Q_t Q_t^{*-1}, \tag{4}$$

where $\bar{Q} = E[\eta_t \eta_t']$, the unconditional covariance of the standardized residuals, is obtained from the first stage of the estimation process and $Q_t^* = (\text{diag}(Q_t))^{-1/2} = \text{diag}(1/\sqrt{q_{11,t}}, \ldots, 1/\sqrt{q_{mm,t}}$ is a diagonal matrix composed of the square root of the diagonal elements of Q_t. In equation (3), θ_1 and θ_2 are scalar parameters, $\eta_t = D_t^{-1}\varepsilon_t$ is the standardized residual matrix, and Q_t is the covariance matrix of η_t. The parameters θ_1 and θ_2 capture the effects of previous shocks and previous dynamic conditional correlations on current dynamic conditional correlations. In the DCC(1,1) case, θ_1 and θ_2 are positive and $\theta_1 + \theta_2 < 1$, ensuring that Q_t is positive and mean-reverting. This implies that, after a shock, the correlation between the underlying assets will return to the long-run unconditional level. The correlation estimators of equation (4) are of the form as (equation (5)):

$$p_{ij,t} = \frac{q_{ij,t}}{\sqrt{q_{ii,t} q_{jj,t}}} \quad \text{for } i, j = 1, 2, \ldots, n \text{ and } i \neq j. \tag{5}$$

The DCC model is estimated by maximization of the following log-likelihood function (equation (6)):

$$L = -\frac{1}{2} \sum_{T=1}^{T} \left(m \log\left(2\pi\right)\right) + 2 \log |D_t| + \log |R_t| + \eta_t' R_t^{-1} \eta_t. \tag{6}$$

4.1.2. The ADCC GARCH Model

A limitation of the standard DCC model is that it does not capture asymmetric effects in conditional asset correlations. The DCC model takes into account the effect of past return shocks on volatility and correlations, however, it ignores the sign. It has been reported that negative returns in financial markets during turbulent periods or downward trends can cause increases in correlations relative to normal market periods (Longin and Solnik, 2001; Garcia and Tsafack, 2011). The ADCC model is a specification that captures asymmetric effects in conditional asset correlations (the ADCC model nests the DCC model). Equation (3) can expand to allow for asymmetries in conditional correlation as (equation (7)):

$$Q_t = (1 - \theta_1 - \theta_2)\overline{Q} - g\overline{\Xi} + \theta_1 \eta_{t-1}\eta'_{t-1} + \theta_2 Q_{t-1} + g\xi_{t-1}\xi'_{t-1}, \tag{7}$$

where the parameter g introduces the asymmetric effects into the model; $\xi_t = I[\eta_t < 0] \circ \eta_t (I[\cdot]$ is a function indicator that takes on value 1 if the residuals are negative and 0 otherwise; $\circ$ denotes the Hadamard product; and $\overline{\Xi} = E[\xi_t \xi'_t]$ is the sample covariance matrix of ξ_t. The ADCC model allows for increases in conditional correlation when returns of the underlying assets are declining rather than rising. The asymmetric response of correlation to equity market shocks can be examined through the notion of the "news impact surface" (Kroner and Ng, 1998) and is a generalization of the "news impact curve" (Engle and Ng, 1993). Since the study time span runs from 2000 to 2013, the ADCC specification can depict risk-return properties and time-varying correlations and interactions between the sample SEE and leading stock markets at upward and downward market phases, including the sub-periods before and after the global financial crisis.

The ADCC model is preferably selected to construct the variance-covariance matrix on the sample SEE stock market performance against other multivariate functional forms for two reasons. First, the ADCC model primarily focuses on dynamic correlations (rather than covariances), which are of core interest to portfolio management practitioners. Second, the ADCC model employs a two-stage estimator of conditional variances and correlations that facilitates the estimation process.

4.2. Empirical Results

4.2.1. The VEC Model

Prior to the estimation of the asymmetric dynamics in conditional correlations of the sample equity markets, the mean specification of the underlying series is modeled. The presence of any cointegrating vectors is tested, in order to identify potential linkages and interrelationships among the equity markets under study. The flexible functional form of a Vector Error Correction model (VECM) is employed, since short-run intertemporal comovements and long-run equilibrium paths can be jointly depicted. The stationarity of the time series was earlier tested on the basis of standard unit-root test statistics. All of the sample equity markets were found to be integrated of order-one, $I(1)$. Two statistically significant cointegration vectors were identified (based on relevant λ_{trace} and λ_{max} tests, not reported).

The VEC model can be stated as:

$$\Delta z_t = \sum_{i=1}^{k-1} \Gamma_i \Delta z_{t-i} + \Pi z_{t-k} + \varepsilon_t, \tag{8}$$

where $\Gamma_i = -(I - A_1 - \cdots - A_i)$, $(I = 1, \ldots, k-1)$, Γ_i are interim multipliers, and $\Pi = -(I - A_1 - \cdots - A_k)$.

The empirical results from the VEC model are summarized in Table 16. The error correction term (ECT) is found to be statistically significant in some of the emerging SEE markets, implying that short-run dynamics ensure reversion back to the common trend. The leading role of the USA and German equity markets is also empirically supported. The causal relationships between the sample equity markets are depicted through the statistically significant lagged terms. The joint significance of the lagged cross-market returns indicates that shifts in leading developed equity markets exert a significant (unidirectional) impact on SEE equity market returns. Test statistics (not reported) on the VECM residuals did not reject the null hypothesis of serial correlation and the presence of heteroskedasticity in the VECM residuals, supporting that multivariate GARCH structures are appropriate for modeling return volatilities and correlations.

4.2.2. The ADCC Model Results

The ADCC model on SEE and leading mature equity markets is estimated in order to gain insight into the dynamic conditional correlations and volatility spillovers between the sample equity markets. To proceed, the standardized residuals of the univariate GARCH(1,1) specification are employed for the estimation of the ADCC model. The α and β coefficients (ARCH and GARCH effects, respectively) were found to be positive and statistically significant in all of the equity markets, indicating reactive and persisting volatility dynamics (Table 17).

The univariate GARCH standardized residuals are incorporated as inputs into the ADCC estimation process. The estimated parameters θ_1 and θ_2 in the ADCC model capture the effects of lagged standardized shocks and lagged dynamic conditional correlations on current dynamic conditional correlations, respectively. The statistical significance of these coefficients indicates the presence of dynamic (time-varying) stock market correlations. The assessment of asymmetric correlation responses to negative returns is examined through the parameter g.

Table 18 summarizes the most important ADCC empirical findings, before and after the 2008 global financial crisis. The dynamic conditional correlation estimates between the sample markets under study are found to exhibit significant asymmetric, time-varying, and mean-reverting properties but are estimated to be rather low, in general. The SEE markets are seen to be predominantly correlated with each other as a peer group rather than with the leading mature markets. In the short-term, cross-market linkages and dynamic correlations may be more important to explain SEE stock market volatility

Table 16 VECM estimates and diagnostics.

	$\Delta z_{S\&P500}$	Δz_{DAX}	$\Delta z_{ASE\text{-}GI}$	$\Delta z_{CYP\text{-}GI}$	$\Delta z_{ISE\text{-}100}$	$\Delta z_{BET\text{-}C}$	Δz_{CROBEX}	Δz_{SOFIX}
C_0	−0.00283	−0.03108	−0.00583	0.003271	0.05232	−0.06507	−0.06088	−0.06375
	(−0.212)	(−1.977)	(−0.340)	(0.064)	(2.723)	(−3.893)	(−4.537)	(−4.731)
$ECT_{S\&P500}$	−0.00016	−0.00001	−0.000274	−0.140136	−0.00026	−0.00137	−0.00136	−0.00150
	(−0.660)	(−0.049)	(−0.868)	(−0.068)	(−0.751)	(−4.483)	(−5.550)	(−6.087)
ECT_{DAX}	−0.00035	−0.00109	−0.00024	−0.140010	−0.00135	−0.00008	−0.00005	−0.00017
	(−1.453)	(−3.784)	(−0.776)	(−0.075)	(−3.835)	(−0.281)	(−0.240)	(−0.705)
$\Delta z_{S\&P500,t-1}$	−0.16909	0.39571	0.39031	0.189207	0.44553	0.37534	0.26695	0.26723
	(−6.539)	(13.007)	(11.763)	(0.092)	(11.984)	(11.606)	(10.282)	(10.247)
$\Delta z_{DAX,t-1}$	0.07367	−0.24054	−0.07070	0.369919	−0.17998	−0.08562	−0.08403	−0.05985
	(3.155)	(−8.756)	(−2.359)	(0.000)	(−5.361)	(−2.932)	(−3.584)	(−2.541)
$\Delta z_{ASE\text{-}GI,t-1}$	0.03007	0.03125	−0.00706	0.076129	−0.01136	0.05072	0.00699	0.02986
	(1.788)	(1.579)	(−0.327)	(0.116)	(−0.469)	(2.411)	(0.414)	(1.760)
$\Delta z_{CYP\text{-}GI,t-1}$	0.029268	0.034259	−0.028950	−0.067336	0.079872	0.018983	−0.001906	0.137650
	(0.110)	(0.156)	(0.218)	(0.081)	(0.113)	(0.314)	(0.479)	(0.010)
$\Delta z_{ISE\text{-}100,t-1}$	−0.01012	−0.01504	0.00837	−0.070399	0.00356	0.03199	0.00132	0.00505
	(−0.700)	(−0.885)	(0.451)	(0.020)	(0.171)	(1.770)	(0.091)	(0.347)
$\Delta z_{BET\text{-}C,t-1}$	0.00313	−0.00288	−0.00411	0.093217	−0.00498	0.03745	0.00091	−0.00649
	(0.192)	(−0.150)	(−0.198)	(0.056)	(−0.213)	(1.841)	(0.055)	(−0.395)
$\Delta z_{CROBEX,t-1}$	−0.03569	−0.02874	−0.05768	−0.084105	−0.05304	0.05806	−0.00720	0.07235
	(−1.730)	(−1.184)	(−2.178)	(0.086)	(−1.787)	(2.250)	(−0.347)	(3.476)
$\Delta z_{SOFIX,t-1}$	0.01212	−0.03013	−0.04038	0.013139	−0.01854	−0.03096	−0.02756	0.08253
	(0.642)	(−1.355)	(−1.665)	(0.410)	(−0.682)	(−1.310)	(−1.453)	(4.331)
$\Delta z_{S\&P500,t-2}$	−0.07958	0.10328	0.08692	0.275777	0.20084	−0.04147	0.06190	−0.00132
	(−2.906)	(3.205)	(2.473)	(0.030)	(5.100)	(−1.210)	(2.251)	(−0.048)
$\Delta z_{DAX,t-2}$	0.02208	−0.04354	−0.00422	0.012737	−0.09079	−0.00984	−0.0506	−0.01830
	(0.959)	(−1.607)	(−0.143)	(0.450)	(−2.743)	(−0.341)	(−2.192)	(−0.788)
$\Delta z_{ASE\text{-}GI,t-2}$	0.00941	0.00758	−0.04056	−0.021142	0.00414	0.02029	0.01000	0.01027
	(0.563)	(0.385)	(−1.890)	(0.373)	(0.172)	(0.970)	(0.595)	(0.609)
$\Delta z_{CYP\text{-}GI,t-2}$	0.023871	0.009193	0.075833	0.058573	0.037255	−0.000219	0.006986	0.012674
	(0.154)	(0.391)	(0.019)	(0.108)	(0.282)	(0.497)	(0.423)	(0.415)
$\Delta z_{ISE\text{-}100,t-2}$	−0.02006	−0.02263	0.01248	−0.014806	0.01714	0.01715	0.02700	−0.00278
	(−1.392)	(−1.334)	(0.675)	(0.334)	(0.826)	(0.951)	(1.865)	(−0.191)
$\Delta z_{BET\text{-}C,t-2}$	−0.02170	−0.02575	−0.01779	−0.033747	−0.01800	−0.05538	−0.03629	−0.00127
	(−1.360)	(−1.371)	(−0.086)	(0.282)	(−0.784)	(−2.774)	(−2.264)	(−0.079)
$\Delta z_{CROBEX,t-2}$	−0.03445	−0.02943	0.01558	−0.046030	−0.02519	−0.01798	−0.00497	−0.02100
	(−1.667)	(−1.211)	(0.587)	(0.228)	(−0.848)	(−0.695)	(−0.239)	(−1.008)
$\Delta z_{SOFIX,t-2}$	0.04895	0.01886	0.05088	0.021807	0.06485	0.06122	0.07548	0.10154
	(2.634)	(0.862)	(2.133)	(0.353)	(2.427)	(2.634)	(4.045)	(5.417)
Diagnostics								
R^2	0.0247	0.0712	0.0657	0.246310	0.0562	0.1058	0.0647	0.1083
R^2-Adjust.	0.0193	0.0660	0.0604	0.198378	0.0509	0.1008	0.0594	0.1033
Log Likelihood	8335.7	7868.2	7626.7	821.9812	7290.6	7700.0	8324.3	8310.6
AIC	−5.814	−5.488	−5.319	−3.259	−5.084	−5.370	−5.806	−5.797
SIC	−5.796	−5.469	−5.300	−3.001	5.066	−5.352	−5.788	−5.778

Notes: the table summarizes the estimates produced by the conditional vector error correction model (VECM) with a constant and two cointegration vectors. The model is used to estimate and test cointegration and common stochastic trends among the sample equity markets. The error correction terms (ECT) measure the response of the equity markets when they diverge from the long-run equilibrium path. The number of lags is set equal to 2 (based on relevant information criteria). The VECM residuals are employed in the estimation of the Conditional Correlation Model. The figures in parentheses denote t-statistic values; AIC and SIC are the Akaike and Schwarz information criteria, respectively.

Table 17 Univariate GARCH(1,1) estimates.

	ω	α	β	$\alpha + \beta$
S&P500	1.48e−06 (0.000)	0.0777 (0.000)	0.9124 (0.000)	0.9901
DAX	2.14e−06 (0.000)	0.0843 (0.000)	0.9080 (0.000)	0.9923
ASE-GI	1.44e−06 (0.000)	0.0832 (0.000)	0.9159 (0.000)	0.9991
CYP-GI	0.00002 (0.0000)	0.2024 (0.0132)	0.7296 (0.0115)	0.932
ISE-100	7.22e−06 (0.000)	0.0811 (0.000)	0.9015 (0.000)	0.9826
BET-C	8.77e−06 (0.000)	0.1419 (0.000)	0.8366 (0.000)	0.9785
CROBEX	2.98e−06 (0.000)	0.0922 (0.000)	0.8916 (0.000)	0.9838
SOFIX	3.50e−06 (0.000)	0.1992 (0.000)	0.7883 (0.000)	0.9875

Notes: the table summarizes the estimated coefficients produced by the univariate GARCH(1,1) model. The univariate variance estimates are introduced as inputs into the estimation process of the ADCC model. The estimated coefficient ω denotes the constant term, α and β are the ARCH and GARCH terms, respectively, in the conditional variance equations. The sum of $\alpha + \beta$ indicates volatility persistence. Figures in $(\cdot)$ are standard errors.

and risk-return trade-offs. In the medium to long term, the dynamic behavior of the SEE markets can be potentially affected by contagion and volatility spillover effects from leading global equity markets.

An important empirical contribution is the evidence that, after the 2008 global financial crisis, the dynamic correlations between the SEE markets themselves as well as between the SEE and the developed markets have increased considerably. This supports the perception of asymmetric stock market reactions, with volatility exhibiting higher sensitivity and persistence to negative news. Furthermore, at crises events, shocks, and downward market phases, stock markets tend to comove closer together, affected by contagion and volatility spillover effects. If this is the case, international portfolio diversification benefits by investing into highly correlated markets may be limited and risk control and dispersion tend to be inefficient.

The dynamic linkages and correlation effects identified between the SEE markets are reasonable, since these neighboring markets have strengthened their commercial, investment, and financial transactions over recent years; have modernized and upgraded their economies with the implementation of extensive structural adjustments; and have promoted deregulation in critical sectors (banking, telecoms, energy), privatization of ailing public sector corporations, and a more flexible and liberal institutional framework, to attract foreign investment inflows.

Table 18 ADCC-GARCH(1,1) estimates: before-after financial crisis.

	Summary statistic of conditional correlations									
	Before financial crisis (January 2000–September 2008)					After financial crisis (October 2008–March 2013)				
	Mean	Median	Min.	Max.	Std.	Mean	Median	Min.	Max.	Std.
S&P500 vs DAX	0.6111	0.6268	0.4773	0.7310	0.0590	0.6884	0.6977	0.5756	0.7538	0.0327
S&P500 vs ASE-GI	0.2746	0.2814	0.8933	0.4755	0.0796	0.3021	0.3013	0.1486	0.4372	0.0685
S&P500 vs CYP-GI	0.1796	0.0102	0.0601	0.8725	0.1139	0.1889	0.2091	0.0095	0.6520	0.1248
S&P500 vs ISE-100	0.2404	0.2177	0.1023	0.4127	0.0723	0.3526	0.3611	0.1958	0.4683	0.0597
S&P500 vs BET-C	0.0821	0.0786	−0.0647	0.2907	0.0543	0.2271	0.2321	0.0730	0.4014	0.0707
S&P500 vs CROBEX	0.1157	0.1171	−0.0811	0.2874	0.0695	0.2519	0.2441	0.1106	0.3907	0.0561
S&P500 vs SOFIX	0.0120	0.0114	−0.1284	0.1483	0.0425	0.0970	0.1022	−0.0355	0.2116	0.0532
DAX vs ASE-GI	0.4486	0.4502	0.2606	0.6405	0.0776	0.4386	0.4495	0.2450	0.6035	0.0830
DAX vs CYP-GI	0.0254	0.0280	0.0185	0.8363	0.1219	0.0366	0.0360	0.0758	0.7250	0.1119
DAX vs ISE-100	0.3471	0.3223	0.0993	0.6384	0.1045	0.4511	0.4580	0.2874	0.5625	0.0626
DAX vs BET-C	0.1329	0.1234	0.0121	0.3818	0.0663	0.2895	0.2884	0.1420	0.4674	0.0631
DAX vs CROBEX	0.1807	0.1737	−0.1427	0.4375	0.0969	0.2992	0.2983	0.0750	0.4730	0.0817
DAX vs SOFIX	0.0546	0.0508	−0.0801	0.2819	0.0622	0.1320	0.1292	0.0333	0.2679	0.0521
ASE-GI vs CYP-GI	0.3090	0.3110	0.0213	0.8545	0.1405	0.3870	0.3890	0.0014	0.3457	0.1210
ASE-GI vs ISE-100	0.3285	0.2943	0.1282	0.5929	0.1160	0.3338	0.3128	0.1628	0.5559	0.0833
ASE-GI vs BET-C	0.1508	0.1219	0.0359	0.3953	0.0800	0.2672	0.2586	0.1165	0.4483	0.0624
ASE-GI vs CROBEX	0.1500	0.1427	−0.0257	0.3568	0.0730	0.2571	0.2467	0.0118	0.4162	0.0823
ASE-GI vs SOFIX	0.0572	0.0360	−0.0499	0.3579	0.0682	0.1239	0.1006	0.0379	0.3159	0.0569
CYP-GI vs ISE-100	0.2864	0.3170	0.0561	0.4649	0.1070	0.3752	0.3876	0.0156	0.4957	0.1035
CYP-GI vs BET-C	0.2930	0.2998	0.0912	0.8602	0.1244	0.3380	0.3400	0.0824	0.6720	0.1128
CYP-GI vs CROBEX	0.0460	0.0501	−0.0952	0.8304	0.1197	0.0665	0.0685	−0.0040	0.0342	0.1145
CYP-GI vs SOFIX	0.0856	0.0920	0.0192	0.6698	0.1065	0.9762	0.9978	0.0280	0.0987	0.1076
ISE-100 vs BET-C	0.1764	0.1561	0.0370	0.4080	0.0740	0.2605	0.2442	0.1495	0.4248	0.0628
ISE-100 vs CROBEX	0.1453	0.1516	−0.4057	0.4450	0.1234	0.2499	0.2467	0.0857	0.4485	0.0863
ISE-100 vs SOFIX	0.0488	0.0460	−0.0862	0.2237	0.0540	0.0927	0.0815	−0.0466	0.2485	0.0594
BET-C vs CROBEX	0.1450	0.1485	−0.3516	0.3621	0.0947	0.2714	0.2713	0.1393	0.4000	0.0475
BET-C vs SOFIX	0.0988	0.1034	−0.1079	0.2390	0.0552	0.1883	0.1836	0.0311	0.3257	0.0582
CROBEX vs SOFIX	0.1053	0.1023	−0.0090	0.2916	0.0525	0.1862	0.1774	0.0522	0.3330	0.0640

Notes: the table summarizes a set of descriptive statistics of the time-varying estimated correlations produced by the ADCC model for the SEE and developed equity markets, including mean, median, maximum, minimum, and standard deviation values. The estimated coefficients, $\theta_1 = 0.02601$ and $\theta_2 = 0.6748$, are positive and statistically significant at the 5% level; $\theta_1 + \theta_2 = 0.70081$, supporting the presence of dynamic correlations over time. Since $\theta_1 + \theta_2 < 1$, the dynamic correlations move around a constant level and the dynamic process appears to be mean-reverting.

5. CONCLUSIONS

This Chapter has undertaken a thorough investigation of major SEE economies, discussing critical recent developments, market trends, and growth prospects. Emphasis was placed on the SEE capital markets, their contribution to domestic economic growth, and the dynamic risk-return properties they exhibit, especially after the 2008 global financial crisis. To better illustrate the empirical findings, the behavioral patterns of the SEE capital markets (Romania, Bulgaria, Croatia, Greece, Cyprus, Turkey) were compared with and contrasted against those of leading mature stock markets (Germany, USA).

The Chapter, more specifically, was developed on three core sections. The first section dealt with the macroeconomic environment in the Eurozone and the SEE economies of interest. Key macroeconomic factors were analyzed and the short-term prospects of the SEE economies were summarized, including an assessment and rating of financial, economic, and political risks. The second section discussed the SEE capital markets, their brief modern historical developments, gradual liberalization and openness, and their risk-return properties that have offered an attractive performance to international investors, especially before the global financial crisis. A concise empirical literature review was also covered, although research on this topic remains thin. The last section applied a set of quantitative models, tools, and statistics to investigate dynamic linkages, comovements, volatility spillovers, and contagion effects between SEE and leading global markets, distinguishing between the recent financial pre-crisis and after-crisis time sub-periods.

The dynamic variance-covariance analysis indicated correlations predominantly between the SEE stock markets rather than with the developed equity markets (ADCC model), which were found to intensify after the financial crisis, in line with similar past findings. The SEE markets were seen to exhibit asymmetric and persisting volatilities at negative news and market crises events. These are useful empirical inputs to international portfolio diversification decisions and efficient risk management.

The SEE economies are currently in a process of extensive structural adjustments to contain the global financial crisis implications and reverse the deep recessionary conditions, moving, at the same time, on a catching-up path toward further integration with their developed European peers. In this setting, dynamic portfolio diversification into the SEE equity markets can still offer potential rewarding investment opportunities and improve investors' return performance. Further empirical research on these issues would be interesting, timely, and useful.

ACKNOWLEDGMENT

Professor Theodore Syriopoulos would like to acknowledge and thank Dr. Efthymios Roumpis for extensive data, quantitative and modeling support, and contribution into this study.

REFERENCES

Alexakis, P., Apergis, N., Xanthakis, E., 1997. Integration of international capital markets: further evidence from EMS and non-EMS membership. Journal of International Financial Markets, Institutions and Money 7, 277–287

Athanassiou, E., Kollias, C., Syriopoulos, T., 2006. Dynamic volatility and external security related shocks: the case of the Athens stock exchange. International Financial Markets, Institutions and Money 16, 411–424

Bauwens, L., Laurent, S., Rombouts, J., 2006. Multivariate GARCH models: a survey. Journal of Applied Econometrics 21 (1), 79–109

Bechev, D., 2012. The periphery of the periphery: the Western Balkans and the Euro crisis. Policy Paper, European Council on Foreign Relations. <www.ecfr.eu>.
Beirne, J., Caporale, G.M., Schultze-Ghattas, M., Spagnolo, N., 2010. Global and regional spillovers in emerging stock markets: a multivariate GARCH-in-mean analysis. Emerging Markets Review 11, 250–260
Bekaert, G., Wu, G., 2000. Asymmetric volatility and risk in equity markets. Review of Financial Studies 13, 1–42
Bessler, D.A., Yang, J., 2003. The structure of interdependence in international stock markets. Journal of International Money and Finance 22, 261–287
Bollerslev, T., 1986. Generalized autoregressive conditional heteroskedasticity. Journal of Econometrics 31 (3), 307–328
Bollerslev, T., Engle, R., Wooldridge, J., 1988. A capital asset pricing model with time varying covariances. Journal of Political Economy 96, 116–131
Bollerslev, T., 1990. Modelling the coherence in short-run nominal exchange rates: a multivariate generalized ARCH Model. Review of Economics and Statistics 72, 498–505
Bonetto, F., Redžepagić, S., Tykhonenko, A., 2009. Balkan countries: catching up and their integration in the European financial system. Paneconomicus 4, 475–489
Buttner, D., Hayo, B., 2011. Determinants of European stock market integration. Economic Systems 35, 574–585
Cappiello, L., Engle, R., Sheppard, K., 2006a. Asymmetric dynamics in the correlations of global equity and bond returns. Journal of Financial Econometrics 4 (4), 537–572
Cappiello, L., Gerard, B., Kaderaja, A., Manganelli, S., 2006b. Financial integration of new EU member states. Working Paper No. 683 (October), European Central Bank.
Cifarelli, G., Paladino, G., 2005. Volatility linkages across three major equity markets: a financial arbitrage approach. Journal of International Money and Finance 24 (3), 413–439
Clausing, K., Dorobantu, C., 2005. Re-entering Europe: does European union candidacy boost foreign direct investment? Economics of Transition 13, 77–103
Dickinson, D.G., 2000. Stock market integration and macroeconomic fundamentals: an empirical analysis, 1980–95. Applied Financial Economics 10 (3), 261–276
Dvorak, T., Podpiera, R., 2006. European union enlargement and equity markets in accession countries. Emerging Markets Review 7, 129–146
Egert, B., Kocenda, E., 2007. Interdependence between Eastern and Western European stock markets: evidence from intraday data. Economic Systems 31 (2), 184–203
Ejara, D., 2009. Comovement of European equity markets after Euro. Working Paper (March), Economics and Finance, University of New Haven.
Engle, R., 1982. Autoregressive conditional heteroskedasticity with estimates of the variance of United Kingdom inflation. Econometrica 50, 987–1007
Engle, R., Ng, V., 1993. Measuring and testing the impact of news on volatility. Journal of Finance 48 (5), 1749–1778
Engle, R., 2002. Dynamic conditional correlation: a new class of multivariate generalized autoregressive conditional heteroskedasticity models. Journal of Business and Economic Statistics 20, 339–350
Engle, R., Kroner, K., 1995. Multivariate simultaneous generalized ARCH. Econometric Theory 11, 122–150
European Commission, 2013. European economic forecasts. Report on the European Economy, January, European Union.
Fernández-Villaverde, J., Rubio-Ramirez, J., 2010. Macroeconomics and volatility: data, models and estimation. Discussion Paper No. 8169, Centre for Economic Policy Research.
Garcia, R., Tsafack, G., 2011. Dependence structure and extreme comovements in international equity and bonds markets. Journal of Banking and Finance 35 (8), 1954–1970
Gelos, G., Sahay, R., 2001. Financial market spillovers in transition economies. Economics of Transition 9 (1), 53–86
Gilmore, C., Lucey, B., McManus, G., 2008. The dynamics of Central European equity market integration. Quarterly Review of Economics and Finance 48 (3), 605–622

Golubović, S., Golubović, N., 2005. Financial sector reform in the Balkan countries in transition. Economics and Organization 2 (3), 229–236

Guidi, F., Ugur, M., 2013. Are South East Europe stock markets integrated with regional and global stock markets? Working Paper (February), University of Greenwich Business School.

Hanousek, J., Kocenda, E., 2011. Foreign news and spillovers in emerging European stock markets. Review of International Economics 19 (1), 170–188

Horvath, R., Petrovski, D., 2012. International stock market integration: Central and South Eastern Europe compared. Working Paper No. 1028 (February). University of Michigan, The William Davidson Institute.

IMF, 2005. Transition Economies: an IMF perspective on progress and prospects. Working Paper, International Monetary Fund. <www.imf.org/external/np/exr/ib/2000//110300.htm>.

IMF, 2012. World economic outlook: coping with high debt and sluggish growth. World Economic and Financial Surveys, Semiannual Report (October), International Monetary Fund.

IMF, 2013. Country Reports. Various Issues, International Monetary Fund. <http://www.imf.org/external/country/>.

Kearney, C., Poti, V., 2006. Correlation dynamics in European equity markets. Research in International Business and Finance 20 (3), 305–321

Kenc, T., Dibooglu, S., 2010. The 2007–2009 financial crisis, global imbalances and capital flows: implications for reform. Economic Systems 34, 3–21

Kekic, L., 2005. Foreign direct investment in the Balkans: recent trends and prospects. Southeast European and Black Sea Studies 5, 171–190

Kenourgios, D., Samitas, A., 2011. Equity market integration in emerging Balkan markets. Research in International Business and Finance 25, 296–307

Koutmos, G., 1996. Modeling the dynamic interdependence of major European stock markets. Journal of Business Finance and Accounting 23, 975–988

Kroner, K., Ng, V., 1998. Modelling asymmetric comovements of assets returns. Review of Financial Studies 11, 817–844

Longin, F., Solnik, B., 2001. Extreme correlation of international equity markets. Journal of Finance 56 (2), 649–676

Marcelo, J., Quiros, J., Quiros, M., 2008. Asymmetric variance and spillover effects: regime shifts in the Spanish stock market. Journal of Financial Markets, Institutions and Money 18 (1), 1–15

Mazzotta, S., 2008. How important is asymmetric covariance for the risk premium of international assets. Journal of Banking and Finance 32 (8), 1636–1647

Middleton, C., Fifield, S., Power, D., 2008. An investigation of the benefits of portfolio investment in Central and Eastern European stock markets. Research in International Business and Finance 22, 162–174

Phylaktis, K., Ravazzolo, F., 2002. Stock market linkages in emerging markets: implications for international portfolio diversification. Journal of International Financial Markets, Institutions and Money 15 (2), 91–106

PRS Group, 2013. International Country Risk Guide. <http://www.prsgroup.com/ICRGMethodology.aspx>.

Samitas, A., Kenourgios, D., Paltalidis, N., 2006. Short and long run parametric dynamics in the Balkans stock markets. International Journal of Business, Management and Economics 2 (8), 5–20

Savva, C., Osborm, D., Gill, L., 2009. Spillovers and correlations between US and major European stock markets: the role of the euro. Applied Financial Economics 19 (19), 1595–1604

Skintzi, V., Refenes, A., 2006. Volatility spillovers and dynamic correlation in European bond markets. Journal of International Financial Markets, Institutions and Money 16 (1), 23–40

Syriopoulos, T., 2004. International portfolio diversification to Central European stock markets. Applied Financial Economics 14 (17), 1–16

Syriopoulos, T., 2006. Risk and return implications from investing in emerging European stock markets. Journal of International Financial Markets, Institutions and Money 16 (3), 283–299

Syriopoulos, T., 2007. Dynamic linkages between emerging European and developed stock markets: has the EMU any impact? International Review of Financial Analysis 16 (1), 41–60

Syriopoulos, T., 2011. Financial integration and portfolio investments to emerging Balkan equity markets. Journal of Multinational Financial Management 21 (1), 40–54

Syriopoulos, T., Roumpis, E., 2009. Dynamic correlations and volatility effects in the Balkan equity markets. Journal of International Financial Markets, Institutions and Money 19 (4), 565–587

UNCTAD, 2013. World investment report: towards a new generation of investment policies. Annual Report, United Nations Conference on Trade and Development.

World Federation of Exchanges, 2013. Country Stock Market Statistics, Various Reports. <http://www.world-exchanges.org/statistics/monthly-reports>.

Yang, J., Min, I., Li, Q., 2003. European stock market integration: does EMU matter? Journal of Business Finance and Accounting 30, 1253–1276

CHAPTER 29

Emerging Market Stocks in Global Portfolios: A Hedging Approach

Imad Moosa and Vikash Ramiah
School of Economics, Finance and Marketing, Royal Melbourne Institute of Technology (RMIT), Melbourne, Australia

1. INTRODUCTION

A consensus view that seems to have been established in the finance literature is that international diversification leads to more efficient portfolios (in terms of the risk-return criterion) than purely domestic portfolios. More specifically, it is envisaged that international diversification provides lower risk or/and higher return than what can be obtained from investment in domestic assets. The underlying idea is that effective diversification requires low return correlations of the constituent components of a diversified portfolio. Since stock returns are less highly correlated across countries than within one country, it follows that international diversification is more effective than diversification within one country.

This proposition made a lot of sense in the 1960s and 1970s when markets were segmented and capital controls as well as other impediments were imposed to restrict capital outflows and foreign ownership of domestic stocks—these factors made cross-country stock returns weakly correlated. Hence, although the scope for international diversification was limited, it was intuitive to suggest that diversification across countries was useful. But things have changed since the advent of globalization and the removal of restrictions on foreign investment in domestic markets and domestic investment in foreign markets. That has made stock returns highly correlated, hence reducing the effectiveness of international diversification, particularly among developed countries. It is for this reason that some advocates of international diversification believe that diversification into emerging markets can be useful, at least relative to diversification into developed markets.

The question that arises here is that if international diversification is as useful as it is typically portrayed to be, why is it then that investors worldwide exhibit very strong home-country bias, the tendency to assign a heavy weight to domestic stocks in any internationally diversified portfolio? Although several explanations have been put forward to resolve the "home-bias puzzle," a more intuitive explanation is that international diversification does not pay off or that it is not effective in reducing risk.

Studies of the benefits of international diversification are typically based on the mean-variance criterion whereby the risk and return on domestic and internationally diversified

Emerging Markets and the Global Economy
http://dx.doi.org/10.1016/B978-0-12-411549-1.00029-6

portfolios are compared, often without testing. Furthermore, the usual assumption is that long positions are taken on stocks, and this is why the emphasis is on low correlation as the conduit to effective international diversification. An alternative approach is found in the hedging literature where emphasis is placed on risk reduction. In their study of international diversification, Coeurdacier and Guibaud (2011) refer to the concept of hedging in conjunction with the concept of home bias. Specifically, they investigate whether or not investors correctly hedge their overexposure to domestic risk by investing in foreign stock markets. However, they emphasize low correlation, implying that the investor always takes similar positions. In the hedging approach, opposite positions are taken on the asset to be hedged and the hedging instrument.

The objective of this study is to find out if diversification into emerging markets produces better results in terms of risk reduction than diversification into developed markets. The portfolios are constructed in such a way as to contain combinations of developed markets only, emerging markets only, and both (mixed portfolios). We also construct two-market and multi-market portfolios and examine returns with and without the foreign exchange factor.

2. THE AVAILABLE EVIDENCE

Early studies of international diversification were conducted in the 1960s and 1970s—they were overwhelmingly supportive of the benefits of international diversification. Grubel (1968), Levy and Sarnat (1970), Grubel and Fander (1971), Solnik (1974), Lassard (1976), and Biger (1979) have demonstrated that international diversification provides US investors with a lower risk for a given level of expected return. For example, Grubel (1968) found that US investors could have achieved better risk-return opportunities by investing part of their portfolios in foreign stock markets during the period 1959–1966. Levy and Sarnat (1970) demonstrated the diversification benefits from investing in both developed and developing stock markets during the period 1951–1967. Grubel and Fander (1971) showed that industry correlations within countries exceed industry correlations across countries. The implication here is that a necessary condition for risk reduction through international diversification is low correlation between stock returns.

A similar story is told by the more recent studies conduced by Bailey and Stulz (1990), Odier and Solnik (1993), Doukas and Yung (1993), Chang et al. (1995), Solnik (1995, 1997), Akdogan (1996), Michaud et al. (1996), De Santis and Gerard (1997), Griffin and Karolyi (1998), Ang and Bekaert (2002), Driessen and Laeven (2007), Yavas (2007), De Santis and Sarno (2008), Coeurdacier and Guibaud (2011), and Fisher (2012). Fisher (2012) argues that since it is nearly impossible to predict which market will be a top performer in a given year, it makes sense to hold a portfolio that is diversified across a number of countries. He further argues that the independent movement of global markets, which react to factors such as different domestic monetary and fiscal policy cycles, provides "considerable diversification benefits."

Diversification into emerging markets is advocated by several scholars. For example, Conover et al. (2002) suggest that emerging equity markets are a worthy addition to a US investor's portfolio of developed market equities. Specifically, they found that portfolio returns increased by approximately 1.5 percentage points a year when emerging country equities were included in the portfolio. A similar idea is put forward by Russel (1998) who states that "even the relatively risky practice of investing in emerging markets has been viewed, by some, as a sound investment strategy for individuals." Goetzmann et al. (2005) argue that globalization has resulted in limiting the benefits of diversification to the extent that it can best be achieved by investing in emerging markets. Driessen and Laeven (2007) find that the benefits of investing abroad are largest for investors in developing countries. The implication of these studies is that the benefits of portfolio diversification accrue to investors from developed countries diversifying into emerging markets and investors from emerging countries diversifying into developed markets.

Several studies have been done on the phenomenon of home bias. Lewis (2006) describes as "one of the most enduring puzzles in international macroeconomics and finance" the tendency of investors to select a disproportionately high weight for domestic securities, thus foregoing the gains of international diversification. French and Poterba (1991) found that the significant home bias cannot be explained in terms of capital controls, tax burden, and transaction costs. Baxter and Jermann (1997) argue that "while recent years have witnessed an increase in international diversification, holdings of domestic assets are still too high to be consistent with the theory of portfolio choice." Some attempts have been made to resolve the home-bias "puzzle" in terms of barriers to international investment (Errunza and Losq, 1985), departures from purchasing power parity (Cooper and Kaplanis, 1994), the hedging of human capital or other nontraded assets (Baxter and Jermann, 1997; Stockman and Dellas, 1989; Obstfeld and Rogoff, 1998; Wheatley, 2001), and in terms of stock market development and familiarity (Chan et al., 2005).

But there are those who cast doubt on the benefits of international diversification and suggest that as an explanation for home bias. For example, Kalra et al. (2004) find that the benefits of international diversification are much smaller than previously thought. Their findings suggest that a small allocation of 10 per cent to international securities may be justified and that even the slight advantage of international diversification may disappear when taxes are incorporated in the evaluation. They also argue that to maintain the intended diversification, periodic rebalancing of the portfolio is necessary to keep the domestic and foreign component weights at target levels as suggested by Rowland (1999) and Laker (2003). However, international investment (particularly in emerging markets) involves nontrivial transaction costs that need to be considered when estimating portfolio performance. Thus, in the presence of periodic rebalancing and associated transaction costs, international diversification does not pay off. On the basis of her results Lewis (2006) concludes that "the benefits to diversification have declined both for stocks inside and outside the US."

3. METHODOLOGY

Financial hedging entails taking an offsetting position on another asset or a hedging instrument—offsetting in the sense that if the unhedged position is long then the position on the hedging instrument must be short, and vice versa. The idea is that if a loss is incurred on the unhedged position, the loss will be offset by profit on the position in the hedging instrument, and vice versa.

3.1. Calculation of the Hedge Ratio

The construction of the portfolios requires the calculation of the hedge ratio by minimizing the variance of the rate of return on the hedged position (the portfolio). The rate of return on the portfolio, R_p, is defined as:

$$R_p = R - hR^*, \quad (1)$$

where R is the rate of return on the domestic asset, R^* is the rate of return on the foreign asset, and h is the hedge ratio. This variance of the rate of return on the portfolio, $\sigma^2(R_p)$, is given by:

$$\sigma^2(R_p) = \sigma^2(R) + h^2\sigma^2(R^*) - 2h\sigma(R, R^*), \quad (2)$$

where $\sigma^2(R)$ is the variance of the rate of return on the domestic asset, $\sigma^2(R^*)$ is the variance of the rate of return on the foreign asset, and $\sigma(R, R^*)$ is the covariance of domestic and foreign returns. The minimum-risk hedge ratio is calculated from the first-order condition:

$$\frac{\partial\sigma^2(R_p)}{\partial h} = 2\sigma^2(R)h - 2\sigma(R, R^*) = 0. \quad (3)$$

Hence:

$$h = \frac{\sigma(R, R^*)}{\sigma^2(R^*)}. \quad (4)$$

Empirically, the minimum-risk hedge ratio can be calculated from historical data by estimating the regression equation:

$$R_t = \alpha + hR_t^* + \varepsilon_t. \quad (5)$$

If the rate of return is taken to be the first log difference (or the percentage change) of the stock price, equation (5) can be re-written as:

$$\Delta p_t = \alpha + h\Delta p_t^* + \varepsilon_t, \quad (6)$$

where p_t and p_t^* are the logarithms of domestic and foreign stock prices, respectively.

To take into account the foreign exchange factor, return on the foreign asset must be converted into domestic currency terms, which gives:

$$\widetilde{R} = (1 + R^*)(1 + \Delta e) - 1, \tag{7}$$

where $\widetilde{R}$ is the return on the foreign asset converted into domestic currency terms and Δe is the percentage change in the exchange rate measured as the domestic currency price of one unit of the foreign currency. An approximation of (7) is obtained when $R^* \Delta e \approx 0$, which is a valid assumption for small values of R^* and Δe. Thus, we have:

$$\widetilde{R} = R^* + \Delta e. \tag{8}$$

The equivalent of equation (6) when we take the exchange rate into consideration is:

$$\Delta p_t = \alpha + h\left(\Delta p_t^* + \Delta e\right) + \varepsilon_t. \tag{9}$$

So far we have dealt with measuring the hedge ratio for a two-stock portfolio (that is, the hedging instrument is one foreign asset). However, a domestic asset can be hedged by taking an opposite position on a number of foreign assets, in which case we have to calculate multiple hedge ratios, one for each foreign asset. The hedge ratio for each of k foreign assets is calculated by regressing domestic return on foreign returns. Without the foreign exchange factor, the regression equation is specified as:

$$\Delta p_t = \alpha + \sum_{i=1}^{k} h_i \Delta p_{it}^* + \varepsilon_t. \tag{10}$$

With the foreign exchange factor, the hedge ratios are calculated from the regression equation:

$$\Delta p_t = \alpha + \sum_{i=1}^{k} h_i\left(\Delta p_{it}^* + \Delta e_{it}\right) + \varepsilon_t. \tag{11}$$

In both cases, the rate of return on the overall portfolio is calculated as:

$$R_p = R - \sum_{i=1}^{k} h_i R_i^*. \tag{12}$$

3.2. Measuring Hedging Effectiveness

Hedging effectiveness can be measured by the variance of the rate of return on the portfolio compared with the variance of the rate of return on the domestic asset. The underlying null hypothesis is:

$$H_0 : \sigma^2(R) = \sigma^2(R_p), \tag{13}$$

whereas the alternative hypothesis of effective hedging is:

$$H_1 : \sigma^2(R) > \sigma^2(R_p). \tag{14}$$

The null is rejected if the variance ratio, VR, is statistically significant—that is if:

$$VR = \frac{\sigma^2(R)}{\sigma^2(R_p)} > F(n-1, n-1), \tag{15}$$

where n is the sample size. This test can be complemented by calculating variance reduction, VD, as follows:

$$VD = 1 - \frac{1}{VR} = 1 - \frac{\sigma^2(R_p)}{\sigma^2(R)} = \frac{\sigma^2(R - hR^*)}{\sigma^2(R)}. \tag{16}$$

The importance of correlation between the rates of return, R and R^*, for hedging effectiveness can be demonstrated by deriving the relation between correlation and the variance ratio. The correlation coefficient, ρ, is defined as:

$$\rho = \frac{\sigma(R, R^*)}{\sigma(R)\sigma(R^*)}, \tag{17}$$

where $\sigma(R)$ and $\sigma(R^*)$ are respectively the standard deviations of the rates of return on the domestic and foreign assets. This gives:

$$\sigma(R, R^*) = \rho\sigma(R)\sigma(R^*). \tag{18}$$

By substituting equation (18) in equation (4), which defines the hedge ratio, we obtain:

$$h = \frac{\rho\sigma(R)\sigma(R^*)}{\sigma^2(R^*)} = \rho\left[\frac{\sigma(R)}{\sigma(R^*)}\right]. \tag{19}$$

Equation (15) can be re-written as:

$$VR = \frac{\sigma^2(R)}{\sigma^2(R) + h^2\sigma^2(R^*) - 2\left[\frac{\rho\sigma(R)\sigma(R^*)}{\sigma^2(R^*)}\right]\rho\sigma(R)\sigma(R^*)} \tag{20}$$

which can be simplified to obtain:

$$VR = \frac{1}{1-\rho^2} \tag{21}$$

implying a positive relation between VR and ρ. It follows that:

$$VD = 1 - \frac{1}{VR} = \rho^2 \tag{22}$$

which shows variance reduction and the correlation coefficient to be related by a positive nonlinear relation.

3.3. Construction of Portfolios

Consider m developed markets and $m - n$ emerging markets with stock price indices $P_1, P_2, \ldots, P_m, P_{m+1}, P_{m+2}, \ldots, P_n$. Without taking into account the foreign exchange factor, the rate of return on any of the possible $n!/2!$ portfolios is:

$$R_p = \Delta p_i - h\Delta p_j, \tag{23}$$

where a lowercase letter implies the logarithm of the corresponding stock price index. For portfolios involving developed markets only, $i = 1, \ldots, m$ and $j = 1, \ldots, m$, such that $i \neq j$. For portfolios involving emerging markets only, $i = m + 1, \ldots, n$ and $j = m+1, \ldots, n$, such that $i \neq j$. For mixed portfolios involving developed and emerging markets, $i = 1, \ldots, m$ and $j = m + 1, \ldots, n$. If the foreign exchange factor is to be accounted for, equation (23) becomes:

$$\widetilde{R}_p = \Delta p_i - h(\Delta p_j + \Delta e_j), \tag{24}$$

where the exchange rate is measured as the price in terms of currency i of one unit of currency j.

For multi-stock mixed portfolios, the rate of return on the portfolio without the foreign exchange rate factor is:

$$R_p = \Delta p_i - \sum_j h_j \Delta p_j, \tag{25}$$

where $i = 1, \ldots, m$ and $1 < j \leq n - m$.

4. AN INFORMAL EXAMINATION OF THE DATA

The empirical results are based on monthly data covering seven developed and seven emerging markets covering the period January 2003 to February 2013. The developed markets are those of the US, UK, Japan, Australia, Canada, Switzerland, and Sweden. The emerging markets are Malaysia, China, Mexico, Thailand, Argentina, Turkey, and Pakistan. Stock prices are proxied by market indices as reported in the *International Financial Statistics* of the International Monetary Fund. There is nothing special about the choice of these countries—the choice was dictated by the availability of data. We actually started with more countries but we had to discard some because of missing observations or similar data problems. The choice of the sample period was dictated by the desire to make the sample as up to date as possible while maintaining a reasonably large sample.

Exchange rates against the US dollar were obtained from the same source. Cross rates between two non-dollar currencies are calculated from the respective dollar rates. For example, the exchange rate between the yen and pound (measured as the yen price of one pound) is calculated by dividing the yen/dollar rate by the pound/dollar rate. This procedure is based on the condition precluding the possibility of triangular arbitrage.

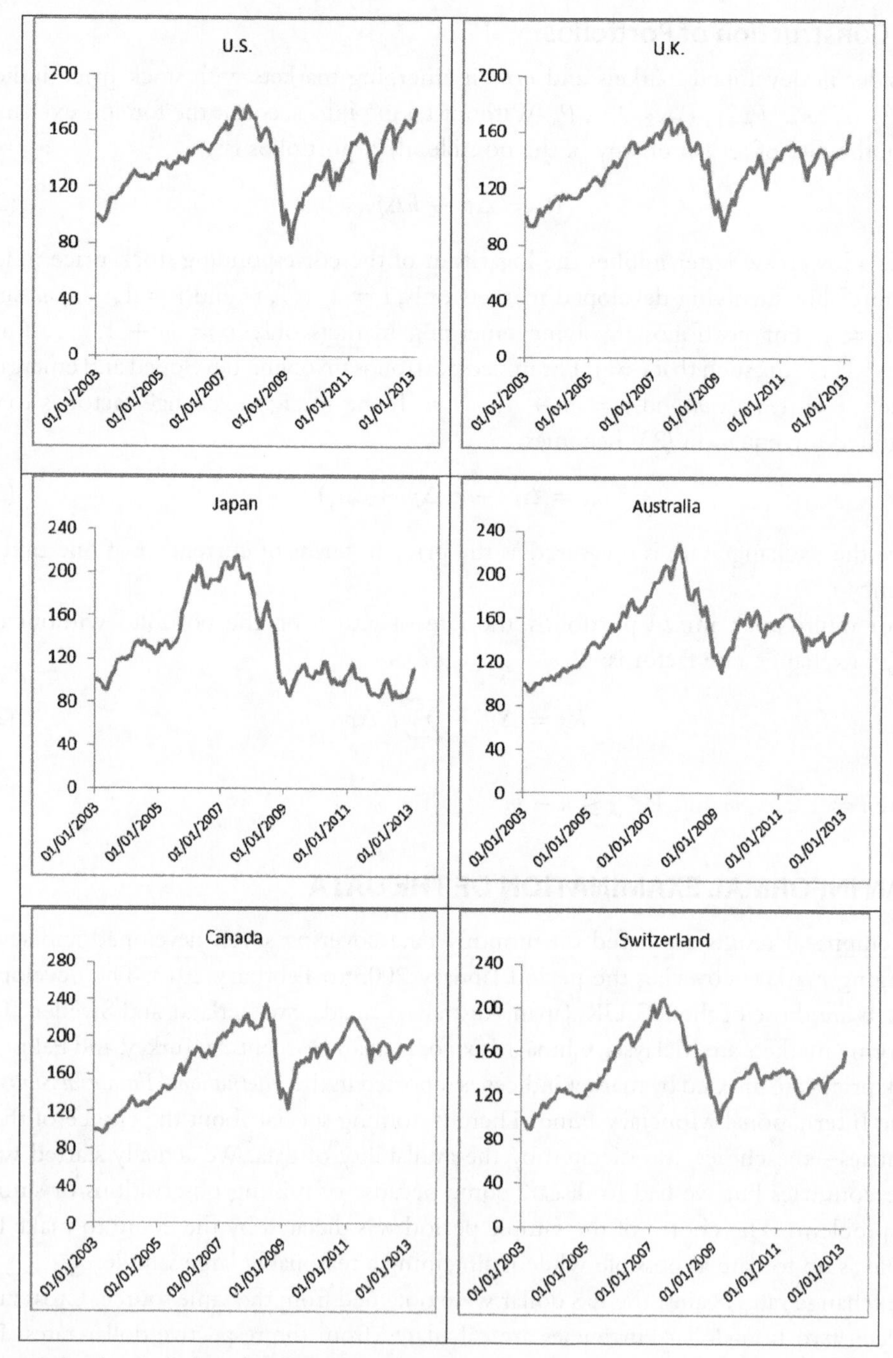

Figure 1 Stock price indices (January 2003 = 100).

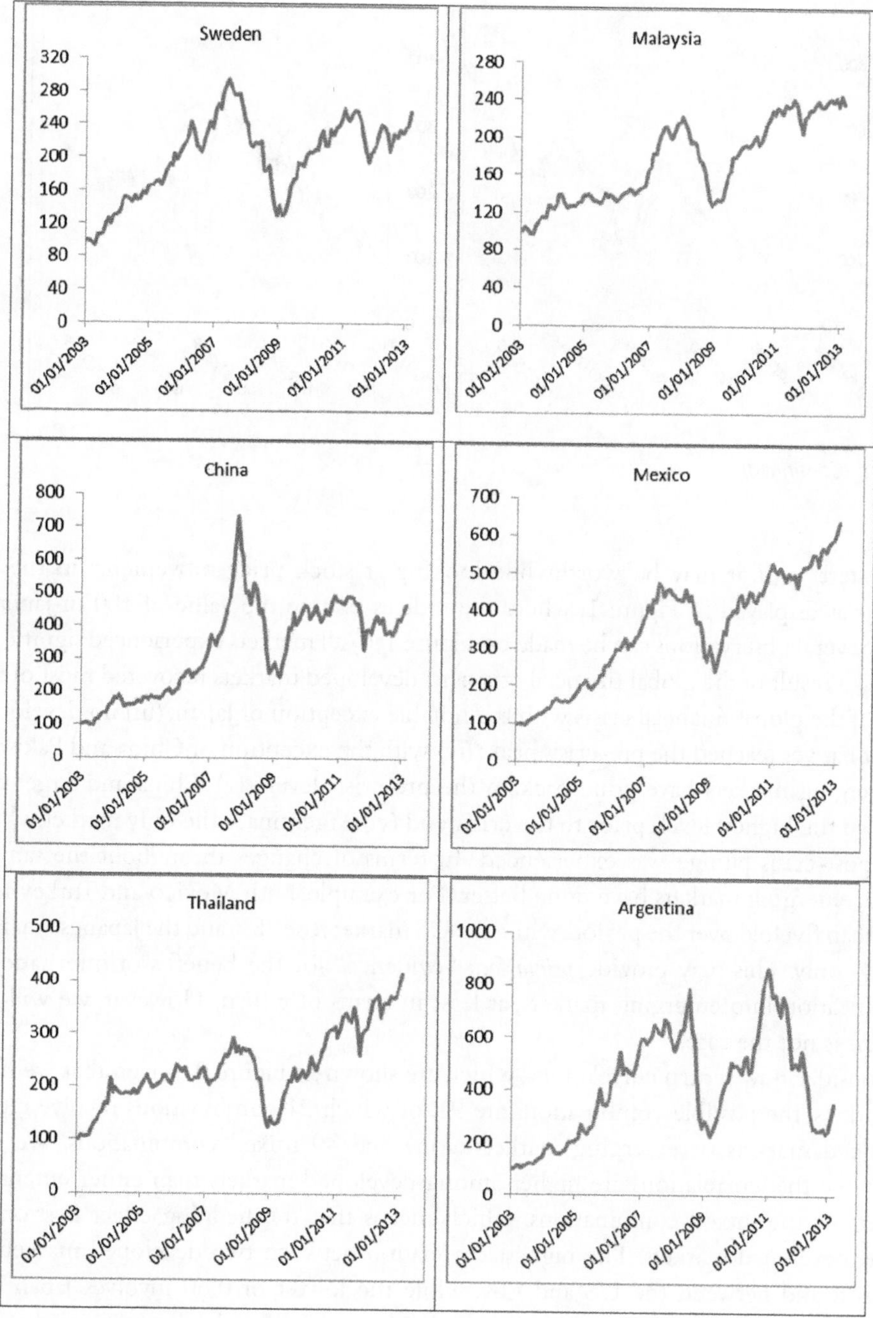

Figure 1 *(Continued)*.

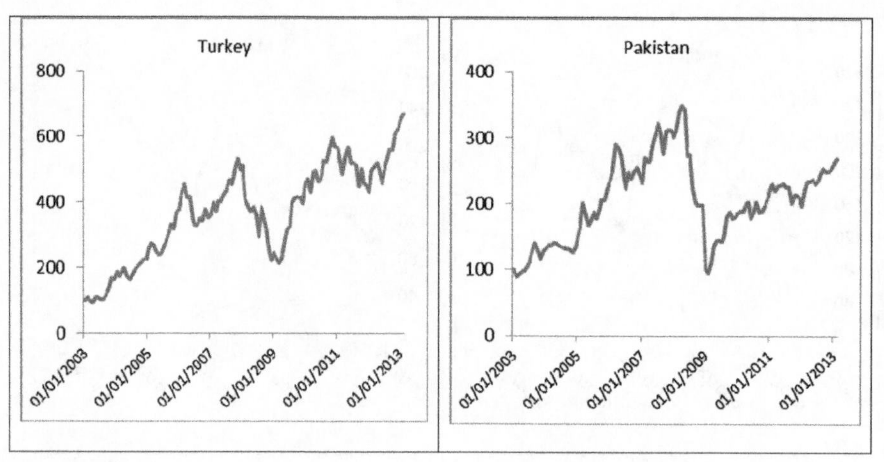

Figure 1 *(Continued).*

To start with, it may be worthwhile looking at stock price movements in the 14 markets as displayed in Figure 1, where the indices assume the value of 100 in January 2003. Several observations can be made on Figure 1: (i) all markets experienced significant drops as a result of the global financial crisis; (ii) developed markets recovered most of the losses of the global financial crisis with the notable exception of Japan; (iii) no developed market has yet reached the pre-crisis peak; (iv) with the exception of China and Pakistan, all emerging markets have gone back to the pre-crisis levels; (v) China and Argentina recorded the highest levels prior to the crisis; and (vi) Argentina is the only market where a big post-crisis plunge was experienced. In terms of changes throughout the sample period, emerging markets have done better. For example, both Mexico and Turkey rose more than fivefold over the period, while the US market rose 75% and the Japanese market by 11% only. This may provide *prima facie* "evidence" for the benefits of international diversification into emerging markets, at least in terms of return. However, we will see that this is not the case.

Consider now return correlations, which are shown in Figure 2. Given that we have 14 markets, the possible combinations are 91, of which 21 combinations involve either developed markets or emerging markets alone and 49 mixed combinations. We can readily see that correlations are higher among developed markets than either emerging markets or the mixed combinations, which means that the hedging effect is stronger among developed markets. The highest correlation between two developed markets of 0.88 is found between the US and UK, while the lowest of 0.60 involves Japan and Switzerland. Low correlations typically involve Japan because the Japanese market has been behaving in a different manner since the boom of the 1980s and the subsequent deflationary conditions prevailing in the Japanese economy. In the mixed portfolios, the highest correlation is to be found between the US and Mexico, which is not surprising,

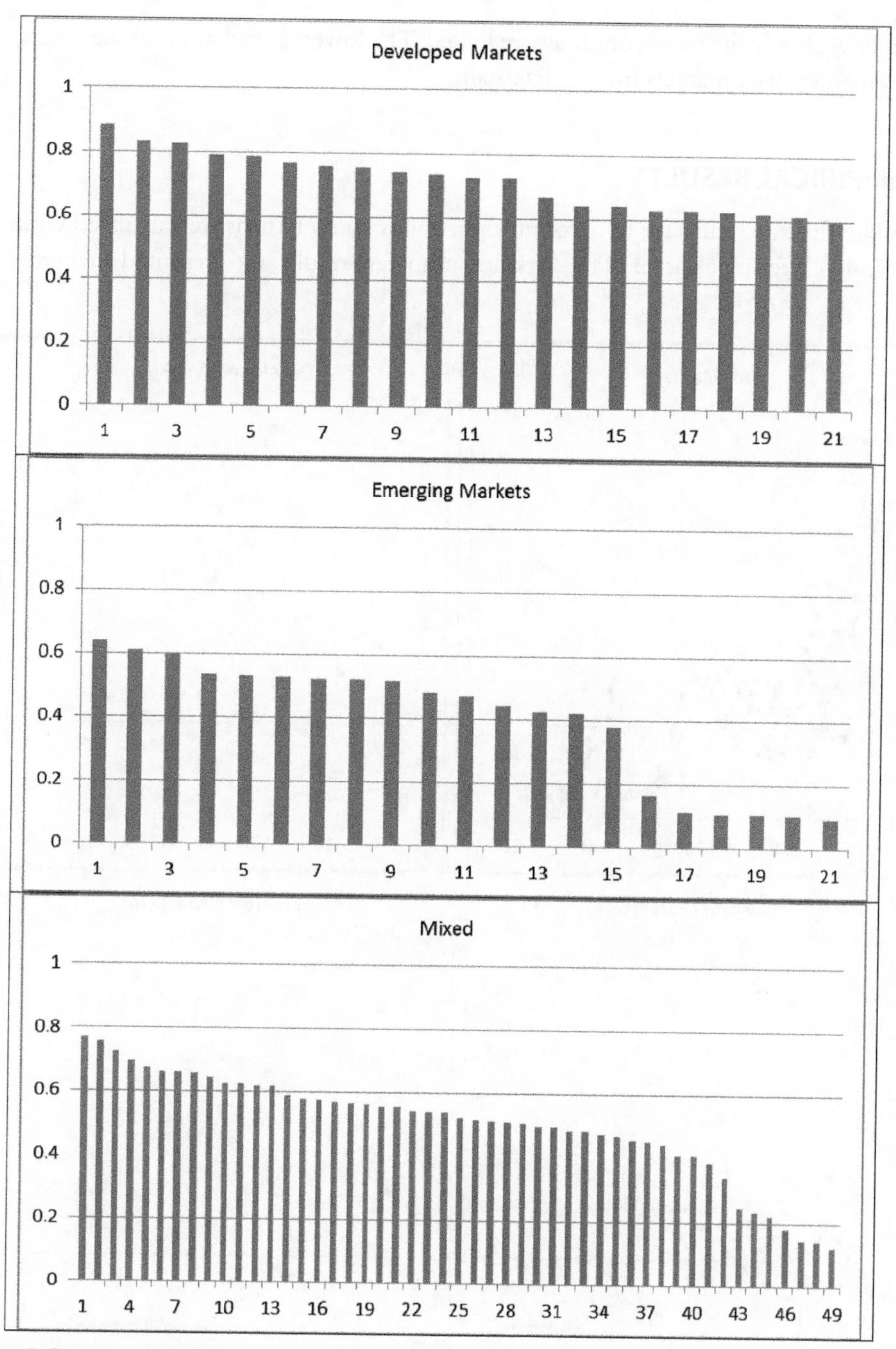

Figure 2 Return correlations.

given how closely the two economies are linked. The lowest correlations in the emerging markets and mixed markets involve Pakistan.

5. EMPIRICAL RESULTS

Consider first the results for two-country portfolios when returns are calculated without the foreign exchange factor. The variance ratio test results are presented in Figure 3,

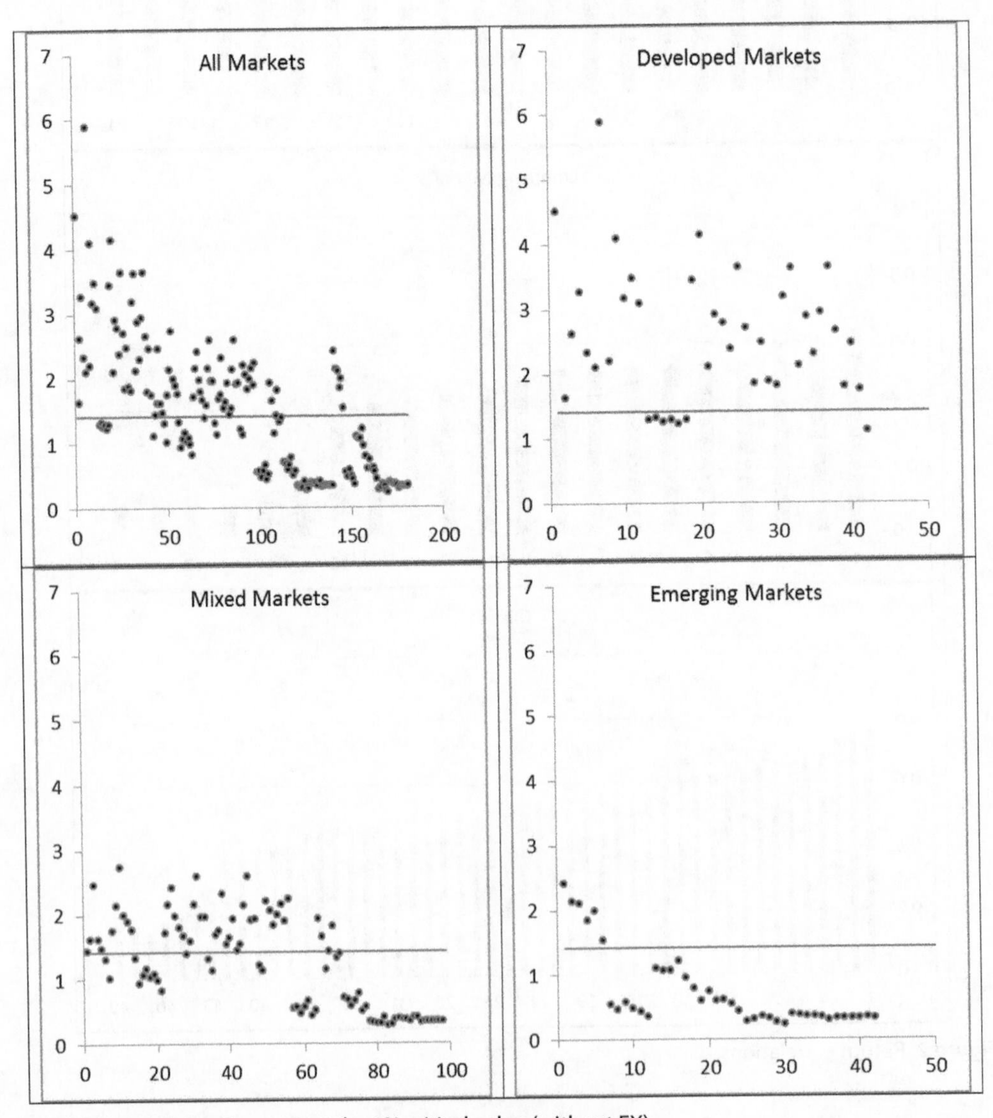

Figure 3 Variance ratios against the 1% critical value (without FX).

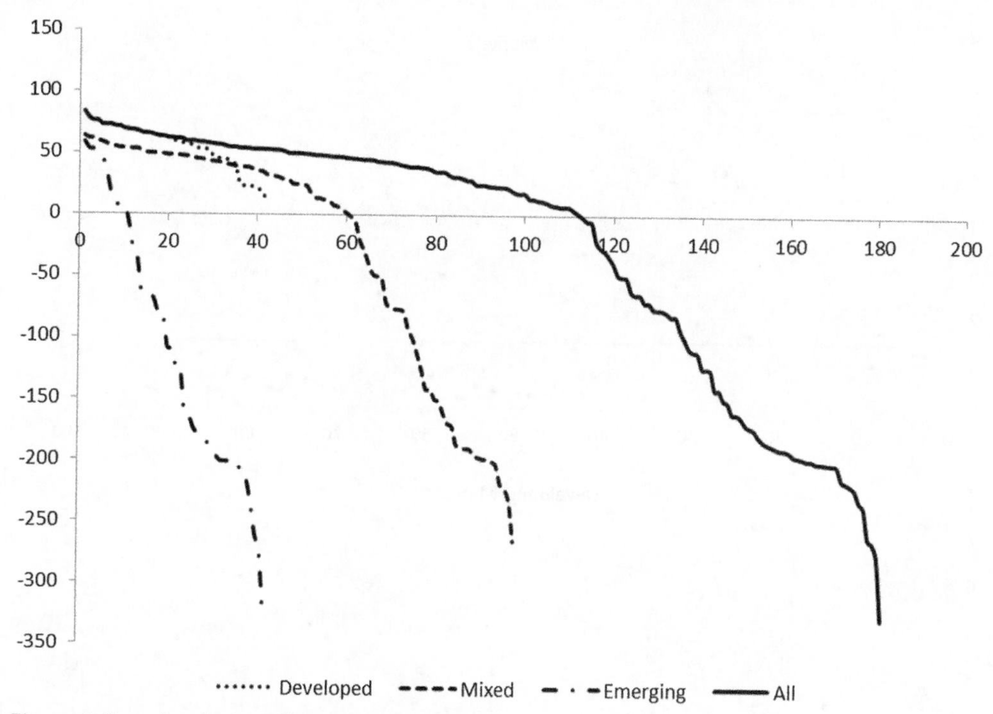

Figure 4 Sorted variance reduction (without FX).

which shows that most portfolios (more than 83%) in developed countries produce effective hedging as the variance ratios corresponding to these portfolios fall above the critical value line. On the contrary, only 14% of the purely emerging portfolios produce effective hedging. About 45% of the mixed portfolios produce effective hedging. In Figure 4, we observe the sorted (highest to lowest) variance reductions corresponding to each portfolio. We can see that in no case does a portfolio of two developed markets produce negative variance reduction, in the sense that the portfolio is more risky than the domestic asset. On the contrary, the majority of mixed portfolios produce negative risk reduction.

The corresponding results when returns are calculated with the foreign exchange factor are presented in Figures 5 and 6. Given the poor performance of emerging market portfolios, this analysis is restricted to developed and mixed portfolios, thus we have 42 developed and 49 mixed portfolios. The results tell the same story, showing that hedging is more effective in developed markets than in mixed markets. Table 1 displays the estimated *VR* and *VD*, showing that positive variance reduction is obtained in every case involving two developed markets. Only 23.8% of the mixed portfolios produce positive variance reduction when the foreign exchange factor is excluded. When it is included in the calculation of returns, 38.8% of the portfolios produce positive risk reduction. The results

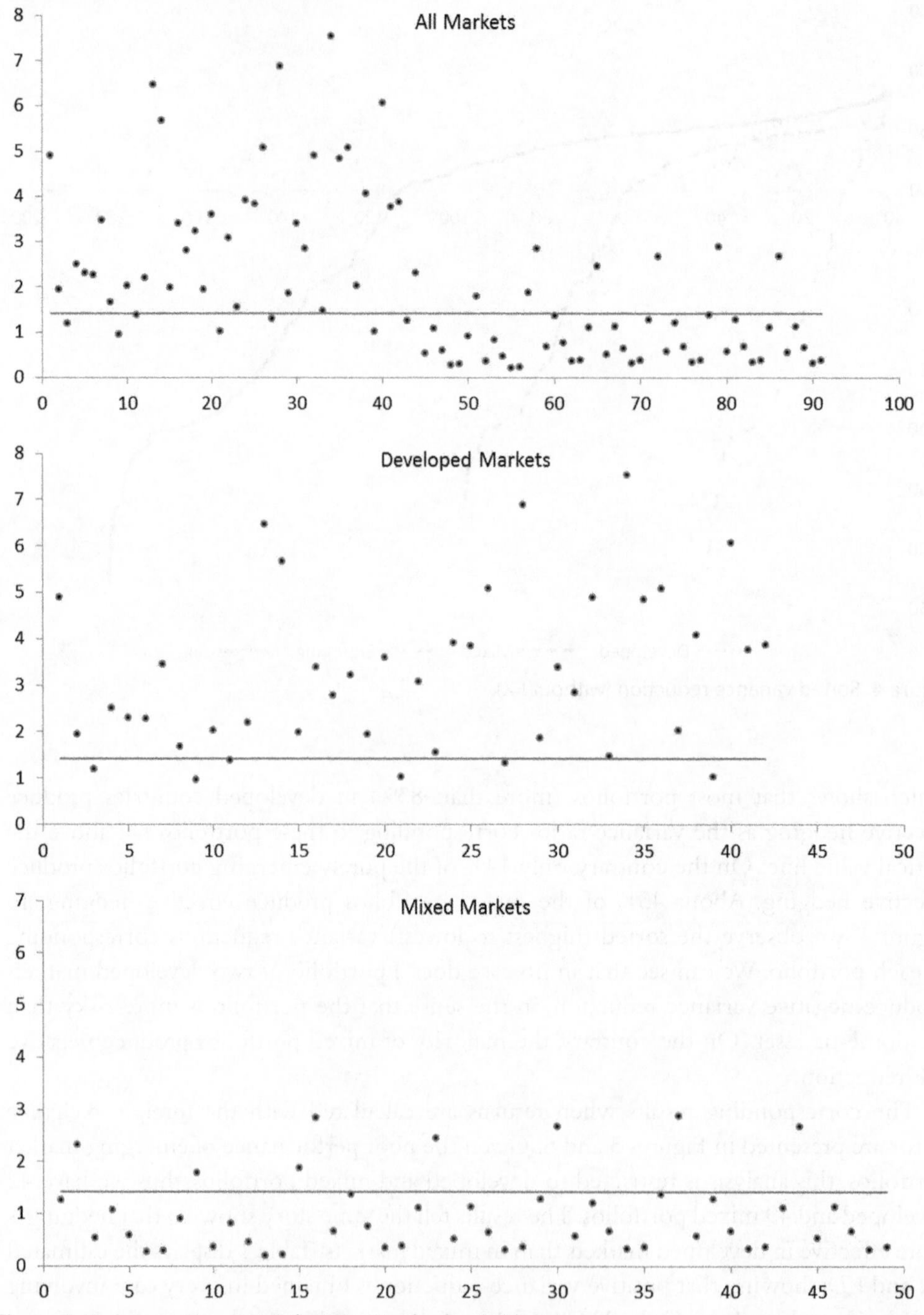

Figure 5 Variance ratio against the 1% critical value (with FX).

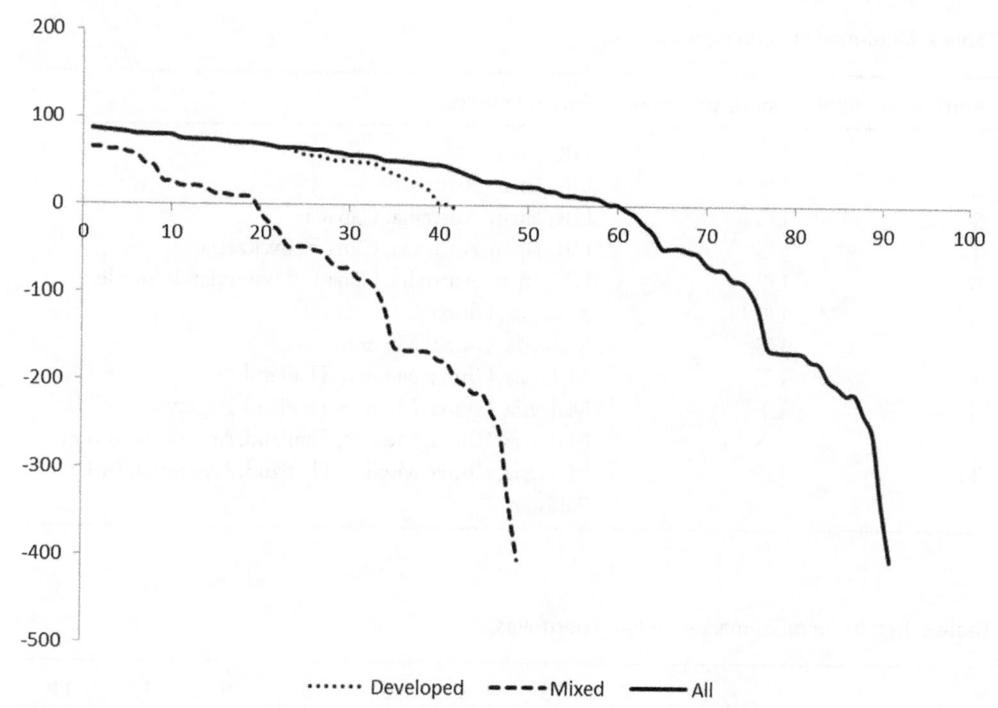

Figure 6 Sorted variance reduction (with FX).

Table 1 Estimated *VR* and *VD* for two-market portfolios.

	Without FX			With FX		
	Portfolios	**Significant *VR***	**Positive *VD* (%)**	**Portfolios**	**Significant *VR***	**Positive *VD* (%)**
Developed	42	83.3	100	42	85.7	100
Emerging	42	14.3	61.2			
Mixed	98	45.9	23.8	49	16.3	38.8
All	182	47.5	61.9	91	48.4	65.9

also tell us that the risk-reduction benefits of international diversification accrue only when opposite positions are taken, unlike the conventional approach. Given the high correlations among developed markets, it is implausible to suggest that risk can be reduced by constructing portfolios involving weighted long positions.

Now we move on to a consideration of multi-market portfolios by restricting the choice to purely developed market portfolios and mixed portfolios, taking the US to be the home country. Table 2 provides a list of 11 portfolios consisting of US stocks and at least two foreign stocks. Portfolios 1–5 involve developed markets only, while portfolios

Table 2 Multi-market hedging portfolios.

Portfolio number	Domestic market	Foreign markets
1	US	UK, Japan
2	US	UK, Japan, Australia
3	US	UK, Japan, Australia, Canada
4	US	UK, Japan, Australia, Canada, Switzerland
5	US	UK, Japan, Australia, Canada, Switzerland, Sweden
6	US	Malaysia, China
7	US	Malaysia, China, Mexico
8	US	Malaysia, China, Mexico, Thailand
9	US	Malaysia, China, Mexico, Thailand, Argentina
10	US	Malaysia, China, Mexico, Thailand, Argentina, Turkey
11	US	Malaysia, China, Mexico, Thailand, Argentina, Turkey, Pakistan

Table 3 Results for multi-market hedging portfolios.

	1	2	3	4	5	6	7	8	9	10	11
A											
$\sigma^2(R_p)$	5.3	17.2	3.9	5.6	3.8	13.9	8.3	7.8	7.8	7.7	7.7
VR	4.7	1.4	6.2	4.4	6.5	1.8	3.0	3.1	3.1	3.2	3.2
VD	78.5	29.9	83.9	77.2	84.6	43.3	66.2	68.1	68.2	68.6	68.7
B											
$\sigma^2(R_p)$	5.5	5.3	3.9	5.6	3.8	13.9	16.9	15.2	15.0	14.5	14.2
VR	4.4	4.7	6.2	4.4	6.5	1.8	1.4	1.6	1.6	1.7	1.7
VD	77.4	78.5	83.9	77.1	84.5	43.3	30.8	37.9	38.9	40.9	42.0
C											
$\sigma^2(R_p)$	4.9	4.6	5.6	3.8	3.5	12.5	5.4	5.2	5.2	5.2	5.2
VR	5.0	5.3	4.4	6.5	7.0	2.0	4.5	4.7	4.7	4.7	4.7
VD	79.8	81.1	77.2	84.6	86.8	49.0	77.8	78.6	78.7	78.8	78.8
D											
$\sigma^2(R_p)$	5.0	4.7	5.6	3.8	3.5	12.5	18.6	17.5	16.2	17.7	17.8
VR	4.9	5.3	4.3	6.5	7.0	2.0	1.3	1.4	1.3	1.4	1.4
VD	79.5	81.0	77.0	84.6	85.7	49.0	24.2	28.3	25.8	27.9	27.5

A: without FX; B: without FX excluding Japan and Mexico; C: with FX; D: with FX excluding Japan and Mexico.

6–11 involve the US and at least two emerging markets. The results of this exercise are presented in Table 3 for the individual portfolios. Starting with the results in Panel A we can see that risk reduction is greater in portfolios 1–5 than in portfolios 6–11. If we exclude the markets of Japan and Mexico, the results presented in Panel B are even stronger. The reason for this change in the results is that the Japanese market has been weakly correlated with other developed markets, while the Mexican market is highly correlated with the US market—hence Japan and Mexico represent anomalies. In Panels C and D, we present the results when returns are calculated with the foreign exchange factor. They tell a similar story: risk reduction is greater within developed markets than what can be obtained by diversifying into emerging markets.

6. ROBUSTNESS TEST 1: THE CONVENTIONAL MEAN-VARIANCE APPROACH

One way to check the robustness of the results derived from the hedging approach suggested here is to use the conventional mean-variance approach whereby weighted portfolios are constructed by taking two long positions on two markets. The weights are chosen such that the variance of the portfolio is minimized. In this case, the return on the portfolio is defined as:

$$R_p = \beta R + (1 - \beta)R^*, \tag{26}$$

where β is the weight assigned to the domestic market. The variance of the portfolio is:

$$\sigma_p^2 = \beta^2\sigma^2 + (1 - \beta)^2\sigma^{*2} + 2\beta(1 - \beta)\rho\sigma\sigma^*. \tag{27}$$

The first-order partial derivative of σ_p^2 with respect to β is:

$$\frac{\partial\left(\sigma_p^2\right)}{\partial\beta} = 2\sigma^2\beta - 2\sigma^{*2} + 2\sigma^{*2}\beta + 2\rho\sigma\sigma^* - 4\rho\beta\sigma\sigma^*. \tag{28}$$

When the partial derivative is equated to zero, we obtain:

$$\beta\left(\sigma^2 + \sigma^{*2} - 2\sigma\sigma^*\right) = -\rho\sigma\sigma^* + \sigma^{*2}. \tag{29}$$

Hence:

$$\beta = \frac{-\rho\sigma\sigma^* + \sigma^{*2}}{\sigma^2 + \sigma^{*2} - 2\sigma\sigma^*}. \tag{30}$$

For illustrative purposes this methodology is applied to the US without the foreign exchange factor—hence 13 portfolios are constructed involving the US and each one of the remaining 13 markets (portfolios 1 to 13). The results are presented in Table 4, showing the mean monthly return of the portfolio, the t statistic for the difference between the mean returns on the US market and each one of the portfolios, the variance of the rate of return on the portfolio, and the associated variance ratio and variance reduction. We can readily see that the results do not support the proposition on the benefits of

Table 4 Results of the mean-variance approach.

Portfolio	Mean return	*t* Statistic*	$\sigma^2(R_p)$	*VR*	*VD*
1	0.48	0.19	18.78	1.00	−0.02
2	0.40	0.31	18.73	0.60	−66.33
3	0.46	0.22	17.85	0.96	−4.08
4	0.62	−0.04	18.44	0.84	−19.09
5	0.52	0.13	16.46	0.92	−9.20
6	0.62	−0.05	18.79	0.62	−60.73
7	0.83	−0.42	15.68	0.98	−2.56
8	0.77	−0.31	15.86	0.22	−346.72
9	1.65	−1.33	51.70	1.65	39.46
10	1.69	−1.63	30.49	0.55	−82.19
11	1.45	−1.04	57.74	0.54	−86.83
12	1.62	−1.00	102.22	1.22	18.24
13	1.82	−1.49	57.68	0.77	−29.50

* The *t* statistic is for the null of the equality of the mean returns (US and portfolio).

international diversification. In no case is the return on the portfolio significantly higher (in a statistical sense) than the return on the US market. And in no case is the variance ratio statistically significant, implying no significant risk reduction. In most cases, risk reduction is negative, implying that diversification leads to a higher level of risk. In the hedging approach, we suggest in this paper international diversification within developed markets leads to significant reduction in risk, but that is only because opposite positions are taken, which makes a lot of sense. When correlation is high, risk is reduced by taking opposite positions. Diversification into emerging markets does not lead to risk reduction, irrespective of whether similar or opposite positions are taken.

7. ROBUSTNESS TEST 2: ALTERNATIVE ESTIMATES OF THE HEDGE RATIO

The second robustness test is to use the hedging approach while calculating the hedge ratio by using various models. It has been argued that one problem with the conventional model of the hedge ratio, as represented by equation (6), is that it ignores short-run dynamics and the long-run relation between stock prices. Specifically, if p and p^* are related by the long-run relation:

$$p_t = a + bp_t^* + \varepsilon_t \tag{31}$$

and if they are cointegrated such that $\varepsilon_t \sim I(0)$, then equation (6) is misspecified and the correctly specified model is an error correction model of the form:

$$\Delta p_t = \alpha + \sum_{i=1}^{n} \beta_i \Delta p_{t-i} + h\Delta p_t^* + \sum_{i=1}^{n} \gamma_i \Delta p_{t-i}^* + \theta \varepsilon_{t-1} + \xi_t, \quad (32)$$

where θ is the coefficient on the error correction term, which should be significantly negative for the model to be valid.

Lien (1996) argues that the estimation of the hedge ratio and hedging effectiveness may change significantly when the possibility of cointegration between prices is ignored. In Lien and Luo (1994) it is shown that, although GARCH may characterize price behavior, the cointegrating relation is the only truly indispensable component when comparing *ex post* performance of various hedging strategies. Ghosh (1993) concluded that a smaller than optimal futures position is undertaken when the cointegrating relation is unduly ignored, attributing the under-hedge results to model misspecification. Lien (1996) provides a theoretical analysis of this proposition, concluding that an errant hedger who mistakenly omits the cointegrating relation always undertakes a smaller than optimal position on the hedging instrument. While Lien's proof is rather elegant, the empirical results derived from an error correction model are typically not that different from those derived from a simple first-difference model (for example, Moosa, 2003).

It is not only about the use of an error correction model as opposed to a first-difference model, as various other model specifications have been suggested to estimate the hedge ratio. Kroner and Sultan (1993) used a bivariate GARCH error correction model to account for both nonstationarity and time-varying moments. Broll et al. (2001) suggested that the hedge ratio should be estimated from a nonlinear model, which can be written in first differences as:

$$\Delta p_t = \alpha + h\Delta p_t^* + \gamma \Delta p_t^{*2} + \varepsilon_t. \quad (33)$$

Nonlinear error correction models have also been suggested (not necessarily for estimating the hedge ratio) by Escribano (1987), and the procedure is applied to a model of the demand for money in Hendry and Ericcson (1991). Nonlinearity in this case is captured by a polynomial in the error correction term. Thus the nonlinear error correction model corresponding to the cointegrating regression (31) is:

$$\Delta p_t = A(L)\Delta p_{t-1} + B(L)\Delta p_t^* + \sum_{i=1}^{k} \gamma_i \varepsilon_{t-i}^i + \xi_t, \quad (34)$$

where $A(L)$ and $B(L)$ are lag polynomials. Hendry and Ericcson (1991) suggest that a polynomial of degree three in the error correction term is sufficient to capture the adjustment process.

Yet another procedure to estimate the hedge ratio is to use an autoregressive distributed lag (ARDL) model of the form:

$$\Delta p_t = \sum_{i=1}^{m} \alpha_i \Delta p_{t-i} + \sum_{i=0}^{n} \beta_i \Delta p^*_{t-i} + \xi_t \tag{35}$$

in which case the hedge ratio may be defined as the coefficient on $\Delta p^*_t (h = \beta_0)$ or as the long-term coefficient, which is calculated as:

$$h = \frac{\sum_{i=0}^{n} \beta_i}{1 - \sum_{i=1}^{m} \alpha_i}. \tag{36}$$

In this exercise, we estimate the hedge ratio from nine combinations of model specifications and estimation methods, which are listed in Table 5. The objective is to find out that if the estimation method or model specification makes any difference for hedging effectiveness. This procedure is applied to two cases in which the US is the domestic market: one producing a highly effective hedge (against the UK) and another producing a less effective hedge (against Japan).

The estimation results are presented in Table 6, which reports the estimated value of the hedge ratio, its t statistic, and the coefficient of determination. Also reported in Table 6 are the variance ratio and variance reduction. No matter which procedure is used, the hedge is highly effective in the case of the UK and ineffective in the case of Japan—the difference lies in return correlations, not the estimation methods. This finding

Table 5 Model specifications and estimation methods.

	Specification	**Estimation method**
1	First difference	OLS
2	First difference	The Cochrane-Orcutt method with an AR(2) process in the residuals
3	First difference	Maximum likelihood with an MA(2) process in the residuals
4	First difference	Instrumental variables with an AR(3) process in the residuals
5	Quadratic first difference	OLS
6	Linear error correction	OLS
7	Nonlinear error correction	OLS
8	Autoregressive distributed lag model in first differences	OLS (the hedge ratio is the coefficient on the contemporaneous explanatory variable)
9	Autoregressive distributed lag model in first differences	OLS (the hedge ratio is the long-run coefficient calculated from the impact coefficients)

Table 6 Estimation results with nine model specifications for the Hedge ratio.

Procedure	Hedge ratio	*t* Statistic	R^2	*VR*	*VD*
US-UK					
1	1.018	20.49	0.78	4.52	77.9
2	1.067	22.32	0.80	4.47	77.6
3	1.054	21.48	0.79	4.49	77.7
4	1.018	18.38	0.78	4.52	77.9
5	0.992	19.32	0.78	4.52	77.9
6	1.039	21.34	0.82	4.51	77.8
7	1.037	20.92	0.82	4.51	77.8
8	1.042	21.56	0.81	4.51	77.8
9	1.175	18.47	0.81	4.30	75.8
US-Japan					
1	0.567	9.07	0.41	0.57	−74.1
2	0.562	9.13	0.41	0.58	−72.6
3	0.565	9.31	0.41	0.57	−73.5
4	0.574	8.87	0.42	0.64	−76.3
5	0.501	7.56	0.44	0.60	−55.4
6	0.538	8.24	0.45	0.61	−65.6
7	0.528	8.01	0.46	0.59	−62.8
8	0.547	8.38	0.42	0.65	−52.8
9	0.491	5.66	0.42	0.68	−47.1

is consistent with the evidence provided by Maharaj et al. (2008) and Moosa (2011). The results, therefore, are robust.

8. CONCLUSION

The literature on the benefits of international diversification has shifted from the proposition that international diversification in general is useful to the proposition that it is more useful, or only useful, if it involves emerging markets. This shift has evolved because of higher correlations among developed markets and weaker correlations between developed and emerging markets. The conventional approach to international portfolio diversification emphasizes the requirement of low correlations to achieve risk reduction, given that the assumption is to construct weighted portfolios involving long positions. The results presented in this study show that the benefit of diversification into emerging markets is a myth, particularly in terms of risk reduction. While taking opposite positions on two developed markets produces significant risk reduction, the hedging effect is weak and even negative when emerging markets are involved. Furthermore, no evidence was found to support the proposition that diversifying into emerging markets boosts return.

What is important here, which is often ignored in the literature, is that diversifying into emerging markets does not only involve market risk, which is what we have been concerned with in this study and what the international diversification literature in general is concerned about. Investment in emerging markets involves other kinds of risks that can be more severe than market risk. It involves political risk, sovereign risk, operational risk, purchasing power risk, etc.—these can be more detrimental than market risk. There is no wonder, then, that home bias is prevalent, particularly when emerging markets are potential diversification outlets. This finding is highly relevant to the work of international portfolio managers. Another point of interest and practical relevance is that more sophistication in the calculation of the hedge ratio does not produce any gains in hedging effectiveness.

The practical implications of the findings of this study are straightforward. The first implication is that attempts to reduce portfolio risk by diversifying into emerging markets is unlikely to bring about the anticipated.

REFERENCES

Akdogan, H., 1996. A suggested approach to country selection in international portfolio diversification. Journal of Portfolio Management 23, 33–39

Ang, A., Bekaert, G., 2002. International asset allocation with regime shifts. Review of Financial Studies 15, 1137–1187

Bailey, W., Stulz, R.M., 1990. Benefits of international diversification: the case of Pacific Basin stock markets. Journal of Portfolio Management 16, 57–61

Baxter, M., Jermann, U.J., 1997. The international diversification puzzle is worse than you think. American Economic Review 87, 170–180

Biger, N., 1979. Exchange risk implications of international portfolio diversification. Journal of International Business Studies 10, 63–74

Broll, U., Chow, K.W., Wong, K.P., 2001. Hedging and nonlinear risk exposure. Oxford Economic Papers 53, 281–296

Chan, K., Covrig, V., Ng, L., 2005. What determines domestic bias and foreign bias? Evidence from mutual fund equity allocation worldwide. Journal of Finance 60, 1495–1534

Chang, E., Eun, C.S., Kolodny, R., 1995. International diversification through closed-end country funds. Journal of Banking and Finance 19, 1237–1263

Coeurdacier, N., Guibaud, S., 2011. International portfolio diversification is better than you think. Journal of International Money and Finance 30, 289–308

Conover, C.M., Jensen, G.R., Johnston, R.R., 2002. Emerging markets: When are they worth it? Financial Analyst Journal March/April, 86–95

Cooper, I., Kaplanis, E., 1994. Home bias in equity portfolios, inflation hedging, and international capital market equilibrium. Review of Financial Studies 7, 45–60

De Santis, G., Gerard, B., 1997. International asset pricing and portfolio diversification with time-varying risk. Journal of Finance 52, 1881–1912

De Santis, R., Sarno, L., 2008. Assessing the benefits of international portfolio diversification in bonds and stocks. European Central Bank Working Papers No. 883, March.

Doukas, J., Yung, K., 1993. Benefits of international diversification: the case of ADRs. Rivista Internazionale di Scienze Economiche e Commerciale 40, 865–880

Driessen, J., Laeven, L., 2007. International portfolio diversification benefits: cross-country evidence from a local perspective. Journal of Banking and Finance 31, 1693–1712
Errunza, V., Losq, E., 1985. International asset pricing and mild segmentation: theory and test. Journal of Finance 40, 105–124
Escribano, A., 1987. Error correction systems: nonlinear adjustment to long-run relationships. CORE Discussion Papers No 8730.
Fisher, G.S., 2012. Why global diversification still makes sense. Forbes 17 January. http://www.forbes.com/sites/greggfisher/2012/01/17/why-global-diversification-still-makes-sense/.
French, K., Poterba, J., 1991. Investor diversification and international equity markets. American Economic Review 81, 222–226
Ghosh, A., 1993. Hedging with stock index futures: estimation and forecasting with error correction model. Journal of Futures Markets 13, 743–752
Goetzmann, W.N., Li, L., Rouwenhorst, K.G., 2005. Long-term global market correlations. Journal of Business 78, 1–38
Griffin, J.M., Karolyi, G.A., 1998. Another look at the role of the industrial structure of markets for international diversification strategies. Journal of Financial Economics 50, 351–373
Grubel, H.G., 1968. Internationally diversified portfolios. American Economic Review 68, 1299–1314
Grubel, H.G., Fander, K., 1971. The interdependence of international equity markets. Journal of Finance 26, 89–94
Hendry, D.F., Ericcson, N., 1991. An econometric analysis of UK money demand in monetary trends in the United States and the United Kingdom by Milton Friedman and Anna J Schwartz. American Economic Review 81, 8–38
Kalra, R., Stoichev, M., Sundaram, S., 2004. Diminishing gains from international diversification. Financial Services Review 13, 199–213
Kroner, K.F., Sultan, J., 1993. Time-varying distributions and dynamic hedging with foreign currency futures. Journal of Financial and Quantitative Analysis 28, 535–551
Laker, D., 2003. Benchmark rebalancing calculations. Journal of Performance Measurement 7, 8–23
Lassard, D.R., 1976. World, country and industry relationships in equity returns: implications for risk reduction through international diversification. Financial Analysts Journal 32, 32–38
Levy, H., Sarnat, M., 1970. International diversification of investment portfolios. American Economic Review 60, 668–675
Lewis, K., 2006. Is the international diversification potential diminishing? Foreign Equity Inside and Outside the U.S. NBER Working Papers No 12697, November.
Lien, D.D., 1996. The effect of the cointegration relationship on futures hedging: a note. Journal of Futures Markets 16, 773–780
Lien, D.D., Luo, X., 1994. Multiperiod hedging in the presence of conditional heteroskedasticity. Journal of Futures Markets 13, 909–920
Maharaj, E.A., Moosa, I.A., Dark, J., Silvapulle, P., 2008. Wavelet estimation of asymmetric hedge ratios: Does econometric sophistication boost hedging effectiveness?. International Journal of Business and Economics 7, 213–230
Michaud, R.O., Bergstorm, G.L., Frashure, R.D., Wolaham, B.K., 1996. Twenty years of international equity investing. Journal of Portfolio Management 22, 9–22
Moosa, I.A., 2003. The sensitivity of the optimal hedge ratio to model specification. Finance Letters 1, 15–20
Moosa, I.A., 2011. The failure of financial econometrics: estimation of the hedge ratio as an illustration. Journal of Financial Transformation 31, 67–71
Obstfeld, M., Rogoff, K., 1998. Foundations of Macroeconomics. MIT Press, Cambridge (MA)
Odier, P., Solnik, B.H., 1993. Lessons from international asset allocation. Financial Analysts Journal 49, 63–77
Rowland, P.F., 1999. Transaction costs and international portfolio diversification. Journal of International Economics 49, 45–170
Russel, J.W., 1998. The international diversification fallacy of exchange-listed securities. Financial Services Review 7, 95–106
Solnik, B.H., 1974. Why not diversify internationally? Financial Analyst Journal 30, 48–54

Solnik, B.H., 1995. Why not diversify internationally rather than domestically? Financial Analyst Journal 51, 89–94

Solnik, B.H., 1997. Going global with equities. Financial Analyst Journal 53, 95–96

Stockman, A.C., Dellas, H., 1989. International portfolio nondiversification and exchange rate variability. Journal of International Economics 26, 271–290

Wheatley, S.M., 2007. Keeping up with the Joneses, Human Capital, and the Home-Equity Biases. University of Melbourne, Working Paper.

Yavas, B.F., 2007. Benefits of international portfolio diversification. Graziado Business Review 10, <http://gbr.pepperdine.edu/2010/08/benefits-of-international-portfolio-diversification/>

CHAPTER 30

The Behavior of International Stock Market Excess Returns in an Increasingly Integrated World*

Michael Donadelli
Department of Economics and Finance, LUISS Guido Carli, Rome, Italy
Center of Excellence SAFE, Goethe, University Frankfurt, Germany

1. INTRODUCTION

There is an extensive literature on empirical finance that studies the behavior of international stock markets. Common empirical regularities are as follows: (i) emerging stock market average excess returns are higher than advanced stock market average excess returns; (ii) emerging stock markets are characterized by higher volatility as well as by higher instability; (iii) international stock markets are increasingly integrated; and (iv) equity market liberalizations reduced the cost of capital (i.e., expected returns). However, most of these findings have been obtained in static context using stock market country indexes in a "pre-2000 world".

This chapter has two main goals. First, it studies the behavior of stock market country indexes as well as the behavior of stock market sector indexes for a large number of emerging and advanced economies. Second, using a robust measure of financial integration, it examines the impact of the global integration process on international stock market excess returns. Differently from previous empirical works, it adopts an updated dataset which allows for a "post-2000 world" analysis. Many investors regard the past decade as an unusual one for international stock market returns. As suggested by Hammond and Leibowitz (2011), investors' view might be based on huge changes in equity market behavior, including much lower than average returns (in advanced economies), much higher than average returns (in emerging economies), much higher volatility, two of the biggest bubbles in stock market history, and rising cross-asset, cross-country, cross-sector, and intra-sector correlations.

The results of this chapter are based on recent empirical works that examine the co-movement between international stock market excess returns impact of the *de jure* and the *de facto* integration on emerging and advanced stock market excess returns.[1] While

*All errors are the author's responsibility.
[1] See Bekaert et al. (2011), Donadelli and Prosperi (2012), and Donadelli (2013a,b).

Emerging Markets and the Global Economy
http://dx.doi.org/10.1016/B978-0-12-411549-1.00030-2

Grootveld and Salomons (2003) examine the behavior of the Equity Risk Premium (ERP), this chapter focuses on the excess returns.[2]

Based on data availability, few works have been devoted to examine the behavior of emerging stock market prices in the pre-1990 era. As data on emerging stock market prices started to be available (i.e., early 1990s), the financial literature started to focus on emerging stock market performances as well as on the predictability of emerging stock market excess returns. Early studies find that local risk factors play a crucial role in explaining emerging excess returns' patterns (i.e., global risk factors have love explanatory power). It turns out that standard asset pricing linear models, such as the world CAPM, do a poor job in explaining variation in emerging excess returns. In contrast, they do a good job in explaining variation in advanced stock market excess returns (Donadelli and Prosperi, 2012). Following equity market liberalizations across emerging economies, the literature started to be interested in examining the impact of liberalized markets on emerging stock prices. Most recent studies show that emerging stock prices are influenced by global risk sources. *Reduction ad absurdum*, under specific time-horizons, the one-factor model is enough to explain variation in emerging stock market excess returns. Nevertheless, Donadelli and Prosperi (2012) and Donadelli (2013a,b) show that model's validity is rarely preserved as well as heavily sample-sensitive. If the last decade is analyzed, in a country-by-country and sector-by-sector contexts, they find that the intercept (or Jensen's alpha or unexpected average excess returns) is positive and statistically different from zero in several emerging stock markets. It turns out that models' validity is also a dynamic concept. A large part of pre-2000 and early 2000s studies argue that stock market liberalization may reduce the liberalizing country's cost of equity capital by allowing for international risk sharing (Stulz, 1999a,b). As a consequence, if the market learns that a stock market liberalization is going to occur, then a country's equity price index should increase (Henry, 2000). As discussed in Donadelli (2013a,b), many studies on emerging stock market liberalizations are developed in a static context. In addition, a large number of empirical works employ stock market country indexes and do not consider sector indexes. While the impact of the *de jure* integration has been largely examined, the real effects of the *de facto* integration on international stock market prices have been rarely discussed. In contrast to early studies, this chapter examines the behavior of international stock market excess returns as well as the impact of the *de facto* integration on stock market indexes, both at the country and sector level, in a pure time-varying context. The key empirical findings of this chapter can be summarized as follows: (i) emerging stock market country and sector indexes (i.e., excess returns) have a strong time-varying component; (ii) during the last 10 years advanced and emerging realized average excess returns (i.e., international stock market country and sector indexes) have largely increased, and emerging stock markets have became increasingly integrated; (iii) existing empirical

[2] The ERP is a long-term concept, and it is often associated to the resolution of the well-known Equity Premium puzzle (Mehra and Prescott, 1985).

findings that examine the impact of financial market liberalizations on emerging stock market prices have been heavily influenced by domestic shocks, such as the Mexican crisis (1994), the Asian financial crisis (1997), the Russian default (1998), the Argentine economic crisis (2001), the 9/11 terrorist attacks (2001), and the subprime crisis (2008)[3]; (iv) there exists a delay between *de jure* and *de facto* integration; (v) the real (i.e., trade-to-GDP ratio) and financial (i.e., the $\bar{R}^2$ of a multi-(*artificial*) factor model) integration processes follow a similar path; and (vi) the intercept (or unexpected excess returns) across emerging stock markets is significantly higher than across advanced (or US) stock markets (i.e., standard linear-factor models do not fully explain variation in emerging stock market excess returns).

2. SUMMARY STATISTICS AND PRELIMINARY ANALYSIS

This section examines the performance of international stock market indexes and degree of co-movement between international stock market excess returns in a dynamic context.[4] In contrast to existing empirical studies, which focus on national stock market indexes, this chapter examines both country and sector indexes.[5] The analysis is conducted over different time-horizons and for different countries/regions.

2.1. Stock Market Country Indexes

Stock market country indexes are represented by the Morgan Stanley Capital International Total Return Indexes (MSCI TRIs). As standard in the literature, all indexes are denominated in US dollars. Returns are computed from MSCI TRIs for 28 emerging and 7 advanced stock markets, as well as for 7 regions.[6] Formally:

$$R_{n,t} = \frac{CI_{n,t}}{CI_{n,t-1}} - 1, \tag{1}$$

where $R_{n,t}$ is the return of country/region n at time t, CI_t represents the MSCI TRI in country/region n at time t. Excess returns are then computed by subtracting from Eq. (1) the one-month T-bill rate.[7] Data are monthly and run from January 1988 (or

[3] For a detailed discussion on emerging financial crises, see Joyce (2011).

[4] A similar analysis can be found in Donadelli and Prosperi (2012), Grootveld and Salomons (2003), and Harvey (1995a,b), among others.

[5] Throughout the chapter the terms "National (industrial) stock market excess returns" and "stock market country (sector) excess returns will be used interchangeably".

[6] Datastream mnemonic for each country contains the following designations: "*TRI*" (i.e., reinvested dividends) and "∼ *U$*" (i.e., the original local currency equity index is converted in US dollars with the Datastream exchange rate conversion facility). The coverage in time and across countries is limited by the availability of all data required. Data starting point limits: Colombia, Peru, Poland, China, India, Pakistan, Sri Lanka, and South Africa (from January 93); Czech Republic, Hungary, Russia, and Egypt (from January 95); Kenya and Nigeria (from June 02); Morocco and Tunisia (from June 04).

[7] The one-month T-bill rate series is from the Kenneth French Data Library.

Table 1 List of employed MSCI TRIs.

Developed countries	Emerging countries				
Advanced	**Latin America**	**Eastern Europe**	**Asia**	**Sub-Saharan Africa**	**North African and ME**
Canada	Argentina	Czech Republic	China	Kenya	Egypt
France	Brazil	Hungary	India	Nigeria	Jordan
Germany	Chile	Poland	Indonesia	South Africa	Morocco
Italy	Colombia	Russia	Korea		Tunisia
Japan	Mexico	Turkey	Malaysia		
United Kingdom	Perù		Pakistan		
United States			Philippines		
			Sri Lanka		
			Taiwan		
			Thailand		

Source: Datastream.

later) to December 2011. The full list of employed stock market country indexes, ordered by geographic area, is presented in Table 1.

Monthly summary statistics for the international stock market excess returns are reported in Table 2. Mean, standard deviation, minimum, maximum, and median values are all expressed in percentage points and computed over the period January 1988-December 2011. The last two lines of Table 2 report the average values of the monthly statistics across the 28 emerging markets and across the 7 advanced markets.

The mean values confirm that emerging stock markets tend to deliver higher average excess returns than advanced markets (i.e., 15.6% vs 5.04%, on annual basis), as well as higher volatility (i.e., 127.92% vs 71.76%, on annual basis). As reported in Bekaert et al. (1998), developed markets tend to display negative skewness over the period January 1988-December 2011. The skewness is negative in 5 out of 7 advanced markets. A similar result is obtained by Grootveld and Salomons (2003), Donadelli and Prosperi (2012). For example, Grootveld and Salomons (2003) find that 5 out of 7 developed stock markets display negative skewness over the period January 1976-December 2001. In contrast, they show that most emerging stock markets display positive skewness. For a shorter sample (i.e., January 2000-December 2010), Donadelli and Prosperi (2012) observe that the skewness is negative in 13 out of 13 developed stock markets. As pointed out by Donadelli (2013a), the result is clearly state-contingent, that is, it strongly depends on macroeconomic scenarios.

Table 3 reports the monthly summary statistics for the excess return of seven regions (i.e., Latin America, Eastern Europe, Asia, Sub-Saharan, North African and Middle East, Emerging, and Advanced). Regional excess returns are obtained by forming equal-,

Table 2 Stock market country excess returns: summary statistics (monthly). Sample: January 1988 (or later)-December 2011.

Country	Mean	Std Dev.	ShR	Max	Min	Median	Kurtosis	Skewness
Emerging economies								
Argentina	2.15	15.85	0.14	95.05	−58.40	1.05	9.46	1.66
Brazil	2.40	15.04	0.16	79.95	−67.19	2.28	4.85	0.25
Chile	1.41	7.25	0.19	21.65	−33.04	1.44	2.33	−0.46
Colombia	1.58	9.75	0.16	30.30	−40.85	1.66	1.62	−0.24
Mexico	1.76	9.55	0.18	28.47	−47.64	2.21	3.13	−0.79
Perú	1.70	9.77	0.17	37.58	−51.56	2.18	4.96	−0.45
Czech Rep.	1.27	9.53	0.13	35.83	−51.77	1.06	5.37	−0.76
Hungary	1.51	12.00	0.13	45.74	−62.24	1.76	4.82	−0.56
Poland	1.77	14.40	0.12	117.07	−52.74	1.31	18.23	2.10
Russia	2.34	16.41	0.14	60.69	−61.07	2.30	2.63	−0.03
Turkey	1.90	16.71	0.11	72.61	−49.38	1.34	2.07	0.54
China	0.28	10.78	0.03	46.44	−43.06	0.24	2.87	0.33
India	0.91	8.99	0.10	32.46	−40.67	1.39	1.64	−0.24
Indonesia	1.69	14.74	0.11	93.79	−45.78	1.03	9.52	1.57
Korea	0.92	11.20	0.08	59.72	−47.15	0.11	3.92	0.43
Malaysia	0.74	8.05	0.09	38.57	−30.61	1.15	3.53	−0.02
Pakistan	0.84	11.27	0.07	36.01	−38.13	0.05	1.68	−0.05
Philippines	0.77	9.66	0.08	43.07	−36.82	0.72	2.35	0.22
Sri Lanka	0.80	10.59	0.08	60.15	−25.58	−0.16	6.74	1.50
Taiwan	0.72	10.62	0.07	46.21	−34.33	0.70	1.63	0.25
Thailand	1.03	11.47	0.09	60.73	−41.97	1.27	4.02	0.32
Kenya	2.05	9.29	0.22	24.44	−33.93	1.81	1.68	−0.42
Nigeria	1.17	9.97	0.12	41.70	−37.37	0.46	3.15	0.14
South Africa	1.12	8.43	0.13	33.77	−44.81	1.29	4.73	−0.75
Egypt	1.40	9.68	0.14	37.17	−33.37	0.65	1.45	0.41
Jordan	0.07	5.49	0.01	22.39	−24.88	−0.43	2.79	−0.05
Morocco	1.15	6.40	0.18	19.49	−23.84	0.72	2.37	−0.42
Tunisia	1.08	5.72	0.19	21.23	−20.94	0.92	3.54	0.03
Advanced economies								
France	0.56	6.10	0.09	20.57	−22.26	0.92	0.75	−0.28
Germany	0.57	6.59	0.09	19.62	−22.83	1.31	1.02	−0.43
Italy	0.26	7.29	0.04	27.29	−23.54	0.24	0.98	0.10
Japan	−0.12	6.79	−0.02	23.58	−23.99	0.14	0.75	0.04
United Kingdom	0.44	5.15	0.09	17.23	−23.24	0.53	1.64	−0.27
United States	0.56	4.34	0.13	13.50	−20.07	1.05	1.90	−0.63
Canada	0.65	5.61	0.12	17.15	−34.22	1.06	5.44	−0.94
Avg. (Emerg)	1.30	10.66	0.12	47.94	−42.11	1.09	4.18	0.16
Avg. (Adv)	0.42	5.98	0.08	19.85	−24.31	0.75	1.78	−0.35

Source: Based on Donadelli (2013a).

Table 3 Regional stock market excess returns: summary statistics (monthly). Sample: January 1988 (or later)–December 2011.

	Latin America	Eastern Europe	Asia Far-East	Sub-Saharan Africa	North African and Middle East	Emerging (All)	Advanced (G7)
Equally weighted portfolios							
Mean	2.04	1.91	0.95	1.10	0.51	1.41	0.42
Std dev.	8.37	13.55	7.07	7.36	5.13	6.44	4.91
ShR	0.24	0.14	0.13	0.15	0.10	0.22	0.08
Max	27.74	72.61	21.60	21.16	18.20	19.75	17.09
Min	−47.42	−55.44	−33.39	−30.90	−25.76	−38.98	−24.31
Median	1.85	1.80	1.09	1.51	0.31	2.06	0.83
Kurtosis	4.60	4.87	2.55	3.03	2.95	5.93	2.46
Skewness	−0.69	0.72	−0.50	−0.77	−0.29	−1.16	−0.56
GDP-weighted portfolios							
Mean	2.06	1.84	0.84	0.97	0.94	1.33	0.37
Std dev.	10.28	14.27	7.94	7.55	7.30	7.28	4.54
ShR	0.20	0.13	0.11	0.13	0.13	0.18	0.08
Max	49.27	72.61	27.70	26.06	34.76	23.64	15.66
Min	−49.80	−56.38	−41.21	−33.51	−28.22	−40.55	−22.30
Median	2.35	0.90	1.03	1.67	0.05	1.51	0.78
Kurtosis	4.20	3.43	2.91	3.29	3.00	4.21	2.34
Skewness	−0.34	0.48	−0.41	−0.68	0.67	−0.73	−0.59
Trade-weighted portfolios							
Mean	1.97	1.94	0.81	0.98	0.95	1.23	0.42
Std dev.	8.90	13.96	7.96	7.52	5.76	7.45	4.77
ShR	0.22	0.14	0.10	0.13	0.17	0.16	0.09
Max	31.18	72.61	25.79	26.43	22.83	20.95	16.41
Min	−48.49	−56.23	−40.36	−31.16	−25.47	−43.99	−23.05
Median	2.33	1.26	1.30	1.54	0.50	1.87	0.88
Kurtosis	4.04	3.98	2.84	3.04	2.39	5.10	2.32
Skewness	−0.86	0.56	−0.42	−0.64	0.13	−1.03	−0.61

Source: Based on Donadelli (2013a).

GDP-, and trade-weighted regional MSCI TRIs (i.e., equal-, GDP-, and trade-weighted portfolios).[8] Mean, standard deviation, minimum, maximum, and median values are expressed in percentage points. Monthly statistics, at the region level, confirm that emerging markets tend to generate higher average excess returns (i.e., ERP) and display higher volatility than developed markets. Results across equal-, GDP, and trade-weighted portfolios are almost identical. In addition, values in Table 3 shows that the average risk premium

[8] For a detailed discussion on the portfolio construction methodology, see Donadelli (2013a).

per unit of risk (i.e., Sharpe ratios) in the advanced world is heavily lower than the average risk premium per unit of risk in the emerging world (i.e., 0.08 vs 0.22, 0.08 vs 0.18, and 0.09 vs 0.16 for the equal-, GDP-, and trade-weighted portfolios, respectively). Statistics confirm also the presence of asymmetry. In fact, the skewness is negative in 6 out of 7 equal-weighted portfolios, and in 5 out of 7 GDP- and trade-weighted portfolios. Such results are heavily driven by the employed sample, which represents a period including many emerging market crises (e.g., Mexican crisis, 1994; Asian crisis, 1997, the 9/11 terrorist attack, and the recent subprime crisis).

2.2. Stock Market Sector Indexes

Stock market sector indexes are represented by Datastream Global Equity Indexes (DGEI). The database breaks down into six levels. Level 1 is the market index, this covers all the sectors in each region or country. Level 2 divides the market into 10 industries and covers all the sectors within each group in each region or country. Levels 3–6 subdivide the level 2 classifications into sector classifications in increasing detail. To have a sufficient number of firms listed in each sector index, it is worth using the 10 sector indexes of level 2 (i.e., Basic Materials, Consumer Goods, Consumer Services, Financials, Healthcare, Industrials, Oil & Gas, Telecommunications, Technology, and Utilities). All series are monthly total return indexes denominated in US dollars and run from January 1994 (or later) to June 2012. The stock market sector excess returns are computed as follows:

$$ExR_{i,t}^{n} = \left(\frac{SI_{i,t}^{n}}{SI_{i,t-1}^{n}} - 1\right) - R_{f,t}, \tag{2}$$

where $ExR_{i,t}$ is the excess return of industry i in country/region n at time t, SI_t is the DGEI of industry i in country/region n at time t, and $R_{f,t}$ is the one-month Treasury bill.

Table 4 reports the mean, standard deviation, and Sharpe ratio values for the 10 sectors. Statistics are provided for 23 emerging stock markets and, for comparison purposes, for the US stock market. For each national stock market, the first two lines report the mean and standard deviation values, respectively. Line 3 reports the Sharpe ratios. Line 4 provides the spread between the average emerging and US stock excess returns. The spread is computed as follows:

$$\text{Spread}_i^{EM} = ExR_{i,avg}^{US} - ExR_{i,avg}^{EM}, \tag{3}$$

where $ExR_{i,avg}^{US}$ is the average excess returns of industry i in the US market, and $ExR_{i,avg}^{EM}$ is the average excess returns of industry i in one of the analyzed emerging stock markets. Values are monthly and expressed in percentage points. The sample goes from January 1995 (or later) to June 2012.

At the sector level, we confirm that emerging markets tend to perform better than advanced markets. Statistics show that the sector-by-sector spread is mostly positive. Focusing on emerging average statistics, the spread ranges from a minimum of 0.04%

Table 4 International stock market sector excess returns: summary statistics (monthly). Statistics are computed for 10 different sectors in 23 different countries. Emerging: emerging average sector-based statistics (i.e., mean, standard deviation, sharpe ratios, and spread are averaged over 22 emerging countries). Sample: January 1995 (or later)-June 2012.

Country	OilGas	BasMats	ConsGds	ConsSvs	Ind.	HC	Financ.	Telec.	Tech.	Utilit.
US	**0.92**	**0.76**	**0.50**	**0.64**	**0.81**	**0.66**	**0.64**	**0.40**	**0.94**	**0.55**
	6.30	7.61	5.66	5.87	6.42	4.70	7.03	6.26	8.45	4.82
	0.15	0.10	0.09	0.11	0.13	0.14	0.09	0.06	0.11	0.11
Arg	0.42	0.96	0.06	0.96	0.77	n/a	0.54	0.41	n/a	−0.11
	12.85	12.13	15.12	12.41	12.37	n/a	13.00	13.47	n/a	10.91
	0.03	0.08	0.00	0.08	0.06	n/a	0.04	0.03	n/a	−0.01
	−0.51	0.21	−0.44	0.32	−0.04	n/a	−0.10	0.01	n/a	−0.66
Brazil	1.87	1.27	1.69	2.12	1.46	0.92	1.08	0.82	2.95	0.83
	12.82	11.91	10.24	12.82	10.69	13.77	10.64	11.43	11.89	11.80
	0.15	0.11	0.16	0.17	0.14	0.07	0.10	0.07	0.25	0.07
	0.94	0.51	1.19	1.48	0.66	0.26	0.44	0.42	2.02	0.28
Chile	0.69	0.95	0.74	1.14	0.51	1.20	0.76	0.50	1.69	0.45
	7.59	8.03	7.15	8.35	8.11	9.54	6.12	8.74	8.66	6.91
	0.09	0.12	0.10	0.14	0.06	0.13	0.12	0.06	0.20	0.07
	−0.23	0.19	0.24	0.50	−0.30	0.53	0.13	0.10	0.76	−0.10
China	1.55	1.84	2.16	0.87	1.52	4.78	1.40	1.32	0.88	1.39
	13.57	15.21	14.84	13.09	14.33	14.36	11.89	10.45	10.34	10.88
	0.11	0.12	0.15	0.07	0.11	0.33	0.12	0.13	0.09	0.13
	0.63	1.08	1.66	0.23	0.71	4.12	0.77	0.92	−0.06	0.83
CzRep	1.47	0.58	0.79	1.44	1.00	n/a	1.53	0.98	n/a	1.41
	1.46	0.58	0.75	1.44	0.95	n/a	1.54	0.98	n/a	1.41
	1.01	0.99	1.06	1.00	1.05	n/a	0.99	1.00	n/a	1.00
	0.55	−0.18	0.29	0.80	0.19	n/a	0.89	0.58	n/a	0.85
HK	3.09	0.50	1.17	0.45	0.72	n/a	0.74	0.92	1.83	0.74
	20.55	10.58	8.12	7.84	8.68	n/a	8.36	9.51	14.35	4.33
	0.15	0.05	0.14	0.06	0.08	n/a	0.09	0.10	0.13	0.17
	2.17	−0.26	0.68	−0.19	−0.09	n/a	0.10	0.52	0.90	0.19
Hun	1.81	0.95	0.62	n/a	−0.46	1.31	2.19	0.50	−0.72	0.59
	12.75	11.66	10.55	n/a	11.15	11.30	13.40	11.07	16.73	10.48
	0.14	0.08	0.06	n/a	−0.04	0.12	0.16	0.05	−0.04	0.06
	0.89	0.19	0.12	n/a	−1.27	0.65	1.55	0.10	−1.65	0.04
India	0.66	1.29	0.97	1.07	n/a	0.77	1.19	0.73	2.79	0.96
	11.19	11.58	8.37	11.52	n/a	7.58	12.43	13.17	16.41	11.21
	0.06	0.11	0.12	0.09	n/a	0.10	0.10	0.06	0.17	0.09
	−0.27	0.54	0.47	0.42	n/a	0.10	0.56	0.33	1.85	0.41
Israel	1.44	1.27	1.37	1.23	0.66	1.08	0.78	0.72	0.36	1.43
	9.48	9.98	10.56	8.22	8.71	7.59	8.03	8.10	10.81	10.56
	0.15	0.13	0.13	0.15	0.08	0.14	0.10	0.09	0.03	0.14
	0.52	0.51	0.88	0.59	−0.15	0.42	0.15	0.32	−0.57	0.88

(*Continued*)

Table 4 (Continued)

Country	OilGas	BasMats	ConsGds	ConsSvs	Ind.	HC	Financ.	Telec.	Tech.	Utilit.
Mal	0.77	0.22	0.64	0.49	0.29	3.47	0.89	0.60	1.64	0.34
	8.10	10.93	9.88	8.69	8.47	9.62	11.09	9.32	16.53	8.41
	0.09	0.02	0.06	0.06	0.03	0.36	0.08	0.06	0.10	0.04
	−0.16	−0.54	0.14	−0.15	−0.51	2.81	0.26	0.20	0.71	−0.21
Mex	n/a	1.87	−0.11	0.73	0.49	2.39	1.27	n/a	n/a	1.42
	n/a	12.14	12.66	9.09	11.92	12.19	11.19	n/a	n/a	9.42
	n/a	0.15	−0.01	0.08	0.04	0.20	0.11	n/a	n/a	0.15
	n/a	1.11	−0.61	0.09	−0.32	1.73	0.64	n/a	n/a	0.86
Pak	1.23	0.74	1.22	0.43	1.66	0.61	1.07	0.11	n/a	0.57
	12.38	9.90	9.97	16.44	30.18	9.75	11.72	12.70	n/a	12.50
	0.10	0.07	0.12	0.03	0.05	0.06	0.09	0.01	n/a	0.05
	0.30	−0.02	0.72	−0.21	0.85	−0.05	0.44	−0.29	n/a	0.01
Peru	1.23	1.09	0.55	4.01	2.28	n/a	1.47	1.60	n/a	0.73
	17.56	7.96	5.99	25.09	21.51	n/a	6.69	16.72	n/a	6.54
	0.07	0.14	0.09	0.16	0.11	n/a	0.22	0.10	n/a	0.11
	0.31	0.33	0.05	3.37	1.47	n/a	0.83	1.20	n/a	0.17
Phil	0.54	0.60	0.44	0.19	0.84	n/a	0.43	0.55	n/a	0.62
	14.66	17.36	8.19	11.56	12.09	n/a	10.23	8.99	n/a	11.47
	0.04	0.03	0.05	0.02	0.07	n/a	0.04	0.06	n/a	0.05
	−0.38	−0.16	−0.05	−0.45	0.03	n/a	−0.20	0.15	n/a	0.07
Pol	1.11	1.79	0.80	1.40	0.30	n/a	1.20	0.64	0.57	1.30
	10.47	12.36	8.54	11.73	10.83	n/a	10.90	10.70	12.66	12.99
	0.11	0.14	0.09	0.12	0.03	n/a	0.11	0.06	0.05	0.10
	0.19	1.03	0.31	0.76	−0.51	n/a	0.56	0.24	−0.36	0.75
Russia	1.99	2.45	2.32	3.91	2.83	1.22	3.50	1.72	n/a	1.82
	14.48	13.34	12.26	15.77	19.60	17.17	21.51	16.10	n/a	18.85
	0.14	0.18	0.19	0.25	0.14	0.07	0.16	0.11	n/a	0.10
	1.07	1.69	1.82	3.27	2.02	0.56	2.87	1.32	n/a	1.27
Sing	1.05	1.21	1.16	0.63	0.64	0.67	0.68	0.43	0.14	3.13
	12.13	14.33	11.19	7.11	7.42	8.03	8.91	7.07	14.58	15.80
	0.09	0.08	0.10	0.09	0.09	0.08	0.08	0.06	0.01	0.20
	0.13	0.45	0.66	−0.01	−0.17	0.01	0.04	0.03	−0.79	2.58
SA	1.26	0.98	1.45	1.03	0.88	1.04	0.95	2.12	n/a	n/a
	10.26	12.40	11.11	10.17	9.83	9.32	9.47	13.89	n/a	n/a
	0.12	0.08	0.13	0.10	0.09	0.11	0.10	0.15	n/a	n/a
	0.34	0.23	0.95	0.39	0.07	0.38	0.31	1.72	n/a	n/a
Sri Lanka	1.78	n/a	0.84	0.48	0.89	n/a	0.59	0.45	n/a	−9.26
	9.59	n/a	8.94	9.72	9.62	n/a	8.85	9.55	n/a	6.98
	0.19	n/a	0.09	0.05	0.09	n/a	0.07	0.05	n/a	−1.33
	0.86	n/a	0.34	−0.16	0.08	n/a	−0.05	0.05	n/a	−9.81

(Continued)

Table 4 (Continued)

Country	OilGas	BasMats	ConsGds	ConsSvs	Ind.	HC	Financ.	Telec.	Tech.	Utilit.
Taiwan	1.20	0.84	0.74	0.03	0.84	n/a	0.01	0.42	1.20	n/a
	6.94	7.91	9.39	8.37	10.89	n/a	10.20	6.42	11.93	n/a
	0.17	0.11	0.08	0.00	0.08	n/a	0.00	0.07	0.10	n/a
	0.27	0.08	0.25	−0.61	0.04	n/a	−0.63	0.02	0.27	n/a
Thai	1.25	0.98	1.02	0.75	1.47	0.82	0.38	0.66	1.26	0.89
	11.04	16.20	13.23	9.41	14.21	8.89	14.34	12.73	15.88	10.26
	0.11	0.06	0.08	0.08	0.10	0.09	0.03	0.05	0.08	0.09
	0.32	0.22	0.52	0.11	0.67	0.16	−0.26	0.26	0.33	0.34
Turkey	1.92	2.32	1.83	1.96	2.08	3.07	2.32	2.05	3.36	2.64
	17.21	16.75	15.58	18.81	17.33	16.69	16.96	19.42	21.29	19.11
	0.11	0.14	0.12	0.10	0.12	0.18	0.14	0.11	0.16	0.14
	0.99	1.56	1.33	1.32	1.27	2.41	1.68	1.65	2.43	2.08
Emerg	**1.35**	**1.18**	**1.02**	**1.20**	**1.03**	**1.67**	**1.13**	**0.87**	**1.38**	**0.59**
	11.77	11.58	10.12	11.32	12.33	11.13	10.79	10.98	14.01	10.54
	0.15	0.14	0.14	0.14	0.12	0.15	0.14	0.12	0.10	0.07
	0.43	0.42	0.52	0.56	0.22	1.00	0.50	0.47	0.45	0.04

Source: Based on Donadelli and Lucchetta (2012).

(utilities) to a maximum of 1.00% (healthcare). It turns out that most of the extra performance has been driven by the healthcare sector over the period January 1995-June 2012.

2.3. International Stock Market Co-Movements

The dynamics of the co-movement between returns is very important in finance. A key ingredient in the mean-variance portfolio optimization world is represented by the variance-covariance matrix of stock returns. In particular, the analysis of the correlation coefficients between international excess returns as well as the study of the co-movement between international returns and leading economic indicators are crucial for portfolio stability and diversification strategies. This subsection examines the unconditional correlation between national stock market excess returns (Figure 1) as well as between emerging stock market sector excess returns and the MSCI World excess return (Figure 2), and the conditional correlation between an indicator of economic policy uncertainty in the US and a set of regional stock market sector excess returns (Figure 3). The unconditional correlation coefficients are estimated using a rolling window of 60 months over the period January 1988 (or later)-December 2011. The dynamic conditional correlation is computed in a DCC-GARCH context. All co-movement measures suggest that cross-country and cross-industry diversification benefits are smaller than in the past (i.e., emerging and advanced stock market indexes tend to move together).

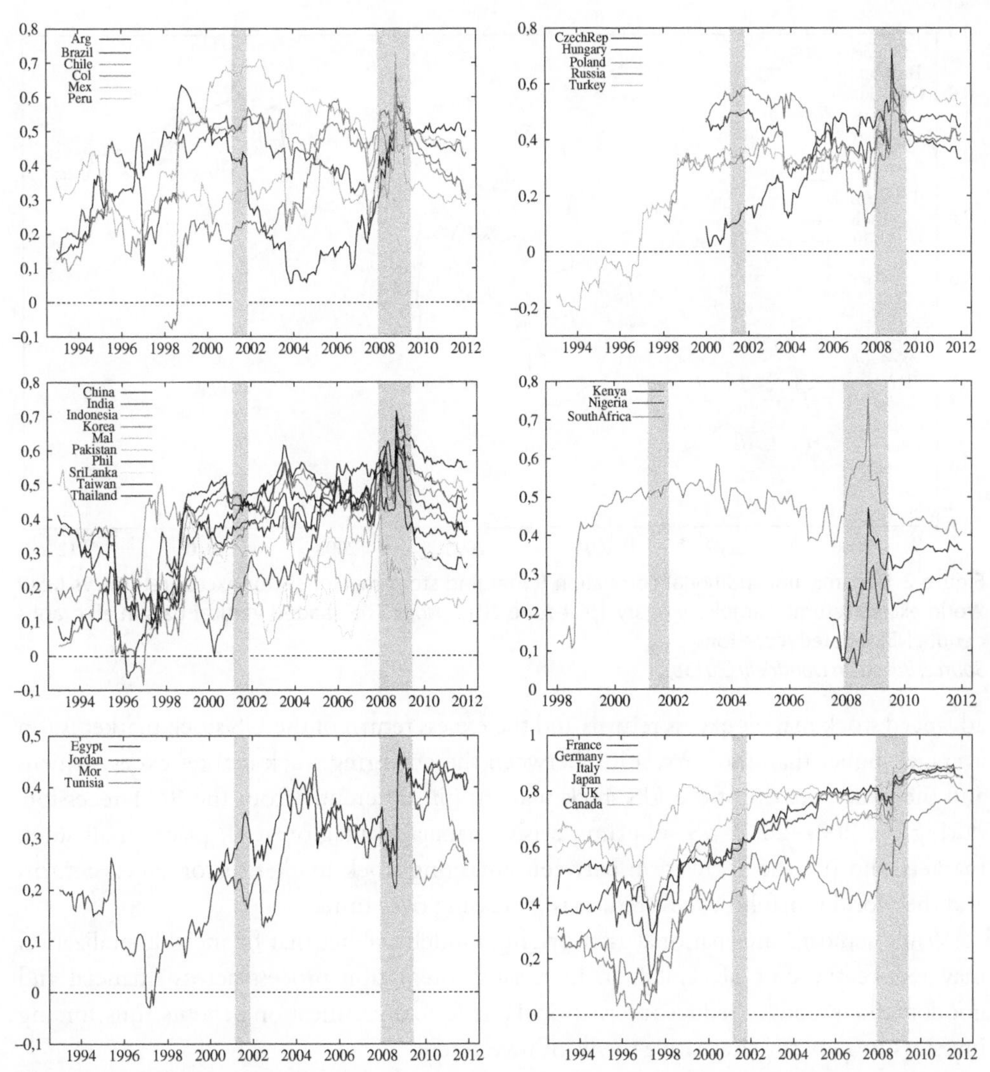

Figure 1 Dynamic unconditional correlation (international stock market excess returns vs US stock market excess return). Sample: January 1988 (or later)-December 2011. *Note*: The shaded vertical bars in all graphs denote NBER-dated recessions.
Source: Based on Donadelli (2013a).

2.3.1. Emerging vs Advanced Stock Market Excess Returns

Figure 1 reports the dynamics of the correlation coefficients between 28 emerging and 6 advanced stock market excess returns, and the excess returns of the US stock market. Figure 2 reports the dynamic unconditional correlation between the excess returns of 10 emerging stock market sector excess returns and the excess returns of the MSCI World. Dynamic unconditional correlations are obtained using a rolling window of 60 months.

Four empirical findings are worth noting: (i) correlation coefficients are increasing both across emerging and advanced stock markets; (ii) the correlation between the

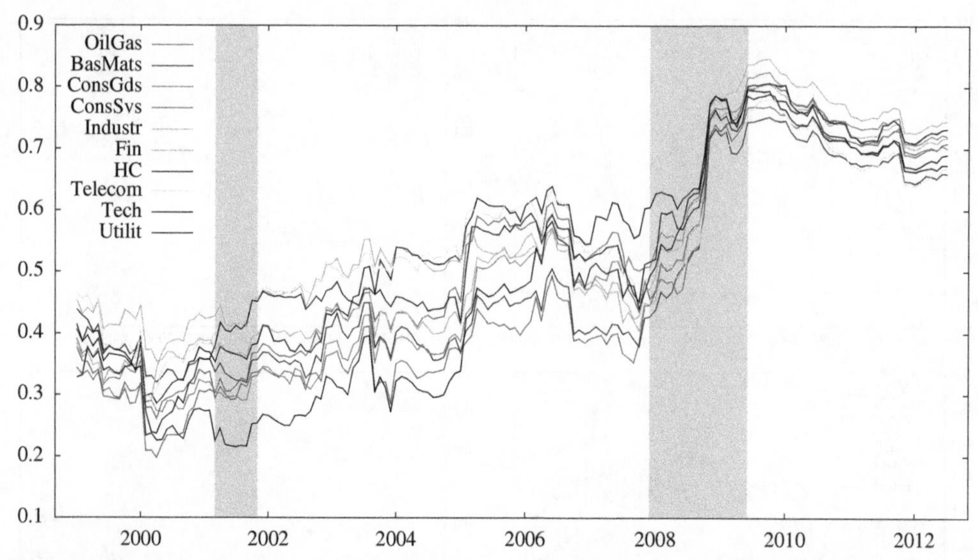

Figure 2 Dynamic unconditional correlation (emerging stock market sector excess returns vs MSCI World excess return). Sample: January 1994-June 2012. *Note*: The shaded vertical bars in all graphs denote NBER-dated recessions.
Source: Based on Donadelli (2013b).

advanced stock market excess returns and the excess return of the US stock market is (on average) higher than the correlation between the emerging stock market excess returns and the excess return of the US stock market; (iii) differently from the 9/11 recession, during the 2007–2009 US subprime crisis financial contagion took place in all stock markets; and (iv) the correlation between emerging stock market sector excess returns and the world portfolio excess return is increasing over time.

While standard international asset pricing models predict that financial liberalization may reduce the cost of capital, an increasing integration process across financial and goods markets tends to reduce international portfolio diversification benefits, thus, forcing investors to look for alternative forms of investment.

2.3.2. Excess Returns vs Macroeconomic Policy Uncertainty

In the spirit of Antonakakis et al. (2012), this subsection examines the extent of time-varying co-movements between stock returns and a newly introduced measure of US economic policy uncertainty. Dynamic correlations are computed in a DCC-GARCH framework.[9] In contrast to Antonakakis et al. (2012), who focus on the US stock market, this subsection focuses also on emerging stock markets. In particular, we rely on four regions in a sector-by-sector context. Figure 3 reports the dynamic conditional correlation between the US economic policy uncertainty index and the excess returns of 10 stock sector indexes in three emerging regions and in the US. The US economic

[9] For a formal discussion on the DCC-GARCH procedure, see Engle (2002).

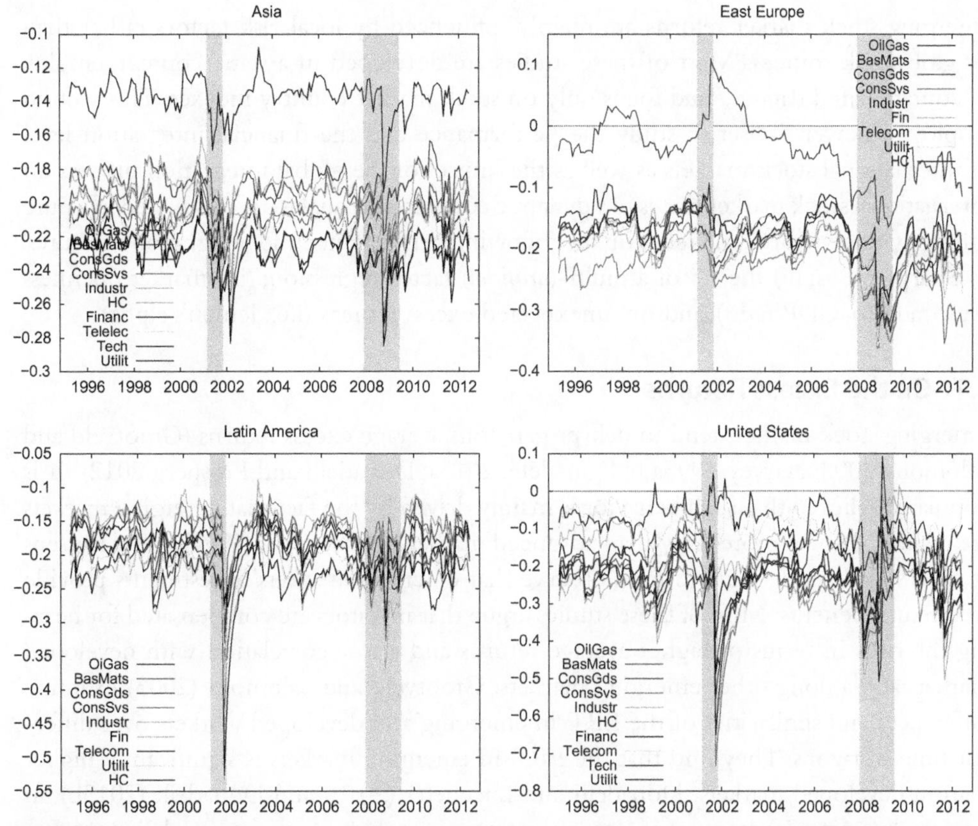

Figure 3 Dynamic conditional correlation (US economic policy uncertainty vs stock market sector excess returns). Sample: January 1995 (or later)-June 2012. *Note*: Shading denotes US recessions as defined by NBER.
Source: Based on Donadelli and Persha (2014).

policy uncertainty measure is from Baker et al. (2012). Regional stock sector indexes have been created as weighted average of country stock market sector indexes. Both in the US and in the emerging world, the time-varying correlation between excess returns and uncertainty is consistently negative over time (i.e., stock excess returns decrease with increasing macro uncertainty). An exception is given by the consumer goods sector in Eastern Europe. Results represented in Figures 2 and 3 confirm that emerging and US stock markets tend to follow similar patterns (i.e., a reduction in international portfolio diversification benefits).

3. A TIME-VARYING ANALYSIS

Early works observe that emerging stock markets tend to display high volatility, low correlations with developed markets and within emerging markets, and high long-horizon returns. Other early studies examining international stock return predictability find that emerging stock market returns are mainly influenced by local risk factors rather than by global risk sources. Most of these studies are developed in a static context, employ a "contaminated dataset," and focus only on stock market country indexes. This section employs a newer dataset to study the performance and the financial integration level of international stock markets as well as the impact of the global integration process on international stock market prices in a dynamic context. The analysis is conducted in a pure rolling-window world, and relies on the following performance and integration measures: (i) Sharpe ratios; (ii) the $\bar{R}^2$ of a multi-(*artificial*) factor regression; (iii) market openness (i.e., trade-to-GDP ratio); and (iv) unexpected excess returns (i.e., Jensen's alpha).

3.1. On the Excess Returns

Emerging stock markets tend to deliver generous average excess returns (Grootveld and Salomons, 2003; Harvey, 1995a,b; Donadelli, 2013a; Donadelli and Prosperi, 2012). It is popularly believed that such behavior is mainly driven by the fact that emerging markets are perceived to be more risky than advanced markets. Barry et al. (1997) and Claessens et al. (1995), among many others, observe that emerging markets' investments provide risk/return benefits. Most of these studies argue that investors are compensated for bearing the risks in terms of higher average returns and a low correlation with developed markets and among other emerging markets. Grootveld and Salomons (2003) examine differences and similarities of the ERP in emerging and developed markets over different time-horizons. They find that the ERP in emerging markets is significantly higher than in developed markets. Donadelli and Lucchetta (2012) and Donadelli (2013b), in a sector-by-sector context, confirm that emerging stock markets tend to deliver higher average excess returns. Via a pure rolling-window analysis, they also show that the first and second moment of the international stock market excess returns are heavily time-varying. Bekaert et al. (1998) observe that the structure of the return distribution of emerging markets is potentially unstable. Grootveld and Salomons (2003) also show that ERP tends to be less stable through time in emerging markets. Using MSCI TRI for 25 emerging national stock markets they argue that much of the instability of emerging ERP is generated by the emerging market crises of the 1990s, the financial market liberalizations, and the higher exposure of emerging stock markets to global business cycles.[10] Figure 4 shows the dynamics of the Sharpe ratio for seven equal- (left panel), GDP- (middle panel), and trade- (right panel) weighted regional indexes (i.e. macro portfolios). Figure 5 shows the dynamics of the Sharpe ratio for 10 emerging (left panel) and US (right panel) stock market sector indexes. Emerging sector indexes are equally weighted averages of countries' sector indexes. Both figures confirm and update most of the existing empirical findings.

The updated empirical results can be summarized as follows: (i) emerging stock markets have provided a higher risk-return performance than advanced stock markets over

[10] Bekaert et al. (1998) develop a similar discussion.

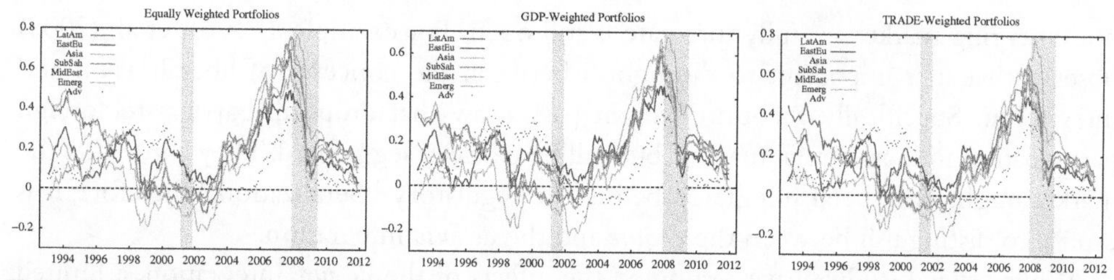

Figure 4 This figure reports the dynamics of the Sharpe ratio for seven macro stock markets. Estimates are computed on rolling basis using a window of 60 months. Sample: January 1988 (or later)-December 2011. *Note*: The shaded vertical bars denote NBER-dated recessions.
Source: Based on Donadelli and Prosperi (2012).

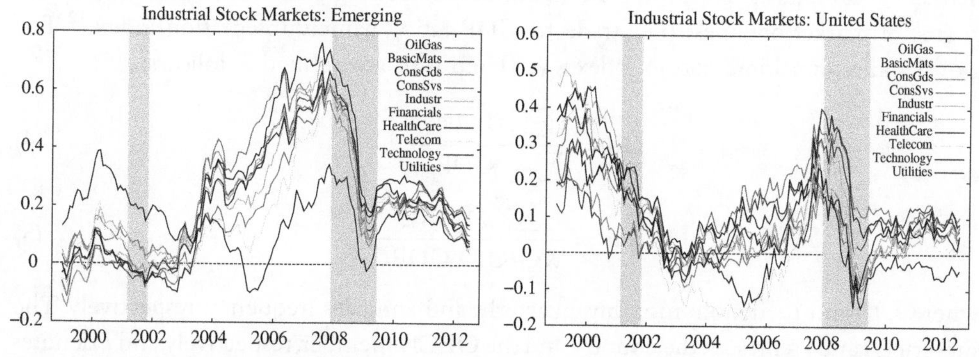

Figure 5 This figure report the dynamics of the Sharpe ratio for 10 US and emerging industrial stock markets. Estimates are computed on rolling basis using a window of 60 months. Sample: January 1994 (or later)-June 2012. *Note*: The shaded vertical bars denote NBER-dated recessions.
Source: Based on Donadelli (2013b).

the last 10 years (see dotted black line of Figure 4); (ii) emerging market performances have been heavily influenced by domestic shocks, such as the Tequila crisis in Mexico and the Asian financial crisis (see the left-hand side of each plot in Figures 4 and 5); (iii) international stock market indexes are increasing during the no-crises period (i.e., between the 9/11 terrorist attacks and the 2007 subprime crisis); and (iv) the joint collapse of international stock market country and sector indexes during the last crisis provides evidence for the existence of contagion.[11]

3.2. On the Global Integration

The effects of equity market liberalizations on international stock market prices and the dynamics of correlations between advanced and emerging stock markets have been largely examined. It is largely accepted that liberalizations and increasing correlations have made emerging stock markets increasingly integrated. However, the debate on whether or

[11] For a detailed discussion on the contagion effects, see Corsetti et al. (2005).

not emerging market are fully integrate is still open. For example, Bekaert et al. (2003) observe that it is important to distinguish between the concepts of liberalization and integration. Specifically, a country might pass a law that drops all barriers to foreign participation in local capital markets but still be partially segmented. They argue that the market might have been integrated before the regulatory liberalization. Therefore, it is crucial to distinguish between the *de jure* and the *de facto* integration.

While several studies have examined the effects of the *de jure* integration, a limited number of works have been devoted to study the effects of the *de facto* integration on international stock market prices. This subsection studies the dynamics of the real and financial integration processes as well as its impact on emerging and advanced stock market excess returns. Real integration, both at local and global level, is captured by the degree of market openness (i.e., trade-to-GDP ratio), namely integration index.[12] The global and regional integration indexes (GII and RII) are defined as follows:

$$\text{GII} = \frac{\sum_{i,t}^{I} \text{Trade}_{i,t}}{\sum_{j,t_4} \text{GDP}_{j,t_4}}, \tag{4}$$

$$\text{RII} = \frac{\sum_{n,t}^{N} \text{Trade}_{n,t}}{\text{WORLD GDP}_{t_{12}}}, \tag{5}$$

where t, t_4, and t_{12} denote monthly, quarterly, and annually frequency, respectively. The subscripts i and j represent the country and the OECD member, respectively, and I denotes the total number of countries.[13] The subscript n denotes a country in each region and N is the total number of countries in a region, and WORLD GDP$_{t_{12}}$ is the annual WORLD GDP—measured in US dollars—of the IMF.

Figure 6 reports the rate of change and the cumulative rate of change of the real integration measure. The dynamics of the emerging integration indexes are reported in Figure 7. All figures suggest that the degree of market openness, both at the global and regional level, has largely increased during the last 10 years. The integration growth across emerging economies in the period 2002–2009 is particularly steep and noteworthy. Not surprisingly, market openness in Asia is higher than in the other emerging regions, and seems to drive real integration in the emerging world.

In the spirit of Pukthuanthong and Roll (2009), *de facto* financial integration is measured by using the $\bar{R}^2$ of a multi-(*artificial*) factor linear model where the risk sources are

[12] A similar measure has been used by de Jong and de Roon (2005), Liao and Santacreu (2012), and Santacreu (2012), among others.

[13] Global trade is represented by the sum of the trade of all regions (i.e., sum imports and exports of goods of 28 emerging and 7 advanced countries). Global GDP is given by the sum of all OECD members GDPs. The OECD Total covers the following 34 countries: Australia, Austria, Belgium, Canada, Chile, Czech Republic, Denmark, Estonia, Finland, France, Germany, Greece, Hungary, Iceland, Ireland, Israel, Italy, Japan, Korea, Luxembourg, Mexico, Netherlands, New Zealand, Norway, Poland, Portugal, Slovak Republic, Slovenia, Spain, Sweden, Switzerland, Turkey, United Kingdom, and United States. Since OECD data can be observed only on quarterly basis, the denominator of the index is assumed to be fixed within a quarter. All variables are denominated in US$.

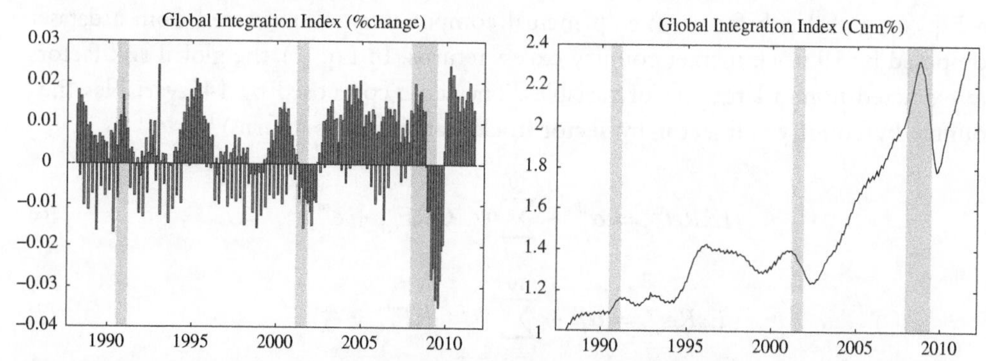

Figure 6 This figure reports the rate of change (%) and the cumulative rate of change (%) of the GII (i.e., global trade-to-GDP ratio). Sample: January 1988-December 2011. The GII is computed as in Eq. (4). *Note*: The shaded vertical bars denote NBER-dated recessions.
Source: Based on Donadelli (2013a).

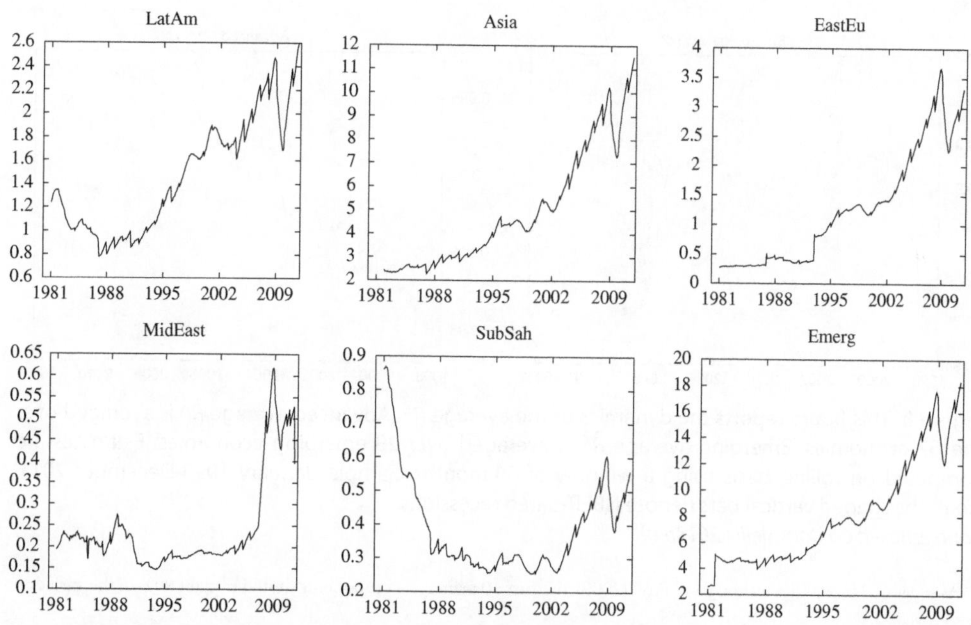

Figure 7 This figure reports the dynamics of the RII (i.e., regional trade-to-GDP ratio) for the following emerging regions: Latin America, Asia, Eastern Europe, Middle East, Sub-Saharan, and Emerging. The RII is computed as in Eq. (5) and expressed in percentage points (vertical axis). Sample: January 1981-December 2011.
Source: Global Financial Data and IMF.

represented by the first 10 principal components extracted from a large set of variables.[14] In Eq. (6), global risk factors (i.e., principal components) are extracted from a dataset composed by 19 stock market country excess returns. In Eq. (7), the global risk factors are extracted from a larger set of variables. The set is composed by 146 variables (i.e., country-by-country and sector-by-sector stock market excess returns):[15]

$$ExRet_{n,t}^{w} = \alpha_n^w + \sum_{c=1}^{10} \psi_c^w GRF_{c,t}^{w} + \epsilon_{n,t}^{w}, \tag{6}$$

$$ExRet_{i,t}^{w} = \alpha_i^w + \sum_{c=1}^{10} \psi_c^w GRF_{c,t}^{w} + \epsilon_{i,t}^{w}. \tag{7}$$

The $\bar{R}^2$s, obtained by estimating Eqs. (6) and (7) in a rolling-window framework, capture the degree of financial openness, both at the country and sector level, across international stock markets. Figure 8 reports the dynamics of the average $\bar{R}^2$ for the international stock markets.[16] Figure 9 reports the dynamics of the $\bar{R}^2$ in a sector-by-sector context.

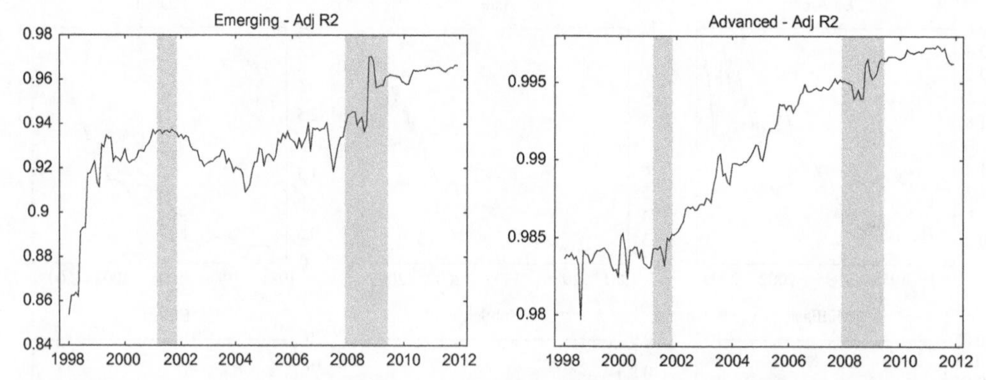

Figure 8 This figure reports the dynamics of the average $\bar{R}^2$. Advanced average $\bar{R}^2$ is averaged over the G7 economies. Emerging average $\bar{R}^2$ is averaged over 28 emerging economies. Estimates are computed on rolling basis using a window of 60 months. Sample: January 1998-December 2011. *Note*: The shaded vertical bars denote NBER-dated recessions.
Source: Based on Donadelli (2013a,b).

[14] As suggested by Pukthuanthong and Roll (2009), the first 10 principal components should explain 90% of the variation across data.

[15] Details on the principal component analysis are given in Donadelli (2013a,b).

[16] The financial integration measure is computed, in each window, for 7 advanced economies and for 28 emerging economies. The average $\bar{R}^2$:

$$\bar{R}^2_{w,avg} = \frac{1}{N}\sum_{n=1}^{N} \bar{R}^2_{w,n}$$

where n denotes the country, N is the total number of countries, and w is the window in which the $\bar{R}^2$ is estimated.

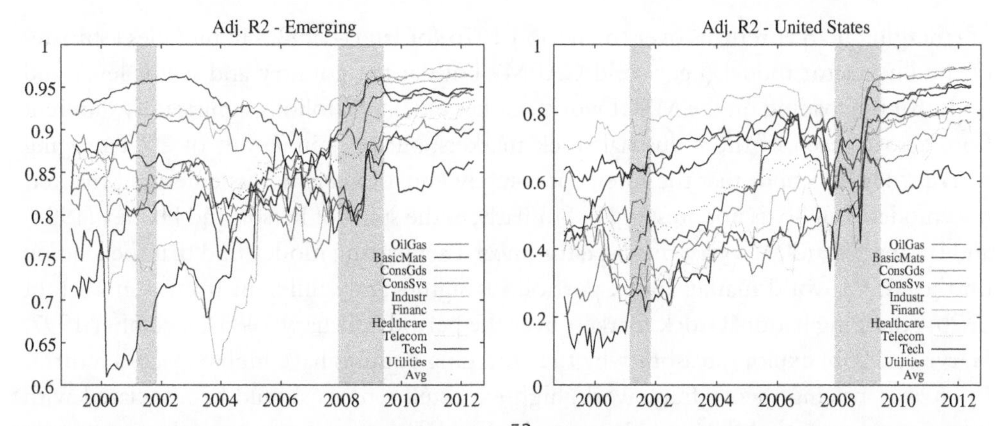

Figure 9 This figure reports the dynamics of the $\bar{R}^2$: A sector-by-sector approach. Emerging stock market sector indexes are computed as weighted average of emerging countries' stock market sector indexes. Estimates are computed on rolling basis using a window of 60 months. Sample: January 1994 (or later)-June 2012. *Note*: The shaded vertical bars denote NBER-dated recessions.
Source: Based on Donadelli (2013b).

The joint analysis of Figures 6–9 suggests that: (i) the real and financial integration processes follow a similar path; (ii) the increasing path of the emerging stock market country and sector indexes during the last two NBER-dated recessions is followed by an increasing financial and real integration process (i.e., emerging excess returns increase as financial openness and the degree of market openness increase); (iii) the financial integration process across emerging economies has been influenced by the emerging crises of the late 1990s and early 2000s; and (iv) while emerging and advanced markets are both increasingly integrated, the integration process across emerging economies is unstable and seems to be influenced by local shocks (see left-panel of Figure 9).

3.3. On "Model's Validity"

The debate on whether or not global factors are the most important source of variation in international stock market excess returns is still widely open. Early studies, based on the high level of segmentation of emerging financial markets, argue that local microeconomic and macroeconomic variables have more explanatory variables than global variables over stock returns. To explain variation in international stock market excess returns, and especially in emerging stock markets, a large part of the empirical finance literature employs multi-factor linear models. On the one hand, early studies assume that emerging markets are segmented. On the other hand, most recent works assume that markets are perfectly integrated. While in a fully integrated environment variation in international stock returns can be fully explained by global risk sources, in a segmented world only local risk sources matter. In addition, few works employ both local and global risk sources to model international stock returns (Bilson et al., 2001). Harvey (1995a) examines the sensitivity of emerging market returns over the period 1976 (or later)-1992. He provides estimates of the one-factor model (i.e., world CAPM), both at the country and sector level, and finds that the loading on the MSCI world market index portfolio is significantly different from zero in each of the industrial stock markets, but only in 7 (out of 20) emerging markets. He also finds that the intercept is rarely equal to zero across emerging markets (i.e., model's validity is not preserved). Similarly, in the spirit of Ferson and Harvey (1994) and Bilson et al. (2001), via a multi-factor linear asset pricing model, find that the loading on the MSCI world market index portfolio is significantly different from 0 in 10 (out of 20) emerging national stock markets over the period February 1985-December 1997. Harvey (1995b) explores reasons why the emerging equities have high expected returns. In an asset pricing theory framework, high expected returns should be associated with large exposures to risk factors. However, he finds that the exposures to the commonly used risk factors are low. Again, standard asset pricing models seem to be unable to explain the cross-section of expected returns. Harvey (1995b) argues that emerging markets are segmented from world capital markets. It turns out that emerging market returns tend to be mainly influenced by local information variables. One possible reason for this failure is that the exposure of emerging markets to risk sources is time-varying.

While many studies have focused on the sensitiveness of emerging stock returns to either local or global risk sources, and employ pre-2000 data, this research focuses also on model's validity (i.e., unexpected excess returns or Jensens' alpha) in an updated international finance environment. Given that emerging markets present a strong time-varying component and have become more integrated, more recent studies find that the sensitivity of emerging market returns to measure of global risk is stronger. In a country-by-country framework, Donadelli and Prosperi (2012) test the validity of the world CAPM for 13 developed and 19 emerging national stock markets, and for 6 macro-area portfolios. They report estimates for two different time-horizons, January 1995-December 2010 and January 2000-December 2010. In contrast to existing empirical findings, they show that the beta of the world CAPM is statistically different from zero in all developed, emerging, and region markets. Given an increasing degree of co-movements between international stock markets, the result seems to be intuitive.

Estimates suggest also that model's validity across emerging markets is rarely preserved (i.e., emerging intercepts are statistically different from zero). In addition, emerging alphas are always larger than advanced alphas, suggesting that emerging stock markets tend to generate higher average unexpected excess returns, namely the *alpha puzzle* (Donadelli and Prosperi, 2012). Donadelli and Prosperi (2012) solve the puzzle by developing a two-country one-period model with quadratic costs. Accounting for time-variation in the risk exposures and the expected returns, in a two-factor conditional version of the CAPM, Donadelli and Prosperi (2012) also show that global liquidity affects both the market price of risk and emerging realized excess returns. As global liquidity proxies, they employ the VIX and the open interest on the US stock market. However, the conditional

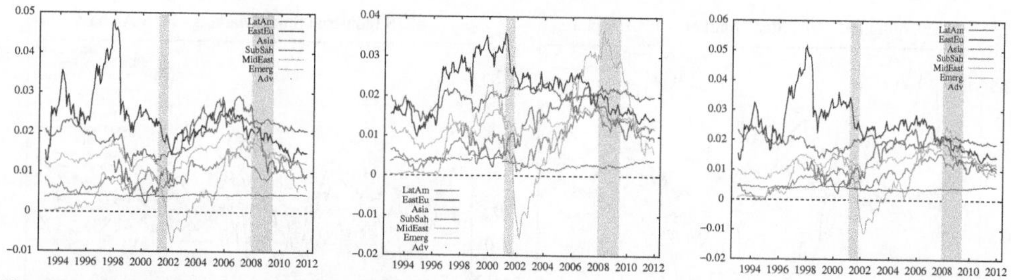

Figure 10 This figure reports the dynamics of the "PCA Alpha" for the equal- (left panel), GDP- (middle panel), and trade- (right panel) weighted portfolios. Estimations are performed on rolling basis using a window of 60 months. Sample: January 1988 (or later)-December 2011. *Note*: The shaded vertical bars denote NBER-dated recessions.
Source: Based on Donadelli (2013a).

version still delivers positive and statistically different from zero alphas. To explain variation across emerging and US industrial stock market returns, Donadelli (2013b) estimates four different linear-factor models using traded and non-traded global risk factors in a sector-by-sector context. Traded risk factors are commonly obtained from Fama & French. Non-traded factors are represented by global macro variables (e.g. US industrial production growth rate, 10Y Italian-German Bund Spread, the steepness of the US yield curve, VIX), and by the principal components extracted from a large set of variables. Results suggest that international stock market excess returns tend to be influenced by the same global risk sources. However, emerging markets contrast with the US market in at least one respect. In practice, emerging markets display are positive and statistically different from zero alphas. The result seems to be consistent across different factor models.

Figure 10 reports the dynamics of the intercept—obtained by estimating Eq. (6) in a rolling-window framework—for seven regional stock markets. Figure 11 reports the dynamics of the intercept—obtained by estimating Eq. (7) in a rolling-window framework—for 10 sectors in the emerging and US stock markets. Not surprisingly, emerging alphas present a strong time-varying component and are significantly larger than advanced stock market alphas. The result confirms the unstable industrial structure of emerging stock markets as well as their ability to deliver higher average unexpected excess returns.

3.4. The Dynamics of International Stock Market Excess Returns: Some Final Remarks

The empirical findings of this chapter can be summarized as follows. First, in contrast to previous empirical findings, the results of this chapter suggest that in the aftermath of equity market liberalizations, emerging stock indexes collapsed (i.e., expected returns increase). Second, it is shown that emerging stock market prices have been largely affected by the crises of the 1990s and early 2000s. Third, *de facto* integration seems to take

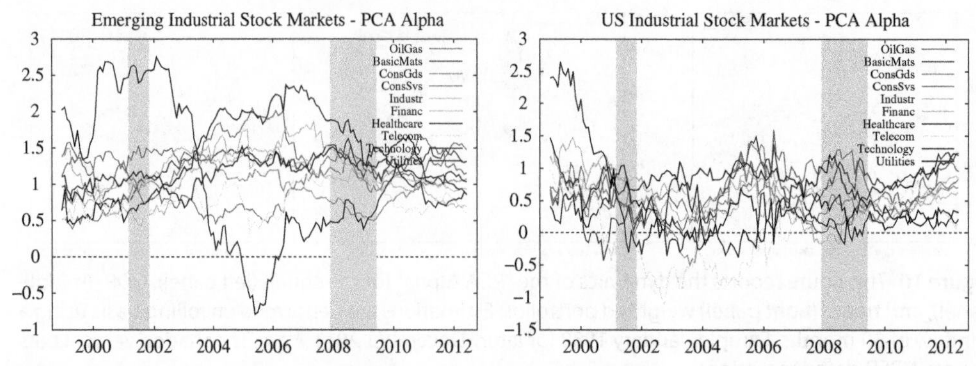

Figure 11 This figure reports the dynamics of the "PCA Alpha" for 10 sectors in the emerging (left panel) and US (right panel) stock markets. Estimates are computed on rolling basis using a window of 60 months. Sample: January 1994 (or later)-June 2012. *Note*: The shaded vertical bars denote NBER-dated recessions.
Source: Based on Donadelli (2013b).

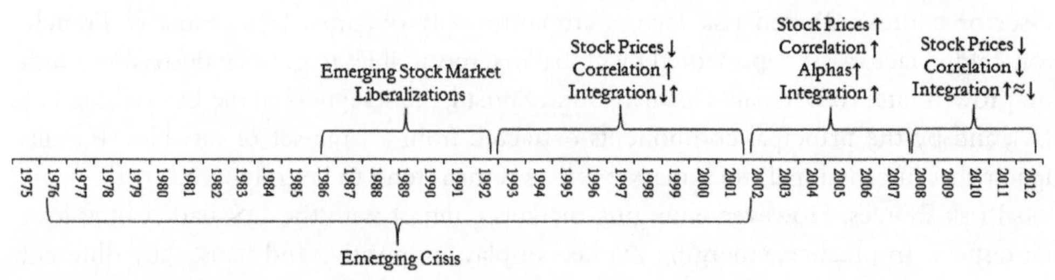

Figure 12 The behavior of emerging stock markets.
Source: Based on Donadelli (2013a,b).

place between the last two NBER-dated recessions. Fourth, emerging expected returns decrease as *de facto* integration increases (see Figure 12).

4. CONCLUSION

This chapter examines the behavior of international stock market excess returns as well as the impact of real and financial integration on emerging stock market indexes in a time-varying context. Summary statistics confirm that emerging stock markets provide higher average excess returns than advanced stock markets and tend to be highly unstable. Early empirical studies observe that the correlation between emerging and advanced stock market excess returns is very low. As a consequence, long position in emerging equity has provided portfolio diversification benefits for many years. However, as recently documented, the equity market liberalizations of the late 1980s and early 1990s, and the subsequent decrease in the level of segmentation have generated an increase in the co-movement between international stock market returns. The impact of liberalizations on emerging stock market prices and the dynamics of the degree of co-movement between international markets have been widely studied. However, most of these studies focus only on stock market country indexes and develop analysis in a static context. In addition they rely on a "contaminated period" (i.e., a period including major emerging crises).

In contrast, this work employs an updated dataset to study the behavior of international stock market excess returns and the impact of *de facto* integration on emerging stock prices in a dynamic context. The main empirical findings are as follows. First, we observe that emerging stock market indexes have been heavily influenced by domestic shocks. Differently from recent studies that examine the impact of financial market liberalizations on emerging stock excess returns, it is shown that liberalizations have affected expected excess returns (as documented) with some delay. It turns out that financial liberalizations do not necessarily imply *de facto* integration. Second, using as a measure of financial integration the $\bar{R}^2$ of a multi-(*artificial*) factor model, we observe that international stock market indexes increase, both at the country and sector level, as the level of *de facto* integration increases. It follows that financial integration seems to be accompanied by economic integration (Phylaktis and Ravazzolo, 2002). Third, it is shown that model's validity is rarely preserved across emerging markets. The latter confirms the emerging markets' ability to generate higher unexpected excess returns. Last, a joint analysis of the dynamics of the co-movement between international stock market returns and the real and financial integration processes indicates that cross-country and cross-industry diversification benefits have largely decreased, thus, forcing international investors to look for alternative forms of investment.

REFERENCES

Antonakakis, N., Chatziantoniou, I., Filis, G., 2012. Dynamic co-movements between stock market returns and policy uncertainty. Unpublished Working Paper.

Baker, S., Bloom, N., Davis, S., 2012. Measuring economic policy uncertainty. Stanford University, Working Paper Series.

Barry, C., Peavy, J., Rodriguez, M., 1997. Emerging stock markets: risk, return, and performance. Research Foundation of the Institute of Chartered Financial Analysts,

Bekaert, G., Erb, C., Harvey, C.R., Viskanta, T., 1998. Distributional characteristics of emerging market returns and asset allocation. Journal of Portfolio Management, 102–116

Bekaert, G., Harvey, C.R., Lundblad, C., 2003. Equity market liberalization in emerging markets. Journal of Financial Research 26 (3), 275–299

Bekaert, G., Harvey, C.R., Lundblad, C., Siegel, S., 2011. What segments equity markets? Review of Financial Studies 24 (12), 3841–3890

Bilson, C.M., Brailsford, T.J., Hooper, V.J., 2001. Selecting macroeconomic variables as explanatory factors of emerging stock market returns. Pacific-Basin Finance Journal 9 (4), 401–426

Claessens, S., Dasgupta, S., Glen, J., 1995. Return behavior in emerging stock markets. World Bank Economic Review 9, 131–151

Corsetti, G., Pericoli, M., Sbracia, M., 2005. Some contagion, some interdependence: more pittfalls in tests of financial contagion. Journal of International Money and Finance 24 (8), 1177–1199 de Jong, F., de Roon, F.A., 2005. Time varying market integration and expected returns in emerging markets. Journal of Financial Economics 78, 583–613

Donadelli, M., 2013a. Global integration and emerging stock market excess returns. Macroeconomics and Finance in Emerging Market Economies

Donadelli, M., 2013b. On the dynamics of industrial stock market excess returns. CASMEF Working Paper Series No. 2013/02.

Donadelli, M., Lucchetta, M., 2012. Emerging stock premia: do industries matter? DSE Working Paper No. 22/12.

Donadelli, M., Persha, L., 2014. Understanding emerging market equity risk premia: industries, governance and macroeconomic policy uncertainty. Research in International Business and Finance 30, 284–309

Donadelli, M., Prosperi, L., 2012. On the role of liquidity in emerging markets stock prices. Research in Economics 66 (4), 320–348

Engle, R., 2002. Dynamic conditional correlation: a simple class of multivariate generalized autoregressive conditional heteroskedasticity models. Journal of Business and Economic Statistics 20 (3), 339–350

Ferson, W.E., Harvey, C.R., 1994. Sources of risk and expected returns in global equity markets. Journal of Banking and Finance 18, 775–803

Grootveld, H., Salomons, R., 2003. The equity risk premium: emerging vs. developed markets. Emerging Markets Review 4 (2), 121–144

Hammond Jr., P.B., Leibowitz, M.L., 2011. In: Hammond Jr., P.B., Leibowitz Jr., M.L., Siegel Jr., L.B. (Eds.), Rethinking the Equity Risk Premium. Research Foundation of CFA Institute

Harvey, C.R., 1995. The risk exposure of emerging equity markets. The World Bank Economic Review 9 (1), 19–50

Harvey, C.R., 1995. Predictable risk and returns in emerging markets. Review of Financial Studies 8, 773–816

Henry, P., 2000. Stock market liberalization, economic reform and emerging market equity prices. Journal of Finance 55, 529–564

Joyce, J.P., 2011. Financial globalization and banking crises in emerging markets. Open Economies Review 22, 875–895

Liao, W., Santacreu, A.M., 2012. The trade co-movement puzzle and the margins of international trade. NYU Working Paper.

Mehra, R., Prescott, E.C., 1985. The equity premium: a puzzle. Journal of Monetary Economics 15 (2), 145–161

Phylaktis, K., Ravazzolo, F., 2002. Measuring financial and economic integration with equity prices in emerging markets. Journal of International Money and Finance 21, 879–903

Pukthuanthong, K., Roll, R., 2009. Global market integration: an alternative measure and its application. Journal of Financial Economics 92 (2), 214–232

Santacreu, A.M., 2012. Innovation, diffusion and trade: theory and measurement. INSEAD Working Paper.

Stulz, R.M., 1999a. International portfolio flows and security markets. Dice Center for Financial Economics, The Ohio State University, Working Paper.

Stulz, R.M., 1999b. Globalization and the cost of equity capital. Working Paper, The New York Stock Exchange.

CHAPTER 31

Determinants of International Financial Integration of GCC Markets

Abdullah R. Alotaibi and Anil V. Mishra
School of Business, University of Western Sydney, Sydney, Australia

1. INTRODUCTION

The rapid increase in international capital flows (foreign direct investment and portfolio investment) is one of the most significant developments among the member countries of the Gulf Cooperation Council (GCC) namely Bahrain, Kuwait, Oman, Qatar, Saudi Arabia, and United Arab Emirates (UAE). For instance, in the GCC region (1980–2010), cross-border portfolio equity assets increased from US$ 4528 million to US$ 483,747 million; FDI assets increased from US$ 1186 million to US$ 162,640 million and total external assets increased from US$ 238,349 million to US$ 2,401,931 million.[1]

The Gulf Cooperation Council (GCC) was established in 1981 with the objective of realizing coordination, integration, and cooperation among member states in various aspects of economic affairs. The GCC signed a preferential trade arrangement that led to the creation of a free trade agreement in agricultural and industrial products (though not petroleum products) and free movement of factors of production. In 2002, GCC decided on implementing gradually a unified economic agreement toward establishing a single market, and forming monetary union at a certain stage. The financial systems in GCC are dominated by commercial banks, which limit the importance of cross-border equity flows. Up to now, member countries of the GCC have taken, or are currently taking, important steps to improve the size and quality of their capital markets. Significant privatizations have occurred, and several countries have built independent and dedicated capital market regulators. In addition, a number of initiatives have been launched to improve the level of integration among stock markets. This would strengthen each of the individual markets, and make the region as a whole a more attractive destination for regional capital relative to external investment options. Furthermore, progress has been made in regional economic integration. The GCC countries have largely unrestricted intraregional mobility of goods, services, national labor, and capital. In 2003, a GCC single common external tariff (CET) rate of 5% was implemented and in early 2008, a common market was established, although not fully implemented. The common market

[1]Lane and Milesi-Ferretti (2007) External Wealth of Nations dataset, International Financial Statistics, Authors' own calculations.

Emerging Markets and the Global Economy
http://dx.doi.org/10.1016/B978-0-12-411549-1.00031-4

would grant GCC citizens equal treatment in all economic activities, capital movement, tax treatment, stock ownership among others. Full implementation of the common market will require changes to national laws, including those pertaining to limits on company ownerships by foreigners. The GCC countries have agreed upon following convergence criteria but not fully adopted: (i) inflation rate should be no higher than the weighted average of all members plus 2 percentage points; (ii) interest rate should not exceed the average of the lowest three interbank rates plus 2 percentage points; (iii) there should be minimum 4 months reserves coverage in terms of imports; (iv) fiscal deficits should not exceed 3% of GDP; and (v) there should be a maximum public debt of 60% of GDP. In 2010, the GCC member countries approved the Statute of the Monetary Council of the Cooperation Council for the Arab States of the Gulf, which focuses on the development and coordination of the monetary policies and exchange rate policies for national currencies until establishment of the Central Bank; preparation for the issuance of the banknotes and coins of the single currency and development of a uniform framework for the introduction and circulation of the single currency in the single currency area.

There has not been a systematic study characterizing GCC member countries, integration[2] with the rest of the world by analyzing external asset and liability positions. This study fills in the gap in financial integration literature by analyzing the degree of financial integration of the GCC member countries with the rest of the world. The study focuses on the development of measures of financial integration in the GCC region, based on foreign assets and liabilities.[3] This chapter employs several quantity-based proxies of international financial integration over the time period from 1980 to 2010. The chapter also contributes to the existing literature by examining the impact of global financial crisis

[2] There are various definitions of financial integration. Adam et al. (2002) state that financial markets are integrated when the law of one price holds. This states that assets generating identical cash flows command the same return, regardless of the domicile of the issuer and of the asset holder. Baele et al. (2004) state that the market for a given set of financial instruments and/or services is fully integrated if all potential market participants with the same relevant characteristics (i) face a single set of rules when they decide to deal with those financial instruments and/or services; (ii) have equal access to the above-mentioned set of financial instruments and/or services; and (iii) are treated equally when they are active in the market. Garcia-Herrero and Woolridge (2007) state that the process of cross-border financial integration involves opening a country's financial markets and institutions to foreign players and permitting local market participants to invest abroad by removing barriers to capital flow, removing obstacles and discrimination of foreign players, harmonization of standards and law.

[3] It is important to develop measures of financial integration that are relatively easy to construct and interpret, based on available data over time. Understanding a country's relative position with respect to the composition of foreign assets and liabilities is important for a number of reasons. First, the composition of foreign assets and liabilities may affect a country's macroeconomic adjustment to shocks. In particular, countries' holdings of foreign assets and liabilities may reduce the volatility of national income by generating investment income streams that are imperfectly correlated with domestic output fluctuations. Second, the size of countries' gross international investment position can be regarded as a volume-based measure of financial openness or the level of integration into international capital markets. Here, the level of financial openness may be important in the diffusion of new financial technologies and in determining the level of productivity in the domestic financial sector (Grossman and Helpman, 1991). Third, a high volume of international asset trade may constrain a country's ability to tax mobile capital and the financial sector (Lane, 2000).

on financial integration measures. On the econometric front, the study employs system GMM Arellano-Bover/Blundell-Bond estimation technique to alleviate bias caused by data, model specification, and endogeneity issues.

The chapter tries to answer the following questions: (i) What are the quantity-based measures of financial integration? (ii) What are the drivers of international financial integration across GCC countries'? (iii) What is the impact of global financial crisis on GCC's financial integration? and (iv) What are the policy implications deriving from the sharp trend toward increasing cross-border asset trade?

The results provide strong evidence that Trade Openness is an important determinant of international financial integration in GCC countries. The results also provide strong evidence that indicators such as financial openness and Domestic Credit have positive and significant impact on GCC countries' international financial integration. The change in financial integration measures due to Trade Openness and Domestic Credit depending on global financial crisis is negative and significant.

The chapter is structured as follows: Section 2 provides a brief literature review. Section 3 discusses measures of international financial integration, data, and stylized facts. Section 4 discusses the theoretical issues related to international financial integration, determinants of international financial integration, impact of global financial crisis on GCC countries, and response to global financial crisis. The section further discusses summary statistics and correlation, methodology, empirical specification, and test results. Finally, Section 5 concludes and furnishes policy implications.

2. LITERATURE REVIEW OF FINANCIAL INTEGRATION

Bekaert and Harvey (2000) employ asset-pricing model to study the integration of emerging market stock exchanges into the global market. Agenor (2003) discusses the benefits and costs of international financial integration. Lane and Milesi-Ferretti (2003) provide a detailed discussion of international financial integration, characterizing its salient features over the last two decades, and examine the relation between foreign assets and liabilities on one side and a set of various regressors on the other side; GDP per capita, Trade Openness, Financial Depth, external liberalization, privatization revenues, stock market capitalization. They state that international trade and stock market capitalization are the most important variables influencing international balance sheets. Baele et al. (2004) propose integration measures to quantify the state and evolution of financial integration in the various segments of euro area including money market, corporate bond market, government bond market, credit market, and capital market. Mishra and Daly (2006) analyze the broad trends in international financial integration for 13 industrial countries. Guerin (2006) finds that the geographical location of a country has a significant role in explaining the spatial allocation of portfolio investment, foreign direct investment, and trade flows, and in determining the degree of financial integration into the world economy. Lane and Milesi-Ferretti (2007) construct estimates of external assets and liabilities and show that the degree of international financial integration has grown dramatically over the last 18 years in both industrialized and developing countries. Baltzer et al. (2008) assess the degree of financial integration of the new EU Member States. They show that financial markets in the new EU Member States are significantly less integrated than those of the euro area. Nevertheless, there is strong evidence that the process of integration is well under way and accelerated following accession to the EU. According to the indicators used, money and banking markets are becoming increasingly integrated both among themselves and vis-à-vis the euro area. Lane and Milesi-Ferretti (2008a) state that GDP per capita and domestic financial development is stronger for external assets than for liabilities. Faria and Mauro (2009) find that equity as a share of countries' total external liabilities is positively and significantly associated with indicators of educational attainment, openness, natural resource abundance, and institutional quality. Kucerová (2009) analyzes the degree of financial integration of the EU-8 countries with the rest of the world by using quantity-based measures of financial integration derived from the countries' international investment positions. The findings suggest a significant linkage between EU-8 foreign assets and liabilities and EU-8 foreign trade. Espinoza et al. (2010) investigate the extent of regional financial integration in the member countries of the Gulf Cooperation Council. The results suggest the development of stock markets in the region will improve the extent of financial integration. Interest rate data show that convergence exists and that interest rate differentials are relatively short-lived—especially compared to the ECCU, another emerging market region sharing a common currency. Equities data using cross-listed stocks confirm that stock markets are fairly integrated compared with other emerging market regions, although financial integration is hampered by market illiquidity. Cavoli et al. (2011) present both stylized facts and panel-data analysis examining relationships between the proportion of foreign listings and other measures of integration in a sample of Asian markets. The results find that higher Trade Openness, higher output growth, and lower inflation are associated with a greater proportion of foreign listings. They also find that FDI openness has a negative relationship to the proportion of foreign listings, suggesting that these aspects of financial integration are substitutes. In addition, the results indicate that unless the appropriate financial liberalization policies are in place, countries may find it difficult to simultaneously attract foreign listings to enhance development of their stock market and to grow their real economy through FDI. Borensztein and Loungani (2011) compare trends in financial integration within Asia with those in industrialized countries and other regional groups. The findings suggest that Asian integration increases when cross-country dispersion in equity returns and interest rate declines. There has been an increase in cross-border equity and bond holdings. Asian countries are more financially integrated with major countries outside the region than with those within the region.

3. MEASURES OF INTERNATIONAL FINANCIAL INTEGRATION

There are three broad categories of measures of integration: price-based, news-based, and quantity-based measures. The price-based measures focus on discrepancies in prices or returns on assets caused by the geographic origin of the assets. These measures can be used to check the law of one price. The cross-sectional variation of interest rates spreads or asset return differentials can be used as an indicator of the deviation of markets from full integration. The speed at which markets integrate can be measured through beta convergence criteria.

News-based measures of integration are based on the notion that the degree of systematic risk is identical across assets in different countries. These measures are designed to distinguish between the information effects and other frictions. The regional news is expected to have little impact on prices as compared with global news.

Quantity-based measures focus on effects of frictions faced by the demand for and supply of investment opportunities. These measures are based on asset quantities and flows. Research in this paper employs quantity-based measures of integration.

The first measure of international financial integration ($IFIA_{it}$) is an asset-based measure:

$$IFIA_{it} = \frac{FA_{it}}{GDP_{it}}, \tag{1}$$

where FA_{it} is the total foreign assets in time t, and GDP_{it} is the nominal GDP of country i in time t, where i represents the particular GCC country. We use GDP as denominator to allow for country size. The ratios relative to GDP enable a direct comparison of countries.

The second is ($IFIL_{it}$) a liability-based measure of international financial integration:

$$IFIL_{it} = \frac{FL_{it}}{GDP_{it}}, \tag{2}$$

where FL_{it} is the total foreign liabilities in time t. The third is a broad indicator of international financial integration based on a volume measure:

$$IFIT_{it} = \frac{FA_{it} + FL_{it}}{GDP_{it}}. \tag{3}$$

The fourth measure of international financial integration ($IFIEDQ_{it}$) is an investment-based measure of financial integration. It contains only FDI and portfolio investments (equity and debt securities). The other categories are dropped from this measure because they are either volatile (other investments) or financial derivatives data may not be available for GCC countries:

$$IFIEDQ_{it} = \frac{FDIA_{it} + PEQA_{it} + PDQA_{it} + FDIL_{it} + PEQL_{it} + PDQL_{it}}{GDP_{it}}, \tag{4}$$

where $FDIA_{it}$ is the stock of FDI assets of country i abroad in time t, $FDIL_{it}$ is the stock of FDI liabilities of the rest of the world in country i in time t, $PEQA_{it}$ is the stock of portfolio equity assets of country i abroad in time t, $PDQA_{it}$ is the stock of portfolio debt assets of country i abroad in time t, $PEQL_{it}$ is the stock of portfolio equity liabilities of the rest of world in country i in time t, and $PDQL_{it}$ is the stock of portfolio debt liabilities of the rest of the world in country i in time t.

The international financial integration measures capture the size of foreign investment globally that is appropriately scaled and consistent over time. The measure of the activity in the global capital market is to consider the total stock of overseas investment at a point in time. The foreign capital stock at each point in time should be normalized by some measure of the size of the world economy, by a denominator in the form of nominal size index. A suitable denominator would probably be the total stock of capital, whether financial or real because the numerator is the stock of foreign-owned capital. The problem with using financial capital measures is that they have greatly multiplied over the long run with the rise in numerous financial intermediaries and financial development has expanded the number of balance sheets in the economy (Goldsmith, 1985). This trend could happen at any point in time without any underlying change in the extent of foreign asset holdings. The problem with using real capital stocks is that only a few countries have a reliable data from which to estimate capital stocks. Most of these estimates are accurate only at benchmark censuses and in between census dates they rely on combinations of interpolation and estimation based on investment flow data and depreciation assumptions. Most of these estimates are calculated in real (constant price) rather than nominal (current price) terms, which make them disproportionate with the nominally measured foreign capital data. This paper utilizes a readily available size of an economy, namely the level of output (GDP) measured in current prices in a common currency unit (Obstfeld and Taylor, 2002).

3.1. Data and Stylized Facts

The data employed in this research is derived from Lane and Milesi-Ferretti (2001, 2007) External Wealth of Nations (EWN) dataset and International Financial Statistics. The EWN dataset is for 145 countries and euro area. The main sources of EWN dataset: International Monetary Fund's Balance of Payments Statistics (BOPs), International Financial Statistics (IFS), Coordinated Portfolio Investment Survey (CPIS), The World Bank's Debt Tables, Global Development Finance, OECD statistics on external indebtedness, and the Bank for International Settlements' data on banks' assets and liabilities by creditor and debtor (BIS). The EWN dataset is based on the 5th revision of Balance of Payments Manual (IMF 1993) methodology. The dataset reports total holdings by domestic residents of financial claims on the rest of the world (external assets) and nonresidents' claims on the domestic economy (external liabilities). The external liabilities are divided into five main categories: portfolio equity investment, portfolio debt investment, foreign direct investment, other investment (debt instruments: loans, deposits, trade credits), and financial derivatives. External assets are divided into six categories: five categories same as external liabilities plus reserve assets. We investigate the level of financial integration and

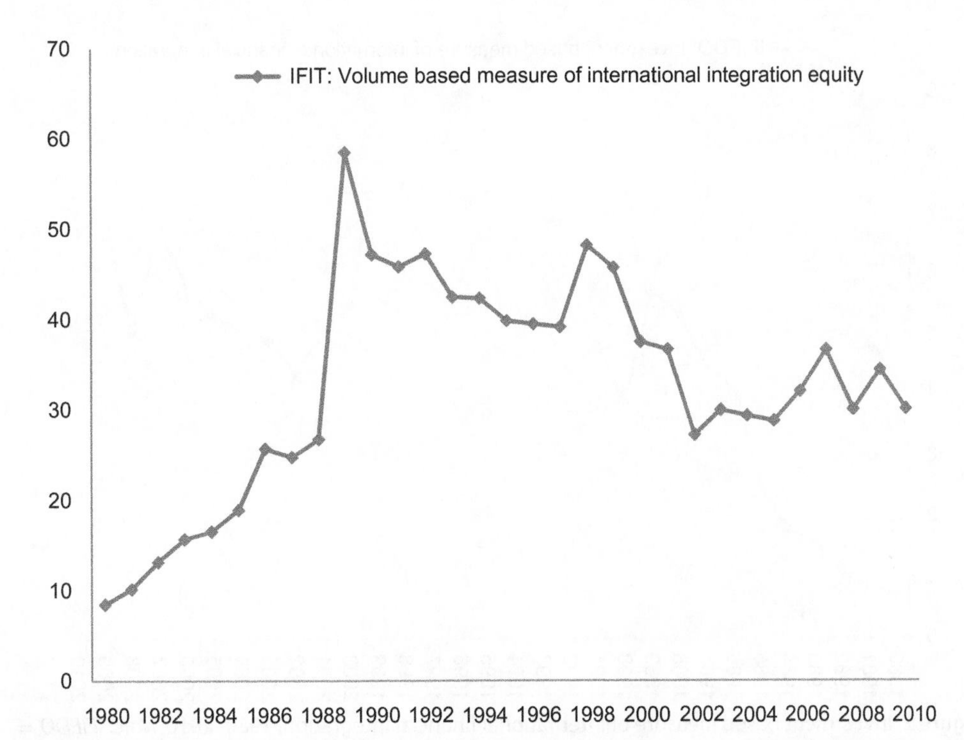

Figure 1 Evolution of international financial integration, 1980–2010. *Note:* $IFIT = \sum_{i=1}^{6} IFIT_{it}$ $\cdot i$ denotes individual GCC country. There are six GCC countries: Bahrain, Kuwait, Oman, Qatar, Saudi Arabia and United Arab Emirates. $IFIT_{it} = \frac{FA_{it}+FL_{it}}{GDP_{it}}$ $\cdot$ FA_{it} is the total foreign assets of country i in time t, FL_{it} is the total foreign liabilities of country i in time t, GDP_{it} is the nominal GDP of country i in time t.

the trend of integration over the period 1980–2010 among the Bahrain, Kuwait, Oman, Qatar, Saudi Arabia, and United Arab Emirates (GCC) and the rest of the world.

Figure 1 plots the evolution of international financial integration measure ($IFIT_{it}$) for GCC over the years 1980–2010. The international financial integration measure rises over the period 1980–1989 and then drops in 1991. The drop in 1991 is due to the Gulf War which took place in Kuwait (2 August 1990 to 28 February 1991). Again in 1990, there was conflict in Saudi Arabia between opposition movement and government. The decline in 2001 reflects the steep fall in world stock markets. The decline in the period 2007–2008 indicates the effect of global financial crisis in GCC.

In Figure 2, the investment measure (ratio of portfolio plus FDI assets and liabilities to GDP) increases over the period from 1980 to 1989 and then the measure drops in 1991. The fall in investment measure over the 1990–1991 period is due to Gulf War. Again the decline in 2001 reflects the fall in world stock markets. The decline in the period 2007–2008 indicates the impact of global financial crisis in GCC.

Overall stylized facts indicate that the GCC region has improved its net external position. Equity instruments (especially FDI) now account for a much larger share of external

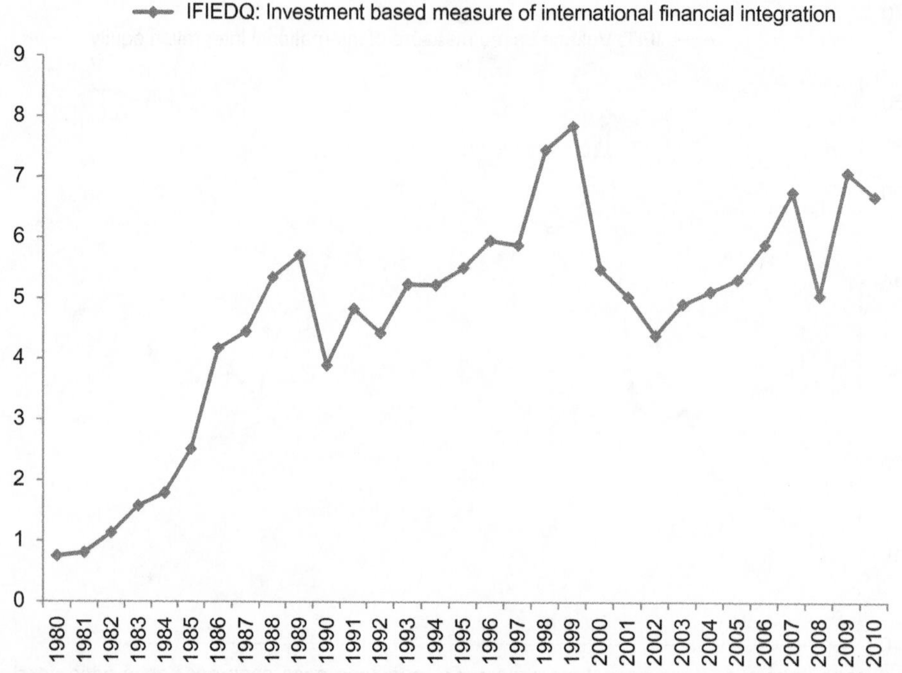

Figure 2 Investment based measure of international financial integration, 1980–2010. *Note:* $IFIEDQ = \sum_{i=1}^{6} IFIEDQ_{it}$ · i denotes individual GCC country. There are six GCC countries: Bahrain, Kuwait, Oman, Qatar, Saudi Arabia and United Arab Emirates.

$$IFIEDQ_{it} = \frac{FDIA_{it} + PEQA_{it} + PDQA_{it} + FDIL_{it} + PEQL_{it} + PDQL_{it}}{GDP_{it}}.$$

$FDIA_{it}$ is the stock of FDI assets of country i abroad in time t, $PEQA_{it}$ is the stock of portfolio equity assets of country i abroad in time t, $PDQA_{it}$ is the stock of portfolio debt assets of country i abroad in time t, $FDIL_{it}$ is the stock of FDI liabilities of the rest of the world in country i in time t, $PEQL_{it}$ is the stock of portfolio equity liabilities of the rest of world in country i in time t, $PDQL_{it}$ is the stock of portfolio debt liabilities of the rest of the world in country i in time t, GDP_{it} is the nominal GDP of country i in time t.

liabilities, such that domestic production risks are now shared to a much greater degree with outside investors. The considerable variation in cross-border positions means that the international financial transmission mechanism is quite complex, with a local shock in one economy having a differential impact on partner countries, according to the level and composition of bilateral investment positions and the nature of co-movements between home and partner financial returns. The heterogeneity in the bilateral transmission of shocks is reinforced by the asymmetries between international financial linkages and international trade linkages, with the degree of trade integration between GCC and world relatively stronger than the degree of financial integration.

4. ANALYSIS OF DETERMINANTS OF INTERNATIONAL FINANCIAL INTEGRATION IN GCC

This section discusses the theoretical issues related to international financial integration, impact of global financial crisis on GCC countries, response to global financial crisis, and determinants of international financial integration. The section further discusses summary statistics and correlation, methodology, empirical specification, and test results.

4.1. Theoretical Issues

International Parity theory suggests that in a world with no borders, the allocation of international asset holdings would take place with no transactions costs; here it is assumed that complete global financial market integration exists. Each country would hold a very high level of foreign assets and liabilities, in line with full diversification. However in the actual world, there are implicit and explicit barriers to full integration and in the gains to international diversification. Martin and Rey (2000, 2004) develop a theoretical model that assumes that investors are risk averse, the number of financial assets is endogenous, assets are imperfect substitutes, and cross-border asset trade entails transactions costs. Under these assumptions, a reduction in international transaction costs stimulates an increase in the demand for (and supply of) assets and an increase in asset prices, leading to higher cross-border diversification. Our empirical specification will be based on the identification of a set of country characteristics that may influence international asset trade.

4.2. Impact of Global Financial Crisis on GCC Countries

During global financial crisis, the GCC countries have been hit by the decline in oil prices and production, as well as by liquidity shortages in global financial markets. GCC region's stock market capitalization fell by 41% ($400 billion) between September 2008 and end-2008 and volatility increased (IMF, 2010). On average, stock market indices of the Arab countries crashed by more than 50% between their peak in mid-2008 and their low in early 2009, thereby causing losses of something between US$200 billion and US$600 billion (Brach and Loewe, 2010). The main channels of transmission of crisis are due to reduction in foreign investment and exports (IMF, 2009).

At the end of 2006, the UAE sovereign funds were about 400% of the country's GDP. The sovereign funds of Kuwait and Saudi Arabia had foreign assets of about 142% and 64% of GDP. Atleast 30% of these assets were temporarily lost during the financial crisis. According to Deutsche Bank and Forbes estimates, the losses of Arab sovereign funds accounted for over US$450 billion, while private investors lost another US$300–500 billion. The losses were very unevenly distributed across the region. The sovereign funds of Kuwait and the UAE (especially Dubai) had invested large shares of their capital into emerging market stocks and bonds, and as a consequence they experienced particularly large losses. The sovereign funds of Saudi Arabia followed a much more conservative investment strategy and therefore fared much better. Out of some US$60 billion accumulated until 2008, Qatar's sovereign wealth fund lost US$10 billion during crisis (Brach and Loewe, 2010).

The GCC financial systems are heavily regulated by state-owned banks, and most banks have easy access to domestic sources of finance. In Bahrain, two banks ran into financial difficulties, but the central bank took control of them to prevent other banks being affected by their problems (Lidstone, 2009; Wigglesworth, 2009a). In Saudi Arabia, several banks were at risk of insolvency (Wigglesworth, 2009b). In Kuwait, two investment companies defaulted; however, they reached restructuring agreement with their creditors. Credit rating agencies have taken several negative rating actions on GCC banks (IMF, 2010).

4.2.1. Response to Global Financial Crisis

Most energy-exporting GCC countries have focused on stabilizing their financial sectors. They have first taken measures to ease and encourage interbank lending and to prevent collapse of national banking institutes. Kuwait, Qatar, Saudi Arabia, and UAE have introduced blanket state guarantees for commercial bank deposits in order to establish confidence among savers and investors, while only Qatar and Saudi Arabia have also established state guarantee funds. All GCC countries have pumped liquidity into local financial markets. Most energy-exporting countries have strengthened their financial market regulations and relaxed monetary policies: reduced key interest rates and minimum reserve requirements (IMF, 2009; Siddiqi, 2009).

Central banks infused liquidity into the financial system through repos and placement of long-term deposits. Saudi Arabia passed a stimulus package that forms part of a five-year $400 billion investment plan that will contribute to the global effort to revive demand (IMF, 2010). Kuwait has also established a fund to assist private enterprises when necessary, but has at the same time announced cuts in public expenditure on social services and infrastructure (Smith, 2009).

4.3. Variables

4.3.1. Trade Openness

Trade Openness is the sum of imports and exports normalized by GDP. Mishra (2007) and Lane and Milesi-Ferretti (2008b) state that bilateral equity investment is strongly correlated with underlying patterns of trade. Investors are better able to attain accounting and regulatory information on foreign markets through trade and thereby invest in foreign assets. Default risk is also ameliorated by tighter trade integration. Finally, trade transactions may directly generate cross-border financial flows including trade credits, export insurance, payment facilitation. The data on Trade Openness are from World Bank's World Development Indicators.

4.3.2. Financial Depth

Financial Depth is the ratio of money supply (M2) to GDP. Money supply (M2) is money and quasi-money which comprises of the sum of currency outside banks, demand deposits other than those of the central government, the time savings, and foreign currency deposits of resident sectors other than the central government. The ratio of M2 to GDP is often used as a measure of the size and liquidity of the financial intermediary sector (King and Levine, 1993). In addition, M2 to GDP, as the inverse value of the velocity of circulation of money, corresponds to the cash holding coefficient and, as such, indicates the confidence that economic agents have in the domestic currency and the banking system. M2 corresponds to lines 34 and 35 in the International Monetary Fund's International Financial Statistics. GDP data are from International Monetary Fund's World Economic Outlook database.

4.3.3. Domestic Credit

Domestic Credit is the ratio of Domestic Credit provided by banking sector to GDP. Levine et al. (2000) employ this measure in their study related to financial intermediation and growth. They find higher levels of Domestic Credit as indicating higher levels of financial services and therefore, greater financial intermediary growth. The development of domestic financial markets facilitates asset trade among local residents and thereby potentially diminishes the role of external financial intermediaries in linking domestic agents. However, domestic financial development may be spurred by foreign investment in the domestic financial system, and the creation of domestic financial products also facilitates foreign demand for domestic liabilities (Martin and Rey, 2004) thus suggesting a positive correlation between financial development and financial globalization. The institutional capability accumulated by investing in domestic markets lowers the barrier to acquiring foreign assets, implying potentially strong complementarities between growth of domestic financial positions and external financial positions.

4.3.4. GDP per capita

The level of economic development is an important factor in explaining domestic residents' propensity to engage in cross-border asset trade. In the presence of fixed costs or less-than-proportional learning costs of international asset trade, we would expect to see higher international financial integration in wealthier economies (Mulligan and Salai-i-Martin, 1996). GDP per capita data is from International Monetary Fund's World Economic Outlook database.

4.4. Summary Statistics and Correlation

Table 1 illustrates summary statistics of variables. Asset measure (ratio of external assets to GDP) ranges from 0.289 to 17.769 and it has mean value of 3.777. Investment measure (ratio of sum of FDI and portfolio assets, and liabilities to GDP) ranges from 0.367 to 33.896 and it has mean value of 5.241. Financial Depth (ratio of M2 to GDP) has mean value of 104.343 and Domestic Credit (ratio of Domestic Credit provided by banking sector to GDP) has mean value of 40.519.

Table 2 illustrates correlation matrix of measures and variables. There is high correlation between measures and therefore they are not taken together in regressions.

Table 1 Summary statistics of variables.

Variables	Observations	Mean	Standard deviation	Minimum	Maximum
Asset measure	186	3.777	4.106	0.289	17.769
Liability measure	186	1.642	3.483	0.061	16.382
Volume measure	186	5.420	7.120	0.463	34.151
Investment measure	186	5.241	7.117	0.367	33.896
Financial depth	186	104.343	91.374	5.433	321.656
Trade openness	186	107.637	38.597	56.47	251.14
GDP per capita	186	17808.58	14064.44	4600	86436
Domestic credit	186	40.519	18.323	6.815	94.517

Note: asset measure is ratio of external assets to GDP. Liability measure is ratio of external liabilities to GDP. Volume measure is ratio of sum of external assets and liabilities to GDP. Investment measure is sum of FDI and portfolio assets and liabilities to GDP. Financial Depth is ratio of M2 to GDP. Trade Openness is ratio of sum of imports and export to GDP. GDP per capita in US$. Domestic Credit is ratio of Domestic Credit provided by banking sector to GDP.

Table 2 Correlation matrix.

	Asset measure	Liability measure	Volume measure	Investment measure	Financial depth	Trade openness	GDP per capita	Domestic credit
Asset measure	1.000							
Liability measure	0.908	1.000						
Volume measure	0.979	0.973	1.000					
Investment measure	0.978	0.974	0.999	1.000				
Financial Depth	0.235	0.033	0.143	0.138	1.000			
Trade Openness	0.072	0.023	0.051	0.048	−0.034	1.000		
GDP per capita	−0.216	−0.043	−0.138	−0.134	−0.411	0.067	1.000	
Domestic Credit	0.108	−0.001	0.058	0.054	0.316	−0.154	−0.227	1.000

Note: asset measure is ratio of external assets to GDP. Liability measure is ratio of external liabilities to GDP. Volume measure is ratio of sum of external assets and liabilities to GDP. Investment measure is sum of FDI and portfolio assets and liabilities to GDP. Financial Depth is ratio of M2 to GDP. Trade Openness is ratio of sum of imports and export to GDP. GDP per capita in US$. Domestic Credit is ratio of Domestic Credit provided by banking sector to GDP. Financial Depth, Trade Openness, and Domestic Credit are expressed in percent.

The correlation matrix indicates that variables are not highly correlated with each other and neither with measures.

4.5. Methodology and Empirical Specification

Financial integration measure may be dynamic in nature and the econometric treatment of dynamic nature of financial integration measure includes lagged values of financial integration measure among the explanatory variables:

$$y_{it} = \delta y_{i,t-1} + x'_{it}\beta + u_{it} \qquad i = 1, \ldots\ldots\ldots, N \qquad t = 2, \ldots\ldots\ldots\ldots\ldots, T, \quad (5)$$

where δ is a scalar, x'_{it} is a $1 \times K$ vector of explanatory variables, and β is a $K \times 1$ vector of parameters to be estimated. The error term u_{it} is composed of an unobserved effect and time-invariant effect μ_i and random disturbance term ν_{it}:

$$u_{it} = \mu_i + \nu_{it}, \quad (6)$$

where $\mu_i \sim IID(0, \sigma_\mu^2)$ and $\nu_{it} \sim IID(0, \sigma_\nu^2)$ independent of each other and among themselves. The dynamic panel-data regressions described in above Eqs. (5) and (6) are characterized by two sources of persistence over time, i.e., autocorrelation due to the presence of a lagged dependent variable among the regressors and individual effects characterizing the heterogeneity among the individuals. Since y_{it} is a function of μ_i, this implies that $y_{i,t-1}$ is also a function of μ_i. Therefore, $y_{i,t-1}$ is correlated with the error term through the presence of μ_i. The OLS estimator for Eq. (5) is biased and inconsistent even if the ν_{it} are not serially correlated. The fixed effect estimator of (5), which eliminates the individual effects μ_i, produces biased and inconsistent estimates (Nickell, 1981; Kiviet, 1995). Anderson and Hsiao (1982) suggested first differencing the model to get rid of the μ_i and then using $\Delta y_{i,t-2} = (y_{i,t-2} - y_{i,t-3})$ as an instrument for $\Delta y_{i,t-1} = (y_{i,t-1} - y_{i,t-2})$. These instruments will not be correlated with $\Delta \nu_{it} = \nu_{i,t} - \nu_{i,t-1}$, so far as the ν_{it} themselves are not serially correlated. This instrumental variable (IV) estimation method leads to consistent but not necessarily efficient estimates of the parameters in the model because it does not make use of all available moment conditions (Ahn and Schmidt, 1995) and it does not take into account the differenced structure on residual disturbances ($\Delta \nu_{it}$). Arellano (1989) states that for simple dynamic error components models, the estimator that uses differences $\Delta y_{i,t-2}$ rather than levels $y_{i,t-2}$ for instruments has a singularity point and very large variances over a significant range of parameter values. On the other hand, the estimator that uses $y_{i,t-2}$ has no singularities and much smaller variances. Arellano and Bond (1991) proposed a generalized method of moments (GMM) estimator of the first differenced model that brings about significant efficiency gains as compared with the estimator by Anderson and Hsiao (1982) through exploiting additional orthogonality conditions associated with higher lags of the endogenous variable in the set of instruments.

To deal with basic problems of endogeneity between variables the regression equation will be based on the Arellano-Bover/Blundell-Bond linear dynamic panel-data estimation. In these models, the unobserved panel level effects are correlated with the lagged dependent variables, making standard estimators inconsistent. Arellano and Bond (1991) derived a one-step and two-step GMM estimators using moment conditions in which lagged levels of the dependent and predetermined variables were instruments for the differenced equations. Blundell and Bond (1998) show that the lagged-level instruments in the Arellano-Bond estimator become weak as the autoregressive process becomes too persistent or the ratio of the variance of the panel-level effect to the variance of the idiosyncratic error becomes too large. Linear dynamic panel-data models include p lags of the dependent variable on covariates and contain unobserved panel level effects, fixed or random. Arellano and Bover (1995) develop a framework for efficient instrumental variable estimators of random effects models with information in levels which can accommodate predetermined variables. Building on the work of Arellano and Bover (1995), Blundell and Bond (1998) proposed a system estimator that uses moment conditions in which lagged differences are used as instruments for the level equation in addition to the moment conditions of lagged levels as instruments for the differenced equation. This estimator is designed for datasets with many panels and few periods. The method assumes that there is no autocorrelation in the idiosyncratic errors and requires the initial condition that the panel-level effects be uncorrelated with the first difference of the first observation of the dependent variable. In a dynamic panel-data GMM estimation, the number of moment conditions increases with T. The moment conditions employed by the Arellano-Bover/Blundell method are valid only if there is no serial correlation in the idiosyncratic error. The Arellano-Bond test is a test for no autocorrelation in linear dynamic panel models. We perform Arellano and Bond test for serial correlation in the first differenced errors at order m.

The determinants of financial integration will be investigated by estimating several empirical specifications. A benchmark specification that includes financial integration variables is given by the following relationship:

$$y_{it} = \delta y_{i,t-1} + x_{it}'\beta + u_{it}, \tag{7}$$

where y_{it} is measure of financial integration as per Eqs. (1)–(4); x_{it}' includes various country characteristics including trade, GDP per capita, ratio of liquid liabilities to GDP, ratio of Domestic Credit provided by banking sector to GDP, and u_{it} is error term. We first difference the data to take into account stationarity.[4]

4.6. Empirical Results

The section presents Arellano-Bover/Blundell-Bond tests (Tables 3–5) regression results upon estimating Eq. (7). Columns (1)–(4) illustrate results over the period from 1980 to

[4] We conduct several panel unit root tests to determine the stationarity of variables and find that variables are stationary upon first difference. Results are available from authors.

Table 3 Asset measure.

	1980–2007				1980–2010			
	(1)	(2)	(3)	(4)	(5)	(6)	(7)	(8)
Financial depth	2.545***	2.533***	1.792***	1.562***	2.070***	2.095***	1.464***	1.299**
	(0.000)	(0.000)	(0.000)	(0.000)	(0.000)	(0.001)	(0.007)	(0.011)
Trade openness		2.243*	2.389*	2.675*		2.050*	2.188*	2.404**
		(0.083)	(0.076)	(0.056)		(0.072)	(0.056)	(0.031)
GDP per capita			−0.000***	−0.000***			−0.000***	−0.000***
			(0.001)	(0.003)			(0.000)	(0.000)
Domestic credit				2.002***				1.529**
				(0.000)				(0.024)
Wald Chi-Square	35.62	145.93	251.21	303.33	24.77	40.32	333.05	1496.56
	(0.00)	(0.00)	(0.000)	(0.000)	(0.000)	(0.000)	(0.000)	(0.000)
Observations	156	156	156	156	174	174	174	174
Arellano-Bond test	−0.926	−0.980	−0.968	−0.966	−0.886	−0.930	−0.911	−0.900
AR(2) *p*-value	(0.354)	(0.326)	(0.332)	(0.333)	(0.375)	(0.352)	(0.362)	(0.368)

Note: asset measure (Ratio of external assets to GDP) is dependent variable. Columns (1)–(4) indicate results over the period 1980–2007 and columns (5)–(8) indicate results over the period 1980–2010. Arellano-Bover/Blundell-Bond estimation with lags(1) and AR(2) tests. Arellano-Bond test for no autocorrelation. Lag value of the dependent variable is not reported. *P*-values in brackets. Constant is not reported. Financial Depth is ratio of M2 to GDP. Trade Openness is ratio of sum of imports and export to GDP. GDP per capita in US$. Domestic Credit is ratio of Domestic Credit provided by banking sector to GDP.

*Significance at 10%.

**Significance at 5%.

***Significance at 1%.

Table 4 Volume measure.

	1980–2007				1980–2010			
	(1)	(2)	(3)	(4)	(5)	(6)	(7)	(8)
Financial depth	2.733***	2.727***	1.908***	1.598***	2.307***	2.367***	1.637***	1.459***
	(0.000)	(0.000)	(0.000)	(0.000)	(0.002)	(0.000)	(0.000)	(0.000)
Trade openness		4.377*	4.492*	4.859*		3.920*	4.053*	4.273**
		(0.072)	(0.068)	(0.057)		(0.060)	(0.053)	(0.033)
GDP per capita			−0.000**	−0.000***			−0.000***	−0.000***
			(0.004)	(0.008)			(0.000)	(0.000)
Domestic credit				2.676***				1.652*
				(0.000)				(0.079)
Wald Chi-Square	158.01	873.36	1777.42	5110.03	136.25	640.48	1143.97	3524.64
	(0.00)	(0.00)	(0.000)	(0.000)	(0.000)	(0.000)	(0.000)	(0.000)
Observations	156	156	156	156	174	174	174	174
Arellano-Bond test	−0.967	−1.023	−1.024	−1.027	−0.961	−1.008	−1.006	−1.003
AR(2) *p*-value	(0.333)	(0.306)	(0.305)	(0.304)	(0.336)	(0.313)	(0.314)	(0.315)

Note: volume measure (Ratio of sum of external assets and external liabilities to GDP) is dependent variable. Columns (1)–(4) indicate results over the period 1980–2007 and columns (5)–(8) indicate results over the period 1980–2010. Arellano-Bover/Blundell-Bond estimation with lags(1) and AR(2) tests. Arellano-Bond test for no autocorrelation. Lag value of the dependent variable is not reported. Constant is not reported. *P*-values in brackets. Financial Depth is ratio of M2 to GDP. Trade Openness is ratio of sum of imports and export to GDP. GDP per capita in US$. Domestic Credit is ratio of Domestic Credit provided by banking sector to GDP.
*Significance at 10%.
**Significance at 5%.
***Significance at 1%.

Table 5 Investment measure.

	1980–2007				1980–2010			
	(1)	(2)	(3)	(4)	(5)	(6)	(7)	(8)
Financial depth	2.627***	2.644***	1.836***	1.500***	2.210***	2.281***	1.613***	1.414***
	(0.000)	(0.000)	(0.000)	(0.000)	(0.003)	(0.000)	(0.001)	(0.003)
Trade openness		4.459*	4.574*	4.948*		3.977*	4.075*	0.043**
		(0.073)	(0.070)	(0.062)		(0.061)	(0.056)	(0.038)
GDP per capita			−0.000***	−0.000***			−0.000***	−0.000***
			(0.003)	(0.009)			(0.000)	(0.000)
Domestic credit				2.970***				1.883***
				(0.002)				(0.005)
Wald Chi-Square	176.83	1091.22	2524.02	16379.76	148.55	778.10	1355.16	4786.67
	(0.000)	(0.00)	(0.000)	(0.000)	(0.000)	(0.000)	(0.000)	(0.000)
Observations	156	156	156	156	174	174	174	174
Arellano-Bond test	−0.966	−1.024	−1.026	−1.032	−0.958	−1.007	−1.007	−1.006
AR(2) *p*-value	(0.333)	(0.305)	(0.304)	(0.301)	(0.337)	(0.313)	(0.313)	(0.314)

Note: investment measure (Ratio of sum of FDI, portfolio asset, and liabilities to GDP) is dependent variable. Columns (1)–(4) indicate results over the period 1980–2007 and columns (5)–(8) indicate results over the period 1980–2010. Arellano-Bover/Blundell-Bond estimation with lags(1) and AR(2) tests. Arellano-Bond test for no autocorrelation. Lag value of the dependent variable is not reported. Constant is not reported. *P*-values in brackets. Financial Depth is ratio of M2 to GDP. Trade Openness is ratio of sum of imports and export to GDP. GDP per capita in US$. Domestic Credit is ratio of Domestic Credit provided by banking sector to GDP.
*Significance at 10%.
**Significance at 5%.
***Significance at 1%.

2007 and columns (5)–(8) illustrate the results over the period from 1980 to 2010 (taking into account global financial crisis). Table 3 illustrates the regression results when the external asset normalized by GDP ($IFIA_{it}$) is dependent variable. Financial Depth appears to be positive and highly significant. This implies that economic agents have confidence in the domestic currency and the banking system. Over the period 1980–2007 (columns (1)–(4)), a 1 percentage point increase in Financial Depth increases $IFIA_{it}$ on average by 2.10 percentage point. Over the period 1980–2010 (columns (5)–(8)), 1 percentage point increase in Financial Depth increases $IFIA_{it}$ on average by 1.73 percentage point. Trade Openness is positive and significant. Trade Openness enables investors to have better accounting and regulatory information on foreign markets and thereby invest in foreign assets. In columns (2)–(4), 1 percentage point increase in Trade Openness increases $IFIA_{it}$ on average by 2.43 percentage points. Over the period 1980–2010, 1 percentage point increase in Trade Openness increases $IFIA_{it}$ on average by 2.21 percentage points. GDP per capita is negative and statistically significant; however, it is economically insignificant. One possible explanation is that an increase in the GDP per capita lowers the rate of return and flow of FDI.

Domestic Credit appears to be positive and significant. The banking institutional capability accumulated by investing in domestic markets lowers the barrier to acquiring foreign assets, implying potentially strong complementarities between the growth of domestic financial positions and external financial positions. One percentage point increase in Domestic Credit increases $IFIA_{it}$ on average by 2 percentage points over the period 1980–2007. One percentage point increase in Domestic Credit increases $IFIA_{it}$ on average by 1.53 percentage point over the period 1980–2010. The Arellano-Bond test for serial correlation in the first differenced errors indicates that there is no autocorrelation of second order.

Table 4 illustrates the regression results when the external asset and liability normalized by GDP ($IFIT_{it}$) is dependent variable. $IFIT_{it}$ is volume-based measure of financial integration. Table 5 illustrates the regression results when the sum of portfolio and FDI assets and liabilities normalized by GDP ($IFIEDQ_{it}$) is dependent variable. $IFIEDQ_{it}$ is investment-based measure of financial integration. In Tables 4 and 5, financial openness, Trade Openness, and Domestic Credit are positive and significant. GDP per capita is negative and significant; however, it is economically insignificant.

Table 6 illustrates the results upon taking into account recent impact of global financial crisis on financial integration measures in GCC. Columns (1)–(3) illustrate Arellano-Bover/Bludell-Bond estimation results and columns (4)–(6) illustrate Arellano-Bond estimation results as a robustness check. In columns (1) and (4), dependent variable is asset-based financial integration measure (ratio of external assets to GDP). In columns (2) and (5), dependent variable is volume-based financial integration measure (ratio of the sum of external assets and liabilities to GDP). Finally in columns (3) and (6), dependent variable is investment-based financial integration measure (ratio of sum of FDI, portfolio

Table 6 Robustness test (1980–2010).

	Arellano-Bover/Blundell-Bond			Arellano-Bond		
	(1)	**(2)**	**(3)**	**(4)**	**(5)**	**(6)**
Financial depth	1.308***	1.368***	1.282***	1.370***	1.452***	1.339***
	(0.000)	(0.000)	(0.000)	(0.005)	(0.001)	(0.002)
Trade openness	2.645*	4.788*	4.852*	2.970**	4.859*	4.817*
	(0.055)	(0.056)	(0.062)	(0.024)	(0.069)	(0.073)
GDP per capita	−0.010***	−0.0109***	−0.010***	−0.009***	−0.010***	−0.010***
	(0.002)	(0.005)	(0.005)	(0.001)	(0.006)	(0.005)
Domestic credit	2.177***	2.840***	3.091***	1.610***	1.931***	1.920***
	(0.000)	(0.000)	(0.001)	(0.000)	(0.000)	(0.001)
GFC	−0.230	−0.814	−0.869	−0.095	−0.534	−0.594
	(0.625)	(0.404)	(0.380)	(0.828)	(0.546)	(0.511)
GFC* financial depth	0.303	0.665	0.680	0.300	0.631	0.640
	(0.201)	(0.157)	(0.156)	(0.221)	(0.181)	(0.181)
GFC* trade openness	−4.887**	−1.029**	−1.017**	−4.776**	−9.606**	−9.282**
	(0.034)	(0.020)	(0.023)	(0.041)	(0.024)	(0.037)
GFC* GDP per capita	0.006**	0.006**	0.006**	0.005	0.004	0.004
	(0.037)	(0.034)	(0.035)	(0.116)	(0.188)	(0.157)
GFC* domestic credit	−1.314***	−1.748***	−1.726***	−1.391***	−1.925***	−1.861***
	(0.001)	(0.005)	(0.006)	(0.001)	(0.005)	(0.007)
Wald Chi-Square	151.49	342.27	334.34	152.99	368.53	376.77
	(0.000)	(0.000)	(0.000)	(0.000)	(0.000)	(0.000)
Observations	174	174	174	168	168	168
Arellano-Bond test	−0.978	−1.036	−1.041	−0.965	−1.037	−1.039
AR(2) *p*-value	(0.327)	(0.300)	(0.297)	(0.334)	(0.299)	(0.298)

Note: in columns (1) and (4), asset measure (ratio of sum of external assets to GDP) is dependent variable. In columns (2) and (5), volume measure (ratio of sum of external assets and external liabilities to GDP) is dependent variable. In columns (3) and (6), investment measure (ratio of sum of FDI, portfolio assets and liabilities to GDP) is dependent variable. Columns (1)–(3) indicate results for Arellano-Bover/Blundell-Bond estimation. Columns (4)–(6) indicate results for Arellano-Bond estimation. Lags(1) and AR(2) tests. Arellano-Bond test for no autocorrelation. Lag value of the dependent variable is not reported. Constant is not reported. *P*-values in brackets. Financial Depth is ratio of M2 to GDP. Trade Openness is ratio of sum of imports and export to GDP. GDP per capita in US$. Domestic Credit is ratio of Domestic Credit provided by banking sector to GDP. GFC is dummy = 1 for global financial crisis period otherwise 0. GFC* Financial Depth is an interaction between GFC and Financial Depth. GFC* Trade Openness is an interaction between GFC and Trade Openness. GFC* GDP per capita is an interaction between GFC and GDP per capita. GFC* Domestic Credit is an interaction between GFC and Domestic Credit.
*Significance at 10%.
**Significance at 5%.
***Significance at 1%.

assets, and liabilities to GDP). We introduce a Dummy variable, which takes the value of 1 over the period of global financial crisis (2008–2010), otherwise 0. We construct several interaction variables to capture the effect of change in financial integration measures due to (Financial Depth, Trade Openness, GDP per capita, Domestic Credit) depending on global financial crisis. The interaction variable between Dummy and Trade Openness (Dummy*Trade Openness) determines change in financial integration measures due to Trade Openness depending on global financial crisis. We expect the interaction variable to be negative due to decline in Trade Openness during global financial crisis, resulting in lower values of integration measures. We find the interaction variable (Dummy*Trade Openness) to be negative and significant.[5]

The coefficient of interaction variable between Dummy and Domestic Credit (Dummy* Domestic Credit) determines the change in financial integration measures that happens in GCC countries due to Domestic Credit depending on global financial crisis. We expect the interaction variable to be negative, resulting in lower values of integration measures. We find the interaction variable (Dummy*Domestic Credit) to be negative and significant.

The interaction variable between Dummy and Financial Depth (Dummy*Financial Depth) and Dummy and GDP per capita (Dummy*GDP per capita) determines the change in financial integration measures that happens in GCC countries during global financial crisis. The interaction variable Dummy*Financial Depth is insignificant in all regressions. The interaction variable Dummy *GDP per capita is insignificant in Arellano-Bond regression results (columns (4)–(6)).

Overall findings in Tables 3–6 indicate that Financial Depth, Trade Openness, and Domestic Credit have positive and significant impact on measures of financial integration. The change in financial integration measures due to Trade Openness and Domestic Credit depending on global financial crisis is negative and significant.

5. CONCLUSIONS AND POLICY IMPLICATIONS

The chapter sheds light on determinants of the degree of GCC's international financial integration. We investigate the degree of international financial integration of the GCC member countries with the rest of the world by constructing several quantity-based measures of financial integration. We use various indicators based on related literature including indicators of Financial Depth, Trade Openness, economic development, and banking sector development. We employ linear dynamic GMM panel estimation techniques (Arellano-Bond and Arellano-Bover/Blundell-Bond) to study the impact of various indicators on measures of financial integration.

The results provide strong evidence that Trade Openness is an important determinant of international financial integration in GCC countries. The positive and significant Trade Openness implies that those factors that stimulate trade in goods and services also

[5] During the period of global financial crisis (2008–2009) exports in goods and services fell in GCC countries. For Bahrain, from 2008 to 2009 Trade Openness (as % of GDP) fell from 171.16 to 166.72; Kuwait (92.08–90.932), Oman (97.24–92.56), Qatar (81.92–77.97), Saudi Arabia (104.88–96.50), and UAE (158.13–155.45). Trade Openness (as % of GDP) data are from World Bank World Development Indicators.

stimulate trade in assets. Trade in goods and services and trade in assets are complementary activities.

The results also provide strong evidence that indicators such as financial openness and Domestic Credit have positive and significant impact on GCC countries' international financial integration. During the process of integration, the size of national financial markets should increase (relative to domestic GDP) starting with those countries with less developed financial markets. Financial integration is likely to increase the efficiency of the financial intermediaries and markets of less financially developed countries by stimulating the demand for funds and for financial services. There will be increased competition with more sophisticated and cheaper financial intermediaries, associated with financial integration. The competition from these intermediaries may reduce the cost of financial services to the firms and households of countries with less developed financial systems, and thus expand the quantity of the local financial markets.

We construct global financial crisis Dummy that takes value 1 during financial crisis period (2008–2010) otherwise 0. We also construct several interaction variables to capture the change in financial integration measures due to Financial Depth, Trade Openness, GDP per capita, and Domestic Credit depending on global financial crisis. We find a negative change in financial integration measures due to Trade Openness and Domestic Credit depending on global financial crisis.

This study has strong policy implication for GCC countries. In 2002, GCC decided on implementing gradually a unified economic agreement toward establishing a single market, and forming monetary union at a certain stage. Understanding of the drivers of international financial integration will provide important insight into the process of monetary and financial integration. In imperfectly integrated markets, regional factors are important in shaping policy decisions and structures of financial markets differ across countries.

The future path for international financial integration in GCC depends on the deepening of domestic financial systems, overall economic development, as well as the pace of trade integration. GCC's financial integration may require improvements in national regulation, i.e., accounting standards, securities law, bank supervision, and corporate governance to bring it in line with the best practice regulation in the integrating area. On public sector front, there is a need for better corporate governance of state-owned/affiliated enterprises, with greater attention given to managing quasi-sovereign balance-sheet risks, transparency, and excessive leverage. A more sophisticated domestic financial sector will give rise to greater private sector capability in the acquisition of foreign assets and sustainable issuance of foreign liabilities.

The development of local debt markets could reduce reliance on banks in financing projects and help lower funding costs. Developing the corporate bond market would help banks reduce their asset/liability maturity mismatches. Harmonization of regulation and supervision within the GCC will also be essential to avoid regulatory arbitrage in both offshore and onshore banking activities. GCC countries may have to attain significant progress in terms of regulation of financial markets and development of robust risk management tools (IMF, 2010).

REFERENCES

Adam, K., Jappelli, T., Menichini, A., Padula, M., Pagano, M., 2002. Analyse, compare, and apply alternative indicators and monitoring methodologies to measure the evolution of capital market integration in the European union. Report to the European commission.

Agenor, P.-R., 2003. Benefits and costs of international financial integration: theory and facts. World Economy 26 (8), 1089–1118

Ahn, S.C., Schmidt, P., 1995. Efficient estimation of models for dynamic panel data. Journal of Econometrics 68, 5–27

Anderson, T.W., Hsiao, C., 1982. Formulation and estimation of dynamic models using panel data. Journal of Econometrics 18, 47–82

Arellano, M., 1989. A note on the Anderson-Hsiao estimator for panel data. Economics Letters 31, 337–341

Arellano, M., Bond, S., 1991. Some tests of specification for panel data: Monte Carlo evidence and an application to employment equations. Review of Economic Studies 58, 277–297

Arellano, M., Bover, O., 1995. Another look at the instrumental variable estimation of error-components models. Journal of Econometrics 68, 29–51

Baele, L., Fernando, A., Hordahl, P., Krylova, E., Monnet, C., 2004. Measuring European financial integration. Oxford Review of Economic Policy 20, 509–530

Baltzer, M., Cappiello, L., De Santis, R., Manganelli, S., 2008. Measuring financial integration in new EU Member States. ECB Occasional Paper No. 81.

Bekaert, G., Harvey, C., 2000. Foreign speculators and emerging equity markets. Journal of Finance 55, 565–614

Blundell, R., Bond, S., 1998. Initial conditions and moment restrictions in dynamic panel-data models. Journal of Econometrics 87, 115–143

Borensztein, E., Loungani, P., 2011. Asian financial integration: trends and interruptions. IMF Working Papers 11/04, International Monetary Fund.

Brach, J., Loewe, M., 2010. The global financial crisis and the Arab world: impact, reactions and consequences. Mediterranean Politics 15 (1), 45–71

Cavoli, T., McIver, R., Nowland, J., 2011. Cross listings and financial integration in Asia. ASEAN Economic Bulletin 28 (2), 241–256

Espinoza, R., Prasad, A., Williams, O., 2010. Regional financial integration in the GCC. IMF Working Papers 10/90, International Monetary Fund.

Faria, A., Mauro, P., 2009. Institutions and the external capital structure of countries. Journal of International Money and Finance 28, 367–391

Garcia-Herrero, A., Woolridge, P., 2007. Global and regional financial integration: progress in emerging markets. BIS Quarterly Review, September.

Goldsmith, R.W., 1985. Comparative National Balance Sheets: A Study of Twenty Countries, 1688–1978. University of Chicago Press, Chicago

Guerin, S., 2006. The role of geography in financial and economic integration: a comparative analysis of foreign direct investment, trade and portfolio investment flows. The World Economy 29 (2), 189–209

Grossman, G., Helpman, E., 1991. Innovation and Growth in the Global Economy. MIT Press, Cambridge, M.A

IMF, 2009. Global economic outlook April 2009: crisis and recovery. International Monetary Fund.

IMF, 2010. Impact of the global financial crisis on the Gulf Cooperation Council countries and challenges ahead. International Monetary Fund.

Kiviet, J.F., 1995. On bias, inconsistency and efficiency of various estimators in dynamic panel data models. Journal of Econometrics 68, 53–78

King, R.G., Levine, R., 1993. Finance and growth: Schumpeter might be right. Quarterly Journal of Economics 108, 717–738

Kucerová, Z., 2009. Measuring financial integration in central Europe through international investment positions. Eastern European Economics 47 (4), 25–41
Lane, P.R., 2000. International investment positions: a cross-sectional analysis. Journal of International Money and Finance 19, 513–534
Lane, R., Milesi-Ferretti, G., 2001. The External Wealth of Nations: measures of foreign assets and liabilities for industrial and developing countries. Journal of International Economics 55, 263–294
Lane, R., Milesi-Ferretti, G., 2003. International financial integration. International Monetary Fund Staff Papers 50 (S), 82–113
Lane, R., Milesi-Ferretti, G., 2007. The External Wealth of Nations mark II: revised and extended estimates of foreign assets and liabilities. Journal of International Economics 73, 223–250
Lane, R., Milesi-Ferretti, G., 2008a. The drivers of financial globalization. American Economic Review: Papers & Proceedings 98 (2), 327–332
Lane, R., Milesi-Ferretti, G., 2008b. International investment patterns. The Review of Economics and Statistics 90 (3), 538–549
Levine, R., Loayza, N., Beck, T., 2000. Financial intermediation and growth: causality and causes. Journal of Monetary Economics 46, 31–77
Lidstone, D., 2009. Sector regaining its confidence after the shock of crisis. Financial Times, 10 November.
Martin, P., Rey, H., 2000. Financial integration and asset returns. European Economic Review 44, 1327–1350
Martin, P., Rey, H., 2004. Financial supermarkets: size matters for asset trade. Journal of International Economics 64, 335–361
Mishra, A., Daly, K., 2006. Multi-country empirical investigation into international financial integration. Journal of Asia Pacific Economy 11 (4), 444–461
Mishra, A.V., 2007. International investment patterns: evidence using a new dataset. Research in International Business and Finance 21 (2), 342–360
Mulligan, C., Salai-i-Martin, X., 1996. The adoption costs of financial technologies: implications for monetary policy. NBER Working Paper No. 5504.
Nickell, S., 1981. Biases in dynamic models with fixed effects. Econometrica 49, 1417–1426
Obstfeld, M., Taylor, A.M., 2002. Globalization and capital markets. NBER Working Paper No. 8846.
Siddiqi, M., 2009. Surviving the international crisis. The Middle East 1, 45–48
Smith, P., 2009. Kuwait tackles its economic issues. The Middle East 3, 40–41
Wigglesworth, R., 2009a. Buffeting for banks from credit crisis. Financial Times, 20 July.
Wigglesworth, R., 2009b. Conservatism and an aversion to lending sprees. Financial Times, 23 September.

CHAPTER 32

Asset Return and Volatility Spillovers Between Big Commodity Producing Countries

Perry Sadorsky
Schulich School of Business, York University, Toronto, Ontario, Canada

1. INTRODUCTION

Citigroup analysts have defined a new group of countries: Canada, Australia, Russia, Brazil, and South Africa and labeled these countries with the acronym CARBS.[1] The CARBS are countries that have large commodity assets and high stock market liquidity. Two of the CARBS are developed economies (Australia and Canada) while the other three (Brazil, Russia, and South Africa) are emerging economies. Because of their dependence on natural resources, the economies of the CARBS tend to exhibit similar patterns over the course of the commodity cycle. The CARBS account for 29% of the world's landmass and 6% of the world's population. These countries produce between one quarter and one half of most of the world's key commodities. Because of their prominence in natural resource production, the CARBS are expected to play an important role in global economic development.

The importance of commodity exports from the CARBS economies is evident, as commodities as a percentage of exports range from a low of 47% (Brazil) to a high of 92% (Russia) (Table 1). Commodities as a percentage of GDP range from a low of 8% (Australia) to a high of 23% (Russia). Given the importance of commodities to the CARBS economies, it is not too surprising that the commodity sector accounts for a large part of stock market capitalization. The commodity sector as a percentage of stock market capitalization ranges from a low of 35% (South Africa) to a high of 74% (Russia).

This chapter makes several important contributions to the literature. First, while there is an extensive literature investigating volatility spillovers between various stock markets (e.g., Bhar and Nikolova, 2009; Cha and Jithendranathan, 2009; Edwards and Susmel, 2001; Engle, 2002, 2009; Engle et al., 1990; Forbes and Rigobon, 2002; Hakin and McAleer, 2010; King et al. 1994), there is little known about return and volatility spillovers between the CARBS, commodity prices, and the important developed stock markets of Japan, the

[1] http://www.businessinsider.com/meet-the-carbs-canada-australia-russia-brazil-south-africa-2011-11?op=1.

Emerging Markets and the Global Economy
http://dx.doi.org/10.1016/B978-0-12-411549-1.00032-6

Table 1 The importance of commodities to the CARBS economies.

	Commodities as a % of exports	Commodities as a % of GDP	Commodity sector as a % of local MSCI index
Canada	74	17	50
Australia	60	8	37
Russia	92	23	74
Brazil	47	15	45
South Africa	64	10	35

United Kingdom (UK), and the United States (US). A good analysis of asset return and volatility spillovers between these markets is needed for an understanding of the co-movements between these markets. These results have implications for derivative pricing, portfolio optimization, risk management, and hedging.

Second the empirical approach in this chapter uses the recently developed techniques of Diebold and Yilmaz (2009, 2012) to estimate asset return and volatility spillovers between the CARBS stock markets and stock markets in the US, UK, and Japan. This new approach, which uses variance decompositions from vector autoregressions (VARs), provides a simple and intuitive way to calculate spillover tables and spillover plots. Diebold and Yilmaz (2009) use their new approach to study volatility spillovers between 19 global equity markets using weekly data from January 1992 to November 2007. They find that while return spillovers display a gently increasing trend but no bursts, volatility spillovers display no trend but clear evidence of bursts. The basic framework of Diebold and Yilmaz (2009) is useful but suffers from two limitations. First, the Diebold and Yilmaz (2009) approach relies on the Cholesky-factor identification of VARs and this means that the variance decompositions depend upon the ordering of the variables. Second, this approach only provides information on total spillovers from or to a market. In response, Diebold and Yilmaz (2012) improve upon their earlier paper by using a generalized vector autoregressive framework in which forecast-error variance decompositions are invariant to the variable ordering, and they explicitly include directional volatility spillovers. Diebold and Yilmaz (2012) apply their new approach to daily data (January 1999–January 2010) on US stocks, bonds, foreign exchange, and commodity markets. They find that cross-market volatility spillovers were limited until 2007. The volatility spillovers increased as the global financial crisis intensified.

Third, while most studies on return and volatility spillovers focus on stock indices, this chapter uses data on exchange traded funds (ETFs). The main advantage of using ETF data is that unlike country-or industry-specific stock indices, which are not investable, ETFs are investable and, therefore, more closely represent the actual investment decisions of individuals and institutions. The disadvantage of using ETF data is that many ETFs have a relatively short trading history.

The purpose of this chapter is to investigate asset return and volatility spillovers between an important group of commodity producing countries (Canada, Australia, Brazil, and South Africa), commodity prices, and the developed stock markets of Japan, the United Kingdom, and the United States. The empirical approach uses recently developed VAR techniques to calculate spillover tables and spillover plots. These results should be useful to investors, policy makers and others interested in how the stock markets, of this new grouping of countries interact with each other and with other important developed stock markets.

This chapter is organized as follows. Section 2 sets out a selected literature review, while Sections 3 and 4 present the econometric model and the data. Sections 5 and 6 report the results for return spillovers and volatility spillovers. The last section of the chapter presents the conclusions.

2. SELECTED LITERATURE REVIEW

Research into volatility spillovers was first conducted in the context of developed stock markets and this research really started to take off after the introduction of GARCH modeling. Today, the literature on volatility modeling and spillovers is huge and this section is only meant to provide a selected literature review. Hamao et al. (1990), King and Wadhani (1990), and Schwert (1990) are well-known papers that investigate stock market dynamics pre and post the 1987 stock market crash. Susmel and Engle (1994), Koutomos and Booth (1995), Bae and Karolyi (1994), Lin et al. (1994) find evidence of asymmetry in volatility spillovers between major developed stock markets. Thedossiou and Lee (1993) find evidence of volatility spillovers between the stock markets in the US, Japan, the UK, Canada, and Germany.

Karolyi (1995) finds that volatility shocks are transmitted from the US to Canadian stock markets. Joeng (2009) finds evidence of bi-directional causality in intra-day returns between the US, Canada, and the UK during concurrent trading hours. In their analysis of ETFs, Krause and Tse (2013) find that price discovery flows from the US to Canada but volatility spillovers are bi-directional.

Brooks and Henry (2000) use weekly data covering the period January 1980–June 1998 to analyze stock market volatility between Australia, Japan, and the US. They find that volatility transmits from the US market to the Australian market. McNelis (1993) and Valadkhani et al. (2008) find evidence of volatility interplay between the Australian stock market and the stock markets of the UK, US, and Singapore.

In a series of papers, Bakaert and Harvey (1995, 1997, 2003, 2005) investigate the impact of stock market integration on emerging stock markets, volatility, and cross-market correlations. In general, they find that emerging stock markets are becoming more integrated with the developed stock markets. Beirne et al. (2010) use trivariate VAR GARCH models to investigate volatility spillovers between 41 emerging stock markets, regional stock markets, and global stock markets. They find strong evidence of volatility spillovers between regional and global stock markets.

Bhar and Nikolova (2009) study return and volatility spillovers between BRIC countries and their respective regions of the world. India has the highest level of regional and global integration of the BRIC countries followed by Brazil, Russia, and China. Lucey and Voronkova (2008) fail to find a long-run relationship between the Russian stock market and other developed stock markets.

Mandaci and Torun (2007) use cointegration and Granger causality to test for stock market integration between Turkey, Russia, Brazil, Korea, South Africa, and Poland over the period January 1996 to August 2006. They find that South Africa is pairwise cointegrated with Russia. Granger causality tests reveal that South Africa causes Brazil and Poland causes South Africa. Alagidede and Panagiotidis (2009) study the stock returns of Egypt, Kenya, Morocco, Nigeria, South Africa, Tunisia, and Zimbabwe. They find that the random walk hypothesis is rejected for all countries. Goldberg and Veitch (2010) estimate a time-varying beta model of country risk for South Africa over the period 1993 to 2008. Using a global CAPM, evidence is presented showing that South Africa's beta is low and dependent upon the exchange rate and gold prices during the pre-integration period (prior to 1998). After integration, the beta is higher and economic fundamentals play a much smaller role indicating that South Africa's stock market is more integrated into the global financial markets. Korkmaz et al. (2012) study return and volatility spillovers between Colombia, Indonesia, Vietnam, Egypt, Turkey, and South Africa (CIVETS) using causality in mean and causality in variance tests. In general, the contemporaneous spillover effect is small. Only 10 out of 30 causality in mean tests reveal statistically significant results. For the causality in variance tests the only statistically significant evidence of pairwise causality is between Vietnam and South Africa.

Investigating volatility spillovers between oil prices and equity prices is currently an active area of research. Malik and Hammoudeh (2007) find evidence of spillovers from oil prices to the Gulf equity markets of Bahrain, Kuwait, and Saudi Arabia. Arouri et al. (2011a) find evidence of a spillover effect from oil to stock markets in Europe and a bidirectional spillover effect between oil and US stock market sectors. Arouri et al. (2011b) find evidence of spillover effects between oil prices and Gulf Cooperation Council (GCC) countries. Arouri et al. (2012) find evidence of volatility spillovers between oil prices and European stock prices measured using a broad index as well as industry-specific sectors. Sadorsky (2012) finds evidence of volatility spillovers between the stock prices of clean energy companies, technology companies, and oil prices.

3. THE ECONOMETRIC MODEL

The econometric model is based on forecast decompositions from a covariance stationary N-variable vector autoregression (VAR) of order p:

$$x_t = \sum_{i=1}^{p} \Phi_i x_{t-i} + \varepsilon_t, \tag{1}$$

where ε is a vector of independently and identically distributed errors. The vector x represents either a vector of asset returns or a vector of asset volatilities. The moving average representation of this VAR can be written as:

$$x_t = \sum_{i=0}^{\infty} A_i \varepsilon_{t-i}. \tag{2}$$

The $N \times N$ coefficient matrix A satisfies a recursive structure. The moving average coefficients are used to calculate variance decompositions and impulse responses. Variance decompositions are used in calculating the fraction of the H-step-ahead error variance in forecasting one variable that is due to shocks to a different variable. The Diebold and Yilmaz (2009, 2012) approach uses variance decompositions to calculate spillovers. The calculation of the variance decompositions requires orthogonal VAR innovations. Diebold and Yilmaz (2009) used Cholesky factorization to achieve orthogonality. The Cholesky factorization, however, may depend upon the ordering of the variables. Koop et al. (1996) and Pesaran and Shin (1998) developed a generalized VAR framework in which the variance decompositions are invariant to the ordering of the variables. Diebold and Yilmaz (2012) use this generalized approach and this is the approach used in this present chapter.

The H-step-ahead forecast-error variance decomposition for $H = 1, 2, \ldots$ is denoted by:

$$\xi_{ij}^{g}(H) = \frac{\sigma_{jj}^{-1} \sum_{h=0}^{H-1} (e_i' A_h \sum e_j)^2}{\sum_{h=0}^{H-1} (e_i' A_h \sum A_h' e_i)}. \tag{3}$$

Here, $\sum$ is the variance matrix for the error vector ε, σ_{jj} is the standard deviation of the error term for the jth equation, and e_i is a selection vector with one as the ith element and zeros elsewhere. The generalized impulse response allows for correlated shocks but since the shocks are not orthogonalized, the sum of contributions to the variance of the forecast error need not equal one. Consequently, each entry of the variance decomposition matrix is normalized by the row sum:

$$\xi_{ij}^{\prime g}(H) = \frac{\xi_{ij}^{g}(H)}{\sum_{j=1}^{N} \xi_{ij}^{g}(H)}. \tag{4}$$

The total spillover index can be constructed as:

$$S^g(H) = \frac{\sum_{i,j=1:i\neq j}^{N} \xi r_{ij}^g(H)}{\sum_{i,j=1}^{N} \xi_{ij}^{\prime g}(H)} \cdot 100 = \frac{\sum_{i,j=1:i\neq j}^{N} \xi r_{ij}^g(H)}{N} \cdot 100. \tag{5}$$

The directional spillovers received by asset i from other assets j are calculated as:

$$S_{i\leftarrow}^g(H) = \frac{\sum_{j=1:i\neq j}^{N} \xi r_{ij}^g(H)}{\sum_{i,j=1}^{N} \xi_{ij}^{\prime g}(H)} \cdot 100 = \frac{\sum_{j=1:i\neq j}^{N} \xi r_{ij}^g(H)}{N} \cdot 100. \tag{6}$$

The directional spillovers transmitted by asset i to other assets j are calculated as:

$$S_{i\rightarrow}^g(H) = \frac{\sum_{j=1:i\neq j}^{N} \xi r_{ji}^g(H)}{\sum_{i,j=1}^{N} \xi_{ji}^{\prime g}(H)} \cdot 100 = \frac{\sum_{j=1:i\neq j}^{N} \xi r_{ji}^g(H)}{N} \cdot 100. \tag{7}$$

The net spillover from asset i to all other markets j can be calculated as:

$$S_i^g(H) = S_{i\rightarrow}^g(H) - S_{i\leftarrow}^g(H). \tag{8}$$

The estimation of the VAR proceeds in two stages. In the first stage, the entire data set is used to calculate a VAR and the variance decompositions used to calculate a spillover table. In the second stage, the VAR is estimated using a rolling window and the variance decompositions are used to calculate time-varying spillovers.

4. DATA

The data set consists of a group of US dollar denominated exchange traded funds (ETFs) that trade on major US exchanges. One advantage of using ETFs is that ETFs are financial products that investors can actually buy and sell. Analysis based on ETFs is very useful because it more closely resembles the investing environment that individuals and institutions face. By comparison, country specific stock indices are not directly investable. ETFs offer a convenient way for investors to gain exposure to these country specific indices. The investment perspective is of a US investor or an international investor with a US dollar trading account. The data series and their respective ticker symbols for US listed ETFs are: Canada (EWC), Australia (EWA), Brazil (EWZ), South Africa (EZA), United States (SPY), Japan (EWJ), United Kingdom (EWU), and the Deutsch Bank Commodity index (DBC). The DBC is mostly focused on energy and metals, and consists of holdings in Brent crude oil, West Texas Intermediate crude oil, heating oil, gasoline, gold, copper, and zinc. The daily data set covers the period February 7, 2006–January 30, 2013 and is determined by the availability of the data. Since a US listed ETF for Russia did not begin trading until 2007, Russia is omitted from the analysis. All stock price data, available from Yahoo Finance, are in US dollars and are adjusted for splits and dividends.

Table 2 Summary statistics for daily % returns.

Series	Obs.	Mean	Std. error	Minimum	Maximum
CAN (EWC)	1757	0.0167	1.7856	−11.6526	11.6754
AUS (EWA)	1757	0.0343	2.2406	−13.1769	18.7876
BRA (EWZ)	1757	0.0295	2.7223	−21.8568	22.7630
ZAF (EZA)	1757	0.0200	2.6013	−22.4044	20.6252
USA (SPY)	1757	0.0180	1.4655	−10.3567	13.5607
JAP (EWJ)	1757	−0.0140	1.5701	−11.0617	14.6543
UK (EWU)	1757	0.0070	1.8571	−12.7745	15.7453
DBC (DBC)	1757	0.0129	1.4447	−6.9341	6.6631

Ticker symbols in parentheses.

Table 3 Correlations for daily % returns.

	CAN	AUS	BRA	ZAF	USA	JAP	UK	DBC
CAN	1	0.8117	0.8300	0.7933	0.8265	0.6933	0.8222	0.6575
AUS	0.8117	1	0.8105	0.7981	0.8523	0.7689	0.8487	0.5320
BRA	0.8300	0.8105	1	0.8415	0.8301	0.7208	0.8226	0.5570
ZAF	0.7933	0.7981	0.8415	1	0.8246	0.7191	0.8245	0.5158
USA	0.8265	0.8523	0.8301	0.8246	1	0.8031	0.8937	0.4693
JAP	0.6933	0.7689	0.7208	0.7191	0.8031	1	0.7840	0.4082
UK	0.8222	0.8487	0.8226	0.8245	0.8937	0.7840	1	0.5222
DBC	0.6575	0.5320	0.5570	0.5158	0.4693	0.4082	0.5222	1

Daily returns for asset *i* are calculated as $100^* \ln (p_{it}/p_{it-1})$ where p_{it} is the daily closing price of asset *i*. Summary statistics for the daily returns show that Australia had the highest average daily return while Japan had a negative average daily return (Table 2). Brazil had the highest standard error while commodities had the lowest standard error. Correlations between the daily returns for country ETFs are very high, generally in excess of 0.70 (Table 3). The correlation between counties and commodities is, for most countries, less than 0.50. Commodities correlate the highest with Canada and the lowest with Japan.

Daily variance is estimated using daily high ($p^{\max}$) and low values ($p^{\min}$) (Parkinson, 1980; Alizadeh et al. 2002):

$$\widetilde{\sigma}_{it}^2 = 0.361[\ln (p_{it}^{\max}) - \ln (p_{it}^{\min})]^2. \tag{9}$$

Annualized daily percent standard deviation is used as the measure of volatility.

$$\widehat{\sigma}_{it} = 100\sqrt{365.\widetilde{\sigma}_{it}^2}. \tag{10}$$

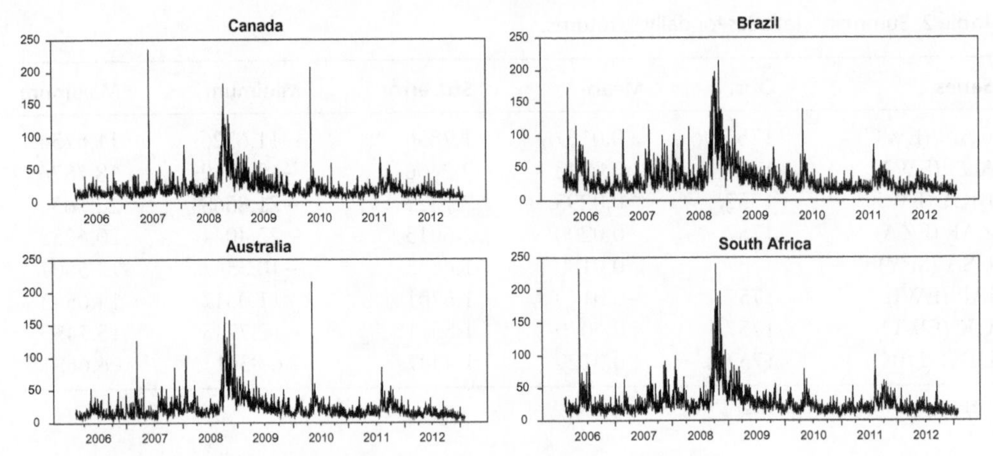

Figure 1a Daily volatilities (annualized standard deviations, percentages).

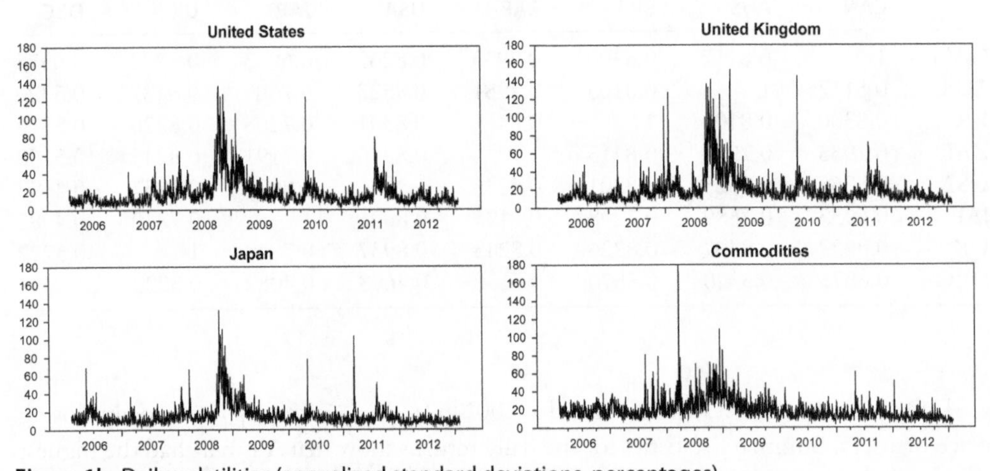

Figure 1b Daily volatilities (annualized standard deviations, percentages).

Plots of daily volatilities show that for each asset there is pronounced volatility clustering in 2008–2009 (Figures 1a and 1b). This time period coincides with the global economic slowdown known as "The Great Recession" (IMF, 2010). For the equity assets, volatility spikes are also observed in the summer of 2010 (American and European debt crises) and 2011 (American and European debt crises). The American and European debt crises events in 2010 and 2011 had little impact on commodity volatility. The highest commodity volatility was recorded in the first quarter of 2008.

Brazil has the highest average daily volatility while Japan has the lowest (Table 4). For each ETF, the minimum and maximum values indicate considerable variability. The correlations between volatilities (Table 5) show a similar pattern as the one found for

Table 4 Summary statistics for daily volatility (annualized standard deviations, %).

Series	Obs.	Mean	Std. error	Minimum	Maximum
CAN (EWC)	1757	22.8246	17.3501	5.1431	235.1164
AUS (EWA)	1757	21.8696	17.4445	3.6083	215.3425
BRA (EWZ)	1757	32.4023	23.7004	6.2533	214.4391
ZAF (EZA)	1757	27.0385	20.6008	5.5653	239.4943
USA (SPY)	1757	17.8407	15.0016	2.7320	136.9729
JAP (EWJ)	1757	15.0838	11.5875	3.5374	131.9421
UK (EWU)	1757	19.1942	15.9179	3.9446	152.4889
DBC (DBC)	1757	19.2771	11.6992	3.3564	179.0258

Ticker symbols in parentheses.

Table 5 Correlations for daily volatility (annualized standard deviations, %).

	CAN	AUS	BRA	ZAF	USA	JAP	UK	DBC
CAN	1	0.8336	0.7767	0.7473	0.8043	0.7716	0.7785	0.5417
AUS	0.8336	1	0.8021	0.8127	0.8629	0.8331	0.8384	0.5190
BRA	0.7767	0.8021	1	0.8229	0.7978	0.7817	0.7538	0.5351
ZAF	0.7473	0.8127	0.8229	1	0.8216	0.8057	0.7914	0.5047
USA	0.8043	0.8629	0.7978	0.8216	1	0.8542	0.8614	0.5057
JAP	0.7716	0.8331	0.7817	0.8057	0.8542	1	0.8182	0.5116
UK	0.7785	0.8384	0.7538	0.7914	0.8614	0.8182	1	0.5012
DBC	0.5417	0.5190	0.5351	0.5047	0.5057	0.5116	0.5012	1

returns. Countries correlate more highly with each other than they do with commodities. Canada has the highest correlation with commodities while the UK has the lowest.

5. EMPIRICAL RESULTS FOR RETURNS SPILLOVERS

Table 6 reports a table of returns spillovers over the entire sample.[2] This table shows how the spillover index can be decomposed into all of the forecast error variance for shocks to variable *i* and from variable *i*. The lower right-hand corner shows a spillover index of 79.1%. This value indicates that 79.1% of forecast error variance comes from return spillovers indicating that for this particular group of ETFs measured over this particular time period, return spillovers are an important source of forecast error variance. One practical implication of these results is that there is little opportunity for diversification.

[2] The order of the VAR was set at 2 as determined by the AIC. The forecast horizon was set at 10. For the rolling window analysis, a 200 day rolling window was used. Consistent with the findings of Diebold and Yilmaz (2009, 2012) the results reported in this paper are robust to small changes in window length and forecast horizon.

Table 6 Returns spillover table.

	CAN	AUS	BRA	ZAF	USA	JAP	UK	DBC	From others
CAN	18.5	12.7	13.1	12.4	13	9.4	13	8	82
AUS	12.8	18.8	12.4	12	13.8	11.1	13.7	5.4	81
BRA	13.3	12.6	18.9	13.4	13.1	9.9	12.8	5.8	81
ZAF	12.9	12.5	13.8	19	13.3	9.9	13.2	5.4	81
USA	12.8	13.4	12.6	12.3	18.3	11.9	14.6	4.2	82
JAP	11.1	12.8	11.4	11	14.3	21.9	13.6	3.8	78
UK	12.7	13.3	12.3	12.2	14.6	11.4	18.2	5.1	82
DBC	14.4	9.7	10.3	9.4	7.6	5.9	9.4	33.2	67
Contribution to others	90	87	86	83	90	69	90	38	633
Contribution including own	109	106	105	102	108	91	109	71	79.10%

The *ij*th entry in Table 6 is the estimated contribution to the forecast error variance of asset i coming from innovations to asset j. The off-diagonal column sums (labeled as Contributions to Others) or row sums (labeled as Contributions from Others) when summed across assets give the numerator of the spillover index. The column sums or row sums (including diagonals) when totaled across assets give the denominator of the spillover index.

The spillover table provides what Diebold and Yilmaz (2009) call an input-output decomposition of the spillover index. For example, innovations to Canadian returns are responsible for 14.4% of the error variance in forecasting 10-day-ahead commodity returns but only 11.1% of the error variance in forecasting 10-day-ahead Japanese returns. Return spillovers from Canada to commodities are larger than return spillovers from Canada to Japan. Total return spillovers from Canada to others (Canada Contributions to Others) are slightly larger than total return spillovers from others to Canada (Contributions from Others). Innovations to Canadian and Brazilian returns have the most impact on the error variance in forecasting 10-day-ahead commodity returns. Notice that for most of the assets, the contributions to others are similar in magnitude to contributions from others. Commodities are the exception where the contribution from others (67%) is much larger than the contribution to others (38%).

Table 6 provides a useful summary of the average spillover index for returns calculated using the entire data set. Spillovers between assets can, however, change across time. For this reason it is desirable to use a rolling window analysis to calculate spillovers to and from different assets. Figure 2 shows how the spillover index for returns has changed across time. Prior to the fall of 2008, the spillover index for returns ranged between 68% and 74%. The spillover index for returns spiked in September of 2008 around the time of the Lehman Brothers crisis. Throughout the first half of 2008, the US banking industry was dealing with the fallout from the subprime mortgage market collapse. The

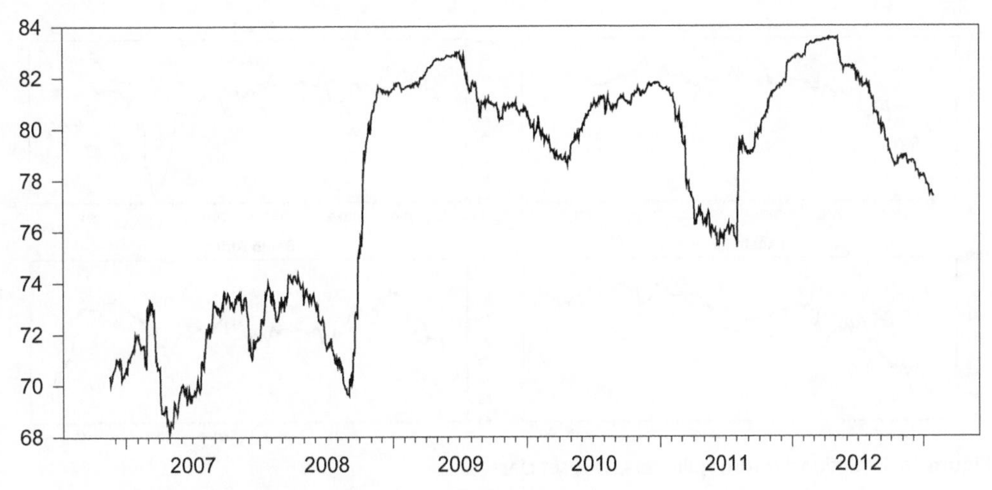

Figure 2 Spillover plot. Returns. 200 day window. Ten-step horizon.

takeover of Bear Sterns in March of 2008 by JP Morgan showed just how vulnerable large heavily leveraged US financial institutions were. The bankruptcy of Lehman Brothers in September of 2008 signaled that a financial crisis that had been mostly confined to the US had now gone global.[3] The spillover index for returns rose quickly to 83%. The spillover index did drop somewhat in 2011 before returning to very high levels in the middle of 2012 (around the time of heightened concerns regarding the debt crises in Europe and America). As of early 2013, the spillover index remains well above its pre-2008 values.

The rows and columns of Table 6 can be estimated dynamically using rolling window analysis to construct directional spillover plots. These directional spillover plots show how contributions to and from each asset changed across time. Directional return spillovers, to asset classes, are shown in Figures 3a and 3b. Canadian, Australian, and commodity returns have shown an increase in their respective contributions to forecast error variance. Brazilian and South African returns have shown a decrease in their respective contributions to forecast error variance. The contributions of the United States and the United Kingdom have remained fairly constant over the estimation period. Directional return spillovers, from asset classes, are shown in Figures 4a and 4b. Canada, Australia, Brazil, and South Africa show similar patterns in how other asset classes affect their returns.

The directional returns spillover plots can be used to create a net directional spillover plot. The net directional spillover plot is calculated as the contribution of asset *i* to all other assets minus the contribution from other assets to asset *i*. Canada, the US, and the UK have mostly positive net directional spillovers (they contribute more to other assets

[3] For a good overview of the subprime mortgage meltdown, see http://www.pbs.org/wgbh/pages/frontline/meltdown/view/.

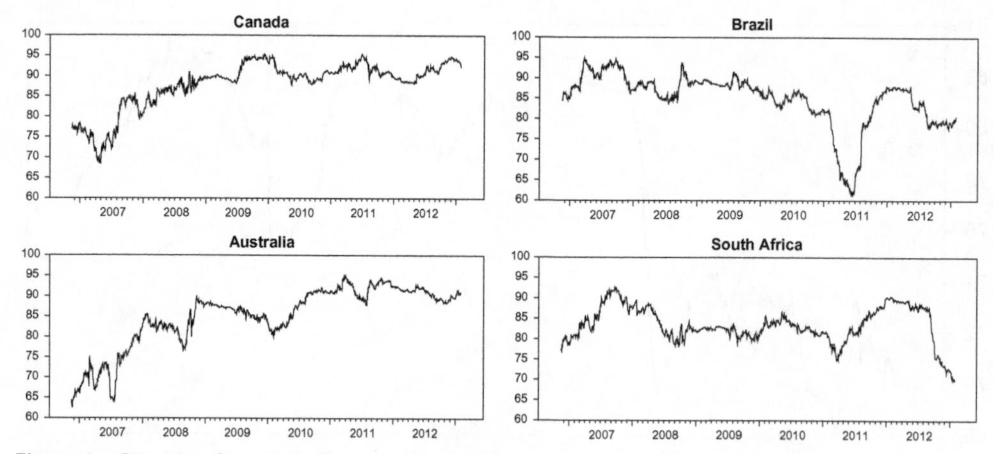

Figure 3a Directional return spillovers, to asset classes.

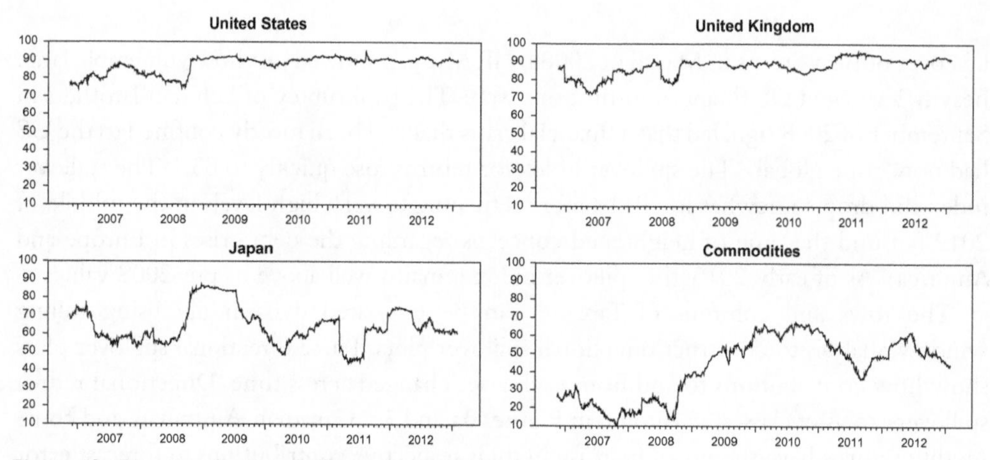

Figure 3b Directional return spillovers, to asset classes.

than other assets contribute to them) (Figures 5a and 5b). Commodities and Japan receive more contributions from other assets than they contribute to others.

6. EMPIRICAL RESULTS FOR VOLATILITY SPILLOVERS

Table 7 reports a table of volatility spillovers over the entire sample.[4] The lower right-hand corner shows a spillover index of 70.5%. This value indicates that 70.5% of forecast error variance comes from volatility spillovers indicating that for this particular group of ETFs,

[4] The order of the VAR was set at 6 as determined by the AIC. The forecast horizon was set at 10. For the rolling window analysis, a 200 day rolling window was used. Consistent with the findings of Diebold and Yilmaz (2009, 2012) the results reported in this paper are robust to small changes in window length and forecast horizon.

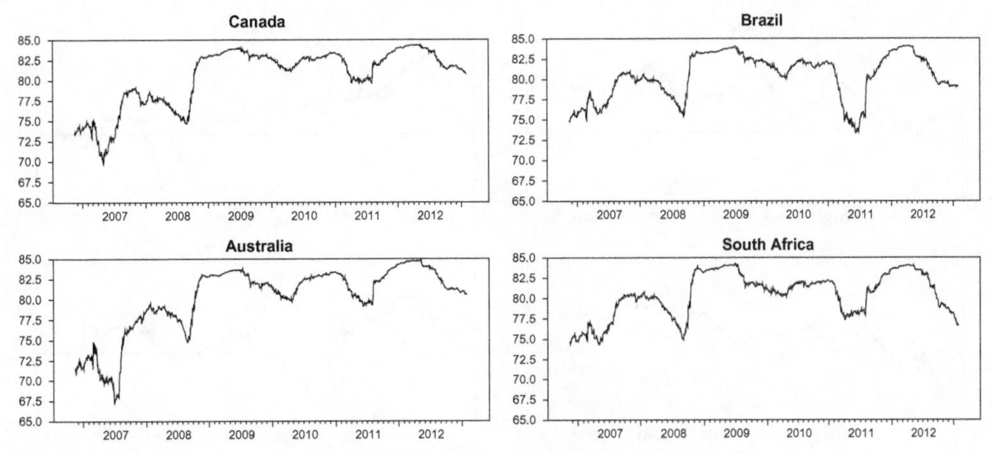

Figure 4a Directional return spillovers, from asset classes.

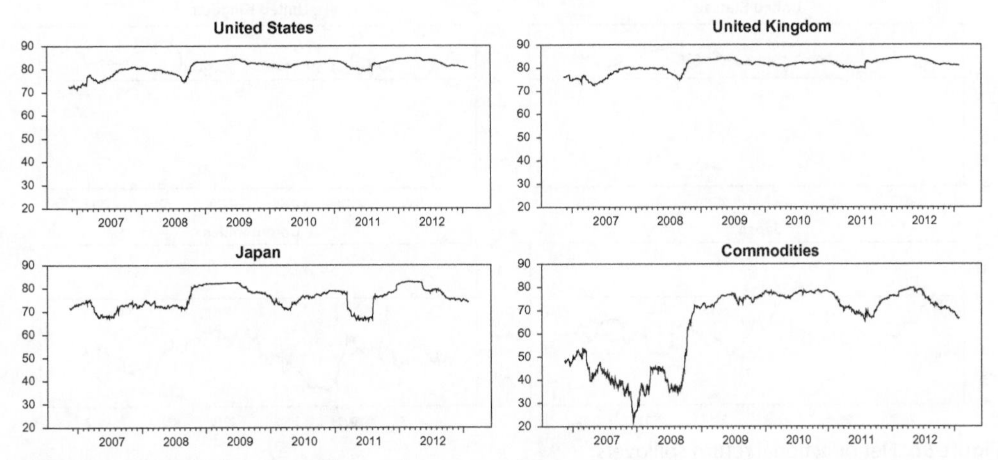

Figure 4b Directional return spillovers, from asset classes.

there are considerable volatility spillovers. Innovations to Brazilian returns are responsible for 15.1% of the error variance in forecasting 10-day-ahead South Africa volatility but only 9% of the error variance in forecasting 10-day-ahead commodity volatility. Notice that for commodities, each country contributes more to commodity volatility than commodity volatility contributes to each asset respectively.

The spillover volatility plot (Figure 6) shows how volatility spillovers increased during March (Bear Sterns takeover by JP Morgan) and September (Lehman Brothers Bankruptcy) of 2008. Volatility spillovers did drop somewhat in 2011 before rising again in 2012 as debt concerns in America and Europe affected financial markets. Since the summer of 2008, volatility spillovers have remained above pre-2008 levels.

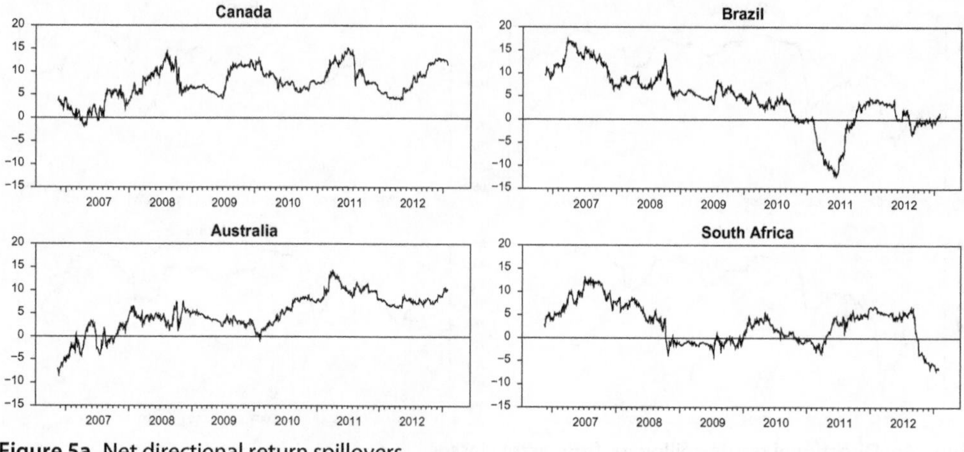

Figure 5a Net directional return spillovers.

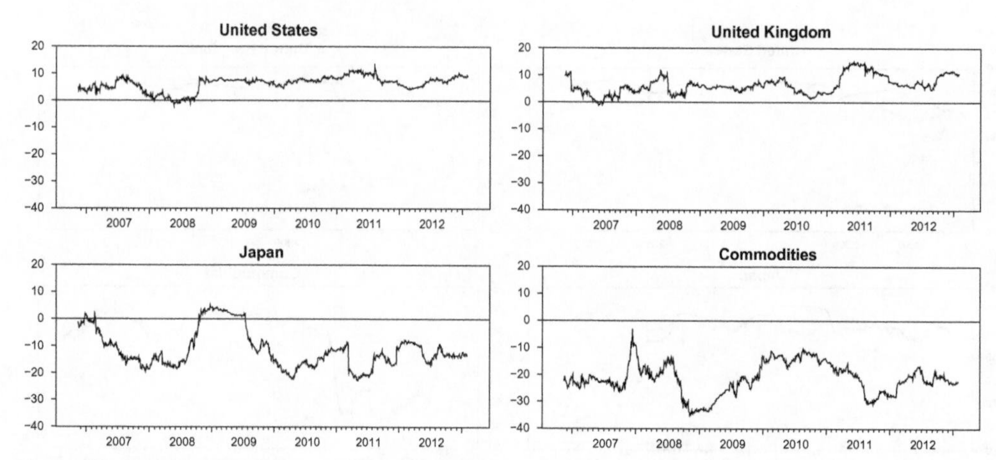

Figure 5b Net directional return spillovers.

Directional volatility spillovers, to asset classes, are shown in Figure 7a and 7b. Canadian and Australian volatility have shown an increase in their respective contributions to forecast error variance. The contributions of the other assets have remained fairly constant over the estimation period. Directional volatility spillovers, from asset classes, are shown in Figures 8a and 8b. Canada and Australia have shown the largest increase in how other asset classes affect their volatility.

The net directional spillover plot is calculated as the contribution of asset i to all other assets minus the contribution from other assets to asset i. Prior to 2008, Canada and Australia had negative net directional volatility spillovers but since 2008 they have mostly positive net directional spillovers (they contribute more to other assets than other assets

Table 7 Volatility spillover table.

	CAN	AUS	BRA	ZAF	USA	JAP	UK	DBC	From others
CAN	25	14.3	13.2	9.7	14.3	10.3	10.2	2.9	75
AUS	11.5	22.9	13	11.1	15.6	11.6	11.7	2.6	77
BRA	9.8	11.8	30.2	14.1	13.2	9.7	8.6	2.6	70
ZAF	8.4	12.5	15.1	26.2	14.4	10.8	10.3	2.2	74
USA	9.7	14.3	12.6	11.2	24.6	12.9	13.2	1.5	75
JAP	9	13	12.4	11.9	15.9	24.3	11.4	2.2	76
UK	9.6	13.5	11.2	10.7	16.3	12.3	24.3	2.1	76
DBC	6.6	4.5	9	5.7	6.6	4.9	4.4	58.4	42
Contribution to others	64	84	86	75	96	73	70	16	564
Contribution including own	90	107	117	101	121	97	94	75	70.50%

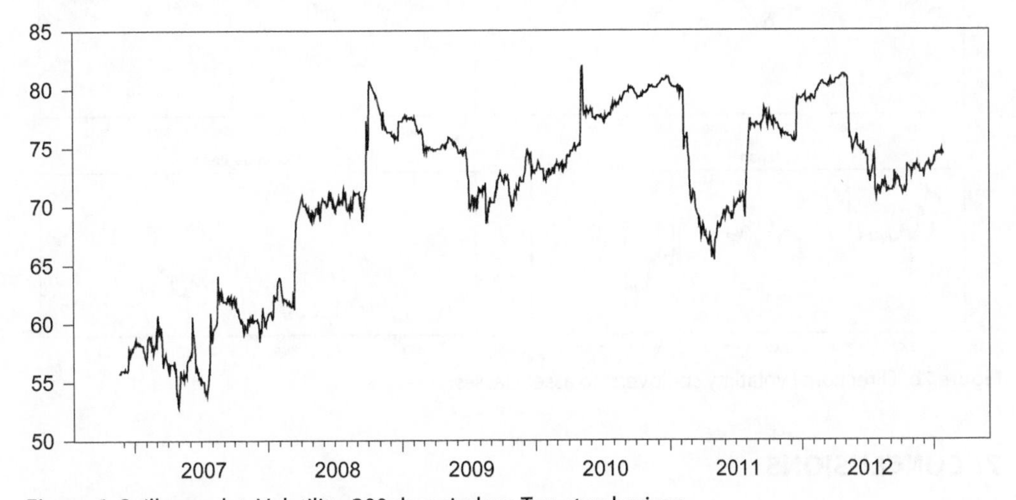

Figure 6 Spillover plot. Volatility. 200 day window. Ten-step horizon.

contribute to them) (Figure 9a). Commodities receive more contributions from other assets than they contribute to others (Figure 9b). Asset price volatility is often used to measure information flow (e.g., Bae and Karolyi, 1994; Clark, 1973; Ross, 1989). Volatility spillovers provide useful information on information transmission between assets. In the context of Figures 9a and 9b, information flows from equities to commodities.

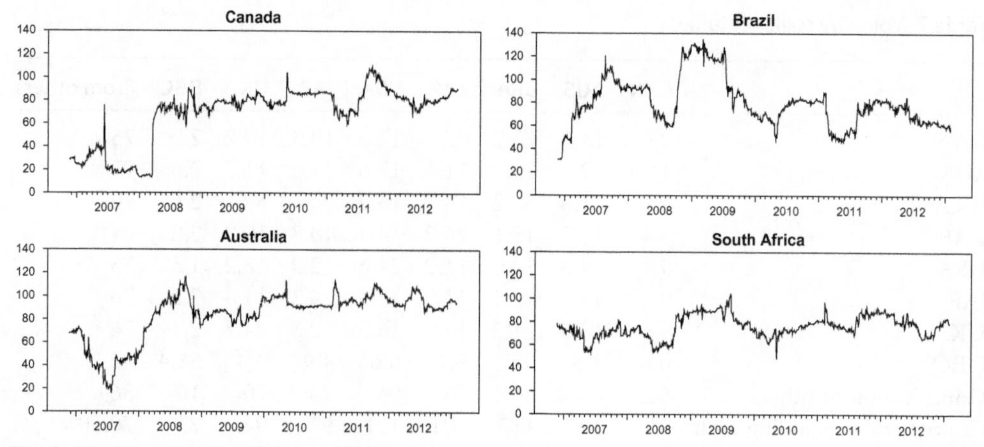

Figure 7a Directional volatility spillovers, to asset classes.

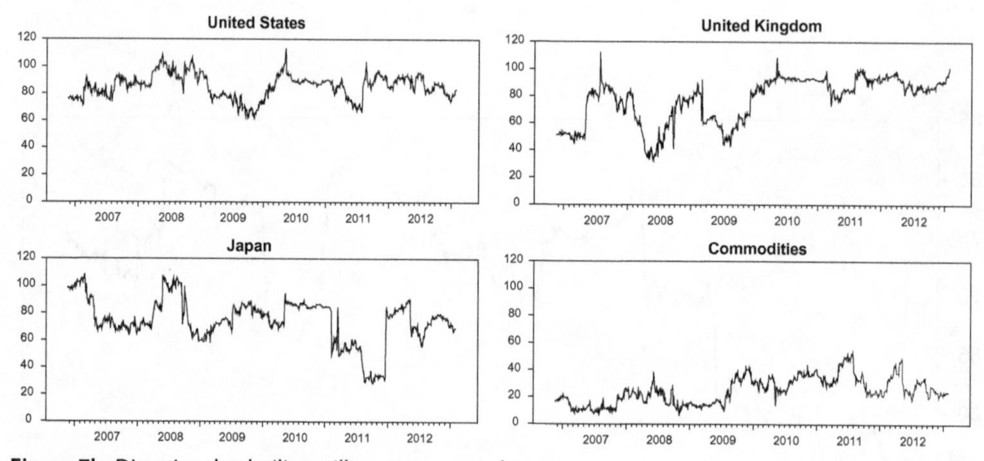

Figure 7b Directional volatility spillovers, to asset classes.

7. CONCLUSIONS

This chapter uses recently developed variance decomposition techniques to analyze return and volatility spillovers between a selection of big commodity producing countries (Canada, Australia, Brazil, and South Africa), commodity prices, and the equity markets in Japan, UK, and US. Asset returns are measured using daily returns and volatility on ETFs because ETFs more closely match actual investment decision making by individuals and institutions.

This analysis of return spillovers yields some interesting results. First, the spillover index for returns increased considerably after the middle of 2008 (Figure 2). Between August 2008 and October 2008, the spillover index jumped from 70% to 82%. Problems in the

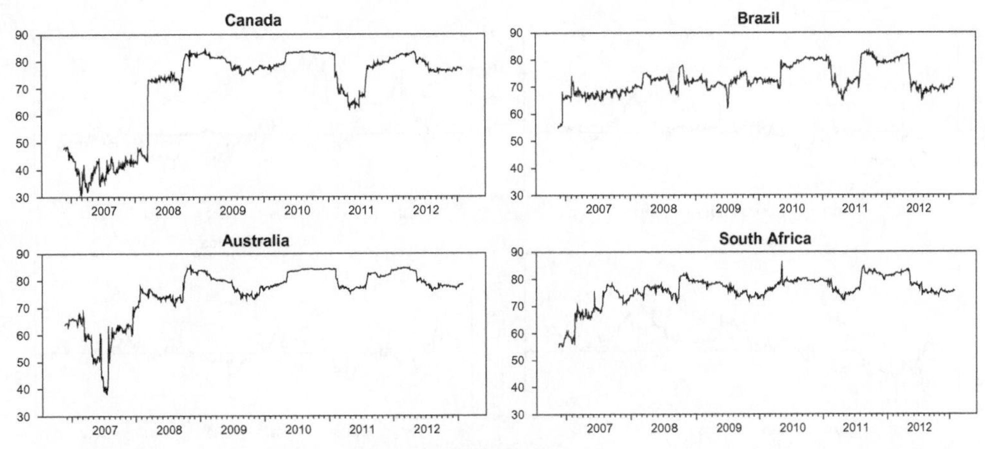

Figure 8a Directional volatility spillovers, from asset classes.

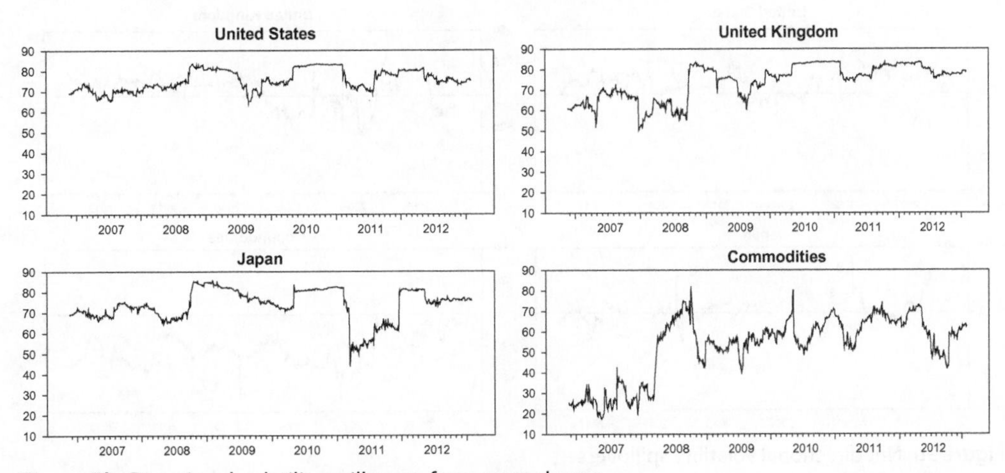

Figure 8b Directional volatility spillovers, from asset classes.

US banking sector resulting from the deterioration of the subprime mortgage market had been accumulating throughout the first half of 2008 but it was the Lehman Brothers bankruptcy in September of 2008 that shook the world's financial markets. A local banking problem had now become a global problem. As the financial crisis spread from one country to another, credit markets quickly dried up and asset correlation increased. Second, as of early 2013, return spillovers between ETFs are still very high and have yet to regain their lower values recorded before the crisis. Third, the high return spillovers between ETFs make it difficult to find diversification opportunities between these assets.

This analysis of volatility spillovers yields similar results to those of return spillovers. First, the volatility spillover index has increased considerably after the middle of 2008

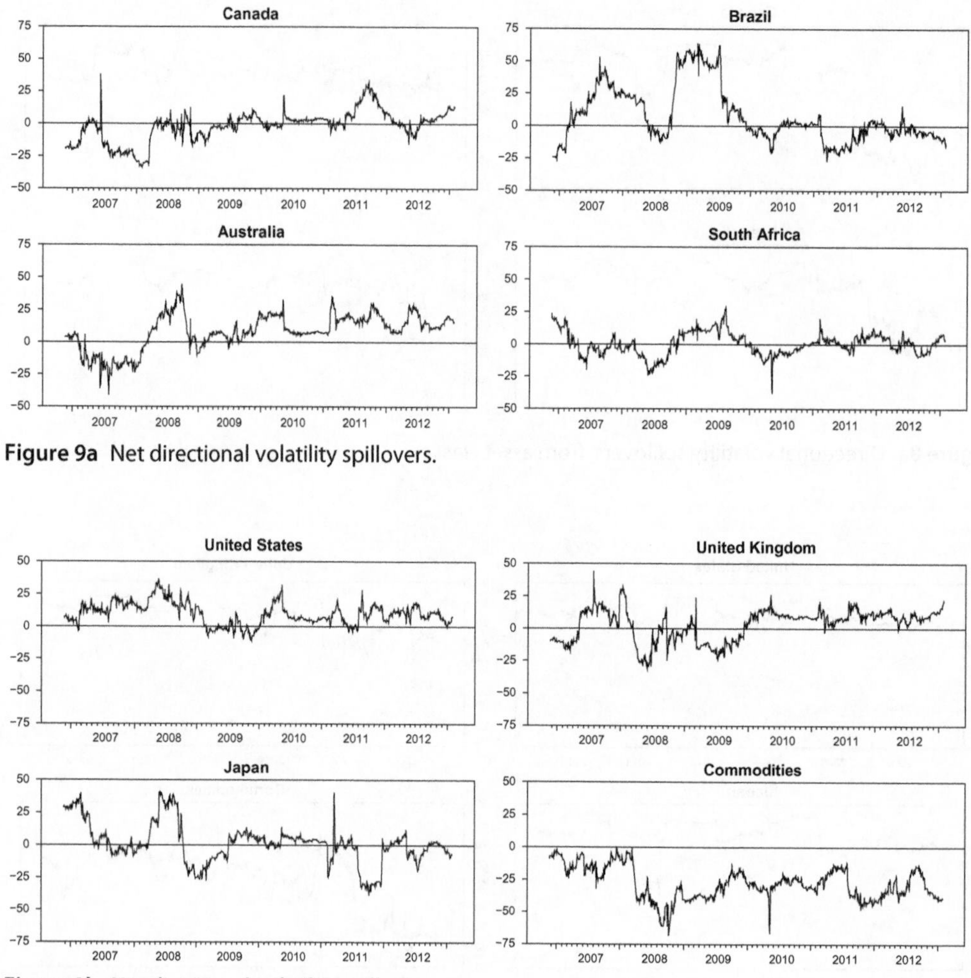

Figure 9a Net directional volatility spillovers.

Figure 9b Net directional volatility spillovers.

(Figure 6). In 2007, the spillover index was in the 55–60% range. By the end of 2008, the spillover index had increased to 80%. Second, volatility spillovers between ETFs are still very high and have yet to regain their pre-2008 values recorded before the crisis. Third, the high volatility spillovers between ETFs make it difficult to find diversification opportunities between these assets.

Spillovers are important in explaining returns and volatility but at any particular point in time their dynamics may be different. Diebold and Yilmaz (2009) observe that major financial crises and events produced large volatility spillovers but the impact of these events on return spillovers was much less. Their analysis covered the period 1995–2007, a period of mostly country specific financial crises, and did not, however, cover the period of the most recent global financial crisis. One possible explanation for this difference in how return and volatility respond to news events is that volatility is more closely associated with information flows than are returns. The return and volatility spillover plots in this present paper (Figures 2 and 6) show similar patterns indicating that at least from the perspective of spillover plots, returns and volatilities responded similarly to news events. This could be due to the fact that the major crisis experienced for the period of study used in this paper was a global financial crisis which affected global financial markets. Nonetheless, for some pairs of assets the directional spillover plots for returns and volatility display different patterns. This may be due to how central banks in different countries responded to the global financial crisis and how secure the banking system in individual countries was.

The results have implications for portfolio optimization and hedging. The equity markets of Canada, Australia, Brazil, and South Africa are much more dependent on the performance of commodity producing companies than are the developed markets of Japan, the UK, and the US. The equity markets in countries with a large reliance on commodities may be driven by different fundamentals than the equity markets in countries with a small reliance on commodities. Different fundamental drivers between countries may indicate different return and volatility spillovers between equity assets. It seems reasonable to expect that the big commodity producers of Canada, Australia, Brazil, and South Africa to have more correlation with each other than with developed equity markets. However, the results of this chapter show that this is not the case. The return and volatility spillovers between the developed and emerging equity assets studied in this chapter have increased since the middle of 2008. This makes portfolio diversification and hedging between these assets more difficult. Investors in emerging markets like Brazil or South Africa need to be aware that these emerging market investments have high return and volatility spillovers with the developed markets of Japan, the UK, and the US. The return and volatility spillovers between equities and commodities have increased since the middle of 2008 but still remain low enough to offer some diversification benefits. This suggests that the most likely avenue for portfolio diversification and hedging would be to combine equity assets with commodities. This suggestion supports the findings of others who have found evidence to show that a portfolio of stocks and commodities can have higher returns and lower risk than a portfolio of stocks only (e.g., Gorton and Rouwenhorst, 2006; Erb and Harvey, 2006; Hillier et al., 2006).

ACKNOWLEDGMENT

I thank an anonymous reviewer for helpful comments.

REFERENCES

Alizadeh, S., Brandt, M.W., Diebold, F.X., 2002. Range-based estimation of stochastic volatility models. Journal of Finance 57, 1047–1092

Alagidede, P., Panagiotidis, T., 2009. Modelling stock returns in Africa's emerging equity markets. International Review of Financial Analysis 18, 1–18

Arouri, M., Jouini, J., Nguyen, D., 2011. Volatility spillovers between oil prices and stock sector returns: implications for portfolio management. Journal of International Money and Finance 30, 1387–1405

Arouri, M., Lahiani, A., Nguyen, D., 2011. Return and volatility transmission between world oil prices and stock markets of the GCC countries. Economic Modelling 28, 1815–1825

Arouri, M., Jouini, J., Nguyen, D., 2012. On the impacts of oil price fluctuations on European equity markets: Volatility spillover and hedging effectiveness. Energy Economics 34, 611–617

Bae, K.-H., Karolyi, G.A., 1994. Good news, bad news and international spillovers of stock returns between Japan and the US. Pacific-Basin Finance Journal 2, 405–438

Beirne, J., Caporale, G.M., Schulze-Ghattas, M., Spagnolo, N., 2010. Global and regional spillovers in emerging stock markets: a multivariate GARCH-in-mean analysis. Emerging Markets Review 11, 250–260

Beirne, J., Caporale, G.M., Schulze-Ghattas, M., Spagnolo, N., 2012. Global and regional spillovers in emerging stock markets: a multivariate GARCH-in-mean analysis. Emerging Markets Review 11, 250–260

Bekaert, G., Harvey, C.R., 1995. Time-varying world market integration. Journal of Finance 50, 403–444

Bekaert, G., Harvey, C., 1997. Emerging equity market volatility. Journal of Financial Economics 43, 29–77

Bekaert, G., Harvey, C.R., 2003. Emerging markets finance. Journal of Empirical Finance 10, 3–55

Bekaert, G., Harvey, C.R., Ng, A., 2005. Market integration and contagion. Journal of Business 78, 39–69

Bhar, R., Nikolova, B., 2009. Return, volatility spillovers and dynamic correlation in the BRIC equity markets: an analysis using a bivariate EGARCH framework. Global Finance Journal 19, 203–218

Brooks, C., Henry, O.T., 2000. Linear and non-linear transmission of equity return volatility: evidence from the US, Japan and Australia. Economic Modeling 17, 497–513

Cha, H.-J., Jithendranathan, T., 2009. Time-varying correlations and optimal allocation in emerging market equities for the US investor. International Journal of Finance and Economics 14, 172–187

Clark, B.K., 1973. A subordinated stochastic process model with finite variance for speculative prices. Econometrica 41, 135–155

Diebold, F.X., Yilmaz, K., 2009. Measuring financial asset return and volatility spillovers, with application to global equity markets. Economic Journal 119, 158–171

Diebold, F.X., Yilmaz, K., 2012. Better to give than to receive: predictive directional measurement of volatility spillovers. International Journal of Forecasting 28, 57–66

Edwards, S., Susmel, R., 2001. Volatility dependence and contagion in emerging equity markets. Journal of Development Economics 66, 505–532

Engle, R.F., 2002. Dynamic conditional correlation: a simple class of multivariate GARCH models. Journal of Business and Economic Statistics 20, 339–350

Engle, R.F., 2009. Anticipating Correlations. Princeton University Press, Princeton

Engle, R.F., Ito, T., Lin, W.L., 1990. Meteor showers or heat waves: heteroskedastic intra-daily volatility in the foreign exchange market. Econometrica 58, 525–542

Erb, C.B., Harvey, C.R., 2006. The strategic and tactical value of commodity futures. Financial Analysts Journal 62, 69–97

Forbes, K.J., Rigobon, R., 2002. No contagion, only interdependence: measuring stock market comovements. Journal of Finance 57, 2223–2261

Goldberg, C.S., Veitch, J.M., 2010. Country risk and financial integration—a case study of South Africa. Research in International Business and Finance 24, 138–145

Gorton, G., Rouwenhorst, K.G., 2006. Facts and fantasies about commodity futures. Financial Analysts Journal 62, 47–68

Hillier, D., Draper, P., Faff, R., 2006. Do precious metal shine? An investment perspective. Financial Analysts Journal 62, 98–106

Hakin, A., McAleer, M., 2010. Modelling the interactions across international stock, bond and foreign exchange markets. Applied Economics 42, 825–850

Hamao, Y., Masulis, R.W., Ng, V., 1990. Correlations in price changes and volatility across international stock markets. Review of Financial Studies 3, 281–307

IMF, 2010. World Economic Outlook: Recovery, Risk, and Rebalancing. International Monetary Fund, Washington, DC

Jeong, J.G., 2009. Cross-Atlantic flow of information during the concurrent trading hours: the case of the U.S., U.K., and Canadian stock markets. Journal of International Finance and Economics 9, 118–125

Karolyi, G.A., 1995. A multivariate GARCH model of international transmission of stock returns and volatility: the case of the United States and Canada. Journal of Business and Economic Statistics 13, 11–25

King, M., Wadhwani, S., 1990. Transmission of volatility between stock markets. Review of Financial Studies 3, 5–33

King, M., Sentana, E., Wadhwani, S., 1994. Volatility and links between national stock markets. Econometrica 62, 901–933

Koop, G., Pesaran, M.H., Potter, S.M., 1996. Impulse response analysis in non-linear multivariate models. Journal of Econometrics 74, 119–147

Korkmaz, T., Cevik, E.I., Atukeren, E., 2012. Return and volatility spillovers among CIVETS stock markets. Emerging Markets Review 13, 230–252

Koutmos, G., Booth, G.G., 1995. Asymmetric volatility transmission in international stock markets. Journal of International Money and Finance 14, 747–762

Krause, T., Tse, Y., 2013. Volatility and return spillovers in Canadian and U.S. industry ETFs. International Review of Economics and Finance 25, 244–259

Lin, W.-L., Engle, R.F., Ito, T., 1994. Do bulls and bears move across borders?. Review of Financial Studies 7, 507–538

Lucey, B., Voronkova, S., 2008. Russian equity market linkages before and after the 1998 crisis: evidence from stochastic and regime switching cointegration tests. Journal of International Money and Finance 27, 1303–1324

Malik, F., Hammoudeh, S., 2007. Shock and volatility transmission in the oil, US and Gulf equity markets. International Review of Economics and Finance 16, 357–368

Mandaci, P.E., Torun, E., 2007. Testing integration between the major emerging markets. Central Bank Review (Turkey) 1, 1–12

McNelis, P., 1993. The response of Australian stock, foreign exchange and bond markets to foreign asset returns and volatilities. Discussion Paper No 9301. Economic Research Department, Reserve Bank of Australia.

Parkinson, M., 1980. The extreme value method for estimating the variance of the rate of return. Journal of Business 53, 61–65

Pesaran, M.H., Shin, Y., 1998. Generalized impulse response analysis in linear multivariate models. Economics Letters 58, 17–29

Ross, S., 1989. Information and volatility: the no-arbitrage Martingale approach to timing and resolution irrelevancy. Journal of Finance 44, 1–17

Sadorsky, P., 2012. Correlations and volatility spillovers between oil prices and the stock prices of clean energy and technology companies. Energy Economics 34, 248–255

Schwert, W., 1990. Stock volatility and the crash of '87. Review of Financial Studies 3, 77–102

Susmel, R., Engle, R.F., 1994. Hourly volatility spillovers between international equity markets. Journal of International Money and Finance 13, 3–25

Theodossiou, P., Lee, U., 1993. Mean and volatility spillovers across major national stock markets: further empirical evidence. Journal of Financial Research 16, 327–350

Valadkhani, A., Chancharat, S., Harvie, C., 2008. A factor analysis of international portfolio diversification. Studies in Economics and Finance 25, 165–174

CHAPTER 33

Correlation and Network Structure of International Financial Markets in Times of Crisis

Leonidas Sandoval
Insper Instituto de Ensino e Pesquisa, Brazil

1. INTRODUCTION

The last two largest global economic crises have their origins in the financial markets: the first one, which reached its peak in 2008, originated from the so-called suprime mortgages. This crisis was triggered by the default of a large number of mortgages in the USA. Subprimes are loans to borrowers who have low credit scores. Most of them had a small initial interest rate, adjustable for future payments, which led to many home foreclosures after the rates climbed substantially. Meanwhile, the loans were transformed in pools that were then resold to interested investors. Since the returns of such investments were high, a financial bubble was created, inflating the subprime mortgage market until the defaults started to pop up.

Because of their underestimation of risk, financial institutions worldwide lost trillions of dollars, and many of them declared bankruptcy, and credit lines tightened around the world, taking the financial crisis to the so-called real economy and hitting many countries in Europe with devastating effects. The so-called Credit Crisis is an ongoing one, and no one knows how much damage to the world economies it is yet to cause.

Other global financial crises that happened fairly recently were the Black Monday (1987), the Asian Crisis (1997), the Russian Crisis (1998), the burst of the dot.com bubble (2000 and 2001), and many minor crises. All of them should not have happened in all of the age of the Universe (about 13 billion years), according to the mainstream financial theory and practice.

Economists have been studying the reasons why markets crash, and why there is propagation of volatility from one market to another, since a long time. After the crash of 1987, many studies have been published on transmission of volatility (contagion) between markets using econometric models, on how the correlation between world markets change with time, and on how the correlation tends to increase in times of high volatility. This issue is of particular importance if one wishes to build portfolios of international assets which can withstand times of crisis.

Emerging Markets and the Global Economy
http://dx.doi.org/10.1016/B978-0-12-411549-1.00033-8

One tool that was first developed in nuclear physics for studying complex systems with unknown correlation structure is random matrix theory (see Mehta, 2004), which confronts the results obtained for the eigenvalues of the correlation matrix of a real system with those of the correlation matrix obtained from a pure random matrix. This approach has been successfully applied to a large number of financial markets. In particular, Maslov (2001) applied Random Matrix Theory to the study of the relations between world markets. This approach has also been used in the construction of hierarchical structures between different assets of financial markets.

In this chapter, we shall focus on the time series of 79 benchmark indices across the world during the 10 years from the beginning of 2003 to the end of 2012. The indices and the countries they belong to are described in Section 2. The other crises listed above have been analyzed by Sandoval and Franca (2012), using basically the same tools as here, and their network structure was studied in Sandoval (2012a) (as Minimum Spanning Trees) and in Sandoval (2013) (as Asset Graphs). Section 3 explains how Random Matrix Theory is applied to the data; Section 4 deals with the connection between the correlation of indices and the volatility of the world market; Section 5 uses the correlation between indices in order to build networks based on asset graphs. Section 6 offers some final conclusions.

2. THE DATA

The data consist on the time series of the closing values of the benchmark indices of 79 stock exchanges across the globe, collected from the beginning of 2003 to the end of 2012. The indices and the countries to which they belong are: S&P 500 (United States of America), S&P/TSX Composite (Canada), IPC (Mexico), Bermuda SX Index (Bermuda), Jamaica SX Market Index (Jamaica), BCT Corp Costa Rica (Costa Rica), Bolsa deValores de Panama General, Merval (Argentina), Ibovespa (Brazil), IPSA (Chile), IGBC (Colombia), IGBVL (Peru), IBC (Venezuela), FTSE 100 (United Kingdom), ISEQ (Ireland), CAC 40 (France), DAX (Germany), ATX (Austria), SMI (Switzerland), BEL 20 (Belgium), AEX (Netherlands), OMX Stockholm 30 (Sweden), OMX Copenhagen 20 (Denmark), OMX Helsinki (Finland), OBX (Norway), OMX Iceland All-Share Index (Iceland), MIB-30 (Italy), IBEX 35 (Spain), PSI 20 (Portugal), Athens SX General Index (Greece), WIG (Poland), PX 50 (Czech Republic), SAX (Slovakia), CROBEX (Croatia), OMXT (Estonia), OMXR (Latvia), Budapest SX Index (Hungary), SOFIX (Bulgaria), PFTS (Ukraine), MICEX (Russia), ISE National 100 (Turkey), KASE (Kazakhstan), Malta SX Index (Malta), Tel Aviv 25 (Israel), Al Quds (Palestine), ASE General Index (Jordan), BLOM (Lebanon), TASI (Saudi Arabia), MSM 30 (Oman), DSM 20 (Qatar), ADX General Index (United Arab Emirates), KSE 100 (Pakistan), SENSEX 30 (India), DSE General Index (Bangladesh), Sri Lanka Colombo Stock Exchange All-Share Index, Nikkei 225 (Japan), Hang Seng (Hong Kong), Shangai SE Composite (China),

TAIEX (Taiwan), KOSPI (South Korea), MSE TOP 20 (Mongolia), Straits Times (Singapore), Jakarta Composite Index (Indonesia), KLCI (Malaysia), SET (Thailand), PSEI (Philippines), VN-Index (Vietnam), S&P/ASX 200 (Australia), NZX 50 (New Zealand), CFG 25 (Morocco), TUNINDEX (Tunisia), EGX 30 (Egypt), Nigeria SX All Share Index (Nigeria), Gaborone (Botswana), GSE All Share Index (Ghana), NSE 20 (Kenya), SEMDEX (Mauritius), and FTSE/JSE Africa All Share (South Africa). The data were collected from a Bloomberg terminal.

Since we are dealing with countries that have different holidays and, in some cases, different weekends, we fixed the dates in which the New York Stock Exchange, by far the most important in terms of volume of negotiations and in influence, operated. If an index was not computed in one of the same dates, its value of the previous working day was repeated; in case one index operated in a day the New York Stock Exchange did not, then the index for that date was deleted. This contrasts with the common method used, which is to delete all days to which one of the time series had no data assigned; that would lead to the deletion of too many days, and we then would have returns that were not true to the real variations of the indices. Indices that were most affected by our method were the ones from Israel, Jordan, Saudi Arabia, Oman, Qatar, the United Arab Emirates, and Egypt, where weekends are not on Saturdays and Sundays. Nevertheless, we think that our choice preserves best the real returns in the major stock markets.

The data were used in order to calculate log-returns, defined as:

$$S_t = \ln(P_t) - \ln(P_{t-1}) \approx \frac{P_t - P_{t-1}}{P_t}, \qquad (1)$$

where P_t is the value of an index on day t and P_{t-1} is the value of the same index on the previous day. Such measure is often used in order to avoid non-stationarity of data.

The log-returns are then used in order to calculate the Spearman rank correlation between each index, and the results are ordered in a correlation matrix. The reason for using the Spearman rank correlation and not the usual Pearson correlation is because the former is better at measuring nonlinear correlations, although both correlation measures yield very similar results.

In order to study the effects of the crisis of 2008 and onwards, we divide the data into two blocks, the first pertaining the 5 years from 2003 to 2007, and the other containing the years from 2008 to 2012. Then, Random Matrix Theory is used in order to find correlations that seem not to be random. This is explained in the next section.

3. RANDOM MATRIX THEORY

Random matrix theory had its origins in 1953, in the work of the Hungarian physicist Eugene Wigner. He was studying the energy levels of complex atomic nuclei, such as uranium, and had no means of calculating the distance between those levels. He then assumed that those distances were random, and arranged the random number in a matrix which expressed the connections between the many energy levels. Surprisingly, he could then be able to make sensible predictions about how the energy levels related to one another.

This method also found connections with the study of the Riemann zeta function, which is of primordial importance to the study of prime numbers, used for coding and decoding information, for example. The theory was later developed, with many and surprising results arising. Today, random matrix theory is applied to quantum physics, nanotechnology, quantum gravity, the study of the structure of crystals, and may have applications in ecology, linguistics, and many other fields where a large amount of apparently unrelated information may be understood as being somehow connected. The theory has also been applied to finance in a series of works dealing with the correlation matrices of stock prices, and to risk management in portfolios.

The first result of the theory that we shall mention is that, given an $L \times N$ matrix with random numbers built on a Gaussian distribution with average zero and standard deviation σ, then, in the limit $L \to \infty$ and $N \to \infty$ such that $Q = L/N$ remains finite and greater than 1, the eigenvalues λ of such a matrix will have the following probability density function, called a Marčenku-Pastur distribution (Marĕnko and Pastur, 1967):

$$\rho(\lambda) = \frac{Q}{2\pi\sigma^2} \frac{\sqrt{(\lambda_+ - \lambda)(\lambda - \lambda_-)}}{\lambda}, \tag{2}$$

where

$$\lambda_- = \sigma^2 \left(1 + \frac{1}{Q} - 2\sqrt{\frac{1}{Q}}\right), \quad \lambda_+ = \sigma^2 \left(1 + \frac{1}{Q} + 2\sqrt{\frac{1}{Q}}\right), \tag{3}$$

and λ is restricted to the interval $[\lambda_-, \lambda_+]$.

Figure 1 shows some Marčenku-Pastur distributions for some values of Q and σ. Since the distribution (2) is only valid for the limit $L \to \infty$ and $N \to \infty$, finite distributions will present differences from this behavior. Another source of deviations is the fact that financial time series are better described by non-Gaussian distributions, such as t Student or Tsallis distribution. Biroli et al. (2007) calculated a probability density function analogous to the Marčenku-Pastur distribution, but based on a t Student distribution for the randomized data. Their results show that there is a longer tale toward higher eigenvalues which decays as a power law.

In Figure 2, we compare the theoretical distribution for $Q = 10$ and $\sigma = 1$ with distributions of the eigenvalues of three correlation matrices generated from finite $L \times N$ matrices such that $Q = L/M = 10$, and the elements of the matrices are random numbers with mean zero and standard deviation 1. Real data will deviate from the theoretical probability distribution. This may be taken into account by randomizing the order of data in each of the time series used so as to preserve its mean and standard deviation, but destroy any correlation between the time series. The result of a large enough number of

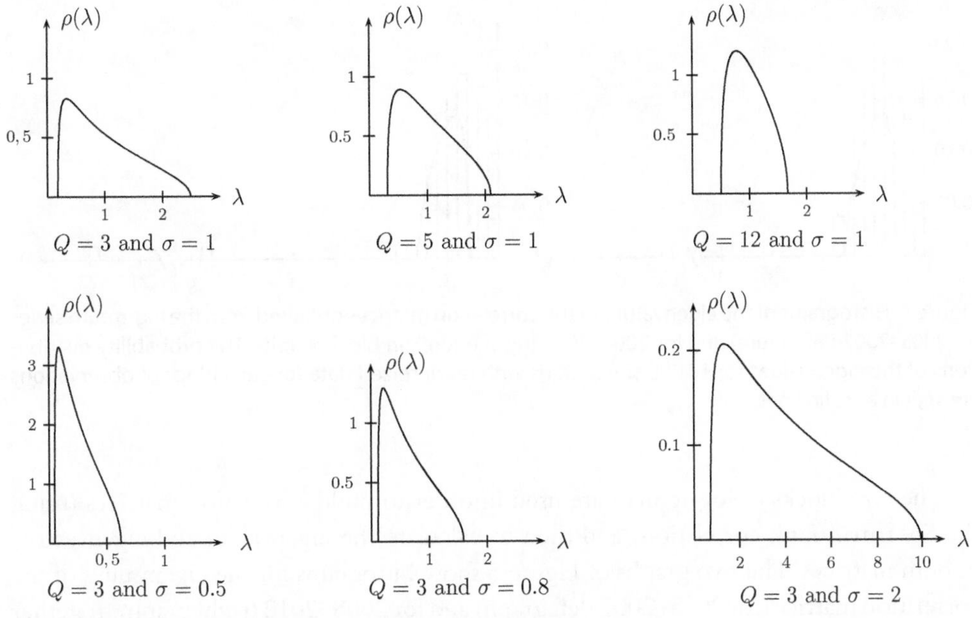

Figure 1 Marčenku-Pastur distribution for fixed values of Q and σ.

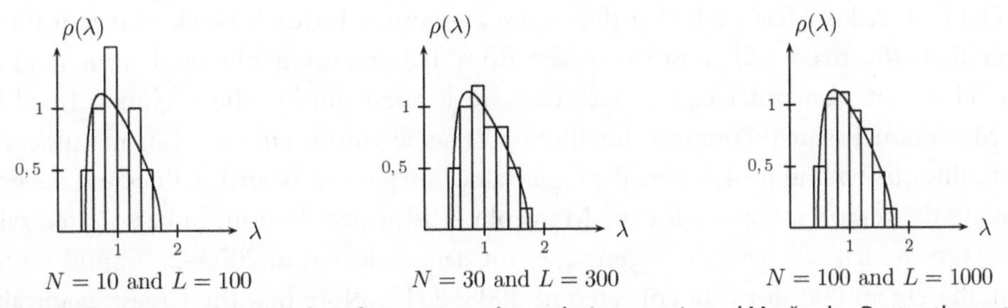

Figure 2 Histograms of eigenvalues for generated correlation matrix and Marčenku-Pastur theoretical distribution (solid line) for $Q = 10$ and $\sigma = 1$.

such simulations may then be compared with the results obtained with the original data instead of comparing the latter with the theoretical Marčenku-Pastur distribution.

In order to apply Random Matrix Theory to the 79 stock exchanges, we divide their time series into two blocks: the first ranging from the beginning of 2003 to the end of 2007, so pre-crisis, and the second encompassing the years from 2008 to 2012 (post-crisis). The first block of time series is formed by 1258 observations (days), so that $Q = L/M = 1258/79 \approx 15,92$; the second block of time series is formed by 1259 observations (days), so that $Q = L/M = 1259/79 \approx 15,94$. For these values, we have $\lambda_- \approx 0.56$ and $\lambda_+ \approx 1.56$ for both blocks of time series.

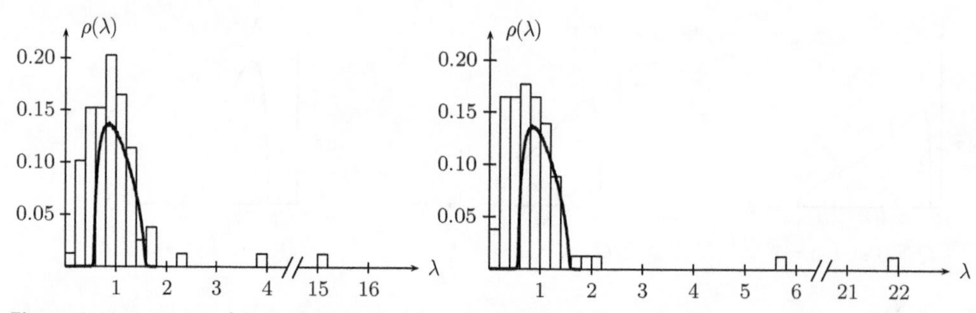

Figure 3 Histograms of the eigenvalues of the correlation matrices obtained from the log-return series for 2003–2007 (left figure) and for 2008–2012 (right figure), in block graphs. The probability distributions of the eigenvalues for 10,000 simulations with randomized data for each block of observations are shown as solid lines.

The two blocks of log-returns are used in order to build correlation matrices (using the Spearman rank correlation) and then to calculate the eigenvalues and eigenvectors of both matrices. The two graphs of Figure 3 show histograms for the eigenvalues of the correlation matrices for 2003–2007 (left graph) and for 2008–2012 (right graph). Together with the graphs are plotted as solid lines the probability distributions of the eigenvalues for 10,000 simulations with randomized data for each block of observations. The results of the simulations are very similar to the theoretical Marčenku-Pastur distributions.

The first striking feature is that the largest eigenvalue for each block of data is much larger than the maximum limit expected from a distribution obtained from random data. There are also other eigenvalues that are located outside the region defined by the Marčenku-Pastur theoretical distribution. This feature is enhanced if one plots the eigenvalues, like in Figure 4, where the eigenvalues are plotted as vertical lines and the gray areas are the region predicted for the Marčenku-Pastur distribution, and associated with noise. On the left, we have the eigenvalues for data collected in 2003–2007, and on the right, the eigenvalues for data collected in 2008–2012. Note that the largest eigenvalue for 2008–2012 is rather larger than the largest eigenvalue for 2003–2007. Also, for 2008–2012, there are three other eigenvalues that detach themselves from the bulk, while for 2003–2007, there are two of them. Besides the eigenvalues that are above the values predicted for a random collection of data, there are many eigenvalues below the same prediction. This happens in both periods being analyzed.

More information on the meaning of the largest eigenvalues may be obtained if one plots the eigenvectors associated with them. Figure 5 shows the components of the eigenvectors, plotted as column bars, associated with the three largest eigenvalues for the data collected in 2003–2007. The eigenvalue associated with the largest eigenvalue (e_1) has a very distinct structure, as nearly all indices appear with positive values. The exceptions are indices from stock markets that are very small in terms of number of stocks and of volume of negotiations. This eigenvector is often associated with a *market mode*, and a

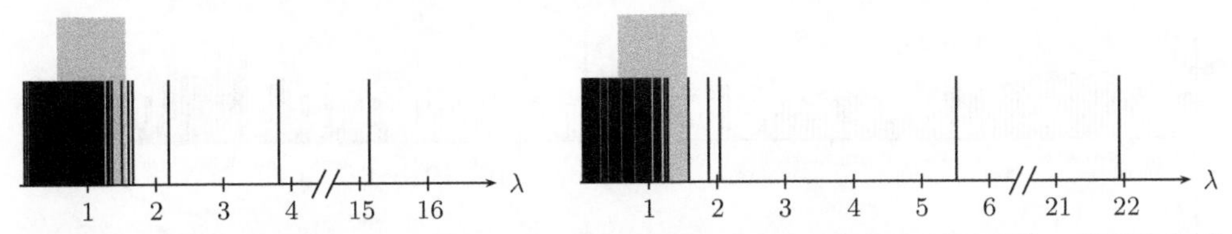

Figure 4 Eigenvalues of the correlation matrices for the log-returns of 2003–2007 (left) and 2008–2012 (right), represented as vertical lines. The gray areas are the regions predicted for the Marčenku-Pastur distributon, and associated with noise.

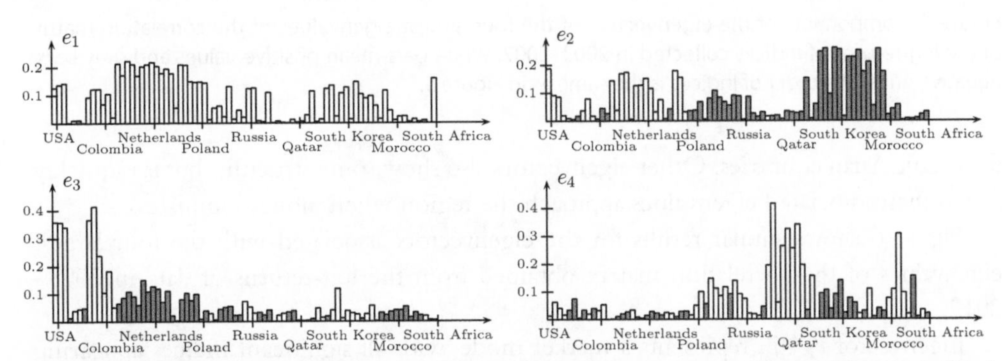

Figure 5 Components of the eigenvectors of the four largest eigenvalues of the correlation matrix of the log-returns of indices collected in 2003–2007. White bars mean positive values and gray bars, negative ones. The order of indices is the following: **USA**, Canada, Mexico, Bermuda, Jamaica, Costa Rica, Panama, Argentina, Brazil, Chile, **Colombia**, Peru, Venezuela, UK, Ireland, France, Germany, Austria, Switzerland, Belgium, **Netherlands**, Sweden, Denmark, Finland, Norway, Iceland, Italy, Spain, Portugal, Greece, **Poland**, Czech Republic, Slovakia, Croatia, Estonia, Latvia, Hungary, Bulgaria, Romania, Ukraine, **Russia**, Turkey, Kazakhstan, Malta, Israel, Palestine, Jordan, Lebanon, Saudi Arabia, Oman, **Qatar**, United Arab Emirates, Pakistan, India, Bangladesh, Sri Lanka, Japan, Hong Kong, China, Taiwan, **South Korea**, Mongolia, Singapore, Indonesia, Malaysia, Thailand, Philippines, Vietnam, Australia, New Zealand, **Morocco**, Tunisia, Egypt, Nigeria, Botswana, Ghana, Kenya, Mauritius, and **South Africa**.

portfolio built by taking the value of each index as its weight would follow very closely the general movements of the international stock market. In fact, when compared with an index of the global stock market, like the MSCI World Index, the portfolio built in terms of eigenvector e_1 has Pearson correlation 0.77.

Eigenvector e_2, related with the second largest eigenvalue, has a structure that is typical of stock markets that do not operate at the same time, as seen in Sandoval (2012b). It generally shows positive values for Western countries and negative values for Eastern ones, defining two basic blocks. Eigenvector e_3, associated with the third largest eigenvalue, shows strong positive peaks in North America and South America, and negative peaks in Europe. Eigenvalue e_4, associated with the fourth largest eigenvalue, has strong positive peaks in Arab countries in the Middle East and North Africa, and smaller negative ones

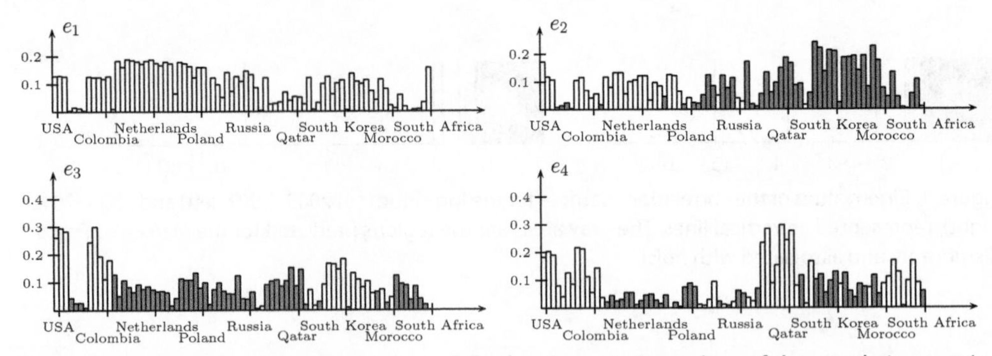

Figure 6 Components of the eigenvectors of the four largest eigenvalues of the correlation matrix of the log-returns of indices collected in 2003–2007. White bars mean positive values and gray bars, negative ones. The order of indices is the same as in Figure 5.

for Pacific Asian countries. Other eigenvectors also show some structure, but it is quickly lost as their associated eigenvalues approach the region where noise dominates.

Figure 6 shows similar results for the eigenvectors associated with the four largest eigenvalues of the correlation matrix obtained from the log-returns of data in 2008–2012.

Eigenvector e_1 still represents a market mode, with all significant indices appearing with positive values, and eigenvector e_2 shows two blocks, a Western and an Eastern one. Eigenvector e_3 shows a block formed by North and South American indices, a block of European indices, probably joined by the African indices that operate at the same hours as the Central European markets, and a third block, of Pacific Asian indices, and it is probably connected with a fine-tuning of the difference in operation hours of markets. Eigenvector e_4 separates indices from the Americas, from Europe, Arab countries, and Pacific Asian ones.

Comparing the eigenvectors in Figures 5 and 6, one may also notice that there were no substantial changes to the structure shown by them from the period 2003–2007 to the period 2008–2012, leading to the belief that there is some stability on the world stock market structure, even during periods of crises.

4. CORRELATION AND VOLATILITY OF THE MARKET

It is a general consensus that, when markets are more volatile, they tend to behave more similarly, so that volatility and correlation of assets or indices should move relatively together. In Sandoval (2013), we made calculations of the average value of correlation matrices and of the volatilities of the market mode for running windows during the periods of some of the major financial crises of the past decades. Here, we come back to that study, but now using our data of 79 indices for the years from 2003 to 2012. The approach is a little different than what has been done before, as we shall compare the

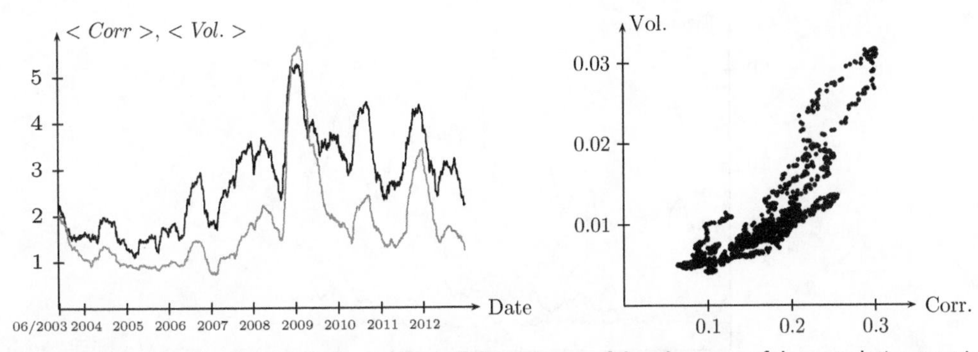

Figure 7 Graph on the left: evolution in time of the average of the elements of the correlation matrix of the log-returns (black line) and of the volatility of the log-returns of the MSCI World Index (gray line), both normalized so as to have standard deviation one. The graph on the right is the dispersion graph of the average correlation and of the average volatility, not normalized.

average correlation of indices with the volatility of the MSCI World Index, which is a stock market index of over 6000 stocks of companies in different stock markets across the globe, and is often used as a benchmark for the global financial market.

The calculations are done in running windows of 100 days each, moving one day at a time. This gives us a total of 2415 windows running from 2003 to 2012. The average correlation is calculated as the mean of the elements of the correlation matrix obtained from each window, and it is assigned to the last day of the window (so, results start from 100 days after the beginning of 2003). We also calculate the standard deviation of the elements of the correlation matrix for each window. The volatility of the MSCI World Index is also calculated in moving windows of 100 days, with steps of one day, and it is computed as the standard deviation of the log-returns of the index for each window. This volatility is also assigned to the last day of the window.

The results are plotted in Figure 7. The graph on the left is the evolution in time of the average of the elements of the correlation matrix of the log-returns (black line) and of the average of the volatility of the MSCI World Index (gray line). In order to best compare both measures, they are both normalized so as to have standard deviation one. The graph on the right is the dispersion graph of the average correlation and of the average volatility, not normalized. The Pearson correlation between both measures is 0.84.

Note that, when volatility rises, mainly during and after the subprime crisis of 2008, the correlation between the indices also rises. This is evidence that correlation and volatility go hand in hand when it concerns world financial markets. This effect is bad news for investors who wish to avoid risk in times of crisis by diversifying their portfolios using assets from different countries.

Another measure that is very much correlated with both the average of the elements of the correlation matrix and the volatility of the MSCI World Index is the largest eigenvalue

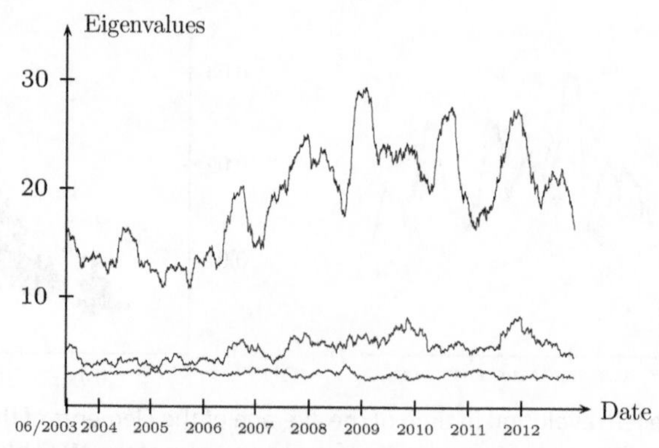

Figure 8 Three largest eigenvalues of the correlation matrix of the log-returns of the indices, calculated in running windows of 100 days with a step of one day.

of the correlation matrix. Figure 8 shows the first three largest eigenvalues of correlation matrices calculated in running windows of 100 days with steps of one day from 2003 to 2012. The first and the second largest eigenvalues are more sensitive to periods of high volatility.

Next, we shall focus on the network structure of the stock market indices that can be derived from their correlations.

5. NETWORK STRUCTURE

The correlation matrix of the time series of financial data encodes a large amount of information, and an even greater amount of noise. That information and noise must be filtered if one is to try to understand how the elements (in our case, indices) relate to each other and how that relation evolves in time. One of the most common filtering procedures is to represent those relations using a *Minimum Spanning Tree* (MST), which is a graph containing all indices, connected by at least one edge, so that the sum of the edges is minimum, and which presents no loops. Another type of representation is that of a *Planar Maximally Filtered Graph* (PMFG), which admits loops but must be representable in two-dimensional graphs without crossings.

Yet another type of representation is obtained by establishing a number which defines how many connections (edges) are to be represented in a graph of the correlations between nodes. There is no limitation with respect to the crossing of edges or to the formation of loops, and if the number is high enough, then one has a graph where all nodes are connected to one another. These are usually called *Asset Trees*, or *Asset Graphs*, since they are not trees in the network sense. Another way to build asset graphs is to establish a value (threshold) such that distances above it are not considered. This eliminates connections (edges) as well as indices (nodes), but also makes the diagrams more understandable by filtering both information and noise. Some previous works using graphic representations of correlations between international assets (indices or otherwise) can be found in the works of Coelho et al. (2007), Coronnello et al. (2007), Ausloos and Lambiotte (2007), and Eryiğit and Eryiğit (2009).

We shall then represent the indices as asset graphs built from the correlation matrices obtained from their log-returns. Given a correlation coefficient c_{ij} in a correlation matrix of all indices, a distance measure, first used in the context of financial markets by Mantegna (1999), may be defined as:

$$d_{ij} = \sqrt{2\left(1 - c_{ij}\right)}. \tag{4}$$

As correlations between indices vary from -1 (anticorrelated) to 1 (completely correlated), the distance between them vary from 0 (totally correlated) to 2 (completely anticorrelated). Totally uncorrelated indices would have distance 1 between them.

Based on the distance measures, two-dimensional coordinates are assigned to each index using an algorithm called Classical Multidimensional Scaling, which is based on minimizing the stress function:

$$S = \left[\frac{\sum_{i=1}^{n}\sum_{j>i}^{n}\left(\delta_{ij} - \bar{d}_{ij}\right)^2}{\sum_{i=1}^{n}\sum_{j>i}^{n} d_{ij}^2}\right]^{1/2}, \tag{5}$$

where δ_{ij} is 1 for $i = j$ and zero otherwise, n is the number of rows of the correlation matrix, and $\bar{d}_{ij}$ is an m-dimensional Euclidean distance (which may be another type of distance for other types of multidimensional scaling) given by:

$$\bar{d}_{ij} = \left[\sum_{a=1}^{m}\left(x_{ia} - x_{ja}\right)^2\right]^{1/2}. \tag{6}$$

The outputs of this optimization problem are the coordinates x_{ij} of each of the nodes, where $i = 1, \ldots, n$ is the number of nodes and $j = 1, \ldots, m$ is the number of each dimension in an m-dimensional space. It is customary for the representation of the network to be well represented in smaller dimensions than m, and in the case of this article we shall consider $m = 2$ for a two-dimensional visualization of the network. The choice is a compromise between fidelity to the original distances and the easiness of representing the networks.

As some correlations may be the result of random noise, we ran some simulations based on randomized data, consisting on randomly reordering the time series of each index so as to destroy any true correlations between them but maintain each frequency distribution intact. The result of 1000 simulations is a distance value above which correlations are probably due to random noise, which, in our case, is $d = 1.36$.

Our asset graphs are built using distance measures as thresholds. As an example, for threshold $T = 0.5$, one builds an asset graph where all distances below 0.5 are represented as edges (connections) between nodes (indices). All distances above this threshold are removed, and all indices that do not connect to any other index below this threshold are also removed.

Before drawing them, there is a further innovation that must be discussed. The particular nature of stock markets that operate at different time zones makes it difficult to make a representation of them that shows the cyclical nature of the rotation of the planet, with markets from the East being more connected with their counterparts in the West from the previous day. A solution to that, developed in Sandoval (2012b), is to build a network based on the stock market indices and on their lagged values of the previous day. So, one now has, instead of the 79 original indices, 79 more indices associated with their lagged values, for a total of 158 indices. Since it has already been shown Sandoval (2013) that the asset graphs of the stock market indices do not change much in time, we shall consider the asset graphs based on the whole period, from 2003 to 2012.

In Figure 9, we plot all indices on their coordinates. The indices are represented by the four first letters of each country, with the exception of Austria, which is written *Autr* so as to differentiate it from Australia, and by three or fours letters in case of countries with multiple words, like CzRe for the Czech Republic or USA for the United States of America. Lagged indices are represented by black boxes and the original ones are represented in white boxes. Note that there is a clear distinction between original and lagged indices, forming two separate clusters with some interaction occurring for indices which are not very correlated to any other indices in the network, like some Arab and African indices. There is also a clear clustering of indices according to geography (or by time zones), particularly for Western European indices, American, and Pacific Asian ones.

Figure 10 shows the asset graphs for the world stock market indices, displaying only the indices that are connected below certain distance thresholds ($T = 0.5$, $T = 0.7$, $T = 0.9$, and $T = 1.1$) and their connections. For $T = 0.5$, the only countries that are connected are France, Germany, the Netherlands, and Italy, original and lagged ones, forming the core of the Central European countries. For $T = 0.7$, the UK, Switzerland, Belgium, Sweden, Finland, and Spain join the European cluster, which is represented in its two versions (original and lagged).

At $T = 0.9$, two more clusters are formed: one of American indices, made by the USA, Canada, Mexico, and Brazil, and one of Pacific Asian indices, made by Japan, Hong Kong, South Korea, Singapore, and Taiwan. For $T = 1.1$, the clusters join and add to themselves many more indices. Something to be noticed is that Israel and South Africa are part of the European cluster, and that Australia and New Zealand join the Pacific Asian cluster. Most important, there are now connections between lagged and original indices, with the lagged indices of the USA, Canada, Mexico, and Brazil forming connections with the next day indices of Japan, Hong Kong, the Philippines, Australia, and New Zealand. If one makes asset graphs including indices that are lagged by two and three days, a

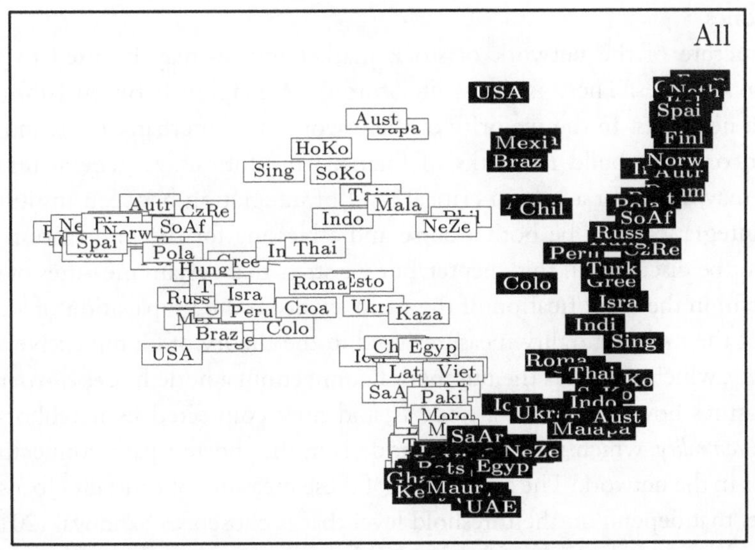

Figure 9 Two-dimensional representation of the node structure (without the connections) of the world stock market indices. White boxes represent the original indices and black boxes represent the lagged indices.

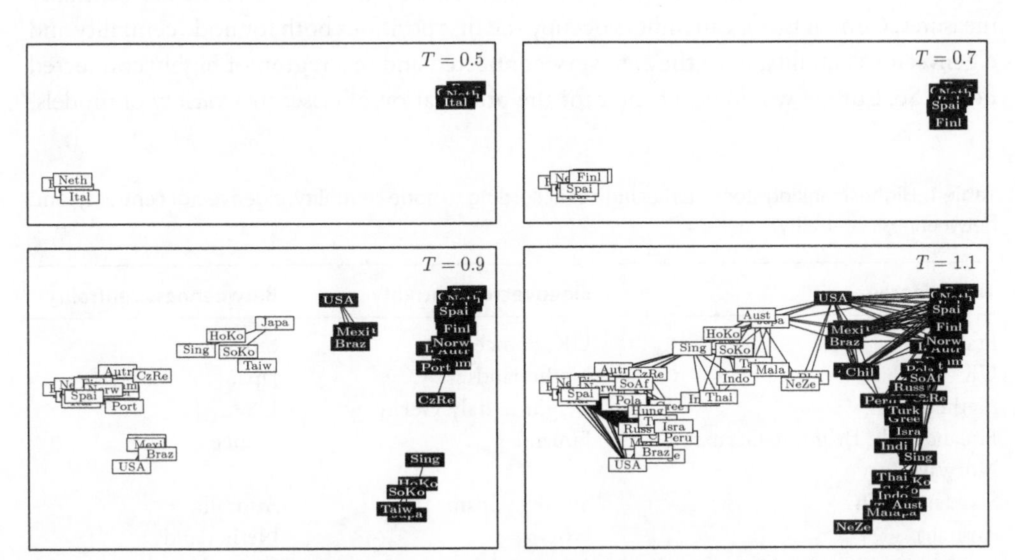

Figure 10 Asset graphs of the world market indices for distance threshold values $T = 0.5$, $T = 0.7$, $T = 0.9$, and $T = 1.1$. White boxes represent the original indices and black boxes represent the lagged indices.

similar structure appears, with American indices being correlated with Pacific Asian and Oceanian ones.

The structure of the network of stock market indices may be used to study the propagation of crises. There is a vast literature on contagion between banks or other markets via networks. In the majority of these works, the interbank loans and liabilities are used in order to build networks of financial institutions. A general result is that contagion may occur for a certain critical level of integration between institutions, and that high integration may be both a curse and a blessing for the propagation of crises. This will not be discussed in this chapter, but we stress that certain measures of centrality may be useful in the identification of the main agents in the propagation of a crisis.

Some of the main centrality measures used in the theory of Complex Networks are *node centrality*, which measures the number of connections a node has, *eigenvector centrality*, which measures how connected a node is, and how connected its neighbors are, and *betweenness centrality*, which measures if a node is in the shortest path connecting all the other nodes in the network. The application of these measures of centrality to asset graphs gives results that depend on the threshold level that is chosen, as Sandoval (2013). As an example, for low enough values of the threshold, there are no connections between nodes, and for high enough threshold values, all nodes are connected to every other node in the network.

If these measures are applied to the asset graph for $T = 1.1$, we obtain the results listed in Table 1, which contains the nodes with the ten best scores in each of the centrality measures. Central European indices occupy the first positions both for node centrality and eigenvector centrality, since they are very connected and in a region of highly connected nodes. So, Europe would be a center for the propagation of crises in a variety of models.

Table 1 Highest ranking stock market indices according to node centrality, eigenvector centrality, and betweenness centrality.

Node degree	Eigenvector centrality	Betweenness centrality
France	UK, France	Singapore
UK	Netherlands	Japan
Netherlands	Belgium, Italy, Germany	USA
Finland, Italy, Belgium, Germany, Norway	Finland	France
Sweden, Spain	Sweden, Spain	Australia
Australia	Norway	Netherlands
Switzerland	Austria	Finland
Denmark, Czech Republic, USA	Switzerland	Hong Kong
Poland	Czech Republic	Austria
South Africa, Hungary, Ireland	Denmark, Poland	Denmark

Now for betweenness centrality, we have Singapore and Japan occupying the first two positions, mainly due to their role as connections between Pacific Asian and European indices to the next day indices of the Americas. The USA also occupies a high rank due to the same reason.

6. CONCLUSION

Based on the time series of 79 stock indices taken from a variety of countries from 2003 to 2012, we built correlation matrices based on the log-returns of those indices, first comparing the results of 2003–2007 (a period of low volatility) with the ones of 2008–2012 (a time of high volatility) under the light of Random Matrix Theory. We identified a large eigenvalue which represents a market mode, which conveys the general behavior of the world stock market, and a second largest one, which highlights the differences between stock markets operating in different time zones. We also use correlation matrices calculated in running windows of 100 days with time step of one day in order to compare the average correlation of stock markets with the volatility of the world stock markets represented by the MSCI World Index, showing there is a strong correlation between them so that, in times of high volatility, stock markets tend to behave in the same way. Next, we built networks of the stock market indices, as represented by asset graphs, in which a structure highly dependent on geographical position and/or on operation hours is clear. We could see that some Central European markets are highly correlated, and that two other cluster, one of American markets, and another of Pacific Asian ones, forms under lower correlation values. We could also see that stock market indices in Pacific Asia are correlated with the previous day's indices of America, and that Central European indices occupy a position of high centrality in a network of stock market indices, and that Singapore and Japan present a high number of betweenness centrality, being the main channels between Eastern and Western indices.

ACKNOWLEDGMENTS

The author acknowledges the support of this work by a grant from Insper, Instituto de Ensino e Pesquisa. This chapter was written using LaTeX, all figures were made using PSTricks, and the calculations were made using Matlab, Excel, and Ucinet. All data and algorithms used are freely available upon request to the author at leonidassj@insper.edu.br.

REFERENCES

Ausloos, M., Lambiotte, R., 2007. Clusters or networks of economies? A macroeconomy study through gross domestic product. Physica A 382, 16–21

Biroli, G., Bouchaud, J.-P., Potters, M., 2007. The student ensemble of correlation matrices: eigenvalue spectrum and Kullback–Leibler entropy. Acta Physica Polonica B 13, 4009–4026

Coelho, R., Gilmore, C.G., Lucey, B., Richmond, P., Hutzler, S., 2007. The evolution of interdependence in world equity markets - evidence from minimum spanning trees. Physica A 376, 455–466

Coronnello, C., Tumminello, M., Lillo, F., Micchichè, S., Mantegna, R.N., 2007. Economic sector identification in a set of stocks traded at the New York Stock Exchange: a comparative analysis. Proceedings of the SPIE 6601, 66010T

Eryiğit, M., Eryiğit, R., 2009. Network structure of cross-correlations among the world market indices. Physica A 388, 3551–3562

Mantegna, R.N., 1999. Hierarchical structure in financial markets. European Physics Journal B 11, 193

Marĕnko, V.A., Pastur, L.A., 1967. USSR-Sb 1, 457–483

Maslov, S., 2001. Measures of globalization based on cross-correlations of world financial indices. Physica A 301, 397–406

Mehta, M.L., 2004. Random Matrices. Academic Press

Sandoval Jr., L., 2012. Pruning a minimum spanning tree. Physica A 391, 2678–2711

Sandoval Jr., L., 2012b. To Lag or Not to Lag? arXiv:1201.4586.

Sandoval Jr., L., 2013. Cluster formation and evolution in networks of financial market indices. Algorithmic Finance 2, 3–43

Sandoval Jr., L., Franca, I.P., 2012. Correlation of financial markets in times of crisis. Physica A 391, 187–208

CHAPTER 34

Financial Development and its Effects on Economic Growth: A Dynamic Analysis

Christophe Rault[*,†], Anamaria Sova[‡,§,¶,‖,], Robert Sova[§], and Guglielmo Maria Caporale[¶]**

[*]Université d'Orléans, Orléans, France
[†]Toulouse Business School, France
[‡]Economic Business Research Centre, Bucharest, Romania
[§]ASE, Bucharest University of Economics Studies, Romania
[¶]Brunel University, London, UK
[‖]CESifo, Munich, Germany
[**]DIW, Berlin, Germany

1. INTRODUCTION

The relationship between financial development and economic growth is a controversial issue. Some authors consider finance as an important element of growth (Levine, 1997, 2005), while for others it is only a minor growth factor (Robinson, 1952; Lucas, 1988). Levine (2005) suggests that financial institutions and markets can foster economic growth through several channels (e.g., by easing the exchange of goods and services through the provision of payment services, mobilizing and pooling savings from a large number of investors, detecting investment opportunities, carrying out corporate governance, diversifying, increasing liquidity, reducing intertemporal risk, etc.). On the contrary, Lucas (1988) argues that the role of finance has been overstressed.

A particular case is represented by the Central and Eastern European countries (CEECs), where the reforms in the banking sector were the first important step toward financial development. From the 1990s, foreign banks were allowed to enter the market, and within a decade they held a majority share in most CEEC banks stimulating economic growth to some extent. Their entry into the market has resulted in considerable benefits for the sector and the economy in general, but they had to face various challenges that arose mostly from the underdevelopment of key institutional support for banking growth.

Although accession to the European Union (EU) has helped the reform process in the CEECs, the real convergence in terms of real GDP per capita remains a challenge. In this context, we are interested to investigate whether financial development can be instrumental in reducing the gap vis-à-vis the other EU members.

The overall objective of this chapter is to investigate the relationship between financial development and economic growth in five economies from Central and Eastern Europe

Emerging Markets and the Global Economy
http://dx.doi.org/10.1016/B978-0-12-411549-1.00034-X

by estimating a dynamic panel data model in the actual context of economic crisis. It is well known that, the massive presence of foreign banks also increases contagion risks, thus, a financial crisis produced in the mature markets of the euro area also reaches the CEECs. A strategy of financial development based on foreign entry from the anchor currency area is no guarantee for a smooth process of finance and growth, an example being the current crisis that started in the mature economies in the summer of 2007 and caused a sudden stop of capital flows to Southeastern Europe (Winkler, 2009).

The achievement of the aim will be realized through the following (objectives):

- It examines the empirical linkages between financial development and economic growth using panel data for five transition countries over the period 1994–2011.
- As the financial development varies considerably across these countries, we split them into two more homogeneous groups: Central European countries (CEE-3) and Southeastern European countries (SEE-2) in order to compare the results.

The layout of the chapter is the following. Section 2 provides a brief review of the literature on the relationship between finance and growth. Section 3 discusses the data and the econometric approach, as well as the panel evidence on the nexus between financial development and economic growth. Section 4 offers some concluding remarks.

2. LITERATURE REVIEW

The relationship between financial development and economic growth has been analyzed in the literature. Most empirical studies conclude that the former, together with a more efficient banking system, accelerates the latter (Levine, 1997, 2005; Wachtel, 2001).

Goldsmith's paper (1969) was the first to show empirically the existence of a positive relationship between financial development and GDP per capita. King and Levine (1993) used mostly monetary indicators and measures of the size and relative importance of banking institutions and found a positive and significant relationship between several financial development indicators and GDP per capita growth. Levine and Zervos (1996) included measures of stock market development and found a positive partial correlation between both stock market and banking development and GDP per capita growth. More precisely, they reported a positive and significant link between the liquidity of stock markets and economic growth, but no robust relationship between the size of stock markets and economic growth. Levine et al. (2000) found that the development of financial intermediation affects growth positively, and that cross-country differences in legal and accounting system largely account for different degrees of financial development. Huang and Lin (2009) revisit the question of whether the finance-growth nexus varies with the stages of economic development. Using a novel threshold regression with the instrumental variable approach, they detect evidence for a positive linkage between financial development and economic growth, but larger in the low-income countries than in the high-income ones. Some authors have suggested that there is a positive relationship between financial deepening and per capita income in the transition economies (Égert et al., 2007; Backé et al., 2007). A positive effect of financial development on economic growth through its sources (capital accumulation and productivity), and even on income inequality and poverty, has also been reported (de Haas, 2001; Levine, 2005).

Hassan et al. (2011) provide evidence on the role of financial development in accounting for economic growth in low- and middle-income countries. They estimate panel regressions in order to examine what proxy measures of financial development are most important in accounting for economic growth over time and how much they contribute to explaining economic growth across geographic regions. The authors find a positive relationship between financial development and economic growth in developing countries. Their results are mixed: a two-way causality relationship between finance and growth for most regions and one-way causality from growth to finance for the two poorest regions.

Zhang et al. (2012) investigate the relationship between financial development and economic growth at the city level in China over the period 2001–2006. The authors using a dynamic panel data find that the most traditional indicators of financial development are positively associated with economic growth. Their findings suggest that the financial reforms that have taken place after China's accession to the World Trade Organization (WTO) are in the right direction.

Arcand et al. (2012) reexamine the relationship between financial depth and economic growth. They find a positive relationship between the size of the financial system and economic growth, but also show that, at high levels of financial depth, more finance is associated with less growth.

Few studies have focused on the transition economies from Central and Eastern Europe (Bonin and Wachtel, 2003; Bonin et al., 2005; Hermes and Lensink, 2000; Berglöf and Bolton, 2002; de Haas, 2001; Fink et al., 2009; Kenourgios and Samitas, 2007; Zagorchev et al., 2011), mostly finding a positive relationship between several financial indicators and economic growth. Hermes and Lensink (2000) provide an overview of the main relevant issues, in particular the role of stock markets in the process of financial intermediation (with an emphasis on the importance of regulation in these markets), and the role of deposit insurance to improve stability of the banking sector. Berglöf and Bolton (2002) find that the link between financial development and economic growth does not appear to be very strong during the first decade of transition, at least when one looks at the ratio of domestic credit to GDP. Kenourgios and Samitas (2007) examined the long-run relationship between finance and economic growth for Poland and concluded that credit to the private sector has been one of the main driving forces of long-run growth. Hagmayr et al. (2007) investigated the finance-growth nexus in four emerging economies of Southeastern Europe for the period 1995–2005 and found a positive and significant effect of bond markets and the capital stock on growth. Fink et al. (2009) investigated the impact of the credit, bond, and stock segments in nine

EU-accession countries for the early transition years (1996–2000) and compared these with mature market economies and to countries at an intermediate stage. They found that the transmission mechanisms differ, and that financial market segments with links to the public sector (but not to stock markets) contributed to stability and growth in the transition economies. Winkler (2009) reviews the process of rapid financial deepening and the associated vulnerability and risks for the Southeastern European countries. He argues that the strategy of pursuing financial development through the entry of foreign banks does not guarantee financial stability. Zagorchev et al. (2011) analyzed the impact of financial development and investment in information and communications technology (ICT) on the economy with a focus on eight CEECs that have passed through a series of macroeconomic structural reforms. Besides, the authors assess the effect of initial stages of financial development on the host country's GDP and economic growth. They find that financial development and investment in ICT have significant positive impacts on GDP per capita in an environment of macroeconomic structural reforms. Financial development contributes to investment in telecommunications technology (TEL) both directly and indirectly, while TEL has a weak direct contribution to financial development and an indirect contribution through a higher GDP per capita.

Finally, a strong consensus has emerged in the last decade that well-functioning financial intermediaries have a significant impact on economic growth (Bonin and Wachtel, 2003).

3. EMPIRICAL ANALYSIS OF THE FINANCIAL DEVELOPMENT AND ECONOMIC GROWTH NEXUS

In this section, we analyze the linkages between financial development/efficiency and economic growth using panel data for five transition countries during the period 1994–2011. First, we estimate the impact of financial indicators over the whole sample. Second, we split the data into subpanels corresponding to two more homogeneous groups of countries and compare the results.

3.1. The Model

To study the relationship between finance and growth, we estimate an augmented Barro-growth regression including financial development variables which takes the following form:

$$\text{GROWTH}_{i,t} = \alpha_i + \beta_i\,[\text{FINANCE}]_{i,t} + \gamma_i[\text{CONDITIONING SET}]_{i,t} + \varepsilon_{i,t}, \quad (1)$$

or

$$g_{i,t} = y_{i,t} - y_{i,t-1} = \alpha_i + \beta_i f_{i,t} + \gamma_i C_{i,t} + \mu_i + \varepsilon_{i,t}, \quad (2)$$

where y is real GDP per capita, $g_{i,t}$ its growth rate, $f_{i,t}$ an indicator of financial development, $C_{i,t}$ a set of conditioning variables, μ_i and $\varepsilon_{i,t}$ error terms, i (where $i = 1, 2, \ldots, N$) the observational unit (country), and t (where $t = 1, 2, \ldots, T$) the time period, while ε is a white noise error with zero mean, and μ a country-specific component of the error term that does not necessarily have a zero mean. The parameter α_i is the country-specific intercept which may vary across countries.

One important issue concerning the link between financial sector development and growth is the difficulty to identify proxies for measuring them. Beck et al. (2000) discuss different indicators of financial development capturing the size, activity, and efficiency of the financial sector, institutions, or markets. In our analysis, we consider several indicators, namely: the ratio of credit to the private sector to GDP as a measure of financial depth; indicators of the size of stock markets as stock market capitalization (as a percentage of GDP); monetization variables such as the ratio of broad money to GDP as a measure of the size of the financial sector; indicators of the efficiency and competitiveness of the financial system such as the margin between lending and deposit interest rates and the EBRD transition index of financial institutional development. Details are provided below.

3.1.1. Activity of the Financial Sector

The ratio of credit to the private sector to GDP (DCPS), which is the value of loans made by banks to private enterprises and households divided by GDP, is used as a measure of financial depth and banking development. This indicator isolates credit issued by banks, as opposed to credit issued by the central bank, and credit to enterprises, as opposed to credit issued to governments (Levine and Zervos, 1996).

3.1.2. Size of the Financial Sector

The stock market capitalisation to GDP ratio (STMC), which is given by the market value of listed shares divided by GDP, is used as an indicator of the size of the financial sector. Although large markets do not necessarily function effectively and taxes may distort incentives to list on the exchange, the market capitalization ratio is frequently used as an indicator of market development.

Liquid liabilities to GDP ratio (LLG), which equals liquid liabilities of the financial system divided by GDP is used as a measure of "financial depth" and thus of the overall size of the financial intermediation sector (King and Levine, 1993a).

3.1.3. Efficiency of the Financial Sector

The interest rate margin (INT), which measures the difference between deposit and lending rates in the banking market, is used to measure the efficiency of the sector.

Levine (1997) suggested several possible indicators for economic growth: real per capita GDP growth, average per capita capital stock growth, and productivity growth. Here we use real per capita GDP growth. Other variables influencing economic growth were introduced in our model, including per capita income, average education, political and stability indicators as well as indicators reflecting trade, fiscal and monetary policy such as government consumption or trade openness and inflation.

In the estimation, we used real GDP per capita with a one-year lag as initial income per capita to control for the steady-state convergence predicted by the neoclassical growth model. For human capital, we introduced a proxy for educational attainment, more precisely the secondary school enrollment ratio whose expected influence on growth is positive through its effect on productivity. International trade openness is proxied by an international trade policy variable, i.e., the trade to GDP ratio, with an expected positive coefficient. Higher openness enhances growth through higher competition and technological progress (see Winter, 2004). Inflation measures the degree of uncertainty about the future market environment, firms becoming more reluctant to make long-run commitments in the presence of higher price variability; the expected sign of this variable is therefore negative.[1]

The estimated model, which includes a proxy for financial development, is the following:

$$\begin{aligned}\mathrm{RGDPC}_{i,t} = \alpha_i &+ \beta_1\mathrm{RGDPC}_{i,t-1} + \beta_2\mathrm{INV}_{i,t} + \beta_3\mathrm{TOP}_{i,t} + \beta_4\mathrm{INFL}_{i,t} + \beta_5\mathrm{GVE}_{i,t}\\ &+\beta_6\mathrm{HC}_{i,t} + \beta_7\mathrm{DCPS}_{i,t} + \beta_8\mathrm{STMC}_{i,t} + \beta_9\mathrm{LLG}_{i,t}\\ &+\beta_{10}\mathrm{RI}_{i,t} + \beta_{11}\mathrm{INT}_{i,t} + u_i + \varepsilon_{i,t},\end{aligned} \tag{3}$$

where: RGDPC = real per capita GDP growth; RGDPC = initial income per capita; INV = investment/GDP (percentage); TOP = trade/GDP (percentage); INFL = inflation, average consumer prices; GVE = government expenditure/GDP; HC = secondary school enrollment ratio; DCPS = domestic credit to the private sector (as a percentage of GDP); STMC = stock market capitalization (as a percentage of GDP); LLG = liquid liabilities (as a percentage of GDP); RI = Reform index of financial institutional development (which is the average of the EBRD's indices of banking sector reform and of reform of non-bank financial institutions); INT = interest rate margin.

3.2. Data

Our panel consists of data for five transition countries from Central and Eastern Europe over the period 1994–2011. The data are annual and the countries included in the sample are: Bulgaria, Czech Republic, Hungary, Poland, and Romania. We also carry out the analysis for two more homogeneous subgroupings: (a) the CEE-3: the Czech Republic, Hungary, and Poland; (b) Southeastern Europe (SEE-2): Bulgaria and Romania. The data were obtained from the EBRD database and the International Monetary Fund (IFS). For more details on data sources and definitions, see the Appendix.

[1] Other study on the finance-growth nexus for the transition economies including inflation as a conditioning variable is Rousseau and Wachtel (2002).

3.3. Methodology

The most common methods for investigating the finance-growth nexus are cross-country regressions and panel data techniques. Note that the estimates of β_i (financial development indicators) can be biased for a variety of reasons, among them measurement error, reverse causation, and omitted variable bias. Therefore, a suitable estimation method should be used in order to obtain unbiased, consistent, and efficient estimates of this coefficient. To deal with these biases, researchers have utilized dynamic panel regressions with lagged values of the explanatory endogenous variables as instruments (see Beck et al., 2000; Rioja and Valev, 2004). Such methods have several advantages over cross-sectional instrumental variable regressions. In particular, they control for endogeneity and measurement error not only of the financial development variables, but also of other explanatory variables. Note also that, in the case of cross-section regressions, the lagged dependent variable is correlated with the error term if it is not instrumented (see Beck, 2008).

The dynamic panel regression takes the following form:

$$g_{i,t} = \alpha_i + \beta f_{i,t} + \gamma_1 C^1_{i,t} + \gamma_2 C^2_{i,t} + \delta y_{i,t-1} + \mu_i + \lambda_t + \varepsilon_{i,t}, \tag{4}$$

where C^1 represents a set of exogenous explanatory variables, C^2 a set of endogenous explanatory variables, and λ a vector of time dummies.

In our analysis, we employ the system GMM estimator developed by Arellano and Bover (1995), which combines a regression in differences with one in levels. Blundell and Bond (1998) present Monte Carlo evidence that the inclusion of the level regression in the estimation reduces the potential bias in finite samples and the asymptotic inaccuracy associated with the difference estimator.

The consistency of the GMM estimator depends on the validity of the instruments used in the model as well as the assumption that the error term does not exhibit serial correlation. In our case, the instruments are chosen from the lagged endogenous and explanatory variables. In order to test the validity of the selected instruments, we perform the Sargan test of overidentifying restrictions proposed by Arellano and Bond (1991). In addition, we also check for the presence of any residual autocorrelation. Finally, we perform stationarity tests belonging to the first- (Levin et al., 2002) and second-generation unit root test (Pesaran, 2007). The results suggest that all series are stationary, and consequently no co-integration analysis is necessary.[2] Therefore we proceed directly to the GMM estimation.

3.4. The Estimation Results

The dynamic panel regressions were run both for the five transition economies as a whole and the two subgroupings mentioned before. The estimation results are presented in Tables 1 and 2. The first regression represents a standard growth equation with the

[2] The results are not reported here.

GDP per capita growth rate as an endogenous variable. The results suggest that capital accumulation, i.e., investment, is the most relevant determinant of the growth process. As expected, human capital and trade openness have a positive and significant impact on economic growth, the former through improved productivity, and the latter (resulting from the signing of regional agreements) through higher competition and technological progress.

To analyze the link between financial sector development and economic growth we added to the standard growth regression (1) three financial indicators, i.e., the ratio to GDP of private credit, liquid liabilities, and stock market capitalization respectively. We find that credit to the private sector has a positive but insignificant effect on economic growth, possibly as a result of the numerous banking crises caused by the large proportion of non-performing loans (and thus unsustainable credit growth) at the beginning of the transition process in the countries of Central and Eastern Europe. However, credit granted to private companies is essential for financing investment projects, which in turn affects positively long-run growth.

Further, the stock market capitalization to GDP ratio has a positive but minor effect on economic growth. Despite an upward trend for this indicator in the CEECs during the period being investigated, their stock markets still have a small size, and it is therefore very important to attract foreign investors. The ratio of liquid liabilities as a proportion of real GDP has a positive and significant coefficient, consistently with the idea that money supply helps growth by facilitating economic activity.

As the size of the financial sector by itself might not be sufficient to estimate the role of financial development in the growth process, we added to the model two indicators of financial efficiency: the interest margin rates between the lending and deposit as a measure of efficiency in the banking sector, and the EBRD index of institutional development which measures the progress in reforming the financial sector. The former variable measures transaction costs within the sector but may also reflect an improvement in the quality of borrowers in the economy. If the margin declines due to a decrease in transaction costs, the share of saving going to investment increases and economic growth accelerates. Both these variables appear to be significant. The margin between lending and deposit interest rates is negatively correlated with economic growth, consistently with theory. This means that a shrinking interest margin rate can increase economic growth. In all transition countries from Central and Eastern Europe, the efficiency increased over time but reached different levels, depending on the privatization methods and the influence of more efficient foreign banks (see Matousek and Taci, 2005; Bonin et al., 2005). The other financial efficiency indicator, i.e., the EBRD index, has a positive effect, implying that reforms in the banking and financial sector, such as market regulation and monitoring, increase economic growth. The results for the two subgroups are reported in Table 2. The private credit to GDP ratio is found to have a positive but insignificant effect in all groups. As for stock market capitalization, this has a positive, small effect in

Table 1 The financial development and economic growth nexus: dynamic panel regression.

Variables	(1) RGDPC	(2) RGDPC	(3) RGDPC
L.RGDPC	0.267	0.215	0.195
	(6.20)***	(5.13)***	(4.11)***
INV	0.325	0.314	0.297
	(5.67)***	(5.13)***	(4.75)***
TOP	0.079	0.071	0.062
	(2.16)**	(2.21)**	(2.37)**
INFL	−0.016	−0.014	−0.011
	(2.61)**	(2.97)***	(3.67)***
GVE	−0.050	−0.051	−0.052
	(2.59)**	(2.79)***	(4.74)***
HC	0.036	0.027	0.018
	(5.65)***	(4.13)***	(3.72)***
DCPS	–	0.007	0.005
		(0.37)	(0.11)
STMC	–	0.025	0.018
		(2.43)**	(2.23)**
LLG	–	0.07	0.011
		(1.97)**	(2.31)**
RI	–	–	0.029
			(1.75)*
INT	–	–	−0.027
			(3.20)***
Constant	0.116	0.211	−0.032
	(6.19)***	(4.12)***	(0.47)
Observations	90	90	90
Arellano-Bond AR(2)	−0.25	0.18	0.39
Prob > z	(0.762)	(0.712)	(0.649)
Sargan test chi2	23.12	27.45	39.20
Prob > chi2	(0.391)	(0.314)	(0.203)

Absolute value of z statistics in parentheses.
*Significant at 10%.
**Significant at 5%.
***Significant at 1%.

the case of the CEE-3 countries, and a still positive but insignificant one in the SEE-2. In the former group, the stock market expanded more rapidly due to early privatization and the entry of foreign investors, but it is still relatively underdeveloped.

Table 2 The financial sector and economic growth nexus in the two subgroups: dynamic panel regression.

Variables	**Subgroup**	
	CEE-3	**SEE-2**
	(1)	**(3)**
	RGDPC	**RGDPC**
L1.RGDPC	0.329	−0.135
	(4.56)***	(0.49)
INV	0.225	0.072
	(5.01)	(7.21)
TOP	0.068	0.059
	(2.63)**	(0.36)
INFL	−0.027	−0.054
	(1.69)*	(3.65)
GVE	−0.045	−0.218
	(1.57)	(3.99)
HC	0.039	0.070
	(2.55)	(1.72)
DCPS	0.089	0.061
	(1.50)	(0.98)
STMC	0.028	0.007
	(2.57)	(1.34)
LLG	0.009	0.005
	(1.95)	(1.73)
RI	1.059	0.293
	(3.71)	(2.26)
INT	−0.041	−0.092
	(2.81)	(5.01)
Constant	0.085	0.142
	(2.35)	(1.22)
Observations	54	36
Arellano-Bond AR (2)	−0.62	−1.15
Prob > z	(0.510)	(0.189)
Sargan test chi2	9.23	6.62
Prob > chi2	(0.179)	(0.205)

Absolute value of z statistics in parentheses.
*Significant at 10%.
**Significant at 5%.
***Significant at 1%.

The index of financial institutional development also has a positive effect in all groups, especially so in the CEE-3, followed by the SEE-2, reforms of the financial system being more advanced in the former group. Monetization is also significantly and positively correlated with real per capita GDP growth in all two cases.

In most high-income countries with developed banking sectors, the ratio of broad money to GDP is at least 60% (Bonin and Wachtel, 2003). In the transition countries, the highest monetization ratio in 2007 was found in Slovenia (75.4), and the lowest in Romania (36.6).[3] The degree of monetization can be seen as an indicator of macroeconomic stability, which represents an incentive for foreign investors.

The efficiency of the banking sector has an important role in economic growth. This indicator is negatively correlated with economic growth in all cases. Achieving higher efficiency remains a challenge for these two groups of countries. The CEE-3 has recorded an increase of this indicator due to the early privatization of the banking sector and the entry of foreign banks. The SEE-2 countries instead have started privatization later and seen high interest rate margins during the transition period (for example, 20.8 in Romania in 2000 in comparison with 7.2 in Poland and 2.1 in Hungary).[4]

Our findings are generally in the line with those of previous studies, i.e., a positive impact of several financial development on economic growth (Kenourgios and Samitas, 2007; Huang and Lin, 2009; Arcand et al., 2012). However, the analysis of two groups of countries allows us to highlight the heterogeneity between countries and how much the proxy measures of financial development vary across regions. Overall, underdevelopment of the stock and credit markets, and therefore lack of financial depth, remains one of the main features of these countries compared with the other EU countries.

4. CONCLUSIONS

In this chapter, we have reviewed the main features of the banking and financial sector in five new EU members, and then investigated the relationship between financial development and economic growth in these economies by estimating a dynamic panel data model over the period 1994–2011. To summarize, financial depth is found to be lacking in all five countries, and therefore the contribution of the relatively underdeveloped credit and stock markets to growth has been rather limited, with only a minor positive effect of some indicators of financial development. This might be a consequence of the large stock of non-performing loans and the banking crises experienced by these economies at the beginning of the transition period. In general, the CEE-3 have more developed financial sectors than the SEE-2 countries. By contrast, the implementation of reforms, the entry of foreign banks, and the privatization of state-owned banks have reduced transaction costs and increased credit availability. This has improved the efficiency of the banking sector (Fries et al., 2006), which has played an important role as an engine of growth. Better regulation and supervision was partly motivated by the European integration process and the need to adopt EU standards. Thus, many of the banking sector weaknesses traditionally characterizing emerging markets have gradually been eliminated. Given the prospect of EU accession, foreign banks, mainly from the euro area, seized the opportunity

[3] European Bank for Reconstruction and Development (EBRD).

[4] Authors' calculation using EBRD database.

and established subsidiaries in all CEECs, seeing them as an extension of the common European market and becoming dominant players in their banking sectors.

However, the massive presence of foreign banks has also increased contagion risks, and the consolidation process (with the majority of banks being foreign-owned) could limit competition. Thus, a financial crisis produced in the mature markets of the euro area could also reach the CEECs. A strategy of financial development based on foreign entry from the anchor currency area is no guarantee for a smooth process of finance and growth, an example being the current crisis which started in the mature economies in the summer of 2007.

APPENDIX

See Table A1.

Table A1 List of variables.

VARIABLE (Series)		Source
CODE	NOM	
BCPS	Bank credit to the public sector as a percentage of GDP	IFS database
DCPS	Domestic credit to private sector (in percent of GDP)	EBRD database
GDPC	GDP per capita (in PPP)	EBRD database
GVE	General government expenditure to GDP	EBRD database
HC	Secondary school enrollment ratio	UNESCO database
HCR	Domestic credit to households (in percent of GDP)	EBRD database
IBR	EBRD index of banking sector reform	EBRD database
INFL	Inflation, average consumer prices	IMF database
INV	Investment/GDP (in percent)	EBRD database
INT	Interest margin rates between lending and deposit (in percent)	Authors' calculation using EBRD database
LLG	Liquid Liabilities (in percent of GDP)	EBRD database
LR	Lending rate (average)	EBRD database
NPL	Non-performing loans (in percent of total loans)	EBRD database
PCFB	Asset share of foreign-owned banks (in percent)	Authors' calculation using EBRD database
RGDPC	Real GDP per capita growth	Authors' calculation using EBRD database
RI	Reform index of financial institutional development	Authors' calculation using EBRD database
STMC	Stock market capitalization (in percent of GDP)	EBRD database
TOP	Trade openness to GDP	EBRD database

ACKNOWLEDGMENT

We are very grateful to an anonymous referee for his useful comments and suggestions.

REFERENCES

Arcand, J.-L., Berkes, E., Panizza, U., 2012. Too much finance? IMF Working Paper WP/12/161. International Monetary Fund, Washington, D.C.

Arellano, M., Bond, S., 1991. Some tests of specification for panel data: Monte Carlo evidence and an application to employment equations. Review of Economic Studies 58 (2), 277–297

Arellano, M., Bover, O., 1995. Another look at the instrumental variable estimation of error-components models. Journal of Econometrics 68 (1), 29–51

Backé, P., Égert, B., Walko, Z., 2007. Credit growth in Central and Eastern Europe. Policy Research Working Paper Series 4638, The World Bank.

Beck, T., 2008. The econometrics of finance and growth. Policy Research Working Paper Series 4608, The World Bank.

Beck, T., Demirgüç-Kunt, A., Levine, R., 2000. A new database on the structure and development of the financial sector. World Bank Economic Review 14 (3), 597–605

Berglöf, E., Bolton, P., 2002. The great divide and beyond: financial architecture in transition. The Journal of Economic Perspectives 16 (1), 77–100

Blundell, R., Bond, S., 1998. Initial conditions and moment restrictions in dynamic panel data models. Journal of Econometrics 87 (1), 115–143

Bonin, J., Wachtel, P., 2003. Financial sector development in transition economies: lessons from the first decade. Financial Markets, Institutions and Instruments 12 (1), 1–66

Bonin, J., Hasan, I., Wachtel, P., 2005. Privatisation matters: bank performance in transition countries. Journal of Banking and Finance 29, 2153–2178

de Haas, R.T.A., 2001. Financial development and economic growth in transition economies. A Survey of the Theoretical and Empirical Literature. Research Series Supervision 35, Netherlands Central Bank.

Égert, B., Backé, P., Zumer, T., 2007. Private-sector credit in Central and Eastern Europe: new (over) shooting stars? Comparative Economic Studies 49 (2), 201–231

Fink, G., Haiss, P., Vuksic, G., 2009. Contribution of financial market segments at different stages of development: transition, cohesion and mature economies compared. Journal of Financial Stability 5 (4), 431–455

Fries, S., Neven, D.J., Seabright, P., Taci, A., 2006. Market entry, privatization and bank performance in transition. Economics of Transition 14 (4), 579–610

Goldsmith, R.W., 1969. Financial Structure and Development. Yale University Press, New Haven

Hagmayr, B., Haiss, P.R., Sumegi, K., 2007. Financial sector development and economic growth–evidence for Southeastern Europe. EuropaInstitut Working Paper.

Hassan, M.K., Sanchez, B., Yu, J., 2011. Financial development and economic growth: new evidence from panel data. Quarterly Review of Economics and Finance 5, 88–104

Hermes, N., Lensink, R., 2000. Financial system development in transition economies. Journal of Banking and Finance 24 (4), 507–524

Huang, H.-C., Lin, S.-C., 2009. Non-linear finance–growth nexus: a threshold with instrumental variable approach. Economics of Transition 17 (3), 439–466

Kenourgios, D., Samitas, A., 2007. Financial development and economic growth in a transition economy: evidence for Poland. Journal of Financial Decision Making 3 (1), 35–48

King, R.G., Levine, R., 1993a. Finance, entrepreneurship, and growth: theory and evidence. Journal of Monetary Economics 32 (3), 513–542

King, R.G., Levine, R., 1993b. Finance and growth: Schumpeter might be right. Quarterly Journal of Economics 108 (3), 717–737

Levine, R., 1997. Financial development and economic growth: views and agenda. Journal of Economic Literature 35 (2), 688–726

Levine, R., 2005. Finance and growth: theory and evidence. In: Aghion, P., Durlauf, S. (Eds.). Handbook of Economic Growth, vol. 1 pp. 865–934

Levine, R., Zervos, S., 1996. Stock market development and long-run growth. World Bank Economic Review 10 (2), 323–339

Levine, R., Loayza, N., Beck, T., 2000. Financial intermediation and growth: causality and causes. Journal of Monetary Economics 46 (1), 31–77

Levin, A., Lin, C.F., Chu, C.S., 2002. Unit root tests in panel data: asymptotic and finite sample properties. Journal of Econometrics 108 (1), 1–24

Lucas, R.E., 1988. On the mechanics of economic development. Journal of Monetary Economics 22 (1), 3–42

Matousek, R., Taci, A., 2005. Efficiency in banking: empirical evidence from the Czech Republic. Economic Change and Restructuring 37 (3), 225–244

Pesaran, H.M., 2007. A simple panel unit root test in the presence of cross-section dependence. Journal of Applied Econometrics 22 (2), 265–312

Rioja, F., Valev, N., 2004. Does one size fit all? A reexamination of the finance and growth relationship. Journal of Development Economics 74 (2), 429–447

Robinson, J., 1952. The generalization of the general theory. In: The Rate of Interest and Other Essays. Macmillan, London, pp. 69–142

Rousseau, P.L., Wachtel, P., 2002. Inflation thresholds and the finance-growth nexus. Journal of International Money and Finance 21 (6), 777–793

Wachtel, P., 2001. Growth and finance: what do we know and how do we know it? International Finance 4 (3), 335–362

Winkler, A., 2009. Southeastern Europe: financial deepening, Foreign banks and sudden stops in capital flows. Focus on European Economic Integration 1, 84–97

Winter, L.A., 2004. Trade liberalization and economic performance: an overview. Economic Journal 114, 4–21

Zagorchev, A., Vasconcellos, G., Bae, Y., 2011. Financial development, technology, growth and performance: evidence from the accession to the EU. Journal of International Financial Markets, Institutions and Money 21 (5), 743–759

Zhang, J., Wang, L., Wang, S., 2012. Financial development and economic growth: recent evidence from China. Journal of Comparative Economics 40 (3), 393–412

CHAPTER 35

Financial Market Integration of ASEAN-5 with China and India

Kee Tuan Teng[*], Siew Hwa Yen[†], Soo Y. Chua[‡], and Hooi Hooi Lean[‡]

[*]Economics & Corporate Administration Department, Faculty of Accountancy, Finance & Business, Tunku Abdul Rahman University College, Penang, Malaysia
[†]Economic Section, School of Distance Education, Universiti Sains Malaysia, Penang, Malaysia
[‡]Economics Programme, School of Social Sciences, Universiti Sains Malaysia, Penang, Malaysia

1. INTRODUCTION

The significant impact of China's stock market correction on February 27, 2007 on the world stock markets has raised concern among the ASEAN-5 investors.[1] On the other hand, little impact was felt by China and India from the plunge in the world stock markets in July–August 2011 as a result of the European sovereign debt crisis, the US economic slowdown, and the downgrading of the US credit rating. This stock market fall, however, had an apparent impact on the US, Japan, and Thailand. Hence, this raised the following questions: "When China and India sneeze, will ASEAN-5 catch cold?" "Will they become more regionally integrated in their financial markets? If yes, since when have these two regions become more integrated naturally?"

The Chinese and Indian stock markets remain isolated from the recent Global financial crisis and the previous 1997 Asian financial crisis, thus, implying the importance of the Chinese and Indian economies at both regional and global levels (McKinnon and Schnabl, 2002; Gupta and Guidi, 2012). Hence, it is vital to look at their foreign portfolio investment inflow as presented in Table 1. A sudden withdrawal of foreign portfolio investment might lead to a crisis in the stock market, which might cause a chain effect on other stock markets.

The inflow of foreign portfolio investments to the Chinese and Indian stock markets has risen noticeably since 1991, with a minimum of sixfold in 2011. Both countries' inflows of portfolio equity remained sustainable with a few significant drops but were able to rebound to the previous level. However, the Indian stock market experienced a negative portfolio equity net inflow in 1998, 2008, and 2011, which coincided with the Asian financial crisis, the US subprime crisis, and the European sovereign debt crisis, respectively. The portfolio equity net inflow in Japan was higher than the US in the 1990s but in the early 2000s, its inflow was significantly lower than the US. Their net

[1] In this study, ASEAN-5 refers to the five founding members of the Association of Southeast Asian Nations, which are Indonesia, Malaysia, the Philippines, Singapore, and Thailand.

Emerging Markets and the Global Economy
http://dx.doi.org/10.1016/B978-0-12-411549-1.00035-1

Table 1 Foreign portfolio equity, net inflows for selected countries (BoP, current US$ million).

	1991	1992	1993	1994	1995	1996	1997	1998	1999	2000	2001	2002	2003	2004	2005	2006	2007	2008	2009	2010	2011
China							5,657	765	612	6,912	849	2,249	7,729	10,923	20,569	42,861	18,478	8,464	29,116	31,357	5,308
India	4	283	1,369	5,491	1,590	3,958	2,555	-601	2,317	2,481	2,949	1,063	8,216	9,053	12,151	9,509	32,862	-15,030	24,688	30,442	-4,137
Japan	46,619	8,878	19,856	48,947	50,597	49,450	27,001	16,114	103,886	-1,285	39,100	-16,689	87,775	98,279	131,315	71,437	45,454	-69,691	12,431	40,328	5,644
United States	10,420	-5,610	20,940	890	16,523	11,057	67,033	41,958	112,289	193,600	121,464	54,067	33,981	61,788	89,258	145,482	275,617	126,805	219,303	177,566	27,350
Indonesia			1,805	1,900	1,493	1,819	-4,987	-4,371	-782	-1,021	442	876	1,130	2,042	-165	1,897	3,558	322	787	2,131	-326
Malaysia												-55	1,339	4,509	-1,199	2,355	-669	-10,715	-448		
Philippines						2,101	-406	264	489	-202	125	227	500	518	1,465	2,525	3,178	-1,289	-1,096	503	1,038
Singapore	-241	1,398	2,759	168	-159	677	-444	1,001	3,118	-1,168	-89	-441	2,785	23,823	4,905	10,062	18,062	-11,657	962	1,181	-3,754
Thailand	37	455	2,678	-393	2,253	1,123	3,867	289	944	900	351	538	1,786	1,319	5,121	5,242	4,268	-3,802	1,694	3,214	874

Source: International Monetary Fund, Balance of Payments database, and World Bank, International Debt Statistics, http://data.worldbank.org/indicator/BX.PEF.TOTL.CD.WD/countries

Remarks: portfolio equity includes net inflows from equity securities other than those recorded as direct investment and including shares, stocks, depository receipts (American or global), and direct purchases of shares in local stock markets by foreign investors. The gray areas indicate that data are not available.

inflow picked up again in 2003 but plunged to a negative value in 2008. As for the US net inflows for portfolio equity were quite stable throughout 1991–2011 but faced a substantial reduction during the bond crisis in 1994, the collapse of Internet bubble, and the subprime crisis. The net inflow of foreign portfolio investments for ASEAN-5 was volatile and most countries in ASEAN-5 experienced prolonged negative value of net inflow during the period of the Asian financial crisis, the stock market meltdown in 2000–2002, and the subprime crisis. In view of the sustainable rise in the foreign portfolio investments' net inflow to China and India, it is worth investigating the level of integration between the Chinese and Indian financial markets with the stock markets in ASEAN-5. Will ASEAN-5 benefit by diversifying their equity portfolios in China and India?

Drawing upon the importance of China and India stock markets highlighted above, this study intends to analyze the possible changes in the direction and degree of financial integration of ASEAN-5 with the four economies, China, India, the US, and Japan using the Dynamic Conditional Correlation Multivariate Generalized Autoregressive Conditional Heteroskedasticity (DCC-MGARCH) model. Alternatively, the Bai and Perron (BP) (1998, 2003) multiple structural breaks test will be adopted to date the significant changes in the level of financial integration among the countries in the study and the events that naturally affect the correlation between the countries.

The DCC-MGARCH model is practical as it is time-variant and generates fewer parameters with the increase in model dimension. It also overcomes the main weaknesses in other MGARCH models such as Vector-GARCH (VEC-GARCH) model by Bollerslev et al. (1988) and Baba-Engle-Kraft-Kroner (BEKK) model by Engle and Kroner (1995). This is because the number of parameters generated by most of the MGARCH models mentioned above will increase with the rise in the model dimension. This problem leads to difficulties in computation, convergence, and result interpretation.[2] The DCC-MGARCH is relatively parsimonious to other MGARCH models (scalar BEKK, diagonal BEKK, exponential smoothing, and orthogonal GARCH) and the empirical results obtained from this model are more sensible (Engle, 2002; Silvennoinen and Teräsvirta, 2008; Arouri and Nguyen, 2009). The DCC-MGARCH is relatively superior to other MGARCH models as it fulfills the four basic objectives (parsimonious, flexibility, no excessive inversion of matrices, and positive definite conditional covariance matrices) of the MGARCH model. In addition, this approach possesses the flexibility of univariate GARCH with its two-step estimation procedure, which makes it practically interesting as it can generate a univariate model as well as a multivariate model with the same set of data input.

Several studies have produced estimates of international stock markets co-movement and integration (Gjerde and Saettem, 1999; Pagan and Harding, 2002; Edwards et al., 2003)

[2] For detail discussion on the MGARCH models, see Engle (2002) and Silvennoinen and Teräsvirta (2008).

with relatively static approaches such as the co-integration test, vector autoregression (VAR), constant conditional correlations-MGARCH (CCC-MGARCH) model, and concordance index. These models are still insufficient in capturing the dynamic feature in the financial markets and failed to quantify the extent of co-movement in the financial series, although it is vastly used in the literature.[3] As an alternative, this study employs the DCC-MGARCH model developed by Engle (2002) due to its suitability in explaining the dynamic features of the cross-market linkages. It is also more relevant and practical to use the DCC-MGARCH model to study international portfolio diversification and risk management.

Another contribution of this study is the endogenous detection of structural break dates in the time-paths of conditional correlation between economies. Most of the studies normally pre-determined the event and tested its significance on the tested pair of countries. This study chose to let the correlation series between countries to tell which event affected them naturally, which is more accurate for assessing the impact of the event on the pairs of countries. Furthermore, economic liberalization occurs gradually in stages and the integration process cannot be identified by a single date. It is important to link the break dates of the pair of markets to what is happening in these markets that eventually makes them more integrated. BP (1998, 2003) multiple structural breaks test answered the difficulty in dating the integration process that links and explains the correlation between two countries.

The rest of this study is structured as follows: Section 2 briefly looks at the empirical studies in financial integration. Section 3 presents the methodology and describes the data. Section 4 reports the results and the last section concludes the study.

2. LITERATURE REVIEW

Since the mid-2000s, the world financial markets were subjected to a series of major financial crises, namely the US subprime crisis in 2008 and the European sovereign debt crisis in 2010. The mentioned financial crises originated from the developed economies and these events seem to affect the developed economies most while the emerging economies were mildly affected (Wong and Li, 2010).[4] It is important to note that the spillover of financial crises from developed countries has the tendency to be swirled around developed countries (Beirne et al., 2009). By looking at the degree of contemporaneous co-movement for countries affected by these crises, financial markets seem to be slowly evolving into regional as well as global integration (Phylaktis and Ravazzolo, 2002).

[3] The constant conditional correlations-MGARCH model is restrictive in its assumption where the conditional correlation is non-time-varying.

[4] The emerging countries involved are ASEAN and China.

McKinnon and Schnabl (2002) and Forbes and Rigobon (2002) found that China stood out to be a natural stabilizer in the Asian region during the 1997 Asian financial crisis, because China was not affected by the crisis. The possibility of external financial turmoil influencing China's stock market is relatively low because China's stock market is still isolated from the rest of the world (Huang et al., 2000; Yu et al., 2010; Huyghebaert and Wang, 2010). This conclusion is also supported by the findings of Beirne et al. (2009) and Azad (2009). Both findings demonstrated that volatility spillover from mature markets (the US and Japan) to emerging markets (China) tends to be incomplete and not contagious. Furthermore, China's stock market is predictable (Azad, 2009). Hence, it is beneficial for international investors to diversify their asset portfolios in China. This piece of recommendation is only practical during the tranquil period in China but not during the period of financial turmoil in the country as shown in Wang et al. (2011), which noted that China's financial instability potentially affects its neighboring country (Japan). Beirne et al. (2009) found that the volatility in emerging markets (ASEAN-5, China and India) during the turbulent period is relatively lower than the mature markets. Nishimura and Men (2010) observed that there is a possibility of China's stock market influencing the G5 stock markets but not the other way around (Huyghebaert and Wang, 2010). The results obtained by Huyghebaert and Wang (2010) contradicted with those of Forbes and Rigobon (2002), which detected that the US stock market volatility has significant spillover to China in the 1990s. The contradictory findings are mainly due to the different time-period when the two studies were conducted. China's economy has been developing rapidly in the last decade (2000–2010) and it has overtaken Japan in 2010 as the second largest economy in the world.

3. DATA AND METHODOLOGY

3.1. Data Description

Monthly data for the stock market indices, which covers the period of January 1991 to June 2010, were obtained from DataStream. The market indices for the emerging and developed economies are Shanghai Stock Exchange Composite Index (SHCI), Bombay Stock Exchange (BSE), Dow Jones Industrial Index (DJII), and Nikkei 225 Stock Average Price Index (NIK). The stock markets indices for the ASEAN-5 are Jakarta Stock Exchange Composite Stock Price Index (JSE), Kuala Lumpur Stock Exchange Composite Price index (KLCI), the Philippines Stock Exchange Composite Price index (PSE), Straits Times Stock Exchange Index of Singapore (SSI) and Bangkok Stock Exchange Price Index (THSE).[5]

To ensure correct model specification and to avoid the possibility of obtaining misleading results, all series used in this study and those series generated by the DCC-MGARCH

[5] Four multivariate models are formed to discuss the stock markets' interdependency: Model 1 = ASEAN-5 with SHCI, model 2 = ASEAN-5 with BSE, model 3 = ASEAN-5 with DJII, and model 4 = ASEAM-5 with NIK.

model are validated by a range of diagnostic tests as shown in Table 2. The stock markets in the emerging economies (China and India) had higher positive average returns compared to the US and ASEAN-5, except Japan showing a negative average market return of 0.43%. The standard deviation of stock market returns was particularly high for China (13.26%), which implies that China's stock market could be highly volatile and has high inherent risk. This indicates that investing in China's stock market could be profitable if one is able to manage his or her risk-adjustment portfolio wisely. If the investors from ASEAN-5 invested in India's stock markets, the risks will be almost halved compared to the risks faced in China's stock market. This is because the values of the standard deviations of ASEAN-5 and India's stock market returns are almost half of China's stock market returns. The data indicate that risk in the US stock market was the lowest followed by Japan's stock market.

Most of the stock returns in this study show negative skewness except for the Philippines, China, and India. This suggests that investment in the Philippines, China, and Indian stock markets may have a high probability of earning positive returns. All stock market returns had a leptokurtic distribution, which means the stock markets might generate either very huge or very small future returns. This is shown by the positive excess kurtosis obtained from the analysis. Investment in these stock markets is highly volatile especially in China.

The Jarque-Bera normality test is highly significant, which means that all the return series are not normally distributed. The null hypothesis of the absence of ARCH effects was rejected at lag 12 for most of the stock return series except at lag 1 for NIK, at lag 10 for PSE, and at lag 16 for SHCI. The results imply that all series indicate the presence of ARCH effects, which justified the choice of the GARCH model.

The Q-statistics of the Ljung-Box test are significant at lag 12 for all series except for the stock market index for India and the US, the Philippines and Thailand. The null hypothesis of no serial correlation for India and the US was rejected at lag 15 and lag 18, respectively. As for the Philippines and Thailand, the null hypothesis could not be rejected up to lag 20. The first-order autocorrelations are low for SHCI, DJII and THSE. This indicates that the first-order autoregressive process, AR(1), needs to be included in the mean equation of GARCH (1,1) model (Hamilton and Gang, 1996; Arouri and Nguyen, 2009).[6]

To ascertain the stationarity of the data, the ADF test was conducted at levels and at first differences of the series. The results in Table 2 show that the null hypothesis of non-stationarity could not be rejected up to lag 12 at levels. We can therefore conclude that all the raw series for this study are non-stationary at levels. The presence of a unit root for all raw series implies the suitability to model the series at the first difference as the series become stationary after first differencing. Hence, this study uses the first

[6] Most studies typically assume the errors of the return series either follow an AR(1) or first-order moving average, MA (1) process.

Table 2 Descriptive statistics.

Panel A	SHCI	BSE	DJII	NIK
Mean	1.25%	1.24%	0.56%	−0.43%
Variance	1.76%	0.73%	0.14%	0.34%
Std dev.	13.26%	8.54%	3.79%	5.80%
Skewness	2.1429***	0.2290	−0.8060***	−0.1666
Excess Kurtosis	13.3622***	1.8808***	1.3881***	0.7053**
Jarque-Bera	1919.9430***	36.5372***	44.1197***	5.9326*
Autocorrelation lag				
1	−0.0031	0.1048	0.0437	0.0947
2	0.1005	0.0857	0.0254	−0.0338
3	−0.0662	−0.0302	0.1195	0.1271
4	−0.0158	0.0201	0.0725	0.0103
5	−0.0215	0.1024	0.0476	0.0245
6	0.0010	0.0654	−0.0361	−0.0656
Ljung-Box Q-statistics	24.8830**	25.4040**	26.2080*	26.4600***
(order)	(12)	(15)	(18)	(12)
Engle ARCH test	60.5455***	37.5687***	19.6939*	3.9464**
(order)	(16)	(12)	(12)	(1)
ADF test statistic	−1.1521	1.1438	0.6927	−1.5595
(Level)	(4)	(0)	(0)	(0)
ADF test statistic	−5.2029 ***	−14.0234 ***	−13.3342 ***	−14.5501 ***
(1st dif)	(0)	(0)	(0)	(0)

Panel B	JSE	KLCI	PSE	SSI	THSE
Mean	0.80%	0.42%	0.71%	0.46%	0.10%
Variance	0.65%	0.49%	0.62%	0.33%	0.80%
Std dev.	8.06%	7.01%	7.89%	5.73%	8.95%
Skewness	−0.9277***	−0.0313	0.3501**	−0.0428	−0.1346
Excess Kurtosis	2.3971***	3.4380***	4.9036***	2.2934***	1.6249***
Jarque-Bera	89.5864***	115.2826***	239.2224***	51.3525***	26.4493**
Autocorrelation lag					
1	0.1800	0.1378	0.1230	0.1755	0.0719
2	−0.0585	0.1492	0.0474	0.1605	0.0437
3	0.0620	−0.1585	−0.0547	0.0027	0.0083
4	0.1299	−0.0251	0.0190	0.1386	0.0027
5	−0.0043	−0.0271	0.0408	−0.0035	−0.0434
6	0.0138	−0.0222	0.0269	−0.0089	0.0011
Ljung-Box Q-statistics	34.5870***	55.5230***	12.6820	26.7590***	11.8930
(order)	(12)	(12)	(12)	(12)	(12)
Engle ARCH test	43.8463***	69.2555***	6.1588**	26.9706***	38.9861***
(order)	(12)	(12)	(10)	(12)	(12)
ADF test statistic	0.4534	0.3630	0.2839	0.2164	−0.5250
(Level)	(3)	(0)	(0)	(1)	(0)
ADF test statistic	−5.9488 ***	−8.2686 ***	−15.0401 ***	−12.2522 ***	−15.3802 ***
(1st dif)	(2)	(1)	(0)	(0)	(0)

Notes: lag length is given in parentheses. For the ADF test, MAXLAG = 14, Automatic based on SIC.
*Significant at 10%.
**Significant at 5%.
***Significant at 1%.

difference of the natural logarithm of the stock market index, which indicates the return of the series.

3.2. Dynamic Conditional Correlation—Multivariate Generalized Autoregressive Conditional Heteroskedasticity (DCC-MGARCH) Model Specification

The DCC-MGARCH approach has been used to reveal the financial interdependency among countries.[7] The DCC-MGARCH model generates the volatility correlation between two markets directly through its conditional variance. The MGARCH model can simultaneously consider the n return series' volatility and correlation on time dependence. The DCC-MGARCH model is a dynamic model with time-varying means, variances, and covariances of the return series, $r_{i,t}$ for country i at time, t with equations as follows:

$$r_{i,t} = \mu_{i,t} + \varepsilon_{i,t},$$
$$\mu_{i,t} = E(r_{i,t}|\Psi_{t-1}) = E_{t-1}(r_{i,t}), \quad \varepsilon_{i,t}|\Psi_{t-1} \sim N(0, \mathrm{H_t}), \tag{1}$$

where Ψ_{t-1} is the set of information available at time $t-1$, at least containing $\{r_{i,t-1}, r_{i,t-2}, \ldots\}$. $H_t = E(\varepsilon_t \varepsilon_t' |\Psi_{t-1})$ is the $(n \times n)$ conditional variance matrix associated with the error vector ε_t' where ε_t' is a $(n \times 1)$ vector with zero mean return error conditional on the set of information available at time $t-1$.

The return series for each individual country follows an autoregressive process (Arouri and Nguyen, 2009; Hamilton and Gang, 1996). The conditional mean equation of the return series for country i is $\mu_{i,t} = \lambda_0 + \lambda_1 r_{i,t-1}$ where λ_0 is a constant term and λ_1 is the coefficient of the lagged return for each market. It is a function of its own past returns and denotes the lagged relationship.

For the DCC-MGARCH model, the conditional variance-covariance matrix, H_t, is written as $H_t = D_t R_t D_t$ where H_t is also denoted as the conditional correlation estimator. D_t is a $(n \times n)$ diagonal matrix of time-varying standard deviations of the returns in the mean equation from the univariate GARCH (1,1) model. $D_t = diag(\sqrt{h_{i,t}})$, where $h_{i,t}$ is the time-varying conditional volatility of the return series for country i at time t (Bollerslev, 1990). Thus, D_t for a multivariate model is expressed as $D_t = diag\left(\sqrt{h_{1,t}}, \ldots, \sqrt{h_{n,t}}\right)$ with $h_{i,t} = \tau_i + \alpha_i \varepsilon_{i,t-1}^2 + \beta_i h_{i,t-1}$ where τ_i is a constant term for the conditional variance equation for country i, α_i is the ARCH effect of the return series, which is the volatility from the previous period on the volatility of the present period due to a shock. β_i is the GARCH effect of the return series, which is the impact of the forecasted variance from the last period. A positive coefficient of β_i, implies volatility clustering and persistency in positive changes in stock market indices. The sum of α_i and β_i of the univariate GARCH indicates the persistency of the volatility shock.

[7] The computer package OxMetrics 5.1 with G@RCH 6.0 module is used for the DCC-MGARCH estimation procedure.

R_t of the DCC model is a $(n \times n)$ time-varying conditional correlation matrix and the conditional variance must be unity.[8] The matrix of R_t contains the coefficients of conditional correlation, given by $R_t = diag(Q_t)^{-1} Q_t diag(Q_t)^{-1}$ where $Q_t \equiv (q_i)_t$ is a conditional covariance matrix; Q_t is a $(n \times n)$ matrix which is symmetric and positive definite given by $Q_t = \left(1 - \alpha_{dcc} + \beta_{dcc}\right)\overline{Q} + \alpha_{dcc}\left(\varepsilon_{t-1}\varepsilon'_{t-1}\right) + \beta_{dcc} Q_{t-1}$ where $\overline{Q}$ denotes the unconditional covariances of the standardized errors matrix, which is a $(n \times n)$ symmetric positive definite matrix, and $\varepsilon_t = (\varepsilon_{1,t}, \ldots, \varepsilon_{n,t})'$ is the standardized residual terms.[9] The model is mean reverting when $(\alpha_{dcc} + \beta_{dcc}) < 1$. If $(\alpha_{dcc} + \beta_{dcc}) = 1$, the model is said to be integrated.

Engle (2002) suggested the estimation of time-varying conditional correlations $(q_{ij,t})$ for any two return series included in R_t by the following GARCH (1, 1) process:

$$q_{ij,t} = \overline{\rho}_{ij} + \alpha_{dcc}(\varepsilon_{i,t-1}\varepsilon_{j,t-1} - \overline{\rho}_{ij}) + \beta_{dcc}(q_{ij,t-1} - \overline{\rho}_{ij}), \tag{2}$$

where $\overline{\rho}_{ij}$ is the unconditional correlation between $\varepsilon_{i,t}$ and $\varepsilon_{j,t}$, and $\overline{q}_{ij,t}$ is the mean value of $q_{ij,t}$. The average variance is unity and the conditional correlation estimator is $\rho_{ij,t} = \frac{q_{ij,t}}{\sqrt{q_{ii,t}q_{jj,t}}}$. Hence the conditional correlation coefficient between $r_{i,t}$ and $r_{j,t}$ is computed as follows:

$$\begin{aligned} q_{ij,t} = \mathrm{E}(\varepsilon_{i,t}\varepsilon_{j,t}|\Psi_{t-1}) &= \frac{E(\varepsilon_{i,t}\varepsilon_{j,t}|\Psi_{t-1})}{\sqrt{E(\varepsilon^2_{i,t}|\Psi_{t-1})E(\varepsilon^2_{j,t}|\Psi_{t-1})}} \\ &= \frac{E(r_{i,t}r_{j,t}|\Psi_{t-1})}{\sqrt{E(r^2_{i,t}|\Psi_{t-1})E(r^2_{j,t}|\Psi_{t-1})}} = Corr(r_{i,t}r_{j,t}|\Psi_{t-1}) = \rho_{ij,t} = [R_t]_{ij}, \end{aligned} \tag{3}$$

$[R_{t,}]_{ij} = \rho_{ij,t}$ is the conditional correlation between the stock return series for country i and j at time t. Hence, $\rho_{ij,t}$ for the DCC (1, 1) can be rewritten as:

$$\rho_{ij,t} = \frac{(1 - \alpha_{dcc} - \beta_{dcc})\overline{q}_{ij} + \alpha_{dcc}\varepsilon_{i,t-1}\varepsilon_{j,t-1} + \beta_{dcc}q_{ij,t-1}}{\sqrt{(1 - \alpha_{dcc} - \beta_{dcc})\overline{q}_{ii} + \alpha_{dcc}\varepsilon^2_{i,t-1} + \beta_{dcc}q_{ii,t-1})(1 - \alpha_{dcc} - \beta_{dcc})\overline{q}_{jj} + \alpha_{dcc}\varepsilon^2_{j,t-1} + \beta_{dcc}q_{jj,t-1})}}. \tag{4}$$

If $\alpha_{dcc} = \beta_{dcc} = 0$ and $\overline{q}_{ij} = 1$, $\rho_{ij,t}$ becomes constant, which is the same as the constant conditional correlation generated by the constant conditional correlation-MGARCH model. The significance of α_{dcc} and β_{dcc} implies the estimators obtained in the DCC-MGARCH are dynamic and time-varying. α_{dcc} measures the short-run volatility impact, which means the persistency of the standardized residuals from the previous period. β_{dcc} measures the lingering effect of a shock impact on the conditional correlations, which means the persistency of the conditional correlation process. $\rho_{ij,t}$ indicates the direction

[8] R_t in the DCC model is time-invariant and is different from the CCC model.

[9] Positive covariance implies the tested variables are strongly linked and moved in the same direction and vice versa.

and strength of the correlation and measures the degree of covariance between two assets in relation to the market's individual variances (Savva, 2009). When the estimated $\rho_{ij,t}$ is positive, the correlation between the return series is rising and moving in the same direction and vice versa.

Two-Step Estimation of the DCC-MGARCH Model

The estimation of the DCC-MGARCH model uses a two-step procedure. Under acceptable uniformity circumstances, the consistency of the second step is dependent on the consistency of the first step. The first step estimates the univariate GARCH (1, 1) model for each return series in the multivariate system. Standardized residuals are obtained by maximizing the likelihood, $\hat{\theta} = \arg\max\{L_v(\theta)\}$. The generated standardized residuals from step 1 are then used to estimate the DCC parameters in step 2 using the following equation, $\max_{\Phi}\{L_c(\hat{\theta}, \Phi)\}$.

DCC-MGARCH Log-Likelihood Estimation

The maximum likelihood technique maximizes the log-likelihood function and computes the most likely values of the parameters and its standard residuals. This study uses Quasi-maximum likelihood (QML) estimation proposed by Bollerslev and Wooldridge (1992).[10]

The log-likelihood of the H_t estimator can be written in the following forms:

$$L = -\frac{1}{2}\sum_{t=1}^{T}(n\log(2\pi) + \log|H_t| + r'_{i,t}H_t^{-1}r_{i,t})$$

$$= -\frac{1}{2}\sum_{t=1}^{T}(n\log(2\pi) + 2\log|D_t| + r'_{i,t}D_t^{-1}D_t^{-1}r_{i,t} - \varepsilon'_t\varepsilon_t + \log|R_t| + \varepsilon'_tR_t^{-1}\varepsilon_t). \quad (5)$$

The log-likelihood function can be broken into two components, which consists of the volatility component and correlation component:

$$L(\theta, \Phi) = L_v(\theta) + L_c(\theta, \Phi),$$

where θ is the parameter for D_t and Φ is the additional parameter in R_t.

The volatility component function can be written as follows:

$$L_v(\theta) = -\frac{1}{2}\sum_t(n\log(2\pi) + \log|D_t|^2 + r'_{i,t}D_t^{-2}r_{i,t}),$$

while the correlation component is as below:

$$L_c(\theta, \Phi) = -\frac{1}{2}\sum_t(\log|R_t| + \varepsilon'_tR_t^{-1}\varepsilon_t - \varepsilon'_t\varepsilon_t).$$

[10] QML is maximum likelihood with robust variance-covariance estimator.

3.3. Bai and Perron Multiple Structural Breaks Test

The Bai and Perron (BP) multiple structural breaks test adopted to detect the structural changes occurring naturally in a time series at time t denoted as y_t can be expressed as follows:

$$y_t = \eta_j x_t + \varepsilon_t, \tag{6}$$

where $t = T_{j-1}+1, \ldots, T_j (j = 1, \ldots, m+1)$, η_j is the coefficient of vectors of covariates, $x_t \cdot \varepsilon_t$ is the error term at time t. The estimation of the model is by minimizing the sum of squared residuals (SSR) in order to find an unknown number of breaks (m) in the model. The estimated break points $(\hat{T}_1 \ldots, \hat{T}_m) = \arg\min_{T_1,\ldots,T_m} S_T(T_1, \ldots, T_m)$ that obtain global minimizers of the SSR where $S_T(T_1, \ldots, T_m)$ denotes the resulting SSR.

The null and alternative hypotheses of the model are as below:

H_0: No structural breaks

H_1: Unknown number of breaks with upper bound of m.

For empirical studies, normally m is set as 5, which means 5 is the maximum number of breaks allowed in the model. The selection of the optimal number of breaks is based on the minimum value of the Bayesian Information Criterion (BIC).

4. FINDINGS

4.1. Empirical Results of the DCC-MGARCH Model and its Diagnostic Tests

Preliminary test on the constant conditional correlation is utilized to detect the existence of dynamic properties in the series before estimating the DCC-MGARCH model to avoid model misspecification. The Tse (2000) Lagrange Multiplier (LM) test was employed to test for the presence of dynamic properties of the conditional correlation series generated by the constant conditional correlation MGARCH model. The null hypothesis of constant correlation against dynamic correlation of LM test was strongly rejected at the one percent level, which implies the existence of dynamic properties in the correlation series for all pairs of countries selected in this study.[11] Hence, we can proceed with the estimation of the DCC-MGARCH model based on the return series of each market.

Table 3 reports the univariate GARCH parameters, which are estimated from step 1 of the DCC-MGARCH model. The AR(1) coefficients are statistically significant for ASEAN-5's stock markets except for Thailand as shown in Table 3 panel A. The AR(1) coefficients are insignificant for all the stock markets in the developed economies (the US and Japan) and emerging economies (China and India) selected in this study as stated in Table 3 panel B.

[11] The LM test was conducted for ASEAN-5 and the reference countries are tested as a group of six countries. The test statistics for each respective group of countries are 55.7462 for ASEAN-5 with SHCI, 55.5559 for ASEAN-5 with BSE, 54.0290 for ASEAN-5 with DJII, and 79.749 ASEAN-5 with NIK.

Table 3 DCC-MGARCH step 1 estimation results for full sample (January 1991–June 2010).

Panel A	JSE	KLCI	PSE	SSI	THSE
Mean equation: AR(1) model:					
Constant: λ_0	0.0123**	0.0086**	0.0098*	0.0073*	0.0077
AR(1): λ_1	0.2159***	0.1991***	0.1491*	0.2297***	0.0308
Variance equation: GARCH (1, 1) model:					
Constant: τ_i	0.0009**	2.0568**	0.0007*	1.1923*	0.0009*
ARCH: α_i	0.1217**	0.2148***	0.1797	0.1029***	0.2560**
GARCH: β_i	0.7298***	0.7443***	0.7181***	0.8609***	0.6288***
$\alpha_i + \beta_i$	0.8515	0.9591	0.8978	0.9639	0.8847
Consistency test:					
Q	17.8476 (8)**	19.0498 (8)**	7.7784 (8)	20.1366 (18)	6.3491 (8)
Q^2	11.6464 (8)	10.2439 (8)	3.6220 (8)	5.7999 (8)	11.6542 (8)
Skewness	−0.60157***	0.12849	0.070859	−0.18477	0.236
Excess Kurtosis	1.5094***	0.73346**	1.7314***	1.1011***	1.19***
Jarque-Bera	36.327***	5.8891*	29.425***	13.153***	15.979***

(continued)

Table 3 (Continued)

Panel B	SHCI	BSE	DJII	NIK
Mean equation: AR(1) model:				
Constant: λ_0	0.0017	0.0137**	0.0065***	−0.0007
AR(1): λ_1	−0.0779	0.0781	−0.00560	0.1079
Variance equation: GARCH (1, 1) model:				
Constant: τ_i	0.0001	0.0015**	0.6048	0.0369
ARCH: α_i	0.1185	0.1852**	0.1279**	0.0254
GARCH: β_i	0.8916***	0.5954***	0.8427***	1.0291
$\alpha_i + \beta_i$	1.0101	0.7806	0.9706	1.0545
Consistency test:				
Q	12.5214 (8)	11.658 (8)	24.8596 (2)	6.6580 (8)
Q^2	0.9850 (8)	9.7201 (8)	4.8833 (8)	5.4236 (8)
Skewness	1.3072***	0.36856**	−0.33576**	0.20099
Excess Kurtosis	8.2807***	0.7435**	1.3471***	0.35495
Jarque-Bera	735.2***	10.687***	22.091***	2.8039

(continued)

Table 3 (Continued)

Panel D	JSE	KLCI	PSE	SSI	THSE	SHCI
Mean equation: ARMA(4,1) model:						
Variance equation: GARCH (1, 1) model:						
$\alpha_i + \beta_i$	0.8612	0.9652	0.9275	0.9793	0.8972	0.9995
Ljung-Box Q-statistics Q	16.3520 (5)	13.6094 (7)	6.6097 (8)	9.3027 (8)	3.6627 (8)	19.8415 (8)**
Engle (1982) ARCH test Q^2	19.0063 (6)	9.4747 (8)	3.4335 (8)	5.0736 (8)	12.6247 (8)	1.9316 (8)
Skewness	−0.4563***	0.0662	0.0620	−0.1907	0.2488	0.7028***
Excess Kurtosis	1.5613***	0.9154***	1.6938***	1.1113***	1.2094***	3.2192***
Jarque-Bera	31.887***	8.3411**	28.122***	13.460***	16.675***	120.30***
	JSE	KLCI	PSE	SSI	THSE	NIK
Mean equation: AR(2) model :						
Variance equation: GARCH (1, 1) model:						
$\alpha_i + \beta_i$	0.8524	0.9653	0.9107	0.9812	0.8867	0.9902
Ljung-Box Q-statistics Q	15.7552 (6)	14.8929 (7)	6.8419 (8)	5.7018 (8)	5.6180 (8)	4.7121 (8)
Engle (1982) ARCH test Q^2	17.5231 (6)	6.8889 (8)	2.7038 (8)	4.0407 (8)	11.5734 (8)	5.5756 (8)
Skewness	−0.5500***	0.1599	0.0565	−0.1843	0.2702*	0.1801
Excess Kurtosis	1.4081***	0.7853**	1.6396***	1.1930***	1.2325***	0.1734
Jarque-Bera	31.115***	7.0090**	26.335***	15.200***	17.658***	1.5582

Remarks: lag length is given in parentheses.
*Significant at 10%.
**Significant at 5%.
***Significant at 1%.

The impact of previous disturbances on the conditional variance is significant for all selected countries except for the stock markets in the Philippines, China, and Japan. The impact of previous disturbances on the conditional variance is denoted by the ARCH coefficient (α) in Table 3. For stock markets, all GARCH coefficients (β) are highly significant except for Japan, which implied persistency in the positive changes in the volatility of the stock index. The sum of ($\alpha + \beta$) for stock markets in the ASEAN-5, India, and the US, indicates the persistence of disturbance over time. Meanwhile, the sum of ($\alpha + \beta$) for China and Japan's stock markets is more than one, which indicates that the disturbance will destabilize the movement of these two stock indices and lead to a permanent change in the future behavior of these two stock markets. Moreover, the impact of the disturbance to these stock markets could be reinforced over time. This condition implies that the conditional variances for these two indices are mildly explosive (Nelson, 1990; Lee and Hansen, 1994). A possible explanation for the explosive conditional variance is the disturbances to volatility are persistent. Lamoureux and Lastrapes (1990) argued that the explosive conditional variance could be due to the misspecification of ARMA models in their conditional means and variances. Hence, in the case of SHCI, the explosive conditional variance disappeared when it was specified as ARMA(4, 1). By using the AR(2) for NIK, the explosive conditional variance had been eliminated. Table 3 panel D shows the results based on the new model. This indicates that a higher order autoregressive structure needs to be included in the mean equation. Similar justification has been done in Wong and Li (2010).

It is vital to perform misspecification tests for the DCC-MGARCH model because the consistency in step 1 estimation will ensure the consistency in the following step 2 estimation. The consistency in step 1 is assessed by the Ljung-Box test on the standardized residuals (Q) and squared standardized residuals (Q^2). The significance of the results could be affected by the number of lags chosen for the test, hence the lag tested is up to 18 lags. The Q-statistic was insignificant for most of the series except JSE, KLCI, and US for the AR(1) model and SHCI for the ARMA(4,1) model. The Q^2 statistic was insignificant for all series for the AR(1), ARMA(4, 1), and AR(2) models. The statistically insignificant results of these two tests indicate the absence of serial correlation and ARCH effects in the conditional means and variances. The majority of the series are consistent, thus passing the misspecification tests. The results of these two tests justified the employment of the DCC-GARCH specification for the selected countries.

The skewness is positive for most stock return indices except for JSE, SSI, and DJII. Excess kurtosis is positive for all indices with a value of 1 and above or −1 and below. This represents a sizable departure from normality. As compared to Table 3 in terms of excess kurtosis, generally, the value is lower, which implies the unconditional distribution of returns became less leptokurtic except for SHCI, which showed a high excess kurtosis of more than 3. Thus, the level of risk for SHCI is low as the past returns yield a leptokurtic distribution. These stocks will have a relatively low amount of variance because return values are usually close to the mean. Investors who wish to avoid large, erratic swings in portfolio returns may wish to structure their investments to produce a leptokurtic distribution.

The normality test strongly rejects the null hypothesis, which means that the indices do not follow a normal distribution except for NIK. The normality test results suggest that the excess kurtosis in the residuals of the return indices was not fully eliminated by the conditionally normal GARCH process. Consequently, the use of QML procedures in the estimation of the DCC-MGARCH model is justifiable by the consistency test results.

4.2. DCC-MGARCH—Time-Varying Patterns (Full Sample) for ASEAN-5's Stock Markets with the Four Economies

The significant results of the DCC-α and -β for models 1 to 4 in Table 4 signify that stock returns in these nine markets were highly dynamic and time-varying. The DCC-α indicates that the impact of recent co-movement on the correlation is significant for all pairs of markets. The highly significant DCC-β displays strong persistence in the dynamic conditional correlation of stock returns among ASEAN-5 with the other four stock markets. The sum of the DCC-α and the DCC-β for models 1 to 4 is all less than unity, which means that the correlations are time-variant.

The average conditional correlation of volatility (ρ_{ij}) for models 2 to 4 is highly significant for all pairs of stock returns in the full sample. However, in model 1 for ASEAN-5 with China, the results obtained are statistically insignificant for all pairs of countries except for KLCI-SHCI that is found to be slightly significant. The statistically significant and high conditional correlations of ASEAN-5 with the US imply that diversification of ASEAN-5's equity portfolios in the US will not benefit ASEAN-5, especially during periods of shocks or financial turmoil. Nevertheless, there is potential for international portfolio diversification by ASEAN-5's stock markets in China, India, and Japan. This is suggested by the relatively low correlation (averaging below 40%) among the ASEAN-5's stock markets with the stock markets in China, India, and Japan.

4.3. Perspective of Structural Changes for ASEAN-5's Stock Markets

Findings based on the DCC-MGARCH model for the full sample show that ASEAN-5's stock markets have low integration with China's stock market. These full sample results differ from that of Nishimura and Men (2010) who stated that China's stock market was no longer isolated from the world market, but the findings in this study are broadly consistent with those of Yu et al. (2010) and Huyghebaert and Wang (2010). The contradictory results might be related to the sample period selected for the pairs of countries in this study namely ASEAN-5 with China, India, the US, and Japan. Azad (2009) and Lean and Ghosh (2010) segregated the sample period in their studies according to important economic

Table 4 DCC-MGARCH Step 2 Estimation results for full sample (January 1991–June 2010).

Model 1 ARMA(4,1)	JSE-SHCI	KLCI-SHCI	PSE-SHCI	SSI-SHCI	THSE-SHCI	α_{dcc}	β_{dcc}	$\alpha_{dcc} + \beta_{dcc}$
ρ_{ij}	−0.0088	0.1436*	0.0500	0.0044	−0.0515	0.0272***	0.8491***	0.8763
Model 2	JSE-BSE	KLCI-BSE	PSE-BSE	SSI-BSE	THSE-BSE	α_{dcc}	β_{dcc}	$\alpha_{dcc} + \beta_{dcc}$
ρ_{ij}	0.3665***	0.3270***	0.2151***	0.3688***	0.3478***	0.0271***	0.8902***	0.9172
Model 3	JSE-DJII	KLCI-DJII	PSI-DJII	SSI-DJII	THSE-DJII	α_{dcc}	β_{dcc}	$\alpha_{dcc} + \beta_{dcc}$
ρ_{ij}	0.4477***	0.4248***	0.4952***	0.5389***	0.4352***	0.0235**	0.8420***	0.8655
Model 4 AR(2)	JSE-NIK	KLCI-NIK	KLCI-JIK	SSI-NIK	THSE-NIK	α_{dcc}	β_{dcc}	$\alpha_{dcc} + \beta_{dcc}$
ρ_{ij}	0.2491***	0.1878**	0.2736***	0.2944***	0.2002**	0.0271*	0.8607***	0.8878

*Significance at 10%.
**Significance at 5%.
***Significance at 1%.

Table 5 Bai and Perron structural break dates for the conditional correlations.

Multivariate model 1:		(JSE, KLCI, PSE, SSI, THSE, SHCI)		
JSE-SHCI	KLCI-SHCI	PSE-SHCI	SSI-SHCI	THSE-SHCI
Nov-93	Aug-94		Oct-95	Nov-93
Oct-96		Apr-97	Sept 98	
Jan-00	May-02			Jan-00
Jan-04		Nov-06	Dec-06	Jul-04
Jul-07	Mar-07			Jul-07
Multivariate model 2:		(JSE, KLCI, PSE, SSI, THSE, BSE)		
JSE-BSE	KLCI-BSE	PSE-BSE	SSI-BSE	THSE-BSE
Nov-93		Nov-96	May-96	Dec-96
Apr-97			Oct-99	Aug-00
Jun-00	Jul-02	Dec-00		Jul-03
Apr-05	Jul-07	Jul-07	May-06	
Multivariate model 3:		(JSE, KLCI, PSE, SSI, THSE, DJII)		
JSE-DJII	KLCI-DJII	PSE-DJII	SSI-DJII	THSE-DJII
Nov-93		Aug-94	Sep-95	Aug-98
Nov-00	Feb-98	Aug-98	Jul-98	
Oct-03	Jun-01	Sep-02		Jul-01
	Jul-07	Jan-07		
Multivariate model 4:		(JSE, KLCI, PSE, SSI, THSE, NIK)		
JSE-NIK	KLCI-NIK	PSE-NIK	SSI-NIK	THSE-NIK
Jan-95	Nov-93		Nov-93	Jul-96
Jan-98	Oct-96	Feb-98	Feb-98	Jul-99
Jan-01	Jun-00			
Dec-03	May-03		May-03	Jun-02
	Jul-07	Jul-07	Jul-07	

events and observed China becoming more integrated financially with the world since the early 2000s. Therefore, the segregation of the sample period must be handled with caution. BP's (1998, 2003) multiple structural breaks test is selected to handle the determination of structural break dates that occurred among the studied markets.

The estimated structural break dates based on the BP (2003) test are reported in Table 5. Generally, the detected structural break dates can be categorized into five major phases, namely the first phase is 1993–1994, second phase is 1995–1996, third phase is 1997–1998, fourth phase is 2000–2002, and the fifth phase is 2006–2007. However, there are structural break dates that do not fall into these five phases as certain events only impact specific pairs of stock markets.

4.3.1. First Phase: 1993–1994

For the first phase, the structural break observed was from November 1993 until November 1994. The breaks between ASEAN-5 with SHCI can be explained by three possible reasons. First, the panic that was provoked when China's government decided to abandon the plan of trading state-owned shares publicly (Xu and Oh, 2010). Second, the treasury bond futures scandal in February 1995, which called for the suspension of regional futures trading centers in China. Third, investors overreacted to the information in the US stock market and this situation was made worst by the institutional investors (Girardin and Liu, 2007). The naïve investors treated the US stock market condition as the major determinant for their investment decisions. During that period, China's stock market was new in the financial world and has yet to be integrated with the rest of the world but there was the possibility of a spillover from China's stock market to the Asian markets. This was because of the establishment of the B-share market since 1992, which allowed foreign investors to purchase the B-share stocks that accounted for 16% of share ownership in the Shanghai Stock Exchange (Naughton, 1998). In addition, Girardin and Liu (2007) mentioned that portfolio investment inflow round tripping happened before the establishment of B-shares.[12] Besides that, China experienced rapid economic growth in the years 1993 and 1994 with an average annual growth rate of 14% and 13.1%, respectively. The booming economic condition contributed toward attracting long-term capital investment inflow from the rest of the world.

The structural breaks for PSE-DJII and SSI-NIK could be explained by the contractionary monetary policy imposed by the Federal Reserve that created havoc in the bond market, which was then followed by the bond market crash in the US Changes in the federal fund rate negatively affected the performance of the stock market in the Philippines and Singapore. This is because the imposition of a higher federal fund rate by the US diverted investors' direction into Asia's stock markets that generated higher returns. In fact, Japan was not affected by the event (Capital Market Review, 1994). Hence, the structural break in the conditional correlation between SSI and NIK was mainly contributed by Singapore. Singapore's stock market lingered with panic as a reaction over the increase in the US interest rates that eventually caused the bond crisis (Capital Market Review, 1994).

The structural breaks observed for the conditional correlation between India and Indonesia, as well as with Malaysia, the Philippines, and Thailand could be explained by the ongoing financial liberalization and reforms occurring in India. The Indian economy had undergone gradual phases of financial reforms by changing to a unified, market-determined exchange rate regime and introducing current account convertibility during that period.

[12] Round-tripping FDI refers to the domestic capital that has fled the home country and then flows back in the form of foreign direct investment.

Most of the breaks detected involved the stock market of Indonesia. The observed breaks in Indonesia were caused by the economic conditions in Indonesia that led to adverse sentiments in its stock market and the domination of foreign investors in the trading in the Jakarta Stock Exchange. The contributing factors are overissuing of initial public offerings (IPO), weakening of oil prices, political and social problems, unexpected rise in inflation rates, and issues related to state banking (Capital Market Review, 1994).

4.3.2. Second Phase: 1995–1996

Four complementary hypotheses can be used to explain the structural changes that had occurred in 1995–1996. First, the break dates observed in the period May 1996–December 1996 for ASEAN-5's stock markets with BSE except JSE-BSE and KLCI-BSE are consistent with the financial liberalization and reforms taking place in India's stock market. The implementation of a new trading system in India's stock market led to a sudden boom in its stock market. The new system promoted efficiency, transparency, and fairness in trading transactions.

4.3.3. Third Phase: 1997–1999

Most of these breaks occurring in this period are the reaction to the Asian financial crisis and the financial reforms, which took place in ASEAN-5 to regain investors' confidence and to speed up the economic recovery. In Indonesia, it is not surprising to find the structural break date for JSE-SHCI in late 1996, which was before the onset of the Asian financial crisis. This is because Indonesia was already facing capital inflows issues in response to its domestic currency appreciation. The central bank of Indonesia's action in appreciating its exchange rate reduced the nation's export competitiveness, which led to a drastic drop in the country's exports. Eventually, the vulnerable Indonesian economy took a plunge because of the financial crisis and entered into an economic recession in 1998, followed by the resignation of President Suharto in May 1998 (ADB). This chain of events can be identified as one of the causes of the structural breaks. This crisis had led to a devaluation of the Indonesia Rupiah by 83.2%. The break date detected in October 1999 could be explained by a series of banking financial reforms, which were implemented in Indonesia. From 1999, Indonesia had actively restructured its banking system by closing down 38 banks and followed by a series of joint recapitalization and merger plans in the banking institutions.

The structural break detected in the conditional correlation between KLCI and DJII on February 1998 was mostly related to the financial reform measures taken by the Malaysian government to revive the economy from the adverse effects of the Asian financial crisis. Since January 1998, a series of financial reforms were implemented to improve the stock markets such as regulations and blanket guarantees for all depositors.[13] This

[13] Legal framework for financial operations was implemented to avoid and minimize financial sector problems. This includes regulation of deposit-taking institutions and supervision of the conduct of these institutions and setting down

was followed by plans to merge financial institutions with the establishment of an asset management company and an agency for bank restructuring and recapitalization, the implementation of the pegged exchange rate and capital controls by Malaysia (Lindgren et al., 1999). The degree of impact of these financial reforms on the conditional correlation was high, which accounted for almost 50% of the correlation with the US. These reforms had brought about a positive rebound in the stock market linkages between Malaysia and the US.

The structural break dates detected in the conditional correlation namely for PSE-SHCI, PSE-DJII, and PSE-NIK during the period of 1997–1999 could be hypothesized to be linked to the intervention by the Philippines government to defend the Peso against the collapse of the Thai Baht. The strategy was very successful in defending the Peso and in restoring the performance of the stock market and the economic activities.

The structural breaks obtained for Thailand were related to its post-crisis reformation. The collapse of the Thai Baht followed by the collapse of the Thai stock market caused a change in government in November 1997 with a wide range of economic reform programs. In August 1998, the government announced numerous restructuring plans in the financial sector to further rescue the Thai economy. The break in July 1999 denoted the establishment of an asset management company by one of the major banks in Thailand.

India was not affected by the Asian financial crisis but Singapore's economy experienced a short downturn. Hence, the structural break detected in the conditional correlation for SSI-BSE during that period could be justified by the ongoing devaluation of the Singaporean dollar to overcome the impact of the crisis on its economy. Singapore's financial measures were very successful in cushioning the impact of the crisis and its economy experienced a fast recovery. In fact, the monetary authorities in India also had taken measures in response to the crisis. The Indian government started with easing monetary policy followed by contractionary monetary policy.

During the period 1997–1999, China's government was engaged in the internal adjustment of its financial market. The government enforced rules and laws to oversee and strengthen the financial market against any external disturbances in view of the financial instability around its neighboring countries (Xu and Oh, 2010). China's economy was still growing even though the economies of its neighboring countries plummeted due to the crisis. Hence, the conditional correlations of China's with ASEAN-5's stock markets are either very low or negative during this phase.

The structural break dates observed between NIK and ASEAN-5's stock markets started from mid-1997 due to the impact of the Asian financial crisis. The crisis caused several big corporations in Japan to file for bankruptcies (Ito, 1999). The Japanese financial market liberalization in 1998 had led to the devaluation of the Japanese Yen.

requirements that limit their risk-taking. The aim of the prudent regulations is to ensure the safety of depositors' funds and to maintain the stability of the financial system.

Overall, the break dates observed among the stock markets in 1998 could be attributed to the exchange rates in Malaysia, the Philippines, Singapore, and Thailand that started to stabilize and this condition was highly correlated with the stock market in the US. This implies that the ASEAN-5's stock markets still co-move and responded positively to the US stock market in general.

4.3.4. Fourth Phase: 2000–2002

A straightforward intuition for the structural breaks in this period is that the dot-com bubble burst and the September 11 terrorist attack in the US had more explanatory power in causing the structural changes in the correlation of ASEAN-5's stock markets with the studied markets. This dot-com burst and its meltdown affected all the selected countries in this study either directly or indirectly. The burst in the US Internet bubble that started in March 2000 was compounded by the terrorist attacks on September 11, 2001. Both of these events caused the stock market condition to deteriorate rapidly. The condition only showed signs of recovery in early 2003.

The structural break dates of the stock market conditional correlations that corresponded with the stock market movement in China in this period are possibly explained by the spillover of the US Internet boom to China's stock market. According to Girardin and Liu (2007), the spillover to China was rather slow because during the US Internet burst, the Internet bubble in China was still expanding until the market became overheated. However, China's government was able to control overvaluation of the stock market by reducing illegal trading, increasing the pace of IPOs, and reviewing how to publicly trade more state-owned shares.[14] (Girardin and Liu, 2007).

4.3.5. Fifth Phase: 2006–2007

It is worth noting that the break date obtained between Malaysia and China at March 2007 was just less than a month after China's financial market correction on February 27, 2007. This unexpected event caused sudden havoc in stock markets worldwide. The impact was felt by Hong Kong, Japan, the UK, the US, and many others. Malaysia's stock market was affected the most among ASEAN-5's stock markets with the change in the closing price of −3.09%.[15] This structural break date obtained by the BP test clearly confirmed that the impact was significant on the Malaysian stock market.

The months of November 2006 and December 2006 are the detected structural break dates in the conditional correlation for PSI-SHCI and SSI-SHCI. These dates could be explained by two reasons. The first possible reason could be the irrational act of China's investors that might have led to a speculative bubble in the stock market in the second half of 2006 (Nishimura and Men, 2010). The second possible reason could be the introduction

[14] China's authorities preventive measures are controlling illegal trading, speeding up IPOs, and discussion on making more State-Owned Enterprises' shares tradable.

[15] For details, refer to Dow Jones, Reuters, http://www.reuters.com/finance/markets/. The table is in Appendix.

of the Qualified Domestic Institutional Investor (QDII) scheme. This scheme was the initial step in liberalizing China's financial markets and relaxing the restriction on local investors who were keen to invest abroad. The first foreign accessed market was Hong Kong and the list of permitted accessed markets has since been expanded to many other countries.

Another interesting finding was July 2007, which had emerged as a common break date for most pairs of correlations. This reveals that the subprime crisis affected all the stock markets in this study, either directly, or indirectly, since the conditional correlation was generated in a multivariate model.

4.3.6. Exceptional Structural Break Dates: 2004

JSE-SHCI observed a structural break in January 2004. This break was signified by the conclusion of the China-ASEAN Free Trade Agreement (CAFTA) in 2003, which accelerated the growth of bilateral trade relations between China and ASEAN.[16] This break is substantiated by the Chow et al. (2005) study, which indicated that financial integration normally moves in tandem with trade integration. The average conditional correlation for ASEAN-5-SHCI was constant around 10% during the pre-January 2004 period. On the contrary, in the post-January 2004 period, the DCC exhibited a significant increasing trend with the average conditional correlation of 20%. Hence, this study re-estimates the DCC-MGARCH model for the period after January 2004 to check for changes in the financial linkages between the selected countries. Lean and Ghosh's (2010) finding of a co-integrating relationship for the Malaysian, PRC, and Indian stock markets, which started from November 2003 lends support to the finding of this study. Lean and Teng (2013) also observed a significant rise in DCC between KLCI and SHCI since April 2004.[17]

4.4. DCC-MGARCH—Time-Varying Patterns for ASEAN-5's Stock Markets with the Four Economies (Pre-January 2004 and Post-January 2004)

Table 6 displays the re-estimation results of the DCC-MGARCH model based on the BP structural break date at January 2004 as per the discussion in the previous section. The two sub-samples are sub-period 1 (January 1991–December 2003) and sub-period 2 (January 2004–June 2010).

For sub-period 1, the stock market average conditional correlations (ρ_{ij}) for China with ASEAN-5 are insignificant except with Thailand. The mean conditional correlations among ASEAN-5's stock markets with stock markets in India, the US, and Japan are significant except for PSE-BSE, KLCI-NIK, and THSE-NIK.

[16] The Framework Agreement on ASEAN-China Comprehensive Economic Cooperation (ACCEC) was signed at the ASEAN + China Summit on November 4, 2002 and the protocol for amendments was signed at the Summit on October 6, 2003. The Framework Agreement sets out how ASEAN and China will cooperate in trade and investment liberalization.

[17] The DCC-MGARCH model for this study is among stock markets in Malaysia, China, India, the US, and Japan.

Table 6 The DCC-MGARCH estimation results for sub-periods.

Model 1 ARMA(4,1)		JSE-SHCI	KLCI-SHCI	PSE-SHCI	SSI-SHCI	THSE-SHCI
DCC-MGARCH: sub-period 1	ρ_{ij}	−0.1238	−0.0040	0.0076	−0.1192	−0.1821**
DCC-MGARCH: sub-period 2	ρ_{ij}	0.2080	0.3929***	0.246**	0.2103*	0.2566***
Model 2		JSE-BSE	KLCI-BSE	PSE-BSE	SSI-BSE	THSE-BSE
DCC-MGARCH: sub-period 1	ρ_{ij}	0.2310***	0.2620***	0.0847	0.1925**	0.2281***
DCC-MGARCH: sub-period 2	ρ_{ij}	0.6214***	0.4481***	0.4562***	0.6581***	0.5208***
Model 3		JSE-DJII	KLCI-DJII	PSE-DJII	SSI-DJII	THSE-DJII
DCC-MGARCH: sub-period 1	ρ_{ij}	0.4407***	0.3941***	0.4684***	0.4856***	0.4131***
DCC-MGARCH: sub-period 2	ρ_{ij}	0.4984***	0.5301***	0.6370***	0.7293***	0.4958***
Model 4 AR(2)		JSE-NIK	KLCI-NIK	PSE-JIK	SSI-NIK	THSE-NIK
DCC-MGARCH: sub-period 1	ρ_{ij}	0.1414***	0.1078	0.1717**	0.1654**	0.1113
DCC-MGARCH: sub-period 2	ρ_{ij}	0.5388***	0.4022***	0.5444***	0.6881***	0.4196***

*Significance at 10%.
**Significance at 5%.
***Significance at 1%.

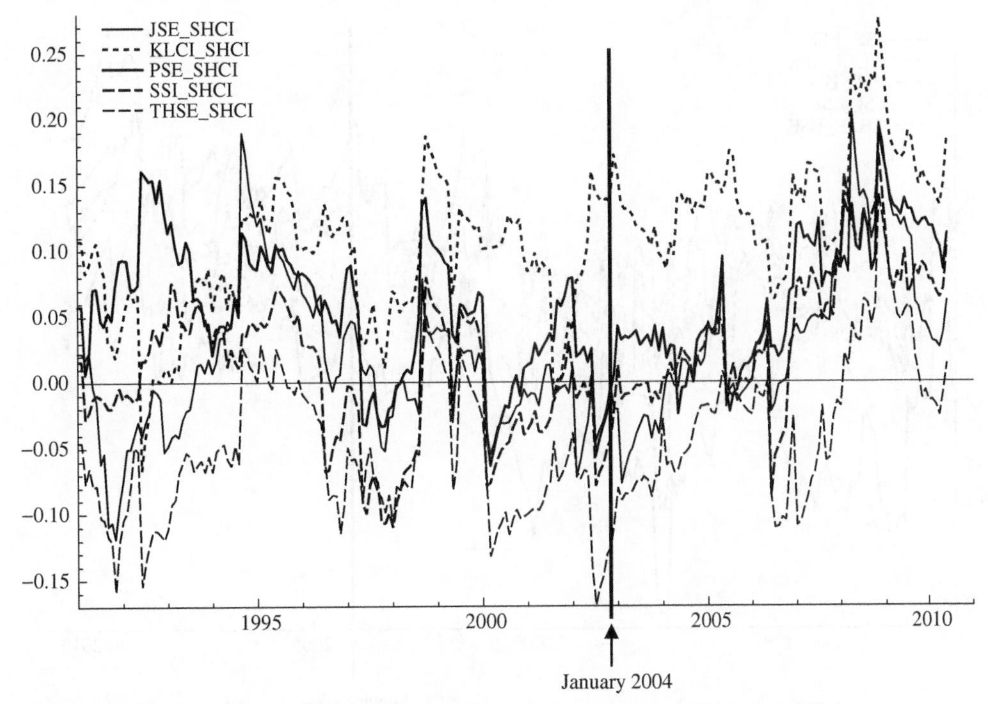

Figure 1 Dynamic conditional correlation between stock markets in ASEAN-5 and China.

For sub-period 2, the mean value of the conditional correlations between ASEAN-5's stock markets and all the other four countries' stock markets is highly significant in particular the correlation with China, which rose at least twofold. The value of the mean conditional correlation between Malaysia and China increased from −0.004 in sub-sample 1 to 0.39 in sub-sample 2 and is significant.

To have a better picture of intra- and inter-regional stock market correlation, the plots for time-varying conditional correlations among ASEAN-5's stock markets with the stock markets of China, India, the US, and Japan are illustrated in Figures 1–4.

Figure 1 shows that the time-varying correlations between ASEAN-5's and China's stock markets remained constant during sub-period 1. A common upward movement is noticeable especially after January 2004 and the degree of correlation between KLCI and SHCI increased by 10% after 2004, which is essentially a doubling in the correlation compared to pre-January 2004. The rise in the degree of correlation infers that the financial integration between ASEAN-5 with China has been increasing since 2004. The change is twofold of that in sub-period 1, but it is still relatively low compared to the correlation with India, the US, and Japan. Figure 1 indicates that the correlations are mostly negative during the Asian financial crisis, subprime crisis, and the bankruptcy of Lehman Brothers in New York on September 15, 2008. This implies that these markets had

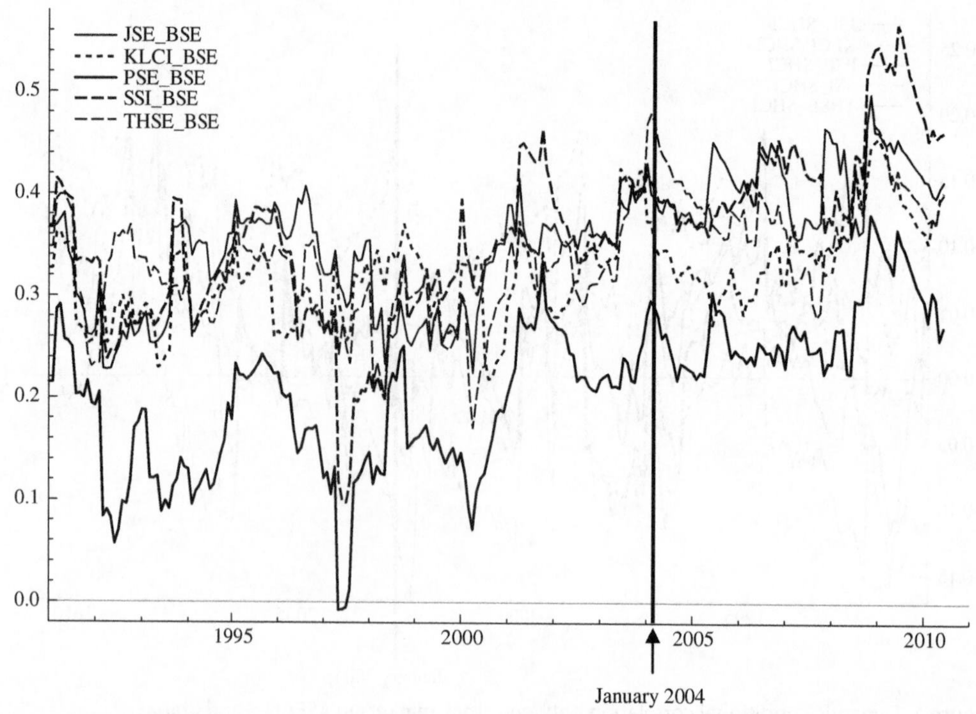

Figure 2 Dynamic conditional correlation between stock markets in ASEAN-5's and India's stock markets.

less synchronized responses to common shocks. This result is consistent with Wong and Li's (2010) findings that the subprime crisis only had a minor impact on China's economy. The benefits gained from portfolio diversification between ASEAN-5's and China's stock markets are that these markets did not co-move during crisis periods, added with the low correlation. Hence, China remains as a good destination to diversify the portfolios of the ASEAN-5's financial assets for risk-loss adjustment.

Figure 2 depicts the rising degree of correlation between ASEAN-5 with BSE, notably during the post period 2004. During sub-period 2, it exhibits a strengthening relationship between India and ASEAN-5 and almost at par with the correlation between ASEAN-5 and Japan (Figure 4). The correlation between India and ASEAN-5 fluctuated around 0.1–0.4 in sub-period 1 and increased to around 0.20–0.55 in sub-period 2. In the diagram, there was a downward movement during the Asian financial crisis but reverted to an increasing positive trend among the markets particularly after January 2004 at a low correlation level below 0.5. In summary, the relationship between India and ASEAN-5 diverged during the financial turmoil in the ASEAN region and their correlation remained at a relatively low level. Thus, India could be a potential market for investors in ASEAN-5 in diversifying their equity portfolios to cushion against shocks.

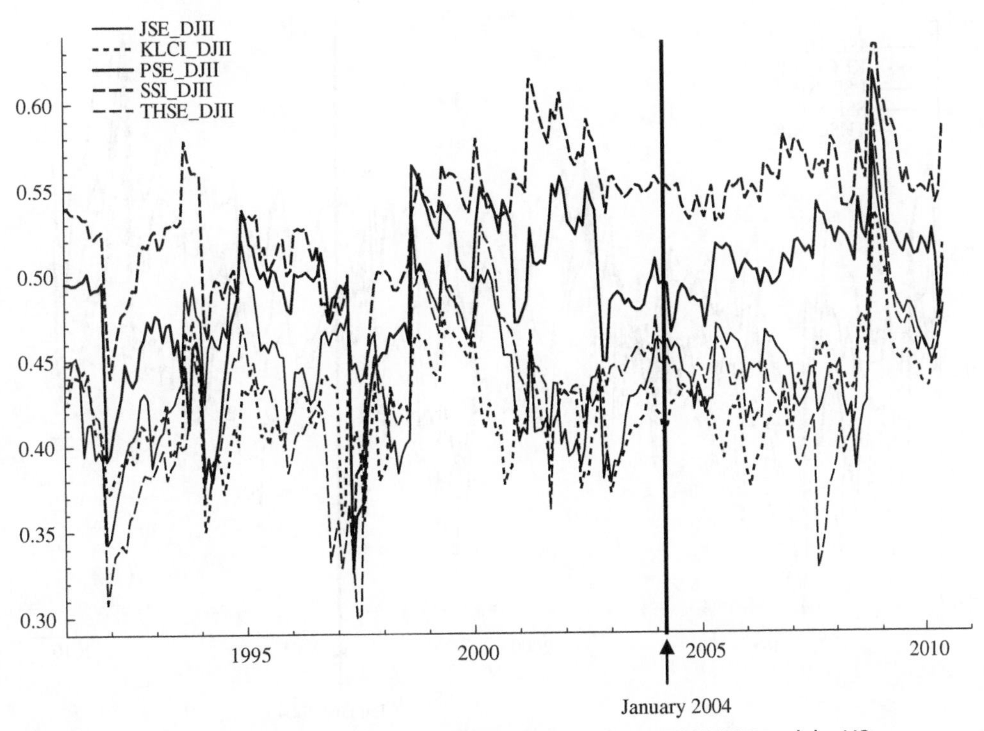

Figure 3 Dynamic conditional correlation between stock markets in ASEAN-5 and the US.

From Figure 3, the conditional correlations for all pairs of ASEAN-5's and DJII stock markets remained consistently strong ranging from 0.4 to 0.6 for the whole period of this study. As for the DCC between NIK and ASEAN-5 given in Figure 4, it was consistently between 0.1 and 0.4 for the full sample. During sub-period 2, Figures 3 and 4 showed that the relationship between the US and Japan with ASEAN-5 did not indicate a clear upward moving trend but illustrated a common temporary upsurge in 2009, which took place during the financial crisis in the US. With the synchronized movement among ASEAN-5 and with the financial turmoil in the US and Japan, it is not advisable to diversify ASEAN-5 equity portfolios into these two markets.

4.4.1. Misspecification Tests for Sub-samples 1 & 2

To support the suitability of using the DCC-MGARCH specification in this study, the test results provided in Table 7 for the sub-samples are sufficient to conclude that the DCC-MGARCH specification is appropriate for this study.[18] The results for the standardized residuals (Q) are mostly insignificant except SSI for the AR(1) model and SHCI for the ARMA(4,1) model for sub-period 1, indicating that serial correlation in the conditional

[18] The univariate tests include test for skewness, normality, serial correlation, and conditional heteroskedasticity.

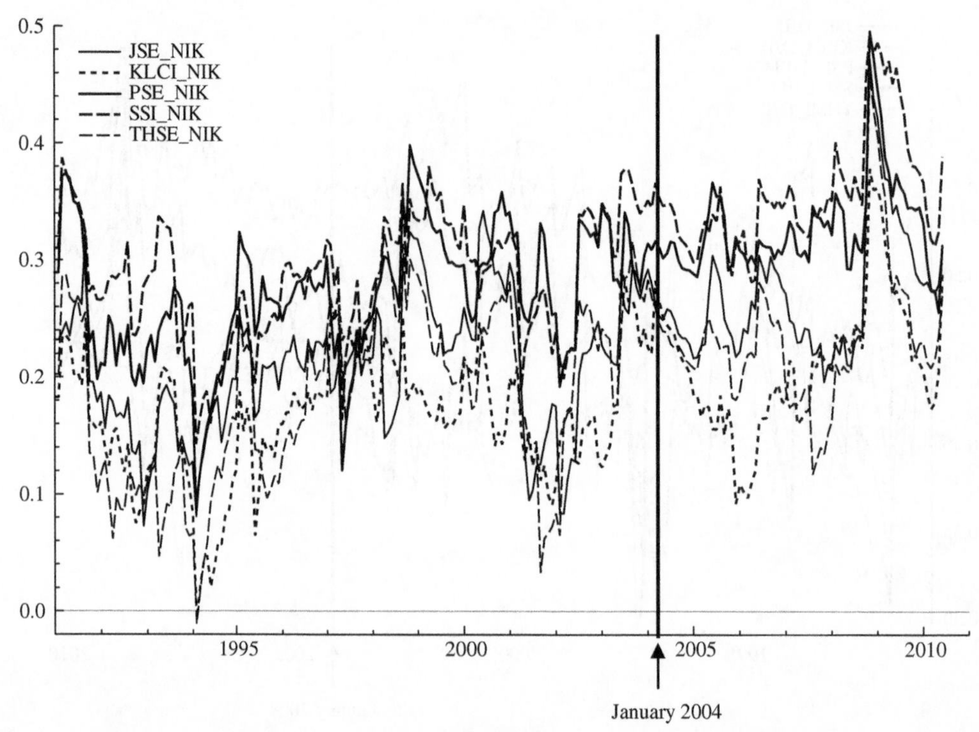

Figure 4 Dynamic conditional correlation between stock markets in ASEAN-5 and Japan.

mean had successfully been eliminated by the GARCH process (Wong and Li, 2010). In addition, no serial correlation in the variance matrix was detected, as the results from the squared standardized residuals (Q^2) are all statistically insignificant.

5. CONCLUSION

This study shows that the stock markets in ASEAN-5 do not react as a whole to external shocks from the four reference nations in this study. The average time-variant correlation obtained from the DCC-MGARCH model for the full sample period reveals that ASEAN-5's stock markets were highly integrated with the BSE and DJII, except for the Philippines, which display a low correlation with BSE. However, ASEAN-5's stock markets were less integrated with NIK. Contrary to expectations, the study did not find a significant correlation between ASEAN-5's and China's stock markets, except for KLCI and SHCI.

The BP (1998, 2003) multiple structural breaks test was used to find the dating of significant economic events in the conditional correlation for all pairs of countries that happened naturally. From the BP multiple structural breaks test, the observed dates mostly coincided with the rapid economic development and rigorous financial liberalization

Table 7 Robust tests for sub-periods model standardized residuals.

Panel A AR(1)	JSE	KLCI	PSE	SSI	THSE	BSE	DJII	NIK
Sub-period 1								
Ljung-Box Q statistics, Q	7.6206 (6)	10.2464 (7)	3.8782 (8)	18.2610 (8)**	4.2041 (8)	6.6700 (5)	4.4185 (5)	5.3100 (8)
Engle (1982) ARCH test, Q^2	9.5921 (7)	6.1726 (8)	6.1223 (8)	6.2383 (8)	9.4040 (8)	9.6823 (8)	4.6239 (8)	4.5384 (8)
Skewness	−0.5073***	0.00467	0.3360*	0.1079	0.2693	0.2983	−0.3811**	0.2947
Excess Kurtosis	0.6773*	0.5194	1.3443***	1.0795***	0.9650**	0.3807	1.1513***	−0.1531
Jarque-Bera	9.6726	1.7541	14.682***	7.8774**	7.9391**	3.2553	12.391***	2.4111
Sub-period 2								
Ljung-Box Q-statistics, Q	7.7016 (8)	10.5821 (8)	11.0811 (8)	6.9409 (8)	8.5601 (5)	2.1363 (8)	9.8893 (8)	10.6209 (8)
Engle (1982) ARCH test, Q^2	6.1221 (8)	13.0250 (8)	9.4546 (8)	5.4954 (8)	10.2822 (8)	8.3446 (8)	4.2863 (8)	10.7751 (8)
Skewness	−0.2692	6.2194	−0.4359	−0.6920**	0.1287	0.3266	−0.2628	0.0747
Excess Kurtosis	1.2743**	−0.1253	1.2567**	1.1734**	0.3328	0.6770	−0.6167	−0.5045
Jarque-Bera	6.2194**	0.4790	7.6017**	10.700***	0.5752	2.8763	2.1333	0.8998

(continued)

Table 7 (Continued)

Panel B ARMA(4,1)	JSE	KLCI	PSE	SSI	THSE	SHCI
Sub-period 1						
Ljung-Box Q-statistics, Q	3.5095 (6)	12.0395 (8	2.1726 (8)	5.5256 (8)	5.6491(8)	30.6382 (8)***
Engle (1982) ARCH test, Q^2	4.7238(6)	10.7167 (8)	6.8334 (8)	9.2098(8)	8.2539 (8)	1.0969 (8)
Skewness	−0.3648*	−0.0932	0.29667	−0.0482	0.2165	0.7270***
Excess Kurtosis	0.7558*	0.7448*	1.9458***	1.2536***	0.9807**	3.6922***
Jarque-Bera	7.1731**	3.8319	26.899***	10.276***	7.4706**	102.35***
Sub-period 2						
Ljung-Box Q-statistics, Q	6.7334 (8)	7.4680 (8)	8.3137 (6)	6.6305 (8)	4.4838 (8)	3.3405 (8)
Engle (1982) ARCH test, Q^2	12.6368 (8)	10.6447 (8)	8.0538 (8)	6.1219 (8)	6.6185 (6)	4.4692 (8)
Skewness	−0.1528	−0.0249	−0.4023	−0.4357	−0.1833	−0.2904
Excess Kurtosis	1.9237***	−0.3754	0.9664*	0.4845	0.3782	0.5135
Jarque-Bera	12.330	0.4660	5.1394*	3.2302	0.9017	1.9535

(continued)

Table 7 (Continued)

Panel C AR(2)	JSE	KLCI	PSE	SSI	THSE	NIK
Sub-period 1						
Ljung-Box Q-statistics, Q	4.7997 (6)	12.6975 (8)	4.3177 (8)	7.4721 (8)	5.0747 (8)	5.2632 (8)
Engle (1982) ARCH test, Q^2	10.8248 (7)	6.6267 (8)	4.7542 (8)	6.8967 (8)	7.9966 (8)	5.2035 (8)
Skewness	−0.4642**	0.0773	0.2980	0.0462	0.3291*	0.2635
Excess Kurtosis	0.6614*	0.6066	1.5662***	1.4625***	1.0772***	−0.20983
Jarque-Bera	8.4454**	2.5474	18.253***	13.959***	10.358***	2.0913
Sub-period 2						
Ljung-Box Q-statistics, Q	6.3807 (8)	8.8672 (8)	10.0877 (8)	8.8193 (8)	11.9142 (8)	9.2738 (8)
Engle (1982) ARCH test, Q^2	10.2813 (8)	9.8281 (8)	9.6008 (8)	7.2529 (8)	9.3195 (8)	9.7577 (8)
Skewness	−0.1893	−0.1741	−0.3096	−0.4050	0.0286	0.1011
Excess Kurtosis	2.2379***	−0.1406	1.0327*	0.4262	0.4270	−0.4099
Jarque-Bera	16.742***	0.4584	4.7118*	2.7228	0.6031	0.6800

Remarks: lag length is given in parentheses.
*Significant at 10% respectively.
**Significant at 5% respectively.
***Significant at 1% respectively.

in China, the conclusion of FTAs, the credibility and expectation of the government's announcement of policy changes, inference and assumption made on information flows, implication related to the reaction of key economic aggregates, internal problem in the financial system, and sudden external disturbance (such as 1994 bond crisis, 1997 Asian financial crisis, collapse of Internet bubble, and 2007–2008 subprime crisis). The single most striking observation to emerge from the dating was January 2004, which stood out to be the date that the stock market in China was no longer isolated from the ASEAN-5 stock markets. This date coincided with the China-ASEAN Free Trade Agreement that was signed in 2004. Thus, this test helps to identify the major drivers in strengthening the linkages among stock markets in ASEAN-5 with China.

In response to the date obtained on the changes in the degree of stock market integration between ASEAN-5 and China, the sample period was divided into two subsamples, namely pre-January 2004, and post-January 2004, in order to observe any significant changes in their dynamic correlation. In the post-January 2004 period, the average dynamic conditional correlation for stock market between ASEAN-5 and China became significant and the degree of correlation rose to around 21% to 34%, which was two times higher than before January 2004. The overall average dynamic correlation of ASEAN-5's stock markets with BSE, DJII, and NIK remained relatively higher than China; approximately twofold. Another important finding is that the stock market DCC between ASEAN-5 and China, India, and Japan dropped noticeably during the Asian financial crisis, the collapse of the Internet bubble, and the subprime crisis. As for the DJII with the ASEAN-5 stock markets, their DCC only fell during the Asian financial crisis. Their correlation mostly increased during the collapse of the Internet bubble and subprime crisis except for the KLCI, which fell during the collapse of the Internet bubble while the JSE and THSE dropped during the subprime crisis.

ASEAN-5's investors should reconsider the choice of destination for international portfolio diversification among the studied markets. Increasing ASEAN-5's portfolio diversification into China and reducing the portfolio diversification in India, the US and Japan would be beneficial for ASEAN-5. This study also suggests that the Asian countries should try to equip themselves for better defence against financial turmoil and progress toward being less reliant on the US dollar. With the weakening of US economy in conjunction with the global financial crisis, massive capital flows were diverted to ASEAN and emerging economies, which gave them better future prospects. ASEAN policy makers should strive to set up a regional capital control cooperation. The think tank and research unit should aid regional leaders in designing and structuring an institutional framework to enhance the regional financial system particularly to avoid an overheating economy and economic bubbles.[19] This team should also explore the possibility of extending the coverage of ASEAN Exchanges by initiating and strengthening financial collaboration

[19] Any sudden capital flight from China, which would have shaken its stock market might have adverse effects on ASEAN stock markets.

with China with the hope to include China's stock market into the ASEAN Exchanges in the near future.[20] The entry of China will boost the market capitalization of the Exchanges and become the next one-stop financial hub in the Asia sub-region for Asian investors.

To promote a more efficient and transparent financial market for investors and portfolio managers in ASEAN-5 and China, policy makers from both regions need to provide a better and more secure market environment for all parties. ASEAN-5 should strengthen their relationship with China by working toward the enhancement of market transparency, informational efficiency, trading mechanisms, and systematic settlement procedures between both regions. Trust among these nations is crucial in developing future economic integration between the two regions.

APPENDIX

Closing prices throughout most of Asia and the Pacific Rim on February 27, 2007.

Asia markets	Price	Change	% change
Australia	5977.60	−44.3	−0.74%
Hong Kong	20147.90	−360.08	−1.76%
India	13478.80	−170.69	−1.25%
Indonesia	1764.01	−19.94	−1.12%
Japan	18119.90	−95.43	−0.52%
Malaysia	234.67	−7.48	−3.09%
Pakistan	11378.00	−15.67	−0.14%
The Philippines	3331.29	−48.71	−1.44%
Singapore	3232.02	−75.9	−2.29%
South Korea	1454.60	−15.43	−1.05%
Sri Lanka	2996.49	−15.83	−0.53%
Taiwan	7901.96	1.76	0.02%
Thailand	683.95	−4.75	−0.69%

Sources; Dow Jones, Reuters; http://www.reuters.com/finance/markets/.

[20] The establishment of ASEAN Exchanges in April 2011 is the starting point of deepening financial integration in Asian intra-regional trading. ASEAN Exchanges consist of ASEAN-5 and Vietnam with market capitalization of $1.98 trillion as of March 2011. Refer to http://www.aseanexchanges.org for details.

REFERENCES

Arouri, M.H., Nguyen, D.K., 2009. Time-varying characteristics of cross-market linkages with empirical application to Gulf stock markets. Managerial Finance 36 (1), 57–70

Azad, A.S.M., 2009. Efficiency, cointegration and contagion in equity markets: Evidence from China, Japan and South Korea. Asian Economic Journal 23 (1), 93–118

Bai, J., Perron, P., 1998. Estimating and testing linear models with multiple structural changes. Econometrica 66 (1), 47–78

Bai, J., Perron, P., 2003. Computation and analysis of multiple structural change models. Journal of Applied Econometrics 18, 1–22

Beirne, J., Caporale, G.M., Schulze-Ghattas, M., Spagnolo, N., 2009. Volatility spillovers and contagion from mature to emerging stock markets. Working Paper Series 1113, European Central Bank. <http://ssrn.com/abstract_id=1502468> (accessed 10.06.10).

Bollerslev, T., 1990. Modelling the coherence in short-run nominal exchange rates: A multivariate generalized ARCH model. Review of Economics and Statistics 72 (3), 498–505

Bollerslev, T., Wooldridge, J., 1992. Quasi-maximum likelihood estimation and inference in dynamic models with time-varying covariances. Econometric Reviews 11 (2), 143–172

Bollerslev, T., Engle, R.F., Wooldridge, J.M., 1988. A capital asset pricing model with time-varying covariances. Journal of Political Economy 96 (1), 116–131

Chow, H.K., Peter, N.K., Roberto, S.M., Augustine, H.H. Tan., 2005. Trade, investment and financial integration in East Asia. Asean+3 Policy Research Group, Singapore Management University.

Edwards, S., Biscarri, J.G., Perez de Gracia, F., 2003. Stock market cycles, financial liberalization and volatility. Journal of International Money and Finance 22 (7), 925–955

Engle, R.F., 1982. Autoregressive conditional heteroskedasticity with estimates of the variance of UK inflation. Econometrica 50, 987–1008

Engle, R.F., 2002. Dynamic conditional correlation – a simple class of multivariate GARCH models. Journal of Business and Economic Statistics 20, 339–350

Engle, R.F., Kroner, K.F., 1995. Multivariate simultaneous generalized ARCH. Econometric Theory 11 (1), 122–150

Forbes, K.J., Rigobon, R., 2002. No contagion, only interdependence: measuring stock market comovements. Journal of Finance 57, 2223–2261

Girardin, E., Liu, Z., 2007. The financial integration of China: new evidence on temporally aggregated data for the A-share market. China Economic Review 18, 354–371

Gjerde, O., Saettem, F., 1999. Causal relations among stock returns and macroeconomic variables in a small, open economy. Journal of International Financial Markets, Institutions and Money 9 (1), 61–74

Gupta, R., Guidi, F., 2012. Cointegration relationship and time varying co-movements among Indian and Asian developed stock markets. International Review of Financial Analysis 21, 10–22

Hamilton, J.D., Gang, L., 1996. Stock market volatility and the business cycle. Journal of Applied Econometrics 11 (5), 573–593

Huang, B.N., Yang, C.W., Hu, J., 2000. Causality and cointegration of stock markets among the United States, Japan and the South China Growth Triangle. International Review of Financial Analysis 9 (3), 281–297

Huyghebaert, N., Wang, L., 2010. The co-movement of stock markets in East Asia did the 1997–1998 Asian financial crisis really strengthen stock market integration? China Economic Review 21, 98–112

Ito, T., 1999. Japan and the Asian financial crisis: the role of financial supervision in restoring growth. Working Paper Series pp. 10–99.

Lamoureux, C.G., Lastrapes, W.D., 1990. Persistence in variance, structural change and the GARCH model. Journal of Business & Economics Statistics 8 (2), 225–234

Lean, H.H., Ghosh, B.N., 2010. Economic integration in Asia: quo vadis Malaysia? International Economic Journal 24 (2), 237–248

Lean, H.H., Teng, K.T., 2013. Integration of world leaders and emerging powers into the Malaysian stock market: A DCC-MGARCH approach. Economic Modelling 32, 333–342

Lee, S.W., Hansen, B.E., 1994. Asymptotic theory for the Garch (1,1) Quasi-maximum likelihood estimator. Econometric Theory 10 (1), 29–52

Lindgren, C.-J., Baliño, T.J.T., Enoch, C., Gulde, A.-M., Quintyn, M., Teo, L., 1999. Financial sector crisis and restructuring. Lessons from Asia. IMF Occasional Paper, 188, International Monetary Fund.

McKinnon, R., Schnabl, G., 2002. Synchronized business cycles in East Asia: fluctuations in the yen/dollar exchange rate and China's stabilizing role. <www.stanford.edu/mckinnon> (accessed September 2010).

Naughton, B., 1998. China's financial reform: achievements and challenges. BRIE Working Paper, 112, Berkeley Roundtable on the International Economy.

Nelson, D.B., 1990. Stationarity and persistence in the GARCH (1,1) model. Econometric Theory 6, 318–334

Nishimura, Y., Men, M., 2010. The paradox of China's international stock market co-movement: Evidence from volatility spillover effects between China and G5 stock markets. Journal of Chinese Economic and Foreign Trade Studies 3 (3), 235–253

Pagan, A.R., Harding, D., 2002. Dissecting the cycle: a methodological investigation. Journal of Monetary Economics 49 (2), 365–381

Phylaktis, K., Ravazzolo, F., 2002. Measuring financial and economic integration with equity prices in emerging markets. Journal of International Money and Finance, Elsevier 21 (6), 879–903

Savva, C., 2009. International stock markets interactions and conditional correlations Journal of International Financial Markets. Institutions & Money 19, 645–661

Silvennoinen, A., Teräsvirta, T., 2008. Multivariate GARCH models. Working Paper Series in Economics and Finance, 669, Stockholm School of Economics.

Tse, Y.K., 2000. A test for constant correlations in a multivariate GARCH model. Journal of Econometrics 98 (1), 107–127

Wang, K., Chen, Y.-H., Huang, S.-W., 2011. The dynamic dependence between the Chinese market and other international stock markets: A time-varying copula approach International Review of Economics and Finance 20 (4), 654–664

Wong, D., Li, K.W., 2010. Comparing the performance of relative stock return differential and real exchange rate in two financial crisis. Applied Financial Economics 20 (1/2), 137–150

Xu, L., Oh, K.B., 2010. The stock market in China: an endogenous adjustment process responding to the demands of economic reform and growth. Journal of Asian Economics 22 (1), 36–47

Yu, I.-W., Fung, K.-P., Tam, C.-S., 2010. Assessing financial market integration in Asia–equity markets. Journal of Banking & Finance 34 (12), 2874–2885

INDEX

2008–2009 crisis, 509
amplifications on, 514
ΔCôVaR Estimates, 300–301
Δ-Rating methodology, 19–20, 47
country-specific fundamental rating, 20
credible weights, 23
market implied rating, 22

A

ADCC GARCH model, 691
ADF (Augmented Dickey-Fuller) test, 450, 653
Adverse-selection hypothesis, 384
Age-dependency ratio, 126
Albeit stress-testing, 424
Algorithmic optimization technique, 433
AR models, 517, 530
Arab Monetary Fund (AMF) database, 162, 166
Arbitrage Pricing Model (APT), 313
ARDL (Autoregressive Distributed Lags) approach, 644, 647–648
Arellano-Bover/Blundell-Bond tests, 761–762
ARMA components, 224
Arrow-Debreu framework, 201
Artificial neural network (ANN), 354, 359
ASEAN markets, 561
ASEAN-5, financial market integration of, 606, 825
data and methodology, 829
Bai and Perron (BP) multiple structural breaks test, 835
data description, 829
DCC-MGARCH model, 832
DCC-MGARCH model, 847
empirical results of, 835
misspecification tests, 851
time-varying patterns, 840
literature review, 828
structural changes, perspective of, 840
exceptional structural break dates, 847
fifth phase, 846
first phase, 843
fourth phase, 846
second phase, 844
third phase, 844
ASEAN-6, 604
ASEAN-China Centre, 608
ASEAN-China Free Trade Area (ACFTA), 604
ASE-General Index (ASE-GI), 679
Asian financial crisis, 845
Asset Graphs, 804
Asset liquidity trading risk, 414, 418
Asset return and volatility spillovers
between big commodity producing countries, 773
data, 778
econometric model, 777
literature review, 775
empirical results for, 781–784
Asset returns, determinants of, 76, 81
bank deposit rates, 77, 82
stock returns, 78, 83
Asset Trees, 804
Association of Southeast Asian Nations (ASEAN), 603
data, 609
empirical specification and methodology, 612
overview of markets and bilateral trade and investment, 607
results, 614
stock market co-movement in, 603
stock market linkages
literature on, 605
theoretical underpinnings of, 605
Asymmetric DCC models, estimation of, 521
Asymmetric DCC-Multivariate GARCH model, 510
Asymmetric dynamic conditional correlation (ADCC) model, 665, 689, 693
Asymmetric information, 179, 384, 390
Asymptotic Mean Squared Error (AMSE), 242, 247, 249–250
Athens Stock Exchange (ASE), 679
Augmented Dickey Fuller (ADF) test, 565
Automated Trading System (ATS), 147
Autoregressive Conditional Duration (ACD) model, 183
Autoregressive Conditional Heteroscedasticity (ARCH) model, 152, 224, 242, 372, 450, 458, 626

Autoregressive Conditional Jump Intensity model, 371
Autoregressive distributed lag (ARDL) model, 720
Available for sale (AFS), 102

B

Baba-Engle-Kraft-Kroner (BEKK) model, 450, 459, 461, 827
Backpropagation neural networks (BPN), 359
Bai and Perron (BP) multiple structural breaks test, 835
Balkan stock markets, 688–689
Bangkok Stock Exchange Price Index (THSE), 829
Bangladeshi stock market, 146
Bank deposit interest rate, 69, 77, 82, 92
Bank license, 54
Bank liquidity crisis, 514
Bank of China, 60
Banks index, 280
Basel-compliant countries, 414
"Basic" regression, 90
Basle I agreement, 271
Basle II agreement, 271
Bassle III agreement, 271–272
Bayesian forecaster, 355
  and case-based optimization, 356
Bayesian Information Criterion (BIC), 835
Bayesian solution, 356
Bear Markets Trend Gaps, 592
Behavioral finance in emerging markets. *See* Cultural behavioral finance in emerging markets
Beirlant criterion, 250
BEKK-GARCH model, 627
BET Index (BET-C), 679
Betweenness centrality, 808
Bid-ask spreads, 29, 32
Big commodity producing countries
  asset return and volatility spillovers between, 773
Bipower variance, 491
Bombay Stock Exchange (BSE), 829
Bond index, 29
Bond yields, 18, 22
Bootstrap panel unit root analysis, 167
Boxing Day 2004 tsunami, 614
Brazil
  market capitalization in, 558
  oil and gas sector in, 205
  real exchange rate, 230
  stock market, 650–652
    during crisis, 574
Brazilian returns, 782–783
Brent crude oil index, 374
Breusch-Godfrey (BG) test, 24, 458
Breusch-Pagan Lagrange Multiplier Test, 20, 24
BRIC countries, 556–557
  during subprime crises, 555
  empirical methodology, 562
    model selection and diagnostic analysis, 564
    Switching-ARCH (SWARCH) model, 563–564
  empirical results, 564
    data and descriptive statistics, 564
    smoothed probabilities and regime classification, 568
    SWARCH results, 566
  implications, 575
  interdependence versus contagion, 570
  related literature, overview of, 560
  return and volatility spillovers between, 776
BRICS, energy sector companies of. *See* Energy sector companies of BRICS
BSE-Sofia Index (SOFIX), 679
Bühlmann-Straub Credibility Theory, 19, 23
Bulgarian economy, 671
Bull and bear markets, 589
Bull Markets Trend Gaps, 592
Business Environment Survey, 383

C

Cairo and Alexandria Stock Exchanges (CASE), 634
Canada, Australia, Russia, Brazil, and South Africa (CARBS), 773
Canadian returns, 782
Capital Asset Pricing Model (CAPM), 313
Case-based reasoning (CBR), 354–355
Cash reserve ratio, 100
CCER database, 314
Central and Eastern Europe (CEE), 627
  volatility and spillover effects of, 449
    autoregressive conditional heteroscedasticity, test for, 458
    constant conditional correlation (CCC) model, 459
    data analysis, 452
    diagonal BEKK, 459

empirical results, 460
literature review, 450
multivariate GARCH models, 458
testing for serial correlation, 458
tests of normality, 453
time series analysis, 453
VARMA AGARCH, 460
VARMA GARCH, 460
Central and Eastern European countries (CEECs), 811
banking industry of, 298
Central European countries, 812
Central European markets, stock market co-movements among, 628
Central Securities Depository System, 147
CEO overconfidence, 338
CEZ, 502
Chicago Board Options Exchange Volatility Index (VIX), 32
China, 557
market capitalization in, 558
oil and gas sector in, 204
stock market, 829
stock market co-movement in, 603–604, 606–609
as trading partner to the world, 604
China-ASEAN Free Trade Agreement (CAFTA), 847
China-owned banks in Hong Kong, 56
data and methodology, 55
empirical results, 58
foreign banks in Hong Kong, 52
hypothesis testing, 53
hypotheses, 54
profitability measures, 54
Chinese Economic Area (CEA) market, 561
Chinese equity markets, 644, 646
Chinese Exchange, 644
Chinese stock markets, 644, 651
Chinese yuan exchange rate, 230
Chittagong Stock Exchange (CSE), 145
Cholesky factorization, 777
CITI bank, 60
CITIC bank, 60
CITIC index, 314
Classical Multidimensional Scaling, 805
Coherency function, estimation of, 633
Collateral in emerging economies, 383, 398
empirical analysis, 391
data, 391
descriptive statistics, 396
model, 392
results, 397
literature on, 384
developed countries, studies in, 384
emerging countries, studies in, 386
policy implication, 408
requirements in large firms, 404
robustness checks, 400
Collateral-based lending, 387
Colombia, Indonesia, Vietnam, Egypt, Turkey, and South Africa (CIVETS), 776
Co-movement, 556, 562
among different financial markets, 511
in asset market returns, 623, 639
between international returns, 734
emerging vs advanced stock market excess returns, 735
excess returns vs macroeconomic policy uncertainty, 736
Comovements and volatility spillovers, 371
data and methodology, 373
data description, 373
estimation of dynamic correlations, 377
empirical results, 378
Co-movements issue between stock–bond markets, 623
empirical analysis and data, 630
data description, 634
evolutionary co-spectral density function, estimation of, 631
theory of evolutionary co-spectral, 630
related literature, 625
results and discussions, 635
CONCENTRATION variable, 395, 402
Conditional correlation, 539
constant, 547
dynamic, 549
Conditional performance measure, 9
Conditional variance-covariance matrix, 649
Conservatism, 334
Constant conditional correlation (CCC) model, 450, 544–545, 547, 689–690
volatility and spillover effects, 459–460
Constant relative risk aversion (CRRA), 5
Consumer price indices (CPI), 100
Contagion, defined, 511
Contagion effect, 538–539, 544

of financial crisis, 509, 511, 665
informational factors, 512
institutional factors, 512
Contagion from US to EMs during crisis period, 510
amplifications on recent crisis, 514
data, 517
descriptive statistics, 518
empirical results, 521
AR model for estimated dynamic conditional correlations, 530
asymmetric DCC models, estimation of, 521
EGARCH specification, 521
implications, 533
methodology, 515
theoretical underpinnings, 511
contagion, 511
economic integration, 513
Contemporaneous bank deposit rates, 82
Contemporaneous inflation coefficient, 88
Control variables, 281
Conventional mean-variance approach, 717
Corruption Perceptions Index (CPI), 24, 28
Co-spectral analysis. *See* Evolutionary co-spectral analysis
Country-specific fundamental rating
rating evaluation, 24
δ-Rating methodology, 20
Country-specific implied and market implied ranks, 43
Country-specific variables, 392, 395, 400, 408
CoVaR (Conditional Value-at-Risk) methodology, 273
data and empirical results, 280
quantile regressions, 281–282
ΔCôVaR Estimates, 300–301
econometric methodology, 277
literature review, 274
"Crash" model, 612
Credibility Theory, 23
Credibility weights, 23, 44
rating evaluation, 37
δ-Rating methodology, 23
Credit Crisis, 795
Credit crunch, 414, 419, 439
Credit default swap (CDS), 18, 22, 510
behavior of, 502
Credit rating agencies (CRAs), 46
Credit risk, 18, 20
CREDITINFO variable, 395, 402, 407
Crisis period (CP), 350
Croatian economy, 672
CROBEX share index (CROBEX), 679
Cross-product ratio (CPR), 317–318
Cultural behavioral finance in emerging markets, 337
cultural variances in psychology, 332
emotions, 339
future of, 341
heuristic simplification, 333
conservatism, 334
framing, 335
representativeness, 334
salience and availability, 336
national culture
conceptualizing, 328
and emerging markets, 330
self-deception, 338
social dynamics, 340
Current account balance (CAB), 24
Cyprus, economy of, 674–675
Cyprus Stock Exchange (CSE), 679
Cyprus-General Index (CYP-GI), 679
Czech Republic, 475, 627
banking industry of, 299

D

Daily returns, 452
Daily volatilities, 431
Data generating processes (DGPs), 242–243, 263
Data source, 125
Datastream Inc., 260
DatastreamGlobal Equity Indexes (DGEI), 731
D-CAPM model, 335
DCC model building, 521
DCC-GARCH model, 372–373, 377, 381, 549, 649, 827, 832, 836–838, 841–842
empirical results of, 835
log-likelihood estimation, 834
time-varying patterns, 840
misspecification tests, 851
two-step estimation of, 834
De facto financial integration, 725, 740
De jure integration, 725–726
Decision making of dealer in equity desk, 106
Decision tree (DT), 354–355
and sequential game, 103
Demand-oriented oil price shocks, 380

Demographic dividend, 117
Demographic transition and savings behavior in Mauritius, 115
literature survey, 117
macroeconomic modeling, 123
data source, 125
demography, 126
government expenditure, 127
income growth, 125
level of financial development, 126
model specification, 124
OLS regression, 132
past savings, 125
VAR approach, 135–136
variable definition, 125
microeconomic modeling, 127, 135
data analysis, 128
expenditure pattern, 130
household debt, 132
income pattern, 128
methodology, 127
model specification, 128
survey data, 127
saving rates, 123
savings trends, 121
Demographics, 126
Dependency effect, 118–119
Deposit-Taking Companies (DTC) license status, 52
Deutsch Bank Commodity index (DBC), 778
Developed and emerging equity market tail risk, 241
empirical application, 260
Monte Carlo experiments, 247
choice of optimal number of extremes, 249
data generating processes, 248
Monte Carlo results, 252
testing structural change in tail behavior, 243
regular variation, 243
structural change in tail behavior, 245
Developed countries, collateral in, 384
bank competition, 386
information asymmetry, 384
risk related to borrower, 384
Dhaka stock exchange (DSE), 145
background of, 145
data, econometric packages, and descriptive statistics, 150
policy implications, 156
results from unit root tests, 152
results from variance-ratio tests, 155
testing methodologies, 148
unit root tests, 148
variance-ratio tests, 149
Direction of Oil and Natural Gas, 205
Diversification into emerging markets, 703
Domestic collateral, 386
Domestic Credit, 759, 766, 768
Dow Jones Industrial Index (DJII), 829
Dubai Financial Market (DFM) General Index, 435
DURATION_LOAN variable, 395
Dynamic conditional correlation (DCC) model, 202, 219, 226, 233, 237, 544, 549, 689–690
Dynamic Conditional Correlation GARCH model (DCC-GARCH), 586

E

Early warning system (EWS) for financial crisis, 347
empirical example and experiment, 357
EWSGII construction, 362
lag-*l* classifier construction, 359
oracle classifier construction, 359
lag-*l* forecasting classifier, 353
definition, 353
machine learning tools, 354
training data set, 354
linking various classifiers, 355
Bayesian forecaster and case-based optimization, 356
oracle classifier, 349, 352
definition, 349
predictor variables, 351
procedure description, 348
East Asian Crisis, 18, 539
East Asian equity markets, 539–540, 542, 544, 549, 551
EBRD index, 818
Econometric model, 777
Economic indicator data, statistics of, 39
Economic indicators
principal component analysis of, 38
score plot of, 25
Economic integration, 513
equalization of rates of return, 513
international financial market completeness, 513
sourcing domestic investment, 513

Economic risk factors, 677
Economic time series, 625
Economic-capital, 413
EGARCH(1,1) model, 516
Egypt
  stock–bond market, dynamic interaction between, 630
Eigenvectors, 802
  centrality, 808
Emerging countries, collateral in, 386
Emerging countries sovereign rating adjustment using market information, 17
  δ-Rating methodology, 20
    country-specific fundamental rating, 20
    credible weights, 23
    market implied rating, 22
  discussion and conclusion, 46
  rating evaluation, 24
    country-specific implied rating, 24
    implied ratings and credibility weights, 37
    market implied rating, 29
Emerging economies, 17
Emerging market developing economy (EDE), 99
Emerging market mutual funds, 3
Emerging market stocks in global portfolios, 701
  available evidence, 702
  conventional mean-variance approach, 717
  data, informal examination of, 707
  empirical results, 712
  hedge ratio, alternative estimates of, 718
  methodology, 704
    construction of portfolios, 707
    hedge ratio, calculation of, 704
    hedging effectiveness, measuring, 705
Emerging markets, 17
Emotions, 332, 339
Energy Information Administration (EIA), 166
Energy sector companies of BRICS, 201
  data, 207
  econometric models, 216
    multivariate GARCH, dynamic conditional correlation, and value at risk, 219
    systematic and specific risks with panel methods, 217
  empirical results, 220
    multivariate GARCH, dynamic conditional correlation, and value at risk, 226
    systematic and specific risks with panel methods, 220
  gas resources, 207
  literature review, 203
  oil resources, 206
  role of gas and oil, 204
Enormous selling period (ESP), 351
Equity desk, decision making of dealer in, 106
Equity market comovements among emerging countries, 643
  data and results, 649
    long-run comovements, 654
    preliminary analysis, 650
    short-run comovements, 658
  empirical method, 647
    ARDL approach to cointegration, 647–648
    DCC-GARCH model, 649
  integration of equity markets, 645
Equity markets, integration of, 645
Equity Multiplier (EM), 55–56
Equity mutual funds performance persistence
  in long term, 320
    non-parametric test, 320
    parametric test, 322
  in short term, 318
    non-parametric test, 318
    parametric test, 319
Equity return, 281
Equity Risk Premium (ERP), 726, 738
Error correction term (ECT), 693
Estate savings, 119
Estimated shape parameter, 192
Estimation procedure and optimal weighting matrix, 11
Estonian stock market, 478
EU expansion, 449
EU-8 foreign assets and liabilities and EU-8 foreign trade, linkage between, 751
Euro Zone sovereign bonds, 22
European Sovereign Debt Crisis, 18, 29, 47
European Systemic Risk Board, 272
Euro-US dollar exchange rate, 202, 237
Euro-US dollar exchange risk, 230
Evolutionary algorithm (EA), 357
Evolutionary co-spectral analysis, 625, 630–631, 638
Evolutionary co-spectral density function, estimation of, 631
EWSGII construction, 348, 357, 362
Ex ante real rate, 71, 74–75
Ex post real rate, 72, 75, 79, 81

Exchange traded funds (ETFs), 496, 774, 778
Exogenous liquidity, 417
Exponential GARCH (EGARCH) model, 516, 609, 612
Exponential weighted moving average (EWMA) model, 689
External assets, 749, 751, 754
External debt (ED), 24
External Wealth of Nations (EWN) dataset, 754
Extreme Value Theory (EVT), 242

F

Fama-French framework, 203
"Fear" index, 208
Financial contagion, 560
Financial Depth, 758
Financial development, 811
- empirical analysis, 814
  - activity of financial sector, 815
  - data, 816
  - efficiency of financial sector, 815
  - estimation results, 817
  - methodology, 817
  - size of financial sector, 815
- level of, 126
- literature review, 812

Financial distress
- Lehman Brothers, case study, 487

Financial hedging, 704
Financial integration, 513
- defined, 750
- literature review of, 751

Financial liberalization, 126, 387
"Financial Risk" index, 677
Financial Sector Assessment Program, 271
Financial Services index, 280
Financial Stability Oversight Council, 272
Financial Times All Shares (FTA) index, 313
Financial volatility, 534
Firm-loan specific variables, 392, 394–395
Firm-specific variables, 393
Fiscal balance (FB), 28
Fisher effect, 74
Fisher equation framework, 68
Fitch Sovereign Historical Ratings, 24, 38
Fixed-effect approach, 24
Fix-effect regression results
- for country-specific model, 26
- of market implied rating model
  - of advanced economies, 34
  - of emerging economies, 35

Flight-to-quality, 514
Forecasting equation, 75
Forecasting liquidity, 103
Foreign banks in Hong Kong, 52
Foreign direct investment (FDI), 668
- in 2006–2011, 670

Foreign investment in a portfolio, 337
Foreign portfolio equity, 21
Four-index alpha, 318–320, 322
Four-index model, 316
Framing effect, 335
Frankfurt Stock Exchange, 680
F-test, 493
FTSE-Global Index, 29, 32

G

GARCH model, 144, 242, 275, 371–372, 516, 626
GARCH(1, 1) model, 545
Gas and oil role in BRICS, 204
GCC financial markets, 414
GDP per capita, 759
General Index ex Financials, 299
Generalized Autoregressive Conditional Heteroskedasticity in mean model (GARCH-M(1, 1) model), 429–430
Generalized method of moments (GMM), 4, 9, 74
Genetic algorithm (GA), 357
Gini Coefficient, 116
GJR-DCC-GARCH models, 373
GJR-GARCH process, 377
Global equity market correlations, 583
Global Financial Crisis (GFC), 537, 603
- data collection, 540
- empirical results, 546
  - constant conditional correlation, 547
  - dynamic conditional correlation, 549
  - volatilities of individual market, 546
- impact on GCC Countries, 757
- literature review, 538
- research methodology, 544

Global Financial Data, 150
Global institutional investors, 347
Global integration indexes, 740
Global portfolio diversification strategies, 584
Global trend indicator, 595
GLOBE cultural measures, 330
Government expenditure to GDP, 127

Gray zone, 348
Greece, economic situation in, 673–674
Gross Domestic Fixed Capital Formation (GDFCF), 123
Gross domestic product (GDP), 17, 28, 116
G-sec dealer, 102
Gulf Cooperation Council (GCC) countries, 161
  empirical investigation, 166
    bootstrap panel unit root analysis, 167
    data, 166
    panel cointegration, 168
    SUR estimates, 171
  policy discussion, 173
  stock markets and oil, 163
  transmission channels, 165
Gulf Cooperation Council (GCC) financial markets, 372, 413–414
  determinants of international financial integration of, 749
    analysis of, 757
    empirical results, 762
    literature review of, 751
    measures of, 753
    methodology and empirical specification, 761
    policy implications, 768
    summary statistics and correlation, 759
    theoretical issues, 757
    variables, 758
  impact of global financial crisis on, 757

H

Hausman test statistic, 73
Hedge ratio
  alternative estimates of, 718
  calculation of, 704
Hedging effectiveness, measuring, 705
Held for trading (HFT), 102
Held to maturity (HTM), 102
Herding behavior, 512
Heteroskedastic and autocorrelation consistent (HAC), 11
Heuristic simplification, 332–333
  conservatism, 334
  framing, 335
  representativeness, 334
  salience and availability, 336
High-dimension low sample-size (HDLSS) classification problem, 355
Hill estimator, 254
Hill statistic, 245, 247, 253
Hindsight bias, 336
Historical simulation method, 420
Ho Chi Minh City Stock Exchange, 604
Hofstede's individualism, 338
Holistic cognition, 333
Home-bias "puzzle," 703
Hong Kong
  banking sector in, 299
  China-owned banks in. *See* China-owned banks in Hong Kong
  financial services in, 300
  licensed banks incorporated in, 53
Hong Kong State Administered Region (HKSAR), 51
Hong Kong Stock Exchange, 180
"Hot hand" phenomenon, 311
Household debt, 132
HTM portfolio, 110
Hungary, 627
Hybrid emerging market mutual funds, 3
  econometric methodology and tests, 9
    estimation procedure and optimal weighting matrix, 11
    general framework, 9
    optimal risky asset allocation specifications, 13
  managed portfolios, performance evaluation of, 7
    conditional setting, 8
    unconditional setting, 7
  stochastic discount factors (SDFs) and benchmark models, 5
    robust performance measures, 7

I

Idiosyncratic risk, 201
Income growth, 125
India, 557
  market capitalization in, 558
  oil and gas sector in, 205
Individualism, 329
Indonesia, 614
  banking industry of, 299
Inflation rate, 69
Inflation rate factor, 28
Inflation uncertainty, 75
Information and communications technology (ICT), 813
Information-sharing institutions, 408

Instantaneous bipower variance, 491
Instantaneous quadratic variance, 491
Insurances index, 280
IntegratedVariation, 486
Interdependence versus contagion, 570
Interest rate margin (INT), 815
INTEREST_LOAN variable, 395, 398
Internal risk models, 413
"International Country Risk Guide" (ICRG) rating system, 676–677
International diversification, 701–702, 710
- conventional mean-variance approach, 717
- hedging approach to, 704

International financial integration, determinants of, 749
- in GCC countries, 757
  - empirical results, 762
  - impact of global financial crisis on, 757
  - methodology and empirical specification, 761
  - summary statistics and correlation, 759
  - theoretical issues, 757
  - variables, 758
- measures of, 753

International financial markets
- correlation and network structure of, 795
  - correlation and volatility of market, 802
  - data, 796
  - network structure, 804
  - random matrix theory, 797

International Financial Statistics, 707
International investment, 703
International Money Fund (IMF) WEO Database, 24
International Parity theory, 757
International portfolio diversification, 644–645, 649, 652
International stock market excess returns, behavior of, 725
- summary statistics and preliminary analysis, 727
  - international stock market co-movements, 734
  - stock market country indexes, 727
  - stock market sector indexes, 731
- time-varying analysis, 737
  - dynamics of international stock market excess returns, 745
  - on excess returns, 738
  - on global integration, 739
  - on "model's validity," 743

Investment Climate Private Enterprise Survey (PICS), 392
ISE-National-100 Index (ISE-100), 634, 679
Israel
- stock–bond market, dynamic interaction between, 630

Istanbul Stock Exchange (ISE), 634, 679

J

Jakarta Stock Exchange Composite Stock Price Index (JSE), 829
Jarque-Bera (JB) test, 427, 651, 830
Jensen single-index alpha, 315
JPM EMBI Global Stripped Spreads returns, 520

K

Kernel-based robust estimator, 12
KPSS (Kwiatkowski, Phillips, Schmidt, and Shin) unit root tests, 450, 653
Kuala Lumpur Stock Exchange Composite Price index (KLCI), 829
Kuwait, 163

L

LAC's banking sector, 510
LACD model, 183
Lagged relative spread coefficient, 192
Lagged volatility coefficient, 192
Lag-*l* classifier construction, 359
Lag-*l* forecasting classifier, 353
- definition, 353
- machine learning tools, 354
- training data set, 354

Lagrange multiplier (LM) test, 152, 168, 458, 835
Latin American markets during 1990s crisis, 562
Lehman Brothers, 492, 514
- financial distress, case study, 487
- and sovereign bond spreads, 528

Lender-borrower relationship, 384
Liberalization, 510, 513
LIBOR, 514
Licensed banks, 52, 54
- in Hong Kong, 53

Life cycle hypothesis (LCH), 115, 117
Life cycle savings, 118
Linear dynamic panel-data models, 761
Liquefied natural gas (LNG), 205
Liquid liabilities to GDP ratio (LLG), 815
Liquidation horizon factor, 434

Liquidity adjustment facility (LAF), 103–104
Liquidity and inflation, relationship between, 90
  decision making of a dealer in the equity desk, 106
  decision tree and sequential game, 103
  economic games, existing literature on, 101
  forecasting liquidity, 103
  Nash equilibrium, 102
  scenario, 100
  zero-sum game, 101
Liquidity spread, 281
Liquidity-adjusted value-at-risk (LVAR)
    mathematical structure, 415, 417–419, 423–424, 431–433
  derivation of, 442
  limit-setting, 425
Ljung-Box test, 188, 651, 830, 839
LLOAN_DURATION variable, 395
Loan characteristics, 393, 395, 398
Log Autoregressive Conditional Duration (LACD) model, 181
Log-likelihood estimation, 834
Log-returns, calculating, 797
Loil, 168
London Interbank Offer rates (LIBOR), 70
Long-run comovements among emerging equity markets, 645–647, 654
Long-term orientation, 330
Lstock, 168

M

Malaysia, China and, 608
Managed portfolios, performance evaluation of, 7
  conditional setting, 8
  unconditional setting, 7
Marčenku-Pastur distribution, 798, 800
MARGIN, 58, 60
Market correlation, measuring, 585–586
Market efficiency, 143
Market Efficiency Hypothesis (MEH), 605
Market implied rating, 22
  δ-Rating methodology, 22
  rating evaluation, 29
Market indicators, statistics of, 42
Market premium, 202, 222
Market requirement indicator, 32
Markov switching model, 562–563
Markowitz theoretical models, 416
Masculinity, degree of
  in national culture, 329
Mauritian economy, 116
MENA countries, 624
  emerging bond markets in, 624
  emerging stock markets in, 624, 628
  stock-bond co-movement, 629
    empirical analysis and data, 630
  stock markets, 628
Mexican banking industry, 281
Mexican crisis, 561
Mexican financial sector, liberalization of, 387
Mexican stock market, 650, 652
Mexico crisis (1994), 539
Micro-prudential regulatory framework, 271
Mid-quote return, 188
Minimum Spanning Tree (MST), 804
Minimum-risk hedge ratio, 704
Mixed-Weibull Log Autoregressive Conditional Duration (LACD) model, 181
Modified Feldstein-Horioka model, 646
Modified information criteria (MIC), 148
Modigliani's life cycle hypothesis, 132, 136
Money supply growth, 69
Monte Carlo experiments, 247
  choice of optimal number of extremes, 249
  data generating processes, 248
  Monte Carlo results, 252
Monte Carlo simulations, 248, 250, 420
Morgan EMBI Global (EMBIG), 518
Morgan Emerging Market Bond Index Global Stripped Spread, 518
Morgan Stanley Capital International (MSCI) index, 518, 649–650
  dataset, 162
  Europe Index, 589
  Japan Index, 589
  USA indexes, 589
  World Index, 803
Morgan Stanley Capital International Total Return Indexes (MSCI TRIs), 727–728
Multi-market portfolios, 715
Multinomial logistic regression (MLR), 354
Multivariate GARCH models, 219, 226, 450
Multivariate generalized autoregressive conditional heteroschedastic (MGARCH) model, 689
Multivariate VARMA models, 474
Mutual fund performance, 316
Mutual fund returns, 315
Mutual funds, 309
  literature review, 310
    mixed results of performance persistence, 313

non-persistence of mutual funds performance, 312
persistence of mutual funds performance, 310
methodology, 314
non-parametric persistence test model, 316
parametric persistence test model, 317
research findings, 318
equity mutual funds performance persistence in long term, 320
equity mutual funds performance persistence in short term, 318
Mutual guarantee societies (MGSs), 408
MVR (multiple variance ratio) tests, 450

N

NAFTA, 645
Nanyang Commercial Bank, 58
NASDAQ stocks, 180
Nash equilibrium, 102
National culture, 328
conceptualizing, 328
and emerging markets, 330
National Oil and Gas Companies in the BRICS, 204
NDTL, 106
New York Stock Exchange (NYSE), 484, 493–494, 496, 797
companies and ETF for, 497
and comparisons, 499
News-based measures of integration, 753
Nikkei 225 Stock Average Price Index (NIK), 829
Node centrality, 808
Nominal equity returns, 69
Nonlinear error correction models, 719
Non-normality
and correlation patterns, 427
testing for, 427
Non-parametric persistence test model, 316
Non-parametric robust estimator, 12
Nonrenewable energy sector, 201
Norway's government bonds, 29
NSC V900, 182
NYSE, 680

O

Oil and Gas Company (ONGC), 205
Oil India Limited, 202, 231
Oil price shocks, demand-oriented, 380
Optimal risky asset allocation, 6
specifications, 13
Optimum risk limits, 433
Oracle classifier, 349, 352
definition, 349
predictor variables, 351
Oracle classifier construction, 359
Oracle lag-zero rule, 348
Ordinary Least Squares (OLS) statistics, 458
estimator, 73
regression, 132, 134
Overconfidence, 338
Overnight Index Swap (OIS), 514

P

Panel model, 19–20
Parametric method, 420
Parametric persistence test model, 317
Paris Stock Exchange, 180
Past information, 90–91
on foreign variables, 90
on inflation, 91–92
on money growth, 90
on nominal stock yields, 91
on rate of growth of money supply, 90
Patriotism, level of, 337
Pearson's correlation coefficients, 371
Pearson's product moment correlation coefficient, 585
Performance measurement, 3–4, 7
Performance persistence, 311
PetroChina Company Limited, 202, 231
Philippines
2004 fiscal crisis, 614
banking industry of, 299
Philippines Stock Exchange Composite Price index (PSE), 829
Planar Maximally Filtered Graph (PMFG), 804
Poland, 627
Political risk index, 678
Portfolio
diversification, 688, 697
equity, 825
policy, 6
Portuguese government bond, 29
Positive sum game, 101
Post-EU
2004–2011 period, 461, 476, 478
2007–2011 period, 461
Post-Lehman failure, 510, 514
Power distance, 329
PP (Phillips-Perron), 450

Prague Stock Exchange (PSE), 484, 493, 495, 498–499
Price jump behavior during financial distress, 483
 data description, 494
  New York Stock Exchange (NYSE), 496
  Prague Stock Exchange, 495
 identification of, 489
 indicators, 489
 Lehman Brothers, case of, 487
 methodology, 492
 motivation for, 485
 regulatory consequences, 501
  emerging markets, specific features of, 503
 results, 497
  New York Stock Exchange and comparisons, 499
  Prague Stock Exchange, 498
Price-based measures, 753
Principal component analysis (PCA) method, 20
Prominent multivariate GARCH models, 450
Pseudo-R^2, 281
Public sector undertaking (PSU) bank, 101
P-values, 32

Q

Qatar, 163
Q-statistics, 830
QuadraticVariation, 486
Qualified Domestic Institutional Investors (QDII) scheme, 846
Quantile regressions, 281–282
Quantity-based measures, 753
Quasi-maximum likelihood estimation, 378, 452, 834

R

Random Matrix Theory, 796–797
Random walk, 143–144, 148
 and efficiency hypothesis. *See* Dhaka stock exchange (DSE)
Random walk hypothesis (RWH), 144
Rate of change in commodity prices, 70
Rate of growth effect, 119
Rate of return on stocks, 96
Rate-of-change variables, 69
Rating agencies, 408
Rating evaluation, 24
 country-specific implied rating, 24
 implied ratings and credibility weights, 37
 market implied rating, 29
Real economy, 795
Real growth, 70
Real rate of return, determinants of, 67
 asset returns, determinants of, 76, 81
  bank deposit rates, 77, 82
  stock returns, 78, 83
 data, 69
 methodology, 71
RealizedVariance, 486
Redistribution effect, 118
Reduction ad absurdum, 726
"Refined" regression results, 83
Regional integration indexes (RII), 740
Regression, 90
Regression method, tests for, 88
"Relative liquidity," 483
Relative spread, 188
Representativeness, 334
Reserve Bank of India (RBI), 99
Restricted Licensed Banks (RLB), 52
Return on Assets (ROA), 54–55, 62
Return on Equities (ROE), 54–55, 62
Ricardian equivalence, 127
Riemann zeta function, 798
Risk appetite, 18, 425
Risk-adjusted returns, 317
Risk-capital, 413
RiskMetricsTM system, 416
Robustness checks, 400
Rolling-window analysis, 738
Romania
 economy of, 669, 671
 stock market, 478
Russia
 market capitalization in, 558
 oil and gas sector in, 205
 ruble exchange rate, 230

S

S&P 500 Composite Index of the United States, 540
S&P 500 index, 518
S&P index, 314
S&P/CITIC indices, 323
Sarbanes-Oxley Act, 46
Saudi Arabia, 163
Saving rates, 125
 for Mauritius and comparators, 123
Savings trends for Mauritius, 121
Schwartz measures, 330

Schwarz Bayesian criterion (SBC), 135
SE All Share Index, 431
Sector-by-sector spread, 731
Securities and Exchange Commission (SEC), 147
Securitization, 513
*See*mingly unrelated regression (SUR) methods, 163
Self-deception, 332, 338
Sequential game, 103
Shanghai Stock Exchange, 180, 604
Shanghai Stock Exchange Composite Index (SHCI), 829
Short-run comovements among emerging equity markets, 645, 658
  DCC-GARCH model, 649
Shuaa Arab index, 429, 431
Shuaa GCC index, 429
Singapore and Hong Kong, relationship between, 542
Single-index alpha, 316, 318–321
Single-index model, 416
SLR (statutory liquidity ratio), 100
Small and medium-size enterprises (SMEs), 383, 402, 408
Smooth transition CC (STCC) models, 627
Social dynamics, 332, 340
South Africa, oil and gas sector in, 205
South African market, 650
South African returns, 783
South-Eastern European (SEE) stock markets, 665
  banking sectors, 667–668
  capital market, 665, 688, 696
  and developed countries, 667
  empirical analysis of, 690
    ADCC GARCH model, 691
    CCC and DCC GARCH models, 690
    correlations, modeling dynamics in, 690
    results, 692
  foreign direct investment (FDI), 668
  growth and prospects, 679
    concise empirical literature review, 687
    data and descriptive statistics, 679
  recent economic developments in, 666
    Bulgaria, 671
    Croatia, 672
    Cyprus, 674
    Greece, 673
    macroeconomic issues, 666
    risk assessment and rating, 676
    Romania, 669
    Turkey, 675
  vs leading mature stock markets, 686–687
South-Eastern European countries (SEE-2), 812
Sovereign bond spreads
  after Lehman Brothers failure, 528
Sovereign credit risk, 18, 20
Sovereign risk, 510, 514, 518, 533
Spillover effects, 450, 478
  in CEE emerging market, 449
SRISK index, 275
Stable period (SP), 350
State of the system, 106
Stochastic discount factor (SDF), 4–5
  and benchmark models, 5
  robust performance measures, 7
Stock and bond markets co-movements, in MENA countries, 623
  empirical analysis and data, 630
    data description, 634
    evolutionary co-spectral density function, estimation of, 631
    theory of evolutionary co-spectral, 630
  related literature, 625
  results and discussions, 635
Stock market capitalization to GDP ratio (STMC), 815
Stock market co-movement, 603
Stock market country excess returns, 729
Stock market country indexes, 727
Stock market integration among emerging countries, 645–646
Stock market liberalization, 726
Stock market linkages
  literature on, 605
  theoretical underpinnings of, 605
Stock market sector indexes, 731
Stock market trends, defining, 588
Stock market volatility and contagion effects, in financial crisis, 665
  SEE countries, recent economic developments in, 666
    macroeconomic issues, 666
    risk assessment and rating, 676
    SE European economies, 669
  SEE stock market growth and prospects, 679
    concise empirical literature review, 687
    data and descriptive statistics, 679
  SEE stock markets, empirical analysis of, 690
    modeling dynamics in correlations, 690
    results, 692

Stock returns, 78, 83
in US and BRIC countries, 575
Stock-bond co-movement, 629
Straits Times Stock Exchange Index of Singapore (SSI), 829
Structural Adjustment Programme, 121
Structural break test, 515
Structural change test, 262, 264
Structured equity portfolios, risk exposure for, 429
Subprime crises
BRIC countries during, 570, 574–575
global financial crisis, 414
Subprimes, 795
Suprime mortgages, 795
SWARCH model, 562–563
Swiss Market Index, 105–106
Switching regimes, 626
Switching-ARCH (SWARCH) model, 562–563, 566
Switzerland bonds, 29
Systemic risk
defined, 272
measuring. *See* CoVaR (Conditional Value-at-Risk) methodology

T

TA-100 index, 634
Tactical risk analysis, 413
findings, 426
algorithmic optimization technique, 433
dataset, 426
non-normality and correlation patterns, statistical inference of, 427
structured equity portfolios, risk exposure for, 429
literature review, 416
methodology and research design, 420
Tail index, 244
TARCH models, 224, 226–227
T-bill rate, 162
Tel-Aviv Stock Exchanges (TASE), 634
Telecommunications technology (TEL), 813
Thai equity market, 650–651
Thailand market, 561
"The Great Recession," 780
Theory of evolutionary co-spectral, 630
Three-month treasury bill spread variation, 281
Threshold, 442
Tick size, 182
Time-fixed effect, 20, 24
Time-series analysis, 624
Time-varying analysis, 737–738
dynamics of international stock market excess returns, 745
on excess returns, 738
on global integration, 739
on "model's validity," 743
Time-varying correlations analysis, 372
Time-varying Weibull mixture model (TVMLACD), 187, 193–194
Timing effect, 118
Trade and Quote database (TAQ), 496
Trade durations, 188
Trade Openness, 751, 758, 762
Trading intensity, 180
Trading risk assessment, modeling of, 431
Transition period (TP), 350
Transmission mechanisms of crises, 538
Transparency International, 24
Trend gaps in assessing equity market correlations, 583
data and descriptive statistics, 589
measuring, 585
results, 590
stock market trends, defining, 588
Tress-testing, 415, 419, 424
T-tests, 32
Tunis Stock Exchange (TSE), 179
econometric models, 183
LACD model, 183
Weibull mixture LACD model, 184
empirical analysis, 187
data, 187
fixed weight mixture LACD estimates, 189
time-varying mixing weights LACD estimates, 193
institutional features of, 182
Turkey
banking industry in, 299
economy of, 675
stock–bond market, dynamic interaction between, 630
Two-sample Wilcoxon test, 493
Two-step estimation of, 834
Type-I error-optimal price jump indicators, 490, 499, 504
Type-II error-optimal price jump indicators, 490, 499, 504

U

Uncertainty avoidance, 330
Unconditional performance measure, 7
Unit root tests, 148
  results from, 152
United States Energy Information Administration, 205
Unstable period (UP), 350
Urbanization ratio, 126
US stock market crisis (1987), 539
US stock market in the aftermath of 2008–2009 crisis, 509
US-based balanced mutual funds, 3

V

Value-at-Risk (VaR) models, 135–136, 273, 413, 416–417, 420, 422
Variance inflation factors (VIF), 24
Variance ratio, 705
Variance reduction, 705, 713
Variance-covariance matrix, 11, 420
Variance-ratio tests, 144–145, 149
  results from, 155
Vector ARMA-asymmetric GARCH (VARMA-AGARCH) model, 450, 460, 478
Vector ARMA-GARCH (VARMA-GARCH) model, 450, 460, 474
Vector autoregressions (VARs), 161, 774, 777
Vector error correction and cointegration model (VECM), 561
Vector Error Correction model (VECM), 692, 694
Vector-GARCH (VEC-GARCH) model, 827
Vietnam equity market, 542, 548
VIX indexes, 29, 32
VIX volatility factor, 230
Volatility in stock prices, 509
Volatility modeling, 450, 453
Volatility shocks, 775
Volatility spillovers, 773–776, 784

W

Wald test, 173
Wavelet coherency, 586
Weibull mixture LACD model, 184
West Texas Intermediate (WTI) oil, 233
Wholesale price index (WPI), 100, 104
Wing Lung Bank (WL), 58
"Winner-picking" strategy, 312
World Business Environment Survey (WBES), 391
World interest rate, 70, 88
World Trade Organization (WTO), 813
Wright's tests, 156

Y

Yield spread change, 281

Z

Zagreb Stock Exchange (ZSE), 679
Zero-sum game, 101
Z-statistics, 493
Z-value of cross-product ratio (CPR), 318